D1023032

COLLINS GEM

GERMAN

DICTIONARY

GERMAN ▶ ENGLISH
ENGLISH ▶ GERMAN

Collins Gem

An Imprint of HarperCollinsPublishers

first published in this edition 1978
fifth edition 1999

© William Collins Sons & Co. Ltd. 1978, 1988
© HarperCollins Publishers 1993, 1997 , 1999

Latest reprint 2000

ISBN 0 00 472357-0

The Collins Gem website address is
www.collins-gem.com

---

contributors
Christine Bahr, Susie Beattie, Anne Dickinson
Helga Holtkamp, Horst Kopleck
Joyce Littlejohn, Val McNulty
John Podbielski, Beate Wengel

based on the first edition by
Ute Nicol, Veronika Schnorr,
Peter Terrell, John Whitlam

---

*A catalogue record for this book
is available from the British Library*

Typeset by Morton Word Processing Ltd, Scarborough

*Printed and bound in Great Britain by Caledonian
International Book Manufacturing Ltd, Glasgow, G64*

INHALT		CONTENTS

EINLEITUNG

Wir freuen uns, dass Sie sich zum Kauf dieses Collins Gem German Wörterbuchs entschlossen haben und hoffen, dass es Ihnen in der Schule, zu Hause, im Urlaub oder im Büro nützlich ist und Freude macht.

Diese Einleitung enthält Tips, wie Sie das Beste aus ihrem Wörterbuch herausholen können — nicht nur aus der umfangreichen Wortliste, sondern auch aus den Informationen, die in jedem Artikel stehen. Das wird Ihnen dabei helfen, modernes Englisch zu lesen und zu verstehen und sich auf Englisch auszudrücken und zu verständigen.

Vorn in diesem Wörterbuch steht eine Liste der im Text verwendeten Abkürzungen und eine Erläuterung der Symbole der Lautschrift. Hinten finden Sie deutsche Verbtabellen und englische unregelmäßige Verben und abschließend einen Abschnitt über Zahlen und Uhrzeit.

ZUM GEBRAUCH IHRES COLLINS GEM WÖRTERBUCHS

Das Wörterbuch enthält eine Fülle von Informationen, die mithilfe von unterschiedlichen Schriften und Schriftgrößen, Symbolen, Abkürzungen und Klammern vermittelt werden. Die dabei verwendeten Regeln und Symbole werden in den folgenden Abschnitten erklärt.

Stichwörter

Die Wörter, die Sie im Wörterbuch nachschlagen — „Stichwörter" — sind alphabetisch geordnet. Sie sind **fett** gedruckt, damit man sie schnell erkennt. Die beiden Stichwörter oben auf jeder Seite geben an das erste und letzte Wort an, das auf der betreffenden Seite behandelt wird.

Informationen zur Verwendung oder zur Form bestimmter Stichwörter stehen in Klammern hinter der Lautschrift. Sie erscheinen meist in abgekürzter Form und sind kursiv gedruckt (z B. (*fam*, (*COMM*)).

Wo es angebracht ist, werden mit dem Stichwort verwandte Wörter im selben Artikel behandelt (z. B. **accept, acceptance**). Sie sind wie das Stichwort fett, aber etwas kleiner gedruckt.
Häufig verwendete Ausdrücke, in denen das Stichwort vorkommt (z. B. **to be cold**), sind in einer anderen Schrift halbfett gedruckt.

Lautschrift

Die Lautschrift für jedes Stichwort (zur Angabe seiner Aussprache) steht in eckigen Klammern direkt hinter dem Stichwort (z. B. **Quark** [kvark], **knead** [niːd]). Die Symbole der Lautschrift sind auf Seite xii erklärt.

Übersetzungen

Die Übersetzungen des Stichworts sind normal gedruckt. Wenn es mehr als eine Bedeutung oder Verwendung des Stichworts gibt, sind diese durch ein Semikolon voneinander getrennt. Vor den Übersetzungen stehen oft andere, kursiv gedruckte Wörter in Klammern. Sie geben an, in welchem Zusammenhang das Stichwort erscheinen könnte (z. B. **rough** (*voice*) oder (*weather*)) oder sie sind Synonyme (z. B. **rough** (*violent*)).

Schlüsselwörter

Besonders behandelt werden bestimmte deutsche und englische Wörter, die man als „Schlüsselwörter" der jeweiligen Sprache betrachten kann. Diese Wörter kommen beispielsweise sehr häufig vor oder werden unterschiedlich verwendet (z. B. **sein**, **auch**; **get that**). Mithilfe von Rauten und Ziffern können Sie die verschiedenen Wortarten und Verwendungen unterscheiden. Weitere nützliche Hinweise finden Sie kursiv und in Klammern in der jeweiligen Sprache des Benutzers.

Grammatische Informationen

Wortarten stehen in abgekürzter Form kursiv gedruckt hinter der Aussprache des Stichworts (z. B. *vt, adv, conj*).

Die unregelmäßigen Formen englischer Substantive und Verben stehen in Klammern vor der Wortart (z. B. **man** (*pl* **men**) *n*, **give** (*pt* **gave**, *pp* **given**) *vt*).

Die deutsche Rechtschreibreform

Dieses Wörterbuch folgt durchweg der reformierten deutschen Rechtschreibung. Alle Stichwörter auf der deutsch-englischen Seite, die von der Rechtschreibreform betroffen sind, sind mit ▲ gekennzeichnet. Alte Schreibungen, die sich wesentlich von der neuen Schreibung unterscheiden und an einem anderen alphabetischen Ort erscheinen, sind jedoch weiterhin aufgeführt und werden zur neuen Schreibung verwiesen. Diese alten Schreibungen sind mit △ gekennzeichnet.

INTRODUCTION

We are delighted you have decided to buy the Collins Gem German Dictionary and hope you will enjoy and benefit from using it at school, at home, on holiday or at work.

This introduction gives you a few tips on how to get the most out of your dictionary — not simply from its comprehensive wordlist but also from the information provided in each entry. This will help you to read and understand modern German, as well as to communicate and express yourself in the language.

The Collins Gem German Dictionary begins by listing the abbreviations used in the text and illustrating the sounds shown by the phonetic symbols. You will find German verb tables and English irregular verbs at the back, followed by a final section on numbers and time expressions.

USING YOUR COLLINS GEM DICTIONARY

A wealth of information is presented in the dictionary, using various typefaces, sizes of type, symbols, abbreviations and brackets. The conventions and symbols used are explained in the following sections.

Headwords

The words you look up in a dictionary — "headwords" — are listed alphabetically. They are printed in **bold type** for rapid identification. The two headwords appearing at the top of each page indicate the first and last word dealt with on the page in question.

Information about the usage or form of certain headwords is given in brackets after the phonetic spelling. This usually appears in abbreviated form and in italics (e.g. (*umg*), (*COMM*)).

Where appropriate, words related to headwords are grouped in the same entry (**Glück, glücken**) in a slightly smaller bold type than the headword.
Common expressions in which the headword appears are shown in a different bold roman type (e.g. **Glück haben**).

Phonetic spellings

The phonetic spelling of each headword (indicating its pronunciation) is given in square brackets immediately after the headword (e.g. **Quark** [kvark]). A list of these symbols is given on page xii.

Meanings

Headword translations are given in ordinary type and, where more than one meaning or usage exists, these are separated by a semi-colon. You will often find other words in italics in brackets before the translations. These offer suggested contexts in which the headword might appear (e.g. **eng** (*Kleidung*) or (*Freundschaft*)) or provide synonyms (e.g. **eng** (*fig: Horizont*)).

"Key" words

Special status is given to certain German and English words which are considered as "key" words in each language. They may, for example, occur very frequently or have several types of usage (e.g. **sein, auch; get, that**). A combination of lozenges and numbers helps you to distinguish different parts of speech and different meanings. Further helpful information is provided in brackets and in italics in the relevant language for the user.

Grammatical information

Parts of speech are given in abbreviated form in italics after the phonetic spellings of headwords (e.g. *vt, adv, konj*).

Genders of German nouns are indicated as follows: m for a masculine and f for a feminine and nt for a neuter noun. The genitive and plural forms of regular nouns are shown on the table on page xi. Nouns which do not follow these rules have the genitive and plural in brackets immediately preceding the gender (e.g. **Spaß**, (-es, ¨-e), *m*).

Adjectives are normally shown in their basic form (e.g. **groß** *adj*), but where they are only used attributively (i.e. before a noun) feminine and neuter endings follow in brackets (hohe (r, s) *adj attrib*).

The German spelling reform

The German spelling reform has been fully implemented in this dictionary. All headwords on the German-English side which are affected by the spelling changes are marked ▲. Old spellings which are significantly different from the new ones and have a different alphabetical position are still listed and are cross-referenced to the new spellings. The old spellings are marked △.

Warenzeichen

Wörter, die unseres Wissens eingetragene Warenzeichen darstellen, sind als solche gekennzeichnet. Es ist jedoch zu beachten, daß weder das Vorhandensein noch das Fehlen derartiger Kennzeichnungen die Rechtslage hinsichtlich eingetragener Warenzeichen berührt.

Note on trademarks

Words which we have reason to believe constitute trademarks have been designated as such. However, neither the presence nor the absence of such designation should be regarded as affecting the legal status of any trademark.

ABKÜRZUNGEN

ABBREVIATIONS

Abkürzung	**abk, abbr**	abbreviation
Adjektiv	**adj**	adjective
Akkusativ	**acc**	accusative
Adverb	**adv**	adverb
Landwirtschaft	**AGR**	agriculture
Akkusativ	**akk**	accusative
Anatomie	**ANAT**	anatomy
Architektur	**ARCHIT**	architecture
Astrologie	**ASTROL**	astrology
Astronomie	**ASTRON**	astronomy
attributiv	**attrib**	attributive
Kraftfahrzeuge	**AUT**	automobiles
Hilfsverb	**aux**	auxiliary
Luftfahrt	**AVIAT**	aviation
besonders	**bes**	especially
Biologie	**BIOL**	biology
Botanik	**BOT**	botany
britisch	**BRIT**	British
Chemie	**CHEM**	chemistry
Film	**CINE**	cinema
Konjunktion	**conj**	conjunction
Handel	**COMM**	commerce
Komparativ	**compar**	comparative
Computer	**COMPUT**	computing
Kochen und Backen	**COOK**	cooking
zusammengesetztes Wort	**cpd**	compound
Dativ	**dat**	dative
bestimmter Artikel	**def art**	definite article
dekliniert	**dekl**	decline
Diminutiv	**dimin**	diminutive
kirchlich	**ECCL**	ecclesiastical
Eisenbahn	**EISENB**	railways
Elektrizität	**ELEK, ELEC**	electricity
besonders	**esp**	especially
und so weiter	**etc**	et cetera
etwas	**etw**	something
Euphemismus, Hüllwort	**euph**	euphemism
Interjektion, Ausruf	**excl**	exclamation
Femininum	**f**	feminine
übertragen	**fig**	figurative
Finanzwesen	**FIN**	finance
nicht getrennt gebraucht	**fus**	(phrasal verb) inseparable
Genitiv	**gen**	genitive
Geografie	**GEOG**	geography
Geologie	**GEOL**	geology
gewöhnlich	**gew**	usually

Grammatik	**GRAM**	grammar
Geschichte	**HIST**	history
unpersönlich	**impers**	impersonal
unbestimmter Artikel	**indef art**	indefinite article
umgangssprachlich (! vulgär)	**inf(!)**	informal (! particularly offensive)
Infinitiv, Grundform	**infin**	infinitive
nicht getrennt gebraucht	**insep**	inseparable
unveränderlich	**inv**	invariable
unregelmäßig	**irreg**	irregular
jemand	**jd**	somebody
jemandem	**jdm**	(to) somebody
jemanden	**jdn**	somebody
jemandes	**jds**	somebody's
Rechtswesen	**JUR**	law
Kochen und Backen	**KOCH**	cooking
Komparativ	**kompar**	comparative
Konjunktion	**konj**	conjunction
Sprachwissenschaft	**LING**	linguistics
Literatur	**LITER**	of literature
Maskulinum	**m**	masculine
Mathematik	**MATH**	mathematics
Medizin	**MED**	medicine
Meteorologie	**MET**	meteorology
Militär	**MIL**	military
Bergbau	**MIN**	mining
Musik	**MUS**	music
Substantiv, Hauptwort	**n**	noun
nautisch, Seefahrt	**NAUT**	nautical, naval
Nominativ	**nom**	nominative
Neutrum	**nt**	neuter
Zahlwort	**num**	numeral
Objekt	**obj**	object
oder	**od**	or
sich	**o.s.**	oneself
Parlament	**PARL**	parliament
abschätzig	**pej**	pejorative
Fotografie	**PHOT**	photography
Physik	**PHYS**	physics
Plural	**pl**	plural
Politik	**POL**	politics
Präfix, Vorsilbe	**pp**	prefix
Präposition	**präp, prep**	preposition
Typografie	**PRINT**	printing
Pronomen, Fürwort	**pron**	pronoun
Psychologie	**PSYCH**	psychology

ABKÜRZUNGEN

ABBREVIATIONS

1. Vergangenheit, Imperfekt	**pt**	past tense
Partizip Perfekt	**pp**	past participle
Radio	**RAD**	radio
Eisenbahn	**RAIL**	railways
Religion	**REL**	religion
jemand(-en, -em)	**sb**	someone, somebody
Schulwesen	**SCH**	school
Naturwissenschaft	**SCI**	science
Singular, Einzahl	**sg**	singular
etwas	**sth**	something
Konjunktiv	**sub**	subjunctive
Subjekt	**subj**	(grammatical) subject
Superlativ	**superl**	superlative
Technik	**TECH**	technology
Nachrichtentechnik	**TEL**	telecommunications
Theater	**THEAT**	theatre
Fernsehen	**TV**	television
Typografie	**TYP**	printing
umgangssprachlich (! vulgär)	**umg(!)**	colloquial (! particularly) offensive)
Hochschulwesen	**UNIV**	university
unpersönlich	**unpers**	impersonal
unregelmäßig	**unreg**	irregular
(nord)amerikanisch	**US**	(North) America
gewöhnlich	**usu**	usually
Verb	**vb**	verb
intransitives Verb	**vi**	intransitive verb
reflexives Verb	**vr**	reflexive verb
transitives Verb	**vt**	transitive verb
Zoologie	**ZOOL**	zoology
zusammengesetztes Wort	**zW**	compound
zwischen zwei Sprechern	**—**	change of speaker
ungefähre Entsprechung	**≈**	cultural equivalent
eingetragenes Warenzeichen	**®**	registered trademark

REGULAR GERMAN NOUN ENDINGS

nom		*gen*	*pl*
-ant	m	-anten	-anten
-anz	f	-anz	-anzen
-ar	m	-ar(e)s	-are
-chen	nt	-chens	-chen
-e	f	-	-n
-ei	f	-ei	-eien
-elle	f	-elle	-ellen
-ent	m	-enten	-enten
-enz	f	-enz	-enzen
-ette	f	-ette	-etten
-eur	m	-eurs	-eure
-euse	f	-euse	-eusen
-heit	f	-heit	-heiten
-ie	f	-ie	-ien
-ik	f	-ik	-iken
-in	f	-in	-innen
-ine	f	-ine	-inen
-ion	f	-ion	-ionen
-ist	m	-isten	-isten
-ium	nt	-iums	-ien
-ius	m	-ius	-iusse
-ive	f	-ive	-iven
-keit	f	-keit	-keiten
-lein	nt	-leins	-lein
-ling	m	-lings	-linge
-ment	nt	-ments	-mente
-mus	m	-mus	-men
-schaft	f	-schaft	-schaften
-tät	f	-tät	-täten
-tor	m	-tors	-toren
-ung	f	-ung	-ungen
-ur	f	-ur	-uren

PHONETIC SYMBOLS / LAUTSCHRIFT

[ː] *length mark   Längezeichen* [ˈ] *stress mark   Betonung*
[ǀ] *glottal stop   Knacklaut*

all vowel sounds are approximate only
alle Vokallaute sind nur ungefähre Entsprechungen

<u>b</u>et	[b]	<u>B</u>all		[e] <u>Me</u>tall
<u>d</u>im	[d]	<u>d</u>ann		[eː] <u>ge</u>ben
<u>f</u>ace	[f]	<u>F</u>ass	<u>se</u>t	[ɛ] <u>hä</u>sslich
<u>g</u>o	[g]	<u>G</u>ast		[ɛ̃ː] <u>Cou</u>sin
<u>h</u>it	[h]	<u>H</u>err	<u>pi</u>ty	[ɪ] <u>Bi</u>schof
<u>y</u>ou	[j]	<u>j</u>a		[i] <u>vi</u>tal
<u>c</u>at	[k]	<u>k</u>alt	<u>gree</u>n	[iː] <u>vie</u>l
<u>l</u>ick	[l]	<u>L</u>ast	<u>ro</u>t	[ɔ] <u>Po</u>st
<u>m</u>ust	[m]	<u>M</u>ast	<u>boar</u>d	[ɔː]
<u>n</u>ut	[n]	<u>N</u>uss		[o] <u>Mo</u>ral
<u>b</u>a<u>ng</u>	[ŋ]	<u>lang</u>		[oː] <u>o</u>ben
<u>p</u>epper	[p]	<u>P</u>akt		[õ] <u>Cha</u>mpignon
<u>r</u>ed	[r]	<u>R</u>egen		[ø] <u>ö</u>konomisch
<u>s</u>it	[s]	<u>R</u>asse		[œ] <u>gö</u>nnen
<u>sh</u>ame	[ʃ]	<u>Sch</u>al	<u>fu</u>ll	[ʊ] <u>ku</u>lant
<u>t</u>ell	[t]	<u>T</u>al	<u>roo</u>t	[uː] <u>Hu</u>t
<u>ch</u>at	[tʃ]	<u>tsch</u>üs	<u>co</u>me	[ʌ]
<u>v</u>ine	[v]	<u>w</u>as		[ʊ] <u>Pu</u>lt
<u>w</u>ine	[w]			[y] <u>phy</u>sisch
<u>loch</u>	[x]	<u>B</u>a<u>ch</u>		[yː] <u>fü</u>r
	[ç]	<u>ich</u>		[ʏ] <u>Mü</u>ll
<u>z</u>ero	[z]	<u>H</u>a<u>s</u>e	<u>a</u>bove	[ə] <u>bi</u>tte
lei<u>s</u>ure	[ʒ]	<u>G</u>enie	<u>gir</u>l	[əː]
<u>j</u>oin	[dʒ]			
<u>th</u>in	[θ]		<u>lie</u>	[aɪ] <u>wei</u>t
<u>th</u>is	[ð]		<u>now</u>	[au]
				[aʊ] <u>Hau</u>t
h<u>a</u>t	[a]	H<u>a</u>st	<u>day</u>	[eɪ]
h<u>a</u>t	[æ]		<u>fair</u>	[ɛə]
		B<u>ah</u>n	<u>beer</u>	[ɪə]
f<u>ar</u>m	[ɑː]		<u>toy</u>	[ɔɪ]
	[ã]	<u>En</u>semble		[ɔʏ] <u>Heu</u>
fian<u>cé</u>	[ɑ̃ː]		<u>pure</u>	[ʊə]

[ʳ] *r can be pronounced before a vowel;*
Bindungs-R

ZAHLEN		NUMBERS
ein(s)	1	one
zwei	2	two
drei	3	three
vier	4	four
fünf	5	five
sechs	6	six
sieben	7	seven
acht	8	eight
neun	9	nine
zehn	10	ten
elf	11	eleven
zwölf	12	twelve
dreizehn	13	thirteen
vierzehn	14	fourteen
fünfzehn	15	fifteen
sechzehn	16	sixteen
siebzehn	17	seventeen
achtzehn	18	eighteen
neunzehn	19	nineteen
zwanzig	20	twenty
einundzwanzig	21	twenty-one
zweiundzwanzig	22	twenty-two
dreißig	30	thirty
vierzig	40	forty
fünfzig	50	fifty
sechzig	60	sixty
siebzig	70	seventy
achtzig	80	eighty
neunzig	90	ninety
hundert	100	a hundred
hunderteins	101	a hundred and one
zweihundert	200	two hundred
zweihunderteins	201	two hundred and one
dreihundert	300	three hundred
dreihunderteins	301	three hundred and one
tausend	1000	a thousand
tausend(und)eins	1001	a thousand and one
fünftausend	5000	five thousand
eine Million	1000000	a million

erste(r, s)	1.	first	1st
zweite(r, s)	2.	second	2nd
dritte(r, s)	3.	third	3rd
vierte(r, s)	4.	fourth	4th
fünfte(r, s)	5.	fifth	5th
sechste(r, s)	6.	sixth	6th
siebte(r, s)	7.	seventh	7th
achte(r, s)	8.	eighth	8th
neunte(r, s)	9.	ninth	9th
zehnte(r, s)	10.	tenth	10th
elfte(r, s)	11.	eleventh	11th
zwölfte(r, s)	12.	twelfth	12th
dreizehnte(r, s)	13.	thirteenth	13th
vierzehnte(r, s)	14.	fourteenth	14th
fünfzehnte(r, s)	15.	fifteenth	15th
sechzehnte(r, s)	16.	sixteenth	16th
siebzehnte(r, s)	17.	seventeenth	17th
achtzehnte(r, s)	18.	eighteenth	18th
neunzehnte(r, s)	19.	nineteenth	19th
zwanzigste(r, s)	20.	twentieth	20th
einundzwanzigste(r, s)	21.	twenty-first	21st
dreißigste(r, s)	30.	thirtieth	30th
hundertste(r, s)	100.	hundredth	100th
hunderterste(r, s)	101.	hundred-and-first	101st
tausendste(r, s)	1000.	thousandth	1000th

Brüche usw.		**Fractions etc.**	
ein Halb	$\frac{1}{2}$	a half	
ein Drittel	$\frac{1}{3}$	a third	
ein Viertel	$\frac{1}{4}$	a quarter	
ein Fünftel	$\frac{1}{5}$	a fifth	
null Komma fünf	0,5	(nought) point five	0.5
drei Komma vier	3,4	three point four	3.4
sechs Komma acht neun	6,89	six point eight nine	6.89
zehn Prozent	10%	ten per cent	
hundert Prozent	100%	a hundred per cent	

Beispiele	**Examples**
er wohnt in Nummer 10	he lives at number 10
es steht in Kapitel 7	it's in chapter 7
auf Seite 7	on page 7
er wohnt im 7. Stock	he lives on the 7th floor
er wurde 7.	he came in 7th
Maßstab eins zu zwanzigtausend	scale one to twenty thousand

UHRZEIT

THE TIME

wie viel Uhr ist es?, wie spät ist es?	what time is it?
es ist ...	it's ...
Mitternacht, zwölf Uhr nachts	midnight, twelve p.m.
ein Uhr (morgens or früh)	one o'clock (in the morning), one (a.m.)
fünf nach eins, ein Uhr fünf	five past one
zehn nach eins, ein Uhr zehn	ten past one
Viertel nach eins, ein Uhr fünfzehn	a quarter past one, one fifteen
fünf vor halb zwei, ein Uhr fünfundzwanzig	twenty-five past one, one twenty-five
halb zwei, ein Uhr dreißig	half past one, one thirty
fünf nach halb zwei, ein Uhr fünfunddreißig	twenty-five to two, one thirty-five
zwanzig vor zwei, ein Uhr vierzig	twenty to two, one forty
Viertel vor zwei, ein Uhr fünfundvierzig	a quarter to two, one forty-five
zehn vor zwei, ein Uhr fünfzig	ten to two, one fifty
zwölf Uhr (mittags), Mittag	twelve o'clock, midday, noon
halb eins (mittags or nachmittags), zwölf Uhr dreißig	half past twelve, twelve thirty (p.m.)
zwei Uhr (nachmittags)	two o'clock (in the afternoon), two (p.m.)
halb acht (abends)	half past seven (in the evening), seven thirty (p.m.)
um wie viel Uhr?	at what time?
um Mitternacht	at midnight
um sieben Uhr	at seven o'clock
in zwanzig Minuten	in twenty minutes
vor fünfzehn Minuten	fifteen minutes ago

DEUTSCH – ENGLISCH
GERMAN – ENGLISH

A, a

Aal [aːl] (-(e)s, -e) *m* eel
Aas [aːs] (-es, -e *od* Äser) *nt* carrion

ab [ap] *präp +dat* from; **Kinder ab 12 Jahren** children from the age of 12; **ab morgen** from tomorrow; **ab sofort** as of now
♦ *adv* **1** off; **links ab** to the left; **der Knopf ist ab** the button has come off; **ab nach Hause!** off you go home
2 (*zeitlich*): **von da ab** from then on; **von heute ab** from today, as of today
3 (*auf Fahrplänen*): **München ab 12.20** leaving Munich 12.20
4: **ab und zu** *od* **an** now and then *od* again

Abänderung ['apˌɛndəʀʊŋ] *f* alteration
Abbau ['apbau] (-(e)s) *m* (+gen) dismantling; (*Verminderung*) reduction (in); (*Verfall*) decline (in); (*MIN*) mining; quarrying; (*CHEM*) decomposition; **a~en** *vt* to dismantle; (*MIN*) to mine; to quarry; (*verringern*) to reduce; (*CHEM*) to break down
abbeißen ['apbaɪsn] (*unreg*) *vt* to bite off
abbekommen ['apbəkɔmən] (*unreg*) *vt* (*Deckel, Schraube, Band*) to loosen; **etwas** ~ (*beschädigt werden*) to get damaged; (*Person*) to get injured
abbestellen ['apbəʃtɛlən] *vt* to cancel
abbezahlen ['apbətsaːlən] *vt* to pay off
abbiegen ['apbiːgən] (*unreg*) *vi* to turn off; (*Straße*) to bend; to bend; (*verhindern*) to ward off

abbilden ['apbɪldən] *vt* to portray; **Abbildung** *f* illustration
abblenden ['apblɛndən] *vt, vi* (*AUT*) to dip (*BRIT*), to dim (*US*)
Abblendlicht ['apblɛntlɪçt] *nt* dipped (*BRIT*) *od* dimmed (*US*) headlights *pl*
abbrechen ['apbrɛçən] (*unreg*) *vt, vi* to break off; (*Gebäude*) to pull down; (*Zelt*) to take down; (*aufhören*) to stop; (*COMPUT*) to abort
abbrennen ['apbrɛnən] (*unreg*) *vt* to burn off; (*Feuerwerk*) to let off ♦ *vi* (*aux sein*) to burn down
abbringen ['apbrɪŋən] (*unreg*) *vt*: **jdn von etw** ~ to dissuade sb from sth; **jdn vom Weg** ~ to divert sb
abbröckeln ['apbrœkəln] *vt, vi* to crumble off *od* away
Abbruch ['apbrʊx] *m* (*von Verhandlungen etc*) breaking off; (*von Haus*) demolition; **jdm/etw** ~ **tun** to harm sb/sth; **a~reif** *adj* only fit for demolition
abbrühen ['apbryːən] *vt* to scald; **abgebrüht** (*umg*) hard-boiled
abbuchen ['apbuːxən] *vt* to debit
abdanken ['apdaŋkən] *vi* to resign; (*König*) to abdicate; **Abdankung** *f* resignation; abdication
abdecken ['apdɛkən] *vt* (*Loch*) to cover; (*Tisch*) to clear; (*Plane*) to uncover
abdichten ['apdɪçtən] *vt* to seal; (*NAUT*) to caulk
abdrehen ['apdreːən] *vt* (*Gas*) to turn off; (*Licht*) to switch off; (*Film*) to shoot ♦ *vi* (*Schiff*) to change course
Abdruck ['apdrʊk] *m* (*Nachdrucken*) reprinting; (*Gedrucktes*) reprint; (*Gipsabdruck, Wachsabdruck*) impression;

(*Fingerabdruck*) print; **a~en** vt to print, to publish

abdrücken ['apdrʏkən] vt (*Waffe*) to fire; (*Person*) to hug, to squeeze

Abend ['a:bənt] (-s, -e) nt evening; **guten ~** good evening; **zu ~ essen** to have dinner od supper; **heute ~** this evening; **~brot** nt supper; **~essen** nt supper; **~garderobe** f evening dress; **~kasse** f box office; **~kleid** nt evening dress; **~kurs** m evening classes pl; **~land** nt (*Europa*) West; **a~lich** adj evening; **~mahl** nt Holy Communion; **~rot** nt sunset; **a~s** adv in the evening

Abenteuer [a:bəntɔyər] (-s, -) nt adventure; **a~lich** adj adventurous; **~urlaub** m adventure holiday

Abenteurer (-s -) m adventurer; **~in** f adventuress

aber ['a:bər] konj but; (*jedoch*) however ♦ adv: **das ist ~ schön** that's really nice; **nun ist ~ Schluss!** now that's enough!; **vielen Dank ~ ~ bitte!** thanks a lot — you're welcome; **A~glaube** m superstition; **~gläubisch** adj superstitious

aberkennen ['ap|ɛrkɛnən] (*unreg*) vt (*JUR*): **jdm etw ~** to deprive sb of sth, to take sth (away) from sb

abermals ['a:bəma:ls] adv once again

abertausend, Abertausend ['a:bərtaʊzant] indef pron: **tausend od Tausend und ~** thousands upon thousands

Abf. abk (= *Abfahrt*) dep.

abfahren ['apfa:rən] (*unreg*) vi to leave, to depart ♦ vt to take od cart away; (*Strecke*) to drive; (*Reifen*) to wear; (*Fahrkarte*) to use

Abfahrt ['apfa:rt] f departure; (*SKI*) descent; (*Piste*) run; **~szeit** f departure time

Abfall ['apfal] m waste; (*von Speisen etc*) rubbish (*BRIT*), garbage (*US*); (*Neigung*) slope; (*Verschlechterung*) decline; **~eimer** m rubbish bin (*BRIT*), garbage can (*US*); **a~en** (*unreg*) vi (*auch fig*) to

fall od drop off; (*sich neigen*) to fall od drop away

abfällig ['apfɛlɪç] adj disparaging, deprecatory

abfangen ['apfaŋən] (*unreg*) vt to intercept; (*Person*) to catch; (*unter Kontrolle bringen*) to check

abfärben ['apfɛrbən] vi to lose its colour; (*Wäsche*) to run; (*fig*) to rub off

abfassen ['apfasən] vt to write, to draft

abfertigen ['apfɛrtigən] vt to prepare for dispatch, to process; (*an der Grenze*) to clear; (*Kundschaft*) to attend to

Abfertigungsschalter m (*Flughafen*) check-in desk

abfeuern ['apfɔyərn] vt to fire

abfinden ['apfɪndən] (*unreg*) vt to pay off ♦ vr to come to terms; **sich mit jdm/~nicht ~** to put up with/not get on with sb

Abfindung f (*von Gläubigern*) payment; (*Geld*) sum in settlement

abflauen ['apflaʊən] vi (*Wind, Erregung*) to die away, to subside; (*Nachfrage, Geschäft*) to fall od drop off

abfliegen ['apfli:gən] (*unreg*) vi (*Flugzeug*) to take off; (*Passagier auch*) to fly ♦ vt (*Gebiet*) to fly over

abfließen ['apfli:sən] (*unreg*) vi to drain away

Abflug ['apflu:k] m departure; (*Start*) take-off; **~halle** f departure lounge; **~zeit** f departure time

Abfluss ▲ ['apflʊs] m draining away; (*Öffnung*) outlet; **~rohr ▲** nt drain pipe; (*von sanitären Anlagen auch*) waste pipe

abfragen ['apfra:gən] vt (*bes SCH*) to test orally (on)

Abfuhr ['apfu:r] (-, -en) f removal; (*fig*) snub, rebuff

abführen ['apfy:rən] vt to lead away; (*Gelder, Steuern*) to pay ♦ vi (*MED*) to have a laxative effect

Abführmittel ['apfy:rmɪtəl] nt laxative, purgative

abfüllen ['apfʏlən] vt to draw off; (in Flaschen) to bottle

Abgabe ['apga:bə] f handing in; (von Ball) pass; (Steuer) tax; (eines Amtes) giving up; (einer Erklärung) giving

Abgang ['apgaŋ] m (von Schule) leaving; (THEAT) exit; (Abfahrt) departure; (der Post, von Waren) dispatch

Abgas ['apga:s] nt waste gas; (AUT) exhaust

abgeben ['apge:bən] (unreg) vt (Gegenstand) to hand od give in; (Ball) to pass; (Wärme) to give off; (Amt) to hand over; (Schuss) to fire; (Erklärung, Urteil) to give; (darstellen, sein) to make ♦ vr: **sich mit jdm/etw ~** to associate with sb/bother with sth; **jdm etw ~** (überlassen) to let sb have sth

abgebrüht ['apgəbry:t] (umg) adj (skrupellos) hard-boiled

abgehen ['apge:ən] (unreg) vi to go away, to leave; (THEAT) to exit; (Knopf etc) to come off; (Straße) to branch off ♦ vt (Strecke) to go od walk along; **etw geht jdm ab** (fehlt) sb lacks sth

abgelegen ['apgəle:gən] adj remote

abgemacht ['apgəmaxt] adj fixed; **~!** done!

abgeneigt ['apgənaikt] adj disinclined

abgenutzt ['apgənʊtst] adj worn

Abgeordnete(r) ['apgəɔrdnətə(r)] f(m) member of parliament; elected representative

abgeschlossen ['apgəʃlɔsən] adj attrib (Wohnung) self-contained

abgeschmackt ['apgəʃmakt] adj tasteless

abgesehen ['apgəze:ən] adj: **es auf jdn/etw ~ haben** to be after sb/sth; **~ von ...** apart from ...

abgespannt ['apgəʃpant] adj tired out

abgestanden ['apgəʃtandən] adj stale; (Bier auch) flat

abgestorben ['apgəʃtɔrbən] adj numb;

(BIOL, MED) dead

abgetragen ['apgətra:gən] adj shabby, worn out

abgewinnen ['apgəvɪnən] (unreg) vt: **einer Sache etw/Geschmack ~** to get sth/pleasure from sth

abgewöhnen ['apgəvø:nən] vt: **jdm/ sich etw ~** to cure sb of sth/give sth up

abgrenzen ['apgrɛntsən] vt (auch fig) to mark off; to fence off

Abgrund ['apgrʊnt] m (auch fig) abyss

abhacken ['aphakən] vt to chop off

abhaken ['apha:kən] vt (auf Papier) to tick off

abhalten ['aphaltən] (unreg) vt (Versammlung) to hold; **jdn von etw ~** (fern halten) to keep sb away from sth; (hindern) to keep sb from sth

abhanden [ap'handən] adj: **~ kommen** to get lost

Abhandlung [ap'handlʊŋ] f treatise, discourse

Abhang ['aphaŋ] m slope

abhängen [ap'hɛŋən] vt (Bild) to take down; (Anhänger) to uncouple; (Verfolger) to shake off ♦ vi (unreg: Fleisch) to hang; **von jdm/etw ~** to depend on sb/sth

abhängig [ap'hɛŋɪç] adj: **~ (von)** dependent (on); **A~keit** f: **A~keit (von)** dependence (on)

abhärten ['aphɛrtən] vt, vr to toughen (o.s.) up; **sich gegen etw ~** to inure o.s. to sth

abhauen ['aphauən] (unreg) vt to cut off; (Baum) to cut down ♦ vi (umg) to clear off od out

abheben ['aphe:bən] (unreg) vt to lift (up); (Karten) to cut; (Geld) to withdraw, to take out ♦ vi (Flugzeug) to take off; (Rakete) to lift off ♦ vr to stand out

abheften ['apheftən] vt (Rechnungen etc) to file away

abhetzen ['aphɛtsən] *vr* to wear *od* tire o.s. out

Abhilfe ['aphılfə] *f* remedy; **~ schaffen** to put things right

abholen ['aphoːlən] *vt* (*Gegenstand*) to fetch, to collect; (*Person*) to call for; (*am Bahnhof etc*) to pick up, to meet

abholzen ['aphɔltsən] *vt* (*Wald*) to clear

abhorchen ['aphɔrçən] *vt* (MED) to listen to a patient's chest

abhören ['aphøːrən] *vt* (*Vokabeln*) to test; (*Telefongespräch*) to tap; (*Tonband etc*) to listen to

Abhörgerät *nt* bug

Abitur [abiˈtuːɐ] (**-s, -e**) *nt* German school-leaving examination; **~i'ent(in**) *m(f)* candidate for school-leaving certificate

---

Abitur

The Abitur is the German school-leaving examination taken in four subjects by pupils at a Gymnasium at the age of 18 or 19. It is necessary for entry to university.

Abk. *abk* (= *Abkürzung*) abbr.

abkapseln ['apkapsəln] *vr* to shut *od* cut o.s. off

abkaufen ['apkaofən] *vt*: **jdm etw ~** (*auch fig*) to buy sth from sb

abkehren ['apkeːrən] *vt* (*Blick*) to avert, to turn away ♦ *vr* to turn away

abklingen ['apklɪŋən] (*unreg*) *vi* to die away; (*Radio*) to fade away

abknöpfen ['apknœpfən] *vt* to unbutton; **jdm etw ~** (*umg*) to get sth off sb

abkochen ['apkɔxən] *vt* to boil

abkommen ['apkɔmən] (*unreg*) *vi* to get away; **von der Straße/von einem Plan ~** to leave the road/give up a plan; **A~ (-s, -)** *nt* agreement

abkömmlich ['apkœmlıç] *adj* available, free

abkratzen ['apkratsən] *vt* to scrape off ♦ *vi* (*umg*) to kick the bucket

abkühlen ['apkyːlən] *vt* to cool down ♦ *vr* (*Mensch*) to cool down *od* off; (*Wetter*) to get cool; (*Zuneigung*) to cool

abkürzen ['apkʏrtsən] *vt* to shorten; (*Wort auch*) to abbreviate; **den Weg ~** to take a short cut

Abkürzung *f* (*Wort*) abbreviation; (*Weg*) short cut

abladen ['aplaːdən] (*unreg*) *vt* to unload

Ablage ['aplaːgə] *f* (*für Akten*) tray; (*für Kleider*) cloakroom

ablassen ['aplasən] (*unreg*) *vt* (*Wasser, Dampf*) to let off; (*vom Preis*) to knock off ♦ *vi*: **von etw ~** to give sth up, to abandon sth

Ablauf ['aplaof] *m* (*Abfluss*) drain; (*von Ereignissen*) course; (*einer Frist, Zeit*) expiry; (BRIT), expiration (US); **a~en** (*unreg*) *vi* (*abfließen*) to drain away; (*Ereignisse*) to happen; (*Frist, Zeit, Pass*) to expire ♦ *vt* (*Sohlen*) to wear (down *od* out)

ablegen ['apleːgən] *vt* to put *od* lay down; (*Kleider*) to take off; (*Gewohnheit*) to get rid of; (*Prüfung*) to take, to sit; (*Zeugnis*) to give

Ableger (-s, -) *m* layer; (*fig*) branch, offshoot

ablehnen ['apleːnən] *vt* to reject; (*Einladung*) to decline, to refuse ♦ *vi* to decline, to refuse

ablehnend *adj* (*Haltung, Antwort*) negative; (*Geste*) disapproving; **ein ~er Bescheid** a rejection

Ablehnung *f* rejection; refusal

ableiten ['aplaitən] *vt* (*Wasser*) to divert; (*deduzieren*) to deduce; (*Wort*) to derive; **Ableitung** *f* diversion; deduction; derivation; (*Wort*) derivative

ablenken ['aplɛŋkən] *vt* to turn away, to deflect; (*zerstreuen*) to distract ♦ *vi* to change the subject; **Ablenkung** *f* distraction

ablesen ['apleːzən] (*unreg*) *vt* (*Messgeräte*) to read

ablichten ['aplıçtən] vt to photocopy

abliefern ['apli:fərn] vt to deliver; **etw bei jdm ~** to hand sth over to sb

Ablieferung f delivery

ablösen ['aplø:zən] vt (abtrennen) to take off, to remove; (in Amt) to take over from; (Wache) to relieve

Ablösung f removal; relieving

abmachen ['apmaxən] vt to take off; (vereinbaren) to agree; **Abmachung** f agreement

abmagern ['apma:gərn] vi to get thinner

Abmagerungskur f diet; **eine ~ machen** to go on a diet

abmarschieren ['apmarʃi:rən] vi to march off

abmelden ['apmɛldən] vt (Zeitungen) to cancel; (Auto) to take off the road ♦ vr to give notice of one's departure; (im Hotel) to check out; **jdn bei der Polizei ~** to register sb's departure with the police

abmessen ['apmɛsən] (unreg) vt to measure; **Abmessung** f measurement

abmontieren ['apmɔnti:rən] vt to take off

abmühen ['apmy:ən] vr to wear o.s. out

Abnahme ['apna:mə] f (+gen) removal; (COMM) buying; (Verringerung) decrease (in)

abnehmen ['apne:mən] (unreg) vt to take off, to remove; (Führerschein) to take away; (Prüfung) to hold; (Maschen) to decrease ♦ vi to decrease; (schlanker werden) to lose weight; **(jdm) etw ~** (Geld) to get sth (out of sb); (kaufen, umg: glauben) to buy sth (from sb); **jdm Arbeit ~** to take work off sb's shoulders

Abnehmer (-s, -) m purchaser, customer

Abneigung ['apnaigʊŋ] f aversion, dislike

abnorm [ap'nɔrm] adj abnormal

abnutzen ['apnʊtsən] vt to wear out; **Abnutzung** f wear (and tear)

Abo ['abo] (umg) nt abk = **Abonnement**

Abonnement [abɔn(ə)'mā:] (-s, -s) nt subscription; **Abonnent(in)** [abɔ'nɛnt(ın)] m(f) subscriber; **abonnieren** vt to subscribe to

Abordnung ['apɔrdnʊŋ] f delegation

abpacken ['appakən] vt to pack

abpassen ['appasən] vt (Person, Gelegenheit) to wait for

Abpfiff ['appfıf] m final whistle

abplagen ['appla:gən] vr to wear o.s. out

abprallen ['appralən] vi to bounce off; to ricochet

abraten ['apra:tən] (unreg) vi: **jdm von etw ~** to advise or warn sb against sth

abräumen ['aprɔymən] vt to clear up od away

abreagieren ['apreagi:rən] vt: **seinen Zorn (an jdm/etw) ~** to work one's anger off (on sb/sth) ♦ vr to calm down

abrechnen ['apreçnən] vt to deduct, to take off ♦ vi to settle up; (fig) to get even

Abrechnung f settlement; (Rechnung) bill

Abrede ['apre:də] f: **etw in ~ stellen** to deny od dispute sth

Abreise ['apraizə] f departure; **a~n** vi to leave, to set off

abreißen ['apraisən] (unreg) vt (Haus) to tear down; (Blatt) to tear off

abrichten ['apriçtən] vt to train

abriegeln ['apri:gəln] vt (Straße, Gebiet) to seal off

Abruf ['apru:f] m: **auf ~** on call; **a~en** (unreg) vt (Mensch) to call away; (COMM: Ware) to request delivery of

abrunden ['aprʊndən] vt to round off

abrupt [a'brʊpt] adj abrupt

abrüsten ['aprʏstən] vi to disarm; **Abrüstung** f disarmament

abrutschen ['aprʊtʃən] vi to slip; (AVIAT) to sideslip

Abs. abk (= Absender) sender, from

Absage ['apza:gə] f refusal; **a~n** vt to cancel, to call off; (Einladung) to turn down ♦ vi to cry off; (ablehnen) to decline

absahnen ['apza:nən] vt to skim ♦ vi (fig) to rake in

Absatz ['apzats] m (COMM) sales pl; (Bodensatz) deposit; (neuer Abschnitt) paragraph; (Treppenabsatz) landing; (Schuhabsatz) heel; **~gebiet** nt (COMM) market

abschaffen ['apʃafən] vt to abolish, to do away with; **Abschaffung** f abolition

abschalten ['apʃaltən] vt, vi (auch umg) to switch off

abschätzen ['apʃɛtsən] vt to estimate; (Lage) to assess; (Person) to size up

abschätzig ['apʃɛtsɪç] adj disparaging, derogatory

Abschaum ['apʃaʊm] (-(e)s) m scum

Abscheu ['apʃɔʏ] (-(e)s) m loathing, repugnance; **~erregend** repulsive, loathsome; **a~lich** [ap'ʃɔʏlɪç] adj abominable

abschicken ['apʃɪkən] vt to send off

abschieben ['apʃi:bən] (unreg) vt to push away; (Person) to pack off; (: POL) to deport

Abschied ['apʃi:t] (-(e)s, -e) m parting; (von Armee) discharge; **(von jdm) ~ nehmen** vr to say goodbye (to sb), to take one's leave (of sb); **seinen ~ nehmen** (MIL) to apply for discharge; **~sbrief** m farewell letter; **~sfeier** f farewell party

abschießen ['apʃi:sən] (unreg) vt (Flugzeug) to shoot down; (Geschoss) to fire

abschirmen ['apʃɪrmən] vt to screen

abschlagen ['apʃla:gən] (unreg) vt (abhacken, COMM) to knock off; (ablehnen, MIL) to repel

abschlägig ['apʃlɛ:gɪç] adj negative

Abschlagszahlung f interim payment

Abschlepp- ['apʃlɛp] zW: **~dienst** m (AUT) breakdown service (BRIT), towing company (US); **a~en** vt (in tow) to take in tow; **~seil** nt towrope

abschließen ['apʃli:sən] (unreg) vt (Tür) to lock; (beenden) to conclude, to finish; (Vertrag, Handel) to conclude ♦ vr (sich isolieren) to cut o.s. off; **~d** adj concluding

Abschluss ▲ ['apʃlʊs] m (Beendigung) close, conclusion; (COMM: Bilanz) balancing; (von Vertrag, Handel) conclusion; **zum ~** in conclusion; **~feier** f (SCH) end of term party; **~prüfung** f final exam

abschneiden ['apʃnaɪdən] (unreg) vt to cut off ♦ vi to do, to come off

Abschnitt ['apʃnɪt] m section; (MIL) sector; (Kontrollabschnitt) counterfoil; (MATH) segment; (Zeitabschnitt) period

abschrauben ['apʃraʊbən] vt to unscrew

abschrecken ['apʃrɛkən] vt to deter, to put off; (mit kaltem Wasser) to plunge in cold water; **~d** adj deterrent; **~des Beispiel** warning

abschreiben ['apʃraɪbən] (unreg) vt to copy; (verloren geben) to write off; (COMM) to deduct

Abschrift ['apʃrɪft] f copy

Abschuss ▲ ['apʃʊs] m (eines Geschützes) firing; (Herunterschießen) shooting down; (Tötung) shooting

abschüssig ['apʃʏsɪç] adj steep

abschwächen ['apʃvɛçən] vt to lessen; (Behauptung, Kritik) to tone down ♦ vr to lessen

abschweifen ['apʃvaɪfən] vi to digress

abschwellen ['apʃvɛlən] (unreg) vi (Geschwulst) to go down; (Lärm) to die down

abschwören ['apʃvø:rən] vi (+dat) to renounce

absehbar [apze:ba:r] adj foreseeable; **in ~er Zeit** in the foreseeable future;

das Ende ist ~ the end is in sight

absehen [ˈapzeːən] (unreg) vt (Ende, Folgen) to foresee ♦ vi: **von etw ~** to refrain from sth; (nicht berücksichtigen) to leave sth out of consideration

abseilen [ˈapzaɪlən] vr (Bergsteiger) to abseil (down)

abseits [ˈapzaɪts] adv out of the way ♦ präp +gen away from; **A~** nt (SPORT) offside

absenden [ˈapzɛndən] (unreg) vt to send off, to dispatch

Absender (-s, -) m sender

absetzen [ˈapzɛtsən] vt (niederstellen, aussteigen lassen) to put down; (abnehmen) to take off; (COMM: verkaufen) to sell; (FIN: abziehen) to deduct; (entlassen) to dismiss; (König) to depose; (streichen) to drop; (hervorheben) to pick out ♦ vr (sich entfernen) to clear off; (sich ablagern) to be deposited

Absetzung f (FIN: Abzug) deduction; (Entlassung) dismissal; (von König) deposing

absichern [ˈapzɪçərn] vt to make safe; (schützen) to safeguard ♦ vr to protect o.s.

Absicht [ˈapzɪçt] f intention; **mit ~** on purpose; **a~lich** adj intentional, deliberate

absinken [ˈapzɪŋkən] (unreg) vi to sink; (Temperatur, Geschwindigkeit) to decrease

absitzen [ˈapzɪtsən] (unreg) vi to dismount ♦ vt (Strafe) to serve

absolut [apzoˈluːt] adj absolute; **A~ismus** m absolutism

absolvieren [apzɔlˈviːrən] vt (SCH) to complete

absonder- [ˈapzɔndər] zW: **~lich** adj odd, strange; **~n** vt to separate; (ausscheiden) to give off, to secrete ♦ vr to cut o.s. off; **A~ung** f separation; (MED) secretion

abspalten [ˈapʃpaltən] vt to split off

abspannen [ˈapʃpanən] vt (Pferde) to unhitch; (Wagen) to uncouple

abspeisen [ˈapʃpaɪzən] vt (fig) to fob sb off

abspenstig [ˈapʃpɛnstɪç] adj: **(jdm) ~ machen** to lure away (from sb)

absperren [ˈapʃpɛrən] vt to block od close off; (Tür) to lock; **Absperrung** f (Vorgang) blocking od closing off; (Sperre) barricade

abspielen [ˈapʃpiːlən] vt (Platte, Tonband) to play; (SPORT: Ball) to pass ♦ vr to happen

Absprache [ˈapʃpraːxə] f arrangement

absprechen [ˈapʃprɛçən] (unreg) vt (vereinbaren) to arrange; **jdm etw ~** to deny sb sth

abspringen [ˈapʃprɪŋən] (unreg) vi to jump down off; (Farbe, Lack) to flake off; (AVIAT) to bale out; (sich distanzieren) to back out

Absprung [ˈapʃprʊŋ] m jump

abspülen [ˈapʃpyːlən] vt to rinse; (Geschirr) to wash up

abstammen [ˈapʃtamən] vi to be descended; (Wort) to be derived; **Abstammung** f descent; derivation

Abstand [ˈapʃtant] m distance; (zeitlich) interval; **davon ~ nehmen, etw zu tun** to refrain from doing sth; **mit ~ der Beste** by far the best

abstatten [ˈapʃtatən] vt (Dank) to give; (Besuch) to pay

abstauben [ˈapʃtaʊbən] vt, vi to dust; (umg: stehlen) to pinch; (:scrounge) to scrounge

Abstecher [ˈapʃtɛçər] (-s, -) m detour

abstehen [ˈapʃteːən] (unreg) vi (Ohren, Haare) to stick out; (entfernt sein) to stand away

absteigen [ˈapʃtaɪgən] (unreg) vi (vom Rad etc) to get off, to dismount; **(in die zweite Liga) ~** to be relegated (to the second division)

abstellen [ˈapʃtɛlən] vt (niederstellen)

to put down; (entfernt stellen) to pull out; (hinstellen: Auto) to park; (ausschalten) to turn od switch off; (Missstand, Unsitte) to stop

Abstellraum m storage room

abstempeln ['apʃtɛmpəln] vt to stamp

absterben ['apʃtɛrbən] (unreg) vi to die; (Körperteil) to go numb

Abstieg ['apʃtiːk] (-(e)s, -e) m descent; (SPORT) relegation; (fig) decline

abstimmen ['apʃtimən] vi to vote ♦ vt: ~ (auf +akk) (Instrument) to tune (to); (Interessen) to match (with); (Termine, Ziele) to fit in (with) ♦ vr to agree

Abstimmung f vote

Abstinenz [apsti'nɛnts] f abstinence; teetotalism; **~ler(in)** (-s, -) m(f) teetotaller

abstoßen ['apʃtoːsən] (unreg) vt to push off od away; (verkaufen) to unload; (anekeln) to repel, to repulse; **~d** adj repulsive

abstrakt [ap'ʃtrakt] adj abstract ♦ adv abstractly, in the abstract

abstreiten ['apʃtraitən] (unreg) vt to deny

Abstrich ['apʃtriç] m (Abzug) cut; (MED) smear; **~e machen** to lower one's sights

abstufen ['apʃtuːfən] vt (Hang) to terrace; (Farben) to shade; (Gehälter) to grade

Absturz ['apʃturts] m fall; (AVIAT) crash

abstürzen ['apʃtyrtsən] vi to fall; (AVIAT) to crash

absuchen ['apzuːxən] vt to scour, to search

absurd [ap'zʊrt] adj absurd

Abszess ▲ [aps'tsɛs] (-es, -e) m abscess

Abt [apt] (-(e)s, ᵉe) m abbot

Abt. abk (= Abteilung) dept.

abtasten ['aptastən] vt to feel, to probe

abtauen ['aptaʊən] vt, vi to thaw

Abtei [ap'taɪ] (-, -en) f abbey

Abteil [ap'taɪl] (-(e)s, -e) nt compart-

ment; **'a~n** vt to divide up; (abtrennen) to divide off; **~ung** f (in Firma, Kaufhaus) department; (in Krankenhaus) section; (MIL) unit

abtippen ['aptipən] vt (Text) to type up

abtransportieren ['aptranspɔrtiːrən] vt to take away, to remove

abtreiben ['aptraibən] (unreg) vt (Boot, Flugzeug) to drive off course; (Kind) to abort ♦ vi to be driven off course; to abort

Abtreibung f abortion

abtrennen ['aptrɛnən] vt (lostrennen) to detach; (entfernen) to take off; (abteilen) to separate off

abtreten ['aptreːtən] (unreg) vt to wear out; (überlassen) to hand over, to cede ♦ vi to go off; (zurücktreten) to step down

Abtritt ['aptrit] m resignation

abtrocknen ['aptrɔknən] vt, vi to dry

abtun ['aptuːn] (unreg) vt (fig) to dismiss

abwägen ['apvɛːgən] (unreg) vt to weigh up

abwälzen ['apvɛltsən] vt (Schuld, Verantwortung): ~ **(auf** +akk) to shift (onto)

abwandeln ['apvandəln] vt to adapt

abwandern ['apvandərn] vi to move away; (FIN) to be transferred

abwarten ['apvartən] vt to wait for ♦ vi to wait

abwärts ['apvɛrts] adv down

Abwasch ['apvaʃ] (-(e)s) m washing-up; **a~en** (unreg) vt (Schmutz) to wash off; (Geschirr) to wash (up)

Abwasser ['apvasər] (-s, -wässer) nt sewage

abwechseln ['apvɛksəln] vi, vr to alternate; (Personen) to take turns; **~d** adj alternate; **Abwechslung** f change; **abwechslungsreich** adj varied

abwegig ['apveːgiç] adj wrong

Abwehr ['apveːr] (-) f defence; (Schutz) protection; (~dienst) counterintelligence (service); **a~en** vt to ward off; (Ball) to stop

bweichen ['apvaɪçən] (unreg) vi to deviate; (Meinung) to differ

bweisen ['apvaɪzən] (unreg) vt to turn away; (Antrag) to turn down; **~d** adj (Haltung) cold

bwenden ['apvɛndən] (unreg) vt to avert ♦ vr to turn away

bwerfen ['apvɛrfən] (unreg) vt to throw off; (Profit) to yield; (aus Flugzeug) to drop; (Spielkarte) to discard

bwerten ['apvɛrtən] vt (FIN) to devalue

bwertend adj (Worte, Sinn) pejorative

bwertung f (von Währung) devaluation

bwesend ['apveːzənt] adj absent

bwesenheit f ['apveːzənhaɪt] f absence

bwickeln ['apvɪkəln] vt to unwind; (Geschäft) to wind up

bwimmeln ['apvɪməln] (umg) vt (Menschen) to get shot of

bwischen ['apvɪʃən] vt to wipe off od away; (putzen) to wipe

bwurf ['apvʊrf] m throwing off; (von Bomben etc) dropping; (von Reiter, SPORT) throw

bwürgen ['apvʏrgən] vt to scotch; (Motor) to stall

bzahlen ['aptsaːlən] vt to pay off

bzählen ['aptsɛːlən] vt, vi to count (up)

bzahlung f repayment; **auf ~ kaufen** to buy on hire purchase

bzapfen ['aptsapfən] vt to draw off; **jdm Blut ~** to take blood from sb

bzäunen ['aptsɔʏnən] vt to fence off

bzeichen ['aptsaɪçən] nt badge; (Orden) decoration

bzeichnen ['aptsaɪçnən] vt to draw, to copy; (Dokument) to initial ♦ vr to stand out; (fig: bevorstehen) to loom

bziehen ['aptsiːən] (unreg) vt to take

off; (Tier) to skin; (Bett) to strip; (Truppen) to withdraw; (subtrahieren) to take away, to subtract; (kopieren) to run off ♦ vi to go away; (Truppen) to withdraw

abzielen ['aptsiːlən] vi: **~ auf** +akk to be aimed at

Abzug ['aptsuːk] m departure; (von Truppen) withdrawal; (Kopie) copy; (Subtraktion) subtraction; (Betrag) deduction; (Rauchabzug) flue; (von Waffen) trigger

abzüglich ['aptsyːklɪç] präp +gen less

abzweigen ['aptsvaɪgən] vi to branch off ♦ vt to set aside

Abzweigung f junction

ach [ax] excl oh; **~ ja!** (oh) yes; **~ so!** I see; **mit A~ und Krach** by the skin of one's teeth

Achse ['aksə] f axis; (AUT) axle

Achsel ['aksəl] (-, -n) f shoulder; **~höhle** f armpit

acht [axt] num eight; **~ Tage** a week; **A~¹** (-, -en) f eight; (beim Eislaufen etc) figure eight

Acht² (-, -en) f: **~ geben (auf** +akk) to pay attention (to); **sich in ~ nehmen (vor** +dat) to be careful (of), to watch out (for); **etw außer ~ lassen** to disregard sth; **a~bar** adj worthy

acht- zW: **~e(r, s)** adj eighth; **A~el** num eighth; **~en** vt to respect ♦ vi: **~en (auf** +akk) to pay attention to; **~en, dass ...** to be careful that ...

ächten ['ɛçtən] vt to outlaw, to ban

Achterbahn ['axtər-] f roller coaster

achter- zW: **~fach** adj eightfold; **~geben** △ (unreg) vi siehe **Acht²**; **~hundert** num eight hundred; **~los** adj careless; **~mal** adv eight times; **~sam** adj attentive

Achtung ['axtʊŋ] f attention; (Ehrfurcht) respect ♦ excl look out!; (MIL) attention!; **alle ~!** good for you/him etc

achtzehn num eighteen

Spelling Reform: ▲ new spelling △ old spelling (to be phased out)

achtzig num eighty

ächzen ['ɛçtsən] vi to groan

Acker ['akər] (-s, ᷓ) m field; **a~n** vt, vi to plough; (umg) to slog away

ADAC [a:de:'a'tse:] abk = Allgemeiner Deutscher Automobil-Club) ≈ AA, RAC

Adapter [a'daptər] (-s, -) m adapter

addieren [a'di:rən] vt to add (up); **Addition** [aditsi'o:n] f addition

Adel ['a:dəl] (-s) m nobility; **a~ig** adj noble; **a~n** vt to raise to the peerage

Ader ['a:dər] (-, -n) f vein

Adjektiv ['atjɛkti:f] (-s, -e) nt adjective

Adler ['a:dlər] (-s, -) m eagle

adlig adj noble

Adopt- zW: **a~ieren** [adɔp'ti:rən] vt to adopt; **~ion** [adɔptsi'o:n] f adoption; **~iveltern** pl adoptive parents; **~ivkind** nt adopted child

Adressbuch ▲ nt directory; (privat) address book

Adress- zW: **~e** [a'drɛsə] f address; **a~ieren** [adrɛ'si:rən] vt: **a~ieren (an** +akk) to address (to)

Adria ['a:dria] (-) f Adriatic

Advent [at'vɛnt] (-(e)s, -e) m Advent; **~skalender** m Advent calendar; **~skranz** m Advent wreath

Adverb [at'vɛrp] nt adverb

Aerobic [ae'ro:bik] nt aerobics sg

Affäre [a'fɛ:rə] f affair

Affe ['afə] (-n, -n) m monkey

Affekt [a'fɛkt] (-(e)s, -e) m: **im ~ han-deln** to act in the heat of the moment; **a~iert** [afɛk'ti:rt] adj affected

Affen- zW: **a~artig** adj like a monkey; **mit a~artiger Geschwindigkeit** like a flash; **a~hitze** (umg) f incredible heat

affig ['afɪç] adj affected

Afrika ['a:frika] (-s) nt Africa; **~ner(in)** [-'ka:nər(ɪn)] (-s, -) m(f) African; **a~nisch** adj African

AG [a:'ge:] abk (= Aktiengesellschaft) = plc (BRIT), ≈ Inc. (US)

Agent [a'gɛnt] m agent; **~ur** f agency

Aggregat [agre'ga:t] (-(e)s, -e) nt aggregate; (TECH) unit

Aggress- zW: **~ion** [agrɛsi'o:n] f aggression; **a~iv** [agrɛ'si:f] adj aggressive; **~ivität** [agrɛsivi'tɛ:t] f aggressiv-ness

Agrarpolitik [a'gra:r-] f agricultur-policy

Ägypten [ɛ'gyptən] (-s) nt Egyp **ägyptisch** adj Egyptian

aha [a'ha:] excl aha

ähneln ['ɛ:nəln] vi +dat to be like, resemble ♦ vr to be alike od similar

ahnen ['a:nən] vt to suspect; (Tod, C fahr) to have a presentiment of

ähnlich ['ɛ:nlɪç] adj (+dat) similar (to **Ä~keit** f similarity

Ahnung ['a:nʊŋ] f idea, suspicion; p sentiment; **a~slos** adj unsuspecting

Ahorn ['a:hɔrn] (-s, -e) m maple

Ähre ['ɛ:rə] f ear

Aids [e:dz] nt AIDS sg

Airbag ['ɛ:əbɛk] (-s, -s) m airbag

Akademie [akade'mi:] f academ **Aka'demiker(in)** (-s, -) m(f) univers graduate; **akademisch** adj academic

akklimatisieren [aklimati'zi:rən] vr become acclimatized

Akkord [a'kɔrt] (-(e)s, -e) m (MU chord); **im ~ arbeiten** to do piecewo

Akkordeon [a'kɔrdeon] (-s, -s) nt a cordion

Akku ['aku] (-s, -s) m rechargeab battery

Akkusativ ['akuzati:f] (-s, -e) m acc sative

Akne ['akna] f acne

Akrobat(in) [akro'ba:t(ɪn)] (-en, -e m(f) acrobat

Akt [akt] (-(e)s, -e) m act; (KUNST) nud **Akte** ['aktə] f file

Akten- zW: **~koffer** m attaché cas **a~kundig** adj on the files; **~schrar** m filing cabinet; **~tasche** f briefcase

Aktie ['aktsiə] f share

Aktien- zW: **~gesellschaft** f pub limited company; **~index** (-(es), -e **-indices**) m share index; **~kurs** share price

ktion [aktsi'o:n] f campaign; (Poli-
zeiaktion, Suchaktion) action

ktionär [aktsio'nɛ:r] (-s, -e) m shareholder

ktiv [ak'ti:f] adj active; (MIL) regular;
~ieren [-'vi:rən] vt to activate; **A~i'tät**
f activity

ktualität [aktuali'tɛ:t] f topicality; (einer Mode) up-to-dateness

ktuell [aktu'ɛl] adj topical; up-to-date

kupunktur [akupuŋk'tu:ər] f acu-
puncture

kustik [a'kʊstik] f acoustics pl

kut [a'ku:t] adj acute

kzent [ak'tsɛnt] m accent; (Betonung)
stress

kzeptabel [aktsɛp'ta:bl] adj acceptable

kzeptieren [aktsɛp'ti:rən] vt to accept

larm [a'larm] (-(e)s, -e) m alarm;
a~bereit adj standing by; **~bereit-
schaft** f stand-by; **a~ieren** [-'mi:rən]
vt to alarm

lbanien [al'ba:niən] (-s) nt Albania

lbanisch adj Albanian

lbern [albərn] adj silly

lbtraum ▲ [alptraʊm] m nightmare

lbum [album] (-s, Alben) nt album

lge [algə] f algae

lgebra [algebra] (-) f algebra

lgerier(in) [al'ge:ri:r] (-s, -) m(f) Algerian

lgerisch adj Algerian

lias [a:lias] adv alias

libi [a:libi] (-s, -s) nt alibi

limente [ali'mɛntə] pl alimony sg

lkohol [alkohɔl] (-s, -e) m alcohol;
a~frei adj non-alcoholic; **~iker(in)**
[alko'ho:likər(in)] (-s, -) m(f) alcoholic;
a~isch adj alcoholic; **~verbot** nt ban
on alcohol

ll [al] (-s) nt universe

ll'abendlich adj every evening

llbekannt adj universally known

---

alle(r, s) ['alə,r,s] adj 1 (sämtliche) all;
wir alle all of us; **alle Kinder waren
da** all the children were there; **alle
Kinder mögen ...** all children like ...;
alle beide both of us/them; **sie kamen alle** they all came; **alles Gute** all
the best; **alles in allem** all in all
2 (mit Zeit- oder Maßangaben) every;
alle vier Jahre every four years; **alle
fünf Meter** every five metres
♦ pron everything; **alles was er sagt**
everything he says, all that he says
♦ adv (zu Ende, aufgebraucht) finished;
die Milch ist alle the milk's all gone,
there's no milk left; **etw alle machen**
to finish sth up

Allee [a'le:] f avenue

allein [a'laɪn] adv alone; (ohne Hilfe) on
one's own, by oneself ♦ konj but, only;
nicht ~ (nicht nur) not only; **~ste-
hend** single; **A~erziehende(r)** f(m)
single parent; **A~gang** m: **im A~gang**
on one's own

allemal ['alə'ma:l] adv (jedes Mal) always; (ohne weiteres) with no bother;
siehe Mal

allenfalls ['alən'fals] adv at all events;
(höchstens) at most

aller- ['alər] zW: **~beste(r, s)** very
best; **~dings** adv (zwar) admittedly;
(gewiss) certainly

Allergie [aler'gi:] f allergy; **al'lergisch**
adj allergic

aller- zW: **~hand** (umg) adj inv all sorts
of; **das ist doch ~hand!** that's a bit
much; **~hand!** (lobend) good show!;
A~heiligen nt All Saints' Day

Allerheiligen (All Saints' Day) is
celebrated on November 1st and is a
public holiday in some parts of Ger-

---

many and in Austria. **Allerseelen**
(All Souls' Day) is celebrated on November 2nd in the Roman Catholic
Church. It is customary to visit cem-
eteries and place lighted candles on
the graves of relatives and friends.

aller- zW: **~höchstens** adv at the very
most; **~lei** adj inv all sorts of; **~letz-**
te(r, s) adj very last; **A~seelen** (-s) nt
All Souls' Day; **~seits** adv on all sides;
prost **~seits!** cheers everyone!

Allerwelts- in zW (Durchschnitts-) common; (nichts sagend) commonplace

alles pron everything; **~** in allem all in
all; **~** Gute! all the best!

Alleskleber (-s, -) m multi-purpose
glue

allgemein ['algəmaɪn] adj general; im
A~en in general; **~** gültig generally
accepted; **A~wissen** nt general
knowledge

Alliierte(r) [ali'i:rtə(r)] m ally

all- zW: **~jährlich** adj annual;
~mächtig adj almighty; **~mählich** adj
gradual; **A~tag** m everyday life;
~täglich adj, adv daily; (gewöhnlich)
commonplace; **~tags** adv on week-
days; **~'wissend** adj omniscient; **~zu**
adv all too; **~** oft all too often; **~** viel
too much

Allzweck- ['altsvɛk-] in zW multi-
purpose

Alm [alm] (-, -en) f alpine pasture

Almosen ['almo:zən] (-s, -) nt alms pl

Alpen ['alpən] pl Alps; **~vorland** nt
foothills pl of the Alps

Alphabet [alfa'be:t] (-(e)s, -e) nt
alphabet; **a~isch** adj alphabetical

Alptraum ['alptraʊm] m = Albtraum

SCHLÜSSELWORT

als [als] konj 1 (zeitlich) when; (gleichzeitig) as; **damals, als ...** in the (days)
when ...; **gerade, als ...** just as ...
  2 (in der Eigenschaft) than; als Antwort as an answer; als Kind as a

child
  3 (bei Vergleichen) than; **ich ka**
später als er I came later than h
(did) od later than him; **lieber ... als**
rather ... than ...; **nichts als Ärg**
nothing but trouble
  4: **als ob/wenn** as if

also ['alzo:] konj so; (folglich) therefor
~ gut od schön! okay then; **~, s**
was! well really!; **na ~!** there you a
then!

Alsterwasser ['alstər-] nt shand
(BRIT), beer and lemonade

Alt [alt] (-s, -e) m (MUS) alto

alt adj old; alles beim A~en lassen t
leave everything as it was

Altar [al'ta:r] (-(e)s, -äre) m altar

Alt- zW: **A~bau** m old buildin
a~bekannt adj long-known; **~bier**
top-fermented German dark beer; **~'e**
sen nt scrap iron

Alten(wohn)heim nt old people
home

Alter ['altər] (-s, -) nt age; (hohes) o
age; im **~** von at the age of; **a~n** vi
grow old, to age

Alters- zW: **~grenze** f age limi
~heim nt old people's home; **~rente**
old age pension; **a~schwach** a
(Mensch) frail; **~versorgung** f old ag
pension

Altertum ['altərtu:m] nt antiquity

alt- zW: **A~glas** nt glass for recycling
A~glascontainer m bottle ban
~klug adj precocious; **~modisch** a
old-fashioned; **A~papier** nt waste pa
per; **A~stadt** f old town

Alufolie ['a:lufo:liə] f aluminium foil

Aluminium [alu'mi:niɔm] (-s) nt al-
minium, aluminum (US)

Alzheimerkrankheit ['alt
haɪmər'kraŋkhaɪt] f Alzheimer's (di
ease)

am [am] = an dem; **~** Schlafen; (um

sleeping; **~ 15. März** on March 15th;
~ besten/schönsten best/most beautiful

mateur [ama'tøːr] *m* amateur

mboss ▲ ['ambɔs] **(-es, -e)** *m* anvil

mbulant [ambu'lant] *adj* outpatient

Ambulanz *f* outpatients *sg*

meise ['aːmaɪzə] *f* ant

meisenhaufen *m* ant hill

merika [a'meːrika] **(-s)** *nt* America;
~ner(in) [-'kaːnər(ɪn)] **(-s, -)** *m(f)*
American; **a~nisch** [-'kaːnɪʃ] *adj*
American

mnestie [amnɛs'tiː] *f* amnesty

mpel ['ampəl] **(-, -n)** *f* traffic lights *pl*

mputieren [ampu'tiːrən] *vt* to amputate

msel ['amzəl] **(-, -n)** *f* blackbird

mt [amt] **(-(e)s, er)** *nt* office; **(Pflicht)**
duty; **(TEL)** exchange; **a~ieren**
[am'tiːrən] *vi* to hold office; **a~lich** *adj*
official

mts- *zW:* **~richter** *m* district judge;
~stunden *pl* office hours; **~zeichen** *nt*
dialling tone; **~zeit** *f* period of office

müsant [amy'zant] *adj* amusing

müsieren [amy'ziːrən] *vt* to amuse
♦ *vr* to enjoy o.s.

müsierviertel *nt* nightclub district

SCHLÜSSELWORT

n [an] *präp +dat* 1 **(räumlich: wo?)** at;
(auf, bei) on; **(nahe bei)** near; **an diesem Ort** in this place; **an der Wand** on the wall; **zu nahe an etw** too near to sth; **unten am Fluss** down by the river; **Köln liegt am Rhein** Cologne is on the Rhine

2 **(zeitlich: wann?)** on; **an diesem Tag** on this day; **an Ostern** at Easter

3: **arm an Fett** low in fat; **an etw sterben** to die of sth; **an (und für) sich** actually

♦ *präp +akk* 1 **(räumlich: wohin?)** to; **er ging ans Fenster** he went (over) to

---

the window; **etw an die Wand hängen/schreiben** to hang/write sth on the wall

2 **(zeitlich: woran?): an etw denken** to think of sth

3 **(gerichtet an)** to; **ein Gruß/eine Frage an dich** greetings/a question to you

♦ *adv* 1 **(ungefähr)** about; **an die hundert** about a hundred

2 **(auf Fahrplänen): Frankfurt an 18.30** arriving Frankfurt 18.30

3 **(ab): von dort/heute an** from there/today onwards

4 **(angeschaltet, angezogen)** on; **das Licht ist an** the light is on; **ohne etwas an** with nothing on; *siehe auch* **am**

---

analog [ana'loːk] *adj* analogous; **A~ie** [-'giː] *f* analogy

Analphabet(in) [an|alfa'beːt(ɪn)] **(-en, -en)** *m(f)* illiterate (person)

Analyse [ana'lyːzə] *f* analysis

analysieren [analy'ziːrən] *vt* to analyse

Ananas ['ananas] **(-, - *od* -se)** *f* pineapple

Anarchie [anar'çiː] *f* anarchy

Anatomie [anato'miː] *f* anatomy

anbahnen ['anbaːnən] *vt, vr* to open up

Anbau ['anbaʊ] *m* **(AGR)** cultivation; **(Gebäude)** extension; **a~en** *vt* **(AGR)** to cultivate; **(Gebäudeteil)** to build on

anbehalten ['anbəhaltən] **(unreg)** *vt* to keep on

anbei [an'baɪ] *adv* enclosed

anbeißen ['anbaɪsən] **(unreg)** *vt* to bite into ♦ *vi* to bite; **(fig)** to swallow the bait; **zum A~ (umg)** good enough to eat

anbelangen ['anbəlaŋən] *vt* to concern; **was mich anbelangt** as far as I am concerned

---

Spelling Reform: ▲ *new spelling* △ *old spelling (to be phased out)*

anbeten ['anbe:tən] vt to worship

Anbetracht ['anbətraxt] m: **in ~** +gen in view of

anbieten ['anbi:tən] (unreg) vt to offer ♦ vr to volunteer

anbinden ['anbındən] (unreg) vt to tie up; **kurz angebunden** (fig) curt

Anblick ['anblık] m sight; **a~en** vt to look at

anbraten ['anbra:tən] vt to brown

anbrechen ['anbrɛçən] (unreg) vt to start; (Vorräte) to break into ♦ vi to start; (Tag) to break; (Nacht) to fall

anbrennen ['anbrɛnən] (unreg) vi to catch fire; (KOCH) to burn

anbringen ['anbrıŋən] (unreg) vt to bring; (Ware) to sell; (festmachen) to fasten

Anbruch ['anbrʊx] m beginning; **~ des Tages/der Nacht** dawn/nightfall

anbrüllen ['anbrʏlən] vt to roar at

Andacht ['andaxt] (-, -en) f devotion; (Gottesdienst) prayers pl; **andächtig** adj ['andɛçtıç] devout

andauern ['andaʊərn] vi to last, to go on; **~d** adj continual

Anden ['andən] pl Andes

Andenken ['andɛŋkən] (-s, -) nt memory; souvenir

andere(r, s) ['andərə(r, z)] adj other; (verschieden) different; **ein ~s Mal** another time; **kein ~r** nobody else; **von etw ~m sprechen** to talk about something else; **~rseits** adv on the other hand

andermal adv: **ein ~** some other time

ändern ['ɛndərn] vt to alter, to change ♦ vr to change

andernfalls ['andərnfals] adv otherwise

anders ['andərs] adj: **~ (als)** differently (from); **wer ~?** who else?; **jd/ irgendwo ~** sb/somewhere else; **~ aussehen/klingen** to look/sound different; **~artig** adj different; **~herum** adv the other way round; **~wo** adv somewhere else; **~woher** adv from

somewhere else

anderthalb ['andərt'halp] adj one and a half

Änderung ['ɛndərʊŋ] f alteration change

Änderungsschneiderei f tailor (wh does alterations)

anderweitig ['andər'vaitıç] adj othe ♦ adv otherwise; (anderswo) elsewhere

andeuten ['andɔYtən] vt to indicate (Wink geben) to hint at; **Andeutung** indication; hint

Andrang ['andraŋ] m crush

andrehen ['andre:ən] vt to turn switch on; **jdm etw ~** (umg) to un load sth onto sb

androhen ['andro:ən] vt: **jdm etw** to threaten sb with sth

aneignen ['an|aignən] vt: **sich dat etw ~** to acquire sth; (widerrechtlich) to ap propriate sth

aneinander [an|ai'nandər] adv at/on to etc one another od each other; **~ g raten** to clash

Anekdote [anɛk'do:tə] f anecdote

anekeln ['an|e:kəln] vt to disgust

anerkannt ['an|ɛrkant] adj recognize acknowledged

anerkennen ['an|ɛrkɛnən] (unreg) vt recognize, to acknowledge; (würdige to appreciate; **~d** adj appreciative

Anerkennung f recognition, acknow edgement; appreciation

anfachen ['anfaxən] vt to fan in flame; (fig) to kindle

anfahren ['anfa:rən] (unreg) vt to deli er; (fahren gegen) to hit; (Hafen) to put into; (fig) to bawl out ♦ vi to drive up (losfahren) to drive off

Anfahrt ['anfa:rt] f (~sweg, ~szeit) jou ney

Anfall ['anfal] m (MED) attack; **a~e** (unreg) vt to attack; (fig) to overcom ♦ vi (Arbeit) to come up; (Produkt) be obtained

anfällig ['anfɛlıç] adj delicate; **~ fü etw** prone to sth

nfang ['anfaŋ] (-(e)s, -fänge) m beginning, start; **von ~ an** right from the beginning; **zu ~** at the beginning; **~ Mai** at the beginning of May; **a~en** (unreg) vt, vi to begin, to start; (machen) to do

nfänger(in) ['anfɛŋər(ɪn)] (-s, -) m(f) beginner

nfänglich ['anfɛŋlɪç] adj initial

nfangs adv at first; **A~buchstabe** m initial od first letter; **A~gehalt** nt starting salary

nfassen ['anfasən] vt to handle; (berühren) to touch ♦ vi to lend a hand ♦ vr to feel

nfechten ['anfɛçtən] (unreg) vt to dispute

nfertigen ['anfɛrtɪgən] vt to make

nfeuern ['anfɔʏərn] vt (fig) to spur on

nflehen ['anfleːən] vt to implore

nfliegen ['anfliːgən] (unreg) vt to fly to

nflug ['anfluːk] m (AVIAT) approach; (Spur) trace

nfordern ['anfɔrdərn] vt to demand; (COMM) to requisition

nforderung f (+gen) demand (for)

nfrage ['anfraːgə] f inquiry; **a~n** vi to inquire

nfreunden ['anfrɔʏndən] vr to make friends

nfügen ['anfyːgən] vt to add; (beifügen) to enclose

nfühlen ['anfyːlən] vt, vr to feel

nführen ['anfyːrən] vt to lead; (zitieren) to quote; (umg: betrügen) to lead up the garden path

nführer m leader

nführungszeichen pl quotation marks, inverted commas

ngabe ['angaːbə] f statement; (TECH) specification; (umg: Prahlerei) boasting; (SPORT) service

ngeben ['angeːbən] (unreg) vt to give; (anzeigen) to inform on; (bestimmen) to set ♦ vi (umg) to boast; (SPORT) to serve

Angeber (-s, -) (umg) m show-off; **Angeberei** (umg) f showing off

angeblich ['angeːplɪç] adj alleged

angeboren ['angəboːrən] adj inborn, innate

Angebot ['angəboːt] nt offer; **~ (an** +dat) (COMM) supply (of)

angebracht ['angəbraxt] adj appropriate, in order

angegriffen ['angəgrɪfən] adj exhausted

angeheitert ['angəhaɪtərt] adj tipsy

angehen ['angeːən] (unreg) vt to concern; (angreifen) to attack; (bitten): **jdn ~ (um)** to approach sb (for) ♦ vi (Feuer) to light; (umg: beginnen) to begin; **~d** adj prospective

angehören ['angəhøːrən] vi (+ dat) to belong to; (Partei) to be a member of

Angehörige(r) ['angəhøːrɪgə(r)] f(m) relative

Angeklagte(r) ['angəklaːkta(r)] f(m) accused

Angel ['aŋəl] (-, -n) f fishing rod; (Türangel) hinge

Angelegenheit ['angələgənhaɪt] f affair, matter

Angel- zW: **~haken** m fish hook; **a~n** vt to catch ♦ vi to fish; **~n (-s)** nt angling, fishing; **~rute** f fishing rod; **~schein** m fishing permit

angemessen ['angəmɛsən] adj appropriate, suitable

angenehm ['angəneːm] adj pleasant; **~!** (bei Vorstellung) pleased to meet you

angeregt [angəreːkt] adj animated, lively

angesehen ['angəzeːən] adj respected

angesichts ['angəzɪçts] präp +gen in view of, considering

angespannt ['angəʃpant] adj (Aufmerksamkeit) close; (Arbeit) hard

Angestellte(r) ['angəʃtɛlta(r)] f(m) employee

angestrengt ['angəʃtrɛŋt] adv as hard as one can

angetan ['angəta:n] adj: **von jdm/etw ~ sein** to be impressed by sb/sth; **es jdm ~ haben** to appeal to sth

angetrunken ['angətruŋkən] adj tipsy

angewiesen ['angəvi:zən] adj: **auf jdn/etw ~ sein** to be dependent on sb/sth

angewöhnen ['angəvø:nən] vt: **jdm/sich etw ~** to get sb/become accustomed to sth

Angewohnheit ['angəvo:nhait] f habit

angleichen ['anglaiçən] (unreg) vt, vr to adjust

Angler ['aŋlər] (-s, -) m angler

angreifen ['angraifən] (unreg) vt to attack; (beschädigen) to damage

Angreifer (-s, -) m attacker

Angriff ['angrif] m attack; **etw in ~ nehmen** to make a start on sth

Angst (-, -e) f fear; **jdm ist a~** sb is afraid od scared; **~ haben (vor** +dat) to be afraid od scared (of); **~ haben um jdn/etw** to be worried about sb/sth; **jdm ~ machen** to scare sb; **~hase** (umg) m chicken, scaredy-cat

ängst- ['ɛŋst] zW: **~igen** vt to frighten ♦ vr: **sich ~igen (vor** +dat od um) to worry (o.s.) (about); **~lich** adj nervous; (besorgt) worried; **A~lichkeit** f nervousness

anhaben ['anha:bən] (unreg) vt to have on; **er kann mir nichts ~** he can't hurt me

anhalt- ['anhalt] zW: **~en** (unreg) vt to stop ♦ vi to stop; (andauern) to persist; **(jdm) etw ~en** to hold sth up (against sb); **jdn zur Arbeit/Höflichkeit ~en** to make sb work/be polite; **~end** adj persistent; **A~er(in)** (-s, -) m(f) hitchhiker; **per A~er fahren** to hitch-hike; **A~spunkt** m clue

anhand [an'hant] präp +gen with

Anhang ['anhaŋ] m appendix; (Leute)

family; supporters pl

anhäng- ['anhɛŋ] zW: **~en** (unreg) vt to hang up; (Wagen) to couple up; (Zusatz) to add (on); **A~er** (-s, -) m supporter; (AUT) trailer; (am Koffer) tag; (Schmuck) pendant; **A~erschaft** f supporters pl; **~lich** adj devoted; **A~lichkeit** f devotion; **A~sel** (-s, -) m appendage

Anhäufung ['anhɔyfuŋ] f accumulation

anheben ['anhe:bən] (unreg) vt to lift up; (Preise) to raise

anheizen ['anhaitsən] vt (Stimmung) to lift; (Moral) to boost

Anhieb ['anhi:b] m: **auf ~** at the very first go; (kurz entschlossen) on the spur of the moment

Anhöhe ['anhø:ə] f hill

anhören ['anhø:rən] vt to listen to; (anmerken) to hear ♦ vr to sound

animieren [ani'mi:rən] vt to encourage, to urge on

Anis [a'ni:s] (-es, -e) m aniseed

Ank. abk (= Ankunft) arr.

Ankauf ['ankauf] m (von Wertpapieren, Devisen, Waren) purchase; **a~en** vt to purchase, to buy

Anker ['aŋkər] (-s, -) m anchor; **vor ~ gehen** to drop anchor

Anklage ['ankla:gə] f accusation; (JUR) charge; **~bank** f dock; **a~n** vt to accuse; **jdn (eines Verbrechens) a~n** (JUR) to charge sb (with a crime)

Ankläger ['anklɛ:gər] m accuser

Anklang ['anklaŋ] m: **bei jdm ~ finden** to meet with sb's approval

Ankleidekabine f changing cubicle

ankleiden ['anklaidən] vt, vr to dress

anklopfen ['anklɔpfən] vi to knock

anknüpfen ['anknypfən] vt to fasten od tie on; (fig) to start ♦ vi (anschließen): **~ an** +akk to refer to

ankommen ['ankɔmən] (unreg) vi to arrive; (näher kommen) to approach; (Anklang finden): **bei jdm (gut) ~** to go down well with sb; **es kommt**

rauf an it depends; (*wichtig sein*) that (is what) matters; **es darauf ~ lassen** to let things take their course; **gegen jdn/etw ~** to cope with sb/sth; **bei jdm schlecht ~** to go down badly with sb

ankreuzen ['ankrɔytsən] *vt* to mark with a cross; (*hervorheben*) to highlight

ankündigen ['ankʏndɪgən] *vt* to announce; **Ankündigung** *f* announcement

Ankunft ['ankʊnft] (-, -künfte) *f* arrival; **~szeit** *f* time of arrival

ankurbeln ['ankʊrbəln] *vt* (*fig*) to boost

Anlage ['anla:gə] *f* disposition; (*Begabung*) talent; (*Park*) gardens *pl*; (*Beilage*) enclosure; (*TECH*) plant; (*FIN*) investment; (*Entwurf*) layout

Anlass ▲ ['anlas] (-es, -lässe) *m*: ~ (**zu**) cause (for); (*Ereignis*) occasion; **aus ~ +gen** on the occasion of; **~ zu etw geben** to give rise to sth; **etw zum ~ nehmen** to take the opportunity of sth

anlassen (*unreg*) *vt* to leave on; (*Motor*) to start ♦ *vr* (*umg*) to start off

Anlasser (-s, -) *m* (*AUT*) starter

anlässlich ▲ ['anlɛslɪç] *präp +gen* on the occasion of

Anlauf ['anlauf] *m* run-up; **a~en** (*unreg*) *vi* to begin; (*neuer Film*) to show; (*SPORT*) to run up; (*Fenster*) to mist up; (*Metall*) to tarnish ♦ *vt* to call at; **rot a~en** to blush; **angelaufen kommen** to come running up

anlegen ['anle:gən] *vt* to put; (*anziehen*) to put on; (*gestalten*) to lay out; (*Geld*) to invest ♦ *vi* to dock; **etw an etw** *akk* **~** to put sth against or on sth; **ein Gewehr ~ (auf** +*akk*) to aim a weapon (at); **es auf etw** *akk* **~ sein** to be out for sth/to do sth; **sich mit jdm ~** (*umg*) to quarrel with sb

Anlegestelle *f* landing place

anlehnen ['anle:nən] *vt* to lean; (*Tür*) to leave ajar; (**sich**) **an etw** *akk* **~** to lean on/against sth

Anleihe ['anlaɪə] *f* (*FIN*) loan

anleiten ['anlaɪtən] *vt* to instruct; **Anleitung** *f* instructions *pl*

anliegen ['anli:gən] *vi* (*unreg*) (*Kleidung*) to cling; **A~** (-s, -) *nt* matter; (*Wunsch*) wish; **~d** *adj* adjacent; (*beigefügt*) enclosed

Anlieger (-s, -) *m* resident; **„~ frei"** "residents only"

anmachen ['anmaxən] *vt* to attach; (*Elektrisches*) to put on; (*Zigarette*) to light; (*Salat*) to dress

anmaßen ['anma:sən] *vt*: **sich** *dat* **etw ~** (*Recht*) to lay claim to sth; **~d** *adj* arrogant

Anmaßung *f* presumption

anmelden ['anmɛldən] *vt* to announce ♦ *vr* (*sich ankündigen*) to make an appointment; (*polizeilich, für Kurs etc*) to register

Anmeldung *f* announcement; appointment; registration

anmerken ['anmɛrkən] *vt* to observe; (*anstreichen*) to mark; **sich** *dat* **nichts ~ lassen** to not give anything away

Anmerkung *f* note

anmieten ['anmi:tən] *vt* to rent; (*auch Auto*) to hire

Anmut ['anmu:t] (-) *f* grace; **a~en** *vt* to give a feeling; **a~ig** *adj* charming

annähen ['annɛ:ən] *vt* to sew on

annähern ['annɛ:ərn] *vr* to get closer; **~d** *adj* approximate

Annäherung *f* approach

Annäherungsversuch *m* advances *pl*

Annahme ['anna:mə] *f* acceptance; (*Vermutung*) assumption

annehm- ['anne:m] *zW*: **~bar** *adj* acceptable; **~en** (*unreg*) *vt* to accept; (*Namen*) to take; (*Kind*) to adopt; (*vermuten*) to suppose, to assume ♦ *vr* (+*gen*) to take care (of); **A~lichkeit** *f*

Spelling Reform: ▲ new spelling △ old spelling (to be phased out)

comfort

Annonce [a'nõːsə] *f* advertisement

annoncieren [anõ'siːrən] *vt, vi* to advertise

annullieren [anʊ'liːrən] *vt* to annul

anonym [ano'nyːm] *adj* anonymous

Anorak ['anorak] (**-s, -s**) *m* anorak

anordnen ['anˌɔrdnən] *vt* to arrange; (*befehlen*) to order

Anordnung *f* arrangement; order

anorganisch ['anˌɔrgaːnɪʃ] *adj* inorganic

anpacken ['anpakən] *vt* to grasp; (*fig*) to tackle; **mit ~** to lend a hand

anpassen ['anpasən] *vt*: **(jdm) ~** to fit (on sb); (*fig*) to adapt ♦ *vr* to adapt

anpassungsfähig *adj* adaptable

Anpfiff ['anpfɪf] *m* (*SPORT*) (starting) whistle; kick-off; (*umg*) rocket

anprallen ['anpralən] *vi*: **~ (gegen** *od* **an** *+akk***)** to collide (with)

anprangern ['anpraŋərn] *vt* to denounce

anpreisen ['anpraɪzən] (*unreg*) *vt* to extol

Anprobe ['anproːbə] *f* trying on

anprobieren ['anprobiːrən] *vt* to try on

anrechnen ['anrɛçnən] *vt* to charge; (*fig*) to count; **jdm etw hoch ~** to think highly of sb for sth

Anrecht ['anrɛçt] *nt*: **~ (auf** *+akk***)** right (to)

Anrede ['anreːdə] *f* form of address; **a~n** *vt* to address; (*belästigen*) to accost

anregen ['anreːgən] *vt* to stimulate; **angeregte Unterhaltung** lively discussion; **~d** *adj* stimulating

Anregung *f* stimulation; (*Vorschlag*) suggestion

anreichern ['anraɪçərn] *vt* to enrich

Anreise ['anraɪzə] *f* journey; **a~n** *vi* to arrive

Anreiz ['anraɪts] *m* incentive

Anrichte ['anrɪçtə] *f* sideboard; **a~n** *vt* to serve up; **Unheil a~n** to make mis-

chief

anrüchig ['anrʏçɪç] *adj* dubious

anrücken ['anrʏkən] *vi* to approach (*MIL*) to advance

Anruf ['anruːf] *m* call; **~beantworter** [-bəʔantvɔrtər] (**-s, -**) *m* answering machine; **a~en** (*unreg*) *vt* to call out to (*bitten*) to call on; (*TEL*) to ring up, to phone, to call

ans [ans] **= an das**

Ansage ['anzaːgə] *f* announcement, **a~n** *vt* to announce ♦ *vr* to say one will come; **~r(in)** (**-s, -**) *m(f)* announcer

ansammeln ['anzaməln] *vt* (*Reichtümer*) to amass ♦ *vr* (*Menschen*) to gather, to assemble; (*Wasser*) to collect; **Ansammlung** *f* collection; (*Leute*) crowd

ansässig ['anzɛsɪç] *adj* resident

Ansatz ['anzats] *m* start; (*Haaransatz*) hairline; (*Halsansatz*) base; (*Verlängerungsstück*) extension; (*Veranschlagung*) estimate; **~punkt** *m* starting point

anschaffen ['anʃafən] *vt* to buy, to purchase; **Anschaffung** *f* purchase

anschalten ['anʃaltən] *vt* to switch on

anschau- ['anʃao] *zW*: **~en** *vt* to look at; **~lich** *adj* illustrative; **A~ung** *f* (*Meinung*) view; **aus eigener A~ung** from one's own experience

Anschein ['anʃaɪn] *m* appearance; **allem ~ nach** to all appearances; **den ~ haben** to seem, to appear; **a~end** *adj* apparent

anschieben ['anʃiːbən] *vt* to push

Anschlag ['anʃlaːk] *m* notice; (*Attentat*) attack; (*COMM*) estimate; (*auf Klavier*) touch; (*Schreibmaschine*) character, **a~en** ['anʃlaːgən] (*unreg*) *vt* to put up, (*beschädigen*) to chip; (*Akkord*) to strike; (*Kosten*) to estimate ♦ *vi* to hit, (*wirken*) to have an effect; (*Glocke*) to ring; **an etw** *akk* **a~en** to hit against sth

anschließen ['anʃliːsən] (*unreg*) *vt* to connect up; (*Sender*) to link up ♦ *vi*:

an etw *akk* ~ to adjoin sth; (*zeitlich*) to follow sth ♦ *vr*: **sich jdm/etw** ~ to join sb/sth; (*beipflichten*) to agree with sb/ sth; **sich an etw** *akk* ~ to adjoin sth; ◆**d** *adj* adjacent; (*zeitlich*) subsequent ♦ *adv* afterwards

Anschluss ▲ ['anʃlʊs] *m* (ELEK, EISENB) connection; (*von Wasser etc*) supply; **im ~ an** +*akk* following; ~ **finden** to make friends; **~flug** *m* connecting flight

anschmiegsam ['anʃmiːkzaːm] *adj* affectionate

anschnallen ['anʃnalən] *vt* to buckle on ♦ *vr* to fasten one's seat belt

anschneiden ['anʃnaɪdən] (*unreg*) *vt* to cut into; (*Thema*) to introduce

anschreiben ['anʃraɪbən] (*unreg*) *vt* to write (up); (*COMM*) to charge up; (*benachrichtigen*) to write to

anschreien ['anʃraɪən] (*unreg*) *vt* to shout at

Anschrift ['anʃrɪft] *f* address

Anschuldigung ['anʃʊldɪgʊŋ] *f* accusation

anschwellen ['anʃvɛlən] (*unreg*) *vi* to swell (up)

anschwindeln ['anʃvɪndəln] *vt* to lie to

ansehen ['anzeːən] (*unreg*) *vt* to look at; **jdm etw** ~ to see sth (from sb's face); **jdn/etw als etw** ~ to look on sb/sth as sth; ~ **für** to consider; **A~** (**-s**) *nt* respect; (*Ruf*) reputation

ansehnlich ['anzeːnlɪç] *adj* fine-looking; (*beträchtlich*) considerable

ansetzen ['anzɛtsən] *vt* (*festlegen*) to fix; (*entwickeln*) to develop; (*Fett*) to put on; (*Blätter*) to grow; (*zubereiten*) to prepare ♦ *vi* (*anfangen*) to start, to begin; (*Entwicklung*) to set in; (*dick werden*) to put on weight ♦ *vr* (*Rost etc*) to start to develop; ~ **an** +*akk* (*anfügen*) to fix on to; (*anlegen, an Mund etc*) to put to

Ansicht ['anzɪçt] *f* (*Anblick*) sight; (*Meinung*) view, opinion; **zur** ~ on approval; **meiner** ~ **nach** in my opinion; **~skarte** *f* picture postcard; **~ssache** *f* matter of opinion

ansonsten [an'zɔnstən] *adv* otherwise

anspannen ['anʃpanən] *vt* to harness; (*Muskel*) to strain; **Anspannung** *f* strain

anspielen ['anʃpiːlən] *vi* (SPORT) to start play; **auf etw** *akk* ~ to refer *od* allude to sth

Anspielung *f*: ~ (**auf** +*akk*) reference (to), allusion (to)

Anspitzer ['anʃpɪtsər] (**-s, -**) *m* pencil sharpener

Ansporn ['anʃpɔrn] (**-(e)s**) *m* incentive

Ansprache ['anʃpraːxə] *f* address

ansprechen ['anʃprɛçən] (*unreg*) *vt* to speak to; (*bitten, gefallen*) to appeal to ♦ *vi*: (**auf etw** *akk*) ~ to react (to sth); **jdn auf etw** *akk* (**hin**) ~ to ask sb about sth; ~**d** *adj* attractive

anspringen ['anʃprɪŋən] (*unreg*) *vi* (AUT) to start ♦ *vt* to jump at

Anspruch ['anʃprʊx] *m* (*Recht*): ~ (**auf** +*akk*) claim (to); **hohe Ansprüche stellen/haben** to demand/expect a lot; **jdn/etw in** ~ **nehmen** to occupy sb/take up sth; **a~slos** *adj* undemanding; **a~svoll** *adj* demanding

anstacheln ['anʃtaxəln] *vt* to spur on

Anstalt ['anʃtalt] (**-, -en**) *f* institution; **~en machen, etw zu tun** to prepare to do sth

Anstand ['anʃtant] *m* decency

anständig ['anʃtɛndɪç] *adj* decent; (*umg*) proper; (*groß*) considerable

anstandslos *adv* without any ado

anstarren ['anʃtarən] *vt* to stare at

anstatt [an'ʃtat] *präp* +*gen* instead of ♦ *konj*: ~ **etw zu tun** instead of doing sth

Ansteck- ['anʃtɛk] *zW*: **a~en** *vt* to pin on; (MED) to infect; (*Pfeife*) to light;

Spelling Reform: ▲ *new spelling* △ *old spelling (to be phased out)*

(*Haus*) to set fire to ♦ *vr:* **ich habe mich bei ihm angesteckt** I caught it from him ♦ *vi* (*fig*) to be infectious; **a~end** *adj* infectious; **~ung** *f* infection

anstehen ['anʃteːən] (*unreg*) *vi* to queue (up) (*BRIT*), to line up (*US*)

ansteigen ['anʃtaɪgən] *vt* (*Straße*) to climb; (*Gelände, Temperatur, Preis*) to rise

anstelle, an Stelle [an'ʃtɛlə] *präp +gen* in place of; **~n** ['an-] *vt* (*einschalten*) to turn on; (*Arbeit geben*) to employ; (*machen*) to do ♦ *vr* to queue (up) (*BRIT*), to line up (*US*); (*umg*) to act

Anstellung *f* employment; (*Posten*) post, position

Anstieg ['anʃtiːk] (**-(e)s, -e**) *m* (*+gen*) climb; (*fig: von Preisen etc*) increase (in)

anstiften ['anʃtɪftən] *vt* (*Unglück*) to cause; **jdn zu etw ~** to put sb up to sth

anstimmen ['anʃtɪmən] *vt* (*Lied*) to strike up with; (*Geschrei*) to set up

Anstoß ['anʃtoːs] *m* impetus; (*Ärgernis*) offence; (*SPORT*) kick-off; **der erste ~** the initiative; **~ nehmen an** +*dat* to take offence at; **a~en** (*unreg*) *vt* to push; (*mit Fuß*) to kick ♦ *vi* to knock, to bump; (*mit der Zunge*) to lisp; (*mit Gläsern*): **a~en (auf** +*akk*) to drink (to), to drink a toast (to)

anstößig ['anʃtøːsɪç] *adj* offensive, indecent

anstreichen ['anʃtraɪçən] (*unreg*) *vt* to paint

anstrengen ['anʃtrɛŋən] *vt* to strain; (*JUR*) to bring ♦ *vr* to make an effort; **~d** *adj* tiring

Anstrengung *f* effort

Anstrich ['anʃtrɪç] *m* coat of paint

Ansturm ['anʃturm] *m* rush; (*MIL*) attack

Antarktis [ant'arktɪs] (**-**) *f* Antarctic

antasten ['antastən] *vt* to touch; (*Recht*) to infringe upon; (*Ehre*) to question

Anteil ['antaɪl] (**-s, -e**) *m* share; (*Mitge-*

fühl) sympathy; **~ nehmen** (an +*dat*) to share (in); (*sich interessieren*) to take a interest (in); **~nahme** *f* sympathy

Antenne [an'tɛnə] *f* aerial

Anti- ['anti] *in zW* anti; **~alko'holike** *m* teetotaller; **~autori'tär** *adj* an authoritarian; **~babypille** *f* contrace tive pill; **~biotikum** [antibi'oːtikun (**-s, -ka**) *nt* antibiotic

antik [an'tiːk] *adj* antique; **A~e** *f* (*Ze alter*) ancient world

Antiquariat [antikvari'aːt] (**-(e)s, -**) *nt* secondhand bookshop

Antiquitäten [antikvi'tɛːtən] *pl* a tiques; **~händler** *m* antique dealer

Antrag ['antraːk] (**-(e)s, -träge**) *m* pr posal; (*PARL*) motion; (*Gesuch*) applica tion; **~steller(in)** (**-s, -**) *m(f)* claiman (*für Kredit*) applicant

antreffen ['antrɛfən] (*unreg*) *vt* to mee

antreiben ['antraɪbən] (*unreg*) *vt* to drive on; (*Motor*) to drive

antreten ['antreːtən] (*unreg*) *vt* (*Amt*) take up; (*Erbschaft*) to come into; (*B weis*) to offer; (*Reise*) to start, to beg ♦ *vi* (*MIL*) to fall in; (*SPORT*) to line u **gegen jdn ~** to play/fight (against) sb

Antrieb ['antriːp] *m* (*auch fig*) drive **aus eigenem ~** of one's own accord

antrinken ['antrɪŋkən] (*unreg*) (*Flasche, Glas*) to start to drink fron **sich** *dat* **Mut/einen Rausch ~** to gi o.s. Dutch courage/get drunk; **ange trunken sein** to be tipsy

Antritt ['antrɪt] *m* beginning, con mencement; (*eines Amts*) taking up

antun ['antuːn] (*unreg*) *vt*: **jdm etw ~** to do sth to sb; **sich** *dat* **Zwang ~** force o.s.; **sich** *dat* **etwas ~** (to try t take one's own life

Antwort ['antvɔrt] (**-, -en**) *f* answer reply; **a~en** *vi* to answer, to reply

anvertrauen ['anfɛrtrauən] *vt*: **jdm** etw ~ to entrust sb with sth; **sich jdm ~** to confide in sb

anwachsen ['anvaksən] (*unreg*) *vi* grow; (*Pflanze*) to take root

Anwalt ['anvalt] (-(e)s, -wälte) *m* solicitor; lawyer; (*fig*) champion

Anwältin ['anveltɪn] *f siehe* **Anwalt**

Anwärter ['anvɛrtər] *m* candidate

anweisen ['anvaɪzən] (*unreg*) *vt* to instruct; (*zuteilen*) to assign

Anweisung *f* instruction; (*COMM*) remittance; (*Postanweisung, Zahlungsanweisung*) money order

anwend- ['anvend] *zW:* **~bar** ['anvent-] *adj* practicable, applicable; **~en** (*unreg*) *vt* to use, to employ; (*Gesetz, Regel*) to apply; **A~ung** *f* use; application

anwesend ['anveːzənt] *adj* present; **die A~en** those present

Anwesenheit *f* presence

anwidern ['anviːdərn] *vt* to disgust

Anwohner(in) ['anvoːnər(ɪn)] (-s, -) *m(f)* neighbour

Anzahl ['antsaːl] *f:* **~ (an** +*dat*) number (of); **a~en** *vt* to pay on account; **~ung** *f* deposit, payment on account

Anzeichen ['antsaɪçən] *nt* sign, indication

Anzeige ['antsaɪgə] *f* (*Zeitungsanzeige*) announcement; (*Werbung*) advertisement; (*bei Polizei*) report; **~ erstatten gegen jdn** to report sb (to the police); **a~n** *vt* (*zu erkennen geben*) to show; (*bekannt geben*) to announce; (*bei Polizei*) to report

anziehen ['antsiːən] (*unreg*) *vt* to attract; (*Kleidung*) to put on; (*Mensch*) to dress; (*Seil*) to pull tight; (*Schraube*) to tighten; (*Knie*) to draw up ♦ *vr* to get dressed; **~d** *adj* attractive

Anziehung (*Reiz*) attraction; **~skraft** *f* power of attraction; (*PHYS*) force of gravitation

Anzug ['antsuːk] *m* suit; (*Herankommen*): **im ~ sein** to be approaching

anzüglich ['antsyːklɪç] *adj* personal; (*anstößig*) offensive; **A~keit** *f* offensiveness; (*Bemerkung*) personal remark

anzünden ['antsʏndən] *vt* to light

anzweifeln ['antsvaɪfəln] *vt* to doubt

apathisch [a'paːtɪʃ] *adj* apathetic

Apfel ['apfəl] (-s, ⸚) *m* apple; **~saft** *m* apple juice; **~sine** [-'ziːnə] *f* orange; **~wein** *m* cider

Apostel [a'pɔstəl] (-s, -) *m* apostle

Apotheke [apo'teːkə] *f* chemist's (shop), drugstore (*US*); **a~npflichtig** [-'pflɪçtɪç] *adj* available only at a chemist's shop (*BRIT*) or pharmacy; **~r(in)** (-s, -) *m(f)* chemist, druggist (*US*)

The Apotheke is a pharmacy selling medicines available only on prescription and toiletries. The pharmacist is qualified to give advice on medicines and treatments.

Apparat [apa'raːt] (-(e)s, -e) *m* piece of apparatus; camera; telephone; (*RADIO, TV*) set; **am ~!** speaking!; **~ur** [-'tuːr] *f* apparatus

Appartement [apart(ə)'maː] (-s, -s) *nt* flat

appellieren [apɛ'liːrən] *vi:* **~ (an** +*akk*) to appeal (to)

Appetit [ape'tiːt] (-(e)s, -e) *m* appetite; **guten ~!** enjoy your meal; **a~lich** *adj* appetizing; **~losigkeit** *f* lack of appetite

Applaus [a'plaʊs] (-es, -e) *m* applause

Aprikose [apri'koːzə] *f* apricot

April [a'prɪl] (-(s), -e) *m* April

Aquarell [akva'rɛl] (-s, -e) *nt* watercolour

Äquator [ɛ'kvaːtɔr] (-s) *m* equator

Arab- ['arab] *zW:* **~er(in)** (-s, -) *m(f)* Arab; **~ien** [a'raːbiən] (-s) *nt* Arabia; **a~isch** [a'raːbɪʃ] *adj* Arabian

Arbeit ['arbaɪt] (-, -en) *f* work *no art*; (*Stelle*) job; (*Erzeugnis*) piece of work; (*wissenschaftliche*) essay; (*Klassenarbeit*) test; **das war eine ~** that was a hard job; **~en** vi to work ♦ vt to work, to make; **~er(in)** (-s, -) m(f) worker; (*ungelernt*) labourer; **~erschaft** f workers pl, labour force; **~geber** (-s, -) m employer; **~nehmer** (-s, -) m employee

Arbeits- in zW labour; **a~am** adj industrious; **~amt** nt employment exchange; **~erlaubnis** f work permit; **a~fähig** adj fit for work, able-bodied; **~gang** m operation; **~kräfte** pl (*Mitarbeiter*) workforce; **a~los** adj unemployed, out-of-work; **~lose(r)** f(m) unemployed person; **~losigkeit** f unemployment; **~markt** m job market; **~platz** m job; place of work; **a~scheu** adj workshy; **~tag** m work(ing) day; **a~unfähig** adj unfit for work; **~zeit** f working hours pl; **~zimmer** nt study

Archäologe [arçɛɔ'lɔːgə] (-n, -n) m archaeologist

Architekt(in) [arçi'tɛkt(ɪn)] (-en, -en) m(f) architect; **~ur** [-'tuːr] f architecture

Archiv [ar'çiːf] (-s, -e) nt archive

arg [ark] adj bad, awful ♦ adv awfully, very

Argentinien [argɛn'tiːniən] (-s) nt Argentina, the Argentine

argentinisch adj Argentinian

Ärger ['ɛrgər] (-s) m (Wut) anger; (*Unannehmlichkeit*) trouble; **ä~lich** adj (*zornig*) angry; (*lästig*) annoying, aggravating; **ä~n** vt to annoy ♦ vr to get annoyed

arg- zW: **~listig** adj cunning, insidious; **~los** adj guileless, innocent

Argument [argu'mɛnt] nt argument

argwöhnisch adj suspicious

Arie ['aːriə] f aria

Aristokrat [aristo'kraːt] (-en, -en) m aristocrat; **~ie** [-'tiː] f aristocracy

Arktis ['arktɪs] (-) f Arctic

Arm [arm] (-(e)s, -e) m arm; (*Flussarm*) branch

arm adj poor

Armatur [arma'tuːr] f (ELEK) armature;

~enbrett nt instrument panel; (AUT) dashboard

Armband nt bracelet; **~uhr** f (wrist)watch

Arme(r) f(m) poor man (woman); **die ~n** the poor

Armee [ar'meː] f army

Ärmel ['ɛrməl] (-s, -) m sleeve; **etw aus dem ~ schütteln** (fig) to produce sth just like that; **~kanal** m English Channel

ärmlich ['ɛrmlɪç] adj poor

armselig adj wretched, miserable

Armut ['armuːt] (-) f poverty

Aroma [a'roːma] (-s, Aromen) nt aroma; **~therapie** f aromatherapy; **a~tisch** [aro'maːtɪʃ] adj aromatic

arrangieren [arãˈʒiːrən] vt to arrange ♦ vr to come to an arrangement

Arrest [a'rɛst] (-(e)s, -e) m detention

arrogant [aro'gant] adj arrogant

Arsch [arʃ] (-es, -e) m (umg!) m arse (BRIT!), ass (US!)

Art [aːrt] (-, -en) f (Weise) way; (Sorte) kind, sort; (BIOL) species; **eine ~ (von) Frucht** a kind of fruit; **Häuser aller ~** houses of all kinds; **es ist nicht seine ~, das zu tun** it's not like him to do that; **ich mache das auf meine ~** I do that my (own) way

Arterie [ar'teːriə] f artery; **~nverkalkung** f arteriosclerosis

artig ['aːrtɪç] adj good, well-behaved

Artikel [ar'tiːkəl] (-s, -) m article

Artillerie [artɪlə'riː] f artillery

Artischocke [artɪ'ʃɔkə] f artichoke

Artist(in) [ar'tɪst(ɪn)] (-en, -en) m(f) (circus/variety) artiste od performer

Arznei [aːrts'naɪ] f medicine; **~mittel** nt medicine, medicament

Arzt [aːrtst] (-es, -e) m doctor; **~helferin** f (doctor's) receptionist

Ärztin ['ɛːrtstɪn] f doctor

ärztlich ['ɛːrtstlɪç] adj medical

As △ [as] (-ses, -se) nt = Ass

Asche ['aʃə] f (-, -n) ash, cinder

Aschen- zW: **~bahn** f cinder track;

~**becher** m ashtray

Aschermittwoch m Ash Wednesday

Äser ['ɛːzər] pl von **Aas**

Asiat(in) [azi'aːt(ɪn)] m(f) Asian; **asiatisch** [-'aːtɪʃ] adj Asian

Asien ['aːzjən] (-s) nt Asia

asozial ['azotsiaːl] adj antisocial; (Familien) asocial

Aspekt [as'pɛkt] (-(e)s, -e) m aspect

Asphalt [as'falt] (-(e)s, -e) m asphalt; **a~ieren** vt to asphalt

Ass ▲ [as] (-es, -e) nt ace

aß etc [aːs] vb siehe **essen**

Assistent(in) [asɪs'tɛnt(ɪn)] m(f) assistant

Assoziation [asotsiatsi'oːn] f association

Ast [ast] (-(e)s, ⁺e) m bough, branch

ästhetisch [ɛs'teːtɪʃ] adj aesthetic

Asthma ['astma] nt asthma; **~tiker(in)** (-s, -) m(f) asthmatic

Astro- [astro] zW: **~loge** (-n, -n) m astrologer; **~lo'gie** f astrology; **~naut** (-en, -en) m astronaut; **~'nom** (-en, -en) m astronomer; **~no'mie** f astronomy

Asyl [a'zyːl] (-s, -e) nt asylum; (Heim) home; (Obdachlosenasyl) shelter; **~ant(in)** [azy'lant(ɪn)] (-en, -en) m(f) asylum-seeker

Atelier [atali'eː] (-s, -s) nt studio

Atem ['aːtəm] (-s) m breath; **den ~ anhalten** to hold one's breath; **außer ~** out of breath; **a~beraubend** adj breathtaking; **a~los** adj breathless; **~not** f difficulty in breathing; **~pause** f breather; **~zug** m breath

Atheismus [ate'ɪsmʊs] m atheism

Atheist m atheist; **a~isch** adj atheistic

Athen [a'teːn] (-s) nt Athens

Äthiopien [ɛti'oːpjən] (-s) nt Ethiopia

Athlet [at'leːt] (-en, -en) m athlete

Atlantik [at'lantɪk] (-s) m Atlantic (Ocean)

Atlas ['atlas] (- od -ses, -se od **Atlan**ten) m atlas

atmen ['aːtmən] vt, vi to breathe

Atmosphäre [atmo'sfɛːrə] f atmosphere; **atmosphärisch** adj atmospheric

Atmung ['aːtmʊŋ] f respiration

Atom [a'toːm] (-s, -e) nt atom; **a~ar** adj atomic; **~bombe** f atom bomb; **~energie** f atomic od nuclear energy; **~kern** m atomic nucleus; **~kraftwerk** nt nuclear power station; **~krieg** m nuclear od atomic war; **~müll** m atomic waste; **~strom** m (electricity generated by) nuclear power; **~versuch** m atomic test; **~waffen** pl atomic weapons; **a~waffenfrei** adj nuclear-free; **~zeitalter** nt atomic age

Attentat [atɛn'taːt] (-(e)s, -e) nt: ~ **(auf** +akk**)** (attempted) assassination (of)

Attentäter [atɛn'tɛːtər] m (would-be) assassin

Attest [a'tɛst] (-(e)s, -e) nt certificate

Attraktion [atraktsi'oːn] f (Tourismus, Zirkus) attraction

attraktiv [atrak'tiːf] adj attractive

Attrappe [a'trapə] f dummy

Attribut [atri'buːt] (-(e)s, -e) nt (GRAM) attribute

ätzen ['ɛtsən] vi to be caustic; **~d** adj (Säure) corrosive; (fig: Spott) cutting

au [au] excl ouch!; **~ ja!** oh yes!

Aubergine [ober'ʒiːnə] f aubergine, eggplant

┌─────────────────────┐
│ SCHLÜSSELWORT   │
└─────────────────────┘

auch [aux] adv 1 (ebenfalls) also, too, as well; **das ist auch schön** that's nice too od as well; **er kommt - ich auch** he's coming - so am I, me too; **auch nicht** not ... either; **ich auch nicht** nor I, me neither; **oder auch** or; **auch das noch!** not that as well!

2 (selbst, sogar) even; **auch wenn das Wetter schlecht ist** even if the

weather is bad; **ohne auch nur zu fragen** without even asking

3 *(wirklich)* really; **du siehst müde aus
- bin ich auch** you look tired - (so) I
am; **so sieht es auch aus** it looks like
it too

4 *(auch immer)*: **wer auch** whoever;
was auch whatever; **wie dem auch
sei** be that as it may; **wie sehr er sich
auch bemühte** however much he
tried

SCHLÜSSELWORT

auf [auf] *präp +dat (wo?)* on; **auf dem
Tisch** on the table; **auf der Reise** on
the way; **auf der Post/dem Fest** at
the post office/party; **auf der Straße**
on the road; **auf dem Land/der ganzen Welt** in the country/the whole
world

♦ *präp +akk (wohin?)* on(to); **auf den
Tisch** on(to) the table; **auf die Post
gehen** go to the post office; **auf das
Land** into the country; **etw auf einen
Zettel schreiben** to write sth on a
piece of paper

2: **auf Deutsch** in German; **auf Le-
benszeit** for my/his lifetime; **bis auf
ihn** except for him; **auf einmal** at
once; **auf seinen Vorschlag (hin)** at
his suggestion

♦ *adv* **1** *(offen)* open; **auf sein** *(umg)*
(Tür, Geschäft) to be open; **das Fenster ist auf** the window is open

2 *(hinauf)* up; **auf und ab** up and
down; **auf und davon** up and away;
auf! *(los!)* come on!

3 *(aufgestanden)* up; **auf sein** to be
up; **ist er schon auf?** is he up yet?

♦ *konj*: **auf dass** (so) that

---

aufatmen ['aufʔaːtmən] *vi* to heave a
sigh of relief

aufbahren ['aufbaːrən] *vt* to lay out

Aufbau ['aufbau] *m (Bauen)* building,
construction; *(Struktur)* structure; *(auf-*

gebautes Teil) superstructure; **a∼en** *vt*
to erect, to build (up); *(Existenz)* to
make; *(gestalten)* to construct; **a∼er**
(auf +dat) (gründen) to found *od* base
(on)

aufbauschen ['aufbauʃən] *vt* to puff
out; *(fig)* to exaggerate

aufbekommen ['aufbəkɔmən] *(unreg)*
vt (öffnen) to get open; *(Hausaufgaben)*
to be given

aufbessern ['aufbɛsərn] *vt (Gehalt)* to
increase

aufbewahren ['aufbəvaːrən] *vt* to
keep; *(Gepäck)* to put in the safekeeping; *(Gepäck)* to put in the
luggage office *(BRIT) od* baggage check
(US)

Aufbewahrung *f (safe)keeping; (Gepäckaufbewahrung)* left-luggage office
(BRIT), baggage check *(US)*

aufbieten ['aufbiːtən] *(unreg) vt (Kraft)*
to summon (up); *(Armee, Polizei)* to
mobilize

aufblasen ['aufblaːzən] *(unreg) vt* to
blow up, to inflate ♦ *vr (umg)* to become bigheaded

aufbleiben ['aufblaɪbən] *(unreg) vi (Laden)* to remain open; *(Person)* to stay
up

aufblenden ['aufblɛndən] *vt (Scheinwerfer)* to switch on full beam ♦ *vi
(Fahrer)* to have the lights on full
beam; *(AUT: Scheinwerfer)* to be on full
beam

aufblicken ['aufblɪkən] *vi* to look up; ∼
zu to look up at; *(fig)* to look up to

aufblühen ['aufblyːən] *vi* to blossom,
to flourish

aufbrauchen ['aufbrauxən] *vt* to use
up

aufbrausen ['aufbrauzən] *vi (fig)* to
flare up; **∼d** *adj* hot-tempered

aufbrechen ['aufbrɛçən] *(unreg) vt* to
break *od* prise *(BRIT)* open ♦ *vi* to burst
open; *(gehen)* to start, to set off

aufbringen ['aufbrɪŋən] *(unreg) vt
(öffnen)* to open; *(in Mode)* to bring
into fashion; *(beschaffen)* to procure,

(FIN) to raise; (ärgern) to irritate; **Verständnis für etw ~** to be able to understand sth

Aufbruch ['aʊfbrɔx] m departure

aufbrühen ['aʊfbryːən] vt (Tee) to make

aufbürden ['aʊfbyrdən] vt: **jdm etw ~** to burden sb with sth

aufdecken ['aʊfdɛkən] vt to uncover

aufdrängen ['aʊfdrɛŋən] vt: **jdm etw ~** to force sth on sb ♦ vr (Mensch): **sich jdm ~** to intrude on sb

aufdrehen ['aʊfdreːən] vt (Wasserhahn etc) to turn on; (Ventil) to open up

aufdringlich ['aʊfdrɪŋlɪç] adj pushy

aufeinander [aʊfaiˈnandər] adv on top of each other; (schießen) at each other; (vertrauen) each other; **~ folgen** to follow one another; **~ folgend** consecutive; **~ prallen** to hit one another

Aufenthalt ['aʊfɛnthalt] m stay; (Verzögerung) delay; (EISENB: Halten) stop; (Ort) haunt

Aufenthaltserlaubnis f residence permit

auferlegen ['aʊfɛrleːgən] vt: (jdm) to impose (upon sb)

Auferstehung ['aʊfɛrʃteːʊŋ] f resurrection

aufessen ['aʊfɛsən] vt to eat up

auffahr- ['aʊfaːr] zW: **~en** (unreg) vi (herankommen) to draw up; (hochfahren) to jump up; (wütend werden) to flare up; (in den Himmel) to ascend ♦ vt (Kanonen, Geschütz) to bring up; **~en auf** +akk (Auto) to run od crash into; **~end** adj hot-tempered; **A~t** f (Hausauffahrt) drive; (Autobahnauffahrt) slip road (BRIT); (freeway) entrance (US); **A~unfall** m pile-up

auffallen ['aʊffalən] (unreg) vi to be noticeable; **jdm ~** to strike sb

auffällig ['aʊffɛlɪç] adj conspicuous, striking

auffangen ['aʊffaŋən] (unreg) vt to catch; (Funkspruch) to intercept; (Preise) to peg

auffassen ['aʊffasən] vt to understand, to comprehend; (auslegen) to see, to view

Auffassung f (Meinung) opinion; (Auslegung) view, concept; (auch: **~sgabe**) grasp

auffindbar ['aʊffɪntbaːr] adj to be found

auffordern ['aʊffɔrdərn] vt (befehlen) to call upon, to order; (bitten) to ask

Aufforderung f (Befehl) order; (Einladung) invitation

auffrischen ['aʊffrɪʃən] vt to freshen up; (Kenntnisse) to brush up; (Erinnerungen) to reawaken ♦ vi (Wind) to freshen

aufführen ['aʊffyːrən] vt (THEAT) to perform; (in einem Verzeichnis) to list, to specify ♦ vr (sich benehmen) to behave

Aufführung f (THEAT) performance; (Liste) specification

Aufgabe ['aʊfgaːbə] f task; (SCH) exercise; (Hausaufgabe) homework; (Verzicht) giving up; (von Gepäck) registration; (von Post) posting; (von Inserat) insertion

Aufgang ['aʊfgaŋ] m ascent; (Sonnenaufgang) rise; (Treppe) staircase

aufgeben ['aʊfgeːbən] (unreg) vt (verzichten) to give up; (Paket) to send, to post; (Bestellung) to register; (Bestellung) to give; (Inserat) to insert; (Rätsel, Problem) to set ♦ vi to give up

Aufgebot ['aʊfgəboːt] nt supply; (Eheaufgebot) banns pl

aufgedunsen ['aʊfgədʊnzən] adj swollen, puffed up

aufgehen ['aʊfgeːən] (unreg) vi (Sonne, Teig) to rise; (sich öffnen) to open; (klar werden) to become clear; (MATH) to come out exactly; **~ (in** +dat) (sich widmen) to be absorbed in); **in Rauch/**

Flammen ~ to go up in smoke/flames

aufgelegt ['aʊfgəleːkt] adj: **gut/schlecht ~ sein** to be in a good/bad mood; **zu etw ~ sein** to be in the mood for sth

aufgeregt ['aʊfgəreːkt] adj excited

aufgeschlossen ['aʊfgəʃlɔsən] adj open, open-minded

aufgeweckt ['aʊfgəvɛkt] adj bright, intelligent

aufgießen ['aʊfgiːsən] (unreg) vt (Wasser) to pour over; (Tee) to infuse

aufgreifen ['aʊfgraɪfən] (unreg) vt (Thema) to take up; (Verdächtige) to pick up, to seize

aufgrund, auf Grund [aʊf'grʊnt] präp +gen on the basis of; (wegen) because of

aufhaben ['aʊfhaːbən] (unreg) vt to have on (Arbeit) to have to do

aufhalsen ['aʊfhalzən] (umg) vt: **jdm etw ~** to saddle or lumber sb with sth

aufhalten ['aʊfhaltən] (unreg) vt (Person) to detain; (Entwicklung) to check; (Tür, Hand) to hold open; (Augen) to keep open ♦ vr (wohnen) to live; (bleiben) to stay; **sich mit etw ~** to waste time over sth

aufhängen ['aʊfhɛŋən] (unreg) vt (Wäsche) to hang up; (Menschen) to hang ♦ vr to hang o.s.

Aufhänger (-s, -) m (am Mantel) loop; (fig) peg

aufheben ['aʊfheːbən] (unreg) vt (hochheben) to raise, to lift; (Sitzung) to wind up; (Urteil) to annul; (Gesetz) to repeal, to abolish; (aufbewahren) to keep ♦ vr to cancel itself out; **bei jdm gut aufgehoben sein** to be well looked after at sb's; **viel A~(s) machen (von)** to make a fuss (about)

aufheitern ['aʊfhaɪtərn] vt, vr (Himmel, Miene) to brighten; (Mensch) to cheer up

aufhellen ['aʊfhɛlən] vt, vr to clear up; (Farbe, Haare) to lighten

aufhetzen ['aʊfhɛtsən] vt to stir up

aufholen ['aʊfhoːlən] vt to make up ♦ vi to catch up

aufhorchen ['aʊfhɔrçən] vi to prick up one's ears

aufhören ['aʊfhøːrən] vi to stop; **~, etw zu tun** to stop doing sth

aufklappen ['aʊfklapən] vt to open

aufklären ['aʊfklɛːrən] vt (Geheimnis etc) to clear up; (Person) to enlighten; (sexuell) to tell the facts of life to; (MIL) to reconnoitre ♦ vr to clear up

Aufklärung f (von Geheimnis) clearing up; (Unterrichtung, Zeitalter) enlightenment; (sexuell) sex education; (MIL, AVIAT) reconnaissance

aufkleben ['aʊfkleːbən] vt to stick on; **Aufkleber** (-s, -) m sticker

aufknöpfen ['aʊfknœpfən] vt to unbutton

aufkommen ['aʊfkɔmən] (unreg) vi (Wind) to come up; (Zweifel, Gefühl) to arise; (Mode) to start; **für jdn/etw ~** to be liable or responsible for sb/sth

aufladen ['aʊflaːdən] (unreg) vt to load

Auflage ['aʊflaːgə] f edition; (Zeitung) circulation; (Bedingung) condition

auflassen ['aʊflasən] (unreg) vt (offen) to leave open; (aufgesetzt) to leave on

auflauern ['aʊflaʊərn] vi: **jdm ~** to lie in wait for sb

Auflauf ['aʊflaʊf] m (KOCH) pudding; (Menschenauflauf) crowd

aufleben ['aʊfleːbən] vi (Mensch, Gespräch) to liven up; (Interesse) to revive

auflegen ['aʊfleːgən] vt, vi to put on; (Telefon) to hang up; (TYP) to print

auflehnen ['aʊfleːnən] vt to lean on ♦ vr to rebel

Auflehnung f rebellion

auflesen ['aʊfleːzən] (unreg) vt to pick up

aufleuchten ['aʊflɔyçtən] vi to light up

auflisten ['aʊflɪstən] vt to list

auflockern ['aʊflɔkərn] vt to loosen; (fig: Eintönigkeit etc) to liven up

auflösen ['aʊfløːzən] vt, vr to dissolve;

(Haare etc) to loosen; *(Missverständnis)* to sort out ♦ *vr* to dissolve; to come undone; to be resolved; **in (Tränen) aufgelöst sein** to be in tears

Auflösung *f* dissolving; *(fig)* solution

aufmachen ['aufmaxən] *vt* to open; *(Kleidung)* to undo; *(zurechtmachen)* to do up ♦ *vr* to set out

Aufmachung *f (Kleidung)* outfit, get-up; *(Gestaltung)* format

aufmerksam ['aufmɛrkza:m] *adj* attentive; **jdn auf etw** *akk* ~ **machen** to point sth out to sb; **A~keit** *f* attention, attentiveness

aufmuntern ['aufmʊntərn] *vt (ermutigen)* to encourage; *(erheitern)* to cheer up

Aufnahme ['aufna:mə] *f* reception; *(Beginn)* beginning; *(in Verein etc)* admission; *(in Liste etc)* inclusion; *(Notieren)* taking down; *(PHOT)* shot; *(auf Tonband)* recording; **a~fähig** *adj* receptive; **~prüfung** *f* entrance test

aufnehmen ['aufne:mən] *(unreg) vt* to receive; *(hochheben)* to pick up; *(beginnen)* to take up; *(in Verein etc)* to admit; *(in Liste etc)* to include; *(fassen)* to hold; *(notieren)* to take down; *(fotografieren)* to photograph; *(auf Tonband, Platte)* take out; **es mit jdm ~ können** to be able to compete with sb

aufopfern ['aufɔpfərn] *vt, vr* to sacrifice; **~d** *adj* selfless

aufpassen ['aufpasən] *vi (aufmerksam sein)* to pay attention; **auf jdn/etw** ~ to look after *od* watch sb/sth; **aufgepasst!** look out!

Aufprall ['aufpral] *(-s, -e) m* impact; **a~en** *vi* to hit, to strike

Aufpreis ['aufprais] *m* extra charge

aufpumpen ['aufpʊmpən] *vt* to pump up

aufräumen ['aufrɔymən] *vt, vi (Dinge)* to clear away; *(Zimmer)* to tidy up

aufrecht ['aufrɛçt] *adj (auch fig)* upright; **~erhalten** *(unreg) vt* to maintain

aufreg- *in zW:* **~en** *vt* to excite ♦ *vr* to get excited; **~end** *adj* exciting; **A~ung** *f* excitement

aufreibend ['aufraibənt] *adj* strenuous

aufreißen ['aufraisən] *(unreg) vt (Umschlag)* to tear open; *(Augen)* to open wide; *(Tür)* to throw open; *(Straße)* to take up

aufreizen ['aufraitsən] *vt* to incite, to stir up; **~d** *adj* exciting, stimulating

aufrichten ['aufrɪçtən] *vt* to put up, to erect; *(moralisch)* to console ♦ *vr* to rise; *(moralisch):* **sich ~ (an** +*dat)* take heart (from)

aufrichtig ['aufrɪçtɪç] *adj* sincere, honest; **A~keit** *f* sincerity

aufrücken ['aufrʏkən] *vi* to move up; *(beruflich)* to be promoted

Aufruf ['aufru:f] *m* summons; *(zur Hilfe)* call; *(des Namens)* calling out; **a~en** *(unreg) vt (Namen)* to call out; *(auffordern):* **jdn a~en (zu)** to call upon sb (for)

Aufruhr ['aufru:r] *(-(e)s, -e) m* uprising, revolt

aufrührerisch ['aufry:rərɪʃ] *adj* rebellious

aufrunden ['aufrʊndən] *vt (Summe)* to round up

Aufrüstung ['aufrʏstʊŋ] *f* rearmament

aufrütteln ['aufrʏtəln] *vt (auch fig)* to shake up

aufs [aufs] = **auf das**

aufsagen ['aufza:gən] *vt (Gedicht)* to recite

aufsässig ['aufzɛsɪç] *adj* rebellious

Aufsatz ['aufzats] *m (Geschriebenes)* essay; *(auf Schrank etc)* top

aufsaugen ['aufzaugən] *(unreg) vt* to soak up

aufschauen ['aufʃauən] *vi* to look up

aufscheuchen ['aufʃɔyçən] *vt* to scare *od* frighten away

aufschieben ['aʊfʃiːbən] (unreg) vt to push open; (verzögern) to put off, postpone

Aufschlag ['aʊfʃlaːk] m (Ärmelaufschlag) cuff; (Jackenaufschlag) lapel; (Hosenaufschlag) turn-up; (Aufprall) impact; (Preisaufschlag) surcharge; (Tennis) service; **a~en** [-gən] (unreg) vt (öffnen) to open; (verwunden) to cut; (hochschlagen) to turn up; (aufbauen: Zelt, Lager) to pitch, to erect; (Wohnsitz) to take up ♦ vi (aufprallen) to hit; (teurer werden) to go up; (Tennis) to serve

aufschließen ['aʊfʃliːsən] (unreg) vt to open up, to unlock ♦ vi (aufrücken) to close up

aufschlussreich ▲ adj informative, illuminating

aufschnappen ['aʊfʃnapən] vt (umg) to pick up ♦ vi to fly open

aufschneiden ['aʊfʃnaɪdən] (unreg) vt (Brot) to cut up; (MED) to lance ♦ vi to brag

Aufschneider (-s, -) m boaster, braggart

Aufschnitt ['aʊfʃnɪt] m (slices of) cold meat

aufschrauben ['aʊfʃraʊbən] vt (festschrauben) to screw on; (lösen) to unscrew

aufschrecken ['aʊfʃrɛkən] vt to startle ♦ vi (unreg) to start up

aufschreiben ['aʊfʃraɪbən] (unreg) vt to write down

aufschreien ['aʊfʃraɪən] (unreg) vi to cry out

Aufschrift ['aʊfʃrɪft] f (Inschrift) inscription; (auf Etikett) label

Aufschub ['aʊfʃuːp] (-(e)s, -schübe) m delay, postponement

Aufschwung ['aʊfʃvʊŋ] m (Elan) boost; (wirtschaftlich) upturn, boom; (SPORT) circle

aufsehen ['aʊfzeːən] (unreg) vi to look up; **~ zu** to look up at; (fig) to look up to; **A~** (-s) nt sensation, stir; **~erre-**gend sensational

Aufseher(in) (-s, -) m(f) guard; (im Betrieb) supervisor; (Museumsaufseher) attendant; (Parkaufseher) keeper

auf sein ▲ siehe auf

aufsetzen ['aʊfzɛtsən] vt to put on; (Dokument) to draw up ♦ vr to sit up(right) ♦ vi (Flugzeug) to touch down

Aufsicht ['aʊfzɪçt] f supervision; **die ~ haben** to be in charge

Aufsichtsrat m (supervisory) board

aufsitzen ['aʊfzɪtsən] (unreg) vi (aufrecht hinsitzen) to sit up; (aufs Pferd, Motorrad) to mount, to get on; (Schiff) to run aground; **jdm ~** (umg) to be taken in by sb

aufsparen ['aʊfʃpaːrən] vt to save (up)

aufsperren ['aʊfʃpɛrən] vt to unlock; (Mund) to open wide

aufspielen ['aʊfʃpiːlən] vr to show off

aufspießen ['aʊfʃpiːsən] vt to spear

aufspringen ['aʊfʃprɪŋən] (unreg) vi (hochspringen) to jump up; (sich öffnen) to spring open; (Hände, Lippen) to become chapped; **auf etw** akk **~** to jump onto sth

aufspüren ['aʊfʃpyːrən] vt to track down, to trace

aufstacheln ['aʊfʃtaxəln] vt to incite

Aufstand ['aʊfʃtant] m insurrection, rebellion; **aufständisch** ['aʊfʃtɛndɪʃ] adj rebellious, mutinous

aufstehen ['aʊfʃteːən] (unreg) vi to get up; (Tür) to be open

aufsteigen ['aʊfʃtaɪgən] (unreg) vi (hochsteigen) to climb; (Rauch) to rise; **auf etw** akk **~** to get onto sth

aufstellen ['aʊfʃtɛlən] vt (aufrecht stellen) to put up; (aufreihen) to line up; (nominieren) to nominate; (formulieren: Programm etc) to draw up; (leisten: Rekord) to set up

Aufstellung f (SPORT) line-up; (Liste) list

Aufstieg ['aʊfʃtiːk] (-(e)s, -e) m (auf Berg) ascent; (Fortschritt) rise; (beruflich, SPORT) promotion

aufstocken ['aʊfʃtɔkən] vt (Kapital) to increase

aufstoßen ['aʊfʃtoːsən] (unreg) vt to push open ♦ vi to belch

aufstützen ['aʊfʃtʏtsən] vt (Körperteil) to prop, to lean; (Person) to prop up ♦ vr: **sich auf etw akk ~** to lean on sth

aufsuchen ['aʊfzuːxən] vt (besuchen) to visit; (konsultieren) to consult

Auftakt ['aʊftakt] m (MUS) upbeat; (fig) prelude

auftanken ['aʊftaŋkən] vi to get petrol (BRIT) od gas (US) ♦ vt to refuel

auftauchen ['aʊftaʊxən] vi to appear; (aus Wasser etc) to emerge; (U-Boot) to surface; (Zweifel) to arise

auftauen ['aʊftaʊən] vt to thaw ♦ vi to thaw; (fig) to relax

aufteilen ['aʊftaɪlən] vt to divide up; (Raum) to partition; **Aufteilung** f division; partition

Auftrag ['aʊftraːk] (-(e)s, -träge) m order; (Anweisung) commission; (Aufgabe) mission; **im ~ von** on behalf of; **a~en** [-gən] (unreg) vt (Essen) to serve; (Farbe) to put on; (Kleidung) to wear out; **jdm etw a~en** to tell sb sth; **dick a~en** (fig) to exaggerate; **~geber (-s, -)** m (COMM) purchaser, customer

auftreiben ['aʊftraɪbən] (unreg) vt (umg: beschaffen) to raise

auftreten ['aʊftreːtən] (unreg) vi to kick open ♦ vi to appear; (mit Füßen) to tread; (sich verhalten) to behave; **A~(-s)** nt (Vorkommen) appearance; (Benehmen) behaviour

Auftrieb ['aʊftriːp] m (PHYS) buoyancy, lift; (fig) impetus

Auftritt ['aʊftrɪt] m (des Schauspielers) entrance; (Szene: auch fig) scene

aufwachen ['aʊfvaxən] vi to wake up

aufwachsen ['aʊfvaksən] (unreg) vi to grow up

Aufwand ['aʊfvant] (-(e)s) m expenditure; (Kosten auch) expense; (Luxus)

show

aufwändig ▲ ['aʊfvɛndɪç] adj costly

aufwärmen ['aʊfvɛrmən] vt to warm up; (alte Geschichten) to rake up

aufwärts ['aʊfvɛrts] adv upwards; **A~entwicklung** f upward trend

Aufwasch ['aʊfvaʃ] m washing-up

aufwecken ['aʊfvɛkən] vt to wake up, to waken up

aufweisen ['aʊfvaɪzən] (unreg) vt to show

aufwenden ['aʊfvɛndən] (unreg) vt to expend; (Geld) to spend; (Sorgfalt) to devote

aufwendig adj siehe **aufwändig**

aufwerfen ['aʊfvɛrfən] (unreg) vt (Fenster etc) to throw open; (Probleme) to throw up, to raise

aufwerten ['aʊfvɛrtən] vt (FIN) to revalue; (fig) to raise in value

aufwickeln ['aʊfvɪkəln] vt (aufrollen) to roll up; (umg: Haar) to put in curlers

aufwiegen ['aʊfviːgən] (unreg) vt to make up for

Aufwind ['aʊfvɪnt] m up-current

aufwirbeln ['aʊfvɪrbəln] vt to whirl up; **Staub ~** (fig) to create a stir

aufwischen ['aʊfvɪʃən] vt to wipe up

aufzählen ['aʊftsɛːlən] vt to list

aufzeichnen ['aʊftsaɪçnən] vt to sketch; (schriftlich) to jot down; (auf Band) to record

Aufzeichnung f (schriftlich) note; (Tonbandaufzeichnung) recording; (Filmaufzeichnung) record

aufzeigen ['aʊftsaɪgən] vt to show, to demonstrate

aufziehen ['aʊftsiːən] (unreg) vt (hochziehen) to raise, to draw up; (öffnen) to pull open; (Uhr) to wind; (umg: necken) to tease; (großziehen: Kinder) to raise, to bring up; (Tiere) to rear

Aufzug ['aʊftsuːk] m (Fahrstuhl) lift, elevator; (Aufmarsch) procession, parade; (Kleidung) get-up; (THEAT) act

aufzwingen ['aʊftsvɪŋən] (unreg) vt: **jdm etw ~** to force sth upon sb

Augapfel ['aʊkʔapfəl] m eyeball; (fig) apple of one's eye

Auge ['aʊgə] (-s, -n) nt eye; (Fettauge) globule of fat; **unter vier ~n** in private

Augen- zW: **~blick** m moment; **im ~blick** at the moment; **a~blicklich** adj (sofort) instantaneous; (gegenwärtig) present; **~braue** f eyebrow; **~opti-ker(in)** m(f) optician; **~weide** f sight for sore eyes; **~zeuge** m eye witness

August [aʊˈɡʊst] (-(e)s od -, -e) m August

Auktion [aʊktsiˈoːn] f auction

Aula ['aʊla] (-, **Aulen** od -s) f assembly hall

aus [aʊs] präp +dat 1 (räumlich) out of; (von ... her) from; **er ist aus Berlin** he's from Berlin; **aus dem Fenster** out of the window

2 (gemacht/hergestellt aus) made of; **ein Herz aus Stein** a heart of stone

3 (auf Ursache deutend) out of; **aus Mitleid** out of sympathy; **aus Erfahrung** from experience; **aus Spaß** for fun

4: **aus ihr wird nie etwas** she'll never get anywhere

♦ adv 1 (zu Ende) finished, over; **aus sein** to be over; **aus und vorbei** over and done with

2 (ausgeschaltet, ausgezogen) out; (Aufschrift an Geräten) off; **aus sein** (nicht brennen) to be out; (abgeschaltet sein: Radio, Herd) to be off; **Licht aus!** lights out!

3 (nicht zu Hause): **aus sein** to be out

4 (in Verbindung mit von): **von Rom aus** from Rome; **vom Fenster aus** out of the window; **von sich aus** (selbst-ständig) of one's own accord; **von ihm aus** as far as he's concerned

ausarbeiten ['aʊsʔarbaɪtən] vt to work

out

ausarten ['aʊsʔartən] vi to degenerate

ausatmen ['aʊsʔaːtmən] vi to breath out

ausbaden ['aʊsbaːdən] (umg) vt: **etw ~ müssen** to carry the can for sth

Ausbau ['aʊsbaʊ] m extension, expan-sion; removal; **a~en** vt to extend, to expand; (herausnehmen) to take out to remove; **a~fähig** adj (fig) worth de-veloping

ausbessern ['aʊsbɛsərn] vt to mend to repair

ausbeulen ['aʊsbɔʏlən] vt to beat out

Ausbeute ['aʊsbɔʏtə] f yield; (Fische catch; **a~n** vt to exploit; (MIN) to work

ausbild- ['aʊsbɪld] zW: **~en** vt to edu cate; (Lehrling, Soldat) to instruct, to train; (Fähigkeiten) to develop; (Ge schmack) to cultivate; **A~er** (-s, -) m in structor; **A~ung** f education; training instruction; development; cultivation

ausbleiben ['aʊsblaɪbən] (unreg) vi (Personen) to stay away, not to come (Ereignisse) to fail to happen, not to happen

Ausblick ['aʊsblɪk] m (auch fig) pro spect, outlook, view

ausbrechen ['aʊsbrɛçən] (unreg) vi to break out ♦ vt to break off; **i Tränen/Gelächter ~** to burst into tears/out laughing

ausbreiten ['aʊsbraɪtən] vt to sprea (out); (Arme) to stretch out ♦ vr to spread; **sich über ein Thema ~** to ex pand od enlarge on a topic

ausbrennen ['aʊsbrɛnən] (unreg) vt to scorch; (Wunde) to cauterize ♦ vi t burn out

Ausbruch ['aʊsbrʊx] m outbreak; (vo Vulkan) eruption; (Gefühlsausbruch outburst; (von Gefangenen) escape

ausbrüten ['aʊsbryːtən] vt (auch fig) t hatch

Ausdauer ['aʊsdaʊər] f perseverance stamina; **a~nd** adj persevering

ausdehnen ['aʊsdeːnən] vt

räumlich) to expand; (*zeitlich, auch Gummi*) to stretch; (*Nebel, fig: Macht*) to extend

usdenken ['ausdɛŋkən] (*unreg*) vt: **ich** *dat* **etw ~** to think sth up

usdruck ['ausdrʊk] m expression, *phrase*; (*Kundgabe, Gesichtsausdruck*) expression; (*COMPUT*) print-out, hard *copy*; **a~en** (*COMPUT*) to print out

usdrücken ['ausdrʏkən] vt (*auch vr: formulieren, zeigen*) to express; (*Zigarette*) to put out; (*Zitrone*) to squeeze

ausdrücklich *adj* express, explicit

ausdrucks- *zW*: **~los** *adj* expressionless, blank; **~voll** *adj* expressive; **A~weise** f mode of expression

useinander [ausʔaɪ'nandər] *adv* (*getrennt*) apart; **~ schreiben** to write as separate words; **~ bringen** to separate; **~ fallen** to fall apart; **~ gehen** (*Menschen*) to separate; (*Meinungen*) to differ; (*Gegenstand*) to fall apart; **~ halten** to tell apart; **~ nehmen** to take to pieces, to dismantle; **~ setzen** (*erklären*) to set forth, to explain; **sich ~ setzen** (*sich verständigen*) to come to terms, to settle; (*sich befassen*) to concern o.s.; **A~setzung** f argument

ausfahren ['ausfaːrən] (*unreg*) vt (*spazieren fahren: im Auto*) to take for a drive; (*: im Kinderwagen*) to take for a walk; (*liefern*) to deliver

usfahrt f (*des Zuges etc*) leaving, departure; (*Autobahnausfahrt*) exit; (*Garagenausfahrt etc*) exit, way out; (*Spazierfahrt*) drive, excursion

usfall ['ausfal] m loss; (*Nichtstattfinden*) cancellation; (*MIL*) sortie; (*radioaktiv*) fall-out; **a~en** (*unreg*) vi (*Zähne, Haare*) to fall out; (*nicht stattfinden*) to be cancelled; (*wegbleiben*) to be omitted; (*Person*) to be stopped; (*nicht funktionieren*) to break down; (*Resultat haben*) to turn out; **~straße** f arterial

---

road

ausfertigen ['ausfɛrtɪgən] vt (*förmlich: Urkunde, Pass*) to draw up; (*Rechnung*) to make out

Ausfertigung ['ausfɛrtɪgʊŋ] f drawing up; making out; (*Exemplar*) copy

ausfinden ['ausfɪndɪç] *adj*: **~ machen** to discover

ausfließen ['ausfliːsən] (*unreg*) vt (*her~*): **~ (aus)** to flow out (of); (*auslaufen: Öl etc*): **~ (aus)** to leak (out of)

Ausflucht ['ausflʊxt] (*-, -flüchte*) f excuse

Ausflug ['ausfluːk] m excursion, outing; **Ausflügler** ['ausflyːklər] (*-s, -*) m tripper

Ausflugslokal nt tourist café

Ausfluss ▲ ['ausflʊs] m outlet; (*MED*) discharge

ausfragen ['ausfraːgən] vt to interrogate, to question

ausfressen ['ausfrɛsən] (*unreg*) vt to eat up; (*aushöhlen*) to corrode; (*umg: anstellen*) to be up to

Ausfuhr ['ausfuːr] (*-, -en*) f export, exportation ▲ ['ausfuːr] f export

ausführ- ['ausfyːr] *zW*: **~en** vt (*verwirklichen*) to carry out; (*Person*) to take out; (*Hund*) to take for a walk; (*COMM: to export*); (*erklären*) to give details of; **~lich** *adj* detailed ♦ *adv* in detail; **A~lichkeit** f detail; **A~ung** f execution, performance; (*Durchführung*) completion; (*Herstellungsart*) version; (*Erklärung*) explanation

ausfüllen ['ausfʏlən] vt to fill up; (*Fragebogen etc*) to fill in; (*Beruf*) to be fulfilling for

Ausgabe ['ausɡaːbə] f (*Geld*) expenditure, outlay; (*Aushändigung*) giving out; (*Gepäckausgabe*) left-luggage office; (*Buch*) edition; (*Nummer*) issue; (*COMPUT*) output

Ausgang ['ausɡaŋ] m way out, exit; (*Ende*) end; (*~spunkt*) starting point;

Spelling Reform: ▲ *new spelling* △ *old spelling (to be phased out)*

(*Ergebnis*) result; (*Ausgehtag*) free time, time off; **kein ~** no exit

Ausgangs- zW: **~punkt** m starting point; **~sperre** f curfew

ausgeben ['ausge:bən] (*unreg*) vt (*Geld*) to spend; (*austeilen*) to issue, to distribute ♦ vr: **sich für etw/jdn ~** to pass o.s. off as sth/sb

ausgebucht ['ausgəbu:xt] adj (*Vorstellung, Flug, Maschine*) fully booked

ausgedient ['ausgədi:nt] adj (*Soldat*) discharged; (*verbraucht*) no longer in use; **~ haben** to have done good service

ausgefallen ['ausgəfalən] adj (*ungewöhnlich*) exceptional

ausgeglichen ['ausgəgliçən] adj (well-)balanced; **A~heit** f balance; (*von Mensch*) even-temperedness

ausgehen ['ausge:ən] (*unreg*) vi to go out; (*zu Ende gehen*) to come to an end; (*Benzin*) to run out; (*Haare, Zähne*) to fall of come out; (*Feuer, Ofen, Licht*) to go out; (*Strom*) to go off; (*Resultat haben*) to turn out; **mir ging das Benzin aus** I ran out of petrol (*BRIT*) od gas (*US*); **von etw ~** (*wegführen*) to lead away from sth; (*herrühren*) to come from sth; (*zugrunde legen*) to proceed from sth; **wir können davon ~, dass ...** we can take as our starting point that ...; **leer ~** to get nothing

ausgelassen ['ausgəlasən] adj boisterous, high-spirited

ausgelastet ['ausgəlastət] adj fully occupied

ausgelernt ['ausgəlɛrnt] adj trained, qualified

ausgemacht ['ausgəmaxt] adj settled; (*umg: Dummkopf etc*) out-and-out, downright; **es war eine ~e Sache, dass ...** it was a foregone conclusion that ...

ausgenommen ['ausgənɔmən] präp +*gen* except ♦ *konj* except; **Anwesende sind ~** present company excepted

ausgeprägt ['ausgəprɛ:kt] adj distinc

ausgerechnet ['ausgərɛçnət] adv ju precisely; **~ du/heute** you of people/today of all days

ausgeschlossen ['ausgəʃlɔsən] a (*unmöglich*) impossible, out of th question

ausgeschnitten ['ausgəʃnitən] a (*Kleid*) low-necked

ausgesprochen ['ausgəʃprɔxən] a (*Faulheit, Lüge etc*) out-and-out, (*u verkennbar*) marked ♦ adv decidedly

ausgezeichnet ['ausgətsaiçnət] adj e cellent

ausgiebig ['ausgi:biç] adj (*Gebrauc* thorough, good; (*Essen*) generous, la ish; **~ schlafen** to have a good sleep

ausgießen ['ausgi:sən] vt to pour ou (*Behälter*) to empty

Ausgleich ['ausglaiç] (-(e)s, -e) m b ance; (*Vermittlung*) reconciliatio (*SPORT*) equalization; **zum ~ einer Si che** gen in order to offset sth; **a~e** (*unreg*) vt to balance (out); to reco cile; (*Höhe*) to even up ♦ vi (*SPORT*) t equalize

ausgraben ['ausgra:bən] (*unreg*) vt dig up; (*Leichen*) to exhume; (*fig*) t unearth

Ausgrabung f excavation; (*Ausgrabe auch*) digging up

Ausguss ▲ ['ausgʊs] m (*Spüle*) sin (*Abfluss*) outlet; (*Tülle*) spout

aushalten ['aushaltən] (*unreg*) vt bear, to stand; (*Geliebte*) to keep ♦ to hold out; **das ist nicht zum A** that is unbearable

aushandeln ['aushandəln] vt to ne gotiate

aushändigen ['aushɛndigən] vt: **jd etw ~** to hand sth over to sb

Aushang ['aushaŋ] m notice

aushängen ['aushɛŋən] (*unreg*) vt (*M dung*) to put up; (*Fenster*) to take o its hinges ♦ vi to be displayed

ausharren ['ausharən] vi to hold out

ausheben ['aushe:bən] (*unreg*) vt (*Era*)

to lift out; (*Grube*) to hollow out; (*Tür*) to take off its hinges; (*Diebesnest*) to clear out; (*MIL*) to enlist

aushecken ['aʊshɛkən] (*umg*) vt to cook up

aushelfen ['aʊshɛlfən] (*unreg*) vi: jdm ~ to help sb out

Aushilfe ['aʊshɪlfə] f help, assistance; (*Person*) (temporary) worker

Aushilfs- zW: **~kraft** f temporary worker; **a~weise** adv temporarily, as a stopgap

ausholen ['aʊshoːlən] vi to swing one's arm back; (*zur Ohrfeige*) to raise one's hand; (*beim Gehen*) to take long strides

aushorchen ['aʊshɔrçən] vt to sound out, to pump

auskennen ['aʊskɛnən] (*unreg*) vr to know a lot; (*an einem Ort*) to know one's way about; (*in Fragen etc*) to be knowledgeable

Ausklang ['aʊsklaŋ] m end

auskleiden ['aʊsklaɪdən] vr to undress ♦ vt (*Wand*) to line

ausklingen ['aʊsklɪŋən] (*unreg*) vi (*Ton, Lied*) to die away; (*Fest*) to peter out

ausklopfen ['aʊsklɔpfən] vt (*Teppich*) to beat; (*Pfeife*) to knock out

auskochen ['aʊskɔxən] vt to boil; (*MED*) to sterilize; **ausgekocht** (*fig*) out-and-out

Auskommen (-s) nt: sein A~ haben to have a regular income; (*umg*) vi: mit jdm a~ to get on with sb; mit etw a~ to get by with sth

auskosten ['aʊskɔstən] vt to enjoy to the full

auskundschaften ['aʊskʊntʃaftən] vt to spy out; (*Gebiet*) to reconnoitre

Auskunft ['aʊskʊnft] (-, **-künfte**) f information; (*nähere*) details pl, particulars pl; (*Stelle*) information office; (*TEL*) directory inquiries sg

auslachen ['aʊslaxən] vt to laugh at,

to mock

ausladen ['aʊslaːdən] (*unreg*) vt to unload; (*umg*: *Gäste*) to cancel an invitation to

Auslage ['aʊslaːgə] f shop window (display); **~n** pl (*Ausgabe*) outlay sg

Ausland ['aʊslant] nt foreign countries pl; im ~ abroad; ins ~ abroad

Ausländer(in) ['aʊslɛndər(ɪn)] (-s, -) m(f) foreigner

ausländisch adj foreign

Auslands- zW: **~gespräch** nt international call; **~reise** f trip abroad; **~schutzbrief** m international travel cover

auslassen ['aʊslasən] (*unreg*) vt to leave out; (*Wort etc auch*) to omit; (*Fett*) to melt; (*Kleidungsstück*) to let out ♦ vr: sich über etw akk ~ to speak one's mind about sth; seine Wut etc an jdm ~ to vent one's rage on sb

Auslassung f omission

Auslauf ['aʊslaʊf] m (*für Tiere*) run; (*Ausfluss*) outflow, outlet; **a~en** (*unreg*) vi to run out; (*Behälter*) to leak; (*NAUT*) to put out (to sea); (*langsam aufhören*) to run down

Ausläufer ['aʊslɔyfər] m (*von Gebirge*) spur; (*Pflanze*) runner; (*MET*: *von Hoch*) ridge; (: *von Tief*) trough

ausleeren ['aʊsleːrən] vt to empty

auslegen ['aʊsleːgən] vt (*Waren*) to lay out; (*Köder*) to put down; (*Geld*) to lend; (*bedecken*) to cover; (*Text etc*) to interpret

Auslegung f interpretation

ausleiern ['aʊslaɪərn] vt (*Gummi*) to wear out

Ausleihe ['aʊslaɪə] f issuing; (*Stelle*) issue desk; **a~n** (*unreg*) vt (*verleihen*) to lend; sich dat etw a~n to borrow sth

Auslese ['aʊsleːzə] f selection; (*Elite*) elite; (*Wein*) choice wine; **a~n** (*unreg*) vt to select; (*umg*: *zu Ende lesen*) to finish

---

Spelling Reform: ▲ new spelling △ old spelling (to be phased out)

ausliefern ['ausli:fərn] vt to deliver
(up), to hand over; (COMM) to deliver;
jdm/etw ausgeliefert sein to be at
the mercy of sb/sth

auslöschen ['auslœʃən] vt to extinguish; (fig) to wipe out, to obliterate

auslosen ['auslo:zən] vt to draw lots
for

auslösen ['auslø:zən] vt (Explosion,
Schuss) to set off; (hervorrufen) to
cause, to produce; (Gefangene) to ransom; (Pfand) to redeem

ausmachen ['ausmaxən] vt (Licht,
Radio) to turn off; (Feuer) to put out;
(entdecken) to make out; (vereinbaren)
to agree; (beilegen) to settle; (Anteil
darstellen, betragen) to represent; (bedeuten) to matter; **macht es Ihnen etwas aus, wenn ...?** would you mind if
...?

ausmalen ['ausma:lən] vt to paint;
(fig) to describe; **sich** dat **etw ~** to
imagine sth

Ausmaß ['ausma:s] nt dimension; (fig
auch) scale

ausmessen ['ausmesən] (unreg) vt to
measure

Ausnahme ['ausna:mə] f exception;
~fall m exceptional case; **~zustand** m
state of emergency

ausnahms- zW: **~los** adv without exception; **~weise** adv by way of exception, for once

ausnehmen ['ausne:mən] (unreg) vt to
take out, to remove; (Tier) to gut;
(Nest) to rob; (umg: Geld abnehmen) to
clean out; (ausschließen) to make an
exception of ♦ vr to look, to appear;
~d adj exceptional

ausnützen ['ausnʏtsən] vt (Zeit, Gelegenheit) to use, to turn to good account; (Einfluss) to use; (Mensch, Gut-
mütigkeit) to exploit

auspacken ['auspakən] vt to unpack

auspfeifen ['auspfaɪfən] (unreg) vt to
hiss/boo at

ausplaudern ['ausplaudərn] vt (Ge-

heimnis) to blab

ausprobieren ['ausprobi:rən] vt to tr
(out)

Auspuff ['auspʊf] (-(e)s, -e) m (TECH
exhaust; **~rohr** nt exhaust (pipe)

ausradieren ['ausradi:rən] vt to erase
to rub out; (fig) to annihilate

ausrangieren ['ausrãʒi:rən] (umg) v
to chuck out

ausrauben ['ausraubən] vt to rob

ausräumen ['ausrɔʏmən] vt (Dinge) to
clear away; (Schrank, Zimmer) to emp
ty; (Bedenken) to dispel

ausrechnen ['ausreçnən] vt to calcu
late, to reckon

Ausrede ['ausre:də] f excuse; **a~n** vi to
have one's say ♦ vt: **jdm etw a~n** to
talk sb out of sth

ausreichen ['ausraɪçən] vi to suffice
to be enough; **~d** adj sufficient, ad
equate; (SCH) adequate

Ausreise ['ausraɪzə] f departure; **be
der ~** when leaving the country; **~er
laubnis** f exit visa; **a~n** vi to leave the
country

ausreißen ['ausraɪsən] (unreg) vt to tea
od pull out ♦ vi (Riss bekommen) to
tear; (umg) to make off, to scram

ausrenken ['ausreŋkən] vt to dislocate

ausrichten ['ausrɪçtən] vt (Botschaft) to
deliver; (Gruß) to pass on; (Hochzei
etc) to arrange; (in gerade Linie bringen)
to get in a straight line; (angleichen) to
bring into line; (TYP) to justify; **ich
werde es ihm ~** I'll tell him; **etwas
nichts bei jdm ~** to get somewhere
nowhere with sb

ausrotten ['ausrɔtən] vt to stamp out
to exterminate

Ausruf ['ausru:f] m (Schrei) cry, excla
mation; (Bekanntmachung) proclama
tion; **a~en** (unreg) vt to cry out, to ex
claim; to call out; **~ezeichen** nt excla
mation mark

ausruhen ['ausru:ən] vt, vr to rest

ausrüsten ['ausrʏstən] vt to equip, to
fit out

Ausrüstung f equipment

ausrutschen ['ausrutʃən] vi to slip

Aussage ['ausza:gə] f (JUR) statement; **a~n** vt to say, to state ♦ vi (JUR) to give evidence

ausschalten ['ausʃaltən] vt to switch off; (fig) to eliminate

Ausschank ['ausʃaŋk] (-(e)s, -schänke) m dispensing, giving out; (COMM) selling; (Theke) bar

Ausschau ['ausʃau] f: ~ halten (nach) to look out (for), to watch (for); **a~en** vi: a~en (nach) to look out (for), to be on the look-out (for)

ausscheiden ['ausʃaidən] (unreg) vt to take out; (MED) to secrete ♦ vi: ~ (aus) to leave; (SPORT) to be eliminated (from) od knocked out (of)

Ausscheidung f separation; secretion; elimination; (aus Amt) retirement

ausschenken ['ausʃeŋkən] vt (Alkohol, Kaffee) to pour out; (COMM) to sell

ausschildern ['ausʃildərn] vt to sign-post

ausschimpfen ['ausʃimpfən] vt to scold, to tell off

ausschlafen ['ausʃla:fən] (unreg) vi, vr to have a good sleep ♦ vt to sleep off; **ich bin nicht ausgeschlafen** I didn't have od get enough sleep

Ausschlag ['ausʃla:k] m (MED) rash; (Pendelausschlag) swing; (Nadelausschlag) deflection; **den ~ geben** (fig) to tip the balance; **a~en** (-ge) (unreg) vt to knock out; (auskleiden) to deck out; (verweigern) to decline ♦ vi (Pferd) to kick out; (BOT) to sprout; **a~gebend** adj decisive

ausschließen ['ausʃli:sən] (unreg) vt to shut od lock out; (fig) to exclude

ausschließlich adj exclusive ♦ adv exclusively ♦ präp +gen exclusive of, excluding

Ausschluss ▲ ['ausʃlus] m exclusion

ausschmücken ['ausʃmykən] vt to decorate; (fig) to embellish

ausschneiden ['ausʃnaidən] (unreg) vt to cut out; (Büsche) to trim

Ausschnitt ['ausʃnit] m (Teil) section; (von Kleid) neckline; (Zeitungsausschnitt) cutting; (aus Film etc) excerpt

ausschreiben ['ausʃraibən] (unreg) vt (ganz schreiben) to write out (in full); (ausstellen) to write (out); (Stelle, Wettbewerb etc) to announce, to advertise

Ausschreitung ['ausʃraituŋ] f (usu pl) riot

Ausschuss ▲ ['ausʃus] m committee, board; (Abfall) waste, scraps pl; (COMM: auch: ~ware) reject

ausschütten ['ausʃytən] vt to pour out; (Eimer) to empty; (Geld) to pay ♦ vr to shake (with laughter)

ausschweifend ['ausʃvaifənt] adj (Leben) dissipated, debauched; (Fantasie) extravagant

aussehen ['ausze:ən] (unreg) vi to look; **es sieht nach Regen aus** it looks like rain; **es sieht schlecht aus** things look bad; **A~** (-s) nt appearance

aus sein △ siehe aus

außen ['ausən] adv outside; (nach ~) outwards; **er ist es** nor it's red on the outside

Außen- zW: ~dienst m: **im ~dienst sein** to work outside the office; **~handel** m foreign trade; **~minister** m foreign minister; **~ministerium** nt foreign ministry; **~politik** f foreign policy; **a~politisch** adj (Entwicklung, Lage) foreign; **~seite** f outside; **~seiter (-s, -)** m outsider; **~stände** pl outstanding debts; **~stehende(r)** f(m) outsider; **~welt** f outside world

außer ['ausər] präp +dat (räumlich) out of; (abgesehen von) except ♦ konj (ausgenommen) except; **~ Gefahr** out of danger; **~ Zweifel** beyond any doubt; **~ Betrieb** out of order; **~ Dienst** retired; **~ Landes** abroad; **~ sich** dat

sein to be beside o.s.; ~ **sich** akk **geraten** to go wild; ~ **wenn** unless; ~ **dass** except; ~**dem** konj besides, in addition

äußere(r, s) ['ɔʏsərə(r,s)] adj outer, external

außergewöhnlich adj unusual

außerhalb präp +gen outside ♦ adv outside

äußerlich adj external

äußern vt to utter, to express; (zeigen) to show ♦ vr to give one's opinion; (Krankheit etc) to show itself

außerordentlich adj extraordinary

außerplanmäßig adj unscheduled

äußerst ['ɔʏsərst] adv extremely, most; ~**e(r, s)** adj utmost; (räumlich) farthest; (Termin) last possible; (Preis) highest

Äußerung f remark, comment

aussetzen ['auszetsən] vt (Kind, Tier) to abandon; (Boote) to lower; (Belohnung) to offer; (Urteil, Verfahren) to postpone ♦ vi (aufhören) to stop; (Pause machen) to have a break; **jdm/etw aussetzen sein** to be exposed to sb/sth; **an jdm/etw etwas** ~ to find fault with sb/sth

Aussicht ['auszɪçt] f view; (in Zukunft) prospect; **etw in** ~ **haben** to have sth in view

a~los adj hopeless; ~**punkt** m viewpoint; **a~reich** adj promising; ~**turm** m observation tower

aussöhnen ['auszø:nən] vt to reconcile ♦ vr to reconcile o.s., to become reconciled

aussondern ['auszəndərn] vt to separate, to select

aussortieren ['auszərti:rən] vt to sort out

ausspannen ['auʃpanən] vt to spread od stretch out; (Pferd) to unharness; (umg: Mädchen): **(jdm) jdn** ~ to steal sb (from sb) ♦ vi to relax

aussperren ['auʃpɛrən] vt to lock out

ausspielen ['auʃpi:lən] vt (Karte) to lead; (Geldprämie) to offer as a prize ♦ vi (KARTEN) to lead; **jdn gegen jdn** ~

to play sb off against sb; **ausgespielt haben** to be finished

Aussprache ['auʃpra:xə] f pronunciation; (Unterredung) (frank) discussion

aussprechen ['auʃprɛçən] (unreg) vt to pronounce; (äußern) to say, to express ♦ vr (sich äußern): **sich** ~ **über** +akk) to speak (about); (sich anvertrauen) to unburden o.s. (about od on); (diskutieren) to discuss ♦ vi (zu Ende sprechen) to finish speaking

Ausspruch ['auʃprɔx] m saying, remark

ausspülen ['auʃpy:lən] vt to wash out; (Mund) to rinse

Ausstand ['auʃtant] m strike; **in den** ~ **treten** to go on strike

ausstatten ['auʃtatən] vt (Zimmer etc) to furnish; (Person) to equip, to kit out

Ausstattung f (Ausstatten) provision; (Kleidung) outfit; (Aufmachung) make up; (Einrichtung) furnishing

ausstechen ['auʃtɛçən] (unreg) vt (Augen, Rasen, Graben) to dig out; (Kekse) to cut out; (übertreffen) to outshine

ausstehen ['auʃte:ən] (unreg) vt to stand, to endure ♦ vi (noch nicht da sein) to be outstanding

aussteigen ['auʃtaigən] (unreg) vi to get out, to alight

ausstellen ['auʃtɛlən] vt to exhibit, to display; (umg: ausschalten) to switch off; (Rechnung etc) to make out; (Pass, Zeugnis) to issue

Ausstellung f exhibition; (FIN) drawing up; (einer Rechnung) making out; (eines Passes etc) issuing

aussterben ['auʃtɛrbən] (unreg) vi to die out

Aussteuer ['auʃtɔʏər] f dowry

Ausstieg ['auʃti:k] (-(e)s, -e) m exit

ausstopfen ['auʃtɔpfən] vt to stuff

ausstoßen ['auʃto:sən] (unreg) vt (Luft, Rauch) to give off, to emit; (aus Verein etc) to expel, to exclude; (Auge) to poke out

ausstrahlen ['auʃtra:lən] vt, vi to radi

ate; (RADIO) to broadcast

Ausstrahlung f radiation; (fig) charisma

ausstrecken ['aʊsʃtrɛkən] vt, vr to stretch out

ausstreichen ['aʊsʃtraɪçən] (unreg) vt to cross out; (glätten) to smooth (out)

ausströmen ['aʊsʃtrøːmən] vi (Gas) to pour out, to escape ♦ vt to give off; (fig) to radiate

aussuchen ['aʊszuːxən] vt to select, to pick out

Austausch ['aʊstaʊʃ] m exchange; **a~bar** adj exchangeable; **a~en** vt to exchange, to swap

austeilen ['aʊstaɪlən] vt to distribute, to give out

Auster ['aʊstər] (-, -n) f oyster

austoben ['aʊstoːbən] vr (Kind) to run wild; (Erwachsene) to sow one's wild oats

austragen ['aʊstraːɡən] (unreg) vt (Post) to deliver; (Streit etc) to decide; (Wettkämpfe) to hold

Australien [aʊsˈtraːliən] (-s) nt Australia; **Australier(in)** (-s, -) m(f) Australian; **australisch** adj Australian

austreiben ['aʊstraɪbən] (unreg) vt to drive out, to expel; (Geister) to exorcize

austreten ['aʊstreːtən] (unreg) vi (aus Toilette) to be excused ♦ vt (Feuer) to tread out, to trample; (Schuhe) to wear out; (Treppe) to wear down; **aus etw ~** to leave sth

austrinken ['aʊstrɪŋkən] (unreg) vt (Glas) to drain; (Getränk) to drink up ♦ vi to finish one's drink, to drink up

Austritt ['aʊstrɪt] m emission; (aus Verein, Partei etc) retirement, withdrawal

austrocknen ['aʊstrɔknən] vt, vi to dry up

ausüben ['aʊsˈyːbən] vt (Beruf) to practise, to carry out; (Funktion) to perform; (Einfluss) to exert; **einen Reiz**

auf jdn ~ to hold an attraction for sb; **eine Wirkung auf jdn ~** to have an effect on sb

Ausverkauf ['aʊsfɛrkaʊf] m sale; **a~en** vt to sell out; (Geschäft) to sell up; **a~t** adj (Karten, Artikel) sold out; (THEAT: Haus) full

Auswahl ['aʊsvaːl] f: **eine ~ (an** +dat) a selection (of), a choice (of)

auswählen ['aʊsvɛːlən] vt to select, to choose

Auswander- ['aʊsvandər] zW: **~er** m emigrant; **a~n** vi to emigrate; **~ung** f emigration

auswärtig ['aʊsvɛrtɪç] adj (nicht am/vom Ort) out-of-town; (ausländisch) foreign

auswärts ['aʊsvɛrts] adv outside; (nach außen) outwards; **~ essen** to eat out; **A~spiel** ['aʊsvɛrtsʃpiːl] nt away game

auswechseln ['aʊsvɛksəln] vt to change, to substitute

Ausweg ['aʊsveːk] m way out; **a~los** adj hopeless

ausweichen ['aʊsvaɪçən] (unreg) vi: **jdm/etw ~** to move aside or make way for sb/sth; (fig) to side-step sb/sth; **~d** adj evasive

ausweinen ['aʊsvaɪnən] vr to have a (good) cry

Ausweis ['aʊsvaɪs] (-es, -e) m identity card; passport; (Mitgliedsausweis, Bibliotheksausweis etc) card; **a~en** [-zən] (unreg) vt to expel, to banish ♦ vr to prove one's identity; **~kontrolle** f identity check; **~papiere** pl identity papers; **~ung** f expulsion

ausweiten ['aʊsvaɪtən] vt to stretch

auswendig ['aʊsvɛndɪç] adv by heart

auswerten ['aʊsvɛrtən] vt to evaluate; **Auswertung** f evaluation, analysis; (Nutzung) utilization

auswirken ['aʊsvɪrkən] vr to have an effect; **Auswirkung** f effect

auswischen ['aʊsvɪʃən] vt to wipe out;

Spelling Reform: ▲ new spelling △ old spelling (to be phased out)

jdm eins ~ (umg) to put one over on sb

Auswuchs ['aʊsvuːks] m (out)growth; (fig) product

auszahlen ['aʊstsaːlən] vt (Lohn, Summe) to pay out; (Arbeiter) to pay off; (Miterbe) to buy out ♦ vr (sich lohnen) to pay

auszählen ['aʊstseːlən] vt (Stimmen) to count

auszeichnen ['aʊstsaɪçnən] vt to honour; (MIL) to decorate; (COMM) to price ♦ vr to distinguish o.s.

Auszeichnung f distinction; (COMM) pricing; (Ehrung) awarding of decoration; (Ehre) honour; (Orden) decoration; **mit ~** with distinction

ausziehen ['aʊstsiːən] (unreg) vt (Kleidung) to take off; (Haare, Zähne, Tisch etc) to pull out; (nachmalen) to trace ♦ vr to undress ♦ vi (aufbrechen) to leave; (aus Wohnung) to move out

Auszubildende(r) ['aʊstsʊbɪldəndə(r)] f(m) trainee

Auszug ['aʊstsuːk] m (aus Wohnung) removal; (aus Buch etc) extract; (Kontoauszug) statement; (Ausmarsch) departure

Auto ['aʊto] (-s, -s) nt (motor)car; ~fahren to drive; **~atlas** m road atlas; **~bahn** f motorway; **~bahndreieck** nt motorway junction; **~bahngebühr** f toll; **~bahnkreuz** nt motorway intersection; **~bus** m bus; **~fähre** f car ferry; **~fahrer(in)** m(f) motorist, driver; **~fahrt** f drive; **a~gen** [-'geːn] adj autogenous; **a~gramm** nt autograph

---

Autobahn

An Autobahn is a motorway. In former West Germany there is a widespread motorway network but in the former DDR the motorways are somewhat less extensive. There is no overall speed limit but a limit of 130 km/hour is recommended and there are lower mandatory limits on certain stretches of road. As yet there are no tolls pay-

able on German Autobahnen. However, a yearly toll is payable in Switzerland and tolls have been introduce in Austria.

Auto- zW: **~'mat** (-en, -en) machine; **~'matik** [aʊto'maːtɪk] f (AU automatic; **a~'matisch** adj automati **a~nom** [-'noːm] adj autonomous

Autor(in) ['aʊtɔr(ɪn)] (-s, -en) m(author

Auto- zW: **~radio** nt car radio; **~reife** m car tyre; **~reisezug** m motora train; **~rennen** nt motor racing

autoritär [aʊtori'tɛːr] adj authoritarian

Autorität f authority

Auto- zW: **~telefon** nt car phone **~unfall** m car od motor accident **~vermietung** m car hire (BRIT) od rent al (US); **~waschanlage** f car wash

Axt [akst] (-, ⁻e) f axe

B, b

Baby ['beːbi] (-s, -s) nt baby; **~nah rung** f baby food; **~sitter** (-s, -) baby-sitter

Bach [bax] (-(e)s, ⁻e) m stream, brook

Backbord (-(e)s, -e) nt (NAUT) port

Backe ['bakə] f cheek

backen ['bakən] (unreg) vt, vi to bake

Backenzahn m molar

Bäcker ['bɛkər(ɪn)] (-s, -) m baker; **~e** f bakery; **(~eiladen)** baker's (shop)

Back- zW: **~form** f baking tin; **~obs** nt dried fruit; **~ofen** m oven; **~pflau me** f prune; **~pulver** nt baking pow der; **~stein** m brick

Bad [baːt] (-(e)s, ⁻er) nt bath; (Schwim men) bathe; (Ort) spa

Bade- ['baːdə] zW: **~anstalt** f (swim ming) baths pl; **~anzug** m bathin suit; **~hose** f bathing od swimmin trunks pl; **~kappe** f bathing cap **~mantel** m bathing) robe; **~meiste** m baths attendant; **b~n** vi to bathe, t have a bath ♦ vt to bathe; **~ort** m spa; **~tuch** nt bath towel; **~wanne** f bath (tub); **~zimmer** nt bathroom

Bagatelle [baga'tɛlə] f trifle

Bagger ['bagər] (-s, -) m excavator; (NAUT) dredger; **b~n** vt, vi to excavate; to dredge

Bahn [ba:n] (-, -en) f railway, railroad (US); (Weg) road, way; (Spur) lane; (Rennbahn) track; (ASTRON) orbit; (Stoffbahn) length; **b~brechend** adj pioneering; **B~Card** ['ba:nka:d] (-, -s) ® f ≈ railcard; **~damm** m railway embankment; **b~en** vt: **sich/jdm einen Weg b~en** to clear a way for sb; **~fahrt** f railway journey; **~fracht** f rail freight; **~hof** (-, -s) m station; **auf dem ~hof** at the station; **~hofshalle** f station concourse; **~linie** f railway line; **~steig** m platform; **~übergang** m level crossing, grade crossing (US)

Bahre ['ba:rə] f stretcher

Bakterien [bak'te:riən] pl bacteria pl

Balance [ba'lã:sə] f balance, equilibrium

balan'cieren vt, vi to balance

bald [balt] adv (zeitlich) soon; (beinahe) almost; **~ig** ['baldiç] adj early, speedy

Baldrian ['baldria:n] (-s, -e) m valerian

Balkan ['balka:n] (-s) m: **der ~** the Balkans pl

Balken ['balkən] (-s, -) m beam; (Tragbalken) girder; (Stützbalken) prop

Balkon [bal'kõː] (-s, -s od -e) m balcony; (THEAT) circle

Ball [bal] (-(e)s, ²e) m ball; (Tanz) dance, ball

Ballast ['balast] (-(e)s, -e) m ballast; (fig) weight, burden

Ballen ['balən] (-s, -) m bale; (ANAT) ball; **b~** vt (formen) to make into a ball; (Faust) to clench ♦ vr (Wolken etc) to build up; (Menschen) to gather

Ballett [ba'lɛt] (-(e)s, -e) nt ballet

Ballkleid nt evening dress

Ballon [ba'lõː] (-s, -s od -e) m balloon

Ballspiel nt ball game

Ballungsgebiet ['baluŋsgəbi:t] nt conurbation

Baltikum ['baltikom] (-s) nt: **das ~** the Baltic States

Banane [ba'na:nə] f banana

Band¹ [bant] (-(e)s, ²e) m (Buchband) volume

Band² (-(e)s, ²er) nt (Stoffband) ribbon, tape; (Fließband) production line; (Tonband) tape; (ANAT) ligament; **etw auf ~ aufnehmen** to tape sth; **am laufenden ~** (umg) non-stop

Band³ (-(e)s, -e) nt (Freundschaftsband etc) bond

Band⁴ [bɛnt] (-, -s) f band, group

band etc vb siehe **binden**

Bandage [ban'da:ʒə] f bandage

banda'gieren vt to bandage

Bande ['bandə] f band; (Straßenbande) gang

bändigen ['bɛndigən] vt (Tier) to tame; (Trieb, Leidenschaft) to control, to restrain

Bandit [ban'di:t] (-en, -en) m bandit

Band- zW: **~nudel** f (KOCH: gew pl) ribbon noodles pl; **~scheibe** f (ANAT) disc; **~wurm** m tapeworm

bange ['baŋə] adj scared; (besorgt) anxious; **jdm wird es ~** sb is becoming scared; **jdm B~ machen** to scare sb; **~n** vi: **um jdn/etw ~n** to be anxious od worried about sb/sth

Bank¹ [baŋk] (-, ²e) f (Sitz~) bench; (Sand~ etc) (sand)bank, (sand)bar

Bank² [baŋk] (-, -en) f (Geldbank) bank; **~anweisung** f banker's order; **~einzug** m direct debit

Bankett [baŋ'kɛt] (-(e)s, -e) nt (Essen) banquet; (Straßenrand) verge (BRIT), shoulder (US)

Bankier [baŋki'e:] (-s, -s) m banker

Bank- zW: **~konto** nt bank account; **~leitzahl** f bank sort code number;

~note f banknote; **~raub** m bank robbery

Bankrott [baŋ'krɔt] (-(e)s, -e) m bankruptcy; **~ machen** to go bankrupt; b~ adj bankrupt

Bankverbindung f banking arrangements pl; **geben Sie bitte Ihre ~** an please give your account details

Bann [ban] (-(e)s, -e) m (HIST) ban; (Kirchenbann) excommunication; (fig: Zauber) spell; **b~en** vt (Geister) to exorcize; (Gefahr) to avert; (bezaubern) to enchant; (HIST) to banish

Banner (-s, -) nt banner, flag

Bar (-, -s) f bar

bar [baːr] adj (+gen) (unbedeckt) bare; (frei von) lacking (in); (offenkundig) utter, sheer; **~e(s) Geld** cash; **etw (in) ~ bezahlen** to pay sth (in) cash; **etw für ~e Münze nehmen** (fig) to take sth at its face value

Bär [bɛːr] (-en, -en) m bear

Baracke [ba'rakə] f hut

barbarisch [bar'baːrɪʃ] adj barbaric, barbarous

Bar- zW: **b~fuß** adj barefoot; **~geld** nt cash, ready money; **b~geldlos** adj non-cash

Barkauf m cash purchase

Barkeeper ['baːrkiːpər] (-s, -) m barman, bartender

barmherzig [barm'hɛrtsɪç] adj merciful, compassionate

Baron [ba'roːn] (-s, -e) m baron; **~in** f baroness

Barren ['barən] (-s, -) m parallel bars pl; (Goldbarren) ingot

Barriere [bari'ɛːrə] f barrier

Barrikade [bari'kaːdə] f barricade

Barsch [barʃ] (-(e)s, -e) m perch

barsch [barʃ] adj brusque, gruff

Bar- zW: **~schaft** f ready money; **~scheck** m open od uncrossed cheque (BRIT), open check (US)

Bart [baːrt] (-(e)s, -e) m beard; (Schlüsselbart) bit; **bärtig** ['bɛːrtɪç] adj bearded

Barzahlung f cash payment

Base ['baːzə] f (CHEM) base; (Kusine cousin

Basel ['baːzəl] nt Basle

Basen pl von Base; Basis

basieren [ba'ziːrən] vt to base ♦ vi t be based

Basis ['baːzɪs] (-, Basen) f basis

Bass ▲ [bas] (-es, ⸗e) m bass

Bassin [ba'sɛ̃ː] (-s, -s) nt pool

basteln ['bastəln] vt to make ♦ vi to d handicrafts

bat etc [baːt] vb siehe bitten

Bataillon [batal'joːn] (-s, -e) nt bat talion

Batik ['baːtɪk] f (Verfahren) batik

Batterie [batə'riː] f battery

Bau [bau] (-(e)s) m (~en) building, con struction; (Aufbau) structure (Körperbau) frame; (~stelle) buildin site; (pl ~e: Tierbau) hole, burrow (: MIN) working(s); (pl ~ten: Gebäude building; **sich im ~ befinden** to b under construction; **~arbeiten** p building od construction work sg; **~a beiter** m building worker

Bauch [baux] (-(e)s, Bäuche) m belly (ANAT auch) stomach, abdomen; **~fe** nt peritoneum; **b~ig** adj bulbous; **~na bel** m navel; **~redner** m ventriloquis **~schmerzen** pl stomachache; **~we** nt stomachache

Baudenkmal nt historical monument

bauen ['bauən] vt, vi to build; (TECH) t construct; **auf jdn/etw ~** to depend od count upon sb/sth

Bauer[1] ['bauər] (-n od -s, -n) m farm er; (Schach) pawn

Bauer[2] ['bauər] (-s, -) nt od r (bird)cage

Bäuerin ['bɔyərɪn] f farmer; (Frau de Bauers) farmer's wife

bäuerlich adj rustic

Bauern- zW: **~haus** nt farmhouse **~hof** m farm(yard)

Bau- zW: **b~fällig** adj dilapidated; **~ge lände** f building site; **~genehmigun**

f building permit; **~gerüst** *nt* scaffolding; **~herr** *m* purchaser; **~kasten** *m* box of bricks; **~land** *nt* building land; **b~lich** *adj* structural

Baum [baʊm] (-(e)s, **Bäume**) *m* tree

baumeln ['baʊməln] *vi* to dangle

bäumen ['bɔymən] *vr* to rear (up)

Baum- *zW*: **~schule** *f* nursery; **~stamm** *m* tree trunk; **~stumpf** *m* tree stump; **~wolle** *f* cotton

Bau- *zW*: **~plan** *m* architect's plan; **~platz** *m* building site

bauspar- *zW*: **~en** *vi* to save with a building society; **B~kasse** *f* building society; **B~vertrag** *m* building society savings agreement

Bau- *zW*: **~stein** *m* building stone, freestone; **~stelle** *f* building site; **~teil** *nt* prefabricated part (of building); **~ten** *pl von* Bau; **~unternehmer** *m* building contractor; **~weise** *f* (method of) construction; **~werk** *nt* building; **~zaun** *m* hoarding

Bayern ['baɪərn] *nt* Bavaria

bayrisch ['baɪrɪʃ] *adj* Bavarian

Bazillus [ba'tsɪlʊs] (-, **Bazillen**) *m* bacillus

beabsichtigen [bə'ʔapzɪçtɪgən] *vt* to intend

beacht- [bə'axt] *zW*: **~en** *vt* to take note of, (*Vorschrift*) to obey; (*Vorfahrt*) to observe; **~lich** *adj* considerable; **B~ung** *f* notice, attention, observation

Beamte(r) [bə'ʔamtə(r)] (-n, -n) *m* official; (*Staatsbeamte*) civil servant; (*Bankbeamte etc*) employee

Beamtin *f siehe* Beamte(r)

beängstigend [bə'ʔɛŋstɪgənt] *adj* alarming

beanspruchen [bə'ʔanʃprʊxən] *vt* to claim; (*Zeit, Platz*) to take up, to occupy; **jdn ~** to take up sb's time

beanstanden [bə'ʔanʃtandən] *vt* to complain about, to object to

beantragen [bə'ʔantragən] *vt* to apply for, to ask for

beantworten [bə'ʔantvɔrtən] *vt* to answer; **Beantwortung** *f* (+*gen*) reply (to)

bearbeiten [bə'ʔarbaɪtən] *vt* to work; (*Material*) to process; (*Thema*) to deal with; (*Land*) to cultivate; (*CHEM*) to treat; (*Buch*) to revise; (*umg: beeinflussen wollen*) to work on

Bearbeitung *f* processing; cultivation; treatment; revision

Bearbeitungsgebühr *f* handling charge

Beatmung [bə'ʔa:tmʊŋ] *f* respiration

beaufsichtigen [bə'ʔaʊfzɪçtɪgən] *vt* to supervise; **Beaufsichtigung** *f* supervision

beauftragen [bə'ʔaʊftragən] *vt* to instruct; **jdn mit etw ~** to entrust sb with sth

Beauftragte(r) *f(m)* representative

bebauen [bə'baʊən] *vt* to build on; (*AGR*) to cultivate

beben ['be:bən] *vi* to tremble, to shake; **B~** (-s, -) *nt* earthquake

Becher ['bɛçər] (-s, -) *m* mug; (*ohne Henkel*) tumbler

Becken ['bɛkən] (-s, -) *nt* basin; (*MUS*) cymbal; (*ANAT*) pelvis

bedacht [bə'daxt] *adj* thoughtful, careful; **auf etw akk ~ sein** to be concerned about sth

bedächtig [bə'dɛçtɪç] *adj* (*umsichtig*) thoughtful, reflective; (*langsam*) slow, deliberate

bedanken [bə'daŋkən] *vr*: **sich (bei jdm) ~** to say thank you (to sb)

Bedarf [bə'darf] (-(e)s) *m* need, requirement; (*COMM*) demand; **je nach ~** according to demand; **bei ~** if necessary; **~ an etw dat haben** to be in need of sth

Bedarfs- *zW*: **~fall** *m* case of need; **~haltestelle** *f* request stop

---

Spelling Reform: ▲ *new spelling* △ *old spelling (to be phased out)*

bedauerlich [bəˈdaʊərlɪç] *adj* regrettable

bedauern [bəˈdaʊərn] *vt* to be sorry for; (*bemitleiden*) to pity; **B~** (**-s**) *nt* regret; **~swert** *adj* (*Zustände*) regrettable; (*Mensch*) pitiable, unfortunate

bedecken [bəˈdɛkən] *vt* to cover

bedeckt *adj* covered; (*Himmel*) overcast

bedenken [bəˈdɛŋkən] (*unreg*) *vt* to think over, to consider

Bedenken (**-s**, **-**) *nt* (*Überlegen*) consideration; (*Zweifel*) doubt; (*Skrupel*) scruple

bedenklich *adj* doubtful; (*bedrohlich*) dangerous, risky

Bedenkzeit *f* time to think

bedeuten [bəˈdɔʏtən] *vt* to mean; to signify; (*wichtig sein*) to be of importance; **~d** *adj* important; (*beträchtlich*) considerable

bedeutsam *adj* (*wichtig*) significant

Bedeutung *f* meaning; significance; (*Wichtigkeit*) importance; **b~slos** *adj* insignificant, unimportant; **b~svoll** *adj* momentous, significant

bedienen [bəˈdiːnən] *vt* to serve; (*Maschine*) to work, to operate ♦ *vr* (*beim Essen*) to help o.s.; **sich jds/ einer Sache ~** to make use of sb/sth

Bedienung *f* service; (*Kellnerin*) waitress; (*Verkäuferin*) shop assistant; (*Zuschlag*) service (charge)

Bedienungsanleitung *f* operating instructions *pl*

bedingen [bəˈdɪŋən] *vt* (*verursachen*) to cause

bedingt *adj* (*Richtigkeit, Tauglichkeit*) limited; (*Zusage, Annahme*) conditional

Bedingung *f* condition; (*Voraussetzung*) stipulation; **b~slos** *adj* unconditional

bedrängen [bəˈdrɛŋən] *vt* to pester, to harass

bedrohen [bəˈdroːən] *vt* to threaten; **Bedrohung** *f* threat, menace

bedrücken [bəˈdrʏkən] *vt* to oppress, to trouble

bedürf- [bəˈdʏrf] *zW*: **~en** (*unreg*) *vi* +*gen* to need, to require; **B~nis** (**-ses, -se**) *nt* need; **~tig** *adj* in need, poor, needy

beeilen [bəˈʔaɪlən] *vr* to hurry

beeindrucken [bəˈʔaɪndrʊkən] *vt* to impress, to make an impression on

beeinflussen [bəˈʔaɪnflʊsən] *vt* to influence

beeinträchtigen [bəˈʔaɪntrɛçtɪgən] *vt* to affect adversely; (*Freiheit*) to infringe upon

beend(ig)en [bəˈʔɛnd(ɪg)ən] *vt* to end, to finish, to terminate

beengen [bəˈʔɛŋən] *vt* to cramp; (*fig*) to hamper, to oppress

beerben [bəˈʔɛrbən] *vt*: **jdn ~** to inherit from sb

beerdigen [bəˈʔeːrdɪgən] *vt* to bury; **Beerdigung** *f* funeral, burial

Beere [ˈbeːrə] *f* berry; (*Traubenbeere*) grape

Beet [beːt] (**-(e)s, -e**) *nt* bed

befähigen [bəˈfɛːɪgən] *vt* to enable

befähigt *adj* (*begabt*) talented; **~ (für)** (*fähig*) capable (of)

Befähigung *f* capability (*Begabung*) talent, aptitude

befahrbar [bəˈfaːrbaːr] *adj* passable; (*NAUT*) navigable

befahren [bəˈfaːrən] (*unreg*) *vt* to use, to drive over; (*NAUT*) to navigate ♦ *adj* used

befallen [bəˈfalən] (*unreg*) *vt* to come over

befangen [bəˈfaŋən] *adj* (*schüchtern*) shy, self-conscious; (*voreingenommen*) biased

befassen [bəˈfasən] *vr* to concern o.s.

Befehl [bəˈfeːl] (**-(e)s, -e**) *m* command, order; **b~en** (*unreg*) *vt* to order ♦ *vi* to give orders; **jdm etw b~en** to order sb to do sth; **~sverweigerung** *f* insubordination

befestigen [bəˈfɛstɪgən] *vt* to fasten; (*stärken*) to strengthen; (*MIL*) to fortify; **~ an** +*dat* to fasten to

Befestigung f fastening; strengthening; (MIL) fortification

befeuchten [bəˈfɔʏçtən] vt to damp(en), to moisten

befinden [bəˈfɪndən] (unreg) vr to be; (sich fühlen) to feel ♦ vt: **jdn/etw für od als etw ~** to deem sb/sth to be sth ♦ vi: **~ (über +akk)** to decide (on), to adjudicate (on); **B~ (-s)** nt health, condition; (Meinung) view, opinion

befolgen [bəˈfɔlɡən] vt to comply with, to follow

befördern [bəˈfœrdərn] vt (senden) to transport, to send; (beruflich) to promote; **Beförderung** f transport; promotion

befragen [bəˈfraːɡən] vt to question

befreien [bəˈfraɪən] vt to set free; (erlassen) to exempt; **Befreiung** f liberation, release; (Erlassen) exemption

befreunden [bəˈfrɔʏndən] vr to make friends; (mit Idee etc) to acquaint o.s.

befreundet adj friendly

befriedigen [bəˈfriːdɪɡən] vt to satisfy; **~d** adj satisfactory

Befriedigung f satisfaction, gratification

befristet [bəˈfrɪstət] adj limited

befruchten [bəˈfrʊxtən] vt to fertilize; (fig) to stimulate

Befruchtung f: **künstliche ~** artificial insemination

Befugnis [bəˈfuːknɪs] (-, -se) f authorization, powers pl

befugt adj authorized, entitled

Befund [bəˈfʊnt] (-(e)s, -e) m findings pl; (MED) diagnosis

befürchten [bəˈfʏrçtən] vt to fear; **Befürchtung** f fear, apprehension

befürworten [bəˈfyːrvɔrtən] vt to speak in favour of; **Befürworter** (-s, -) m supporter, advocate

begabt [bəˈɡaːpt] adj gifted

Begabung [bəˈɡaːbʊŋ] f talent, gift

begann etc [bəˈɡan] vb siehe **beginnen**

begeben [bəˈɡeːbən] (unreg) vr (gehen) to betake o.s.; (geschehen) to occur; **sich ~ nach od zu** to proceed to(wards); **B~heit** f occurrence

begegnen [bəˈɡeːɡnən] vi: **jdm ~** to meet sb; (behandeln) to treat sb; **einer Sache** dat **~** to meet with sth

Begegnung f meeting

begehen [bəˈɡeːən] (unreg) vt (Straftat) to commit; (abschreiten) to cover; (Straße etc) to use, to negotiate; (Feier) to celebrate

begehren [bəˈɡeːrən] vt to desire

begehrt adj in demand; (Junggeselle) eligible

begeistern [bəˈɡaɪstərn] vt to fill with enthusiasm, to inspire ♦ vr: **sich für etw ~** to get enthusiastic about sth

begeistert adj enthusiastic

Begierde [bəˈɡiːrdə] f desire, passion

begierig [bəˈɡiːrɪç] adj eager, keen

begießen [bəˈɡiːsən] (unreg) vt to water; (mit Alkohol) to drink to

Beginn [bəˈɡɪn] (-(e)s) m beginning; **zu ~** at the beginning; **b~en** (unreg) vt, vi to start, to begin

beglaubigen [bəˈɡlaʊbɪɡən] vt to countersign; **Beglaubigung** f countersignature

begleichen [bəˈɡlaɪçən] (unreg) vt to settle, to pay

Begleit- [bəˈɡlaɪt] zW: **b~en** vt to accompany; (MIL) to escort; **~er (-s, -)** m companion; (Freund) escort; (MUS) accompanist; **~schreiben** nt covering letter; **~umstände** pl concomitant circumstances; **~ung** f company; (MIL) escort; (MUS) accompaniment

beglücken [bəˈɡlʏkən] vt to make happy, to delight

beglückwünschen [bəˈɡlʏkvʏnʃən] vt: **~ (zu)** to congratulate (on)

begnadigen [bəˈɡnaːdɪɡən] vt to pardon; **Begnadigung** f pardon, am-

Spelling Reform: ▲ new spelling △ old spelling (to be phased out)

nesty

begnügen [bəˈgnyːgən] *vr* to be satisfied, to content o.s.

begonnen *etc* [bəˈgɔnən] *vb siehe* **beginnen**

begraben [bəˈgraːbən] (*unreg*) *vt* to bury; **Begräbnis** (**-ses, -se**) [bəˈgrɛːpnɪs] *nt* burial, funeral

begreifen [bəˈgraɪfən] (*unreg*) *vt* to understand, to comprehend

begreiflich [bəˈgraɪflɪç] *adj* understandable

begrenzen [bəˈgrɛntsən] *vt* (*beschränken*) to limit

Begrenztheit [bəˈgrɛntsthaɪt] *f* limitation, restriction; (*fig*) narrowness

Begriff [bəˈgrɪf] (**-(e)s, -e**) *m* concept, idea; **im ~ sein, etw zu tun** to be about to do sth; **schwer von ~** (*umg*) slow, dense

begriffsstutzig *adj* slow, dense

begründ- [bəˈgrʏnd] *zW:* **~en** *vt* (*Gründe geben*) to justify; **~et** *adj* well-founded, justified; **B~ung** *f* justification, reason

begrüßen [bəˈgryːsən] *vt* to greet, to welcome; **Begrüßung** *f* greeting, welcome

begünstigen [bəˈgʏnstɪgən] *vt* (*Person*) to favour; (*Sache*) to further, to promote

begutachten [bəˈguːtʔaxtən] *vt* to assess

begütert [bəˈgyːtərt] *adj* wealthy, well-to-do

behaart [bəˈhaːrt] *adj* hairy

behagen [bəˈhaːgən] *vi:* **das behagt ihm nicht** he does not like it

behaglich [bəˈhaːklɪç] *adj* comfortable, cosy; **B~keit** *f* comfort, cosiness

behalten [bəˈhaltən] (*unreg*) *vt* to keep, to retain; (*im Gedächtnis*) to remember

Behälter [bəˈhɛltər] (**-s, -**) *m* container, receptacle

behandeln [bəˈhandəln] *vt* to treat; (*Thema*) to deal with; (*Maschine*) to handle

Behandlung *f* treatment; (*vor Maschine*) handling

beharren [bəˈharən] *vi:* **auf etw** *dat* ~ to stick od keep to sth

beharrlich [bəˈharlɪç] *adj* (*ausdauernd*) steadfast, unwavering; (*hartnäckig*) tenacious, dogged; **B~keit** *f* steadfastness; tenacity

behaupten [bəˈhaʊptən] *vt* to claim, to assert, to maintain; (*sein Recht*) to defend ♦ *vr* to assert o.s.

Behauptung *f* claim, assertion

beheben [bəˈheːbən] (*unreg*) *vt* to remove

behelfen [bəˈhɛlfən] (*unreg*) *vr:* **sich mit etw ~** to make do with sth

behelfsmäßig *adj* improvised, makeshift; (*vorübergehend*) temporary

behelligen [bəˈhɛlɪgən] *vt* to trouble, to bother

beherbergen [bəˈhɛrbɛrgən] *vt* to put up, to house

beherrsch- [bəˈhɛrʃ] *zW:* **~en** *vt* (*Volk*) to rule, to govern; (*Situation*) to control; (*Sprache, Gefühle*) to master ♦ *vr* to control o.s.; **~t** *adj* controlled; **B~ung** *f* rule; control; mastery

beherzigen [bəˈhɛrtsɪgən] *vt* to take to heart

beherzt *adj* courageous, brave

behilflich [bəˈhɪlflɪç] *adj* helpful; **jdm ~ sein (bei)** to help sb (with)

behindern [bəˈhɪndərn] *vt* to hinder, to impede

Behinderte(r) *f(m)* disabled person

Behinderung *f* hindrance; (*Körperbehinderung*) handicap

Behörde [bəˈhøːrdə] *f* (*auch pl*) authorities *pl*

behördlich [bəˈhøːrtlɪç] *adj* official

behüten [bəˈhyːtən] *vt* to guard; **jdn vor etw** *dat* ~ to preserve sb from sth

behutsam [bəˈhuːtzaːm] *adj* cautious, careful; **B~keit** *f* caution, carefulness

SCHLÜSSELWORT

bei [baɪ] *präp* +*dat* **1** (*nahe bei*) near;

(zum Aufenthalt) at, with; (unter, zwischen) among; **bei München** near Munich; **bei uns** at our place; **beim Friseur** at the hairdresser's; **bei seinen Eltern wohnen** to live with one's parents; **bei einer Firma arbeiten** to work for a firm; **etw bei sich haben** to have sth on one; **jdn bei sich haben** to have sb with one; **bei Goethe** in Goethe; **bei Militär** in the army 2 (zeitlich) at, on; (während) during; (Zustand, Umstand) in; **bei Nacht** at night; **bei Nebel** in fog; **bei Regen** if it rains; **bei solcher Hitze** in such heat; **bei meiner Ankuft** on my arrival; **bei der Arbeit** when I'm etc working; **beim Fahren** while driving

beibehalten ['baɪbəhaltən] (unreg) vt to keep, to retain

beibringen ['baɪbrɪŋən] (unreg) vt (Beweis, Zeugen) to bring forward; (Gründe) to adduce; **jdm etw ~** (lehren) to teach sb sth; (zu verstehen geben) to make sb understand sth; (zufügen) to inflict sth on sb

Beichte ['baɪçtə] f confession; **b~n** vi to confess ♦ vi to go to confession

beide(s) ['baɪdə(s)] pron, adj both; **meine ~n Brüder** my two brothers, both my brothers; **die ersten ~n** the first two; **wir ~** we two; **einer von ~n** one of the two; **alles ~s** both (of them)

beider- ['baɪdər] zW: **~lei** adj inv of both; **~seitig** adj mutual, reciprocal; **~seits** adv mutually ♦ präp +gen on both sides of

beieinander [baɪaɪ'nandər] adv together

Beifahrer ['baɪfaːrər] m passenger

Beifall ['baɪfal] (-(e)s) m applause; (Zustimmung) approval

beifügen ['baɪfyːgən] vt to enclose

beige ['beːʒ] adj beige, fawn

beigeben ['baɪgeːbən] (unreg) vt (zu-

fügen) to add; (mitgeben) to give ♦ vi (nachgeben) to give in

Beihilfe ['baɪhɪlfə] f aid, assistance; (Studienbeihilfe) grant; (JUR) aiding and abetting

beikommen ['baɪkɔmən] (unreg) vi +dat to get at; (einem Problem) to deal with

Beil [baɪl] (-(e)s, -e) nt axe, hatchet

Beilage ['baɪlaːgə] f (Buchbeilage etc) supplement; (KOCH) vegetables and potatoes pl

beiläufig ['baɪlɔyfɪç] adj casual, incidental ♦ adv casually, by the way

beilegen ['baɪleːgən] vt (hinzufügen) to enclose, to add; (beimessen) to attribute, to ascribe; (Streit) to settle

Beileid ['baɪlaɪt] nt condolence, sympathy; **herzliches ~** deepest sympathy

beiliegend ['baɪliːgənt] adj (COMM) enclosed

beim [baɪm] = bei dem

beimessen ['baɪmɛsən] (unreg) vt (+dat) to attribute (to), to ascribe (to)

Bein [baɪn] (-(e)s, -e) nt leg

beinah(e) ['baɪnaː(ə)] adv almost, nearly

Beinbruch m fracture of the leg

beinhalten [bə'ɪnhaltən] vt to contain

Beipackzettel ['baɪpaktsetəl] m instruction leaflet

beipflichten ['baɪpflɪçtən] vi: **jdm/etw ~** to agree with sb/sth

beisammen [baɪ'zamən] adv together; **B~sein** (-s) nt get-together

Beischlaf ['baɪʃlaːf] m sexual intercourse

Beisein ['baɪzaɪn] (-s) nt presence

beiseite ['baɪzaɪtə] adv to one side, aside; (stehen) to one side, aside; **etw ~ legen** (sparen) to put sth by

beisetzen ['baɪzetsən] vt to bury; **Beisetzung** f funeral

Beisitzer ['baɪzɪtsər] (-s, -) m (bei

Prüfung) assessor

Beispiel ['baɪʃpiːl] (-(e)s, -e) *nt* example; **sich** +*dat* **an jdm ein ~ nehmen** to take sb as an example; **zum ~** for example; **b~haft** *adj* exemplary; **b~los** *adj* unprecedented; **b~sweise** *adv* for instance ♦ *adv* example

beißen ['baɪsən] (*unreg*) *vt, vi* to bite; (*stechen: Rauch, Säure*) to burn ♦ *vr* (*Farben*) to clash; **~d** *adj* biting, caustic; (*fig auch*) sarcastic

Beistand ['baɪʃtant] (-(e)s, =e) *m* support, help; (*JUR*) adviser

beistehen ['baɪʃteːən] (*unreg*) *vi:* **jdm ~** to stand by sb

beisteuern ['baɪʃtɔʏɐn] *vt* to contribute

Beitrag ['baɪtraːk] (-(e)s, =e) *m* contribution; (*Zahlung*) fee, subscription; (*Versicherungsbeitrag*) premium; **b~en** ['baɪtraːgən] (*unreg*) *vt, vi:* **b~en (zu)** to contribute (to); (*mithelfen*) to help (with)

beitreten ['baɪtreːtən] (*unreg*) *vi* +*dat* to join

Beitritt ['baɪtrɪt] *m* joining, membership

Beiwagen ['baɪvaːgən] *m* (*Motorradbeiwagen*) sidecar

beizeiten [baɪˈtsaɪtən] *adv* in time

bejahen [bəˈjaːən] *vt* (*Frage*) to say yes to, to answer in the affirmative; (*gutheißen*) to agree with

bekämpfen [bəˈkɛmpfən] *vt* (*Gegner*) to fight; (*Seuche*) to combat ♦ *vr* to fight; **Bekämpfung** *f* fight, struggle

bekannt [bəˈkant] *adj* (well-)known; (*nicht fremd*) familiar; **~ geben** to announce publicly; **mit jdm ~ sein** to know sb; **~ machen** to announce; **jdn mit jdm ~ machen** to introduce sb to sb; **das ist mir ~** I know that; **es/sie kommt mir ~ vor** it/she seems familiar; **B~e(r)** *f(m)* acquaintance; friend; **B~enkreis** *m* circle of friends; **~lich** *adv* as is well known, as you know; **B~machung** *f* publication; announce-

ment; **B~schaft** *f* acquaintance

bekehren [bəˈkeːrən] *vt* to convert ♦ *vr* to be *od* become converted

bekennen [bəˈkɛnən] (*unreg*) *vt* to confess; (*Glauben*) to profess; **Farbe ~** (*umg*) to show where one stands

Bekenntnis [bəˈkɛntnɪs] (-ses, -se) *nt* admission, confession; (*Religion*) confession, denomination

beklagen [bəˈklaːgən] *vt* to deplore, to lament ♦ *vr* to complain

bekleiden [bəˈklaɪdən] *vt* to clothe; (*Amt*) to occupy, to fill

Bekleidung *f* clothing

beklemmen [bəˈklɛmən] *vt* to oppress

beklommen [bəˈklɔmən] *adj* anxious, uneasy

bekommen [bəˈkɔmən] (*unreg*) *vt* to get, to receive; (*Kind*) to have; (*Zug*) to catch, to get ♦ *vi:* **jdm ~** to agree with sb

bekömmlich [bəˈkœmlɪç] *adj* easily digestible

bekräftigen [bəˈkrɛftɪgən] *vt* to confirm, to corroborate

bekreuzigen [bəˈkrɔʏtsɪgən] *vr* to cross o.s.

bekunden [bəˈkundən] *vt* (*sagen*) to state; (*zeigen*) to show

belächeln [bəˈlɛçəln] *vt* to laugh at

beladen [bəˈlaːdən] (*unreg*) *vt* to load

Belag [bəˈlaːk] (-(e)s, =e) *m* covering, coating; (*Brotbelag*) spread; (*Zahnbelag*) tartar; (*auf Zunge*) fur; (*Bremsbelag*) lining

belagern [bəˈlaːgɐn] *vt* to besiege; **Belagerung** *f* siege

Belang [bəˈlaŋ] (-(e)s) *m* importance; **~e** *pl* (*Interessen*) interests, concerns; **b~los** *adj* trivial, unimportant

belassen [bəˈlasən] (*unreg*) *vt* (*in Zustand, Glauben*) to leave; (*in Stellung*) to retain

belasten [bəˈlastən] *vt* to burden; (*fig: bedrücken*) to trouble, to worry; (*COMM: Konto*) to debit; (*JUR*) to incriminate ♦ *vr* to weigh o.s. down;

(JUR) to incriminate o.s.; **~d** adj (JUR) incriminating

belästigen [bə'lɛstɪgən] vt to annoy, to pester; **Belästigung** f annoyance, pestering

Belastung [bə'lastʊŋ] f load; (fig: Sorge etc) weight; (COMM) charge, debit(ing); (JUR) incriminatory evidence

belaufen [bə'laʊfən] (unreg) vr: **sich ~ auf** +akk to amount to

beleben [bə'le:bən] vt (anregen) to liven up; (Konjunktur, jds Hoffnungen) to stimulate ♦ vr (Augen) to light up; (Stadt) to come to life

belebt [bə'le:pt] adj (Straße) busy

Beleg [bə'le:k] (-(e)s, -e) m (COMM) receipt; (Beweis) documentary evidence, proof; (Beispiel) example; **b~en** vt to cover; (Kuchen, Brot) to spread; (Platz) to reserve, to book; (Kurs, Vorlesung) to register for; (beweisen) to verify, to prove; (MIL: mit Bomben) to bomb; **~schaft** f personnel, staff; **b~t** adj: **b~tes Brot** open sandwich

belehren [bə'le:rən] vt to instruct, to teach; **Belehrung** f instruction

beleibt [bə'laɪpt] adj stout, corpulent

beleidigen [bə'laɪdɪgən] vt to insult, to offend; **Beleidigung** f insult; (JUR) slander, libel

beleuchten [bə'lɔʏçtən] vt to light, to illuminate; (fig) to throw light on

Beleuchtung f lighting, illumination

Belgien ['bɛlgiən] nt Belgium; **Belgier(in)** m(f) Belgian; **belgisch** adj Belgian

belichten [bə'lɪçtən] vt to expose

Belichtung f exposure; **~smesser** m exposure meter

Belieben [bə'li:bən] nt: (ganz) nach ~ (just) as you wish

beliebig [bə'li:bɪç] adj any you like ♦ adv as you like; **ein ~es Thema** any subject you like od want; **~ viel/viele** as much/many as you like

beliebt [bə'li:pt] adj popular; **sich bei jdm ~ machen** to make o.s. popular with sb; **B~heit** f popularity

beliefern [bə'li:fərn] vt to supply

bellen ['bɛlən] vi to bark

belohnen [bə'lo:nən] vt to reward; **Belohnung** f reward

Belüftung [bə'lʏftʊŋ] f ventilation

belügen [bə'ly:gən] (unreg) vt to lie to, to deceive

belustigen [bə'lʊstɪgən] vt to amuse; **Belustigung** f amusement

bemalen [bə'ma:lən] vt to paint

bemängeln [bə'mɛŋəln] vt to criticize

bemerk- [bə'mɛrk] zW: **~bar** adj perceptible, noticeable; **sich ~bar machen** (Person) to make od get o.s. noticed; (Unruhe) to become noticeable; **~en** vt (wahrnehmen) to notice, to observe; (sagen) to say, to mention; **~enswert** adj remarkable, noteworthy; **B~ung** f remark; (schriftlich auch) note

bemitleiden [bə'mɪtlaɪdən] vt to pity

bemühen [bə'my:ən] vr to take trouble od pains; **Bemühung** f trouble, pains pl, effort

benachbart [bə'naxba:rt] adj neighbouring

benachrichtigen [bə'naxrɪçtɪgən] vt to inform; **Benachrichtigung** f notification, information

benachteiligen [bə'naxtaɪlɪgən] vt to put at a disadvantage; to victimize

benehmen [bə'ne:mən] (unreg) vr to behave; **B~ (-s)** nt behaviour

beneiden [bə'naɪdən] vt to envy; **~swert** adj enviable

benennen [bə'nɛnən] (unreg) vt to name

Bengel ['bɛŋəl] (-s, -) m (little) rascal od rogue

benommen [bə'nɔmən] adj dazed

benoten [bə'no:tən] vt to mark

benötigen [bə'nø:tɪgən] vt to need

Spelling Reform: ▲ new spelling △ old spelling (to be phased out)

benutzen [bə'nʊtsən] vt to use
Benutzer (-s, -) m user
Benutzung f utilization, use
Benzin [bɛnt'siːn] (-s, -e) nt (AUT) petrol (BRIT), gas(oline) (US); **~kanister** m petrol (BRIT) od gas (US) can; **~tank** m petrol tank (BRIT), gas tank (US); **~uhr** f petrol (BRIT) od gas (US) gauge
beobachten [bə'loːbaxtən] vt to observe; **Beobachter** (-s, -) m observer; (eines Unfalls) witness; (PRESSE, TV) correspondent; **Beobachtung** f observation
bepacken [bə'pakən] vt to load, to pack
bequem [bə'kveːm] adj comfortable; (Ausrede) convenient; (Person) lazy, indolent; **~en** vr: **sich ~en(, etw zu tun)** to condescend (to do sth); **B~lichkeit** [-'lɪçkaɪt] f convenience, comfort; (Faulheit) laziness, indolence
beraten [bə'raːtən] (unreg) vt to advise; (besprechen) to discuss, to debate ♦ vr to consult; **gut/schlecht ~ sein** to be well/ill advised; **sich ~ lassen** to get advice
Berater (-s, -) m adviser
Beratung f advice; (Besprechung) consultation; **~sstelle** f advice centre
berauben [bə'raʊbən] vt to rob
berechenbar [bə'rɛçənbaːr] adj calculable
berechnen [bə'rɛçnən] vt to calculate; (COMM: anrechnen) to charge; **~d** adj (Mensch) calculating, scheming
Berechnung f calculation; (COMM) charge
berechtigen [bə'rɛçtɪgən] vt to entitle; to authorize; (fig) to justify
berechtigt [bə'rɛçtɪçt] adj justifiable, justified
Berechtigung f authorization; (fig) justification
bereden [bə'reːdən] vt (besprechen) to discuss; (überreden) to persuade ♦ vr to discuss
Bereich [bə'raɪç] (-(e)s, -e) m (Bezirk)

area; (PHYS) range; (Ressort, Gebiet) sphere
♦ **bereichern** [bə'raɪçərn] vt to enrich ♦ vr to get rich
bereinigen [bə'raɪnɪgən] vt to settle
bereisen [bə'raɪzən] vt (Land) to travel through
bereit [bə'raɪt] adj ready, prepared; **zu etw ~ sein** to be ready for sth; **sich ~erklären** to declare o.s. willing; **~en** vt to prepare, to make ready; (Kummer, Freude) to cause; **~halten** (unreg) vt to keep in readiness; **~legen** vt to lay out; **~machen** vt, vr to prepare, to get ready; **~s** adv already; **B~schaft** f readiness; (Polizei) alert; **B~schaftsdienst** m emergency service; **~stehen** (unreg) vi (Person) to be prepared; (Ding) to be ready; **~stellen** vt (Kisten, Pakete etc) to put ready; (Geld etc) to make available; (Truppen, Maschinen) to put at the ready; **~willig** adj willing, ready; **B~willigkeit** f willingness, readiness
bereuen [bə'rɔʏən] vt to regret
Berg [bɛrk] (-(e)s, -e) m mountain; hill; **b~ab** adv downhill; **~arbeiter** m miner; **b~auf** adv uphill; **~bahn** f mountain railway; **~bau** m mining
bergen ['bɛrgən] (unreg) vt (retten) to rescue; (Ladung) to salvage; (enthalten) to contain
Berg- zW: **~führer** m mountain guide; **~gipfel** m peak, summit; **b~ig** ['bɛrgɪç] adj mountainous; hilly; **~kette** f mountain range; **~mann** (pl **~leute**) m miner; **~rettungsdienst** m mountain rescue team; **~rutsch** m landslide; **~steigen** nt mountaineering; **~steiger(in)** m(f) mountaineer, climber; **~tour** f mountain climb
Bergung ['bɛrgʊŋ] f (von Menschen) rescue; (von Material) recovery; (NAUT) salvage
Berg- zW: **~wacht** f mountain rescue service; **~wanderung** f hike in the mountains; **~werk** nt mine

Bericht [bəˈrɪçt] (-(e)s, -e) m report, account; **b~en** vt, vi to report; **~erstatter** (-s, -) m reporter; (newspaper) correspondent

berichtigen [bəˈrɪçtɪgən] vt to correct; **Berichtigung** f correction

Bernstein [ˈbɛrnʃtaɪn] m amber

bersten [ˈbɛrstən] (unreg) vi to burst, to split

berüchtigt [bəˈrʏçtɪçt] adj notorious, infamous

berücksichtigen [bəˈrʏkzɪçtɪgən] vt to consider, to bear in mind; **Berücksichtigung** f consideration

Beruf [bəˈruːf] (-(e)s, -e) m occupation, profession; (Gewerbe) trade; **b~en** (unreg) vt: **b~en zu** to appoint to ♦ vr: **sich auf jdn/etw b~en** to refer od appeal to sb/sth ♦ adj competent, qualified; **b~lich** adj professional

Berufs- zW: **~ausbildung** f job training; **~berater** m careers adviser; **~beratung** f vocational guidance; **~geheimnis** nt professional secret; **~leben** nt professional life; **~schule** f vocational od trade school; **~sportler** [-ʃpɔrtlər] m professional (sportsman); **b~tätig** adj employed; **b~unfähig** adj unfit for work; **~verkehr** m rush-hour traffic

Berufung f vocation, calling; (Ernennung) appointment; (JUR) appeal; **~ einlegen** to appeal

beruhen [bəˈruːən] vi: **auf etw** dat **~** to be based on sth; **etw auf sich ~ lassen** to leave sth at that

beruhigen [bəˈruːɪgən] vt to calm, to pacify, to soothe ♦ vr (Mensch) to calm (o.s.) down; (Situation) to calm down

Beruhigung f soothing; (der Nerven) calming; **zu jds ~** (in order) to reassure sb; **~smittel** nt sedative

berühmt [bəˈryːmt] adj famous; **B~heit** f (Ruf) fame; (Mensch) celebrity

berühren [bəˈryːrən] vt to touch; (gefühlsmäßig bewegen) to affect; (flüchtig erwähnen) to mention, to touch on ♦ vr to meet, to touch

Berührung f contact

besagen [bəˈzaːgən] vt to mean

besänftigen [bəˈzɛnftɪgən] vt to soothe, to calm

Besatz [bəˈzats] (-es, ⁺e) m trimming, edging

Besatzung f garrison; (NAUT, AVIAT) crew

Besatzungsmacht f occupying power

beschädigen [bəˈʃɛːdɪgən] vt to damage; **Beschädigung** f damage; (Stelle) damaged spot

beschaffen [bəˈʃafən] vt to get, to acquire ♦ adj: **das ist so ~, dass** that is such that; **B~heit** f (von Mensch) constitution, nature

Beschaffung f acquisition

beschäftigen [bəˈʃɛftɪgən] vt to occupy; (beruflich) to employ ♦ vr to occupy od concern o.s.

beschäftigt adj busy, occupied

Beschäftigung f (Beruf) employment; (Tätigkeit) occupation; (Befassen) concern

beschämen [bəˈʃɛːmən] vt to put to shame; **~d** adj shameful; (Hilfsbereitschaft) shaming

beschämt adj ashamed

Bescheid [bəˈʃaɪt] (-(e)s, -e) m information; (Weisung) directions pl; **~ wissen (über +akk)** to be well-informed (about); **ich weiß ~** I know; **jdm ~ geben** od **sagen** to let sb know

bescheiden [bəˈʃaɪdən] (unreg) vr to content o.s. ♦ adj modest; **B~heit** f modesty

bescheinen [bəˈʃaɪnən] (unreg) vt to shine on

bescheinigen [bəˈʃaɪnɪgən] vt to certify; (bestätigen) to acknowledge

Bescheinigung f certificate; (Quittung)

Spelling Reform: ▲ new spelling △ old spelling (to be phased out)

receipt

beschenken [bəˈʃɛŋkən] vt: **jdn mit etw ~** to give sb sth as a present

bescheren [bəˈʃeːrən] vt: **jdm etw ~** to give sb sth as a Christmas present; **jdn ~** to give Christmas presents to sb

Bescherung f giving of Christmas presents; (umg) mess

beschildern [bəˈʃɪldərn] vt to put signs/a sign on

beschimpfen [bəˈʃɪmpfən] vt to abuse; **Beschimpfung** f abuse; insult

Beschlag ▲ [bəˈʃlaːk] (-(e)s, ⁻e) m (tallband) fitting; (auf Fenster) condensation; (auf Metall) tarnish; finish; (Hufeisen) horseshoe; **jdn/etw in ~ nehmen** od **mit ~ belegen** to monopolize sb/sth; **b~en** [bəˈʃlaːgən] (unreg) vt to cover; (Pferd) to shoe ♦ vi, vr (Fenster etc) to mist over; **b~en sein (in** auf +dat) to be well versed (in); **b~nahmen** vt to seize, to confiscate, to requisition; **~nahmung** f confiscation, sequestration

beschleunigen [bəˈʃlɔʏnɪgən] vt to accelerate, to speed up ♦ vi (AUT) to accelerate; **Beschleunigung** f acceleration

beschließen [bəˈʃliːsən] (unreg) vt to decide on; (beenden) to end, to close

Beschluss ▲ [bəˈʃlʊs] (-es, ⁻e) m decision, conclusion; (Ende) conclusion, end

beschmutzen [bəˈʃmʊtsən] vt to dirty, to soil

beschönigen [bəˈʃøːnɪgən] vt to gloss over

beschränken [bəˈʃrɛŋkən] vt, vr: **(sich) ~ (auf** +akk) to limit od restrict (o.s.) (to)

beschränk- zW: **~t** adj confined, restricted; (Mensch) limited, narrow-minded; **B~ung** f limitation

beschreiben [bəˈʃraɪbən] (unreg) vt to describe; (Papier) to write on **Beschreibung** f description

beschriften [bəˈʃrɪftən] vt to mark, to label; **Beschriftung** f lettering

beschuldigen [bəˈʃʊldɪgən] vt to accuse; **Beschuldigung** f accusation

Beschuss ▲ [bəˈʃʊs] m: **jdn/etw unter ~ nehmen** (MIL) to open fire on sb/sth

beschützen [bəˈʃʏtsən] vt: **~ (vor** +dat) to protect (from); **Beschützer (-s, -)** m protector

Beschwerde f complaint; (Mühe) hardship; **~n** pl (Leiden) trouble

beschweren [bəˈʃveːrən] vt to weigh down; (fig) to burden ♦ vr to complain

beschwerlich adj tiring, exhausting

beschwichtigen [bəˈʃvɪçtɪgən] vt to soothe, to pacify

beschwindeln [bəˈʃvɪndəln] vt (betrügen) to cheat; (belügen) to fib to

beschwingt [bəˈʃvɪŋt] adj in high spirits

beschwipst [bəˈʃvɪpst] (umg) adj tipsy

beschwören [bəˈʃvøːrən] (unreg) vt (Aussage) to swear to; (anflehen) to implore; (Geister) to conjure up

beseitigen [bəˈzaɪtɪgən] vt to remove; **Beseitigung** f removal

Besen [ˈbeːzən] (-s, -) m broom; **~stiel** m broomstick

besessen [bəˈzɛsən] adj possessed

besetz- [bəˈzɛts] zW: **~en** vt (Haus, Land) to occupy; (Platz) to take, to fill; (Posten) to fill; (Rolle) to cast; (mit Edelsteinen) to set; **~t** adj full; (TEL) engaged, busy; (Platz) taken; (WC) engaged; **B~tzeichen** nt engaged tone; **B~ung** f occupation; filling; (von Rolle) casting; (die Schauspieler) cast

besichtigen [bəˈzɪçtɪgən] vt to visit, to have a look at; **Besichtigung** f visit

besiegen [bəˈziːgən] vt to defeat, to overcome

besinn- [bəˈzɪn] zW: **~en** (unreg) vt (nachdenken) to think, to reflect; (erinnern) to remember; **sich anders ~** to change one's mind; **B~ung** f consciousness; **zur B~ung kommen** to recover consciousness; *(fig)* to come to one's senses; **~ungslos** *adj* unconscious

Besitz [bəˈzɪts] (**-es**) *m* possession; *(Eigentum)* property; **b~en** *(unreg)* *vt* to possess, to own; *(Eigenschaft)* to have; **~er(in)** (**-s**, **-**) *m(f)* owner, proprietor; **~ergreifung** *f* occupation, seizure

besoffen [bəˈzɔfən] *(umg)* *adj* drunk, stoned

besohlen [bəˈzoːlən] *vt* to sole

Besoldung [bəˈzɔldʊŋ] *f* salary, pay

besondere(r, s) [bəˈzɔndərə(r, s)] *adj* special; *(eigen)* particular; *(gesondert)* separate; *(eigentümlich)* peculiar

Besonderheit [bəˈzɔndərhaɪt] *f* peculiarity

besonders [bəˈzɔndərs] *adv* especially, particularly; *(getrennt)* separately

besonnen [bəˈzɔnən] *adj* sensible, level-headed

besorg- [bəˈzɔrg] *zW*: **~en** *vt* *(beschaffen)* to acquire; *(kaufen auch)* to purchase; *(erledigen: Geschäfte)* to deal with; *(sich kümmern um)* to take care of; **B~nis** (**-**, **-se**) *f* anxiety, concern; **~t** [bəˈzɔrçt] *adj* anxious, worried; **B~ung** *f* acquisition; *(Kauf)* purchase

bespielen [bəˈʃpiːlən] *vt* to record

bespitzeln [bəˈʃpɪtsəln] *vt* to spy on

besprechen [bəˈʃprɛçən] *(unreg)* *vt* to discuss; *(Tonband etc)* to record, to speak onto; *(Buch)* to review ♦ *vr* to discuss, to consult; **Besprechung** *f* meeting, discussion; *(von Buch)* review

besser [ˈbɛsər] *adj* better; **es geht ihm ~** he is feeling better; **~n** *vt* to make better, to improve ♦ *vr* to improve; *(Menschen)* to improve; **B~ung** *f* improvement; **gute B~ung!** get well soon!; **B~wisser** (**-s**, **-**) *m* know-all

Bestand [bəˈʃtant] (**-(e)s**, **-e**) *m* *(Fortbestehen)* duration, stability; *(Kassenbestand)* amount, balance; *(Vorrat)* stock; **~ haben, von ~ sein** to last long, to

endure

beständig [bəˈʃtɛndɪç] *adj* *(ausdauernd: auch fig)* constant; *(Wetter)* settled; *(Stoffe)* resistant; *(Klagen etc)* continual

Bestandsaufnahme [bəˈʃtantsaʊfnaːmə] *f* stocktaking

Bestandteil *m* part, component; *(Zutat)* ingredient

bestärken [bəˈʃtɛrkən] *vt*: **jdn in etw** *dat* ~ to strengthen *od* confirm sb in sth

bestätigen [bəˈʃtɛːtɪgən] *vt* to confirm; *(anerkennen, COMM)* to acknowledge; **Bestätigung** *f* confirmation; acknowledgement

bestatten [bəˈʃtatən] *vt* to bury

Bestattung *f* funeral

Bestattungsinstitut *nt* funeral director's

bestaunen [bəˈʃtaʊnən] *vt* to marvel at, gaze at in wonder

beste(r, s) [ˈbɛstə(r, s)] *adj* best; **so ist es am ~n** it's best that way; **am ~n gehst du gleich** you'd better go at once; **jdn zum B~n haben** to pull sb's leg; **einen Witz** *etc* **zum B~n geben** to tell a joke *etc*; **aufs B~** *od* **~ in** the best possible way; **zu jds B~n** for the benefit of sb

bestechen [bəˈʃtɛçən] *(unreg)* *vt* to bribe; **bestechlich** *adj* corruptible; **Bestechung** *f* bribery, corruption

Besteck [bəˈʃtɛk] (**-(e)s**, **-e**) *nt* knife, fork and spoon, cutlery; *(MED)* set of instruments

bestehen [bəˈʃteːən] *(unreg)* *vi* to be; to exist; *(andauern)* to last ♦ *vt* *(Kampf, Probe, Prüfung)* to pass; **~ auf** +*dat* to insist on; **~ aus** to consist of

bestehlen [bəˈʃteːlən] *(unreg)* *vt*: **jdn (um etw)** ~ to rob sb (of sth)

besteigen [bəˈʃtaɪgən] *(unreg)* *vt* to climb, to ascend; *(Pferd)* to mount; *(Thron)* to ascend

Bestell- [bəˈʃtɛl] *zW*: **~buch** *nt* order

book; **b~en** vt to order; (kommen lassen) to arrange to see; (nominieren) to name; (Acker) to cultivate; (Grüße, Auftrag) to pass on; **~formular** nt order form; **~nummer** f order code; **~ung** f (COMM) order; (~en) ordering

bestenfalls ['bɛstən'fals] adv at best

bestens ['bɛstəns] adv very well

besteuern [bə'ʃtɔʏərn] vt (jdn, Waren) to tax

Bestie ['bɛstiə] f (auch fig) beast

bestimm- zW: **~en** vt (Regeln) to lay down; (Tag, Ort) to fix; (beherrschen) to characterize; (vorsehen) to mean; (ernennen) to appoint; (definieren) to define; (veranlassen) to induce; **~t** adj (entschlossen) firm; (gewiss) certain, definite; (Artikel) definite ♦ adv (gewiss) definitely, for sure; **suchen Sie etwas B~tes?** are you looking for something in particular?; **B~theit** f firmness; certainty; **B~ung** f (Verordnung) regulation; (Festsetzen) determining; (Verwendungszweck) purpose; (Schicksal) fate; (Definition) definition; **B~ungsland** nt (country of) destination; **B~ungsort** m (place of) destination

Bestleistung f best performance

bestmöglich adj best possible

bestrafen [bə'ʃtra:fən] vt to punish; **Bestrafung** f punishment

bestrahlen [bə'ʃtra:lən] vt to shine on; (MED) to treat with X-rays

Bestrahlung f (MED) X-ray treatment, radiotherapy

Bestreben [bə'ʃtre:bən] (-s) nt endeavour, effort

bestreiten [bə'ʃtraitən] (unreg) vt (abstreiten) to dispute; (finanzieren) to pay for, to finance

bestreuen [bə'ʃtrɔʏən] vt (mit Fragen, Bitten etc) to sprinkle, to dust; (Straße) to grit

bestürmen [bə'ʃtʏrmən] vt (mit Fragen, Bitten etc) to overwhelm, to swamp

bestürzend [bə'ʃtʏrtsənd] adj (Nachrichten) disturbing

bestürzt [bə'ʃtʏrtst] adj dismayed

Bestürzung f consternation

Besuch [bə'zu:x] (-(e)s, -e) m visit; (Person) visitor; **einen ~ machen bei jdm** to pay a visit od call; **~ haben** to have visitors; **bei jdm auf od zu ~ sein** to be visiting sb; **b~en** vt to visit; (SCH etc) to attend; **gut b~t** well attended; **~er(in)** (-s, -) m(f) visitor guest; **~szeit** f visiting hours pl

betätigen [bə'tɛ:tɪgən] vt (bedienen) to work, to operate ♦ vr to involve o.s.; **sich als etw ~** to work as sth

Betätigung f activity; (beruflich) occupation; (TECH) operation

betäuben [bə'tɔʏbən] vt to stun; (fig Gewissen) to still; (MED) to anaesthetize

Betäubung f (Narkose): **örtliche ~** local anaesthetic

Betäubungsmittel nt anaesthetic

Bete ['be:tə] f: **Rote ~** beetroot (BRIT) beet (US)

beteilig- [bə'tailɪg] zW: **~en** vr: **sich ~en (an** +dat) to take part (in), to participate (in), to share (in); (an Geschäft: finanziell) to have a share (in) ♦ vt: **jdn ~en (an** +dat) to give sb a share (in); **B~te(r)** f(m) (Mitwirkender) partner; (finanziell) shareholder **B~ung** f participation; (Anteil) share, interest; (Besucherzahl) attendance

beten ['be:tən] vt, vi to pray

beteuern [bə'tɔʏərn] vt to assert; (Unschuld) to protest

Beton [be'tõ:] (-s, -s) m concrete

betonen [bə'to:nən] vt to stress

betonieren [betoni:rən] vt to concrete

Betonung f stress, emphasis

betr. abk (= betrifft) re

Betracht [bə'traxt] m: **in ~ kommen** to be considered od relevant; **etw in ~ ziehen** to take sth into consideration; **außer ~ bleiben** not to be considered; **b~en** vt to look at; (fig) to look at, to consider; **~er(in)** (-s, -) m(f) observer

beträchtlich [bəˈtrɛçtlɪç] adj considerable

Betrachtung f (Ansehen) examination; (Erwägung) consideration

Betrag [bəˈtraːk] (-(e)s, -e) m amount; **b~en** (unreg) vt to amount to ♦ vr to behave; **~en** (-s) nt behaviour

Betreff m: **~ Ihr Schreiben vom ...** re your letter of ...

betreffen [bəˈtrɛfən] (unreg) vt to concern, to affect; **was mich betrifft** as for me; **~d** adj relevant, in question

betreffs [bəˈtrɛfs] präp +gen concerning, regarding; (COMM) re

betreiben [bəˈtraɪbən] (unreg) vt (ausüben) to practise; (Politik) to follow; (Studien) to pursue; (vorantreiben) to push ahead; (TECH: antreiben) to drive

betreten [bəˈtreːtən] (unreg) vt to enter; (Bühne etc) to step onto ♦ adj embarrassed; **B~ verboten** keep off/out

Betreuer(in) [bəˈtrɔʏər(ɪn)] (-s, -) m(f) (einer Person) minder; (eines Gebäudes, Arbeitsgebiets) caretaker; (SPORT) coach

Betreuung f care

Betrieb [bəˈtriːp] (-(e)s, -e) m (Firma) firm, concern; (Anlage) plant; (Tätigkeit) operation; (Treiben) traffic; **außer ~ sein** to be out of order; **in ~ sein** to be in operation

Betriebs- zW: **~ausflug** m works outing; **b~bereit** adj operational; **b~fähig** adj in working order; **~ferien** pl company holidays (BRIT), company vacation sg (US); **~klima** nt (working) atmosphere; **~kosten** pl running costs; **~rat** m workers' council; **~sicher** adj safe (to operate); **~störung** f breakdown; **~system** nt (COMPUT) operating system; **~unfall** m industrial accident; **~wirtschaft** f economics

betrinken [bəˈtrɪŋkən] (unreg) vr to get drunk

betroffen [bəˈtrɔfən] adj (bestürzt) full of consternation; **von etw ~ werden** od **sein** to be affected by sth

betrüben [bəˈtryːbən] vt to grieve

betrübt [bəˈtryːpt] adj sorrowful, grieved

Betrug [bəˈtruːk] (-(e)s) m deception; (JUR) fraud

betrügen [bəˈtryːgən] (unreg) vt to cheat; (JUR) to defraud; (Ehepartner) to be unfaithful to ♦ vr to deceive o.s.

Betrüger (-s, -) m cheat, deceiver; **b~isch** adj deceitful; (JUR) fraudulent

betrunken [bəˈtrʊŋkən] adj drunk

Bett [bɛt] (-(e)s, -en) nt bed; **ins** od **zu ~ gehen** to go to bed; **~bezug** m duvet cover; **~decke** f blanket; (Daunenbett) quilt; (Überwurf) bedspread

Bettel- [ˈbɛtəl] zW: **b~arm** adj very poor, destitute; **~ei** [bɛtəˈlaɪ] f begging; **b~n** vi to beg

bettlägerig [ˈbɛtlɛːgərɪç] adj bedridden

Bettlaken nt sheet

Bettler(in) [ˈbɛtlər(ɪn)] (-s, -) m(f) beggar

Bett- zW: **~tuch** ▲ nt sheet; **~vorleger** m bedside rug; **~wäsche** f bed linen; **~zeug** nt bed linen pl

beugen [ˈbɔʏgən] vt to bend; (GRAM) to inflect ♦ vr (sich fügen) to bow

Beule [ˈbɔʏlə] f bump, swelling

beunruhigen [bəˈʔʊnruːɪgən] vt to disturb, to alarm ♦ vr to become worried

Beunruhigung f worry, alarm

beurlauben [bəˈʔuːrlaʊbən] vt to give leave od a holiday to (BRIT), to grant vacation time to (US)

beurteilen [bəˈʔɔʏrtaɪlən] vt to judge; (Buch etc) to review

Beurteilung f judgement; review; (Note) mark

Beute [ˈbɔʏtə] (-) f booty, loot

Beutel (-s, -) m bag; (Geldbeutel) purse; (Tabakbeutel) pouch

Bevölkerung [bəˈfœlkərʊŋ] f population

---

bevollmächtigen [bə'fɔlmɛçtɪgən] vt
to authorize

Bevollmächtigte(r) f(m) authorized
agent

bevor [bə'foːr] konj before; ~**munden**
vt insep to treat like a child; ~**stehen**
(unreg) vi: (**jdm**) ~**stehen** to be in store
(for sb); ~**stehend** adj imminent, approaching; ~**zugen** vt insep to prefer

bewachen [bə'vaxən] vt to watch, to
guard

Bewachung f (Bewachen) guarding;
(Leute) guard, watch

bewaffnen [bə'vafnən] vt to arm

Bewaffnung f (Vorgang) arming; (Ausrüstung) armament, arms pl

bewahren [bə'vaːrən] vt to keep; **jdn**
vor jdm/etw ~ to save sb from sth/sth

bewähren [bə'vɛːrən] vr to prove o.s.;
(Maschine) to prove its worth

bewahrheiten [bə'vaːrhaɪtən] vr to
come true

bewährt adj reliable

Bewährung f (JUR) probation

bewältigen [bə'vɛltɪgən] vt to overcome; (Arbeit) to finish; (Portion) to
manage

bewandert [bə'vandərt] adj expert,
knowledgeable

bewässern [bə'vɛsərn] vt to irrigate

Bewässerung f irrigation

bewegen [bə'veːgən] vt, vr to move;
jdn zu etw ~ to induce sb to do sth;
~**d** adj touching, moving

Beweg- [bə'veːk] zW: ~**grund** m motive; **b~lich** adj movable, mobile;
(flink) quick; **b~t** adj (Leben) eventful;
(Meer) rough; (ergriffen) touched

Bewegung f movement, motion; (innere) emotion; (körperlich) exercise;
~**sfreiheit** f freedom of movement;
(fig) freedom of action; **b~ungslos** adj
motionless

Beweis [bə'vaɪs] (-es, -e) m proof;
(Zeichen) sign; **b~en** [-zən] (unreg) vt to
prove; (zeigen) to show; ~**mittel** nt
evidence

Bewerb- [bə'vɛrb] zW: **b~en** (unreg) vr
to apply (for); ~**er(in)** (-s, -) m(f) applicant; ~**ung** f application

bewerkstelligen [bə'vɛrkʃtelɪgən] vt
to manage, to accomplish

bewerten [bə'veːrtən] vt to assess

bewilligen [bə'vɪlɪgən] vt to grant, to
allow

Bewilligung f granting

bewirken [bə'vɪrkən] vt to cause, to
bring about

bewirten [bə'vɪrtən] vt to feed, to entertain (to a meal)

bewirtschaften [bə'vɪrtʃaftən] vt to
manage

Bewirtung f hospitality

bewog etc [bə'voːk] vb siehe **bewegen**

bewohn- [bə'voːn] zW: ~**bar** adj habitable; ~**en** vt to inhabit, to live in;
B~er(in) (-s, -) m(f) inhabitant; (von
Haus) resident

bewölkt [bə'vœlkt] adj cloudy, overcast

Bewölkung f clouds pl

Bewunder- [bə'vʊndər] zW: ~**er** (-s, -)
m admirer; **b~n** vt to admire;
b~nswert adj admirable, wonderful;
~**ung** f admiration

bewusst ▲ [bə'vʊst] adj conscious;
(absichtlich) deliberate; **sich** dat **einer**
Sache gen ~ **sein** to be aware of sth;
~**los** adj unconscious; **B~losigkeit** f
unconsciousness; **B~sein** nt consciousness; **bei B~sein** conscious

bezahlen [bə'tsaːlən] vt to pay for

Bezahlung f payment

bezaubern [bə'tsaʊbərn] vt to enchant, to charm

bezeichnen [bə'tsaɪçnən] vt (kennzeichnen) to mark; (nennen) to call;
(beschreiben) to describe; (zeigen) to
show, to indicate; ~**d** adj: ~**d (für)**
characteristic (of), typical (of)

Bezeichnung f (Zeichen) mark, sign;
(Beschreibung) description

bezeugen [bə'tsɔygən] vt to testify to

Bezichtigung [bə'tsɪçtɪgʊŋ] f accusa-

beziehen 55 **Bindung**

tion

beziehen [bəˈtsiːən] (unreg) vt (mit Überzug) to cover; (Bett) to make; (Haus, Position) to move into; (Standpunkt) to take up; (erhalten) to receive; (Zeitung) to subscribe to, to take ♦ vr (Himmel) to cloud over; **etw auf jdn/ etw ~** to relate sth to sb/sth; **sich ~ auf** +akk to refer to

Beziehung f (Verbindung) connection; (Zusammenhang) relation; (Verhältnis) relationship; (Hinsicht) respect; **~en haben** (vorteilhaft) to have connections or contacts; **b~sweise** adv or; (genauer gesagt auch) that is, or rather

Bezirk [bəˈtsɪrk] (-(e)s, -e) m district

Bezug [bəˈtsuːk] (-(e)s, -e) m (Hülle) covering; (COMM) ordering; (Gehalt) income, salary; (Beziehung): **~ (zu)** relation(ship) (to); **in ~ auf** +akk with reference to; **~ nehmen auf** +akk to refer to

bezüglich [bəˈtsyːklɪç] präp +gen concerning, referring to ♦ adj (GRAM) relative; **auf etw** akk **~** relating to sth

bezwecken [bəˈtsvɛkən] vt to aim at

bezweifeln [bəˈtsvaɪfəln] vt to doubt, to query

BH m abk von Büstenhalter

Bhf. abk (= Bahnhof) station

Bibel [ˈbiːbəl] (-, -n) f Bible

Biber [ˈbiːbər] (-s, -) m beaver

Biblio- [biːblio] zW: **~grafie** ▲ [-graˈfiː] f bibliography; **~thek** [-ˈteːk] (-, -en) f library; **~thekar(in)** [-teˈkaːr(ɪn)] (-s, -e) m(f) librarian

biblisch [ˈbiːblɪʃ] adj biblical

bieder [ˈbiːdər] adj upright, worthy; (Kleid etc) plain

bieg- [ˈbiːg] zW: **~en** (unreg) vt, vr to bend ♦ vi to turn; **~sam** [ˈbiːk-] adj flexible; **B~ung** f bend, curve

Biene [ˈbiːnə] f bee

Bienenhonig m honey

Bienenwachs nt beeswax

Bier [biːr] (-(e)s, -e) nt beer; **~deckel** m beer mat; **~garten** m beer garden; **~krug** m beer mug; **~zelt** nt beer tent

Biest [biːst] (-(e)s, -er) (umg: pej) nt (Tier) beast, creature; (Mensch) beast

bieten [ˈbiːtən] (unreg) vt to offer; (bei Versteigerung) to bid ♦ vr (Gelegenheit): **sich jdm ~** to present itself to sb; **sich auf etw ~ lassen** to put up with sth

Bikini [biˈkiːni] (-s, -s) m bikini

Bilanz [biˈlants] f balance; (fig) outcome; **~ ziehen (aus)** to take stock (of)

Bild [bɪlt] (-(e)s, -er) nt (auch fig) picture; photo; (Spiegelbild) reflection; **~bericht** m photographic report

bilden [ˈbɪldən] vt to form; (erziehen) to educate; (ausmachen) to constitute ♦ vr to arise; (erziehen) to educate o.s.

Bilderbuch nt picture book

Bilderrahmen m picture frame

Bild- zW: **~fläche** f screen; (fig) scene; **~hauer** (-s, -) m sculptor; **b~hübsch** adj lovely, pretty as a picture; **b~lich** adj figurative; pictorial; **~schirm** m television screen; (COMPUT) monitor; **~schirmschoner** m (COMPUT) screen saver; **b~schön** adj lovely

Bildung [ˈbɪldʊŋ] f formation; (Wissen, Benehmen) education

Billard [ˈbɪljart] (-s, -e) nt billiards sg; **~kugel** f billiard ball

billig [ˈbɪlɪç] adj cheap; (gerecht) fair, reasonable; **~en** [ˈbɪlɪgən] vt to approve of

Binde [ˈbɪndə] f bandage; (Armbinde) band; (MED) sanitary towel; **~gewebe** nt connective tissue; **~glied** nt connecting link; **~hautentzündung** f conjunctivitis; **b~n** (unreg) vt to bind, to tie; **~strich** m hyphen

Bindfaden [ˈbɪnt-] m string

Bindung f bond, tie; (Skibindung) binding

Spelling Reform: ▲ *new spelling* △ *old spelling (to be phased out)*

binnen ['bɪnən] *präp* (+*dat od gen*) within; **B~hafen** *m* river port; **B~handel** *m* internal trade

Bio- [bio-] *in zW* bio-; **~chemie** *f* biochemistry; **~grafie** ▲ [-'gra:fi:] *f* biography; **~laden** *m* wholefood shop; **~loge** [-'lo:gə] (-n, -n) *m* biologist; **~logie** [-lo:'gi:] *f* biology; **b~logisch** [-'lo:gɪʃ] *adj* biological; **~top** *nt od nt* biotope

---

Bioladen

A *Bioladen* is a shop specializing in environmentally-friendly products such as phosphate-free washing powders, recycled paper and organically-grown vegetables.

Birke ['bɪrkə] *f* birch
Birne ['bɪrnə] *f* pear; (*ELEK*) (light) bulb

SCHLÜSSELWORT

bis [bɪs] *präp* +*akk*, *adv* **1** (*zeitlich*) till, until; (*bis spätestens*) by; **Sie haben bis Dienstag Zeit** you have until *od* till Tuesday; **bis Dienstag muss es fertig sein** it must be ready by Tuesday; **bis auf weiteres** until further notice; **bis in die Nacht** into the night; **bis bald/gleich** see you later/soon

2 (*räumlich*) (up) to; **ich fahre bis Köln** I'm going to *od* I'm going as far as Cologne; **bis an unser Grundstück** (right *od* up) to our plot; **bis hierher** this far

3 (*bei Zahlen*) up to; **bis zu** up to

4: bis auf etw (*akk*) (*außer*) except sth; (*einschließlich*) including sth

♦ *konj* **1** (*mit Zahlen*) to; **10 bis 20** 10 to 20

2 (*zeitlich*) till, until; **bis es dunkel wird** till *od* until it gets dark; **von ... bis ...** from ... to ...

Bischof ['bɪʃɔf] (-s, *=*e) *m* bishop; **bischöflich** ['bɪʃø:flɪç] *adj* episcopal
bisher [bɪs'he:r] *adv* till now, hitherto;

~ig *adj* till now
Biskuit [bɪs'kvi:t] (-(e)s, -s *od* -e) *m od nt* (fatless) sponge
Biss ▲ [bɪs] (-es, -e) *m* bite
biss ▲ *etc vb siehe* **beißen**
bisschen ▲ ['bɪsçən] *adj, adv* bit
Bissen ['bɪsən] (-s, -) *m* bite, morsel
bissig ['bɪsɪç] *adj* (*Hund*) snappy; (*Bemerkung*) cutting, biting
bist [bɪst] *vb siehe* **sein**
bisweilen [bɪs'vaɪlən] *adv* at times, occasionally
Bitte ['bɪtə] *f* request; **b~** *excl* please; (*wie b~?*) (I beg your) pardon? ♦ *interj* (*als Antwort auf Dank*) you're welcome; **darf ich? – aber b~!** may I? – please do; **b~ schön!** it was a pleasure; **b~n** (*unreg*) *vt, vi:* **b~n (um)** to ask (for); **b~nd** *adj* pleading, imploring
bitter ['bɪtər] *adj* bitter; **~böse** *adj* very angry; **B~keit** *f* bitterness; **~lich** *adj* bitter
Blähungen ['blɛ:ɔŋən] *pl* (*MED*) wind *sg*
blamabel [bla'ma:bəl] *adj* disgraceful
Blamage [bla'ma:ʒə] *f* disgrace
blamieren [bla'mi:rən] *vt* to make a fool of o.s., to disgrace o.s. ♦ *vr* to let down, to disgrace
blank [blaŋk] *adj* bright; (*unbedeckt*) bare; (*sauber*) clean, polished; (*umg: ohne Geld*) broke; (*offensichtlich*) blatant
blanko ['blaŋko] *adv* blank; **B~scheck** *m* blank cheque
Blase ['bla:zə] *f* bubble; (*MED*) blister; (*ANAT*) bladder; **b~balg (-(e)s, -bälge)** *m* bellows *pl*; **b~n** (*unreg*) *vt, vi* to blow; **~nentzündung** *f* cystitis
Blas- ['bla:s] *zW:* **~instrument** *nt* wind instrument; **~kapelle** *f* brass band
blass ▲ [blas] *adj* pale
Blässe ['blɛsə] (-) *f* paleness, pallor
Blatt [blat] (-(e)s, *=*er) *nt* leaf; (*von Papier*) sheet; (*Zeitung*) newspaper; (*KARTEN*) hand
blättern ['blɛtərn] *vi:* **in etw** *dat* **~** to

leaf through sth

Blätterteig m flaky od puff pastry

blau [blaʊ] adj blue; (umg) drunk, stoned; (KOCH) boiled; (Auge) black; **~er Fleck** bruise; **Fahrt ins B~e** mystery tour; **~äugig** adj blue-eyed

Blech [blɛç] (-(e)s, -e) nt tin, sheet metal; (Backblech) baking tray; **~büchse** f tin, can; **~dose** f tin, can; **b~en** (umg) vi, vt to fork out; **~schaden** m (AUT) damage to bodywork

Blei [blaɪ] (-(e)s, -e) nt lead

bleibe ['blaɪbə] f roof over one's head; **l~** (unreg) vi to stay, to remain; **~lassen** to leave alone; **b~nd** adj (Erinnerung) lasting; (Schaden) permanent

bleich [blaɪç] adj faded, pale; **~en** vt to bleach

Blei- zW: **b~ern** adj leaden; **b~frei** adj (Benzin) lead-free; **~stift** m pencil

Blende ['blɛndə] f (PHOT) aperture; **b~n** vt to blind, to dazzle; (fig) to hoodwink; **b~nd** (umg) adj grand; **b~nd aussehen** to look smashing

Blick [blɪk] (-(e)s, -e) m (kurz) glance, glimpse; (Anschauen) look; (Aussicht) view; **b~en** vi to look; **sich b~en lassen** to put in an appearance; **~fang** m eye-catcher

blieb etc [bliːp] vb siehe **bleiben**

blind [blɪnt] adj blind; (Glas etc) dull; **~er Passagier** stowaway; **B~darm** m appendix; **B~darmentzündung** f appendicitis; **B~enschrift** ['blɪndən-] f Braille; **B~heit** f blindness; **~lings** adv blindly

blink- ['blɪŋk] zW: **~en** vi to twinkle, to sparkle; (Licht) to flash, to signal; (AUT) to indicate ♦ vt to flash, to signal; **B~er (-s, -)** m (AUT) indicator; **B~licht** nt (AUT) indicator; (an Bahnübergängen usw) flashing light

blinzeln ['blɪntsəln] vi to blink, to wink

Blitz [blɪts] (-es, -e) m (flash of) lightning; **~ableiter** m lightning conduc-

tor; **b~en** vi (aufleuchten) to flash, to sparkle; **es b~t** (MET) there's a flash of lightning; **~licht** nt flashlight; **b~schnell** adj lightning ♦ adv (as) quick as a flash

Block [blɔk] (-(e)s, ⁿe) m block; (von Papier) pad; **~ade** [blɔ'kaːdə] f blockade; **~flöte** f recorder; **b~frei** adj (POL) unaligned; **~haus** nt log cabin; **b~ieren** [blɔ'kiːrən] vt to block ♦ vi (Räder) to jam; **~schrift** f block letters pl

blöd [bløːt] adj silly, stupid; **~eln** [bløːdəln] (umg) vi to act the goat (fam), to fool around; **B~sinn** m nonsense; **~sinnig** adj silly, idiotic

blond [blɔnt] adj blond, fair-haired

SCHLÜSSELWORT

---

bloß [bloːs] **adj 1** (unbedeckt) bare; (nackt) naked; **mit der bloßen Hand** with one's bare hand; **mit bloßem Auge** with the naked eye

2 (alleinig, nur) mere; **der bloße Gedanke** the very thought; **bloßer Neid** sheer envy

♦ adv only, merely; **lass das bloß!** just don't do that!; **wie ist das bloß passiert?** how on earth did that happen?

Blöße ['bløːsə] f bareness; nakedness; (fig) weakness

bloßstellen vt to show up

blühen ['blyːən] vi to bloom (lit), to be in bloom; (fig) to flourish; **~d** adj (Pflanze) blooming; (Aussehen) blooming, radiant; (Handel) thriving, booming

Blume ['bluːmə] f flower; (von Wein) bouquet

Blumen- zW: **~kohl** m cauliflower; **~topf** m flowerpot; **~zwiebel** f bulb

Bluse ['bluːzə] f blouse

Blut [bluːt] (-(e)s) nt blood; **b~arm** adj anaemic; (fig) penniless; **b~befleckt**

adj bloodstained; **~bild** *nt* blood count; **~druck** *m* blood pressure

Blüte ['bly:tə] *f* blossom; *(fig)* prime

Blut- *zW:* **b~en** *vi* to bleed; **~er** *m* (*MED*) haemophiliac; **~erguss ▲** *m* haemorrhage; *(auf Haut)* bruise

Blütezeit *f* flowering period; *(fig)* prime

Blut- *zW:* **~gruppe** *f* blood group; **b~ig** *adj* bloody; **b~jung** *adj* very young; **~probe** *f* blood test; **~spender** *m* blood donor; **~transfusion** *f* (*MED*) blood transfusion; **~ung** *f* bleeding, haemorrhage; **~vergiftung** *f* blood poisoning; **~wurst** *f* black pudding

Bö [bø:] *f* (-, -en) *f* squall

Bock [bɔk] *m* (-(e)s, *-e) m* buck, ram; *(Gestell)* trestle, support; *(SPORT)* buck; **~wurst** *f* type of pork sausage

Boden ['bo:dən] *m* (-s, *-) m* ground; *(Fußboden)* floor; *(Meeresboden, Fassboden)* bottom; *(Speicher)* attic; **b~los** *adj* bottomless; *(umg)* incredible; **~nebel** *m* ground mist; **~personal** *nt* (*AVIAT*) ground staff; **~schätze** *pl* mineral resources; **~see** *m*: **der ~see** Lake Constance; **~turnen** *nt* floor exercises *pl*

Böe ['bø:ə] *f* squall

Bogen ['bo:gən] *m* (-s, *-) m* (*Biegung*) curve; (*ARCHIT*) arch; *(Waffe, MUS)* bow; *(Papier)* sheet

Bohne ['bo:nə] *f* bean

bohnern *vt* to wax, to polish

Bohnerwachs *nt* floor polish

Bohr- ['bo:r] *zW:* **b~en** *vt* to bore; **~er** (-s, *-) m* drill; **~insel** *f* oil rig; **~maschine** *f* drill; **~turm** *m* derrick

Boiler ['bɔylər] *m* (-s, *-) m* (hot-water) tank

Boje ['bo:jə] *f* buoy

Bolzen ['bɔltsən] *m* (-s, *-) m* bolt

bombardieren [bɔmbar'di:rən] *vt* to bombard; *(aus der Luft)* to bomb

Bombe ['bɔmbə] *f* bomb

Bombenangriff *m* bombing raid

Bombenerfolg *(umg) m* smash hit

Bon [bɔŋ] (-s, -s) *m* voucher, chit

Bonbon [bõ'bõ:] (-s, -s) *m* od *nt* sweet

Boot [bo:t] (-(e)s, *-e) nt* boat

Bord [bɔrt] (-(e)s, *-e) m* (*AVIAT, NAU*) board ♦ *nt* (*Brett*) shelf; **an ~** on board

Bordell [bɔr'dɛl] (-s, *-e) nt* brothel

Bordstein *m* kerb(stone)

borgen ['bɔrgən] *vt* to borrow; **jd** etw ~ to lend sb sth

borniert [bɔr'ni:rt] *adj* narrow-minded

Börse ['bœrzə] *f* stock exchange; *(Geldbörse)* purse; **~nmakler** *m* stock broker

Borte ['bɔrtə] *f* edging; *(Band)* trim ming

bös [bø:s] *adj* = **böse**

bösartig ['bø:z-] *adj* malicious

Böschung ['bœʃʊŋ] *f* slope; *(Ufer böschung etc)* embankment

böse ['bø:zə] *adj* bad, evil; *(zornig)* an gry

boshaft ['bo:shaft] *adj* malicious, spite ful

Bosheit *f* malice, spite

Bosnien ['bɔsniən] (-s) *nt* Bosnia; **~ und Herzegowina** [-hɛrtsə'go:vina] *nt* Bosnia (and) Herzegowina

böswillig ['bø:svɪlɪç] *adj* malicious

bot *etc* [bo:t] *vb siehe* **bieten**

Botanik [bo'ta:nɪk] *f* botany; **b~ nisch** *adj* botanical

Bot- [bo:t] *zW:* **~e** (-n, -n) *m* messen ger; **~schaft** *f* message; news; *(PO* embassy; **~schafter** (-s, -) *m* ambassa dor

Bottich ['bɔtɪç] (-(e)s, *-e) m* vat, tub

Bouillon [bʊl'jõ:] (-s, -s) *f* consommé

Bowle ['bo:lə] *f* punch

Box- ['bɔks] *zW:* **b~en** *vi* to box; **~e** (-s, -) *m* boxer; **~kampf** *m* boxin match

boykottieren [bɔykɔ'ti:rən] *vt* to boy cott

brach *etc* [bra:x] *vb siehe* **brechen**

brachte *etc* ['braxtə] *vb siehe* **bringen**

Branche ['brã:ʃə] *f* line of business

Branchenverzeichnis *nt* Yellow Page

® pl

Brand [brant] (-(e)s, ⸗e) m fire; (MED) gangrene; **b~en** ['brandən] vt i to surge; (Meer) to break; **~marken** vt to brand; (fig) to stigmatize; **~salbe** f ointment for burns; **~stifter** [-ˈʃtɪftər] m arsonist, fire raiser; **~stiftung** f arson; **~ung** f surf

Branntwein ['brantvaɪn] m brandy

Brasilien [braˈziːliən] nt Brazil

Brat- ['braːt] zW: **~apfel** m baked apple; **b~en** (unreg) vt to roast; to fry; **~en** (-s, -) m roast, joint; **~hähnchen** nt roast chicken; **~huhn** nt roast chicken; **~kartoffeln** pl fried od roast potatoes; **~pfanne** f frying pan

Bratsche ['braːtʃə] f viola

Bratspieß m spit

Bratwurst f grilled/fried sausage

Brauch [braux] (-(e)s, Bräuche) m custom; **b~bar** adj usable, serviceable; (Person) capable; **b~en** vt (bedürfen) to need; (müssen) to have to; (umg: verwenden) to use

Braue ['brauə] f brow

brauen ['brauən] vt to brew

Brauerei ['brauən] f brewery

braun [braun] adj brown; (von Sonne auch) tanned; **~ gebrannt** tanned

Bräune ['brɔynə] f brownness; (Sonnenbräune) tan; **b~n** vt to make brown; (Sonne) to tan

Brause ['brauzə] f shower bath; (von Gießkanne) rose; (Getränk) lemonade; **b~n** vi to roar; (auch vr: duschen) to take a shower

Braut [braut] (-, Bräute) f bride; (Verlobte) fiancée

Bräutigam ['brɔytɪgam] (-s, -e) m bridegroom; fiancé

Brautpaar nt bride and (bride)groom, bridal pair

brav [braːf] adj (artig) good; (ehrenhaft) worthy, honest

bravo ['braːvo] excl well done

BRD [beːˈɛrˈdeː] (-) f abk = Bundesrepublik Deutschland

The BRD (Bundesrepublik Deutschland) is the official name for the Federal Republic of Germany. It comprises 16 Länder (see Land). It was formerly the name given to West Germany as opposed to East Germany (the DDR). The two Germanies were reunited on 3rd October 1990.

Brech- ['brɛç] zW: **~eisen** nt crowbar; **b~en** (unreg) vt, vi to break; (Licht) to refract; (fig: Mensch) to crush; (speien) to vomit; **~reiz** m nausea, retching

Brei [braɪ] (-(e)s, -e) m (Masse) pulp; (KOCH) gruel; (Haferbrei) porridge

breit [braɪt] adj wide, broad; **sich ~ machen** to spread o.s. out; **B~e** f width; (bes bei Maßangaben) breadth; (GEOG) latitude; **~en** vt: **etw über etw akk ~en** to spread sth over sth; **B~engrad** m degree of latitude; **~treten** (unreg) (umg) vt to go on about

Brems- ['brɛms] zW: **~belag** m brake lining; **~e** [-zə] f brake; (ZOOL) horsefly; **b~en** [-zən] vi to brake ♦ vt (Auto) to brake; (fig) to slow down; **~flüssigkeit** f brake fluid; **~licht** nt brake light; **~pedal** nt brake pedal; **~spur** f skid mark(s pl); **~weg** m braking distance

Brenn- ['brɛn] zW: **b~bar** adj inflammable; **b~en** (unreg) vi to burn, to be on fire; (Licht, Kerze etc) to burn ♦ vt (Holz etc) to burn; (Ziegel, Ton) to fire; (Kaffee) to roast; **darauf b~en, etw zu tun** to be dying to do sth; **~nessel** ▲ f stinging nettle; **~punkt** m (PHYS) focal point; (Mittelpunkt) focus; **~stoff** m fuel

brenzlig ['brɛntslɪç] adj (fig) precarious

Bretagne [brəˈtanjə] f: **die ~** Brittany

Brett [brɛt] (-(e)s, -er) nt board, plank; (Bord) shelf; (Spielbrett) board; **~er** pl (SKI) skis; (THEAT) boards; **schwarzes ~** notice board; **~erzaun** m wooden fence; **~spiel** nt board game

Brezel ['breːtsəl] (-, -n) f pretzel

brichst etc [brɪçst] vb siehe **brechen**

Brief [briːf] (-(e)s, -e) m letter; **~freund** m penfriend; **~kasten** m letterbox; **b~lich** adj, adv by letter; **~marke** f (postage) stamp; **~papier** nt notepaper; **~tasche** f wallet; **~träger** m postman; **~umschlag** m envelope; **~waage** f letter scales; **~wechsel** m correspondence

briet etc [briːt] vb siehe **braten**

Brikett [brɪ'kɛt] (-s, -s) nt briquette

brillant [brɪl'jant] adj (fig) brilliant; **B~** (-en, -en) m brilliant, diamond

Brille ['brɪlə] f spectacles pl; (Schutzbrille) goggles pl; (Toilettenbrille) (toilet) seat; **~ngestell** nt (spectacle) frames

bringen ['brɪŋən] (unreg) vt to bring; (mitnehmen, begleiten) to take; (einbringen: Profit) to bring in; (veröffentlichen) to publish; (THEAT, CINE) to show; (RADIO, TV) to broadcast; (in einen Zustand versetzen) to get; (umg: tun können) to manage; **jdn dazu ~, etw zu tun** to make sb do sth; **jdn nach Hause ~** to take sb home; **jdn um etw ~** to make sb lose sth; **jdn auf eine Idee ~** to give sb an idea

Brise ['briːzə] f breeze

Brit- ['brɪt] zW: **~e** m Briton; **~in** f Briton, **b~isch** adj British

bröckelig ['brœkəlɪç] adj crumbly

Brocken ['brɔkən] (-s, -) m piece, bit; (Felsbrocken) lump of rock

brodeln ['broːdəln] vi to bubble

Brokkoli ['brɔkoli] pl (BOT) broccoli

Brombeere ['brɔmbeːrə] f blackberry, bramble (BRIT)

Bronchien ['brɔnçiən] pl bronchia(l tubes) pl

Bronchitis [brɔn'çiːtɪs] (-) f bronchitis

Bronze ['brõːsə] f bronze

Brosche ['brɔʃə] f brooch

Broschüre [brɔ'ʃyːrə] f pamphlet

Brot [broːt] (-(e)s, -e) nt bread; (Laib) loaf

Brötchen ['brøːtçən] nt roll

Bruch [brʊx] (-(e)s, ¨e) m breakage; (zerbrochene Stelle) break; (fig) split, breach; (MED: Eingeweidebruch) rupture, hernia; (Beinbruch etc) fracture; (MATH) fraction

brüchig ['brʏçɪç] adj brittle, fragile; (Haus) dilapidated

Bruch- zW: **~landung** f crash landing; **~strich** m (MATH) line; **~stück** nt fragment; **~teil** m fraction; **~zahl** [brʊxtsaːl] f (MATH) fraction

Brücke ['brʏkə] f bridge; (Teppich) rug

Bruder ['bruːdər] (-s, ¨) m brother

brüderlich adj brotherly

Brühe ['bryːə] f broth, stock; (pej) muck

brüllen ['brʏlən] vi to bellow, to roar

brummen ['brʊmən] vi (Bär, Mensch etc) to growl; (Insekt) to buzz; (Motoren) to roar; (murren) to grumble

brünett [brʏ'nɛt] adj brunette, dark-haired

Brunnen ['brʊnən] (-s, -) m fountain; (tief) well; (natürlich) spring

Brust [brʊst] (-, ¨e) f breast; (Männerbrust) chest

brüsten ['brʏstən] vr to boast

Brust- zW: **~kasten** m chest; **~schwimmen** nt breast-stroke

Brüstung ['brʏstʊŋ] f parapet

Brut [bruːt] (-, -en) f brood; (Brüten) hatching

brutal [bru'taːl] adj brutal; **B~ität** f brutality

brüten ['bryːtən] vi (auch fig) to brood

Brutkasten m incubator

brutto ['brʊto] adv gross; **B~einkommen** nt gross salary; **B~gehalt** nt gross salary; **B~gewicht** nt gross weight; **B~lohn** m gross wages pl; **B~sozialprodukt** nt gross national product

BSE f abk (= Bovine Spongiforme Enzephalopathie) BSE

Bube ['buːbə] m (-n, -n) m (Schurke) rogue; (KARTEN) jack

Buch [buːx] (-(e)s, ⁼er) nt book; (COMM) account book; **~binder** m bookbinder; **~drucker** m printer

Buche f beech tree

buchen vt to book; (Betrag) to enter

Bücher- ['byːçər] zW: **~brett** nt bookshelf; **~ei** [-'rai] f library; **~regal** nt bookshelves pl, bookcase; **~schrank** m bookcase

Buch- zW: **~führung** f book-keeping, accounting; **~halter(in)** (-s, -) m(f) book-keeper; **~handel** m book trade; **~händler(in)** m(f) bookseller; **~handlung** f bookshop

Büchse ['byksə] f tin, can; (Holzbüchse) box; (Gewehr) rifle; **~nfleisch** nt tinned meat; **~nmilch** f (KOCH) evaporated milk, tinned milk; **~nöffner** m tin opener

Buch- zW: **~stabe** (-ns, -n) m letter of the alphabet; **b~stabieren** [buːxʃtaˈbiːrən] vt to spell; **b~stäblich** ['buːxʃtɛːplɪç] adj literal

Bucht ['buxt] (-, -en) f bay

Buchung ['buːxʊŋ] f booking; (COMM) entry

Buckel ['bukəl] (-s, -) m hump

bücken ['bykən] vr to bend

Bude ['buːdə] f booth, stall; (umg) digs pl (BRIT)

Büfett [byˈfet] (-s, -s) nt (Anrichte) sideboard; (Geschirrschrank) dresser; **kaltes ~** cold buffet

Büffel ['byfəl] (-s, -) m buffalo

Bug [buːk] (-(e)s, -e) m (NAUT) bow; (AVIAT) nose

Bügel ['byːɡəl] (-s, -) m (Kleider~) hanger; (Steig~) stirrup; (Brillen~) arm; **~brett** nt ironing board; **~eisen** nt iron; **~falte** f crease; **b~frei** adj crease-resistant, noniron; **b~n** vt, vi to

iron

Bühne ['byːnə] f stage; **~nbild** nt set, scenery

Buhruf ['buːruːf] m boo

buk etc [buːk] vb siehe **backen**

Bulgarien [bulˈɡaːriən] nt Bulgaria

Bull- ['bʊl] zW: **~auge** nt (NAUT) porthole; **~dogge** f bulldog; **~dozer** ['buldoːzər] (-s, -) m bulldozer; **~e** (-n, -n) m bull

Bumerang ['buːməraŋ] (-s, -e) m boomerang

Bummel ['bʊməl] (-s, -) m stroll; (Schaufensterbummel) window-shopping; **~ant** [-'lant] m slowcoach; **~ei** [-'lai] f wandering; dawdling; skiving; **b~n** vi to wander, to stroll; (trödeln) to dawdle; (faulenzen) to skive, to loaf around; **~streik** ['bʊməlʃtraik] m go-slow

Bund¹ [bʊnt] (-(e)s, ⁼e) m (Freundschaftsbund etc) bond; (Organisation) union; (POL) confederacy; (Hosenbund, Rockbund) waistband

Bund² (-(e)s, -e) nt bunch; (Strohbund) bundle

Bündel ['byndəl] (-s, -) nt bundle, bale; **b~n** vt to bundle

Bundes- ['bʊndəs] in zW Federal; **~bürger** m German citizen; **~hauptstadt** f Federal capital; **~kanzler** m Federal Chancellor; **~land** nt Land; **~liga** f football league; **~präsident** m Federal President; **~rat** m upper house of German Parliament; **~regierung** f Federal government; **~republik** f Federal Republic (of Germany); **~staat** m Federal state; **~straße** f Federal road; **~tag** m German Parliament; **~wehr** f German Armed Forces pl; **b~weit** adj nationwide

---

Bundespräsident

The **Bundespräsident** *is the head of state of the Federal Republic of Ger-*

---

many. He is elected every 5 years - no-one can be elected more than twice - by the members of the Bundesversammlung, a body formed especially for this purpose. His role is to represent Germany at home and abroad. In Switzerland the Bundespräsident is the head of the government, known as the Bundesrat.

The Bundesrat is the Upper House of the German Parliament whose 68 members are nominated by the parliaments of the Länder. Its most important function is to approve federal laws concerned with the jurisdiction of the Länder, and it can raise objections to other laws, but can be outvoted by the Bundestag. In Austria the Länder are also represented in the Bundesrat.

Bundestag

The Bundestag is the Lower House of the German Parliament and is elected by the people by proportional representation. There are 672 MPs, half of them elected directly from the first vote (Erststimme), and half from the regional list of parliamentary candidates resulting from the second vote (Zweitstimme). The Bundestag exercises parliamentary control over the government.

Bündnis ['byntnɪs] (-ses, -se) nt alliance

bunt [bʊnt] adj coloured; (gemischt) mixed; **jdm wird es zu ~** it's getting too much for sb; **B~stift** m coloured pencil, crayon

Burg [bʊrk] (-, -en) f castle, fort

Bürge ['byrgə] (-n, -n) m guarantor; **b~n** vi: **b~n für** to vouch for

Bürger(in) ['byrgər(ɪn)] (-s, -) m(f) citizen; member of the middle class; **~krieg** m civil war; **b~lich** adj (Rechte) civil; (Klasse) middle-class; (pej) bour-

geois; **~meister** m mayor; **~recht** n civil rights pl; **~schaft** f (Vertretung) City Parliament; **~steig** m pavement

Bürgschaft f surety; **~ leisten** to give security

Büro [by'ro:] (-s, -s) nt office; **~angestellte(r)** f(m) office worker; **~klammer** f paper clip; **~kratie** f bureaucracy; **b~kratisch** adj bureaucratic, **~schluss ▲** m office closing time

Bursche ['bʊrʃə] (-n, -n) m lad, fellow; (Diener) servant

Bürste ['byrstə] f brush; **b~n** vt to brush

Bus [bʊs] (-ses, -se) m bus; **~bahnhof** m bus/coach (BRIT) station

Busch [bʊʃ] (-(e)s, *e) m bush, shrub

Büschel ['byʃəl] (-s, -) nt tuft

buschig adj bushy

Busen ['bu:zən] (-s, -) m bosom; (Meerbusen) inlet, bay

Bushaltestelle f bus stop

Buße ['bu:sə] f atonement, penance; (Geld) fine

büßen ['by:sən] vi to do penance, to atone ♦ vt to do penance for, to atone for

Bußgeld ['bu:sgɛlt] nt fine; **~bescheid** m notice of payment due (for traffic offence etc)

Büste ['bystə] f bust; **~nhalter** m bra

Butter ['bʊtər] (-) f butter; **~blume** f buttercup; **~brot** nt (piece of) bread and butter; (umg) sandwich; **~brotpapier** nt greaseproof paper; **~dose** f butter dish; **~milch** f buttermilk; **b~weich** ['bʊtərvaiç] adj soft as butter; (fig, umg) soft

b. w. abk (= bitte wenden) p.t.o.

bzgl. abk (= bezüglich) re

bzw. abk = beziehungsweise

C, c

ca. [ka] abk (= circa) approx.

Café [ka'fe:] (-s, -s) nt café

Cafeteria [kafete'ri:a] (-, -s) f cafeteria

Camcorder [-s, -] m camcorder

Camp- ['kɛmp] zW: **c~en** vi to camp; **~er** (-s, -) m camper; **~ing** (-s) nt camping; **~ingführer** m camping guide (book); **~ingkocher** m camping stove; **~ingplatz** m camp(ing) site

CD-Spieler m CD (player)

Cello ['tʃɛlo] (-s, -s od Celli) nt cello

Celsius ['tsɛlziʊs] (-) nt centigrade

Champagner [ʃam'panjər] (-s, -) m champagne

Champignon ['ʃampinjõ] (-s, -s) m button mushroom

Chance ['ʃã:s(ə)] f chance, opportunity

Chaos ['ka:ɔs] (-, -) nt chaos; **chaotisch** [ka'o:tiʃ] adj chaotic

Charakter [ka'raktər, pl karak'te:rə] (-s, -e) m character; **c~fest** adj of firm character, strong; **c~i'sieren** vt to characterize; **c~istisch** [karakte'rɪstɪʃ] adj: **c~istisch (für)** characteristic (of), typical (of); **c~los** adj unprincipled; **~losigkeit** f lack of principle; **~schwäche** f weakness of character; **~stärke** f strength of character; **~zug** m characteristic, trait

charmant [ʃar'mant] adj charming

Charme [ʃarm] (-s) m charm

Charterflug ['tʃartərflu:k] m charter flight

Chauffeur [ʃɔ'føːr] m chauffeur

Chauvinist [ʃovi'nɪst] m chauvinist, jingoist

Chef [ʃɛf] (-s, -s) m head; (umg) boss; **~arzt** m senior consultant; **~in** (umg) f boss

Chemie [çe'mi:] (-) f chemistry; **~faser** f man-made fibre

Chemikalie [çemi'ka:liə] f chemical

Chemiker ['çe:mikər] (-s, -) m (industrial) chemist

chemisch ['çe:mɪʃ] adj chemical; **~e Reinigung** dry cleaning

Chicorée ['ʃikore:] (-s) m od f chicory

Chiffre ['ʃifrə] f (Geheimzeichen) cipher; (in Zeitung) box number

Chile ['tʃi:le] nt Chile

Chin- ['çi:n] zW: **~a** nt China; **~akohl** m Chinese leaves; **~ese** [-'ne:zə] m Chinese; **~esin** f Chinese; **c~esisch** adj Chinese

Chip [tʃip] (-s, -s) m (Kartoffelchips) crisp (BRIT), chip (US); (COMPUT) chip; **~karte** f smart card

Chirurg [çi'rʊrg] (-en, -en) m surgeon; **~ie** [-'gi:] f surgery; **c~isch** adj surgical

Chlor [klo:r] (-s) nt chlorine; **~o'form** (-s) nt chloroform

cholerisch [ko'le:rɪʃ] adj choleric

Chor [ko:r] (-(e)s, ⁺e) m choir; (Musikstück, THEAT) chorus; **~al** [ko'ra:l] (-s, -äle) m chorale

Choreograf ▲ [koreo'gra:f] (-en, -en) m choreographer

Christ [krɪst] (-en, -en) m Christian; **~baum** m Christmas tree; **~entum** nt Christianity; **~in** f Christian; **~kind** nt = Father Christmas; (Jesus) baby Jesus; **c~lich** adj Christian; **~us** (-) m Christ

Chrom [kro:m] (-s) nt (CHEM) chromium; chrome

Chron- ['kro:n] zW: **~ik** f chronicle; **c~isch** adj chronic; **c~ologisch** [-o'lo:gɪʃ] adj chronological

circa ['tsɪrka] adv about, approximately

Clown [klaʊn] (-s, -s) m clown

Cocktail ['kɔkteːl] (-s, -s) m cocktail

Cola ['ko:la] (-, -s) f Coke ®

Computer [kɔm'pju:tər] (-s, -) m computer; **~spiel** nt computer game

Cord [kɔrt] (-s) m cord, corduroy

Couch [kaʊtʃ] (-, -es od -en) f couch

Coupon [ku'põ] (-s, -s) m = Kupon

Spelling Reform: ▲ new spelling △ old spelling (to be phased out)

Cousin [ku'zɛː] (-s, -s) m cousin; **~e** [ku'ziːnə] f cousine

Creme [kreːm] (-, -s) f cream; (Schuhcreme) polish; (Zahncreme) paste; (KOCH) mousse; **c~farben** adj cream(-coloured)

cremig ['kreːmɪç] adj creamy

Curry ['karɪ] (-s) m od nt curry powder; **~pulver** nt curry powder; **~wurst** f curried sausage

D, d

da [daː] adv **1** (örtlich) there; (hier) here; **da draußen** out there; **da sein** to be there; **da bin ich** here I am; **da, wo** where; **ist noch Milch da?** is there any milk left?

2 (zeitlich) then; (folglich) so

3: **da haben wir Glück gehabt** we were lucky there; **da kann man nichts machen** nothing can be done about it ♦ konj (weil) as, since

dabehalten (unreg) vt to keep

dabei [da'baɪ] adv (räumlich) close to it; (noch dazu) besides; (zusammen mit) with them; (zeitlich) during this; (obwohl doch) but, however; **was ist schon ~?** what of it?; **es ist doch nichts ~, wenn ...** it doesn't matter if ...; **bleiben wir ~** let's leave it at that; **es bleibt ~** that's settled; **das Dumme/Schwierige ~** the stupid/difficult part of it; **er war gerade ~ zu gehen** he was just leaving; **~ sein** (anwesend) to be present; (beteiligt) to be involved; **~stehen** (unreg) vi to stand around

Dach [dax] (-(e)s, ⁻er) nt roof; **~boden** m attic, loft; **~decker** (-s, -) m slater, tiler; **~fenster** nt skylight; **~gepäckträger** m roof rack; **~luke** f skylight; **~pappe** f roofing felt; **~rinne** f gutter

Dachs [daks] (-es, -e) m badger

dachte etc ['daxtə] vb siehe **denken**

Dackel ['dakəl] (-s, -) m dachshund

dadurch [da'dʊrç] adv (räumlich) through it; (durch diesen Umstand) thereby, in that way; (deshalb) because of that, for that reason ♦ konj: **~ dass** because

dafür [da'fyːr] adv for it; (anstatt) instead; **er kann nichts ~** he can't help it; **er ist bekannt ~** he is well-known for that; **was bekomme ich ~?** what will I get for it?

dagegen [da'geːgən] adv against it; (im Vergleich damit) in comparison with it; (bei Tausch) for it/them ♦ konj however; **ich habe nichts ~** I don't mind; **ich war ~** I was against it; **~ kann man nichts tun** one can't do anything about it; **~halten** (unreg) vt (vergleichen) to compare with it; (entgegnen) to object to it; **~sprechen** (unreg) vi: **es spricht nichts ~** there's no reason why not

daheim [da'haɪm] adv at home; **D~** (-s) nt home

daher [da'heːr] adv (räumlich) from there; (Ursache) from that ♦ konj (deshalb) that's why

dahin [da'hɪn] adv (räumlich) there; (zeitlich) then; (vergangen) gone; **~ gehend** on this matter; **~gegen** konj on the other hand; **~gestellt** adv: **~gestellt bleiben** to remain to be seen; **~gestellt sein lassen** to leave open od undecided

dahinten [da'hɪntən] adv over there

dahinter [da'hɪntər] adv behind it; **~kommen** to get to the bottom of it

dalli ['dali] (umg) adv chop chop

damalig ['daːmaːlɪç] adj of that time, then

damals ['daːmaːls] adv at that time, then

Dame ['daːmə] f lady; (SCHACH, KARTEN)

queen; (Spiel) draughts sg; **~nbinde** f sanitary towel od napkin (US); **d~nhaft** adj ladylike; **~ntoilette** f ladies' toilet od restroom (US); **~nwahl** f ladies' excuse-me

damit [da'mɪt] adv with it; (begründend) by that ♦ konj in order to; **was meint er ~?** what does he mean by that?; **genug ~!** that's enough!

dämlich ['dɛːmlɪç] (umg) adj silly, stupid

Damm [dam] (-(e)s, ⸚e) m dyke; (Staudamm) dam; (Hafendamm) mole; (Bahndamm, Straßendamm) embankment

dämmen ['dɛmən] vt (Wasser) to dam up; (Schmerzen) to keep back

dämmer- zW: **~ig** adj dim, faint; **~n** vi (Tag) to dawn; (Abend) to fall; **D~ung** f twilight; (Morgendämmerung) dawn; (Abenddämmerung) dusk

Dampf [dampf] (-(e)s, ⸚e) m steam; (Dunst) vapour; **d~en** vi to steam

dämpfen ['dɛmpfən] vt (KOCH) to steam; (bügeln) to iron with a damp cloth; (fig) to dampen, to subdue

Dampf- zW: **~schiff** nt steamship; **~walze** f steamroller

danach [da'naːx] adv after that; (zeitlich) after that, afterwards; (gemäß) accordingly; according to which; according to that; **er sieht ~ aus** he looks it

Däne ['dɛːnə] (-n, -n) m Dane

daneben [da'neːbən] adv beside it; (im Vergleich) in comparison; **~benehmen** (unreg) vr to misbehave; **~gehen** (unreg) vi to miss; (Plan) to fail

Dänemark ['dɛːnəmark] nt Denmark; **Dänin** f Dane; **dänisch** adj Danish

Dank [daŋk] (-(e)s) m thanks pl; **vielen od schönen ~** many thanks; **jdm ~ sagen** to thank sb; **d~** präp (+dat od gen) thanks to; **d~bar** adj grateful; (Auf-

gabe) rewarding; **~barkeit** f gratitude; **d~e** excl thank you, thanks; **d~en** vi (+dat to thank; **d~enswert** adj (Arbeit) worthwhile; rewarding; (Bemühung) kind; rewarding; **d~sagen** vi to express one's thanks

dann [dan] adv then; **~ und wann** now and then

daran [da'ran] adv on it; (stoßen) against it; **es liegt ~, dass ...** the cause of it is that ...; **gut/schlecht ~ sein** to be well-/badly off; **das Beste/ Dümmste ~** the best/stupidest thing about it; **ich war nahe ~ zu ...** I was on the point of ...; **er ist ~ gestorben** he died from it od of it; **~gehen** (unreg) vi to start; **~setzen** vt to stake

darauf [da'rauf] adv (räumlich) on it; (zielgerichtet) towards it; (danach) afterwards; **es kommt ganz ~ an, ob ...** it depends whether ...; **die Tage ~** the days following od thereafter; **am Tag ~** the next day; **~folgend** (Tag, Jahr) next, following; **~legen** to lay od put on top

daraus [da'raus] adv from it; **was ist ~ geworden?** what became of it?; **~ geht hervor, dass ...** this means that ...

Darbietung ['daːrbiːtʊŋ] f performance

darf etc [darf] vb siehe **dürfen**

darin [da'rɪn] adv in (there), in it

darlegen ['daːrleːgən] vt to explain, to expound, to set forth; **Darlegung** f explanation

Darlehen [(e)n] (-s, -) nt loan

Darm [darm] (-(e)s, ⸚e) m intestine; (Wurstdarm) skin; **~grippe** f (MED) gastric influenza od flu

darstell- ['daːrʃtɛl] zW: **~en** vt (abbilden, bedeuten) to represent; (THEAT) to act; (beschreiben) to describe ♦ vr to appear to be; **D~er(in)** (-s, -) m(f) actor (actress); **D~ung** f portrayal, depiction

darüber [da'ry:bər] *adv (räumlich)* over it, above it; *(fahren)* over it; *(mehr)* more; *(währenddessen)* meanwhile; *(sprechen, streiten)* about it; **~ geht nichts** there's nothing like it

darum [da'rʊm] *adv (räumlich)* round it ♦ *konj* that's why; **er bittet ~** he is pleading for it; **es geht ~, dass ...** the thing is that ...; **er würde viel ~ geben, wenn ...** he would give a lot to ...; **ich tue es ~, weil ...** I am doing it because ...

darunter [da'rʊntər] *adv (räumlich)* under it; *(dazwischen)* among them; *(weniger)* less; **ein Stockwerk ~** one floor below (it); **was verstehen Sie ~?** what do you understand by that?

das [das] *def art* the ♦ *pron* that

Dasein ['da:zaɪn] *(-s) nt (Leben)* life; *(Anwesenheit)* presence; *(Bestehen)* existence

da sein ▲ *siehe* **da**

dass ▲ [das] *konj* that

dasselbe [das'zɛlbə] *art, pron* the same

dastehen ['da:ʃteːən] *(unreg) vi* to stand there

Datei [da'taɪ] *f* file

Daten- ['da:tən] *zW:* **~bank** *f* data base; **~schutz** *m* data protection; **~verarbeitung** *f* data processing

datieren [da'tiːrən] *vt* to date

Dativ ['da:ti:f] *(-s, -e) m* dative (case)

Dattel ['datəl] *(-, -n) f* date

Datum ['da:tʊm] *(-s, Daten) nt* date; **Daten** *pl (Angaben)* data *pl*

Dauer ['daʊər] *(-, -n) f* duration; *(gewisse Zeitspanne)* length; *(Bestand, Fortbestehen)* permanence; **es war nur von kurzer ~** it didn't last long; **auf die ~** in the long run; *(auf längere Zeit)* indefinitely; **~auftrag** *m* standing order; **d~haft** *adj* lasting, durable; **~karte** *f* season ticket; **~lauf** *m* jog(ging); **d~n** *vi* to last; **es hat sehr lang gedauert, bis er ...** it took him a long time to ...; **d~nd** *adj* constant;

~parkplatz *m* long-stay car park; **~welle** *f* perm, permanent wave; **~wurst** *f* German salami; **~zustand** *m* permanent condition

Daumen ['daʊmən] *(-s, -) m* thumb

Daune ['daʊnə] *f* down; **~ndecke** *f* down duvet, down quilt

davon [da'fɔn] *adv* of it; *(räumlich)* away; *(weg von)* from it; *(Grund)* because of it; **das kommt ~!** that's what you get; **~ abgesehen** apart from that; **~ sprechen/wissen** to talk/know of *od* about it; **was habe ich ~?** what's the point?; **~kommen** *(unreg) vi* to escape; **~laufen** *(unreg) vi* to run away

davor [da'foːr] *adv (räumlich)* in front of it; *(zeitlich)* before (that); **~ warnen** to warn about it

dazu [da'tsuː] *adv (legen, stellen)* by it; *(essen, singen)* with it; **und ~ noch** and in addition; **ein Beispiel/seine Gedanken ~** one example for/his thoughts on this; **wie komme ich denn ~?** why should I?; **~ fähig sein** to be capable of it; **sich ~ äußern** to say something on it; **~gehören** *vi* to belong to it; **~kommen** *(unreg) vi (Ereignisse)* to happen too; *(an einen Ort)* to come along

dazwischen [da'tsvɪʃən] *adv* in between; *(räumlich)* among (them); *(zusammen mit)* among them; **~kommen** *(unreg) vi (hineingeraten)* to get caught in it; **es ist etwas ~gekommen** something cropped up; **~reden** *vi (unterbrechen)* to interrupt; *(sich einmischen)* to interfere; **~treten** *(unreg) vi* to intervene

---

DDR

The DDR *(Deutsche Demokratische Republik)* was the name by which the former Communist German Democratic Republic was known. It was founded in 1949 from the Soviet-occupied zone. After the Berlin Wall was built in 1961 it was virtually sealed off from the West. Mass demonstrations and demands for reform forced the opening of the borders in 1989 and the DDR merged in 1990 with the BRD.

Debatte [de'batə] f debate

Deck [dɛk] (-(e)s, -s od -e) nt deck; **an ~ gehen** to go on deck

Decke f cover; (Bettdecke) blanket; (Tischdecke) tablecloth; (Zimmerdecke) ceiling; **unter einer ~ stecken** to be hand in glove; **~l** (-s, -) nt lid; **d~n** vt to cover ♦ vr to coincide

Deckung f (Schützen) covering; (Schutz) cover; (SPORT) defence; (Übereinstimmen) agreement

Defekt [de'fɛkt] (-(e)s, -e) m fault, defect; **d~** adj faulty

defensiv [defɛn'si:f] adj defensive

definieren [defi'ni:rən] vt to define; **Definition** [definitsi'o:n] f definition

Defizit ['de:fitsɪt] (-s, -e) nt deficit

deftig ['dɛftɪç] adj (Essen) large; (Witz) coarse

Degen ['de:gən] (-s, -) m sword

degenerieren [degene'ri:rən] vi to degenerate

dehnbar ['de:nba:r] adj elastic; (fig: Begriff) loose

dehnen vt, vr to stretch

Deich [daɪç] (-(e)s, -e) m dyke, dike

deichseln (umg) vt (fig) to wangle

dein(e) [daɪn(ə)] adj your; **~e(r, s)** pron yours; **~er** (gen von du) pron of you; **~erseits** adv on your part; **~esgleichen** pron people like you; **~etwegen** adv (für dich) for your sake; (wegen dir) on your account; **~etwillen** adv: um **~etwillen** = deinetwegen; **~ige** pron: **der/die/das ~ige** od **D~ige** yours

Deklination [deklinatsi'o:n] f declension

deklinieren [dekli'ni:rən] vt to decline

Dekolleté, Dekolletee ▲ [dekɔl'te:]

(-s, -s) nt low neckline

Deko- [deko] zW: **~rateur** [-ra'tø:r] m window dresser; **~ration** [-ratsi'o:n] f decoration; (in Laden) window dressing; **d~rativ** [-ra'ti:f] adj decorative; **d~rieren** [-'ri:rən] vt to decorate; (Schaufenster) to dress

Delegation [delegatsi'o:n] f delegation

delegieren [dele'gi:rən] vt: **~ an** +akk (Aufgaben) to delegate to

Delfin ▲ [dɛl'fi:n] (-s, -e) m dolphin

delikat [deli'ka:t] adj (zart, heikel) delicate; (köstlich) delicious

Delikatesse [delika'tesə] f delicacy; **~n** pl (Feinkost) delicatessen food; **~ngeschäft** f delicatessen

Delikt [de'lɪkt] (-(e)s, -e) nt (JUR) offence

Delle ['dɛlə] (umg) f dent

Delphin △ [dɛl'fi:n] (-s, -e) m = **Delfin**

dem [de(:)m] art dat von **der**

Demagoge [dema'go:gə] (-n, -n) m demagogue

dementieren [demɛn'ti:rən] vt to deny

dem- zW: **~gemäß** adv accordingly; **~nach** adv accordingly; **~nächst** adv shortly

Demokrat [demo'kra:t] (-en, -en) m democrat; **~ie** [-'ti:] f democracy; **d~isch** adj democratic; **d~isieren** [-i'zi:rən] vt to democratize

demolieren [demo'li:rən] vt to demolish

Demon- [demɔn] zW: **~strant(in)** [-'strant(ɪn)] m(f) demonstrator; **~stration** [stratsi'o:n] f demonstration; **d~strativ** [-stra'ti:f] adj demonstrative; (Protest) pointed; **d~strieren** [-'stri:rən] vt, vi to demonstrate

Demoskopie [demosko'pi:] f public opinion research

Demut ['de:mu:t] (-) f humility

demütig ['de:my:tɪç] adj humble; **~en**

demzufolge

deuten

['deːmyːtɪgən] vt to humiliate; **D~ung** f humiliation

demzufolge ['deːmtsuˈfɔlɡə] adv accordingly

den [deː)n] art akk von **der**

denen ['deːnən] pron dat pl von **der**; **die**; **das**

Denk- ['dɛŋk] zW: **d~bar** adj conceivable; **~en** (-s) nt thinking; **d~en** (unreg) vt, vi to think; **d~faul** adj lazy; **~fehler** m logical error; **~mal** (-s, -er) nt monument; **~malschutz** m protection of historical monuments; **unter ~malschutz stehen** to be classified as a historical monument; **d~würdig** adj memorable; **~zettel** m: **jdm einen ~zettel verpassen** to teach sb a lesson

denn [dɛn] konj for ♦ adv then; (nach Komparativ) than; **warum ~?** why?

dennoch ['dɛnɔx] konj nevertheless

Denunziant [denʊntsiˈant(ɪn)] m informer

Deodorant [deˈodoˈrant] (-s, -s od -e) nt deodorant

Deponie [depoˈniː] f dump

deponieren [depoˈniːrən] vt (COMM) to deposit

Depot [deˈpoː] (-s, -s) nt warehouse; (Busdepot, EISENB) depot; (Bankdepot) strongroom, safe (US)

Depression [depresiˈoːn] f depression; **depres'siv** adj depressive

deprimieren [depriˈmiːrən] vt to depress

SCHLÜSSELWORT

der [deː)r] (f **die**, nt **das**, gen **des**, **der**, **des**, dat **dem**, **der**, **dem**, akk **den**, **die**, **das**, pl **die**) def art the; **der Rhein** the Rhine; **der Klaus** (umg) Klaus; **die Frau** (im Allgemeinen) women; **der Tod/das Leben** death/life; **der Fuß des Berges** the foot of the hill; **gib es der Frau** give it to the woman; **er hat sich die Hand verletzt** he has hurt his hand

♦ relativ pron (bei Menschen) who, that; (bei Tieren, Sachen) which, that; **der Mann, den ich gesehen habe** the man who od whom od that I saw

♦ demonstrativ pron he/she/it; (jener, dieser) that; (pl) those; **der/die war es** it was him/her; **der mit der Brille** the one with glasses; **ich will den (da)** I want that one

derart ['deːrˈart] adv so; (solcher Art) such; **~ig** adj such, this sort of

derb [dɛrp] adj sturdy; (Kost) solid; (grob) coarse

der- zW: **'~'gleichen** pron such; **'~jenige** pron he; she; it; the one (who); that (which); **'~'maßen** adv to such an extent, so; **~'selbe** art, pron the same; **'~'weil(en)** adv in the meantime; **'~'zeitig** adj present, current; (damalig) then

des [dɛs] art gen von **der**

desertieren [dezɛrˈtiːrən] vi to desert

desgleichen ['dɛsˈɡlaɪçən] adv likewise, also

deshalb ['dɛsˈhalp] adv therefore, that's why

Desinfektion [dɛzɪnfɛktsiˈoːn] f disinfection; **~smittel** nt disinfectant

desinfizieren [dɛzɪnfiˈtsiːrən] vt to disinfect

dessen ['dɛsən] pron gen von **der**; **das**; **~ ungeachtet** nevertheless, regardless

Dessert [deˈseːr] (-s, -s) nt dessert

destillieren [dɛstɪˈliːrən] vt to distil

desto ['dɛsto] adv all the, so much the; **~ besser** all the better

deswegen ['dɛsˈveːɡən] konj therefore, hence

Detail [deˈtaɪ] (-s, -s) nt detail

Detektiv [detɛkˈtiːf] (-s, -e) m detective

deut- ['dɔʏt] zW: **~en** vt to interpret, to explain ♦ vi: **~en auf** (+akk) to point (to od at); **~lich** adj clear; (Unterschied) distinct; **D~lichkeit** f clarity; distinctness

Deutsch [dɔytʃ] *nt* German

deutsch *adj* German; **auf D~** in German; **D~e Demokratische Republik** (*HIST*) German Democratic Republic, East Germany; **~es Beefsteak** ≈ hamburger; **D~e(r)** *mf* German; **ich bin D~er** I am German; **D~land** *nt* Germany

Devise [de'vi:zə] *f* motto, device; **~n** *pl* (*FIN*) foreign currency, foreign exchange

Dezember [de'tsɛmbər] (**-s, -**) *m* December

dezent [de'tsɛnt] *adj* discreet

dezimal [detsi'ma:l] *adj* decimal; **D~system** *nt* decimal system

d. h. *abk* (= *das heißt*) i.e.

Dia ['di:a] (**-s, -s**) *nt* (*PHOT*) slide, transparency

Diabetes [dia'be:tes] (**-, -**) *m* (*MED*) diabetes

Diagnose [dia'gno:zə] *f* diagnosis

diagonal [diago'na:l] *adj* diagonal

Dialekt [dia'lɛkt] (**-(e)s, -e**) *m* dialect; **d~isch** *adj* dialectal; (*Logik*) dialectical

Dialog [dia'lo:k] (**-(e)s, -e**) *m* dialogue

Diamant [dia'mant] *m* diamond

Diaprojektor ['di:aprojɛktɔr] *m* slide projector

Diät [di'ɛːt] (**-, -en**) *f* diet

dich [dɪç] (*akk von du*) *pron* you; yourself

dicht [dɪçt] *adj* dense; (*Nebel*) thick; (*Gewebe*) close; (*undurchlässig*) (water)tight; (*fig*) concise ♦ *adv:* **~ an/bei** close to; **~ bevölkert** densely *od* heavily populated; **D~e** *f* density; thickness; closeness; (water)tightness; (*fig*) conciseness

dichten *vt* (*dicht machen*) to make watertight, to seal; (*NAUT*) to caulk; (*LITER*) to compose, to write ♦ *vi* to compose, to write

Dichter(in) (**-s, -**) *m(f)* poet; (*Autor*) writer; **d~isch** *adj* poetical

dichthalten (*unreg*) (*umg*) *vi* to keep one's mouth shut

Dichtung *f* (*TECH*) washer; (*AUT*) gasket; (*Gedichte*) poetry; (*Prosa*) (piece of) writing

dick [dɪk] *adj* thick; (*fett*) fat; **durch ~ und dünn** through thick and thin; **D~darm** *m* (*ANAT*) colon; **D~e** *f* thickness; fatness; **~flüssig** *adj* viscous; **D~icht** (**-s, -e**) *nt* thicket; **D~kopf** *m* mule; **D~milch** *f* soured milk

die [di:] *def art siehe* **der**

Dieb(in) [di:p, 'di:bɪn] (**-(e)s, -e**) *m(f)* thief; **d~isch** *adj* thieving; (*umg*) immense; **~stahl** (**-(e)s, *e**) *m* theft; **~stahlversicherung** *f* insurance against theft

Diele ['di:lə] *f* (*Brett*) board; (*Flur*) hall, lobby

dienen ['di:nən] *vi:* (*jdm*) **~** to serve (sb)

Diener (**-s, -**) *m* servant; **~in** *f* (maid)servant; **~schaft** *f* servants *pl*

Dienst [di:nst] (**-(e)s, -e**) *m* service; **außer ~** retired; **~ haben** to be on duty; **~ habend** (*Arzt*) on duty

Dienstag ['di:nsta:k] *m* Tuesday; **d~s** *adv* on Tuesdays

Dienst- *zW:* **~bote** *m* servant; **~geheimnis** *nt* official secret; **~gespräch** *nt* business call; **~leistung** *f* service; **~lich** *adj* official; **~mädchen** *nt* (house)maid; **~reise** *f* business trip; **~stelle** *f* office; **~vorschrift** *f* official regulations *pl*; **~weg** *m* official channels *pl*; **~zeit** *f* working hours *pl*; (*MIL*) period of service

dies [di:s] *pron* (*demonstrativ: sg*) this; (*: pl*) these; **~bezüglich** *adj* (*Frage*) on this matter; **~e(r, s)** ['di:zə(r, s)] *pron* this (one)

Diesel ['di:zəl] *m* (*Kraftstoff*) diesel

dieselbe [di:'zɛlbə] *pron, art* the same

Dieselmotor *m* diesel engine

dies- *zW:* **~jährig** *adj* this year's; **~mal**

Spelling Reform: ▲ *new spelling* △ *old spelling (to be phased out)*

adv this time; **~seits** *präp +gen* on this side; **D~seits** (-) *nt* this life

Dietrich ['di:trɪç] (-s, -e) *m* picklock

diffamieren [dɪfa'mi:rən] (*pej*) *vt* to defame

Differenz [dɪfe'rɛnts] (-, -en) *f* (*Unterschied*) difference; **~en** *pl* (*Meinungsverschiedenheit*) difference (of opinion); **d~ieren** *vt* to make distinctions in; **d~iert** *adj* (*Mensch etc*) complex

differenzial ▲ [dɪferɛntsia:l] *adj* differential; **D~rechnung** ▲ *f* differential calculus

digital [digi'ta:l] *adj* digital; **D~fernsehen** *f* digital TV

Dikt- [dɪkt] *zW:* **~afon**, **~aphon** [-a'fo:n] *nt* dictaphone; **~at** [-'ta:t] (-(e)s, -e) *nt* dictation; **~ator** [-'ta:tɔr] *m* dictator; **d~atorisch** [-a'to:rɪʃ] *adj* dictatorial; **~atur** [-a'tu:r] *f* dictatorship; **d~ieren** [-'ti:rən] *vt* to dictate

Dilemma [di'lema] (-s, -s *od* -ta) *nt* dilemma

Dilettant [dile'tant] *m* dilettante, amateur; **d~isch** *adj* amateurish, dilettante

Dimension [dimenzi'o:n] *f* dimension

DIN *f abk* (= *Deutsche Industrie-Norm*) German Industrial Standard

Ding [dɪŋ] (-(e)s, -e) *nt* thing, object; **d~lich** *adj* real, concrete; **~s(bums)** ['dɪŋks(bʊms)] (-) (*umg*) *nt* thingummybob

Diplom [di'plo:m] (-(e)s, -e) *nt* diploma, certificate; **~at** [-'ma:t] (-en, -en) *m* diplomat; **~atie** [-a'ti:] *f* diplomacy; **d~atisch** [-'ma:tɪʃ] *adj* diplomatic; **~ingenieur** *m* qualified engineer

dir [di:r] (*dat von* **du**) *pron* (to) you

direkt [di'rɛkt] *adj* direct; **D~flug** *m* direct flight; **D~or** *m* director; (*SCH*) principal, headmaster; **D~übertragung** *f* live broadcast

Dirigent [diri'gɛnt(ɪn)] *m* conductor

dirigieren [diri'gi:rən] *vt* to direct; (*MUS*) to conduct

Diskette [dɪs'kɛtə] *f* diskette, floppy disk

Diskont [dɪs'kɔnt] (-s, -e) *m* discount; **~satz** *m* rate of discount

Diskothek [dɪsko'te:k] (-, -en) *f* disco(theque)

diskret [dɪs'kre:t] *adj* discreet; **D~ion** *f* discretion

diskriminieren [dɪskrimi'ni:rən] *vt* to discriminate against

Diskussion [dɪskusi'o:n] *f* discussion; debate; **zur ~** **stehen** to be under discussion

diskutieren [dɪsku'ti:rən] *vt, vi* to discuss; to debate

Distanz [dɪs'tants] *f* distance; **distan'zieren** *vr:* **sich von jdm/etw d~ieren** to distance o.s. from sb/sth

Distel ['dɪstəl] (-, -n) *f* thistle

Disziplin [dɪstsi'pli:n] *f* discipline

Dividende [divi'dɛndə] *f* dividend

dividieren [divi'di:rən] *vt:* (**durch etw**) **~** to divide (by sth)

DM [de:'ʔɛm] *abk* (= *Deutsche Mark*) German Mark

D-Mark ['de:mark] *f* D Mark, German Mark

doch [dɔx] *adv* **1** (*dennoch*) after all; (*sowieso*) anyway; **er kam doch noch** he came after all; **du weißt es ja doch besser** you know better than I do anyway; **und doch ...** and yet ...

2 (*als bejahende Antwort*) yes I do/it does *etc*; **das ist nicht wahr - doch!** that's not true - yes it is!

3 (*auffordernd*): **komm doch** do come; **lass ihn doch** just leave him; **nicht doch!** oh no!

4: **sie ist doch noch so jung** but she's still so young; **Sie wissen doch, wie das ist** you know how it is(, don't you?); **wenn doch** if only

♦ *konj* (*aber*) but; (*trotzdem*) all the same; **und doch hat er es getan** but still he did it

Docht [dɔxt] (-(e)s, -e) *m* wick

Dock [dɔk] (-s, -s od -e) nt dock

Dogge ['dɔgə] f bulldog

Dogma ['dɔgma] (-s, -men) nt dogma; **d~tisch** adj dogmatic

Doktor ['dɔktɔr, pl -'toːrən] (-s, -en) m doctor

Dokument [doku'mɛnt] nt document

Dokumentar- [dokumɛn'taːr] zW: **~bericht** m documentary; **~film** m documentary (film); **d~isch** adj documentary

Dolch [dɔlç] (-(e)s, -e) m dagger

dolmetschen ['dɔlmɛtʃən] vt, vi to interpret; **Dolmetscher(in)** (-s, -) m(f) interpreter

Dom [doːm] (-(e)s, -e) m cathedral

dominieren [domi'niːrən] vt to dominate ♦ vi to predominate

Donau ['doːnau] f Danube

Donner ['dɔnər] (-s, -) m thunder; **d~n** vi unpers to thunder

Donnerstag ['dɔnərstaːk] m Thursday

doof [doːf] (umg) adj daft, stupid

Doppel ['dɔpəl] (-s, -) nt duplicate; (SPORT) doubles; **~bett** nt double bed; **d~deutig** adj ambiguous; **~fenster** nt double glazing; **~gänger** (-s, -) m double; **~punkt** m colon; **~stecker** m two-way adaptor; **d~t** adj double; **in d~ter Ausführung** in duplicate; **~verdiener** m person with two incomes; (pl: Paar) two-income family; **~zentner** m 100 kilograms; **~zimmer** nt double room

Dorf [dɔrf] (-(e)s, ⁼er) nt village; **~bewohner** m villager

Dorn [dɔrn] (-(e)s, -en) m (BOT) thorn; **d~ig** adj thorny

Dörrobst ['dœrɔpst] nt dried fruit

Dorsch [dɔrʃ] (-(e)s, -e) m cod

dort [dɔrt] adv there; **~ drüben** over there; **~her** adv from there; **~hin** adv (to) there; **~ig** adj of that place; in that town

Dose ['doːzə] f box; (Blechdose) tin, can

Dosen pl von **Dose**; **Dosis**

Dosenöffner m tin od can opener

Dosis ['doːzɪs] (-, Dosen) f dose

Dotter ['dɔtər] (-s, -) m (egg) yolk

Drache ['draxə] (-n, -n) m (Tier) dragon

Drachen ['draxən] m kite; **~fliegen** (-s) nt hang-gliding

Draht [draːt] (-(e)s, ⁼e) m wire; **auf ~ sein** to be on the ball; **d~ig** adj (Mann) wiry; **~seil** nt cable; **~seilbahn** f cable railway, funicular

Drama ['draːma] (-s, Dramen) nt drama, play; **~tiker** [-'maːtikər] (-s, -) m dramatist; **d~tisch** [-'maːtɪʃ] adj dramatic

dran [dran] (umg) adv: **jetzt bin ich ~!** it's my turn now; siehe **daran**

Drang [draŋ] (-(e)s, ⁼e) m (Trieb): **~ (nach)** impulse (for), urge (for), desire (for); (Druck) pressure

drängeln ['drɛŋəln] vt, vi to push, to jostle

drängen ['drɛŋən] vt (schieben) to push, to press; (antreiben) to urge ♦ vi (eilig sein) to be urgent; (Zeit) to press; **auf etw akk ~** to press for sth

drastisch ['drastɪʃ] adj drastic

drauf [drauf] (umg) adv = **darauf**; **D~gänger** (-s, -) m daredevil

draußen ['drausən] adv outside, out-of-doors

Dreck [drɛk] (-(e)s) m mud, dirt; **d~ig** adj dirty, filthy

Dreh- ['dreː] zW: **~arbeiten** pl (CINE) shooting sg; **~bank** f lathe; **~buch** nt (CINE) script; **d~en** vt to turn, to rotate; (Zigaretten) to roll; (Film) to shoot ♦ vi to turn, to rotate ♦ vr to turn; (handeln von): **es d~t sich um ...** it's about ...; **~orgel** f barrel organ; **~tür** f revolving door; **~ung** f (Rotation) rotation; (Umdrehung, Wendung) turn; **~zahl** f rate of revolutions; **~zahlmesser** m rev(olution) counter

drei [draɪ] *num* three; **~ viertel** three quarters; **D~eck** *nt* triangle; **~eckig** *adj* triangular; **~einhalb** *num* three and a half; **~erlei** *adj inv* of three kinds; **~fach** *adj* triple, treble ♦ *adv* three times; **~hundert** *num* three hundred; **D~'königsfest** *nt* Epiphany; **~mal** *adv* three times; **~malig** *adj* three times

dreinreden ['draɪnreːdən] *vi:* **jdm ~** (*dazwischenreden*) to interrupt sb; (*sich einmischen*) to interfere with sb

Dreirad *nt* tricycle

dreißig ['draɪsɪç] *num* thirty

dreist [draɪst] *adj* bold, audacious

drei- *zW:* **~viertel** △ *num siehe* **drei**; **D~viertelstunde** *f* three-quarters of an hour; **~zehn** *num* thirteen

dreschen ['drɛʃən] (*unreg*) *vt* (*Getreide*) to thresh; (*umg: verprügeln*) to beat up

dressieren [drɛ'siːrən] *vt* to train

drillen ['drɪlən] *vt* (*bohren*) to drill, to bore; (*MIL*) to drill; (*fig*) to train

Drilling *m* triplet

drin [drɪn] (*umg*) *adv* = **darin**

dringen ['drɪŋən] (*unreg*) *vi* (*Wasser, Licht, Kälte*): **~ (durch/in +akk)** to penetrate (through/into); **auf etw** *akk* **~** to insist on sth

dringend ['drɪŋənt] *adj* urgent

Dringlichkeit *f* urgency

drinnen ['drɪnən] *adv* inside, indoors

dritte(r, s) ['drɪtə(r, s)] *adj* third; **D~ Welt** Third World; **D~s Reich** Third Reich; **D~l** (**-s, -**) *nt* third; **~ns** *adv* thirdly

DRK [deː|ɛr'kaː] *nt abk* (= *Deutsches Rotes Kreuz*) German Red Cross

droben ['droːbən] *adv* above, up there

Droge ['droːgə] *f* drug

drogen *zW:* **~abhängig** *adj* addicted to drugs; **D~händler** *m* drug pedlar, pusher

Drogerie [droːgə'riː] *f* chemist's shop

┌─────────────┐
│ **Drogerie** │
└─────────────┘

The **Drogerie** as opposed to the **Apotheke** sells medicines not requir-

ing a prescription. It tends to be cheaper and also sells cosmetics, perfume and toiletries.

Drogist [dro'gɪst] *m* pharmacist, chemist

drohen ['droːən] *vi:* (**jdm**) **~** to threaten (sb)

dröhnen ['drøːnən] *vi* (*Motor*) to roar; (*Stimme, Musik*) to ring, to resound

Drohung ['droːʊŋ] *f* threat

drollig ['drɔlɪç] *adj* droll

Drossel ['drɔsəl] (**-, -n**) *f* thrush

drüben ['dryːbən] *adv* over there, on the other side

drüber ['dryːbər] (*umg*) *adv* = **darüber**

Druck [drʊk] (**-(e)s, -e**) *m* (*PHYS: Zwang*) pressure; (*TYP: Vorgang*) printing; (*: Produkt*) print; (*fig: Belastung*) burden, weight; **~buchstabe** *m* block letter

drücken ['drʏkən] *vt* (*Knopf, Hand*) to press; (*zu eng sein*) to pinch; (*fig: Preise*) to keep down; (*: belasten*) to oppress, to weigh down ♦ *vi* to press; to pinch ♦ *vr:* **sich vor etw** *dat* **~** to get out of (doing) sth; **~d** *adj* oppressive

Drucker (**-s, -**) *m* printer

Drücker (**-s, -**) *m* button; (*Türdrücker*) handle; (*Gewehrdrücker*) trigger

Druck- *zW:* **~e'rei** *f* printing works, press; **~erschwärze** *f* printer's ink; **~fehler** *m* misprint; **~knopf** *m* press stud, snap fastener; **~sache** *f* printed matter; **~schrift** *f* block *od* printed letters *pl*

drum [drʊm] (*umg*) *adv* = **darum**

drunten ['drʊntən] *adv* below, down there

Drüse ['dryːzə] *f* gland

Dschungel ['dʒʊŋəl] (**-s, -**) *m* jungle

du [duː] (*nom*) *pron* you; **~ sagen** = **duzen**

Dübel ['dyːbəl] (**-s, -**) *m* Rawlplug ®

ducken ['dʊkən] *vt* (*Kopf, Person*) to duck; (*fig*) to take down a peg or two ♦ *vr* to duck

Duckmäuser ['dʊkmɔʏzər] (**-s, -**) *m*

ves man

udelsack ['duːdəlzak] *m* bagpipes *pl*

uell [du'el] (**-s, -e**) *nt* duel

uft [doft] (**-(e)s, -e**) *m* scent, odour; **d~en** *vi* to smell, to be fragrant; **d~ig** *adj* (*Stoff, Kleid*) delicate, diaphanous

ulden ['dɔldən] *vt* to suffer; (*zulassen*) to tolerate ♦ *vi* to suffer

umm [dɔm] *adj* stupid; (*ärgerlich*) annoying; **der D~e** sein to be the loser; **~erweise** *adv* stupidly; **D~heit** *f* stupidity; (*Tat*) blunder, stupid mistake; **D~kopf** *m* blockhead

umpf [dʊmpf] *adj* (*Ton*) hollow, dull; (*Luft*) musty; (*Erinnerung, Schmerz*) vague

üne ['dyːnə] *f* dune

üngen ['dyŋən] *vt* to manure

ünger (**-s, -**) *m* dung, manure; (*künstlich*) fertilizer

unkel ['dʊŋkəl] *adj* dark; (*Stimme*) deep; (*Ahnung*) vague; (*rätselhaft*) obscure; (*verdächtig*) dubious, shady; im **D~n tappen** (*fig*) to grope in the dark

Dunkel- *zW:* **~heit** *f* darkness; (*fig*) obscurity; **~kammer** *f* (*PHOT*) darkroom; **d~n** *vi unpers* to grow dark; **~ziffer** *f* estimated number of unreported cases

ünn [dʏn] *adj* thin; **~flüssig** *adj* watery, thin

unst [dʊnst] (**-es, ²e**) *m* vapour; (*Wetter*) haze

ünsten ['dʏnstən] *vt* to steam

unstig ['dʊnstɪç] *adj* vaporous; (*Wetter*) hazy, misty

uplikat [dupli'kaːt] (**-(e)s, -e**) *nt* duplicate

Dur [duːr] (**-, -**) *nt* (*MUS*) major

SCHLÜSSELWORT

durch [dɔrç] *präp +akk* **1** (*hindurch*) through; **durch den Urwald** through the jungle; **durch die ganze Welt reisen** to travel all over the world

2 (*mittels*) through, by (means of);

(*aufgrund*) due to, owing to; **Tod durch Herzschlag/den Strang** death from a heart attack/by hanging; **durch die Post** by post; **durch seine Bemühungen** through his efforts

♦ *adv* **1** (*hindurch*) through; **die ganze Nacht durch** all through the night; **den Sommer durch** during the summer; **8 Uhr durch** past 8 o'clock; **durch und durch** completely

2 (*durchgebraten etc*): (**gut**) **durch** well-done

durch- *zW:* **~arbeiten** *vt, vi* to work through ♦ *vr* to work one's way through; **~'aus** *adv* completely; (*unbedingt*) definitely; **~aus nicht** absolutely not

Durchblick ['dɔrçblɪk] *m* view; (*fig*) comprehension; **d~en** *vi* to look through; (*umg: verstehen*): (**bei etw**) **d~en** to understand (sth); **etw d~en lassen** (*fig*) to hint at sth

durchbrechen ['dɔrçbreçən] (*unreg*) *vt, vi* to break through

durch'brechen [dɔrç'breçən] (*unreg*) *vt insep* (*Schranken*) to break through; (*Schallmauer*) to break; (*Gewohnheit*) to break free from

durchbrennen ['dɔrçbrenən] (*unreg*) *vi* (*Draht, Sicherung*) to burn through; (*umg*) to run away

durchbringen ['dɔrçbrɪŋən] (*unreg*) *vt* (*Kranken*) to pull through; (*umg: Familie*) to support; (*durchsetzen: Antrag, Kandidat*) to get through; (*vergeuden: Geld*) to get through, to squander

Durchbruch ['dɔrçbrox] *m* (*Öffnung*) opening; (*MIL*) breach; (*von Gefühlen etc*) eruption; (*der Zähne*) cutting; (*fig*) breakthrough; **zum ~ kommen** to break through

durch- *zW:* **~dacht** [-'daxt] *adj* well thought-out; **~'denken** (*unreg*) *vt* to think out; **~drehen** *vt* (*Fleisch*) to

---

mince ♦ vi (umg) to crack up

durcheinander [dʊrçaɪ'nandər] adv in a mess, in confusion; (umg: verwirrt) confused; ~ **bringen** to mess up; (verwirren) to confuse; ~ **reden** to talk at the same time; **D~** (-s) nt (Verwirrung) confusion; (Unordnung) mess

durch- zW: **~fahren** (unreg) vi (~ Tunnel usw) to drive through; (ohne Unterbrechung) to drive straight through; (ohne anzuhalten): **der Zug fährt bis Hamburg ~** the train runs direct to Hamburg; (ohne Umsteigen): **können wir ~fahren?** can we go direct?, can we go non-stop?; **D~fahrt** f transit; (Verkehr) thoroughfare; **D~fall** m (MED) diarrhoea; **~fallen** (unreg) vi to fall through; (in Prüfung) to fail; **~finden** (unreg) vr to find one's way through; **~fragen** vr to find one's way by asking

durchführ- ['dʊrçfyːr] zW: **~bar** adj feasible, practicable; **~en** vt to carry out; **D~ung** f execution, performance

Durchgang ['dʊrçgaŋ] m passage(way); (bei Produktion, Versuch) run; (SPORT) round; (bei Wahl) ballot; **„~ verboten"** "no thoroughfare"

Durchgangsverkehr m through traffic

durchgefroren ['dʊrçgəfroːrən] adj (Mensch) frozen stiff

durchgehen ['dʊrçgeːən] (unreg) vt (behandeln) to go over ♦ vi to go through; (ausreißen: Pferd) to break loose; (Mensch) to run away; **mein Temperament ging mit mir durch** my temper got the better of me; **jdm etw ~ lassen** to let sb get away with sth; **~d** adj (Zug) through; (Öffnungszeiten) continuous

durch- zW: **~greifen** (unreg) vi to take strong action; **~halten** (unreg) vi to last out ♦ vt to keep up; **~kommen** (unreg) vi (auch: überleben) to pull through; **~kreuzen** vt insep to thwart, to frustrate; **~lassen** (unreg) vt

(Person) to let through; (Wasser) to let in; **~lesen** (unreg) vt to read through; **~leuchten** vt insep to X-ray; **~machen** vt to go through; **die Nacht ~machen** to make a night of it

Durchmesser (-s, -) m diameter

durch- zW: **~nässen** vt insep to soak (through); **~nehmen** (unreg) vt to go over; **~nummerieren ▲** vt to number consecutively; **~queren** [dʊrç'kveːrən] vt insep to cross; **D~reise** f transit; auf der **D~reise** passing through; (Güter) in transit; **~ringen** (unreg) vr to reach decision after a long struggle

durchs [dʊrçs] = **durch das**

Durchsage ['dʊrçzaːgə] f intercom od radio announcement

durchschauen ['dʊrçʃaʊən] vi to look od see through; (Person, Lüge) to see through

durchscheinen ['dʊrçʃaɪnən] (unreg) vi to shine through; **~d** adj translucent

Durchschlag ['dʊrçʃlaːk] m (Doppel) carbon copy; (Sieb) strainer; **d~en** [-gən] (unreg) vt (entzweischlagen) to split (in two); (sieben) to sieve ♦ vr (zum Vorschein kommen) to emerge, to come out ♦ vi to get by

durchschlagend adj resounding

durchschneiden ['dʊrçʃnaɪdən] (unreg) vt to cut through

Durchschnitt ['dʊrçʃnɪt] m (Mittelwert) average; **über/unter dem ~** above/below average; **im ~** on average; **d~lich** adj average ♦ adv on average; **Durchschnittswert** m average

durch- zW: **D~schrift** f copy; **~sehen** (unreg) vt to look through; **~setzen** to enforce ♦ vr (Erfolg haben) to succeed; (sich behaupten) to get one's way; **seinen Kopf ~setzen** to get one's way; **~'setzen** vt insep to mix

Durchsicht ['dʊrçzɪçt] f looking through, checking; **d~ig** adj transparent

durch- zW: **~sprechen** (unreg) vt to talk over; **~stehen** (unreg) vt to live through; **~stellen** vt (an Telefon) to put through; **~stöbern** (auch untr) vt (Kisten) to rummage through, to rifle through; (Haus, Wohnung) to ransack; **~streichen** (unreg) vt to cross out; **~suchen** vt insep to search; **D~suchung** f search; **~wachsen** (Speck) streaky; (fig: mittelmäßig) so-so; **D~wahl** f (TEL) direct dialling; **~weg** adv throughout, completely; **~ziehen** (unreg) vt (Faden) to draw through ♦ vi to pass through; **D~zug** m (Luft) draught; (von Truppen, Vögeln) passage

SCHLÜSSELWORT

dürfen ['dyrfən] (unreg) vt 1 (Erlaubnis haben) to be allowed to; **ich darf das** I'm allowed to (do that); **darf ich?** may I?; **darf ich ins Kino?** can od may I go to the cinema?; **es darf geraucht werden** you may smoke

2 (in Verneinungen): **er darf das nicht** he's not allowed to (do that); **das darf nicht geschehen** that must not happen; **da darf sie sich nicht wundern** that shouldn't surprise her

3 (in Höflichkeitsformeln): **darf ich Sie bitten, das zu tun?** may od could I ask you to do that?; **was darf es sein?** what can I do for you?

4 (können): **das dürfen Sie mir glauben** you can believe me

5 (Möglichkeit): **das dürfte genug sein** that should be enough; **es dürfte Ihnen bekannt sein, dass ...** as you will probably know ...

dürftig ['dyrftiç] adj (ärmlich) needy, poor; (unzulänglich) inadequate

dürr [dyr] adj dried-up; (Land) arid; (mager) skinny, gaunt; **D~e** f aridity; (Zeit) drought; (Magerkeit) skinniness

Durst [dʊrst] (-(e)s) m thirst; ~ **haben** to be thirsty; **d~ig** adj thirsty

Dusche ['dʊʃə] f shower; **d~en** vi, vr to have a shower

Düse ['dy:zə] f nozzle; (Flugzeugdüse) jet

Düsen- zW: **~antrieb** m jet propulsion; **~flugzeug** nt jet (plane); **~jäger** m jet fighter

Dussel ['dʊsəl] (-s, -) (umg) m twit

düster ['dy:stər] adj dark; (Gedanken, Zukunft) gloomy

Dutzend ['dʊtsənt] (-s, -e) nt dozen; **~(e)** od **d~(e) Mal(e)** a dozen times

duzen ['du:tsən] vt: (jdn) ~ to use the familiar form of address "du" (to od with sb)

duzen

There are two different forms of address in Germany: du and Sie. Duzen means addressing someone as 'du' - used with children, family and close friends - and siezen means addressing someone as 'Sie' - used for all grown-ups and older teenagers. Students almost always use 'du' to each other.

Dynamik [dy'na:mɪk] f (PHYS) dynamics sg; (fig: Schwung) momentum; (von Mensch) dynamism; **dynamisch** adj (auch fig) dynamic

Dynamit [dyna'mi:t] (-s) nt dynamite

Dynamo [dy'na:mo] (-s, -s) m dynamo

DZ nt abk = **Doppelzimmer**

D-Zug ['de:tsu:k] m through train

E, e

Ebbe ['ɛbə] f low tide

eben ['e:bən] adj level, flat; (glatt) smooth ♦ adv (bestätigend) exactly; ~ **deswegen** just because of that; **~bürtig** adj: **jdm ~bürtig sein** to be sb's equal; **E~e** f plain; (fig) level; **~falls** adv likewise; **~so** adv just as

Eber ['eːbɐr] (-s, -) m boar

ebnen ['eːbnən] vt to level

Echo ['ɛço] (-s, -s) nt echo

echt [ɛçt] adj genuine; (typisch) typical;
E~heit f genuineness

Eck- ['ɛk] zW: **e~ball** m corner (kick); **~e**
f corner; (MATH) angle; **e~ig** adj angular; **~zahn** m eye tooth

ECU [eˈkyː] (-, -s) m (FIN) ECU

edel ['eːdəl] adj noble; **E~metall** nt
rare metal; **E~stahl** m high-grade
steel; **E~stein** m precious stone

EDV [eːdeˈfau] (-) f abk (= elektronische
Datenverarbeitung) electronic data processing

Efeu ['eːfɔy] (-s) m ivy

Effekt [ɛˈfɛkt] (-s, -e) m effect

Effekten [ɛˈfɛktən] pl stocks

effektiv [ɛfɛkˈtiːf] adj effective, actual

EG ['eːˈgeː] f abk (= Europäische Gemeinschaft) EC

egal [eˈgaːl] adj all the same

Ego- [eːgo] zW: **~ismus** [-ˈɪsmʊs] m
selfishness, egoism; **~ist** [-ˈɪst] m ego-
ist; **e~istisch** adj selfish, egoistic

Ehe ['eːə] f marriage

ehe konj before

Ehe- zW: **e~beratung** f marriage guidance (counselling); **~bruch** m adultery;
~frau f married woman; wife; **~leute** pl
married people; **e~lich** adj matrimonial;
(Kind) legitimate

ehemalig ['eːəmaːlɪç] adj former

ehemals adv formerly

Ehe- zW: **~mann** m married man; husband; **~paar** nt married couple

eher ['eːɐr] adv (früher) sooner; (lieber)
rather, sooner; (mehr) more

Ehe- zW: **~ring** m wedding ring;
~schließung f marriage ceremony

eheste(r, s) ['eːəstə(r, s)] adj (früheste)
first, earliest; **am ~n** (liebsten) soonest;
(meist) most; (wahrscheinlichst) most
probably

Ehr- ['eːr] zW: **e~bar** adj honourable,
respectable; **~e** f honour; **e~en** vt to
honour

Ehren- ['eːrən] zW: **e~amtlich** adj
honorary; **~gast** m guest of honour;
e~haft adj honourable; **~platz** m
place of honour and (US) honor; **~run...**
f lap of honour; **~sache** f point of
honour; **e~voll** adj honourable;
~wort nt word of honour

Ehr- zW: **~furcht** f awe, deep respec...
e~fürchtig adj reverent; **~gefühl** nt
sense of honour; **~geiz** m ambition;
e~geizig adj ambitious; **e~lich** adj
honest; **~lichkeit** f honesty; **e~los** adj
dishonourable; **~ung** f honour(ing...
e~würdig adj venerable

Ei [aɪ] (-(e)s, -er) nt egg

Eich- zW: **~e** f [ˈaɪçə] f oak (tree); **~el** (-
-n) f acorn; **~hörnchen** nt squirrel

Eichmaß nt standard

Eid [aɪt] (-(e)s, -e) m oath

Eidechse ['aɪdɛksə] f lizard

eidesstattlich adj: **~e Erklärung** aff...
davit

Eidgenosse m Swiss

Eier- zW: **~becher** m eggcup; **~ku...**
chen m omelette; pancake; **~likör** m
advocaat; **~schale** f eggshell; **~stoc...**
m ovary; **~uhr** f egg timer

Eifer ['aɪfɐr] (-s) m zeal, enthusiasm...
~sucht f jealousy; **e~süchtig** adj
e~süchtig (auf +akk) jealous (of)

eifrig ['aɪfrɪç] adj zealous, enthusiastic

Eigelb ['aɪgɛlp] (-(e)s, -) nt egg yolk

eigen ['aɪgən] adj own; (~artig) peculiar; **mit der/dem ihm ~en ...** wit...
that ... peculiar to him; **sich zu ~...**
zu E~ machen to make sth one...
own; **E~art** f peculiarity; characteristic; **e~artig** adj peculiar; **E~bedarf** m
zum **E~bedarf** for (one's own) personal use/domestic requirements; **de...**
Vermieter machte **E~bedarf** geltend...
the landlord showed he needed the
house/flat for himself; **~händig** ad...
with one's own hand; **E~heim** nt
owner-occupied house; **E~heit** f peculiarity; **~mächtig** adj high-handed...
E~name m proper name; **~s** adv ex...

pressly, on purpose; **E~schaft** f quality, property, attribute; **E~sinn** m obstinacy; **~sinnig** adj obstinate; **~tlich**
adj actual, real ♦ adv actually, really;
E~tor nt own goal; **E~tum** nt property; **E~tümer(in)** (-s, -) m(f) owner,
proprietor; **~tümlich** adj peculiar;
E~tümlichkeit f peculiarity; **E~tums-
wohnung** f freehold flat

ignen ['aignən] vr to be suited; **Eignung** f suitability

il- ['aɪl] zW: **~bote** m courier; **~brief**
m express letter; **~e** f haste; **es hat
keine ~e** there's no hurry; **~en** vi
(Mensch) to hurry; (dringend sein) to be
urgent; **~ends** adv hastily; **~gut** nt
express goods pl, fast freight (US);
~ig adj hasty, hurried; (dringlich) urgent; **es ~ig haben** to be in a hurry;
~zug m semi-fast train, limited stop
train

imer ['aɪmər] (-s, -) m bucket, pail

in ['aɪn] adv: **nicht ~ noch aus wissen** not to know what to do

in(e) ['aɪn(ə)] num one ♦ indef art a, an

inander [aɪ'nandər] pron one another,
each other

inarbeiten ['aɪnarbaɪtən] vt to train
♦ vr: **sich in etw** akk **~** to familiarize
o.s. with sth

inatmen ['aɪnaːtmən] vt, vi to inhale,
to breathe in

inbahnstraße ['aɪnbaːnʃtraːsə] f one-
way street

inband ['aɪnbant] m binding, cover

inbauen ['aɪnbaʊən] vt to build in;
(Motor) to install, to fit

inbaumöbel pl built-in furniture sg

inbegriffen ['aɪnbəɡrɪfən] adj included

inberufen ['aɪnbəruːfən] (unreg) vt to
convene; (MIL) to call up

inbettzimmer nt single room

inbeziehen ['aɪnbətsiːən] (unreg) vt to
include

einbiegen ['aɪnbiːɡən] (unreg) vi to
turn

einbilden ['aɪnbɪldən] vt: **sich** dat **etw
~** to imagine sth

Einbildung f imagination; (Dünkel)
conceit; **~skraft** f imagination

Einblick ['aɪnblɪk] m insight

einbrechen ['aɪnbreçən] (unreg) vi (in
Haus) to break in; (Nacht) to fall; (Winter) to set in; (durchbrechen) to break;
~ in +akk (MIL) to invade

Einbrecher (-s, -) m burglar

einbringen ['aɪnbrɪŋən] (unreg) vt to
bring in; (Geld, Vorteil) to yield; (mit-
bringen) to contribute

Einbruch ['aɪnbrʊx] m (Hauseinbruch)
break-in, burglary; (Eindringen) invasion; (des Winters) onset; (Durchbrechen) break; (MET) approach; (MIL)
penetration; **(bei/vor) ~ der Nacht**
at/before nightfall; **e~sicher** adj
burglar-proof

einbürgern ['aɪnbʏrɡərn] vt to natural-
ize ♦ vr to become adopted

einbüßen ['aɪnbyːsən] vt to lose, to
forfeit

einchecken ['aɪntʃekən] vt, vi to check
in

eincremen ['aɪnkreːmən] vt to put
cream on

eindecken ['aɪndekən] vr: **sich (mit
etw) ~** to lay in stocks (of sth); to
stock up (with sth)

eindeutig ['aɪndɔʏtɪç] adj unequivocal

eindringen ['aɪndrɪŋən] (unreg) vi: **~
(in** +akk) to force one's way in(to); (in
Haus) to break in(to); (in Land) to invade; (Gas, Wasser) to penetrate; **(auf
jdn) ~** (mit Bitten) to pester (sb)

eindringlich adj forcible, urgent

Eindringling m intruder

Eindruck ['aɪndrʊk] m impression

eindrücken ['aɪndrʏkən] vt to press in

eindrucksvoll adj impressive

eine(r, s) pron one; (jemand) someone

eineiig ['aɪn|aɪɪç] adj (Zwillinge) identical

eineinhalb ['aɪn|aɪn'halp] num one and a half

einengen ['aɪn|ɛŋən] vt to confine, to restrict

einer- ['aɪnər] zW: '**E~'lei** (-s) nt sameness; '**~'lei** adj (gleichartig) the same kind of; **es ist mir ~lei** it is all the same to me; **~seits** adv on the one hand

einfach ['aɪnfax] adj simple; (nicht mehrfach) single ♦ adv simply; **E~heit** f simplicity

einfädeln ['aɪnfɛːdəln] vt (Nadel, Faden) to thread; (fig) to contrive

einfahren ['aɪnfaːrən] (unreg) vt to bring in; (Barriere) to knock down; (Auto) to run in ♦ vi to drive in; (Zug) to pull in; (MIN) to go down

Einfahrt f (Vorgang) driving in; pulling in; (MIN) descent; (Ort) entrance

Einfall ['aɪnfal] m (Idee) idea, notion; (Lichteinfall) incidence; (MIL) raid; **e~en** (unreg) vi (Licht) to fall; (MIL) to raid; (einstürzen) to fall in, to collapse; (einstimmen): **(in etw** akk**) e~en** to join in (with sth); **etw fällt jdm ein** sth occurs to sb; **das fällt mir gar nicht ein** I wouldn't dream of it; **sich** dat **etw e~en lassen** to have a good idea

einfältig ['aɪnfɛltɪç] adj simple(-minded)

Einfamilienhaus [aɪnfa'miːliənhaʊs] nt detached house

einfarbig ['aɪnfarbɪç] adj all one colour; (Stoff etc) self-coloured

einfetten ['aɪnfɛtən] vt to grease

einfließen ['aɪnfliːsən] (unreg) vi to flow in

einflößen ['aɪnfløːsən] vt: **jdm etw ~** to give sb sth; (fig) to instil sth in sb

Einfluss ▲ ['aɪnflʊs] m influence; **~bereich** m sphere of influence

einförmig ['aɪnfœrmɪç] adj uniform; **E~keit** f uniformity

einfrieren ['aɪnfriːrən] (unreg) vi to

freeze (up) ♦ vt to freeze

einfügen ['aɪnfyːgən] vt to fit in; (zusätzlich) to add

Einfuhr ['aɪnfuːr] (-) f import; **~be schränkung** f import restrictions **~bestimmungen** pl import regulatio

einführen ['aɪnfyːrən] vt to bring i (Mensch, Sitten) to introduce; (War to import

Einführung f introduction

Eingabe ['aɪngaːbə] f petition; (co PUT) input

Eingang ['aɪngaŋ] m entrance; (COMM Ankunft) arrival; (Erhalt) receipt

eingeben ['aɪngeːbən] (unreg) vt (Ar nei) to give; (Daten etc) to enter

eingebildet ['aɪngəbɪldət] adj imag nary; (eitel) conceited

Eingeborene(r) ['aɪngəboːrənə(r)] f(n native

Eingebung f inspiration

eingefleischt ['aɪngəflaɪʃt] adj (G wohnheit, Vorurteile) deep-rooted

eingehen ['aɪngeːən] (unreg) vi (Ai nahme finden) to come in; (Sendun Geld) to be received; (Tier, Pflanze) die; (Firma) to fold; (schrumpfen) shrink ♦ vt to enter into; (Wette make; **auf etw** akk **~** to go onto st **auf jdn ~** to respond to sb; **jdm** (verständlich) machen to be compreh sible to sb; **~d** adj exhaustive, thoroug

Eingemachte(s) ['aɪngəmaːxtə(s)] preserves pl

eingenommen ['aɪngənɔmən] adj (von) fond (of), partial (to); **~ (gege** prejudiced (against)

eingeschrieben ['aɪngəʃriːbən] registered

eingespielt ['aɪngəʃpiːlt] adj: **aufe nander ~ sein** to be in tune with eac other

Eingeständnis ['aɪngəʃtɛntnɪs] (-ses -se) nt admission, confession

eingestehen ['aɪngəʃteːən] (unreg) to confess

eingestellt ['aɪngəʃtɛlt] adj: **auf etw**

sein to be prepared for sth

ingetragen ['aɪngətraːgən] adj (COMM) registered

ingeweide ['aɪngəvaɪdə] (-s, -) nt innards pl, intestines pl

ingeweihte(r) ['aɪngəvaɪtə(r)] f(m) initiate

ingewöhnen ['aɪngəvøːnən] vr: **sich ~ in** +akk to settle (down) in

ingleisig ['aɪnglaɪzɪç] adj single-track

ingreifen ['aɪngraɪfən] (unreg) vi to intervene, to interfere; (Zahnrad) to mesh

ingriff ['aɪngrɪf] m intervention, interference; (Operation) operation

inhaken ['aɪnhaːkən] vt ♦ vr: **sich bei jdm ~** to link arms with sb ♦ vi (sich einmischen) to intervene

inhalt ['aɪnhalt] m: ~ **gebieten** +dat to put a stop to; **e~en** (unreg) vt (Regel) to keep ♦ vi to stop

inhändigen ['aɪnhɛndɪgən] vt to hand in

inhängen ['aɪnhɛŋən] vt to hang; (Telefon) to hang up ♦ vi (TEL) to hang up; **sich bei jdm ~** to link arms with sb

inheimisch ['aɪnhaɪmɪʃ] adj native; **E~e(r)** f(m) local

Einheit ['aɪnhaɪt] f unity; (Maß, MIL) unit; **e~lich** adj uniform; **~spreis** m standard price

inholen ['aɪnhoːlən] vt (Tau) to haul in; (Fahne, Segel) to lower; (Vorsprung aufholen) to catch up with; (Verspätung) to make up; (Rat, Erlaubnis) to ask ♦ vi (einkaufen) to shop

inhüllen ['aɪnhʏlən] vt to wrap up

inhundert ['aɪn'hʊndərt] num one hundred, a hundred

inig ['aɪnɪç] adj (vereint) united; ~ **gehen** to agree; **sich dat ~ sein** to be in agreement; ~ **werden** to agree

inige(r, s) ['aɪnɪgə(r, s)] adj, pron some ♦ pl some; (mehrere) several; ~ **Mal** a

few times

einigen vt to unite ♦ vr: **sich ~ (auf** +akk) to agree (on)

einigermaßen adv somewhat; (leidlich) reasonably

einig- zW: **E~keit** f unity; (Übereinstimmung) agreement; **E~ung** f agreement; (Vereinigung) unification

einkalkulieren ['aɪnkalkuliːrən] vt to take into account, to allow for

Einkauf ['aɪnkaʊf] m purchase; **e~en** vt to buy ♦ vi to shop; **e~en gehen** to go shopping

Einkaufs- zW: **~bummel** m shopping spree; **~korb** m shopping basket; **~wagen** m shopping trolley; **~zentrum** nt shopping centre

einklammern ['aɪnklamərn] vt to put in brackets, to bracket

Einklang ['aɪnklaŋ] m harmony

einklemmen ['aɪnklɛmən] vt to jam

einkochen ['aɪnkɔxən] vt to boil down; (Obst) to preserve, to bottle

Einkommen ['aɪnkɔmən] (-s, -) nt income; **~(s)steuer** f income tax

Einkünfte ['aɪnkʏnftə] pl income sg, revenue sg

einladen ['aɪnlaːdən] (unreg) vt (Person) to invite; (Gegenstände) to load; **jdn ins Kino ~** to take sb to the cinema

Einladung f invitation

Einlage ['aɪnlaːgə] f (Programmeinlage) interlude; (Spareinlage) deposit; (Schuheinlage) insole; (Fußstütze) support; (Zahneinlage) temporary filling; (KOCH) noodles pl, vegetables pl etc in soup

einlagern ['aɪnlaːgərn] vt to store

Einlass ▲ ['aɪnlas] (-es, ≃e) m (Zutritt) admission

einlassen ['aɪnlasən] (unreg) vt to let in; (einsetzen) to set in ♦ vr: **sich mit jdm/auf etw** akk ~ to get involved with sb/sth

Einlauf ['aɪnlaʊf] m arrival; (von Pferden) finish; (MED) enema; **e~en** (unreg)

vi to arrive, to come in; (*in Hafen*) to enter; (SPORT) to finish; (*Wasser*) to run in; (*Stoff*) to shrink ♦ *vt* (*Schuhe*) to break in ♦ *vr* (SPORT) to warm up; (*Motor, Maschine*) to run in; **jdm das Haus e~en** to invade sb's house

einleben ['ainle:bən] *vr* to settle down

einlegen ['ainle:gən] *vt* (*einfügen: Blatt, Sohle*) to insert; (KOCH) to pickle; (*Pause*) to have; (*Protest*) to make; (*Veto*) to use; (*Berufung*) to lodge; (AUT: *Gang*) to engage

einleiten ['ainlaitən] *vt* to introduce, to start; (*Geburt*) to induce; **Einleitung** *f* introduction; induction

einleuchten ['ainløyçtən] *vi*: **(jdm)** ~ to be clear *od* evident (to sb); **~d** *adj* clear

einliefern ['ainli:fərn] *vt*: ~ **(in** +*akk*) take (into)

Einlieferungsschein *m* certificate of posting

Einliegerwohnung ['ainli:gərvo:nʊn] *f* self-contained flat; (*für Eltern, Großeltern*) granny flat

einlösen ['ainlø:zən] *vt* (*Scheck*) to cash; (*Schuldschein, Pfand*) to redeem; (*Versprechen*) to keep

einmachen ['ainmaxən] *vt* to preserve

einmal ['ainma:l] *adv* once; (*erstens*) first; (*zukünftig*) sometime; **nehmen wir ~ an** just let's suppose; **noch ~** once more; **nicht ~** not even; **auf ~** all at once; **es war ~** once upon a time there was/were; **E~eins** *nt* multiplication tables *pl*; **~ig** *adj* unique; (*nur einmal erforderlich*) single; (*prima*) fantastic

Einmarsch ['ainmarʃ] *m* entry; (MIL) invasion; **e~ieren** *vi* to march in

einmischen ['ainmɪʃən] *vr*: **sich ~ (in** +*akk*) to interfere (with)

einmütig ['ainmy:tɪç] *adj* unanimous

Einnahme ['ainna:mə] *f* (*von Medizin*) taking; (MIL) capture, taking; **~n** *pl* (*Geld*) takings, revenue *sg*; **~quelle** *f* source of income

einnehmen ['ainne:mən] (*unreg*) *vt* to take; (*Stellung, Raum*) to take up; ~ **für/gegen** to persuade in favour of/ against; **~d** *adj* charming

einordnen ['ain|ɔrdnən] *vt* to arrange, to fit in ♦ *vr* to adapt; (AUT) to get into lane

einpacken ['ainpakən] *vt* to pack (up)

einparken ['ainparkən] *vt* to park

einpendeln ['ainpendəln] *vr* to even out

einpflanzen ['ainpflantsən] *vt* to plant; (MED) to implant

einplanen ['ainpla:nən] *vt* to plan for

einprägen ['ainpre:gən] *vt* to impress, to imprint; (*beibringen*): **(jdm)** ~ to impress (on sb); **sich** *dat* **etw** ~ to memorize sth

einrahmen ['ainra:mən] *vt* to frame

einräumen ['ainrɔymən] *vt* (*ordnend*) to put away; (*überlassen: Platz*) to give up; (*zugestehen*) to admit, to concede

einreden ['ainre:dən] *vt*: **jdm/sich etw** ~ to talk sb/o.s. into believing sth

einreiben ['ainraibən] (*unreg*) *vt* to rub in

einreichen ['ainraiçən] *vt* to hand in, (*Antrag*) to submit

Einreise ['ainraizə] *f* entry; **~bestimmungen** *pl* entry regulations; **~erlaubnis** *f* entry permit; **~genehmigung** *f* entry permit; **e~n** *vi*: (**in ein Land**) **e~n** to enter (a country)

einrichten ['ainrɪçtən] *vt* (*Haus*) to furnish; (*schaffen*) to establish, to set up; (*arrangieren*) to arrange; (*möglich machen*) to manage ♦ *vr* (*in Haus*) to furnish one's house; **sich ~ (auf** +*akk*) (*sich vorbereiten*) to prepare o.s. (for), (*sich anpassen*) to adapt (to)

Einrichtung *f* (*Wohnungseinrichtung*) furnishings *pl*; (*öffentliche Anstalt*) organization; (*Dienste*) service

einrosten ['ainrɔstən] *vi* to get rusty

einrücken ['ainrʏkən] *vi* (MIL: *in Land*) to move in

Eins [aıns] (-, -en) f one; **e~** num one; **es ist mir alles e~** it's all one to me

einsam ['aınzaːm] adj lonely, solitary; **E~keit** f loneliness, solitude

einsammeln ['aınzaməln] vt to collect

Einsatz ['aınzats] m (Teil) inset; (an Kleid) insertion; (Verwendung) use, employment; (Spieleinsatz) stake; (Risiko) risk; (MIL) operation; (MUS) entry; **im ~** in action; **e~bereit** adj ready for action

einschalten ['aınʃaltən] vt (einfügen) to insert; (Pause) to make; (ELEK) to switch on; (Anwalt) to bring in ♦ vr (dazwischentreten) to intervene

einschärfen ['aınʃɛrfən] vt: **jdm etw ~** to impress sth (up)on sb

einschätzen ['aınʃɛtsən] vt to estimate, to assess ♦ vr to rate o.s.

einschenken ['aınʃɛŋkən] vt to pour out

einschicken ['aınʃıkən] vt to send in

einschl. abk (= einschließlich) incl.

einschlafen ['aınʃlaːfən] (unreg) vi to fall asleep, to go to sleep

einschläfernd ['aınʃlɛːfərnt] adj (MED) soporific; (langweilig) boring; (Stimme) lulling

Einschlag ['aınʃlaːk] m impact; (fig: Beimischung) touch, hint; **e~en** [-gən] (unreg) vt to knock in; (Fenster) to smash, to break; (Zähne, Schädel) to smash in; (AUT: Räder) to turn; (kürzer machen) to take up; (Ware) to pack, to wrap up; (Weg, Richtung) to take ♦ vt to hit; (sich einigen) to agree; (Anklang finden) to work, to succeed; **in etw akk/auf jdn e~en** to hit sth/sb

einschlägig ['aınʃlɛːgıç] adj relevant

einschließen ['aınʃliːsən] (unreg) vt (Kind) to lock in; (Häftling) to lock up; (Gegenstand) to lock away; (Bergleute) to cut off; (umgeben) to surround; (MIL) to encircle; (fig: beinhalten) to include, to comprise ♦ vr to lock o.s. in

einschließlich adv inclusive ♦ präp +gen inclusive of, including

einschmeicheln ['aınʃmaıçəln] vr: **sich ~ (bei)** to ingratiate o.s. (with)

einschnappen ['aınʃnapən] vi (Tür) to click to; (fig) to be touchy; **eingeschnappt sein** to be in a huff

einschneidend ['aınʃnaıdənt] adj drastic

Einschnitt ['aınʃnıt] m cutting; (MED) incision; (Ereignis) decisive point

einschränken ['aınʃrɛŋkən] vt to limit, to restrict; (Kosten) to cut down, to reduce ♦ vr to cut down (on expenditure); **Einschränkung** f restriction, limitation; reduction; (von Behauptung) qualification

Einschreib- ['aınʃraıb] zW: **~(e)brief** m recorded delivery letter; **e~en** (unreg) vt to write in; (Post) to send recorded delivery ♦ vr to register; (UNIV) to enrol; **~en** nt recorded delivery letter

einschreiten ['aınʃraıtən] (unreg) vi to step in, to intervene; **~ gegen** to take action against

einschüchtern ['aınʃʏçtərn] vt to intimidate

einschulen ['aınʃuːlən] vt: **eingeschult werden** (Kind) to start school

einsehen ['aınzeːən] (unreg) vt (hineinsehen in) to realize; (Akten) to have a look at; (verstehen) to see; **E~ (-s)** nt understanding; **ein E~ haben** to show understanding

einseitig ['aınzaıtıç] adj one-sided

Einsend- ['aınzɛnt] zW: **e~en** (unreg) vt to send in; **~er (-s, -)** m sender, contributor; **~ung** f sending in

einsetzen ['aınzɛtsən] vt to put (in); (in Amt) to appoint, to install; (Geld) to stake; (verwenden) to use; (MIL) to employ ♦ vi (beginnen) to set in; (MUS) to enter, to come in ♦ vr to work hard; **sich für jdn/etw ~** to support sb/sth

Einsicht ['aɪnzɪçt] f insight; (in Akten) look, inspection; **zu der ~ kommen, dass ...** to come to the conclusion that ...; **e~ig** adj (Mensch) judicious; **e~slos** adj unreasonable; **e~svoll** adj understanding

einsilbig ['aɪnzɪlbɪç] adj (auch fig) monosyllabic; (Mensch) uncommunicative

einspannen ['aɪnʃpanən] vt (Papier) to insert; (Pferde) to harness; umg: Person) to rope in

Einsparung ['aɪnʃpaːrʊŋ] f economy, saving

einsperren ['aɪnʃpɛrən] vt to lock up

einspielen ['aɪnʃpiːlən] vr (SPORT) to warm up ♦ vt (Film: Geld) to bring in; (Instrument) to play in; **sich aufeinander ~** to become attuned to each other; **gut eingespielt** running smoothly

einsprachig ['aɪnʃpraːxɪç] adj monolingual

einspringen ['aɪnʃprɪŋən] vi (unreg) (aushelfen) to help out, to step into the breach

Einspruch ['aɪnʃprʊx] m protest, objection; **~srecht** nt veto

einspurig ['aɪnʃpuːrɪç] adj (EISENB) single-track; (AUT) single-lane

einst [aɪnst] adv once; (zukünftig) one day, some day

einstecken ['aɪnʃtɛkən] vt to stick in, to insert; (Brief) to post; (ELEK: Stecker) to plug in; (Geld) to pocket; (mitnehmen) to take; (überlegen sein) to put in the shade; (hinnehmen) to swallow

einstehen ['aɪnʃteːən] (unreg) vi: **für jdn/etw ~** to guarantee sb/sth; (verantworten): **für etw ~** to answer for sth

einsteigen ['aɪnʃtaɪgən] vi (unreg) vi to get in od on; (in Schiff) to go on board; (sich beteiligen) to come in; (hineinklettern) to climb in

einstellen ['aɪnʃtɛlən] vt (aufhören) to stop; (Geräte) to adjust; (Kamera etc)

to focus; (Sender, Radio) to tune in; (unterstellen) to put; (in Firma) to employ, to take on ♦ vi (Firma) to take on staff/workers ♦ vr (anfangen) to set in; (kommen) to arrive; **sich auf jdn ~** to adapt to sb; **sich auf etw** akk **~** to prepare o.s. for sth

Einstellung f (Aufhören) suspension; adjustment; focusing; (von Arbeiter etc) appointment; (Haltung) attitude

Einstieg ['aɪnʃtiːk] (-(e)s, -e) m entry; (fig) approach

einstig [aɪnstɪç] adj former

einstimmig ['aɪnʃtɪmɪç] adj unanimous; (MUS) for one voice

einstmals adv once, formerly

einstöckig ['aɪnʃtœkɪç] adj twostoreyed

Einsturz ['aɪnʃtʊrts] m collapse

einstürzen ['aɪnʃtʏrtsən] vi to fall in, to collapse

einst- zW: **~weilen** adv meanwhile; (vorläufig) temporarily, for the time being; **~weilig** adj temporary

eintägig ['aɪntɛːgɪç] adj one-day

eintauschen ['aɪntaʊʃən] vt: **~ (gegen** od **für)** to exchange (for)

eintausend ['aɪntaʊzənt] num one thousand

einteilen ['aɪntaɪlən] vt (in Teile) to divide (up); (Menschen) to assign

einteilig adj one-piece

eintönig ['aɪntøːnɪç] adj monotonous

Eintopf ['aɪntɔpf] m stew

Eintracht ['aɪntraxt] (-) f concord, harmony; **einträchtig** ['aɪntrɛçtɪç] adj harmonious

Eintrag ['aɪntraːk] (-(e)s, *e) m entry; **amtlicher ~** entry in the register; **e~en** [-gən] (unreg) vt (in Buch) to enter; (Profit) to yield ♦ vr to put one's name down

einträglich ['aɪntrɛːklɪç] adj profitable

eintreffen ['aɪntrɛfən] vi (unreg) vi to happen; (ankommen) to arrive

eintreten ['aɪntreːtən] (unreg) vi to occur; (sich einsetzen) to intercede ♦ vt

(Tür) to kick open; **~ in** +*akk* to enter; *(in Klub, Partei)* to join

Eintritt ['aıntrıt] *m (Betreten)* entrance; *(Anfang)* commencement; *(in Klub etc)* joining

Eintritts- *zW:* **~geld** *nt* admission charge; **~karte** *f* (admission) ticket; **~preis** *m* admission charge

einüben ['aınly:bən] *vt* to practise

Einvernehmen ['aınfernɛ:mən] *(-s, -)* *nt* agreement, harmony

einverstanden ['aınferʃtandən] *excl* agreed, okay ♦ *adj:* **~ sein** to agree, to be agreed

Einverständnis ['aınferʃtɛntnıs] *nt* understanding; *(gleiche Meinung)* agreement

Einwand ['aınvant] *(-(e)s, ⁼e)* *m* objection

Einwand- *zW:* **~erer** *m* ['aınvandərər] immigrant; **e~ern** *vi* to immigrate; **~erung** *f* immigration

einwandfrei *adj* perfect ♦ *adv* absolutely

Einweg- ['aınve:g-] *zW:* **~flasche** *f* no-deposit bottle; **~spritze** *f* disposable syringe

einweichen ['aınvaıçən] *vt* to soak

einweihen ['aınvaıən] *vt (Kirche)* to consecrate; *(Brücke)* to open; *(Gebäude)* to inaugurate; **~ in** +*akk (Person)* to initiate (in); **Einweihung** *f* consecration; opening; inauguration; initiation

einweisen ['aınvaızən] *(unreg) vt (in Amt)* to install; *(in Arbeit)* to introduce; *(in Anstalt)* to send

einwenden ['aınvɛndən] *(unreg) vt:* **etwas ~ gegen** to object to, to oppose

einwerfen ['aınvɛrfən] *(unreg) vt* to throw in; *(Brief)* to post; *(Geld)* to put in, to insert; *(Fenster)* to smash; *(äußern)* to interpose

einwickeln ['aınvıkəln] *vt* to wrap up; *(fig: umg)* to outsmart

einwilligen ['aınvılıgən] *vi:* **~ (in** +*akk)* to consent (to), to agree (to); **Einwilligung** *f* consent

einwirken ['aınvırkən] *vi:* **auf jdn/etw ~** to influence sb/sth

Einwohner ['aınvo:nər] *(-s, -)* *m* inhabitant; **~/meldeamt** *nt* registration office; **~schaft** *f* population, inhabitants *pl*

Einwurf ['aınvorf] *m (Öffnung)* slot; *(von Münze)* insertion; *(von Brief)* posting; *(Einwand)* objection; *(SPORT)* throw-in

Einzahl ['aıntsa:l] *f* singular; **e~en** *vt* to pay in; **~ung** *f* paying in; **~ungsschein** *m* paying-in slip, deposit slip

einzäunen ['aıntsɔynən] *vt* to fence in

Einzel ['aıntsəl] *(-s, -)* *nt (TENNIS)* singles; **~fahrschein** *m* one-way ticket; **~fall** *m* single instance, individual case; **~handel** *m* retail trade; **~handelspreis** *m* retail price; **~heit** *f* particular, detail; **~kind** *nt* only child; **e~n** *adj* single; *(vereinzelt)* the odd ♦ *adv* singly; **e~n angeben** to specify; **der/die E~ne** the individual; **das E~ne** the particular; **ins E~ne gehen** to go into detail(s); **~teil** *nt* component (part); **~zimmer** *nt* single room; **~zimmerzuschlag** *m* single room supplement

einziehen ['aıntsi:ən] *(unreg) vt* to draw in, to take in; *(Kopf)* to duck; *(Fühler, Antenne, Fahrgestell)* to retract; *(Steuern, Erkundigungen)* to collect; *(MIL)* to draft, to call up; *(aus dem Verkehr ziehen)* to withdraw; *(konfiszieren)* to confiscate ♦ *vi* to move in; *(Friede, Ruhe)* to come; *(Flüssigkeit)* to penetrate

einzig ['aıntsıç] *adj* only; *(ohnegleichen)* unique; **das E~e** the only thing; **der/die E~e** the only one; **~artig** *adj* unique

Einzug ['aıntsu:k] *m* entry, moving in

Eis [aɪs] (-es, -) nt ice; (*Speiseeis*) ice cream; ~**bahn** f ice od skating rink; ~**bär** m polar bear; ~**becher** m sundae; ~**bein** nt pig's trotters pl; ~**berg** m iceberg; ~**café** nt ice-cream parlour (BRIT) od parlor (US); ~**decke** f sheet of ice; ~**diele** f ice-cream parlour

Eisen ['aɪzən] (-s, -) nt iron

Eisenbahn f railway, railroad (US); ~**er** (-s, -) m railwayman, railway employee, railroader (US); ~**schaffner** m railway guard; ~**wagen** m railway carriage

Eisenerz nt iron ore

eisern ['aɪzərn] adj iron; (*Gesundheit*) robust; (*Energie*) unrelenting; (*Reserve*) emergency

Eis- zW: **e~frei** adj clear of ice; ~**hockey** nt ice hockey; **e~ig** ['aɪzɪç] adj icy; **e~kalt** adj icy cold; ~**kunstlauf** m figure skating; ~**laufen** nt ice skating; ~**pickel** m ice axe; ~**schrank** m fridge, icebox (US); ~**würfel** m ice cube; ~**zapfen** m icicle; ~**zeit** f ice age

eitel ['aɪtəl] adj vain; **E~keit** f vanity

Eiter ['aɪtər] (-s) m pus; **e~ig** adj suppurating; **e~n** vi to suppurate

Eiweiß (-es, -e) nt white of an egg; (CHEM) protein

Ekel[1] ['eːkəl] (-s, -) m nausea, disgust; ~ **erregend** adj nauseating, disgusting; **e~haft** adj nauseating, disgusting; **e~ig** adj nauseating, disgusting; **e~n** vt to disgust ♦ vr: **sich e~n (vor** +dat) to loathe, to be disgusted (at); **es e~t jdn** od **jdm** sb is disgusted; **eklig** adj nauseating, disgusting

Ekstase [ɛk'staːzə] f ecstasy

Ekzem [ɛk'tseːm] (-s, -e) nt (MED) eczema

Elan [e'lãː] (-s) m elan

elastisch [e'lastɪʃ] adj elastic

Elastizität [elastitsi'tɛːt] f elasticity

Elch [ɛlç] (-(e)s, -e) m elk

Elefant [ele'fant] m elephant

elegant [ele'gant] adj elegant

Eleganz [ele'gants] f elegance

Elek- [e'lɛk] zW: ~**triker** [-trikər] (-s, -) m electrician; **e~trisch** [-trɪʃ] adj electric; **e~trisieren** [-tri'ziːrən] vt (auch fig) to electrify; (*Mensch*) to give an electric shock to ♦ vr to get an electric shock; **e~trizität** [tritsi'tɛːt] f electricity; **e~trizitätswerk** nt power station; (*Gesellschaft*) electric power company

Elektro- [e'lɛktro] zW: ~**de** [-'troːdə] f electrode; ~**gerät** nt electrical appliance; ~**herd** m electric cooker; ~**n** (-s, -en) nt electron; ~**nenrechner** [elɛk'troːnən-] m computer; ~**nik** f electronics sg; **e~nisch** adj electronic; ~**rasierer** m electric razor; ~**technik** f electrical engineering

Element [ele'mɛnt] (-s, -e) nt element; (ELEK) cell, battery; **e~ar** [-'taːr] adj elementary; (*naturhaft*) elemental

Elend ['eːlɛnt] (-(e)s) nt misery; **e~** adj miserable; **e~sviertel** nt slum

elf [ɛlf] num eleven; **E~** (-, -en) f (SPORT) eleven

Elfe f elf

Elfenbein nt ivory

Elfmeter m (SPORT) penalty (kick)

Elite [e'liːtə] f elite

Ell- zW: ~**bogen** m elbow; ~**e** ['ɛlə] f ell; (*Maß*) yard; ~**enbogen** m elbow; ~**(en)bogenfreiheit** f (fig) elbow room

Elsass ▲ ['ɛlzas] (- od -es) nt: **das ~** Alsace

Elster ['ɛlstər] (-, -n) f magpie

Eltern ['ɛltərn] pl parents; ~**beirat** (SCH) m PTA (BRIT), parents' council; ~**haus** nt home; **e~los** adj parentless

E-Mail ['iːmeɪl] (-, -s) f E-mail

Emaille [e'maljə] (-, -s) nt enamel

emaillieren [ema'jiːrən] vt to enamel

Emanzipation [emantsipatsi'oːn] f emancipation

emanzi'pieren vt to emancipate

Embryo ['ɛmbryo] (-s, -s od **Embryonen**) m embryo

Emi- zW: **~'grant(in)** m(f) emigrant; **~gration** f emigration; **e~grieren** vi to emigrate

Emissionen [emisi'o:nən] fpl emissions

Empfang [ɛm'pfaŋ] (-(e)s, ÷e) m reception; (Erhalten) receipt; **in ~ nehmen** to receive; **e~en** (unreg) vt to receive ♦ vi (schwanger werden) to conceive

Empfäng- [ɛm'pfɛŋ] zW: **~er** (-s, -) m receiver; (COMM) addressee, consignee; **~erabschnitt** m receipt slip; **e~lich** adj receptive, susceptible; **~nis** (-, -se) f conception; **~nisverhütung** f contraception

Empfangs- zW: **~bestätigung** f acknowledgement; **~dame** f receptionist; **~schein** m receipt; **~zimmer** nt reception room

empfehlen [ɛm'pfe:lən] (unreg) vt to recommend ♦ vr to take one's leave; **~swert** adj recommendable

Empfehlung f recommendation

empfiehlst etc [ɛm'pfi:lst] vb siehe **empfehlen**

empfind- [ɛm'pfɪnt] zW: **~en** [-dən] (unreg) vt to feel; **~lich** adj sensitive; (Stelle) sore; (reizbar) touchy; **~sam** adj sentimental; **E~ung** [-dʊŋ] f feeling, sentiment

empfohlen etc [ɛm'pfo:lən] vb siehe **empfehlen**

empor [ɛm'po:r] adv up, upwards

empören [ɛm'po:rən] vt to make indignant; to shock ♦ vr to become indignant; **~d** adj outrageous

Emporkömmling [ɛm'po:rkœmlɪŋ] m upstart, parvenu

Empörung f indignation

emsig ['ɛmzɪç] adj diligent, busy

End- ['ɛnt] m zW final; **~e** (-s, -n) nt end; **am ~e** at the end; (schließlich) in the end; **am ~e sein** to be at the end of one's tether; **~e Dezember** at the end of December; **zu ~e sein** to be finished; **e~en** vi to end; **e~gültig** ['ɛnt-] adj final, definite

Endivie [ɛn'di:viə] f endive

End- zW: **e~lich** adj final; (MATH) finite ♦ adv finally; **e~lich!** at last!; **komm e~lich!** come on!; **e~los** adj endless, infinite; **~spiel** nt final(s); **~spurt** m (SPORT) final spurt; **~station** f terminus; **~ung** f ending

Energie [enɛr'gi:] f energy; **~bedarf** m energy requirement; **e~los** adj lacking in energy, weak; **~verbrauch** m energy consumption; **~versorgung** f supply of energy; **~wirtschaft** f energy industry

energisch [e'nɛrgɪʃ] adj energetic

eng [ɛŋ] adj narrow; (Kleidung) tight; (fig: Horizont) narrow, limited; (Freundschaft, Verhältnis) close; **~ an etw** dat close to sth

Engagement [ãgaʒə'mã:] (-s, -s) nt engagement; (Verpflichtung) commitment

engagieren [ãga'ʒi:rən] vt to engage ♦ vr to commit o.s.

Enge ['ɛŋə] f (auch fig) narrowness; (Landenge) defile; (Meerenge) straits pl; **jdn in die ~ treiben** to drive sb into a corner

Engel ['ɛŋəl] (-s, -) m angel; **e~haft** adj angelic

England ['ɛŋlant] nt England; **Engländer(in)** m(f) Englishman(-woman); **englisch** adj English

Engpass ▲ m defile, pass; (fig, Verkehr) bottleneck

en gros [ã'gro] adv wholesale

engstirnig ['ɛŋʃtɪrnɪç] adj narrow-minded

Enkel ['ɛŋkəl] (-s, -) m grandson; **~in** f granddaughter; **~kind** nt grandchild

enorm [e'nɔrm] adj enormous

Ensemble [ã'sãbəl] (-s, -s) nt company, ensemble

entbehr- [ɛnt'beːr-] zW: **~en** vt to do without, to dispense with; **~lich** adj superfluous; **E~ung** f deprivation

entbinden [ɛnt'bɪndən] (unreg) vt (+gen) to release (from); (MED) to deliver ♦ vi (MED) to give birth; **Entbindung** f (MED) confinement; **Entbindungsheim** nt maternity hospital

entdeck- [ɛnt'dɛk] zW: **~en** vt to discover; **E~er** (-s, -) m discoverer; **E~ung** f discovery

Ente ['ɛntə] f duck; (fig) canard, false report

enteignen [ɛnt'|aignən] vt to expropriate; (Besitzer) to dispossess

enterben [ɛnt'|ɛrbən] vt to disinherit

entfallen [ɛnt'falən] (unreg) vi to drop, to fall; (wegfallen) to be dropped; **jdm ~** (vergessen) to slip sb's memory; **auf jdn ~** to be allotted to sb

entfalten [ɛnt'faltən] vt to unfold; (Talente) to develop ♦ vr to open; (Mensch) to develop one's potential; **Entfaltung** f unfolding; (von Talenten) development

entfern- [ɛnt'fɛrn] zW: **~en** vt to remove; (hinauswerfen) to expel ♦ vr to go away, to withdraw; **~t** adj distant; **weit davon ~t sein, etw zu tun** to be far from doing sth; **E~ung** f distance; (Wegschaffen) removal

entfremden [ɛnt'frɛmdən] vt to estrange, to alienate; **Entfremdung** f alienation, estrangement

entfrosten [ɛnt'frɔstən] vt to defrost

Entfroster (-s, -) m (AUT) defroster

entführ- [ɛnt'fyːr] zW: **~en** vt to carry off, to abduct; to kidnap; **E~er** m kidnapper; **E~ung** f abduction; kidnapping

entgegen [ɛnt'geːgən] präp +dat contrary to, against ♦ adv towards; **~bringen** (unreg) vt to bring; **jdm etw ~bringen** (fig) to show sb sth; **~gehen** (unreg) vi +dat to go to meet, to go towards; **~gesetzt** adj opposite; (widersprechend) opposed; **~halten**

(unreg) vt (fig) to object; **E~kommen** nt obligingness; **~kommen** (unreg) vi +dat to approach; to meet; (fig) to accommodate; **~kommend** adj obliging; **~nehmen** (unreg) vt to receive, to accept; **~sehen** (unreg) vi +dat to await; **~setzen** vt to oppose; **~treten** (unreg) vi +dat to step up to; (fig) to oppose, to counter; **~wirken** (fig) vi +dat to counteract

entgegnen [ɛnt'geːgnən] vt to reply, to retort

entgehen [ɛnt'geːən] (unreg) vi (fig): **jdm ~** to escape sb's notice; **sich** dat **etw ~ lassen** to miss sth

Entgelt [ɛnt'gɛlt] (-(e)s, -e) nt compensation, remuneration

entgleisen [ɛnt'glaizən] vi (EISENB) to be derailed; (fig: Person) to misbehave; **~ lassen** to derail

entgräten [ɛnt'grɛːtən] vt to fillet, to bone

Enthaarungscreme [ɛnt'haːrʊŋs-] f hair-removing cream

enthalten [ɛnt'haltən] (unreg) vt to contain ♦ vr: **sich (von etw) ~** to abstain (from sth), to refrain (from sth)

enthaltsam [ɛnt'haltzaːm] adj abstinent, abstemious

enthemmen [ɛnt'hɛmən] vt: **jdn ~** to free sb from his inhibitions

enthüllen [ɛnt'hʏlən] vt to reveal, to unveil

Enthusiasmus [ɛntuzi'asmʊs] m enthusiasm

entkommen [ɛnt'kɔmən] (unreg) vi: **~ (aus** od +dat**)** to get away (from), to escape (from)

entkräften [ɛnt'krɛftən] vt to weaken, to exhaust; (Argument) to refute

entladen [ɛnt'laːdən] (unreg) vt to unload; (ELEK) to discharge ♦ vr (ELEK: Gewehr) to discharge; (Ärger etc) to vent itself

entlang [ɛnt'laŋ] adv along; **~ dem Fluss, den Fluss ~** along the river; **~gehen** (unreg) vi to walk along

entlarven [ɛnt'larfən] vt to unmask, to expose

entlassen [ɛnt'lasən] (unreg) vt to discharge; (Arbeiter) to dismiss; **Entlassung** f discharge; dismissal

entlasten [ɛnt'lastən] vt to relieve; (Achse) to relieve the load on; (Angeklagten) to exonerate; (Konto) to clear

Entlastung f relief; (COMM) crediting

Entlastungszug m relief train

entlegen [ɛnt'le:gən] adj remote

entlocken [ɛnt'lɔkən] vt: (jdm etw) ~ to elicit (sth from sb)

entmutigen [ɛnt'mu:tɪgən] vt to discourage

entnehmen [ɛnt'ne:mən] (unreg) vt (+dat) to take out (of), to take (from); (folgern) to infer (from)

entreißen [ɛnt'raɪsən] (unreg) vt: **jdm etw ~** to snatch sth (away) from sb

entrichten [ɛnt'rɪçtən] vt to pay

entrosten [ɛnt'rɔstən] vt to remove rust from

entrümpeln [ɛnt'rʏmpəln] vt to clear out

entrüst- [ɛnt'rʏst] zW: **~en** vt to incense, to outrage ♦ vr to be filled with indignation; **~et** adj indignant, outraged; **E~ung** f indignation

entschädigen [ɛnt'ʃɛːdɪgən] vt to compensate; **Entschädigung** f compensation

entschärfen [ɛnt'ʃɛrfən] vt to defuse; (Kritik) to tone down

Entscheid [ɛnt'ʃaɪt] (-(e)s, -e) m decision; **e~en** [-dən] (unreg) vt, vi, vr to decide; **e~end** adj decisive; (Stimme) casting; **~ung** f decision

entschieden [ɛnt'ʃiːdən] adj decided; (entschlossen) resolute; **E~heit** f firmness, determination

entschließen [ɛnt'ʃliːsən] (unreg) vr to decide

entschlossen [ɛnt'ʃlɔsən] adj determined, resolute; **E~heit** f determination

Entschluss ▲ [ɛnt'ʃlʊs] m decision; **e~freudig** adj decisive; **~kraft** f determination, decisiveness

entschuldigen [ɛnt'ʃʊldɪgən] vt to excuse ♦ vr to apologize

Entschuldigung f apology; (Grund) excuse; **jdn um ~ bitten** to apologize to sb; **~!** excuse me; (Verzeihung) sorry

entsetz- [ɛnt'zɛts] zW: **~en** vt to horrify; (MIL) to relieve ♦ vr to be horrified od appalled; **E~en** (-s) nt horror, dismay; **~lich** adj dreadful, appalling; **~t** adj horrified

Entsorgung [ɛnt'zɔrgʊn] f (von Kraftwerken, Chemikalien) (waste) disposal

entspannen [ɛnt'ʃpanən] vt, vr (Körper) to relax; (POL: Lage) to ease

Entspannung f relaxation, rest; (POL) détente; **~spolitik** f policy of détente

entsprechen [ɛnt'ʃprɛçən] (unreg) vi +dat to correspond to; (Anforderungen, Wünschen) to meet, to comply with; **~d** adj appropriate ♦ adv accordingly

entspringen [ɛnt'ʃprɪŋən] (unreg) vi (+dat) to spring (from)

entstehen [ɛnt'ʃteːən] (unreg) vi: **(aus** od **durch)** to arise (from), to result (from)

Entstehung f genesis, origin

entstellen [ɛnt'ʃtɛlən] vt to disfigure; (Wahrheit) to distort

entstören [ɛnt'ʃtøːrən] vt (RADIO) to eliminate interference from

enttäuschen [ɛnt'tɔʏʃən] vt to disappoint; **Enttäuschung** f disappointment

entwaffnen [ɛnt'vafnən] vt (lit, fig) to disarm

entwässern [ɛnt'vɛsərn] vt to drain; **Entwässerung** f drainage

entweder [ɛnt've:dər] konj either

entwenden [ɛnt'vɛndən] (unreg) vt to purloin, to steal

entwerfen [ɛnt'vɛrfən] (unreg) vt

(*Zeichnung*) to sketch; (*Modell*) to design; (*Vortrag, Gesetz etc*) to draft

entwerten [ɛntˈveːrtən] *vt* to devalue; (*stempeln*) to cancel

Entwerter (**-s, -**) *m* ticket punching machine

entwickeln [ɛntˈvɪkəln] *vt, vr* (*auch* PHOT) to develop; (*Mut, Energie*) to show (o.s.), to display (o.s.)

Entwicklung [ɛntˈvɪklʊŋ] *f* development; (PHOT) developing

Entwicklungs- *zW:* **~hilfe** *f* aid for developing countries; **~land** *nt* developing country

entwöhnen [ɛntˈvøːnən] *vt* to wean; (*Süchtige*) (**einer Sache** *dat od* **von etw**) **~** to cure (of sth)

Entwöhnung *f* weaning; cure, curing

entwürdigend [ɛntˈvʏrdɪɡənt] *adj* degrading

Entwurf [ɛntˈvʊrf] *m* outline, design; (*Vertragsentwurf, Konzept*) draft

entziehen [ɛntˈtsiːən] (*unreg*) *vt* (+*dat*) to withdraw (from), to take away (from); (*Flüssigkeit*) to draw (from), to extract (from) ♦ *vr* (+*dat*) to escape (from); (*jds Kenntnis*) to be outside of beyond; (*der Pflicht*) to shirk (from)

Entziehung *f* withdrawal; **~sanstalt** *f* drug addiction/alcoholism treatment centre; **~skur** *f* treatment for drug addiction/alcoholism

entziffern [ɛntˈtsɪfərn] *vt* to decipher; to decode

entzücken [ɛntˈtsʏkən] *vt* to delight; **E~** (**-s**) *nt* delight; **~d** *adj* delightful, charming

entzünden [ɛntˈtsʏndən] *vt* to light, to set light to; (*fig*, MED) to inflame; (*Streit*) to spark off ♦ *vr* (*auch fig*) to catch fire; (*Streit*) to start; (MED) to become inflamed

Entzündung *f* (MED) inflammation

entzwei [ɛntˈtsvai] *adv* broken; in two; **~brechen** (*unreg*) *vt, vi* to break in two; **~en** *vt* to set at odds ♦ *vr* to fall out; **~gehen** (*unreg*) *vi* to break (in

two)

Enzian [ˈɛntsiːən] (**-s, -e**) *m* gentian

Epidemie [epideˈmiː] *f* epidemic

Epilepsie [epilɛˈpsiː] *f* epilepsy

Episode [epiˈzoːdə] *f* episode

Epoche [eˈpɔxə] *f* epoch; **~ machend** epoch-making

Epos [ˈeːpɔs] (**-s, Epen**) *nt* epic (poem)

er [eːr] (*nom*) *pron* he; it

erarbeiten [ɛrˈarbaitən] *vt* to work for, to acquire; (*Theorie*) to work out

erbarmen [ɛrˈbarmən] *vr* (+*gen*) to have pity *od* mercy (on); **E~** (**-s**) *nt* pity

erbärmlich [ɛrˈbɛrmlɪç] *adj* wretched, pitiful; **E~keit** *f* wretchedness

erbarmungslos [ɛrˈbarmʊŋsloːs] *adj* pitiless, merciless

erbau- [ɛrˈbau] *zW:* **~en** *vt* to build, to erect; (*fig*) to edify; **E~er** (**-s, -**) *m* builder; **~lich** *adj* edifying

Erbe¹ [ˈɛrbə] (**-n, -n**) *m* heir

Erbe² [ˈɛrbə] *nt* inheritance; (*fig*) heritage

erben *vt* to inherit

erbeuten [ɛrˈbɔytən] *vt* to carry off; (MIL) to capture

Erb- [ɛrb] *zW:* **~faktor** *m* gene; **~folge** *f* (line of) succession; **~in** *f* heiress

erbittern [ɛrˈbɪtərn] *vt* to embitter; (*erzürnen*) to incense

erbittert [ɛrˈbɪtərt] *adj* (*Kampf*) fierce, bitter

erblassen [ɛrˈblasən] *vi* to (turn) pale

erblich [ˈɛrplɪç] *adj* hereditary

erblinden [ɛrˈblɪndən] *vi* to go blind

erbrechen [ɛrˈbrɛçən] (*unreg*) *vt, vr* to vomit

Erbschaft *f* inheritance, legacy

Erbse [ˈɛrpsə] *f* pea

Erbstück *nt* heirloom

Erd- [eːrt] *zW:* **~achse** *f* earth's axis; **~atmosphäre** *f* earth's atmosphere; **~beben** *nt* earthquake; **~beere** *f* strawberry; **~boden** *m* ground; **~e** *f* earth; **zu ebener ~e** at ground level; **e~en** *vt* (ELEK) to earth

erdenklich [ɛrˈdɛŋklɪç] *adj* conceivable

Erd- zW: **~gas** nt natural gas; **~geschoss** ▲ nt ground floor; **~kunde** f geography; **~nuss** ▲ f peanut; **~öl** nt (mineral) oil

erdrosseln [er'drɔsəln] vt to strangle, to throttle

erdrücken [er'drʏkən] vt to crush

Erd- zW: **~rutsch** m landslide; **~teil** m continent

erdulden [er'dʊldən] vt to endure, to suffer

ereignen [er'aignən] vr to happen

Ereignis [er'aignıs] (**-ses, -se**) nt event; **e~los** adj uneventful; **e~reich** adj eventful

ererbt [er'erpt] adj (Haus) inherited; (Krankheit) hereditary

erfahren [er'fa:rən] (unreg) vt to learn, to find out; (erleben) to experience ♦ adj experienced

Erfahrung f experience; **e~sgemäß** adv according to experience

erfassen [er'fasən] vt to seize; (einbeziehen) to include, to register; (verstehen) to grasp

erfind- [er'fınd] zW: **~en** (unreg) vt to invent; **E~er** (**-s, -**) m inventor; **~erisch** adj inventive; **E~ung** f invention

Erfolg [er'fɔlk] (**-(e)s, -e**) m success; (Folge) result; **~ versprechend** promising; **e~en** [-gən] vi to follow; (sich ergeben) to result; (stattfinden) to take place; (Zahlung) to be effected; **e~los** adj unsuccessful; **~losigkeit** f lack of success; **e~reich** adj successful

erforderlich adj requisite, necessary

erfordern [er'fɔrdərn] vt to require, to demand

erforschen [er'fɔrʃən] vt (Land) to explore; (Problem) to investigate; (Gewissen) to search; **Erforschung** f exploration; investigation; searching

erfreuen [er'frɔyən] vr: **sich ~ an** +dat to enjoy ♦ vt to delight; **sich einer Sa-**

che gen~ to enjoy sth

erfreulich [er'frɔyliç] adj pleasing, gratifying; **~erweise** adv happily, luckily

erfrieren [er'fri:rən] (unreg) vi to freeze (to death); (Glieder) to get frostbitten; (Pflanzen) to be killed by frost

erfrischen [er'frıʃən] vt to refresh; **Erfrischung** f refreshment

Erfrischungs- zW: **~getränk** nt (liquid) refreshment; **~raum** m snack bar, cafeteria

erfüllen [er'fʏlən] vt (Raum etc) to fill; (fig: Bitte etc) to fulfil ♦ vr to come true

ergänzen [er'gɛntsən] vt to supplement, to complete ♦ vr to complement one another; **Ergänzung** f completion; (Zusatz) supplement

ergeben [er'ge:bən] (unreg) vt to yield, to produce ♦ vr to surrender; (folgen) to result ♦ adj devoted, humble

Ergebnis [er'ge:pnıs] (**-ses, -se**) nt result; **e~los** adj without result, fruitless

ergehen [er'ge:ən] (unreg) vi to be issued, to go out ♦ vi unpers: **es ergeht ihm gut/schlecht** he's faring od getting on well/badly ♦ vr: **sich in etw** dat ~ to indulge in sth; **etw über sich ~ lassen** to put up with sth

ergiebig [er'gi:bıç] adj productive

Ergonomie [ergono'mi:] f ergonomics sg

Ergonomik [ergo'no:mık] f = **Ergonomie**

ergreifen [er'graifən] (unreg) vt (auch fig) to seize; (Beruf) to take up; (Maßnahmen) to resort to; (rühren) to move; **~d** adj moving, touching

ergriffen [er'grıfən] adj deeply moved

Erguss ▲ [er'gʊs] m discharge; (fig) outpouring, effusion

erhaben [er'ha:bən] adj raised, embossed; (fig) exalted, lofty; **über etw** akk ~ **sein** to be above sth

erhalten [er'haltən] (unreg) vt to receive; (bewahren) to preserve, to maintain; **gut ~** in good condition

erhältlich [erˈhɛltliç] *adj* obtainable, available

Erhaltung *f* maintenance, preservation

erhärten [ɛrˈhɛrtən] *vt* to harden; *(These)* to substantiate, to corroborate

erheben [ɛrˈheːbən] *(unreg) vt* to raise; *(Protest, Forderungen)* to make; *(Fakten)* to ascertain, to establish ♦ *vr* to rise (up)

erheblich [ɛrˈheːpliç] *adj* considerable

erheitern [ɛrˈhaɪtərn] *vt* to amuse, to cheer (up)

Erheiterung *f* exhilaration; **zur allgemeinen ~** to everybody's amusement

erhitzen [ɛrˈhɪtsən] *vt* to heat ♦ *vr* to heat up; *(fig)* to become heated

erhoffen [ɛrˈhɔfən] *vt* to hope for

erhöhen [ɛrˈhøːən] *vt* to raise; *(verstärken)* to increase

erhol- [ɛrˈhoːl] *zW:* **~en** *vt* to recover; *(entspannen)* to have a rest; **~sam** *adj* restful; **E~ung** *f* recovery; relaxation, rest; **~ungsbedürftig** *adj* in need of a rest, run-down; **E~ungsgebiet** *nt* ≈ holiday area; **E~ungsheim** *nt* convalescent home

erhören [ɛrˈhøːrən] *vt (Gebet etc)* to hear; *(Bitte etc)* to yield to

erinnern [ɛrˈʔɪnɐn] *vt:* **~ (an** +*akk*) to remind (of) ♦ *vr:* **sich (an** *akk* **etw) ~** to remember (sth)

Erinnerung *f* memory; *(Andenken)* reminder

erkältet [ɛrˈkɛltət] *adj* with a cold; **~ sein** to have a cold

Erkältung *f* cold

erkennbar *adj* recognizable

erkennen [ɛrˈkɛnən] *(unreg) vt* to recognize; *(sehen, verstehen)* to see

erkennt- *zW:* **~lich** *adj:* **sich ~lich zeigen** to show one's appreciation; **E~lichkeit** *f* gratitude; *(Geschenk)* token of one's gratitude; **E~nis** (-, -se) *f* knowledge; *(das Erkennen)* recognition; *(Einsicht)* insight; **zur E~nis kommen** to realize

Erkennung *f* recognition

Erkennungszeichen *nt* identification

Erker [ˈɛrkɐ] (-s, -) *m* bay

erklär- [ɛrˈklɛːr] *zW:* **~bar** *adj* explicable; **~en** *vt* to explain; **~lich** *adj* explicable; *(verständlich)* understandable; **E~ung** *f* explanation; *(Aussage)* declaration

erkranken [ɛrˈkraŋkən] *vi* to fall ill; **Erkrankung** *f* illness

erkund- [ɛrˈkʊnd] *zW:* **~en** *vt* to find out, to ascertain; *(bes MIL)* to reconnoitre, to scout; **~igen** *vr:* **sich ~igen (nach)** to inquire (about); **E~igung** *f* inquiry; **E~ung** *f* reconnaissance, scouting

erlahmen [ɛrˈlaːmən] *vi* to tire; *(nachlassen)* to flag, to wane

erlangen [ɛrˈlaŋən] *vt* to attain, to achieve

Erlass ▲ (-es, ¤e) *m* decree; *(Aufhebung)* remission

erlassen *(unreg) vt (Verfügung)* to issue; *(Gesetz)* to enact; *(Strafe)* to remit; **jdm etw ~** to release sb from sth

erlauben [ɛrˈlaʊbən] *vt:* **(jdm etw) ~** to allow *od* permit (sb (to do) sth) ♦ *vr* to permit o.s., to venture

Erlaubnis [ɛrˈlaʊpnɪs] (-, -se) *f* permission; *(Schriftstück)* permit

erläutern [ɛrˈlɔʏtɐn] *vt* to explain; **Erläuterung** *f* explanation

erleben [ɛrˈleːbən] *vt* to experience; *(Zeit)* to live through; *(miterleben)* to witness; *(noch miterleben)* to live to see

Erlebnis [ɛrˈleːpnɪs] (-ses, -se) *nt* experience

erledigen [ɛrˈleːdɪgən] *vt* to take care of, to deal with; *(Antrag etc)* to process; *(umg: erschöpfen)* to wear out; *(: ruinieren)* to finish; *(: umbringen)* to do in

erleichtern [ɛrˈlaɪçtɐn] *vt* to make easier; *(fig: Last)* to lighten; *(lindern, beruhigen)* to relieve; **Erleichterung** *f* facilitation; lightening; relief

erleiden [ɛrˈlaɪdən] *(unreg) vt* to suffer,

to endure

erlernen [ɛr'lɛrnən] *vt* to learn, to acquire

erlesen [ɛr'le:zən] *adj* select, choice

erleuchten [ɛr'lɔʏçtən] *vt* to illuminate; (*fig*) to inspire

Erleuchtung *f* (*Einfall*) inspiration

Erlös [ɛr'lø:s] (-es, -e) *m* proceeds *pl*

erlösen [ɛr'lø:zən] *vt* to redeem, to save; **Erlösung** *f* release; (*REL*) redemption

ermächtigen [ɛr'mɛçtɪgən] *vt* to authorize, to empower; **Ermächtigung** *f* authorization; authority

ermahnen [ɛr'ma:nən] *vt* to exhort, to admonish; **Ermahnung** *f* admonition, exhortation

ermäßigen [ɛr'mɛsɪgən] *vt* to reduce; **Ermäßigung** *f* reduction

ermessen [ɛr'mɛsən] (*unreg*) *vt* to estimate, to gauge; **E~** (-s) *nt* estimation; discretion; **in jds E~ liegen** to lie within sb's discretion

ermitteln [ɛr'mɪtəln] *vt* to determine; (*Täter*) to trace ♦ *vi*: **gegen jdn ~** to investigate sb

Ermittlung *f* determination; (*Polizeiermittlung*) investigation

ermöglichen [ɛr'mø:klɪçən] *vt* (+*dat*) to make possible (for)

ermorden [ɛr'mɔrdən] *vt* to murder

ermüden [ɛr'my:dən] *vt*, *vi* to tire; (*TECH*) to fatigue; **~d** *adj* tiring; (*fig*) wearisome

Ermüdung *f* fatigue

ermutigen [ɛr'mu:tɪgən] *vt* to encourage

ernähr- [ɛr'nɛ:r] *zW*: **~en** *vt* to feed, to nourish; (*Familie*) to support ♦ *vr* to support o.s., to earn a living; **sich ~en von** to live on; **E~er** (-s, -) *m* breadwinner; **E~ung** *f* nourishment; nutrition; (*Unterhalt*) maintenance

ernennen [ɛr'nɛnən] (*unreg*) *vt* to ap-

point; **Ernennung** *f* appointment

erneu- [ɛr'nɔʏ] *zW*: **~ern** *vt* to renew; to restore; to renovate; **E~erung** *f* renewal; restoration; renovation; **~t** *adj* renewed, fresh ♦ *adv* once more

ernst [ɛrnst] *adj* serious; **~ gemeint** meant in earnest, serious; **E~** (-es) *m* seriousness; **das ist mein E~** I'm quite serious; **im E~** in earnest; **E~ machen mit etw** to put sth into practice; **E~fall** *m* emergency; **~haft** *adj* serious; **E~haftigkeit** *f* seriousness; **~lich** *adj* serious

Ernte [ˈɛrntə] *f* harvest; **e~n** *vt* to harvest; (*Lob etc*) to earn

ernüchtern [ɛr'nʏçtərn] *vt* to sober up; (*fig*) to bring down to earth

Erober- [ɛr'oːbər] *zW*: **~er** (-s, -) *m* conqueror; **e~n** *vt* to conquer; **~ung** *f* conquest

eröffnen [ɛr'œfnən] *vt* to open ♦ *vr* to present itself; **jdm etw ~** to disclose sth to sb

Eröffnung *f* opening

erörtern [ɛr'œrtərn] *vt* to discuss

Erotik [ɛ'roːtɪk] *f* eroticism; **erotisch** *adj* erotic

erpress- [ɛr'prɛs] *zW*: **~en** *vt* (*Geld etc*) to extort; (*Mensch*) to blackmail; **E~er** (-s, -) *m* blackmailer; **E~ung** *f* extortion; blackmail

erprobt [ɛr'proːpt] *adj* (*Gerät, Medikamente*) proven, tested

erraten [ɛr'raːtən] (*unreg*) *vt* to guess

erreg- [ɛr'reːg] *zW*: **~en** *vt* to excite; (*ärgern*) to infuriate; (*hervorrufen*) to arouse, to provoke ♦ *vr* to get excited od worked up; **E~er** (-s, -) *m* causative agent; **E~ung** *f* excitement

erreichbar *adj* accessible, within reach

erreichen [ɛr'raɪçən] *vt* to reach; (*Zweck*) to achieve; (*Zug*) to catch

errichten [ɛr'rɪçtən] *vt* to erect, to put up; (*gründen*) to establish, to set up

erringen [ɛr'rɪŋən] (*unreg*) *vt* to gain,

to win

erröten [ɛrˈrøːtən] vi to blush, to flush

Errungenschaft [ɛrˈrʊŋənʃaft] f achievement; (umg: Anschaffung) acquisition

Ersatz [ɛrˈzats] (-es) m substitute; replacement; (Schadenersatz) compensation; (MIL) reinforcements pl; ~dienst m (MIL) alternative service; ~reifen m (AUT) spare tyre; ~teil nt spare (part)

erschaffen [ɛrˈʃafən] (unreg) vt to create

erscheinen [ɛrˈʃaɪnən] (unreg) vi to appear; **Erscheinung** f appearance; (Geist) apparition; (Gegebenheit) phenomenon; (Gestalt) figure

erschießen [ɛrˈʃiːsən] (unreg) vt to shoot (dead)

erschlagen [ɛrˈʃlaːgən] (unreg) vt to strike dead

erschöpf- [ɛrˈʃœpf] zW: **~en** vt to exhaust; **~end** adj exhaustive, thorough; **E~ung** f exhaustion

erschrecken [ɛrˈʃrɛkən] vt to startle, to frighten ♦ vi to be frightened od startled; **~d** adj alarming, frightening

erschrocken [ɛrˈʃrɔkən] adj frightened, startled

erschüttern [ɛrˈʃʏtərn] vt to shake; (fig) to move deeply; **Erschütterung** f shaking; shock

erschweren [ɛrˈʃveːrən] vt to complicate

erschwinglich adj within one's means

ersetzen [ɛrˈzɛtsən] vt to replace; **jdm Unkosten** etc ~ to pay sb's expenses etc

ersichtlich [ɛrˈzɪçtlɪç] adj evident, obvious

ersparen [ɛrˈʃpaːrən] vt (Ärger etc) to spare; (Geld) to save

Ersparnis (-, -se) f saving

SCHLÜSSELWORT

erst [eːrst] adv 1 first; **mach erst mal die Arbeit fertig** finish your work first; **wenn du das erst mal hinter dir hast** once you've got that behind you

2 (nicht früher als, nur) only; (nicht bis) not till; **erst gestern** only yesterday; **erst morgen** not until tomorrow; **erst als** only when, not until; **wir fahren erst später** we're not going until later; **er ist (gerade) erst angekommen** he's only just arrived

3: **wäre er doch erst zurück!** if only he were back!

erstatten [ɛrˈʃtatən] vt (Kosten) to (re)pay; **Anzeige** etc **gegen jdn** ~ to report sb; **Bericht** ~ to make a report

Erstattung f (von Kosten) refund

Erstaufführung [ˈeːrstˈʔaʊfyːrʊŋ] f first performance

erstaunen [ɛrˈʃtaʊnən] vt to astonish ♦ vi to be astonished; **E~** (-s) nt astonishment

erstaunlich adj astonishing

erst- [eːrst] zW: **E~ausgabe** f first edition; **~beste(r, s)** adj first that comes along; **~e(r, s)** adj first

erstechen [ɛrˈʃtɛçən] (unreg) vt to stab (to death)

erstehen [ɛrˈʃteːən] (unreg) vt to buy ♦ vi to (a)rise

erstens [ˈeːrstəns] adv firstly, in the first place

ersticken [ɛrˈʃtɪkən] vt (auch fig) to stifle; (Mensch) to suffocate; (Flammen) to smother ♦ vi (Mensch) to suffocate; (Feuer) to be smothered; **in Arbeit** ~ to be snowed under with work

erst- zW: **~klassig** adj first-class; **~malig** adj first; **~mals** adv for the first time

erstrebenswert [ɛrˈʃtreːbənsveːrt] adj desirable, worthwhile

erstrecken [ɛrˈʃtrɛkən] vr to extend, to stretch

ersuchen [ɛrˈzuːxən] vt to request

ertappen [ɛrˈtapən] vt to catch, to detect

erteilen [ɛrˈtaɪlən] vt to give

Ertrag [ɛrˈtraːk] (-(e)s, -e) m yield; (Gewinn) proceeds pl

ertragen [ɛr'traːɡən] (unreg) vt to bear, to stand

erträglich [ɛr'trɛːklɪç] adj tolerable, bearable

ertrinken [ɛr'trɪŋkən] (unreg) vi to drown; **E~ (-s)** nt drowning

erübrigen [ɛr'yːbrɪɡən] vt to spare ♦ vr to be unnecessary

erwachen [ɛr'vaxən] vi to awake

erwachsen [ɛr'vaksən] adj grown-up; **E~e(r)** f(m) adult; **E~enbildung** f adult education

erwägen [ɛr'vɛːɡən] (unreg) vt to consider; **Erwägung** f consideration

erwähn- [ɛr've-] zW: **~en** vt to mention; **~enswert** adj worth mentioning; **E~ung** f mention

erwärmen [ɛr'vɛrmən] vt to warm, to heat ♦ vr to get warm, to warm up; **sich ~ für** to warm to

Erwarten nt: **über meinen/unseren usw ~** beyond my/our etc expectations; **wider ~** contrary to expectations

erwarten [ɛr'vartən] vt to expect; (warten auf) to wait for; **etw kaum ~ können** to be hardly able to wait for sth

Erwartung f expectation

erwartungsgemäß adv as expected

erwartungsvoll adj expectant

erwecken [ɛr'vɛkən] vt to rouse, to awake; **den Anschein ~** to give the impression

Erweis [ɛr'vais] **(-es, -e)** m proof; **e~en** (unreg) vt to prove ♦ vr: **sich e~en (als)** to prove (to be); **jdm einen Gefallen/Dienst e~en** to do sb a favour/service

Erwerb [ɛr'vɛrp] **(-(e)s, -e)** m acquisition; (Beruf) trade; **e~en** [-bən] (unreg) vt to acquire

erwerbs- zW: **~los** adj unemployed; **E~quelle** f source of income; **~tätig** (gainfully) employed

erwidern [ɛr'viːdərn] vt to reply; (vergelten) to return

erwischen [ɛr'vɪʃən] (umg) vt to catch, to get

erwünscht [ɛr'vʏnʃt] adj desired

erwürgen [ɛr'vʏrɡən] vt to strangle

Erz [ɛrts] **(-es, -e)** nt ore

erzähl- [ɛr'tsɛ:l] zW: **~en** vt to tell ♦ vi: **sie kann gut ~en** she's a good storyteller; **Er~er (-s, -)** m narrator; **E~ung** f story, tale

Erzbischof m archbishop

erzeug- [ɛr'tsɔʏɡ] zW: **~en** vt to produce; (Strom) to generate; **E~nis (-ses, -se)** nt product, produce; **E~ung** f production; generation

erziehen [ɛr'tsiːən] (unreg) vt to bring up; (bilden) to educate, to train; **Er~zieher(in) (-s, -)** m(f) (Berufsbezeichnung) teacher; **Erziehung** f bringing up; (Bildung) education; **Erziehungsbeihilfe** f educational grant; **Erziehungsberechtigte(r)** f(m) parent; guardian

erzielen [ɛr'tsiːlən] vt to achieve, to obtain; (Tor) to score

erzwingen [ɛr'tsvɪŋən] (unreg) vt to force, to obtain by force

es [ɛs] (nom, akk) pron it

Esel ['eːzəl] **(-s, -)** m donkey, ass

Eskalation [ɛskalatsi'oːn] f escalation

ess- ▲ ['ɛs] zW: **~bar** ['ɛsbaːr] adj eatable, edible; **E~besteck** nt knife, fork and spoon; **E~ecke** f dining area

essen ['ɛsən] (unreg) vt, vi to eat; **E~ (-s, -)** nt meal; food

Essig ['ɛsɪç] **(-s, -e)** m vinegar

Ess- ▲ zW: **~kastanie** f sweet chestnut; **~löffel** m tablespoon; **~tisch** m dining table; **~waren** pl foodstuffs, provisions; **~zimmer** nt dining room

etablieren [eta'bliːrən] vr to become established, to set up in business

Etage [e'taːʒə] f floor, storey; **~nbetten** pl bunk beds; **~nwohnung** f flat

Etappe [e'tapə] f stage

Etat [e'ta:] (-s, -s) m budget

etc abk (= et cetera) etc

Ethik ['e:tɪk] f ethics sg; **ethisch** adj ethical

Etikett [eti'kɛt] (-(e)s, -e) nt label; tag; **~e** f etiquette, manners pl

etliche ['ɛtlɪçə] pron pl some, quite a few; **~s** pron a thing or two

Etui [ɛt'vi:] (-s, -s) nt case

etwa ['ɛtva] adv (ungefähr) about; (vielleicht) perhaps; (beispielsweise) for instance; **nicht ~** by no means; **~ig** ['ɛtvaɪç] adj possible

etwas pron something; anything; (ein wenig) a little ♦ adv a little

euch [ɔyç] pron (akk von ihr) you; yourselves; (dat von ihr) (to) you

euer ['ɔyər] pron (gen von ihr) of you ♦ adj your

Eule ['ɔylə] f owl

eure ['ɔyrə] adj f siehe euer

eure(r, s) ['ɔyrə(r, s)] pron yours; **~rseits** adv on your part; **~s** adj nt siehe euer; **~sgleichen** pron people like you; **~twegen** adv (für euch) for your sakes; (wegen euch) on your account; **~twillen** adv: **um ~twillen** = euretwegen

eurige ['ɔyrigə] pron: **der/die/das ~** od **E~** yours

Euro ['ɔyro:] (-s, -s) m (FIN) euro

Euro- zW: **~pa** [ɔy'ro:pa] nt Europe; **~päer(in)** [ɔyro'pɛːər(ɪn)] m(f) European; **e~päisch** adj European; **~pa-meister** [ɔy'ro:pa-] m European champion; **~paparlament** nt European Parliament; **~scheck** m (FIN) eurocheque

Euter ['ɔytər] (-s, -) nt udder

ev. abk = evangelisch

evakuieren [evaku'i:rən] vt to evacuate

evangelisch [evaŋ'ge:lɪʃ] adj Protestant

Evangelium [evaŋ'ge:liʊm] nt gospel

eventuell [eventu'ɛl] adj possible ♦ adv

possibly, perhaps

evtl. abk = eventuell

EWG [e:ve:'ge:] (-) f abk (= Europäische Wirtschaftsgemeinschaft) EEC, Common Market

ewig ['e:vɪç] adj eternal; **E~keit** f eternity

EWU [e:ve:'u:] f abk (= Europäische Währungsunion) EMU

exakt [ɛ'ksakt] adj exact

Examen [ɛ'ksa:mən] (-s, - od Examina) nt examination

Exemplar [ɛksɛm'pla:r] (-s, -e) nt specimen; (Buchexemplar) copy; **e~isch** adj exemplary

Exil [ɛ'ksi:l] (-s, -e) nt exile

Existenz [ɛksɪs'tɛnts] f existence; (Unterhalt) livelihood, living; (pej: Mensch) character; **~minimum** (-s) nt subsistence level

existieren [ɛksɪs'ti:rən] vi to exist

exklusiv [ɛksklu'zi:f] adj exclusive; **~e** adv exclusive of, not including ♦ präp **+gen** exclusive of, not including

exotisch [ɛ'kso:tɪʃ] adj exotic

Expedition [ɛkspeditsi'o:n] f expedition

Experiment [ɛksperi'mɛnt] nt experiment; **e~ell** [-'tɛl] adj experimental; **e~ieren** [-'ti:rən] vi to experiment

Experte [ɛks'pɛrtə] (-n, -n) m expert, specialist

Expertin f expert, specialist

explo- [ɛksplo] zW: **~dieren** [-'di:rən] vi to explode; **E~sion** [-zi'o:n] f explosion; **~siv** [-'zi:f] adj explosive

Export [ɛks'pɔrt] (-(e)s, -e) m export; **~eur** [-'tøːr] m exporter; **~handel** m export trade; **e~ieren** [-'ti:rən] vt to export; **~land** nt exporting country

Express- ▲ [ɛks'prɛs] zW: **~gut** n express goods pl, express freight; **~zug** m express (train)

extra ['ɛkstra] adj inv (umg: gesondert) separate; (besondere) extra ♦ adv (gesondert) separately; (speziell) specially; (absichtlich) on purpose; (vor Adjektiven, zusätzlich) extra; **E~** (-s, -s) nt extra; **E~ausgabe** f special edition; **E~blatt** nt special edition

Extrakt [eks'trakt] (-(e)s, -e) m extract

extravagant [ekstrava'gant] adj extravagant

extrem [eks'tre:m] adj extreme; **~istisch** [-'mɪstɪʃ] adj (POL) extremist; **E~itäten** [-mi'tɛ:tən] pl extremities

exzentrisch [eks'tsɛntrɪʃ] adj eccentric

EZ nt abk = Einzelzimmer

F, f

Fa. abk (= Firma) firm; (in Briefen) Messrs

Fabel ['fa:bəl] (-, -n) f fable; **f~haft** adj fabulous, marvellous

Fabrik [fa'bri:k] f factory; **~ant** [-'kant] m (Hersteller) manufacturer; (Besitzer) industrialist; **~arbeiter** m factory worker; **~at** [-'ka:t] (-(e)s, -e) nt manufacture, product; **~gelände** nt factory site

Fach [fax] (-(e)s, ⁻er) nt compartment; (Sachgebiet) subject; **ein Mann vom ~** an expert; **~arbeiter** m skilled worker; **~arzt** m (medical) specialist; **~ausdruck** m technical term

Fächer ['fɛçər] (-s, -) m fan

Fach- zW: **~geschäft** nt specialist shop; **~hochschule** f technical college; **~kraft** f skilled worker, trained employee; **f~kundig** adj expert, specialist; **f~lich** adj professional; expert; **~mann** (pl **-leute**) m specialist; **f~männisch** adj professional; **~schule** f technical college; **f~simpeln** vi to talk shop; **~werk** nt timber frame

Fackel ['fakəl] (-, -n) f torch

fad(e) [fa:t, 'fa:də] adj insipid; (langweilig) dull

Faden ['fa:dən] (-s, ⁻) m thread; **f~scheinig** adj (auch fig) threadbare

fähig ['fɛ:ɪç] adj: **~ (zu od +gen)** capable

(of); able (to); **F~keit** f ability

fahnden ['fa:ndən] vi: **~ nach** to search for; **Fahndung** f search

Fahndungsliste f list of wanted criminals, wanted list

Fahne ['fa:nə] f flag, standard; **eine ~ haben** (umg) to smell of drink; **~nflucht** f desertion

Fahr- zW: **~ausweis** m ticket; **~bahn** f carriageway (BRIT), roadway

Fähre ['fɛ:rə] f ferry

fahren ['fa:rən] (unreg) vt to drive; (Rad) to ride; (befördern) to drive, to take; (Rennen) to drive in ♦ vi (sich bewegen) to go; (Schiff) to sail; (abfahren) to leave; **mit dem Auto/Zug ~** to go od travel by car/train; **mit der Hand ~ über** +akk to pass one's hand over

Fahr- zW: **~er(in)** (-s, -) m(f) driver; **~erflucht** f hit-and-run; **~gast** m passenger; **~geld** nt fare; **~karte** f ticket; **~kartenausgabe** f ticket office; **~kartenautomat** m ticket machine; **~kartenschalter** m ticket office; **f~lässig** adj negligent; **f~lässige Tötung** manslaughter; **~lehrer** m driving instructor; **~plan** m timetable; **f~planmäßig** adj scheduled; **~preis** m fare; **~prüfung** f driving test; **~rad** nt bicycle; **~radweg** m cycle lane; **~schein** m ticket; **~scheinentwerter** m (automatic) ticket stamping machine

Fährschiff ['fɛ:rʃɪf] nt ferry(boat)

Fahr- zW: **~schule** f driving school; **~spur** f lane; **~stuhl** m lift (BRIT), elevator (US)

Fahrt [fa:rt] (-, -en) f journey; (kurz) trip; (AUTO) drive; (Geschwindigkeit) speed; **gute ~!** I have a good journey

Fährte ['fɛ:rtə] f track, trail

Fahrt- zW: **~kosten** pl travelling expenses; **~richtung** f course, direction

Fahrzeit f time for the journey

Fahrzeug nt vehicle; **~brief** m log

book; **~papiere** pl vehicle documents

fair [feːr] adj fair

Fakt [fakt] nt (-(e)s, -en) m fact

Faktor ['faktɔr] m factor

Fakultät [fakʊl'tɛːt] f faculty

Falke ['falkə] (-n, -n) m falcon

Fall [fal] (-(e)s, -e) m (Sturz) fall; (Sachverhalt, JUR, GRAM) case; **auf jeden ~, auf alle Fälle** in any case; (bestimmt) definitely; **auf keinen ~!** no way!

Falle f trap

fallen (unreg) vi to fall; **etw ~ lassen** to drop sth; (Bemerkung) to make sth; (Plan) to abandon sth, to drop sth

fällen ['fɛlən] vt (Baum) to fell; (Urteil) to pass

fällig ['fɛlɪç] adj due

falls [fals] adv in case, if

Fallschirm m parachute; **~springer** m parachutist

falsch [falʃ] adj false; (unrichtig) wrong

fälschen ['fɛlʃən] vt to forge

fälsch- zW: **~lich** adj false; **~licherweise** adv mistakenly; **F~ung** f forgery

Falte ['faltə] f (Knick) fold, crease; (Hautfalte) wrinkle; (Rockfalte) pleat; **f~n** vt to fold; (Stirn) to wrinkle

faltig ['faltɪç] adj (Hände, Haut) wrinkled; (zerknittert: Rock) creased

familiär [famɪli'ɛːr] adj familiar

Familie [fa'miːliə] f family

Familien- zW: **~betrieb** m family business; **~kreis** m family circle; **~mitglied** nt member of the family; **~name** m surname; **~stand** m marital status

Fanatiker [fa'naːtikər] (-s, -) m fanatic; **fanatisch** adj fanatical

fand etc [fant] vb siehe **finden**

Fang [faŋ] (-(e)s, -e) m catch; (Jagen) hunting; (Kralle) talon, claw; **f~en** (unreg) vt to catch ♦ vr to get caught; (Flugzeug) to level out; (Mensch: nicht fallen) to steady o.s.; (fig) to regain o.s.; (in Leistung) to get back on form

Fantasie ▲ [fanta'ziː] f imagination;

f~los adj unimaginative; **f~ren** vi to fantasize; **f~voll** adj imaginative

fantastisch ▲ [fan'tastɪʃ] adj fantastic

Farb- ['farb] zW: **~abzug** m colour print; **~aufnahme** f colour photograph; **~band** nt typewriter ribbon; **~e** f colour; (zum Malen etc) paint; (Stofffarbe) dye; **f~echt** adj colourfast

färben ['fɛrbən] vt to colour; (Stoff, Haar) to dye

farben- ['farbən] zW: **~blind** adj colour-blind; **~freudig** adj colourful; **~froh** adj colourful, gay

Farb- zW: **~fernsehen** nt colour television; **~film** m colour film; **~foto** nt colour photograph; **f~ig** adj coloured; **~ige(r)** f(m) coloured (person); **~kasten** m paintbox; **f~lich** adj colour; **f~los** adj colourless; **~stift** m coloured pencil; **~stoff** m dye; **~ton** m hue, tone

Färbung ['fɛrbʊŋ] f colouring; (Tendenz) bias

Farn [farn] (-(e)s, -e) m fern; bracken

Fasan [fa'zaːn] (-(e)s, -e(n)) m pheasant

Fasching ['faʃɪŋ] (-s, -e od -s) m carnival

Faschismus [fa'ʃɪsmʊs] m fascism

Faschist m fascist

Faser ['faːzər] (-, -n) f fibre; **f~n** vi to fray

Fass ▲ [fas] (-es, -er) nt vat, barrel; (für Öl) drum; **Bier vom ~** draught beer

Fassade [fa'saːdə] f façade

fassen ['fasən] vt (ergreifen) to grasp, to take; (inhaltlich) to hold; (Entschluss etc) to take; (verstehen) to understand; (Ring etc) to set; (formulieren) to formulate, to phrase ♦ vr to calm down; **nicht zu ~** unbelievable

Fassung ['fasʊŋ] f (Umrahmung) mounting; (Lampenfassung) socket; (Wortlaut) version; (Beherrschung) composure; **jdn aus der ~ bringen** to upset sb; **f~slos** adj speechless

fast [fast] *adv* almost, nearly

fasten ['fastən] *vi* to fast; **F~zeit** *f* Lent

Fastnacht *f* Shrove Tuesday; carnival

faszinieren [fastsi'ni:rən] *vt* to fascinate

fatal [fa'ta:l] *adj* fatal; (*peinlich*) embarrassing

faul [faʊl] *adj* rotten; (*Person*) lazy; (*Ausreden*) lame; **daran ist etwas ~** there's something fishy about it; **~en** *vi* to rot; **~enzen** *vi* to idle; **F~enzer** (*-s, -*) *m* idler, loafer; **F~heit** *f* laziness; **~ig** *adj* putrid

Faust ['faʊst] (*-, Fäuste*) *f* fist; **auf eigene ~** off one's own bat; **~handschuh** *m* mitten

Favorit [favo'ri:t] (*-en, -en*) *m* favourite

Fax [faks] (*-, -(e)*) *nt* fax

faxen ['faksən] *vt* to fax; **jdm etw ~** to fax sth to sb

FCKW *m abk* (= *Fluorchlorkohlenwasserstoff*) CFC

Februar ['fe:brua:r] (*-(s), -e*) *m* February

fechten ['fɛçtən] (*unreg*) *vi* to fence

Feder ['fe:dər] (*-, -n*) *f* feather; (*Schreibfeder*) pen nib; (*TECH*) spring; **~ball** *m* shuttlecock; **~bett** *nt* continental quilt; **~halter** *m* penholder, pen; **f~leicht** *adj* light as a feather; **f~n** *vi* (*nachgeben*) to be springy; (*sich bewegen*) to bounce ♦ *vt* to spring; **~ung** *f* (*AUT*) suspension

Fee [fe:] *f* fairy

fegen ['fe:gən] *vt* to sweep

fehl [fe:l] *adj*: **~ am Platz** *od* **Ort** out of place; **F~betrag** *m* deficit; **~en** *vi* to be wanting *od* missing; (*abwesend sein*) to be absent; **etw ~t jdm** sb lacks sth; **du ~st mir** I miss you; **was ~t ihm?** what's wrong with him?; **F~er** (*-s, -*) *m* mistake, error; (*Mangel, Schwäche*) fault; **~erfrei** *adj* faultless; without any mistakes; **~erhaft** *adj* incorrect; faulty;

~erlos *adj* flawless, perfect; **F~geburt** *f* miscarriage; **~gehen** (*unreg*) *vi* to go astray; **~griff** *m* blunder; **F~konstruktion** *f* badly designed thing; **~schlagen** (*unreg*) *vi* to fail; **~start** *m* (*SPORT*) false start; **F~zündung** *f* (*AUT*) misfire, backfire

Feier ['faɪər] (*-, -n*) *f* celebration; **~abend** *m* time to stop work; **~abend machen** to stop, to knock off; **jetzt ist ~abend!** that's enough!; **f~lich** *adj* solemn; **~lichkeit** *f* solemnity; **~lichkeiten** *pl* (*Veranstaltungen*) festivities; **f~n** *vt, vi* to celebrate; **~tag** *m* holiday

feig(e) [faɪk, 'faɪgə] *adj* cowardly

Feige ['faɪgə] *f* fig

Feigheit *f* cowardice

Feigling *m* coward

Feile ['faɪlə] *f* file

feilschen ['faɪlʃən] *vi* to haggle

fein [faɪn] *adj* fine; (*vornehm*) refined; (*Gehör etc*) keen; **~! great!

Feind [faɪnt] (*-(e)s, -e*) *m* enemy; **f~lich** *adj* hostile; **~schaft** *f* enmity; **~selig** *adj* hostile

Fein- *zW*: **f~fühlig** *adj* sensitive; **~gefühl** *nt* delicacy, tact; **~heit** *f* fineness; refinement; keenness; **~kostgeschäft** *nt* delicatessen (shop); **~schmecker** (*-s, -*) *m* gourmet; **~wäsche** *f* delicate clothing (*when washing*); **~waschmittel** *nt* mild detergent

Feld [fɛlt] (*-(e)s, -er*) *nt* field; (*SCHACH*) square; (*SPORT*) pitch; **~herr** *m* commander; **~stecher** (*-s, -*) *m* binoculars *pl*; **~weg** *m* path; **~zug** *m* (*fig*) campaign

Felge ['fɛlgə] *f* (*wheel*) rim

Fell [fɛl] (*-(e)s, -e*) *nt* fur; coat; (*von Schaf*) fleece; (*von toten Tieren*) skin

Fels [fɛls] (*-en, -en*) *m* rock; (*Klippe*) cliff

Felsen ['fɛlzən] (*-s, -*) *m* = **Fels**; **f~fest** *adj* firm

feminin [femi'ni:n] *adj* feminine

Fenster ['fɛnstər] (-s, -) nt window; ~**bank** f windowsill; ~**laden** m shutter; ~**leder** nt chamois (leather); ~**scheibe** f windowpane

Ferien ['feːriən] pl holidays, vacation sg (US); ~ **haben** to be on holiday; ~**bungalow** [-bʊŋgalo] (-s, -s) m holiday bungalow; ~**haus** nt holiday home; ~**kurs** m holiday course; ~**lager** nt holiday camp; ~**reise** f holiday; ~**wohnung** f holiday apartment

Ferkel ['fɛrkəl] (-s, -) nt piglet

fern [fɛrn] adj, adv far-off, distant; ~ **von hier** a long way (away) from here; **der F~e Osten** the Far East; ~**halten** to keep away; **F~bedienung** f remote control; **F~e** f distance; ~**er** adj further ♦ adv further; (weiterhin) in future; **F~gespräch** nt trunk call; **F~glas** nt binoculars pl; **F~licht** nt (AUT) full beam; **F~rohr** nt telescope; **F~ruf** m (förmlich) telephone number; **F~schreiben** nt telex; **F~sehapparat** m television set; **F~sehen** (-s) nt television; **im F~sehen** on television; ~**sehen** (unreg) vi to watch television; **F~seher** m television; **F~sehturm** m television tower; **F~sprecher** m telephone; **F~steuerung** f remote control; **F~straße** f ≈ 'A' road (BRIT), highway (US); **F~verkehr** m long-distance traffic

Ferse ['fɛrzə] f heel

fertig ['fɛrtɪç] adj (bereit) ready; (beendet) finished; (gebrauchsfertig) readymade; ~ **bringen** (fähig sein) to be capable of; ~ **machen** (beenden) to finish; (umg: Person) to finish; (: körperlich) to exhaust; (: moralisch) to get down; **sich ~ machen** to get ready; ~ **stellen** to complete; **F~gericht** nt precooked meal; **F~haus** nt kit house, prefab; **F~keit** f skill

Fessel ['fɛsəl] (-, -n) f fetter; **f~n** vt to bind; (mit ~n) to fetter; (fig) to spellbind; **f~nd** adj fascinating, captivating

Fest (-(e)s, -e) nt party; festival; frohes ~! Happy Christmas!

fest [fɛst] adj firm; (Nahrung) solid; (Gehalt) regular; ~**e Kosten** fixed cost ♦ adv (schlafen) soundly; ~ **angestellt** permanently employed; ~**binden** (unreg) vt to tie, to fasten; ~**bleiben** (unreg) vi to stand firm; **F~essen** nt banquet; ~**halten** (unreg) vt to seize, to hold fast; (Ereignis) to record ♦ vr: **sich ~halten (an** +dat) to hold on (to); ~**igen** vt to strengthen; **F~igkeit** f strength; **F~ival** ['fɛstival] (-s, -s) nt festival; **F~land** nt mainland; ~**legen** vt to fix ♦ vr to commit o.s.; ~**lich** adj festive; ~**liegen** (unreg) vi (~stehen: Termin) to be confirmed, be fixed; ~**machen** vt to fasten; (Termin etc) to fix; **F~nahme** f arrest; ~**nehmen** (unreg) vt to arrest; **F~preis** m (COMM) fixed price; **F~rede** f address; ~**setzen** vt to fix, to settle; **F~spiele** pl (Veranstaltung) festival sg; ~**stehen** (unreg) vi to be certain; ~**stellen** vt to establish; (sagen) to remark; **F~tag** m feast day, holiday; **F~ung** f fortress; **F~wochen** pl festival sg

Fett (-(e)s, -e) nt fat, grease

fett adj fat; (Essen etc) greasy; (TYP) bold; ~**arm** adj low fat; ~**en** vt to grease; **F~fleck** m grease stain; ~**ig** adj greasy, fatty

Fetzen ['fɛtsən] (-s, -) m scrap

feucht [fɔʏçt] adj damp; (Luft) humid; **F~igkeit** f dampness; humidity; **F~igkeitscreme** f moisturizing cream

Feuer ['fɔʏər] (-s, -) nt fire; (zum Rauchen) a light; (fig: Schwung) spirit; ~**alarm** m fire alarm; **f~fest** adj fireproof; **f~gefahr** f danger of fire; **f~gefährlich** adj inflammable; ~**leiter** f fire escape ladder; ~**löscher** (-s, -) m fire extinguisher; ~**melder** (-s, -) m fire alarm; **f~n** vt, vi (auch fig) to fire; ~**stein** m flint; ~**treppe** f fire escape; ~**wehr** (-, -en) f fire brigade; ~**wehrauto** nt fire engine; ~**wehrmann** m fireman; **~werk** nt fireworks pl; **~zeug** nt (cigarette) lighter

Fichte ['fɪçtə] f spruce, pine

Fieber ['fiːbər] (-s, -) nt fever, temperature; **f~haft** adj feverish; **~thermometer** nt thermometer; **fiebrig** adj (Erkältung) feverish

fiel etc [fiːl] vb siehe **fallen**

fies [fiːs] (umg) adj nasty

Figur [fi'guːr] (-, -en) f figure; (Schachfigur) chessman, chess piece

Filet [fi'leː] (-s, -s) nt (KOCH) fillet

Filiale [fili'aːlə] f (COMM) branch

Film [fɪlm] (-(e)s, -e) m film; **~aufnahme** f shooting; **f~en** vt, vi to film; **~kamera** f cine camera

Filter ['fɪltər] (-s, -) m filter; **f~n** vt to filter; **~papier** nt filter paper; **~zigarette** f tipped cigarette

Filz [fɪlts] (-es, -e) m felt; **f~en** vt (umg) to frisk ♦ vi (Wolle) to mat; **~stift** m felt-tip pen

Finale [fi'naːlə] (-s, -(s)) nt finale; (SPORT) final(s)

Finanz [fi'nants] f finance; **~amt** nt Inland Revenue office; **~beamte(r)** m revenue officer; **f~iell** [-tsi'ɛl] adj financial; **f~ieren** [-'tsiːrən] vt to finance; **f~kräftig** adj financially strong; **~minister** m Chancellor of the Exchequer (BRIT), Minister of Finance

Find- [fɪnt] zW: ~**en** (unreg) vt to find; (meinen) to think ♦ vt to be (found); (sich fassen) to compose o.s.; **ich f~e nichts dabei, wenn ...** I don't see what's wrong if ...; **das wird sich f~en** things will work out; **~er** (-s, -) m finder; **~erlohn** m reward (for sb who finds sth); **f~ig** adj resourceful

fing etc [fɪŋ] vb siehe **fangen**

Finger ['fɪŋər] (-s, -) m finger; **~abdruck** m fingerprint; **~nagel** m fingernail; **~spitze** f fingertip

fingiert adj made-up, fictitious

Fink [fɪŋk] (-en, -en) m finch

Finn- [fɪn] zW: ~**e** (-n, -n) m Finn; **~in** f Finn; **f~isch** adj Finnish; **~land** nt Finland

finster ['fɪnstər] adj dark, gloomy; (verdächtig) dubious; (verdrossen) grim; (Gedanke) dark; **F~nis** (-) f darkness, gloom

Firma ['fɪrma] (-, -men) f firm

Firmen- ['fɪrmən] zW: ~**inhaber** m owner of firm; **~schild** nt (shop) sign; **~wagen** m company car; **~zeichen** nt trademark

Fisch [fɪʃ] (-(e)s, -e) m fish; ~**e** pl (ASTROL) Pisces sg; **f~en** vt, vi to fish; **~er** (-s, -) m fisherman; **~e'rei** f fishing, fishery; **~fang** m fishing; **~geschäft** nt fishmonger's (shop); **~gräte** f fishbone; **~stäbchen** [-ʃtɛːpçən] nt fish finger (BRIT), fish stick (US)

fit [fɪt] adj fit; **F~ness** ▲ (-, -) f (physical) fitness

fix [fɪks] adj fixed; (Person) alert, smart; ~ **und fertig** finished; (erschöpft) done in; **F~er(in)** m(f) (umg) junkie; **F~erstube** f (umg) junkies' centre; **f~ieren** [fɪ'ksiːrən] vt to fix; (anstarren) to stare at

flach [flax] adj flat; (Gefäß) shallow

Fläche ['flɛçə] f area; (Oberfläche) surface

Flachland nt lowland

flackern ['flakərn] vi to flare, to flicker

Flagge ['flagə] f flag; **f~n** vi to fly a flag

flämisch ['flɛːmɪʃ] adj (LING) Flemish

Flamme ['flamə] f flame

Flandern ['flandərn] nt Flanders

Flanke ['flaŋkə] f flank; (SPORT: Seite) wing

Flasche ['flaʃə] f bottle; (umg: Versager) wash-out

Flaschen- ['flaʃən] zW: ~**bier** nt bottled beer; **~öffner** m bottle opener; **~zug** m pulley

flatterhaft adj flighty, fickle

flattern ['flatərn] vi to flutter

flau [flaʊ] *adj* weak, listless; *(Nachfrage)* slack; **jdm ist ~** sb feels queasy

Flaum [flaʊm] *m (Feder)* down; *(Haare)* fluff

flauschig ['flaʊʃɪç] *adj* fluffy

Flaute ['flaʊtə] *f* calm; *(COMM)* recession

Flechte ['flɛçtə] *f* plait; *(MED)* dry scab; *(BOT)* lichen; **f~n** *(unreg) vt* to plait; *(Kranz)* to twine

Fleck [flɛk] *(-(e)s, -e)* *m* spot; *(Schmutzfleck)* stain; *(Stofffleck)* patch; *(Makel)* blemish; **nicht vom ~ kommen** *(auch fig)* not to get any further; **vom ~ weg** straight away

Flecken *(-s, -)* *m* = Fleck; **f~los** *adj* spotless; **~mittel** *nt* stain remover; **~wasser** *nt* stain remover

fleckig *adj* spotted; stained

Fledermaus ['fleːdɐmaʊs] *f* bat

Flegel ['fleːgəl] *(-s, -)* *m (Mensch)* lout; **f~haft** *adj* loutish, unmannerly; **~jahre** *pl* adolescence *sg*

flehen ['fleːən] *vi* to implore; **~tlich** *adj* imploring

Fleisch [flaɪʃ] *(-(e)s)* *nt* flesh; *(Essen)* meat; **~brühe** *f* beef tea, meat stock; **~er** *(-s, -)* *m* butcher; **~e'rei** *f* butcher's (shop); **f~ig** *adj* fleshy; **f~los** *adj* meatless, vegetarian

Fleiß [flaɪs] *(-es)* *m* diligence, industry; **f~ig** *adj* diligent, industrious

fletschen ['flɛtʃən] *vt (Zähne)* to show

flexibel [flɛ'ksiːbəl] *adj* flexible

Flicken ['flɪkən] *(-s, -)* *m* patch; **f~** *vt* to mend

Flieder ['fliːdɐ] *(-s, -)* *m* lilac

Fliege ['fliːgə] *f* fly; *(Kleidung)* bow tie; **f~n** *(unreg) vt, vi* to fly; **auf jdn/etw f~n** *(umg)* to be mad about sb/sth; **~npilz** *m* toadstool; **~r** *(-s, -)* *m* flier, airman

fliehen ['fliːən] *(unreg) vi* to flee

Fliese ['fliːzə] *f* tile

Fließ- ['fliːs] *zW:* **~band** *nt* production *od* assembly line; **f~en** *(unreg) vi* to flow; **f~end** *adj* flowing; *(Rede,*

Deutsch) fluent; *(Übergänge)* smooth

flimmern ['flɪmɐn] *vi* to glimmer

flink [flɪŋk] *adj* nimble, lively

Flinte ['flɪntə] *f* rifle; shotgun

Flitterwochen *f* honeymoon *sg*

flitzen ['flɪtsən] *vi* to flit

Flocke ['flɔkə] *f* flake

flog *etc* [floːk] *vb siehe* **fliegen**

Floh [floː] *(-(e)s, ⸚e)* *m* flea; **~markt** *m* flea market

florieren [floˈriːrən] *vi* to flourish

Floskel ['flɔskəl] *(-, -n)* *f* set phrase

Floß [floːs] *(-es, ⸚e)* *nt* raft, float

floss ▲ *etc vb siehe* **fließen**

Flosse ['flɔsə] *f* fin

Flöte ['fløːtə] *f* flute; *(Blockflöte)* recorder

flott [flɔt] *adj* lively; *(elegant)* smart; *(NAUT)* afloat; **F~e** *f* fleet, navy

Fluch [fluːx] *(-(e)s, ⸚e)* *m* curse; **f~en** *vi* to curse, to swear

Flucht [flʊxt] *(-, -en)* *f* flight; *(Fensterflucht)* row; *(Zimmerflucht)* suite; **f~artig** *adj* hasty

flücht- ['flʏçt] *zW:* **~en** *vi, vr* to flee, to escape; **~ig** *adj* fugitive; *(vergänglich)* transitory; *(oberflächlich)* superficial; *(eilig)* fleeting; **F~igkeitsfehler** *m* careless slip; **F~ling** *m* fugitive, refugee

Flug [fluːk] *(-(e)s, ⸚e)* *m* flight; **~blatt** *nt* pamphlet

Flügel ['flyːgəl] *(-s, -)* *m* wing; *(MUS)* grand piano

Fluggast *m* airline passenger

Flug- *zW:* **~gesellschaft** *f* airline (company); **~hafen** *m* airport; **~lärm** *m* aircraft noise; **~linie** *f* airline; **~plan** *m* flight schedule; **~platz** *m* airport; *(klein)* airfield; **~reise** *f* flight; **~schein** *m (Ticket)* plane ticket; *(Pilotenschein)* pilot's licence; **~steig** *[-staɪk]* *(-(e)s, -e)* *m* gate; **~verbindung** *f* air connection; **~verkehr** *m* air traffic; **~zeug** *nt (aero)plane*, airplane *(US)*; **~zeugentführung** *f* hijacking of a plane; **~zeughalle** *f* hangar; **~zeugträger**

aircraft carrier

Flunder ['flʊndər] (-, -n) f flounder

flunkern ['flʊŋkərn] vi to fib, to tell stories

Fluor ['fluːɔr] (-s) nt fluorine

Flur [fluːr] (-(e)s, -e) m hall; (Treppenflur) staircase

Fluss ▲ [flʊs] (-es, ⁼e) m river; (Fließen) flow

flüssig ['flʏsɪç] adj liquid; ~ machen (Geld) to make available; **F~keit** f liquid; (Zustand) liquidity

flüstern ['flʏstərn] vt, vi to whisper

Flut [fluːt] (-, -en) f (auch fig) flood; (Gezeiten) high tide; ~en vi to flood; **~licht** nt floodlight

Fohlen ['foːlən] (-s, -) nt foal

Föhn¹ [føːn] (-(e)s, -e) m (warmer Fallwind) föhn

Föhn² (-(e)s, -e) ▲ (Haartrockner) hair-dryer; **F~en** ▲ vt to (blow) dry; **~frisur** ▲ f blow-dry hairstyle

Folge ['fɔlɡə] f series, sequence; (Fortsetzung) instalment; (Auswirkung) result; **in rascher ~** in quick succession; **etw zur ~ haben** to result in sth; **~n haben** to have consequences; **einer Sache** dat **~ leisten** to comply with sth; **f~n** vi +dat to follow; (gehorchen) to obey; **jdm f~n können** (fig) to follow od understand sb; **f~nd** adj following; **f~ndermaßen** adv as follows, in the following way; **f~n** vt: **f~n (aus)** to conclude (from); **~rung** f conclusion

folglich ['fɔlklɪç] adv consequently

folgsam ['fɔlkzaːm] adj obedient

Folie ['foːliə] f foil

Folklore ['fɔlkloːər] f folklore

Folter ['fɔltər] (-, -n) f torture; (Gerät) rack; **f~n** vt to torture

Fön [føːn] (-(e)s, -e) ® m hair dryer

Fondue [fõdyː] (-s, -s od -, -s) nt od f (KOCH) fondue

fönen △ siehe **föhnen**

Fönfrisur △ f siehe **Föhnfrisur**

Fontäne [fɔn'tɛːnə] f fountain

Förder- ['fœrdər] zW: **~band** nt conveyor belt; **~korb** m pit cage; **f~lich** adj beneficial

fordern ['fɔrdərn] vt to demand

fördern ['fœrdərn] vt to promote; (unterstützen) to help; (Kohle) to extract

Forderung ['fɔrdəruŋ] f demand

Förderung ['fœrdəruŋ] f promotion; help; extraction

Forelle [fo'rɛlə] f trout

Form [fɔrm] (-, -en) f shape; (Gestaltung) form; (Guss~) mould; (Back~) baking tin; **in ~ sein** to be in good form od shape; **in ~ von** in the shape of

Formalität f formality

Format [fɔr'maːt] (-(e)s, -e) nt format; (fig) distinction

formbar adj malleable

Formblatt nt form

Formel [fɔr'mɛl] (-, -n) f formula

formell [fɔr'mɛl] adj formal

formen vt to form, to shape

Formfehler m faux pas, gaffe; (JUR) irregularity

formieren [fɔr'miːrən] vt to form ♦ vr to form up

förmlich ['fœrmlɪç] adj formal; (umg) real; **F~keit** f formality

formlos adj shapeless; (Benehmen etc) informal

Formular [fɔrmu'laːr] (-s, -e) nt form

formulieren [fɔrmu'liːrən] vt to formulate

forsch [fɔrʃ] adj energetic, vigorous

forsch- ['fɔrʃ] zW: **~en** vi: **~en (nach)** to search (for); (wissenschaftlich) to (do) research; **~end** adj searching; **F~er** (-s, -) m research scientist; (Naturforscher) explorer; **F~ung** f research

Forst [fɔrst] (-(e)s, -e) m forest

Förster ['fœrstər] (-s, -) m forester; (für Wild) gamekeeper

fort [fɔrt] adv away; (verschwunden)

Spelling Reform: ▲ new spelling △ old spelling (to be phased out)

gone; (*vorwärts*) on; **und so ~** and so on; **in einem ~** on and on; **~bestehen** (*unreg*) *vi* to survive; **~bewegen** *vt, vr* to move away; **~bilden** *vr* to continue one's education; **~bleiben** (*unreg*) *vi* to stay away; **F~dauer** *f* continuance; **~fahren** (*unreg*) *vi* to depart; (*~setzen*) to go on, to continue; **~führen** *vt* to continue, to carry on; **~gehen** (*unreg*) *vi* to go away; **~geschritten** *adj* advanced; **~pflanzen** *vr* to reproduce; **F~pflanzung** *f* reproduction

fort- *zW:* **~schaffen** *vt* to remove; **~schreiten** (*unreg*) *vi* to advance

Fortschritt ['fɔrtʃrɪt] *m* advance; **~e machen** to make progress; **f~lich** *adj* progressive

fort- *zW:* **~setzen** *vt* to continue; **F~setzung** *f* continuation; (*folgender Teil*) instalment; **F~setzung folgt** to be continued; **~während** *adj* incessant, continual

Foto ['foːto] (*-s, -s*) *nt* photo(graph); **~apparat** *m* camera; **~ graf** *m* photographer; **~gra'fie** *f* photography; (*Bild*) photograph; **f~gra'fieren** *vt* to photograph ♦ *vi* to take photographs; **~kopie** *f* photocopy

Fr. *abk* (*= Frau*) Mrs, Ms

Fracht [fraxt] *f* (*-, -en*) *f* freight; (*NAUT*) cargo; (*Preis*) carriage; **~ zahlt Empfänger** (*COMM*) carriage forward; **~er** (*-s, -*) *m* freighter, cargo boat; **~gut** *nt* freight

Frack [frak] (*-(e)s, ⁼e*) *m* tails *pl*

Frage ['fraːgə] (*-, -n*) *f* question; **jdm eine ~ stellen** to ask sb a question, to put a question to sb; **eine infrage**; **~bogen** *m* questionnaire; **f~n** *vt, vi* to ask; **~zeichen** *nt* question mark

fraglich *adj* questionable, doubtful

fraglos *adv* unquestionably

Fragment [fra'gmɛnt] *nt* fragment

fragwürdig ['fraːkvʏrdɪç] *adj* questionable, dubious

Fraktion [fraktsi'oːn] *f* parliamentary

party

frankieren [fraŋ'kiːrən] *vt* to stamp, to frank

franko ['fraŋko] *adv* post-paid; carriage paid

Frankreich ['fraŋkraɪç] (*-s*) *nt* France

Franzose [fran'tsoːzə] *m* Frenchman; **Französin** [fran'tsøːzɪn] *f* Frenchwoman; **französisch** *adj* French

fraß *etc* [fraːs] *vb siehe* **fressen**

Fratze ['fratsə] *f* grimace

Frau [frau] (*-, -en*) *f* woman; (*Ehefrau*) wife; (*Anrede*) Mrs, Ms; **~ Doktor** Doctor

Frauen- *zW:* **~arzt** *m* gynaecologist; **~bewegung** *f* feminist movement; **~haus** *nt* women's refuge; **~zimmer** *nt* female, broad (*US*)

Fräulein ['frɔʏlaɪn] *nt* young lady; (*Anrede*) Miss, Ms

fraulich ['fraulɪç] *adj* womanly

frech [frɛç] *adj* cheeky, impudent; **F~heit** *f* cheek, impudence

frei [frai] *adj* free; (*Stelle, Sitzplatz*) free, vacant; (*Mitarbeiter*) freelance; (*unbekleidet*) bare; **von etw ~ sein** to be free of sth; **im F~en** in the open air; **~ sprechen** to talk without notes; **~ Haus** (*COMM*) carriage paid; **~er Wettbewerb** (*COMM*) fair/open competition; **F~bad** *nt* open-air swimming pool; **~bekommen** (*unreg*) *vt*: **einen Tag ~bekommen** to get a day off; **~beruflich** *adj* self-employed; **~gebig** *adj* generous; **~halten** (*unreg*) *vt* to keep free; **~händig** *adv* (*fahren*) with no hands; **F~heit** *f* freedom; **~heitlich** *adj* liberal; **F~heitsstrafe** *f* prison sentence; **F~karte** *f* free ticket; **~lassen** (*unreg*) *vt* to (set) free; **~legen** *vt* to expose; **~lich** *adv* certainly, admittedly; **ja ~lich** yes of course; **F~lichtbühne** *f* open-air theatre; **F~lichtmuseum** *nt* open-air museum; **~machen** *vt* (*Post*) to frank ♦ *vr* to arrange to be free; (*entkleiden*) to undress; **Tage ~machen** to take days off;

~nehmen ▲ (unreg) vt: **sich** dat **einen Tag ~nehmen** to take a day off; **~sprechen** (unreg) vt: **~sprechen (von)** to acquit (of); **F~spruch** m acquittal; **~stehen** (unreg) vi: **es steht dir ~, das zu tun** you're free to do that; (leer stehen: Wohnung, Haus) to lie/stand empty; **~stellen** vt: **jdm etw ~stellen** to leave sth (up) to sb; **F~stoß** m free kick

Freitag m Friday; **~s** adv on Fridays

frei- zW: **~willig** adj voluntary; **F~zeit** f spare od free time; **F~zeitpark** m amusement park; **F~zeitzentrum** nt leisure centre; **~zügig** adj liberal, broad-minded; (mit Geld) generous

fremd [frɛmt] adj (unvertraut) strange; (ausländisch) foreign; (nicht eigen) someone else's; **etw ist jdm ~** sth is foreign to sb; **~artig** adj strange; **F~enführer** ['frɛmdən-] m (tourist) guide; **F~enverkehr** m tourism; **F~enverkehrsamt** nt tourist board; **F~enzimmer** nt guest room; **F~körper** m foreign body; **~ländisch** adj foreign; **F~sprache** f foreign language; **F~wort** nt foreign word

Frequenz [fre'kvɛnts] f (RADIO) frequency

fressen ▲ [frɛsn] (unreg) vt, vi to eat

Freude ['frɔydə] f joy, delight

freudig adj joyful, happy

freuen ['frɔyən] vt unpers to make happy od pleased ♦ vr to be glad od happy; **freut mich!** pleased to meet you; **sich auf etw** akk **~** to look forward to sth; **sich über etw** akk **~** to be pleased about sth

Freund ['frɔynt] (-(e)s, -e) m friend; boyfriend; **~in** [-dɪn] f friend; girlfriend; **f~lich** adj kind, friendly; **f~licherweise** adv kindly; **~lichkeit** f friendliness, kindness; **~schaft** f friendship; **f~schaftlich** adj friendly

Frieden ['fri:dən] (-s, -) m peace; **im ~**

in peacetime

Friedens- zW: **~schluss** ▲ m peace agreement; **~vertrag** m peace treaty; **~zeit** f peacetime

fried- ['fri:t] zW: **~fertig** adj peaceable; **F~hof** m cemetery; **~lich** adj peaceful

frieren ['fri:rən] (unreg) vt, vi to freeze; **ich friere, es friert mich** I'm freezing, I'm cold

Frikadelle [frika'dɛlə] f rissole

Frikassee [frika'se:] (-s, -s) nt (KOCH) fricassee

frisch [frɪʃ] adj fresh; (lebhaft) lively; **~ gestrichen!** wet paint!; **sich ~ machen** to freshen (o.s.) up; **F~e** f freshness; liveliness; **F~haltefolie** f cling film

Friseur [fri'zø:r] m hairdresser

Friseuse [fri'zø:zə] f hairdresser

frisieren [fri'zi:rən] vt to do (one's) hair; (fig: Abrechnung) to fiddle, to doctor ♦ vr to do one's hair

Frisiersalon m hairdressing salon

frisst ▲ [frɪst] vb siehe **fressen**

Frist [frɪst] (-, -en) f period; (Termin) deadline; **f~gerecht** adj within the stipulated time od period; **f~los** adj (Entlassung) instant

Frisur [fri'zu:r] f hairdo, hairstyle

frivol [fri'vo:l] adj frivolous

froh [fro:] adj happy, cheerful; **ich bin ~, dass ...** I'm glad that ...

fröhlich ['frø:lɪç] adj merry, happy; **F~keit** f merriness, gaiety

fromm [frɔm] adj pious, good; (Wunsch) idle; **Frömmigkeit** ['frœmɪçkaɪt] f piety

Fronleichnam [fro:n'laɪçna:m] (-(e)s) m Corpus Christi

Front [frɔnt] (-, -en) f front; **f~al** [frɔn'ta:l] adj frontal

fror etc [fro:r] vb siehe **frieren**

Frosch [frɔʃ] (-(e)s, -e) m frog; (Feuerwerk) squib; **~mann** m frogman; **~schenkel** m frog's leg

Frost [frɔst] (-(e)s, ⁼e) m frost; **~beule** f chilblain

frösteln ['frœstəln] vi to shiver

frostig adj frosty

Frostschutzmittel nt antifreeze

Frottier(hand)tuch [frɔ'tiːr(hant)tuːx] nt towel

Frucht [fruxt] (-, ⁼e) f (auch fig) fruit; (Getreide) corn; **f~bar** adj fruitful, fertile; **~barkeit** f fertility; **f~ig** adj (Geschmack) fruity; **f~los** adj fruitless; **~saft** m fruit juice

früh [fryː] adj, adv early; **heute ~** this morning; **F~aufsteher** (-s, -) m early riser; **F~e** f early morning; **~er** adj earlier; (ehemalig) former ♦ adv formerly; **~er war das anders** that used to be different; **~estens** adv at the earliest; **F~jahr** nt, **F~ling** m spring; **~reif** adj precocious; **F~stück** nt breakfast; **~stücken** vi to (have) breakfast; **F~stücksbüfett** nt breakfast buffet; **~zeitig** adj early; (pej) untimely

frustrieren [frʊs'triːrən] vt to frustrate

Fuchs [fʊks] (-es, ⁼e) m fox; **f~en** (umg) vt to rile, to annoy; **f~teufelswild** adj hopping mad

Fuge ['fuːgə] f joint; (MUS) fugue

fügen ['fyːgən] vt to place, to join ♦ vr: **sich ~ (in +akk)** to be obedient (to); (anpassen) to adapt oneself (to); ♦ vr unpers to happen

fühl- zW: **~bar** adj perceptible, noticeable; **~en** vt, vi, vr to feel; **F~er** (-s, -) m feeler

fuhr etc [fuːr] vb siehe **fahren**

führen ['fyːrən] vt to lead; (Geschäft) to run; (Name) to bear; (Buch) to keep ♦ vi to lead ♦ vr to behave

Führer ['fyːrər] (-s, -) m leader; (Fremdenführer) guide; **~schein** m driving licence

Führung ['fyːrʊŋ] f leadership; (eines Unternehmens) management; (MIL) command; (Benehmen) conduct; (Museumsführung) conducted tour; **~szeugnis** nt certificate of good conduct

Fülle ['fʏlə] f wealth, abundance; **f~n** vt to fill; (KOCH) to stuff ♦ vr to fill (up)

Füll- zW: **~e** f (durch KOCH) m fountain pen; **~federhalter** m fountain pen; **~ung** f filling; (Holzfüllung) panel

fummeln ['fʊməln] (umg) vi to fumble

Fund [fʊnt] (-(e)s, -e) m find

Fundament [fʊnda'mɛnt] nt foundation; **fundamen'tal** adj fundamental

Fund- zW: **~büro** nt lost property office, lost and found (US); **~grube** f (fig) treasure trove

fundiert [fʊn'diːrt] adj sound

fünf [fʏnf] num five; **~hundert** num five hundred; **~te(r, s)** adj fifth; **f~tel** (-s, -) nt fifth; **~zehn** num fifteen; **~zig** num fifty

Funk [fʊŋk] (-s) m radio, wireless; **~e** (-ns, -n) m (auch fig) spark; **f~eln** vi to sparkle; **~en** (-s, -) m (auch fig) spark; **f~en** vi (durch Funk) to signal, to radio; (umg: richtig funktionieren) to work ♦ vi (Funken sprühen) to shower with sparks; **~er** (-s, -) m radio operator; **~gerät** nt radio set; **~rufempfänger** m pager, paging device; **~streife** f police radio patrol; **~telefon** nt cellphone

Funktion [fʊŋktsi'oːn] f function; **f~ieren** [-'niːrən] vi to work, to function

für [fyːr] präp +akk for; **was ~** what kind of sort of; **das F~ und Wider** the pros and cons pl; **Schritt ~ Schritt** step by step

Furche ['fʊrçə] f furrow

Furcht [fʊrçt] (-) f fear; **f~bar** adj terrible, frightful

fürchten ['fʏrçtən] vt to be afraid of, to fear ♦ vr: **sich ~ (vor +dat)** to be afraid (of)

fürchterlich adj awful

furchtlos adj fearless

füreinander [fyːr|aɪ'nandər] adv for each other

Furnier [fʊr'niːr] (-s, -e) nt veneer

fürs [fyːrs] = **für das**

Fürsorge ['fy:ɐzɔrgə] f care; (*Sozialfürsorge*) welfare; **~r(in)** (-s, -) m(f) welfare worker; **~unterstützung** f social security, welfare benefit (US); **fürsorglich** adj attentive, caring

Fürsprache f recommendation; (um *Gnade*) intercession

Fürsprecher m advocate

Fürst [fyrst] (-en, -en) m prince; **~entum** nt principality; **~in** f princess; **f~lich** adj princely

Fuß [fu:s] (-es, ²e) m foot; (von *Glas, Säule etc*) base; (von *Möbel*) leg; zu ~ on foot; **~ball** m football; **~ballplatz** m football pitch; **~ballspiel** nt football match; **~ballspieler** m footballer; **~boden** m floor; **~bremse** f (AUT) footbrake; **~ende** nt foot; **~gänger(in)** (-s, -) m(f) pedestrian; **~gängerzone** f pedestrian precinct; **~nagel** m toenail; **~note** f footnote; **~spur** f footprint; **~tritt** m kick; (Spur) footstep; **~weg** m footpath

Futter ['fʊtɐ] (-s, -) nt fodder, feed; (*Stoff*) lining; **~al** [-'raːl] (-s, -e) nt case

füttern ['fʏtɐn] vt to feed; (*Kleidung*) to line

Futur [fu'tuːr] (-s, -e) nt future

G, g

g abk = Gramm

gab etc [gaːp] vb siehe geben

Gabe ['gaːbə] f gift

Gabel ['gaːbəl] (-, -n) f fork; **~ung** f fork

gackern ['gakɐn] vi to cackle

gaffen ['gafən] vi to gape

Gage ['gaːʒə] f fee; salary

gähnen ['gɛːnən] vi to yawn

Galerie [galə'riː] f gallery

Galgen ['galgən] (-s, -) m gallows sg; **~frist** f respite; **~humor** m macabre humour

Galle ['galə] f gall; (*Organ*) gall bladder; **~nstein** m gallstone

gammeln ['gaməln] (umg) vi to bum around; **Gammler(in)** (-s, -) (pej) m(f) layabout, loafer (inf)

Gämse ▲ ['gɛmzə] f chamois

Gang [gaŋ] (-(e)s, ²e) m walk; (*Botengang*) errand; (~art) gait; (*Abschnitt eines Vorgangs*) operation; (*Essensgang, Ablauf*) course; (*Flur etc*) corridor; (*Durchgang*) passage; (TECH) gear; **in ~ bringen** to start up; (fig) to get off the ground; **in ~ sein** to be in operation; (fig) to be under way

gang adj: **~ und gäbe** usual, normal

gängig ['gɛŋɪç] adj common, current; (*Ware*) in demand, selling well

Gangschaltung f gears pl

Ganove [ga'noːvə] (-n, -n) (umg) m crook

Gans [gans] (-, ²e) f goose

Gänse- ['gɛnzə] zW: **~blümchen** nt daisy; **~füßchen** (umg) pl (*Anführungszeichen*) inverted commas; **~haut** f goose pimples pl; **~marsch** m: **im ~marsch** in single file; **~rich** (-s, -e) m gander

ganz [gants] adj whole; (*vollständig*) complete ♦ adv quite; (*völlig*) completely; **~ Europa** all Europe; **~es Geld** all his money; **~ und gar nicht** not at all; **es sieht ~ so aus** it really looks like it; **aufs G~e gehen** to go for the lot

gänzlich ['gɛntslɪç] adj complete, entire ♦ adv completely, entirely

Ganztagsschule f all-day school

gar [gaːr] adj cooked, done ♦ adv quite: **~ nicht/nichts/keiner** not/nothing/nobody at all; **~ nicht schlecht** not bad at all

Garage [ga'raːʒə] f garage

Garantie [garan'tiː] f guarantee; **g~ren** vt to guarantee; **er kommt g~rt** he's guaranteed to come

---

Spelling Reform: ▲ *new spelling* △ *old spelling (to be phased out)*

Garbe ['garbə] f sheaf

Garde ['gardə] f guard

Garderobe [gardə'ro:bə] f wardrobe; (Abgabe) cloakroom; **~nfrau** f cloakroom attendant

Gardine [gar'di:nə] f curtain

gären ['gɛːrən] vt, vi to cook

gären ['gɛːrən] (unreg) vi to ferment

Garn [garn] (-(e)s, -e) nt thread; yarn (auch fig)

Garnele [gar'ne:lə] f shrimp, prawn

garnieren [gar'ni:rən] vt to decorate; (Speisen, fig) to garnish

Garnison [garni'zo:n] (-, -en) f garrison

Garnitur [garni'tu:r] f (Satz) set; (Unterwäsche) set of (matching) underwear; **erste ~** (fig) top rank; **zweite ~** (fig) second rate

garstig ['garstɪç] adj nasty, horrid

Garten ['gartən] (-s, ") m garden; **~arbeit** f gardening; **~gerät** nt gardening tool; **~lokal** nt beer garden; **~tür** f garden gate

Gärtner(in) ['gɛrtnər(ɪn)] (-s, -) m(f) gardener; **~ei** [-'raɪ] f nursery; (Gemüsegärtnerei) market garden (BRIT), truck farm (US)

Gärung ['gɛːrʊŋ] f fermentation

Gas [ga:s] (-es, -e) nt gas; **~ geben** (AUT) to accelerate, to step on the gas; **~hahn** m gas tap; **~herd** m gas cooker; **~kocher** m gas cooker; **~leitung** f gas pipe; **~pedal** nt accelerator, gas pedal

Gasse ['gasə] f lane, alley

Gast [gast] (-es, -e) m guest; (in Lokal) patron; **bei jdm zu ~ sein** to be sb's guest; **~arbeiter(in)** m(f) foreign worker

Gäste- ['gɛstə] zW: **~buch** nt visitors' book, guest book; **~zimmer** nt guest od spare room

Gast- zW: **g~freundlich** adj hospitable; **g~geber** (-s, -) m host; **~geberin** f hostess; **~haus** nt hotel, inn; **~hof** m hotel, inn; **g~ieren** [-'ti:rən] vi (THEAT)

to (appear as a) guest; **g~lich** adj hospitable; **~rolle** f guest role; **~spiel** nt (THEAT) guest performance; **~stätte** f restaurant; pub; **~wirt** m innkeeper; **~wirtschaft** f hotel, inn

Gaswerk nt gasworks sg

Gaszähler m gas meter

Gatte ['gatə] (-n, -n) m husband, spouse

Gattin f wife, spouse

Gattung ['gatʊŋ] f genus; kind

Gaudi ['gaʊdi] (umg: SÜDD, ÖSTERR) nt od f fun

Gaul [gaʊl] (-(e)s, Gäule) m horse; nag

Gaumen ['gaʊmən] (-s, -) m palate

Gauner ['gaʊnər] (-s, -) m rogue; **~ei** [-'raɪ] f swindle

geb. abk = **geboren**

Gebäck [gə'bɛk] (-(e)s, -e) nt pastry

gebacken [gə'bakən] adj baked; (gebraten) fried

Gebälk [gə'bɛlk] (-(e)s) nt timberwork

Gebärde [gə'bɛːrdə] f gesture; **g~n** vr to behave

gebären [gə'bɛːrən] (unreg) vt to give birth to, to bear

Gebärmutter f uterus, womb

Gebäude [gə'bɔʏdə] (-s, -) nt building; **~komplex** m (building) complex

geben ['ge:bən] (unreg) vt, vi to give; (Karten) to deal ♦ vb unpers: **es gibt** there is/are; there will be ♦ vr (sich verhalten) to behave, to act; (aufhören) to abate; **jdm etw ~** to give sth od sth to sb; **was gibts?** what's up?; **was gibt es im Kino?** what's on at the cinema?; **sich geschlagen ~** to admit defeat; **das wird sich schon ~** that'll soon sort itself out

Gebet [gə'be:t] (-(e)s, -e) nt prayer

gebeten [gə'be:tən] vb siehe **bitten**

Gebiet [gə'bi:t] (-(e)s, -e) nt area; (Hoheitsgebiet) territory; (fig) field; **g~en** (unreg) vt to command, to demand; **g~erisch** adj imperious

Gebilde [gə'bɪldə] (-s, -) nt object

gebildet adj cultured, educated

Gebirge [gə'bɪrgə] (-s, -) *nt* mountain chain

Gebiss [gə'bɪs] (-es, -e) *nt* teeth *pl*; (*künstlich*) dentures *pl*

gebissen *vb siehe* **beißen**

geblieben [gə'bli:bən] *vb siehe* **bleiben**

geblümt [gə'bly:mt] *adj* (*Kleid, Stoff, Tapete*) floral

geboren [gə'bo:rən] *adj* born; (*Frau*) née

geborgen [gə'bɔrgən] *adj* secure, safe

Gebot [gə'bo:t] (-(e)s, -e) *nt* command; (*REL*) commandment; (*bei Auktion*) bid

geboten [gə'bo:tən] *vb siehe* **bieten**

Gebr. *abk* (= *Gebrüder*) Bros.

gebracht [gə'braxt] *vb siehe* **bringen**

gebraten [gə'bra:tən] *adj* fried

Gebrauch [gə'braux] (-(e)s, Gebräuche) *m* use; (*Sitte*) custom; **g~en** *vt* to use

gebräuchlich [gə'brɔʏçlɪç] *adj* usual, customary

Gebrauchs- *zW:* **~anweisung** *f* directions *pl* for use; **g~fertig** *adj* ready for use; **~gegenstand** *m* commodity

gebraucht [gə'brauxt] *adj* used; **G~wagen** *m* secondhand od used car

gebrechlich [gə'breçlɪç] *adj* frail

Gebrüder [gə'bry:dər] *pl* brothers

Gebrüll [gə'brʏl] (-(e)s) *nt* roaring

Gebühr [gə'by:r] (-, -en) *f* charge, fee; **nach ~** fittingly; **über ~** unduly; **g~en** *vi:* **jdm g~en** to be sb's due *od* due to sb ♦ *vr* to be fitting; **g~end** fitting, appropriate ♦ *adv* fittingly, appropriately

Gebühren- *zW:* **~einheit** *f* (*TEL*) unit; **~erlass** ▲ *m* remission of fees; **~ermäßigung** *f* reduction of fees; **g~frei** *adj* free of charge; **~ordnung** *f* scale of charges, tariff; **g~pflichtig** *adj* subject to a charge

gebunden [gə'bʊndən] *vb siehe* **binden**

Geburt [gə'bu:rt] (-, -en) *f* birth

Geburtenkontrolle *f* birth control

Geburtenregelung *f* birth control

gebürtig [gə'bʏrtɪç] *adj* born in, native of; **~e Schweizerin** native of Switzerland

Geburts- *zW:* **~anzeige** *f* birth notice; **~datum** *nt* date of birth; **~jahr** *nt* year of birth; **~ort** *m* birthplace; **~tag** *m* birthday; **~urkunde** *f* birth certificate

Gebüsch [gə'bʏʃ] (-(e)s, -e) *nt* bushes *pl*

gedacht [gə'daxt] *vb siehe* **denken**

Gedächtnis [gə'dɛçtnɪs] (-ses, -se) *nt* memory; **~feier** *f* commemoration

Gedanke [gə'daŋkə] (-ns, -n) *m* thought; **sich über etw** *akk* **~n machen** to think about sth

Gedanken- *zW:* **~austausch** *m* exchange of ideas; **~los** *adj* thoughtless; **~strich** *m* dash; **~übertragung** *f* thought transference, telepathy

Gedeck [gə'dɛk] (-(e)s, -e) *nt* cover(ing); (*Speisenfolge*) menu; **ein ~ auflegen** to lay a place

gedeihen [gə'daɪən] (*unreg*) *vi* to thrive, to prosper

Gedenken *nt:* **zum ~ an jdn** in memory of sb

gedenken [gə'dɛŋkən] (*unreg*) *vi* +*gen* (*beabsichtigen*) to intend; (*sich erinnern*) to remember

Gedenk- *zW:* **~feier** *f* commemoration; **~minute** *f* minute's silence; **~stätte** *f* memorial; **~tag** *m* remembrance day

Gedicht [gə'dɪçt] (-(e)s, -e) *nt* poem

gediegen [gə'di:gən] *adj* (*good*) quality; (*Mensch*) reliable, honest

Gedränge [gə'drɛŋə] (-s) *nt* crush, crowd

gedrängt *adj* compressed; **~ voll** packed

gedrückt [gə'drʏkt] *adj* (*deprimiert*) low, depressed

Spelling Reform: ▲ new spelling △ old spelling (to be phased out)

gedrungen [gə'drʊnən] adj thickset, stocky

Geduld [gə'dʊlt] f patience; **g~en** [gə'dʊldən] vr to be patient; **g~ig** adj patient, forbearing; **~sprobe** f trial of (one's) patience

gedurft [gə'dʊrft] vb siehe **dürfen**

geehrt [gə'eːrt] adj: **Sehr ~e Frau X!** Dear Mrs X

geeignet [gə'laignət] adj suitable

Gefahr [gə'faːr] f (-, -en) f danger; ~ **laufen, etw zu tun** to run the risk of doing sth; **auf eigene ~** at one's own risk

gefährden [gə'fɛːrdən] vt to endanger

Gefahren- zW: **~quelle** f source of danger; **~zulage** f danger money

gefährlich [gə'fɛːrlɪç] adj dangerous

Gefährte [gə'fɛːrtə] (-n, -n) m companion; (*Lebenspartner*) partner

Gefährtin [gə'fɛːrtɪn] f (female) companion; (*Lebenspartner*) (female) partner

Gefälle [gə'fɛlə] (-s, -) nt gradient, incline

Gefallen[1] [gə'falən] (-s, -) m favour

Gefallen[2] [gə'falən] (-s) nt pleasure; **an etw** dat **~ finden** to derive pleasure from sth

gefallen pp von **fallen** ♦ vi: **jdm ~** to please sb; **er/es gefällt mir** I like him/it; **das gefällt mir an ihm** that's one thing I like about him; **sich** dat **etw ~ lassen** to put up with sth

gefällig [gə'fɛlɪç] adj (*hilfsbereit*) obliging; (*erfreulich*) pleasant; **G~keit** f favour; helpfulness; **etw aus G~keit tun** to do sth out of the goodness of one's heart

gefangen [gə'faŋən] adj captured; (*fig*) captivated; **~ halten** to keep prisoner; **~ nehmen** to take prisoner; **G~e(r)** f(m) prisoner, captive; **G~nahme** f capture; **G~schaft** f captivity

Gefängnis [gə'fɛŋnɪs] (-ses, -se) nt prison; **~strafe** f prison sentence; **~wärter** m prison warder; **~zelle** f

prison cell

Gefäß [gə'fɛːs] (-es, -e) nt vessel; (*auch ANAT*) container

gefasst ▲ [gə'fast] adj composed, calm; **auf etw** akk **~ sein** to be prepared od ready for sth

Gefecht [gə'fɛçt] (-(e)s, -e) nt fight; (*MIL*) engagement

Gefieder [gə'fiːdər] (-s, -) nt plumage, feathers pl

gefleckt [gə'flɛkt] adj spotted, mottled

geflogen [gə'floːgən] vb siehe **fliegen**

geflossen [gə'flɔsən] vb siehe **fließen**

Geflügel [gə'flyːgəl] (-s) nt poultry

Gefolgschaft [gə'fɔlkʃaft] f following

gefragt [gə'fraːkt] adj in demand

gefräßig [gə'frɛːsɪç] adj voracious

Gefreite(r) [gə'fraitə(r)] m lance corporal; (*NAUT*) able seaman; (*AVIAT*) aircraftman

Gefrierbeutel m freezer bag

gefrieren [gə'friːrən] (*unreg*) vi to freeze

Gefrier- zW: **~fach** nt icebox; **~fleisch** nt frozen meat; **g~getrocknet** [-gətrɔknət] adj freeze-dried; **~punkt** m freezing point; **~schutzmittel** nt antifreeze; **~truhe** f deep-freeze

gefroren [gə'froːrən] vb siehe **frieren**

Gefühl [gə'fyːl] (-(e)s, -e) nt feeling; **etw im ~ haben** to have a feel for sth; **g~los** adj unfeeling

gefühls- zW: **~betont** adj emotional; **G~duselei** [-duːzə'lai] f oversentimentality; **~mäßig** adj instinctive

gefüllt [gə'fʏlt] adj (*KOCH*) stuffed

gefunden [gə'fʊndən] vb siehe **finden**

gegangen [gə'gaŋən] vb siehe **gehen**

gegeben [gə'geːbən] vb siehe **geben** ♦ adj given; **zu ~er Zeit** in good time

gegebenenfalls [gə'geːbənənfals] adv if need be

┌─────────────────────┐
│ *SCHLÜSSELWORT* │
└─────────────────────┘

gegen ['geːgən] präp +akk **1** against; **nichts gegen jdn haben** to have nothing against sb; **X gegen Y** (*SPORT*,

JUR) X versus Y; **ein Mittel gegen Schnupfen** something for colds

2 (*in Richtung auf*) towards; **gegen Osten** to(wards) the east; **gegen Abend** towards evening; **gegen einen Baum fahren** to drive into a tree

3 (*ungefähr*) round about; **gegen 3 Uhr** around 3 o'clock

4 (*gegenüber*) towards; (*ungefähr*) around; **gerecht gegen alle** fair to all

5 (*im Austausch für*) for; **gegen bar** for cash; **gegen Quittung** against a receipt

6 (*verglichen mit*) compared with

Gegenangriff m counter-attack
Gegenbeweis m counter-evidence
Gegend ['ge:gənt] (-, -en) f area, district
Gegen- zW: **g~ei'nander** adv against one another; **~fahrbahn** f oncoming carriageway; **~frage** f counter-question; **~gewicht** nt counterbalance; **~gift** nt antidote; **~leistung** f service in return; **~maßnahme** f countermeasure; **~mittel** nt antidote, cure; **~satz** m contrast; **~sätze überbrücken** to overcome differences; **g~sätzlich** adj contrary, opposite; (*widersprüchlich*) contradictory; **g~seitig** adj mutual, reciprocal; **sich g~seitig helfen** to help each other; **~spieler** m opponent; **~sprechanlage** f (two-way) intercom; **~stand** m object; **~stimme** f vote against; **~stoß** m counterblow; **~stück** nt counterpart; **~teil** nt opposite; **im ~teil** on the contrary; **g~teilig** adj opposite, contrary

gegenüber [ge:gən'|y:bər] präp +dat opposite; (*zu*) to(wards); (*angesichts*) in the face of ♦ adv opposite; **G~** (-s, -) nt person opposite; **~liegen** (unreg) vr to face each other; **~stehen** (unreg) vr to be opposed to (each other);

JUR) X versus Y; **ein Mittel gegen Schnupfen** something for colds

2 (*in Richtung auf*) towards; **gegen Osten** to(wards) the east; **gegen Abend** towards evening; **gegen einen Baum fahren** to drive into a tree

~stellen vt to confront; (*fig*) to contrast; **G~stellung** f confrontation; (*fig*) contrast; **~treten** (unreg) vi +dat to face

Gegen- zW: **~verkehr** m oncoming traffic; **~vorschlag** m counterproposal; **~wart** f present; **g~wärtig** adj present ♦ adv at present; **das ist mir nicht mehr g~wärtig** that has slipped my mind; **~wert** m equivalent; **~wind** m headwind; **g~zeichnen** vt, vi to countersign

gegessen [gə'gɛsən] vb siehe **essen**

Gegner ['ge:gnər] (-s, -) m opponent; **g~isch** adj opposing

gegr. abk (= *gegründet*) est.

gegrillt [gə'grɪlt] adj grilled

Gehacke(s) [gə'haktə(s)] nt mince(d meat)

Gehalt¹ [gə'halt] (-(e)s, -e) m content

Gehalt² [gə'halt] (-(e)s, ⁻er) nt salary

Gehalts- zW: **~empfänger** m salary earner; **~erhöhung** f salary increase; **~zulage** f salary increment

gehaltvoll [gə'haltfɔl] adj (*nahrhaft*) nutritious

gehässig [gə'hɛsɪç] adj spiteful, nasty

Gehäuse [gə'hɔʏzə] (-s, -) nt case; casing; (*von Apfel etc*) core

Gehege [gə'he:gə] (-s, -) nt reserve; (*im Zoo*) enclosure

geheim [gə'haɪm] adj secret; **~ halten** to keep secret; **G~dienst** m secret service, intelligence service; **G~nis** (-ses, -se) nt secret; mystery; **~nisvoll** adj mysterious; **G~polizei** f secret police

gehemmt [gə'hɛmt] adj inhibited, self-conscious

gehen ['ge:ən] (unreg) vt, vi to go; (zu Fuß —) to walk ♦ vb unpers: **wie geht es (dir)?** how are you ♦ (of things?; **~ nach** (Fenster) to face; **mir/ihm geht es gut** I'm/he's (doing) fine; **geht das?** is that possible?; **gehts noch?** can you manage?; **es geht** not too bad, O.K.; **das geht nicht** that's not on; **es geht**

um etw it has to do with sth, it's about sth; **sich ~ lassen** (*unbeherrscht sein*) to lose control (of o.s.); **jdn ~ lassen** to let/leave sb alone; **lass mich ~!** leave me alone!

geheuer [gəˈhɔʏər] *adj:* **nicht ~** eerie; (*fragwürdig*) dubious

Gehilfe [gəˈhɪlfə] (**-n, -n**) *m* assistant; **Gehilfin** *f* assistant

Gehirn [gəˈhɪrn] (**-(e)s, -e**) *nt* brain; **~erschütterung** *f* concussion; **~hautentzündung** *f* meningitis

gehoben [gəˈhoːbən] *pp von* **heben** ♦ *adj* (*Position*) elevated; high

geholfen [gəˈhɔlfən] *vb siehe* **helfen**

Gehör [gəˈhøːr] (**-(e)s**) *nt* hearing; **musikalisches ~** ear; **~ finden** to gain a hearing; **jdm ~ schenken** to give sb a hearing

gehorchen [gəˈhɔrçən] *vi +dat* to obey

gehören [gəˈhøːrən] *vi* to belong ♦ *vr unpers* to be right *od* proper

gehörig *adj* proper; **~ zu** *od +dat* belonging to; part of

gehörlos *adj* deaf

gehorsam [gəˈhoːrzaːm] *adj* obedient; **G~** (**-s**) *m* obedience

Geh- ['geː-] *zW:* **~steig** *m* pavement, sidewalk (*US*); **~weg** *m* pavement, sidewalk (*US*)

Geier ['gaɪər] (**-s, -**) *m* vulture

Geige ['gaɪgə] *f* violin; **~r** (**-s, -**) *m* violinist

geil [gaɪl] *adj* randy (*BRIT*), horny (*US*)

Geisel ['gaɪzəl] (**-, -n**) *f* hostage

Geist [gaɪst] (**-(e)s, -er**) *m* spirit; (*Gespenst*) ghost; (*Verstand*) mind

geisterhaft *adj* ghostly

Geistes- *zW:* **g~abwesend** *adj* absent-minded; **~blitz** *m* brainwave; **~gegenwart** *f* presence of mind; **g~krank** *adj* mentally ill; **~kranke(r)** *f(m)* mentally ill person; **~krankheit** *f* mental illness; **~wissenschaften** *pl* the arts; **~zustand** *m* state of mind

geist- *zW:* **~ig** *adj* intellectual; mental; (*Getränke*) alcoholic; **~ig behindert**

mentally handicapped; **~lich** *adj* spiritual, religious; clerical; **G~liche(r)** *m* clergyman; **G~lichkeit** *f* clergy; **~los** *adj* uninspired, dull; **~reich** *adj* clever; witty; **~voll** *adj* intellectual; (*weise*) wise

Geiz [gaɪts] (**-es**) *m* miserliness, meanness; **g~en** *vi* to be miserly; **~hals** *m* miser; **g~ig** *adj* miserly; mean; **~kragen** *m* miser

gekannt [gəˈkant] *vb siehe* **kennen**

gekonnt [gəˈkɔnt] *adj* skilful ♦ *vb siehe* **können**

gekünstelt [gəˈkʏnstəlt] *adj* artificial, affected

Gel [geːl] (**-s, -e**) *nt* gel

Gelächter [gəˈlɛçtər] (**-s, -**) *nt* laughter

geladen [gəˈlaːdən] *adj* loaded; (*ELEK*) live; (*fig*) furious

gelähmt [gəˈlɛːmt] *adj* paralysed

Gelände [gəˈlɛndə] (**-s, -**) *nt* land, terrain; (*von Fabrik, Sportgelände*) grounds *pl;* (*Baugelände*) site; **~lauf** *m* crosscountry race

Geländer [gəˈlɛndər] (**-s, -**) *nt* railing; (*Treppengeländer*) banister(s)

gelangen [gəˈlaŋən] *vi:* **~ (an** *+akk od* **zu)** to reach; (*erwerben*) to attain; **in jds Besitz** *akk* **~** to come into sb's possession

gelangweilt [gəˈlaŋvaɪlt] *adj* bored

gelassen [gəˈlasən] *adj* calm, composed; **G~heit** *f* calmness, composure

Gelatine [ʒelaˈtiːnə] *f* gelatine

geläufig [gəˈlɔʏfɪç] *adj* (*üblich*) common; **das ist mir nicht ~** I'm not familiar with that

gelaunt [gəˈlaʊnt] *adj:* **schlecht/gut ~** in a bad/good mood; **wie ist er ~?** what sort of mood is he in?

gelb [gɛlp] *adj* yellow; (*Ampellicht*) amber; **~lich** *adj* yellowish; **G~sucht** *f* jaundice

Geld [gɛlt] (**-(e)s, -er**) *nt* money; **etw zu ~ machen** to sell sth off; **~anlage** *f* investment; **~automat** *m* cash dispenser; **~beutel** *m* purse; **~börse**

purse; **~geber** (-s, -) m financial backer; **g~gierig** adj avaricious; **~schein** m banknote; **~schrank** m safe, strongbox; **~strafe** f fine; **~stück** nt coin; **~wechsel** m exchange (of money)

Gelee [ʒeˈleː] (-s, -s) nt od m jelly

gelegen [ɡəˈleːɡən] adj situated; (passend) convenient, opportune ♦ vb siehe **liegen**; etw kommt jdm ~ sth is convenient for sb

Gelegenheit [ɡəˈleːɡənhait] f opportunity; (Anlaß) occasion; **bei jeder ~** at every opportunity; **~sarbeit** f casual work; **~skauf** m bargain

gelegentlich [ɡəˈleːɡəntlɪç] adj occasional ♦ adv sometimes; (bei Gelegenheit) some time (or other) ♦ präp +gen on the occasion of

gelehrt [ɡəˈleːrt] adj learned; **G~e(r)** f(m) scholar; **G~heit** f scholarliness

Geleise [ɡəˈlaɪzə] (-s, -) nt = **Gleis**

Geleit [ɡəˈlait] (-(e)s, -e) nt escort; **g~en** vt to escort

Gelenk [ɡəˈlɛŋk] (-(e)s, -e) nt joint; **g~ig** adj supple

gelernt [ɡəˈlɛrnt] adj skilled

Geliebte(r) [ɡəˈliːptə(r)] f(m) sweetheart, beloved

geliehen [ɡəˈliːən] vb siehe **leihen**

gelind(e) [ɡəˈlɪnd(ə)] adj mild, light; (fig: Wut) fierce; **~ gesagt** to put it mildly

gelingen [ɡəˈlɪŋən] (unreg) vi to succeed; **es ist mir gelungen, etw zu tun** I succeeded in doing sth

geloben [ɡəˈloːbən] vt, vi to vow, to swear

gelten [ˈɡɛltən] (unreg) vt (wert sein) to be worth ♦ vi (gültig sein) to hold; (erlaubt sein) to be allowed ♦ vb unpers: **es gilt, etw zu tun** it is necessary to do sth; **jdm viel/wenig ~** to mean a lot/not to mean much to sb; **was gilt die Wette?** do you bet?; **etw ~ lassen** to accept sth; **als od für etw ~**

to be considered to be sth; **jdm od für jdn ~** (betreffen) to apply to od for sb; **~d** adj prevailing; **etw ~d machen** to assert sth; **sich ~d machen** to make itself/o.s. felt

Geltung [ˈɡɛltʊŋ] f: **~ haben** to have validity; **sich/etw dat ~ verschaffen** to establish one's position/the position of sth; **etw zur ~ bringen** to show sth to its best advantage; **zur ~ kommen** to be seen/heard etc to its best advantage

Geltungsbedürfnis nt desire for admiration

Gelübde [ɡəˈlʏpdə] (-s, -) nt vow

gelungen [ɡəˈlʊŋən] adj successful

gemächlich [ɡəˈmɛːçlɪç] adj leisurely

Gemahl [ɡəˈmaːl] (-(e)s, -e) m husband; **~in** f wife

Gemälde [ɡəˈmɛːldə] (-s, -) nt picture, painting

gemäß [ɡəˈmɛːs] präp +dat in accordance with ♦ adj (+dat) appropriate (to)

gemäßigt adj moderate; (Klima) temperate

gemein [ɡəˈmain] adj common; (niederträchtig) mean; **etw ~ haben (mit)** to have sth in common (with)

Gemeinde [ɡəˈmaində] f district, community; (Pfarrgemeinde) parish; (Kirchengemeinde) congregation; **~steuer** f local rates pl; **~verwaltung** f local administration; **~wahl** f local election

Gemein- zW: **g~gefährlich** adj dangerous to the public; **~heit** f commonness; mean thing to do/to say; **g~nützig** adj charitable; **g~nütziger Verein** non-profit-making organization; **g~sam** adj joint, common (AUCH MATH) ♦ adv together, jointly; **g~same Sache mit jdm machen** to be in cahoots with sb; **etw g~sam haben** to have sth in common; **~samkeit** f community, having in common; **~schaft** f community; **in ~schaft mit** jointly od together with; **g~schaftlich** adj = **gemeinsam**; **~schaftsarbeit** f teamwork; team effort; **~sinn** m public spirit

Gemenge [gə'mɛŋə] (-s, -) nt mixture; (Handgemenge) scuffle

gemessen [gə'mɛsən] adj measured

Gemetzel [gə'mɛtsəl] (-s, -) nt slaughter, carnage, butchery

Gemisch [gə'mɪʃ] (-es, -e) nt mixture; **g~t** adj mixed

gemocht [gə'mɔxt] vb siehe **mögen**

Gemse △ ['gɛmzə] f siehe **Gämse**

Gemurmel [gə'mʊrməl] (-s) nt murmur(ing)

Gemüse [gə'my:zə] (-s, -) nt vegetables pl; **~garten** m vegetable garden; **~händler** m greengrocer

gemusst ▲ [gə'mʊst] vb siehe **müssen**

gemustert [gə'mʊstɐt] adj patterned

Gemüt [gə'my:t] (-(e)s, -er) nt disposition, nature; person; **sich dat etw zu ~e führen** (umg) to indulge in sth; **die ~er erregen** to arouse strong feelings; **g~lich** adj comfortable, cosy; (Person) good-natured; **~lichkeit** f comfortableness, cosiness; amiability

Gemüts- zW: **~mensch** m sentimental person; **~ruhe** f composure; **~zustand** m state of mind

Gen [geːn] (-s, -e) nt gene

genannt [gə'nant] vb siehe **nennen**

genau [gə'nau] adj exact, precise ♦ adv exactly, precisely; **etw ~ nehmen** to take sth seriously; **~ genommen** strictly speaking; **G~igkeit** f exactness, accuracy; **~so** adv just the same; **~so gut** just as good

genehm [gə'neːm] adj agreeable, acceptable; **~igen** vt to approve, to authorize; **sich dat etw ~igen** to indulge in sth; **G~igung** f approval, authorization; (Schriftstück) permit

General [gene'raːl] (-s, -e od ~e) m general; **~direktor** m director general;

~konsulat nt consulate general; **~probe** f dress rehearsal; **~streik** m general strike; **g~überholen** vt to overhaul thoroughly; **~versammlung** f general meeting

Generation [generatsi'oːn] f generation

Generator [gene'raːtɔr] m generator, dynamo

generell [genə'rɛl] adj general

genesen [ge'neːzən] (unreg) vi to convalesce, to recover; **Genesung** f recovery, convalescence

genetisch [ge'neːtɪʃ] adj genetic

Genf ['gɛnf] nt Geneva; **der ~er See** Lake Geneva

genial [gen'iaːl] adj brilliant

Genick [gə'nɪk] (-(e)s, -e) nt (back of the) neck

Genie [ʒe'niː] (-s, -s) nt genius

genieren [ʒe'niːrən] vt to bother ♦ vr to feel awkward od self-conscious

genießen zW: **~bar** adj edible; drinkable; **~en** [gə'niːsən] (unreg) vt to enjoy; to eat; to drink; **G~er** (-s, -) m epicure; pleasure lover; **~erisch** adj appreciative ♦ adv with relish

genmanipuliert ['geːnmanipuliːrt] adj genetically modified

genommen [gə'nɔmən] vb siehe **nehmen**

Genosse [gə'nɔsə] (-n, -n) m (bes POL) comrade, companion; **~nschaft** f cooperative (association)

Genossin f (bes POL) comrade, companion

Gentechnik ['geːntɛçnɪk] f genetic engineering

genug [gə'nuːk] adv enough

Genüge [gə'nyːgə] f: **jdm/etw ~ tun** od **leisten** to satisfy sb/sth; **g~n** vi (+dat) to be enough (for); **g~nd** adj sufficient

genügsam [gə'nyːkzaːm] adj modest, easily satisfied; **G~keit** f moderation

Genugtuung [gə'nuːktuːʊŋ] f satisfaction

Genuss ▲ {gə'nʊs} (-es, ꞏe) m pleasure; (*Zusichnehmen*) consumption; **in den ~ von etw kommen** to receive the benefit of sth; **genüsslich** ▲ {gə'nʏslɪç} adv with relish

Genussmittel ▲ pl (semi-)luxury items

geöffnet {gə'œfnət} adj open

Geograf {geo'graːf} (-en, -en) m geographer; **Geograꞏfie** f geography; **g~isch** adj geographical

Geologe {geo'loːgə} (-n, -n) m geologist; **Geoꞏloꞏgie** f geology

Geometrie {geome'triː} f geometry

Gepäck {gə'pɛk} (-(e)s) nt luggage, baggage; **~abfertigung** f luggage office; **~annahme** f luggage office; **~aufbewahrung** f left-luggage office (BRIT), baggage check (US); **~aufgabe** f luggage office; **~ausgabe** f luggage reclaim; **~netz** nt luggage rack; **~träger** m porter; (*Fahrrad*) carrier; **~versicherung** f luggage insurance; **~wagen** m luggage van (BRIT), baggage car (US)

gepflegt {gə'pfleːkt} adj well-groomed; (*Park etc*) well looked after

Gerade {gə'raːdə} f straight line; **g~aus** adv straight ahead; **g~heꞏraus** adv straight out, bluntly; **g~stehen** (*unreg*) vi: **für jdn/etw g~stehen** to be answerable for sb('s actions)/sth; **g~wegs** adv direct, straight; **g~zu** adv (*beinahe*) virtually, almost

gerade {gə'raːdə} adj straight; (*aufrecht*) upright; **eine gerade Zahl** an even number

♦ adv 1 (*genau*) just, exactly; (*speziell*) especially; **gerade deshalb** that's just od exactly why; **das ist es ja gerade!** that's just it!; **gerade du** you especially; **warum gerade ich?** why me (of all people)?; **jetzt gerade nicht!** not

now!; **gerade neben** right next to

2 (*eben, soeben*) just; **er wollte gerade aufstehen** he was just about to get up; **gerade erst** only just; **gerade noch** (only) just

gerannt {gə'rant} vb siehe **rennen**

Gerät {gə'rɛːt} (-(e)s, -e) nt device; (*Werkzeug*) tool; (SPORT) apparatus; (*Zubehör*) equipment no pl

geraten {gə'raːtən} (*unreg*) vi (*gedeihen*) to thrive; (*gelingen*): **gut/schlecht ~** to turn out well (for sb); **gut/schlecht ~** to turn out well/badly; **an jdn ~** to come across sb; **in etw** akk **~** to get into sth; **nach jdm ~** to take after sb

Geratewohl {gəraːtə'voːl} nt: **aufs ~** on the off chance; (*bei Wahl*) at random

geräuchert {gə'rɔʏçərt} adj smoked

geräumig {gə'rɔʏmɪç} adj roomy

Geräusch {gə'rɔʏʃ} (-(e)s, -e) nt sound, noise; **g~los** adj silent

gerben {'gɛrbən} vt to tan

gerecht {gə'rɛçt} adj just, fair; **jdm/etw ~ werden** to do justice to sb/sth; **G~igkeit** f justice, fairness

Gerede {gə'reːdə} (-s) nt talk, gossip

geregelt {gə'reːgəlt} adj (*Arbeit*) steady, regular; (*Mahlzeiten*) regular, set

gereizt {gə'raɪtst} adj irritable; **G~heit** f irritation

Gericht {gə'rɪçt} (-(e)s, -e) nt court; (*Essen*) dish; **mit jdm ins ~ gehen** (*fig*) to judge sb harshly; **das Jüngste ~** the Last Judgement; **g~lich** adj judicial, legal ♦ adv judicially, legally

Gerichts- zW: **~barkeit** f jurisdiction; **~hof** m court (of law); **~kosten** pl costs; **~medizin** f forensic medicine; **~saal** m courtroom; **~verfahren** nt legal proceedings pl; **~verhandlung** f trial; **~vollzieher** m bailiff

gerieben {gə'riːbən} adj grated; (*umg: schlau*) smart, wily ♦ vb siehe **reiben**

gering [gǝ'rɪŋ] *adj* slight, small; (*niedrig*) low; (*Zeit*) short; **~fügig** *adj* slight, trivial; **~schätzig** *adj* disparaging

geringste(r, s) *adj* slightest, least; **~nfalls** *adv* at the very least

gerinnen [gǝ'rɪnǝn] (*unreg*) *vi* to congeal; (*Blut*) to clot; (*Milch*) to curdle

Gerippe [gǝ'rɪpǝ] (**-s, -**) *nt* skeleton

gerissen [gǝ'rɪsǝn] *adj* wily, smart

geritten [gǝ'rɪtǝn] *vb siehe* **reiten**

gern(e) ['gɛrn(ǝ)] *adv* willingly, gladly; **~ haben, ~ mögen** to like; **etwas ~ tun** to like doing something; **ich möchte ~ ...** I'd like ...; **ja, ~** yes, please; yes, I'd like to ...; **~ geschehen** it's a pleasure

gerochen [gǝ'rɔxǝn] *vb siehe* **riechen**

Geröll [gǝ'rœl] (**-(e)s, -e**) *nt* scree

Gerste ['gɛrstǝ] *f* barley; **~nkorn** *nt* (*im Auge*) stye

Geruch [gǝ'rʊx] (**-(e)s, =e**) *m* smell, odour; **g~los** *adj* odourless

Gerücht [gǝ'rʏçt] (**-(e)s, -e**) *nt* rumour

geruhsam [gǝ'ruːzaːm] *adj* (*Leben*) peaceful; (*Nacht, Zeit*) peaceful, restful; (*langsam: Arbeitsweise, Spaziergang*) leisurely

Gerümpel [gǝ'rʏmpǝl] (**-s**) *nt* junk

Gerüst [gǝ'rʏst] (**-(e)s, -e**) *nt* (*Baugerüst*) scaffold(ing); frame

gesalzen [gǝ'zaltsǝn] *pp von* **salzen**
♦ *adj* (*umg: Preis, Rechnung*) steep

gesamt [gǝ'zamt] *adj* whole, entire; (*Kosten*) total; (*Werke*) complete; **im G~en** all in all; **G~ausgabe** *f* complete edition; **G~deutsch** *adj* all-German; **G~eindruck** *m* general impression; **G~heit** *f* totality, whole; **G~schule** *f* ≃ comprehensive school

---

Gesamtschule

The Gesamtschule is a comprehensive school for pupils of different abilities. Traditionally pupils go to either a Gymnasium, Realschule or Hauptschule, depending on ability. The Gesamtschule seeks to avoid the

---

elitism of many Gymnasien. However, these schools are still very controversial, with many parents still preferring the traditional education system.

---

gesandt [gǝ'zant] *vb siehe* **senden**

Gesandte(r) [gǝ'zantǝ(r)] *m* envoy

Gesandtschaft [gǝ'zantʃaft] *f* legation

Gesang [gǝ'zaŋ] (**-(e)s, =e**) *m* song; (*Singen*) singing; **~buch** *nt* (*REL*) hymn book

Gesäß [gǝ'zɛːs] (**-es, -e**) *nt* seat, bottom

Geschäft [gǝ'ʃɛft] (**-(e)s, -e**) *nt* business; (*Laden*) shop; (*~sabschluß*) deal; **g~ig** *adj* active, busy; (*pej*) officious; **g~lich** *adj* commercial ♦ *adv* on business

Geschäfts- *zW*: **~bedingungen** *pl* terms *pl* of business; **~bericht** *m* financial report; **~frau** *f* businesswoman; **~führer** *m* manager (*Klub*) secretary; **~geheimnis** *nt* trade secret; **~jahr** *nt* financial year; **~lage** *f* business conditions *pl*; **~mann** *m* businessman; **g~mäßig** *adj* businesslike; **~partner** *m* business partner; **~reise** *f* business trip; **~schluss ▲** *m* closing time; **~stelle** *f* office, place of business; **g~tüchtig** *adj* business-minded; **~viertel** *nt* business quarter; shopping centre; **~wagen** *m* company car; **~zeit** *f* business hours *pl*

geschehen [gǝ'ʃeːǝn] (*unreg*) *vi* to happen; **es war um ihn ~** that was the end of him

gescheit [gǝ'ʃait] *adj* clever

Geschenk [gǝ'ʃɛŋk] (**-(e)s, -e**) *nt* present, gift

Geschichte [gǝ'ʃɪçtǝ] *f* story; (*Sache*) affair; (*Historie*) History

geschichtlich *adj* historical

Geschick [gǝ'ʃɪk] (**-(e)s, -e**) *nt* aptitude; (*Schicksal*) fate; **~lichkeit** *f* skill, dexterity; **g~t** *adj* skilful

geschieden [gǝ'ʃiːdǝn] *adj* divorced

geschienen [gǝ'ʃiːnǝn] *vb siehe* **schei-**

nen

Geschirr [gə'ʃɪr] (-(e)s, -e) nt crockery; pots and pans pl; (Pferdegeschirr) harness; **~spülmaschine** f dishwasher; **~spülmittel** nt washing-up liquid; **~tuch** nt dish cloth

Geschlecht [gə'ʃlɛçt] (-(e)s, -er) nt sex; (GRAM) gender; (Gattung) race; family; **g~lich** adj sexual

Geschlechts- zW: **~krankheit** f venereal disease; **~teil** nt genitals pl; **~verkehr** m sexual intercourse

geschlossen [gə'ʃlɔsən] adj shut ♦ vb siehe **schließen**

Geschmack [gə'ʃmak] (-(e)s, =e) m taste; **nach jds ~** to sb's taste; **~ finden an etw** dat to (come to) like sth; **g~los** adj tasteless; (fig) in bad taste; **~ssinn** m sense of taste; **g~voll** adj tasteful

geschmeidig [gə'ʃmaɪdɪç] adj supple; (formbar) malleable

Geschnetzelte(s) [gə'ʃnɛtsəltə(s)] nt (KOCH) strips of meat stewed to produce a thick sauce

geschnitten [gə'ʃnɪtən] vb siehe **schneiden**

Geschöpf [gə'ʃœpf] (-(e)s, -e) nt creature

Geschoss ▲ [gə'ʃɔs] (-es, -e) nt (MIL) projectile, missile; (Stockwerk) floor

geschossen [gə'ʃɔsən] vb siehe **schießen**

geschraubt [gə'ʃraʊpt] adj stilted, artificial

Geschrei [gə'ʃraɪ] (-s) nt cries pl, shouting; (fig: Aufhebom) noise, fuss

geschrieben [gə'ʃriːbən] vb siehe **schreiben**

Geschütz [gə'ʃʏts] (-es, -e) nt gun, cannon; **ein schweres ~ auffahren** (fig) to bring out the big guns

geschützt adj protected

Geschw. abk siehe **Geschwister**

Geschwätz [gə'ʃvɛts] (-es) nt chatter,

gossip; **g~ig** adj talkative

geschweige [gə'ʃvaɪgə] adv: **~ (denn)** let alone, not to mention

geschwind [gə'ʃvɪnt] adj quick, swift; **G~igkeit** [-dɪçkaɪt] f speed, velocity; **G~igkeitsbeschränkung** f speed limit; **G~igkeitsüberschreitung** f exceeding the speed limit

Geschwister [gə'ʃvɪstər] pl brothers and sisters

geschwommen [gə'ʃvɔmən] vb siehe **schwimmen**

Geschworene(r) [gə'ʃvoːrənə(r)] f(m) juror; **~n** pl jury

Geschwulst [gə'ʃvʊlst] (-, =e) f swelling; growth, tumour

geschwungen [gə'ʃvʊŋən] pp von **schwingen** ♦ adj curved, arched

Geschwür [gə'ʃvyːr] (-(e)s, -e) nt ulcer

Gesell- [gə'zɛl] zW: **~e** (-n, -n) m fellow; (Handwerkgeselle) journeyman; **g~ig** adj sociable; **~igkeit** f sociability; **~schaft** f society; (Begleitung, comm) company; (Abendgesellschaft etc) party; **g~schaftlich** adj social; **~schaftsordnung** f social structure; **~schaftsschicht** f social stratum

gesessen [gə'zɛsən] vb siehe **sitzen**

Gesetz [gə'zɛts] (-es, -e) nt law; **~buch** nt statute book; **~entwurf** m (draft) bill; **~gebung** f legislation; **g~lich** adj legal, lawful; **g~licher Feiertag** statutory holiday; **g~los** adj lawless; **g~mäßig** adj lawful; **g~t** adj (Mensch) sedate; **g~widrig** adj illegal, unlawful

Gesicht [gə'zɪçt] (-(e)s, -er) nt face; **das zweite ~** second sight; **das ist mir nie zu ~ gekommen** I've never laid eyes on that

Gesichts- zW: **~ausdruck** m (facial) expression; **~creme** f face cream; **~farbe** f complexion; **~punkt** m point of view; **~wasser** nt face lotion; **~züge** pl features

Gesindel [gə'zɪndəl] (-s) nt rabble

gesinnt [gə'zɪnt] adj disposed, minded

Gesinnung [gə'zɪnʊŋ] f disposition; (Ansicht) views pl

gesittet [gə'zɪtət] adj well-mannered

Gespann [gə'ʃpan] (-(e)s, -e) nt team; (umg) couple

gespannt adj tense, strained; (begierig) eager; **ich bin ~, ob** I wonder if od whether; **auf etw/jdn ~ sein** to look forward to sth/meeting sb

Gespenst [gə'ʃpɛnst] (-(e)s, -er) nt ghost, spectre

gesperrt [gə'ʃpɛrt] adj closed off

Gespött [gə'ʃpœt] (-(e)s) nt mockery; **zum ~ werden** to become a laughing stock

Gespräch [gə'ʃprɛːç] (-(e)s, -e) nt conversation; discussion(s); (Anruf) call; **g~ig** adj talkative

gesprochen [gə'ʃprɔxən] vb siehe **sprechen**

gesprungen [gə'ʃprʊŋən] vb siehe **springen**

Gespür [gə'ʃpyːr] (-s) nt feeling

Gestalt [gə'ʃtalt] (-, -en) f form, shape; (Person) figure; **in ~ von** in the form of; **~ annehmen** to take shape; **g~en** vt (formen) to shape, to form; (organisieren) to arrange, to organize ♦ vr: **sich g~en (zu)** to turn out (to be); **~ung** f formation; organization

gestanden [gə'ʃtandən] vb siehe **stehen**

Geständnis [gə'ʃtɛntnɪs] (-ses, -se) nt confession

Gestank [gə'ʃtaŋk] (-(e)s) m stench

gestatten [gə'ʃtatən] vt to permit, to allow; **~ Sie?** may I?; **sich dat ~, etw zu tun** to take the liberty of doing sth

Geste ['gɛstə] f gesture

gestehen [gə'ʃteːən] (unreg) vt to confess

Gestein [gə'ʃtaɪn] (-(e)s, -e) nt rock

Gestell [gə'ʃtɛl] (-(e)s, -e) nt frame; (Regal) rack, stand

gestern ['gɛstərn] adv yesterday; **~ Abend/Morgen** yesterday evening/morning

Gestirn [gə'ʃtɪrn] (-(e)s, -e) nt star; (Sternbild) constellation

gestohlen [gə'ʃtoːlən] vb siehe **stehlen**

gestorben [gə'ʃtɔrbən] vb siehe **sterben**

gestört [gə'ʃtøːrt] adj disturbed

gestreift [gə'ʃtraɪft] adj striped

gestrichen [gə'ʃtrɪçən] adj cancelled

gestrig ['gɛstrɪç] adj yesterday's

Gestrüpp [gə'ʃtrʏp] (-(e)s, -e) nt undergrowth

Gestüt [gə'ʃtyːt] (-(e)s, -e) nt stud farm

Gesuch [gə'zuːx] (-(e)s, -e) nt petition; (Antrag) application; **g~t** adj (COMM) in demand; wanted; (fig) contrived

gesund [gə'zʊnt] adj healthy; **wieder ~ werden** to get better; **G~heit** f health(iness); **G~heit!** bless you!; **~heitlich** adj health attrib, physical ♦ adv: **wie geht es Ihnen ~heitlich?** how's your health?; **~heitsschädlich** adj unhealthy; **G~heitswesen** nt health service; **G~heitszustand** m state of health

gesungen [gə'zʊŋən] vb siehe **singen**

getan [gə'taːn] vb siehe **tun**

Getöse [gə'tøːzə] (-s) nt din, racket

Getränk [gə'trɛŋk] (-(e)s, -e) nt drink; **~ekarte** f wine list

getrauen [gə'traʊən] vr to dare, to venture

Getreide [gə'traɪdə] (-s, -) nt cereals pl, grain; **~speicher** m granary

getrennt [gə'trɛnt] adj separate

Getriebe [gə'triːbə] (-s, -) nt (Leute) bustle; (AUT) gearbox

getrieben vb siehe **treiben**

getroffen [gə'trɔfən] vb siehe **treffen**

getrost [gə'troːst] adv without any bother

getrunken [gə'trʊŋkən] vb siehe **trinken**

Getue [gə'tuːə] (-s) nt fuss

geübt [gə'yːpt] adj experienced

Gewächs [gə'vɛks] (-es, -e) nt growth;

(*Pflanze*) plant

gewachsen [gə'vaksən] *adj*: jdm/etw ~ **sein** to be sb's equal/equal to sth

Gewächshaus *nt* greenhouse

gewagt [gə'vaːkt] *adj* daring, risky

gewählt [gə'vɛːlt] *adj* (*Sprache*) refined, elegant

Gewähr [gə'vɛːr] (-) *f* guarantee; **keine** ~ **übernehmen für** to accept no responsibility for; **g~en** *vt* to grant; (*geben*) to provide; **g~leisten** *vt* to guarantee

Gewahrsam [gə'vaːrzaːm] (-s, -e) *m* safekeeping; (*Polizeigewahrsam*) custody

Gewalt [gə'valt] (-, -en) *f* power; (*große Kraft*) force; (~*taten*) violence; **mit aller** ~ with all one's might; **~anwendung** *f* use of force; **g~ig** *adj* tremendous; (*Irrtum*) huge; **~marsch** *m* forced march; **g~sam** *adj* forcible; **g~tätig** *adj* violent

Gewand [gə'vant] (-(e)s, ⁻er) *nt* gown, robe

gewandt [gə'vant] *adj* deft, skilful; (*erfahren*) experienced; **G~heit** *f* dexterity, skill

gewann *etc* [gə'van] *vb siehe* **gewinnen**

Gewässer [gə'vɛsər] (-s, -) *nt* waters *pl*

Gewebe [gə'veːbə] (-s, -) *nt* (*Stoff*) fabric; (BIOL) tissue

Gewehr [gə'veːr] (-(e)s, -e) *nt* gun; rifle; **~lauf** *m* rifle barrel

Geweih [gə'vaɪ] (-(e)s, -e) *nt* antlers *pl*

Gewerb- [gə'vɛrb] *zW*: **~e** (-s, -) *nt* trade, occupation; **Handel und ~e** trade and industry; **~eschule** *f* technical school; **~ezweig** *m* line of trade

Gewerkschaft [gə'vɛrkʃaft] *f* trade union; **~ler** (-s, -) *m* trade unionist; **~sbund** *m* trade unions federation

gewesen [gə'veːzən] *pp von* **sein**

Gewicht [gə'vɪçt] (-(e)s, -e) *nt* weight; (*fig*) importance

gewieft [gə'viːft] *adj* shrewd, cunning

gewillt [gə'vɪlt] *adj* willing, prepared

Gewimmel [gə'vɪməl] (-s) *nt* swarm

Gewinde [gə'vɪndə] (-s, -) *nt* (*Kranz*) wreath; (*von Schraube*) thread

Gewinn [gə'vɪn] (-(e)s, -e) *m* profit; (*bei Spiel*) winnings *pl*; ~ **bringend** profitable; **etw mit** ~ **verkaufen** to sell sth at a profit; **~- und Verlustrechnung** (COMM) profit and loss account; **~beteiligung** *f* profit-sharing; **g~en** (*unreg*) *vt* to win; (*erwerber*) to gain; (*Kohle, Öl*) to extract ♦ *vi* to win; (*profitieren*) to gain; **an etw** *dat* **g~en** to gain (in) sth; **g~end** *adj* (*Lächeln, Aussehen*) winning, charming; **~er(in)** (-s, -) *m(f)* winner; **~spanne** *f* profit margin; **~ung** *f* winning; gaining; (*von Kohle etc*) extraction

Gewirr [gə'vɪr] (-(e)s, -e) *nt* tangle; (*von Straßen*) maze

gewiss ▲ [gə'vɪs] *adj* certain ♦ *adv* certainly

Gewissen [gə'vɪsən] (-s, -) *nt* conscience; **g~haft** *adj* conscientious; **g~los** *adj* unscrupulous

Gewissens- *zW*: **~bisse** *pl* pangs of conscience, qualms; **~frage** *f* matter of conscience; **~konflikt** *m* moral conflict

gewissermaßen [gəvɪsər'maːsən] *adv* more or less, in a way

Gewissheit ▲ [gə'vɪshaɪt] *f* certainty

Gewitter [gə'vɪtər] (-s, -) *nt* thunderstorm; **g~n** *unpers*: **es g~t** there's a thunderstorm

gewitzt [gə'vɪtst] *adj* shrewd, cunning

gewogen [gə'voːgən] *adj* (+*dat*) well-disposed (towards)

gewöhnen [gə'vøːnən] *vt*: jdn **an etw** *akk* ~ to accustom sb to sth; (*erziehen zu*) to teach sb sth ♦ *vr*: **sich an etw** *akk* ~ to get used *od* accustomed to sth

Gewohnheit [gə'voːnhaɪt] *f* habit;

(*Brauch*) custom; **aus ~** from habit; **zur ~ werden** to become a habit

Gewohnheits- *zW:* **~mensch** *m* creature of habit; **~recht** *nt* common law

gewöhnlich [gə'vøːnlɪç] *adj* usual; ordinary; (*pej*) common; **wie ~** as usual

gewohnt [gə'voːnt] *adj* usual; **etw ~ sein** to be used to sth

Gewöhnung *f:* **~ (an** +*akk***)** getting accustomed (to)

Gewölbe [gə'vœlbə] (**-s, -**) *nt* vault

gewollt [gə'vɔlt] *adj* affected, artificial

gewonnen [gə'vɔnən] *vb siehe* **gewinnen**

geworden [gə'vɔrdən] *vb siehe* **werden**

geworfen [gə'vɔrfən] *vb siehe* **werfen**

Gewühl [gə'vyːl] (**-(e)s**) *nt* throng

Gewürz [gə'vʏrts] (**-es, -e**) *nt* spice, seasoning; **g~t** *adj* spiced

gewusst ▲ *adj siehe* **wissen**

Gezeiten [gə'tsaitən] *pl* tides

gezielt [gə'tsiːlt] *adj* with a particular aim in mind, purposeful; (*Kritik*) pointed

gezogen [gə'tsoːgən] *vb siehe* **ziehen**

Gezwitscher [gə'tsvɪtʃər] (**-s**) *nt* twitter(ing), chirping

gezwungen [gə'tsvʊŋən] *adj* forced; **~ermaßen** *adv* of necessity

ggf. *abk von* **gegebenenfalls**

gibst *etc* [gɪːpst] *vb siehe* **geben**

Gicht [gɪçt] (**-**) *f* gout

Giebel ['giːbəl] (**-s, -**) *m* gable; **~dach** *nt* gable(d) roof; **~fenster** *nt* gable window

Gier [giːr] (**-**) *f* greed; **g~ig** *adj* greedy

gießen ['giːsən] (*unreg*) *vt* to pour; (*Blumen*) to water; (*Metall*) to cast; (*Wachs*) to mould

Gießkanne *f* watering can

Gift [gɪft] (**-(e)s, -e**) *nt* poison; **g~ig** *adj* poisonous; (*fig: boshaft*) venomous; **~müll** *m* toxic waste; **~stoff** *m* toxic substance; **~zahn** *m* fang

ging *etc* [gɪŋ] *vb siehe* **gehen**

Gipfel ['gɪpfəl] (**-s, -**) *m* summit, peak; (*fig: Höhepunkt*) height; **g~n** *vi* to cul-

minate; **~treffen** *nt* summit (meeting)

Gips [gɪps] (**-es, -e**) *m* plaster; (*MED*) plaster (of Paris); **~abdruck** *m* plaster cast; **g~en** *vt* to plaster; **~verband** *m* plaster (cast)

Giraffe [gi'rafə] *f* giraffe

Girlande [gɪr'landə] *f* garland

Giro ['ʒiːro] (**-s, -s**) *nt* giro; **~konto** *nt* current account

Gitarre [gi'tarə] *f* guitar

Gitter ['gɪtər] (**-s, -**) *nt* grating, bars *pl*; (*für Pflanzen*) trellis; (*Zaun*) railing(s); **~bett** *nt* cot; **~fenster** *nt* barred window; **~zaun** *m* railing(s)

Glanz [glants] (**-es**) *m* shine, lustre; (*fig*) splendour

glänzen ['glɛntsən] *vi* to shine (*also fig*), to gleam ♦ *vt* to polish; **~d** *adj* shining; (*fig*) brilliant

Glanz- *zW:* **~leistung** *f* brilliant achievement; **g~los** *adj* dull; **~zeit** *f* heyday

Glas [glaːs] (**-es, -er**) *nt* glass; **~er** (**-s, -**) *m* glazier; **~faser** *f* fibreglass; **g~ieren** [gla'ziːrən] *vt* to glaze; **g~ig** *adj* glassy; **~scheibe** *f* pane; **~ur** [gla'zuːr] *f* glaze; (*KOCH*) icing

glatt [glat] *adj* smooth; (*rutschig*) slippery; (*Absage*) flat; (*Lüge*) downright; **Glätte** *f* smoothness; slippery

Glatteis *nt* (black) ice; **jdn aufs ~ führen** (*fig*) to take sb for a ride

glätten *vt* to smooth out

Glatze ['glatsə] *f* bald head; **eine ~ bekommen** to go bald

Glaube ['glaubə] (**-ns, -n**) *m:* **~ (an** +*akk***)** faith (in); belief (in); **g~n** *vt, vi* to believe; to think; **jdm g~n** to believe sb; **an etw akk g~n** to believe in sth; **daran g~n müssen** (*umg*) to be for it

glaubhaft ['glaubhaft] *adj* credible

gläubig ['glɔybɪç] *adj* (*REL*) devout; (*vertrauensvoll*) trustful; **G~e(r)** *f(m)* believer; **die G~en** the faithful; **G~er** (**-s, -**) *m* creditor

glaubwürdig ['glaubvʏrdɪç] *adj* credible; (*Mensch*) trustworthy; **G~keit** *f* credibility; trustworthiness

gleich [glaɪç] *adj* equal; (*identisch*) (the) same, identical ♦ *adv* equally; (*sofort*) straight away; (*bald*) in a minute; **es ist mir ~** it's all the same to you; **~ bleibend** constant; **~ gesinnt** like-minded; **2 mal 2 ~ 4** 2 times 2 is od equals 4; **~ groß** the same size; **~ nach/an** right after/at; **~altrig** *adj* of the same age; **~bedeutend** *adj* synonymous; **G~berechtigung** *f* equal rights *pl*; **~en** (*unreg*) *vi*: **jdm/etw ~en** to be like sb/sth ♦ *vr* to be alike; **~falls** *adv* likewise; **danke ~falls!** the same to you; **G~förmigkeit** *f* uniformity; **G~gewicht** *nt* equilibrium, balance; **~gültig** *adj* indifferent; (*unbedeutend*) unimportant; **G~gültigkeit** *f* indifference; **G~heit** *f* equality; **~kommen** (*unreg*) *vi* +*dat* to be equal to; **~mäßig** *adj* even, equal; **~sam** *adv* as it were; **G~schritt** *m*: **im G~schritt gehen** to walk in step; **~stellen** *vt* (*rechtlich etc*) to treat as (an) equal; **G~strom** *m* (*ELEK*) direct current; **~tun** (*unreg*) *vi*: **es jdm ~tun** to match sb; **G~ung** *f* equation; **~viel** *adv* no matter; **~wertig** *adj* (*Geld*) of the same value; (*Gegner*) evenly matched; **~zeitig** *adj* simultaneous

Gleis [glaɪs] (**-es, -e**) *nt* track, rails *pl*; (*Bahnsteig*) platform

gleiten ['glaɪtən] (*unreg*) *vi* to glide; (*rutschen*) to slide

Gleitzeit *f* flex(i)time

Gletscher ['glɛtʃər] (**-s, -**) *m* glacier; **~spalte** *f* crevasse

Glied [gliːt] (**-(e)s, -er**) *nt* member; (*Arm, Bein*) limb; (*von Kette*) link; (*MIL*) rank(s); **g~ern** [-dərn] *vt* to organize, to structure; **~erung** *f* structure, organization

glimmen ['glɪmən] (*unreg*) *vi* to glow, to gleam

glimpflich ['glɪmpflɪç] *adj* mild, lenient; **~ davonkommen** to get off lightly

glitschig ['glɪtʃɪç] *adj* (*Fisch, Weg*) slippery

glitzern ['glɪtsərn] *vi* to glitter; to twinkle

global [glo'baːl] *adj* global

Globus ['gloːbʊs] (**- od -ses, Globen od -se**) *m* globe

Glocke ['glɔkə] *f* bell; **etw an die große ~ hängen** (*fig*) to shout sth from the rooftops

Glocken- *zW*: **~blume** *f* bellflower; **~geläut** *nt* peal of bells; **~spiel** *nt* chimes; (*MUS*) glockenspiel; **~turm** *m* bell tower

Glosse ['glɔsə] *f* comment

glotzen ['glɔtsən] (*umg*) *vi* to stare

Glück [glʏk] (**-(e)s**) *nt* luck, fortune; (*Freude*) happiness; **~ haben** to be lucky; **viel ~!** good luck!; **zum ~** fortunately; **g~en** *vi* to succeed; **es g~te ihm, es zu bekommen** he succeeded in getting it

gluckern ['glʊkərn] *vi* to glug

glück- *zW*: **~lich** *adj* fortunate; (*froh*) happy; **~licherweise** *adv* fortunately; **~'selig** *adj* blissful

Glücks- *zW*: **~fall** *m* stroke of luck; **~kind** *nt* lucky person; **~sache** *f* matter of luck; **~spiel** *nt* game of chance

Glückwunsch *m* congratulations *pl*, best wishes *pl*

Glüh- ['glyː] *zW*: **~birne** *f* light bulb; **g~en** *vi* to glow; **~wein** *m* mulled wine; **~würmchen** *nt* glow-worm

Glut [gluːt] (**-, -en**) *f* (*Röte*) glow; (*Feuersglut*) fire; (*Hitze*) heat; (*fig*) ardour

GmbH [geː|ɛmbeː'haː] *f abk* (= *Gesellschaft mit beschränkter Haftung*) limited company, Ltd

Gnade ['gnaːdə] *f* (*Gunst*) favour; (*Erbarmen*) mercy; (*Milde*) clemency

---

Spelling Reform: ▲ *new spelling* △ *old spelling (to be phased out)*

Gnaden- zW: **~frist** f reprieve, respite; **g~los** adj merciless; **~stoß** m coup de grâce

gnädig ['gnɛːdɪç] adj gracious; (voll Erbarmen) merciful

Gold [gɔlt] (-(e)s) nt gold; **g~en** adj golden; **~fisch** m goldfish; **~grube** f goldmine; **g~ig** ['gɔldɪç] (umg) adj (fig: allerliebst) sweet, adorable; **~regen** m laburnum; **~schmied** m goldsmith

Golf¹ [gɔlf] (-(e)s, -e) m gulf

Golf² [gɔlf] (-s) nt golf; **~platz** m golf course; **~schläger** m golf club

Golfstrom m Gulf Stream

Gondel ['gɔndəl] (-, -n) f gondola; (Seilbahn) cable car

gönnen ['gœnən] vt: jdm etw ~ not to begrudge sb sth; **sich** dat **etw** ~ to allow o.s. sth

Gönner (-s, -) m patron; **g~haft** adj patronizing

Gosse ['gɔsə] f gutter

Gott [gɔt] (-es, ⁻er) m god; **mein** ~! for heaven's sake!; **um** ~**es willen!** for heaven's sake!; **grüß** ~! hello; **~ sei Dank!** thank God!; **g~heit** f deity

Göttin ['gœtɪn] f goddess

göttlich adj divine

gottlos adj godless

Götze ['gœtsə] (-n, -n) m idol

Grab [graːp] (-(e)s, ⁻er) nt grave; **g~en** ['graːbən] (unreg) vt to dig; **~en** (-s, ⁻) m ditch; (MIL) trench; **~stein** m gravestone

Grad [graːt] (-(e)s, -e) m degree

Graf [graːf] (-en, -en) m count, earl

Grafiker(in) ▲ [ɡraːfɪkər(ɪn)] (-s, -) m(f) graphic designer

grafisch ▲ ['ɡraːfɪʃ] adj graphic

Gram [ɡraːm] (-(e)s) m grief, sorrow

grämen ['ɡrɛːmən] vr to grieve

Gramm [ɡram] (-s, -e) nt gram(me)

Grammatik [ɡra'matɪk] f grammar

Granat [ɡraˈnaːt] (-(e)s, -e) m (Stein) garnet

Granate f (MIL) shell; (Handgranate) grenade

Granit [ɡraˈniːt] (-s, -e) m granite

Gras [ɡraːs] (-es, ⁻er) nt grass; **g~en** ['graːzən] vi to graze; **~halm** m blade of grass

grassieren [ɡraˈsiːrən] vi to be rampant, to rage

grässlich ▲ ['ɡrɛslɪç] adj horrible

Grat [ɡraːt] (-(e)s, -e) m ridge

Gräte ['ɡrɛːtə] f fishbone

gratis ['ɡraːtɪs] adj, adv free (of charge); **G~probe** f free sample

Gratulation [ɡratulatsiˈoːn] f congratulation(s)

gratulieren [ɡratu'liːrən] vi: jdm ~ (zu etw) to congratulate sb (on sth); (ich) **gratuliere!** congratulations!

grau [ɡrau] adj grey

Gräuel ▲ ['ɡrɔyəl] (-s, -) m horror, revulsion; **etw ist jdm ein** ~ sb loathes sth

Grauen (-s) nt horror; **g~** vi unpers: **es graut jdm vor etw** sb dreads sth, sb is afraid of sth ♦ vr: **sich g~ vor** to dread, to have a horror of; **g~haft** adj horrible

grauhaarig adj grey-haired

gräulich ▲ ['ɡrɔylɪç] adj horrible

grausam ['ɡrauzaːm] adj cruel; **G~keit** f cruelty

Grausen ['ɡrauzən] (-s) nt horror; **g~** = **grauen**

gravieren [ɡraˈviːrən] vt to engrave; **~d** adj grave

graziös [ɡratsiˈøːs] adj graceful

greifbar adj tangible, concrete; **in ~er Nähe** within reach

greifen ['ɡraɪfən] (unreg) vt to seize; to grip; **nach etw** ~ to reach for sth; **um sich** ~ (fig) to spread; **zu etw** ~ (fig) to turn to sth

Greis [ɡraɪs] (-es, -e) m old man; **g~enhaft** adj senile; **~in** f old woman

grell [ɡrɛl] adj harsh

Grenz- ['ɡrɛnts] zW: **~beamte(r)** m frontier official; **~e** f boundary; (Staatsgrenze) frontier; (Schranke) limit; **g~en** vi: **g~en (an** +akk) to border on;

g~enlos adj boundless; **~fall** m borderline case; **~kontrolle** f border control; **~übergang** m frontier crossing

Greuel △ ['grɔʏəl] (-s, -) m siehe **Gräuel**

greulich △ adj siehe **gräulich**

Griech- ['griːç] zW: **~e** (-n, -n) m Greek; **~enland** nt Greece; **~in** f Greek; **g~isch** adj Greek

griesgrämig ['griːsgrɛːmɪç] adj grumpy

Grieß [griːs] (-es, -e) m (KOCH) semolina

Griff [grɪf] (-(e)s, -e) m grip; (Vorrichtung) handle; **g~bereit** adj handy

Grill [grɪl] m grill; **~e** f cricket; **g~en** vt to grill; **~fest** nt barbecue party

Grimasse [grɪ'masə] f grimace

grimmig ['grɪmɪç] adj furious; (heftig) fierce, severe

grinsen ['grɪnzən] vi to grin

Grippe ['grɪpə] f influenza, flu

grob [grɔp] adj coarse, gross; (Fehler, Verstoß) gross; **G~heit** f coarseness; coarse expression

grölen ['grøːlən] (pej) vt to bawl, to bellow

Groll [grɔl] (-(e)s) m resentment; **g~en** vi (Donner) to rumble; **g~en (mit** od **+dat)** to bear ill with (towards)

groß [groːs] adj big, large; (hoch) tall; (fig) great ♦ adv greatly; **im Großen und Ganzen** on the whole; **bei jdm ~ geschrieben werden** to be high on sb's list of priorities; **~artig** adj great, splendid; **G~aufnahme** f (CINE) close-up; **G~britannien** nt Great Britain

Größe ['grøːsə] f size; (Höhe) height; (fig) greatness

Groß- zW: **~einkauf** m bulk purchase; **~eltern** pl grandparents; **g~enteils** adv mostly; **~format** nt large size; **~handel** m wholesale trade; **~händler** m wholesaler; **~macht** f great power; **~mutter** f grandmother; **~rechner** m

mainframe (computer); **g~schreiben** (unreg) vt (Wort) to write in block capitals; siehe **groß**; **g~spurig** adj pompous; **~stadt** f city, large town

größte(r, s) [grøːstə(r, s)] adj superl von **groß**; **~nteils** adv for the most part

Groß- zW: **g~tun** (unreg) vi to boast; **~vater** m grandfather; **g~ziehen** (unreg) vt to raise; **g~zügig** adj generous; (Planung) on a large scale

grotesk [gro'tɛsk] adj grotesque

Grotte ['grɔtə] f grotto

Grübchen ['gryːpçən] nt dimple

Grube ['gruːbə] f pit; mine

grübeln ['gryːbəln] vi to brood

grün [gryːn] adj green; **der ~e Punkt** green spot symbol on recyclable packaging

---

grüner Punkt

The grüner Punkt is a green spot which appears on packaging that should be kept separate from normal household refuse to be recycled through the recycling company, DSD (Duales System Deutschland). The recycling is financed by licences bought by the packaging manufacturer from DSD. These costs are often passed on to the consumer.

Grünanlage f park

Grund [grʊnt] (-(e)s, ⁓e) m ground; (von See, Gefäß) bottom; (fig) reason; **im ~e genommen** basically; siehe **aufgrund**; **~ausbildung** f basic training; **~besitz** m land(ed property), real estate; **~buch** nt land register

gründen ['grʏndən] vt to found ♦ vr: **sich ~ (auf +dat)** to be based (on); **~ auf +akk** to base on

Gründer- zW: **(-s, -)** m founder

Grund- zW: **~gebühr** f basic charge; **~gesetz** nt constitution; **~lage** f foundation; **g~legend** adj fundamental

gründlich adj thorough

Grund- zW: **g~los** adj groundless; **~regel** f basic rule; **~riss** ▲ m plan; (fig) outline; **~satz** m principle; **g~sätzlich** adj fundamental; (Frage) of principle ♦ adv fundamentally; (prinzipiell) on principle; **~schule** f elementary school; **~stein** m foundation stone; **~stück** nt estate; plot

Grundwasser nt ground water

<u>Grundschule</u>

The Grundschule is a primary school which children attend for 4 years from the age of 6 to 10. There are no formal examinations in the Grundschule but parents receive a report on their child's progress twice a year. Many children attend a Kindergarten from 3-6 years before going to the Grundschule, though no formal instruction takes place in the Kindergarten.

Grünstreifen m central reservation

grunzen ['grʊntsən] vi to grunt

Gruppe ['grʊpə] f group; **~nermäßigung** f group reduction; **g~nweise** adv in groups

gruppieren [grʊ'pi:rən] vt, vr to group

gruselig adj creepy

gruseln ['gru:zəln] vi unpers: **es gruselt jdm vor etw** sth gives sb the creeps ♦ vr to have the creeps

Gruß [gru:s] m (-es, ¨e) m greeting; (MIL) salute; **viele Grüße** best wishes; **mit freundlichen Grüßen** yours sincerely; **Grüße an** +akk regards to

grüßen ['gry:sən] vt to greet; (MIL) to salute; **jdn von jdm ~** to give sb sb's regards; **jdn ~ lassen** to send sb one's regards

gucken ['gʊkən] vi to look

gültig ['gʏltɪç] adj valid; **G~keit** f validity

Gummi ['gʊmi] (-s, -s) nt od m rubber;

(~harze) gum; **~band** nt rubber od elastic band; (Hosenband) elastic; **~bärchen** nt ≈ jelly baby (BRIT); **~baum** m rubber plant; **g~eren** [gu'mi:rən] vt to gum; **~stiefel** m rubber boot

günstig ['gʏnstɪç] adj convenient; (Gelegenheit) favourable; **das habe ich ~ bekommen** it was a bargain

Gurgel ['gʊrgəl] (-,-) f throat; **g~n** vi to gurgle; (im Mund) to gargle

Gurke ['gʊrkə] f cucumber; **saure ~** pickled cucumber, gherkin

Gurt [gʊrt] (-(e)s, -e) m belt

Gürtel ['gʏrtəl] (-s, -) m belt; (GEOG) zone; **~reifen** m radial tyre

GUS f abk (= Gemeinschaft unabhängiger Staaten) CIS

Guss ▲ [gʊs] (-es, ¨e) m casting; (Regenguß) downpour; (KOCH) glazing; **~eisen** nt cast iron

gut adj good; **alles Gute** all the best; **also gut** all right then
♦ adv well; **gut gehen** to work, to come off; **es geht jdm gut** sb's doing fine; **gut gemeint** well meant; **gut schmecken** to taste good; **jdm gut tun** to do sb good; **gut, aber ...** OK, but ...; **(na) gut, ich komme** all right, I'll come; **gut drei Stunden** a good three hours; **das kann gut sein** that may well be; **lass es gut sein** that'll do

Gut [gu:t] (-(e)s, ¨er) nt (Besitz) possession; **Güter** pl (Waren) goods; **~achten** (-s, -) nt (expert) opinion; **~achter** (-s, -) m expert; **g~artig** adj good-natured; (MED) benign; **g~bürgerlich** adj (Küche) (good) plain; **~dünken** nt: **nach ~dünken** at one's discretion

Güte ['gy:tə] f goodness, kindness; (Qualität) quality

Güter- zW: **~abfertigung** f (EISENB)

Gütezeichen

goods office; **~bahnhof** m goods station; **~wagen** m goods waggon (BRIT), freight car (US); **~zug** m goods train (BRIT), freight train (US)

Gütezeichen nt quality mark; ≈ kite mark

gut- zW: **~gehen** △ (unreg) vi unpers siehe **gut**; **~gemeint** △ adj siehe **gut**; **~gläubig** adj trusting; **G~haben** (-s) nt credit; **~heißen** (unreg) vt to approve (of)

gütig ['gy:tɪç] adj kind

Gut- zW: **g~mütig** adj good-natured; **~schein** m voucher; **g~schreiben** (unreg) vt to credit; **~schrift** f (Betrag) credit; **g~tun** △ (unreg) vi siehe **gut**; **g~willig** adj willing

Gymnasium [gym'na:zɪʊm] nt grammar school (BRIT), high school (US)

Gymnasium

The Gymnasium is a selective secondary school. After nine years of study pupils sit the Abitur so they can go on to higher education. Pupils who successfully complete six years at a Gymnasium automatically gain the mittlere Reife.

Gymnastik [gym'nastɪk] f exercises pl, keep fit

H, h

Haag [ha:k] m: **Den ~** the Hague

Haar [ha:r] (-(e)s, -e) nt hair; **um ein ~** nearly; **an den ~en herbeigezogen** (umg: Vergleich) very far-fetched; **~bürste** f hairbrush; **h~en** vi, vr to lose hair; **~esbreite** f: **um ~esbreite** by a hair's-breadth; **~festiger** (-s, -) m (hair) setting lotion; **h~genau** adv precisely; **h~ig** adj hairy; (fig) nasty; **~klammer** f hairgrip; **~nadel** f hair-

pin; **h~scharf** adv (beobachten) very sharply; (daneben) by a hair's breadth; **~schnitt** m haircut; **~spange** f hair slide; **h~sträubend** adj hair-raising; **~teil** nt hairpiece; **~waschmittel** nt shampoo

Habe ['ha:bə] (-) f property

haben ['ha:bən] (unreg) vt, vb aux to have; **Hunger/Angst ~** to be hungry/afraid; **woher hast du das?** where did you get that from?; **was hast du denn?** what's the matter (with you)?; **du hast zu schweigen** you're to be quiet; **ich hätte gern** I would like; **H~** (-s, -) nt credit

Habgier f avarice; **h~ig** adj avaricious

Habicht ['ha:bɪçt] (-s, -e) m hawk

Habseligkeiten ['ha:pze:lɪçkaɪtən] pl belongings

Hachse ['haksə] f (KOCH) knuckle

Hacke ['hakə] f hoe; (Ferse) heel; **h~n** vt to hack, to chop; (Erde) to hoe

Hackfleisch nt mince, minced meat

Hafen ['ha:fən] (-s, ¨) m harbour, port; **~arbeiter** m docker; **~rundfahrt** f boat trip round the harbour; **~stadt** f port

Hafer ['ha:fər] (-s, -) m oats pl; **~flocken** pl rolled oats; **~schleim** m gruel

Haft [haft] (-) f custody; **h~bar** adj liable, responsible; **~befehl** m warrant (for arrest); **h~en** vi to stick, to cling; **h~en für** to be liable od responsible for; **h~en bleiben** (an +dat) to stick (to); **~häftling** m prisoner; **~pflicht** f liability; **~pflichtversicherung** f (AUT) third party insurance; **~schalen** pl contact lenses; **~ung** f liability; **~ungsbeschränkung** f limitation of liability

Hagebutte ['ha:gəbʊtə] f rose hip

Hagel ['ha:gəl] (-s) m hail; **h~n** vi unpers to hail

hager ['ha:gər] adj gaunt

Hahn [ha:n] (-(e)s, ¨e) m cock; (Wasser-

hahn) tap, faucet (US)

Hähnchen ['hɛːnçən] nt cockerel; (KOCH) chicken

Hai(fisch) ['haɪ(fɪʃ)] (-(e)s, -e) m shark

häkeln ['hɛːkəln] vt to crochet

Haken ['haːkən] (-s, -) m hook; (fig) catch; **~kreuz** nt swastika; **~nase** f hooked nose

halb [halp] adj half; **~ eins** half past twelve; **~ offen** half-open; **ein ~es Dutzend** half a dozen; **H~dunkel** nt semi-darkness

halber ['halbər] präp +gen (wegen) on account of; (für) for the sake of

Halb- zW: **~heit** f half-measure; **h~ieren** vt to halve; **~insel** f peninsula; **~jahr** nt six months; (auch: KOMM) half-year; **h~jährlich** adj half-yearly; **~kreis** m semicircle; **~leiter** m semiconductor; **~mond** m half-moon; (fig) crescent; **~pension** f half-board; **~rechte(r)** mf (SPORT) inside right; **~schuh** m shoe; **h~tags** adv: **h~tags arbeiten** to work part-time, to work mornings/afternoons; **h~wegs** adv halfway; **h~wegs besser** more or less better; **~zeit** f (SPORT) half; (Pause) half-time

Halde ['haldə] f (Kohlen) heap

half [half] vb siehe **helfen**

Hälfte ['hɛlftə] f half

Halfter ['halftər] (-s, -) m od nt (für Tiere) halter

Halle ['halə] f hall; (AVIAT) hangar; **h~n** vi to echo, to resound; **~nbad** nt indoor swimming pool

hallo [ha'loː] excl hello

Halluzination [halutsinatsi'oːn] f hallucination

Halm [halm] (-(e)s, -e) m blade; stalk

Halogenlampe [halo'geːnlampə] f halogen lamp

Hals [hals] (-es, -e) m neck; (Kehle) throat; **~ über Kopf** in a rush; **~band** nt (von Hund) collar; **~kette** f necklace; **~-Nasen-Ohren-Arzt** m ear, nose and throat specialist; **~schmerzen** pl

sore throat sg; **~tuch** nt scarf

Halt [halt] (-(e)s, -e) m stop; (fester ~) hold; (innerer ~) stability; **~ od h~!** stop!, halt!; **~ machen** to stop; **h~bar** adj durable; (Lebensmittel) nonperishable; (MIL, fig) tenable; **~barkeit** f durability; (non-)perishability

halten ['haltən] (unreg) vt to keep; (festhalten) to hold ♦ vi to hold; (frisch bleiben) to keep; (stoppen) to stop ♦ vr (frisch bleiben) to keep; (sich behaupten) to hold out; **~ für** to regard as; **~ von** to think of; **an sich ~** to restrain o.s.; **sich rechts/links ~** to keep to the right/left

Halte- zW: **~stelle** f stop; **~verbot** nt: **hier ist ~verbot** there's no waiting here

Halt- zW: **h~los** adj unstable; **h~machen** △ vi siehe **Halt**; **~ung** f posture; (fig) attitude; (Selbstbeherrschung) composure

Halunke [ha'lʊŋkə] (-n, -n) m rascal

hämisch ['hɛːmɪʃ] adj malicious

Hammel ['haməl] (-s, = od -) m wether; **~fleisch** nt mutton

Hammer ['hamər] (-s, =) m hammer

hämmern ['hɛmərn] vt, vi to hammer

Hämor(rho)iden [hɛmɔro'iːdən, hɛmɔ'riːdən] pl haemorrhoids

Händedruck ['hɛndədrʊk] m handshake

Handel ['handəl] (-s) m trade; (Geschäft) transaction

Handeln ['handəln] (-s) nt action

handeln vi to trade; (agieren) to act ♦ vr unpers: **sich ~ um** to be a question of, to be about; **~ von** to be about

Handels- zW: **~bilanz** f balance of

Hand [hant] (-, =e) f hand; **~arbeit** f manual work; (Nadelarbeit) needlework; **~ball** m (SPORT) handball; **~bremse** f handbrake; **~buch** nt handbook, manual

Hamster ['hamstər] (-s, -) m hamster; **~ei** [-'raɪ] f hoarding; **h~n** vi to hoard

trade; **~kammer** f chamber of commerce; **~reisende(r)** m commercial traveller; **~schule** f business school; **h~üblich** adj customary; (Preis) going attrib; **~vertreter** m sales representative

Hand- zW: **~feger** (-s, -) m hand brush; **h~fest** adj hefty; **h~gearbeitet** adj handmade; **~gelenk** nt wrist; **~gemenge** nt scuffle; **~gepäck** nt hand luggage; **h~geschrieben** adj handwritten; **h~greiflich** adj palpable; **h~greiflich werden** to become violent; **~griff** m flick of the wrist; **h~haben** vt insep to handle

Händler ['hɛndlər] (-s, -) m trader, dealer

handlich ['hantlɪç] adj handy

Handlung ['handlʊŋ] f act(ion); (in Buch) plot; (Geschäft) shop

Hand- zW: **~schelle** f handcuff; **~schrift** f handwriting; (Text) manuscript; **~schuh** m glove; **~stand** m (SPORT) handstand; **~tasche** f handbag; **~tuch** nt towel; **~umdrehen** nt: **im ~umdrehen** in the twinkling of an eye; **~werk** nt trade, craft; **~werker** (-s, -) m craftsman, artisan; **~werkzeug** nt tools pl

Handy ['hɛndɪ] (-s, -s) nt mobile (telephone)

Hanf [hanf] (-(e)s) m hemp

Hang [haŋ] (-(e)s, ⁻e) m inclination; (Abhang) slope

Hänge- ['hɛŋə] in zW hanging; **~brücke** f suspension bridge; **~matte** f hammock

hängen ['hɛŋən] (unreg) vi to hang ♦ vt: **etw (an etw akk) ~** to hang sth (on sth); **sich ~ an** +dat (fig) to be attached to; **sich ~ an** +akk to hang on to, to cling to; **~ bleiben** to be caught; (fig) to remain, to stick; **~ bleiben an** +dat to catch od get caught on; **~ lassen** (vergessen) to leave; **den Kopf ~ las-**

sen to get downhearted

Hannover [ha'noːfər] (-s) nt Hanover

hänseln ['hɛnzəln] vt to tease

Hansestadt ['hanzəʃtat] f Hanse town

hantieren [han'tiːrən] vi to work, to be busy; **mit etw ~** to handle sth

hapern ['haːpərn] vi unpers: **es hapert an etw** dat there is a lack of sth

Happen ['hapən] (-s, -) m mouthful

Harfe ['harfə] f harp

Harke ['harkə] f rake; **h~n** vt, vi to rake

harmlos ['harmloːs] adj harmless; **H~igkeit** f harmlessness

Harmonie [harmo'niː] f harmony; **h~ren** vi to harmonize

harmonisch [har'moːnɪʃ] adj harmonious

Harn [harn] (-(e)s, -e) m urine; **~blase** f bladder

Harpune [har'puːnə] f harpoon

harren ['harən] vi: **~ (auf** +akk) to wait (for)

hart [hart] adj hard; (fig) harsh; **~ gekocht** hard-boiled

Härte ['hɛrtə] f hardness; (fig) harshness

hart- zW: **~herzig** adj hard-hearted; **~näckig** adj stubborn

Harz [haːrts] (-es, -e) nt resin

Haschee [ha'ʃeː] (-s, -s) nt hash

Haschisch ['haʃɪʃ] (-) nt hashish

Hase ['haːzə] (-n, -n) m hare

Haselnuss ▲ ['haːzəlnʊs] f hazelnut

Hasenscharte f harelip

Hass ▲ [has] (-es) m hate, hatred

hassen ['hasən] vt to hate

hässlich ▲ ['hɛslɪç] adj ugly; (gemein) nasty; **H~keit** f ugliness; nastiness

Hast [hast] f haste

hast vb siehe **haben**

hasten vi to hurry

hastig adj hasty

hat [hat] vb siehe **haben**

hatte ['hatə] vb siehe **haben**

Haube ['haubə] f hood; (Mütze) cap;

Spelling Reform: ▲ new spelling △ old spelling (to be phased out)

(AUT) bonnet, hood (US)

Hauch [haux] (-(e)s, -e) m breath; (Lufthauch) breeze; (fig) trace; **h~dünn** adj extremely thin

Haue ['haʊə] f hoe, pick; (umg) hiding; **h~n** (unreg) vt to hew, to cut; (umg) to thrash

Haufen ['haʊfən] (-s, -) m heap; (Leute) crowd; **ein ~ (x)** (umg) loads od a lot (of x); **auf einem ~** in one heap

häufen ['hɔyfən] vt to pile up ♦ vr to accumulate

haufenweise adv in heaps; in droves; **etw ~ haben** to have piles of sth

häufig ['hɔyfıç] adj frequent ♦ adv frequently; **H~keit** f frequency

Haupt [haʊpt] (-(e)s, Häupter) nt head; (Oberhaupt) chief ♦ in zW main; **~bahnhof** m central station; **h~beruflich** adv as one's main occupation; **~darsteller(in)** m(f) leading actor (actress); **~fach** nt (SCH, UNIV) main subject, major (US); **~gericht** nt (KOCH) main course

Häuptling ['hɔyptlıŋ] m chief(tain)

Haupt- zW: **~mann** (pl **-leute**) m (MIL) captain; **~person** f central figure; **~quartier** nt headquarters pl; **~rolle** f leading part; **~sache** f main thing; **h~sächlich** adj chief ♦ adv chiefly; **~saison** f high season, peak season; **~schule** f ≃ secondary school; **~stadt** f capital; **~straße** f main street; **~verkehrszeit** f rush-hour, peak traffic hours pl

---
Hauptschule

The Hauptschule is a non-selective school which pupils may attend after the Grundschule. They complete five years of study and most go on to do some vocational training.

Haus [haʊs] (-es, Häuser) nt house; **h~halten** (sparen) to economize; **nach ~e** home; **zu ~e** at home; **~apotheke** f medicine cabinet; **~arbeit** f house-

work; (SCH) homework; **~arzt** m family doctor; **~aufgabe** f (SCH) homework; **~besitzer(in)** m(f) house owner; **~besuch** m (von Arzt) house call; **~durchsuchung** f police raid; **h~eigen** adj belonging to a/the hotel/firm

Häuser- ['hɔyzər] zW: **~block** m block (of houses); **~makler** m estate agent (BRIT), real estate agent (US)

Haus- zW: **~flur** m hallway; **~frau** f housewife; **h~gemacht** adj homemade; **~halt** m household; (POL) budget; **h~halten** (unreg) vi △ siehe **Haus**; **~hälterin** f housekeeper; **~haltsgeld** nt housekeeping (money); **~haltsgerät** nt domestic appliance; **~herr** m host; (Vermieter) landlord; **h~hoch** adj: **h~hoch verlieren** to lose by a mile

hausieren [haʊ'ziːrən] vi to peddle

Hausierer (-s, -) m pedlar (BRIT), peddler (US)

häuslich ['hɔyslıç] adj domestic

Haus- zW: **~meister** m caretaker, janitor; **~nummer** f street number; **~ordnung** f house rules pl; **~putz** m house cleaning; **~schlüssel** m front door key; **~schuh** m slipper; **~tier** nt pet; **~tür** f front door; **~wirt** m landlord; **~wirtschaft** f domestic science; **~zelt** nt frame tent

Haut [haʊt] (-, Häute) f skin; (Tierhaut) hide; **~creme** f skin cream; **h~eng** adj skin-tight; **~farbe** f complexion; **~krebs** m skin cancer

Haxe ['haksə] f = Hachse

Hbf. abk = Hauptbahnhof

Hebamme ['heːpamə] f midwife

Hebel ['heːbəl] (-s, -) m lever

heben ['heːbən] (unreg) vt to raise, to lift

Hecht [hɛçt] (-(e)s, -e) m pike

Heck [hɛk] (-(e)s, -e) nt stern; (von Auto) rear

Hecke ['hɛkə] f hedge

Heckenschütze m sniper

Heckscheibe f rear window

Heer [he:r] (-(e)s, -e) nt army

Hefe ['he:fə] f yeast

Heft [heft] (-(e)s, -e) nt exercise book; (*Zeitschrift*) number; (*von Messer*) haft; **h~en** vt: **h~en (an** +akk**)** to fasten (to); (*nähen*) to tack ((on) to); **etw an etw** akk **h~en** to fasten sth to sth; **~er** (-s, -) m folder

heftig adj fierce, violent; **H~keit** f fierceness, violence

Heft- zW: **~klammer** f paper clip; **~pflaster** nt sticking plaster; **~zwecke** f drawing pin

hegen ['he:gən] vt (*Wild, Bäume*) to care for, to tend; (*fig, geh: empfinden: Wunsch*) to cherish; (: *Misstrauen*) to feel

Hehl [he:l] m od nt: **kein(en) ~ aus etw machen** to make no secret of sth; **~er** (-s, -) m receiver (of stolen goods), fence

Heide[1] ['haɪdə] (-n, -n) m heathen, pagan

Heide[2] ['haɪdə] f heath, moor; **~kraut** nt heather

Heidelbeere f bilberry

Heidentum nt paganism

Heidin f heathen, pagan

heikel ['haɪkəl] adj awkward, thorny

Heil [haɪl] (-(e)s) nt well-being; (*Seelenheil*) salvation; **h~** in one piece, intact; **~and** (-(e)s, -e) m saviour; **h~bar** adj curable; **h~en** vt to cure ♦ vi to heal; **h~froh** adj very relieved

heilig ['haɪlɪç] adj holy; **~ sprechen** to canonize; **H~abend** m Christmas Eve; **H~e(r)** f(m) saint; **~en** vt to sanctify, to hallow; **H~enschein** m halo; **H~keit** f holiness; **H~tum** nt shrine; (*Gegenstand*) relic

Heil- zW: **h~los** adj unholy; (*fig*) hopeless; **~mittel** nt remedy; **~praktiker(in)** m(f) non-medical practitioner; **h~sam** adj (*fig*) salutary; **~sarmee** f Salvation Army; **~ung** f cure

Heim [haɪm] (-(e)s, -e) nt home; **h~** adv home

Heimat ['haɪmaːt] (-, -en) f home (town/country etc); **~land** nt homeland; **h~lich** adj native, home attrib; (*Gefühle*) nostalgic; **h~los** adj homeless; **~ort** m home town/area

Heim- zW: **~computer** m home computer; **h~fahren** (unreg) vi to drive home; **~fahrt** f journey home; **h~gehen** vi to go home; (*sterben*) to pass away; **h~isch** adj (*gebürtig*) native; **sich h~isch fühlen** to feel at home; **~kehr** (-, -en) f homecoming; **h~kehren** vi to return home; **h~lich** adj secret; **~lichkeit** f secrecy; **~reise** f journey home; **~spiel** nt (*SPORT*) home game; **h~suchen** vt to afflict; (*Geist*) to haunt; **~trainer** m exercise bike; **h~tückisch** adj malicious; **~weg** m way home; **~weh** nt homesickness; **~werker** (-s, -) m handyman; **h~zahlen** vt: **jdm etw h~zahlen** to pay sb back for sth

Heirat ['haɪraːt] (-, -en) f marriage; **h~en** vt to marry ♦ vi to marry, to get married ♦ vr to get married; **~santrag** m proposal

heiser ['haɪzər] adj hoarse; **H~keit** f hoarseness

heiß [haɪs] adj hot; **~e(s) Eisen** (umg) hot potato; **h~blütig** adj hot-blooded

heißen ['haɪsən] (unreg) vi to be called; (*bedeuten*) to mean ♦ vt to command; (*nennen*) to name ♦ vi unpers: **es heißt** it says; it is said; **das heißt** that is (to say)

Heiß- zW: **~hunger** m ravenous hunger; **h~laufen** (unreg) vi, vr to overheat

heiter ['haɪtər] adj cheerful; (*Wetter*) bright; **H~keit** f cheerfulness; (*Belustigung*) amusement

Heiz- ['haɪts] zW: **h~bar** adj heated; (*Raum*) with heating; **h~en** vt to heat; **~körper** m radiator; **~öl** nt fuel oil;

Spelling Reform: ▲ new spelling △ old spelling (to be phased out)

~sonne f electric fire; **~ung** f heating
hektisch ['hɛktɪʃ] adj hectic
Held [hɛlt] (-en, -en) m hero; **h~enhaft** adj heroic; **~in** f heroine
helfen ['hɛlfən] (unreg) vi to help; (nützen) to be of use ♦ vb unpers: **es hilft nichts, du musst ...** it's no use, you'll have to ...; **jdm (bei etw) ~** to help sb (with sth); **sich** dat **zu ~ wissen** to be resourceful
Helfer (-s, -) m helper, assistant; **~shelfer** m accomplice
hell [hɛl] adj clear, bright; (Farbe, Bier) light; (Farbe, Bier) light; **~blau** adj light blue; **~blond** adj ash blond; **H~e** (-) f clearness, brightness; **~hörig** adj (Wand) paper-thin; **~hörig werden** (fig) to prick up one's ears; **H~seher** m clairvoyant; **~wach** adj wide-awake
Helm ['hɛlm] (-(e)s, -e) m helmet
Hemd [hɛmt] (-(e)s, -en) nt shirt; (Unterhemd) vest; **~bluse** f blouse
hemmen ['hɛmən] vt to check, to hold up; **gehemmt sein** to be inhibited; **Hemmung** f check; (PSYCH) inhibition; **hemmungslos** adj unrestrained, without restraint
Hengst [hɛŋst] (-es, -e) m stallion
Henkel ['hɛŋkəl] (-s, -) m handle
Henker (-s, -) m hangman
Henne ['hɛnə] f hen

<hr>
SCHLÜSSELWORT

her [heːr] adv **1** (Richtung): **komm her zu mir** come here (to me); **von England her** from England; **von weit her** from a long way away; **her damit!** hand it over!; **wo hat er das her?** where did he get that from?
2 (Blickpunkt): **von der Form her** as far as the form is concerned
3 (zeitlich): **das ist 5 Jahre her** that was 5 years ago; **wo bist du her?** where do you come from?; **ich kenne ihn von früher her** I know him from before

herab [he'rap] adv down(ward)(s); **~hängen** (unreg) vi to hang down; **~lassen** (unreg) vt to let down ♦ vr to condescend; **~lassend** adj condescending; **~setzen** vt to lower, to reduce; (fig) to belittle, to disparage

heran [he'ran] adv: **näher ~!** come up closer!; **~ zu mir!** come up to me!; **~bringen (an** +akk) to bring up (to); **~fahren** (unreg) vi: **~fahren (an** +akk) to drive up (to); **~kommen** (unreg) vi: **(an jdn/etw) ~kommen** to approach (sb/sth), to come near (to sb/sth); **~machen** vr: **sich an jdn ~machen** to make up to sb; **~treten** (unreg) vi: **mit etw an jdn ~treten** to approach sb with sth; **~wachsen** (unreg) vi to grow up; **~ziehen** (unreg) vt to pull nearer; (aufziehen) to raise; (ausbilden) to train; **jdn zu etw ~ziehen** to call upon sb to help in sth

herauf [he'raof] adv up(ward)(s), up here; **~beschwören** (unreg) vt to conjure up, to evoke; **~bringen** (unreg) vt to bring up; **~setzen** vt (Preise, Miete) to raise, put up

heraus [he'raos] adv out; **~bekommen** (unreg) vt to get out; (fig) to find out (figure out); **~bringen** (unreg) vt to bring out; (Geheimnis) to elicit; **~finden** (unreg) vt to find out; **~fordern** vt to challenge; **H~forderung** f challenge; provocation; **~geben** (unreg) vt to hand over, to surrender; (zurückgeben) to give back; (Buch) to edit; (veröffentlichen) to publish; **H~geber** (-s, -) m editor; (Verleger) publisher; **~gehen** (unreg) vi: **aus sich ~gehen** to come out of one's shell; **~halten** (unreg) vr: **sich aus etw ~halten** to keep out of sth; **~hängen**[1] vt to hang out; **~hängen**[2] (unreg) vi to hang out; **~holen** (aus) **~holen** (aus) to get out (of); **~kommen** (unreg) vi to come out; **dabei kommt nichts ~** nothing

will come of it; **~nehmen** (unreg) vt to
remove (from), take out (of); **sich** dat
etw **~nehmen** to take liberties; **~rei-**
ßen (unreg) vt to tear out; to pull out;
~rücken vt (Geld) to fork out, to hand
over; **mit etw ~rücken** (fig) to come
out with sth; **~stellen** vr: **sich ~stel-**
len (als) to turn out (to be); **~suchen**
vt: **sich** dat **jdn/etw ~suchen** to pick
sb/sth out; **~ziehen** (unreg) vt to pull
out, to extract

herb [hɛrp] adj (slightly) bitter, acid;
(Wein) dry; (fig: schmerzlich) bitter

herbei [hɛr'bai] adv (over) here;
~führen vt to bring about; **~schaffen**
vt to procure

herbemühen ['hɛːrbəmyːən] vr to
take the trouble to come

Herberge ['hɛrbɛrgə] f shelter; hostel,
inn

Herbergsmutter f warden

Herbergsvater m warden

herbitten (unreg) vt to ask to come
(here)

Herbst [hɛrpst] (-(e)s, -e) m autumn,
fall (US); **h~lich** adj autumnal

Herd [heːrt] (-(e)s, -e) m cooker; (fig,
MED) focus, centre

Herde ['heːrdə] f herd; (Schafherde)
flock

herein [hɛ'rain] adv in (here), here; **~!**
come in!; **~bitten** (unreg) vt to ask in;
~brechen (unreg) vi to set in; **~brin-**
gen (unreg) vt to bring in; **~fallen** (unreg) vi to be caught, to be taken in;
~fallen auf +akk to fall for; **~kommen**
(unreg) vi to come in; **~lassen** (unreg)
vt to admit; **~legen** vt: **jdn ~legen** to
take sb in; **~platzen** (umg) vi to burst
in

Her- zW: **~fahrt** f journey here;
h~fallen (unreg) vi: **h~fallen über** +akk
to fall upon; **~gang** m course of
events; **h~geben** (unreg) vt to give, to
hand (over); **sich zu etw h~geben** to

lend one's name to sth; **h~gehen** (unreg) vi: **hinter jdm h~gehen** to follow
sb; **es geht hoch h~** there are a lot of
goings-on; **h~halten** (unreg) vt to hold
out; **h~halten müssen** (umg) to have
to suffer; **h~hören** vi to listen

Hering ['heːrɪŋ] (-s, -e) m herring

her- [hɛr] zW: **~kommen** (unreg) vi to
come; **komm mal ~!** come here!;
~kömmlich adj traditional; **H~kunft**
(-, **-künfte**) f origin; **H~kunftsland** nt
country of origin; **H~kunftsort** m
place of origin; **~laufen** (unreg) vi:
~laufen hinter +dat to run after

hermetisch [hɛr'meːtɪʃ] adj hermetic
♦ adv hermetically

her'nach adv afterwards

Heroin [hero'iːn] (-s) nt heroin

Herr [hɛr] (-(e)n, -en) m master;
(Mann) gentleman; (REL) Lord; (vor
Namen) Mr.; **mein ~!** sir!; **meine ~en!**
gentlemen!

Herren- zW: **~haus** nt mansion; **~kon-**
fektion f menswear; **h~los** adj owner-
less; **~toilette** f men's toilet od restroom (US)

herrichten ['hɛrrɪçtən] vt to prepare

Herr- zW: **~in** f mistress; **h~isch** adj
domineering; **h~lich** adj marvellous,
splendid; **~lichkeit** f splendour, magnificence; **~schaft** f power, rule; (~
und ~in) master and mistress; **meine
~schaften!** ladies and gentlemen!

herrschen ['hɛrʃən] vi to rule; (bestehen) to prevail, to be

Herrscher(in) (-s, -) m(f) ruler

her- zW: **~rühren** vi to arise, to origi-
nate; **~sagen** vt to recite; **~stellen** vt
to make, to manufacture; **H~steller**
(-s, -) m manufacturer; **H~stellung** f
manufacture

herüber [hɛ'ryːbər] adv over (here),
across

herum [hɛ'rom] adv about, (a)round;
um etw ~ around sth; **~führen** vt to

show around; **~gehen** (*unreg*) *vi* to walk about; **um etw ~gehen** to walk *od* go round *lit*; **~kommen** (*unreg*) *vi* (*um Kurve etc*) to come round, to turn (round); **~kriegen** (*umg*) *vt* to bring *od* talk around; **~lungern** (*umg*) *vi* to hang about *od* around; **~sprechen** (*unreg*) *vt* to get around, to be spread; **~treiben** *vi*, *vr* to drift about; **~ziehen** *vi*, *vr* to wander about

herunter [hɛˈrʊntɐr] *adv* downward(s), down (there); **~gekommen** *adj* rundown; **~kommen** (*unreg*) *vi* to come down; (*fig*) to come down in the world; **~machen** *vt* to take down; (*schimpfen*) to have a go at

hervor [hɛrˈfoːr] *adv* out, forth; **~bringen** (*unreg*) *vt* to produce; (*Wort*) to utter; **~gehen** (*unreg*) *vi* to emerge, to result; **~heben** (*unreg*) *vt* to stress; (*als Kontrast*) to set off; **~ragend** *adj* (*fig*) excellent; **~rufen** (*unreg*) *vt* to cause, to give rise to; **~treten** (*unreg*) *vi* to come out (from *behind/between/ below*); (*Adern*) to be prominent

Herz [hɛrts] (**-ens, -en**) *nt* heart; (*KARTEN*) hearts *pl*; **~anfall** *m* heart attack; **~fehler** *m* heart defect; **h~haft** *adj* hearty

herziehen [ˈhɛːrtsiːən] (*unreg*) *vi*: **über jdn/etw ~** (*umg: auch fig*) to pull sb/ sth to pieces (*inf*)

Herz- *zW*: **~infarkt** *m* heart attack; **~klopfen** *nt* palpitation; **h~lich** *adj* cordial; **h~lichen Glückwunsch** congratulations *pl*; **h~liche Grüße** best wishes; **h~los** *adj* heartless

Herzog [ˈhɛrtsoːk] (**-(e)s, ̈e**) *m* duke; **~tum** *nt* duchy

Herz- *zW*: **~schlag** *m* heartbeat; (*MED*) heart attack; **~stillstand** *m* cardiac arrest; **h~zerreißend** *adj* heartrending

Hessen [ˈhɛsən] (**-s**) *nt* Hesse

hessisch *adj* Hessian

Hetze [ˈhɛtsə] *f* (*Eile*) rush; **h~n** *vt* to hunt; (*verfolgen*) to chase ♦ *vi* (*eilen*) to rush; **jdn/etw auf jdn/etw h~n** to set

sb/sth on sb/sth; **h~n gegen** to stir up feeling against; **h~n zu** to agitate for

Heu [hɔy] (**-(e)s**) *nt* hay; **Geld wie ~** stacks of money

Heuch- [ˈhɔyç] *zW*: **~elei** [-əˈlaɪ] *f* hypocrisy; **h~eln** *vt* to pretend, to feign ♦ *vi* to be hypocritical; **~ler(in)** (**-s, -**) *m(f)* hypocrite; **h~lerisch** *adj* hypocritical

heulen [ˈhɔylən] *vi* to howl; to cry

Heurige(r) [ˈhɔyrɪgə(r)] *m* new wine

Heu- *zW*: **~schnupfen** *m* hay fever; **~schrecke** *f* grasshopper; locust

heute [ˈhɔytə] *adv* today; **~ Abend/ früh** this evening/morning

heutig [ˈhɔytɪç] *adj* today's

heutzutage [ˈhɔytʦutaːgə] *adv* nowadays

Hexe [ˈhɛksə] *f* witch; **h~n** *vi* to practise witchcraft; **ich kann doch nicht h~n** I can't work miracles; **~nschuss** ▲ *m* lumbago; **~rei** *f* witchcraft

Hieb [hiːp] (**-(e)s, -e**) *m* blow; (*Wunde*) cut, gash; (*Stichelei*) cutting remark; **~e bekommen** to get a thrashing

hielt *etc* [hiːlt] *vb siehe* **halten**

hier [hiːr] *adv* here; **~ behalten** to keep here; **~ bleiben** to stay here; **~ lassen** to leave here; **~ auf** *adv* thereupon; (*danach*) after that; **~bei** *adv* herewith, enclosed; **~durch** *adv* by this means; (*örtlich*) through here; **~her** *adv* this way, here; **~hin** *adv* here; **~mit** *adv* hereby; **~nach** *adv* hereafter; **~von** *adv* about this, hereof; **~zulande, ~ zu Lande** *adv* in this country

hiesig [ˈhiːzɪç] *adj* of this place, local

hieß *etc* [hiːs] *vb siehe* **heißen**

Hilfe [ˈhɪlfə] *f* help; aid; **erste ~** first aid; **~!** help!

Hilf- *zW*: **h~los** *adj* helpless; **~losigkeit** *f* helplessness; **h~reich** *adj* helpful

Hilfs- *zW*: **~arbeiter** *m* labourer; **h~bedürftig** *adj* needy; **h~bereit** *adj* ready to help; **~kraft** *f* assistant, helper

hilfst [hɪlfst] *vb siehe* **helfen**

Himbeere ['hɪmbeːrə] f raspberry
Himmel ['hɪməl] (-s, -) m sky; (REL,
auch fig) heaven; h~**bett** nt four-poster
bed; h~**blau** adj sky-blue; ~**fahrt** f As-
cension; ~**srichtung** f direction
himmlisch ['hɪmlɪʃ] adj heavenly

─────────────────
│ SCHLÜSSELWORT │
─────────────────

hin [hɪn] adv **1** (*Richtung*): **hin und zurück** there and back; **hin und her** to
and fro; **bis zur Mauer hin** up to the
wall; **wo ist er hin?** where has he
gone?; **Geld hin, Geld her** money or
no money

2 (*auf ... hin*): **auf meine Bitte hin** at
my request; **auf seinen Rat hin** on
the basis of his advice

3: mein Glück ist hin my happiness
has gone

hinab [hɪ'nap] adv down; ~**gehen** (*unreg*) vi to go down; ~**sehen** (*unreg*) vi
to look down

hinauf [hɪ'nauf] adv up; ~**arbeiten** vr
to work one's way up; ~**steigen** (*unreg*) vi to climb

hinaus [hɪ'naus] adv out; ~**gehen** (*unreg*) vi to go out; ~**gehen über** +akk to
exceed; ~**laufen** (*unreg*) vi to run out;
~**laufen auf** +akk to come to, to
amount to; ~**schieben** (*unreg*) vt to
put off, to postpone; ~**werfen** (*unreg*)
vt (*Gegenstand, Person*) to throw out;
~**wollen** vi to want to go out; ~**wollen auf** +akk to drive at, to get at

Hinblick ['hɪnblɪk] m: **in od im ~ auf**
+akk in view of

hinder- ['hɪndər] zW: ~**lich** adj: ~**lich
sein** to be a hindrance od nuisance;
~**n** vt to hinder, to hamper; **jdn an
etw** dat ~**n** to prevent sb from doing
sth; **H~nis** (-ses, -se) nt obstacle;
H~nisrennen nt steeplechase

hindeuten ['hɪndɔytən] vi: ~ **auf** +akk
to point to

hindurch [hɪn'dʊrç] adv through;
across; (*zeitlich*) through(out)

hinein [hɪ'naɪn] adv in; ~**fallen** (*unreg*)
vi to fall in; ~**fallen in** +akk to fall into;
~**gehen** (*unreg*) vi to go in; ~**gehen in**
+akk to go into, to enter; ~**geraten**
(*unreg*): ~**geraten in** +akk to get into;
~**passen** vi to fit in; ~**passen in** +akk
to fit into; (*fig*) to fit in with; ~**steigern** vr to get worked up; ~**versetzen** vr: **sich ~versetzen in** +akk to put
o.s. in the position of; ~**ziehen** (*unreg*)
vt to pull in ♦ vi to go in

hin- ['hɪn] zW: ~**fahren** (*unreg*) vi to
go; to drive ♦ vt to take; to drive;
H~fahrt f journey there; ~**fallen** (*unreg*) vi to fall (down); ~**fällig** adj frail;
(*fig: ungültig*) invalid; **H~flug** m outward flight; **H~gabe** f devotion; ~**geben** (*unreg*) vr +dat to give o.s. up to,
to devote o.s. to; ~**gehen** (*unreg*) vi to
go; (*Zeit*) to pass; ~**halten** (*unreg*) vt to
hold out; (*warten lassen*) to put off, to
stall

hinken ['hɪŋkən] vi to limp; (*Vergleich*)
to be unconvincing

hinkommen (*unreg*) vi (*an Ort*) to arrive

hin- ['hɪn] zW: ~**legen** vt to put down
♦ vr to lie down; ~**nehmen** (*unreg*) vt
(*fig*) to put up with, to take; **H~reise** f
journey out; ~**reißen** (*unreg*) vt to carry away, to enrapture; **sich ~reißen
lassen, etw zu tun** to get carried
away and do sth; ~**richten** vt to execute; **H~richtung** f execution; ~**set-
zen** vr to sit down; ~**sichtlich** präp +gen with regard to;
~**stellen** vt to put (down) ♦ vr to
place o.s.

hinten ['hɪntən] adv at the back; behind; ~**herum** adv round the back;
(*fig*) secretly

hinter ['hɪntər] präp (+dat od akk) behind; (*: nach*) after; ~ **jdm her sein** to

─────────────────

Spelling Reform: ▲ new spelling △ old spelling (to be phased out)

be after sb; **H~achse** f rear axle; **H~bliebene(r)** f(m) surviving relative; **~e(r, s)** adj rear, back; **~einander** adv one after the other; **~gedanke** m ulterior motive; **~gehen** (unreg) vt to deceive; **H~grund** m background; **H~halt** m ambush; **~hältig** adj underhand, sneaky; **~her** adv afterwards, after; **H~hof** m backyard; **H~kopf** m back of one's head; **~lassen** (unreg) vt to leave; **~ legen** vt to deposit; **H~list** f cunning, trickery; (Handlung) trick, dodge; **~listig** adj cunning, crafty; **H~mann** m person behind; **H~rad** nt back wheel; **H~radantrieb** m (AUT) rear wheel drive; **~rücks** adv from behind; **H~tür** f back door; (fig: Ausweg) loophole; **~ ziehen** (unreg) vt (Steuern) to evade

hinüber [hɪ'ny:bər] adv across, over; **~gehen** (unreg) vi to go over od across

hinunter [hɪ'nʊntər] adv down; **~bringen** (unreg) vt to take down; **~schlucken** vt (auch fig) to swallow; **~steigen** (unreg) vi to descend

Hinweg ['hɪnvɛk] m journey out

hinweghelfen [hɪn'vɛk-] (unreg) vi: **jdm über etw** akk **~** to help sb to get over sth

hinwegsetzen [hɪn'vɛk-] vr: **sich ~ über** +akk to disregard

hin- ['hɪn] zW: **H~weis** (**-es**, **-e**) m (Andeutung) hint; (Anweisung) instruction; (Verweis) reference; **~weisen** (unreg) vi: **~weisen auf** +akk (anzeigen) to point to; (sagen) to point out, to refer to; (Verweis) to throw down; **~ziehen** (unreg) vr (fig) to drag on

hinzu [hɪn'tsu:] adv in addition; **~fügen** vt to add; **~kommen** (unreg) vi (Mensch) to arrive, to turn up; (Umstand) to ensue

Hirn [hɪrn] (**-(e)s**, **-e**) nt brain(s); **~gespinst** (**-(e)s**, **-e**) nt fantasy

Hirsch [hɪrʃ] (**-(e)s**, **-e**) m stag

Hirt ['hɪrt] (**-en**, **-en**) m herdsman; (Schafhirt) m shepherd

hissen ['hɪsən] vt to hoist

Historiker [hɪs'to:rikər] (**-s**, **-**) m historian

historisch [hɪs'to:rɪʃ] adj historical

Hitze ['hɪtsə] (**-**) f heat; **h~beständig** adj heat-resistant; **h~frei** adj: **h~frei haben** to have time off school because of excessively hot weather; **~welle** f heat wave

hitzig ['hɪtsɪç] adj hot-tempered; (Debatte) heated

Hitzkopf m hothead

Hitzschlag m heatstroke

hl. abk von **heilig**

H-Milch ['ha:mɪlç] f long-life milk

Hobby ['hɔbi] (**-s**, **-s**) nt hobby

Hobel ['ho:bəl] (**-s**, **-**) m plane; **~bank** f carpenter's bench; **h~n** vt, vi to plane; **~späne** pl wood shavings

Hoch (**-s**, **-s**) nt (Ruf) cheer; (MET) anticyclone

hoch [ho:x] (attrib **hohe(r, s)**) adj high; ♦ adv: **~ achten** to respect; **~ begabt** extremely gifted; **~ dotiert** highly paid; **H~achtung** f respect, esteem; **~achtungsvoll** adv yours faithfully; **H~amt** nt high mass; **~arbeiten** vr to work one's way up; **H~betrieb** m intense activity; (COMM) peak time; **H~burg** f stronghold; **H~deutsch** nt High German; **H~druck** m high pressure; **H~ebene** f plateau; **H~form** f top form; **H~gebirge** nt high mountains pl; **H~glanz** m (PHOT) high gloss print; **etw** auf **H~glanz bringen** to make sth sparkle like new; **~halten** (unreg) vt to hold up; (fig) to uphold, to cherish; **H~haus** nt multi-storey building; **~heben** (unreg) vt to lift (up); **H~konjunktur** f boom; **H~land** nt highlands pl; **~leben** vi: **jdn ~leben lassen** to give sb three cheers; **H~mut** m pride; **~mütig** adj proud, haughty; **~näsig** adj stuck-up, snooty; **H~ofen** m blast furnace; **~prozentig** adj (Alkohol) strong; **H~rechnung** f projection; **H~saison** f high season;

H~schule f college; university; difference in altitude
H~sommer m middle of summer; **Höhepunkt** m climax
H~spannung f high tension; **höher** adj, adv higher
H~sprung m high jump **hohl** [hoːl] adj hollow
höchst [høːçst] adv highly, extremely **Höhle** ['høːlə] f cave, hole; (Mundhöhle) cavity; (fig, ZOOL) den
Hochstapler ['hoːxstaːplər] (-s, -) m swindler **Hohlmaß** nt measure of volume
höchste(r, s) adj highest; (äußerste) **Hohn** [hoːn] (-(e)s) m scorn
extreme **höhnisch** adj scornful, taunting
Höchst- zW: **h~ens** adv at the most; **holen** ['hoːlən] vt to get, to fetch; **~geschwindigkeit** f maximum (Atem) to take; **jdn/etw ~ lassen** to speed; **h~persönlich** adv in person; send for sb/sth
~preis m maximum price; **Holland** ['hɔlant] nt Holland; **Holländer** ['hɔlɛndər] m Dutchman; **holländisch** adj Dutch
Hoch- zW: **~verrat** m high treason; **Hölle** ['hœlə] f hell
~wasser nt high water; (Überschwemmung) floods pl **höllisch** ['hœlɪʃ] adj hellish, infernal
Hochzeit ['hɔxtsaɪt] (-, -en) f wedding; **holperig** ['hɔlpərɪç] adj rough, bumpy
~sreise f honeymoon **Holunder** [ho'lʊndər] (-s, -) m elder
hocken ['hɔkən] vi, vt to squat, to **Holz** [hɔlts] (-es, ⁻er) nt wood
crouch **hölzern** ['hœltsərn] adj (auch fig)
Hocker (-s, -) m stool wooden
Höcker ['hœkər] (-s, -) m hump **Holz-** zW: **~fäller** (-s, -) m lumberjack,
Hoden ['hoːdən] (-s, -) m testicle woodcutter; **h~ig** adj woody; **~kohle**
Hof [hoːf] (-(e)s, ⁻e) m (Hinterhof) yard; f charcoal; **~schuh** m clog; **~weg** m
(Bauernhof) farm; (Königshof) court (fig) wrong track; **~wolle** f fine wood
hoff- ['hɔf] zW: **~en** vi: **~en (auf** +akk) shavings pl
to hope (for); **~entlich** adv I hope, **Homöopathie** [homøopa'tiː] f
hopefully; **H~nung** f hope homeopathy
Hoffnungs- zW: **h~los** adj hopeless; **homosexuell** [homozɛksu'ɛl] adj
~losigkeit f hopelessness; **h~voll** adj homosexual
hopeful **Honig** ['hoːnɪç] (-s, -e) m honey; **~melone** (BOT, KOCH) honeydew melon;
höflich ['høːflɪç] adj polite, courteous; **~wabe** f honeycomb
H~keit f courtesy, politeness **Honorar** [hono'raːr] (-s, -e) nt fee
hohe(r, s) adj attrib siehe **Hopfen** ['hɔpfən] (-s, -) m hops pl
hoch **hopsen** ['hɔpsən] vi to hop
Höhe ['høːə] f height; (Anhöhe) hill **Hörapparat** m hearing aid
Hoheit ['hoːhaɪt] f (POL) sovereignty; **hörbar** adj audible
(Titel) Highness **horchen** ['hɔrçən] vi to listen; (pej) to
Hoheits- zW: **~gebiet** nt sovereign eavesdrop
territory; **~gewässer** nt territorial wa- **Horde** ['hɔrdə] f horde
ters pl **hör-** ['høːr] zW: **~en** vt, vi to hear;
Höhen- ['høːən] zW: **~luft** f mountain Musik/Radio **~en** to listen to music/
air; **~messer** (-s, -) m altimeter; the radio; **H~er** (-s, -) m hearer;
~sonne f sun lamp; **~unterschied** m

(RADIO) listener; *(UNIV)* student; *(Telefonhörer)* receiver; **H~funk** (-s) *m* radio; **~geschädigt** [-gəʃɛːdɪçt] *adj* hearing-impaired

Horizont [hori'tsɔnt] (-(e)s, -e) *m* horizon; **h~al** [-'taːl] *adj* horizontal

Hormon [hɔr'moːn] (-s, -e) *nt* hormone

Hörmuschel *f (TEL)* earpiece

Horn [hɔrn] (-(e)s, "er) *nt* horn; **~haut** *f* horny skin

Hornisse [hɔr'nɪsə] *f* hornet

Horoskop [horo'skoːp] (-s, -e) *nt* horoscope

Hörspiel *nt* radio play

Hort [hɔrt] (-(e)s, -e) *m (SCH)* day centre for schoolchildren whose parents are at work

horten ['hɔrtən] *vt* to hoard

Hose ['hoːzə] *f* trousers *pl*, pants *pl (US)*

Hosen- *zW:* **~anzug** *m* trouser suit; **~rock** *m* culottes *pl*; **~tasche** *f* (trouser) pocket; **~träger** *m* braces *pl (BRIT)*, suspenders *pl (US)*

Hostie ['hɔstiə] *f (REL)* host

Hotel [ho'tɛl] (-s, -s) *nt* hotel; **~ier** (-s, -s) [hoteli'eː] *m* hotelkeeper, hotelier; **~verzeichnis** *nt* hotel register

Hubraum ['huːp-] *m (AUT)* cubic capacity

hübsch [hʏpʃ] *adj* pretty, nice

Hubschrauber ['huːpʃraubɐ] (-s, -) *m* helicopter

Huf [huːf] (-(e)s, -e) *m* hoof; **~eisen** *nt* horseshoe

Hüft- ['hʏft] *zW:* **~e** *f* hip; **~gürtel** *m* girdle; **~halter** (-s, -) *m* girdle

Hügel ['hyːgəl] (-s, -) *m* hill; **h~ig** *adj* hilly

Huhn [huːn] (-(e)s, "er) *nt* hen; *(KOCH)* chicken

Hühner- ['hyːnɐr] *zW:* **~auge** *nt* corn; **~brühe** *f* chicken broth

Hülle ['hʏlə] *f* cover(ing); wrapping; **in ~ und Fülle** galore; **h~n** *vt:* **h~n (in** +*akk*) to cover (with); to wrap (in)

Hülse ['hʏlzə] *f* husk, shell; **~nfrucht** *f*

pulse

human [hu'maːn] *adj* humane; **~i'tär** *adj* humanitarian; **H~i'tät** *f* humanity

Hummel ['hʊməl] (-, -n) *f* bumblebee

Hummer ['hʊmɐ] (-s, -) *m* lobster

Humor [hu'moːr] (-s, -e) *m* humour; **~ haben** to have a sense of humour; **~ist** [-'rɪst] *m* humorist; **h~voll** *adj* humorous

humpeln ['hʊmpəln] *vi* to hobble

Humpen ['hʊmpən] (-s, -) *m* tankard

Hund [hʊnt] (-(e)s, -e) *m* dog

Hunde- *zW:* **~hütte** *f* (dog) kennel; **h~müde** *(umg)* *adj* dog-tired

hundert ['hʊndɐt] *num* hundred; **H~'jahrfeier** *f* centenary; **~prozentig** *adj*, *adv* one hundred per cent

Hundesteuer *f* dog licence fee

Hündin ['hʏndɪn] *f* bitch

Hunger ['hʊŋɐr] (-s) *m* hunger; **~ haben** to be hungry; **h~n** *vi* to starve; **~snot** *f* famine

hungrig ['hʊŋrɪç] *adj* hungry

Hupe ['huːpə] *f* horn; **h~n** *vi* to hoot, to sound one's horn

hüpfen ['hʏpfən] *vi* to hop; to jump

Hürde ['hʏrdə] *f* hurdle; *(für Schafe)* pen; **~nlauf** *m* hurdling

Hure ['huːrə] *f* whore

hurtig ['hʊrtɪç] *adj* brisk, quick ♦ *adv* briskly, to scurry

huschen ['hʊʃən] *vi* to flit; to scurry

Husten ['huːstən] (-s) *m* cough; **h~** *vi* to cough; **~anfall** *m* coughing fit; **~bonbon** *m od nt* cough drop; **~saft** *m* cough mixture

Hut¹ [huːt] (-(e)s, "e) *m* hat

Hut² [huːt] (-) *f* care; **auf der ~ sein** to be on one's guard

hüten ['hyːtən] *vt* to guard ♦ *vr* to watch out; **sich ~, zu** to take care not to; **sich ~ (vor)** to beware (of), to be on one's guard (against)

Hütte ['hʏtə] *f* hut; cottage; *(Eisenhütte)* forge

Hütten- *zW:* **~käse** *m (KOCH)* cottage cheese; **~schuh** *m* slipper sock

Hydrant [hy'drant] *m* hydrant
hydraulisch [hy'draulɪʃ] *adj* hydraulic
Hygiene [hygi'e:nə] *f* hygiene
hygienisch [hygi'e:nɪʃ] *adj* hygienic
Hymne ['hʏmnə] *f* hymn; anthem
Hypno- [hʏp'no:] *zW:* **~se** *f* hypnosis;
h~tisch *adj* hypnotic; **~tiseur**
[-ti'zø:r] *m* hypnotist; **h~tisieren** *vt* to
hypnotize
Hypothek [hypo'te:k] (-, -en) *f* mortgage
Hypothese [hypo'te:zə] *f* hypothesis
Hysterie [hyste'ri:] *f* hysteria
hysterisch [hʏs'te:rɪʃ] *adj* hysterical

I, i

ICE [i:tse:'|e:] *m abk =* **Intercity-Expresszug**
Ich (-(s), -(s)) *nt* self; *(PSYCH)* ego
ich [ɪç] *pron* I; ~ **bins!** it's me!
Ideal [ide'a:l] (-s, -e) *nt* ideal; **ideal** *adj*
ideal; **idealistisch** [-'lɪstɪʃ] *adj* idealistic
Idee [i'de:, *pl* i'de:ən] *f* idea
identifizieren [identifi'tsi:rən] *vt* to
identify
identisch [i'dɛntɪʃ] *adj* identical
Identität [identi'tɛːt] *f* identity
Ideo- [ideo] *zW:* **~loge** [-'lo:gə] (-n, -n)
m ideologist; **~logie** [-lo'gi:] *f* ideology; **ideologisch** [-'lo:gɪʃ] *adj* ideological
Idiot [idi'o:t] (-en, -en) *m* idiot; **idiotisch** *adj* idiotic
idyllisch [i'dʏlɪʃ] *adj* idyllic
Igel ['i:gəl] (-s, -) *m* hedgehog
ignorieren [ɪgno'ri:rən] *vt* to ignore
ihm [i:m] *(dat von* er, es) *pron* (to) him;
(to) it
ihn [i:n] *(akk von* er, es) *pron* him; it;
~**en** *(dat von* sie *pl) pron* (to) them; **Ih-nen** *(dat von* Sie *pl) pron* (to) you

ihr [i:r] *pron* **1** *(nom pl)* you; **ihr seid es**
it's you
2 *(dat von* sie*)* to her; **gib es ihr** give it
to her; **er steht neben ihr** he is standing beside her
♦ *possessiv pron* **1** *(sg)* her; *(: bei Tieren,*
Dingen) its; **ihr Mann** her husband
2 *(pl)* their; **die Bäume und ihre**
Blätter the trees and their leaves

ihr(e) [i:r] *adj (sg)* her, its; *(pl)* their;
Ihr(e) *adj* your
ihre(r, s) *pron (sg)* hers, its; *(pl)* theirs;
Ihre(r, s) *pron* yours; ~**r** *(gen von* sie
sg/pl) pron of her/them; **Ihrer** *(gen von*
Sie*) pron* of you; ~**rseits** *adv* for her/
their part; ~**sgleichen** *pron* people like
her/them; *(von Dingen)* others like it;
~**twegen** *adv (für sie)* for her/its/their
sake; *(wegen ihr)* on her/its/their account; ~**twillen** *adv:* **um ~twillen =**
ihretwegen
ihrige ['i:rɪgə] *pron:* **der/die/das ~** *od* **l~**
hers; its; theirs
illegal [ɪ'lega:l] *adj* illegal
Illusion [ɪluzi'o:n] *f* illusion
illusorisch [ɪlu'zo:rɪʃ] *adj* illusory
illustrieren [ɪlʊs'triːrən] *vt* to illustrate
Illustrierte *f* magazine
im [ɪm] = in dem
Imbiss ▲ ['ɪmbɪs] (-es, -e) *m* snack;
~**stube** *f* snack bar
imitieren [imi'ti:rən] *vt* to imitate
Imker ['ɪmkər] (-s, -) *m* beekeeper
immatrikulieren [ɪmatriku'li:rən] *vi,*
vt to register
immer ['ɪmər] *adv* always; ~ **wieder**
again and again; ~ **noch** still; ~ **noch**
nicht still not; **für** ~ forever; ~ **wenn**
ich ... every time I ...; ~ **schöner/**
trauriger more and more beautiful/
sadder and sadder; **was/wer (auch)** ~
whatever/whoever; ~**hin** *adv* all the

same; **~zu** adv all the time

Immobilien [ımo'biːliən] pl real estate
sg; **~makler** m estate agent (BRIT), realtor (US)

immun [ı'muːn] adj immune; **Immunität** [-i'tɛːt] f immunity; **Immun-
system** nt immune system

Imperfekt ['ımpɛrfɛkt] (-s, -e) nt imperfect (tense)

Impf- ['ımpf] zW: **impfen** vt to vaccinate; **~stoff** m vaccine, serum; **~ung** f
vaccination

imponieren [ımpo'niːrən] vi +dat to
impress

Import [ım'pɔrt] (-(e)s, -e) m import;
~eur m importer; **importieren** vt to
import

imposant [ımpo'zant] adj imposing

impotent ['ımpotɛnt] adj impotent

imprägnieren [ımprɛ'gniːrən] vt to
(water)proof

improvisieren [ımprovi'ziːrən] vt, vi
to improvise

Impuls [ım'pʊls] (-es, -e) m impulse;
impulsiv [-'ziːf] adj impulsive

imstande, im Stande [ım'ʃtandə]
adj: **~ sein** to be in a position; (fähig)
to be able

in [ın] präp +akk 1 (räumlich: wohin?)
into; **in die Stadt** into town; **in die
Schule gehen** to go to school
2 (zeitlich): **bis ins 20. Jahrhundert**
into od up to the 20th century
♦ präp +dat 1 (räumlich: wo) in; **in der
Stadt** in town; **in der Schule sein** to
be at school
2 (zeitlich: wann): **in diesem Jahr** this
year; (in jenem Jahr) in that year; **heute in zwei Wochen** two weeks today

Inanspruchnahme
[ın'ʔanʃprʊxnaːmə] f (+gen) demands pl
(on)

Inbegriff ['ınbəgrıf] m embodiment,
personification; **inbegriffen** adv in-

cluded

indem [ın'deːm] konj while; **~ man
etw macht** (dadurch) by doing sth

Inder(in) ['ındər(ın)] m(f) Indian

indes(sen) [ın'dɛs(ə)n)] adv however;
(inzwischen) meanwhile ♦ konj while

Indianer(in) [ındi'aːnər(ın)] (-s, -) m(f)
American Indian, native American; **in-
dianisch** adj Red Indian

Indien ['ındiən] nt India

indirekt ['ındirɛkt] adj indirect

indisch ['ındıʃ] adj Indian

indiskret ['ındıskreːt] adj indiscreet

indiskutabel ['ındıskutaːbəl] adj out of
the question

individuell [ındividu'ɛl] adj individual

Individuum [ındi'viːduʊm] (-s, -en) nt
individual

Indiz [ın'diːts] (-es, -ien) nt (JUR) clue; **~
(für)** sign (of)

industrialisieren [ındʊstriali'ziːrən] vt
to industrialize

Industrie [ındʊs'triː] f industry ♦ in zW
industrial; **~gebiet** nt industrial area;
~- und Handelskammer f chamber
of commerce; **~zweig** m branch of industry

ineinander [ınʔaı'nandər] adv in(to)
one another od each other

Infarkt [ın'farkt] (-(e)s, -e) m coronary
(thrombosis)

Infektion [ınfɛktsi'oːn] f infection;
~skrankheit f infectious disease

Infinitiv ['ınfinitiːf] (-s, -e) m infinitive

infizieren [ınfi'tsiːrən] vt to infect ♦ vr:
sich (bei jdm) ~ to be infected (by
sb)

Inflation [ınflatsi'oːn] f inflation

inflationär [ınflatsio'nɛːr] adj inflationary

infolge [ın'fɔlgə] präp +gen as a result
of, owing to; **~dessen** [-'dɛsən] adv
consequently

Informatik [ınfɔr'maːtık] f information
studies pl

Information [ınfɔrmatsi'oːn] f information no pl

informieren [ɪnfɔr'miːrən] vt to inform ♦ vr: **sich ~ (über** +akk) to find out (about)

in Frage, in Frage adv: **~ stellen** to question sth; **nicht ~ kommen** to be out of the question

Ingenieur [ɪnʒeni'øːr] m engineer; **~schule** f school of engineering

Ingwer ['ɪŋvər] (-s) m ginger

Inh. abk (= Inhaber) prop.; (= Inhalt) contents

Inhaber(in) ['ɪnhaːbər(ɪn)] (-s, -) m(f) owner; (Hausinhaber) occupier; (Lizenzinhaber) licensee, holder; (FIN) bearer

inhaftieren [ɪnhaf'tiːrən] vt to take into custody

inhalieren [ɪnha'liːrən] vt, vi to inhale

Inhalt ['ɪnhalt] (-(e)s, -e) m contents pl; (eines Buchs etc) content; (MATH) area; volume; **inhaltlich** adj as regards content

Inhalts- zW: **~angabe** f summary; **~verzeichnis** nt table of contents

inhuman ['ɪnhuma:n] adj inhuman

Initiative [initsia'tiːvə] f initiative

inklusive [ɪnklu'ziːvə] präp +gen inclusive of ♦ adv inclusive

In-Kraft-Treten [ɪn'krafttreːtən] (-s) nt coming into force

Inland ['ɪnlant] (-(e)s) nt (GEOG) inland; (POL, COMM) home (country); **~flug** m domestic flight

inmitten [ɪn'mɪtən] präp +gen in the middle of; **~ von** amongst

innehaben ['ɪnəhaːbən] (unreg) vt to hold

innen ['ɪnən] adv inside; **Innenarchitekt** m interior designer; **Inneneinrichtung** f (interior) furnishings pl; **Innenhof** m inner courtyard; **Innenminister** m minister of the interior, Home Secretary (BRIT); **Innenpolitik** f domestic policy; **~politisch** adj (Entwicklung, Lage) internal, domestic; **Innenstadt** f town/city centre

inner- ['ɪnər] zW: **~e(r, s)** adj inner; (im Körper, inländisch) internal; **Innere(s)** nt inside; (Mitte) centre; (fig) heart; **Innereien** [-'raɪən] pl innards; **~halb** adv within; (räumlich) inside ♦ präp +gen within; inside; **~lich** adj internal; (geistig) inward; **~ste(r, s)** adj innermost; **Innerste(s)** nt heart

innig ['ɪnɪç] adj (Freundschaft) close

inoffiziell ['ɪnʔɔfitsiɛl] adj unofficial

ins [ɪns] = in das

Insasse ['ɪnzasə] (-n, -n) m (Anstalt) inmate; (AUT) passenger

Insassenversicherung f passenger insurance

insbesondere [ɪnsbə'zɔndərə] adv (e)specially

Inschrift ['ɪnʃrɪft] f inscription

Insekt [ɪn'zɛkt] (-(e)s, -en) nt insect

Insektenschutzmittel nt insect repellent

Insel ['ɪnzəl] (-, -n) f island

Inser- zW: **~at** [ɪnze'raːt] (-(e)s, -e) nt advertisement; **~ent** [ɪnze'rɛnt] m advertiser; **inserieren** [ɪnze'riːrən] vt, vi to advertise

insgeheim [ɪnsgə'haɪm] adv secretly

insgesamt [ɪnsgə'zamt] adv altogether, all in all

insofern [ɪnzo'fɛrn] adv in this respect ♦ konj if; (deshalb) (and) so; **~ als** in so far as

insoweit [ɪnzo'vaɪt] = **insofern**

Installateur [ɪnstala'tøːr] m electrician; plumber

Instandhaltung [ɪn'ʃtanthaltʊŋ] f maintenance

inständig [ɪn'ʃtɛndɪç] adj urgent

Instandsetzung [ɪn'ʃtant-] f overhaul; (eines Gebäudes) restoration

Instanz [ɪn'ʃtants] f authority; (JUR) court

Instinkt [ɪn'stɪŋkt] (-(e)s, -e) m instinct; **instinktiv** [-'tiːf] adj instinctive

Institut [ɪnsti'tuːt] (-(e)s, -e) nt insti-

tute
Instrument [instru'mɛnt] nt instrument
Intell- [ɪn'tɛl-] zW: **intellektuell** [-ɛk-
tu'ɛl] adj intellectual; **intelligent**
[-i'gɛnt] adj intelligent; **~igenz**
[-i'gɛnts] f intelligence; (Leute) intelligentsia pl
Intendant [ɪntɛn'dant] m director
intensiv [ɪntɛn'ziːf] adj intensive; **Intensivstation** f intensive care unit
Intercity [ɪntər'sɪti] zW: **~-
Expresszug** ▲ m high-speed train;
~-Zug m intercity (train); **~-Zuschlag**
m intercity supplement
Interess- zW: **interessant**
[ɪntɛrɛ'sant] adj interesting; **interes-
santerweise** adv interestingly
enough; **~e** [ɪntɛ'rɛsə] (-s, -n) nt interest; **~e haben an** +dat to be interested
in; **~ent** [ɪntɛrɛ'sɛnt] m interested party; **interessieren** [ɪntɛrɛ'siːrən] vt to
interest ♦ vr: **sich interessieren für** to
be interested in
intern [ɪn'tɛrn] adj (Angelegenheiten, Regelung) internal; (Besprechung) private
Internat [ɪntɛr'naːt] (-(e)s, -e) nt
boarding school
inter- [ɪntɛr] zW: **~national** [-natsio-
'naːl] adj international; **I~net** ▲
['ɪntanɛt] (-s) nt: **das I~net** the Internet; **I~net-Café** nt Internet café;
~pretieren [-pre'tiːrən] vt to interpret;
Intervall [-'val] (-s, -e) nt interval; **Interview** [-'vjuː] (-s, -s) nt interview;
~viewen [-'vjuːən] vt to interview
intim [ɪn'tiːm] adj intimate; **Intimität** f
intimacy
intolerant ['ɪntolɛrant] adj intolerant
Intrige [ɪn'triːgə] f intrigue, plot
Invasion [ɪnvazi'oːn] f invasion
Inventar [ɪnvɛn'taːr] (-s, -e) nt inventory
Inventur [ɪnvɛn'tuːr] f stocktaking; **~
machen** to stocktake
investieren [ɪnvɛs'tiːrən] vt to invest
inwie- [ɪnvi'] zW: **~fern** adv how far,
to what extent; **~weit** adv how far, to

what extent
inzwischen [ɪn'tsvɪʃən] adv meanwhile
Irak [i'raːk] (-s) m: **der ~** Iraq; **irakisch**
adj Iraqi
Iran [i'raːn] (-s) m: **der ~** Iran; **iranisch** adj Iranian
irdisch ['ɪrdɪʃ] adj earthly
Ire ['iːrə] (-n, -n) m Irishman
irgend ['ɪrgɛnt] adv at all; **wann/was/
wer ~** whenever/whatever/whoever;
~etwas pron something/anything;
~jemand pron somebody/anybody;
~ein(e, s) adj some, any; **~einmal** adv
sometime or other; (fragend) ever;
~wann adv sometime; **~wie** adv
somehow; **~wo** adv somewhere; anywhere; **~wohin** adv somewhere; anywhere
Irin ['iːrɪn] f Irishwoman
Irland ['ɪrlant] (-s) nt Ireland
Ironie [iro'niː] f irony; **ironisch**
[i'roːnɪʃ] adj ironic(al)
irre ['ɪrə] adj crazy, mad; **Irre(r)** f(m) lunatic; **~führen** vt to mislead; **~ma-
chen** vt to confuse; **~n** vi to be mistaken; (umherirren) to wander, to stray
♦ vr to be mistaken; **Irrenanstalt** f lunatic asylum
Irr- zW: **~garten** m maze; **i~ig** ['ɪrɪç]
adj incorrect, wrong; **i~itieren**
[ɪri'tiːrən] vt (verwirren) to confuse;
(ärgern) to irritate; (stören) to annoy;
i~sinnig adj mad, crazy; (umg) terrific; **i~tum** (-s, -tümer) m mistake, error; **irrtümlich** adj mistaken
Island ['iːslant] (-s) nt Iceland
Isolation [izolatsi'oːn] f isolation; (ELEK)
insulation
Isolier- [izo'liːr] zW: **~band** nt insulating tape; **isolieren** vt to isolate; (ELEK)
to insulate; **~station** f (MED) isolation
ward; **~ung** f isolation; (ELEK) insulation
Israel ['ɪsraeːl] (-s) nt Israel; **~i** (-s, -s)
[-'eːli] m Israeli; **israelisch** adj Israeli
isst ▲ [ɪst] vb siehe **essen**
ist [ɪst] vb siehe **sein**

Italien [i'ta:liən] (-s) nt Italy; **~er(in)** (-s) m(f) Italian; **italienisch** adj Italian

I. V. abk = in Vertretung

J, j

ja [ja:] adv 1 yes; **haben Sie das gesehen? - ja** did you see it? - yes, (yes, I did); **ich glaube ja** (yes) I think so

2 (fragend) really?; **ich habe gekündigt - ja?** I've quit - have you?; **du kommst, ja?** you're coming, aren't you?

3: **sei ja vorsichtig** do be careful; **Sie wissen ja, dass ...** as you know, ...; **tu das ja nicht!** don't do that!; **ich habe es ja gewusst** I just knew it!; **ja, also** ... well you see ...

Jacht [jaxt] (-, -en) f yacht

Jacke ['jakə] f jacket; (Wolljacke) cardigan

Jackett [ʒa'kɛt] (-s, -s od -e) nt jacket

Jagd [ja:kt] (-, -en) f hunt; (Jagen) hunting; **~beute** f kill; **~flugzeug** nt fighter; **~hund** m hunting dog

jagen ['ja:gən] vi to hunt; (eilen) to race ♦ vt to hunt; (wegjagen) to drive (off); (verfolgen) to chase

Jäger ['jɛːgər] (-s, -) m hunter; **~schnitzel** nt (KOCH) pork in a spicy sauce with mushrooms

jäh [jɛː] adj sudden, abrupt; (steil) steep, precipitous

Jahr [ja:r] (-(e)s, -e) nt year; **j~elang** adv for years

Jahres- zW: **~abonnement** nt annual subscription; **~abschluss** ▲ m end of the year; (COMM) annual statement of account; **~beitrag** m annual subscription; **~karte** f yearly season ticket;

~tag m anniversary; **~wechsel** m turn of the year; **~zahl** f date; year; **~zeit** f season

Jahr- zW: **~gang** m age group; (von Wein) vintage; **~hundert** (-s, -e) nt century; **jährlich** ['jɛːrlɪç] adj, adv yearly; **~markt** m fair; **~tausend** nt millennium; **~'zehnt** nt decade

Jähzorn ['jɛːtsɔrn] m sudden anger; hot temper; **j~ig** adj hot-tempered

Jalousie [ʒalu'zi:] f venetian blind

Jammer ['jamər] (-s) m misery; **es ist ein ~, dass ...** it is a crying shame that ...

jämmerlich ['jɛmərlɪç] adj wretched, pathetic

jammern vi to wail ♦ vt unpers: **es jammert mich** it makes sb feel sorry

Januar ['januaːr] (-(s), -e) m January

Japan ['ja:pan] (-s) nt Japan; **~er(in)** [-'pa:nər(ɪn)] (-s) m(f) Japanese; **j~isch** adj Japanese

jäten ['jɛːtən] vt: **Unkraut ~** to weed

jauchzen ['jauxtsən] vi to rejoice

jaulen ['jaulən] vi to howl

jawohl [ja'vo:l] adv yes (of course)

Jawort ['ja:vɔrt] nt consent

Jazz [dʒæz] (-) m Jazz

je [je:] adv 1 (jemals) ever; **hast du so was je gesehen?** did you ever see anything like it?

2 (jeweils) every, each; **sie zahlten je 3 Mark** they paid 3 marks each

♦ konj 1: **je nach** depending on; **je nachdem** it depends; **je nachdem, ob** ... depending on whether ...

2: **je eher, desto** od **umso besser** the sooner the better

Jeans [dʒi:nz] pl jeans

jede(r, s) ['je:də(r, s)] adj every, each ♦ pron everybody; (~ Einzelne) each; **~s Mal** every time, each time; **ohne ~ x**

without any x

jedenfalls *adv* in any case

jedermann *pron* everyone

jederzeit *adv* at any time

jedoch [je'dɔx] *adv* however

jeher ['je:he:r] *adv*: **von/seit ~** always

jemals ['je:ma:ls] *adv* ever

jemand ['je:mant] *pron* somebody; anybody

jene(r, s) ['je:nə(r, s)] *adj* that ♦ *pron* that one

jenseits ['je:nzaɪts] *adv* on the other side ♦ *präp* +gen on the other side of, beyond

Jenseits *nt*: **das ~** the hereafter, the beyond

jetzig ['jɛtsɪç] *adj* present

jetzt [jɛtst] *adv* now

jeweilig *adj* respective

jeweils *adv*: **~ zwei zusammen** two at a time; **zu ~ 5 DM** at 5 marks each; **~ das Erste** the first each time

Jh. *abk* = **Jahrhundert**

Job [dʒɔp] (**-s, -s**) *m* (*umg*) job; **j~ben** ['dʒɔbən] *vi* (*umg*) to work

Jockei ['dʒɔke] (**-s, -s**) *m* jockey

Jod [jo:t] (**-(e)s**) *nt* iodine

jodeln ['jo:dəln] *vi* to yodel

joggen ['dʒɔgən] *vi* to jog

Jog(h)urt ['jo:gʊrt] (**-s, -s**) *m od nt* yogurt

Johannisbeere [jo'hanɪsbe:rə] *f* red-currant; **schwarze ~** blackcurrant

johlen ['jo:lən] *vi* to yell

jonglieren [ʒõˈgli:rən] *vi* to juggle

Journal- [ʒɔrnal] *zW*: **~ismus** [-ˈlɪsmʊs] *m* journalism; **~ist(in)** [-ˈlɪst(ɪn)] *m(f)* journalist; **jour-na'listisch** *adj* journalistic

Jubel ['ju:bəl] *m* rejoicing; **j~n** *vi* to rejoice

Jubiläum [jubi'lɛ:ɔm] (**-s, Jubiläen**) *nt* anniversary; jubilee

jucken ['jʊkən] *vi* to itch ♦ *vt*: **es juckt mich am Arm** my arm is itching

Juckreiz ['jʊkraɪts] *m* itch

Jude ['ju:də] (**-n, -n**) *m* Jew

Juden- *zW*: **~tum** (**-**) *nt* Judaism; Jew-ry; **~verfolgung** *f* persecution of the Jews

Jüdin ['jy:dɪn] *f* Jewess

jüdisch ['jy:dɪʃ] *adj* Jewish

Jugend ['ju:gənt] (**-**) *f* youth; **j~frei** *adj* (*CINE*) U (*BRIT*), G (*US*), suitable for children; **~herberge** *f* youth hostel; **~herbergsausweis** *m* youth hostel-ling card; **j~lich** *adj* youthful; **~liche(r)** *f(m)* teenager, young person

Jugoslaw- [jugo'sla:v] *zW*: **~ien** (**-s**) *nt* Yugoslavia; **j~isch** *adj* Yugoslavian

Juli ['ju:li] (**-(s), -s**) *m* July

jun. *abk* (= *junior*) jr.

jung [jʊŋ] *adj* young; **J~e** (**-n, -n**) *m* boy, lad ♦ *nt* young animal; **J~en** *pl* (*von Tier*) young *pl*

Jünger ['jʏŋər] (**-s, -**) *m* disciple

jünger *adj* younger

Jung- *zW*: **~frau** *f* virgin; (*ASTROL*) Vir-go; **~geselle** *m* bachelor; **~gesellin** *f* unmarried woman

jüngst [jʏŋst] *adv* lately, recently; **~e(r, s)** *adj* youngest; (*neueste*) latest

Juni ['ju:ni] (**-(s), -s**) *m* June

Junior ['ju:ni:or] (**-s, -en**) *m* junior

Jurist ['ju'rɪst] *m* jurist, lawyer; **j~isch** *adj* legal

Justiz [jʊs'ti:ts] (**-**) *f* justice; **~beam-te(r)** *m* judicial officer; **~irrtum** *m* mis-carriage of justice; **~minister** *m* ≈ Lord (High) Chancellor (*BRIT*), ≈ Attor-ney General (*US*)

Juwel [ju've:l] (**-s, -en**) *nt od m* jewel

Juwelier [juve'li:r] (**-s, -e**) *m* jeweller; **~geschäft** *nt* jeweller's (shop)

Jux [jʊks] (**-es, -e**) *m* joke, lark

K, k

Kabarett [kaba'rɛt] (**-s, -e** *od* **-s**) *nt* cabaret; **~ist** [-'tɪst] *m* cabaret artiste

Kabel ['ka:bəl] (**-s, -**) *nt* (*ELEK*) wire; (*stark*) cable; **~fernsehen** *nt* cable television

Kabeljau [ˈkaːbəljaʊ] (-s, -e od -s) m cod

Kabine [ka'biːnə] f cabin; (Zelle) cubicle

Kabinenbahn f cable railway

Kabinett [kabi'nɛt] (-s, -e) nt (POL) cabinet

Kachel [ˈkaxəl] (-, -n) f tile; **k~n** vt to tile; **~ofen** m tiled stove

Käfer [ˈkɛːfər] (-s, -) m beetle

Kaffee [ˈkafe] (-s, -s) m coffee; **~haus** nt café; **~kanne** f coffeepot; **~löffel** m coffee spoon

Käfig [ˈkɛːfɪç] (-s, -e) m cage

kahl [kaːl] adj bald; **~ geschoren** shaven, shorn; **~köpfig** adj bald-headed

Kahn [kaːn] (-(e)s, ᵉe) m boat, barge

Kai [kaɪ] (-s, -e od -s) m quay

Kaiser [ˈkaɪzər] (-s, -) m emperor; **~in** f empress; **k~lich** adj imperial; **~reich** nt empire; **~schnitt** m (MED) Caesarian (section)

Kakao [ka'kaːo] (-s, -s) m cocoa

Kaktee [kak'teː(ə)] (-, -n) f cactus

Kaktus [ˈkaktʊs] (-, -teen) m cactus

Kalb [kalp] (-(e)s, ᵉer) nt calf; **k~en** [ˈkalbən] vi to calve; **~fleisch** nt veal; **~sleder** nt calf(skin)

Kalender [ka'lɛndər] (-s, -) m calendar; (Taschenkalender) diary

Kaliber [ka'liːbər] (-s, -) nt (auch fig) calibre

Kalk [kalk] (-(e)s, -e) m lime; (BIOL) calcium; **~stein** m limestone

kalkulieren [kalku'liːrən] vt to calculate

Kalorie [kalo'riː] f calorie

kalt [kalt] adj cold; **mir ist (es) ~** I am cold; **~ bleiben** (fig) to remain unmoved; **~ stellen** to chill; **~blütig** adj cold-blooded; (ruhig) cool

Kälte [ˈkɛltə] (-) f cold; coldness; **~grad** m degree of frost od below zero; **~welle** f cold spell

kalt- zW: **~herzig** adj cold-hearted;

~schnäuzig adj cold, unfeeling; **~stellen** vt (fig) to leave out in the cold

kam etc [kaːm] vb siehe **kommen**

Kamel [kaˈmeːl] (-(e)s, -e) nt camel

Kamera [ˈkamera] (-, -s) f camera

Kamerad [kamaˈraːt] (-en, -en) m comrade, friend; **~schaft** f comradeship; **k~schaftlich** adj comradely

Kameramann (-(e)s, -männer) m cameraman

Kamille [ka'mɪlə] f camomile; **~ntee** m camomile tea

Kamin [ka'miːn] (-s, -e) m (außen) chimney; (innen) fireside, fireplace; **~kehrer** (-s, -) m chimney sweep

Kamm [kam] (-(e)s, ᵉe) m comb; (Bergkamm) ridge; (Hahnenkamm) crest

kämmen [ˈkɛmən] vt to comb; **~** vr to comb one's hair

Kammer [ˈkamər] (-, -n) f chamber; small bedroom; **~diener** m valet

Kampagne [kamˈpanjə] f campaign

Kampf [kampf] (-(e)s, ᵉe) m fight, battle; (Wettbewerb) contest; (fig: Anstrengung) struggle; **k~bereit** adj ready for action

kämpfen [ˈkɛmpfən] vi to fight

Kämpfer (-s, -) m fighter, combatant

Kampf- zW: **~handlung** f action; **k~los** adj without a fight; **~richter** m (SPORT) referee; (TENNIS) umpire; **~stoff** m: **chemischer/biologischer ~stoff** chemical/biological weapon

Kanada [ˈkanada] (-s) nt Canada; **Kanadier(in)** (-s, -) [ka'naːdiər(ɪn)] m(f) Canadian; **k~nadisch** adj Canadian

Kanal [ka'naːl] (-s, Kanäle) m (Fluss) canal; (Rinne, Armelkanal) channel; (für Abfluss) drain; **~inseln** pl Channel Islands; **~isation** f [-izatsi'oːn] f sewage system; **~tunnel** m: **der ~tunnel** the Channel Tunnel

Kanarienvogel [ka'naːriənfoːgəl] m canary

kanarisch [ka'na:rɪʃ] adj: **K~e Inseln** Canary Islands, Canaries

Kandi- [kandi] zW: **~dat** f ['da:t] (-en, -en) m candidate; **~datur** [-da'tu:r] f candidature, candidacy; **k~dieren** [-'di:rən] vi to stand, to run

Kandis(zucker) ['kandɪs(tsʊkər)] (-) m candy

Känguru ▲ ['kɛŋguru] (-s, -s) nt kangaroo

Kaninchen [ka'ni:nçən] nt rabbit

Kanister [ka'nɪstər] (-s, -) m can, canister

Kännchen ['kɛnçən] nt pot

Kanne ['kanə] f (Krug) jug; (Kaffeekanne) pot; (Milchkanne) churn; (Gießkanne) can

kannst etc [kanst] vb siehe **können**

Kanone [ka'no:nə] f gun; (HIST) cannon; (fig: Mensch) ace

Kante ['kantə] f edge

Kantine [kan'ti:nə] f canteen

Kanton [kan'to:n] (-s, -e) m canton

┌─────────────────────────────┐
│ Kanton   │
└─────────────────────────────┘

Kanton is the term for a state or region of Switzerland. Under the Swiss constitution the Kantone enjoy considerable autonomy. The Swiss Kantone are Aargau, Appenzell, Basel, Bern, Fribourg, Geneva, Glarus, Graubünden, Luzern, Neuchâtel, St. Gallen, Schaffhausen, Schwyz, Solothurn, Ticino, Thurgau, Unterwalden, Uri, Valais, Vaud, Zug and Zürich.

Kanu ['ka:nu] (-s, -s) nt canoe

Kanzel ['kantsəl] (-, -n) f pulpit

Kanzler ['kantslər] (-s, -) m chancellor

Kap [kap] (-s, -s) nt cape (GEOG)

Kapazität [kapatsi'tɛ:t] f capacity; (Fachmann) authority

Kapelle [ka'pɛlə] f (Gebäude) chapel; (MUS) band

kapieren [ka'pi:rən] (umg) vt, vi to get, to understand

Kapital [kapi'ta:l] (-s, -e od -ien) nt

capital; ~anlage f investment; **~ismus** [-'lɪsmʊs] m capitalism; **~ist** [-'lɪst] m capitalist; **k~istisch** adj capitalist

Kapitän [kapi'tɛ:n] (-s, -e) m captain

Kapitel [ka'pɪtəl] (-s, -) nt chapter

Kapitulation [kapitulatsi'o:n] f capitulation

kapitulieren [kapitu'li:rən] vi to capitulate

Kappe ['kapə] f cap; (Kapuze) hood

kappen vt to cut

Kapsel ['kapsəl] (-, -n) f capsule

kaputt [ka'put] (umg) adj kaput, broken; (Person) exhausted, finished; **am Auto ist etwas ~** there's something wrong with the car; **~gehen** (unreg) vi to break; (Schuhe) to fall apart; (Firma) to go bust; (Stoff) to wear out; (sterben) to cop it (umg); **~machen** vt to break; (Mensch) to exhaust, to wear out

Kapuze [ka'pu:tsə] f hood

Karamell ▲ [kara'mɛl] (-s) m caramel; **~bonbon** m od nt toffee

Karate [ka'ra:tə] (-s) nt karate

Karawane [kara'va:nə] f caravan

Kardinal [kardi'na:l] (-s, **Kardinäle**) m cardinal; **~zahl** f cardinal number

Karfreitag [ka:r'fraita:k] m Good Friday

karg [kark] adj (Landschaft, Boden) barren; (Lohn) meagre

kärglich ['kɛrklɪç] adj poor, scanty

Karibik [ka'ri:bik] (-) f: **die ~** the Caribbean

karibisch [ka'ri:bɪʃ] adj: **K~e Inseln** Caribbean Islands

kariert [ka'ri:rt] adj (Stoff) checked; (Papier) squared

Karies ['ka:ri̯ɛs] (-) f caries

Karikatur [karika'tu:r] f caricature; **~ist** [-'rɪst] m cartoonist

Karneval ['karnəval] (-s, -e od -s) m carnival

┌─────────────────────────────┐
│ Karneval   │
└─────────────────────────────┘

Karneval is the time immediately be-

fore Lent when people gather to eat, drink and generally have fun before the fasting begins. Rosenmontag, the day before Shrove Tuesday, is the most important day of Karneval on the Rhine. Most firms take a day's holiday on that day to enjoy the celebrations. In South Germany and Austria Karneval is called Fasching.

Karo ['ka:ro] (-s, -s) nt square; (KARTEN) diamonds

Karosserie [karɔsə'ri:] f (AUT) body(work)

Karotte [ka'rɔtə] f carrot

Karpfen ['karpfən] (-s, -) m carp

Karre ['karə] f cart, barrow

Karren (-s, -) m cart, barrow

Karriere [kari'ɛ:rə] f career; ~ **machen** to get on, to get to the top; **~macher** (-s, -) m careerist

Karte ['kartə] f card; (Landkarte) map; (Speisekarte) menu; (Eintrittskarte, Fahrkarte) ticket; **alles auf eine ~ setzen** to put all one's eggs in one basket

Kartei [kar'tai] f card index; **~karte** f index card

Kartell [kar'tel] (-s, -e) nt cartel

Karten- zW: **~spiel** nt card game; pack of cards; **~telefon** nt cardphone; **~vorverkauf** m advance booking office

Kartoffel [kar'tɔfəl] (-, -n) f potato; **~brei** m mashed potatoes pl; **~mus** nt mashed potatoes pl; **~püree** nt mashed potatoes pl; **~salat** m potato salad

Karton [kar'tõ:] (-s, -s) m cardboard; (Schachtel) cardboard box; **k~iert** [kartõ'ni:rt] adj hardback

Karussell [karu'sel] (-s, -s) nt roundabout (BRIT), merry-go-round

Karwoche ['ka:rvɔxə] f Holy Week

Käse ['kɛ:zə] (-s, -) m cheese; **~glocke**

f cheese (plate) cover; **~kuchen** m cheesecake

Kaserne [ka'zɛrnə] f barracks pl; **~nhof** m parade ground

Kasino [ka'zi:no] (-s, -s) nt club; (MIL) officers' mess; (Spielkasino) casino

Kaskoversicherung ['kasko-] f (Teilkasko) ≈ third party, fire and theft insurance; (Vollkasko) ≈ fully comprehensive insurance

Kasse ['kasə] f (Geldkasten) cashbox; (in Geschäft) till, cash register; cash desk, checkout; (Kinokasse, Theaterkasse etc) box office; ticket office; (Krankenkasse) health insurance; (Sparkasse) savings bank; **~ machen** to count the money; **getrennte ~ führen** to pay separately; **an der ~** (in Geschäft) at the desk; **gut bei ~ sein** to be in the money

Kassen- zW: **~arzt** m panel doctor (BRIT); **~bestand** m cash balance; **~patient** m panel patient (BRIT); **~prüfung** f audit; **~sturz** m: **~sturz machen** to check one's money; **~zettel** m receipt

Kassette [ka'setə] f small box; (Tonband, PHOT) cassette; (Bücherkassette) case

Kassettenrekorder (-s, -) m cassette recorder

kassieren [ka'si:rən] vt to take ♦ vi: **darf ich ~?** would you like to pay now?

Kassierer [ka'si:rər] (-s, -) m cashier; (von Klub) treasurer

Kastanie [kas'ta:niə] f chestnut; (Baum) chestnut tree

Kasten ['kastən] (-s, ⁻) m (auch SPORT) box; case; (Truhe) chest

kastrieren [kas'tri:rən] vt to castrate

Katalog [kata'lo:k] (-(e)s, -e) m catalogue

Katalysator [kataly'za:tɔr] m catalyst; (AUT) catalytic converter

katastrophal [katastro'fa:l] adj catastrophic

Katastrophe [kata'stro:fə] f catastrophe, disaster

Kat-Auto ['kat|aʊto] nt car fitted with a catalytic converter

Kategorie [katego'ri:] f category

kategorisch [kate'go:rɪʃ] adj categorical

Kater ['ka:tər] (-s, -) m tomcat; (umg) hangover

kath. abk (= katholisch) Cath.

Kathedrale [kate'dra:lə] f cathedral

Katholik [kato'li:k] (-en, -en) m Catholic

katholisch [ka'to:lɪʃ] adj Catholic

Kätzchen ['kɛtsçən] nt kitten

Katze ['katsə] f cat; **für die Katz** (umg) in vain, for nothing

Katzen- zW: **~auge** nt cat's eye; (Fahrrad) rear light; **~sprung** (umg) m stone's throw; short journey

Kauderwelsch ['kaʊdərvɛlʃ] (-(s)) nt jargon; (umg) double Dutch

kauen ['kaʊən] vt, vi to chew

kauern ['kaʊərn] vi to crouch down; (furchtsam) to cower

Kauf [kaʊf] (-(e)s, Käufe) m purchase, buy; (~en) buying; **ein guter ~** a bargain; **etw in ~ nehmen** to put up with sth; **k~en** vt to buy

Käufer(in) ['kɔʏfər(ɪn)] (-s, -) m(f) buyer

Kauf- zW: **~frau** f businesswoman; **~haus** nt department store; **~kraft** f purchasing power

käuflich ['kɔʏflɪç] adj purchasable, for sale; (pej) venal ♦ adv: **~ erwerben** to purchase

Kauf- zW: **k~lustig** adj interested in buying; **~mann** (pl -leute) m businessman; shopkeeper; **k~männisch** adj commercial; **k~männische Angestellte** office worker; **~preis** m purchase price; **~vertrag** m bill of sale

Kaugummi ['kaʊgʊmi] m chewing gum

Kaulquappe ['kaʊlkvapə] f tadpole

kaum [kaʊm] adv hardly, scarcely

Kaution [kaʊtsi'o:n] f deposit; (JUR) bail

Kauz [kaʊts] (-es, Käuze) m owl; (fig) queer fellow

Kavalier [kava'li:r] (-s, -e) m gentleman, cavalier; **~sdelikt** nt peccadillo

Kaviar ['ka:viar] m caviar

keck [kɛk] adj daring, bold

Kegel ['ke:gəl] (-s, -) m skittle; (MATH) cone; **~bahn** f skittle alley; bowling alley; **k~n** vi to play skittles

Kehle ['ke:lə] f throat

Kehlkopf m larynx

Kehre ['ke:rə] f turn(ing), bend; **k~n** vt, vi (wenden) to turn; (mit Besen) to sweep; **sich an etw dat nicht k~n** not to heed sth

Kehricht ['ke:rɪçt] (-s) m sweepings pl

Kehrseite f reverse, other side; wrong side; bad side

kehrtmachen vi to turn about, to about-turn

keifen ['kaɪfən] vi to scold, to nag

Keil [kaɪl] (-(e)s, -e) m wedge; (MIL) arrowhead; **~riemen** m (AUT) fan belt

Keim [kaɪm] (-(e)s, -e) m bud; (MED, fig) germ; **k~en** vi to germinate; **k~frei** adj sterile; **~zelle** f (fig) nucleus

kein [kaɪn] adj no, not ... any; **~e(r, s)** pron no one, nobody; none; **~erlei** adj attrib no ... whatsoever

keinesfalls adv on no account

keineswegs adv by no means

keinmal adv not once

Keks [ke:ks] (-es, -e) m od nt biscuit

Kelch [kɛlç] (-(e)s, -e) m cup, goblet, chalice

Kelle ['kɛlə] f (Suppenkelle) ladle; (Maurerkelle) trowel

Keller ['kɛlər] (-s, -) m cellar

Kellner(in) ['kɛlnər(ɪn)] (-s, -) m(f) waiter(-tress)

keltern ['kɛltərn] vt to press

kennen ['kɛnən] (unreg) vt to know; **~ lernen** to get to know; **sich ~ lernen** to get to know each other; (zum ersten

Mal) to meet

Kenner (-s, -) *m* connoisseur

kenntlich *adj* distinguishable, discernible; **etw ~ machen** to mark sth

Kenntnis (-, -se) *f* knowledge *no pl*; **etw zur ~ nehmen** to note sth; **von etw ~ nehmen** to take notice of sth; **jdn in ~ setzen** to inform sb

Kenn- *zW*: **~zeichen** *nt* mark, characteristic; **k~zeichnen** *vt insep* to characterize; **~ziffer** *f* reference number

kentern ['kɛntərn] *vi* to capsize

Keramik [ke'ra:mɪk] (-, -en) *f* ceramics *pl*, pottery

Kerbe ['kɛrbə] *f* notch, groove

Kerker ['kɛrkər] (-s, -) *m* prison

Kerl [kɛrl] (-s, -e) *m* chap, bloke (*BRIT*), guy

Kern [kɛrn] (-(e)s, -e) *m* (*Obstkern*) pip, stone; (*Nusskern*) kernel; (*Atomkern*) nucleus; (*fig*) heart, core; **~energie** *f* nuclear energy; **~forschung** *f* nuclear research; **~frage** *f* central issue; **k~gesund** *adj* thoroughly healthy, fit as a fiddle; **k~ig** *adj* (*kraftvoll*) robust; (*Ausspruch*) pithy; **~kraftwerk** *nt* nuclear power station; **k~los** *adj* seedless, without pips; **~physik** *f* nuclear physics *sg*; **~spaltung** *f* nuclear fission; **~waffen** *pl* nuclear weapons

Kerze ['kɛrtsə] *f* candle; (*Zündkerze*) plug; **k~ngerade** *adj* straight as a die; **~nständer** *m* candle holder

kess ▲ [kɛs] *adj* saucy

Kessel ['kɛsəl] (-s, -) *m* kettle; (*von Lokomotive etc*) boiler; (*GEOG*) depression; (*MIL*) encirclement

Kette ['kɛtə] *f* chain; **k~n** *vt* to chain; **~nrauchen** (-s) *nt* chain smoking; **~nreaktion** *f* chain reaction

Ketzer ['kɛtsər] (-s, -) *m* heretic

keuchen ['kɔʏçən] *vi* to pant, to gasp

Keuchhusten *m* whooping cough

Keule ['kɔʏlə] *f* club; (*KOCH*) leg

keusch [kɔʏʃ] *adj* chaste; **K~heit** *f*

chastity

kfm. *abk* = **kaufmännisch**

Kfz [ka:|ɛf'tsɛt] *nt abk* = **Kraftfahrzeug**

KG [ka:'ge:] (-, -s) *f abk* (= *Kommanditgesellschaft*) limited partnership

kg *abk* = **Kilogramm**

kichern ['kɪçərn] *vi* to giggle

kidnappen ['kɪtnɛpən] *vt* to kidnap

Kiefer[1] ['ki:fər] (-s, -) *m* jaw

Kiefer[2] ['ki:fər] (-, -n) *f* pine; **~nzapfen** *m* pine cone

Kiel [ki:l] (-(e)s, -e) *m* (*Federkiel*) quill; (*NAUT*) keel

Kieme ['ki:mə] *f* gill

Kies [ki:s] (-es, -e) *m* gravel

Kilo ['ki:lo] *nt* kilo; **~gramm** [kilo'gram] *nt* kilogram; **~meter** [kilo'me:tər] *m* kilometre; **~meterzähler** *m* milometer

Kind [kɪnt] (-(e)s, -er) *nt* child; **von ~ auf** from childhood

Kinder- ['kɪndər] *zW*: **~betreuung** *f* crèche; **~ei** [-'raɪ] *f* childishness; **~garten** *m* nursery school, playgroup; **~gärtnerin** *f* nursery school teacher; **~geld** *nt* child benefit (*BRIT*); **~heim** *nt* children's home; **~krippe** *f* crèche; **~lähmung** *f* poliomyelitis; **k~leicht** *adj* childishly easy; **k~los** *adj* childless; **~mädchen** *nt* nursemaid; **k~reich** *adj* with a lot of children; **~sendung** *f* (*RADIO, TV*) children's programme; **~sicherung** *f* (*AUT*) childproof safety catch; **~spiel** *nt* (*fig*) child's play; **~tagesstätte** *f* day nursery; **~wagen** *m* pram, baby carriage (*US*); **~zimmer** *nt* (*für* ~) children's room; (*für Säugling*) nursery

---

Kindergarten

A *Kindergarten* is a nursery school for children aged between 3 and 6 years. The children sing and play but do not receive any formal instruction. Most *Kindergärten* are financed by the *town or the church with parents paying a monthly contribution towards the cost.*

Kind- *zW:* **~heit** *f* childhood; **k~isch** *adj* childish; **k~lich** *adj* childlike

Kinn [kɪn] (-(e)s, -e) *nt* chin; **~haken** *m* (BOXEN) uppercut

Kino ['kiːno] (-s, -s) *nt* cinema; **~besucher** *m* cinema-goer; **~programm** *nt* film programme

Kiosk [ki'ɔsk] (-(e)s, -e) *m* kiosk

Kippe ['kɪpə] *f* cigarette end; (umg) fag; **auf der ~ stehen** (fig) to be touch and go

kippen *vi* to topple over, to overturn ♦ *vt* to tilt

Kirch- ['kɪrç] *zW:* **~e** *f* church; **~enlied** *nt* hymn; **~ensteuer** *f* church tax; **~gänger(-s, -)** *m* churchgoer; **~hof** *m* churchyard; **k~lich** *adj* ecclesiastical

Kirmes ['kɪrmɛs] (-, -sen) *f* fair

Kirsche ['kɪrʃə] *f* cherry

Kissen ['kɪsən] (-s, -) *nt* cushion; (Kopfkissen) pillow; **~bezug** *m* pillowslip

Kiste ['kɪstə] *f* box; chest

Kitsch [kɪtʃ] (-(e)s, -) *m* kitsch; **k~ig** *adj* kitschy

Kitt [kɪt] (-(e)s, -e) *m* putty

Kittel (-s, -) *m* overall, smock

kitten *vt* to putty; (fig: Ehe etc) to cement

kitzelig ['kɪtsəlɪç] *adj* (auch fig) ticklish

kitzeln *vi* to tickle

Kiwi ['kiːvi] (-, -s) *f* (BOT, KOCH) kiwi fruit

KKW [kaːkaːˈveː] *nt* abk = **Kernkraftwerk**

Klage ['klaːgə] *f* complaint; (JUR) action; **k~n** *vi* (wehklagen) to lament, to wail; (sich beschweren) to complain; (JUR) to take legal action

Kläger(in) ['klɛːgər(ɪn)] (-s, -) *m(f)* plaintiff

kläglich ['klɛːklɪç] *adj* wretched

klamm [klam] *adj* (Finger) numb; (feucht) damp

Klammer ['klamər] (-, -n) *f* clamp; (in

Text) bracket; (Büroklammer) clip; (Wäscheklammer) peg; (Zahnklammer) brace; **k~n** *vr:* **sich k~n an** +akk to cling to

Klang [klaŋ] (-(e)s, "e) *m* sound; **k~voll** *adj* sonorous

Klappe ['klapə] *f* valve; (Ofenklappe) damper; (umg: Mund) trap; **k~n** *vi* (Geräusch) to click; (Sitz etc) to tip ♦ *vi* to tip ♦ *vb unpers* to work

Klapper ['klapər] (-, -n) *f* rattle; **k~ig** *adj* run-down, worn-out; **k~n** *vi* to clatter, to rattle; **~schlange** *f* rattlesnake; **~storch** *m* stork

Klapp- *zW:* **~messer** *nt* jackknife; **~rad** *nt* collapsible bicycle; **~stuhl** *m* folding chair; **~tisch** *m* folding table

Klaps [klaps] (-es, -e) *m* slap

klar [klaːr] *adj* clear; (NAUT) ready for sea; (MIL) ready for action; **sich dat (über etw akk) ~ werden** to get (sth) clear in one's mind; **sich dat im K~en sein über** +akk to be clear about; **ins K~e kommen** to get clear; **(na) ~!** of course!; **~ sehen** to see clearly

Kläranlage *f* purification plant

klären ['klɛːrən] *vt* (Flüssigkeit) to purify; (Probleme) to clarify ♦ *vr* to clear (itself) up

Klarheit *f* clarity

Klarinette [klari'nɛtə] *f* clarinet

klar- *zW:* **~machen** *vt* to clear up, to explain; **~machen** *vt* (Schiff) to get ready for sea; **jdm etw ~machen** to make sth clear to sb; **~sehen** △ (unreg) *vi siehe* **klar**; **K~sichtfolie** *f* transparent film; **~stellen** *vt* to clarify

Klärung ['klɛːrʊŋ] *f* (von Flüssigkeit) purification; (von Probleme) clarification

klarwerden △ (unreg) *vi siehe* **klar**

Klasse ['klasə] *f* class; (SCH) class, form

klasse (umg) *adj* smashing

Klassen- *zW:* **~arbeit** *f* test; **~gesellschaft** *f* class society; **~lehrer** *m* form master; **k~los** *adj* classless; **~sprecher(in)** *m(f)* form prefect; **~zimmer**

nt classroom

klassifizieren [klasifi'tsiːrən] *vt* to classify

Klassik ['klasɪk] *f (Zeit)* classical period; *(Stil)* classicism; **~er** (-s, -) *m* classic

klassisch *adj (auch fig)* classical

Klatsch [klatʃ] (-(e)s, -e) *m* smack, crack; *(Gerede)* gossip; **~base** *f* gossip, scandalmonger; **~e** *(umg) f* crib; **k~en** *vi (Geräusch)* to clash; *(reden)* to gossip; *(applaudieren)* to applaud, to clap ♦ *vt*: **jdm Beifall k~en** to applaud sb; **~mohn** *m (corn)* poppy; **k~nass** ▲ *adj* soaking wet

Klaue ['klauə] *f* claw; *(umg: Schrift)* scrawl; **k~n** *(umg) vt* to pinch

Klausel ['klauzəl] (-, -n) *f* clause

Klausur [klau'zuːr] *f* seclusion; **~arbeit** *f* examination paper

Klavier [kla'viːr] (-s, -e) *nt* piano

Kleb- [kleːb] *zW:* **k~en** ['kleːbən] *vt, vi:* **k~en (an +akk)** to stick (to); **k~rig** *adj* sticky; **~stoff** *m* glue; **~streifen** *m* adhesive tape

kleckern ['klɛkərn] *vi* to make a mess ♦ *vt* to spill

Klecks [klɛks] (-es, -e) *m* blot, stain

Klee [kleː] (-s) *m* clover; **~blatt** *nt* cloverleaf; *(fig)* trio

Kleid [klaɪt] (-(e)s, -er) *nt* garment; *(Frauenkleid)* dress; **~er** *pl (~ung)* clothes; **k~en** ['klaɪdən] *vt* to clothe, to dress; to suit ♦ *vr* to dress

Kleider- ['klaɪdər] *zW:* **~bügel** *m* coat hanger; **~bürste** *f* clothes brush; **~schrank** *m* wardrobe

Kleid- *zW:* **k~sam** *adj* flattering; **~ung** *f* clothing; **~ungsstück** *nt* garment

klein [klaɪn] *adj* little, small; **~ hacken** to chop, to mince; **~ schneiden** to chop up; **K~e(r, s)** *mf* little one; **K~format** *nt* small size; **im K~format** small-scale; **K~geld** *nt* small change; **K~kind** *nt* infant; **K~igkeit** *f* trifle; **K~kram** *m* details *pl*; **~laut** *adj* de-

jected, quiet; **~lich** *adj* petty, paltry; **K~od** ['klaɪnoːt] (-s, -odien) *nt* gem, jewel; treasure; **K~stadt** *f* small town; **~städtisch** *adj* provincial; **~stmöglich** *adj* smallest possible

Kleister ['klaɪstər] (-s, -) *m* paste

Klemme ['klɛmə] *f* clip; *(MED)* clamp; *(fig)* jam; **k~n** *vt (festhalten)* to jam; *(quetschen)* to pinch, to nip ♦ *vr* to catch o.s.; *(sich hineinzwängen)* to squeeze o.s. ♦ *vi (Tür)* to stick, to jam; **sich hinter jdn/etw k~n** to get on to sb/down to sth

Klempner ['klɛmpnər] (-s, -) *m* plumber

Klerus ['kleːrʊs] (-) *m* clergy

Klette ['klɛtə] *f* burr

Kletter- ['klɛtər] *zW:* **~er** (-s, -) *m* climber; **k~n** *vi* to climb; **~pflanze** *f* creeper

Klient(in) [kli'ɛnt(ɪn)] *m(f)* client

Klima ['kliːma] (-s, -s *od* -te) *nt* climate; **~anlage** *f* air conditioning; **~wechsel** *m* change of air

klimpern ['klɪmpərn] *(umg) vi (mit Münzen, Schlüsseln)* to jingle; *(auf Klavier)* to plonk (away)

Klinge ['klɪŋə] *f* blade; sword

Klingel ['klɪŋəl] (-, -n) *f* bell; **~beutel** *m* collection bag; **k~n** *vi* to ring

klingen ['klɪŋən] *(unreg) vi* to sound; *(Gläser)* to clink

Klinik ['kliːnɪk] *f* hospital, clinic

Klinke ['klɪŋkə] *f* handle

Klippe ['klɪpə] *f* cliff; *(im Meer)* reef; *(fig)* hurdle

klipp und klar ['klɪp'ʊntklaːr] *adj* clear and concise

klirren ['klɪrən] *vi* to clank, to jangle; *(Gläser)* to clink; **~de Kälte** biting cold

Klischee [kli'ʃeː] (-s, -s) *nt (Druckplatte)* plate, block; *(fig)* cliché; **~vorstellung** *f* stereotyped idea

Klo [kloː] (-s, -s) *(umg) nt* loo *(BRIT)*, john *(US)*

Kloake [klo'a:kə] f sewer

klobig ['klo:bɪç] adj clumsy

Klopapier (umg) nt loo paper (BRIT)

klopfen ['klɔpfən] vi to knock; (Herz) to thump ♦ vt to beat; **es klopft** somebody's knocking; **jdm auf die Schulter ~** to tap sb on the shoulder

Klopfer (-s, -) m (Teppichklopfer) beater; (Türklopfer) knocker

Klops [klɔps] (-es, -e) m meatball

Klosett [klo'zɛt] (-s, -e od -s) nt lavatory, toilet; **~papier** nt toilet paper

Kloß [klo:s] (-es, -e) m (im Hals) lump; (KOCH) dumpling

Kloster ['klo:stər] (-s, =) nt (Männerkloster) monastery; (Frauenkloster) convent; **klösterlich** ['klø:stərlɪç] adj monastic; convent çyd

Klotz [klɔts] (-es, -e) m log; (Hackklotz) block; **ein ~ am Bein** (fig) a drag, a millstone round (sb's) neck

Klub [klʊp] (-s, -s) m club; **~sessel** m easy chair

Kluft [klʊft] (-, -e) f cleft, gap; (GEOG) gorge, chasm

klug [klu:k] adj clever, intelligent; **K~heit** f cleverness, intelligence

Klumpen ['klʊmpən] (-s, -) m (Erdklumpen) clod; (Blutklumpen) clot; (Goldklumpen) nugget; (KOCH) lump

km abk = **Kilometer**

knabbern ['knabərn] vt, vi to nibble

Knabe ['kna:bə] (-n, -n) m boy

Knäckebrot ['knɛkəbro:t] nt crispbread

knacken ['knakən] vt, vi (auch fig) to crack

Knacks [knaks] (-es, -e) m crack; (fig) defect

Knall [knal] (-(e)s, -e) m bang; (Peitschenknall) crack; **~ und Fall** (umg) unexpectedly; **~bonbon** nt cracker; **k~en** vi to bang; to crack; **k~rot** adj bright red

knapp [knap] adj tight; (Geld) scarce; (Sprache) concise; **eine ~e Stunde** just under an hour; **~ unter/neben** just

under/by; **K~heit** f tightness; scarcity; conciseness

knarren ['knarən] vi to creak

Knast [knast] (-(e)s) (umg) m (Haftstrafe) porridge (inf), time (inf); (Gefängnis) slammer (inf), clink (inf)

knattern ['knatərn] vi to rattle; (Maschinengewehr) to chatter

Knäuel ['knɔyəl] (-s, -) m od n (Wollknäuel) ball; (Menschenknäuel) knot

Knauf [knaʊf] (-(e)s, Knäufe) m knob; (Schwertknauf) pommel

Knebel ['kne:bəl] (-s, -) m gag

kneifen ['knaɪfən] (unreg) vt to pinch ♦ vi to pinch; (sich drücken) to back out; **vor etw ~** to dodge sth

Kneipe ['knaɪpə] (umg) f pub

kneten ['kne:tən] vt to knead; (Wachs) to mould

Knick [knɪk] (-(e)s, -e) m (Sprung) crack; (Kurve) bend; (Falte) fold; **k~en** vt, vi (springen) to crack; (brechen) to break; (Papier) to fold; **geknickt sein** to be downcast

Knicks [knɪks] (-es, -e) m curtsey

Knie [kni:] (-s, -) nt knee; **~beuge** f knee bend; **~bundhose** m knee breeches; **~gelenk** nt knee joint; **~kehle** f back of the knee; **k~n** vi to kneel; **~scheibe** f kneecap; **~strumpf** m knee-length sock

Kniff [knɪf] (-(e)s, -e) m (fig) trick, knack; **k~elig** adj tricky

knipsen ['knɪpsən] vt (Fahrkarte) to punch; (PHOT) to take a snap of, to snap ♦ vi to take a snap od snaps

Knirps [knɪrps] (-es, -e) m little chap; (® Schirm) telescopic umbrella

knirschen ['knɪrʃən] vi to crunch; **mit den Zähnen ~** to grind one's teeth

knistern ['knɪstərn] vi to crackle

Knitter- ['knɪtər] zW: **~falte** f crease; **k~frei** adj non-crease; **k~n** vi to crease

Knoblauch ['kno:plaʊx] (-(e)s) m garlic; **~zehe** f (KOCH) clove of garlic

Knöchel ['knœçəl] (-s, -) m knuckle;

(*Fußknöchel*) ankle

Knochen ['knɔxən] (-s, -) m bone;
~**bruch** m fracture; ~**gerüst** nt skeleton; ~**mark** nt bone marrow

knöchern ['knœçərn] adj bone

knochig ['knɔxɪç] adj bony

Knödel ['knøːdəl] (-s, -) m dumpling

Knolle ['knɔlə] f tuber

Knopf [knɔpf] (-(e)s, -e) m button;
(*Kragenknopf*) stud

knöpfen ['knœpfən] vt to button

Knopfloch nt buttonhole

Knorpel ['knɔrpəl] (-s, -) m cartilage,
gristle; **k~ig** adj gristly

Knospe ['knɔspə] f bud

Knoten ['knoːtən] (-s, -) m knot; (BOT)
node; (MED) lump; **k~** vt to knot;
~**punkt** m junction

Knüller ['knʏlər] (-s, -) (*umg*) m hit;
(*Reportage*) scoop

knüpfen ['knʏpfən] vt to tie; (*Teppich*)
to knot; (*Freundschaft*) to form

Knüppel ['knʏpəl] (-s, -) m cudgel;
(*Polizeiknüppel*) baton, truncheon;
(AVIAT) (joy)stick

knurren ['knʊrən] vi (*Hund*) to snarl,
to growl; (*Magen*) to rumble; (*Mensch*)
to mutter

knusperig ['knʊspərɪç] adj crisp; (*Keks*)
crunchy

k. o. [kaːˈoː] adj knocked out; (*fig*) done
in

Koalition [koalitsiˈoːn] f coalition

Kobold ['koːbɔlt] (-(e)s, -e) m goblin,
imp

Koch [kɔx] (-(e)s, -e) m cook; ~**buch** nt
cook(ery) book; **k~en** vt, vi to cook;
(*Wasser*) to boil; ~**er** (-s, -) m stove,
cooker; ~**gelegenheit** f cooking facilities pl

Köchin ['kœçɪn] f cook

Koch- zW: ~**löffel** m kitchen spoon;
~**nische** f kitchenette; ~**platte** f hotplate; ~**salz** nt cooking salt; ~**topf** m
saucepan, pot

Köder ['køːdər] (-s, -) m bait, lure

ködern vt (*Tier*) to trap with bait; (*Person*) to entice, to tempt

Koexistenz [koɛksɪsˈtɛnts] f coexistence

Koffein [kɔfeˈiːn] (-s) nt caffeine;
k~frei adj decaffeinated

Koffer ['kɔfər] (-s, -) m suitcase;
(*Schrankkoffer*) trunk; ~**kuli** m (luggage) trolley; ~**radio** nt portable
radio; ~**raum** m (AUT) boot (BRIT),
trunk (US)

Kognak ['kɔnjak] (-s, -s) m brandy,
cognac

Kohl [koːl] (-(e)s, -e) m cabbage

Kohle ['koːlə] f coal; (*Holzkohle*) charcoal; (CHEM) carbon; ~**hydrat** (-(e)s,
-e) nt carbohydrate

Kohlen- zW: ~**dioxid** (-s, -e) nt carbon dioxide; ~**händler** m coal
merchant, coalman; ~**säure** f carbon
dioxide; ~**stoff** m carbon

Kohlepapier nt carbon paper

Koje ['koːjə] f cabin; (*Bett*) bunk

Kokain [kokaˈiːn] (-s) nt cocaine

kokett [koˈkɛt] adj coquettish, flirtatious

Kokosnuss ▲ ['koːkɔsnʊs] f coconut

Koks [koːks] (-es, -e) m coke

Kolben ['kɔlbən] (-s, -) m (*Gewehrkolben*) rifle butt; (*Keule*) club; (CHEM)
flask; (TECH) piston; (*Maiskolben*) cob

Kolik ['koːlɪk] f colic, the gripes pl

Kollaps [kɔˈlaps] (-es, -e) m collapse

Kolleg [kɔˈleːk] (-s, -s od -ien) nt lecture course; ~**e** [kɔˈleːgə] (-n, -n) m
colleague; ~**in** f colleague; ~**ium** nt
working party; (SCH) staff

Kollekte [kɔˈlɛktə] f (REL) collection

kollektiv [kɔlɛkˈtiːf] adj collective

Köln [kœln] (-s) nt Cologne

Kolonie [koloˈniː] f colony

kolonisieren [koloniˈziːrən] vt to colonize

Kolonne [koˈlɔnə] f column; (*von Fahr-*

zeugen) convoy

Koloss ▲ [ko'lɔs] (-es, -e) m colossus; **kolo'ssal** adj colossal

Kölsch [kœlʃ] (-, -) nt (Bier) ≈ (strong) lager

Kombi- ['kɔmbi] zW: **~nation** [-natsi'oːn] f combination; (Vermutung) conjecture; (Hemdhose) combinations pl; **k~nieren** [-'niːrən] vt to combine ♦ vi to deduce, to work out; (vermuten) to guess; **~wagen** m station wagon; **~zange** f (pair of) pliers pl

Komet [ko'meːt] (-en, -en) m comet

Komfort [kɔm'foːr] (-s) m luxury

Komik ['koːmik] f humour, comedy; **~er** (-s, -) m comedian

komisch ['koːmiʃ] adj funny

Komitee [komi'teː] (-s, -s) nt committee

Komma ['kɔma] (-s, -s od -ta) nt comma; **2 ~ 3** 2 point 3

Kommand- [ko'mand] zW: **~ant** [-'dant] m commander, commanding officer; **k~ieren** [-'diːrən] vt, vi to command; **~o** (-s, -s) nt command, order; (Truppe) detachment, squad; **auf ~o** to order

kommen ['kɔmən] (unreg) vi to come; (näher kommen) to approach; (passieren) to happen; (gelangen, geraten) to get; (Blumen, Zähne, Tränen etc) to appear; (in die Schule, das Zuchthaus etc) to go; **~ lassen** to send for; **das kommt in den Schrank** that goes in the cupboard; **zu sich ~** to come round od to; **zu etw ~** to acquire sth; **um etw ~** to lose sth; **nichts auf jdn/etw ~ lassen** to have nothing said against sb/sth; **jdm frech ~** to get cheeky with sb; **auf jeden vierten kommt ein Platz** there's one place for every fourth person; **wer kommt zuerst?** who's first?; **unter ein Auto ~** to be run over by a car; **wie hoch kommt das?** what does that cost?; **komm gut nach Hause!** safe journey (home); **~den Sonntag** next Sunday;

K~ (-s) nt coming

Kommentar [kɔmɛn'taːr] m commentary; **kein ~** no comment; **k~los** adj without comment

Kommentator [kɔmɛn'taːtɔr] m (TV) commentator

kommentieren [kɔmɛn'tiːrən] vt to comment on

kommerziell [kɔmɛrtsi'ɛl] adj commercial

Kommilitone [kɔmili'toːnə] (-n, -n) m fellow student

Kommissar [kɔmɪ'saːr] m police inspector

Kommission [kɔmisi'oːn] f (COMM) commission; (Ausschuss) committee

Kommode [kɔ'moːdə] f (chest of) drawers

kommunal [kɔmu'naːl] adj local; (von Stadt auch) municipal

Kommune [kɔ'muːnə] f commune

Kommunikation [kɔmunikatsi'oːn] f communication

Kommunion [kɔmuni'oːn] f communion

Kommuniqué, Kommunikee ▲ [kɔmyni'keː] (-s, -s) nt communiqué

Kommunismus [kɔmu'nɪsmʊs] m communism

Kommunist(in) [kɔmu'nɪst(ɪn)] m(f) communist; **k~isch** adj communist

kommunizieren [kɔmuni'tsiːrən] vi to communicate

Komödie [ko'møːdiə] f comedy

Kompagnon [kɔmpan'jõː] (-s, -s) m (COMM) partner

kompakt [kɔm'pakt] adj compact

Kompanie [kɔmpa'niː] f company

Kompass ▲ [kɔm'pas] (-es, -e) m compass

kompatibel [kɔmpa'tiːbəl] adj compatible

kompetent [kɔmpe'tɛnt] adj competent

Kompetenz f competence, authority

komplett [kɔm'plɛt] adj complete

Komplex [kɔm'plɛks] (-es, -e) m (Ge-

bäudekomplex) complex

Komplikation [kɔmplikatsiˈoːn] *f* complication

Kompliment [kɔmpliˈmɛnt] *nt* compliment

Komplize [kɔmˈpliːtsə] (*-n, -n*) *m* accomplice

kompliziert [kɔmpliˈtsiːrt] *adj* complicated

komponieren [kɔmpoˈniːrən] *vt* to compose

Komponist [kɔmpoˈnɪst(ɪn)] *m* composer

Komposition [kɔmpozitsiˈoːn] *f* composition

Kompost [kɔmˈpɔst] (*-(e)s, -e*) *m* compost

Kompott [kɔmˈpɔt] (*-(e)s, -e*) *nt* stewed fruit

Kompromiss ▲ [kɔmproˈmɪs] (*-es, -e*) *m* compromise; **k~bereit** *adj* willing to compromise

Kondens- [kɔnˈdɛns] *zW:* **~ation** [kɔndɛnzatsiˈoːn] *f* condensation; **k~ieren** [kɔndɛnˈziːrən] *vt* to condense; **~milch** *f* condensed milk

Kondition [kɔndɪtsiˈoːn] *f* (COMM, FIN) condition; *(Durchhaltevermögen)* stamina; *(körperliche Verfassung)* physical condition, state of health

Konditionstraining [kɔndɪtsiˈoːnstreːnɪŋ] *nt* fitness training

Konditor [kɔnˈdiːtɔr] *m* pastry cook; **~ei** [-ˈraɪ] *f* café; cake shop

Kondom [kɔnˈdoːm] (*-s, -e*) *nt* condom

Konferenz [kɔnfeˈrɛnts] *f* conference, meeting

Konfession [kɔnfɛsiˈoːn] *f* (religious) denomination; **k~ell** [-ˈnɛl] *adj* denominational; **k~slos** *adj* nondenominational

Konfirmand [kɔnfɪrˈmant] *m* candidate for confirmation

Konfirmation [kɔnfɪrmatsiˈoːn] *f* (REL) confirmation

konfirmieren [kɔnfɪrˈmiːrən] *vt* to confirm

konfiszieren [kɔnfɪsˈtsiːrən] *vt* to confiscate

Konfitüre [kɔnfiˈtyːrə] *f* jam

Konflikt [kɔnˈflɪkt] (*-(e)s, -e*) *m* conflict

konfrontieren [kɔnfrɔnˈtiːrən] *vt* to confront

konfus [kɔnˈfuːs] *adj* confused

Kongress ▲ [kɔnˈɡrɛs] (*-es, -e*) *m* congress; **~zentrum** *nt* conference centre

Kongruenz [kɔŋɡruˈɛnts] *f* agreement, congruence

König [ˈkøːnɪç] (*-(e)s, -e*) *m* king; **~in** [ˈkøːnɪɡɪn] *f* queen; **k~lich** *adj* royal; **~reich** *nt* kingdom

Konjugation [kɔnjuɡatsiˈoːn] *f* conjugation

konjugieren [kɔnjuˈɡiːrən] *vt* to conjugate

Konjunktion [kɔnjʊŋktsiˈoːn] *f* conjunction

Konjunktiv [ˈkɔnjʊŋktiːf] (*-s, -e*) *m* subjunctive

Konjunktur [kɔnjʊŋkˈtuːr] *f* economic situation; *(Hochkonjunktur)* boom

konkret [kɔnˈkreːt] *adj* concrete

Konkurrent(in) [kɔnkʊˈrɛnt(ɪn)] *m(f)* competitor

Konkurrenz [kɔnkʊˈrɛnts] *f* competition; **k~fähig** *adj* competitive; **~kampf** *m* competition; rivalry, competitive situation

konkurrieren [kɔnkʊˈriːrən] *vi* to compete

Konkurs [kɔnˈkʊrs] (*-es, -e*) *m* bankruptcy

Können (*-s*) *nt* ability

SCHLÜSSELWORT

können [ˈkœnən] (*pt* konnte, *pp* gekonnt *od (als Hilfsverb)* können) *vt, vi*

1 to be able to; **ich kann es machen** I can do it, I am able to do it; **ich kann es nicht machen** I can't do it, I'm not able to do it; **ich kann nicht ...** I can't ..., I cannot ...; **ich kann nicht mehr** I can't go on

2 (*wissen, beherrschen*) to know; **können Sie Deutsch?** can you speak German?; **er kann gut Englisch** he speaks English well; **sie kann keine Mathematik** she can't do mathematics

3 (*dürfen*) to be allowed to; **kann ich gehen?** can I go?; **könnte ich ...?** could I ...?; **kann ich mit?** (*umg*) can I come with you?

4 (*möglich sein*): **Sie könnten Recht haben** you may be right; **das kann sein** that's possible; **kann sein** maybe

Könner *m* expert

konnte *etc* ['kɔntə] *vb siehe* **können**

konsequent [kɔnze'kvɛnt] *adj* consistent

Konsequenz [kɔnze'kvɛnts] *f* consistency; (*Folgerung*) conclusion

Konserv- [kɔn'zɛrv] *zW:* **k~ativ** [-a'tiːf] *adj* conservative; **~ative(r)** [-a'tiːvə(r)] *f(m)* (*POL*) conservative; **~e** *f* tinned food; **~enbüchse** *f* tin, can; **k~ieren** [-'viːrən] *vt* to preserve; **~ierung** *f* preservation; **~ierungsstoff** *m* preservatives

Konsonant [kɔnzo'nant] *m* consonant

konstant [kɔn'stant] *adj* constant

konstru- *zW:* **~ieren** [kɔnstru'iːrən] *vt* to construct; **K~kteur** [kɔnstrʊk'tøːr] *m* designer; **K~ktion** [kɔnstrʊktsi'oːn] *f* construction; **~ktiv** [kɔnstrʊk'tiːf] *adj* constructive

Konsul ['kɔnzul] (*-s, -n*) *m* consul; **~at** [-'laːt] *nt* consulate

konsultieren [kɔnzʊl'tiːrən] *vt* to consult

Konsum [kɔn'zuːm] (*-s*) *m* consumption; **~artikel** *m* consumer article; **~ent** [-'mɛnt] *m* consumer; **k~ieren**

['miːrən] *vt* to consume

Kontakt [kɔn'takt] (*-(e)s, -e*) *m* contact; **k~arm** *adj* unsociable; **k~freudig** *adj* sociable; **~linsen** *pl* contact lenses

kontern ['kɔntərn] *vt, vi* to counter

Kontinent [kɔnti'nɛnt] *m* continent

Kontingent [kɔntɪŋ'gɛnt] (*-(e)s, -e*) *nt* quota; (*Truppenkontingent*) contingent

kontinuierlich [kɔntinu'iːrlɪç] *adj* continuous

Konto ['kɔnto] (*-s, Konten*) *nt* account; **~auszug** *m* statement (of account); **~inhaber(in)** *m(f)* account holder; **~stand** *m* balance

Kontra ['kɔntra] (*-s, -s*) *nt* (*KARTEN*) double; **jdm ~ geben** (*fig*) to contradict sb; **~bass** ▲ *m* double bass; **~hent** *m* (*COMM*) contracting party; **~punkt** *m* counterpoint

Kontrast [kɔn'trast] (*-(e)s, -e*) *m* contrast

Kontroll- [kɔn'trɔl] *zW:* **~e** *f* control, supervision; (*Passkontrolle*) passport control; **~eur** [-'løːr] *m* inspector; **k~ieren** [-'liːrən] *vt* to control, to supervise; (*nachprüfen*) to check

Konvention [kɔnvɛntsi'oːn] *f* convention; **k~ell** [-'nɛl] *adj* conventional

Konversation [kɔnverzatsi'oːn] *f* conversation; **~slexikon** *nt* encyclop(a)edia

Konvoi ['kɔnvɔy] (*-s, -s*) *m* convoy

Konzentration [kɔntsɛntratsi'oːn] *f* concentration

Konzentrationslager *nt* concentration camp

konzentrieren [kɔntsɛn'triːrən] *vt, vr* to concentrate

konzentriert *adj* concentrated ♦ *adv* (*zuhören, arbeiten*) intently

Konzern [kɔn'tsɛrn] (*-s, -e*) *m* combine

Konzert [kɔn'tsɛrt] (*-(e)s, -e*) *nt* concert; (*Stück*) concerto; **~saal** *m* concert hall

Konzession [kɔntsɛsi'oːn] *f* licence; (*Zugeständnis*) concession

Konzil [kɔnˈtsiːl] (-s, -e od -ien) nt council

kooperativ [koʔoperaˈtiːf] adj cooperative

koordinieren [koʔɔrdiˈniːrən] vt to co-ordinate

Kopf [kɔpf] (-(e)s, ᵉe) m head; **~haut** f scalp; **~hörer** m headphones pl; **~kissen** nt pillow; **k~los** adj panic-stricken; **k~rechnen** vi to do mental arithmetic; **~salat** m lettuce; **~schmerzen** pl headache sg; **~sprung** m header, dive; **~stand** m headstand; **~stütze** f (im Auto etc) headrest, head restraint; **~tuch** nt headscarf; **~weh** nt headache; **~zerbrechen** nt: **jdm ~zerbrechen machen** to be a headache for sb

Kopie [koˈpiː] f copy; **k~ren** vt to copy

Kopiergerät nt photocopier

Koppel¹ [ˈkɔpəl] (-, -n) f (Weide) enclosure

Koppel² [ˈkɔpəl] (-s, -) nt (Gürtel) belt

koppeln vt to couple

Koppelung f coupling

Koralle [koˈralə] f coral

Korb [kɔrp] (-(e)s, ᵉe) m basket; **jdm einen ~ geben** (fig) to turn sb down; **~ball** m basketball; **~stuhl** m wicker chair

Kord [kɔrt] (-(e)s, -e) m cord, corduroy

Kordel [ˈkɔrdəl] (-, -n) f cord, string

Kork [kɔrk] (-(e)s, -e) m cork; **~en** (-s, -) m stopper, cork; **~enzieher** (-s, -) m corkscrew

Korn [kɔrn] (-(e)s, ᵉer) nt corn, grain; (Gewehr) sight

Körper [ˈkœrpər] (-s, -) m body; **~bau** m build; **k~behindert** adj disabled; **~geruch** m body odour; **~gewicht** nt weight; **~größe** f height; **k~lich** adj physical; **~pflege** f personal hygiene; **~schaft** f corporation; **~schaftssteuer** f corporation tax; **~teil** m part of the body; **~verletzung** f bodily od physical injury

Kot [koːt] (-(e)s) m excrement

Kotelett [kotəˈlɛt] (-(e)s, -e od -s) nt

korpulent [kɔrpuˈlɛnt] adj corpulent

korrekt [kɔˈrɛkt] adj correct; **K~ur** [-ˈtuːr] f (eines Textes) proofreading; (Text) proof; (SCH) marking, correction

Korrespond– [kɔrɛspɔnd] zW: **~ent(in)** [-ˈdɛnt(ɪn)]m(f) correspondent; **~enz** [-ˈdɛnts] f correspondence; **k~ieren** [-ˈdiːrən] vi to correspond

Korridor [ˈkɔridoːr] (-s, -e) m corridor

korrigieren [kɔriˈgiːrən] vt to correct

Korruption [kɔrʊptsiˈoːn] f corruption

Kose– [ˈkoːzə] zW: **~form** f pet form; **~name** m pet name; **~wort** nt term of endearment

Kosmetik [kɔsˈmeːtɪk] f cosmetics pl; **~erin** f beautician

kosmetisch adj cosmetic; (Chirurgie) plastic

kosmisch [ˈkɔsmɪʃ] adj cosmic

Kosmo– [kɔsmo] zW: **~naut** [-ˈnaʊt] (-en, -en) m cosmonaut; **k~politisch** adj cosmopolitan; **~s** (-) m cosmos

Kost [kɔst] (-) f (Nahrung) food; (Verpflegung) board; **k~bar** adj precious; (teuer) costly, expensive; **~barkeit** f preciousness; costliness, expensiveness; (Wertstück) valuable

kosten f cost(s); (Ausgaben) expenses; **auf ~ von** at the expense of; **k~** vt to cost; (versuchen) to taste ♦ vi to taste; **was kostet ...?** what does ... cost?, how much is ...?; **~anschlag** m estimate; **k~los** adj free (of charge)

köstlich [ˈkœstlɪç] adj precious; (Essen) delicious; **sich ~ amüsieren** to have a marvellous time

Kostprobe f taste; (fig) sample

kostspielig adj expensive

Kostüm [kɔsˈtyːm] (-s, -e) nt costume; (Damenkostüm) suit; **~fest** nt fancy-dress party; **k~ieren** [kɔsty'miːrən] vt, vr to dress up; **~verleih** m costume agency

---

cutlet, chop; **~en** pl (Bart) sideboards

Köter ['køːtər] (-s, -) m cur

Kotflügel m (AUT) wing

kotzen ['kɔtsən] (umg!) vi to puke (umg), to throw up (umg)

Krabbe ['krabə] f shrimp; **k~ln** vi to crawl

Krach [krax] (-(e)s, -s od -e) m crash; (andauernd) noise; (umg: Streit) quarrel, argument; (umg) to crash; (beim Brechen) to crack ♦ vr (umg) to argue, to quarrel

krächzen ['krɛçtsən] vi to croak

Kraft [kraft] (-, -e) f strength; power; force; (Arbeitskraft) worker; **in ~ treten** to come into force; **k~** präp +gen by virtue of; **~fahrer** m (motor) driver; **~fahrzeug** nt motor vehicle; **~fahrzeugbrief** m logbook; **~fahrzeugsteuer** f = road tax; **~fahrzeugversicherung** f car insurance

kräftig ['krɛftɪç] adj strong; **~en** vt to strengthen

Kraft- zW: **k~los** adj weak; powerless; (JUR) invalid; **~probe** f trial of strength; **~stoff** m fuel; **k~voll** adj vigorous; **~werk** nt power station

Kragen ['kraːgən] (-s, -) m collar; **~weite** f collar size

Krähe ['krɛːə] f crow; **k~n** vi to crow

Kralle ['kralə] f claw; (Vogelkralle) talon; **k~n** vt to clutch; (krampfhaft) to claw

Kram [kraːm] (-(e)s) m stuff, rubbish; **k~en** vi to rummage; **~laden** (pej) m small shop

Krampf [krampf] (-(e)s, -e) m cramp; (zuckend) spasm; **~ader** f varicose vein; **k~haft** adj convulsive; (fig: Versuche) desperate

Kran [kraːn] (-(e)s, -e) m crane; (Wasserkran) tap, faucet (US)

krank [kraŋk] adj ill, sick; **K~e(r)** f(m) sick person, invalid; patient; **~en** vi: **an etw dat ~en** (fig) to suffer from sth

kränken ['krɛŋkən] vt to hurt

Kranken- zW: **~geld** nt sick pay; **~gymnastik** f physiotherapy; **~haus**

nt hospital; **~kasse** f health insurance; **~pfleger** m nursing orderly; **~schein** m health insurance card; **~schwester** f nurse; **~versicherung** f health insurance; **~wagen** m ambulance

Krank- zW: **k~haft** adj diseased; (Angst etc) morbid; **~heit** f illness; disease; **~heitserreger** m disease-causing agent

kränklich ['krɛŋklɪç] adj sickly

Kränkung f insult, offence

Kranz [krants] (-es, -e) m wreath, garland

krass ▲ [kras] adj crass

Krater ['kraːtər] (-s, -) m crater

Kratz- ['krats] zW: **~bürste** f (fig) crosspatch; **k~en** vt, vi to scratch; **~er** (-s, -) m scratch; (Werkzeug) scraper

Kraul [kraʊl] (-s) nt crawl; **~ schwimmen** to do the crawl; **k~en** vi (schwimmen) to do the crawl ♦ vt (streicheln) to fondle

kraus [kraʊs] adj crinkly; (Haar) frizzy; (Stirn) wrinkled

Kraut [kraʊt] (-(e)s, Kräuter) nt plant; (Gewürz) herb; (Gemüse) cabbage

Krawall [kra'val] (-s, -e) m row, uproar

Krawatte [kra'vatə] f tie

kreativ [krea'tiːf] adj creative

Krebs [kreːps] (-es, -e) m crab; (MED, ASTROL) cancer; **k~krank** adj suffering from cancer

Kredit [kre'diːt] (-(e)s, -e) m credit; **~institut** nt bank; **~karte** f credit card

Kreide ['kraɪdə] f chalk; **k~bleich** adj as white as a sheet

Kreis [kraɪs] (-es, -e) m circle; (Stadtkreis etc) district; **im ~ gehen** (auch fig) to go round in circles

kreischen ['kraɪʃən] vi to shriek, to screech

Kreis- zW: **~el** ['kraɪzəl] (-s, -) m top; (~verkehr) roundabout (BRIT), traffic circle (US); **k~en** ['kraɪzən] vi to spin; **~lauf** m (MED) circulation; (fig: der Natur etc) cycle; **~säge** f circular saw; **~stadt** f county town; **~verkehr** m roundabout traffic

Krematorium [krema'to:riəm] nt crematorium

Kreml ['krɛml] (-s) m Kremlin

krepieren [kre'pi:rən] (umg) vi (sterben) to die, to kick the bucket

Krepp [krɛp] (-s, -s od -e) m crepe; **~papier** ▲ nt crepe paper

Kresse ['krɛsə] f cress

Kreta ['kre:ta] (-s) nt Crete

Kreuz [krɔyts] (-es, -e) nt cross; (ANAT) small of the back; (KARTEN) clubs; **k~en** vt, vr to cross ♦ vi (NAUT) to cruise; **~er** (-s, -) m (Schiff) cruiser; **~fahrt** f cruise; **~feuer** nt (fig): **ins ~feuer geraten** to be under fire from all sides; **~igen** vt to crucify; **~igung** f crucifixion; **~ung** f (Verkehrskreuzung) crossing, junction; (Züchten) cross; **~verhör** nt cross-examination; **~weg** m crossroads; (REL) Way of the Cross; **~worträtsel** nt crossword puzzle; **~zug** m crusade

Kriech- ['kri:ç] zW: **k~en** (unreg) vi to crawl, to creep; (pej) to grovel, to crawl; **~er** (-s, -) m crawler; **~spur** f crawler lane; **~tier** nt reptile

Krieg [kri:k] (-(e)s, -e) m war

kriegen ['kri:gən] (umg) vt to get

Kriegs- zW: **~erklärung** f declaration of war; **~fuß** m: **mit jdm/etw auf ~fuß stehen** to be at loggerheads with sb/to have difficulties with sth; **~gefangene(r)** m prisoner of war; **~gefangenschaft** f captivity; **~gericht** nt court-martial; **~schiff** nt warship; **~verbrecher** m war criminal; **~versehrte(r)** m person disabled in the war; **~zustand** m state of war

Krim [krɪm] (-) f Crimea

Krimi ['kri:mi] (-s, -s) (umg) m thriller

Kriminal- [krimi'na:l] zW: **~beamte(r)** m detective; **~i'tät** f criminality; **~polizei** f ≈ Criminal Investigation Department (BRIT), Federal Bureau of

Investigation (US); **~ro'man** m detective story

kriminell [krimi'nɛl] adj criminal; **K~e(r)** m criminal

Krippe ['krɪpə] f crib; (Kinderkrippe) crèche

Krise ['kri:zə] f crisis; **k~ln** vi: **es k~lt** there's a crisis

Kristall [krɪs'tal] (-s, -e) m crystal ♦ nt (Glas) crystal

Kriterium [kri'te:riəm] nt criterion

Kritik [kri'ti:k] f criticism; (Zeitungskritik) review, write-up; **~er** ['kri:tikər] (-s, -) m critic; **k~los** adj uncritical

kritisch ['kri:tɪʃ] adj critical

kritisieren [kriti'zi:rən] vt, vi to criticize

kritzeln ['krɪtsəln] vt, vi to scribble, to scrawl

Kroatien [kro'a:tsiən] nt Croatia

Krokodil [kroko'di:l] (-s, -e) nt crocodile

Krokus ['kro:kʊs] (-, -od -se) m crocus

Krone ['kro:nə] f crown; (Baumkrone) top

krönen ['krø:nən] vt to crown

Kron- zW: **~korken** m bottle top; **~leuchter** m chandelier; **~prinz** m crown prince

Krönung ['krø:nʊŋ] f coronation

Kropf [krɔpf] (-(e)s, ²e) m (MED) goitre; (von Vogel) crop

Kröte ['krø:tə] f toad

Krücke ['krʏkə] f crutch

Krug [kru:k] (-(e)s, ²e) m jug; (Bierkrug) mug

Krümel ['kry:məl] (-s, -) m crumb; **k~n** vt, vi to crumble

krumm [krʊm] adj (auch fig) crooked; (kurvig) curved; **jdm etw ~ nehmen** to take sth amiss; **~beinig** adj bandylegged; **~lachen** (umg) vr to laugh o.s. silly

Krümmung ['krʏmʊŋ] f bend, curve

Krüppel ['krʏpəl] (-s, -) m cripple

Kruste ['krʊstə] f crust

Kruzifix [krutsi'fiks] (-es, -e) nt crucifix

Kübel ['ky:bəl] (-s, -) m tub; (Eimer) pail

Kubikmeter [ku'bi:kme:tər] m cubic metre

Küche ['kyçə] f kitchen; (Kochen) cooking, cuisine

Kuchen ['ku:xən] (-s, -) m cake; ~**form** f baking tin; ~**gabel** f pastry fork

Küchen- zW: ~**herd** m cooker, stove; ~**schabe** f cockroach; ~**schrank** m kitchen cabinet

Kuckuck ['kʊkʊk] (-s, -e) m cuckoo; ~**suhr** f cuckoo clock

Kugel ['ku:gəl] (-, -n) f ball; (MATH) sphere; (MIL) bullet; (Erdkugel) globe; (SPORT) shot; **k~förmig** adj spherical; ~**lager** nt ball bearing; **k~rund** adj (Gegenstand) round; (umg: Person) tubby; ~**schreiber** m ball-point (pen), Biro ®; **k~sicher** adj bulletproof; ~**stoßen** (-s) nt shot put

Kuh [ku:] (-, ⁻e) f cow

kühl [ky:l] adj (auch fig) cool; **K~anlage** f refrigeration plant; **K~e** (-) f coolness; ~**en** vt to cool; **K~er** (-s, -) m (AUT) radiator; **K~erhaube** f (AUT) bonnet (BRIT), hood (US); **K~raum** m cold storage chamber; **K~schrank** m refrigerator; **K~truhe** f freezer; **K~ung** f cooling; **K~wasser** nt radiator water

kühn [ky:n] adj bold, daring; **K~heit** f boldness

Kuhstall m byre, cattle shed

Küken ['ky:kən] (-s, -) nt chicken

kulant [ku'lant] adj obliging

Kuli ['ku:li] (-s, -s) m coolie; (umg: Kugelschreiber) Biro ®

Kulisse [ku'lɪsə] f scenery

kullern ['kʊlərn] vi to roll

Kult [kʊlt] (-(e)s, -e) m worship, cult; **mit etw einen ~ treiben** to make a cult out of sth

kultivieren [kʊlti'vi:rən] vt to cultivate

kultiviert adj cultivated, refined

Kultur [kʊl'tu:r] f culture; civilization;

(des Bodens) cultivation; ~**banause** (umg) m philistine, low-brow; ~**beutel** m toilet bag; **k~ell** [-u'rɛl] adj cultural; ~**ministerium** nt ministry of education and the arts

Kümmel ['kyməl] (-s, -) m caraway seed; (Branntwein) kümmel

Kummer ['kʊmər] (-s) m grief, sorrow

kümmerlich ['kymərlɪç] adj miserable, wretched

kümmern ['kymərn] vt to concern ♦ vr: **sich um jdn ~** to look after sb; **das kümmert mich nicht** that doesn't worry me; **sich um etw ~** to see to sth

Kumpel ['kʊmpəl] (-s, -) (umg) m mate

kündbar ['kyntba:r] adj redeemable, recallable; (Vertrag) terminable

Kunde¹ ['kʊndə] (-n, -n) m customer

Kunde² ['kʊndə] f (Botschaft) news

Kunden- zW: ~**dienst** m after-sales service; ~**konto** nt charge account; ~**nummer** f customer number

Kund- zW: **k~geben** (unreg) vt to announce; ~**gebung** f announcement; (Versammlung) rally

Künd- ['kynd] zW: **k~igen** vi to give in one's notice ♦ vt to cancel; **jdm k~igen** to give sb his notice; **die Stellung/Wohnung k~igen** to give notice that one is leaving one's job/house; **jdm die Stellung/Wohnung k~igen** to give sb notice to leave his/her job/house; ~**igung** f notice; ~**igungsfrist** f period of notice; ~**igungsschutz** m protection against wrongful dismissal

Kundin f customer

Kundschaft f customers pl, clientele

künftig ['kynftɪç] adj future ♦ adv in future

Kunst [kʊnst] (-, ⁻e) f art; (Können) skill; **das ist doch keine ~** it's easy; ~**dünger** m artificial manure; ~**faser** f synthetic fibre; ~**fertigkeit** f skilfulness; ~**gegenstand** m art object; ~**gerecht** adj skilful; ~**geschichte** f history of art; **~gewerbe** nt arts and crafts pl; **~griff** m trick, knack; **~händler** m art dealer

Künstler(in) ['kʏnstlər(ɪn)] (-s, -) m(f) artist; **k~isch** adj artistic; **~name** m pseudonym

künstlich ['kʏnstlɪç] adj artificial

Kunst- zW: **~sammler** (-s, -) m art collector; **~seide** f artificial silk; **~stoff** m synthetic material; **~stück** nt trick; **~turnen** nt gymnastics sg; **k~voll** adj artistic; **~werk** nt work of art

kunterbunt ['kʊntərbʊnt] adj higgledy-piggledy

Kupee ▲ [ku'pe:] (-s, -s) nt coupé

Kupfer ['kʊpfər] (-s) nt copper; **k~n** adj copper

Kupon [ku'põː, ku'pɔŋ] (-s, -s) m coupon; (Stoff~) length of cloth

Kuppe ['kʊpə] f (Berg~) top; (Finger~) tip

Kuppel (-, -n) f dome; **k~n** vi (JUR) to procure; (AUT) to declutch ♦ vt to join

Kupplung f coupling; (AUT) clutch

Kur [kuːr] (-, -en) f cure, treatment

Kür [kyːr] (-, -en) f (SPORT) free exercises pl

Kurbel ['kʊrbəl] (-, -n) f crank, winder; (AUT) starting handle; **~welle** f crankshaft

Kürbis ['kʏrbɪs] (-ses, -se) m pumpkin; (exotisch) gourd

Kurgast m visitor (to a health resort)

kurieren [ku'riːrən] vt to cure

kurios [kuri'oːs] adj curious, odd; **K~i'tät** f curiosity

Kurort m health resort

Kurs [kʊrs] (-es, -e) m course; (FIN) rate; **~buch** nt timetable; **k~ieren** [kʊr'ziːrən] vi to circulate; **k~iv** [kʊr'ziːf] adv in italics; **~us** ['kʊrzʊs] (-, Kurse) m course; **~wagen** m (EISENB) through carriage

Kurtaxe [-taksə] (-, -n) f visitors' tax (at health resort or spa)

Kurve ['kʊrvə] f curve; (Straßenkurve) curve, bend; **kurvig** adj (Straße) bendy

kurz [kʊrts] adj short; **~ gesagt** in short; **~ halten** to keep short; **zu ~ kommen** to come off badly; **den Kürzeren ziehen** to get the worst of it; **K~arbeit** f short-time work; **~arm(e)lig** adj short-sleeved

Kürze ['kʏrtsə] f shortness, brevity; **k~n** vt to cut short; (in der Länge) to shorten; (Gehalt) to reduce

kurz- zW: **~erhand** adv on the spot; **~fristig** adj short-term; **K~geschichte** f short story; **~halten** △ (unreg) vt siehe kurz; **~lebig** adj short-lived

kürzlich ['kʏrtslɪç] adv lately, recently

Kurz- zW: **~schluss** ▲ m (ELEK) short circuit; **k~sichtig** adj short-sighted

Kürzung f (eines Textes) abridgement; (eines Theaterstück, des Gehalts) cut

Kurzwelle f short wave

kuscheln ['kʊʃəln] vr to snuggle up

Kusine [ku'ziːnə] f cousin

Kuss ▲ [kʊs] (-es, ⁼e) m kiss

küssen ['kʏsən] vt, vr to kiss

Küste ['kʏstə] f coast, shore

Küstenwache f coastguard

Küster ['kʏstər] (-s, -) m sexton, verger

Kutsche ['kʊtʃə] f coach, carriage; **~r** (-s, -) m coachman

Kutte ['kʊtə] f habit

Kuvert [ku'vert] (-s, -e od -s) nt envelope; cover

KZ nt abk von **Konzentrationslager**

L, l

l. abk = **Liter**

labil [la'biːl] adj (MED: Konstitution) delicate

Labor [la'boːr] (-s, -e od -s) nt lab; **~ant(in)** m(f) lab(oratory) assistant

Labyrinth [laby'rɪnt] (-s, -e) nt labyrinth

Lache

158

Landhaus

Lache ['laxə] f (Flüssigkeit) puddle; (von Blut, Benzin etc) pool

lächeln ['lɛçəln] vi to smile; **L~** (-s) nt smile

lachen ['laxən] vi to laugh

lächerlich ['lɛçərlɪç] adj ridiculous

Lachgas nt laughing gas

lachhaft adj laughable

Lachs [laks] (-es, -e) m salmon

Lack [lak] (-(e)s, -e) m lacquer, varnish; (von Auto) paint; **l~ieren** [la'ki:rən] vt to varnish; (Auto) to spray; **~ierer** [la'ki:rər] (-s, -) m varnisher

Laden ['la:dən] (-s, ⁻) m shop; (Fensterladen) shutter

laden ['la:dən] (unreg) vt (Lasten) to load; (JUR) to summon; (einladen) to invite

Laden- zW: **~dieb** m shoplifter; **~diebstahl** m shoplifting; **~schluss** ▲ m closing time; **~tisch** m counter

Laderaum m freight space; (AVIAT, NAUT) hold

Ladung ['la:dʊŋ] f (Last) cargo, load; (Beladen) loading; (JUR) summons; (Einladung) invitation; (Sprengladung) charge

Lage ['la:gə] f position, situation; (Schicht) layer; **in der ~ sein** to be in a position

Lageplan m ground plan

Lager ['la:gər] (-s, -) nt camp; (COMM) warehouse; (Schlaflager) bed; (von Tier) lair; (TECH) bearing; **~bestand** m stocks pl; **~feuer** nt campfire; **~haus** nt warehouse, store

lagern ['la:gərn] vi (Dinge) to be stored; (Menschen) to camp ♦ vt to store; (betten) to lay down; (Maschine) to bed

Lagune [la'gu:nə] f lagoon

lahm [la:m] adj lame; **~ legen** to paralyse

lahmen vi to be lame

Lähmung f paralysis

Laib [laɪp] (-s, -e) m loaf

Laie ['laɪə] (-n, -n) m layman; **l~nhaft** adj amateurish

Laken ['la:kən] (-s, -) nt sheet

Lakritze [la'krɪtsə] f liquorice

lallen ['lalən] vt, vi to slur; (Baby) to babble

Lamelle [la'mɛlə] f lamella; (ELEK) lamina; (TECH) plate

Lametta [la'mɛta] (-s) nt tinsel

Lamm [lam] (-(e)s, ⁻er) nt lamb

Lampe ['lampə] f lamp

Lampen- zW: **~fieber** nt stage fright; **~schirm** m lampshade

Lampion [lampi'ŏ:] (-s, -s) m Chinese lantern

Land [lant] (-(e)s, ⁻er) nt land; (Nation, nicht Stadt) country; (Bundesland) state; **auf dem ~(e)** in the country; siehe hierzulande; **~besitz** m landed property; **~ebahn** f runway; **l~en** ['landən] vt, vi to land

---

Land

A Land (plural Länder) is a member state of the BRD and of Austria. There are 16 Länder in Germany, namely Baden-Württemberg, Bayern, Berlin, Brandenburg, Bremen, Hamburg, Hessen, Mecklenburg-Vorpommern, Niedersachsen, Nordrhein-Westfalen, Rheinland-Pfalz, Saarland, Sachsen, Sachsen-Anhalt, Schleswig-Holstein and Thüringen. Each Land has its own parliament and constitution. The 9 Länder of Austria are Vorarlberg, Tirol, Salzburg, Oberösterreich, Niederösterreich, Kärnten, Steiermark, Burgenland and Wien.

Landes- ['landəs] zW: **~farben** pl national colours; **~innere(s)** nt inland region; **~sprache** f national language; **l~üblich** adj customary; **~verrat** m high treason; **~währung** f national currency; **l~weit** adj nationwide

Land- zW: **~haus** nt country house; **~karte** f map; **~kreis** m administrative region; **l~läufig** adj customary

ländlich ['lɛntlɪç] adj rural

Land- zW: **~schaft** f countryside; (KUNST) landscape; **~schaftsschutz-gebiet** nt nature reserve; **~sitz** m country seat; **~straße** f country road; **~streicher** (-s, -) m tramp; **~strich** m region

Landung ['landʊŋ] f landing; **~sbrücke** f jetty, pier

Land- zW: **~weg** m: **etw auf dem ~weg befördern** to transport sth by land; **~wirt** m farmer; **~wirtschaft** f agriculture; **~zunge** f spit

lang [laŋ] adj long; (Mensch) tall; **~at-mig** adj long-winded; **~e** adv for a long time; (dauern, brauchen) a long time

Länge ['lɛŋə] f length; (GEOG) longitude

langen ['laŋən] vi (ausreichen) to do, to suffice; (fassen): **~ (nach)** to reach (for) ♦ vt: **jdm etw ~** to hand od pass sb sth; **es langt mir** I've had enough

Längengrad m longitude

Längenmaß nt linear measure

lang- zW: **L~eweile** f boredom; **~fris-tig** adj long-term; **~jährig** (Freundschaft, Gewohnheit) long-standing; **L~lauf** m (SKI) cross-country skiing

länglich adj longish

längs [lɛŋs] präp (+gen od dat) along ♦ adv lengthwise

lang- zW: **~sam** adj slow; **L~samkeit** f slowness; **L~schläfer(in)** m(f) late riser

längst [lɛŋst] adv: **das ist ~ fertig** that was finished a long time ago, that has been finished for a long time; **~e(r, s)** adj longest

lang- zW: **~weilen** vt to bore ♦ vr to be bored; **~weilig** adj boring, tedious; **L~welle** f long wave; **~wierig** adj lengthy, drawn-out

Lanze ['lantsə] f lance

Lappalie [la'pa:liə] f trifle

Lappen ['lapən] (-s, -) m cloth, rag; (ANAT) lobe

läppisch ['lɛpɪʃ] adj foolish

Lapsus ['lapsʊs] (-, -) m slip

Laptop ['lɛptɔp] (-s, -s) m laptop (computer)

Lärche ['lɛrçə] f larch

Lärm [lɛrm] (-(e)s) m noise; **l~en** vi to be noisy, to make a noise

Larve ['larfə] f (BIOL) larva

lasch [laʃ] adj slack

Laser ['le:zɐ] (-s, -) m laser

SCHLÜSSELWORT

lassen ['lasən] (ließ, pp gelassen od (als Hilfsverb) lassen) vt 1 (unterlassen) to stop; (momentan) to leave; **lass das (sein)!** don't (do it)!; (hör auf) stop it!; **lass mich!** leave me alone; **lassen wir das!** let's leave it; **er kann das Trinken nicht lassen** he can't stop drinking

2 (zurücklassen) to leave; **etw lassen, wie es ist** to leave sth (just) as it is

3 (überlassen): **jdn ins Haus lassen** to let sb into the house

♦ vi: **lass mal, ich mache das schon** leave it, I'll do it

♦ Hilfsverb **1** (veranlassen): **etw machen lassen** to have od get sth done; **sich etw schicken lassen** to have sth sent (to one)

2 (zulassen): **jdn etw wissen lassen** to let sb know sth; **das Licht brennen lassen** to leave the light on; **jdn warten lassen** to keep sb waiting; **das lässt sich machen** that can be done

3: lass uns gehen let's go

---

lässig ['lɛsɪç] adj casual; **L~keit** f casualness

Last [last] (-, -en) f load, burden; (NAUT, AVIAT) cargo; (meist pl: Gebühr) charge; **jdm zur ~ fallen** to be a burden to sb;

~auto nt lorry; truck; **l~en** vi: **l~en auf** +dat to weigh on; **~enaufzug** m goods lift od elevator (US)

Laster ['lastər] (**-s**, **-**) nt vice

lästern ['lɛstərn] vt, vi (Gott) to blaspheme; (schlecht sprechen) to mock

Lästerung f jibe; (Gotteslästerung) blasphemy

lästig ['lɛstɪç] adj troublesome, tiresome

Last- zW: **~kahn** m barge; **~kraftwagen** m heavy goods vehicle; **~schrift** f debit; **~wagen** m lorry; truck; **~zug** m articulated lorry

Latein [la'taın] (**-s**) nt Latin; **~amerika** nt Latin America

latent [la'tɛnt] adj latent

Laterne [la'tɛrnə] f lantern; (Straßenlaterne) lamp, light; **~npfahl** m lamppost

latschen ['la:tʃən] (umg) vi (gehen) to wander, to go; (lässig) to slouch

Latte ['latə] f lath; (SPORT) goalpost; (quer) crossbar

Latzhose ['latsho:zə] f dungarees pl

lau [lau] adj (Nacht) balmy; (Wasser) lukewarm

Laub [laup] (**-(e)s**) nt foliage; **~baum** m deciduous tree; **~frosch** m tree frog; **~säge** f fretsaw

Lauch [laux] (**-(e)s, -e**) m leek

Lauer ['lauər] f: **auf der ~ sein** od **liegen** to lie in wait; **l~n** vi to lie in wait; (Gefahr) to lurk

Lauf [lauf] (**-(e)s, Läufe**) m run; (Wettlauf) race; (Entwicklung, ASTRON) course; (Gewehrlauf) barrel; **einer Sache** dat **ihren ~ lassen** to let sth take its course; **~bahn** f career

laufen ['laufən] (unreg) vt, vi to run; (umg: gehen) to walk; **~d** adj running; (Monat, Ausgaben) current; **auf dem ~den sein/halten** to be/keep up to date; **am ~den Band** (fig) continuously

Läufer ['lɔyfər] (**-s, -**) m (Teppich, SPORT) runner; (Fußball) half-back; (Schach)

bishop

Lauf- zW: **~masche** f run, ladder (BRIT); **~pass ▲** m: **jdm den ~pass geben** (umg) to send sb packing (inf); **~stall** m playpen; **~steg** m catwalk; **~werk** nt (COMPUT) disk drive

Lauge ['laugə] f soapy water; (CHEM) alkaline solution

Laune ['launə] f mood, humour; (Einfall) caprice; (schlechte) temper; **l~nhaft** adj capricious, changeable

launisch adj moody; bad-tempered

Laus [laus] (**-, Läuse**) f louse

lauschen ['lauʃən] vi to eavesdrop, to listen in

lauschig ['lauʃɪç] adj snug

lausig ['lauzɪç] (umg: pej) adj measly; (Kälte) perishing

laut [laut] adj loud ♦ adv loudly; (lesen) aloud ♦ präp (+gen od dat) according to; **L~** (**-(e)s, -e**) m sound

Laute ['lautə] f lute

lauten ['lautən] vi to say; (Urteil) to be

läuten ['lɔytən] vt, vi to ring, to sound

lauter ['lautər] adj (Wasser) clear, pure; (Wahrheit, Charakter) honest ♦ adj inv (Freude, Dummheit etc) sheer ♦ adv nothing but, only

laut- zW: **~hals** adv at the top of one's voice; **~los** adj noiseless, silent; **L~schrift** f phonetics pl; **L~sprecher** m loudspeaker; **~stark** adj vociferous; **L~stärke** f (RADIO) volume

lauwarm ['lauvarm] adj (auch fig) lukewarm

Lavendel [la'vɛndəl] (**-s, -**) m lavender

Lawine [la'vi:nə] f avalanche; **~ngefahr** f danger of avalanches

lax [laks] adj lax

Lazarett [latsa'rɛt] (**-(e)s, -e**) nt (MIL) hospital, infirmary

leasen ['li:zən] vt to lease

Leben (**-s, -**) nt life

leben ['le:bən] vt, vi to live; **~d** adj living; **~dig** [le'bɛndɪç] adj living, alive; (lebhaft) lively; **L~digkeit** f liveliness

Lebens- zW: **~art** f way of life; **~er-**

wartung f life expectancy; **l~fähig** adj able to live; **~freude** f zest for life; **~gefahr** f: **~gefahr!** danger!; **in ~gefahr** dangerously ill; **~gefährlich** adj dangerous; (Verletzung) critical; **haltungskosten** pl cost of living sg; **~jahr** nt year of life; **l~länglich** adj (Strafe) for life; **~lauf** m curriculum vitae; **~mittel** pl food sg; **~mittelgeschäft** nt grocer's (shop); **~mittelvergiftung** f (MED) food poisoning; **l~müde** adj tired of life; **~retter** m lifesaver; **~standard** m standard of living; **~unterhalt** m livelihood; **~versicherung** f life insurance; **~wandel** m way of life; **~weise** f lifestyle, way of life; **l~wichtig** adj vital, essential; **~zeichen** nt sign of life

Leber ['le:bər] f (-, -n) f liver; **~fleck** m mole; **~tran** m cod-liver oil; **~wurst** f liver sausage

Lebewesen nt creature

leb- ['le:p] zW: **l~haft** adj lively, vivacious; **L~kuchen** m gingerbread; **~los** adj lifeless

Leck [lɛk] (-(e)s, -e) nt leak; **l~** adj leaky, leaking; **l~en** vi (Loch haben) to leak; (schlecken) to lick ♦ vt to lick

lecker ['lɛkər] adj delicious, tasty; **L~bissen** m dainty morsel

Leder ['le:dər] (-s, -) nt leather; **~hose** f lederhosen; **l~n** adj leather; **~waren** pl leather goods

ledig ['le:dɪç] adj single; einer Sache gen **~ sein** to be free of sth; **~lich** adv merely, solely

leer [le:r] adj empty; vacant; **~ machen** to empty; **~ stehend** empty; **L~e** (-) f emptiness; **~en** vt, vr to empty; **L~gewicht** nt weight when empty; **L~gut** nt empties pl; **L~lauf** m neutral; **L~ung** f emptying; (Post) collection

legal [le'ga:l] adj legal, lawful; **~isieren** vt to legalize

legen ['le:gən] vt to lay, to put, to

place; (Ei) to lay ♦ vr to lie down; (fig) to subside

Legende [le'gɛndə] f legend

leger [le'ʒe:r] adj casual

Legierung [le'gi:rʊŋ] f alloy

Legislative [legɪsla'ti:və] f legislature

legitim [legi'ti:m] adj legitimate

legitimieren [legiti'mi:rən] vt to legitimate ♦ vr to prove one's identity

Lehm [le:m] (-(e)s, -e) m loam; **l~ig** adj loamy

Lehne ['le:nə] f arm; back; **l~n** vt, vr to lean

Lehnstuhl m armchair

Lehr- zW: **~amt** nt teaching profession; **~buch** nt textbook

Lehre ['le:rə] f teaching, doctrine; (beruflich) apprenticeship; (moralisch) lesson; (TECH) gauge; **l~n** vt to teach

Lehrer(in) (-s, -) m(f) teacher; **~zimmer** nt staff room

Lehr- zW: **~gang** m course; **~jahre** pl apprenticeship sg; **~kraft** f (förmlich) teacher; **~ling** m apprentice; **~plan** m syllabus; **~reich** adj instructive; **~stelle** f apprenticeship; **~zeit** f apprenticeship

Leib [laɪp] (-(e)s, -er) m body; **halt ihn mir vom ~!** keep him away from me!; **l~haftig** adj personified; (Teufel) incarnate; **l~lich** adj bodily; (Vater etc) own; **~schmerzen** pl stomach pains; **~wache** f bodyguard

Leiche ['laɪçə] f corpse; **~nhalle** f mortuary; **~nwagen** m hearse

Leichnam ['laɪçna:m] (-(e)s, -e) m corpse

leicht [laɪçt] adj light; (einfach) easy; **jdm ~ fallen** to be easy for sb; **es sich** dat **~ machen** to make things easy for o.s.; **L~athletik** f athletics sg; **~fertig** adj frivolous; **~gläubig** adj gullible, credulous; **~hin** adv lightly; **L~igkeit** f easiness; **mit L~igkeit** with ease; **L~sinn** m carelessness; **~sinnig** adj careless

Leid [laɪt] (-(e)s) nt grief, sorrow; **es tut mir/ihm ~** I am/he is sorry; **er/ das tut mir ~** I am sorry for him/it; **l~** adj: **etw l~ haben** od **sein** to be tired of sth; **l~en** (unreg) vt to suffer; (erlauben) to permit ♦ vi to suffer; **jdn/etw nicht l~en können** not to be able to stand sb/sth; **~en** [ˈlaɪdən] (-s, -) nt suffering; (Krankheit) complaint; **~enschaft** f passion; **l~enschaftlich** adj passionate

leider [ˈlaɪdər] adv unfortunately; **ja, ~** yes, I'm afraid so; **~ nicht** I'm afraid not

leidig [ˈlaɪdɪç] adj worrying, troublesome

leidlich [ˈlaɪtlɪç] adj tolerable ♦ adv tolerably

Leid- zW: **~tragende(r)** f(m) bereaved; (Benachteiligter) one who suffers; **~wesen** nt: **zu jds ~wesen** to sb's disappointment

Leier [ˈlaɪər] (-, -n) f lyre; (fig) old story; **~kasten** m barrel organ

Leihbibliothek f lending library

Leihbücherei f lending library

leihen [ˈlaɪən] (unreg) vt to lend; **sich** dat **etw ~** to borrow sth

Leih- zW: **~gebühr** f hire charge; **~haus** nt pawnshop; **~wagen** m hired car

Leim [laɪm] (-(e)s, -e) m glue; **l~en** to glue

Leine [ˈlaɪnə] f line, cord; (Hundeleine) leash, lead

Leinen nt linen; **l~** adj linen

Leinwand f (KUNST) canvas; (CINE) screen

leise [ˈlaɪzə] adj quiet; (sanft) soft, gentle

Leiste [ˈlaɪstə] f ledge; (Zierleiste) strip; (ANAT) groin

leisten [ˈlaɪstən] vt (Arbeit) to do; (Gesellschaft) to keep; (Ersatz) to supply; (vollbringen) to achieve; **sich** dat **etw ~ können** to be able to afford sth

Leistung f performance; (gute) achievement; **~sdruck** m pressure; **l~sfähig** adj efficient

Leitartikel m leading article

Leitbild nt model

leiten [ˈlaɪtən] vt to lead; (Firma) to manage; (in eine Richtung) to direct; (ELEK) to conduct

Leiter¹ [ˈlaɪtər] (-s, -) m leader, head; (ELEK) conductor

Leiter² [ˈlaɪtər] (-, -n) f ladder

Leitfaden m guide

Leitplanke f crash barrier

Leitung f (Führung) direction; (CINE, THEAT etc) production; (von Firma) management; directors pl; (Wasserleitung) pipe; (Kabel) cable; **eine lange ~ haben** to be slow on the uptake

Leitungs- zW: **~draht** m wire; **~rohr** nt pipe; **~wasser** nt tap water

Lektion [lɛktsiˈoːn] f lesson

Lektüre [lɛkˈtyːrə] f (Lesen) reading; (Lesestoff) reading matter

Lende [ˈlɛndə] f loin; **~nstück** nt fillet

lenk- [ˈlɛŋk] zW: **~bar** adj (Fahrzeug) steerable; (Kind) manageable; **~en** vt to steer; (Kind) to guide; (Blick, Aufmerksamkeit): **~en (auf** +akk) to direct (at); **L~rad** nt steering wheel; **L~radschloss ▲** nt steering (wheel) lock; **L~stange** f handlebars pl; **L~ung** f steering

Lepra [ˈleːpra] (-) f leprosy

Lerche [ˈlɛrçə] f lark

lernbegierig adj eager to learn

lernen [ˈlɛrnən] vt to learn

lesbar [ˈlɛsbaːr] adj legible

Lesbierin [ˈlɛsbiərɪn] f lesbian

lesbisch [ˈlɛsbɪʃ] adj lesbian

Lese [ˈleːzə] f (Wein) harvest

Lesebrille f reading glasses

Lesebuch nt reading book, reader

lesen (unreg) vt, vi to read; (ernten) to gather, to pick

Leser(in) (-s, -) m(f) reader; **~brief** m reader's letter; **l~lich** adj legible

Lesezeichen nt bookmark

Lesung ['le:zʊŋ] f (PARL) reading

letzte(r, s) ['lɛtstə(r, s)] adj last; (neueste) latest; **zum ~n Mal** for the last time; **~ns** adv lately; **~re(r, s)** adj latter

Leuchte ['lɔʏçtə] f lamp, light; **l~n** vi to shine, to gleam; **~r (-s, -)** m candlestick

Leucht- zW: **~farbe** f fluorescent colour; **~rakete** f flare; **~reklame** f neon sign; **~röhre** f strip light; **~turm** m lighthouse

leugnen ['lɔʏgnən] vt to deny

Leukämie [lɔʏkɛ'mi:] f leukaemia

Leukoplast [lɔʏko'plast] (®), **(-[e]s, -e)** nt Elastoplast ®

Leumund ['lɔʏmʊnt] (-[e]s, -e) m reputation

Leumundszeugnis nt character reference

Leute ['lɔʏtə] pl people pl

Leutnant ['lɔʏtnant] (-s, -s od -e) m lieutenant

leutselig ['lɔʏtze:lɪç] adj amiable

Lexikon ['lɛksikɔn] (-s, **Lexiken** od **Lexika**) nt encyclop(a)edia

Libelle [li'bɛlə] f dragonfly; (TECH) spirit level

liberal [libe'ra:l] adj liberal; **L~e(r)** f(m) liberal

Licht [lɪçt] (-[e]s, -er) nt light; **~bild** nt photograph; (Dia) slide; **~blick** m cheering prospect; **l~empfindlich** adj sensitive to light; **l~en** vt to clear; (Anker) to weigh ♦ vr to clear up; (Haar) to thin; **l~erloh** adv: **l~erloh brennen** to be ablaze; **~hupe** f flashing of headlights; **~jahr** nt light year; **~maschine** f dynamo; **~schalter** m light switch; **~schutzfaktor** m protection factor

Lichtung f clearing, glade

Lid [li:t] (-[e]s, -er) nt eyelid; **~schatten** m eyeshadow

lieb [li:p] adj dear; **das ist ~ von dir**

that's kind of you; **~ gewinnen** to get fond of; **~ haben** to be fond of; **~äugeln** ['li:bɔʏgəln] vi insep: **mit etw ~äugeln** to have one's eye on sth; **mit dem Gedanken ~äugeln, etw zu tun** to toy with the idea of doing sth

Liebe ['li:bə] f love; **l~bedürftig** adj: **l~bedürftig sein** to need love; **l~n** vt to love; to like

liebens- zW: **~wert** adj loveable; **~würdig** adj kind; **~würdigerweise** adv kindly; **L~würdigkeit** f kindness

lieber ['li:bər] adv rather, preferably; **ich gehe ~ nicht** I'd rather not go; siehe auch **gern**; **lieb**

Liebes- zW: **~brief** m love letter; **~kummer** m: **~kummer haben** to be lovesick; **~paar** nt courting couple, lovers pl

liebevoll adj loving

lieb- [li:p] zW: **~gewinnen** △ (unreg) vt siehe **lieb**; **~haben** △ (unreg) vt siehe **lieb**; **L~haber (-s, -)** m lover; **L~haberei** [li:phabə'raɪ] f hobby; **~kosen** [li:p'ko:zən] vt insep to caress; **~lich** adj lovely, charming; **L~ling** m darling; **L~lings-** in zW favourite; **~los** adj unloving; **L~schaft** f love affair

Lied [li:t] (-[e]s, -er) nt song; (REL) hymn; **~erbuch** ['li:dər-] nt songbook; hymn book

liederlich ['li:dərlɪç] adj slovenly; (Lebenswandel) loose, immoral; **L~keit** f slovenliness; immorality

Lieferant [li:fə'rant] m supplier

Lieferbedingungen pl terms of delivery

liefern ['li:fərn] vt to deliver; (versorgen mit) to supply; (Beweis) to produce

Liefer- zW: **~schein** m delivery note; **~termin** m delivery date; **~ung** f delivery; supply; **~wagen** m van; **~zeit** f delivery period

Liege ['li:gə] f bed

liegen ['liːgən] (unreg) vi to lie; (sich befinden) to be; **mir liegt nichts/viel daran** it doesn't matter to me/it matters a lot to me; **es liegt bei Ihnen, ob ... it's up to you whether ...; Sprachen ~ mir nicht** languages are not my line; **woran liegt es?** what's the cause?; ~ **bleiben** (im Bett) to stay in bed; (nicht aufstehen) to stay lying down; (vergessen werden) to be left (behind); ~ **lassen** (vergessen) to leave behind

Liege- zW: **~sitz** m (AUT) reclining seat; **~stuhl** m deck chair; **~wagen** m (EISENB) couchette

Lift [lɪft] (-(e)s, -e od -s) m lift

Likör [liˈkøːr] (-s, -e) m liqueur

lila ['liːla] adj inv purple, lilac; **L~** (-s, -s) nt (Farbe) purple, lilac

Lilie ['liːliə] f lily

Limonade [limoˈnaːdə] f lemonade

Limone [liˈmoːnə] f lime

Linde ['lɪndə] f lime tree, linden

lindern ['lɪndərn] vt to alleviate, to soothe; **Linderung** f alleviation

Lineal [lineˈaːl] (-s, -e) nt ruler

Linie ['liːniə] f line

Linien- zW: **~blatt** nt ruled sheet; **~flug** m scheduled flight; **~richter** m linesman

linieren [liˈniːrən] vt to line

Linke ['lɪŋkə] f left side; left hand; (POL) left

linkisch adj awkward, gauche

links [lɪŋks] adv left; to od on the left; ~ **von mir** on od to my left; **L~händer(in)** (-s, -) m(f) left-handed person; **L~kurve** f left-hand bend; **L~verkehr** m driving on the left

Linoleum [liˈnoːleʊm] (-s) nt lino(leum)

Linse ['lɪnzə] f lentil; (optisch) lens sg

Lippe ['lɪpə] f lip; **~nstift** m lipstick

lispeln ['lɪspəln] vi to lisp

Lissabon ['lɪsabɔn] (-s) nt Lisbon

List [lɪst] (-, -en) f cunning; trick, ruse

Liste ['lɪstə] f list

listig ['lɪstɪç] adj cunning, sly

Liter ['liːtər] (-s, -) nt od m litre

literarisch [liteˈraːrɪʃ] adj literary

Literatur [literaˈtuːr] f literature

Litfaßsäule ['lɪtfasˌzɔylə] f advertising pillar

Liturgie [litʊrˈgiː] f liturgy

liturgisch [liˈtʊrgɪʃ] adj liturgical

Litze ['lɪtsə] f braid; (ELEK) flex

Lizenz [liˈtsɛnts] f licence

Lkw [ɛlkaːˈveː] (-(s), -(s)) m abk = Lastkraftwagen

Lob [loːp] (-(e)s) nt praise

Lobby ['lɔbi] f lobby

loben ['loːbən] vt to praise; **~swert** adj praiseworthy

löblich ['løːplɪç] adj praiseworthy, laudable

Loch [lɔx] (-(e)s, ⁻er) nt hole; **l~en** vt to punch holes in; **~er** (-s, -) m punch

löcherig ['lœçərɪç] adj full of holes

Lochkarte f punch card

Lochstreifen m punch tape

Locke ['lɔkə] f lock, curl; **l~n** vt to entice; (Haare) to curl; **~nwickler** (-s, -) m curler

locker ['lɔkər] adj loose; **~lassen** (unreg) vi: **nicht ~lassen** not to let up; **~n** vt to loosen

lockig ['lɔkɪç] adj curly

lodern ['loːdərn] vi to blaze

Löffel ['lœfəl] (-s, -) m spoon

löffeln vt to spoon

Loge ['loːʒə] f (THEAT) box; (Freimaurer) (masonic) lodge; (Pförtnerloge) office

Logik ['loːgɪk] f logic

logisch ['loːgɪʃ] adj logical

Logopäde [logoˈpɛːdə] (-n, -n) m speech therapist

Lohn [loːn] (-(e)s, ⁻e) m reward; (Arbeitslohn) pay, wages pl; **~büro** nt wages office; **~empfänger** m wage earner

lohnen ['loːnən] vr unpers to be worth it ♦ vt: (jdm etw) ~ to reward (sb for sth); **~d** adj worthwhile

Lohn- zW: **~erhöhung** f pay rise;

~steuer f income tax; **~steuerkarte** f (income) tax card; **~streifen** m pay slip; **~tüte** f pay packet

Lokal [lo'ka:l] (-(e)s, -e) nt pub(lic house)

lokal adj local; **~i'sieren** vt to localize

Lokomotive [lokomo'ti:və] f locomotive

Lokomotivführer m engine driver

Lorbeer ['lɔrbeːr] (-s, -en) m (auch fig) laurel; **~blatt** nt (KOCH) bay leaf

Los [lo:s] (-es, -e) nt (Schicksal) lot, fate; (Lotterielos) lottery ticket

los adj (locker) loose; **~!** go on!; **etw ~ sein** to be rid of sth; **was ist ~?** what's the matter?; **dort ist nichts/viel ~** there's nothing/a lot going on there; **~binden** (unreg) vt to untie

Löschblatt ['lœʃblat] nt sheet of blotting paper

löschen ['lœʃən] vt (Feuer, Licht) to put out, to extinguish; (Durst) to quench; (COMM) to cancel; (COMPUT) to delete; (Tonband) to erase; (Fracht) to unload ♦ vi (Feuerwehr) to put out a fire; (Tinte) to blot

Lösch- zW: **~fahrzeug** nt fire engine; fire boat; **~gerät** nt fire extinguisher; **~papier** nt blotting paper

lose ['lo:zə] adj loose

Lösegeld nt ransom

losen ['lo:zən] vi to draw lots

lösen ['lø:zən] vt to loosen; (Rätsel etc) to solve; (Verlobung) to call off; (CHEM) to dissolve; (Partnerschaft) to break up; (Fahrkarte) to buy ♦ vr (aufgehen) to come loose; (Zucker etc) to dissolve; (Problem, Schwierigkeit) to (re)solve itself

los- zW: **~fahren** (unreg) vi to leave; **~gehen** (unreg) vi to set out; (anfangen) to start; (Bombe) to go off; **auf jdn ~gehen** to go for sb; **~kaufen** vt (Gefangene, Geiseln) to pay ransom for; **~kommen** vi: **von etw**

~kommen to get away from sth; **~lassen** (unreg) vt (Seil) to let go of; (Schimpfe) to let loose; **~laufen** (unreg) vi to run off

löslich ['lø:slɪç] adj soluble; **L~keit** f solubility

los- zW: **(sich) ~lösen** to free (o.s.); **~machen** to loosen; (Boot) to unmoor vr to get away; **~schrauben** vt to unscrew

Losung ['lo:zʊŋ] f watchword, slogan

Lösung ['lø:zʊŋ] f (Lockermachen) loosening; (eines Rätsels, CHEM) solution; **~smittel** nt solvent

los- zW: **~werden** (unreg) vt to get rid of; **~ziehen** (unreg) (umg) vi (sich aufmachen) to set off

Lot [lo:t] (-(e)s, -e) nt plumbline; **im ~** vertical; (fig) on an even keel

löten ['lø:tən] vt to solder

Lothringen ['lo:trɪŋən] (-s) nt Lorraine

Lotse ['lo:tsə] (-n, -n) m pilot; (AVIAT) air traffic controller; **l~n** vt to pilot; (umg) to lure

Lotterie [lɔta'ri:] f lottery

Lotto ['lɔto] (-s, -s) nt national lottery; **~zahlen** pl winning lottery numbers

Löwe ['lø:və] (-n, -n) m lion; (ASTROL) Leo; **~nanteil** m lion's share; **~nzahn** m dandelion

loyal [loa'ja:l] adj loyal; **L~ität** f loyalty

Luchs [lʊks] (-es, -e) m lynx

Lücke ['lʏkə] f gap

Lücken- zW: **~büßer** (-s, -) m stopgap; **l~haft** adj full of gaps; (Versorgung, Vorräte etc) inadequate; **l~los** adj complete

Luft [lʊft] (-, ̈e) f air; (Atem) breath; **in der ~ liegen** to be in the air; **jdn wie ~ behandeln** to ignore sb; **~angriff** m air raid; **~ballon** m balloon; **~blase** f air bubble; **l~dicht** adj airtight; **~druck** m atmospheric pressure

lüften ['lʏftən] vt to lift, to raise ♦ vi to let some air in

Luft- zW: **~fahrt** f aviation; **~fracht** f air freight; **l~gekühlt** adj air-cooled; **~gewehr** nt air rifle, airgun; **l~ig** adj (Ort) breezy; (Raum) airy; (Kleider) summery; **~kissenfahrzeug** nt hovercraft; **~kurort** m health resort; **l~leer** adj: **l~leerer Raum** vacuum; **~linie** f: **in der ~linie** as the crow flies; **~loch** nt air hole; (AVIAT) air pocket; **~matratze** f Lilo ® (BRIT), air mattress; **~pirat** m hijacker; **~post** f airmail; **~pumpe** f air pump; **~röhre** f (ANAT) windpipe; **~schlange** f streamer; **~schutzkeller** m air-raid shelter; **~verkehr** m air traffic; **~verschmutzung** f air pollution; **~waffe** f air force; **~zug** m draught

Lüge ['ly:gə] f lie; **jdn/etw ~n strafen** to give the lie to sb/sth; **l~n** (unreg) vi to lie

Lügner(in) (-s, -) m(f) liar

Luke ['lu:kə] f dormer window; hatch

Lump [lʊmp] (-en, -en) m scamp, rascal

Lumpen ['lʊmpən] (-s, -) m rag

lumpen ['lʊmpən] vi: **sich nicht ~ lassen** not to be mean

lumpig ['lʊmpɪç] adj shabby

Lupe ['lu:pə] f magnifying glass; **unter die ~ nehmen** (fig) to scrutinize

Lust [lʊst] (-, ¨e) f joy, delight; (Neigung) desire; **~ haben zu od auf etw akk/etw zu tun** to feel like sth/doing sth

lüstern ['lʏstərn] adj lustful, lecherous

lustig ['lʊstɪç] adj (komisch) amusing, funny; (fröhlich) cheerful

Lust- zW: **l~los** adj unenthusiastic; **~mord** m sex(ual) murder; **~spiel** nt comedy

lutschen ['lʊtʃən] vt, vi to suck; **am Daumen ~** to suck one's thumb

Lutscher (-s, -) m lollipop

luxuriös [lʊksuri'ø:s] adj luxurious

Luxus ['lʊksʊs] (-) m luxury; **~artikel** pl luxury goods; **~hotel** nt luxury hotel

Luzern [lu'tsɛrn] (-s) nt Lucerne

Lymphe ['lʏmfə] f lymph

lynchen ['lʏnçən] vt to lynch

Lyrik ['ly:rɪk] f lyric poetry; **~er** (-s, -) m lyric poet

lyrisch ['ly:rɪʃ] adj lyrical

M, m

m abk = **Meter**

Machart f make

machbar adj feasible

machen ['maxən] vt **1** to do; (herstellen, zubereiten) to make; **was machst du da?** what are you doing (there)?; **das ist nicht zu machen** that can't be done; **das Radio leiser machen** to turn the radio down; **aus Holz gemacht** made of wood

2 (verursachen, bewirken) to make; **jdm Angst machen** to make sb afraid; **das macht die Kälte** it's the cold that does that

3 (ausmachen) to matter; **das macht nichts** that doesn't matter; **die Kälte macht mir nichts** I don't mind the cold

4 (kosten, ergeben) to be; **3 und 5 macht 8** 3 and 5 is od are 8; **was od wie viel macht das?** how much does that make?

5: was macht die Arbeit? how's the work going?; **was macht dein Bruder?** how is your brother doing?; **das Auto machen lassen** to have the car done; **machs gut!** take care!; (viel Glück) good luck!

♦ vi: **mach schnell!** hurry up!; **Schluss machen** to finish (off); **mach schon!** come on!; **das macht müde** it makes you tired; **in etw** dat **machen** to be od deal in sth

♦ vr to come along (nicely); **sich an etw** akk **machen** to set about sth; **sich verständlich machen** to make o.s.

understood; **sich** dat **viel aus jdm/
etw machen** to like sb/sth

Macht [maxt] (-, -e) f power; **~haber**
(-s, -) m ruler

mächtig ['mɛçtɪç] adj powerful,
mighty; (umg: ungeheuer) enormous

Macht- zW: **m~los** adj powerless;
~probe f trial of strength; **~wort** nt:
ein ~wort sprechen to exercise one's
authority

Mädchen ['mɛːtçən] nt girl; **m~haft**
adj girlish; **~name** m maiden name

Made ['maːdə] f maggot

madig ['maːdɪç] adj maggoty; **jdm etw
~ machen** to spoil sth for sb

mag etc [maːk] vb siehe **mögen**

Magazin [maga'tsiːn] (-s, -e) nt magazine

Magen ['maːgən] (-s, - od ⸚) m stomach; **~geschwür** nt (MED) stomach ulcer; **~schmerzen** pl stomachache sg

mager ['maːgər] adj lean; (dünn) thin;
M~keit f leanness; thinness

Magie [ma'giː] f magic

magisch ['maːgɪʃ] adj magical

Magnet [ma'gneːt] (-s od -en, -en) m
magnet; **m~isch** adj magnetic; **~na-
del** f magnetic needle

mähen ['mɛːən] vt, vi to mow

Mahl [maːl] (-(e)s, -e) nt meal; **m~en**
(unreg) vt to grind; **~zeit** f meal ♦ excl
enjoy your meal

Mahnbrief m reminder

Mähne ['mɛːnə] f mane

mahn- ['maːn] zW: **~en** vt to remind;
(warnend) to warn; (wegen Schuld) to
demand payment from; **M~mal** nt
memorial; **M~ung** f reminder; admonition, warning

Mai [maɪ] (-(e)s, -e) m May;
~glöckchen nt lily of the valley

Mailand ['maɪlant] nt Milan

mailändisch adj Milanese

Mais [maɪs] (-es, -e) m maize, corn

(US); **~kolben** m corncob; **~mehl** nt
(KOCH) corn meal

Majestät [majɛs'tɛːt] f majesty;
m~isch adj majestic

Majonäse [majo'nɛːzə] f mayonnaise

Major [ma'joːr] (-s, -e) m (MIL) major;
(AVIAT) squadron leader

Majoran [majo'raːn] (-s, -e) m marjo-
ram

makaber [ma'kaːbər] adj macabre

Makel ['maːkəl] (-s, -) m blemish; (moralisch) stain; **m~los** adj immaculate,
spotless

mäkeln ['mɛːkəln] vi to find fault

Makler(in) ['maːklər(ɪn)] (-s, -) m(f)
broker

Makrele [ma'kreːlə] f mackerel

Mal [maːl] (-(e)s, -e) nt mark, sign;
(Zeitpunkt) time; **ein für alle ~** once
and for all; **m~** adv times; (umg) siehe
einmal ♦ suffix: **-m~** -times

malen vt, vi to paint

Maler (-s, -) m painter; **Male'rei** f
painting; **m~isch** adj picturesque

Malkasten m paintbox

Mallorca [ma'jɔrka, ma'lɔrka] (-s) nt
Majorca

malnehmen (unreg) vt, vi to multiply

Malz [malts] (-es) nt malt; **~bier** nt
(KOCH) malt beer; **~bonbon** nt cough
drop; **~kaffee** m malt coffee

Mama ['mama:] (-, -s) (umg) f
mum(my) (BRIT), mom(my) (US)

Mami ['mami] (-, -s) f = **Mama**

Mammut ['mamʊt] (-s, -e od -s) nt
mammoth

man [man] pron one, you; **~ sagt, ...**
they od people say ...; **wie schreibt ~
das?** how do you write it?, how is it
written?

Manager(in) ['mɛnɪdʒər(ɪn)] (-s, -)
m(f) manager

manch [manç] (unver) pron many a

manche(r, s) ['mançə(r, s)] adj many

a; (pl: einige) a number of ♦ pron some

mancherlei [man'çar'laɪ] adj inv various
♦ pron inv a variety of things

manchmal adv sometimes

Mandant(in) [man'dant(ɪn)] m(f) (JUR) client

Mandarine [manda'ri:nə] f mandarin, tangerine

Mandat [man'da:t] (-(e)s, -e) nt mandate

Mandel ['mandəl] (-, -n) f almond; (ANAT) tonsil; **~entzündung** f (MED) tonsillitis

Manege [ma'ne:ʒə] f ring, arena

Mangel ['maŋəl] (-s, ⁰) m lack; (Knappheit) shortage; (Fehler) defect, fault; **~** an +dat shortage of; **~erscheinung** f deficiency symptom; **m~haft** adj poor; (fehlerhaft) defective, faulty; **m~n** vi unpers: es m~t jdm an etw dat sb lacks sth ♦ vt (Wäsche) to mangle

mangels präp +gen for lack of

Manie [ma'ni:] f mania

Manier [ma'ni:r] (-) f manner; style; (pej) mannerism; **~en** pl (Umgangsformen) manners; **m~lich** adj well-mannered

Manifest [mani'fɛst] (-es, -e) nt manifesto

Maniküre [mani'ky:rə] f manicure

manipulieren [manipu'li:rən] vt to manipulate

Manko ['maŋko] (-s, -s) nt deficiency; (COMM) deficit

Mann [man] (-(e)s, ⁰er) m man; (Ehemann) husband; (NAUT) hand; **seinen ~ stehen** to hold one's own

Männchen ['mɛnçən] nt little man; (Tier) male

Mannequin ['manə'kɛ̃:] (-s, -s) nt fashion model

männlich ['mɛnlɪç] adj (BIOL) male; (fig, GRAM) masculine

Mannschaft f (SPORT, fig) team; (AVIAT, NAUT) crew; (MIL) other ranks pl

Manöver [ma'nø:vər] (-s, -) nt manoeuvre

manövrieren [manø'vri:rən] vt, vi to manoeuvre

Mansarde [man'zardə] f attic

Manschette [man'ʃetə] f cuff; (TECH) collar; sleeve; **~nknopf** m cufflink

Mantel ['mantəl] (-s, ⁰) m coat; (TECH) casing, jacket

Manuskript [manu'skrɪpt] (-(e)s, -e) nt manuscript

Mappe ['mapə] f briefcase; (Aktenmappe) folder

Märchen ['mɛ:rçən] nt fairy tale; **m~haft** adj fabulous; **~prinz** m Prince Charming

Margarine [marga'ri:nə] f margarine

Margerite [margə'ri:tə] f (BOT) marguerite

Marienkäfer [ma'ri:ənke:fər] m ladybird

Marine [ma'ri:nə] f navy; **m~blau** adj navy blue

marinieren [mari'ni:rən] vt to marinate

Marionette [mario'netə] f puppet

Mark¹ [mark] (-, -) f (Münze) mark

Mark² [mark] (-(e)s) nt (Knochenmark) marrow; **jdm durch ~ und Bein gehen** to go right through sb

markant [mar'kant] adj striking

Marke ['markə] f mark; (Warensorte) brand; (Fabrikat) make; (Rabattmarke, Briefmarke) stamp; (Essenmarke) ticket; (aus Metall etc) token, disc

Markenartikel m proprietary article

markieren [mar'ki:rən] vt to mark; (umg) to act ♦ vi (umg) to act it

Markierung f marking

Markise [mar'ki:zə] f awning

Markstück nt one-mark piece

Markt [markt] (-(e)s, ⁰e) m market; **~forschung** f market research; **~lücke** f (COMM) opening, gap in the market; **~platz** m market place; **m~üblich** adj (Preise, Mieten) standard, usual; **~wert** m (COMM) market value; **~wirtschaft** f market economy

Marmelade [marmə'la:də] f jam

Marmor ['marmɔr] (-s, -e) m marble;
m~ieren [-'ri:rən] vt to marble

Marokko [ma'rɔko] (-s) nt Morocco

Marone [ma'ro:nə] (-, -n od **Maroni**) f
chestnut

Marotte [ma'rɔtə] f fad, quirk

Marsch[1] [marʃ] (-, -en) f marsh

Marsch[2] [marʃ] (-(e)s, ‿e) m march
♦ excl march!; **~befehl** m marching orders pl; **m~bereit** adj ready to move;
m~ieren [mar'ʃi:rən] vi to march

Märtyrer(in) ['mɛrtyrər(ɪn)] (-s, -) m(f)
martyr

März [mɛrts] (-(es), -e) m March

Marzipan [martsi'pa:n] (-s, -e) nt marzipan

Masche ['maʃə] f mesh; (Strickmasche)
stitch; **das ist die neueste ~** that's
the latest thing; **~ndraht** m wire
mesh; **m~nfest** adj run-resistant

Maschine [ma'ʃi:nə] f machine; (Motor) engine; (Schreibmaschine) typewriter; **~ schreiben** to type; **m~ll**
[maʃi'nɛl] adj machine(-made); mechanical

Maschinen- zW: **~bauer** m mechanical engineer; **~gewehr** nt machine
gun; **~pistole** f submachine gun;
~schaden m mechanical fault;
~schlosser m fitter; **~schrift** f typescript

Maschinist [maʃi'nɪst] m engineer

Maser ['ma:zər] (-, -n) f (von Holz)
grain; **~n** pl (MED) measles sg

Maske ['maskə] f mask; **~nball** m
fancy-dress ball

maskieren [mas'ki:rən] vt to mask;
(verkleiden) to dress up ♦ vr to disguise
o.s.; to dress up

Maskottchen [mas'kɔtçən] nt (lucky)
mascot

Maß[1] [ma:s] (-es, -e) nt measure;
(Mäßigung) moderation; (Grad) degree, extent; **~ halten** to exercise
moderation

Maß[2] [ma:s] (-, -(e)) f litre of beer

Massage [ma'sa:ʒə] f massage

Maßanzug m made-to-measure suit

Maßarbeit f (fig) neat piece of work

Masse ['masə] f mass

Maßeinheit f unit of measurement

Massen- zW: **~artikel** m mass-produced article; **~grab** nt mass
grave; **m~haft** adj loads of; **~medien**
pl mass media pl; **~veranstaltung** f
mass meeting; **m~weise** adv on a
large scale

Masseur [ma'sørr] m masseur; **~in** f
masseuse

maßgebend adj authoritative

maßhalten △ (unreg) vi siehe **Maß**[1]

massieren [ma'si:rən] vt to massage;
(MIL) to mass

massig ['masɪç] adj massive; (umg)
massive amount of

mäßig ['mɛ:sɪç] adj moderate; **~en**
['mɛ:sɪgən] vt to restrain, to moderate;
M~keit f moderation

Massiv (-s, -e) nt massif

massiv [ma'si:f] adj solid; (fig) heavy,
rough

Maß- zW: **~krug** m tankard; **m~los** adj
extreme; **~nahme** f measure, step;
~stab m rule, measure; (fig) standard;
(GEOG) scale; **m~voll** adj moderate

Mast [mast] (-(e)s, -(e)n) m mast; (ELEK)
pylon

mästen ['mɛstən] vt to fatten

Material [materi'a:l] (-s, -ien) nt material(s); **~fehler** m material defect;
~ismus [-'lɪsmɔs] m materialism;
m~istisch [-'lɪstɪʃ] adj materialistic

Materie [ma'te:riə] f matter, substance

materiell [materi'ɛl] adj material

Mathematik [matema'ti:k] f mathematics sg; **~er(in)** [mate'ma:tikər(ɪn)]
(-s, -) m(f) mathematician

mathematisch [mate'ma:tɪʃ] adj
mathematical

Matjeshering ['matjəshe:rɪŋ] m (KOCH)
young herring

Matratze [ma'tratsə] f mattress

Matrixdrucker ['ma:trıks-] m dotmatrix printer

Matrose [ma'tro:zə] (-n, -n) m sailor

Matsch [matʃ] (-(e)s) m mud; (Schneematsch) slush; **m~ig** adj muddy; slushy

matt [mat] adj weak; (glanzlos) dull; (PHOT) matt; (SCHACH) mate

Matte ['matə] f mat

Mattscheibe f (TV) screen

Mauer ['mauər] (-, -n) f wall; **m~n** vi to build; to lay bricks ♦ vt to build

Maul [maul] (-(e)s, Mäuler) nt mouth; **m~en** (umg) vi to grumble; **~esel** m mule; **~korb** m muzzle; **~sperre** f lockjaw; **~tasche** f (KOCH) pasta envelopes stuffed and used in soup; **~tier** nt mule; **~wurf** m mole

Maurer ['maurər] (-s, -) m bricklayer

Maus [maus] (-, Mäuse) f (auch COMPUT) mouse

Mause- ['mauzə] zW: **~falle** f mousetrap; **m~n** vi to catch mice ♦ vt (umg) to pinch; **m~tot** adj stone dead

Maut- ['maut] zW: **~gebühr** f toll (charge); **~straße** f toll road

maximal [maksi'ma:l] adj maximum ♦ adv at most

Mayonnaise [majɔ'nɛ:zə] f mayonnaise

Mechan- [meça:n] zW: **~ik** f mechanics sg; (Getriebe) mechanics pl; **~iker** (-s, -) m mechanic, engineer; **m~isch** adj mechanical; **~ismus** m mechanism

meckern ['mekərn] vi to bleat; (umg) to moan

Medaille [me'daljə] f medal

Medaillon [medal'jõ:] (-s, -s) nt (Schmuck) locket

Medikament [medika'mɛnt] nt medicine

Meditation [meditatsi'o:n] f meditation

meditieren [medi'ti:rən] vi to meditate

Medizin [medi'tsi:n] (-, -en) f medicine; **m~isch** adj medical

Meer [me:r] (-(e)s, -e) nt sea; **~enge** f straits pl; **~esfrüchte** pl seafood sg; **~esspiegel** m sea level; **~rettich** m horseradish; **~schweinchen** nt guinea-pig

Mehl [me:l] (-(e)s, -e) nt flour; **m~ig** adj floury; **~schwitze** f (KOCH) roux; **~speise** f (KOCH) flummery

mehr [me:r] adv more; **~deutig** adj ambiguous; **~ere** pron several; **~eres** pron several things; **~fach** adj multiple; (wiederholt) repeated; **M~fahrtenkarte** f multi-journey ticket; **M~heit** f majority; **m~malig** adj repeated; **~mals** adv repeatedly; **~stimmig** adj for several voices; **~stimmig singen** to harmonize; **M~wertsteuer** f value added tax; **M~zahl** f majority; (GRAM) plural

Mehrzweck- in zW multipurpose

meiden ['maidən] (unreg) vt to avoid

Meile ['mailə] f mile; **~nstein** m milestone; **m~nweit** adj for miles

mein(e) [main] adj my; **~e(r, s)** pron mine

Meineid ['main|ait] m perjury

meinen ['mainən] vi to think ♦ vt to think; (sagen) to say; (sagen wollen) to mean; **das will ich ~** I should think so

mein- zW: **~erseits** adv for my part; **~etwegen** adv (für mich) for my sake; (wegen mir) on my account; (von mir aus) as far as I'm concerned; I don't care od mind; **~etwillen** adv: **um ~etwillen** for my sake, on my account

Meinung ['mainuŋ] f opinion; **ganz meine ~** I quite agree; **jdm die ~ sagen** to give sb a piece of one's mind

Meinungs- zW: **~austausch** m exchange of views; **~umfrage** f opinion poll; **~verschiedenheit** f difference of opinion

Meise ['maizə] f tit(mouse)

Meißel ['maisəl] (-s, -) m chisel

meist [maist] adj most ♦ adv mostly; **am ~en** the most; **~ens** adv generally, usually

Meister ['maɪstər] (-s, -) m master; (SPORT) champion; **m~haft** adj masterly; **m~n** vt (Schwierigkeiten etc) to overcome, conquer; **~schaft** f mastery; (SPORT) championship; **~stück** nt masterpiece; **~werk** nt masterpiece

Melancholie [melaŋkoˈliː] f melancholy; **melancholisch** [melanˈkoːlɪʃ] adj melancholy

Melde- ['meldə] zW: **~frist** f registration period; **m~n** vt to report ♦ vr to report; (SCH) to put one's hand up; (freiwillig) to volunteer; (auf etw, am Telefon) to answer; **sich m~n bei** to report to; to register with; **sich zu Wort m~n** to ask to speak; **~pflicht** f obligation to register with the police; **~schluss** ▲ m closing date; **~stelle** f registration office

Meldung ['meldʊŋ] f announcement; (Bericht) report

meliert [meˈliːrt] adj (Haar) greying; (Wolle) flecked

melken ['mɛlkən] (unreg) vt to milk

Melodie [meloˈdiː] f melody, tune

melodisch [meˈloːdɪʃ] adj melodious, tuneful

Melone [meˈloːnə] f melon; (Hut) bowler (hat)

Membran [mɛmˈbraːn] (-, -en) f (TECH) diaphragm

Memoiren [memoˈaːrən] pl memoirs

Menge ['mɛŋə] f quantity; (Menschenmenge) crowd; (große Anzahl) lot (of); **m~n** vt to mix ♦ vr: **sich m~n in** +akk to meddle with; **~nlehre** f (MATH) set theory; **~nrabatt** m bulk discount

Mensch [mɛnʃ] (-en, -en) m human being, man; person ♦ excl hey!; **kein ~** nobody

Menschen- zW: **~affe** m (ZOOL) ape; **m~freundlich** adj philanthropic; **~kenner** m judge of human nature; **m~leer** adj deserted; **m~möglich** adj

humanly possible; **~rechte** pl human rights; **~unwürdig** adj beneath human dignity; **~verstand** m: **gesunder ~verstand** common sense

Mensch- **~heit** f humanity, mankind; **m~lich** adj human; (human) humane; **~lichkeit** f humanity

Menstruation [mɛnstruatsiˈoːn] f menstruation

Mentalität [mɛntaliˈtɛːt] f mentality

Menü [meˈnyː] (-s, -s) nt (auch COMPUT) menu

Merk- ['mɛrk] zW: **~blatt** nt instruction sheet od leaflet; **m~en** vt to notice; **sich dat etw m~en** to remember sth; **m~lich** adj noticeable; **~mal** nt sign, characteristic; **m~würdig** adj odd

messbar ▲ ['mɛsbaːr] adj measurable

Messbecher ▲ m measuring jug

Messe ['mɛsə] f fair; (ECCL) mass; **~gelände** nt exhibition centre; **~halle** f pavilion at a fair

messen (unreg) vt to measure ♦ vr to compete

Messer ['mɛsər] (-s, -) nt knife; **~spitze** f knife point; (in Rezept) pinch

Messestand m stall at a fair

Messgerät ▲ nt measuring device, gauge

Messing ['mɛsɪŋ] (-s) nt brass

Metall [meˈtal] (-s, -e) nt metal; **m~isch** adj metallic

Meter ['meːtər] (-s, -) nt od m metre; **~maß** nt tape measure

Methode [meˈtoːdə] f method; **methodisch** adj methodical

Metropole [metroˈpoːlə] f metropolis

Metzger ['mɛtsɡər] (-s, -) m butcher; **~ei** [-ˈraɪ] f butcher's (shop)

Meute ['mɔʏtə] f pack; **~rei** f mutiny; **m~rn** vi to mutiny

miauen [miˈaʊən] vi to miaow

mich [mɪç] (akk von ich) pron me; myself

Miene ['miːnə] f look, expression

mies [miːs] (umg) adj lousy

Miet- ['miːt] zW: **~auto** nt hired car; **~e** f rent; **zur ~e wohnen** to live in rented accommodation; **m~en** vt to rent; (Auto) to hire; **~er(in)** (-s, -) m(f) tenant; **~shaus** nt tenement, block of (rented) flats; **~vertrag** m lease

Migräne [mi'grɛːnə] f migraine

Mikro- ['mikro] zW: **~fon**, **~phon** [-'foːn] (-s, -e) nt microphone; **~skop** [-'skoːp] (-s, -e) nt microscope; **m~skopisch** adj microscopic; **~wellenherd** m microwave (oven)

Milch [mɪlç] (-) f milk; **~glas** nt frosted glass; **m~ig** adj milky; **~kaffee** m white coffee; **~mann** (pl -männer) m milkman; **~mixgetränk** nt (KOCH) milkshake; **~pulver** nt powdered milk; **~straße** f Milky Way; **~zahn** m milk tooth

mild [mɪlt] adj mild; (Richter) lenient; (freundlich) kind, charitable; **M~e** f mildness; leniency; **~ern** vt to mitigate, to soften; (Schmerz) to alleviate; **~ernde Umstände** extenuating circumstances

Milieu [mili'øː] (-s, -s) nt background, environment; **m~geschädigt** adj maladjusted

Mili- [mili] zW: **m~tant** [-'tant] adj militant; **~tär** [-'tɛːr] (-s) nt military, army; **~tärgericht** nt military court; **m~tärisch** adj military

Milli- ['mɪli] zW: **~ardär** [-ar'dɛːr] m multimillionaire; **~arde** [-'ardə] f milliard; billion (BES US); **~meter** m millimetre; **~meterpapier** nt graph paper

Million [mili'oːn] (-, -en) f million; **~är** [-o'nɛːr] m millionaire

Milz [mɪlts] (-, -en) f spleen

Mimik ['miːmɪk] f mime

Mimose [mi'moːzə] f mimosa; (fig) sensitive person

minder ['mɪndər] adj inferior ♦ adv less; **M~heit** f minority; **~jährig** adj minor; **M~jährige(r)** f(m) minor; **~n** vt, vr to decrease, to diminish; **M~ung** f decrease;

~wertig adj inferior; **M~wertigkeitskomplex** m inferiority complex

Mindest- ['mɪndəst] zW: **~alter** nt minimum age; **~betrag** m minimum amount; **m~e(r, s)** adj least; **zum ~en** od **m~en** adv at least; **~haltbarkeitsdatum** nt best-before date; **~lohn** m minimum wage; **~maß** nt minimum

Mine ['miːnə] f mine; (Bleistiftmine) lead; (Kugelschreibermine) refill

Mineral [mine'raːl] (-s, -e od -ien) nt mineral; **m~isch** adj mineral; **~wasser** nt mineral water

Miniatur [minia'tuːr] f miniature

Mini- zW: **~golf** ['miniɡɔlf] nt miniature golf, crazy golf; **m~mal** [mini'maːl] adj minimal; **~mum** ['minimʊm] nt minimum; **~rock** nt miniskirt

Minister [mi'nɪstər] (-s, -) m minister; **m~iell** adj ministerial; **~ium** nt ministry; **~präsident** m prime minister

Minus ['miːnʊs] (-, -) nt deficit

minus adv minus; **M~zeichen** nt minus sign

Minute [mi'nuːtə] f minute

Minze ['mɪntsə] f mint

mir [miːr] (dat von ich) pron (to) me; **~ nichts, dir nichts** just like that

Misch- [mɪʃ] zW: **~brot** nt bread made from more than one kind of flour; **~ehe** f mixed marriage; **m~en** vt to mix; **~ling** m half-caste; mongrel; **~ung** f mixture

miserabel [miza'raːbəl] (umg) adj (Essen, Film) dreadful

Miss- ▲ [mɪs] zW: **~behagen** nt discomfort, uneasiness; **~bildung** f deformity; **m~billigen** vt insep to disapprove of; **~brauch** m abuse; (falscher Gebrauch) misuse; **m~brauchen** vt insep to abuse; **jdn** zu od **für etw m~brauchen** to use sb for od to do sth; **~erfolg** m failure; **m~fallen** (-s) nt displeasure; **m~fallen** (unreg) vt insep:

jdm m~fallen to displease sb; **~geschick** nt misfortune; **m~glücken** [mɪsˈɡlʏkən] vi insep to fail; **jdm m~glückt etw** sb does not succeed with sth; **~griff** m mistake; **~gunst** f envy; **m~günstig** adj envious; **m~handeln** vt insep to ill-treat; **~'handlung** f ill-treatment

Mission [mɪsiˈoːn] f mission; **~ar(in)** m(f) missionary

Miss- ▲ zW: **~klang** m discord; **~kredit** m discredit; **m~lingen** [mɪsˈlɪŋən] (unreg) vi insep to fail; **m~mut** m sullenness; **m~mutig** adj sullen; **m~raten** (unreg) vi insep to turn out badly ♦ adj ill-bred; **~stand** m bad state of affairs; abuse; **m~trauen** vi insep to mistrust; **~trauen (-s)** nt distrust, suspicion; **~trauensantrag** m (POL) motion of no confidence; **m~trauisch** adj distrustful, suspicious; **~verhältnis** nt disproportion; **~verständnis** nt misunderstanding; **m~verstehen** (unreg) vt insep to misunderstand; **~wirtschaft** f mismanagement

Mist [mɪst] (-(e)s) m dung; dirt; (umg) rubbish

Mistel (-, -n) f mistletoe

Misthaufen m dungheap

mit [mɪt] präp +dat with; (~tels) by ♦ adv along, too; **~ der Bahn** by train; **~ 10 Jahren** at the age of 10; **wollen Sie ~?** do you want to come along?

Mitarbeit [ˈmɪtʔarbaɪt] f cooperation; **m~en** vi to cooperate, to collaborate; **~er(in)** m(f) collaborator; co-worker ♦ pl (Personal) staff

Mit- zW: **~bestimmung** f participation in decision-making; **m~bringen** (unreg) vt to bring along

miteinander [mɪtʔaɪˈnandər] adv together, with one another

miterleben vt to see, to witness

Mitesser [ˈmɪtʔɛsər] (-s, -) m blackhead

mitfahr- zW: **~en** vi to accompany;

(auf Reise auch) to travel with; **M~gelegenheit** f lift; **M~zentrale** f agency for arranging lifts

mitfühlend adj sympathetic, compassionate

Mit- zW: **m~geben** (unreg) vt to give; **~gefühl** nt sympathy; **m~gehen** (unreg) vi to go/come along; **m~genommen** adj done in, in a bad way; **~gift** f dowry

Mitglied [ˈmɪtɡliːt] nt member; **~sbeitrag** m membership fee; **~schaft** f membership

Mitleid nt sympathy; (Erbarmen) compassion; **m~ig** adj sympathetic; **m~slos** adj pitiless, merciless

Mit- zW: **m~machen** vt to join in, to take part in; **~mensch** m fellow man; **m~nehmen** (unreg) vt to take along/away; (anstrengen) to wear out, to exhaust; **zum ~nehmen** to take away; **m~reden** vi: **bei etw m~reden** to have a say in sth; **m~reißen** (unreg) vt to carry away/along; (fig) to thrill, captivate

mitsamt [mɪtˈzamt] präp +dat together with

Mitschuld f complicity; **m~ig** adj: **m~ig (an** +dat) implicated (in); (an Unfall) partly responsible (for)

Mit- zW: **~schüler(in)** m(f) schoolmate; **m~spielen** vi to join in, to take part; **~spieler(in)** m(f) partner

Mittag [ˈmɪtaːk] (-(e)s, -e) m midday, lunchtime; **(zu) ~ essen** to have lunch; **heute/morgen ~** today/tomorrow at lunchtime od noon; **~essen** nt lunch, dinner

mittags adv at lunchtime od noon;
M~pause f lunch break; **M~schlaf** m
early afternoon nap, siesta
Mittäter(in) ['mɪtɛːtər(ɪn)] m(f) accomplice
Mitte ['mɪtə] f middle; (POL) centre;
aus unserer ~ from our midst
mitteilen ['mɪttaɪlən] vt: **jdm etw ~**
to inform sb of sth, to communicate
sth to sb
Mitteilung f communication
Mittel ['mɪtəl] (-s -) nt means; method;
(MATH) average; (MED) medicine; **ein ~
zum Zweck** a means to an end; **~al-
ter** nt Middle Ages pl; **m~alterlich** adj
mediaeval; **~ding** nt cross; **~europa**
nt Central Europe; **~gebirge** nt low
mountain range; **m~mäßig** adj mediocre, middling; **~mäßigkeit** f medi-
ocrity; **~meer** nt Mediterranean; **~ohr-
entzündung** f inflammation of the
middle ear; **~punkt** m centre; **~stand**
m middle class; **~streifen** m central
reservation; **~stürmer** m centre-
forward; **~weg** m middle course;
~welle f (RADIO) medium wave
mitten ['mɪtən] adv in the middle; **~
auf der Straße/in der Nacht** in the
middle of the street/night
Mitternacht ['mɪtərnaxt] f midnight
mittlere(r, s) ['mɪtlərə(r, s)] adj middle; (durchschnittlich) medium, average; **~ Reife ≈** O-levels

---
mittlere Reife

The **mittlere Reife** *is the standard
certificate gained at a Realschule or
Gymnasium on successful completion of 6 years' education there. If a
pupil at a Realschule attains good results in several subjects he is allowed
to enter the 11th class of a Gymnasium to study for the Abitur.*

---

mittlerweile ['mɪtlər'vaɪlə] adv meanwhile
Mittwoch ['mɪtvɔx] (-(e)s, -e) m

Wednesday; **m~s** adv on Wednesdays
mitunter [mɪt'|ʊntər] adv occasionally,
sometimes
Mit- zW: **m~verantwortlich** adj jointly
responsible; **m~wirken** vi: **m~wirken
(bei)** to contribute (to); (THEAT) to take
part (in); **~wirkung** f contribution;
participation
Mobbing ['mɔbɪŋ] (-s) nt workplace
bullying
Möbel ['møːbəl] pl furniture sg; **~wa-
gen** m furniture od removal van
mobil [mo'biːl] adj mobile; (MIL) mobi-
lized; **M~iar** [mobi'laːr] (-s, -e) nt furnishings pl; **M~machung** f mobiliza-
tion; **M~telefon** nt mobile phone
möblieren [mø'bliːrən] vt to furnish;
möbliert wohnen to live in furnished
accommodation
möchte etc ['mœçtə] vb siehe **mögen**
Mode ['moːdə] f fashion
Modell [mo'dɛl] (-s, -e) nt model;
m~ieren [-'liːrən] vt to model
Modenschau f fashion show
moderig ['moːdərɪç] adj (Keller) musty;
(Luft) stale
modern [mo'dɛrn] adj modern; (modisch) fashionable; **~isieren** vt to
modernize
Mode- zW: **~schau** f fashion show;
~schmuck m fashion jewellery;
~schöpfer(in) m(f) fashion designer;
~wort nt fashionable word, buzz
word
modisch ['moːdɪʃ] adj fashionable
Mofa ['moːfa] (-s, -s) nt small moped
mogeln ['moːgəln] (umg) vi to cheat

SCHLÜSSELWORT

mögen ['møːgən] (pt **mochte**, pp **gemocht** od (als Hilfsverb) **mögen**) vt, vi to
like; **magst du/mögen Sie ihn?** do
you like him?; **ich möchte ...** I would
like ...; **I'd like ...; er möchte in die
Stadt** he'd like to go into town; **ich
möchte nicht, dass du ...** I wouldn't
like you to ...; **ich mag nicht mehr**

I've had enough
♦ *Hilfsverb* to like to; *(wollen)* to want; **möchtest du etwas essen?** would you like something to eat?; **sie mag nicht bleiben** she doesn't want to stay; **das mag wohl sein** that may well be; **was mag das heißen?** what might that mean?; **Sie möchten zu Hause anrufen** could you please call home?

möglich ['møːklɪç] *adj* possible; **~erweise** *adv* possibly; **M~keit** *f* possibility; **nach M~keit** if possible; **~st** *adv* as ... as possible

Mohn [moːn] (-(e)s, -e) *m* (~*blume*) poppy; (~*samen*) poppy seed

Möhre ['møːrə] *f* carrot

Mohrrübe ['moːrryːbə] *f* carrot

mokieren [mo'kiːrən] *vr*: **sich ~ über** +*akk* to make fun of

Mole ['moːlə] *f* (harbour) mole

Molekül [mole'kyːl] (-s, -e) *nt* molecule

Molkerei [mɔlkə'raɪ] *f* dairy

Moll [mɔl] (-, -) *nt* (MUS) minor (key)

mollig *adj* cosy; *(dicklich)* plump

Moment [mo'mɛnt] (-(e)s, -e) *m* moment ♦ *nt* factor; **im ~** at the moment; **~ (mal)!** just a moment; **m~an** [-'tan] *adj* momentary ♦ *adv* at the moment

Monarch [mo'narç] (-en, -en) *m* monarch; **~ie** [monar'çiː] *f* monarchy

Monat ['moːnat] (-(e)s, -e) *m* month; **m~elang** *adv* for months; **m~lich** *adj* monthly

Monats- *zW*: **~gehalt** *nt*: **das dreizehnte ~gehalt** Christmas bonus *(of one month's salary)*; **~karte** *f* monthly ticket

Mönch [mœnç] (-(e)s, -e) *m* monk

Mond [moːnt] (-(e)s, -e) *m* moon; **~finsternis** *f* eclipse of the moon; **m~hell** *adj* moonlit; **~landung** *f*

moon landing; **~schein** *m* moonlight

Mono- [mono] *in zW* mono; **~log** [-'loːk] (-s, -e) *m* monologue; **~pol** [-'poːl] (-s, -e) *nt* monopoly; **m~polisieren** [-poli'ziːrən] *vt* to monopolize; **m~ton** [-'toːn] *adj* monotonous; **~tonie** [-to'niː] *f* monotony

Montag ['moːntaːk] (-(e)s, -e) *m* Monday

Montage [mɔn'taːʒə] *f* (PHOT etc) montage; (TECH) assembly; *(Einbauen)* fitting

Monteur [mɔn'tøːr] *m* fitter

montieren [mɔn'tiːrən] *vt* to assemble

Monument [monu'mɛnt] *nt* monument; **m~al** [-'taːl] *adj* monumental

Moor [moːr] (-(e)s, -e) *nt* moor

Moos [moːs] (-es, -e) *nt* moss

Moped ['moːpɛt] (-s, -s) *nt* moped

Moral [mo'raːl] (-, -en) *f* morality; *(einer Geschichte)* moral; **m~isch** *adj* moral

Morast [mo'rast] (-(e)s, -e) *m* morass, mire; **m~ig** *adj* boggy

Mord [mɔrt] (-(e)s, -e) *m* murder; **~anschlag** *m* murder attempt

Mörder(in) ['mœrdər(ɪn)] (-s, -) *m(f)* murderer (murderess)

mörderisch *adj* (fig: schrecklich) terrible, dreadful ♦ *adv* (umg: entsetzlich) terribly, dreadfully

Mord- *zW*: **~kommission** *f* murder squad; **~sglück** (umg) *nt* amazing luck; **m~smäßig** (umg) *adj* terrific, enormous; **~sverdacht** *m* suspicion of murder; **~waffe** *f* murder weapon

morgen ['mɔrgən] *adv* tomorrow; **~ früh** tomorrow morning; **M~** (-s, -) *m* morning; **M~mantel** *m* dressing gown; **M~rock** *m* dressing gown; **M~röte** *f* dawn; **~s** *adv* in the morning

morgig ['mɔrgɪç] *adj* tomorrow's; **der ~e Tag** tomorrow

Morphium ['mɔrfiʊm] *nt* morphine

morsch [mɔrʃ] *adj* rotten

Morsealphabet ['mɔrzəʔalfabeːt] *nt* Morse code

morsen *vi* to send a message by Morse code

Mörtel ['mœrtəl] (*-s*, *-*) *m* mortar

Mosaik [moza'iːk] (*-s*, *-en* *od* *-e*) *nt* mosaic

Moschee [mɔ'ʃeː] (*-*, *-n*) *f* mosque

Moskito [mɔs'kiːto] (*-s*, *-s*) *m* mosquito

Most [mɔst] (*-(e)s*, *-e*) *m* (unfermented) fruit juice; (*Apfelwein*) cider

Motel [mo'tɛl] *nt* motel

Motiv [mo'tiːf] (*-s*, *-e*) *nt* motive; (*Mus*) theme; **~ation** [-vatsi'oːn] *f* motivation; **m~ieren** [moti'viːrən] *vt* to motivate

Motor ['moːtɔr, *pl* mo'toːrən] (*-s*, *-en*) *m* engine; (*bes ELEK*) motor; **~boot** *nt* motorboat; **~haube** *f* (*von Auto*) bonnet (*BRIT*), hood (*US*); **m~isieren** *vt* to motorize; **~öl** *nt* engine oil; **~rad** *nt* motorcycle; **~roller** *m* (motor) scooter; **~schaden** *m* engine trouble *od* failure

Motte ['mɔtə] *f* moth; **~nkugel** *f* mothball(s)

Motto ['mɔto] (*-s*, *-s*) *nt* motto

Möwe ['møːvə] *f* seagull

Mücke ['mʏkə] *f* midge, gnat; **~nstich** *m* midge *od* gnat bite

müde ['myːdə] *adj* tired

Müdigkeit ['myːdɪçkaɪt] *f* tiredness

Muffel (*-s*, *-*) (*umg*) *m* killjoy, sourpuss

muffig *adj* (*Luft*) musty

Mühe ['myːə] *f* trouble, pains *pl*; **mit Müh und Not** with great difficulty; **sich** *dat* **~ geben** to go to a lot of trouble; **m~los** *adj* without trouble, easy; **m~voll** *adj* laborious, arduous

Mühle ['myːlə] *f* mill; (*Kaffeemühle*) grinder

Müh- *zW*: **~sal** (*-*, *-e*) *f* tribulation; **m~sam** *adj* arduous, troublesome; **m~selig** *adj* arduous, laborious

Mulde ['mʊldə] *f* hollow, depression

Mull [mʊl] (*-(e)s*, *-e*) *m* thin muslin

Müll [mʏl] (*-(e)s*) *m* refuse; **~abfuhr** *f* rubbish disposal; (*Leute*) dustmen *pl*; **~abladeplatz** *m* rubbish dump; **~eimer** *m* dustbin, garbage can (*US*); **~haufen** *m* rubbish heap; **~schlucker** (*-s*, *-*) *m* garbage disposal unit; **~tonne** *f* dustbin; **~verbrennungsanlage** *f* incinerator

mulmig ['mʊlmɪç] *adj* rotten; (*umg*) dodgy; **jdm ist ~** sb feels funny

multiplizieren [mʊltipli'tsiːrən] *vt* to multiply

Mumie ['muːmiə] *f* mummy

Mumm [mʊm] (*-s*) (*umg*) *m* gumption, nerve

Mumps [mʊmps] (*-*) *m* *od* *f* (*MED*) mumps

München ['mʏnçən] (*-s*) *nt* Munich

Mund [mʊnt] (*-(e)s*, *ᵘer*) *m* mouth; **~art** *f* dialect

münden ['mʏndən] *vi*: **~ in** *+akk* to flow into

Mund- *zW*: **m~faul** *adj* taciturn; **~geruch** *m* bad breath; **~harmonika** *f* mouth organ

mündig ['mʏndɪç] *adj* of age; **M~keit** *f* majority

mündlich ['mʏntlɪç] *adj* oral

Mundstück *nt* mouthpiece; (*Zigarettenmundstück*) tip

Mündung ['mʏndʊŋ] *f* (*von Fluss*) mouth; (*Gewehr*) muzzle

Mund- *zW*: **~wasser** *nt* mouthwash; **~werk** *nt*: **ein großes ~werk haben** to have a big mouth; **~winkel** *m* corner of the mouth

Munition [munitsi'oːn] *f* ammunition; **~slager** *nt* ammunition dump

munkeln ['mʊŋkəln] *vi* to whisper, to mutter

Münster ['mʏnstər] (*-s*, *-*) *nt* minster

munter ['mʊntər] *adj* lively

Münze ['mʏntsə] *f* coin; **m~n** *vt* to coin, to mint; **auf jdn gemünzt sein**

to be aimed at sb

Münzfernsprecher ['mʏntsfɛrnʃprɛ-çər] m callbox (BRIT), pay phone

mürb(e) ['mʏrb(ə)] adj (Gestein) crumbly; (Holz) rotten; (Gebäck) crisp; **jdn ~ machen** to wear sb down; **M~eteig** ['mʏrbataɪç] m shortcrust pastry

murmeln ['mʊrməln] vt, vi to murmur, to mutter

murren ['mʊrən] vi to grumble, to grouse

mürrisch ['mʏrɪʃ] adj sullen

Mus [muːs] (-es, -e) nt purée

Muschel ['mʊʃəl] (-, -n) f mussel; (~schale) shell; (Telefonmuschel) receiver

Muse ['muːzə] f muse

Museum [muˈzeːʊm] nt museum

Musik [muˈziːk] f music; (Kapelle) band; **m~alisch** [-ˈkaːlɪʃ] adj musical; **~ant(in)** [-ˈkant(ɪn)] (-en, -en) m(f) musician; **~box** f jukebox; **~er** (-s, -) m musician; **~hochschule** f college of music; **~instrument** nt musical instrument

musisch ['muːzɪʃ] adj (Mensch) artistic

musizieren [muziˈtsiːrən] vi to make music

Muskat [mʊsˈkaːt] (-(e)s, -e) m nutmeg

Muskel ['mʊskəl] (-s, -n) m muscle; **~kater** m: **~kater haben** to be stiff

Muskulatur [mʊskulaˈtuːr] f muscular system

muskulös [mʊskuˈløːs] adj muscular

Müsli ['myːsli] (-s, -) nt (KOCH) muesli

Muss ▲ [mʊs] (-) nt necessity, must

Muße ['muːsə] (-) f leisure

SCHLÜSSELWORT

müssen ['mʏsən] (pt **musste**, pp **gemusst** od (als Hilfsverb) **müssen**) vi

1 (Zwang) must (nur im Präsens), to have to; **ich muss es tun** I must do it, I have to do it; **ich musste es tun** I had to do it; **er muss es nicht tun** he doesn't have to do it; **muss ich?** must I?, do I have to?; **wann müsst ihr zur Schule?** when do you have to go to school?; **er hat gehen müssen** he (has) had to go; **muss das sein?** is that really necessary?; **ich muss mal** (umg) I need the toilet

2 (sollen): **das musst du nicht tun!** you oughtn't to od shouldn't do that; **Sie hätten ihn fragen müssen** you should have asked him

3: **es muss geregnet haben** it must have rained; **es muss nicht wahr sein** it needn't be true

müßig ['myːsɪç] adj idle

Muster ['mʊstər] (-s, -) nt model; (Dessin) pattern; (Probe) sample; **m~gültig** adj exemplary; **m~n** vt (Tapete) to pattern; (fig, MIL) to examine; (Truppen) to inspect; **~ung** f (von Stoff) pattern; (MIL) inspection

Mut [muːt] m courage; **nur ~!** cheer up!; **jdm ~ machen** to encourage sb; **m~ig** adj courageous; **m~los** adj discouraged, despondent

mutmaßlich ['muːtmaːslɪç] adj presumed ♦ adv probably

Mutprobe f test od trial of courage

Mutter¹ ['mʊtər] (-, ¨) f mother

Mutter² ['mʊtər] (-, -n) f (Schraubenmutter) nut

mütterlich ['mʏtərlɪç] adj motherly; **~erseits** adv on the mother's side

Mutter- zW: **~liebe** f motherly love; **~mal** nt birthmark; **~milch** f mother's milk; **~schaft** f motherhood, maternity; **~schutz** m maternity regulations; **'~seelenallein** adj all alone; **~sprache** f native language; **~tag** m Mother's Day

Mutti ['mʊti] (-, -s) f mum(my) (BRIT), mom(my) (US)

mutwillig ['muːtvɪlɪç] adj malicious, deliberate

Mütze ['mʏtsə] f cap

MwSt abk (= Mehrwertsteuer) VAT

mysteriös [mʏsteriˈøːs] adj mysterious

Mythos ['myːtɔs] (-, **Mythen**) m myth

N, n

na [na] excl well; **~ gut** okay then

Nabel ['naːbəl] (-s, -) m navel; **~schnur** f umbilical cord

SCHLÜSSELWORT

nach [naːx] präp +dat **1** (örtlich) to; **nach Berlin** to Berlin; **nach links/ rechts** (to the) left/right; **nach oben/ hinten** up/back
2 (zeitlich) after; **einer nach dem anderen** one after the other; **nach Ihnen!** after you!; **zehn (Minuten) nach drei** ten (minutes) past three
3 (gemäß) according to; **nach dem Gesetz** according to the law; **dem Namen nach** judging by his/her name; **nach allem, was ich weiß** as far as I know

♦ adv: **ihm nach!** after him!; **nach und nach** gradually, little by little; **nach wie vor** still

nachahmen ['naːxʔaːmən] vt to imitate

Nachbar(in) ['naːxbaːr(ɪn)] (-s, -n) m(f) neighbour; **~haus** nt: **im ~haus** next door; **n~lich** adj neighbourly; **~schaft** f neighbourhood; **~staat** m neighbouring state

nach- zW: **~bestellen** vt: **50 Stück ~bestellen** to order another 50; **N~bestellung** f (COMM) repeat order; **N~bildung** f imitation, copy; **~blicken** vi to gaze after; **~datieren** vt to postdate

nachdem [naːxˈdeːm] konj after; (weil) since; **je ~ (ob)** it depends (whether)

nachdenken (unreg) vi: **~ über** +akk to think about; **N~** (-s) nt reflection, meditation

nachdenklich adj thoughtful, pensive

Nachdruck ['naːxdrɔk] m emphasis; (TYP) reprint, reproduction

nachdrücklich ['naːxdrʏklɪç] adj emphatic

nacheinander [naːxʔaɪˈnandər] adv one after the other

nachempfinden ['naːxʔɛmpfɪndən] (unreg) vt: **jdm etw ~** to feel sth with sb

Nacherzählung ['naːxʔɛrtseːlʊŋ] f reproduction (of a story)

Nachfahr ['naːxfaːr] (-s, -en) m descendant

Nachfolge ['naːxfɔlɡə] f succession; **n~n** vi +dat to follow; **~r(in)** (-s, -) m(f) successor

nachforschen vt, vi to investigate

Nachforschung f investigation

Nachfrage ['naːxfraːɡə] f inquiry; (COMM) demand; **n~n** vi to inquire

nach- zW: **~füllen** vt to refill; **~geben** (unreg) vi to give way, to yield; **N~gebühr** f (POST) excess postage

nachgehen ['naːxɡeːən] (unreg) vi (+dat) to follow; (erforschen) to inquire (into); (Uhr) to be slow

Nachgeschmack ['naːxɡəʃmak] m aftertaste

nachgiebig ['naːxɡiːbɪç] adj soft, accommodating; **N~keit** f softness

nachhaltig ['naːxhaltɪç] adj lasting; (Widerstand) persistent

nachhause adv (österreichisch, schweizerisch) home

nachhelfen ['naːxhɛlfən] (unreg) vi +dat to assist, to help

nachher [naːxˈheːr] adv afterwards

Nachhilfeunterricht ['naːxhɪlfəʔʊntərrɪçt] m extra tuition

nachholen ['naːxhoːlən] vt to catch up with; (Versäumtes) to make up for

Nachkomme [ˈnaːkɔmə] (-, -n) *m* descendant

nachkommen (*unreg*) *vi* to follow; (*einer Verpflichtung*) to fulfil; **N~schaft** *f* descendants *pl*

Nachkriegszeit *f* postwar period

Nach- *zW:* **~lass ▲** (-es, -lässe) *m* (*COMM*) discount, rebate; (*Erbe*) estate; **n~lassen** (*unreg*) *vt* (*Strafe*) to remit; (*Summe*) to take off; (*Schulden*) to cancel ♦ *vi* to decrease, to ease off; (*Sturm*) to die down, to ease off; (*schlechter werden*) to deteriorate; **er hat n~gelassen** he has got worse; **n~lässig** *adj* negligent, careless

nachlaufen [ˈnaːklaufən] (*unreg*) *vi +dat* to run after, to chase

nachlösen [ˈnaːkløːzən] *vi* (*Zuschlag*) to pay on the train, pay at the other end; (*zur Weiterfahrt*) to pay the supplement

nachmachen [ˈnaːxmaxən] *vt* to imitate, to copy; (*fälschen*) to counterfeit

Nachmittag [ˈnaːxmɪtaːk] *m* afternoon; **am ~** in the afternoon; **n~s** *adv* in the afternoon

Nach- *zW:* **~nahme** *f* cash on delivery; **per ~nahme** C.O.D.; **~name** *m* surname; **~porto** *nt* excess postage

nachprüfen [ˈnaːxpryːfən] *vt* to check, to verify

nachrechnen [ˈnaːxrɛçnən] *vt* to check

nachreichen [ˈnaːxraiçən] *vt* (*Unterlagen*) to hand in later

Nachricht [ˈnaːxrɪçt] (-, -en) *f* (piece of) news; (*Mitteilung*) message; **~en** *pl* (*Neuigkeiten*) news

Nachrichten- *zW:* **~agentur** *f* news agency; **~dienst** *m* (*MIL*) intelligence service; **~sprecher(in)** *m(f)* newsreader; **~technik** *f* telecommunications *sg*

Nachruf [ˈnaːxruːf] *m* obituary

nachsagen [ˈnaːxzaːɡən] *vt* to repeat;

jdm etw ~ to say sth of sb

Nachsaison [ˈnaːxzɛzõ] *f* off-season

nachschicken [ˈnaːxʃɪkən] *vt* to forward

nachschlagen [ˈnaːxʃlaːɡən] (*unreg*) *vt* to look up

Nachschlagewerk *nt* reference book

Nachschlüssel *m* duplicate key

Nachschub [ˈnaːxʃuːp] *m* supplies *pl*; (*Truppen*) reinforcements *pl*

nachsehen [ˈnaːxzeːən] (*unreg*) *vt* (*prüfen*) to check ♦ *vi* (*erforschen*) to look and see; **jdm etw ~** to forgive sb sth; **das N~ haben** to come off worst

Nachsendeantrag *m* application to have one's mail forwarded

nachsenden [ˈnaːxzɛndən] (*unreg*) *vt* to send on, to forward

nachsichtig *adj* indulgent, lenient

nachsitzen [ˈnaːxzɪtsən] (*unreg*) *vi:* **(müssen)** (*SCH*) to be kept in

Nachspeise [ˈnaːxʃpaizə] *f* dessert, sweet, pudding

Nachspiel [ˈnaːxʃpiːl] *nt* epilogue; (*fig*) sequel

nachsprechen [ˈnaːxʃprɛçən] (*unreg*) *vt:* **(jdm) ~** to repeat (after sb)

nächst [nɛːçst] *präp +dat* (*räumlich*) next to; (*außer*) apart from; **~beste(r, s)** *adj* first that comes along; (*zweitbeste*) next best; **N~e(r)** *f(m)* neighbour; **~e(r, s)** *adj* next; (*~gelegen*) nearest

nachstellen [ˈnaːxʃtɛlən] *vt* (*TECH: neu einstellen*) to adjust

nächst *zW:* **N~enliebe** *f* love for one's fellow men; **~ens** *adv* shortly, soon; **~liegend** *adj* nearest; (*fig*) obvious; **~möglich** *adj* next possible

Nacht [naxt] (-, ⁻e) *f* night; **~dienst** *m* night shift

Nachteil [ˈnaːxtail] *m* disadvantage; **n~ig** *adj* disadvantageous

Nachthemd *nt* (*Herrennachthemd*) nightshirt; (*Damennachthemd*) nightdress

---

Spelling Reform: ▲ *new spelling* △ *old spelling (to be phased out)*

Nachtigall ['naxtɪgal] (-, -en) f nightingale

Nachtisch ['na:xtɪʃ] m = **Nachspeise**

Nachtklub m night club

Nachtleben nt nightlife

nächtlich ['nɛçtlɪç] adj nightly

Nachtlokal nt night club

Nach- zW: **~trag** (-(e)s, -träge) m supplement; **n~tragen** (unreg) vt to carry; (zufügen) to add; **jdm etw n~tragen** to hold sth against sb; **n~träglich** adj later, subsequent; additional ♦ adv later, subsequently; additionally; **n~trauern** vi: **jdm/etw n~trauern** to mourn the loss of sb/sth

Nacht- zW: **n~s** adv at od by night; **~schicht** f nightshift; **~schwester** f night nurse; **~tarif** m off-peak tariff; **~tisch** m bedside table; **~wächter** m night watchman

Nach- zW: **~untersuchung** f checkup; **n~wachsen** (unreg) vi to grow again; **~wahl** f (POL) ≈ by-election

Nachweis ['na:xvaɪs] (-es, -e) m proof; **n~bar** adj provable, demonstrable; **n~en** (unreg) vt to prove; **jdm etw n~en** to point sth out to sb; **n~lich** adj evident, demonstrable

nach- zW: **~wirken** vi to have aftereffects; **N~wirkung** f aftereffect; **N~wort** nt epilogue; **N~wuchs** m offspring; (beruflich etc) new recruits pl; **~zahlen** vt, vi to pay extra; **N~zahlung** f additional payment; (zurückdatiert) back pay; **~ziehen** (unreg) vt (hinter sich herziehen: Bein) to drag; **N~zügler** (-s, -) m straggler

Nacken ['nakən] (-s, -) m nape of the neck

nackt [nakt] adj naked; (Tatsachen) plain, bare; **N~badestrand** m nudist beach; **N~heit** f nakedness

Nadel ['na:dəl] (-, -n) f needle; (Stecknadel) pin; **~öhr** nt eye of a needle; **~wald** m coniferous forest

Nagel ['na:gəl] (-s, ") m nail; **~bürste** f nailbrush; **~feile** f nailfile; **~lack** m

varnish od polish (BRIT); **n~n** vt, vi to nail; **n~neu** adj brand-new; **~schere** f nail scissors pl

nagen ['na:gən] vt, vi to gnaw

Nagetier ['na:gəti:r] nt rodent

nah(e) ['na:(ə)] adj (räumlich) near(by); (Verwandte) near; (Freunde) close; (zeitlich) near, close ♦ adv near(by); near; close; (verwandt) closely ♦ präp (+dat) near (to), close to; **der Nahe Osten** the Near East; **~ gehen** (+dat) to grieve; **~ kommen** (+dat) to get close (to); **jdm etw ~ legen** to suggest sth to sb; **~ liegen** to be obvious; **~ liegend** obvious; **~ stehen** (+dat) to be close (to); **einer Sache ~ stehen** to sympathize with sb/sth; **~ stehend** close; **jdm (zu) ~ treten** to offend sb

Nahaufnahme f close-up

Nähe ['nɛ:ə] (-) f nearness, proximity; (Umgebung) vicinity; **in der ~** close by; at hand; **aus der ~** from close to

nah(e)bei adv nearby

nahen vi, vr to approach, to draw near

nähen ['nɛ:ən] vt, vi to sew

näher adj, adv nearer; (Erklärung, Erkundigung) more detailed; **(sich) ~ kommen** to get closer; **N~e(s)** nt details pl, particulars pl

Naherholungsgebiet nt recreational area (close to a town)

nähern vr to approach

nahezu adv nearly

Nähgarn nt thread

Nahkampf m hand-to-hand fighting

Nähkasten m sewing basket, workbox

nahm etc [na:m] vb siehe **nehmen**

Nähmaschine f sewing machine

Nähnadel f needle

nähren ['nɛ:rən] vt to feed ♦ vr (Person) to feed o.s.; (Tier) to feed

nahrhaft ['na:rhaft] adj nourishing, nutritious

Nahrung ['na:rʊŋ] f food; (fig auch) sustenance

Nahrungs- zW: **~mittel** nt foodstuffs pl; **~mittelindustrie** f food industry;

~suche f search for food

Nährwert m nutritional value

Naht [naːt] (-, -e) f seam; (MED) suture; (TECH) join; **n~los** adj seamless; **n~los ineinander übergehen** to follow without a gap

Nah- zW: **~verkehr** m local traffic; **~verkehrszug** m local train; **~ziel** nt immediate objective

Name ['naːmə] (-ns, -n) m name; **im ~n von** on behalf of; **n~ns** adv by the name of; **~nstag** m name day, saint's day; **n~ntlich** adj by name ♦ adv particularly, especially

┌─────────────────┐
│ **Namenstag**   │
└─────────────────┘

In Catholic areas of Germany the Namenstag is often a more important celebration than a birthday. This is the day dedicated to the saint after whom a person is called, and on that day the person receives presents and invites relatives and friends round to celebrate.

namhaft ['naːmhaft] adj (berühmt) famed, renowned; (beträchtlich) considerable; **~ machen** to name

nämlich ['nɛːmlɪç] adv that is to say, namely; (denn) since

nannte etc ['nantə] vb siehe **nennen**

Napf [napf] (-(e)s, ⁻e) m bowl, dish

Narbe ['narbə] f scar; **narbig** adj scarred

Narkose [nar'koːzə] f anaesthetic

Narr [nar] (-en, -en) m fool; **n~en** vt to fool; **Närrin** ['nɛrɪn] f fool; **närrisch** adj foolish, crazy

Narzisse [nar'tsɪsə] f narcissus; daffodil

naschen ['naʃən] vt, vi to nibble; (heimlich kosten) to pinch a bit

naschhaft adj sweet-toothed

Nase ['naːzə] f nose

Nasen- zW: **~bluten** (-s) nt nosebleed; **~loch** nt nostril; **~tropfen** pl nose drops

naseweis adj pert, cheeky; (neugierig) nosey

Nashorn ['naːshɔrn] nt rhinoceros

nass ▲ [nas] adj wet

Nässe ['nɛsə] (-) f wetness; **n~n** vt to wet

nasskalt ▲ adj wet and cold

Nassrasur ▲ f wet shave

Nation [natsi'oːn] f nation

national [natsio'naːl] adj national; **N~feiertag** m national holiday; **N~hymne** f national anthem; **~isieren** [-i'ziːrən] vt to nationalize; **N~ismus** [-'lɪsmʊs] m nationalism; **~istisch** [-'lɪstɪʃ] adj nationalistic; **N~ität** f nationality; **N~mannschaft** f national team; **N~sozialismus** m national socialism

Natron ['naːtrɔn] (-s) nt soda

Natter ['natər] (-, -n) f adder

Natur [na'tuːr] f nature; (körperlich) constitution; **~ell** (-es, -e) nt disposition; **~erscheinung** f natural phenomenon or event; **n~farben** adj natural coloured; **n~gemäß** adj natural; **~gesetz** nt law of nature; **n~getreu** adj true to life; **~katastrophe** f natural disaster

natürlich [na'tyːrlɪç] adj natural ♦ adv naturally; **ja, ~!** yes, of course; **N~keit** f naturalness

Natur- zW: **~park** m ≈ national park; **~produkt** nt natural product; **n~rein** adj natural, pure; **~schutz** m nature conservation; **unter ~schutz stehen** to be legally protected; **~schutzgebiet** nt nature reserve; **~wissenschaft** f natural science; **~wissenschaftler(in)** m(f) scientist

nautisch ['nautɪʃ] adj nautical

Nazi ['naːtsi] (-s, -s) m Nazi

NB abk (= nota bene) NB

n. Chr. abk (= nach Christus) A.D.

Nebel ['neːbəl] (-s, -) m fog, mist; **n~ig**

---

adj foggy, misty; **~scheinwerfer** *m* fog lamp

neben ['ne:bən] *präp (+akk od dat)* next to; (+*dat:* außer) apart from, besides; **~an** [ne:bən'an] *adv* next door; **N~anschluss** ▲ *m* (TEL) extension; **N~ausgang** *m* side exit; **~bei** [ne:bən'bai] *adv* at the same time; (außerdem) additionally; (beiläufig) incidentally; **~beruf** *m* second job; **N~beschäftigung** *f* second job; **N~buhler(in)** (-, -) *m(f)* rival; **~einander** [ne:bən'ai'nandər] *adv* side by side; **~einander legen** to put next to each other; **~eingang** *m* side entrance; **N~fach** *nt* subsidiary subject; **N~fluss** ▲ *m* tributary; **N~gebäude** *nt* annexe; **N~geräusch** *nt* (RADIO) interference; **~her** [ne:bən'he:r] *adv* (zusätzlich) besides; (gleichzeitig) at the same time; (daneben) alongside; **N~kosten** *pl* extra charges, extras; **N~produkt** *nt* by-product; **N~sache** *f* trifle, side issue; **~sächlich** *adj* minor, peripheral; **N~saison** *f* low season; **N~straße** *f* side street; **N~verdienst** *m* secondary income; **N~wirkung** *f* side effect; **N~zimmer** *nt* adjoining room

neblig ['ne:blɪç] *adj* foggy, misty

Necessaire [nesɛ'sɛ:r] (-s, -s) *nt* (Nähnecessaire) needlework box; (Nagelnecessaire) manicure case

necken ['nɛkən] *vt* to tease

Neckerei [nɛkə'rai] *f* teasing

Neffe ['nɛfə] (-n, -n) *m* nephew

negativ ['ne:gati:f] *adj* negative; **N~** (-s, -e) *nt* (PHOT) negative

Neger ['ne:gər] (-s, -) *m* negro; **~in** *f* negress

nehmen ['ne:mən] (unreg) *vt* to take; **jdn zu sich ~** to take sb in; **sich ernst ~** to take o.s. seriously; **nimm dir doch bitte** please help yourself

Neid [nait] (-(e)s) *m* envy; **~er** (-s, -) *m* envier; **n~isch** ['naidɪʃ] *adj* envious, jealous

neigen ['naigən] *vt* to incline, to lean; (Kopf) to bow ♦ *vi:* **zu etw ~** to tend to sth

Neigung *f* (des Geländes) slope; (Tendenz) tendency, inclination; (Vorliebe) liking; (Zuneigung) affection

nein [nain] *adv* no

Nektarine [nɛkta'ri:nə] *f* (Frucht) nectarine

Nelke ['nɛlkə] *f* carnation, pink; (Gewürz) clove

Nenn- ['nɛn] zW: **n~en** (unreg) *vt* to name; (mit Namen) to call; **wie n~t man ...?** what do you call ...?; **n~enswert** *adj* worth mentioning; **~er** (-s, -) *m* denominator; **~wert** *m* nominal value; (COMM) par

Neon ['ne:ɔn] (-s) *nt* neon; **~licht** *nt* neon light; **~röhre** *f* neon tube

Nerv [nɛrf] (-s, -en) *m* nerve; **jdm auf die ~en gehen** to get on sb's nerves; **n~enaufreibend** *adj* nerve-racking; **~enbündel** *nt* bundle of nerves; **~enheilanstalt** *f* mental home; **n~enkrank** *adj* mentally ill; **~ensäge** (umg) *f* pain (in the neck) (umg); **~ensystem** *nt* nervous system; **~enzusammenbruch** *m* nervous breakdown; **n~lich** *adj* (Belastung) affecting the nerves; **n~ös** [nɛr'vø:s] *adj* nervous; **~osität** *f* nervousness; **n~tötend** *adj* nerve-racking; (Arbeit) soul-destroying

Nerz [nɛrts] (-es, -e) *m* mink

Nessel ['nɛsəl] (-, -n) *f* nettle

Nessessär ▲ [nese'sɛ:r] (-s, -s) *nt* = Necessaire

Nest [nɛst] (-(e)s, -er) *nt* nest; (umg: Ort) dump

nett [nɛt] *adj* nice; (freundlich) nice, kind; **~erweise** *adv* kindly

netto ['nɛto:] *adv* net

Netz [nɛts] (-es, -e) *nt* net; (Gepäcknetz) rack; (Einkaufsnetz) string bag; (Spinnennetz) web; (System) network; **jdm ins ~ gehen** (fig) to fall into sb's trap; **~anschluss** ▲ *m* mains connection; **~haut** f retina

neu [nɔʏ] adj new; (Sprache, Geschichte) modern; **seit ~estem** (since) recently; **die ~esten Nachrichten** the latest news; **~ schreiben** to rewrite, to write again; **N~anschaffung** f new purchase od acquisition; **~artig** adj new kind of; **N~bau** m new building; **N~e(r)** f(m) the new man/woman; **~erdings** adv (kürzlich) (since) recently; (von ~em) again; **N~erscheinung** f (Buch) new publication; (Schallplatte) new release; **N~erung** f innovation, new departure; **N~gier** f curiosity; **~gierig** adj curious; **N~heit** f newness; novelty; **N~igkeit** f news sg; **N~jahr** nt New Year; **~lich** adv recently, the other day; **N~ling** m novice; **N~mond** m new moon

neun [nɔʏn] num nine; **~zehn** num nineteen; **~zig** num ninety

neureich adj nouveau riche; **N~e(r)** f(m) nouveau riche

neurotisch adj neurotic

Neuseeland [nɔʏ'zeːlant] nt New Zealand; **Neuseeländer(in)** [nɔʏ'zeːlɛndər(ɪn)] m(f) New Zealander

neutral [nɔʏ'traːl] adj neutral; **~i'sieren** vt to neutralize

Neutrum ['nɔʏtrʊm] (-s, -a od -en) nt neuter

Neu- zW: **~wert** m purchase price; **n~wertig** adj (as) new, not used; **~zeit** f modern age; **n~zeitlich** adj modern, recent

─────────

SCHLÜSSELWORT

nicht [nɪçt] adv **1** (Verneinung) not; **er ist es nicht** it's not him, it isn't him; **er raucht nicht** (gerade) he isn't smoking; (gewöhnlich) he doesn't smoke; **ich kann das nicht - ich auch nicht** I can't do it - neither od nor can I; **es regnet nicht mehr** it's not raining any

more; **nicht rostend** stainless

2 (Bitte, Verbot): **nicht!** don't!, no!; **nicht berühren!** do not touch!; **nicht doch!** don't!

3 (rhetorisch): **du bist müde, nicht (wahr)?** you're tired, aren't you?; **das ist schön, nicht (wahr)?** it's nice, isn't it?

4: was du nicht sagst! the things you say!

Nichtangriffspakt [nɪçt'|angrɪfspakt] m non-aggression pact

nichtig ['nɪçtɪç] adj (ungültig) null, void; (wertlos) futile; **N~keit** f nullity, invalidity; (Sinnlosigkeit) futility

Nichtraucher(in) m(f) non-smoker

nichts [nɪçts] pron nothing; **für ~ und wieder ~** for nothing at all; **~ sagend** meaningless; **N~ (-)** nt nothingness; (pej: Person) nonentity

Nichtschwimmer m non-swimmer

nichts- zW: **~desto'weniger** adv nevertheless; **N~nutz (-es, -e)** m good-for-nothing; **~nutzig** adj worthless, useless; **N~tun (-s)** nt idleness

Nichtzutreffende(s) nt: **~s** od nicht Zutreffendes (bitte) streichen! (please) delete where appropriate

Nickel ['nɪkəl] (-s) nt nickel

nicken ['nɪkən] vi to nod

Nickerchen ['nɪkərçən] nt nap

nie [niː] adv never; **~ wieder** od **mehr** never again; **~ und nimmer** never ever

nieder ['niːdər] adj low; (gering) inferior ♦ adv down; **N~gang** m decline; **~gedrückt** adj (deprimiert) dejected, depressed; **~gehen** (unreg) vi to descend; (AVIAT) to come down; (Regen) to fall; (Boxer) to go down; **~geschlagen** adj depressed, dejected; **N~lage** f defeat; **N~lande** pl Netherlands; **N~länder(in)** m(f) Dutchman(-

─────────

Spelling Reform: ▲ new spelling △ old spelling (to be phased out)

woman); **~ländisch** adj Dutch; **~las-sen** (unreg) vr (sich setzen) to sit down; (an Ort) to settle (down); (Arzt, Rechtsanwalt) to set up a practice; **N~lassung** f settlement; (COMM) branch; **~legen** vt to lay down; (Arbeit) to stop; (Amt) to resign; **N~sachsen** nt Lower Saxony; **N~schlag** m (MET) precipitation; rainfall; **~schlagen** vt (Gegner) to beat down; (Gegenstand) to knock down; (Augen) to lower; (Aufstand) to put down ♦ vr (CHEM) to precipitate; **~trächtig** adj base, mean; **N~trächtigkeit** f meanness, baseness; outrage; **N~ung** f (GEOG) depression; (Mündungsgebiet) flats pl

niedlich ['ni:tlɪç] adj sweet, cute
niedrig ['ni:drɪç] adj low; (Stand) lowly, humble; (Gesinnung) mean
niemals ['ni:ma:ls] adv never
niemand ['ni:mant] pron nobody, no-one
Niemandsland ['ni:mantslant] nt no-man's-land
Niere ['ni:rə] f kidney
nieseln ['ni:zəln] vi to drizzle
niesen ['ni:zən] vi to sneeze
Niete ['ni:tə] f (TECH) rivet; (Los) blank; (Reinfall) flop; (Mensch) failure; **n~n** vt to rivet

---

St. Nikolaus

On December 6th, St. Nikolaus visits German children to reward those who have been good by filling shoes they have left out with sweets and small presents.

Nikotin [niko'ti:n] (-s) nt nicotine
Nilpferd [ni:l-] nt hippopotamus
Nimmersatt ['nɪmɐzat] (-(e)s, -e) m glutton
nimmst etc [nɪmst] vb siehe **nehmen**
nippen ['nɪpən] vt, vi to sip
nirgend- ['nɪrgənt] zW: **~s** adv nowhere; **~wo** adv nowhere; **~wohin**

adv nowhere
Nische ['ni:ʃə] f niche
nisten ['nɪstən] vi to nest
Niveau [ni'vo:] (-s, -s) nt level
Nixe ['nɪksə] f water nymph
nobel ['no:bəl] adj (großzügig) generous; (elegant) posh (inf)

---

noch [nɔx] adv 1 (weiterhin) still; **noch nicht** not yet; **noch nie** never (yet); **noch immer** od **immer noch** still; **bleiben Sie doch noch** stay a bit longer 2 (in Zukunft) still, yet; **das kann noch passieren** that might still happen; **er wird noch kommen** he'll still come (yet) 3 (nicht später als): **noch vor einer Woche** only a week ago; **noch am selben Tag** the very same day; **noch im 19. Jahrhundert** as late as the 19th century; **noch heute** today 4 (zusätzlich): **wer war noch da?** who else was there?; **noch einmal** once more, again; **noch dreimal** three more times; **noch einer** another one 5 (bei Vergleichen): **noch größer** even bigger; **das ist noch besser** that's better still; **und wenn es noch so schwer ist** however hard it is 6: **Geld noch und noch** heaps and heaps of money; **sie hat noch und noch versucht, ...** she tried again and again to ...

♦ konj: **weder A noch B** neither A nor B

---

noch- zW: **~mal** ['nɔxma:l] adv again, once more; **~malig** ['nɔxma:lɪç] adj repeated; **~mals** adv again, once more
Nominativ ['no:minati:f] (-s, -e) m nominative
nominell [nomi'nɛl] adj nominal
Nonne ['nɔnə] f nun
Nord(en) ['nɔrd(ən)] (-s) m north
Nordirland nt Northern Ireland
nordisch adj northern

nördlich ['nœrtlɪç] adj northerly, northern ♦ präp +gen (to the) north of; ~ **von** (to the) north of

Nord- zW: ~**pol** m North Pole; ~**rhein-Westfalen** nt North Rhine-Westphalia; ~**see** f North Sea; **n~wärts** adv northwards

nörgeln ['nœrgəln] vi to grumble; **Nörgler** (-s, -) m grumbler

Norm [nɔrm] (-, -en) f norm; (Größenvorschrift) standard; **n~al** [nɔr'maːl] adj normal; **n~al(benzin** nt ≈ 2-star petrol (BRIT), regular petrol (US); **n~alerweise** adv normally; **n~ali'sieren** vt to normalize ♦ vt to return to normal

normen vt to standardize

Norwegen ['nɔrveːgən] nt Norway; **norwegisch** adj Norwegian

Nostalgie [nɔstal'giː] f nostalgia

Not [noːt] (-, ⸚e) f need; (Mangel) want; (Mühe) trouble; (Zwang) necessity; **zur ~** if necessary; **n~leidend** needy; **zur ~** if necessary; (gerade noch) just about

Notar [no'taːr] (-s, -e) m notary; **n~i'ell** adj notarial

Not- zW: ~**arzt** m emergency doctor; ~**ausgang** m emergency exit; ~**behelf** (-s, -e) m makeshift; ~**bremse** f emergency brake; ~**dienst** m (Bereitschaftsdienst) emergency service; **n~dürftig** adj scanty; (behelfsmäßig) makeshift

Note ['noːtə] f note; (SCH) mark (BRIT), grade (US)

Noten- zW: ~**blatt** nt sheet of music; ~**schlüssel** m clef; ~**ständer** m music stand

Not- zW: ~**fall** m (case of) emergency; **n~falls** adv if need be; **n~gedrungen** adj necessary, unavoidable; **etw n~gedrungen machen** to be forced to do sth

notieren [no'tiːrən] vt to note; (COMM) to quote

Notierung f (COMM) quotation

nötig ['nøːtɪç] adj necessary; **etw ~ haben** to need sth; **n~en** [-gən] vt to compel, to force; **n~enfalls** adv if necessary

Notiz [no'tiːts] (-, -en) f note; (Zeitungsnotiz) item; **~ nehmen** to take notice; ~**block** m notepad; ~**buch** nt notebook

Not- zW: ~**lage** f crisis, emergency; **n~landen** vi to make a forced od emergency landing; **n~leidend** △ adj siehe **Not**; ~**lösung** f temporary solution; ~**lüge** f white lie

notorisch [no'toːrɪʃ] adj notorious

Not- zW: ~**ruf** m emergency call; ~**rufsäule** f emergency telephone; ~**stand** m state of emergency; ~**unterkunft** f emergency accommodation; ~**verband** m emergency dressing; ~**wehr** (-) f self-defence; **n~wendig** adj necessary; **n~wendigkeit** f necessity

Novelle [no'vɛlə] f short novel; (JUR) amendment

November [no'vɛmbər] (-s, -) m November

Nu [nuː] m: **im ~** in an instant

Nuance [ny'ãːsə] f nuance

nüchtern ['nyçtərn] adj sober; (Magen) empty; (Urteil) prudent; **N~heit** f sobriety

Nudel ['nuːdəl] (-, -n) f noodle; ~**n** pl (Teigwaren) pasta sg; (in Suppe) noodles

Null [nʊl] (-, -en) f nought, zero; (pej: Mensch) washout; **n~** num zero; (Fehler) no; **n~ Uhr** midnight; **n~ und nichtig** null and void; ~**punkt** m zero; **auf dem ~punkt** at zero

numerisch [nu'meːrɪʃ] adj numerical

Nummer ['nʊmər] (-, -n) f number; (Größe) size; **n~ieren** ▲ vt to number; ~**nschild** nt (AUT) number od license (US) plate

nun [nuːn] adv now ♦ excl well; **das ist**

~ mal so that's the way it is

nur [nuːr] *adv* just, only; **wo bleibt er ~?** (just) where is he?

Nürnberg ['nʏrnbɛrk] (-s) *nt* Nuremberg

Nuss ▲ [nʊs] (-, ⸚e) *f* nut; **~baum** *m* walnut tree; **~knacker** (-s, -) *m* nutcracker

nutz [nʊts] *adj*: **zu nichts ~ sein** to be no use for anything; **~bringend** *adj* (*Verwendung*) profitable

nütze ['nʏtsə] *adj* = **nutz**

Nutzen (-s) *m* usefulness; (*Gewinn*) profit; **von ~ useful**; **n~** *vi* to use ♦ *vt*: **etw zu etw n~** to use sth for sth; **was nutzt es?** what's the use?, what use is it?

nützen *vi, vt* = **nutzen**

nützlich ['nʏtslɪç] *adj* useful; **N~keit** *f* usefulness

Nutz- *zW*: **n~los** *adj* useless; **~losigkeit** *f* uselessness; **~nießer** (-s, -) *m* beneficiary

Nylon ['naɪlɔn] (-(s)) *nt* nylon

O, o

Oase [o'aːzə] *f* oasis

ob [ɔp] *konj* if, whether; **~ das wohl wahr ist?** can that be true?; **und ~!** you bet!

obdachlos *adj* homeless

Obdachlose(r) *f(m)* homeless person; **~nasyl** *nt* shelter for the homeless

Obduktion [ɔpdʊktsi'oːn] *f* postmortem

obduzieren [ɔpdu'tsiːrən] *vt* to do a post-mortem on

O-Beine ['oːbaɪnə] *pl* bow *od* bandy legs

oben ['oːbən] *adv* above; (*in Haus*) upstairs; **~ erwähnt**, **~ genannt** above-mentioned; **nach ~** up; **von ~** down; **~ ohne** topless; **jdn von ~ bis unten ansehen** to look sb up and down; **~an** *adv* at the top; **~auf** *adv* up

above, on the top ♦ *adj* (*munter*) in form; **~drein** *adv* into the bargain

Ober ['oːbər] (-s, -) *m* waiter; **die ~en** *pl* (*umg*) the bosses; (*ECCL*) the superiors; **~arm** *m* upper arm; **~arzt** *m* senior physician; **~aufsicht** *f* supervision; **~bayern** *nt* Upper Bavaria; **~befehl** *m* supreme command; **~befehlshaber** *m* commander-in-chief; **~bekleidung** *f* outer clothing; **~bürgermeister** *m* lord mayor; **~deck** *nt* upper *od* top deck; **o~e(r, s)** *adj* upper; **~fläche** *f* surface; **o~flächlich** *adj* superficial; **~geschoss** ▲ *nt* upper storey; **o~halb** *adv* above ♦ *präp +gen* above; **~haupt** *nt* head, chief; **~haus** *nt* (*POL*) upper house, House of Lords (*BRIT*); **~hemd** *nt* shirt; **~herrschaft** *f* supremacy, sovereignty; **~in** *f* matron; (*ECCL*) Mother Superior; **~kellner** *m* head waiter; **~kiefer** *m* upper jaw; **~körper** *m* upper part of body; **~leitung** *f* direction; (*ELEK*) overhead cable; **~licht** *nt* skylight; **~lippe** *f* upper lip; **~schenkel** *m* thigh; **~schicht** *f* upper classes *pl*; **~schule** *f* grammar school (*BRIT*), high school (*US*); **~schwester** *f* (*MED*) matron

Oberst ['oːbərst] (-en *od* -s, -en *od* -e) *m* colonel; **o~e(r, s)** *adj* very top, topmost

Ober- *zW*: **~stufe** *f* upper school; **~teil** *nt* upper part; **~weite** *f* bust/chest measurement

obgleich [ɔp'glaɪç] *konj* although

Obhut ['ɔphuːt] (-) *f* care, protection; **in jds ~ sein** to be in sb's care

obig ['oːbɪç] *adj* above

Objekt [ɔp'jɛkt] (-(e)s, -e) *nt* object; **~iv** [-'tiːf] (-s, -e) *nt* lens; **o~iv** *adj* objective

Objektivi'tät *f* objectivity

Oblate [o'blaːtə] *f* (*Gebäck*) wafer; (*ECCL*) host

obligatorisch [ɔbliga'toːrɪʃ] *adj* compulsory, obligatory

Obrigkeit ['oːbrɪçkaɪt] f (Behörden) authorities pl, administration; (Regierung) government

obschon [ɔp'ʃoːn] konj although

Observatorium [ɔpzɛrvaˈtoːriʊm] nt observatory

obskur [ɔpsˈkuːr] adj obscure; (verdächtig) dubious

Obst [oːpst] (-(e)s) nt fruit; **~baum** m fruit tree; **~garten** m orchard; **~händler** m fruiterer, fruit merchant; **~kuchen** m fruit tart

obszön [ɔpsˈtsøːn] adj obscene; **O~i'tät** f obscenity

obwohl [ɔpˈvoːl] konj although

Ochse ['ɔksə] (-n, -n) m ox; **o~n** (umg) vt, vi to cram, to swot (BRIT)

Ochsenschwanzsuppe f oxtail soup

Ochsenzunge f oxtongue

öd(e) ['øːd(ə)] adj (Land) waste, barren; (fig) dull; **Ö~** f desert, waste(land); (fig) tedium

oder ['oːdər] konj or; **das stimmt, ~?** that's right, isn't it?

Ofen ['oːfən] (-s, -) m oven; (Heizofen) fire, heater; (Kohlenofen) stove; (Hochofen) furnace; (Herd) cooker, stove; **~rohr** nt stovepipe

offen ['ɔfən] adj open; (aufrichtig) frank; (Stelle) vacant; **~ bleiben** (Frage, Entscheidung) to remain open; **~ halten** to keep open; **~ lassen** to leave open; **~ stehen** to be open; (Rechnung) to be unpaid; **es steht Ihnen ~, es zu tun** you are at liberty to do it; **~ gesagt** to be honest; **~bar** adj obvious; **~baren** [ɔfənˈbaːrən] vt to reveal, to manifest; **O~'barung** f (REL) revelation; **O~heit** f candour, frankness; **~herzig** adj candid, frank; (Kleid) revealing; **~kundig** adj well-known; (klar) evident; **~sichtlich** adj evident, obvious

offensiv [ɔfɛnˈziːf] adj offensive; **O~e** [-'ziːvə] f offensive

öffentlich ['œfəntlɪç] adj public; **Ö~keit** f (Leute) public; (einer Versammlung etc) public nature; **in aller Ö~keit** in public; **an die Ö~keit dringen** to reach the public ear

offiziell [ɔfiˈtsiɛl] adj official

Offizier [ɔfiˈtsiːr] (-s, -e) m officer; **~skasino** nt officers' mess

öffnen ['œfnən] vt, vr to open; **jdm die Tür ~** to open the door for sb

Öffner ['œfnər] (-s, -) m opener

Öffnung ['œfnʊŋ] f opening; **~szeiten** pl opening times

oft [ɔft] adv often

öfter ['œftər] adv more often od frequently; **~s** adv often, frequently

oh [oː] excl oh; **~ je!** oh dear

OHG abk (= Offene Handelsgesellschaft) general partnership

ohne ['oːnə] präp +akk without ♦ konj without; **das ist nicht ~** (umg) it's not bad; **~ weiteres** without a second thought; (sofort) immediately; **~ zu fragen** without asking; **~ dass er es wusste** without him knowing it; **~dies** [oːnəˈdiːs] adv anyway; **~gleichen** [oːnəˈglaɪçən] adj unsurpassed, without equal; **~hin** [oːnəˈhɪn] adv anyway, in any case

Ohnmacht ['oːnmaxt] f faint; (fig) impotence; **in ~ fallen** to faint

ohnmächtig ['oːnmɛçtɪç] adj in a faint, unconscious; (fig) weak, impotent; **sie ist ~** she has fainted

Ohr [oːr] (-(e)s, -en) nt ear

Öhr [øːr] (-(e)s, -e) nt eye

Ohren- zW: **~arzt** m ear specialist; **o~betäubend** adj deafening; **~schmalz** nt earwax; **~schmerzen** pl earache sg

Ohr- zW: **~feige** f slap on the face; box on the ears; **o~feigen** vt: **jdn o~feigen** to slap sb's face; to box sb's ears; **~läppchen** nt ear lobe; **~ring** m earring; **~wurm** m earwig; (MUS)

---

catchy tune

Öko- [øko] zW: **~laden** m wholefood shop; **ö~logisch** [-'lo:gɪʃ] adj ecological; **ö~nomisch** [-'no:mɪʃ] adj economical

Oktober [ɔk'to:bar] (-s, -) m October; **~fest** nt Munich beer festival

---

Oktoberfest

The annual beer festival, the Oktoberfest, takes place in Munich at the end of September in a huge area where beer tents and various amusements are set up. People sit at long wooden tables, drink beer from enormous beer mugs, eat pretzels and listen to brass bands. It is a great attraction for tourists and locals alike.

ökumenisch [øku'me:nɪʃ] adj ecumenical

Öl [ø:l] (-(e)s, -e) nt oil; **~baum** m olive tree; **ö~en** vt to oil; (TECH) to lubricate; **~farbe** f oil paint; **~feld** nt oilfield; **~film** m film of oil; **~heizung** f oil-fired central heating; **ö~ig** adj oily; **~industrie** f oil industry

oliv [o'li:f] adj olive-green; **O~e** f olive

Öl- zW: **~messstab** m dipstick; **~sardine** f sardine; **~stand** m oil level; **~standzeiger** m (AUT) oil gauge; **~tanker** m oil tanker; **~ung** f lubrication; oiling; (ECCL) anointment; **die Letzte ~ung** Extreme Unction; **~wechsel** m oil change

Olymp- [o'lymp] zW: **~iade** [olympi'a:də] f Olympic Games pl; **~iasieger(in)** [-'azi:gar(ɪn)] m(f) Olympic champion; **~iateilnehmer(in)** m(f) Olympic competitor; **o~isch** adj Olympic

Ölzeug nt oilskins pl

Oma ['o:ma] (-, -s) (umg) f granny

Omelett [ɔm(ə)'lɛt] (-(e)s, -s) nt omelet(te)

ominös [omi'nø:s] adj (unheilvoll) ominous

Onanie [ona'ni:] f masturbation; **o~ren** vi to masturbate

Onkel ['ɔŋkəl] (-s, -) m uncle

Opa ['o:pa] (-s, -s) (umg) m grandpa

Oper ['o:par] (-, -n) f opera; opera house

Operation [operatsi'o:n] f operation; **~ssaal** m operating theatre

Operette [ope'rɛtə] f operetta

operieren [ope'ri:rən] vt to operate on ♦ vi to operate

Opern- zW: **~glas** nt opera glasses pl; **~haus** nt opera house

Opfer ['ɔpfar] (-s, -) nt sacrifice; (Mensch) victim; **o~n** vt to sacrifice; **~ung** f sacrifice

opponieren [ɔpo'ni:rən] vi: **gegen jdn/etw ~** to oppose sb/sth

Opportunist [ɔpɔrtu'nɪst] m opportunist

Opposition [ɔpozitsi'o:n] f opposition; **o~ell** adj opposing

Optik ['ɔptɪk] f optics sg; **~er** (-s, -) m optician

optimal [ɔpti'ma:l] adj optimal, optimum

Optimismus [ɔpti'mɪsmʊs] m optimism

Optimist [ɔpti'mɪst] m optimist; **o~isch** adj optimistic

optisch ['ɔptɪʃ] adj optical

Orakel [o'ra:kəl] (-s, -) nt oracle

oral [o'ra:l] adj (MED) oral

Orange [o'rã:ʒə] f orange; **o~** adj orange; **~ade** [orã'ʒa:də] f orangeade; **~at** [orã'ʒa:t] (-s, -e) nt candied peel

Orchester [ɔr'kɛstar] (-s, -) nt orchestra

Orchidee [ɔrçi'de:ə] f orchid

Orden ['ɔrdən] (-s, -) m (ECCL) order; (MIL) decoration; **~sschwester** f nun

ordentlich ['ɔrdəntlɪç] adj (anständig) decent, respectable; (geordnet) tidy, neat; (umg: annehmbar) not bad; (: tüchtig) real, proper ♦ adv properly; **~er Professor** (full) professor; **O~keit** f respectability; tidiness, neatness

ordinär [ɔrdiˈnɛːr] adj common, vulgar

ordnen [ˈɔrdnən] vt to order, to put in order

Ordner (-s, -) m steward; (COMM) file

Ordnung f order; (Ordnen) ordering; (Geordnetsein) tidiness; ~ **machen** to tidy up; **in** ~! okay!

Ordnungs- zW: **o~gemäß** proper, according to the rules; **o~liebend** adj orderly, methodical; **~strafe** f fine; **o~widrig** adj contrary to the rules, irregular; **~widrigkeit** f infringement (of law or rule); **~zahl** f ordinal number

Organ [ɔrˈgaːn] (-s, -e) nt organ; (Stimme) voice; **~isation** f organization; **~isator** [iˈzaːtɔr] m organizer; **o~isch** adj organic; **o~isieren** [-ˈziːrən] vt to organize, to arrange; (umg: beschaffen) to acquire ♦ vr to organize; **~ismus** [-ˈnɪsmʊs] m organism; **~ist** [-ˈnɪst] m organist; **~spende** f organ donation; **~spenderausweis** m donor card

Orgasmus [ɔrˈgasmʊs] m orgasm

Orgel [ˈɔrgəl] (-, -n) f organ

Orgie [ˈɔrgiə] f orgy

Orient [ˈoːriɛnt] (-s) m Orient, east; **o~alisch** [-ˈtaːlɪʃ] adj oriental

orientier- zW: **~en** [-ˈtiːrən] vt (örtlich) to locate; (fig) to inform ♦ vr to find one's way od direction; to inform o.s.; **O~ung** [-ˈtiːrʊŋ] f orientation; (fig) information; **O~ungssinn** m sense of direction; **O~ungsstufe** f period during which pupils are selected for different schools

---

Orientierungsstufe

The **Orientierungsstufe** is the name given to the first two years spent in a **Realschule** or **Gymnasium**, during which a child is assessed as to his or her suitability for that type of school. At the end of two years it may be decided to transfer the child to a school more suited to his or her ability.

---

original [origiˈnaːl] adj original; **O~** (-s, -e) nt original; **O~fassung** f original version; **O~ität** f originality

originell [origiˈnɛl] adj original

Orkan [ɔrˈkaːn] (-(e)s, -e) m hurricane; **o~artig** adj (Wind) gale-force; (Beifall) thunderous

Ornament [ɔrnaˈmɛnt] nt decoration, ornament; **o~al** [-ˈtaːl] adj decorative, ornamental

Ort [ɔrt] (-(e)s, -e od ⸗er) m place; **an** ~ **und Stelle** on the spot; **o~en** vt to locate

ortho- [ɔrto] zW: **~dox** [-ˈdɔks] adj orthodox; **O~grafie** ▲ [-graˈfiː] f spelling, orthography; **~'grafisch** ▲ adj orthographic; **O~päde** [-ˈpɛːdə] (-n, -n) m orthopaedist; **O~pädie** [-pɛˈdiː] f orthopaedics sg; **~'pädisch** adj orthopaedic

örtlich [ˈœrtlɪç] adj local; **Ö~keit** f locality

ortsansässig adj local

Ortschaft f village, small town

Orts- zW: **o~fremd** adj non-local; **~gespräch** nt local (phone)call; **~name** m place name; **~netz** nt (TEL) local telephone exchange area; **~tarif** m (TEL) tariff for local calls; **~zeit** f local time

Ortung f locating

Öse [ˈøːzə] f loop, eye

Ostasien [ɔsˈtaːziən] nt Eastern Asia

Osten [ˈɔstən] (-s) m east

Oster- [ˈoːstər] zW: **~ei** nt Easter egg; **~fest** nt Easter; **~glocke** f daffodil; **~hase** m Easter bunny; **~montag** m Easter Monday; **~n** (-s, -) nt Easter

Österreich [ˈøːstəraɪç] (-s) nt Austria; **~er(in)** (-s, -) m(f) Austrian; **ö~isch** adj Austrian

Ostküste f east coast

östlich [ˈœstlɪç] adj eastern, easterly

Ostsee f: die ~ the Baltic (Sea)
Ouvertüre [uver'ty:rə] f overture
oval [o'va:l] adj oval
Ovation [ovatsi'o:n] f ovation
Oxid, Oxyd [ɔ'ksy:t] (-(e)s, -e) nt oxide; **o~ieren** vt, vi to oxidize; **~ierung** f oxidization
Ozean ['o:tsea:n] (-s, -e) m ocean; **~dampfer** m (ocean-going) liner
Ozon [o'tso:n] (-s) nt ozone; **~loch** nt ozone hole; **~schicht** f ozone layer

P, p

Paar [pa:r] (-(e)s, -e) nt pair; (Ehepaar) couple; **ein p~** a few; **ein p~ Mal** a few times; **p~en** vt, vr to couple; (Tiere) to mate; **~lauf** m pair skating; **~ung** f combination; mating; **p~weise** adv in pairs; in couples
Pacht [paxt] (-, -en) f lease; **p~en** vt to lease
Pächter ['pɛçtər] (-s, -) m leaseholder, tenant
Pack¹ [pak] (-(e)s, -e od ⁼e) m bundle, pack
Pack² [pak] (-(e)s) nt (pej) mob, rabble
Päckchen ['pɛkçən] nt small package; (Zigaretten) packet; (Postpäckchen) small parcel
Pack- zW: **p~en** vt to pack; (fassen) to grasp, to seize; (umg: schaffen) to manage; (fig: fesseln) to grip; **~en** (-s, -) m bundle; (fig: Menge) heaps of; **~esel** m (auch fig) packhorse; **~papier** nt brown paper, wrapping paper; **~ung** f packet; (Pralinenpackung) box; (MED) compress; **~ungsbeilage** f enclosed instructions pl for use
Pädagog- [peda'go:g] zW: **~e** (-n, -n) m teacher; **~ik** f education; **p~isch** adj educational, pedagogical
Paddel ['padəl] (-s, -) nt paddle; **~boot** nt canoe; **p~n** vi to paddle
Page [pa:ʒə] (-n, -n) m page

Paket [pa'ke:t] (-(e)s, -e) nt packet; (Postpaket) parcel; **~karte** f dispatch note; **~post** f parcel post; **~schalter** m parcels counter
Pakt [pakt] (-(e)s, -e) m pact
Palast [pa'last] (-es, Paläste) m palace
Palästina [palɛ'sti:na] (-s) nt Palestine
Palme ['palmə] f palm (tree)
Pampelmuse ['pampəlmu:zə] f grapefruit
panieren [pa'ni:rən] vt (KOCH) to bread
Paniermehl [pa'ni:rme:l] nt breadcrumbs pl
Panik ['pa:nɪk] f panic
panisch ['pa:nɪʃ] adj panic-stricken
Panne ['panə] f (AUT etc) breakdown; (Missgeschick) slip; **~nhilfe** f breakdown service
panschen ['panʃən] vi to splash about ♦ vt to water down
Pantoffel [pan'tɔfəl] (-s, -n) m slipper
Pantomime [panto'mi:mə] f mime
Panzer ['pantsər] (-s, -) m (Platte) armour plate; (Fahrzeug) tank; **~glas** nt bulletproof glass; **p~n** vt to armour ♦ vr (fig) to arm o.s.
Papa [pa'pa:] (-s, -s) (umg) m dad, daddy
Papagei [papa'gai] (-s, -en) m parrot
Papier [pa'pi:r] (-s, -e) nt paper; (Wertpapier) security; **~fabrik** f paper mill; **~geld** nt paper money; **~korb** m wastepaper basket; **~taschentuch** nt tissue
Papp- ['pap] zW: **~deckel** m cardboard; **~e** f cardboard; **~el** (-, -n) f poplar; **p~en** (umg) vt, vi to stick; **p~ig** adj sticky
Paprika ['paprika] (-s, -s) m (Gewürz) paprika; (~schote) pepper
Papst [pa:pst] (-(e)s, -e) m pope
päpstlich ['pɛ:pstlɪç] adj papal
Parabel [pa'ra:bəl] (-, -n) f parable; (MATH) parabola
Parabolantenne [para'bo:lantenə] f satellite dish
Parade [pa'ra:də] f (MIL) parade, re-

view; (SPORT) parry

Paradies [para'di:s] (-es, -e) nt paradise; **p~isch** adj heavenly

Paradox [para'dɔks] (-es, -e) nt paradox; **p~** adj paradoxical

Paragraf ▲ [para'gra:f] (-en, -en) m paragraph; (JUR) section

parallel [para'le:l] adj parallel; **P~e** f parallel

Parasit [para'zi:t] (-en, -en) m (auch fig) parasite

parat [pa'ra:t] adj ready

Pärchen ['pɛːrçən] nt couple

Parfüm [par'fy:m] (-s, -s od -e) nt perfume; **~erie** [-ə'ri:] f perfumery; **p~frei** adj non-perfumed; **p~ieren** vt to scent, to perfume

parieren [pa'ri:rən] vt to parry ♦ vi (umg) to obey

Paris [pa'ri:s] (-) nt Paris; **~er** adj Parisian ♦ m Parisian; **~erin** f Parisian

Park [park] (-s, -s) m park; **~anlage** f park; (um Gebäude) grounds pl; **p~en** vt, vi to park; **~ett** (-(e)s, -e) nt parquet (floor); (THEAT) stalls pl; **~gebühr** f parking fee; **~haus** nt multi-storey car park; **~lücke** f parking space; **~platz** m parking place; car park, parking lot (US); **~scheibe** f parking disc; **~schein** m car park ticket; **~uhr** f parking meter; **~verbot** nt parking ban

Parlament [parla'mɛnt] nt parliament; **~arier** [-'ta:riɐ] (-s, -) m parliamentarian; **p~arisch** [-'ta:rɪʃ] adj parliamentary

Parlaments- zW: **~beschluss** ▲ m vote of parliament; **~mitglied** nt member of parliament; **~sitzung** f sitting (of parliament)

Parodie [paro'di:] f parody; **p~ren** vt to parody

Parole [pa'ro:lə] f password; (Wahlspruch) motto

Partei [par'tai] f party; **~ ergreifen für**

jdn to take sb's side; **p~isch** adj partial, bias(s)ed; **p~los** adj neutral, impartial; **~mitglied** nt party member; **~programm** nt (party) manifesto; **~tag** m party conference

Parterre [par'tɛr] (-s, -s) nt ground floor; (THEAT) stalls pl

Partie [par'ti:] f part; (Spiel) game; (Ausflug) outing; (Mann, Frau) catch; (COMM) lot; **mit von der ~** sein to join in

Partizip [parti'tsi:p] (-s, -ien) nt participle

Partner(in) ['partnər(ɪn)] (-s, -) m(f) partner; **~schaft** f partnership; (von Städten) twinning; **p~schaftlich** adj as partners; **~stadt** f twin town

Party ['pa:rti] (-, -s) f party

Pass ▲ [pas] (-es, -e) m pass; (Ausweis) passport

passabel [pa'sa:bəl] adj passable, reasonable

Passage [pa'sa:ʒə] f passage

Passagier [pasa'ʒi:r] (-s, -e) m passenger; **~flugzeug** nt airliner

Passamt ▲ nt passport office

Passant [pa'sant] m passer-by

Passbild ▲ nt passport photograph

passen ['pasən] vi to fit; (Farbe) to go; (auf Frage, KARTEN, SPORT) to pass; **das passt mir nicht** that doesn't suit me; **~ zu** (Farbe, Kleider) to go with; **er passt nicht zu dir** he's not right for you; **~d** adj suitable; (zusammenpassend) matching; (angebracht) fitting; (Zeit) convenient

passier- zW: **~bar** adj passable; **~en** vt to pass; (durch Sieb) to strain ♦ vi to happen; **P~schein** m pass, permit

Passion [pasi'o:n] f passion; **p~iert** [-'ni:rt] adj enthusiastic, passionate; **~sspiel** nt Passion Play

passiv ['pasi:f] adj passive; **P~** (-s, -e) nt passive; **P~a** pl (COMM) liabilities;

P~i'tät f passiveness; **P~rauchen** nt passive smoking

Pass- ▲ zW: **~kontrolle** f passport control; **~stelle** f passport office; **~straße** f (mountain) pass

Paste ['pastə] f paste

Pastete [pas'te:tə] f pie

pasteurisieren [pastøri'zi:rən] vt to pasteurize

Pastor ['pastor] m vicar; pastor, minister

Pate ['pa:tə] (-n, -n) m godfather; **~nkind** nt godchild

Patent [pa'tɛnt] (-(e)s, -e) nt patent; (MIL) commission; **p~** adj clever; **~amt** nt patent office

Patentante f godmother

patentieren [patɛn'ti:rən] vt to patent

Patentinhaber m patentee

pathetisch [pa'te:tiʃ] adj emotional; bombastic

Pathologe [pato'lo:gə] (-n, -n) m pathologist

pathologisch adj pathological

Pathos ['pa:tɔs] (-) nt emotiveness, emotionalism

Patient(in) [patsi'ɛnt(in)] m(f) patient

Patin ['pa:tin] f godmother

Patriot [patri'o:t] (-en, -en) m patriot; **p~isch** adj patriotic; **~ismus** [-'tismus] m patriotism

Patrone [pa'tro:nə] f cartridge

Patrouille [pa'truljə] f patrol

patrouillieren [patrol'ji:rən] vi to patrol

patsch [patʃ] excl splash; **P~e** (umg) f (Bedrängnis) mess, jam; **~en** vi to smack, to slap; (im Wasser) to splash; **~nass** ▲ adj soaking wet

patzig [patsiç] (umg) adj cheeky, saucy

Pauke ['pauka] f kettledrum; **auf die ~ hauen** to live it up

pauken vt (intensiv lernen) to swot up (inf) ♦ vi to swot (inf), cram (inf)

pausbäckig ['pausbɛkiç] adj chubby-cheeked

pauschal [pau'ʃa:l] adj (Kosten) inclu-

sive; (Urteil) sweeping; **P~e** f flat rate; **P~gebühr** f flat rate; **P~preis** m all-in price; **P~reise** f package tour; **P~summe** f lump sum

Pause ['pauzə] f break; (THEAT) interval; (Innehalten) pause; (Kopie) tracing

pausen vt to trace; **~los** adj non-stop; **P~zeichen** nt call sign; (MUS) rest

Pauspapier nt tracing paper

Pavillon ['paviljõ] (-s, -s) m pavilion

Pazif- [pa'tsi:f] zW: **~ik** (-s) m Pacific; **p~istisch** adj pacifist

Pech [pɛç] (-s, -e) nt pitch; (fig) bad luck; **~ haben** to be unlucky; **p~schwarz** adj pitch-black; **~strähne** (umg) m unlucky patch; **~vogel** (umg) m unlucky person

Pedal [pe'da:l] (-s, -e) nt pedal

Pedant [pe'dant] m pedant; **~e'rie** f pedantry; **p~isch** adj pedantic

Pediküre [pedi'ky:rə] f (Fußpflege) pedicure

Pegel ['pe:gəl] (-s, -) m water gauge; **~stand** m water level

peilen ['pailən] vt to get a fix on

Pein [pain] (-) f agony, pain; **p~igen** vt to torture; (plagen) to torment; **p~lich** adj (unangenehm) embarrassing, awkward, painful; (genau) painstaking

Peitsche ['paitʃə] f whip; **p~n** vt to whip; (Regen) to lash

Pelle ['pɛlə] f skin; **p~n** vt to skin, to peel

Pellkartoffeln pl jacket potatoes

Pelz [pɛlts] (-es, -e) m fur

Pendel ['pɛndəl] (-s, -) nt pendulum; **p~n** vi (Zug, Fähre etc) to operate a shuttle service; (Mensch) to commute; **~verkehr** m shuttle traffic; (für Pendler) commuter traffic

Pendler ['pɛndlər] (-s, -) m commuter

penetrant [pene'trant] adj sharp; (Person) pushing

Penis ['pe:nis] (-, -se) m penis

pennen ['pɛnən] (umg) vi to kip

Penner (umg; pej) m (Landstreicher)

tramp

Pension [pɛnzi'oːn] f (Geld) pension; (Ruhestand) retirement; (für Gäste) boarding od guesthouse; **~är(in)** [-'nɛːr(ɪn)] (-s, -e) m(f) pensioner; **p~ieren** vt to pension off; **p~iert** adj retired; **~ierung** f retirement; **~sgast** m boarder, paying guest

Pensum ['pɛnzom] (-s, Pensen) nt quota; (SCH) curriculum

per [pɛr] präp +akk by, per; (pro) per; (bis) by

Perfekt ['pɛrfɛkt] (-(e)s, -e) nt perfect; **p~** adj perfect

perforieren [pɛrfo'riːrən] vt to perforate

Pergament [pɛrga'mɛnt] nt parchment; **~papier** nt greaseproof paper

Periode [peri'oːdə] f period; **periodisch** adj periodic; (dezimal) recurring

Perle ['pɛrlə] f (auch fig) pearl; **p~n** vi to sparkle; (Tropfen) to trickle

Perl- ['pɛrl] zW: **~mutt** (-s) nt mother-of-pearl; **~wein** m sparkling wine

perplex [pɛr'plɛks] adj dumbfounded

Person [pɛr'zoːn] (-, -en) f person; **ich für meine ~** ... personally I ...

Personal [pɛrzoˈnaːl] (-s) nt personnel; (Bedienung) servants pl; **~ausweis** m identity card; **~computer** m personal computer; **~ien** [-iən] pl particulars; **~mangel** m undermanning; **~pronomen** nt personal pronoun

personell [pɛrzoˈnɛl] adj (Veränderungen) personnel

Personen- zW: **~aufzug** m lift, elevator (US); **~kraftwagen** m private motorcar; **~schaden** m injury to persons; **~zug** m stopping train; passenger train

personifizieren [pɛrzonifi'tsiːrən] vt to personify

persönlich [pɛr'zøːnlɪç] adj personal ♦ adv in person; P~keit f personality

Perspektive [pɛrspɛk'tiːvə] f perspective

Perücke [pe'rʏkə] f wig

pervers [pɛr'vɛrs] adj perverse

Pessimismus [pɛsi'mɪsmos] m pessimism

Pessimist [pɛsi'mɪst] m pessimist; **p~isch** adj pessimistic

Pest [pɛst] (-) f plague

Petersilie [petər'ziːliə] f parsley

Petroleum [pe'troːleum] (-s) nt paraffin, kerosene (US)

Pfad [pfaːt] (-(e)s, -e) m path; **~finder** (-s, -) m boy scout; **~finderin** f girl guide

Pfahl [pfaːl] (-(e)s, ⁓e) m post, stake

Pfand [pfant] (-(e)s, ⁓er) nt pledge, security; (Flaschenpfand) deposit; (im Spiel) forfeit; **~brief** m bond

pfänden ['pfɛndən] vt to seize, to distrain

Pfänderspiel nt game of forfeits

Pfandflasche f returnable bottle

Pfandschein m pawn ticket

Pfändung ['pfɛndoŋ] f seizure, distraint

Pfanne ['pfanə] f (frying) pan

Pfannkuchen m pancake; (Berliner) doughnut

Pfarr- ['pfar] zW: **~ei** f parish; **~er** (-s, -) m priest; (evangelisch) vicar; minister; **~haus** nt vicarage; manse

Pfau [pfau] (-(e)s, -en) m peacock; **~enauge** nt peacock butterfly

Pfeffer ['pfɛfər] (-s, -) m pepper; **~kuchen** m gingerbread; **~minz** (-es, -e) nt peppermint; **~mühle** f pepper mill; **p~n** vt to pepper; (umg: werfen) to fling; **gepfefferte Preise/Witze** steep prices/spicy jokes

Pfeife ['pfaɪfə] f whistle; (Tabakpfeife, Orgelpfeife) pipe; **p~n** (unreg) vt, vi to whistle; **~r** (-s, -) m piper

Pfeil [pfaɪl] (-(e)s, -e) m arrow

Pfeiler ['pfaɪlər] (-s, -) m pillar; prop;

Spelling Reform: ▲ new spelling △ old spelling (to be phased out)

(*Brückenpfeiler*) pier

Pfennig ['pfɛnɪç] (-(e)s, -e) *m* pfennig (*hundredth part of a mark*)

Pferd [pfeːrt] (-(e)s, -e) *nt* horse

Pferde- ['pfeːrdə] *zW:* **~rennen** *nt* horse race; horse racing; **~schwanz** *m* (*Frisur*) ponytail; **~stall** *m* stable

Pfiff [pfɪf] (-(e)s, -e) *m* whistle

Pfifferling ['pfɪfərlɪŋ] *m* yellow chanterelle (*mushroom*); **keinen ~ wert** not worth a thing

pfiffig *adj* sly, sharp

Pfingsten ['pfɪŋstən] (-, -) *nt* Whitsun (*BRIT*), Pentecost

Pfirsich ['pfɪrzɪç] (-s, -e) *m* peach

Pflanz- ['pflants] *zW:* **~e** *f* plant; **p~en** *vt* to plant; **~enfett** *nt* vegetable fat; **p~lich** *adj* vegetable; **~ung** *f* plantation

Pflaster ['pflastər] (-s, -) *nt* plaster; (*Straße*) pavement; **p~n** *vt* to pave; **~stein** *m* paving stone

Pflaume ['pflaumə] *f* plum

Pflege ['pfleːgə] *f* care; (*von Idee*) cultivation; (*Krankenpflege*) nursing; **in ~ sein** (*Kind*) to be fostered out; **p~bedürftig** *adj* needing care; **~eltern** *pl* foster parents; **~heim** *nt* nursing home; **~kind** *nt* foster child; **p~leicht** *adj* easy-care; **~mutter** *f* foster mother; **p~n** *vt* to look after; (*Kranke*) to nurse; (*Beziehungen*) to foster; **~r** (-s, -) *m* orderly; male nurse; **~rin** *f* nurse, attendant; **~vater** *m* foster father

Pflicht [pflɪçt] (-, -en) *f* duty; (*SPORT*) compulsory section; **p~bewusst ▲** *adj* conscientious; **~fach** *nt* (*SCH*) compulsory subject; **~gefühl** *nt* sense of duty; **p~gemäß** *adj* dutiful ♦ *adv* as in duty bound; **~versicherung** *f* compulsory insurance

pflücken ['pflʏkən] *vt* to pick; (*Blumen*) to pick, to pluck

Pflug [pfluːk] (-(e)s, ̈e) *m* plough

pflügen ['pflyːgən] *vt* to plough

Pforte ['pfɔrtə] *f* gate; door

Pförtner ['pfœrtnər] (-s, -) *m* porter, doorkeeper, doorman

Pfosten ['pfɔstən] (-s, -) *m* post

Pfote ['pfoːtə] *f* paw; (*umg: Schrift*) scrawl

Pfropfen (-s, -) *m* (*Flaschenpfropfen*) stopper; (*Blutpfropfen*) clot

pfui [pfʊɪ] *excl* ugh!

Pfund [pfʊnt] (-(e)s, -e) *nt* pound

pfuschen ['pfʊʃən] (*umg*) *vi* to be sloppy; **jdm ins Handwerk ~** *vi* to interfere in sb's business

Pfuscher ['pfʊʃər] (-s, -) (*umg*) *m* sloppy worker; (*Kurpfuscher*) quack; **~ei** (*umg*) *f* sloppy work; quackery

Pfütze ['pfʏtsə] *f* puddle

Phänomen [fɛno'meːn] (-s, -e) *nt* phenomenon; **p~al** [-'naːl] *adj* phenomenal

Phantasie *etc* [fanta'ziː] *f* = **Fantasie** *etc*

phantastisch [fan'tastɪʃ] *adj* = **fantastisch**

Phase ['faːzə] *f* phase

Philologie [filolo'giː] *f* philology

Philosoph [filo'zoːf] (-en, -en) *m* philosopher; **~ie** [-'fiː] *f* philosophy; **p~isch** *adj* philosophical

phlegmatisch [flɛ'gmaːtɪʃ] *adj* lethargic

Phonetik [fo'neːtɪk] *f* phonetics *sg*

phonetisch *adj* phonetic

Phosphor ['fɔsfɔr] (-s) *m* phosphorus

Photo *etc* ['foːto] (-s, -s) *nt* = **Foto** *etc*

Phrase ['fraːzə] *f* phrase; (*pej*) hollow phrase

pH-Wert [peː'haːveːrt] *m* pH-value

Physik [fy'ziːk] *f* physics *sg*; **p~alisch** [-'kaːlɪʃ] *adj* of physics; **~er(in)** ['fyːzɪkər(ɪn)] (-s, -) *m(f)* physicist

Physiologie [fyziolo'giː] *f* physiology

physisch ['fyːzɪʃ] *adj* physical

Pianist(in) [pia'nɪst(ɪn)] *m(f)* pianist

Pickel ['pɪkəl] (-s, -) *m* pimple; (*Werkzeug*) pickaxe; (*Bergpickel*) ice axe; **p~ig** *adj* pimply, spotty

picken ['pɪkən] vi to pick, to peck

Picknick ['pɪknɪk] (-s, -e od -s) nt picnic; ~ **machen** to have a picnic

piepen ['pi:pən] vi to chirp

piepsen ['pi:psən] vi to chirp

Piepser (umg) m pager, paging device

Pier [pi:ɐ] (-s, -s od -e) m od f pier

Pietät [pie'tɛːt] f piety, reverence; **p~los** adj impious, irreverent

Pigment [pɪg'mɛnt] nt pigment

Pik [pi:k] (-s, -s) nt (KARTEN) spades

pikant [pi'kant] adj spicy, piquant; (anzüglich) suggestive

Pilger ['pɪlgɐ] (-s, -) m pilgrim; ~**fahrt** f pilgrimage

Pille ['pɪlə] f pill

Pilot [pi'lo:t] (-en, -en) m pilot

Pilz [pɪlts] (-es, -e) m fungus; (essbar) mushroom; (giftig) toadstool; ~**krankheit** f fungal disease

Pinguin ['pɪŋguiːn] (-s, -e) m penguin

Pinie ['pi:niə] f pine

pinkeln ['pɪŋkəln] (umg) vi to pee

Pinnwand ['pɪnvant] f noticeboard

Pinsel ['pɪnzəl] (-s, -) m paintbrush

Pinzette [pɪn'tsɛtə] f tweezers pl

Pionier [pio'niːɐ] (-s, -e) m pioneer; (MIL) sapper, engineer

Pirat [pi'raːt] (-en, -en) m pirate

Piste ['pɪstə] f (SKI) run, piste; (AVIAT) runway

Pistole [pɪs'toːlə] f pistol

Pizza ['pɪtsa] (-, -s) f pizza

Pkw [peːkaːveː] (-(s), -(s)) m abk = Personenkraftwagen

plädieren [plɛ'diːrən] vi to plead

Plädoyer [plɛdoaˈjeː] (-s, -s) nt speech for the defence; (fig) plea

Plage ['plaːgə] f (Mühe) nuisance; ~**geist** m pest, nuisance; **p~n** vt to torment ♦ vr to toil, to slave

Plakat [pla'kaːt] (-(e)s, -e) nt placard; poster

Plan [plaːn] (-(e)s, ⁺e) m plan; (Karte) map

Plane f tarpaulin

planen vt to plan; (Mord etc) to plot

Planer (-s, -) m planner

Planet [pla'neːt] (-en, -en) m planet

planieren [pla'niːrən] vt to plane, to level

Planke ['plaŋkə] f plank

plan- ['plaːn] zW: ~**los** adj (Vorgehen) unsystematic; (Umherlaufen) aimless; ~**mäßig** adj according to plan; systematic; (EISENB) scheduled

Plansoll nt output target

Plantage [plan'taːʒə] f plantation

Plan(t)schbecken ['plan(t)ʃbɛkən] nt paddling pool

plan(t)schen ['plan(t)ʃən] vi to splash

Planung f planning

Planwirtschaft f planned economy

plappern ['plapɐn] vi to chatter

plärren ['plɛrən] vi (Mensch) to cry, to whine; (Radio) to blare

Plasma ['plasma] (-s, Plasmen) nt plasma

Plastik¹ ['plastɪk] f sculpture

Plastik² ['plastɪk] (-s) nt (Kunststoff) plastic; ~**beutel** m plastic bag, carrier bag; ~**folie** f plastic film

plastisch ['plastɪʃ] adj plastic; **stell dir das ~ vor!** just picture it!

Platane [pla'taːnə] f plane (tree)

Platin ['plaːtiːn] (-s) nt platinum

platonisch [pla'toːnɪʃ] adj platonic

platsch [platʃ] excl splash; **~en** vi to splash

plätschern ['plɛtʃɐn] vi to babble

platschnass ▲ adj drenched

platt [plat] adj flat; (umg: überrascht) flabbergasted; (fig: geistlos) flat, boring; ~**deutsch** adj low German; **P~e** f (Speisenplatte, PHOT, TECH) plate; (Steinplatte) flag; (Kachel) tile; (Schallplatte) record; **P~enspieler** m record player; **P~enteller** m turntable

Platz [plats] (-es, ⁺e) m place; (Sitzplatz) seat; (Raum) space, room; (in

Stadt) square; (*Sportplatz*) playing field; **~ nehmen** to take a seat; **jdm ~ machen** to make room for sb; **~angst** *f* claustrophobia; **~anweiser(in) (-s, -)** *m(f)* usher(ette)

Plätzchen ['plɛtsçən] *nt* spot; (*Gebäck*) biscuit

platz- *zW:* **p~en** *vi* to burst; (*Bombe*) to explode; **vor Wut p~en** (*umg*) to be bursting with anger

platzieren ▲ [pla'tsi:rən] *vt* to place ♦ *vr* (*SPORT*) to be placed; (*TENNIS*) to be seeded

Platz- *zW:* **~karte** *f* seat reservation; **~mangel** *m* lack of space; **~patrone** *f* blank cartridge; **~regen** *m* downpour; **~reservierung** *f* [-rezɛrvi:ruŋ] *f* seat reservation; **~wunde** *f* cut

Plauderei [plaudə'rai] *f* chat, conversation; (*RADIO*) talk

plaudern ['plaudərn] *vi* to chat, to talk

plausibel [plau'zi:bəl] *adj* plausible

plazieren △ *vt, vr siehe* **platzieren**

Pleite ['plaitə] *f* bankruptcy; (*umg: Reinfall*) flop; **~ machen** to go bust; **p~** (*umg*) *adj* broke

Plenum ['ple:nʊm] **(-s)** *nt* plenum

Plombe ['plɔmbə] *f* lead seal; (*Zahnplombe*) filling

plombieren [plɔm'bi:rən] *vt* to seal; (*Zahn*) to fill

plötzlich ['plœtslɪç] *adj* sudden ♦ *adv* suddenly

plump [plʊmp] *adj* clumsy; (*Hände*) coarse; (*Körper*) shapeless; **~sen** (*umg*) *vi* to plump down, to fall

Plunder ['plʊndər] **(-s)** *m* rubbish

plündern ['plʏndərn] *vt* to plunder; (*Stadt*) to sack ♦ *vi* to plunder; **Plünderung** *f* plundering, sack, pillage

Plural ['plu:ra:l] **(-s, -e)** *m* plural; **p~istisch** *adj* pluralistic

Plus [plʊs] **(-, -)** *nt* plus; (*FIN*) profit; (*Vorteil*) advantage; **p~** *adv* plus

Plüsch [ply:ʃ] **(-(e)s, -e)** *m* plush

Plus- [plʊs] *zW:* **~pol** *m* (*ELEK*) positive

pole; **~punkt** *m* point; (*fig*) point in sb's favour

Plutonium [plu'to:niʊm] **(-s)** *nt* plutonium

PLZ *abk* = **Postleitzahl**

Po [po:] **(-s, -s)** (*umg*) *m* bottom, bum

Pöbel ['pø:bəl] **(-s)** *m* mob, rabble; **~ei** *f* vulgarity; **p~haft** *adj* low, vulgar

pochen ['pɔxən] *vi* to knock; (*Herz*) to pound; **auf etw akk ~** (*fig*) to insist on sth

Pocken ['pɔkən] *pl* smallpox *sg*

Podium ['po:diʊm] *nt* podium; **~sdiskussion** *f* panel discussion

Poesie [poe'zi:] *f* poetry

Poet [po'e:t] **(-en, -en)** *m* poet; **p~isch** *adj* poetic

Pointe [po'ɛ:tə] *f* point

Pokal [po'ka:l] **(-s, -e)** *m* goblet; (*SPORT*) cup; **~spiel** *nt* cup tie

pökeln ['pø:kəln] *vt* to pickle, to salt

Poker ['po:kər] **(-s)** *nt od m* poker

Pol [po:l] **(-s, -e)** *m* pole; **p~ar** *adj* polar; **~arkreis** *m* Arctic circle

Pole ['po:lə] **(-n, -n)** *m* Pole

polemisch [po'le:mɪʃ] *adj* polemical

Polen ['po:lən] **(-s)** *nt* Poland

Police [po'li:s(ə)] *f* insurance policy

Polier [po'li:r] **(-s, -e)** *m* foreman

polieren *vt* to polish

Poliklinik [poli'kli:nɪk] *f* outpatients (department) *sg*

Polin *f* Pole

Politik [poli'ti:k] *f* politics *sg*; (*eine bestimmte*) policy; **~er(in)** [po'li:tikar(ɪn)] **(-s, -)** *m(f)* politician

politisch [po'li:tɪʃ] *adj* political

Politur [poli'tu:r] *f* polish

Polizei [poli'tsai] *f* police; **~beamte(r)** *m* police officer; **p~lich** *adj* police; **sich p~lich melden** to register with the police; **~revier** *nt* police station; **~staat** *m* police state; **~streife** *f* police patrol; **~stunde** *f* closing time; **~wache** *f* police station

Polizist(in) [poli'tsɪst(ɪn)] **(-en, -en)** *m(f)* policeman(-woman)

Pollen ['pɔlən] (-s, -) *m* pollen; **~flug** *m* pollen count

polnisch ['pɔlnɪʃ] *adj* Polish

Polohemd ['poːlohemt] *nt* polo shirt

Polster ['pɔlstər] (-s, -) *nt* cushion; (*~ung*) upholstery; (*in Kleidung*) padding; (*fig: Geld*) reserves *pl*; **~er** (-s, -) *m* upholsterer; **~möbel** *nt* upholstered furniture *sg*; **p~n** *vt* to upholster; to pad

Polterabend ['pɔltəraːbənt] *m* party on eve of wedding

poltern *vi* (*Krach machen*) to crash; (*schimpfen*) to rant

Polyp [po'lyːp] (-en, -en) *m* polyp; (*umg*) cop; **~en** *pl* (*MED*) adenoids

Pomade [po'maːdə] *f* pomade

Pommes frites [pɔm'frɪt] *pl* chips, French fried potatoes

Pomp [pɔmp] (-(e)s) *m* pomp; **p~ös** [pɔm'pøːs] *adj* (*Auftritt, Fest, Haus*) ostentatious, showy

Pony ['pɔni] (-s, -s) *nt* (*Pferd*) pony ♦ *m* (*Frisur*) fringe

Popmusik ['pɔpmuːzɪk] *f* pop music

Popo [po'poː] (-s, -s) (*umg*) *m* bottom, bum

poppig ['pɔpɪç] *adj* (*Farbe etc*) gaudy

populär [popu'lɛːr] *adj* popular

Popularität [populari'tɛːt] *f* popularity

Pore ['poːrə] *f* pore

Pornografie ▲ [pɔrnogra'fiː] *f* pornography; **pornografisch** [pɔrno'graːfɪʃ] *adj* pornographic

porös [po'røːs] *adj* porous

Porree ['pɔre] (-s, -s) *m* leek

Portefeuille [pɔrt(ə)'føːj] *nt* (*POL, FIN*) portfolio

Portemonnaie [pɔrtmɔ'neː] (-s, -s) *nt* purse

Portier [pɔrti'eː] (-s, -s) *m* porter

Portion [pɔrtsi'oːn] *f* portion, helping; (*umg: Anteil*) amount

Portmonee [pɔrtmɔ'neː] (-s, -s) *nt* = Portemonnaie

Porto ['pɔrto] (-s, -s) *nt* postage; **p~frei** *adj* post-free, (postage) prepaid

Porträt [pɔr'trɛː] (-s, -s) *nt* = Porträt; **p~ieren** *vt* = porträtieren

Porträt [pɔr'trɛː] (-s, -s) *nt* portrait; **p~ieren** *vt* to paint, to portray

Portugal ['pɔrtugal] (-s) *nt* Portugal; **Portugiese** [pɔrtu'giːzə] (-n, -n) *m* Portuguese; **Portu'giesin** *f* Portuguese; **portu'giesisch** *adj* Portuguese

Porzellan [pɔrtsə'laːn] (-s, -e) *nt* china, porcelain; (*Geschirr*) china

Posaune [po'zaunə] *f* trombone

Pose ['poːzə] *f* pose

Position [pozitsi'oːn] *f* position

positiv ['poːzitiːf] *adj* positive; **P~** (-s, -e) *nt* (*PHOT*) positive

possessiv ['pɔsesiːf] *adj* possessive; **P~pronomen** (-s, -e) *nt* possessive pronoun

possierlich [pɔ'siːrlɪç] *adj* funny

Post [pɔst] (-, -en) *f* post (office); (*Briefe*) mail; **~amt** *nt* post office; **~anweisung** *f* postal order, money order; **~bote** *m* postman; **~en** (-s, -) *m* post, position; (*COMM*) item; (*auf Liste*) entry; (*MIL*) sentry; (*Streikposten*) picket; **~er** (-s, -(s)) *nt* poster; **~fach** *nt* post office box; **~karte** *f* postcard; **p~lagernd** *adv* poste restante (*BRIT*), general delivery (*US*); **~leitzahl** *f* postal code; **~scheckkonto** *nt* post office giro account; **~sparbuch** *nt* post office savings book; **~sparkasse** *f* post office savings bank; **~stempel** *m* postmark; **p~wendend** *adv* by return of post; **~wertzeichen** *nt* postage stamp

potent [po'tɛnt] *adj* potent

Potential △ [potɛntsi'aːl] (-s, -e) *nt* siehe Potenzial

potentiell △ [potɛntsi'ɛl] *adj* siehe potenziell

Potenz [po'tɛnts] *f* power; (*eines Mannes*) potency

Potenzial ▲ [potɛn'tsiaːl] (-s, -e) *nt*

Spelling Reform: ▲ *new spelling* △ *old spelling (to be phased out)*

potential

potenziell ▲ [poten'tsiɛl] *adj* potential

Pracht [praxt] (-) *f* splendour, magnificence; **prächtig** ['prɛçtɪç] *adj* splendid

Prachtstück *nt* showpiece

prachtvoll *adj* splendid, magnificent

Prädikat [predi'ka:t] (-(e)s, -e) *nt* title; (GRAM) predicate; (Zensur) distinction

prägen ['prɛːɡən] *vt* to stamp; (Münze) to mint; (Ausdruck) to coin; (Charakter) to form

prägnant [prɛ'ɡnant] *adj* precise, terse

Prägung ['prɛːɡʊŋ] *f* minting; forming; (Eigenart) character, stamp

prahlen ['praːlən] *vi* to boast, to brag; **Prahlerei** *f* boasting

Praktik ['praktɪk] *f* practice; **p~abel** [-'kaːbəl] *adj* practicable; **~ant(in)** [-'kant(ɪn)] *m(f)* trainee; **~um** (-s, Praktika *od* Praktiken) *nt* practical training

praktisch ['praktɪʃ] *adj* practical, handy; **~er Arzt** general practitioner

praktizieren [prakti'tsiːrən] *vt, vi* to practise

Praline [pra'liːnə] *f* chocolate

prall [pral] *adj* firmly rounded; (Segel) taut; (Arme) plump; (Sonne) blazing; **~en** *vi* to bounce, to rebound; (Sonne) to blaze

Prämie ['prɛːmiə] *f* premium; (Belohnung) award, prize; **p~ren** *vt* to give an award to

Präparat [prɛpa'raːt] (-(e)s, -e *od* (BIOL) preparation; (MED) medicine

Präposition [prɛpozi'tsioːn] *f* preposition

Prärie [prɛ'riː] *f* prairie

Präsens ['prɛːzɛns] (-) *nt* present tense

präsentieren [prɛzɛn'tiːrən] *vt* to present

Präservativ [prɛzɛrva'tiːf] (-s, -e) *nt* contraceptive

Präsident(in) [prɛzi'dɛnt(ɪn)] *m(f)* president; **~schaft** *f* presidency

Präsidium [prɛ'ziːdiʊm] *nt* presidency, chair(manship); (Polizeipräsidium) police headquarters *pl*

prasseln ['prasəln] *vi* (Feuer) to crackle; (Hagel) to drum; (Wörter) to rain down

Praxis ['praksɪs] (-, **Praxen**) *f* practice; (Behandlungsraum) surgery; (von Anwalt) office

Präzedenzfall [prɛtse'dɛnts-] *m* precedent

präzis [prɛ'tsiːs] *adj* precise; **P~ion** [prɛtsizi'oːn] *f* precision

predigen ['preːdɪɡən] *vt, vi* to preach; **Prediger** (-s, -) *m* preacher

Predigt ['preːdɪçt] (-, -en) *f* sermon

Preis [prais] (-es, -e) *m* price; (Siegespreis) prize; **um keinen ~** not at any price; **p~bewusst** ▲ *adj* priceconscious

Preiselbeere *f* cranberry

preis- ['prais] *zW*: **~en** (unreg) *vi* to praise; **~geben** (unreg) *vt* to abandon; (opfern) to sacrifice; (zeigen) to expose; **~gekrönt** *adj* prizewinning; **P~gericht** *nt* jury; **~günstig** *adj* inexpensive; **P~lage** *f* price range; **~lich** *adj* (Lage, Unterschied) price, in price; **P~liste** *f* price list; **P~richter** *m* judge (in a competition); **P~schild** *nt* price tag; **P~träger(in)** *m(f)* prizewinner; **~wert** *adj* inexpensive

Prell- [prɛl] *zW*: **~bock** *m* buffers *pl*; **p~en** *vt* to bounce; (fig) to cheat, to swindle; **~ung** *f* bruise

Premiere [prəmi'ɛːrə] *f* premiere

Premierminister [prəmi'eːmɪnɪstər] *m* prime minister, premier

Presse ['prɛsə] *f* press; **~agentur** *f* press agency; **~freiheit** *f* freedom of the press; **p~n** *vt* to press

Pressluft ▲ ['prɛslʊft] *f* compressed air; **~bohrer** *m* pneumatic drill

Prestige [prɛs'tiːʒə] (-s) *nt* prestige

prickeln ['prɪkəln] *vt, vi* to tingle; to tickle

Priester ['priːstər] (-s, -) *m* priest

prima [ˈpriːma] *adj inv* first-class, excellent

primär [pri'mɛːr] *adj* primary

Primel ['priːməl] (-, -n) *f* primrose

primitiv [primi'ti:f] *adj* primitive

Prinz [prɪnts] (-en, -en) *m* prince; **~essin** *f* princess

Prinzip [prɪn'tsi:p] (-s, -ien) *nt* principle; **p~iell** [-i'ɛl] *adj, adv* on principle; **p~ienlos** *adj* unprincipled

Priorität [priori'tɛːt] *f* priority

Prise ['pri:zə] *f* pinch

Prisma ['prɪsma] (-s, Prismen) *nt* prism

privat [pri'vaːt] *adj* private; **P~besitz** *m* private property; **P~fernsehen** *nt* commercial television; **P~patient(in)** *m(f)* private patient; **P~schule** *f* public school

Privileg [privi'le:k] (-(e)s, -ien) *nt* privilege

Pro [pro:] (-) *nt* pro

pro *präp +akk* per

Probe ['pro:bə] *f* test; (*Teststück*) sample; (*THEAT*) rehearsal; **jdn auf die ~ stellen** to put sb to the test; **~exemplar** *nt* specimen copy; **~fahrt** *f* test drive; **p~n** *vt* to try; (*THEAT*) to rehearse; **p~weise** *adv* on approval; **~zeit** *f* probation period

probieren [pro'bi:rən] *vt* to try; (*Wein, Speise*) to taste, to sample ♦ *vi* to try; to taste

Problem [pro'ble:m] (-s, -e) *nt* problem; **~atik** [-'ma:tɪk] *f* problem; **p~atisch** [-'ma:tɪʃ] *adj* problematic; **p~los** *adj* problem-free

Produkt [pro'dʊkt] (-(e)s, -e) *nt* product; (*AGR*) produce *no pl*; **~ion** [produktsi'o:n] *f* production; output; **p~iv** [-'ti:f] *adj* productive; **~ivität** [-'tɛːt] *f* productivity

Produzent [produ'tsɛnt] *m* manufacturer; (*Film*) producer

produzieren [produ'tsi:rən] *vt* to produce

Professor [pro'fɛsɔr] *m* professor

Profi ['pro:fi] (-s, -s) *m* (*umg, SPORT*) pro

Profil [pro'fi:l] (-s, -e) *nt* profile; (*fig*) image

Profit [pro'fi:t] (-(e)s, -e) *m* profit; **p~ieren** *vi*: **p~ieren (von)** to profit (from)

Prognose [pro'gno:zə] *f* prediction, prognosis

Programm [pro'gram] (-s, -e) *nt* programme; (*COMPUT*) program; **p~ieren** [-'mi:rən] *vt* to programme; (*COMPUT*) to program; **~ierer(in)** (-s, -) *m(f)* programmer

progressiv [progrɛ'si:f] *adj* progressive

Projekt [pro'jɛkt] (-(e)s, -e) *nt* project; **~or** [pro'jɛktɔr] *m* projector

proklamieren [prokla'mi:rən] *vt* to proclaim

Prokurist(in) [proku'rɪst(ɪn)] *m(f)* ≈ company secretary

Prolet [pro'le:t] (-en, -en) *m* prole, pleb; **~arier** [-'ta:riər] (-s, -) *m* proletarian

Prolog [pro'lo:k] (-(e)s, -e) *m* prologue

Promenade [promə'na:də] *f* promenade

Promille [pro'mɪlə] (-(s), -) *nt* alcohol level

prominent [promi'nɛnt] *adj* prominent

Prominenz [promi'nɛnts] *f* VIPs *pl*

Promotion [promotsi'o:n] *f* doctorate, Ph.D.

promovieren [promo'vi:rən] *vi* to do a doctorate *od* Ph.D.

prompt [prɔmpt] *adj* prompt

Pronomen [pro'no:mɛn] (-s, -) *nt* pronoun

Propaganda [propa'ganda] (-) *f* propaganda

Propeller [pro'pɛlər] (-s, -) *m* propeller

Prophet [pro'fe:t] (-en, -en) *m* prophet

prophezeien [profe'tsaiən] *vt* to prophesy; **Prophezeiung** *f* prophecy

Proportion [proportsi'o:n] *f* proportion; **p~al** [-'na:l] *adj* proportional

proportioniert [proportsio'ni:rt] *adj*:

gut/schlecht ~ well-/badly-proportioned

Prosa ['pro:za] (-) *f* prose; **p~isch** [pro'za:ɪʃ] *adj* prosaic

prosit ['pro:zɪt] *excl* cheers

Prospekt [pro'spɛkt] (-(e)s, -e) *m* leaflet, brochure

prost [pro:st] *excl* cheers

Prostituierte [prostitu'i:rtə] *f* prostitute

Prostitution [prostitutsi'o:n] *f* prostitution

Protest [pro'tɛst] (-(e)s, -e) *m* protest; **~ant(in)** [protɛs'tant(ɪn)] *m(f)* Protestant; **p~antisch** [protɛs'tantɪʃ] *adj* Protestant; **p~ieren** [protɛs'ti:rən] *vi* to protest

Prothese [pro'te:zə] *f* artificial limb; (*Zahnprothese*) dentures *pl*

Protokoll [proto'kɔl] (-s, -e) *nt* register; (*von Sitzung*) minutes *pl*; (*diplomatisch*) protocol; (*Polizeiprotokoll*) statement; **p~ieren** [-'li:rən] *vt* to take down in the minutes

protzen ['prɔtsən] *vi* to show off

Proviant [provi'ant] (-s, -e) *m* provisions *pl*, supplies *pl*

Provinz [pro'vɪnts] (-, -en) *f* province; **p~i'ell** [-a'ɛl] *adj* provincial

Provision [provizi'o:n] *f* (*COMM*) commission

provisorisch [provi'zo:rɪʃ] *adj* provisional

Provokation [provokatsi'o:n] *f* provocation

provozieren [provo'tsi:rən] *vt* to provoke

Prozedur [protse'du:r] *f* procedure; (*pej*) carry-on

Prozent [pro'tsɛnt] (-(e)s, -e) *nt* per cent, percentage; **~satz** *m* percentage; **p~ual** [-u'a:l] *adj* percentage *cpd*; as a percentage

Prozess ▲ [pro'tsɛs] (-es, -e) *m* trial, case

Prozession [protsesi'o:n] *f* procession

prüde ['pry:də] *adj* prudish; **P~rie**

[-'ri:] *f* prudery

Prüf- ['pry:f] *zW:* **p~en** *vt* to examine, to test; (*nachprüfen*) to check; **~er** (-s, -) *m* examiner; **~ling** *m* examinee; **~ung** *f* examination; checking; **~ungsausschuss ▲** *m* examining board

Prügel ['pry:gəl] (-s, -) *m* cudgel ♦ *pl* (*Schläge*) beating; **~ei** [-'laɪ] *f* fight; **p~n** *vt* to beat ♦ *vr* to fight; **~strafe** *f* corporal punishment

Prunk [prʊŋk] (-(e)s) *m* pomp, show; **p~voll** *adj* splendid, magnificent

PS [pe:'ɛs] *abk* (= *Pferdestärke*) H.P.

Psych- ['psyç] *zW:* **~iater** [-i'a:tər] (-s, -) *m* psychiatrist; **p~iatrisch** *adj* (*MED*) psychiatric; **p~isch** *adj* psychological; **~oanalyse** [-o|ana'ly:zə] *f* psychoanalysis; **~ologe** (-n, -n) *m* psychologist; **~olo'gie** *f* psychology; **p~ologisch** *adj* psychological; **~otherapeut(in)** (-en, -en) *m(f)* psychotherapist

Pubertät [puber'tɛ:t] *f* puberty

Publikum ['pu:blikum] (-s) *nt* audience; (*SPORT*) crowd

publizieren [publi'tsi:rən] *vt* to publish, to publicize

Pudding ['pʊdɪŋ] (-s, -e *od* -s) *m* blancmange

Pudel ['pu:dəl] (-s, -) *m* poodle

Puder ['pu:dər] (-s, -) *m* powder; **~dose** *f* powder compact; **p~n** *vt* to powder; **~zucker** *m* icing sugar

Puff¹ [pʊf] (-s, -e) *m* (*Wäschepuff*) linen basket; (*Sitzpuff*) pouf

Puff² [pʊf] (-s, **ᵉe**) (*umg*) *m* (*Stoß*) push

Puff³ [pʊf] (-s, -) (*umg*) *m od nt* (*Bordell*) brothel

Puffer (-s, -) *m* buffer

Pullover [pʊ'lo:vər] (-s, -) *m* pullover, jumper

Puls [pʊls] (-es, -e) *m* pulse; **~ader** *f* artery; **p~ieren** *vi* to throb, to pulsate

Pult [pʊlt] (-(e)s, -e) *nt* desk

Pulver ['pʊlfər] (-s, -) *nt* powder; **p~ig** *adj* powdery; **~schnee** *m* powdery snow

pummelig ['pʊməlɪç] *adj* chubby

Pumpe ['pʊmpə] *f* pump; **p~n** *vt* to pump; (*umg*) to lend; to borrow

Punkt [pʊŋkt] (-(e)s, -e) *m* point; (*bei Muster*) dot; (*Satzzeichen*) full stop; **p~ieren** [-'tiːrən] *vt* to dot; (*MED*) to aspirate

pünktlich ['pʏŋktlɪç] *adj* punctual; **P~keit** *f* punctuality

Punktsieg *m* victory on points

Punktzahl *f* score

Punsch [pʊnʃ] (-(e)s, -e) *m* punch

Pupille [pu'pɪlə] *f* pupil

Puppe ['pʊpə] *f* doll; (*Marionette*) puppet; (*Insektenpuppe*) pupa, chrysalis

Puppen- *zW:* **~spieler** *m* puppeteer; **~stube** *f* doll's house; **~theater** *nt* puppet theatre

pur [puːr] *adj* pure; (*völlig*) sheer; (*Whisky*) neat

Püree [py're:] (-s, -s) *nt* mashed potatoes *pl*

Purzelbaum ['pʊrtsəlbaʊm] *m* somersault

purzeln ['pʊrtsəln] *vi* to tumble

Puste ['puːstə] (-) (*umg*) *f* puff; (*fig*) steam; **p~n** *vi* to puff, to blow

Pute ['puːtə] *f* turkey hen; **~r** (-s, -) *m* turkey cock

Putsch [pʊtʃ] (-(e)s, -e) *m* revolt, putsch

Putz [pʊts] (-es) *m* (*Mörtel*) plaster, roughcast

putzen *vt* to clean; (*Nase*) to wipe, to blow ♦ *vr* to clean o.s.; to dress o.s. up

Putz- *zW:* **~frau** *f* charwoman; **p~ig** *adj* quaint, funny; **~lappen** *m* cloth

Puzzle ['pasəl] (-s, -s) *nt* jigsaw

PVC *nt abk* PVC

Pyjama [pi'dʒaːma] (-s, -s) *nt* pyjamas *pl*

Pyramide [pyra'miːdə] *f* pyramid

Pyrenäen [pyre'nɛːən] *pl* Pyrenees

Q, q

Quacksalber ['kvakzalbər] (-s, -) *m* quack (doctor)

Quader ['kvaːdər] (-s, -) *m* square stone; (*MATH*) cuboid

Quadrat [kva'draːt] (-(e)s, -e) *nt* square; **q~isch** *adj* square; **~meter** *m* square metre

quaken ['kvaːkən] *vi* to croak; (*Ente*) to quack

quäken ['kvɛːkən] *vi* to screech

Qual [kvaːl] (-, -en) *f* pain, agony; (*seelisch*) anguish; **quälen** *vt* to torment ♦ *vr* to struggle; (*geistig*) to torment o.s.; **Quälerei** *f* torture, torment

Qualifikation [kvalifikatsi'oːn] *f* qualification

qualifizieren [kvalifi'tsiːrən] *vt* to qualify; (*einstufen*) to label ♦ *vr* to qualify

Qualität [kvali'tɛːt] *f* quality; **~sware** *f* article of high quality

Qualle ['kvalə] *f* jellyfish

Qualm [kvalm] (-(e)s) *m* thick smoke; **q~en** *vt, vi* to smoke

qualvoll ['kvaːlfɔl] *adj* excruciating, painful, agonizing

Quant- ['kvant] *zW:* **~ität** [-i'tɛːt] *f* quantity; **q~itativ** [-ita'tiːf] *adj* quantitative; **~um** (-s) *nt* quantity, amount

Quarantäne [karan'tɛːnə] *f* quarantine

Quark [kvark] (-s) *m* curd cheese

Quartal [kvar'taːl] (-s, -e) *nt* quarter (year)

Quartier [kvar'tiːr] (-s, -e) *nt* accommodation; (*MIL*) quarters *pl*; (*Stadtquartier*) district

Quarz [kvaːrts] (-es, -e) *m* quartz

quasseln ['kvasəln] (*umg*) *vi* to natter

Quatsch [kvatʃ] (-es) *m* rubbish; **q~en** *vi* to chat, to natter

Quecksilber ['kvɛkzɪlbər] *nt* mercury

Quelle ['kvɛlə] *f* spring; (*eines Flusses*)

Spelling Reform: ▲ new spelling △ old spelling (to be phased out)

source; **q~n** (unreg) vi (hervorquellen) to pour od gush forth; (schwellen) to swell

quer [kveːr] adv crossways, diagonally; (rechtwinklig) at right angles; **~ auf dem Bett** across the bed; **Q~balken** m crossbeam; **Q~flöte** f flute; **Q~format** nt (PHOT) oblong format; **Q~schnitt** m cross-section; **~schnittsgelähmt** adj paralysed below the waist; **Q~straße** f intersecting road

quetschen ['kvɛtʃən] vt to squash, to crush; (MED) to bruise

Quetschung f bruise, contusion

quieken ['kviːkən] vi to squeak

quietschen ['kviːtʃən] vi to squeak

Quintessenz ['kvɪntɛsɛnts] f quintessence

Quirl [kvɪrl] (-(e)s, -e) m whisk

quitt [kvɪt] adj quits, even

Quitte f quince

quittieren [kvɪtiːrən] vt to give a receipt for; (Dienst) to leave

Quittung f receipt

Quiz [kvɪs] (-, -) nt quiz

quoll etc [kvɔl] vb siehe **quellen**

Quote ['kvoːtə] f number, rate

R, r

Rabatt [ra'bat] (-(e)s, -e) m discount

Rabattmarke f trading stamp

Rabe ['raːbə] (-n, -n) m raven

rabiat [rabi'aːt] adj furious

Rache ['raxə] f revenge, vengeance

Rachen (-s, -) m throat

rächen ['rɛçən] vt to avenge, to revenge ♦ vr to take (one's) revenge; **das wird sich ~** you'll pay for this

Rad [raːt] (-(e)s, "er) nt wheel; (Fahrrad) bike; **~ fahren** to cycle

Radar [ra'daːr] (-s) m od nt radar; **~falle** f speed trap; **~kontrolle** f radar-controlled speed trap

Radau [ra'dau] (-s) (umg) m row

radeln ['raːdəln] (umg) vi to cycle

Radfahr- zW: **r~en** △ (unreg) vi siehe **Rad**; **~er(in)** m(f) cyclist; **~weg** m cycle track od path

Radier- [ra'diːr] zW: **r~en** vt to rub out, to erase; (KUNST) to etch; **~gummi** m rubber, eraser; **~ung** f etching

Radieschen [ra'diːsçən] nt radish

radikal [radi'kaːl] adj radical

Radio ['raːdio] (-s, -s) nt radio, wireless; **r~ak'tiv** adj radioactive; **~aktivi'tät** f radioactivity; **~apparat** m radio, wireless set

Radius ['raːdios] (-, **Radien**) m radius

Rad- zW: **~kappe** f (AUT) hub cap; **~ler(in)** (umg) m(f) cyclist; **~rennen** nt cycle race; cycle racing; **~sport** m cycling; **~weg** m cycleway

raffen ['rafən] vt to snatch, to pick up; (Stoff) to gather (up); (Geld) to pile up, to rake in

raffi'niert adj crafty, cunning

ragen ['raːgən] vi to tower, to rise

Rahm [raːm] (-s) m cream

Rahmen (-s, -) m frame(work); **im ~ des Möglichen** within the bounds of possibility; **r~** vt to frame

räkeln ['rɛːkəln] vr = **rekeln**

Rakete [ra'keːtə] f rocket; **~nstützpunkt** m missile base

rammen ['ramən] vt to ram

Rampe ['rampə] f ramp; **~nlicht** nt (THEAT) footlights pl

ramponieren [rampo'niːrən] (umg) vt to damage

Ramsch [ramʃ] (-(e)s, -e) m junk

ran [ran] (umg) adv = **heran**

Rand [rant] (-(e)s, "er) m edge; (von Brille, Tasse etc) rim; (Hutrand) brim; (auf Papier) margin; (Schmutzrand, unter Augen) ring; (fig) verge, brink; **außer ~ und Band** wild; **am ~e bemerkt** mentioned in passing

randalieren [randa'liːrən] vi to (go on the) rampage

Rang [raŋ] (-(e)s, "e) m rank; (Stand) standing; (Wert) quality; (THEAT) circle

Rangier- [rãˈʒiːr] zW: **~bahnhof** m

marshalling yard; **r~en** vt (EISENB) to shunt, to switch (US) ♦ vi to rank, to be classed; **~gleis** nt siding

Ranke ['raŋkə] f tendril, shoot

ranzig ['rantsiç] adj rancid

Rappen ['rapən] m (FIN) rappen, centime

rar [raːr] adj rare; **sich ~ machen** (umg) to keep o.s. to o.s.; **R~i'tät** f rarity; (Sammelobjekt) curio

rasant [ra'zant] adj quick, rapid

rasch [raʃ] adj quick

rascheln vi to rustle

Rasen ['raːzən] (-s, -) m lawn; grass

rasen vi to rave; (schnell) to race; **~d** adj furious; **~de Kopfschmerzen** a splitting headache

Rasenmäher (-s, -) m lawnmower

Rasier- [ra'ziːr] zW: **~apparat** m shaver; **~creme** f shaving cream; **r~en** vt, vr to shave; **~klinge** f razor blade; **~messer** nt razor; **~pinsel** m shaving brush; **~schaum** m shaving foam; **~seife** f shaving soap od stick; **~wasser** nt shaving lotion

Rasse ['rasə] f race; (Tierrasse) breed; **~hund** m thoroughbred dog

rasseln ['rasəln] vi to clatter

Rassen- zW: **~hass ▲** m race od racial hatred; **~trennung** f racial segregation

Rassismus [ra'sɪsmʊs] m racism

Rast [rast] (-, -en) f rest; **r~en** vi to rest; **~hof** m (AUT) service station; **r~los** adj tireless; (unruhig) restless; **~platz** m (AUT) layby; **~stätte** f (AUT) service station

Rasur [ra'zuːr] f shaving

Rat [raːt] (-(e)s, -schläge) m advice no pl; **ein ~** a piece of advice; **keinen ~ wissen** not to know what to do; siehe zurate

Rate f instalment

raten (unreg) vt, vi to guess; (empfehlen): **jdm ~** to advise sb

Ratenzahlung f hire purchase

Ratgeber (-s, -) m adviser

Rathaus nt town hall

ratifizieren [ratifi'tsiːrən] vt to ratify

Ration [ratsi'oːn] f ration; **r~al** [-'naːl] adj rational; **r~ali'sieren** vt to rationalize; **r~ell** [-'nɛl] adj efficient; **r~ieren** [-'niːrən] vt to ration

Rat- zW: **r~los** adj at a loss, helpless; **r~sam** adj advisable; **~schlag** m (piece of) advice

Rätsel ['rɛːtsəl] (-s, -) nt puzzle; (Worträtsel) riddle; **r~haft** adj mysterious; **es ist mir ~haft** it's a mystery to me

Ratte ['ratə] f rat; **~nfänger** (-s, -) m ratcatcher

rau [rau] adj rough, coarse; (Wetter) harsh

Raub [raup] (-(e)s) m robbery (Beute) loot, booty; **~bau** m ruthless exploitation; **r~en** ['raubən] vt to rob; (Mensch) to kidnap, to abduct

Räuber ['rɔybər] (-s, -) m robber

Raub- zW: **~mord** m robbery with murder; **~tier** nt predator; **~überfall** m robbery with violence; **~vogel** m bird of prey

Rauch [raux] (-(e)s) m smoke; **r~en** vt, vi to smoke; **~er(in)** m(f) smoker; **~erabteil** nt (EISENB) smoker; **räuchern** vt to smoke, to cure; **~fleisch** nt smoked meat; **r~ig** adj smoky

rauf [rauf] (umg) adv = herauf; hinauf

raufen vt (Haare) to pull out ♦ vi, vr to fight; **Raufe'rei** f brawl, fight

rauh △ etc [rau] adj siehe rau etc

Raum [raum] (-(e)s, Räume) m space; (Zimmer, Platz) room; (Gebiet) area

räumen ['rɔymən] vt to clear; (Wohnung, Platz) to vacate; (wegbringen) to shift, to move; (in Schrank etc) to put away

Raum- zW: **~fähre** f space shuttle;

~fahrt f space travel; **~inhalt** m cubic capacity, volume

räumlich ['rɔymlɪç] adj spatial; **R~keiten** pl premises

Raum- zW: **~pflegerin** f cleaner; **~schiff** nt spaceship; **~schifffahrt ▲** f space travel

Räumung ['rɔymʊŋ] f vacating, evacuation; clearing (away)

Räumungs- zW: **~arbeiten** pl clearance operations; **~verkauf** m clearance sale; (bei Geschäftsaufgabe) closing down sale

raunen ['raʊnən] vt, vi to whisper

Raupe ['raʊpə] f caterpillar; (~nkette) (caterpillar) track

Raureif ▲ ['raʊraɪf] m hoarfrost

raus [raʊs] (umg) adv = **heraus; hinaus**

Rausch [raʊʃ] (-(e)s, Räusche) m intoxication

rauschen vi (Wasser) to rush; (Baum) to rustle; (Radio etc) to hiss; (Mensch) to sweep, to sail; **~d** adj (Beifall) thunderous; (Fest) sumptuous

Rauschgift nt drug; **~süchtige(r)** f(m) drug addict

räuspern ['rɔyspərn] vr to clear one's throat

Razzia ['ratsia] (-, Razzien) f raid

Reagenzglas [rea'gɛntsglɑːs] nt test tube

reagieren [rea'giːrən] vi: **~ (auf +akk)** to react (to)

Reakt- zW: **~ion** [reaktsi'oːn] f reaction; **r~io'när** adj reactionary; **~or** [re'aktɔr] m reactor

real [re'aːl] adj real, material

reali'sieren vt (verwirklichen: Pläne) to carry out

Realismus [rea'lɪsmʊs] m realism

rea'listisch adj realistic

Realschule f secondary school

The Realschule is one of the secondary schools a German schoolchild may attend after the Grundschule. On the successful completion of six years of schooling in the Realschule pupils gain the mittlere Reife and usually go on to vocational training or further education.

Rebe ['reːbə] f vine

rebellieren [rebe'liːrən] vi to rebel; **Rebelli'on** f rebellion; **re'bellisch** adj rebellious

Rebhuhn ['rɛphuːn] nt (KOCH, ZOOL) partridge

Rechen ['rɛçən] (-s, -) m rake

Rechen- zW: **~fehler** m miscalculation; **~maschine** f calculating machine; **~schaft** f account; **für etw ~schaft ablegen** to account for sth; **~schieber** m slide rule

Rech- [rɛç] zW: **r~nen** vt, vi to calculate; **jdn/etw r~nen zu** to count sb/ sth among; **r~nen mit** to reckon with; **r~nen auf** +akk to count on; **~nen** nt arithmetic; **~ner** (-s, -) m calculator; (COMPUT) computer; **~nung** f calculation(s); (COMM) bill, check (US); **jdm/ etw ~nung tragen** to take sb/sth into account; **~nungsbetrag** m total amount of a bill/invoice; **~nungsjahr** nt financial year; **~nungsprüfer** m auditor

Recht [rɛçt] (-(e)s, -e) nt right; (JUR) law; **mit ~** rightly, justly; **R~ haben** to be right; **jdm R~ geben** to agree with sb; **von ~s wegen** by rights

recht adj right ♦ adv (vor Adjektiv) really, quite; **das ist mir ~** that suits me; **jetzt erst ~** now more than ever

Rechte f right (hand); (POL) Right; **r~(r, s)** adj right; (POL) right-wing; **ein ~r** a right-winger; **~(s)** nt right thing; **etwas/nichts ~s** something/nothing proper

recht- zW: **~eckig** adj rectangular; **~fertigen** vt insep to justify ♦ vr insep to justify o.s.; **R~fertigung** f justification; **~haberisch** (pej) adj (Mensch) opinionated; **~lich** adj (gesetzlich: Gleichstel-

lung, Anspruch) legal; **~los** *adj* with no rights; **~mäßig** *adj* legal, lawful

rechts [reçts] *adv* on/to the right; **R~anwalt** *m* lawyer, barrister; **R~anwältin** *f* lawyer, barrister

Rechtschreibung *f* spelling

Rechts- *zW:* **~fall** *m* (law) case; **~händer** (-s, -) *m* right-handed person; **r~kräftig** *adj* valid, legal; **~kurve** *f* right-hand bend; **r~verbindlich** *adj* legally binding; **r~verkehr** *m* driving on the right; **r~widrig** *adj* illegal; **~wissenschaft** *f* jurisprudence

rechtwinklig *adj* right-angled

rechtzeitig *adj* timely ♦ *adv* in time

Reck [rɛk] (-(e)s, -e) *nt* horizontal bar; **r~en** *vt, vr* to stretch

recyceln [riːˈsaikəln] *vt* to recycle; **Re-cycling** [riːˈsaiklɪŋ] (-s) *nt* recycling

Redakteur [redakˈtøːr] *m* editor

Redaktion [redaktsiˈoːn] *f* editing; (*Leute*) editorial staff; (*Büro*) editorial office(s)

Rede [ˈreːdə] *f* speech; (*Gespräch*) talk; **jdn zur ~ stellen** to take sb to task; **~freiheit** *f* freedom of speech; **r~gewandt** *adj* eloquent; **r~n** *vi* to talk, to speak ♦ *vt* to say; (*Unsinn etc*) to talk; **~nsart** *f* set phrase

redlich [ˈreːtlɪç] *adj* honest

Redner (-s, -) *m* speaker, orator

redselig [ˈreːtzeːlɪç] *adj* talkative, loquacious

reduzieren [reduˈtsiːrən] *vt* to reduce

Reede [ˈreːdə] *f* protected anchorage; **~r** (-s, -) *m* shipowner; **~'rei** *f* shipping line *od* firm

reell [reˈɛl] *adj* fair, honest; (*MATH*) real

Refer- *zW:* **~at** [refeˈraːt] (-(e)s, -e) *nt* report; (*Vortrag*) paper; (*Gebiet*) section; **~ent** [refeˈrɛnt] *m* speaker; (*Berichterstatter*) reporter; (*Sachbearbeiter*) expert; **r~ieren** [refeˈriːrən] *vi:* **r~ieren über** +*akk* to speak *od* talk on

reflektieren [reflɛkˈtiːrən] *vt* (*Licht*) to reflect

Reflex [reˈflɛks] (-es, -e) *m* reflex; **r~iv** [-ˈksiːf] *adj* (*GRAM*) reflexive

Reform [reˈfɔrm] (-, -en) *f* reform; **~ati'on** *f* reformation; **~ationstag** *m* Reformation Day; **~haus** *nt* health food shop; **r~ieren** [-ˈmiːrən] *vt* to reform

Regal [reˈgaːl] (-s, -e) *nt* (book)shelves *pl*, bookcase; stand, rack

rege [ˈreːgə] *adj* (*lebhaft: Treiben*) lively; (*wach, lebendig: Geist*) keen

Regel [ˈreːgəl] (-, -n) *f* rule; (*MED*) period; **r~mäßig** *adj* regular; **~mäßigkeit** *f* regularity; **r~n** *vt* to regulate, to control; (*Angelegenheit*) to settle ♦ *vr:* **sich von selbst r~n** to take care of itself; **r~recht** *adj* regular, proper, thorough; **~ung** *f* regulation; settlement; **r~widrig** *adj* irregular, against the rules

Regen [ˈreːgən] (-s, -) *m* rain; **~bogen** *m* rainbow; **~bogenpresse** *f* tabloids *pl*

regenerierbar [regeneˈriːrbaːr] *adj* renewable

Regen- *zW:* **~mantel** *m* raincoat, mac(kintosh); **~schauer** *m* shower (of rain); **~schirm** *m* umbrella; **~wald** *m* (*GEOG*) rainforest; **~wurm** *m* earthworm; **~zeit** *f* rainy season

Regie [reˈʒiː] *f* (*Film etc*) direction; (*THEAT*) production

Regier- [reˈgiːr] *zW:* **r~en** *vt, vi* to govern, to rule; **~ung** *f* government; (*Monarchie*) reign; **~ungssitz** *m* seat of government; **~ungswechsel** *m* change of government; **~ungszeit** *f* period in government; (*von König*) reign

Regiment [regiˈmɛnt] (-s, -er) *nt* regiment

Region [regiˈoːn] *f* region

Regisseur [reʒiˈsøːr] *m* director; (*THEAT*) (stage) producer

---

Spelling Reform: ▲ *new spelling* △ *old spelling (to be phased out)*

Register [re'ɡɪstər] (**-s, -**) nt register; (in Buch) table of contents, index

registrieren [reɡɪs'triːrən] vt to register

Regler ['reːɡlər] (**-s, -**) m regulator, governor

reglos ['reːkloːs] adj motionless

regnen ['reːɡnən] vi unpers to rain

regnerisch adj rainy

regulär [reɡu'lɛːr] adj regular

regulieren [reɡu'liːrən] vt to regulate; (COMM) to settle

Regung ['reːɡʊŋ] f motion; (Gefühl) feeling, impulse; **r~slos** adj motionless

Reh [reː] (**-(e)s, -e**) nt deer, roe; **~bock** m roebuck; **~kitz** nt fawn

Reib- ['raɪb] zW: **~e** f grater; **~eisen** nt grater; **r~en** (unreg) vt to rub; (KOCH) to grate; **~fläche** f rough surface; **~ung** f friction; **r~ungslos** adj smooth

Reich (**-(e)s, -e**) nt empire, kingdom; (fig) realm; **das Dritte R~** the Third Reich

reich [raɪç] adj rich

reichen vi (genügen) to be enough ♦ vt to hold out; (geben) to pass, to hand; (anbieten) to offer; **jdm ~** to be enough od sufficient for sb

reich- zW: **~haltig** adj ample, rich; **~lich** adj ample, plenty of; **R~tum** (**-s**) m wealth; **R~weite** f range

Reif (**-(e)s, -e**) m (Ring) ring, hoop

reif [raɪf] adj ripe; (Mensch, Urteil) mature

Reife (**-**) f ripeness; maturity; **r~n** vi to mature; to ripen

Reifen (**-s, -**) m ring, hoop; (Fahrzeugreifen) tyre; **~druck** m tyre pressure; **~panne** f puncture

Reihe ['raɪə] f row; (von Tagen etc, umg: Anzahl) series sg; **der ~ nach** in turn; **er ist an der ~** it's his turn; **an die ~ kommen** to have one's turn

Reihen- zW: **~folge** f sequence; alphabetische **~folge** alphabetical order; **~haus** nt terraced house

reihum [raɪ'ʔʊm] adv: **es geht/wir machen das ~** we take turns

Reim [raɪm] (**-(e)s, -e**) m rhyme; **r~en** vt to rhyme

rein1 [raɪn] (umg) adv = herein; hinein

rein2 [raɪn] adj pure; (sauber) clean ♦ adv purely; **etwas ins R~e schreiben** to make a fair copy of sth; **etw ins R~e bringen** to clear up sth; **R~fall** (umg) m let-down; **R~gewinn** m net profit; **R~heit** f purity; cleanness; **~igen** vt to clean; (Wasser) to purify; **R~igung** f cleaning; purification; (Geschäft) cleaner's; **chemische R~igung** dry cleaning; dry cleaner's; **R~igungsmittel** nt cleansing agent; **~rassig** adj pedigree; **R~schrift** f fair copy

Reis [raɪs] (**-es, -e**) m rice

Reise ['raɪzə] f journey; (Schiffsreise) voyage; **~n** pl (Herumreisen) travels; **gute ~!** have a good journey; **~apotheke** f first-aid kit; **~büro** nt travel agency; **r~fertig** adj ready to start; **~führer** m guide(book); (Mensch) travel guide; **~gepäck** nt luggage; **~gesellschaft** f party of travellers; **~kosten** pl travelling expenses; **~leiter** m courier; **~lektüre** f reading matter for the journey; **r~n** vi to travel; **nach** to go to; **~nde(r)** f(m) traveller; **~pass** ▲ m passport; **~proviant** m food and drink for the journey; **~route** f route, itinerary; **~ruf** m personal message; **~scheck** m traveller's cheque; **~veranstalter** m tour operator; **~versicherung** f travel insurance; **~ziel** nt destination

Reißbrett nt drawing board

reißen ['raɪsən] (unreg) vt to tear; (ziehen) to pull, to drag; (Witz) to crack ♦ vi to tear; to pull, to drag; **etw an sich ~** to snatch sth up; (fig) to take over sth; **sich um etw ~** to scramble for sth; **~d** adj (Fluss) raging; (WIRTS: Verkauf) rapid

Reiß- zW: **~verschluss** ▲ m zip(per), zip fastener; **~zwecke** m drawing pin

(BRIT), thumbtack *(US)*

Reit- ['raɪt] *zW*: **r~en** *(unreg)* *vt, vi* to ride; **~er (-s, -)** *m* rider; *(MIL)* cavalryman, trooper; **~erin** *f* rider; **~hose** *f* riding breeches *pl*; **~pferd** *nt* saddle horse; **~stiefel** *m* riding boot; **~weg** *n* bridle path; **~zeug** *nt* riding outfit

Reiz [raɪts] **(-es, -e)** *m* stimulus; *(angenehm)* charm; *(Verlockung)* attraction; **r~bar** *adj* irritable; **~barkeit** *f* irritability; **r~en** *vt* to stimulate; *(unangenehm)* to irritate; *(verlocken)* to appeal to, to attract; **r~end** *adj* charming; **r~voll** *adj* attractive

rekeln ['reːkəln] *vr* to stretch out; *(lümmeln)* to lounge *od* loll about

Reklamation [reklamatsi'oːn] *f* complaint

Reklame [re'klaːmə] *f* advertising; advertisement; **~ machen für etw** to advertise sth

rekonstruieren [rekɔnstru'iːrən] *vt* to reconstruct

Rekord [re'kɔrt] **(-(e)s, -e)** *m* record; **~leistung** *f* record performance

Rektor ['rɛktɔr] *m* *(UNIV)* rector, vicechancellor; *(SCH)* headteacher *(BRIT)*, principal *(US)*; **~at [-'raːt] (-(e)s, -e)** *nt* rectorate, vice-chancellorship; headship; *(Zimmer)* rector's *etc* office

Relais [rə'leː] **(-, -)** *nt* relay

relativ [rela'tiːf] *adj* relative; **r~en** *adj* relative; **R~ität [-lativi'tɛːt]** *f* relativity

relevant [rele'vant] *adj* relevant

Relief [reli'ɛf] **(-s, -s)** *nt* relief

Religion [religi'oːn] *f* religion

religiös [religi'øːs] *adj* religious

Reling ['reːlɪŋ] **(-, -s)** *f (NAUT)* rail

Remoulade [remu'laːdə] *f* remoulade

Rendezvous [rãde'vuː] **(-, -)** *nt* rendezvous

Renn- ['rɛn] *zW*: **~bahn** *f* racecourse; *(AUT)* circuit, race track; **r~en** *(unreg)* *vt, vi* to run, to race; **~en (-s, -)** *nt* running; *(Wettbewerb)* race; **~fahrer** *m*

racing driver; **~pferd** *nt* racehorse; **~wagen** *m* racing car

renommiert [reno'miːrt] *adj* renowned

renovieren [reno'viːrən] *vt* to renovate; **Renovierung** *f* renovation

rentabel [rɛn'taːbəl] *adj* profitable, lucrative

Rentabilität [rɛntabili'tɛːt] *f* profitability

Rente ['rɛntə] *f* pension

Rentenversicherung *f* pension scheme

rentieren [rɛn'tiːrən] *vr* to pay, to be profitable

Rentner(in) ['rɛntnər(ɪn)] **(-s, -)** *m(f)* pensioner

Reparatur [repara'tuːr] *f* repairing; repair; **~werkstatt** *f* repair shop; *(AUT)* garage

reparieren [repa'riːrən] *vt* to repair

Reportage [repɔr'taːʒə] *f* (on-the-spot) report; *(TV, RADIO)* live commentary *od* coverage

Reporter [re'pɔrtər] **(-s, -)** *m* reporter, commentator

repräsentativ [reprɛzenta'tiːf] *adj (stellvertretend, typisch: Menge, Gruppe)* representative; *(beeindruckend: Haus, Auto etc)* impressive

repräsentieren [reprɛzen'tiːrən] *vt (Staat, Firma)* to represent; *(darstellen: Wert)* to constitute ♦ *vi (gesellschaftlich)* to perform official duties

Repressalie [repre'saːliə] *f* reprisal

Reprivatisierung [reprivati'ziːrʊŋ] *f* denationalization

Reproduktion [reprodʊktsi'oːn] *f* reproduction

reproduzieren [reprodu'tsiːrən] *vt* to reproduce

Reptil [rep'tiːl] **(-s, -ien)** *nt* reptile

Republik [repu'bliːk] *f* republic; **r~anisch** *adj* republican

Reservat [rezɛr'vaːt] **(-(e)s, -e)** *nt* reservation

Reserve [re'zɛrvə] f reserve; **~rad** nt (AUT) spare wheel; **~spieler** m reserve; **~tank** m reserve tank

reservieren [rezɛr'viːrən] vt to reserve

Reservoir [rezɛrvo'aːr] (-s, -e) nt reservoir

Residenz [rezi'dɛnts] f residence, seat

resignieren [rezi'gniːrən] vi to resign

resolut [rezo'luːt] adj resolute

Resonanz [rezo'nants] f resonance; (fig) response

Resozialisierung [rezotsiali'ziːroŋ] f rehabilitation

Respekt [re'spɛkt] (-(e)s) m respect; **r~ieren** [-'tiːrən] vt to respect; **r~los** adj disrespectful; **r~voll** adj respectful

Ressort [rɛ'soːr] (-s, -s) nt department

Rest [rɛst] (-(e)s, -e) m remainder, rest; (Überrest) remains pl

Restaurant [rɛstoˈrãː] (-s, -s) nt restaurant

restaurieren [rɛstauˈriːrən] vt to restore

Rest- zW: **~betrag** m remainder, outstanding sum; **r~lich** adj remaining; **r~los** adj complete

Resultat [rezul'taːt] (-(e)s, -e) nt result

Retorte [re'tɔrtə] f retort

Retouren [re'tuːrən] pl (COMM) returns

retten ['rɛtən] vt to save, to rescue

Retter(in) m(f) rescuer

Rettich ['rɛtiç] (-s, -e) m radish

Rettung f rescue; (Hilfe) help; **seine letzte ~** his last hope

Rettungs- zW: **~boot** nt lifeboat; **~dienst** m rescue service; **r~los** adj hopeless; **~ring** m lifebelt, life preserver (US); **~wagen** m ambulance

retuschieren [retu'ʃiːrən] vt (PHOT) to retouch

Reue ['rɔʏə] (-) f remorse; (Bedauern) regret; **r~n** vt: **es reut ihn** he regrets (it) od is sorry (about it)

Revanche [re'vãːʃə] f revenge; (SPORT) return match

revanchieren [revã'ʃiːrən] vr (sich

rächen) to get one's own back, to have one's revenge; (erwidern) to reciprocate, to return the compliment

Revier [re'viːr] (-s, -e) nt district; (Jagdrevier) preserve; (Polizeirevier) police station; beat

Revolte [re'vɔltə] f revolt

revol'tieren vi (gegen jdn/etw) to rebel

Revolution [revolutsi'oːn] f revolution; **~är** [-'nɛːr] (-s, -e) m revolutionary; **r~ieren** [-'niːrən] vt to revolutionize

Revolver [re'vɔlvər] (-s, -) m revolver

Rezept [re'tsɛpt] (-(e)s, -e) nt recipe; (MED) prescription; **r~frei** adj available without prescription; **~ion** f reception; **r~pflichtig** adj available only on prescription

R-Gespräch ['ɛrgəʃprɛːç] nt reverse charge call (BRIT), collect call (US)

Rhabarber [ra'barbər] (-s) m rhubarb

Rhein [rain] (-s) m Rhine; **r~isch** adj Rhenish

Rheinland-Pfalz nt (GEOG) Rheinland-Pfalz, Rhineland-Palatinate

Rhesusfaktor ['reːzusfaktoːr] m rhesus factor

rhetorisch [re'toːriʃ] adj rhetorical

Rheuma ['rɔʏma] (-s) nt rheumatism; **r~tisch** [-'maːtiʃ] adj rheumatic

rhythmisch ['rʏtmiʃ] adj rhythmical

Rhythmus ['rʏtmɔs] m rhythm

richt- ['rɪçt] zW: **~en** vt to direct; (Waffe) to aim; (einstellen) to adjust; (instandsetzen) to repair; (zurechtmachen) to prepare; (bestrafen) to pass judgement on ♦ vr: **sich ~en nach** to go by; **~en an** +akk to direct at; (fig) to direct to; **~en auf** +akk to aim at; **R~er(in)** m(f) judge; **~erlich** adj judicial; **R~geschwindigkeit** f recommended speed

richtig adj right, correct; (echt) proper ♦ adv (umg: sehr) really; **bin ich hier ~?** am I in the right place?; **der/die R~e** the right one/person; **das R~e** the right thing; **etw ~ stellen** to correct sth; **R~keit** f correctness

Richt- zW: **~linie** f guideline; **~preis** m recommended price

Richtung f direction; tendency, orientation

rieb etc [ri:p] vb siehe **reiben**

riechen ['ri:çən] (unreg) vt, vi to smell; **an etw** dat **~** to smell sth; **nach etw ~** to smell of sth; **ich kann das/ihn nicht ~** (umg) I can't stand it/him

rief etc [ri:f] vb siehe **rufen**

Riegel ['ri:gəl] (-s, -) m bolt; (Schokolade usw) bar

Riemen ['ri:mən] (-s, -) m strap; (Gürtel, TECH) belt; (NAUT) oar

Riese ['ri:zə] (-n, -n) m giant

rieseln vi to trickle; (Schnee) to fall gently

Riesen- zW: **~erfolg** m enormous success; **r~groß** adj colossal, gigantic, huge; **~rad** nt big wheel

riesig ['ri:zıç] adj enormous, huge, vast

riet etc [ri:t] vb siehe **raten**

Riff [rıf] (-(e)s, -e) nt reef

Rille ['rılə] f groove

Rind [rınt] (-(e)s, -er) nt ox; cow; cattle pl; (KOCH) beef

Rinde ['rındə] f rind; (Baumrinde) bark; (Brotrinde) crust

Rind- [rınt] zW: **~fleisch** nt beef; **~vieh** nt cattle pl; (umg) blockhead, stupid oaf

Ring [rıŋ] (-(e)s, -e) m ring; **~buch** nt ring binder; **r~en** (unreg) vi to wrestle; **~en** (-s) nt wrestling; **~finger** m ring finger; **~kampf** m wrestling bout; **~richter** m referee; **r~s** adv: **r~s um** round; **r~sherum** adv round about; **~straße** f ring road; **r~sum** adv (rundherum) round about; (überall) all round; **r~sumher** adv = **ringsum**

Rinn- [rın] zW: **~e** f gutter, drain; **r~en** (unreg) vi to run; to trickle; **~stein** m gutter

Rippchen ['rıpçən] nt small rib; cutlet

Rippe ['rıpə] f rib

Risiko ['ri:ziko] (-s, -s od **Risiken**) nt risk

riskant [rıs'kant] adj risky, hazardous

riskieren [rıs'ki:rən] vt to risk

Riss ▲ [rıs] (-es, -e) m tear; (in Mauer, Tasse etc) crack; (in Haut) scratch; (TECH) design

rissig ['rısıç] adj torn; cracked; scratched

Ritt [rıt] (-(e)s, -e) m ride

ritt etc vb siehe **reiten**

Ritter (-s, -) m knight; **r~lich** adj chivalrous

Ritze ['rıtsə] f crack, chink

Rivale [ri'va:lə] (-n, -n) m rival

Rivalität [rivali'tɛ:t] f rivalry

Robbe ['rɔbə] f seal

Roboter ['rɔbɔtər] (-s, -) m robot

robust [ro'bʊst] adj (kräftig: Mensch, Gesundheit) robust

roch etc [rɔx] vb siehe **riechen**

Rock [rɔk] (-(e)s, -e) m skirt; (Jackett) jacket; (Uniformrock) tunic

Rodel ['ro:dəl] (-s, -) m toboggan; **~bahn** f toboggan run; **r~n** vi to toboggan

Rogen ['ro:gən] (-s, -) m roe, spawn

Roggen ['rɔgən] (-s, -) m rye; **~brot** nt (KOCH) rye bread

roh [ro:] adj raw; (Mensch) coarse, crude; **R~bau** m shell of a building; **R~material** nt raw material; **R~öl** nt crude oil

Rohr [ro:r] (-(e)s, -e) nt pipe, tube; (BOT) cane; (Schilf) reed; (Gewehrrohr) barrel; **~bruch** m burst pipe

Röhre ['rø:rə] f tube, pipe; (RADIO etc) valve; (Backröhre) oven

Rohr- zW: **~leitung** f pipeline; **~zucker** m cane sugar

Rohstoff m raw material

Rokoko ['rɔkoko] (-s) nt rococo

Rollladen △ m siehe **Rollladen**

Rollbahn ['rɔlba:n] f (AVIAT) runway

Rolle ['rɔlə] f roll; (THEAT, soziologisch) role; (Garnrolle etc) reel, spool; (Walze) roller; (Wäscherolle) mangle; **keine ~ spielen** to not matter; **eine (wichtige) ~ spielen bei** to play a (major) part od role in; **r~n** vt, vi to roll; (AVIAT) to taxi; **~r (-s, -)** m scooter; (Welle) roller

Roll- zW: **~kragen** m rollneck, polo neck; **~laden ▲** m shutter; **~mops** m pickled herring; **~schuh** m roller skate; **~stuhl** m wheelchair; **~stuhlfahrer(in)** m(f) wheelchair user; **~treppe** f escalator

Rom [rɔːm] (-s) nt Rome

Roman [ro'maːn] (-s, -e) m novel; **~tik** f romanticism; **~tiker** [ro'mantɪkər] (-s, -) m romanticist; **r~tisch** [ro'mantɪʃ] adj romantic; **~ze** [ro'mantsə] f romance

Römer ['røːmər] (-s, -) m wineglass; (Mensch) Roman

römisch ['røːmɪʃ] adj Roman; **~-katholisch** adj (REL) Roman Catholic

röntgen ['rœntgən] vt to X-ray; **R~bild** nt X-ray; **R~strahlen** pl X-rays

rosa ['roːza] adj inv pink, rose(-coloured)

Rose ['roːzə] f rose

Rosen- zW: **~kohl** m Brussels sprouts pl; **~kranz** m rosary; **~montag** m Monday before Ash Wednesday

rosig ['roːzɪç] adj rosy

Rosine [ro'ziːnə] f raisin, currant

Ross ▲ [rɔs] (-es, -e) nt horse, steed; **~kastanie** f horse chestnut

Rost [rɔst] (-(e)s, -e) m rust; (Gitter) grill, gridiron; (Bettrost) springs pl; **~braten** m roast(ed) meat, roast; **r~en** vi to rust

rösten ['rœstən] vt to roast; to toast; to grill

Rost- zW: **r~frei** adj rust-free; rustproof; stainless; **r~ig** adj rusty; **~schutz** m rust-proofing

rot [roːt] adj red; **in den ~en Zahlen** in the red

Röte ['røːtə] (-) f redness; **~ln** pl Ger-

man measles sg; **r~n** vt, vr to redden

rothaarig adj red-haired

rotieren [ro'tiːrən] vi to rotate

Rot- zW: **~kehlchen** nt robin; **~stift** m red pencil; **~wein** m red wine

Rouge [ruːʒ] nt blusher

Roulade [ru'laːdə] f (KOCH) beef olive

Route ['ruːtə] f route

Routine [ru'tiːnə] f experience; routine

Rübe ['ryːbə] f turnip; **Gelbe ~** carrot; **Rote ~** beetroot (BRIT), beet (US)

rüber ['ryːbər] (umg) adv = herüber; hinüber

Rubrik [ru'briːk] f heading; (Spalte) column

Ruck [rʊk] (-(e)s, -e) m jerk, jolt

Rück- zW: **~antwort** f reply, answer; **r~bezüglich** adj reflexive

Rücken ['rʏkən] (-s, -) m back; (Bergrücken) ridge

rücken vt, vi to move

Rücken- zW: **~mark** nt spinal cord; **~schwimmen** nt backstroke

Rück- zW: **~erstattung** f return, restitution; **~fahrkarte** f return (ticket); **~fahrt** f return journey; **~fall** m relapse; **r~fällig** adj relapsing; **r~fällig werden** to relapse; **~flug** m return flight; **~frage** f question; **r~fragen** vi to check, to inquire (further); **~gabe** f return; **~gaberecht** nt right of return; **~gang** m decline, fall; **r~gängig** adj; **etw r~gängig machen** to cancel sth; **~grat** (-(e)s, -e) nt spine, backbone; **~halt** m (Unterstützung) backing, support; **~kehr** (-, -en) f return; **~licht** nt back light; **r~lings** adv from behind; backwards; **~nahme** f taking back; **~porto** nt return postage; **~reise** f return journey; (NAUT) home voyage; **~reiseverkehr** m homebound traffic; **~ruf** m recall

Rucksack ['rʊkzak] m rucksack; **~tourist(in)** m(f) backpacker

Rück- zW: **~schau** f reflection; **~schlag** m (plötzliche Verschlechterung) setback; **~schluss ▲** m conclusion;

~schritt m retrogression;
r~schrittlich adj reactionary; retrograde; **~seite** f back; (von Münze etc) reverse; **~sicht** f consideration; **~sicht nehmen auf** +akk to show consideration for; **r~sichtslos** adj inconsiderate; (Fahren) reckless; (unbarmherzig) ruthless; **r~sichtsvoll** adj considerate; **~sitz** m back seat; **~spiegel** m (AUT) rear-view mirror; **~spiel** nt return match; **~sprache** f further discussion od talk; **~stand** m arrears pl; **r~ständig** adj backward, out-of-date; (Zahlungen) in arrears; **~strahler** (-s, -) m rear reflector; **~tritt** m resignation; **~trittbremse** f pedal brake; **~vergütung** f repayment; (COMM) refund; **~versicherung** f reinsurance; **r~wärtig** adj rear; **r~wärts** adv backward(s), back; **~wärtsgang** m (AUT) reverse gear; **~weg** m return journey, way back; **r~wirkend** adj retroactive; **~wirkung** f reaction; retrospective effect; **~zahlung** f repayment; **~zug** m retreat

Rudel ['ruːdəl] (-s, -) nt pack; herd
Ruder ['ruːdər] (-s, -) nt oar; (Steuer) rudder; **~boot** nt rowing boat; **r~n** vt, vi to row
Ruf [ruːf] (-(e)s, -e) m call, cry; (Ansehen) reputation; **r~en** (unreg) vt, vi to call; to cry; **~name** m usual (first) name; **~nummer** f (tele)phone number; **~säule** f (an Autobahn) emergency telephone; **~zeichen** nt (RADIO) call sign; (TEL) ringing tone
rügen ['ryːgən] vt to rebuke
Ruhe ['ruːə] (-) f rest; (Ungestörtheit) peace, quiet; (Gelassenheit, Stille) calm; (Schweigen) silence; **jdn in ~ lassen** to leave sb alone; **sich zur ~ setzen** to retire; **~!** be quiet!, silence!; **r~n** vi to rest; **~pause** f break; **~stand** m retirement; **~stätte** f: **letzte ~stätte** final resting place; **~störung** f breach of

the peace; **~tag** m (von Geschäft) closing day
ruhig ['ruːɪç] adj quiet; (bewegungslos) still; (Hand) steady; (gelassen, friedlich) calm; (Gewissen) clear; **kommen Sie ~ herein** just come on in; **tu das ~** feel free to do that
Ruhm [ruːm] (-(e)s) m fame, glory
rühmen ['ryːmən] vt to praise ♦ vr to boast
Rühr- [ryːr] zW: **~ei** nt scrambled egg; **r~en** vt, vr (auch fig) to move, to stir ♦ vi: **r~en von** to come od stem from; **r~en an** +akk to touch; (fig) to touch on; **r~end** adj touching, moving; **r~selig** adj sentimental, emotional; **~ung** f emotion
Ruin [ru'iːn] (-s, -e) m ruin; **~e** f ruin; **r~ieren** [-'niːrən] vt to ruin
rülpsen ['rʏlpsən] vi to burp, to belch
Rum [rʊm] (-s, -s) m rum
Rumän- [ru'mɛːn] zW: **~ien** (-s) nt Ro(u)mania; **r~isch** adj Ro(u)manian
Rummel ['rʊməl] (-s) (umg) m hubbub; (Jahrmarkt) fair; **~platz** m fairground, fair
Rumpf [rʊmpf] (-(e)s, ⁼e) m trunk, torso; (AVIAT) fuselage; (NAUT) hull
rümpfen ['rʏmpfən] vt (Nase) to turn up
rund [rʊnt] adj round ♦ adv (etwa) around; **~ um etw** round sth; **R~brief** m circular; **R~e** ['rʊndə] f round; (in Rennen) lap; (Gesellschaft) circle; **R~fahrt** f (round) trip
Rundfunk ['rʊntfʊŋk] (-(e)s) m broadcasting; **im ~** on the radio; **~gerät** nt wireless set; **~sendung** f broadcast, radio programme
Rund- zW: **r~heraus** adv straight out, bluntly; **r~herum** adv round about; all round; **r~lich** adj plump, rounded; **~reise** f round trip; **~schreiben** nt (COMM) circular; **r~(wander)weg** m circular path od route
runter ['rʊntər] (umg) adv = herunter;

hinunter

Runzel ['rʊntsəl] (-, -n) f wrinkle; **r~ig** adj wrinkled; **r~n** vt to wrinkle; **die Stirn r~n** to frown

rupfen ['rʊpfən] vt to pluck

ruppig ['rʊpɪç] adj rough, gruff

Rüsche ['ry:ʃə] f frill

Ruß [ru:s] (-es) m soot

Russe ['rʊsə] (-n, -n) m Russian

Rüssel ['rʏsəl] (-s, -) m snout; (Elefantenrüssel) trunk

rußig ['ru:sɪç] adj sooty

Russin ['rʊsɪn] f Russian

russisch adj Russian

Russland ▲ ['rʊslant] (-s) nt Russia

rüsten ['rʏstən] vt to prepare ♦ vi to prepare; (MIL) to arm ♦ vr to prepare (o.s.); to arm o.s.

rüstig ['rʏstɪç] adj sprightly, vigorous

Rüstung ['rʏstʊŋ] f preparation; arming; (Ritterrüstung) armour; (Waffen etc) armaments pl; **~skontrolle** f arms control

Rute ['ru:tə] f rod

Rutsch [rʊtʃ] (-(e)s, -e) m slide; (Erdrutsch) landslide; **~bahn** f slide; **r~en** vi to slide; (ausrutschen) to slip; **r~ig** adj slippery

rütteln ['rʏtəln] vt, vi to shake, to jolt

S, s

S. abk (= Seite) p.; = Schilling

s. abk (= siehe) see

Saal [za:l] (-(e)s, Säle) m hall; room

Saarland ['za:rlant] nt: **das ~** the Saar(land)

Saat [za:t] (-, -en) f seed; (Pflanzen) crop; (Säen) sowing

Säbel ['zɛ:bəl] (-s, -) m sabre, sword

Sabotage [zabo'ta:ʒə] f sabotage

Sach- ['zax] zW: **~bearbeiter** m specialist; **s~dienlich** adj relevant, helpful; **~e** f thing; (Angelegenheit) affair, business; (Frage) matter; (Pflicht) task; **zur ~e** to the point; **s~kundig** adj ex-

pert; **s~lich** adj matter-of-fact; objective; (Irrtum, Angabe) factual

sächlich ['zɛxlɪç] adj neuter

Sachschaden m material damage

Sachsen ['zaksən] (-s) nt Saxony

sächsisch ['zɛksɪʃ] adj Saxon

sacht(e) [zaxt(ə)] adv softly, gently

Sachverständige(r) f(m) expert

Sack [zak] (-(e)s, -e) m sack; **~gasse** f cul-de-sac, dead-end street (US)

Sadismus [za'dɪsmʊs] m sadism

Sadist [za'dɪst] m sadist

säen ['zɛ:ən] vt, vi to sow

Safersex ▲, **Safer Sex** m safe sex

Saft [zaft] (-(e)s, ²e) m juice; (BOT) sap; **s~ig** adj juicy; **s~los** adj dry

Sage ['za:gə] f saga

Säge ['zɛ:gə] f saw; **~mehl** nt sawdust

sagen ['za:gən] vt, vi to say; (mitteilen): **jdm ~** to tell sb; ▶ **Sie ihm, dass ...** tell him ...

sägen vt, vi to saw

sagenhaft adj legendary; (umg) great, smashing

sah etc [za:] vb siehe **sehen**

Sahne ['za:nə] (-) f cream

Saison [zɛ'zõ:] (-, -s) f season

Saite ['zaɪtə] f string

Sakko ['zako] (-s, -s) m od nt jacket

Sakrament [zakra'mɛnt] nt sacrament

Sakristei [zakrɪs'taɪ] f sacristy

Salat [za'la:t] (-(e)s, -e) m salad; (Kopfsalat) lettuce; **~soße** f salad dressing

Salbe ['zalbə] f ointment

Salbei ['zalbaɪ] (-s od -) m od f sage

Saldo ['zaldo] (-s, **Salden**) m balance

Salmiak [zalmi'ak] (-s) m sal ammoniac; **~geist** m liquid ammonia

Salmonellenvergiftung [zalmo-'nɛlən-] f salmonella (poisoning)

salopp [za'lɔp] adj casual

Salpeter [zal'pe:tər] (-s) m saltpetre; **~säure** f nitric acid

Salz [zalts] (-es, -e) nt salt; **s~en** (unreg) vt to salt; **s~ig** adj salty; **~kartoffeln** pl boiled potatoes; **~säure** f hydrochloric acid; **~streuer** m salt cellar; **~wasser** nt (Meerwasser) m seed water

Samen ['zaːmən] (-s, -) m seed; (ANAT) sperm

Sammel- ['zamǝl] zW: **~band** m anthology; **~fahrschein** m multi-journey ticket; (für mehrere Personen) group ticket

sammeln ['zamǝln] vt to collect ♦ vr to assemble, to gather; (konzentrieren) to concentrate

Sammlung ['zamlʊŋ] f collection; assembly, gathering; concentration

Samstag ['zamstaːk] m Saturday; **s~s** adv (on) Saturdays

Samt [zamt] (-(e)s, -e) m velvet; **s~** präp +dat (along) with, together with; **s~ und sonders** each and every one (of them)

sämtlich ['zɛmtlɪç] adj all (the), entire

Sand [zant] (-(e)s, -e) m sand

Sandale [zanˈdaːlǝ] f sandal

Sand- zW: **~bank** f sandbank; **s~ig** ['zandɪç] adj sandy; **~kasten** m sandpit; **~kuchen** m Madeira cake; **~papier** nt sandpaper; **~stein** m sandstone; **s~strahlen** vt, vi insep to sandblast; **~strand** m sandy beach

sandte etc ['zantǝ] vb siehe **senden**

sanft [zanft] adj soft, gentle; **~mütig** adj gentle, meek

sang etc [zaŋ] vb siehe **singen**

Sänger(in) ['zɛŋǝr(ɪn)] (-s, -) m(f) singer

Sani- zW: **s~eren** [zaˈniːrən] vt to redevelop; (Betrieb) to make financially sound ♦ vr to line one's pockets; to become financially sound; **s~tär** [zaniˈtɛːr] adj sanitary; **s~täre Anlagen** sanitation sg; **~täter** [zaniˈtɛːtər] (-s, -) m first-aid attendant; (MIL) (medical) orderly

sanktionieren [zaŋktsioˈniːrən] vt to sanction

Sardelle [zarˈdɛlǝ] f anchovy

Sardine [zarˈdiːnǝ] f sardine

Sarg [zark] (-(e)s, ⁺e) m coffin

Sarkasmus [zarˈkasmʊs] m sarcasm

saß etc [zaːs] vb siehe **sitzen**

Satan ['zaːtan] (-s, -e) m Satan; devil

Satellit [zateˈliːt] (-en, -en) m satellite; **~enfernsehen** nt satellite television

Satire [zaˈtiːrǝ] f satire; **satirisch** adj satirical

satt [zat] adj full; (Farbe) rich, deep; **jdn/etw ~ sein** od **haben** to be fed up with sb/sth; **sich ~ hören/sehen an** +dat to hear/see enough of; **sich ~ essen** to eat one's fill; **~ machen** to be filling

Sattel ['zatǝl] (-s, ⁺) m saddle; (Berg) ridge; **s~n** vt to saddle; **~schlepper** m articulated lorry

sättigen ['zɛtɪɡǝn] vt to satisfy; (CHEM) to saturate

Satz [zats] (-es, ⁺e) m (GRAM) sentence; (Nebensatz, Adverbialsatz) clause; (Theorem) theorem; (MUS) movement; (TENNIS: Briefmarken etc) set; (Kaffee) grounds pl; (COMM) rate; (Sprung) jump; **~teil** m part of a sentence; **~ung** f (Statut) statute, rule; **~zeichen** nt punctuation mark

Sau [zau] (-, Säue) f sow; (umg) dirty pig

sauber ['zaubǝr] adj clean; (ironisch) fine; **~ halten** to keep clean; **S~keit** f cleanness; (einer Person) cleanliness

säuberlich ['zɔybǝrlɪç] adv neatly

säubern vt to clean; (POL etc) to purge; **Säuberung** f cleaning; purge

Sauce ['zoːsǝ] f sauce, gravy

sauer ['zauǝr] adj sour; (CHEM) acid; (umg) cross; **saurer Regen** acid rain; **S~braten** m braised beef marinated in vinegar

Sauerei [zauǝˈrai] (umg) f rotten state of affairs, scandal; (Schmutz etc) mess; (Unanständigkeit) obscenity

Sauerkraut nt sauerkraut, pickled cab-

---

bage

säuerlich ['zɔyɐlɪç] adj (Geschmack) sour; (missvergnügt: Gesicht) dour

Sauer- zW: **~milch** f sour milk; **~rahm** m (KOCH) sour cream; **~stoff** m oxygen; **~teig** m leaven

saufen ['zaʊfən] (unreg) (umg) vt, vi to drink, to booze; **Säufer** ['zɔyfɐ] (-s, -) (umg) m boozer

saugen ['zaʊɡən] (unreg) vt, vi to suck

säugen ['zɔyɡən] vt to suckle

Sauger ['zaʊɡɐ] (-s, -) m dummy, comforter (BRIT); (auf Flasche) teat

Säugetier ['zɔyɡə-] nt mammal

Säugling m infant, baby

Säule ['zɔylə] f column, pillar

Saum [zaʊm] (-(e)s, Säume) m hem; (Naht) seam

säumen ['zɔymən] vt to hem; to seam ◆ vi to delay, to hesitate

Sauna ['zaʊna] (-, -s) f sauna

Säure ['zɔyrə] f acid

sausen ['zaʊzən] vi to blow; (umg: eilen) to rush; (Ohren) to buzz; **etw ~ lassen** (umg) not to bother with sth

Saxofon, Saxophon [zakso'fo:n] (-s, -e) nt saxophone

SB abk = **Selbstbedienung**

S-Bahn f abk (= Schnellbahn) high speed railway; (= Stadtbahn) suburban railway

schaben ['ʃa:bən] vt to scrape

schäbig ['ʃɛːbɪç] adj shabby

Schablone [ʃa'blo:nə] f stencil; (Muster) pattern; (fig) convention

Schach [ʃax] (-s, -s) nt chess; (Stellung) check; **~brett** nt chessboard; **~figur** f chessman; **~matt** adj checkmate; **~spiel** nt game of chess

Schacht [ʃaxt] (-(e)s, ̈e) m shaft

Schachtel (-, -n) f box

schade ['ʃa:də] adj a pity od shame ◆ excl: (wie) ~! what a pity od shame; **sich** dat **zu ~ sein für etw** to consider o.s. too good for sth

Schädel ['ʃɛːdəl] (-s, -) m skull; **~bruch** m fractured skull

Schaden ['ʃa:dən] (-s, ̈) m damage; (Verletzung) injury; (Nachteil) disadvantage; **s~** vi +dat to hurt; **einer Sache s~** to damage sth; **~ersatz** m compensation, damages pl; **~freude** f malicious glee; **s~froh** adj (Mensch, Lachen) gloating; **~sfall** m: **im ~sfall** in the event of a claim

schadhaft ['ʃa:thaft] adj faulty, damaged

schäd- ['ʃɛːt] zW: **~igen** ['ʃɛːdɪɡən] vt to damage; (Person) to do harm to, to harm; **~lich** adj: **~lich (für)** harmful (to); **~lichkeit** f harmfulness; **S~ling** m pest

Schadstoff ['ʃa:tʃtɔf] m harmful substance; **s~arm** adj: **s~arm sein** to contain a low level of harmful substances

Schaf [ʃa:f] (-(e)s, -e) nt sheep

Schäfer ['ʃɛːfɐ] (-s, -e) m shepherd; **~hund** m Alsatian (dog) (BRIT), German shepherd (dog) (US)

schaffen¹ ['ʃafən] (unreg) vt to create; (Platz) to make

schaffen² ['ʃafən] vt (erreichen) to manage, to do; (erledigen) to finish; (Prüfung) to pass; (transportieren) to take ◆ vi (umg: arbeiten) to work; **sich** dat **etw ~** to get o.s. sth; **sich an etw** dat **zu ~ machen** to busy o.s. with sth

Schaffner(in) ['ʃafnɐ(ɪn)] (-s, -) m(f) (Busschaffner) conductor(-tress); (EISENB) guard

Schaft [ʃaft] (-(e)s, ̈e) m shaft; (von Gewehr) stock; (von Stiefel) leg; (BOT) stalk; tree trunk

Schal [ʃa:l] (-s, -e od -s) m scarf

schal adj flat; (fig) insipid

Schälchen ['ʃɛːlçən] nt cup, bowl

Schale ['ʃa:lə] f skin; (abgeschält) peel; (Nussschale, Muschelschale, Eischale) shell; (Geschirr) dish, bowl

schälen ['ʃɛːlən] vt to peel; to shell ◆ vr to peel

Schall [ʃal] (-(e)s, -e) m sound; ~**dämpfer** (-s, -) m (AUT) silencer; s~**dicht** adj soundproof; s~**en** vi to (re)sound; s~**end** adj resounding, loud; ~**mauer** f sound barrier; ~**platte** f (gramophone) record

Schalt- [ʃalt] zW: ~**bild** nt circuit diagram; ~**brett** nt switchboard; s~**en** vi to switch, to turn ♦ vi (AUT) to change (gear); (umg: begreifen) to catch on; ~**er** (-s, -) m counter; (an Gerät) switch; ~**erbeamte(r)** m counter clerk; ~**erstunden** pl hours of business; ~**hebel** m switch; (AUT) gear lever; ~**jahr** nt leap year; ~**ung** f switching; (ELEK) circuit; (AUT) gear change

Scham [ʃa:m] (-) f shame; (~gefühl) modesty; (Organe) private parts pl

schämen [ˈʃɛːmən] vr to be ashamed

schamlos adj shameless

Schande [ˈʃandə] (-) f disgrace

schändlich [ˈʃɛntlɪç] adj disgraceful, shameful

Schändung [ˈʃɛndʊŋ] f violation, defilement

Schanze [ˈʃantsə] f (Sprungschanze) ski jump

Schar [ʃaːr] (-, -en) f band, company; (Vögel) flock; (Menge) crowd; **in ~en** in droves; s~**en** vr to assemble, to rally

scharf [ʃarf] adj sharp; (Essen) hot, spicy; (Munition) live; ~ **nachdenken** to think hard; **auf etw** akk ~ **sein** (umg) to be keen on sth

Schärfe [ˈʃɛrfə] f sharpness; (Strenge) rigour; s~**n** vt to sharpen

Scharf- zW: s~**machen** (umg) vt to stir up; ~**richter** m executioner; ~**schütze** m marksman, sharpshooter; s~**sinnig** adj astute, shrewd

Scharlach [ˈʃarlax] (-s, -e) m (~fieber) scarlet fever

Scharnier [ʃarˈniːr] (-s, -e) nt hinge

scharren [ˈʃarən] vt, vi to scrape, to scratch

Schaschlik [ˈʃaʃlɪk] (-s, -s) m od nt (shish) kebab

Schatten [ˈʃatən] (-s, -) m shadow; ~**riss** ▲ m silhouette; ~**seite** f shady side, dark side

schattieren [ʃaˈtiːrən] vt, vi to shade

schattig [ˈʃatɪç] adj shady

Schatulle [ʃaˈtʊlə] f casket; (Geldschatulle) coffer

Schatz [ʃats] (-es, ⸚e) m treasure; (Person) darling

schätz- [ʃɛts] zW: ~**bar** adj assessable; **S~chen** nt darling, love; ~**en** vt (abschätzen) to estimate; (Gegenstand) to value; (würdigen) to value, to esteem; (vermuten) to reckon; **S~ung** f estimate; estimation; valuation; **nach meiner S~ung** ... I reckon that ...

Schau [ʃaʊ] (-) f show; (Ausstellung) display, exhibition; **etw zur ~ stellen** to make a show of sth, to show off; ~**bild** nt diagram

Schauder [ˈʃaʊdər] (-s, -) m shudder; (wegen Kälte) shiver; s~**haft** adj horrible; s~**n** vi to shudder; to shiver

schauen [ˈʃaʊən] vi to look

Schauer [ˈʃaʊər] (-s, -) m (Regenschauer) shower; (Schreck) shudder; ~**geschichte** f horror story; s~**lich** adj horrific, spine-chilling

Schaufel [ˈʃaʊfəl] (-, -n) f shovel; (NAUT) paddle; (TECH) scoop; s~**n** vt to shovel, to scoop

Schau- zW: ~**fenster** nt shop window; ~**fensterbummel** m window shopping (expedition); ~**kasten** m showcase

Schaukel [ˈʃaʊkəl] (-, -n) f swing; s~**n** vi to swing, to rock; ~**pferd** nt rocking horse; ~**stuhl** m rocking chair

Schaulustige(r) [ˈʃaʊlʊstɪɡə(r)] f(m) onlooker

Schaum [ʃaʊm] (-(e)s, Schäume) m foam; (Seifenschaum) lather; ~**bad** nt bubble bath

schäumen ['ʃɔʏmən] vi to foam

Schaum- zW: **~festiger** (-s, -) m mousse; **~gummi** m foam (rubber); **s~ig** adj frothy, foamy; **~stoff** m foam material; **~wein** m sparkling wine

Schauplatz m scene

schaurig ['ʃaʊrɪç] adj horrific, dreadful

Schauspiel nt spectacle; (THEAT) play; **~er(in)** m(f) actor (actress); **s~ern** vi insep to act; **Schauspielhaus** nt theatre

Scheck [ʃɛk] (-s, -s) m cheque; **~gebühr** f encashment fee; **~heft** m cheque book; **~karte** f cheque card

scheffeln ['ʃɛfəln] vt to amass

Scheibe ['ʃaɪbə] f disc; (Glasscheibe) pane; (MIL) target

Scheiben- zW: **~bremse** f (AUT) disc brake; **~wischer** m (AUT) windscreen wiper

Scheide ['ʃaɪdə] f sheath; (Grenze) boundary; (ANAT) vagina; **s~n** (unreg) vt to separate; (Ehe) to dissolve ♦ vi to depart; to part; **sich s~n lassen** to get a divorce

Scheidung f (Ehescheidung) divorce

Schein [ʃaɪn] (-(e)s, -e) m light; (Anschein) appearance; (Geld) (bank)note; (Bescheinigung) certificate; **zum ~** in pretence; **s~bar** apparent; **s~en** (unreg) vi to shine; (Anschein haben) to seem; **s~heilig** adj hypocritical; **~werfer** (-s, -) m floodlight; spotlight; (Suchscheinwerfer) searchlight; (AUT) headlamp

Scheiß- [ʃaɪs] (-(e)s) (umg) in zW bloody

Scheiße ['ʃaɪsə] (-) (umg) f shit

Scheitel ['ʃaɪtl] (-s, -) m top; (Haarscheitel) parting; **s~n** vt to part

scheitern ['ʃaɪtərn] vi to fail

Schelle ['ʃɛlə] f small bell; **s~n** vi to ring

Schellfisch ['ʃɛlfɪʃ] m haddock

Schelm [ʃɛlm] (-(e)s, -e) m rogue; **s~isch** adj mischievous, roguish

Schelte ['ʃɛltə] f scolding; **s~n** (unreg) vt to scold

Schema ['ʃeːma] (-s, -s od -ta) nt scheme, plan; (Darstellung) schema; **nach ~** quite mechanically; **s~tisch** [ʃeˈmaːtɪʃ] adj schematic; (pej) mechanical

Schemel ['ʃeːml] (-s, -) m (foot)stool

Schenkel ['ʃɛŋkl] (-s, -) m thigh

schenken ['ʃɛŋkən] vt (auch fig) to give; (Getränk) to pour; **sich dat etw ~** (umg) to skip sth; **das ist geschenkt!** (billig) that's a giveaway!; (nichts wert) that's worthless!

Scherbe ['ʃɛrbə] f broken piece, fragment; (archäologisch) potsherd

Schere ['ʃeːrə] f scissors pl; (groß) shears pl; **s~n** (unreg) vt to cut; (Schaf) to shear; (kümmern) to bother ♦ vr to care; **scher dich zum Teufel!** get lost!; **~rei** (umg) f bother, trouble

Scherz [ʃɛrts] (-es, -e) m joke; fun; **~frage** f conundrum; **s~haft** adj joking, jocular

Scheu [ʃɔʏ] (-) f shyness; (Angst) fear; (Ehrfurcht) awe; **s~** adj shy; **s~en** vr: **sich s~en vor** +dat to be afraid of, to shrink from ♦ vt to shun ♦ vi (Pferd) to shy

scheuern ['ʃɔʏərn] vt to scour, to scrub

Scheune ['ʃɔʏnə] f barn

Scheusal ['ʃɔʏzaːl] (-s, -e) nt monster

scheußlich ['ʃɔʏslɪç] adj dreadful, frightful

Schi [ʃiː] m = Ski

Schicht [ʃɪçt] (-, -en) f layer; (Klasse) class, level; (in Fabrik etc) shift; **~arbeit** f shift work; **s~en** vt to layer, to stack

schick [ʃɪk] adj stylish, chic

schicken ['ʃɪkən] vt to send ♦ vr: **sich ~ (in** +akk) to resign o.s. (to) ♦ vb unpers (anständig sein) to be fitting

schicklich adj proper, fitting

Schicksal (-s, -e) nt fate; **~sschlag** m great misfortune, blow

Schieb- [ʃiːb] zW: **~edach** nt (AUT) sun roof; **s~en** (unreg) vt (auch Drogen) to push; (Schuld) to put ♦ vi to push;

~etür f sliding door; **~ung** f fiddle

Schieds- ['ʃiːts] zW: **~gericht** nt court of arbitration; **~richter** m referee; umpire; (Schlichter) arbitrator

schief [ʃiːf] adj crooked; (Ebene) sloping; (Turm) leaning; (Winkel) oblique; (Blick) funny; (Vergleich) distorted ♦ adv crooked(ly); (ansehen) askance; **etw ~ stellen** to slope sth; **~ gehen** (umg) to go wrong

Schiefer ['ʃiːfər] (-s, -) m slate

schielen ['ʃiːlən] vi to squint; **nach etw ~** (fig) to eye sth

schien etc siehe **scheinen**

Schienbein nt shinbone

Schiene ['ʃiːnə] f rail; (MED) splint; **s~n** vt to put in splints

schier [ʃiːr] adj (fig) sheer ♦ adv nearly, almost

Schieß- ['ʃiːs] zW: **~bude** f shooting gallery; **s~en** (unreg) vt to shoot; (Ball) to kick; (Geschoss) to fire ♦ vi to shoot; (Salat etc) to run to seed; **s~en auf** +akk to shoot at; **~e'rei** f shooting incident, shoot-out; **~pulver** nt gunpowder; **~scharte** f embrasure

Schiff [ʃɪf] (-(e)s, -e) nt ship, vessel; (Kirchenschiff) nave; **s~bar** adj (Fluss) navigable; **~bruch** m shipwreck; **s~brüchig** adj shipwrecked; **~chen** nt small boat; (Weben) shuttle; (Mütze) forage cap; **~er** (-s, -) m bargeman, boatman; **~fahrt** f shipping; (Reise) voyage

Schikane [ʃi'kaːnə] f harassment; dirty trick; **mit allen ~n** with all the trimmings

schikanieren [ʃika'niːrən] vt to harass, to torment

Schikoree ▲ ['ʃikore] (-s) m od f = **Chicorée**

Schild¹ [ʃɪlt] (-(e)s, -e) m shield; **etw im ~e führen** to be up to sth

Schild² [ʃɪlt] (-(e)s, -er) nt sign; nameplate; (Etikett) label

Schilddrüse f thyroid gland

schildern ['ʃɪldərn] vt to depict, to portray

Schildkröte f tortoise; (Wasserschildkröte) turtle

Schilf [ʃɪlf] (-(e)s, -e) nt (Pflanze) reed; (Material) reeds pl, rushes pl; **~rohr** nt (Pflanze) reed

schillern ['ʃɪlərn] vi to shimmer; **~d** adj iridescent

Schilling ['ʃɪlɪŋ] m schilling

Schimmel ['ʃɪməl] (-s, -) m mould; (Pferd) white horse; **s~ig** adj mouldy; **s~n** vi to get mouldy

Schimmer ['ʃɪmər] (-s) m (Lichtsein) glimmer; (Glanz) shimmer; **s~n** vi to glimmer, to shimmer

Schimpanse [ʃɪm'panzə] (-n, -n) m chimpanzee

schimpfen ['ʃɪmpfən] vt to scold ♦ vi to curse, to complain; to scold

Schimpfwort nt term of abuse

schinden ['ʃɪndən] (unreg) vt to maltreat, to drive too hard ♦ vr: **sich ~ (mit)** to sweat and strain (at), to toil away (at); **Eindruck ~** (umg) to create an impression

Schinderei f grind, drudgery

Schinken ['ʃɪŋkən] (-s, -) m ham

Schirm [ʃɪrm] (-(e)s, -e) m (Regenschirm) umbrella; (Sonnenschirm) parasol, sunshade; (Wandschirm, Bildschirm) screen; (Lampenschirm) (lamp)shade; (Mützenschirm) peak; (Pilzschirm) cap; **~mütze** f peaked cap; **~ständer** m umbrella stand

schizophren [ʃitso'freːn] adj schizophrenic

Schlacht [ʃlaxt] (-, -en) f battle; **s~en** vt to slaughter, to kill; **~er** (-s, -) m butcher; **~feld** nt battlefield; **~hof** m slaughterhouse, abattoir; **~schiff** nt battleship; **~vieh** nt animals kept for meat; beef cattle

Schlaf [ʃlaːf] (-(e)s) m sleep; **~anzug** m

---

pyjamas *pl*

Schläfe *f* (ANAT) temple

schlafen ['ʃlaːfən] (*unreg*) *vi* to sleep; ~ **gehen** to go to bed; **S~szeit** *f* bedtime

schlaff [ʃlaf] *adj* slack; (*energielos*) limp; (*erschöpft*) exhausted

Schlaf- *zW*: ~**gelegenheit** *f* sleeping accommodation; ~**lied** *nt* lullaby; **s~los** *adj* sleepless; ~**losigkeit** *f* sleeplessness, insomnia; ~**mittel** *nt* sleeping pill

schläfrig ['ʃlɛːfrɪç] *adj* sleepy

Schlaf- *zW*: ~**saal** *m* dormitory; ~**sack** *m* sleeping bag; ~**tablette** *f* sleeping pill; ~**wagen** *m* sleeping car, sleeper; **s~wandeln** *vi insep* to sleepwalk; ~**zimmer** *nt* bedroom

Schlag [ʃlaːk] (-(e)s, ⁻e) *m* (*auch fig*) blow; (*auch* MED) stroke; (*Pulsschlag, Herzschlag*) beat; (ELEK) shock; (*Blitzschlag*) bolt, stroke; (*Autotür*) car door; (*umg*: *Portion*) helping; (*Art*) kind, type; **Schläge** *pl* (*Tracht Prügel*) beating *sg*; **mit einem** ~ all at once; ~ **auf** ~ in rapid succession; ~**ader** *f* artery; ~**anfall** *m* stroke; **s~artig** *adj* sudden, without warning; ~**baum** *m* barrier

Schlägel ['ʃlɛːgəl] (-s, -) *m* (drum)stick; (*Hammer*) mallet, hammer

schlagen ['ʃlaːgən] (*unreg*) *vt, vi* to strike, to hit; (*wiederholt* ~, *besiegen*) to beat; (*Glocke*) to ring; (*Stunde*) to strike; (*Sahne*) to whip; (*Schlacht*) to fight ♦ *vr* to fight; **nach jdm** ~ (*fig*) to take after sb; **sich gut** ~ (*fig*) to do well

Schlager ['ʃlaːgər] (-s, -) *m* (*auch fig*) hit

Schläger ['ʃlɛːgər] *m* brawler; (SPORT) bat; (TENNIS etc) racket; (GOLF) club; (*hockey*) stick; (*Waffe*) rapier; **Schläge'rei** *f* fight, punch-up

Schlagersänger(in) *m(f)* pop singer

Schlag- *zW*: **s~fertig** *adj* quick-witted; ~**fertigkeit** *f* ready wit, quickness of repartee; ~**loch** *nt* pothole; ~**obers**

(ÖSTERR) *nt* = **Schlagsahne**; ~**sahne** *f* (whipped) cream; ~**seite** *f* (NAUT) list; ~**wort** *nt* slogan, catch phrase; ~**zeile** *f* headline; ~**zeug** *nt* percussion; drums *pl*; ~**zeuger** (-s, -) *m* drummer

Schlamassel [ʃla'masəl] (-s, -) (*umg*) *m* mess

Schlamm [ʃlam] (-(e)s, -e) *m* mud; **s~ig** *adj* muddy

Schlamp- *zW*: ~**e** (*umg*) *f* slut; **s~en** (*umg*) *vi* to be sloppy; ~**e'rei** (*umg*) *f* disorder, untidiness; sloppy work; **s~ig** (*umg*) *adj* (*Mensch, Arbeit*) sloppy, messy

Schlange ['ʃlaŋə] *f* snake; (*Menschenschlange*) queue (BRIT), line-up (US); ~ **stehen** to (form a) queue, to line up

schlängeln ['ʃlɛŋəln] *vr* (*Schlange*) to wind; (*Weg*) to wind, twist; (*Fluss*) to meander

Schlangen- *zW*: ~**biss** ▲ *m* snake bite; ~**gift** *nt* snake venom; ~**linie** *f* wavy line

schlank [ʃlaŋk] *adj* slim, slender; **S~heit** *f* slimness, slenderness; **S~heitskur** *f* diet

schlapp [ʃlap] *adj* limp; (*locker*) slack; **S~e** (*umg*) *f* setback

Schlaraffenland [ʃla'rafənlant] *nt* land of milk and honey

schlau [ʃlau] *adj* crafty, cunning

Schlauch [ʃlaux] (-(e)s, Schläuche) *m* hose; (*in Reifen*) inner tube; (*umg*: *Anstrengung*) grind; ~**boot** *nt* rubber dinghy; **s~en** (*umg*) *vt* to tell on, to exhaust

Schläue ['ʃlɔyə] (-) *f* cunning

Schlaufe ['ʃlaufə] *f* loop; (*Aufhänger*) hanger

Schlauheit *f* cunning

schlecht [ʃlɛçt] *adj* bad ♦ *adv* badly; ~ **gelaunt** in a bad mood; ~ **und recht** after a fashion; **jdm ist** ~ sb feels sick *od* bad; **jdm geht es** ~ sb is in a bad way; ~ **machen** to run down; **S~igkeit** *f* badness; bad deed

schlecken ['ʃlɛkən] *vt, vi* to lick

Schlegel ['ʃleːgəl] (-s, -) m (KOCH) leg; siehe **Schlägel**

schleichen ['ʃlaɪçən] (unreg) vi to creep, to crawl; **~d** adj gradual; creeping

Schleichwerbung f (COMM) plug

Schleier ['ʃlaɪər] (-s, -) m veil; **s~haft** (umg) adj: **jdm s~haft sein** to be a mystery to sb

Schleif- ['ʃlaɪf] zW: **~e** f loop; (Band) bow; **s~en¹** vt, vi to drag; **s~en²** (unreg) vt to grind; (Edelstein) to cut; **~stein** m grindstone

Schleim [ʃlaɪm] (-(e)s, -e) m slime; (MED) mucus; (KOCH) gruel; **~haut** f (ANAT) mucous membrane; **s~ig** adj slimy

Schlemm- ['ʃlɛm] zW: **s~en** vi to feast; **~er** (-s, -) m gourmet; **s~erei** f gluttony, feasting

schlendern ['ʃlɛndərn] vi to stroll

schlenkern ['ʃlɛŋkərn] vt, vi to swing, to dangle

Schlepp- ['ʃlɛp] zW: **~e** f train; **s~en** vt to drag; (Auto, Schiff) to tow; (tragen) to lug; **s~end** adj dragging, slow; **~er** (-s, -) m tractor; (Schiff) tug

Schlesien ['ʃleːziən] (-s) nt Silesia

Schleuder ['ʃlɔydər] (-, -n) f catapult; (Wäscheschleuder) spin-drier; (Butterschleuder etc) centrifuge; **~gefahr** f risk of skidding; „Achtung **~gefahr**" "slippery road ahead"; **s~n** vt to hurl; (Wäsche) to spin-dry ♦ vi (AUT) to skid; **~preis** m give-away price; **~sitz** m (AVIAT) ejector seat; (fig) hot seat; **~ware** f cheap or cut-price goods pl

schleunigst ['ʃlɔynɪçst] adv straight away

Schleuse ['ʃlɔyzə] f lock; (~ntor) sluice

schlicht [ʃlɪçt] adj simple, plain; **s~en** vt (glätten) to smooth, to dress; (Streit) to settle; **S~er** (-s, -) m mediator, arbitrator; **S~ung** f settlement; arbitration

Schlick [ʃlɪk] (-(e)s, -e) m mud;

(Ölschlick) slick

schlief etc [ʃliːf] vb siehe **schlafen**

Schließ- ['ʃliːs] zW: **s~en** (unreg) vt to close, to shut; (beenden) to close; (Freundschaft, Bündnis, Ehe) to enter into; (folgern): **s~en (aus)** to infer (from) ♦ vi, vr to close, to shut; **etw in sich s~en** to include sth; **~fach** nt locker; **s~lich** adv finally; **s~lich doch** after all

Schliff [ʃlɪf] (-(e)s, -e) m cut(ting); (fig) polish

schlimm [ʃlɪm] adj bad; **~er** adj worse; **~ste(r, s)** adj worst; **~stenfalls** adv at (the) worst

Schlinge ['ʃlɪŋə] f loop; (bes Henkersschlinge) noose; (Falle) snare; (MED) sling; **s~n** (unreg) vt to wind; (essen) to bolt, to gobble ♦ vi (essen) to bolt one's food, to gobble

schlingern vi to roll

Schlips [ʃlɪps] (-es, -e) m tie

Schlitten ['ʃlɪtən] (-s, -) m sledge, sleigh; **~fahren** (-s) nt tobogganing

schlittern ['ʃlɪtərn] vi to slide

Schlittschuh ['ʃlɪtʃuː] m skate; **~ laufen** to skate; **~bahn** f skating rink; **~läufer(in)** m(f) skater

Schlitz [ʃlɪts] (-es, -e) m slit; (für Münze) slot; (Hosenschlitz) flies pl; **s~äugig** adj slant-eyed

Schloss [ʃlɔs] (-es, **=er**) nt lock; (an Schmuck etc) clasp; (Bau) castle; chateau

schloss ▲ etc vb siehe **schließen**

Schlosser ['ʃlɔsər] (-s, -) m (Autoschlosser) fitter; (für Schlüssel etc) locksmith

Schlosserei [-'raɪ] f metal (working) shop

Schlot [ʃloːt] (-(e)s, -e) m chimney; (NAUT) funnel

schlottern ['ʃlɔtərn] vi to shake, to tremble; (Kleidung) to be baggy

Schlucht [ʃluxt] (-, -en) f gorge, ravine

schluchzen ['ʃluxtsən] vi to sob

Schluck [ʃlʊk] (-(e)s, -e) m swallow; (Menge) drop; **~auf** (-s, -s) m hiccups pl; **s~en** vt, vi to swallow

schludern ['ʃluːdərn] vi to skimp, to do sloppy work

schlug etc [ʃluːk] vb siehe **schlagen**

Schlummer ['ʃlʊmər] (-s) m slumber; **s~n** vi to slumber

Schlund [ʃlʊnt] (-(e)s, ˥e) m gullet; (fig) jaw

schlüpfen ['ʃlʏpfən] vi to slip; (Vogel etc) to hatch (out)

Schlüpfer ['ʃlʏpfər] (-s, -) m panties pl, knickers pl

schlüpfrig ['ʃlʏpfrɪç] adj slippery; (fig) lewd; **S~keit** f slipperiness; (fig) lewdness

schlurfen ['ʃlʊrfən] vi to shuffle

schlürfen ['ʃlʏrfən] vt, vi to slurp

Schluss ▲ [ʃlʊs] (-es, ˥e) m end; (~folgerung) conclusion; am ~ at the end; ~ machen mit to finish with

Schlüssel ['ʃlʏsəl] (-s, -) m (auch fig) key; (Schraubenschlüssel) spanner, wrench; (MUS) clef; **~bein** nt collarbone; **~blume** f cowslip, primrose; **~bund** m bunch of keys; **~dienst** m key cutting service; **~loch** nt keyhole; **~position** f key position; **~wort** nt keyword

schlüssig ['ʃlʏsɪç] adj conclusive

Schluss- ▲ zW: **~licht** nt taillight; (fig) tailender; **~strich** m (fig) final stroke; **~verkauf** m clearance sale

schmächtig ['ʃmɛçtɪç] adj slight

schmackhaft ['ʃmakhaft] adj tasty

schmal [ʃmaːl] adj narrow; (Person, Buch etc) slender, slim; (karg) meagre

schmälern ['ʃmɛːlərn] vt to diminish; (fig) to belittle

Schmalfilm m cine film

Schmalz [ʃmalts] (-es, -e) nt dripping, lard; (fig) sentiment, schmaltz; **s~ig** adj (fig) schmaltzy

schmarotzen [ʃmaˈrɔtsən] vi to sponge; (BOT) to be parasitic; **Schmarotzer** (-s, -) m parasite; sponger

Schmarren ['ʃmarən] (-s, -) m (ÖSTERR) small piece of pancake; (fig) rubbish, tripe

schmatzen ['ʃmatsən] vi to smack one's lips; to eat noisily

schmecken ['ʃmɛkən] vt, vi to taste; es schmeckt ihm he likes it

Schmeichel- ['ʃmaɪçəl] zW: **~ei** [-'laɪ] f flattery; **s~haft** adj flattering; **s~n** vi to flatter

schmeißen ['ʃmaɪsən] (unreg) (umg) vt to throw, to chuck

Schmelz [ʃmɛlts] (-es, -e) m enamel; (Glasur) glaze; (von Stimme) melodiousness; **s~en** (unreg) vi to melt; (Erz) to smelt ♦ vi to melt; **~punkt** m melting point; **~wasser** nt melted snow

Schmerz [ʃmɛrts] (-es, -en) m pain; (Trauer) grief; **s~empfindlich** adj sensitive to pain; **s~en** vt, vi to hurt; **~ensgeld** nt compensation; **s~haft** adj painful; **s~lich** adj painful; **s~los** adj painless; **~mittel** nt painkiller; **~tablette** f painkiller

Schmetterling ['ʃmɛtərlɪŋ] m butterfly

schmettern ['ʃmɛtərn] vt (werfen) to hurl; (TENNIS: Ball) to smash; (singen) to belt out (inf)

Schmied [ʃmiːt] (-(e)s, -e) m blacksmith; **~e** ['ʃmiːdə] f smithy, forge; **~eeisen** nt wrought iron; **s~en** to forge; (Pläne) to devise, to concoct

schmiegen ['ʃmiːgən] vt to press, to nestle ♦ vr: **sich ~ (an +akk)** to cuddle up (to), to nestle (up to)

Schmier- ['ʃmiːr] zW: **~e** f grease; (THEAT) greasepaint, make-up; **s~en** vt to smear; (ölen) to lubricate, to grease; (bestechen) to bribe; (schreiben) to scrawl ♦ vi (schreiben) to scrawl; **~fett** nt grease; **~geld** nt bribe; **s~ig** adj greasy; **~seife** f soft soap

Schminke ['ʃmɪŋkə] f make-up; **s~n** vt, vr to make up

schmirgeln ['ʃmɪrgəln] vt to sand (down)

Schmirgelpapier nt emery paper

schmollen ['ʃmɔlən] vi to sulk, to pout

Schmorbraten m stewed od braised meat

schmoren ['ʃmoːrən] vt to stew, to braise

Schmuck [ʃmʊk] (-(e)s, -e) m jewellery; (Verzierung) decoration

schmücken ['ʃmʏkən] vt to decorate

Schmuck- zW: **s~los** adj unadorned, plain; **~sachen** pl jewels, jewellery sg

Schmuggel ['ʃmʊgəl] (-s) m smuggling; **s~n** vt, vi to smuggle

Schmuggler (-s, -) m smuggler

schmunzeln ['ʃmʊntsəln] vi to smile benignly

schmusen ['ʃmuːzən] (umg) vi (zärtlich sein) to cuddle, to canoodle (inf)

Schmutz [ʃmʊts] (-es) m dirt, filth; **~fink** m filthy creature; **~fleck** m stain; **s~ig** adj dirty

Schnabel ['ʃnaːbəl] (-s, ") m beak, bill; (Ausguss) spout

Schnalle ['ʃnalə] f buckle, clasp; **s~n** vt to buckle

Schnapp- ['ʃnap] zW: **s~en** vt to grab, to catch ♦ vi to snap; **~schloss** ▲ nt spring lock; **~schuss** ▲ m (PHOT) snapshot

Schnaps [ʃnaps] (-es, "e) m spirits pl; schnapps

schnarchen ['ʃnarçən] vi to snore

schnattern ['ʃnatərn] vi (Gänse) to gabble; (Ente) to quack

schnauben ['ʃnaʊbən] vi to snort ♦ vr to blow one's nose

schnaufen ['ʃnaʊfən] vi to puff, to pant

Schnauze f snout, muzzle; (Ausguss) spout; (umg) gob

schnäuzen ▲ ['ʃnɔʏtsən] vr to blow one's nose

Schnecke ['ʃnɛkə] f snail; **~nhaus** nt snail's shell

Schnee [ʃneː] (-s) m snow; (Eischnee)

beaten egg white; **~ball** m snowball; **~flocke** f snowflake; **s~frei** adj free of snow; **~gestöber** nt snowstorm; **~glöckchen** nt snowdrop; **~grenze** f snow line; **~kette** f (AUT) snow chain; **~mann** m snowman; **~pflug** m snowplough; **~regen** m sleet; **~schmelze** f thaw; **~wehe** f snowdrift

Schneide ['ʃnaɪdə] f edge; (Klinge) blade; **s~n** (unreg) vt to cut; (kreuzen) to cross, to intersect with ♦ vr to cut o.s.; to cross, to intersect; **s~nd** adj cutting; **~r** (-s, -) m tailor; **~rei** f (Geschäft) tailor's; **~rin** f dressmaker; **s~rn** vt to make ♦ vi to be a tailor; **~zahn** m incisor

schneien ['ʃnaɪən] vi unpers to snow

Schneise ['ʃnaɪzə] f clearing

schnell [ʃnɛl] adj quick, fast ♦ adv quick, quickly, fast; **S~hefter** (-s, -) m loose-leaf binder; **S~igkeit** f speed; **S~imbiss** ▲ m (Lokal) snack bar; **S~kochtopf** m (Dampfkochtopf) pressure cooker; **S~reinigung** f dry cleaner's; **~stens** adv as quickly as possible; **S~straße** f expressway; **S~zug** m fast od express train

schneuzen △ ['ʃnɔʏtsən] vr siehe **schnäuzen**

schnippeln ['ʃnɪpəln] (umg) vt: **~** (an +dat) to snip (at)

schnippisch ['ʃnɪpɪʃ] adj sharp-tongued

Schnitt (-(e)s, -e) m cut(ting); (~punkt) intersection; (Querschnitt) (cross) section; (Durchschnitt) average; (~muster) pattern; (an Buch) edge; (umg: Gewinn) profit

Schnitt- zW: **~blumen** pl cut flowers; **~e** f slice; (belegt) sandwich; **~fläche** f section; **~lauch** m chive; **~punkt** m (point of) intersection; **~stelle** f (COMPUT) interface; **~wunde** f cut

Schnitz- ['ʃnɪts] zW: **~arbeit** f wood

Spelling Reform: ▲ new spelling △ old spelling (to be phased out)

carving; **~el** (-s, -) *nt* chip; (KOCH) escalope; **s~en** *vt* to carve; **~er** (-s, -) *m* carver; (umg) blunder; **~e'rei** *f* carving; carved woodwork

schnodderig ['ʃnɔdərɪç] (umg) adj snotty

Schnorchel ['ʃnɔrçəl] (-s, -) *m* snorkel

Schnörkel ['ʃnœrkəl] (-s, -) *m* flourish; (ARCHIT) scroll

schnorren ['ʃnɔrən] *vt, vi* to cadge

schnüffeln ['ʃnyfəln] *vi* to sniff

Schnüffler (-s, -) *m* snooper

Schnuller ['ʃnʊlər] (-s, -) *m* dummy, comforter (US)

Schnupfen ['ʃnʊpfən] (-s, -) *m* cold

schnuppern ['ʃnʊpərn] *vi* to sniff

Schnur [ʃnuːr] (-, ⁼e) *f* string, cord; (ELEK) flex

schnüren ['ʃnyːrən] *vt* to tie

schnurgerade adj straight (as a die)

Schnurrbart ['ʃnʊrbaːrt] *m* moustache

schnurren ['ʃnʊrən] *vi* to purr; (Kreisel) to hum

Schnürschuh *m* lace-up (shoe)

Schnürsenkel *m* shoelace

schnurstracks adv straight (away)

Schock [ʃɔk] (-(e)s, -e) *m* shock; **s~ieren** [ʃɔˈkiːrən] *vt* to shock, to outrage

Schöffe ['ʃœfə] (-n, -n) *m* lay magistrate; **Schöffin** *f* lay magistrate

Schokolade [ʃokoˈlaːdə] *f* chocolate

Scholle ['ʃɔlə] *f* clod; (Eisscholle) ice floe; (Fisch) plaice

schon [ʃoːn] adv 1 (bereits) already; **er ist schon da** he's there already, he's already there; **ist er schon da?** is he there yet?; **warst du schon einmal da?** have you ever been there?; **ich war schon einmal da** I've been there before; **das war schon immer so** that has always been the case; **schon oft** often; **hast du schon gehört?** have you heard?

2 (bestimmt) all right; **du wirst schon**

sehen you'll see (all right); **das wird schon noch gut** that'll be OK

3 (bloß) just; **allein schon das Gefühl ...** just the very feeling ...; **schon der Gedanke** the very thought; **wenn ich das schon höre** I only have to hear that

4 (einschränkend): **ja schon, aber ...** yes (well), but ...

5: **schon möglich** possible; **schon gut!** OK!; **du weißt schon** you know; **komm schon!** come on!

schön [ʃøːn] adj beautiful; (nett) nice; **~e Grüße** best wishes; **~e Ferien** have a nice holiday; **~en Dank** (many) thanks; **sich ~ machen** to make o.s. look nice

schonen ['ʃoːnən] *vt* to look after ♦ *vr* to take it easy; **~d** adj careful, gentle

Schön- *zW:* **~heit** *f* beauty; **~heitsfehler** *m* blemish, flaw; **~heitsoperation** *f* cosmetic surgery

Schonkost (-) *f* light diet; (Spezialdiät) special diet

Schon- *zW:* **~ung** *f* good care; (Nachsicht) consideration; (Forst) plantation of young trees; **s~ungslos** adj unsparing, harsh; **~zeit** *f* close season

Schöpf- ['ʃœpf] *zW:* **s~en** *vt* to scoop, to ladle; (Mut) to summon up; (Luft) to breathe in; **~er** (-s, -) *m* creator; **s~erisch** adj creative; **~kelle** *f* ladle; **~ung** *f* creation

Schorf [ʃɔrf] (-(e)s, -e) *m* scab

Schornstein ['ʃɔrnʃtaɪn] *m* chimney; (NAUT) funnel; **~feger** (-s, -) *m* chimney sweep

Schoß [ʃoːs] (-es, ⁼e) *m* lap

schoss ▲ *etc vb siehe* **schießen**

Schoßhund *m* pet dog, lapdog

Schote ['ʃoːtə] *f* pod

Schotte ['ʃɔtə] *m* Scot, Scotsman

Schotter ['ʃɔtər] (-s) *m* broken stone, road metal; (EISENB) ballast

Schott- [ʃɔt] *zW:* **~in** *f* Scot, Scotswoman; **s~isch** adj Scottish, Scots;

~**land** nt Scotland

schraffieren [ʃra'fi:rən] vt to hatch

schräg [ʃrɛːk] adj slanting, not straight; etw ~ **stellen** to put sth at an angle; ~ **gegenüber** diagonally opposite; **S~e** ['ʃrɛːgə] f slant; **S~strich** m oblique stroke

Schramme ['ʃramə] f scratch; **s~n** vt to scratch

Schrank [ʃraŋk] (-(e)s, ⁼e) m cupboard; (Kleiderschrank) wardrobe; ~**e** f barrier; ~**koffer** m trunk

Schraube ['ʃraubə] f screw; **s~n** vt to screw; ~**nschlüssel** m spanner; ~**nzieher** (-s, -) m screwdriver

Schraubstock ['ʃraupʃtɔk] m (TECH) vice

Schreck [ʃrɛk] (-(e)s, -e) m terror; fright; ~**en** (-s, -) m terror; fright; **s~en** vt to frighten; to scare; ~**gespenst** nt spectre, nightmare; **s~haft** adj jumpy, easily frightened; **s~lich** adj terrible, dreadful

Schrei [ʃrai] (-(e)s, -e) m scream; (Ruf) shout

Schreib- ['ʃraib] zW: ~**block** m writing pad; **s~en** (unreg) vt, vi to write; (buchstabieren) to spell; ~**en** (-s, -) nt letter, communication; **s~faul** adj bad about writing letters; ~**kraft** f typist; ~**maschine** f typewriter; ~**papier** nt notepaper; ~**tisch** m desk; ~**ung** f spelling; ~**waren** pl stationery sg; ~**weise** f spelling; way of writing; ~**zentrale** f typing pool; ~**zeug** nt writing materials pl

schreien ['ʃraiən] (unreg) vt, vi to scream; (rufen) to shout; ~**d** adj (fig) glaring; (Farbe) loud

Schrein [ʃrain] (-(e)s, -e) m shrine

Schreiner ['ʃrainər] (-s, -) m joiner; (Zimmermann) carpenter; (Möbelschreiner) cabinetmaker; ~**ei** [-'rai] f joiner's workshop

schreiten ['ʃraitən] (unreg) vi to stride

schrieb etc [ʃri:p] vb siehe **schreiben**

Schrift [ʃrift] (-, -en) f writing; handwriting; (~art) script; (Gedrucktes) pamphlet, work; ~**deutsch** nt written German; ~**führer** m secretary; **s~lich** adj written ♦ adv in writing; ~**sprache** f written language; ~**steller(in)** (-s, -) m(f) writer; ~**stück** nt document; ~**wechsel** m correspondence

schrill [ʃril] adj shrill

Schritt [ʃrit] (-(e)s, -e) m step; (Gangart) walk; (Tempo) pace; (von Hose) crutch; ~ **fahren** to drive at walking pace; ~**macher** (-s, -) m pacemaker; ~**tempo** ▲ nt: im ~**tempo** at a walking pace

schroff [ʃrɔf] adj steep; (zackig) jagged; (fig) brusque

schröpfen ['ʃrœpfən] vt (fig) to fleece

Schrot [ʃro:t] (-(e)s, -e) m od nt (Blei) (small) shot; (Getreide) coarsely ground grain, groats pl; ~**flinte** f shotgun

Schrott [ʃrɔt] (-(e)s, -e) m scrap metal; ~**haufen** m scrap heap; **s~reif** adj ready for the scrap heap

schrubben ['ʃrubən] vt to scrub

Schrubber (-s, -) m scrubbing brush

schrumpfen ['ʃrumpfən] vi to shrink; (Apfel) to shrivel

Schub- ['ʃu:b] zW: ~**fach** nt drawer; ~**karren** m wheelbarrow; ~**lade** f drawer

Schubs [ʃu:ps] (-es, -e) (umg) m shove (inf), push

schüchtern ['ʃʏçtərn] adj shy; **S~heit** f shyness

Schuft [ʃoft] (-(e)s, -e) m scoundrel

schuften (umg) vi to graft, to slave away

Schuh [ʃu:] (-(e)s, -e) m shoe; ~**band** nt shoelace; ~**creme** f shoe polish; ~**größe** f shoe size; ~**löffel** m shoehorn; ~**macher** m shoemaker

Schul- zW: ~**arbeit** f homework (no

pl); **~aufgaben** pl homework sg; **~be-**
such m school attendance; **~buch** nt
school book

Schuld [ʃʊlt] (-, -en) f guilt; (FIN) debt;
(Verschulden) fault; **~ haben** (an +dat)
to be to blame (for); **er hat ~** it's his
fault; **jdm ~ geben** to blame sb; **siehe**
zuschulden; **s~** adj: **s~ sein** (an +dat)
to be to blame (for); **er ist s~** it's his
fault; **s~en** [ʃɔldən] vt to owe;
s~enfrei adj free from debt; **~gefühl**
nt feeling of guilt; **s~ig** adj guilty; (ge-
bührend) due; **s~ig an etw** dat **sein** to
be guilty of sth; **jdm etw s~ig sein** to
owe sb sth; **jdm etw s~ig bleiben** not
to provide sb with sth; **s~los** adj innocent, without guilt; **~ner** (-s, -) m
debtor; **~schein** m promissory note,
IOU

Schule [ʃuːlə] f school; **s~n** vt to train,
to school

Schüler(in) [ʃyːlər(ɪn)] (-s, -) m(f) pupil; **~austausch** m school or student
exchange; **~ausweis** m (school) student card

Schul- zW: **~ferien** pl school holidays;
s~frei adj: **s~freier Tag** holiday; **s~frei**
sein to be a holiday; **~hof** m playground; **~jahr** nt school year; **~kind**
nt schoolchild; **s~pflichtig** adj of
school age; **~schiff** nt (NAUT) training
ship; **~stunde** f period, lesson; **~ta-**
sche f school bag

Schulter [ʃʊltər] (-, -n) f shoulder;
~blatt nt shoulder blade; **s~n** vt to
shoulder

Schulung f education, schooling

Schulzeugnis nt school report

Schund [ʃʊnt] (-(e)s) m trash, garbage

Schuppe [ʃʊpə] f scale; **~n** pl
(Haarschuppen) dandruff sg

Schuppen (-s, -) m shed

schuppig [ʃʊpɪç] adj scaly

Schur [ʃuːr] (-, -en) f shearing

schüren [ʃyːrən] vt to rake; (fig) to stir
up

schürfen [ʃyrfən] vt, vi to scrape, to

scratch; (MIN) to prospect

Schurke [ʃʊrkə] (-n, -n) m rogue

Schurwolle f: „reine ~" "pure new
wool"

Schürze [ʃyrtsə] f apron

Schuss ▲ [ʃʊs] (-es, ‸e) m shot; (WE-
BEN) woof; **~bereich** m effective range

Schüssel [ʃysəl] (-, -n) f bowl

Schuss- ▲ zW: **~linie** f line of fire;
~verletzung f bullet wound; **~waffe** f
firearm

Schuster [ʃuːstər] (-s, -) m cobbler,
shoemaker

Schutt [ʃʊt] (-(e)s) m rubbish;
(Bauschutt) rubble

Schüttelfrost m shivering

schütteln [ʃʏtəln] vt, vr to shake

schütten [ʃʏtən] vt to pour; (Zucker,
Kies etc) to tip; (verschütten) to spill ♦ vi
unpers to pour (down)

Schutthalde f dump

Schutthaufen m heap of rubble

Schutz [ʃʊts] (-es) m protection; (Unterschlupf) shelter; **jdn in ~ nehmen** to
stand up for sb; **~anzug** m overalls pl;
~blech nt mudguard

Schütze [ʃʏtsə] (-n, -n) m gunman;
(Gewehrschütze) rifleman; (Scharf-
schütze, Sportschütze) marksman;
(ASTROL) Sagittarius

schützen [ʃʏtsən] vt to protect; **~ vor**
+dat od **gegen** to protect from

Schützenfest nt fair featuring shooting
matches

Schutz- zW: **~engel** m guardian angel; **~gebiet** nt protectorate; (Naturschutzgebiet) reserve; **~hütte** f shelter, refuge; **~impfung** f immunisation

Schützling [ʃʏtslɪŋ] m protégé(e);
(bes Kind) charge

Schutz- zW: **s~los** adj defenceless;
~mann m policeman; **~patron** m patron saint

Schwaben [ʃvaːbən] nt Swabia;
schwäbisch adj Swabian

schwach [ʃvax] adj weak, feeble

Schwäche [ʃvɛçə] f weakness; **s~n** vt

to weaken
Schwachheit *f* weakness
schwächlich *adj* weakly, delicate
Schwächling *m* weakling
Schwach- zW: **~sinn** *m* imbecility; **s~sinnig** *adj* mentally deficient; (*Idee*) idiotic; **~strom** *m* weak current
Schwächung ['ʃvɛçʊŋ] *f* weakening
Schwager ['ʃvaːgər] (**-s**, **ᵂ**) *m* brother-in-law; **Schwägerin** ['ʃvɛːgərɪn] *f* sister-in-law
Schwalbe ['ʃvalbə] *f* swallow
Schwall [ʃval] (**-(e)s**, **-e**) *m* surge; (*Worte*) flood, torrent
Schwamm [ʃvam] (**-(e)s**, **ᵂe**) *m* sponge; (*Pilz*) fungus
schwamm *etc vb siehe* **schwimmen**
schwammig *adj* spongy; (*Gesicht*) puffy
Schwan [ʃvaːn] (**-(e)s**, **ᵂe**) *m* swan
schwanger ['ʃvaŋər] *adj* pregnant; **S~schaft** *f* pregnancy
schwanken *vi* to sway; (*taumeln*) to stagger, to reel; (*Preise, Zahlen*) to fluctuate; (*zögern*) to hesitate, to vacillate
Schwankung *f* fluctuation
Schwanz [ʃvants] (**-es**, **ᵂe**) *m* tail
schwänzen ['ʃvɛntsən] (*umg*) *vt* to skip, to cut ♦ *vi* to play truant
Schwarm [ʃvarm] (**-(e)s**, **ᵂe**) *m* swarm; (*umg*) heart-throb, idol
schwärm- ['ʃvɛrm] zW: **~en** *vi* to swarm; **~en für** to be mad *od* wild about; **S~erei** [-əˈraɪ] *f* enthusiasm; **~erisch** *adj* impassioned, effusive
Schwarte ['ʃvartə] *f* hard skin; (*Speckschwarte*) rind
schwarz [ʃvarts] *adj* black; **~es Brett** notice board; **ins S~e treffen** (*auch fig*) to hit the bull's eye; **~ in den ~en Zahlen** in the black; **~ sehen** (*umg*) to see the gloomy side of things; **S~arbeit** *f* illicit work, moonlighting; **S~brot** *nt* black bread; **S~e(r)** *f(m)*

black (man/woman)
Schwärze ['ʃvɛrtsə] *f* blackness; (*Farbe*) blacking; (*Druckerschwärze*) printer's ink; **s~n** *vt* to blacken
Schwarz- zW: **s~fahren** (*unreg*) *vi* to travel without paying; to drive without a licence; **~handel** *m* black market (trade); **~markt** *m* black market; **~wald** *m* Black Forest; **s~weiß**, **s~weiß** *adj* black and white
schwatzen ['ʃvatsən] *vi* to chatter
schwätzen ['ʃvɛtsən] *vi* to chatter
Schwätzer ['ʃvɛtsər] (**-s**, **-**) *m* gasbag
schwatzhaft *adj* talkative, gossipy
Schwebe ['ʃveːbə] *f*: **in der ~** (*fig*) in abeyance; **~bahn** *f* overhead railway; **s~n** *vi* to drift, to float; (*hoch*) to soar
Schwed- ['ʃveːd] zW: **~e** *m* Swede; **~en** *nt* Sweden; **~in** *f* Swede; **s~isch** *adj* Swedish
Schwefel ['ʃveːfəl] (**-s**) *m* sulphur; **s~ig** *adj* sulphurous; **~säure** *f* sulphuric acid
Schweig- ['ʃvaɪg] zW: **~egeld** *nt* hush money; **~en** (**-s**) *nt* silence; **s~en** (*unreg*) *vi* to be silent; to stop talking; **~epflicht** *f* pledge of secrecy; (*von Anwalt*) requirement of confidentiality; **s~sam** ['ʃvaɪkzaːm] *adj* silent, taciturn; **~samkeit** *f* taciturnity, quietness
Schwein [ʃvaɪn] (**-(e)s**, **-e**) *nt* pig; (*umg*) (good) luck
Schweine- zW: **~fleisch** *nt* pork; **~rei** *f* mess; (*Gemeinheit*) dirty trick; **~stall** *m* pigsty
schweinisch *adj* filthy
Schweinsleder *nt* pigskin
Schweiß [ʃvaɪs] (**-es**) *m* sweat, perspiration; **s~en** *vt, vi* to weld; **~er** (**-s**, **-**) *m* welder; **~füße** *pl* sweaty feet; **~naht** *f* weld
Schweiz [ʃvaɪts] *f* Switzerland; **~er(in)** *m(f)* Swiss; **s~erisch** *adj* Swiss
schwelgen ['ʃvɛlgən] *vi* to indulge

Spelling Reform: ▲ new spelling △ old spelling (to be phased out)

Schwelle ['ʃvɛlə] f (auch fig) threshold; doorstep; (EISENB) sleeper (BRIT), tie (US)

schwellen (unreg) vi to swell

Schwellung f swelling

Schwemme ['ʃvɛmə] f (WIRTS: Überangebot) surplus

Schwenk- ['ʃvɛŋk] zW: **~bar** adj swivel-mounted; **s~en** vt to swing; (Fahne) to wave; (abspülen) to rinse ♦ vi to turn, to swivel; (MIL) to wheel; **~ung** f turn; wheel

schwer [ʃveːr] adj heavy; (schwierig) difficult, hard; (schlimm) serious, bad ♦ adv (sehr) very (much); (verletzt etc) seriously, badly; **~ erziehbar** difficult (to bring up); **jdm ~ machen** to make sth difficult for sb/o.s.; **~ nehmen** to take to heart; **sich dat od akk ~ tun** to have difficulties; **~ verdaulich** indigestible, heavy; **~ wiegend** weighty, important; **S~arbeiter** m manual worker, labourer; **S~behinderte(r)** f(m) seriously handicapped person; **S~e** f weight, heaviness; (PHYS) gravity; **~elos** adj weightless; (Kammer) zero-G; **~fällig** adj ponderous; **S~gewicht** nt heavyweight; (fig) emphasis; **~hörig** adj hard of hearing; **S~industrie** f heavy industry; **S~kraft** f gravity; **S~kranke(r)** f(m) person who is seriously ill; **~lich** adv hardly; **~mütig** adj melancholy; **S~punkt** m centre of gravity; (fig) emphasis, crucial point

Schwert [ʃveːrt] (-(e)s, -er) nt sword; **~lilie** f iris

schwer- zW: **S~verbrecher(in)** m(f) criminal, serious offender; **S~verletzte(r)** f(m) serious casualty; (bei Unfall usw auch) seriously injured person

Schwester ['ʃvɛstər] (-, -n) f sister; (MED) nurse; **~lich** adj sisterly

Schwieger- ['ʃviːɡər] zW: **~eltern** pl parents-in-law; **~mutter** f mother-in-law; **~sohn** m son-in-law; **~tochter** f daughter-in-law; **~vater** m father-in-law

schwierig ['ʃviːrɪç] adj difficult, hard; **S~keit** f difficulty

Schwimm- ['ʃvɪm] zW: **~bad** nt swimming baths pl; **~becken** nt swimming pool; **s~en** (unreg) vi to swim; (treiben nicht sinken) to float; (fig: unsicher sein) to be all at sea; **~er (-s, -)** m swimmer; (Angeln) float; **~erin** f (female) swimmer; **~lehrer** m swimming instructor; **~weste** f life jacket

Schwindel ['ʃvɪndəl] (-s) m giddiness; dizzy spell; (Betrug) swindle, fraud, (Zeug) stuff; **s~frei** adj: **s~frei sein** to have a good head for heights; **s~n** (umg) vi (lügen) to fib; **jdm s~t es** sb feels dizzy

schwinden ['ʃvɪndən] (unreg) vi to disappear; (sich verringern) to decrease; (Kräfte) to decline

Schwindler ['ʃvɪndlər] m swindler; (Lügner) liar

schwindlig adj dizzy; **mir ist ~** I feel dizzy

Schwing- ['ʃvɪŋ] zW: **s~en** (unreg) vt to swing; (Waffe etc) to brandish ♦ vi to swing; (vibrieren) to vibrate; (klingen) to sound; **~tür** f swing door(s); **~ung** f vibration; (PHYS) oscillation

Schwips [ʃvɪps] (-es, -e) m: **einen ~ haben** to be tipsy

schwirren ['ʃvɪrən] vi to buzz

schwitzen ['ʃvɪtsən] vi to sweat, to perspire

schwören ['ʃvøːrən] (unreg) vt, vi to swear

schwul [ʃvuːl] (umg) adj gay, queer

schwül [ʃvyːl] adj sultry, close; **S~e (-)** f sultriness

Schwule(r) (umg) f(m) gay (man/woman)

Schwung [ʃvʊŋ] (-(e)s, -̈e) m swing; (Triebkraft) momentum; (fig: Energie) verve, energy; (umg: Menge) batch; **s~haft** adj brisk, lively; **s~voll** adj vigorous

Schwur [ʃvuːr] (-(e)s, ˸e) *m* oath; **~gericht** *nt* court with a jury

sechs [zɛks] *num* six; **~hundert** *num* six hundred; **~te(r, s)** *adj* sixth; **S~tel** (-s, -) *nt* sixth

sechzehn ['zɛçtseːn] *num* sixteen

sechzig ['zɛçtsɪç] *num* sixty

See¹ [zeː] (-, -n) *f* sea

See² [zeː] (-s, -n) *m* lake

See- [zeː] *zW:* **~bad** *nt* seaside resort; **~hund** *m* seal; **~igel** ['zeːʔiːgəl] *m* sea urchin; **s~krank** *adj* seasick; **~krankheit** *f* seasickness; **~lachs** *m* rock salmon

Seele ['zeːlə] *f* soul; **s~nruhig** *adv* calmly

Seeleute ['zeːlɔytə] *pl* seamen

Seel- *zW:* **s~isch** *adj* mental; **~sorge** *f* pastoral duties *pl*; **~sorger** (-s, -) *m* clergyman

See- *zW:* **~macht** *f* naval power; **~mann** (*pl* -leute) *m* seaman, sailor; **~meile** *f* nautical mile; **~möwe** *f* (*ZOOL*) seagull; **~not** *f* distress; **~räuber** *m* pirate; **~rose** *f* water lily; **~stern** *m* starfish; **s~tüchtig** *adj* seaworthy; **~weg** *m* sea route; **auf dem ~weg** by sea; **~zunge** *f* sole

Segel ['zeːgəl] (-s, -) *nt* sail; **~boot** *nt* yacht; **~fliegen** (-s) *nt* gliding; **~flieger** *m* glider pilot; **~flugzeug** *nt* glider; **s~n** *vt, vi* to sail; **~schiff** *nt* sailing vessel; **~sport** *m* sailing; **~tuch** *nt* canvas

Segen ['zeːgən] (-s, -) *m* blessing

Segler ['zeːglər] (-s, -) *m* sailor, yachtsman

segnen ['zeːgnən] *vt* to bless

Seh- ['zeː] *zW:* **s~behindert** *adj* partially sighted; **s~en** (*unreg*) *vt, vi* to see; (*in bestimmte Richtung*) to look; **mal s~en(, ob ...)** let's see (if ...); **siehe Seite 5** see page 5; **s~enswert** *adj* worth seeing; **~enswürdigkeiten** *pl* sights (of a town); **~fehler** *m* sight de-

fect

Sehne ['zeːnə] *f* sinew; (*an Bogen*) string

sehnen *vr:* **sich ~ nach** to long for, yearn for

sehnig *adj* sinewy

Sehn- *zW:* **s~lich** *adj* ardent; **~sucht** *f* longing; **s~süchtig** *adj* longing

sehr [zeːr] *adv* very; (*mit Verben*) a lot, (very) much; **zu ~** too much; **~ geehrte(r) ... dear ...**

seicht [zaɪçt] *adj* (*auch fig*) shallow

Seide ['zaɪdə] *f* silk; **s~n** *adj* silk; **~npapier** *nt* tissue paper

seidig ['zaɪdɪç] *adj* silky

Seife ['zaɪfə] *f* soap

Seifen- *zW:* **~lauge** *f* soapsuds *pl*; **~schale** *f* soap dish; **~schaum** *m* lather

seihen ['zaɪən] *vt* to strain, to filter

Seil [zaɪl] (-(e)s, -e) *nt* rope; cable; **~bahn** *f* cable railway; **~hüpfen** (-s) *nt* skipping; **~springen** (-s) *nt* skipping; **~tänzer(in)** *m(f)* tightrope walker

---

sein [zaɪn] (*pt* **war**, *pp* **gewesen**) *vi*
1 to be; **ich bin** I am; **du bist** you are; **er/sie/es ist** he/she/it is; **wir sind/ihr seid/sie sind** we/you/they are; **wir waren** we were; **wir sind gewesen** we have been

2: seien Sie nicht böse don't be angry; **sei so gut und ...** be so kind as to ...; **das wäre gut** that would *od* that'd be a good thing; **wenn ich Sie wäre** if I were *od* was you; **das wärs** that's all, that's it; **morgen bin ich in Rom** tomorrow I'll *od* I will *od* I shall be in Rome; **waren Sie mal in Rom?** have you ever been to Rome?

3: wie ist das zu verstehen? how is that to be understood?; **er ist nicht zu ersetzen** he cannot be replaced;

---

mit ihr ist nicht zu reden you can't talk to her

4: mir ist kalt I'm cold; **was ist? was?** what's the matter?, what is it?; **ist was?** is something the matter?; **es sei denn, dass ... unless ...; wie dem auch sei** be that as it may; **wie wäre es mit ...?** how od what about ...?; **lass das sein!** stop that!

sein(e) [ˈzaɪn(ə)] adj his; its; **~e(r, s)** pron his; its; **~er** (gen von **er**) pron of him; **~erseits** adv for his part; **~erzeit** adv in those days, formerly; **~esgleichen** pron people like him; (wegen ihm) on his account; (von ihm aus) as far as he is concerned; (um seinetwillen) **~etwillen** adv: **um ~etwillen = seinetwegen; ~ige** pron: **der/die/das ~ige** od **S~ige** his

seit [zaɪt] präp +dat since ♦ konj since; **er ist ~ einer Woche hier** he has been here for a week; **~ langem** for a long time; **~dem** [zaɪtˈdeːm] adv, konj since

Seite [ˈzaɪtə] f side; (Buchseite) page; (MIL) flank

Seiten- zW: **~ansicht** f side view; **~hieb** m (fig) passing shot, dig; **s~s** präp +gen on the part of; **~schiff** nt aisle; **~sprung** m extramarital escapade; **~stechen** nt (a) stitch; **~straße** f side road; **~streifen** m verge; (der Autobahn) hard shoulder

seither [zaɪtˈheːr] adv, konj since (then)

seit- zW: **~lich** adj on one od the side; side cpd; **~wärts** adv sidewards

Sekretär [zekreˈtɛːr] m secretary; (Möbel) bureau

Sekretariat [zekretaˈriaːt] (-(e)s, -e) nt secretary's office, secretariat

Sekretärin f secretary

Sekt [zɛkt] (-(e)s, -e) m champagne

Sekte [ˈzɛktə] f sect

Sekunde [zeˈkʊndə] f second

selber [ˈzɛlbər] = **selbst**

Selbst [zɛlpst] (-) nt self

selbst [zɛlpst] pron 1: **ich/er/wir selbst** I myself/he himself/we ourselves; **sie ist die Tugend selbst** she's virtue itself; **er braut sein Bier selbst** he brews his own beer; **wie geht's? - gut, und selbst?** how are things? - fine, and yourself?

2 (ohne Hilfe) alone, on my/his/one's etc own; own; **von selbst** by itself; **er kam von selbst** he came of his own accord; **selbst gemacht** home-made ♦ adv even; **selbst wenn** even if; **selbst Gott** even God (himself)

selbständig etc [ˈzɛlpʃtɛndɪç] = **selbständig** etc

Selbst- zW: **~auslöser** m (PHOT) delayed-action shutter release; **~bedienung** f self-service; **~befriedigung** f masturbation; **~beherrschung** f self-control; **~bestimmung** f (POL) self-determination; **~beteiligung** f (VERSICHERUNG: bei Kosten) (voluntary) excess; **s~bewusst** ▲ adj (self-)confident; **~bewusstsein** ▲ nt self-confidence; **~erhaltung** f self-preservation; **~erkenntnis** f self-knowledge; **s~gefällig** adj smug, self-satisfied; **~gespräch** nt conversation with o.s.; **~kostenpreis** m cost price; **s~los** adj unselfish, selfless; **~mord** m suicide; **~mörder(in)** m(f) suicide; **s~mörderisch** adj suicidal; **s~sicher** adj self-assured; **s~ständig** ▲ adj independent; **~ständigkeit** f independence; **s~süchtig** adj (Mensch) selfish; **~versorger** (-s, -) m (im Urlaub etc) self-caterer; **s~verständlich** [ˈzɛlpstfɛrˈʃtɛntlɪç] adj obvious ♦ adv naturally; **ich halte das für s~verständlich** I take that for granted; **~verteidigung** f self-defence; **~vertrauen** nt self-confidence; **~verwaltung** f autonomy, self-government

selig ['ze:lɪç] *adj* happy, blissful; (REL) blessed; (tot) late; **S~keit** *f* bliss

Sellerie ['zɛləri:] (-s, -(s) od -, -) *m* od *f* celery

selten ['zɛltən] *adj* rare ♦ *adv* seldom, rarely; **S~heit** *f* rarity

Selterswasser ['zɛltərsvasər] *nt* soda water

seltsam ['zɛltza:m] *adj* strange, curious; **S~keit** *f* strangeness

Semester [ze'mɛstər] (-s, -) *nt* semester; **~ferien** *pl* vacation *sg*

Semi- [zemi] *zW* semi-; **~kolon** [-'ko:lɔn] *nt* semicolon

Seminar [zemi'na:r] (-s, -e) *nt* seminary; (*Kurs*) seminar; (UNIV: *Ort*) department building

Semmel ['zɛməl] (-, -n) *f* roll

Senat [ze'na:t] (-(e)s, -e) *m* senate, council

Sende- ['zɛndə] *zW*: **~bereich** *m* transmission range; **~folge** *f* (*Serie*) series; **s~n** (*unreg*) *vt* to send; (RADIO, TV) to transmit, to broadcast ♦ *vi* to transmit, to broadcast; **~r** (-s, -) *m* station; (*Anlage*) transmitter; **~reihe** *f* series (of broadcasts)

Sendung ['zɛndʊŋ] *f* consignment; (*Aufgabe*) mission; (RADIO, TV) transmission; (*Programm*) programme

Senf [zɛnf] (-(e)s, -e) *m* mustard

senil [ze'ni:l] (*pej*) *adj* senile

Senior(in) ['ze:niɔr(ɪn)] (-s, -en) *m(f)* (*Mensch im Rentenalter*) (old age) pensioner

Seniorenheim [zeni'o:rənhaɪm] *nt* old people's home

Senk- ['zɛŋk] *zW*: **~blei** *nt* plumb; **~e** *f* depression; **s~en** *vt* to lower ♦ *vr* to sink, to drop gradually; **s~recht** *adj* vertical, perpendicular; **~rechte** *f* perpendicular; **~rechtstarter** *m* (AVIAT) vertical take-off plane; (*fig*) high-flyer

Sensation [zɛnzatsi'o:n] *f* sensation; **s~ell** [-'nɛl] *adj* sensational

sensibel [zɛn'zi:bəl] *adj* sensitive

sentimental [zɛntimɛn'ta:l] *adj* sentimental; **S~ität** *f* sentimentality

separat [zepa'ra:t] *adj* separate

September [zɛp'tɛmbər] (-(s), -) *m* September

Serie ['ze:riə] *f* series

serien- *zW*: **~mäßig** *adj* standard; **S~mörder(in)** *m(f)* serial killer; **~weise** *adv* in series

seriös [zeri'ø:s] *adj* serious, bona fide

Service[1] [zɛr'vi:s] (-(s), -) *nt* (*Geschirr*) set, service

Service[2] (-, -s) *m* service

servieren [zɛr'vi:rən] *vt, vi* to serve

Serviererin [zɛr'vi:rərɪn] *f* waitress

Serviette [zɛrvi'ɛtə] *f* napkin, serviette

Servo- ['zɛrvo] *zW*: **~bremse** *f* (AUT) servo(-assisted) brake; **~lenkung** *f* (AUT) power steering

Sessel ['zɛsəl] (-s, -) *m* armchair; **~lift** *m* chairlift

sesshaft ▲ ['zɛshaft] *adj* settled; (*ansässig*) resident

setzen ['zɛtsən] *vt* to put, to set; (*Baum etc*) to plant; (*Segel, TYP*) to set ♦ *vr* to settle; (*Person*) to sit down ♦ *vi* (*springen*) to leap; (*wetten*) to bet

Setz- ['zɛts] *zW*: **~er** (-s, -) *m* (TYP) compositor; **~ling** *m* young plant

Seuche ['zɔyçə] *f* epidemic; **~ngebiet** *nt* infected area

seufzen ['zɔyftsən] *vt, vi* to sigh

Seufzer ['zɔyftsər] (-s, -) *m* sigh

Sex [zɛks] (-(es)) *m* sex; **~ualität** [-uali'tɛt] *f* sex, sexuality; **~ualkunde** [zɛksu'a:l-] *f* (SCH) sex education; **s~uell** [-u'ɛl] *adj* sexual

Shampoo [ʃam'pu:] (-s) *nt* shampoo

Sibirien [zi'bi:riən] *nt* Siberia

SCHLÜSSELWORT

sich [zɪç] *pron* 1 (*akk*): **er/sie/es ... sich** he/she/it ... himself/herself/itself; **sie**

---

pl/man they/one ... themselves/ oneself; **Sie ... sich** you ... yourself/ yourselves pl; **sich wiederholen** to repeat oneself/itself

2 (dat): **er/sie/es ... sich** he/she/it ... to himself/herself/itself; **sie** pl/**man ... sich** they/one ... to themselves/ oneself; **Sie ... sich** you ... to yourself/yourselves pl; **sie hat sich einen Pullover gekauft** she bought herself a jumper; **sich die Haare waschen** to wash one's hair

3 (mit Präposition): **haben Sie Ihren Ausweis bei sich?** do you have your pass on you?; **er hat nichts bei sich** he's got nothing on him; **sie bleiben gern unter sich** they keep themselves to themselves

4 (einander) each other, one another; **sie bekämpfen sich** they fight each other and one another

5: **dieses Auto fährt sich gut** this car drives well; **hier sitzt es sich gut** it's good to sit here

Sichel ['zıçəl] (-, -n) f sickle; (Mondsichel) crescent

sicher ['zıçər] adj safe; (gewiss) certain; (zuverlässig) secure, reliable; (selbstsicher) confident; **vor jdm/etw ~ sein** to be safe from sb/sth; **ich bin nicht ~** I'm not sure of certain; **~ nicht** surely not; **aber ~!** of course!; **~gehen** (unreg) vi to make sure

Sicherheit ['zıçərhaıt] f safety; (auch FIN) security; (Gewissheit) certainty; (Selbstsicherheit) confidence

Sicherheits– zW: **~abstand** m safe distance; **~glas** nt safety glass; **~gurt** m safety belt; **s~halber** adv for safety; to be on the safe side; **~nadel** f safety pin; **~schloss** ▲ nt safety lock; **~vorkehrung** f safety precaution

sicher– zW: **~lich** adv certainly, surely; **~n** vt to secure; (schützen) to protect; (Waffe) to put the safety catch on; **jdm etw ~n** to secure sth for sb; **sich**

dat etw ~n to secure sth (for o.s.); **~stellen** vt to impound; (COMPUT) to save; **S~ung** f (S~n) securing; (Vorrichtung) safety device; (an Waffen) safety catch; (ELEK) fuse; **S~ungskopie** f back-up copy

Sicht [zıçt] (-) f sight; (Aussicht) view; **auf o nach ~** (FIN) at sight; **auf lange ~** on a long-term basis; **s~bar** adj visible; **s~en** vt to sight; (auswählen) to sort out; **s~lich** adj evident, obvious; **~verhältnisse** pl visibility sg; **~vermerk** m visa; **~weite** f visibility

sickern ['zıkərn] vi to trickle, to seep

Sie [zi:] (nom, akk) pron you

sie [zi:] pron (sg: nom) she, it; (: akk) her, it; (pl: nom) they; (: akk) them

Sieb [zi:p] (-(e)s, -e) nt sieve; (KOCH) strainer; **s~en¹** ['zi:bən] vt or sift; (Flüssigkeit) to strain

sieben² num seven; **~hundert** num seven hundred; **S~sachen** pl belongings

siebte(r, s) ['zi:ptə(r, s)] adj seventh; **S~l** (-s, -) nt seventh

siebzehn ['zi:ptse:n] num seventeen

siebzig ['zi:ptsıç] num seventy

siedeln ['zi:dəln] vi to settle

sieden ['zi:dən] vt, vi to boil, to simmer

Siedepunkt m boiling point

Siedler (-s, -) m settler

Siedlung f settlement; (Häusersiedlung) housing estate

Sieg [zi:k] (-(e)s, -e) m victory

Siegel ['zi:gəl] (-s, -) nt seal; **~ring** m signet ring

Sieg– zW: **s~en** vi to be victorious; (SPORT) to win; **~er** (-s, -) m victor; (SPORT etc) winner; **s~reich** adj victorious

siehe etc ['zi:ə] vb siehe sehen

siezen ['zi:tsən] vt to address as "Sie"

Signal [zı'gna:l] (-s, -e) nt signal

Silbe ['zılbə] f syllable

Silber ['zılbər] (-s) nt silver; **~hochzeit** f silver wedding (anniversary); **s~n** adj

silver; **~papier** nt silver paper
Silhouette [zilu'etə] f silhouette
Silvester [zil'vestər] **(-s, -)** nt New Year's Eve, Hogmanay (SCOTTISH); **~abend** m = Silvester

---

Silvester

Silvester is the German word for New Year's Eve. Although not an official holiday most businesses close early and shops shut at midday. Most Germans celebrate in the evening, and at midnight they let off fireworks and rockets, the revelry usually lasts until the early hours of the morning.

---

simpel ['zimpəl] adj simple
Sims [zims] **(-es, -e)** nt od m (Kaminsims) mantelpiece; (Fenstersims) (window)sill
simulieren [zimu'li:rən] vt to simulate; (vortäuschen) to feign ♦ vi to feign illness
simultan [zimol'ta:n] adj simultaneous
Sinfonie [zɪnfo'ni:] f symphony
singen ['zɪŋən] (unreg) vt, vi to sing
Singular ['zɪŋgula:r] m singular
Singvogel ['zɪŋfo:gəl] m songbird
sinken ['zɪŋkən] (unreg) vi to sink; (Preise etc) to fall, to go down
Sinn [zin] **(-(e)s, -e)** m mind; (Wahrnehmungssinn) sense; (Bedeutung) sense, meaning; **~ für etw** sense of sth; **von ~en sein** to be out of one's mind; **es hat keinen ~** there's no point; **~bild** nt symbol; **s~en** (unreg) vi to ponder; **auf etw akk s~en** to contemplate sth; **~estäuschung** f illusion; **s~gemäß** adj (Wiedergabe) in one's own words; **s~ig** adj clever; **s~lich** adj sensual, sensuous; (Wahrnehmung) sensory; **~lichkeit** f sensuality; **s~los** adj senseless; meaningless; **~losigkeit** f senselessness; meaninglessness; **s~voll** adj meaning-

ful; (vernünftig) sensible
Sintflut ['zintflu:t] f Flood
Sippe ['zɪpə] f clan, kin
Sippschaft ['zɪpʃaft] (pej) f relations pl, tribe; (Bande) gang
Sirene [zi're:nə] f siren
Sirup ['zi:rup] **(-s, -e)** m syrup
Sitt- ['zɪt] zW: **~e** f custom; **~en** pl (~lichkeit) morals; **~enpolizei** f vice squad; **s~sam** adj modest, demure
Situation [zituatsi'o:n] f situation
Sitz [zɪts] **(-es, -e)** m seat; der Anzug hat einen guten ~ the suit is a good fit; **s~en** (unreg) vi to sit; (Bemerkung, Schlag) to strike home, to tell; (Gelerntes) to have sunk in; **s~en bleiben** to remain seated; (SCH) to have to repeat a year; **auf etw dat s~en bleiben** to be lumbered with sth; **s~en lassen** (SCH) to make (sb) repeat a year; (Mädchen) to jilt; (Wartenden) to stand up; **etw auf sich dat s~en lassen** to take sth lying down; **s~end** adj (Tätigkeit) sedentary; **~gelegenheit** f place to sit down; **~platz** m seat; **~streik** m sit-down strike; **~ung** f meeting
Sizilien [zi'tsi:liən] nt Sicily
Skala ['ska:la] **(-, Skalen)** f scale
Skalpell [skal'pɛl] **(-s, -e)** nt scalpel
Skandal [skan'da:l] **(-s, -e)** m scandal; **s~ös** [-'lø:s] adj scandalous
Skandinav- [skandi'na:v] zW: **~ien** nt Scandinavia; **~ier(in)** m(f) Scandinavian; **s~isch** adj Scandinavian
Skelett [ske'lɛt] **(-(e)s, -e)** nt skeleton
Skepsis ['skɛpsis] **(-)** f scepticism
skeptisch ['skɛptɪʃ] adj sceptical
Ski [ʃi:] **(-s, -er)** m ski; **~ laufen** od **fahren** to ski; **~fahrer** m skier; **~gebiet** nt ski(ing) area; **~läufer** m skier; **~lehrer** m ski instructor; **~lift** m ski-lift; **s~springen** nt ski-jumping; **~stock** m ski-pole
Skizze ['skɪtsə] f sketch
skizzieren [skɪ'tsi:rən] vt, vi to sketch

Spelling Reform: ▲ new spelling △ old spelling (to be phased out)

Sklave

Sklave ['skla:və] (-n, -n) m slave; **~'rei** f slavery; **Sklavin** f slave

Skonto ['skɔnto] (-s, -s) m od nt discount

Skorpion [skɔrpi'o:n] (-s, -e) m scorpion; (ASTROL) Scorpio

Skrupel ['skru:pəl] (-s, -) m scruple; **s~los** adj unscrupulous

Skulptur [skʊlp'tu:r] f sculpture

S-Kurve ['ɛskʊrvə] f S-bend

Slip [slɪp] (-s, -s) m (under)pants; **~einlage** f panty liner

Slowakei [slova'kaɪ] f: **die ~** Slovakia

Slowenien [slo've:niən] nt Slovenia

Smaragd [sma'rakt] (-(e)s, -e) m emerald

Smoking ['smo:kɪŋ] (-s, -s) m dinner jacket

---

so [zo:] adv 1 (so sehr) so; **so groß/schön** etc so big/nice etc; **so groß/schön wie** ... as big/nice as ...; **so viel (wie)** as much as; **rede nicht so viel** don't talk so much; **so weit sein** to be ready; **so weit wie** od **als möglich** as far as possible; **bis so weit zufrieden** by and large I'm quite satisfied; **so wenig (wie)** as little (as); **das hat ihn so geärgert, dass** ... that annoyed him so much that ...; **so einer wie ich** somebody like me; **na so was!** well, well!

2 (auf diese Weise) like this; **mach es nicht so** don't do it like that; **so oder so** in one way or the other; **und so weiter** and so on; ... **oder so was** ... or something like that; **das ist gut so** that's fine; **so genannt** so-called

3 (umg: umsonst): **ich habe es so bekommen** I got it for nothing

♦ konj: **so dass, sodass** so that; **so wie es jetzt ist** as things are at the moment

♦ excl: **so?** really?; **so, das wärs** so, that's it then

---

s. o. abk = **siehe oben**

Söckchen ['zœkçən] nt ankle socks

Socke ['zɔkə] f sock

Sockel ['zɔkəl] (-s, -) m pedestal, base

sodass ▲ [zo'das] konj so that

Sodawasser ['zo:davasər] nt soda water

Sodbrennen ['zo:tbrɛnən] (-s, -) nt heartburn

soeben [zo'e:bən] adv just (now)

Sofa ['zo:fa] (-s, -s) nt sofa

sofern [zo'fɛrn] konj if, provided (that)

sofort [zo'fɔrt] adv immediately, at once; **~ig** adj immediate

Sog [zo:k] (-(e)s, -e) m (Strömung) undertow

sogar [zo'ga:r] adv even

sogleich [zo'glaɪç] adv straight away, at once

Sohle ['zo:lə] f sole; (Talsohle etc) bottom; (MIN) level

Sohn [zo:n] (-(e)s, ⁼e) m son

Solar- [zo'la:r] in ZW solar; **~zelle** f solar cell

solch [zɔlç] pron such; **ein ~e(r, s)** ... such a ...

Soldat [zɔl'da:t] (-en, -en) m soldier

Söldner ['zœldnar] (-s, -) m mercenary

solidarisch [zoli'da:rɪʃ] adj in od with solidarity; **sich ~ erklären** to declare one's solidarity

Solidari'tät f solidarity

solid(e) [zo'li:d(ə)] adj solid; (Leben, Person) respectable

Solist(in) [zo'lɪst(ɪn)] m(f) soloist

Soll [zɔl] (-s, -(s)) nt (FIN) debit (side); (Arbeitsmenge) quota, target

---

sollen ['zɔlən] (pt **sollte**, pp **gesollt** od (als Hilfsverb) **sollen**) Hilfsverb 1 (Pflicht, Befehl) to be supposed to; **du hättest nicht gehen sollen** you shouldn't have gone, you oughtn't to have gone; **soll ich?** shall I?; **soll ich dir helfen?** shall I help you?; **sag ihm, er**

soll warten tell him he's to wait; **was soll ich machen?** what should I do? **2** (*Vermutung*): **sie soll verheiratet sein** she's said to be married; **was soll das heißen?** what's that supposed to mean?; **man sollte glauben, dass ...** you would think that ...; **sollte das passieren, ...** if that should happen ...

♦ *vt, vi:* **was soll das?** what's all this?; **das sollst du nicht** you shouldn't do that; **was solls?** what the hell?

Solo ['zoːlo] (**-s, -s** *od* **Soli**) *nt* solo

somit [zoˈmɪt] *konj* and so, therefore

Sommer ['zɔmər] (**-s, -**) *m* summer; **s~lich** *adj* summery; summer; **~reifen** *m* normal tyre; **~schlussverkauf** ▲ *m* summer sale; **~sprossen** *f* freckles

Sonde ['zɔndə] *f* probe

Sonder- ['zɔndər] *in zW* special; **~angebot** *nt* special offer; **s~bar** *adj* strange, odd; **~fahrt** *f* special trip; **~fall** *m* special case; **s~lich** *adj* particular; (*außergewöhnlich*) remarkable; (*eigenartig*) peculiar; **~marke** *f* special issue stamp; **s~n** *konj* but ♦ *vt* to separate; **nicht nur ..., s~n auch** not only ..., but also; **~preis** *m* special reduced price; **~zug** *m* special train

Sonnabend ['zɔnʔaːbənt] *m* Saturday

Sonne ['zɔnə] *f* sun; **s~n** *vr* to sun o.s.

Sonnen- *in zW:* **~aufgang** *m* sunrise; **s~baden** *vi* to sunbathe; **~brand** *m* sunburn; **~brille** *f* sunglasses *pl*; **~creme** *f* suntan lotion; **~energie** *f* solar energy, solar power; **~finsternis** *f* solar eclipse; **~kollektor** *m* solar panel; **~schein** *m* sunshine; **~schirm** *m* parasol, sunshade; **~schutzfaktor** *m* protection factor; **~stich** *m* sunstroke; **~uhr** *f* sundial; **~untergang** *m* sunset; **~wende** *f* solstice

sonnig ['zɔnɪç] *adj* sunny

Sonntag ['zɔntaːk] *m* Sunday

sonst [zɔnst] *adv* otherwise; (*mit pron, in Fragen*) else; (*zu anderer Zeit*) at other times, normally ♦ *konj* otherwise; **~ noch etwas?** anything else?; **~ nichts** nothing else; **~ jemand** anybody (at all); **~ wo** somewhere else; **~ woher** from somewhere else; **~ wohin** somewhere else; **~ig** *adj* other

sooft [zoˈʔɔft] *konj* whenever

Sopran [zoˈpraːn] (**-s, -e**) *m* soprano

Sorge ['zɔrgə] *f* care, worry

sorgen *vi:* **für jdn ~** to look after sb ♦ *vr:* **sich ~ (um)** to worry (about); **für etw ~** to take care of *od* see to sth; **~frei** *adj* carefree; **~voll** *adj* troubled, worried

Sorgerecht *nt* custody (of a child)

Sorg- [zɔrk] *zW:* **~falt** (**-**) *f* care(fulness); **s~fältig** *adj* careful; **s~los** *adj* careless; (*ohne ~en*) carefree; **s~sam** *adj* careful

Sorte ['zɔrtə] *f* sort; (*Warensorte*) brand; **~n** *pl* (*FIN*) foreign currency *sg*

sortieren [zɔrˈtiːrən] *vt* to sort (out)

Sortiment [zɔrtiˈmɛnt] *nt* assortment

sosehr [zoˈzeːr] *konj* as much as

Soße ['zoːsə] *f* sauce; (*Bratensoße*) gravy

soufflieren [zuˈfliːrən] *vt, vi* to prompt

Souterrain [zuteˈrɛː] (**-s, -s**) *nt* basement

souverän [zuvəˈrɛːn] *adj* sovereign; (*überlegen*) superior

so- *zW:* **~viel** [zoˈfiːl] *konj:* **~viel ich weiß** as far as I know; *siehe so;* **~weit** [zoˈvait] *konj* as far as; *siehe so;* **~wenig** [zoˈveːnɪç] *konj* little as; *siehe so;* **~wie** [zoˈviː] *konj* (*~bald*) as soon as; (*ebenso*) as well as; **~wieso** [zoviˈzoː] *adv* anyway

sowjetisch [zɔˈvjɛtɪʃ] *adj* Soviet

Sowjetunion *f* Soviet Union

sowohl [zoˈvoːl] *konj:* **~ ... als** *od* **wie auch** both ... and

sozial [zotsiˈaːl] *adj* social; **S~abgaben**

pl national insurance contributions;
S~arbeiter(in) *m(f)* social worker;
S~demokrat *m* social democrat; **~demokratisch** *adj* social democratic; **S~hilfe** *f* income support (BRIT), welfare (aid) (US); **~i'sieren** *vt* to socialize; **S~ismus** ['lɪsmʊs] *m* socialism; **S~ist** [-'lɪst] *m* socialist; **~istisch** *adj* socialist; **S~politik** *f* social welfare policy; **S~produkt** *nt* (net) national product; **S~staat** *m* welfare state; **S~versicherung** *f* national insurance (BRIT), social security (US); **S~wohnung** *f* council flat

soziologisch [zotsio:'loːgɪʃ] *adj* sociological

sozusagen [zotsu'zaːgən] *adv* so to speak

Spachtel ['ʃpaxtəl] (-s, -) *m* spatula

spähen ['ʃpeːən] *vi* to peep, to peek

Spalier [ʃpa'liːr] (-s, -e) *nt* (Gerüst) trellis; (Leute) guard of honour

Spalt [ʃpalt] (-(e)s, -e) *m* crack; (Türspalt) chink; (fig: Kluft) split; **~e** *f* crack, fissure; (Gletscherspalte) crevasse; (in Text) column; **s~en** *vt, vr* (auch fig) to split; **~ung** *f* splitting

Span [ʃpaːn] (-(e)s, ᵆe) *m* shaving

Spanferkel *nt* sucking pig

Spange ['ʃpaŋə] *f* clasp; (Haarspange) hair slide; (Schnalle) buckle

Spanien [ʃpaːniən] *nt* Spain; **Spanier(in)** *m(f)* Spaniard; **spanisch** *adj* Spanish

Spann- ['ʃpan] *zW:* **~beton** *m* prestressed concrete; **~betttuch** ▲ *nt* fitted sheet; **~e** *f* (Zeitspanne) space; (Differenz) gap; **s~en** *vt* (straffen) to tighten, to tauten; (befestigen) to brace ♦ *vi* to be tight; **s~end** *adj* exciting, gripping; **~ung** *f* tension; (ELEK) voltage; (fig) suspense; (unangenehm) tension

Spar- ['ʃpaːr] *zW:* **~buch** *nt* savings book; **~büchse** *f* money box; **s~en** *vt, vi* to save; **sich** *dat* **etw s~en** to save o.s. sth; (Bemerkung) to keep sth to

o.s.; **mit etw s~en** to be sparing with sth; **an etw** *dat* **s~en** to economize on sth; **~er** (-s, -) *m* saver

Spargel ['ʃpargəl] (-s, -) *m* asparagus

Sparkasse *f* savings bank

Sparkonto *nt* savings account

spärlich ['ʃpeːrlɪç] *adj* meagre; (Bekleidung) scanty

Spar- *zW:* **~preis** *m* economy price; **s~sam** *adj* economical, thrifty; **~samkeit** *f* thrift, economizing; **~schwein** *nt* piggy bank

Sparte ['ʃpartə] *f* field; line of business; (PRESSE) column

Spaß [ʃpaːs] (-es, ᵆe) *m* joke; (Freude) fun; **jdm ~ machen** to be fun (for sb); **viel ~!** have fun!; **s~en** *vi* to joke; **mit ihm ist nicht zu s~en** you can't take liberties with him; **s~haft** *adj* funny, droll; **s~ig** *adj* funny, droll

spät [ʃpeːt] *adj, adv* late; **wie ~ ist es?** what's the time?

Spaten ['ʃpaːtən] (-s, -) *m* spade

später *adj, adv* later

spätestens *adv* at the latest

Spätvorstellung *f* late show

Spatz [ʃpats] (-en, -en) *m* sparrow

spazier- [ʃpa'tsiːr] *zW:* **~en** *vi* to stroll, to walk; **~en fahren** to go for a drive; **~en gehen** to go for a walk; **S~gang** *m* walk; **S~stock** *m* walking stick; **S~weg** *m* path, walk

Specht [ʃpɛçt] (-(e)s, -e) *m* woodpecker

Speck [ʃpɛk] (-(e)s, -e) *m* bacon

Spediteur [ʃpedi'tøːr] *m* carrier; (Möbelspediteur) furniture remover

Spedition [ʃpeditsi'oːn] *f* carriage; (~sfirma) road haulage contractor; removal firm

Speer [ʃpeːr] (-(e)s, -e) *m* spear; (SPORT) javelin

Speiche ['ʃpaiçə] *f* spoke

Speichel ['ʃpaiçəl] (-s) *m* saliva, spit(tle)

Speicher ['ʃpaiçər] (-s, -) *m* storehouse; (Dachspeicher) attic, loft; (Korn-

speien *(speicher)* granary; *(Wasserspeicher)* tank; *(TECH)* store; *(COMPUT)* memory; **s~n** vt to store; *(COMPUT)* to save

speien ['ʃpaɪən] *(unreg)* vt, vi to spit; *(erbrechen)* to vomit; *(Vulkan)* to spew

Speise ['ʃpaɪzə] f food; **~eis** [-ʔaɪs] nt ice-cream; **~kammer** f larder, pantry; **~karte** f menu; **s~n** vt to feed; to eat ♦ vi to dine; **~röhre** f gullet, oesophagus; **~saal** m dining room; **~wagen** m dining car

Speku- ['ʃpeku] zW: **~lant** m speculator; **~lation** [-latsi'o:n] f speculation; **s~lieren** [-'li:rən] vi (fig) to speculate; **auf etw** akk **s~lieren** to have hopes of sth

Spelunke [ʃpe'luŋkə] f dive

Spende ['ʃpɛndə] f donation; **s~n** vt to donate, to give; **~r (-s, -)** m donor, donator

spendieren [ʃpɛn'di:rən] vt to pay for, to buy; **jdm etw ~** to treat sb to sth, to stand sb sth

Sperling ['ʃpɛrlɪŋ] m sparrow

Sperma ['ʃpɛrma] (-s, **Spermen**) nt sperm

Sperr- ['ʃpɛr] zW: **~e** f barrier; *(Verbot)* ban; **s~en** vt to block; *(SPORT)* to suspend, to bar; *(vom Ball)* to obstruct; *(einschließen)* to lock; *(verbieten)* to ban ♦ vt to baulk, to jib(e); **~gebiet** nt prohibited area; **~holz** nt plywood; **s~ig** adj bulky; **~müll** m bulky refuse; **~sitz** m *(THEAT)* stalls pl; **~stunde** f closing time

Spesen ['ʃpe:zən] pl expenses

Spezial [ʃpetsi'a:l] in zW special; **~gebiet** nt specialist field; **s~i'sieren** vr to specialize; **~i'sierung** f specialization; **~ist** [-'lɪst] m specialist; **~i'tät** f speciality

speziell [ʃpetsi'ɛl] adj special

spezifisch [ʃpe'tsi:fɪʃ] adj specific

Sphäre ['sfɛ:rə] f sphere

Spiegel ['ʃpi:gəl] m mirror; *(Was-*

serspiegel) level; *(MIL)* tab; **~bild** nt reflection; **s~bildlich** adj reversed; **~ei** nt fried egg; **s~n** vt to mirror, to reflect ♦ vr to be reflected ♦ vi to gleam; *(widerspiegeln)* to be reflective; **~ung** f reflection

Spiel [ʃpi:l] **(-(e)s, -e)** nt game; *(Schauspiel)* play; *(Tätigkeit)* play(ing); *(KARTEN)* deck; *(Freies)* (free) play; **s~en** vt, vi to play; *(um Geld)* to gamble; *(THEAT)* to perform, to act; **s~end** adv easily; **~er (-s, -)** m player; *(um Geld)* gambler; **~erei** f trifling pastime; **~feld** nt pitch, field; **~film** m feature film; **~kasino** nt casino; **~plan** m *(THEAT)* programme; **~platz** m playground; **~raum** m room to manoeuvre, scope; **~regel** f rule; **~sachen** pl toys; **~uhr** f musical box; **~verderber (-s, -)** m spoilsport; **~waren** pl toys; **~zeug** nt toy(s)

Spieß [ʃpi:s] **(-es, -e)** m spear; *(Bratspieß)* spit; **~bürger** m bourgeois; **~er (-s, -)** *(umg)* m bourgeois; **s~ig** *(pej)* adj (petit) bourgeois

Spinat [ʃpi'na:t] **(-(e)s, -e)** m spinach

Spind [ʃpɪnt] **(-(e)s, -e)** m od nt locker

Spinn- ['ʃpɪn] zW: **~e** f spider; **s~en** *(unreg)* vt, vi to spin; *(umg)* to talk rubbish; *(verrückt sein)* to be crazy od mad; **~e'rei** f spinning mill; **~rad** nt spinning wheel; **~webe** f cobweb

Spion [ʃpi'o:n] **(-s, -e)** m spy; *(in Tür)* spyhole; **~age** [ʃpio'na:ʒə] f espionage; **s~ieren** [ʃpio'ni:rən] vi to spy; **~in** f (female) spy

Spirale [ʃpi'ra:lə] f spiral

Spirituosen [ʃpiritu'o:zən] pl spirits

Spiritus ['ʃpi:rɪtus] **(-, -se)** m (methylated) spirit

Spital [ʃpi'ta:l] **(-s, ²er)** nt hospital

spitz [ʃpɪts] adj pointed; *(Winkel)* acute; *(fig: Zunge)* sharp; *(: Bemerkung)* caustic

Spitze f point, tip; *(Bergspitze)* peak;

Spitzel (-s, -) *m* police informer

spitzen *vt* to sharpen

Spitzenmarke *f* brand leader

spitzfindig *adj* (over)subtle

Spitzname *m* nickname

Splitter ['ʃplɪtər] (-s, -) *m* splinter

sponsern ['ʃpɔnzərn] *vt* to sponsor

spontan [ʃpɔn'taːn] *adj* spontaneous

Sport [ʃpɔrt] (-(e)s, -e) *m* sport; (*fig*) hobby; **~lehrer(in)** *m(f)* games or P.E. teacher; **~ler(in)** (-s, -) *m(f)* sportsman(-woman); **s~lich** *adj* sporting; (*Mensch*) sporty; **~platz** *m* playing *od* sports field; **~schuh** *m* (*Turnschuh*) training shoe, trainer; **~stadion** *nt* sports stadium; **~verein** *m* sports club; **~wagen** *m* sports car

Spott [ʃpɔt] (-(e)s) *m* mockery, ridicule; **s~billig** *adj* dirt-cheap; **s~en** *vi* to mock; **s~en** (**über** +*akk*) to mock (at), to ridicule

spöttisch ['ʃpœtɪʃ] *adj* mocking

sprach *etc* [ʃpraːx] *vb siehe* **sprechen**

Sprach- *zW:* **s~begabt** *adj* good at languages; **~e** *f* language; **~enschule** *f* language school; **~fehler** *m* speech defect; **~führer** *m* phrasebook; **~gefühl** *nt* feeling for language; **~kenntnisse** *pl* linguistic proficiency *sg;* **~kurs** *m* language course; **~labor** *nt* language laboratory; **s~lich** *adj* linguistic; **s~los** *adj* speechless

sprang *etc* [ʃpraŋ] *vb siehe* **springen**

Spray [spreː] (-s, -s) *m od nt* spray

Sprech- ['ʃprɛç] *zW:* **~anlage** *f* intercom; **s~en** (*unreg*) *vi* to speak, to talk ♦ *vt* to say; (*Sprache*) to speak; (*Person*) to speak to; **mit jdm s~en** to speak to sb; **das spricht für ihn** that's a point in his favour; **~er(in)** (-s, -) *m(f)* speaker; (*für Gruppe*) spokesman(-woman); (*RADIO, TV*) announcer; **~stunde** *f* consultation (hour); (*doctor's*) surgery; **~stundenhilfe** *f* (*doctor's*) receptionist; **~zimmer** *nt* consulting room, surgery, office (*US*)

spreizen ['ʃpraɪtsən] *vt* (*Beine*) to open, to spread; (*Finger, Flügel*) to spread

Spreng- ['ʃprɛŋ] *zW:* **s~en** *vt* to sprinkle; (*mit ~stoff*) to blow up; (*Gestein*) to blast; (*Versammlung*) to break up; **~stoff** *m* explosive(s)

spricht *etc* [ʃprɪçt] *vb siehe* **sprechen**

Sprichwort *nt* proverb; **sprichwörtlich** *adj* proverbial

Spring- ['ʃprɪŋ] *zW:* **~brunnen** *m* fountain; **s~en** (*unreg*) *vi* to jump; (*Glas*) to crack; (*mit Kopfsprung*) to dive; **~er** (-s, -) *m* jumper; (*Schach*) knight

Sprit [ʃprɪt] (-(e)s, -e) (*umg*) *m* juice, gas

Spritz- ['ʃprɪts] *zW:* **~e** *f* syringe; injection; (*an Schlauch*) nozzle; **s~en** *vt* to spray; (*MED*) to inject ♦ *vi* to splash; (*herausspritzen*) to spurt; (*MED*) to give injections; **~pistole** *f* spray gun; **~tour** *f* (*umg*) spin

spröde ['ʃprøːdə] *adj* brittle; (*Person*) reserved, coy

Sprosse ['ʃprɔsə] *f* rung

Sprössling ▲ ['ʃprœslɪŋ] (*umg*) *m* (*Kind*) offspring (*pl inv*)

Spruch [ʃprʊx] (-(e)s, ⁼e) *m* saying, maxim; (*JUR*) judgement

Sprudel ['ʃpruːdəl] (-s, -) *m* mineral water; lemonade; **s~n** *vi* to bubble; **~wasser** *nt* (*KOCH*) sparkling *od* fizzy mineral water

Sprüh- ['ʃpryː] *zW:* **~dose** *f* aerosol (can); **s~en** *vi* to spray; (*fig*) to sparkle ♦ *vt* to spray; **~regen** *m* drizzle

Sprung [ʃprʊŋ] (-(e)s, ⁼e) *m* jump; (*Riss*) crack; **~brett** *nt* springboard; **s~haft** *adj* erratic; (*Aufstieg*) rapid; **~schanze** *f* ski jump

Spucke ['ʃpʊkə] (-) *f* spit; **s~n** *vt, vi* to spit

Spuk [ʃpuːk] (-(e)s, -e) *m* haunting; (*fig*) nightmare; **s~en** *vi* (*Geist*) to walk; **hier s~t es** this place is haunted

Spülbecken ['ʃpyːlbɛkən] *nt* (*in Küche*)

sink

Spule [ˈʃpuːlə] f spool; (ELEK) coil

Spül- [ˈʃpyːl] zW: **~e** f (kitchen) sink; **s~en** vt, vi to rinse; (Geschirr) to wash up; (Toilette) to flush; **~maschine** f dishwasher; **~mittel** nt washing-up liquid; **~stein** m sink; **~ung** f rinsing; flush; (MED) irrigation

Spur [ʃpuːr] (-, -en) f trace; (Fußspur, Radspur, Tonbandspur) track; (Fährte) trail; (Fahrspur) lane

spürbar adj noticeable, perceptible

spüren [ˈʃpyːrən] vt to feel

spurlos adv without (a) trace

Spurt [ʃpʊrt] (-(e)s, -s od -e) m spurt; **s~en** vi to spurt

sputen [ˈʃpuːtən] vr to make haste

St. abk = Stück; = Sankt

Staat [ʃtaːt] (-(e)s, -en) m state; (Prunk) show; (Kleidung) finery; **s~enlos** adj stateless; **s~lich** adj state(-); state-run

Staats- zW: **~angehörige(r)** f(m) national; **~angehörigkeit** f nationality; **~anwalt** m public prosecutor; **~bürger** m citizen; **~dienst** m civil service; **~examen** nt (UNIV) state exam(ination); **s~feindlich** adj subversive; **~mann** (pl -männer) m statesman; **~oberhaupt** nt head of state

Stab [ʃtaːp] (-(e)s, "-e) m rod; (Gitterstab) bar; (Menschen) staff; **~hochsprung** m pole vault

stabil [ʃtaˈbiːl] adj stable; (Möbel) sturdy; **~isieren** vt to stabilize

Stachel [ˈʃtaxəl] (-s, -n) m spike; (von Tier) spine; (von Insekten) sting; **~beere** f gooseberry; **~draht** m barbed wire; **s~ig** adj prickly; **~schwein** nt porcupine

Stadion [ˈʃtaːdiɔn] (-s, Stadien) nt stadium

Stadium [ˈʃtaːdiʊm] nt stage, phase

Stadt [ʃtat] (-, "-e) f town; **~autobahn** f urban motorway; **~bahn** f suburban railway; **~bücherei** f municipal library

Städt- [ʃtɛt] zW: **~ebau** m town planning; **~epartnerschaft** f town twinning; **~er(in)** (-s, -) m(f) town dweller; **s~isch** adj municipal; (nicht ländlich) urban

Stadt- zW: **~kern** m town centre, city centre; **~mauer** f city wall(s); **~mitte** f town centre; **~plan** m street map; **~rand** m outskirts pl; **~rat** m (Behörde) town council, city council; **~rundfahrt** f tour of a/the city; **~teil** m district, part of town; **~zentrum** nt town centre

Staffel [ˈʃtafəl] (-, -n) f rung; (SPORT) relay (team); (AVIAT) squadron; **~lauf** m (SPORT) relay (race); **s~n** vt to graduate

Stahl [ʃtaːl] (-(e)s, "-e) m steel

stak etc [ʃtaːk] vb siehe **stecken**

Stall [ʃtal] (-(e)s, "-e) m stable; (Kaninchenstall) hutch; (Schweinestall) sty; (Hühnerstall) henhouse

Stamm [ʃtam] (-(e)s, "-e) m (Baumstamm) trunk; (Menschenstamm) tribe; (GRAM) stem; **~baum** m family tree; (von Tier) pedigree; **s~eln** vt, vi to stammer; **s~en** vi: **s~en von** od **aus** to come from; **~gast** m regular (customer)

stämmig [ˈʃtɛmɪç] adj sturdy; (Mensch) stocky

Stammtisch [ˈʃtamtɪʃ] m table for the regulars

stampfen [ˈʃtampfən] vt, vi to stamp; (stapfen) to tramp; (mit Werkzeug) to pound

Stand [ʃtant] (-(e)s, "-e) m position; (Wasserstand, Benzinstand etc) level; (Stehen) standing position; (Zustand) state; (Spielstand) score; (Messestand etc) stand; (Klasse) class; (Beruf) profession; siehe **imstande**, **zustande**

stand etc vb siehe **stehen**

Standard [ˈʃtandart] (-s, -s) m standard

Ständer ['ʃtɛndər] (-s, -) m stand

Standes- ['ʃtandəs] zW: **~amt** nt registry office; **~beamte(r)** m registrar; **s~gemäß** adj, adv according to one's social position; **~unterschied** m social difference

Stand- zW: **~haft** adj steadfast; **s~halten** (unreg) vi: (jdm/etw) **s~halten** to stand firm (against sb/sth), to resist (sb/sth)

ständig ['ʃtɛndɪç] adj permanent; (ununterbrochen) constant, continual

Stand- zW: **~licht** nt sidelights pl, parking lights pl (US); **~ort** m location; (MIL) garrison; **~punkt** m standpoint; **~spur** f hard shoulder

Stange ['ʃtaŋə] f stick; (Stab) pole, bar; rod; (Zigaretten) carton; **von der ~** (COMM) off the peg; **eine ~ Geld** (umg) quite a packet

Stängel ▲ ['ʃtɛŋəl] (-s, -) m stalk

Stapel ['ʃtaːpəl] (-s, -) m pile; (NAUT) stocks pl; **~lauf** m launch; **s~n** vt to pile (up)

Star¹ [ʃtaːr] (-(e)s, -e) m starling; (MED) cataract

Star² [ʃtaːr] (-s, -s) m (Filmstar etc) star

starb etc [ʃtarp] vb siehe **sterben**

stark [ʃtark] adj strong; (heftig, groß) heavy; (Maßangabe) thick

Stärke ['ʃtɛrkə] f strength; heaviness; thickness; (KOCH: Wäschestärke) starch; **s~n** vt to strengthen; (Wäsche) to starch

Starkstrom m heavy current

Stärkung ['ʃtɛrkʊŋ] f strengthening; (Essen) refreshment

starr [ʃtar] adj stiff; (unnachgiebig) rigid; (Blick) staring; **~en** vi to stare; **~en vor od von** to be covered in; (Waffen) to be bristling with; **S~heit** f rigidity; **~köpfig** adj stubborn; **S~sinn** m obstinacy

Start [ʃtart] (-(e)s, -e) m start; (AVIAT) takeoff; **~automatik** f (AUT) automatic choke; **~bahn** f runway; **s~en** vi to start ♦ vi to start; to take off; **~er** (-s,

-) m starter; **~erlaubnis** f takeoff clearance; **~hilfekabel** nt jump leads pl

Station [ʃtatsi̯oːn] f station; hospital ward; **s~är** [ʃtatsi̯oːnɛːr] adj (MED) inpatient attr; **s~ieren** [-'niːrən] vt to station

Statist [ʃta'tɪst] m extra, supernumerary

Statistik f statistics sg; **~er** (-s, -) m statistician

statistisch adj statistical

Stativ [ʃta'tiːf] (-s, -e) nt tripod

statt [ʃtat] konj instead of ♦ präp (+gen od dat) instead of

Stätte ['ʃtɛtə] f place

statt- zW: **s~finden** (unreg) vi to take place; **~haft** adj admissible; **~lich** adj imposing, handsome

Statue ['ʃtaːtu̯ə] f statue

Status ['ʃtaːtʊs] (-, -) m status

Stau [ʃtau] (-(e)s, -e) m blockage; (Verkehrsstau) (traffic) jam

Staub [ʃtaup] (-(e)s) m dust; **~saugen** to vacuum, to hoover ®; **s~en** ['ʃtaubən] vi to be dusty; **s~ig** adj dusty; **s~saugen** vi to vacuum, to hoover ®; **~sauger** m vacuum cleaner; **~tuch** nt duster

Staudamm m dam

Staude ['ʃtaudə] f shrub

stauen ['ʃtauən] vt (Wasser) to dam up; (Blut) to stop the flow of ♦ vr (Wasser) to become dammed up; (MED: Verkehr) to become congested; (Menschen) to collect; (Gefühle) to build up

staunen ['ʃtaunən] vi to be astonished; **S~** (-s) nt amazement

Stausee ['ʃtauzeː] (-s, -n) m reservoir, man-made lake

Stauung ['ʃtauʊŋ] f (von Wasser) damming-up; (von Blut, Verkehr) congestion

Std. abk (= Stunde) hr.

Steak [ʃteːk] nt steak

Stech- ['ʃtɛç] zW: **s~en** (unreg) vt (mit Nadel etc) to prick; (mit Messer) to stab; (mit Finger) to poke; (Biene etc) to sting; (*Mücke*) to bite; (*Sonne*) to burn; (*KARTEN*) to take; (*ART*) to engrave; (*Torf, Spargel*) to cut; **in See s~en** to put to sea; **~en** (*-s, -*) *nt* (*SPORT*) play-off; jump-off; **s~end** *adj* piercing, stabbing; (*Geruch*) pungent; **~palme** *f* holly; **~uhr** *f* time clock

Steck- ['ʃtɛk] *zW*: **~brief** *m* "wanted" poster; **~dose** *f* (wall) socket; **s~en** *vt* to put, to insert; (*Nadel*) to stick; (*Pflanzen*) to plant; (*beim Nähen*) to pin ♦ *vi* (*auch unreg*) to be; (*festsitzen*) to be stuck; (*Nadeln*) to stick; **s~en bleiben** to get stuck; **s~en lassen** to leave in; **~enpferd** *nt* hobby-horse; **~er** (*-s, -*) *m* plug; **~nadel** *f* pin

Steg [ʃteːk] (*-(e)s, -e*) *m* small bridge; (*Anlegesteg*) landing stage; **~reif** *m*: **aus dem ~reif** just like that

stehen ['ʃteːən] (*unreg*) *vi* to stand; (*sich befinden*) to be; (*in Zeitung*) to be; (*stillstehen*) to have stopped ♦ *vi unpers*: **es steht schlecht um jdn/etw** things are bad for sb/sth; **zu jdm/etw ~** to stand by sb/sth; **jdm ~** to suit sb; **wie stehts?** how are things?; (*SPORT*) what's the score?; **~ bleiben** to remain standing; (*Uhr*) to stop; (*Fehler*) to stay as it is; **~ lassen** to leave; (*Bart*) to grow

Stehlampe ['ʃteːlampə] *f* standard lamp

stehlen ['ʃteːlən] (*unreg*) *vt* to steal

Stehplatz ['ʃteːplats] *m* standing place

steif [ʃtaɪf] *adj* stiff; **S~heit** *f* stiffness

Steig- ['ʃtaɪk] *zW*: **~bügel** *m* stirrup; **s~en** ['ʃtaɪgən] (*unreg*) *vi* to rise; (*klettern*) to climb; **s~en in** +*akk*/**auf** +*akk* to get in/on; **s~ern** *vt* to raise; (*Auktion*) to bid ♦ *vr* to increase; **~erung** *f* raising; (*GRAM*) comparison; **~ung** *f* incline, gradient, rise

steil [ʃtaɪl] *adj* steep; **S~küste** *f* steep coast; (*Klippen*) cliffs *pl*

Stein [ʃtaɪn] (*-(e)s, -e*) *m* stone; (*in Uhr*) jewel; **~bock** *m* (*ASTROL*) Capricorn; **~bruch** *m* quarry; **s~ern** *adj* (*made of*) stone; (*fig*) stony; **~gut** *nt* stoneware; **s~ig** ['ʃtaɪnɪç] *adj* stony; **s~igen** *vt* to stone; **~kohle** *f* mineral coal; **~zeit** *f* Stone Age

Stelle ['ʃtɛlə] *f* place; (*Arbeit*) post, job; (*Amt*) office; **an Ihrer/meiner ~** in your/my place; *siehe* **anstelle**

stellen ['ʃtɛlən] *vt* to put; (*Uhr etc*) to set; (*zur Verfügung ~*) to supply; (*fassen: Dieb*) to apprehend ♦ *vr* (*sich aufstellen*) to stand; (*sich einfinden*) to present o.s.; (*bei Polizei*) to give o.s. up; (*vorgeben*) to pretend (to be); **sich zu etw ~** to have an opinion of sth

Stellen- *zW*: **~angebot** *nt* offer of a post; (*in Zeitung*) "vacancies"; **~anzeige** *f* job advertisement; **~gesuch** *nt* application for a post; **~vermittlung** *f* employment agency

Stell- **~ung** *f* position; (*MIL*) line; **~ung nehmen zu** to comment on; **~ungnahme** *f* comment; **s~vertretend** *adj* deputy, acting; **~vertreter** *m* deputy

Stelze ['ʃtɛltsə] *f* stilt

stemmen ['ʃtɛmən] *vt* to lift (up); (*drücken*) to press; **sich ~ gegen** (*fig*) to resist, to oppose

Stempel ['ʃtɛmpəl] (*-s, -*) *m* stamp; (*BOT*) pistil; **~kissen** *nt* ink pad; **s~n** *vt* to stamp; (*Briefmarke*) to cancel; **s~n gehen** (*umg*) to be *od* go on the dole

Stengel △ ['ʃtɛŋəl] (*-s, -*) *m* = **Stängel**

Steno- ['ʃteno] *zW*: **~gramm** ['gram] *nt* shorthand report; **~grafie** ▲ ['gra-fiː] *f* shorthand; **s~grafieren** ▲ ['gra-fiːrən] *vt, vi* to write (in) shorthand; **~typist(in)** [-ty'pɪst(ɪn)] *m(f)* shorthand typist

Stepp- ['ʃtɛp] *zW*: **~decke** *f* quilt; **~e** *f* prairie; steppe; **s~en** *vt* to stitch ♦ *vi* to tap-dance

---

Spelling Reform: ▲ new spelling △ old spelling (to be phased out)

Sterb- ['ʃtɛrb] zW: **~efall** m death; **~ehilfe** f euthanasia; **s~en** (unreg) vi to die; **~lich** ['ʃtɛrplɪç] adj mortal; **~lichkeit** f mortality; **~lichkeitsziffer** f death rate

stereo- ['ʃteːreo] in zW stereo(-); **S~anlage** f stereo (system); **~typ** [ʃtereoˈtyːp] adj stereotype

steril [ʃteˈriːl] adj sterile; **~isieren** vt to sterilize; **S~isierung** f sterilization

Stern [ʃtɛrn] (-(e)s, -e) m star; **~bild** n constellation; **~schnuppe** f meteor, falling star; **~stunde** f historic moment; **~zeichen** nt sign of the zodiac

stet [ʃteːt] adj steady; **~ig** adj constant, continual; **~s** adv continually, always

Steuer¹ ['ʃtɔyər] (-s, -) nt (NAUT) helm; (~ruder) rudder; (AUT) steering wheel

Steuer² ['ʃtɔyər] (-, -n) f tax; **~berater(in)** m(f) tax consultant

Steuerbord nt (NAUT, AVIAT) starboard

Steuer- ['ʃtɔyər] zW: **~erklärung** f tax return; **s~frei** adj tax-free; **~freibetrag** m tax allowance; **~klasse** f tax group; **~knüppel** m control column; (AVIAT, COMPUT) joystick; **~mann** (-(e)s, pl -männer od -leute) m helmsman; **s~n** vt, vi to steer; (Flugzeug) to pilot; (Entwicklung, Tonstärke) to control; **s~pflichtig** [-pflɪçtɪç] adj taxable; **~rad** nt steering wheel; **~ung** f (auch AUT) steering; piloting; control; (Vorrichtung) controls pl; **~zahler** (-s, -) m taxpayer

Steward ['stjuːərt] (-s, -s) m steward; **~ess ▲** ['stjuːərdes] (-, -en) f stewardess; air hostess

Stich [ʃtɪç] (-(e)s, -e) m (Insektenstich) sting; (Messerstich) stab; (beim Nähen) stitch; (Färbung) tinge; (KARTEN) trick; (ART) engraving; **jdn im ~ lassen** to leave sb in the lurch; **s~eln** vi (fig) to jibe; **s~haltig** adj sound, tenable; **~probe** f spot check; **~straße** f cul-de-sac; **~wahl** f final ballot; **~wort** nt cue; (in Wörterbuch) headword; (für Vortrag) note

sticken ['ʃtɪkən] vt, vi to embroider

Sticke'rei f embroidery

stickig adj stuffy, close

Stickstoff m nitrogen

Stief- ['ʃtiːf] zW: **~el** (-s, -) m boot

Stief- zW: **~kind** nt stepchild; (fig) Cinderella; **~mutter** f stepmother; **~mütterchen** nt pansy; **s~mütterlich** adj (fig): **jdn/etw s~mütterlich behandeln** to pay little attention to sb/sth; **~vater** m step-father

stiehlst etc [ʃtiːlst] vb siehe **stehlen**

Stiel [ʃtiːl] (-(e)s, -e) m handle; (BOT) stalk

Stier (-(e)s, -e) m bull; (ASTROL) Taurus

stieren vi to stare

Stierkampf m bullfight

Stierkämpfer m bullfighter

Stift [ʃtɪft] (-(e)s, -e) m peg; (Nagel) tack; (Farbstift) crayon; (Bleistift) pencil **♦** nt (charitable) foundation; (ECCL) religious institution; **s~en** vt to found; (Unruhe) to cause; (spenden) to contribute; **~er(in)** (-s, -) m(f) founder; **~ung** f donation; (Organisation) foundation; **~zahn** m post crown

Stil [ʃtiːl] (-(e)s, -e) m style

still [ʃtɪl] adj quiet, (unbewegt) still; (heimlich) secret; **S~er Ozean** Pacific; **~ halten** to keep still; **~ stehen** to stand still; **S~e** f stillness, quietness; **in aller S~e** quietly; **~en** vt to stop; (befriedigen) to satisfy; (Säugling) to breast-feed; **~legen ▲** vt to close down; **~schweigen** (unreg) vi to be silent; **S~schweigen** nt silence; **~schweigend** adj (Einverständnis) tacit **♦** adv silently; tacitly; **S~stand** m standstill

Stimm- ['ʃtɪm] zW: **~bänder** pl vocal cords; **s~berechtigt** adj entitled to vote; **~e** f voice; (Wahlstimme) vote; **s~en** vt (MUS) to tune **♦** vi to be right; **das s~te ihn traurig** that made him feel sad; **s~en für/gegen** to vote for/

against; **s~t so!** that's right; **~enmehrheit** f majority (of votes); **~enthaltung** f abstention; **~gabel** f tuning fork; **~recht** nt right to vote; **~ung** f mood; atmosphere; **s~ungsvoll** adj enjoyable; full of atmosphere; **~zettel** m ballot paper

stinken ['ʃtɪŋkən] (unreg) vi to stink

Stipendium [ʃtiˈpɛndiʊm] nt grant

stirbst etc [ʃtɪrpst] vb siehe **sterben**

Stirn [ʃtɪrn] (-, -en) f forehead, brow; (Frechheit) impudence; **~band** nt headband; **~höhle** f sinus

stöbern ['ʃtøːbərn] vi to rummage

stochern ['ʃtɔxərn] vi to poke (about)

Stock¹ [ʃtɔk] (-(e)s, ⸚e) m stick; (BOT) stock

Stock² [ʃtɔk] (-(e)s, - od Stockwerke) m storey

stocken vi to stop, to pause; **~d** adj halting

Stockung f stoppage

Stockwerk nt storey, floor

Stoff [ʃtɔf] (-(e)s, -e) m (Gewebe) material, cloth; (Materie) matter; (von Buch etc) subject (matter); **s~lich** adj material; **~tier** nt soft toy; **~wechsel** m metabolism

stöhnen ['ʃtøːnən] vi to groan

Stollen ['ʃtɔlən] (-s, -) m (MIN) gallery; (KOCH) cake eaten at Christmas; (von Schuhen) stud

stolpern ['ʃtɔlpərn] vi to stumble, to trip

Stolz [ʃtɔlts] (-es) m pride; **s~** adj proud; **s~ieren** [ʃtɔlˈtsiːrən] vi to strut

stopfen ['ʃtɔpfən] vt (hineinstopfen) to stuff; (voll stopfen) to fill (up); (nähen) to darn ♦ vi (MED) to cause constipation

Stopfgarn nt darning thread

Stoppel ['ʃtɔpəl] (-, -n) f stubble

Stopp- ['ʃtɔp] zW: **~en** vt to stop; (mit Uhr) to time ♦ vi to stop; **~schild** nt stop sign; **~uhr** f stopwatch

Stöpsel ['ʃtœpsəl] (-s, -) m plug; (für Flaschen) stopper

Storch [ʃtɔrç] (-(e)s, ⸚e) m stork

Stör- ['ʃtøːr] zW: **s~en** vt to disturb; (behindern, RADIO) to interfere with ♦ vr: **sich an etw** dat **s~en** to let sth bother one; **s~end** adj disturbing, annoying; **~enfried** (-(e)s, -e) m troublemaker

stornieren [ʃtɔrˈniːrən] vt (Auftrag) to cancel; (Buchung) to reverse

Stornogebühr [ʃtɔrno-] f cancellation fee

störrisch ['ʃtœrɪʃ] adj stubborn, perverse

Störung f disturbance; interference

Stoß [ʃtoːs] (-es, ⸚e) m (Schub) push; (Schlag) blow; kick; (mit Schwert) thrust; (mit Fuß) kick; (Erdstoß) shock; (Haufen) pile; **~dämpfer** (-s, -) m shock absorber; **s~en** (unreg) vt (mit Druck) to shove, to push; (mit Schlag) to knock, to bump; (mit Fuß) to kick; (Schwert etc) to thrust; (anstoßen: Kopf etc) to bump ♦ vr to get a knock ♦ vi: **s~en an od auf** +akk to bump into; (finden) to come across; (angrenzen) to be next to; **sich s~en an** +dat (fig) to take exception to; **~stange** f (AUT) bumper

stottern ['ʃtɔtərn] vt, vi to stutter

Str. abk (= Straße) St.

Straf- ['ʃtraːf] zW: **~anstalt** f penal institution; **~arbeit** f (SCH) punishment; lines pl; **s~bar** adj punishable; **~e** f punishment; (JUR) penalty; (Gefängnisstrafe) sentence; (Geldstrafe) fine; **s~en** vt to punish

straff [ʃtraf] adj tight; (streng) strict; (Stil etc) concise; (Haltung) erect; **~en** vt to tighten, to tauten

Strafgefangene(r) f(m) prisoner, convict

Strafgesetzbuch nt penal code

sträflich ['ʃtrɛːflɪç] adj criminal

Spelling Reform: ▲ *new spelling* △ *old spelling (to be phased out)*

Sträfling m convict

Straf- zW: **~porto** nt excess postage (charge); **~predigt** f telling-off; **~raum** m (SPORT) penalty area; **~recht** nt criminal law; **~stoß** m (SPORT) penalty (kick); **~tat** f punishable act; **~zettel** m ticket

Strahl [ʃtraːl] (-s, -en) m ray, beam; (Wasserstrahl) jet; **s~en** vi to radiate; (fig) to beam; **~ung** f radiation

Strähne ['ʃtrɛːnə] f strand

stramm [ʃtram] adj tight; (Haltung) erect; (Mensch) robust

strampeln ['ʃtrampəln] vi to kick (about), to fidget

Strand [ʃtrant] (-(e)s, =e) m shore; (mit Sand) beach; **~bad** nt open-air swimming pool, lido; **s~en** ['ʃtrandən] vi to run aground; (fig: Mensch) to fail; **~gut** nt flotsam; **~korb** m beach chair

Strang [ʃtraŋ] (-(e)s, =e) m cord, rope; (Bündel) skein

Strapaz- zW: **~e** [ʃtra'paːtsə] f strain, exertion; **s~ieren** [ʃtrapa'tsiːrən] vt (Material) to treat roughly, to punish; (Mensch, Kräfte) to wear out, to exhaust; **s~ierfähig** adj hard-wearing; **s~iös** [ʃtrapatsi'øːs] adj exhausting, tough

Straße ['ʃtraːsə] f street, road

Straßen- zW: **~bahn** f tram, streetcar (US); **~glätte** f slippery road surface; **~karte** f road map; **~kehrer** (-s, -) m roadsweeper; **~sperre** f roadblock; **~verkehr** m (road) traffic; **~verkehrsordnung** f highway code

Strateg- [ʃtra'teːg] zW: **~e** (-n, -n) m strategist; **~ie** [ʃtrate'giː] f strategy; **s~isch** adj strategic

sträuben ['ʃtrɔybən] vt to ruffle ♦ vr to bristle; (Mensch): **sich (gegen etw)** ~ to resist (sth)

Strauch [ʃtraux] (-(e)s, Sträucher) m bush, shrub

Strauß[1] [ʃtraus] (-es, Sträuße) m bunch; bouquet

Strauß[2] [ʃtraus] (-es, -e) m ostrich

Streb- [ʃtreːb] zW: **s~en** vi to strive, to endeavour; **s~en nach** to strive for; **~er** (-s, -) (pej) m pusher, climber; (SCH) swot (BRIT)

Strecke ['ʃtrɛkə] f stretch; (Entfernung) distance; (EISENB, MATH) line; **s~n** vt to stretch; (Waffen) to lay down; (KOCH) to eke out ♦ vr to stretch (o.s.)

Streich [ʃtraɪç] (-(e)s, -e) m trick, prank; (Hieb) blow; **s~eln** vt to stroke; **s~en** (unreg) vt (berühren) to stroke; (auftragen) to spread; (anmalen) to paint; (durchstreichen) to delete; (nicht genehmigen) to cancel ♦ vi (berühren) to brush; (schleichen) to prowl; **~holz** nt match; **~instrument** nt string instrument

Streif- [ʃtraɪf] zW: **~e** f patrol; **s~en** vt (leicht berühren) to brush against, to graze; (Blick) to skim over; (Thema, Problem) to touch on; (abstreifen) to take off ♦ vi (gehen) to roam; **~en** (-s, -) m (in Linie) stripe; (Stück) strip; (Film) film; **~enwagen** m patrol car; **~schuss** ▲ m graze, grazing shot; **~zug** m scouting trip

Streik [ʃtraɪk] (-(e)s, -s) m strike; **~brecher** (-s, -) m blackleg, strikebreaker; **s~en** vi to strike; **~posten** m (strike) picket

Streit [ʃtraɪt] (-(e)s, -e) m argument; dispute; **s~en** (unreg) vi, vr to argue; to dispute; **~frage** f point at issue; **s~ig** adj: **jdm etw s~ig machen** to dispute sb's right to sth; **~igkeiten** pl quarrel sg, dispute sg; **~kräfte** pl (MIL) armed forces

streng [ʃtrɛŋ] adj severe; (Lehrer, Maßnahme) strict; (Geruch etc) sharp; **~genommen** strictly speaking; **S~e** (-) f severity, strictness, sharpness; **~gläubig** adj orthodox, strict; **~stens** adv strictly

Stress ▲ [ʃtrɛs] (-es, -e) m stress

stressen vt to put under stress

streuen ['ʃtrɔyən] vt to strew, to scatter, to spread

Strich [ʃtrɪç] (-(e)s, -e) *m* (*Linie*) line;
(*Federstrich, Pinselstrich*) stroke; (*von
Geweben*) nap; (*von Fell*) pile; **auf den
~ gehen** (*umg*) to walk the streets;
jdm gegen den ~ gehen to rub sb up
the wrong way; **einen ~ machen
durch** to cross out; (*fig*) to foil; **~kode**
m (*auf Waren*) bar code; **~mädchen** *nt*
streetwalker; **s~weise** *adv* here and
there

Strick [ʃtrɪk] (-(e)s, -e) *m* rope; **s~en**
vt, vi to knit; **s~jacke** *f* cardigan; **~lei-
ter** *f* rope ladder; **~nadel** *f* knitting
needle; **~waren** *pl* knitwear *sg*

strikt [strɪkt] *adj* strict

strittig [ˈʃtrɪtɪç] *adj* disputed, in dispute

Stroh [ʃtroː] (-(e)s) *nt* straw; **~blume** *f*
everlasting flower; **~dach** *nt* thatched
roof; **~halm** *m* (*drinking*) straw

Strom [ʃtroːm] (-(e)s, ⸚e) *m* river; (*fig*)
stream; (*ELEK*) current; **s~abwärts** *adv*
downstream; **s~aufwärts** *adv* upstream; **~ausfall** *m* power failure

strömen [ˈʃtrøːmən] *vi* to stream, to
pour

Strom-   *zW:*   **~kreis** *m* circuit;
s~linienförmig *adj* streamlined;
~sperre *f* power cut

Strömung [ˈʃtrøːmʊŋ] *f* current

Strophe [ˈʃtroːfə] *f* verse

strotzen [ˈʃtrɔtsən] *vi:* **~ vor** *od* **von** to
abound in, to be full of

Strudel [ˈʃtruːdəl] (-s, -) *m* whirlpool,
vortex; (*KOCH*) strudel

Struktur [ʃtrʊkˈtuːr] *f* structure

Strumpf [ʃtrʊmpf] (-(e)s, ⸚e) *m* stocking; **~band** *nt* garter; **~hose** *f* (*pair of*)
tights

Stube [ˈʃtuːbə] *f* room

Stuben- *zW:* **~arrest** *m* confinement
to one's room; (*MIL*) confinement to
quarters; **~hocker** (*umg*) *m* stay-at-
home; **s~rein** *adj* house-trained

Stuck [ʃtʊk] (-(e)s) *m* stucco

Stück [ʃtʏk] (-(e)s, -e) *nt* piece; (*etwas*)

bit; (*THEAT*) play; **~chen** *nt* little piece;
~lohn *m* piecework wages *pl*;
s~weise *adv* bit by bit, piecemeal;
(*COMM*) individually

Student(in) [ʃtuˈdɛnt(ɪn)] *m(f)* student;
s~isch *adj* student, academic

Studie [ˈʃtuːdiə] *f* study

Studienfahrt *f* study trip

studieren [ʃtuˈdiːrən] *vt, vi* to study

Studio [ˈʃtuːdio] (-s, -s) *nt* studio

Studium [ˈʃtuːdiʊm] *nt* studies *pl*

Stufe [ˈʃtuːfə] *f* step; (*Entwicklungsstufe*)
stage; **s~nweise** *adv* gradually

Stuhl [ʃtuːl] (-(e)s, ⸚e) *m* chair; **~gang**
m bowel movement

stülpen [ˈʃtʏlpən] *vt* (*umdrehen*) to
turn upside down; (*bedecken*) to put

stumm [ʃtʊm] *adj* silent; (*MED*) dumb

Stummel [ˈʃtʊməl] (-s, -) *m* stump;
(*Zigarettenstummel*) stub

Stummfilm *m* silent film

Stümper [ˈʃtʏmpər] (-s, -) *m* incompetent, duffer; **s~haft** *adj* bungling, incompetent; **s~n** *vi* to bungle

Stumpf [ʃtʊmpf] (-(e)s, ⸚e) *m* stump;
s~ *adj* blunt; (*teilnahmslos, glanzlos*)
dull; (*Winkel*) obtuse; **~sinn** *m* tedious-
ness; **s~sinnig** *adj* dull

Stunde [ˈʃtʊndə] *f* hour; (*SCH*) lesson

stunden *vt:* **jdm etw ~** to give sb
time to pay sth; **S~geschwindigkeit**
f average speed per hour;
S~kilometer *pl* kilometres per hour;
~lang *adj* for hours; **S~lohn** *m* hourly
wage; **S~plan** *m* timetable; **~weise**
adj by the hour; every hour

stündlich [ˈʃtʏntlɪç] *adj* hourly

Stups [ʃtʊps] (-es, -e) (*umg*) *m* push;
~nase *f* snub nose

stur [ʃtuːr] *adj* obstinate, pigheaded

Sturm [ʃtʊrm] (-(e)s, ⸚e) *m* storm,
gale; (*MIL etc*) attack, assault

stürm- [ʃtʏrm] *zW:* **~en** *vi* (*Wind*) to
blow hard, to rage; (*rennen*) to storm
♦ *vt* (*MIL, fig*) to storm ♦ *vb unpers:* **es ~t**

Spelling Reform: ▲ *new spelling* △ *old spelling* (*to be phased out*)

there's a gale blowing; **S~er** (-s, -) *m*
(SPORT) forward, striker; **~isch** *adj*
stormy

Sturmwarnung *f* gale warning

Sturz [ʃtʊrts] (-es, ²e) *m* fall; (POL) overthrow

stürzen [ʃtʏrtsən] *vt* (werfen) to hurl;
(POL) to overthrow; (umkehren) to
overturn ♦ *vr* to rush; (hineinstürzen) to
plunge ♦ *vi* to fall; (AVIAT) to dive;
(rennen) to dash

Sturzflug *m* nose dive

Sturzhelm *m* crash helmet

Stute [ʃtuːtə] *f* mare

Stützbalken *m* brace, joist

Stütze [ʃtʏtsə] *f* support; help

stutzen [ʃtʊtsən] *vt* to trim; (Ohr,
Schwanz) to dock; (Flügel) to clip ♦ *vi*
to hesitate; to become suspicious

stützen *vt* (auch fig) to support; (Ellbogen etc) to prop up

stutzig *adj* perplexed, puzzled; (misstrauisch) suspicious

Stützpunkt *m* point of support; (von
Hebel) fulcrum; (MIL, fig) base

Styropor [ʃtyroˈpoːr] (®; -s) *nt* polystyrene

s. u. *abk* = **siehe unten**

Subjekt [zʊpˈjɛkt] (-(e)s, -e) *nt* subject;
s~iv [-tiːf] *adj* subjective; **~ivi'tät** *f*
subjectivity

Subsidiarität *f* subsidiarity

Substantiv [zʊpstanˈtiːf] (-s, -e) *nt*
noun

Substanz [zʊpˈstants] *f* substance

subtil [zʊpˈtiːl] *adj* subtle

subtrahieren [zʊptraˈhiːrən] *vt* to subtract

subtropisch [ˈzʊptroːpɪʃ] *adj* subtropi-
cal

Subvention [zʊpvɛntsiˈoːn] *f* subsidy;
s~ieren *vt* to subsidize

Such- [ˈzuːx] *zW:* **~aktion** *f* search; **~e**
f search; **s~en** *vt* to look (for), to seek;
(versuchen) to try ♦ *vi* to seek, to
search; **~er** (-s, -) *m* seeker, searcher;
(PHOT) viewfinder

Sucht [zʊxt] (-, ²e) *f* mania; (MED) ad-
diction, craving

süchtig [ˈzʏçtɪç] *adj* addicted; **S~e(r)**
f(m) addict

Süd- [ˈzyːt] *zW:* **~en** [ˈzyːdən] (-s) *m*
south; **~früchte** *pl* Mediterranean fruit
sg; **s~lich** *adj* southern; **s~lich von** (to
the) south of; **~pol** *m* South Pole;
s~wärts *adv* southwards

süffig [ˈzʏfɪç] *adj* (Wein) pleasant to the
taste

süffisant [zʏfiˈzant] *adj* smug

suggerieren [zʊɡeˈriːrən] *vt* to suggest

Sühne [ˈzyːnə] *f* atonement, expiation;
s~n *vt* to atone for, to expiate

Sultan [ˈzʊltan] (-s, -e) *m* sultan; **~ine**
[zʊltaˈniːnə] *f* sultana

Sülze [ˈzʏltsə] *f* brawn

Summe [ˈzʊmə] *f* sum, total

summen *vt, vi* to buzz; (Lied) to hum

Sumpf [zʊmpf] (-(e)s, ²e) *m* swamp,
marsh; **s~ig** *adj* marshy

Sünde [ˈzʏndə] *f* sin; **~nbock** (umg) *m*
scapegoat; **~r(in)** (-s, -) *m(f)* sinner;
sündigen *vi* to sin

Super [ˈzuːpər] (-s) *nt* (Benzin) four star
(petrol) (BRIT), premium (US); **~lativ**
[-latiːf] (-s, -e) *m* superlative; **~macht**
f superpower; **~markt** *m* supermarket

Suppe [ˈzʊpə] *f* soup; **~nteller** *m* soup
plate

süß [zyːs] *adj* sweet; **S~e** (-) *f* sweetness; **~en** *vt* to sweeten; **S~igkeit** *f*
sweetness; (Bonbon etc) sweet (BRIT),
candy (US); **~lich** *adj* sweetish; (fig)
sugary; **~sauer** *adj* (Gurke) pickled;
(Sauce etc) sweet-and-sour; **S~speise**
f pudding, sweet; **S~stoff** *m* sweet-
ener; **S~waren** *pl* confectionery
(sing); **S~wasser** *nt* fresh water

Symbol [zʏmˈboːl] (-s, -e) *nt* symbol;
s~isch *adj* symbolic(al)

Symmetrie [zʏmeˈtriː] *f* symmetry

symmetrisch [zʏˈmeːtrɪʃ] *adj* sym-
metrical

Sympathie [zʏmpaˈtiː] *f* liking, sympathy; **sympathisch** [zɪmˈpaːtɪʃ] adj likeable; **er ist mir ~** I like him; **sympathisieren** vi to sympathize

Symphonie [zymfoˈniː] f (MUS) symphony

Symptom [zympˈtoːm] (-s, -e) nt symptom; **s~atisch** [zymptoˈmaːtɪʃ] adj symptomatic

Synagoge [zynaˈɡoːɡə] f synagogue

synchron [zynˈkroːn] adj synchronous; **~i'sieren** vt to synchronize; (Film) to dub

Synonym [zynoˈnyːm] (-s, -e) nt synonym; **s~** adj synonymous

Synthese [zynˈteːzə] f synthesis

synthetisch adj synthetic

System [zʏsˈteːm] (-s, -e) nt system; **s~atisch** adj systematic; **s~ati'sieren** vt to systematize

Szene [ˈstseːnə] f scene; **~rie** [stsenəˈriː] f scenery

T, t

t abk (= Tonne) t

Tabak [ˈtaːbak] (-s, -e) m tobacco

Tabell- [taˈbɛl] zW: **t~arisch** [tabɛˈlaːrɪʃ] adj tabular; **~e** f table

Tablett [taˈblɛt] nt tray; **~e** f tablet, pill

Tabu [taˈbuː] nt taboo; **t~** adj taboo

Tachometer [taxoˈmeːtər] (-s, -) m (AUT) speedometer

Tadel [ˈtaːdəl] (-s, -) m censure; scolding; (Fehler) fault, blemish; **t~los** adj faultless, irreproachable; **t~n** vt to scold

Tafel [ˈtaːfəl] (-, -n) f (auch MATH) table; (Anschlagtafel) board; (Wandtafel) blackboard; (Schiefertafel) slate; (Gedenktafel) plaque; (Illustration) plate; (Schalttafel) panel; (Schokolade etc) bar

Tag [taːk] (-(e)s, -e) m day; **unter/über ~e** (MIN) underground/on the surface; **an den ~ kommen** to

come to light; **guten ~!** good morning/afternoon!; **siehe zutage**; **t~aus** adv: **t~aus, ~ein** day in, day out; **~dienst** m day duty

Tage- [ˈtaːɡə] zW: **~buch** [ˈtaːɡəbuːx] nt diary, journal; **~geld** nt daily allowance; **t~lang** adv for days; **t~n** vi to sit, to meet ♦ vb unpers: **es tagt** dawn is breaking

Tages- zW: **~ablauf** m course of the day; **~anbruch** m dawn; **~fahrt** f day trip; **~karte** f menu of the day; (Fahrkarte) day ticket; **~licht** nt daylight; **~ordnung** f agenda; **~zeit** f time of day; **~zeitung** f daily (paper)

täglich [ˈtɛːklɪç] adj, adv daily

tagsüber [ˈtaːksyːbər] adv during the day

Tagung f conference

Taille [ˈtaljə] f waist

Takt [takt] (-(e)s, -e) m tact; (MUS) time; **~gefühl** nt tact

Taktik f tactics pl; **taktisch** adj tactical

Takt- zW: **t~los** adj tactless; **~losigkeit** f tactlessness; **~stock** m (conductor's) baton; **t~voll** adj tactful

Tal [taːl] (-(e)s, ̈er) nt valley

Talent [taˈlɛnt] (-(e)s, -e) nt talent; **t~iert** [talɛnˈtiːrt] adj talented, gifted

Talisman [ˈtaːlɪsman] (-s, -e) m talisman

Talsohle f bottom of a valley

Talsperre f dam

Tampon [ˈtampɔn] (-s, -s) m tampon

Tandem [ˈtandɛm] (-s, -s) nt tandem

Tang [taŋ] (-(e)s, -e) m seaweed

Tank [taŋk] (-s, -s) m tank; **~anzeige** f fuel gauge; **t~en** vt to fill up with petrol (BRIT) od gas (US); (AVIAT) to (re)fuel; **~er** (-s, -) m tanker; **~schiff** nt tanker; **~stelle** f petrol (BRIT) od gas (US) station; **~wart** m petrol pump (BRIT) od gas station (US) attendant

Tanne [ˈtanə] f fir

Tannen- zW: **~baum** m fir tree; **~zap-**

fen m fir cone

Tante ['tantə] f aunt

Tanz [tants] (-es, ⸚e) m dance; **t~en** vt, vi to dance

Tänzer(in) ['tɛntsər(ɪn)] (-s, -) m(f) dancer

Tanzfläche f (dance) floor

Tanzschule f dancing school

Tapete [ta'peːtə] f wallpaper; **~nwechsel** m (fig) change of scenery

tapezieren [tape'tsiːrən] vt to (wall)paper; **Tapezierer** [tape'tsiːrər] (-s, -) m (interior) decorator

tapfer ['tapfər] adj brave; **T~keit** f courage, bravery

Tarif [ta'riːf] (-s, -e) m tariff, (scale of) fares od charges; **~lohn** m standard wage rate; **~verhandlungen** pl wage negotiations; **~zone** f fare zone

Tarn- ['tarn] zW: **t~en** vt to camouflage; (Person, Absicht) to disguise; **~ung** f camouflaging; disguising

Tasche ['taʃə] f pocket; handbag

Taschen- in zW pocket; **~buch** nt paperback; **~dieb** m pickpocket; **~geld** nt pocket money; **~lampe** f (electric) torch, flashlight (US); **~messer** nt penknife; **~tuch** nt handkerchief

Tasse ['tasə] f cup

Tastatur [tasta'tuːr] f keyboard

Taste ['tastə] f push-button control (an Schreibmaschine) key; **t~n** vt to feel, to touch ♦ vi to feel, to grope ♦ vr to feel one's way

Tat [taːt] (-, -en) f act, deed, action; **in der ~** indeed, as a matter of fact; **etc** vb siehe tun; **~bestand** m facts of the case; **t~enlos** adj inactive

Tät- ['tɛːt] zW: **~er(in)** (-s, -) m(f) perpetrator, culprit; **t~ig** adj active; **in einer Firma t~ig sein** to work for a firm; **~igkeit** f activity; (Beruf) occupation; **t~lich** adj violent; **~lichkeiten** pl (Schläge) blows

tätowieren [tɛto'viːrən] vt to tattoo

Tatsache f fact

tatsächlich adj actual ♦ adv really

Tau¹ [tau] (-(e)s, -e) nt rope

Tau² [tau] (-(e)s) m dew

taub [taup] adj deaf; (Nuss) hollow

Taube ['taubə] f dove; pigeon; **~nschlag** m dovecote; **hier geht es zu wie in einem ~nschlag** it's a hive of activity here

taub- zW: **T~heit** f deafness; **~stumm** adj deaf-and-dumb

Tauch- ['taux] zW: **t~en** vt to dip ♦ vi to dive; (NAUT) to submerge; **~er** (-s, -) m diver; **~eranzug** m diving suit; **~erbrille** f diving goggles pl; **~sieder** (-s, -) m immersion coil (for boiling water)

tauen ['tauən] vt, vi to thaw ♦ vb unpers: **es taut** it's thawing

Tauf- ['tauf] zW: **~becken** nt font; **~e** f baptism; **t~en** vt to christen, to baptize; **~pate** m godfather; **~patin** f godmother; **~schein** m certificate of baptism

taug- ['taug] zW: **~en** vi to be of use; **t~en für** to do for, to be good for; **nicht ~en** to be no good od useless; **T~enichts** (-es, -e) m good-for-nothing; **~lich** ['tauklɪç] adj suitable; (MIL) fit (for service)

Taumel ['tauməl] (-s) m dizziness; (fig) frenzy; **t~n** vi to reel, to stagger

Tausch [tauʃ] (-(e)s, -e) m exchange; **t~en** vt to exchange, to swap

täuschen ['tɔyʃən] vt to deceive ♦ vi to be deceptive ♦ vr to be wrong; **~d** adj deceptive

Tauschhandel m barter

Täuschung f deception; (optisch) illusion

tausend ['tauzənt] num (a) thousand

Tauwetter nt thaw

Taxi ['taksi] (-(s), -(s)) nt taxi; **~fahrer** m taxi driver; **~stand** m taxi rank

Tech- ['tɛç] zW: **~nik** f technology; (Methode, Kunstfertigkeit) technique; **~niker** (-s, -) m technician; **~nisch** adj technical; **~nolo'gie** f technology; **t~no'logisch** adj technological

Tee [teː] (-s, -s) m tea; **~beutel** m tea

bag; **~kanne** f teapot; **~löffel** m tea-spoon

Teer [te:r] (-(e)s, -e) m tar; **t~en** vt to tar

Teesieb nt tea strainer

Teich [taɪç] (-(e)s, -e) m pond

Teig [taɪk] (-(e)s, -e) m dough; **t~ig** ['taɪgɪç] adj doughy; **~waren** pl pasta sg

Teil [taɪl] (-(e)s, -e) m od nt part; (Anteil) share; (Bestandteil) component; **zum ~** partly; **t~bar** adj divisible; **~betrag** m instalment; **~chen** nt (atomic) particle; **t~en** vt, vr to divide; (mit jdm) to share; **t~haben** (unreg) vi: **t~haben an** +dat to share in; **~haber** (-s, -) m partner; **~kaskoversicherung** f third party, fire and theft insurance; **t~möbliert** adj partially furnished; **~nahme** f participation; (Mitleid) sympathy; **t~nahmslos** adj disinterested, apathetic; **t~nehmen** (unreg) vi: **t~nehmen an** +dat to take part in; **~nehmer** (-s, -) m participant; **t~s** adv partly; **~ung** f division; **t~weise** adv partially, in part; **~zahlung** f payment by instalments; **~zeitarbeit** f part-time work

Teint [tɛ̃:] (-s, -s) m complexion

Telearbeit ['te:leʔarbaɪt] f teleworking

Telefax ['te:lefaks] nt fax

Telefon [tele'fo:n] (-s, -e) nt tele-phone; **~anruf** m (tele)phone call; **~at** [telefo'na:t] (-(e)s, -e) nt (tele)phone call; **~buch** nt telephone directory; **~hörer** m (telephone) receiver; **t~ieren** vi to telephone; **t~isch** [-ɪʃ] adj telephone; (Benachrichtigung) by telephone; **~ist(in)** [telefo'nɪst(ɪn)] m(f) telephonist; **~karte** f phonecard; **~nummer** f (tele)phone number; **~zelle** f telephone kiosk, callbox; **~zentrale** f telephone exchange

Telegraf [tele'gra:f] (-en, -en) m tele-graph; **~enmast** m telegraph pole;

~ie [-'fi:] f telegraphy; **t~ieren** [-'fi:rən] vt, vi to telegraph, to wire

Telegramm [tele'gram] (-s, -e) nt tele-gram, cable; **~adresse** f telegraphic address

Tele- zW: **~objektiv** ['te:leʔɔpjɛkti:f] nt telephoto lens; **t~pathisch** [tele'pa:tɪʃ] adj telepathic; **~skop** [tele'sko:p] (-s, -e) nt telescope

Teller ['tɛlər] (-s, -) m plate; **~gericht** nt (KOCH) one-course meal

Tempel ['tɛmpəl] (-s, -) m temple

Temperament [tɛmpera'mɛnt] nt temperament; (Schwung) vivacity, live-liness; **t~voll** adj high-spirited, lively

Temperatur [tɛmpera'tu:r] f tempera-ture

Tempo¹ ['tɛmpo] (-s, Tempi) nt (MUS) tempo

Tempo² ['tɛmpo] (-s, -s) nt speed, pace; **~!** I get a move on!; **~limit** [-lɪmɪt] (-s, -s) nt speed limit; **~ta-schentuch** ® nt tissue

Tendenz [tɛn'dɛnts] f tendency; (Absicht) intention; **t~iös** [-i'ø:s] adj biased, tendentious

tendieren [tɛn'di:rən] vi: **~ zu** to show a tendency to, to incline towards

Tennis ['tɛnɪs] (-, -) nt tennis; **~ball** m tennis ball; **~platz** m tennis court; **~schläger** m tennis racket; **~schuh** m tennis shoe; **~spieler(in)** m(f) tennis player

Tenor [te'no:r] (-s, ⁻e) m tenor

Teppich ['tɛpɪç] (-s, -e) m carpet; **~bo-den** m wall-to-wall carpeting

Termin [tɛr'mi:n] (-s, -e) m (Zeitpunkt) date; (Frist) time limit, deadline; (Arzt-termin etc) appointment; **~kalender** m diary, appointments book; **~planer** m personal organizer

Terrasse [tɛ'rasə] f terrace

Terrine [tɛ'ri:nə] f tureen

territorial [tɛritori'a:l] adj territorial

Territorium [tɛri'to:riom] nt territory

Terror ['tɛrɔr] (-s) m terror; reign of terror; **t~isieren** [terori'zi:rən] vt to terrorize; **~ismus** [-'rɪsmus] m terrorism; **~ist** [-'rɪst] m terrorist

Tesafilm ['te:zafɪlm] ® m Sellotape ® (BRIT), Scotch tape ® (US)

Tessin [tɛ'si:n] (-s) nt: **das ~** Ticino

Test [tɛst] (-s, -s) m test

Testament [tɛsta'mɛnt] nt will, testament; (REL) Testament; **t~arisch** [-'ta:rɪʃ] adj testamentary

Testamentsvollstrecker m executor (of a will)

testen vt to test

Tetanus ['te:tanus] (-) m tetanus; **~impfung** f (anti-)tetanus injection

teuer ['tɔyər] adj dear, expensive; **T~ung** f increase in price; **T~ungszulage** f cost of living bonus

Teufel ['tɔyfəl] (-s, -) m devil; **teuflisch** ['tɔyflɪʃ] adj fiendish, diabolical

Text [tɛkst] (-(e)s, -e) m text; (Liedertext) words pl; **t~en** vi to write the words

textil [tɛks'ti:l] adj textile; **T~ien** pl textiles; **T~industrie** f textile industry; **T~waren** pl textiles

Textverarbeitung f word processing

Theater [te'a:tər] (-s, -) nt theatre; (umg) fuss; **~ spielen** (auch fig) to playact; **~besucher** m playgoer; **~kasse** f box office; **~stück** nt (stage) play

Theke ['te:kə] f (Schanktisch) bar; (Ladentisch) counter

Thema [te:ma] (-s, Themen od -ta) nt theme, topic, subject

Themse ['tɛmzə] f Thames

Theo- [teo] zW: **~loge** [-'lo:gə] (-n, -n) m theologian; **~logie** [-lo'gi:] f theology; **t~logisch** [-'lo:gɪʃ] adj theological; **~retiker** [-'re:tikər] (-s, -) m theorist; **t~retisch** [-'re:tɪʃ] adj theoretical; **~rie** [-'ri:] f theory

Thera- [tera] zW: **~peut** [-'pɔyt] (-en, -en) m therapist; **t~peutisch** [-'pɔytɪʃ] adj therapeutic; **~pie** [-'pi:] f therapy

Therm- zW: **~albad** [tɛr'ma:lba:t] nt thermal bath; thermal spa; **~odrucker** [tɛrmo-] m thermal printer; **~ometer** [tɛrmo'me:tər] (-s, -) nt thermometer; **~osflasche** ['tɛrmosflaʃə] ® f Thermos ® flask

These ['te:zə] f thesis

Thrombose [trɔm'bo:zə] f thrombosis

Thron [tro:n] (-(e)s, -e) m throne; **t~en** vi to sit enthroned; (fig) to sit in state; **~folge** f succession (to the throne); **~folger(in)** (-s, -) m(f) heir to the throne

Thunfisch ['tu:nfɪʃ] m tuna

Thüringen ['ty:rɪŋən] (-s) nt Thuringia

Thymian ['ty:mia:n] (-s, -e) m thyme

Tick [tɪk] (-(e)s, -e) m tic; (Eigenart) quirk; (Fimmel) craze

ticken vi to tick

tief [ti:f] adj deep; (~sinnig) profound; (Ausschnitt, Preis, Ton) low; **~ greifend** far-reaching; **~ schürfend** profound; **T~** (-s, -s) nt (MET) depression; **T~druck** m low pressure; **T~e** f depth; **T~ebene** f plain; **T~enschärfe** f (PHOT) depth of focus; **T~garage** f underground garage; **~gekühlt** adj frozen; **T~kühlfach** nt deepfreeze compartment; **T~kühlkost** f (deep) frozen food; **T~kühltruhe** f deep-freeze, freezer; **T~punkt** m low point; (fig) low ebb; **T~schlag** m (BOXEN, fig) blow below the belt; **T~see** f deep sea; **~sinnig** adj profound; melancholy; **T~stand** m low level; **T~stwert** m minimum od lowest value

Tier [ti:r] (-(e)s, -e) nt animal; **~arzt** m vet(erinary surgeon); **~garten** m zoo(logical gardens pl); **~heim** nt cat/dog home; **t~isch** adj animal; (auch fig) brutish; (fig: Ernst etc) deadly; **~kreis** m zodiac; **~kunde** f zoology; **t~liebend** adj fond of animals; **~park** m zoo; **~quälerei** [-kvɛ:lə'raɪ] f cruelty to animals; **~schutzverein** m society for the prevention of cruelty to animals

Tiger(in) ['ti:gər(ɪn)] (-s, -) m(f) tiger (-gress)

tilgen ['tɪlgən] vt to erase; (Sünden) to expiate; (Schulden) to pay off

Tinte ['tɪntə] f ink

Tintenfisch m cuttlefish

Tipp ▲ [tɪp] (-s, -e) m tip; **~en** vt, vi to tap, to touch; (umg: schreiben) to type; (im Lotto etc) to bet (on); **auf jdn ~en** (umg: raten) to tip sb, to put one's money on sb (fig)

Tipp- ['tɪp] zW: **~fehler** (umg) m typing error; **t~topp** (umg) adj tip-top; **~zettel** m (pools) coupon

Tirol [ti'ro:l] nt the Tyrol; **~er(in)** m(f) Tyrolean; **t~isch** adj Tyrolean

Tisch [tɪʃ] (-(e)s, -e) m table; **bei ~** at table; **vor/nach ~** before/after eating; **unter den ~ fallen** (fig) to be dropped; **~decke** f tablecloth; **~ler** (-s, -) m carpenter, joiner; **~le'rei** f joiner's workshop; (Arbeit) carpentry, joinery; **t~lern** vi to do carpentry etc; **~rede** f after-dinner speech; **~tennis** nt table tennis; **~tuch** nt tablecloth

Titel ['ti:təl] (-s, -) m title; **~bild** nt cover (picture); (von Buch) frontispiece; **~rolle** f title role; **~seite** f cover; (Buchtitelseite) title page; **~verteidiger** m defending champion, title holder

Toast [to:st] (-(e)s, -e od -s) m toast; **~brot** nt bread for toasting; **~er** (-s, -) m toaster

tob- ['to:b] zW: **~en** vi (Kinder) to romp about; **~süchtig** adj maniacal

Tochter ['tɔxtər] (-, ˙) f daughter; **~gesellschaft** f subsidiary (company)

Tod [to:t] (-(e)s, -e) m death; **t~ernst** adj deadly serious ♦ adv in dead earnest

Todes- ['to:dəs] zW: **~angst** [-aŋst] f mortal fear; **~anzeige** f obituary (notice); **~fall** m death; **~strafe** f death penalty; **~ursache** f cause of death; **~urteil** nt death sentence; **~verach-**

tung f utter disgust

todkrank adj dangerously ill

tödlich ['tø:tlɪç] adj deadly, fatal

tod- zW: **~müde** adj dead tired; **~schick** (umg) adj smart, classy; **~sicher** (umg) adj dead certain; **T~sünde** f deadly sin

Toilette [toa'lɛtə] f toilet, lavatory; (Frisiertisch) dressing table

Toiletten- zW: **~artikel** pl toiletries, toilet articles; **~papier** nt toilet paper; **~tisch** m dressing table

toi, toi, toi ['tɔy'tɔy'tɔy] excl touch wood

tolerant [tole'rant] adj tolerant

Toleranz [tole'rants] f tolerance

tolerieren [tole'ri:rən] vt to tolerate

toll [tɔl] adj mad; (Treiben) wild; (umg) terrific; **~en** vi to romp; **T~kirsche** f deadly nightshade; **~kühn** adj daring; **T~wut** f rabies

Tomate [to'ma:tə] f tomato; **~nmark** nt tomato purée

Ton¹ [to:n] (-(e)s, -e) m (Erde) clay

Ton² [to:n] (-(e)s, ˙e) m (Laut) sound; (MUS) note; (Redeweise) tone; (Farbton, Nuance) shade; (Betonung) stress; **t~angebend** adj leading; (MUS) **~art** f (musical) key; **~band** nt tape; **~bandgerät** nt tape recorder

tönen ['tø:nən] vi to sound ♦ vt to shade; (Haare) to tint

tönern ['tø:nərn] adj clay

Ton- zW: **~fall** m intonation; **~film** m sound film; **~leiter** f (MUS) scale; **t~los** adj soundless

Tonne ['tɔnə] f barrel; (Maß) ton

Ton- zW: **~taube** f clay pigeon; **~waren** pl pottery sg, earthenware sg

Topf [tɔpf] (-(e)s, ˙e) m pot; **~blume** f pot plant

Töpfer ['tœpfər] (-s, -) m potter; **~ei** [-'rai] f piece of pottery; potter's workshop; **~scheibe** f potter's wheel

topografisch [topo'gra:fɪʃ] adj

---

topographic

Tor¹ [toːr] (-en, -en) *m* fool

Tor² [toːr] (-(e)s, -e) *nt* gate; *(SPORT)* goal; **~bogen** *m* archway

Torf [tɔrf] (-(e)s) *m* peat

Torheit *f* foolishness; foolish deed

töricht ['tøːrɪçt] *adj* foolish

torkeln ['tɔrkəln] *vi* to stagger, to reel

Torte ['tɔrtə] *f* cake; *(Obsttorte)* flan, tart

Tortur [tɔr'tuːr] *f* ordeal

Torwart (-(e)s, -e) *m* goalkeeper

tosen ['toːzən] *vi* to roar

tot [toːt] *adj* dead; **~ geboren** stillborn; **sich ~ stellen** to pretend to be dead

total [to'taːl] *adj* total; **~itär** [totali'tɛːr] *adj* totalitarian; **T~schaden** *m (AUT)* complete write-off

Tote(r) *f(m)* dead person

töten ['tøːtən] *vt, vi* to kill

Toten- *zW:* **~bett** *nt* death bed; **t~blass ▲** *adj* deathly pale, white as a sheet; **~kopf** *m* skull; **~schein** *m* death certificate; **~stille** *f* deathly silence

tot- *zW:* **~fahren** *(unreg) vt* to run over; **~geboren △** *siehe tot;* **~lachen** *(umg) vr* to laugh one's head off

Toto ['toːto] (-s, -s) *m od nt* pools *pl;* **~schein** *m* pools coupon

tot- *zW:* **T~schlag** *m* manslaughter; **~schlagen** *(unreg) vt (auch fig)* to kill; **~schweigen** *(unreg) vt* to hush up; **~stellen △** *vr siehe* **tot**

Tötung ['tøːtʊŋ] *f* killing

Toupet [tu'peː] (-s, -s) *nt* toupee

toupieren [tu'piːrən] *vt* to backcomb

Tour [tuːr] (-, -en) *f* tour, trip; *(Umdrehung)* revolution; *(Verhaltensart)* way; **in einer ~** incessantly; **~enzähler** *m* rev counter; **~ismus** [tu'rɪsmʊs] *m* tourism; **~ist** [tu'rɪst] *m* tourist; **~istenklasse** *f* tourist class; **~nee** [tʊr'neː] (-, -n) *f (THEAT etc)* tour; **auf ~nee gehen** to go on tour

Trab [traːp] (-(e)s) *m* trot

Trabantenstadt *f* satellite town

traben ['traːbən] *vi* to trot

Tracht [traxt] (-, -en) *f (Kleidung)* costume, dress; **eine ~ Prügel** a sound thrashing; **t~en** *vi:* **t~en (nach)** to strive (for); **jdm nach dem Leben t~en** to seek to kill sb; **danach t~en, etw zu tun** to strive *od* endeavour to do sth

trächtig ['trɛçtɪç] *adj (Tier)* pregnant

Tradition [traditsi'oːn] *f* tradition; **t~ell** [-'nɛl] *adj* traditional

traf *etc* [traːf] *vb siehe* **treffen**

Tragbahre *f* stretcher

tragbar *adj (Gerät)* portable; *(Kleidung)* wearable; *(erträglich)* bearable

träge ['trɛːgə] *adj* sluggish, slow; *(PHYS)* inert

tragen ['traːgən] *(unreg) vt* to carry; *(Kleidung, Brille)* to wear; *(Namen, Früchte)* to bear; *(erdulden)* to endure ♦ *vi (schwanger sein)* to be pregnant; *(Eis)* to hold; **sich mit einem Gedanken ~** to have an idea in mind; **zum T~ kommen** to have an effect

Träger ['trɛːgər] (-s, -) *m* carrier; wearer; bearer; *(Ordensträger)* holder; *(an Kleidung)* (shoulder) strap; *(Körperschaft etc)* sponsor

Tragetasche *f* carrier bag

Tragfläche *f (AVIAT)* wing

Tragflügelboot *nt* hydrofoil

Trägheit ['trɛːkhaɪt] *f* laziness; *(PHYS)* inertia

Tragik ['traːgɪk] *f* tragedy; **tragisch** *adj* tragic

Tragödie [tra'gøːdiə] *f* tragedy

Tragweite *f* range; *(fig)* scope

Train- ['trɛːn] *zW:* **~er** (-s, -) *m (SPORT)* trainer, coach; *(Fußball)* manager; **t~ieren** [trɛ'niːrən] *vt, vi* to train; *(Mensch)* to train, to coach; *(Übung)* to practise; **~ing** (-s, -s) *nt* training; **~ingsanzug** *m* track suit

Traktor ['traktɔr] *m* tractor; *(von Drucker)* tractor feed

trällern ['trɛlərn] *vt, vi* to trill, to sing

Tram [tram] (-, -s) *f* tram

trampeln ['trampəln] *vt, vi* to trample, to stamp

trampen ['trɛmpən] *vi* to hitch-hike

Tramper(in) [trɛmpər(in)] (**-s, -**) *m(f)* hitch-hiker

Tran [traːn] (**-(e)s, -e**) *m* train oil, blubber

tranchieren [trã'ʃiːrən] *vt* to carve

Träne ['trɛːnə] *f* tear; **t~n** *vi* to water; **~ngas** *nt* teargas

trank *etc* [traŋk] *vb siehe* **trinken**

tränken ['trɛŋkən] *vt (Tiere)* to water

transchieren ▲ [tran'ʃiːrən] *vt* to carve

Trans- *zW:* **~formator** [transfɔr-'maːtɔr] *m* transformer; **~istor** [tran'zistɔr] *m* transistor; **~itverkehr** [tran'ziːtfɛrkeːr] *m* transit traffic; **~itvisum** *nt* transit visa; **t~parent** adj transparent; **~parent** (**-(e)s, -e**) *nt (Bild)* transparency; *(Spruchband)* banner; **~plantation** [transplantatsi'oːn] *f* transplantation; *(Hauttransplantation)* graft(ing)

Transport [trans'pɔrt] (**-(e)s, -e**) *m* transport; **t~ieren** [transpɔr'tiːrən] *vt* to transport; **~kosten** *pl* transport charges, carriage *sg*; **~mittel** *nt* means *sg* of transportation; **~unternehmen** *nt* carrier

Traube ['traubə] *f* grape; bunch (of grapes); **~nzucker** *m* glucose

trauen ['trauən] *vi:* jdm/etw **~** to trust sb/sth ♦ *vt* to dare ♦ *vr* to marry

Trauer ['trauər] (**-**) *f* sorrow; *(für Verstorbenen)* mourning; **~fall** *m* death, bereavement; **~feier** *f* funeral service; **~kleidung** *f* mourning; **t~n** *vi* to mourn; **um** jdn **t~n** to mourn (for) sb; **~rand** *m* black border; **~spiel** *nt* tragedy

traulich ['traulɪç] adj cosy, intimate

Traum [traum] (**-(e)s, Träume**) *m* dream

Trauma (**-s, -men**) *nt* trauma

träum- ['trɔym] *zW:* **~en** *vt, vi* to dream; **T~er** (**-s, -**) *m* dreamer; **T~e'rei** *f* dreaming; **~erisch** adj dreamy

traumhaft adj dreamlike; *(fig)* wonderful

traurig ['trauʁɪç] adj sad; **T~keit** *f* sadness

Trau- ['trau] *zW:* **~ring** *m* wedding ring; **~schein** *m* marriage certificate; **~ung** *f* wedding ceremony; **~zeuge** *m* witness (to a marriage); **~zeugin** *f* witness (to a marriage)

treffen ['trɛfən] (*unreg*) *vt* to strike, to hit; *(Bemerkung)* to hurt; *(begegnen)* to meet; *(Entscheidung etc)* to make; *(Maßnahmen)* to take ♦ *vi* to hit ♦ *vr* to meet; **er hat es gut getroffen** he did well; **~ auf** +*akk* to come across, to meet with; **es traf sich, dass ...** it so happened that ...; **es trifft sich gut** it's convenient; **wie es so trifft** as these things happen; **T~** (**-s, -**) *nt* meeting; **~d** adj pertinent, apposite

Treffer (**-s, -**) *m* hit; *(Tor)* goal; *(Los)* winner

Treffpunkt *m* meeting place

Treib- [traib] *zW:* **~eis** *nt* drift ice; **t~en** (*unreg*) *vt* to drive; *(Studien etc)* to pursue; *(Sport)* to do, to go in for ♦ *vi (Schiff etc)* to drift; *(Pflanzen)* to sprout; *(KOCH: aufgehen)* to rise; *(Tee, Kaffee)* to be diuretic; **~haus** *nt* greenhouse; **~hauseffekt** *m* greenhouse effect; **~hausgas** *nt* greenhouse gas; **~stoff** *m* fuel

trenn- ['trɛn] *zW:* **~bar** adj separable; **~en** *vt* to separate; *(teilen)* to divide ♦ *vr* to separate; **sich ~en von** to part with; **T~ung** *f* separation; **T~wand** *f* partition (wall)

Trepp- ['trɛp] *zW:* **t~ab** adv downstairs; **t~auf** adv upstairs; **~e** *f* stair(case); **~engeländer** *nt* banister; **~enhaus** *nt* staircase

Tresor [tre'zo:r] (-s, -e) m safe

Tretboot nt pedalo, pedal boat

treten ['tre:tən] (unreg) vi to step; (Tränen, Schweiß) to appear ♦ vt (mit Fußtritt) to kick; (niedertreten) to tread, to trample; **~ nach** to kick at; **~ in** +akk to step in(to); **in Verbindung ~** to get in contact; **in Erscheinung ~** to appear

treu [trɔy] adj faithful, true; **T~e** (-) f loyalty, faithfulness; **T~händer** (-s, -) m trustee; **T~handanstalt** f trustee organization; **T~handgesellschaft** f trust company; **~herzig** adj innocent; **~los** adj faithless

---

The Treuhandanstalt was the organization set up in 1990 to take over the nationally-owned companies of the former DDR, break them down into smaller units and privatize them. It was based in Berlin and had nine branches. Many companies were closed down by the Treuhandanstalt because of their outdated equipment and inability to compete with Western firms which resulted in rising unemployment. Having completed its initial task, the Treuhandanstalt was closed down in 1995.

Tribüne [tri'by:nə] f grandstand; (Rednertribüne) platform

Trichter ['trɪçtər] (-s, -) m funnel; (in Boden) crater

Trick [trɪk] (-s, -e od -s) m trick; **~film** m cartoon

Trieb [tri:p] (-(e)s, -e) m urge, drive; (Neigung) inclination; (an Baum etc) shoot; **t~** etc vb siehe **treiben**; **~kraft** f (fig) drive; **~täter** m sex offender; **~werk** nt engine

triefen ['tri:fən] vi to drip

triffst etc [trɪfst] vb siehe **treffen**

triftig ['trɪftɪç] adj good, convincing

Trikot [tri'ko:] (-s, -s) nt vest; (SPORT) shirt

Trimester [tri'mɛstər] (-s, -) nt term

trimmen ['trɪmən] vr to do keep fit exercises

trink- ['trɪŋk] zW: **~bar** adj drinkable; **~en** (unreg) vt, vi to drink; **T~er** (-s, -) m drinker; **T~geld** nt tip; **T~halle** f refreshment kiosk; **T~wasser** nt drinking water

Tripper ['trɪpər] (-s, -) m gonorrhoea

Tritt [trɪt] (-(e)s, -e) m step; (Fußtritt) kick; **~brett** nt (EISENB) step; (AUT) running board

Triumph [tri'ʊmf] (-(e)s, -e) m triumph; **~bogen** m triumphal arch; **t~ieren** [triʊm'fi:rən] vi to triumph; (jubeln) to exult

trocken ['trɔkən] adj dry; **T~element** nt dry cell; **T~haube** f hair dryer; **T~heit** f dryness; **~legen** vt (Sumpf) to drain; (Kind) to put a clean nappy on; **T~milch** f dried milk; **T~rasur** f dry shave, electric shave

trocknen ['trɔknən] vt, vi to dry

Trödel ['trø:dəl] (-s) (umg) m junk; **~markt** m flea market; **t~n** (umg) vi to dawdle

Trommel ['trɔməl] (-, -n) f drum; **~fell** nt eardrum; **t~n** vt, vi to drum

Trompete [trɔm'pe:tə] f trumpet; **~r** (-s, -) m trumpeter

Tropen ['tro:pən] pl tropics; **~helm** m sun helmet

tröpfeln ['trœpfəln] vi to drop, to trickle

Tropfen ['trɔpfən] (-s, -) m drop; **t~** vt, vi to drip ♦ vb unpers: **es tropft** a few raindrops are falling; **t~weise** adv in drops

Tropfsteinhöhle f stalactite cave

tropisch ['tro:pɪʃ] adj tropical

Trost [tro:st] (-es) m consolation, comfort

trösten ['trø:stən] vt to console, to comfort

trost- zW: **~los** adj bleak; (Verhältnisse) wretched; **T~preis** m consolation prize; **~reich** adj comforting

Trott [trɔt] (-(e)s, -e) m trot; (Routine) routine; **~el** (-s, -) (umg) m fool, dope; **t~en** vi to trot

Trotz [trɔts] (-es) m pigheadedness; etw aus ~ tun to do sth just to show them; **jdm zum** ~ in defiance of sth; **t~** präp (+gen od dat) in spite of; **t~dem** adv nevertheless, all the same ♦ konj although; **t~en** vi (+dat) to defy; (der Kälte, Klima etc) to withstand; (der Gefahr) to brave; (t~ig sein) to be awkward; **t~ig** adj defiant, pig-headed; **~kopf** m obstinate child

trüb [try:p] adj dull; (Flüssigkeit, Glas) cloudy; (fig) gloomy

Trubel ['tru:bəl] (-s) m hurly-burly

trüb- zW: **~en** ['try:bən] vt to cloud ♦ vr to become clouded; **T~heit** f dullness; (cloudiness); gloom; **T~sal** (-, -e) f distress; **~selig** adj sad, melancholy; **T~sinn** m depression; **~sinnig** adj depressed, gloomy

Trüffel ['tryfəl] (-, -n) f truffle

trug etc [tru:k] vb siehe **tragen**

trügen ['try:gən] (unreg) vt to deceive ♦ vi to be deceptive

trügerisch adj deceptive

Trugschluss ▲ ['tru:gʃlʊs] m false conclusion

Truhe ['tru:ə] f chest

Trümmer ['trymər] pl wreckage sg; (Bautrümmer) ruins; **~haufen** m heap of rubble

Trumpf [trʊmpf] (-(e)s, ⁻e) m (auch fig) trump; **t~en** vt, vi to trump

Trunk [trʊŋk] (-(e)s, ⁻e) m drink; **t~en** adj intoxicated; **~enheit** f intoxication; **~enheit am Steuer** drunken driving; **~sucht** f alcoholism

Trupp [trʊp] (-s, -s) m troop; **~e** f troop; (Waffengattung) force; (Schauspieltruppe) troupe; **~en** pl (MIL) troops; **~enübungsplatz** m training area

Truthahn ['tru:tha:n] m turkey

Tschech- ['tʃɛç] zW: **~e** m Czech; **~ien** (-s) nt the Czech Republic; **~in** f Czech; **t~isch** adj Czech; **~oslowakei** [-oslova'kaɪ] f: **die ~oslowakei** Czechoslovakia; **t~oslowakisch** [-oslo'va:kɪʃ] adj Czechoslovak(ian)

tschüs(s) [tʃys] excl cheerio

T-Shirt ['ti:ʃœt] nt T-shirt

Tube ['tu:bə] f tube

Tuberkulose [tuberku'lo:zə] f tuberculosis

Tuch [tu:x] (-(e)s, ⁻er) nt cloth; (Halstuch) scarf; (Kopftuch) headscarf; (Handtuch) towel

tüchtig ['tʏçtɪç] adj efficient, (cap)able; (umg: kräftig) good, sound; **T~keit** f efficiency, ability

Tücke ['tʏkə] f (Arglist) malice; (Trick) trick; (Schwierigkeit) difficulty, problem

tückisch ['tʏkɪʃ] adj treacherous; (böswillig) malicious

Tugend ['tu:gənt] (-, -en) f virtue; **t~haft** adj virtuous

Tülle f spout

Tulpe ['tʊlpə] f tulip

Tumor ['tu:mɔr] (-s, -e) m tumour

Tümpel ['tʏmpəl] (-s, -) m pool, pond

Tumult [tu'mʊlt] (-(e)s, -e) m tumult

tun [tu:n] (unreg) vt (machen) to do; (legen) to put ♦ vi to act ♦ vr: **es tut sich etwas/viel** something/a lot is happening; **jdm etw ~** (antun) to do sth to sb; **etw tut es auch** sth will do; **das tut nichts** that doesn't matter; **das tut nichts zur Sache** that's neither here nor there; **so ~ als ob** to act as if

tünchen ['tʏnçən] vt to whitewash

Tunfisch ▲ ['tu:nfɪʃ] m = **Thunfisch**

Tunke ['tʊŋkə] f sauce; **t~n** vt to dip, to dunk

tunlichst ['tu:nlɪçst] adv if at all possible; **~ bald** as soon as possible

Tunnel ['tʊnəl] (-s, -s od -s) m tunnel

Tupfen ['tʊpfən] (-s, -) m dot, spot; **t~**

vt, vi to dab; *(mit Farbe)* to dot

Tür [ty:r] (-, -en) *f* door

Turbine [tʊrˈbiːnə] *f* turbine

Türk- [tʏrk] *zW:* **~e** *m* Turk; **~ei** [tʏrˈkaɪ] *f:* **die ~ei** Turkey; **~in** *f* Turk

Türkis [tʏrˈkiːs] (-es, -e) *m* turquoise; **t~** *adj* turquoise

türkisch [ˈtʏrkɪʃ] *adj* Turkish

Türklinke *f* doorknob, door handle

Turm [tʊrm] (-(e)s, ⁼e) *m* tower; *(Kirchturm)* steeple; *(Sprungturm)* diving platform; *(SCHACH)* castle, rook

türmen [ˈtʏrmən] *vr* to tower up ♦ *vt* to heap up ♦ *vi (umg)* to scarper, to bolt

Turn- [ˈtʊrn] *zW:* **t~en** *vi* to do gymnastic exercises ♦ *vt* to perform; **~en** (-s) *nt* gymnastics; *(SCH)* physical education, P.E.; **~er(in)** (-s, -) *m(f)* gymnast; **~halle** *f* gym(nasium); **~hose** *f* gym shorts *pl*

Turnier [tʊrˈniːr] (-s, -e) *nt* tournament

Turn- *zW:* **~schuh** *m* gym shoe; **~verein** *m* gymnastics club; **~zeug** *nt* gym things *pl*

Tusche [ˈtʊʃə] *f* Indian ink

tuscheln [ˈtʊʃəln] *vt, vi* to whisper

Tuschkasten *m* paintbox

Tüte [ˈtyːtə] *f* bag

tuten [ˈtuːtən] *vi (AUT)* to hoot *(BRIT)*, to honk *(US)*

TÜV [tʏf] (-s, -s) *m abk* (= *Technischer Überwachungs-Verein*) ≃ MOT

Typ [typ] (-s, -en) *m* type; **~e** *f (TYP)* type

Typhus [ˈtyːfʊs] (-) *m* typhoid (fever)

typisch [ˈtyːpɪʃ] *adj:* **~ (für)** typical (of)

Tyrann [tyˈran] (-en, -en) *m* tyrant; **~ei** [-ˈnaɪ] *f* tyranny; **t~isch** *adj* tyrannical; **t~isieren** *vt* to tyrannize

U, u

u. a. *abk* = unter anderem

U-Bahn [ˈuːbaːn] *f* underground, tube

übel [ˈyːbəl] *adj* bad; *(moralisch)* bad, wicked; **jdm ist ~** sb feels sick; **~ gelaunt** bad-tempered; **jdm eine Bemerkung ~ nehmen** to be offended at sb's remark; **Ü~** (-s, -) *nt* evil; *(Krankheit)* disease; **Ü~keit** *f* nausea

üben [ˈyːbən] *vt, vi* to exercise, to practise

über [ˈyːbər] *präp +dat* **1** *(räumlich)* over, above; *(höher als)* above; **zwei Grad über null** two degrees above zero

2 *(zeitlich)* over; **über der Arbeit einschlafen** to fall asleep over one's work ♦ *präp +akk* **1** *(räumlich)* over; *(hoch über auch)* above; *(quer über auch)* across

2 *(zeitlich)* over; **über Weihnachten** over Christmas; **über kurz oder lang** sooner or later

3 *(mit Zahlen)* **Kinder über 12 Jahren** children over *od* above 12 years of age; **ein Scheck über 200 Mark** a cheque for 200 marks

4 *(auf dem Wege)* via; **nach Köln über Aachen** to Cologne via Aachen; **ich habe es über die Auskunft erfahren** I found out from information

5 *(betreffend)* about; **ein Buch über ...** a book about *od* on ...; **über jdn/etw lachen** to laugh about *od* at sb/sth

6: **Macht über jdn haben** to have power over sb; **sie liebt ihn über alles** she loves him more than everything

♦ *adv* over; **über und über** over and over; **den ganzen Tag über** all day long; **jdm in etw** *dat* **über sein** to be superior to sb in sth

überall [y:bər'|al] *adv* everywhere; ~ **hin** *adv* everywhere

überanstrengen [y:bər'|anʃtrɛŋən] *vt insep* to overexert ♦ *vr insep* to overexert o.s.

überarbeiten [y:bər'|arbaitən] *vt insep* to revise, to rework ♦ *vr insep* to overwork (o.s.)

überaus ['y:bər|aus] *adv* exceedingly

überbelichten ['y:bərbəlıçtən] *vt* (PHOT) to overexpose

über'bieten (*unreg*) *vt insep* to outbid; (*übertreffen*) to surpass; (*Rekord*) to break

Überbleibsel [y:bərblaipsəl] (**-s**, **-**) *nt* residue, remainder

Überblick ['y:bərblık] *m* view; (*fig:* Darstellung) survey, overview; (*Fähigkeit*) : ~ (**über** +*akk*) grasp (of), overall view (of); **ü~en** [-'blıkən] *vt insep* to survey

überbring'en [y:bər'brıŋ] *zW:* ~**en** (*unreg*) *vt insep* to deliver, to hand over; **Ü~er** (**-s**, **-**) *m* bearer

überbrücken [y:bər'brykən] *vt insep* to bridge (over)

überbuchen [y:bər'bu:xən] *vt insep* to overbook

über'dauern *vt insep* to outlast

über'denken (*unreg*) *vt insep* to think over

überdies [y:bər'di:s] *adv* besides

überdimensional ['y:bərdimenziona:l] *adj* oversize

Überdruss ▲ ['y:bərdrus] (**-es**) *m* weariness; **bis zum ~** ad nauseam

überdurchschnittlich ['y:bərdurçʃnıtlıç] *adj* above-average ♦ *adv* exceptionally

übereifrig ['y:bər|aifrıç] *adj* over-keen

übereilt [y:bər'|ailt] *adj* (over)hasty, premature

überein- [y:bər'|ain] *zW:* ~**ander** [y:bər|ai'nandər] *adv* one upon the other; (*sprechen*) about each other;

~kommen (*unreg*) *vi* to agree; **Ü~kunft** (**-**, **-künfte**) *f* agreement; **~stimmen** *vi* to agree; **Ü~stimmung** *f* agreement

überempfindlich ['y:bər|empfıntlıç] *adj* hypersensitive

über'fahren [y:bər'fa:rən] (*unreg*) *vt insep* (AUT) to run over; (*fig*) to walk all over

Überfahrt ['y:bərfa:rt] *f* crossing

Überfall ['y:bərfal] *m* (Banküberfall, MIL) raid; (*auf jdn*) assault; **ü~en** [-'falən] (*unreg*) *vt insep* to attack; (*Bank*) to raid; (*besuchen*) to drop in on, to descend on

überfällig ['y:bərfɛlıç] *adj* overdue

über'fliegen (*unreg*) *vt insep* to fly over, to overfly; (*Buch*) to skim through

Überfluss ▲ ['y:bərflus] *m:* ~ (**an** +*dat*) (super)abundance (of), excess (of)

überflüssig ['y:bərflysıç] *adj* superfluous

über'fordern *vt insep* to demand too much of; (*Kräfte etc*) to overtax

über'führen *vt insep* (*Leiche etc*) to transport; (*Täter*) to have convicted

Über'führung *f* transport; conviction; (*Brücke*) bridge, overpass

über'füllt *adj* (Schulen, Straßen) overcrowded; (*Kurs*) oversubscribed

Übergabe ['y:bərga:bə] *f* handing over; (MIL) surrender

Übergang ['y:bərgaŋ] *m* crossing; (*Wandel, Überleitung*) transition

Übergangs- *zW:* ~**lösung** *f* provisional solution, stopgap; ~**zeit** *f* transitional period

über'geben (*unreg*) *vt insep* to hand over; (MIL) to surrender ♦ *vr insep* to be sick

übergehen ['y:bərge:ən] *vi* (*in Besitz*) to pass; (*zum Feind etc*) to go over, to defect; ~ **in** +*akk* to turn into; **über'gehen** (*unreg*) *vt insep* to pass

---

Spelling reform: ▲ new spelling △ old spelling (to be phased out)

over, to omit

Übergewicht ['y:bərgəvɪçt] nt excess weight; (fig) preponderance

überglücklich ['y:bərɡlyklɪç] adj overjoyed

Übergröße ['y:bərɡrø:sə] f oversize

überhaupt [y:bər'haupt] adv at all; (im Allgemeinen) in general; (besonders) especially; ~ **nicht/keine** not/none at all

überheblich [y:bər'he:plɪç] adj arrogant; **Ü~keit** f arrogance

überholen vt insep to overtake; (TECH) to overhaul

über'holt adj out-of-date, obsolete

Überholverbot [y:bər'ho:lfɛrbo:t] nt restriction on overtaking

über'hören vt insep not to hear; (absichtlich) to ignore

überirdisch ['y:bər|ɪrdɪʃ] adj supernatural, unearthly

über'laden (unreg) vt insep to overload ♦ adj (fig) cluttered

über'lassen (unreg) vt insep: **jdm etw ~** to leave sth to sb ♦ vr insep: **sich einer Sache** dat ~ to give o.s. over to sth

über'lasten vt insep to overload; (Mensch) to overtax

überlaufen ['y:bərlaufən] (unreg) vi (Flüssigkeit) to flow over; (zum Feind etc) to go over, to defect; ~ **sein** to be inundated od besieged; **über'laufen** (unreg) vt insep (Schauer etc) to come over

über'leben vt insep to survive; **Überlebende(r)** f(m) survivor

über'legen vt insep to consider ♦ adj superior; **ich muss es mir ~** I'll have to think about it; **Überlegenheit** f superiority

Überlegung f consideration, deliberation

über'liefern vt insep to hand down, to transmit

Überlieferung f tradition

überlisten [y:bər'lɪstən] vt insep to outwit

überm ['y:bərm] = **über dem**

Übermacht ['y:bərmaxt] f superior force, superiority; **übermächtig** ['y:bərmɛçtɪç] adj superior (in strength); (Gefühl etc) overwhelming

übermäßig ['y:bərmɛ:sɪç] adj excessive

Übermensch ['y:bərmɛnʃ] m superman; **ü~lich** adj superhuman

übermitteln [y:bər'mɪtəln] vt insep to convey

übermorgen ['y:bərmɔrɡən] adv the day after tomorrow

Übermüdung [y:bər'my:dʊŋ] f fatigue, overtiredness

Übermut ['y:bərmu:t] m exuberance

übermütig ['y:bərmy:tɪç] adj exuberant, high-spirited; ~ **werden** to get overconfident

übernächste(r, s) ['y:bərnɛ:çstə(r, s)] adj (Jahr) next but one

übernachten [y:bər'naxt] zW: ~**en** vi insep: **(bei jdm)** ~**en** to spend the night (at sb's place); **Ü~ung** f overnight stay; **Ü~ung mit Frühstück** bed and breakfast; **Ü~ungsmöglichkeit** f overnight accommodation no pl

Übernahme [y:bər'na:mə] f taking over od on, acceptance

über'nehmen (unreg) vt insep to take on, to accept; (Amt, Geschäft) to take over ♦ vr insep to take on too much

über'prüfen vt insep to examine, to check

überqueren [y:bər'kve:rən] vt insep to cross

über'ragen [y:bər'ra:ɡən] vt insep to tower above; (fig) to surpass

überraschen [y:bər'raʃən] vt insep to surprise

Überraschung f surprise

überreden [y:bər're:dən] vt insep to persuade

überreichen [y:bər'raɪçən] vt insep to present, to hand over

'Überrest m remains, remnants

überrumpeln [y:bər'rompəln] vt insep to take by surprise

überrunden [y:bər'rʊndən] vt insep to lap

übers ['y:bərs] = **über das**

Überschall- ['y:bərʃal] zW: **~flugzeug** nt supersonic jet; **~geschwindigkeit** f supersonic speed

über'schätzen vt insep to overestimate

'überschäumen vi (Bier) to foam over, bubble over; (Temperament) to boil over

Überschlag ['y:bərʃla:k] m (FIN) estimate; (SPORT) somersault; **ü~en** [-'ʃla:gən] (unreg) vt (berechnen) to estimate; (auslassen: Seite) to omit ♦ vr insep to somersault; (Stimme) to crack; (AVIAT) to loop the loop; **'überschlagen** (unreg) vt (Beine) to cross ♦ vi (Wellen) to break; (Funken) to flash

überschnappen ['y:bərʃnapən] vi (Stimme) to crack; (umg: Mensch) to flip one's lid

über'schneiden (unreg) vr insep (auch fig) to overlap; (Linien) to intersect

über'schreiben (unreg) vt insep to provide with a heading; **jdm etw ~** to transfer od make over sth to sb

über'schreiten (unreg) vt insep to cross over; (fig) to exceed; (verletzen) to transgress

Überschrift ['y:bərʃrɪft] f heading, title

Überschuss ▲ ['y:bərʃʊs] m: **~ (an** +dat) surplus (of); **überschüssig** ['y:bərʃʏsɪç] adj surplus, excess

über'schütten vt insep: **jdn/etw mit etw ~** to pour sth over sb/sth; **jdn mit etw ~** (fig) to shower sb with sth

überschwänglich ▲ ['y:bərʃvɛŋlɪç] adj effusive

überschwemmen [y:bər'ʃvɛmən] vt insep to flood

Überschwemmung f flood

Übersee ['y:bərze:] f: **nach/in ~** overseas; **ü~isch** adj overseas

über'sehen (unreg) vt insep to look (out) over; (fig: Folgen) to see, to get an overall view of; (: nicht beachten) to overlook

über'senden (unreg) vt insep to send, to forward

übersetz- zW: **~en** (übersetzen) vi insep to translate; **'übersetzen** vi to cross; **Ü~er(in)** [-'zɛtsər(ɪn)] (-s, -) m(f) translator; **Ü~ung** [-'zɛtsʊŋ] f translation; (TECH) gear ratio

Übersicht ['y:bərzɪçt] f overall view; (Darstellung) survey; **ü~lich** adj clear; (Gelände) open; **~lichkeit** f clarity, lucidity

übersiedeln ['y:bərzi:dəln] vi sep to move; **über'siedeln** vi to move

über'spannt adj eccentric; (Idee) wild, crazy

überspitzt [y:bər'ʃpɪtst] adj exaggerated

über'springen (unreg) vt insep to jump over; (fig) to skip

über'stehen (unreg) vt insep to overcome, to get over; (Winter etc) to survive, to get through; **'überstehen** (unreg) vi to project

über'steigen (unreg) vt insep to climb over; (fig) to exceed

über'stimmen vt insep to outvote

Überstunden ['y:bərʃtʊndən] pl overtime sg

über'stürzen vt insep to rush ♦ vr insep to follow (one another) in rapid succession

überstürzt adj (over)hasty

Übertrag ['y:bərtra:k] (-(e)s, -(e)) m (COMM) amount brought forward; **ü~bar** [-'tra:kba:r] adj transferable; (MED) infectious; **ü~en** [-'tra:gən] (unreg) vt insep to transfer; (RADIO) to broadcast; (übersetzen) to render; (Krankheit) to transmit ♦ vr insep to spread ♦ adj figurative; **etw auf jdn ~en** to transfer sth to sb; **jdm etw ü~en** to assign sth to sb; **sich ü~en auf** +akk to spread to; **~ung** ['-tra:gʊŋ] f transfer(ence); (RADIO) broadcast; rendering; transmission

über'treffen (unreg) vt insep to surpass

über'treiben (unreg) vt to exaggerate; **Übertreibung** f exaggeration

übertreten [y:bər'tre:tən] (unreg) vt insep to cross; (Gebot etc) to break; **'übertreten** [y:bər'tre:tən] vi (über Linie, Gebiet) to step (over); (SPORT) to overstep; (zu anderem Glauben) to be converted; **'übertreten** (in +akk) (POL) to go over (to)

Über'tretung f violation, transgression

übertrieben [y:bər'tri:bən] adj exaggerated, excessive

übervölkert [y:bər'fœlkərt] adj overpopulated

übervoll ['y:bərfɔl] adj overfull

übervorteilen [y:bər'fɔrtaɪlən] vt insep to dupe, to cheat

über'wachen vt insep to supervise; (Verdächtigen) to keep under surveillance; **Überwachung** f supervision; surveillance

überwältigen [y:bər'vɛltigən] vt insep to overpower; **~d** adj overwhelming

überweisen [y:bər'vaɪzən] (unreg) vt insep to transfer

Überweisung f transfer; **~sauftrag** m (credit) transfer order

über'wiegen (unreg) vi insep to predominate; **~d** adj predominant

über'winden (unreg) vt insep to overcome ♦ vr insep to make an effort, to bring o.s. (to do sth)

Überwindung f effort, strength of mind

Überzahl ['y:bərtsa:l] f superiority, superior numbers pl; **in der ~ sein** to be numerically superior

überzählig ['y:bərtsɛ:lɪç] adj surplus

über'zeugen vt insep to convince; **~d** adj convincing

Überzeugung f conviction

überziehen [y:bər'tsi:ən] (unreg) vt to put on; **über'ziehen** (unreg) vt insep to

cover; (Konto) to overdraw

Überziehungskredit m overdraft provision

Überzug ['y:bərtsu:k] m cover; (Belag) coating

üblich ['y:plɪç] adj usual

U-Boot ['u:bo:t] nt submarine

übrig ['y:brɪç] adj remaining; **für jdn etwas ~ haben** (umg) to be fond of sb; **die Ü~en** the others; **das Ü~e** the rest; **im Ü~en** besides; **~ bleiben** to remain, to be left (over); **~ lassen** to leave (over); **~ens** ['y:brɪgəns] adv besides; (nebenbei bemerkt) by the way

Übung ['y:bʊŋ] f practice; (Turnübung, Aufgabe etc) exercise; **~ macht den Meister** practice makes perfect

Ufer ['u:fər] (-s, -) nt bank; (Meeresufer) shore

Uhr [u:r] (-, -en) f clock; (Armbanduhr) watch; **wie viel ~ ist es?** what time is it?; **1 ~** 1 o'clock; **20 ~** 8 o'clock, 20.00 (twenty hundred) hours; **~(arm)band** nt watch strap; **~band** nt watch strap; **~macher** (-s, -) m watchmaker; **~werk** nt clockwork; works of a watch; **~zeiger** m hand; **~zeigersinn** m: **im ~zeigersinn** clockwise; **entgegen dem ~zeigersinn** anticlockwise; **~zeit** f time (of day)

Uhu ['u:hu] (-s, -s) m eagle owl

UKW [u:ka:'ve:] abk (= Ultrakurzwelle) VHF

ulkig ['ʊlkɪç] adj funny

Ulme ['ʊlmə] f elm

Ultimatum [ʊlti'ma:tʊm] (-s, Ultimaten) nt ultimatum

Ultra- ['ʊltra] zW: **~schall** m (PHYS) ultrasound; **u~violett** adj ultraviolet

SCHLÜSSELWORT

um [ʊm] präp +akk **1** (um herum) (a)round; **um Weihnachten** around Christmas; **er schlug um sich** he hit about him

2 (mit Zeitangabe) at; **um acht (Uhr)** at eight (o'clock)

3 (*mit Größenangabe*) by; **etw um 4 cm kürzen** to shorten sth by 4 cm; **um 10% teurer** 10% more expensive; **um vieles besser** better by far; **um nichts besser** not in the least bit better

4: **der Kampf um den Titel** the battle for the title; **um Geld spielen** to play for money; **Stunde um Stunde** hour after hour; **Auge um Auge** an eye for an eye

♦ *präp +gen*: **um ... willen** for the sake of ...; **um Gottes willen** for goodness' *od* (*stärker*) God's sake

♦ *konj*: **um ... zu** (in order) to ...; **zu klug, um ... zu ...** too clever to ...; *siehe* **umso**

♦ *adv* 1 (*ungefähr*) about; **um (die) 30 Leute** about *od* around 30 people

2 (*vorbei*): **die 2 Stunden sind um** the two hours are up

---

umändern ['ʊmʔɛndərn] *vt* to alter
Umänderung *f* alteration
umarbeiten ['ʊmʔarbaitən] *vt* to remodel; (*Buch etc*) to revise, to rework
umarmen [ʊm'ʔarmən] *vt insep* to embrace
Umbau ['ʊmbaʊ] (*-(e)s, -e od -ten*) *m* reconstruction, alteration(s); **u~en** *vt* to rebuild, to reconstruct
umbilden ['ʊmbɪldən] *vt* to reorganize; (*POL: Kabinett*) to reshuffle
umbinden ['ʊmbɪndən] (*unreg*) *vt* (*Krawatte etc*) to put on
umblättern ['ʊmblɛtərn] *vt* to turn over
umblicken ['ʊmblɪkən] *vr* to look around
umbringen ['ʊmbrɪŋən] (*unreg*) *vt* to kill
umbuchen ['ʊmbuːxən] *vi* to change one's reservation/flight *etc* ♦ *vt* to change
umdenken ['ʊmdɛŋkən] (*unreg*) *vi* to adjust one's views
umdrehen ['ʊmdreːən] *vt* to turn (round); (*Hals*) to wring ♦ *vr* to turn (round)
Um'drehung *f* revolution; rotation
umeinander [ʊmʔaɪˈnandər] *adv* round one another; (*füreinander*) for one another
umfahren ['ʊmfaːrən] (*unreg*) *vt* to run over; **um'fahren** (*unreg*) *vt insep* to drive round; (*Schiff*) to sail round
umfallen ['ʊmfalən] (*unreg*) *vi* to fall down *od* over
Umfang ['ʊmfaŋ] *m* extent; (*von Buch*) size; (*Reichweite*) range; (*Fläche*) area; (*MATH*) circumference; **u~reich** *adj* extensive; (*Buch etc*) voluminous
um'fassen *vt insep* to embrace; (*umgeben*) to surround; (*enthalten*) to include; **um'fassend** *adj* comprehensive, extensive
umformen ['ʊmfɔrmən] *vi* to transform
Umfrage ['ʊmfraːgə] *f* poll
umfüllen ['ʊmfʏlən] *vt* to transfer; (*Wein*) to decant
umfunktionieren ['ʊmfʊŋktsioniːrən] *vt* to convert, to transform
Umgang ['ʊmgaŋ] *m* company; (*mit jdm*) dealings *pl*; (*Behandlung*) way of behaving
umgänglich ['ʊmgɛŋlɪç] *adj* sociable
Umgangs- *zW*: **~formen** *pl* manners; **~sprache** *f* colloquial language
umgeben [ʊmˈgeːbən] (*unreg*) *vt insep* to surround
Umgebung *f* surroundings *pl*; (*Milieu*) environment; (*Personen*) people in one's circle
umgehen ['ʊmgeːən] (*unreg*) *vi* to go (a)round; **im Schlosse ~** to haunt the castle; **mit jdm grob** *etc* **~** to treat sb roughly *etc*; **mit Geld sparsam ~** to be careful with one's money; **um'gehen** *vt insep* to bypass; (*MIL*) to

---

outflank; (*Gesetz etc*) to circumvent; (*vermeiden*) to avoid; '**umgehend** *adj* immediate

Um'gehung *f* bypassing; outflanking; circumvention; avoidance; **~sstraße** *f* bypass

umgekehrt ['ʊmgəkeːrt] *adj* reverse(d); (*gegenteilig*) opposite ♦ *adv* the other way around; **und ~** and vice versa

umgraben ['ʊmgraːbən] (*unreg*) *vt* to dig up

Umhang ['ʊmhaŋ] *m* wrap, cape

umhauen ['ʊmhaʊən] *vt* to fell; (*fig*) to bowl over

umher [ʊm'heːr] *adv* about, around; **~gehen** (*unreg*) *vi* to walk about; **~ziehen** (*unreg*) *vi* to wander from place to place

umhinkönnen [ʊm'hɪnkœnən] (*unreg*) *vi*: **ich kann nicht umhin, das zu tun** I can't help doing it

umhören ['ʊmhøːrən] *vr* to ask around

Umkehr ['ʊmkeːr] (-) *f* turning back; (*Änderung*) change; **u~en** *vi* to turn back ♦ *vt* to turn round, to reverse; (*Tasche etc*) to turn inside out; (*Gefäß etc*) to turn upside down

umkippen ['ʊmkɪpən] *vt* to tip over ♦ *vi* to overturn; (*umg: Mensch*) to keel over; (*fig: Meinung ändern*) to change one's mind

Umkleide- ['ʊmklaɪdə] *zW*: **~kabine** *f* (*im Schwimmbad*) (changing) cubicle; **~raum** *m* changing od dressing room

umkommen ['ʊmkɔmən] (*unreg*) *vi* to die, to perish; (*Lebensmittel*) to go bad

Umkreis ['ʊmkraɪs] *m* neighbourhood; **im ~ von** within a radius of

Umlage ['ʊmlaːgə] *f* share of the costs

Umlauf ['ʊmlaʊf] *m* (*Geldumlauf*) circulation; (*von Gestirn*) revolution; **~bahn** *f* orbit

Umlaut ['ʊmlaʊt] *m* umlaut

umlegen ['ʊmleːgən] *vt* to put on; (*verlegen*) to move, to shift; (*Kosten*) to

share out; (*umkippen*) to tip over; (*umg: töten*) to bump off

umleiten ['ʊmlaɪtən] *vt* to divert

Umleitung *f* diversion

umliegend ['ʊmliːgənt] *adj* surrounding

um'randen *vt insep* to border, to edge

umrechnen ['ʊmrɛçnən] *vt* to convert

Umrechnung *f* conversion; **~skurs** *m* rate of exchange

um'reißen (*unreg*) *vt insep* to outline, to sketch

Umriss ▲ ['ʊmrɪs] *m* outline

umrühren ['ʊmryːrən] *vt, vi* to stir

ums [ʊms] = **um das**

Umsatz ['ʊmzats] *m* turnover; **~steuer** *f* sales tax

umschalten ['ʊmʃaltən] *vt* to switch

Umschlag ['ʊmʃlaːk] *m* cover; (*Buchumschlag auch*) jacket; (*MED*) compress; (*Briefumschlag*) envelope; (*Wechsel*) change; (*von Hose*) turn-up; **u~en** [-gən] (*unreg*) *vi* to change; (*NAUT*) to capsize ♦ *vt* to knock over; (*Ärmel*) to turn up; (*Seite*) to turn over; (*Waren*) to transfer; **~platz** *m* (*COMM*) distribution centre

umschreiben ['ʊmʃraɪbən] (*unreg*) *vt* (*neu schreiben*) to rewrite; (*übertragen*) to transfer; **~ auf** +*akk* to transfer to; **um'schreiben** *vt insep* to paraphrase; (*abgrenzen*) to define

umschulen ['ʊmʃuːlən] *vt* to retrain; (*Kind*) to send to another school

Umschweife ['ʊmʃvaɪfə] *pl*: **ohne ~** without beating about the bush, straight out

Umschwung ['ʊmʃvʊŋ] *m* change (around), revolution

umsehen ['ʊmzeːən] (*unreg*) *vr* to look around *od* about; (*suchen*): **sich ~ (nach)** to look out (for)

umseitig ['ʊmzaɪtɪç] *adv* overleaf

umsichtig ['ʊmzɪçtɪç] *adj* cautious, prudent

umso ▲ ['ʊmzo] *konj*: **~ besser/**

schlimmer so much the better/worse

umsonst [ʊm'zɔnst] *adv* in vain; *(gratis)* for nothing

umspringen ['ʊmʃprɪŋən] *(unreg)* *vi* to change; *(Wind auch)* to veer; **mit jdm ~** to treat sb badly

Umstand ['ʊmʃtant] *m* circumstance; **Umstände** *pl* *(fig: Schwierigkeiten)* fuss; **in anderen Umständen sein** to be pregnant; **Umstände machen** to go to a lot of trouble; **unter Umständen** possibly

umständlich ['ʊmʃtɛntlɪç] *adj* *(Methode)* cumbersome, complicated; *(Ausdrucksweise, Erklärung)* long-winded; *(Mensch)* ponderous

Umstandskleid *nt* maternity dress

Umstehende(n) ['ʊmʃteːəndə(n)] *pl* bystanders

umsteigen ['ʊmʃtaɪgən] *(unreg)* *vi* (**ELEK SENB**) to change

umstellen ['ʊmʃtɛlən] *vt* *(an anderen Ort)* to change round, to rearrange; *(TECH)* to convert ♦ *vr* to adapt (o.s.); **sich auf etw akk ~** to adapt to sth; **um'stellen** *vt insep* to surround

Umstellung ['ʊmʃtɛlʊŋ] *f* change; *(Umgewöhnung)* adjustment; *(TECH)* conversion

umstimmen ['ʊmʃtɪmən] *vt* (**MUS**) to retune; **jdn ~** to make sb change his mind

umstoßen ['ʊmʃtoːsən] *(unreg)* *vt* to overturn; *(Plan etc)* to change, to upset

umstritten [ʊm'ʃtrɪtən] *adj* disputed

Umsturz ['ʊmʃtʊrts] *m* overthrow

umstürzen ['ʊmʃtʏrtsən] *(umwerfen)* to overturn ♦ *vi* to collapse, to fall down; *(Wagen)* to overturn

Umtausch ['ʊmtaʊʃ] *m* exchange; **u~en** *vt* to exchange

Umverpackung ['ʊmfɛrpakʊŋ] *f* packaging

umwandeln ['ʊmvandəln] *vt* to

change, to convert; (**ELEK**) to transform

umwechseln ['ʊmvɛksəln] *vt* to change

Umweg ['ʊmveːk] *m* detour, roundabout way

Umwelt ['ʊmvɛlt] *f* environment; **u~freundlich** *adj* not harmful to the environment, environment-friendly; **u~schädlich** *adj* ecologically harmful; **~schutz** *m* environmental protection; **~schützer** *m* environmentalist; **~verschmutzung** *f* environmental pollution

umwenden ['ʊmvɛndən] *(unreg)* *vt*, *vr* to turn (round)

umwerfen ['ʊmvɛrfən] *(unreg)* *vt* to upset, to overturn; *(fig: erschüttern)* to upset, to throw; **~d** (* umg*) *adj* fantastic

umziehen ['ʊmtsiːən] *(unreg)* *vt*, *vr* to change ♦ *vi* to move

Umzug ['ʊmtsuːk] *m* procession; *(Wohnungsumzug)* move, removal

unab- ['ʊn|ap] *zW:* **~änderlich** *adj* irreversible, unalterable; **~hängig** *adj* independent; **U~hängigkeit** *f* independence; **~kömmlich** *adj* indispensable; **zur Zeit ~kömmlich** not free at the moment; **~lässig** *adj* incessant, constant; **~sehbar** *adj* immeasurable; *(Folgen)* unforeseeable; *(Kosten)* incalculable; **~sichtlich** *adj* unintentional; **~'wendbar** *adj* inevitable

unachtsam ['ʊn|axtzaːm] *adj* careless; **U~keit** *f* carelessness

unan- ['ʊn|an] *zW:* **~'fechtbar** *adj* indisputable; **~gebracht** *adj* uncalled-for; **~gemessen** *adj* inadequate; **~genehm** *adj* unpleasant; **U~nehmlichkeit** *f* inconvenience; **U~nehmlichkeiten** *pl* *(Ärger)* trouble *sg;* **~sehnlich** *adj* unsightly; **~ständig** *adj* indecent, improper

unappetitlich ['ʊn|apetiːtlɪç] *adj* unsavoury

Unart ['ʊn|aːrt] *f* bad manners *pl;* *(An-*

gewohnheit) bad habit; **u~ig** *adj* naughty, badly behaved

unauf- ['ʊn|aʊf] *zW:* **~fällig** *adj* unobtrusive; *(Kleidung)* inconspicuous; **~'findbar** *adj* not to be found; **~gefordert** *adj* unasked ♦ *adv* spontaneously; **~haltsam** *adj* irresistible; **~'hörlich** *adj* incessant, continuous; **~merksam** *adj* inattentive; **~richtig** *adj* insincere

unaus- ['ʊn|aʊs] *zW:* **~geglichen** *adj* unbalanced; **~'sprechlich** *adj* inexpressible; **~'stehlich** *adj* intolerable

unbarmherzig ['ʊnbarmhɛrtsɪç] *adj* pitiless, merciless

unbeabsichtigt ['ʊnbə|apzɪçtɪçt] *adj* unintentional

unbeachtet ['ʊnbə|axtət] *adj* unnoticed, ignored

unbedenklich ['ʊnbədɛŋklɪç] *adj* *(Plan)* unobjectionable

unbedeutend ['ʊnbədɔʏtənt] *adj* insignificant, unimportant; *(Fehler)* slight

unbedingt ['ʊnbədɪŋt] *adj* unconditional ♦ *adv* absolutely; **musst du ~ gehen?** do you really have to go?

unbefangen ['ʊnbəfaŋən] *adj* impartial, unprejudiced; *(ohne Hemmungen)* uninhibited; **U~heit** *f* impartiality; uninhibitedness

unbefriedigend ['ʊnbəfri:dɪgənd] *adj* unsatisfactory

unbefriedigt ['ʊnbəfri:dɪçt] *adj* unsatisfied, dissatisfied

unbefugt ['ʊnbəfu:kt] *adj* unauthorized

unbegreiflich [ʊnbə'graɪflɪç] *adj* inconceivable

unbegrenzt ['ʊnbəgrɛntst] *adj* unlimited

unbegründet ['ʊnbəgrʏndət] *adj* unfounded

Unbehagen ['ʊnbəha:gən] *nt* discomfort; **unbehaglich** ['ʊnbəha:klɪç] *adj* uncomfortable; *(Gefühl)* uneasy

unbeholfen ['ʊnbəhɔlfən] *adj* awkward, clumsy

unbekannt ['ʊnbəkant] *adj* unknown

unbekümmert ['ʊnbəkʏmərt] *adj* unconcerned

unbeliebt ['ʊnbəli:pt] *adj* unpopular

unbequem ['ʊnbəkve:m] *adj* *(Stuhl)* uncomfortable; *(Mensch)* bothersome; *(Regelung)* inconvenient

unberechenbar [ʊnbə'rɛçənba:r] *adj* incalculable; *(Mensch, Verhalten)* unpredictable

unberechtigt ['ʊnbərɛçtɪçt] *adj* unjustified; *(nicht erlaubt)* unauthorized

unberührt ['ʊnbərʏrt] *adj* untouched, intact; **sie ist noch ~** she is still a virgin

unbescheiden ['ʊnbəʃaɪdən] *adj* presumptuous

unbeschreiblich [ʊnbə'ʃraɪplɪç] *adj* indescribable

unbeständig ['ʊnbəʃtɛndɪç] *adj* *(Mensch)* inconstant; *(Wetter)* unsettled; *(Lage)* unstable

unbestechlich [ʊnbə'ʃtɛçlɪç] *adj* incorruptible

unbestimmt ['ʊnbəʃtɪmt] *adj* indefinite; *(Zukunft auch)* uncertain

unbeteiligt [ʊnbə'taɪlɪçt] *adj* unconcerned, indifferent

unbeweglich ['ʊnbəve:klɪç] *adj* immovable

unbewohnt ['ʊnbəvo:nt] *adj* uninhabited; *(Wohnung)* unoccupied

unbewusst ▲ ['ʊnbəvʊst] *adj* unconscious

unbezahlt ['ʊnbətsa:lt] *adj* *(Rechnung)* outstanding, unsettled; *(Urlaub)* unpaid

unbrauchbar ['ʊnbrauxba:r] *adj* *(Arbeit)* useless; *(Gerät auch)* unusable

und [ʊnt] *konj* and; **~ so weiter** and so on

Undank ['ʊndaŋk] *m* ingratitude; **u~bar** *adj* ungrateful

undefinierbar [ʊndefi'ni:rba:r] *adj* indefinable

undenkbar [ʊn'dɛŋkba:r] *adj* inconceivable

undeutlich ['ʊndɔʏtlɪç] adj indistinct

undicht ['ʊndɪçt] adj leaky

Unding ['ʊndɪŋ] nt absurdity

undurch- ['ʊndʊrç] zW: **~führbar** [-'fy:rbaːr] adj impracticable; **~lässig** [-'lɛsɪç] adj waterproof, impermeable; **~sichtig** [-'zɪçtɪç] adj opaque; (fig) obscure

uneben ['ʊnʔeːbən] adj uneven

unecht ['ʊnʔɛçt] adj (Schmuck) fake; (vorgetäuscht: Freundlichkeit) false

unehelich ['ʊnʔeːəlɪç] adj illegitimate

uneinig ['ʊnʔaɪnɪç] adj divided; **~ sein** to disagree; **U~keit** f discord, dissension

uneins ['ʊnʔaɪns] adj at variance, at odds

unempfindlich ['ʊnʔɛmpfɪntlɪç] adj insensitive; (Stoff) practical

unendlich [ʊnʔɛntlɪç] adj infinite

unent- ['ʊnʔɛnt] zW: **~behrlich** [-'beːrlɪç] adj indispensable; **~geltlich** [-gɛltlɪç] adj free (of charge); **~schieden** [-ʃiːdən] adj undecided; **~schieden enden** (SPORT) to end in a draw; **~schlossen** [-ʃlɔsən] adj undecided; irresolute; **~wegt** [-'veːkt] adj unswerving; (unaufhörlich) incessant

uner- ['ʊnʔeːr] zW: **~bittlich** [-'bɪtlɪç] adj unyielding, inexorable; **~fahren** [-faːrən] adj inexperienced; **~freulich** [-frɔʏlɪç] adj unpleasant; **~gründlich** adj unfathomable; **~hört** [-høːrt] adj unheard-of; (Bitte) outrageous; **~lässlich** ▲ [-'lɛslɪç] adj indispensable; **~laubt** adj unauthorized; **~messlich** ▲ adj immeasurable, immense; **~reichbar** adj (Ziel) unattainable; (Ort) inaccessible; (telefonisch) unobtainable; **~schöpflich** [-'ʃœpflɪç] adj inexhaustible; **~schwinglich** [-'ʃvɪŋlɪç] adj (Preis) exorbitant; too expensive; **~träglich** [-'trɛːklɪç] adj unbearable; (Frechheit) insufferable; **~wartet** adj unexpected; **~wünscht**

adj undesirable, unwelcome

unfähig ['ʊnfɛːɪç] adj incapable, incompetent; **zu etw ~ sein** to be incapable of sth; **U~keit** f incapacity; incompetence

unfair ['ʊnfeːr] adj unfair

Unfall ['ʊnfal] m accident; **~flucht** f hit-and-run (driving); **~schaden** m damages pl; **~station** f emergency ward; **~stelle** f scene of the accident; **~versicherung** f accident insurance

unfassbar ▲ [ʊn'fasbaːr] adj inconceivable

unfehlbar [ʊn'feːlbaːr] adj infallible ♦ adv inevitably; **U~keit** f infallibility

unförmig ['ʊnfœrmɪç] adj (formlos) shapeless

unfrei ['ʊnfraɪ] adj not free, unfree; (Paket) unfranked; **~willig** adj involuntary, against one's will

unfreundlich ['ʊnfrɔʏntlɪç] adj unfriendly; **U~keit** f unfriendliness

Unfriede(n) ['ʊnfriːdə(n)] m dissension, strife

unfruchtbar ['ʊnfrʊxtbaːr] adj infertile; (Gespräche) unfruitful; **U~keit** f infertility; unfruitfulness

Unfug ['ʊnfuːk] (-s) m (Benehmen) mischief; (Unsinn) nonsense; **grober ~** (JUR) gross misconduct; malicious damage

Ungar(in) ['ʊŋgar(ɪn)] m(f) Hungarian; **u~isch** adj Hungarian; **~n** nt Hungary

ungeachtet ['ʊngəʔaxtət] präp +gen notwithstanding

ungeahnt ['ʊngəʔaːnt] adj unsuspected, undreamt-of

ungebeten ['ʊngəbeːtən] adj uninvited

ungebildet ['ʊngəbɪldət] adj uneducated; uncultured

ungedeckt ['ʊngədɛkt] adj (Scheck) uncovered

Ungeduld ['ʊngədʊlt] f impatience; **u~ig** [-dɪç] adj impatient

ungeeignet ['ʊngəʔaɪɡnət] adj unsuitable

ungefähr ['ʊngəfɛːr] *adj* rough, approximate; **das kommt nicht von ~** that's hardly surprising

ungefährlich ['ʊngəfɛːrlɪç] *adj* not dangerous, harmless

ungehalten ['ʊngəhaltən] *adj* indignant

ungeheuer ['ʊngəhɔyər] *adj* huge ♦ *adv* (*umg*) enormously; **U~** (-s, -) *nt* monster; **~lich** [-'hɔyərlɪç] *adj* monstrous

ungehörig ['ʊngəhøːrɪç] *adj* impertinent, improper

ungehorsam ['ʊngəhoːrzaːm] *adj* disobedient; **U~** *m* disobedience

ungeklärt ['ʊngəklɛːrt] *adj* not cleared up; (*Rätsel*) unsolved

ungeladen ['ʊngəlaːdən] *adj* not loaded; (*Gast*) uninvited

ungelegen ['ʊngəleːgən] *adj* inconvenient

ungelernt ['ʊngəlɛrnt] *adj* unskilled

ungelogen ['ʊngəloːgən] *adv* really, honestly

ungemein ['ʊngəmaɪn] *adj* uncommon

ungemütlich ['ʊngəmyːtlɪç] *adj* uncomfortable; (*Person*) disagreeable

ungenau ['ʊngənau] *adj* inaccurate; **U~igkeit** *f* inaccuracy

ungenießbar ['ʊngəniːsbaːr] *adj* inedible; undrinkable; (*umg*) unbearable

ungenügend ['ʊngənyːgənt] *adj* insufficient, inadequate

ungepflegt ['ʊngəpfleːkt] *adj* (*Garten etc*) untended; (*Person*) unkempt; (*Hände*) neglected

ungerade ['ʊngəraːdə] *adj* uneven, odd

ungerecht ['ʊngərɛçt] *adj* unjust; **~fertigt** *adj* unjustified; **U~igkeit** *f* injustice, unfairness

ungern ['ʊngərn] *adv* unwillingly, reluctantly

ungeschehen ['ʊngəʃeːən] *adj*: **~ machen** to undo

Ungeschicklichkeit ['ʊngəʃɪklɪçkaɪt] *f* clumsiness

ungeschickt *adj* awkward, clumsy

ungeschminkt ['ʊngəʃmɪŋkt] *adj* without make-up; (*fig*) unvarnished

ungesetzlich ['ʊngəzɛtslɪç] *adj* illegal

ungestört ['ʊngəʃtøːrt] *adj* undisturbed

ungestraft ['ʊngəʃtraːft] *adv* with impunity

ungestüm ['ʊngəʃtyːm] *adj* impetuous; tempestuous

ungesund ['ʊngəzʊnt] *adj* unhealthy

ungetrübt ['ʊngətryːpt] *adj* clear; (*fig*) untroubled; (*Freude*) unalloyed

Ungetüm ['ʊngətyːm] *nt* (-(e)s, -e) monster

ungewiss ▲ ['ʊngəvɪs] *adj* uncertain; **U~heit** *f* uncertainty

ungewöhnlich ['ʊngəvøːnlɪç] *adj* unusual

ungewohnt ['ʊngəvoːnt] *adj* unaccustomed

Ungeziefer ['ʊngətsiːfər] *nt* (-s) vermin

ungezogen ['ʊngətsoːgən] *adj* rude, impertinent; **U~heit** *f* rudeness, impertinence

ungezwungen ['ʊngətsvʊŋən] *adj* natural, unconstrained

unglaublich [ʊn'glaʊplɪç] *adj* incredible

ungleich ['ʊnglaɪç] *adj* dissimilar; unequal ♦ *adv* incomparably; **~artig** *adj* different; **U~heit** *f* dissimilarity; inequality; **~mäßig** *adj* irregular, uneven

Unglück ['ʊnglyk] *nt* (-(e)s, -e) *nt* misfortune; (*Pech*) bad luck; (~*sfall*) calamity, disaster; (*Verkehrsunglück*) accident; **u~lich** *adj* unhappy; (*erfolglos*) unlucky; (*unerfreulich*) unfortunate; **u~licherweise** [-'vaɪzə] *adv* unfortunately; **~sfall** *m* accident, calamity

ungültig ['ʊngyltɪç] *adj* invalid; **U~keit** *f* invalidity

ungünstig ['ʊngynstɪç] *adj* unfavourable

ungut ['ʊnguːt] *adj* (*Gefühl*) uneasy; nichts für ~ no offence

unhaltbar ['ʊnhaltbaːr] *adj* untenable

Unheil ['ʊnhaɪl] *nt* evil; (*Unglück*) misfortune; ~ anrichten to cause mischief; **u~bar** *adj* incurable

unheimlich ['ʊnhaɪmlɪç] *adj* weird, uncanny ♦ *adv* (*umg*) tremendously

unhöflich ['ʊnhøːflɪç] *adj* impolite; **U~keit** *f* impoliteness

unhygienisch ['ʊnhygieːnɪʃ] *adj* unhygienic

Uni ['ʊni] (-, -s) (*umg*) *f* university

Uniform [uni'fɔrm] *f* uniform; **u~iert** [-'miːrt] *adj* uniformed

uninteressant ['ʊnɪntɛresant] *adj* uninteresting

Uni- *zW*: ~**versität** [univɛrzi'tɛːt] *f* university; ~**versum** [uni'vɛrzʊm] (-s) *nt* universe

unkenntlich ['ʊnkɛntlɪç] *adj* unrecognizable

Unkenntnis ['ʊnkɛntnɪs] *f* ignorance

unklar ['ʊnklaːr] *adj* unclear; im U~en sein über +*akk* to be in the dark about; **U~heit** *f* unclarity; (*Unentschiedenheit*) uncertainty

unklug ['ʊnkluːk] *adj* unwise

Unkosten ['ʊnkɔstən] *pl* expense(s); ~**beitrag** *m* contribution to costs *od* expenses

Unkraut ['ʊnkraʊt] *nt* weed; weeds *pl*

unkündbar ['ʊnkʏntbaːr] *adj* (*Stelle*) permanent; (*Vertrag*) binding

unlauter ['ʊnlaʊtər] *adj* unfair

unleserlich ['ʊnleːzərlɪç] *adj* illegible

unlogisch ['ʊnloːgɪʃ] *adj* illogical

unlösbar ['ʊnløːsbaːr] *adj* insoluble

Unlust ['ʊnlʊst] *f* lack of enthusiasm

Unmenge ['ʊnmɛŋə] *f* tremendous number, hundreds *pl*

Unmensch ['ʊnmɛnʃ] *m* ogre, brute; **u~lich** *adj* inhuman, brutal; (*ungeheuer*) awful

unmerklich [ʊn'mɛrklɪç] *adj* imperceptible

unmissverständlich ▲ ['ʊnmɪsfɛrʃtɛntlɪç] *adj* unmistakable

unmittelbar ['ʊnmɪtəlbaːr] *adj* immediate

unmodern ['ʊnmoːdɛrn] *adj* old-fashioned

unmöglich ['ʊnmøːklɪç] *adj* impossible; **U~keit** *f* impossibility

unmoralisch ['ʊnmoraːlɪʃ] *adj* immoral

Unmut ['ʊnmuːt] *m* ill humour

unnachgiebig ['ʊnnaːxgiːbɪç] *adj* unyielding

unnahbar [ʊn'naːbaːr] *adj* unapproachable

unnötig ['ʊnnøːtɪç] *adj* unnecessary

unnütz ['ʊnnʏts] *adj* useless

unordentlich ['ʊnɔrdəntlɪç] *adj* untidy

Unordnung ['ʊnɔrdnʊŋ] *f* disorder

unparteiisch ['ʊnpartaɪʃ] *adj* impartial; **U~e(r)** *f(m)* umpire; (*FUSSBALL*) referee

unpassend ['ʊnpasɛnt] *adj* inappropriate; (*Zeit*) inopportune

unpässlich ▲ ['ʊnpɛslɪç] *adj* unwell

unpersönlich ['ʊnpɛrzøːnlɪç] *adj* impersonal

unpolitisch ['ʊnpoliːtɪʃ] *adj* apolitical

unpraktisch ['ʊnpraktɪʃ] *adj* unpractical

unpünktlich ['ʊnpʏŋktlɪç] *adj* unpunctual

unrationell ['ʊnratsionɛl] *adj* inefficient

unrealistisch ['ʊnrealɪstɪʃ] *adj* unrealistic

unrecht ['ʊnrɛçt] *adj* wrong; **U~** *nt* wrong; zu U~ wrongly; U~ haben to be wrong; ~**mäßig** *adj* unlawful, illegal

unregelmäßig ['ʊnreːgəlmɛːsɪç] *adj* irregular; **U~keit** *f* irregularity

unreif ['ʊnraɪf] *adj* (*Obst*) unripe; (*fig*)

immature

unrentabel [ˈʊnrɛntaːbəl] adj unprofitable

unrichtig [ˈʊnrɪçtɪç] adj incorrect, wrong

Unruhe [ˈʊnruːə] f unrest; **~stifter** m troublemaker

unruhig [ˈʊnruːɪç] adj restless

uns [ʊns] (akk, dat von **wir**) pron us; ourselves

unsachlich [ˈʊnzaxlɪç] adj not to the point, irrelevant

unsagbar [ʊnˈzaːkbaːr] adj indescribable

unsanft [ˈʊnzanft] adj rough

unsauber [ˈʊnzaʊbər] adj unclean, dirty; (fig) crooked; (MUS) fuzzy

unschädlich [ˈʊnʃɛːtlɪç] adj harmless; **jdn/etw ~ machen** to render sb/sth harmless

unscharf [ˈʊnʃarf] adj indistinct; (Bild etc) out of focus, blurred

unscheinbar [ˈʊnʃaɪnbaːr] adj insignificant; (Aussehen, Haus etc) unprepossessing

unschlagbar [ʊnˈʃlaːkbaːr] adj invincible

unschön [ˈʊnʃøːn] adj (hässlich: Anblick) ugly, unattractive; (unfreundlich: Benehmen) unpleasant, ugly

Unschuld [ˈʊnʃʊlt] f innocence; **u~ig** [-dɪç] adj innocent

unselbst(st)ändig [ˈʊnzɛlpʃtɛndɪç] adj dependent, over-reliant on others

unser(e) [ˈʊnzər(ə)] adj our; **~e(r, s)** pron ours; **~einer** pron people like us; **~eins** pron = unsereiner; **~erseits** adv on our part; **~etwegen** adv (für uns) for our sake; (wegen uns) on our account; **~twillen** adv: **um ~twillen = unsertwegen**

unsicher [ˈʊnzɪçər] adj uncertain; (Mensch) insecure; **U~heit** f uncertainty; insecurity

unsichtbar [ˈʊnzɪçtbaːr] adj invisible

Unsinn [ˈʊnzɪn] m nonsense; **u~ig** adj nonsensical

Unsitte [ˈʊnzɪtə] f deplorable habit

unsozial [ˈʊnzotsiaːl] adj (Verhalten) antisocial

unsportlich [ˈʊnʃpɔrtlɪç] adj not sporty; unfit; (Verhalten) unsporting

unsre [ˈʊnzrə] = **unsere**

unsterblich [ˈʊnʃtɛrplɪç] adj immortal

Unstimmigkeit [ˈʊnʃtɪmɪçkaɪt] f inconsistency; (Streit) disagreement

unsympathisch [ˈʊnzʏmpatɪʃ] adj unpleasant; **er ist mir ~** I don't like him

untätig [ˈʊntɛːtɪç] adj idle

untauglich [ˈʊntaʊklɪç] adj unsuitable; (MIL) unfit

unteilbar [ʊnˈtaɪlbaːr] adj indivisible

unten [ˈʊntən] adv below; (im Haus) downstairs; (an der Treppe etc) at the bottom; **nach ~** down; **~ am Berg** etc at the bottom of the mountain etc; **ich bin bei ihm ~ durch** (umg) he's through with me

---

SCHLÜSSELWORT

unter [ˈʊntər] präp +dat **1** (räumlich, mit Zahlen) under; (drunter) underneath, below; **unter 18 Jahren** under 18 years

2 (zwischen) among(st); **sie waren unter sich** they were by themselves; **einer unter ihnen** one of them; **unter anderem** among other things

♦ präp +akk under, below

Unterarm [ˈʊntərarm] m forearm

unter- zW: **~belichten** vt (PHOT) to underexpose; **U~bewusstsein** ▲ nt subconscious; **~bezahlt** adj underpaid

unterbieten [ʊntərˈbiːtən] (unreg) vt insep (COMM) to undercut; (Rekord) to lower

unterbrechen [ʊntərˈbrɛçən] (unreg) vt insep to interrupt

Unterbrechung f interruption

unterbringen [ˈʊntərbrɪŋən] (unreg) vt (in Koffer) to stow; (in Zeitung) to place; (Person: in Hotel etc) to accommodate, to put up

unterdessen [ʊntɐˈdɛsən] *adv* meanwhile

Unterdruck [ˈʊntɐdrʊk] *m* low pressure

unterdrücken [ʊntɐˈdrʏkən] *vt insep* to suppress; (*Leute*) to oppress

untere(r, s) [ˈʊntərə(r, s)] *adj* lower

untereinander [ʊntɐʔaɪˈnandɐ] *adv* with each other; among themselves *etc*

unterentwickelt [ˈʊntɐʔɛntvɪkəlt] *adj* underdeveloped

unterernährt [ˈʊntɐʔɛrnɛːrt] *adj* undernourished, underfed

Unterernährung *f* malnutrition

Unterführung *f* subway, underpass

Untergang [ˈʊntɐgaŋ] *m* (down)fall, decline; (*NAUT*) sinking; (*von Gestirn*) setting

untergeben *adj* subordinate

untergehen [ˈʊntɐgeːən] (*unreg*) *vi insep* to happen ♦ *adj*: **mit Blut ~** suffused with blood; (*Augen*) bloodshot

unterlegen [ʊntɐˈleːgən] *vt* to lay *od* put under; **unter'legen** *adj* inferior; (*besiegt*) defeated

Unterleib [ˈʊntɐlaɪp] *m* abdomen

unter'liegen (*unreg*) *vi insep* (+*dat*) to be defeated *od* overcome (by); (*unterworfen sein*) to be subject to

Untermiete [ˈʊntɐmiːtə] *f*: **zur ~ wohnen** to be a subtenant *od* lodger; **~r(in)** *m(f)* subtenant, lodger

unter'nehmen (*unreg*) *vt insep* to undertake; **Unter'nehmen** (**-s, -**) *nt* undertaking, enterprise (*auch* COMM)

Unternehmer [ʊntɐˈneːmɐ] (**-s, -**) *m* entrepreneur, businessman

'unterordnen [ˈʊntɐʔɔrdnən] *vr* +*dat* to submit o.s. (to), to give o.s. second place to

Unterredung [ʊntɐˈreːdʊŋ] *f* discussion, talk

Unterricht [ˈʊntɐrɪçt] (**-(e)s, -e**) *m* instruction, lessons *pl*; **u~en** [ʊntɐˈrɪçtən] *vt insep* to instruct; (*SCH*) to teach ♦ *vr insep*: **sich u~en** (**über** +*akk*) to inform o.s. (about), to obtain information (about); **~sfach** *nt* subject (on school *etc* curriculum)

---

unterkommen [ˈʊntɐkɔmən] (*unreg*) *vi* to find shelter; to find work; **das ist mir noch nie untergekommen** I've never met with that

unterkühlt [ʊntɐˈkyːlt] *adj* (*Körper*) affected by hypothermia

Unterkunft [ˈʊntɐkʊnft] (**-, -künfte**) *f* accommodation

Unterlage [ˈʊntɐlaːgə] *f* foundation; (*Beleg*) document; (*Schreibunterlage etc*) pad

unterlassen (*unreg*) *vt insep* (*versäumen*) to fail to do; (*sich enthalten*) to refrain from

unterlaufen [ʊntɐˈlaʊfən] (*unreg*) *vi insep* to happen ♦ *adj*: **mit Blut ~** suffused with blood; (*Augen*) bloodshot

Untergeschoss ▲ [ˈʊntɐgəʃɔs] *nt* basement

'Untergewicht *nt* underweight

unter'gliedern *vt insep* to subdivide

Untergrund [ˈʊntɐgrʊnt] *m* foundation; (*POL*) underground; **~bahn** *f* underground, tube, subway (*US*)

unterhalb [ˈʊntɐhalp] *präp* +*gen* below ♦ *adv* below; **~ von** below

Unterhalt [ˈʊntɐhalt] *m* maintenance; **u~en** (*unreg*) *vt insep* to maintain; (*belustigen*) to entertain ♦ *vr insep* to talk; (*sich belustigen*) to enjoy o.s.; **u~sam** *adj* (*Abend, Person*) entertaining, amusing; **~ung** *f* maintenance; (*Belustigung*) entertainment, amusement; (*Gespräch*) talk

Unterhändler [ˈʊntɐhɛntlɐ] *m* negotiator

Unter- *zW*: **~hemd** *nt* vest, undershirt (*US*); **~hose** *f* underpants *pl*; **~kiefer** *m* lower jaw

---

Spelling Reform: ▲ *new spelling* △ *old spelling (to be phased out)*

Unterrock ['ʊntərɔk] m petticoat, slip

unter'sagen vt insep to forbid; **jdm etw ~** to forbid sb to do sth

Untersatz ['ʊntərzats] m coaster, saucer

unter'schätzen vt insep to underestimate

unter'scheiden (unreg) vt insep to distinguish ♦ vr insep to differ

Unter'scheidung f (Unterschied) distinction; (Unterscheiden) differentiation

Unterschied ['ʊntərʃiːt] (-(e)s, -e) m difference, distinction; **im ~ zu** as distinct from; **u~lich** adj varying, differing; (diskriminierend) discriminatory

unterschiedslos adj indiscriminately

unter'schlagen (unreg) vt insep to embezzle; (verheimlichen) to suppress

Unter'schlagung f embezzlement

Unterschlupf ['ʊntərʃlʊpf] (-(e)s, -schlüpfe) m refuge

unter'schreiben (unreg) vt insep to sign

Unterschrift ['ʊntərʃrɪft] f signature

Unterseeboot ['ʊntərzeːboːt] nt submarine

Untersetzer ['ʊntərzɛtsər] m tablemat; (für Gläser) coaster

untersetzt [ʊntərˈzɛtst] adj stocky

unterste(r, s) ['ʊntərstə(r, s)] adj lowest, bottom

unterstehen [ʊntərˈʃteːən] (unreg) vi insep (+dat) to be under ♦ vr insep to dare; **'unterstehen** (unreg) vi to shelter

unterstellen [ʊntərˈʃtɛlən] vt insep to subordinate; (fig) to impute ♦ vt (Auto) to garage, to park ♦ vr to take shelter

unter'streichen (unreg) vt insep (auch fig) to underline

Unterstufe ['ʊntərʃtuːfə] f lower grade

unter'stützen vt insep to support

Unter'stützung f support, assistance

unter'suchen vt insep (MED) to examine; (Polizei) to investigate

Unter'suchung f examination; investigation, inquiry; **~sausschuss** ▲ m committee of inquiry; **~shaft** f im-

prisonment on remand

Untertasse ['ʊntərtasə] f saucer

untertauchen ['ʊntərtaʊxən] vi to dive; (fig) to disappear, to go underground

Unterteil ['ʊntərtaɪl] nt od m lower part, bottom; **u~en** [ʊntərˈtaɪlən] vt insep to divide up

Untertitel ['ʊntərtiːtəl] m subtitle

Unterwäsche ['ʊntərvɛʃə] f underwear

unterwegs [ʊntərˈveːks] adv on the way

unter'werfen (unreg) vt insep to subject; (Volk) to subjugate ♦ vr insep (+dat) to submit (to)

unter'zeichnen vt insep to sign

unter'ziehen (unreg) vt insep to subject ♦ vr insep (+dat) to undergo; (einer Prüfung) to take

untragbar [ʊnˈtraːkbaːr] adj unbearable, intolerable

untreu ['ʊntrɔy] adj unfaithful; **U~e** f unfaithfulness

untröstlich [ʊnˈtrøːstlɪç] adj inconsolable

unüberlegt ['ʊnlyːbərleːkt] adj illconsidered ♦ adv without thinking

unübersichtlich adj (Gelände) broken; (Kurve) blind

unumgänglich [ʊnʊmˈɡɛŋlɪç] adj indispensable, vital; absolutely necessary

ununterbrochen ['ʊnʊntərbrɔxən] adj uninterrupted

unver- ['ʊnfɛr] zW: **~änderlich** [-ˈɛndərlɪç] adj unchangeable; **~antwortlich** [-ˈantvɔrtlɪç] adj irresponsible; (unentschuldbar) inexcusable; **~besserlich** adj incorrigible; **~bindlich** adj not binding; (Antwort) curt ♦ adv (COMM) without obligation; **~bleit** adj (Benzin usw) unleaded; **ich fahre ~bleit** I use unleaded; **~blümt** [-ˈblyːmt] adj plain, blunt ♦ adv plainly, bluntly; **~daulich** adj indigestible; **~einbar** adj incompatible; **~fänglich** [-ˈfɛŋlɪç] adj harmless; **~froren** adj pudent; **~gesslich** ▲ adj (Tag, Erlebnis) unforgettable; **~hofft** [-'hɔft] adj unexpected; **~meidlich** [-'maitlɪç] adj unavoidable; **~mutet** adj unexpected; **~nünftig** [-'nynftɪç] adj foolish; **~schämt** adj impudent; **U~schämtheit** f impudence, insolence; **~sehrt** adj uninjured; **~söhnlich** [-'zø:nlɪç] adj irreconcilable; **~ständlich** [-'ʃtɛntlɪç] adj unintelligible; **~träglich** adj quarrelsome; (Meinungen, MED) incompatible; **~zeihlich** adj unpardonable; **~züglich** [-'tsy:klɪç] adj immediate

unvollkommen [ʊnfɔlkɔmən] adj imperfect

unvollständig adj incomplete

unvor- [ʊnfoːr] zW: **~bereitet** adj unprepared; **~eingenommen** adj unbiased; **~hergesehen** [-heːrgəzeːən] adj unforeseen; **~sichtig** [-zɪçtɪç] adj careless, imprudent; **~stellbar** [-'ʃtɛlbaːr] adj inconceivable; **~teilhaft** adj disadvantageous

unwahr ['ʊnvaːr] adj untrue; **~scheinlich** adj improbable, unlikely ♦ adv (umg) incredibly

unweigerlich [ʊn'vaigərlɪç] adj unquestioning ♦ adv without fail

Unwesen ['ʊnveːzən] nt nuisance; (Unfug) mischief; **sein ~ treiben** to wreak havoc

unwesentlich adj inessential, unimportant; **~ besser** marginally better

Unwetter ['ʊnvɛtər] nt thunderstorm

unwichtig [ʊnvɪçtɪç] adj unimportant

unwider- [ʊnviːdər] zW: **~legbar** adj irrefutable; **~ruflich** adj irrevocable; **~stehlich** adj irresistible

unwill- ['ʊnvɪl] zW: **U~e(n)** m indignation; **~ig** adj indignant; (widerwillig) reluctant; **~kürlich** [-kyːrlɪç] adj involuntary ♦ adv instinctively; (lachen) involuntarily

unwirklich ['ʊnvɪrklɪç] adj unreal

unwirksam ['ʊnvɪrkzaːm] adj (Mittel, Methode) ineffective

unwirtschaftlich ['ʊnvɪrtʃaftlɪç] adj uneconomical

unwissen- ['ʊnvɪsən] zW: **~d** adj ignorant; **U~heit** f ignorance; **~tlich** adv unknowingly, unwittingly

unwohl ['ʊnvoːl] adj unwell, ill; **U~sein (-s)** nt indisposition

unwürdig ['ʊnvʏrdɪç] adj unworthy

unzählig [ʊn'tseːlɪç] adj innumerable, countless

unzer- [ʊntser] zW: **~brechlich** adj unbreakable; **~störbar** adj indestructible; **~trennlich** adj inseparable

Unzucht ['ʊntsʊxt] f sexual offence

unzüchtig ['ʊntsʏçtɪç] adj immoral, lewd

unzu- ['ʊntsu] zW: **~frieden** adj dissatisfied; **U~friedenheit** f discontent; **~länglich** adj inadequate; **~lässig** adj inadmissible; **~rechnungsfähig** adj irresponsible; **~treffend** adj incorrect; **~verlässig** adj unreliable

unzweideutig ['ʊntsvaidɔytɪç] adj unambiguous

üppig ['ʏpɪç] adj (Frau) curvaceous; (Busen) full, ample; (Essen) sumptuous; (Vegetation) luxuriant, lush

Ur- ['uːr] in zW original

uralt ['uːralt] adj ancient, very old

Uran [u'raːn] (-s) nt uranium

Ur- zW: **~aufführung** f first performance; **~einwohner** m original inhabitant; **~eltern** pl ancestors; **~enkel(in)** m(f) great-grandchild, great-grandson(-daughter); **~großeltern** pl great-grandparents; **~heber (-s, -)** m originator; (Autor) author; **~heberrecht** nt copyright

Urin [u'riːn] (-s, -e) m urine

Urkunde ['uːrkʊndə] f document, deed

Urlaub ['uːrlaʊp] (-(e)s, -e) m holiday(s pl) (BRIT), vacation (US); (MIL etc) leave;

~er [-'laubər] (**-s,** -) *m* holiday-maker (*BRIT*), vacationer (*US*); **~sort** *m* holiday resort; **~szeit** *f* holiday season

Urne ['ʊrnə] *f* urn

Ursache ['u:rzaxə] *f* cause; **keine ~** that's all right

Ursprung ['u:rʃprʊŋ] *m* origin, source; (*von Fluss*) source

ursprünglich ['u:rʃprʏŋlɪç] *adj* original ♦ *adv* originally

Ursprungsland *nt* country of origin

Urteil ['ʊrtail] (**-s,** -e) *nt* opinion; (*JUR*) sentence, judgement; **u~en** *vi* to judge; **~sspruch** *m* sentence, verdict

Urwald *m* jungle

Urzeit *f* prehistoric times *pl*

USA [u:'ɛs'ɑ:] *pl abk* (= Vereinigte Staaten von Amerika) USA

usw. *abk* (= und so weiter) etc

Utensilien [uten'zi:liən] *pl* utensils

Utopie [uto'pi:] *f* pipe dream

utopisch [u'to:pɪʃ] *adj* utopian

V, v

vag(e) [va:k, 'va:gə] *adj* vague

Vagina [va'gi:na] (-, **Vaginen**) *f* vagina

Vakuum ['va:kuʊm] (**-s, Vakua** *od* **Vakuen**) *nt* vacuum

Vampir [vam'pi:r] (**-s,** -e) *m* vampire

Vanille [va'nɪljə] (-) *f* vanilla

Variation [variatsi'o:n] *f* variation

variieren [vari'i:rən] *vt, vi* to vary

Vase ['va:zə] *f* vase

Vater ['fa:tər] (**-s,** ˙) *m* father; **~land** *nt* native country; Fatherland

väterlich ['fɛ:tərlɪç] *adj* fatherly

Vaterschaft *f* paternity

Vaterunser (**-s,** -) *nt* Lord's Prayer

Vati ['fa:ti] *m* daddy

v. Chr. *abk* (= vor Christus) B.C.

Vegetarier(in) [vege'ta:riər(ın)] (**-s,** -) *m(f)* vegetarian

vegetarisch [vege'ta:rɪʃ] *adj* vegetarian

Veilchen ['failçən] *nt* violet

Vene ['ve:nə] *f* vein

Ventil [vɛn'ti:l] (**-s,** -e) *nt* valve

Ventilator [vɛnti'la:tɔr] *m* ventilator

verab- [fɛr'ap] *zW:* **~reden** *vt* to agree, to arrange ♦ *vr:* **sich mit jdm ~reden** to arrange to meet sb; **mit jdm ~redet sein** to have arranged to meet sb; **V~redung** *f* arrangement; (*Treffen*) appointment; **~scheuen** *vt* to detest, to abhor; **~schieden** *vt* (*Gäste*) to say goodbye to; (*entlassen*) to discharge; (*Gesetz*) to pass ♦ *vr* to take one's leave; **V~schiedung** *f* leavetaking; discharge; passing

ver- [fɛr] *zW:* **~achten** *vt* to despise; **~ächtlich** [-'ɛçtlıç] *adj* contemptuous; (*~achtenswert*) contemptible; **jdn ~ächtlich machen** to run sb down; **V~achtung** *f* contempt

verallgemeinern [fɛralgə'mainərn] *vt* to generalize; **Verallgemeinerung** *f* generalization

veralten [fɛr'altən] *vi* to become obsolete *od* out-of-date

Veranda

Veranda [ve'randa] (-, **Veranden**) *f* veranda

veränder- [fɛr'ɛndər] *zW:* **~lich** *adj* changeable; **~n** *vt, vr* to change, to alter; **V~ung** *f* change, alteration

veran- [fɛr'an] *zW:* **~lagt** *adj* with a … nature; **V~lagung** *f* disposition; **~lassen** *vt* to cause; **Maßnahmen ~lassen** to take measures; **sich ~lasst sehen** to feel prompted; **~schaulichen** *vt* to illustrate; **~schlagen** *vt* to estimate; **~stalten** *vt* to organize; to arrange; **V~stalter** (**-s,** -) *m* organizer; **V~staltung** *f* (*V~stalten*) organizing; (*Konzert etc*) event, function

verantwort- [fɛr'antvɔrt] *zW:* **~en** *vt* to answer for ♦ *vr* to justify o.s.; **~lich** *adj* responsible; **V~ung** *f* responsibility; **~ungsbewusst ▲** *adj* responsible; **~ungslos** *adj* irresponsible

verarbeiten [fɛr'arbaitən] *vt* to process; (*geistig*) to assimilate; **etw zu etw ~** to make sth into sth; **Verarbeitung** *f* processing; assimilation

verärgern [fɛrˈʔɛrgərn] vt to annoy

verausgaben [fɛrˈʔaʊsɡaːbən] vr to run out of money; (fig) to exhaust o.s.

Verb [vɛrp] (-s, -en) nt verb

Verband [fɛrˈbant] (-(e)s, =e) m (MED) bandage, dressing; (Bund) association, society; (MIL) unit; **~kasten** m medicine chest, first-aid box; **~zeug** nt bandage

verbannen [fɛrˈbanən] vt to banish

verbergen [fɛrˈbɛrgən] (unreg) vt, vr: (sich) ~ (vor +dat) to hide (from)

verbessern [fɛrˈbɛsərn] vt, vr to improve; (berichtigen) to correct (o.s.)

Verbesserung f improvement; correction

verbeugen [fɛrˈbɔygən] vr to bow

Verbeugung f bow

ver'biegen (unreg) vi to bend

ver'bieten (unreg) vt to forbid; **jdm etw ~** to forbid sb to do sth

verbilligen [fɛrˈbɪlɪgən] vt to reduce the cost of; (Preis) to reduce

ver'binden (unreg) vt to connect; (kombinieren) to combine; (MED) to bandage ♦ vr (auch CHEM) to combine, to join; **jdm die Augen ~** to blindfold sb

verbindlich [fɛrˈbɪntlɪç] adj binding; (freundlich) friendly

Ver'bindung f connection; (Zusammensetzung) combination; (CHEM) compound; (UNIV) club

verbissen [fɛrˈbɪsən] adj (Kampf) bitter; (Gesichtsausdruck) grim

ver'bitten (unreg) vt: **sich** dat **etw ~** not to tolerate sth, not to stand for sth

Verbleib [fɛrˈblaɪp] (-(e)s) m whereabouts; **v~en** (unreg) vi to remain

verbleit [fɛrˈblaɪt] adj (Benzin) leaded

verblüffen [fɛrˈblʏfən] vt to stagger, to amaze; **Verblüffung** f stupefaction

ver'blühen vi to wither, to fade

ver'bluten vi to bleed to death

verborgen [fɛrˈbɔrgən] adj hidden

Verbot [fɛrˈboːt] (-(e)s, -e) nt prohibition, ban; **v~en** adj forbidden; **Rauchen v~en!** no smoking; **~sschild** nt prohibitory sign

Verbrauch [fɛrˈbraʊx] (-(e)s) m consumption; **v~en** vt to use up; **~er** (-s, -) m consumer; **v~t** adj used up, finished; (Luft) stale; (Mensch) worn-out

Verbrechen [fɛrˈbrɛçən] (-s, -) nt crime

Verbrecher [fɛrˈbrɛçər] (-s, -) m criminal; **v~isch** adj criminal

ver'breiten vt, vr to spread; **sich über etw** akk ~ to expound on sth

verbreitern [fɛrˈbraɪtərn] vt to broaden

Verbreitung f spread(ing), propagation

verbrenn- [fɛrˈbrɛn] zW: **~bar** adj combustible; **~en** (unreg) vt to burn; (Leiche) to cremate; **V~ung** f burning; (in Motor) combustion; (von Leiche) cremation; **V~ungsmotor** m internal combustion engine

verbringen [fɛrˈbrɪŋən] (unreg) vt to spend

verbrühen [fɛrˈbryːən] vt to scald

verbuchen [fɛrˈbuːxən] vt (FIN) to register; (Erfolg) to enjoy; (Misserfolg) to suffer

verbunden [fɛrˈbʊndən] adj connected; **jdm ~ sein** to be obliged od indebted to sb; „**falsch ~**" (TEL) "wrong number"

verbünden [fɛrˈbʏndən] vr to ally o.s.; **Verbündete(r)** f(m) ally

ver'bürgen vr: **sich ~ für** to vouch for

ver'büßen vt: **eine Strafe ~** to serve a sentence

Verdacht [fɛrˈdaxt] (-(e)s) m suspicion

verdächtig [fɛrˈdɛçtɪç] adj suspicious, suspect; **~en** [fɛrˈdɛçtɪgən] vt to suspect

verdammen [fɛrˈdamən] vt to damn,

verdammt to condemn; **verdammt!** damn!

verdammt (*umg*) *adj, adv* damned; ~ **noch mal!** damn!, dammit!

ver'dampfen *vi* to vaporize, to evaporate

ver'danken *vt*: **jdm etw** ~ to owe sb sth

verdau- [fɛr'dau] *zW:* ~**en** *vt* (*auch fig*) to digest; ~**lich** *adj* digestible; **das ist schwer ~lich** that is hard to digest; **V~ung** *f* digestion

Verdeck [fɛr'dɛk] (-(e)s, -e) *nt* (*AUT*) hood; (*NAUT*) deck; **v~en** *vt* to cover (up); (*verbergen*) to hide

Verderb- [fɛr'dɛrp] *zW:* ~**en** [-'dɛrbən] (-s) *nt* ruin; **v~en** (*unreg*) *vt* to spoil; (*schädigen*) to ruin; (*moralisch*) to corrupt ♦ *vi* (*Essen*) to spoil, to rot; (*Mensch*) to go to the bad; **es mit jdm v~en** to get into sb's bad books; **v~lich** *adj* (*Einfluss*) pernicious; (*Lebensmittel*) perishable

verdeutlichen [fɛr'dɔytlɪçən] *vt* to make clear

ver'dichten *vt, vr* to condense

ver'dienen *vt* to earn; (*moralisch*) to deserve

Ver'dienst (-(e)s, -e) *m* earnings *pl* ♦ *nt* merit; (*Leistung*): ~ (**um**) service (to)

verdient [fɛr'di:nt] *adj* well-earned; (*Person*) deserving of esteem; **sich um etw ~ machen** to do a lot for sth

verdoppeln [fɛr'dɔpəln] *vt* to double

verdorben [fɛr'dɔrbən] *adj* spoilt; (*geschädigt*) ruined; (*moralisch*) corrupt

verdrängen [fɛr'drɛŋən] *vt* to oust, to displace (*auch PHYS*); (*PSYCH*) to repress

ver'drehen *vt* (*auch fig*) to twist; (*Augen*) to roll; **jdm den Kopf** ~ (*fig*) to turn sb's head

verdrießlich [fɛr'dri:slɪç] *adj* peevish, annoyed

Verdruss [fɛr'drʊs] ▲ (-es, -e) *m* annoyance, worry

verdummen [fɛr'dʊmən] *vt* to make stupid ♦ *vi* to grow stupid

verdunkeln [fɛr'dʊŋkəln] *vt* to darken;

(*fig*) to obscure ♦ *vr* to darken

Verdunk(e)lung *f* blackout; (*fig*) obscuring

verdünnen [fɛr'dʏnən] *vt* to dilute

verdunsten [fɛr'dʊnstən] *vi* to evaporate

verdursten [fɛr'dʊrstən] *vi* to die of thirst

verdutzt [fɛr'dʊtst] *adj* nonplussed, taken aback

verehr- [fɛr'|e:r] *zW:* ~**en** *vt* to venerate, to worship (*auch REL*); **jdm etw ~en** to present sb with sth; **V~er(in)** (-s, -) *m(f)* admirer, worshipper (*auch REL*); ~**t** *adj* esteemed; **V~ung** *f* respect; (*REL*) worship

Verein [fɛr'|ain] (-(e)s, -e) *m* club, association; **v~bar** *adj* compatible; **v~baren** *vt* to agree upon; ~**barung** *f* agreement; **v~en** *vt* (*Menschen, Länder*) to unite; (*Prinzipien*) to reconcile; **mit v~ten Kräften** having pooled resources, having joined forces; ~**te Nationen** United Nations; **v~fachen** *vt* to simplify; **v~heitlichen** [-'haitlɪçən] *vt* to standardize; **v~igen** *vt, vr* to unite; **v~igung** *f* union; (*Verein*) association; **v~t** *adj* united; **v~zelt** *adj* isolated

ver'eitern *vi* to suppurate, to fester

verengen [fɛr'|ɛŋən] *vr* to narrow

vererb- [fɛr'|ɛrb] *zW:* ~**en** *vt* to bequeath; (*BIOL*) to transmit ♦ *vr* to be hereditary; **V~ung** *f* bequeathing; (*BIOL*) transmission; (*Lehre*) heredity

verewigen [fɛr'|e:vɪgən] *vt* to immortalize ♦ *vr* (*umg*) to immortalize o.s.

ver'fahren (*unreg*) *vi* to act ♦ *vr* to get lost ♦ *adj* tangled; ~ **mit** to deal with; **Ver'fahren** (-s, -) *nt* procedure; (*TECH*) process; (*JUR*) proceedings *pl*

Verfall [fɛr'fal] (-(e)s) *m* decline; (*von Haus*) dilapidation; (*FIN*) expiry; **v~en** (*unreg*) *vi* to decline; (*Haus*) to be falling down; (*FIN*) to lapse; **v~en in** +*akk* to lapse into; **v~en auf** +*akk* to hit upon; **einem Laster v~en sein** to be addicted to a vice; **~sdatum** nt expiry date; (der Haltbarkeit) sell-by date

ver'färben vt to change colour

ver'fassen [fɛr'fasən] vt (Rede) to prepare, work out

Verfasser(in) [fɛr'fasər(ɪn)] (-s, -) m(f) author, writer

Verfassung f (auch POL) constitution

Verfassungs- zW: **~gericht** nt constitutional court; **v~widrig** adj unconstitutional

ver'faulen vi to rot

ver'fehlen vt to miss; **etw für verfehlt halten** to regard sth as mistaken

verfeinern [fɛr'faɪnərn] vt to refine

ver'filmen vt to film

ver'flixt [fɛr'flɪkst] (umg) adj damned, damn

ver'fluchen vt to curse

verfolg- [fɛr'fɔlg] zW: **~en** vt to pursue; (gerichtlich) to prosecute; (grausam, bes POL) to persecute; **V~er** (-s, -) m pursuer; **V~ung** f pursuit; prosecution; persecution

verfrüht [fɛr'fry:t] adj premature

verfüg- [fɛr'fy:g] zW: **~bar** adj available; **~en** vt to direct, to order ♦ vi: **~en über** +akk to have at one's disposal; **V~ung** f direction, order; **zur V~ung** at one's disposal; **jdm zur V~ung stehen** to be available to sb

verführ- [fɛr'fy:r] zW: **~en** vt to tempt; (sexuell) to seduce; **V~er** m tempter; seducer; **~erisch** adj seductive; **V~ung** f seduction; (Versuchung) temptation

ver'gammeln (umg) vi to go to seed; (Nahrung) to go off

vergangen [fɛr'gaŋən] adj past; **V~heit** f past

vergänglich [fɛr'gɛŋlɪç] adj transitory

vergasen [fɛr'ga:zən] vt (töten) to gas

Vergaser (-s, -) m (AUT) carburettor

vergaß etc [fɛr'ga:s] vb siehe **vergessen**

vergeb- [fɛr'ge:b] zW: **~en** (unreg) vt (verzeihen) to forgive; (weggeben) to give away; **jdm etw ~en** to forgive sb (for) sth; **~ens** adv in vain; **~lich** [fɛr'ge:plɪç] adv in vain ♦ adj vain, futile; **V~ung** f forgiveness

ver'gehen (unreg) vi to pass by od away ♦ vr to commit an offence; **jdm vergeht etw** sb loses sth; **sich an jdm ~** to (sexually) assault sb; **Ver'gehen** (-s, -) nt offence

ver'gelten (unreg) vt: **jdm etw ~** to pay sb back for sth, to repay sb for sth

Ver'geltung f retaliation, reprisal

vergessen [fɛr'gɛsən] (unreg) vt to forget; **V~heit** f oblivion

vergesslich ▲ [fɛr'gɛslɪç] adj forgetful; **V~keit** f forgetfulness

vergeuden [fɛr'gɔydən] vt to squander, to waste

vergewaltigen [fɛrgə'valtɪgən] vt to rape; (fig) to violate

Vergewaltigung f rape

vergewissern [fɛrgə'vɪsərn] vr to make sure

ver'gießen (unreg) vt to shed

vergiften [fɛr'gɪftən] vt to poison

Vergiftung f poisoning

Vergissmeinnicht ▲ [fɛr'gɪsmaɪnnɪçt] (-(e)s, -e) nt forget-me-not

vergisst ▲ etc [fɛr'gɪst] vb siehe **vergessen**

Vergleich [fɛr'glaɪç] (-(e)s, -e) m comparison; (JUR) settlement; **im ~ mit** od **zu** compared with od to; **v~bar** adj comparable; **v~en** (unreg) vt to compare ♦ vr to reach a settlement

vergnügen [fɛr'gny:gən] vr to enjoy od amuse o.s.; **V~** (-s, -e) nt pleasure; **viel V~!** enjoy yourself!

vergnügt [fɛr'gny:kt] adj cheerful

Vergnügung f pleasure, amusement; **~spark** m amusement park

vergolden [fɛr'gɔldən] vt to gild

ver'graben vt to bury

ver'greifen (unreg) vr: **sich an jdm ~** to lay hands on sb; **sich an etw ~** to misappropriate sth; **sich im Ton ~** to say the wrong thing

vergriffen [fɛr'ɡrɪfən] adj (Buch) out of print; (Ware) out of stock

vergrößern [fɛr'ɡrøːsərn] vt to enlarge; (mengenmäßig) to increase; (Lupe) to magnify

Vergrößerung f enlargement; increase; magnification; **~sglas** nt magnifying glass

Vergünstigung [fɛr'ɡʏnstɪɡʊŋ] f concession, privilege

Vergütung f compensation

verhaften [fɛr'haftən] vt to arrest

Verhaftung f arrest

ver'halten (unreg) vr to be, to stand; (sich benehmen) to behave ♦ vt to hold od retain back; (Schritt) to check; **sich ~ (zu)** (MATH) to be in proportion (to); **Ver'halten (-s)** nt behaviour

Verhältnis [fɛr'hɛltnɪs] (-ses, -se) nt relationship; (MATH) proportion, ratio; **~se** pl (Umstände) conditions; **über seine ~se leben** to live beyond one's means; **v~mäßig** adj relative, comparative ♦ adv relatively, comparatively

verhandeln [fɛr'handəln] vi to negotiate; (JUR) to hold proceedings ♦ vt to discuss; (JUR) to hear; **über etw akk ~** to negotiate sth od about sth

Verhandlung f negotiation; (JUR) proceedings pl; **~sbasis** f (FIN) basis for negotiations

ver'hängen vt (fig) to impose, to inflict

Verhängnis [fɛr'hɛŋnɪs] (-ses, -se) nt fate, doom; **jdm zum ~ werden** to be sb's undoing; **v~voll** adj fatal, disastrous

verharmlosen [fɛr'harmloːzən] vt to make light of, to play down

verhärten [fɛr'hɛrtən] vr to harden

verhasst ▲ [fɛr'hast] adj odious, hateful

verhauen [fɛr'hauən] (unreg; umg) vt (verprügeln) to beat up

verheerend [fɛr'heːrənt] adj disastrous, devastating

verheimlichen [fɛr'haimlɪçən] vt: **jdm etw ~** to keep sth secret from sb

verheiratet [fɛr'hairaːtət] adj married

ver'helfen (unreg) vi: **jdm ~ zu** to help sb to get

ver'hindern vt to prevent; **verhindert sein** to be unable to make it

verhöhnen [fɛr'høːnən] vt to mock, to sneer at

Verhör [fɛr'høːr] (-(e)s, -e) nt interrogation; (gerichtlich) (cross-)examination; **v~en** vt to interrogate; to (cross-)examine ♦ vr to misunderstand, to mishear

ver'hungern vi to starve, to die of hunger

ver'hüten vt to prevent, to avert

Ver'hütung f prevention; **~smittel** nt contraceptive

verirren [fɛr'ɪrən] vr to go astray

ver'jagen vt to drive away od out

verkalken [fɛr'kalkən] vi to calcify; (umg) to become senile

Verkauf [fɛr'kauf] m sale; **v~en** vt to sell

Verkäufer(in) [fɛr'kɔyfər(ɪn)] (-s, -) m(f) seller; salesman(-woman); (in Laden) shop assistant

verkaufsoffen adj: **~er Samstag** Saturday when the shops stay open all day

Verkehr [fɛr'keːr] (-s, -e) m traffic; (Umgang, bes sexuell) intercourse; (Umlauf) circulation; **v~en** vi (Fahrzeug) to ply, to run ♦ vt, vr to turn, to transform; **v~en mit** to associate with; **bei jdm v~en** (besuchen) to visit sb regularly

Verkehrs- zW: **~ampel** f traffic lights pl; **~aufkommen** nt volume of traffic; **~beruhigung** f traffic calming; **~delikt** nt traffic offence; **~funk** m radio traffic service; **v~günstig** adj convenient; **~mittel** nt means of transport; **~schild** nt road sign; **~stauung** f traffic jam, stoppage; **~unfall** m traffic accident; **~verein** m tourist information office; **~zeichen** nt traffic sign

verkehrt adj wrong; (umgekehrt) the wrong way round

ver'kennen (unreg) vt to misjudge, not to appreciate

ver'klagen vt to take to court

verkleiden [fer'klaidən] vr to disguise (o.s.); (sich kostümieren) to get dressed up ♦ vt (Wand) to cover

Verkleidung f disguise; (ARCHIT) wainscoting

verkleinern [fer'klainərn] vt to make smaller, to reduce in size

ver'kneifen (umg) vt: **sich dat etw ~** (Lachen) to stifle sth; (Schmerz) to hide sth; (sich versagen) to do without sth

verknüpfen [fer'knypfən] vt to tie (up), to knot; (fig) to connect

ver'kommen (unreg) vi to deteriorate, to decay; (Mensch) to go downhill, to come down in the world ♦ adj (moralisch) dissolute, depraved

verkörpern [fer'kœrpərn] vt to embody, to personify

ver'kraften [fer'kraftən] vt to cope with

ver'kriechen (unreg) vr to creep away, to creep into a corner

verkrüppelt [fer'krypəlt] adj crippled

ver'kühlen vr to get a chill

ver'kümmern vi to waste away

verkünden [fer'kyndən] vt to proclaim; (Urteil) to pronounce

verkürzen [fer'kyrtsən] vt to shorten; (Wort) to abbreviate; **sich dat die Zeit ~** to while away the time

Verkürzung f shortening; abbreviation

verladen [fer'la:dən] (unreg) vt (Waren, Vieh) to load; (Truppen) to embark, entrain, enplane

Verlag [fer'la:k] (-(e)s, -e) m publishing firm

verlangen [fer'laŋən] vt to demand; to desire ♦ vi: **~ nach** to ask for, to desire; **~ Sie Herrn X** ask for Mr X; **V~** (-s, -) nt: **V~ (nach)** desire (for); **auf jds V~ (hin)** at sb's request

verlängern [fer'lɛŋərn] vt to extend; (länger machen) to lengthen

Verlängerung f extension; (SPORT) extra time; **~sschnur** f extension cable

verlangsamen [fer'laŋzaːmən] vt, vr to decelerate, to slow down

Verlass ▲ [fer'las] m: **auf ihn/das ist kein ~** he/it cannot be relied upon

ver'lassen (unreg) vt to leave ♦ vr: **sich ~ auf** +akk to depend on ♦ adj desolate; (Mensch) abandoned

verlässlich ▲ [fer'lɛslıç] adj reliable

Verlauf [fer'lauf] m course; **v~en** (unreg) vi (zeitlich) to pass; (Farben) to run ♦ vr to get lost; (Menschenmenge) to disperse

ver'lauten vi: **etw ~ lassen** to disclose sth; **wie verlautet** as reported

ver'legen vt to move; (verlieren) to mislay; (Buch) to publish ♦ vr: **sich auf etw akk ~** to take up od to sth ♦ adj embarrassed; **nicht ~ um** never at a loss for; **Ver'legenheit** f embarrassment; (Situation) difficulty, scrape

Verleger [fer'leːgər] (-s, -) m publisher

Verleih [fer'lai] (-(e)s, -e) m hire service; **v~en** (unreg) vt to lend; (Kraft, Anschein) to confer, to bestow; (Preis, Medaille) to award; **~ung** f lending; bestowal; award

ver'leiten vt to lead astray; **~ zu** to talk into, to tempt into

ver'lernen vt to forget, to unlearn

ver'lesen (unreg) vt to read out; (aussondern) to sort out ♦ vr to make a mistake in reading

verletz- [fer'lɛts] zW: **~en** vt (auch fig)

to injure, to hurt; (*Gesetz etc*) to violate; **~end** *adj* (*fig: Worte*) hurtful; **~lich** *adj* vulnerable, sensitive; **V~te(r)** *f(m)* injured person; **V~ung** *f* injury; (*Verstoß*) violation, infringement

verleugnen [fɛr'lɔygnən] *vt* (*Herkunft, Glauben*) to belie; (*Menschen*) to disown

verleumden [fɛr'lɔymdən] *vt* to slander; **Verleumdung** *f* slander, libel

ver'lieben *vr*: **sich ~** (**in** +*akk*) to fall in love (with)

verliebt [fɛr'li:pt] *adj* in love

verlieren [fɛr'li:rən] (*unreg*) *vt, vi* to lose ♦ *vr* to get lost

Verlierer *m* loser

verlob- [fɛr'lo:b] *zW*: **~en** *vr*: **sich ~en** (**mit**) to get engaged (to); **V~te(r)** [fɛr'lo:ptə(r)] *f(m)* fiancé *m*, fiancée *f*; **V~ung** *f* engagement

ver'locken *vt* to entice, to lure

Ver'lockung *f* temptation, attraction

verlogen [fɛr'lo:gən] *adj* untruthful

verlor *etc vb siehe* **verlieren**

verloren [fɛr'lo:rən] *adj* lost; (*Eier*) poached ♦ *vb siehe* **verlieren**; **etw ~ geben** to give sth up for lost; **~ gehen** to get lost

verlosen [fɛr'lo:zən] *vt* to raffle, to draw lots for; **Verlosung** *f* raffle, lottery

Verlust [fɛr'lʊst] (**-(e)s, -e**) *m* loss; (*MIL*) casualty

ver'machen *vt* to bequeath, to leave

Vermächtnis [fɛr'mɛçtnɪs] (**-ses, -se**) *nt* legacy

Vermählung [fɛr'mɛːlʊŋ] *f* wedding, marriage

vermarkten [fɛr'marktən] *vt* (*COMM: Artikel*) to market

vermehren [fɛr'meːrən] *vt, vr* to multiply; (*Menge*) to increase

Vermehrung *f* multiplying; increase

ver'meiden (*unreg*) *vt* to avoid

vermeintlich [fɛr'maɪntlɪç] *adj* supposed

Vermerk [fɛr'mɛrk] (**-(e)s, -e**) *m* note;

(*in Ausweis*) endorsement; **v~en** *vt* to note

ver'messen (*unreg*) *vt* to survey ♦ *adj* presumptuous, bold; **Ver'messenheit** *f* presumptuousness; recklessness

Ver'messung *f* survey(ing)

vermiet- [fɛr'miːt] *zW*: **ver'mieten** *vt* to let, to rent (out); (*Auto*) to hire out, to rent; **Ver'mieter(in)** (**-s, -**) *m(f)* landlord(-lady); **Ver'mietung** *f* letting, renting (out); (*von Autos*) hiring (out)

vermindern [fɛr'mɪndərn] *vt, vr* to lessen, to decrease; (*Preise*) to reduce

Verminderung *f* reduction

ver'mischen *vt, vr* to mix, to blend

vermissen [fɛr'mɪsən] *vt* to miss

vermitt- [fɛr'mɪt] *zW*: **~eln** *vi* to mediate ♦ *vt* (*Gespräch*) to connect; **jdm etw ~eln** to help sb to obtain sth; **V~ler** (**-s, -**) *m* (*Schlichter*) agent, mediator; **V~lung** *f* procurement; (*Stellenvermittlung*) agency; (*TEL*) exchange; (*Schlichtung*) mediation; **V~lungsgebühr** *f* commission

ver'mögen (*unreg*) *vt* to be capable of; **~ zu** to be able to; **Ver'mögen** (**-s, -**) *nt* wealth; (*Fähigkeit*) ability; **ein V~kosten** to cost a fortune; **ver'mögend** *adj* wealthy

vermuten [fɛr'muːtən] *vt* to suppose, to guess; (*argwöhnen*) to suspect

vermutlich *adj* supposed, presumed ♦ *adv* probably

Vermutung *f* supposition; suspicion

vernachlässigen [fɛr'naːxlɛsɪgən] *vt* to neglect

ver'nehmen (*unreg*) *vt* to perceive, to hear; (*erfahren*) to learn; (*JUR*) to (cross-)examine; **dem V~ nach** from what I/we *etc* hear

Vernehmung *f* (cross-)examination

verneigen [fɛr'naɪgən] *vr* to bow

verneinen [fɛr'naɪnən] *vt* (*Frage*) to answer in the negative; (*ablehnen*) to deny; (*GRAM*) to negate; **~d** *adj* negative

Verneinung *f* negation

vernichten [fɛr'nɪçtən] *vt* to annihilate, to destroy; **~d** *adj* (*fig*) crushing; (*Blick*) withering; (*Kritik*) scathing

Vernunft [fɛr'nʊnft] (-) *f* reason, understanding

vernünftig [fɛr'nʏnftɪç] *adj* sensible, reasonable

veröffentlichen [fɛr'œfəntlɪçən] *vt* to publish; **Veröffentlichung** *f* publication

verordnen [fɛr'ɔrdnən] *vt* (*MED*) to prescribe

Verordnung *f* order, decree; (*MED*) prescription

ver'pachten *vt* to lease (out)

ver'packen *vt* to pack

Ver'packung *f* packing, wrapping; **~smaterial** *nt* packing, wrapping

ver'passen *vt* to miss; **jdm eine Ohrfeige ~** (*umg*) to give sb a clip round the ear

verpfänden [fɛr'pfɛndən] *vt* (*Besitz*) to mortgage

ver'pflanzen *vt* to transplant

ver'pflegen *vt* to feed, to cater for

Ver'pflegung *f* feeding, catering; (*Kost*) food; (*in Hotel*) board

verpflichten [fɛr'pflɪçtən] *vt* to oblige, to bind; (*anstellen*) to engage ♦ *vr* to undertake; (*MIL*) to sign on ♦ *vi* to carry obligations; **jdm zu Dank verpflichtet sein** to be obliged to sb

Verpflichtung *f* obligation, duty

verpönt [fɛr'pøːnt] *adj* disapproved (of), taboo

ver'prügeln (*umg*) *vt* to beat up, to do over

Verputz [fɛr'pʊts] *m* plaster, roughcast; **v~en** *vt* to plaster; (*umg: Essen*) to put away

Verrat [fɛr'raːt] (-(e)s) *m* treachery; (*POL*) treason; **v~en** (*unreg*) *vt* to betray; (*Geheimnis*) to divulge ♦ *vr* to

give o.s. away

Verräter [fɛr'rɛːtər] (-s, -) *m* traitor(-tress); **v~isch** *adj* treacherous

ver'rechnen *vt*: **~ mit** to set off against ♦ *vr* to miscalculate

Verrechnungsscheck [fɛr'rɛçnʊŋsʃɛk] *m* crossed cheque

verregnet [fɛr'reːgnət] *adj* spoilt by rain, rainy

ver'reisen *vi* to go away (on a journey)

verrenken [fɛr'rɛŋkən] *vt* to contort; (*MED*) to dislocate; **sich** *dat* **den Knöchel ~** to sprain one's ankle

ver'richten *vt* to do, to perform

verriegeln [fɛr'riːgəln] *vt* to bolt up, to lock

verringern [fɛr'rɪŋərn] *vt* to reduce ♦ *vr* to diminish

Verringerung *f* reduction; lessening

ver'rinnen (*unreg*) *vi* to run out *od* away; (*Zeit*) to elapse

ver'rosten *vi* to rust

verrotten [fɛr'rɔtən] *vi* to rot

ver'rücken *vt* to move, to shift

verrückt [fɛr'rʏkt] *adj* crazy, mad; **V~e(r)** *f(m)* lunatic; **V~heit** *f* madness, lunacy

Verruf [fɛr'ruːf] *m*: **in ~ geraten/bringen** to fall/bring into disrepute; **v~en** *adj* notorious, disreputable

Vers [fɛrs] (-es, -e) *m* verse

ver'sagen *vt*: **jdm/sich etw ~** to deny sb/o.s. sth ♦ *vi* to fail; **Ver'sagen** (-s) *nt* failure

ver'salzen (*unreg*) *vt* to put too much salt in; (*fig*) to spoil

ver'sammeln *vt*, *vr* to assemble, to gather

Ver'sammlung *f* meeting, gathering

Versand [fɛr'zant] (-(e)s) *m* forwarding; dispatch; (*~abteilung*) dispatch department; **~haus** *nt* mail-order firm

versäumen [fɛr'zɔymən] *vt* to miss; (*unterlassen*) to neglect, to fail

ver'schaffen vt: jdm/sich etw ~ to get od procure sth for sb/o.s.

verschämt [fɛr'ʃɛːmt] adj bashful

verschandeln [fɛr'ʃandəln] (umg) vt to spoil

verschärfen [fɛr'ʃɛrfən] vt to intensify; (Lage) to aggravate ♦ vr to intensify; to become aggravated

ver'schätzen vr to be out in one's reckoning

ver'schenken vt to give away

verscheuchen [fɛr'ʃɔʏçən] vt (Tiere) to chase off od away

ver'schicken vt to send off

ver'schieben (unreg) vt to shift; (EISENB) to shunt; (Termin) to postpone

verschieden [fɛr'ʃiːdən] adj different; (pl: mehrere) various; **sie sind ~ groß** they are of different sizes; **~tlich** adv several times

verschimmeln [fɛr'ʃiməln] vi (Nahrungsmittel) to go mouldy

ver'schlafen [fɛr'ʃlaːfən] (unreg) vt to sleep through; (fig: versäumen) to miss ♦ vi, vr to oversleep ♦ adj sleepy

Verschlag [fɛr'ʃlaːk] m shed; **v~en** [-gən] (unreg) vt to board up ♦ adj cunning; **jdm den Atem v~en** to take sb's breath away; **an einen Ort v~en werden** to wind up in a place

verschlechtern [fɛr'ʃlɛçtərn] vt to make worse ♦ vr to deteriorate, to get worse; **Verschlechterung** f deterioration

Verschleiß [fɛr'ʃlaɪs] (-es, -e) m wear and tear; **v~en** (unreg) vt to wear out

ver'schleppen vt to carry off, to abduct; (Krankheit) to protract; (zeitlich) to drag out

ver'schleudern vt to squander; (COMM) to sell dirt-cheap

verschließbar adj lockable

verschließen [fɛr'ʃliːsən] (unreg) vt to close; to lock ♦ vr: **sich einer Sache** dat ~ to close one's mind to sth

verschlimmern [fɛr'ʃlɪmərn] vt to make worse, to aggravate ♦ vr to get worse, to deteriorate

verschlingen [fɛr'ʃlɪŋən] (unreg) vt to devour, to swallow up; (Fäden) to twist

verschlossen [fɛr'ʃlɔsən] adj locked; (fig) reserved; **V~heit** f reserve

ver'schlucken vt to swallow ♦ vr to choke

Verschluss ▲ [fɛr'ʃlʊs] m lock; (von Kleid etc) fastener; (PHOT) shutter; (Stöpsel) plug

verschlüsseln [fɛr'ʃlʏsəln] vt to encode

verschmieren [fɛr'ʃmiːrən] vt (verstreichen: Gips, Mörtel) to apply, spread on; (schmutzig machen: Wand etc) to smear

verschmutzen [fɛr'ʃmʊtsən] vt to soil; (Umwelt) to pollute

verschneit [fɛr'ʃnaɪt] adj snowed up, covered in snow

verschollen [fɛr'ʃɔlən] adj lost, missing

ver'schonen vt: **jdn mit etw** ~ to spare sb sth

verschönern [fɛr'ʃøːnərn] vt to decorate; (verbessern) to improve

ver'schreiben (unreg) vt (MED) to prescribe ♦ vr to make a mistake (in writing); **sich einer Sache** dat ~ to devote o.s. to sth

verschreibungspflichtig adj (Medikament) available on prescription only

verschrotten [fɛr'ʃrɔtən] vt to scrap

verschuld- [fɛr'ʃʊld] zW: **~en** vt to be guilty of; **V~en** (-s) nt fault, guilt; **~et** adj in debt; (Geld) debts pl

ver'schütten vt to spill; (zuschütten) to fill; (unter Trümmern) to bury

ver'schweigen (unreg) vt to keep secret; **jdm etw** ~ to keep sth from sb

verschwend- [fɛr'ʃvɛnd] zW: **~en** vt to squander; **V~er** (-s, -) m spendthrift; **~erisch** adj wasteful, extravagant; **V~ung** f waste; extravagance

verschwiegen [fɛr'ʃviːgən] adj discreet; (Ort) secluded; **V~heit** f discretion

tion; seclusion

ver'schwimmen (*unreg*) *vi* to grow hazy, to become blurred

ver'schwinden (*unreg*) *vi* to disappear, to vanish; **Ver'schwinden** (*-s*) *nt* disappearance

verschwitzt [fɛr'ʃvɪtst] *adj* (*Mensch*) sweaty

verschwommen [fɛr'ʃvɔmən] *adj* hazy, vague

verschwör- [fɛr'ʃvøːr] *zW:* **~en** (*unreg*) *vr* to plot, to conspire; **V~ung** *f* conspiracy, plot

ver'sehen (*unreg*) *vt* to supply, to provide; (*Pflicht*) to carry out; (*Amt*) to fill; (*Haushalt*) to keep; **ehe er (es) sich ~ hatte** ... before he knew it ...; **Ver'sehen** (*-s, -*) *nt* oversight; **aus V~** by mistake; **~tlich** *adv* by mistake

Versehrte(r) [fɛr'zeːrtə(r)] *f(m)* disabled person

ver'senden (*unreg*) *vt* to forward, to dispatch

ver'senken *vt* to sink ♦ *vr:* **sich ~ in** *+akk* to become engrossed in

versessen [fɛr'zɛsən] *adj:* **~ auf** *+akk* mad about

ver'setzen *vt* to transfer; (*verpfänden*) to pawn; (*umg*) to stand up ♦ *vr:* **sich in jdn** *od* **in jds Lage ~** to put o.s. in sb's place; **jdm einen Tritt/Schlag ~** to kick/hit sb; **etw mit etw ~** to mix sth with sth; **jdn in gute Laune ~** to put sb in a good mood

Ver'setzung *f* transfer

verseuchen [fɛr'zɔʏçən] *vt* to contaminate

versichern [fɛr'zɪçərn] *vt* to assure; (*mit Geld*) to insure

Versicherung *f* assurance; insurance

Versicherungs- *zW:* **~gesellschaft** *f* insurance company; **~karte** *f* insurance card; **die grüne ~karte** the green card; **~police** *f* insurance policy

ver'sinken (*unreg*) *vi* to sink

versöhnen [fɛr'zøːnən] *vt* to reconcile ♦ *vr* to become reconciled

Versöhnung *f* reconciliation

ver'sorgen *vt* to provide, to supply; (*Familie etc*) to look after

Ver'sorgung *f* provision; (*Unterhalt*) maintenance; (*Altersversorgung etc*) benefit, assistance

ver'späten [fɛr'ʃpɛːtən] *vr* to be late

verspätet *adj* (*Zug, Abflug, Ankunft*) late; (*Glückwünsche*) belated

Verspätung *f* delay; **~ haben** to be late

ver'sperren *vt* to bar, to obstruct

verspielt [fɛr'ʃpiːlt] *adj* (*Kind, Tier*) playful

ver'spotten *vt* to ridicule, to scoff at

ver'sprechen (*unreg*) *vt* to promise; **sich dat etw von etw ~** to expect sth from sth; **Ver'sprechen** (*-s, -*) *nt* promise

verstaatlichen [fɛr'ʃtaːtlɪçən] *vt* to nationalize

Verstand [fɛr'ʃtant] *m* intelligence; mind; **den ~ verlieren** to go out of one's mind; **über jds ~ gehen** to go beyond sb

verständig [fɛr'ʃtɛndɪç] *adj* sensible; **~en** [fɛr'ʃtɛndɪgən] *vt* to inform ♦ *vr* to communicate; (*sich einigen*) to come to an understanding; **V~ung** *f* communication; (*Benachrichtigung*) informing; (*Einigung*) agreement

verständ- [fɛr'ʃtɛnt] *zW:* **~lich** *adj* understandable, comprehensible; **V~lichkeit** *f* clarity, intelligibility; **V~nis** (*-ses, -se*) *nt* understanding; **~nislos** *adj* uncomprehending; **~nisvoll** *adj* understanding, sympathetic

verstärk- [fɛr'ʃtɛrk] *zW:* **~en** *vt* to strengthen; (*Ton*) to amplify; (*erhöhen*) *vt* to intensify ♦ *vr* to intensify; **V~er** (*-s, -*) *m* amplifier; **V~ung** *f* strengthening; (*Hilfe*) reinforcements *pl*; (*von Ton*) am-

---

verstauchen 280 **vertreten**

plification

verstauchen [fɛrˈʃtauxən] *vt* to sprain

verstauen [fɛrˈʃtauən] *vt* to stow away

Versteck [fɛrˈʃtɛk] (-(e)s, -e) *nt* hiding (place); **v~en** *vt*, *vr* to hide; **v~t** *adj* hidden

ver'stehen (*unreg*) *vt* to understand ♦ *vr* to get on; **das versteht sich (von selbst)** that goes without saying

versteigern [fɛrˈʃtaigərn] *vt* to auction; **Versteigerung** *f* auction

verstell- [fɛrˈʃtɛl] *zW:* **~bar** *adj* adjustable, variable; **~en** *vt* to move, to shift; (*Uhr*) to adjust; (*versperren*) to block; (*fig*) to disguise ♦ *vr* to pretend, to put on an act; **V~ung** *f* pretence

versteuern [fɛrˈʃtɔyərn] *vt* to pay tax on

verstimmt [fɛrˈʃtimt] *adj* out of tune; (*fig*) cross, put out; (*Magen*) upset

ver'stopfen *vt* to block, to stop up; (*MED*) to constipate

Ver'stopfung *f* obstruction; (*MED*) constipation

verstorben [fɛrˈʃtɔrbən] *adj* deceased, late

verstört [fɛrˈʃtøːrt] *adj* (*Mensch*) distraught

Verstoß [fɛrˈʃtoːs] *m:* **~ (gegen)** infringement (of), violation (of); **v~en** (*unreg*) *vt* to disown, to reject ♦ *vi:* **v~en gegen** to offend against

ver'streichen (*unreg*) *vt* to spread ♦ *vi* to elapse

ver'streuen *vt* to scatter (about)

verstümmeln [fɛrˈʃtYməln] *vt* to maim, to mutilate (*auch fig*)

verstummen [fɛrˈʃtumən] *vi* to go silent; (*Lärm*) to die away

Versuch [fɛrˈzuːx] (-(e)s, -e) *m* attempt; (*SCI*) experiment; **v~en** *vt* to try; (*verlocken*) to tempt ♦ *vr:* **sich an etw** *dat* **v~en** to try one's hand at sth; **~skaninchen** *nt* (*fig*) guinea-pig; **~ung** *f* temptation

vertagen [fɛrˈtaːgən] *vt*, *vi* to adjourn

ver'tauschen *vt* to exchange; (*verse-*

hentlich) to mix up

verteidig- [fɛrˈtaidig] *zW:* **~en** *vt* to defend; **V~er** (-s, -) *m* defender; (*JUR*) defence counsel; **V~ung** *f* defence

ver'teilen *vt* to distribute; (*Rollen*) to assign; (*Salbe*) to spread

Verteilung *f* distribution, allotment

vertiefen [fɛrˈtiːfən] *vt* to deepen ♦ *vr:* **sich in etw** *akk* **~** to become engrossed *od* absorbed in sth

Vertiefung *f* depression

vertikal [vɛrtiˈkaːl] *adj* vertical

vertilgen [fɛrˈtilgən] *vt* to exterminate; (*umg*) to eat up, to consume

vertonen [fɛrˈtoːnən] *vt* to set to music

Vertrag [fɛrˈtraːk] (-(e)s, **̈e**) *m* contract, agreement; (*POL*) treaty; **v~en** [-gən] (*unreg*) *vt* to tolerate, to stand ♦ *vr* to get along; (*sich aussöhnen*) to become reconciled; **v~lich** *adj* contractual

verträglich [fɛrˈtrɛːkliç] *adj* goodnatured, sociable; (*Speisen*) easily digested; (*MED*) easily tolerated; **V~keit** *f* sociability; good nature; digestibility

Vertrags- *zW:* **~bruch** *m* breach of contract; **~händler** *m* appointed retailer; **~partner** *m* party to a contract; **~werkstatt** *f* appointed repair shop; **v~widrig** *adj* contrary to contract

vertrauen [fɛrˈtrauən] *vi:* **jdm ~** to trust sb; **~ auf** *+akk* to rely on; **V~** (-s) *nt* confidence; **V~ erweckend** inspiring trust; **v~svoll** *adj* trustful; **v~swürdig** *adj* trustworthy

vertraulich [fɛrˈtrauliç] *adj* familiar; (*geheim*) confidential

vertraut [fɛrˈtraut] *adj* familiar; **V~heit** *f* familiarity

vertreiben (*unreg*) *vt* to drive away; (*aus Land*) to expel; (*COMM*) to sell; (*Zeit*) to pass

vertret- [fɛrˈtreːt] *zW:* **~en** (*unreg*) *vt* to represent; (*Ansicht*) to hold, to advocate; **sich** *dat* **die Beine ~en** to stretch one's legs; **V~er** (-s, -) *m* representative; (*Verfechter*) advocate; **V~ung** *f* representation; advocacy

Vertrieb [fɛr'triːp] (-(e)s, -e) *m* marketing (department)

ver'trocknen *vi* to dry up

ver'trösten *vt* to put off

vertun [fɛr'tuːn] (*unreg*) *vt* to waste ♦ *vr* (*umg*) to make a mistake

vertuschen [fɛr'tʊʃən] *vt* to hush *od* cover up

verübeln [fɛr'yːbəln] *vt*: **jdm etw ~** to be cross *od* offended with sb on account of sth

verüben [fɛr'yːbən] *vt* to commit

verun- [fɛr'ʊn] *zW*: **~glimpfen** *vt* to disparage; **~glücken** *vi* to have an accident; **tödlich ~glücken** to be killed in an accident; **~reinigen** *vt* to soil; (*Umwelt*) to pollute; **~sichern** *vt* to rattle; **~treuen** [-trɔyən] *vt* to embezzle

verur- [fɛr'uːr] *zW*: **~sachen** *vt* to cause; **~teilen** [-taɪlən] *vt* to condemn; **V~teilung** *f* condemnation; (*JUR*) sentence

verviel- [fɛr'fiːl] *zW*: **~fachen** *vt* to multiply; **~fältigen** [-fɛltɪgən] *vt* to duplicate, to copy; **V~fältigung** *f* duplication, copying

vervollkommnen [fɛr'fɔlkɔmnən] *vt* to perfect

vervollständigen [fɛr'fɔlʃtɛndɪgən] *vt* to complete

ver'wackeln *vt* (*Foto*) to blur

ver'wählen *vr* (*TEL*) to dial the wrong number

verwahren [fɛr'vaːrən] *vt* to keep, to lock away ♦ *vr* to protest

verwalt- [fɛr'valt] *zW*: **~en** *vt* to manage; to administer; **V~er** (-s, -) *m* manager; (*Vermögensverwalter*) trustee; **V~ung** *f* management

ver'wandeln *vt* to change, to transform ♦ *vr* to change; to be transformed; **Ver'wandlung** *f* change,

transformation

verwandt [fɛr'vant] *adj*: **~ (mit)** related (to); **V~e(r)** *f(m)* relative, relation; **V~schaft** *f* relationship; (*Menschen*) relations *pl*

ver'warnen *vt* to caution

Ver'warnung *f* caution

ver'wechseln *vt*: **~ mit** to confuse with; to mistake for; **zum V~ ähnlich** as like as two peas

Ver'wechslung *f* confusion, mixing up

Ver'wehung [fɛr'veːʊŋ] *f* snowdrift; sand drift

verweichlicht [fɛr'vaɪçlɪçt] *adj* effeminate, soft

ver'weigern *vt*: **jdm etw ~** to refuse sb sth; **den Gehorsam/die Aussage ~** to refuse to obey/testify

Ver'weigerung *f* refusal

Verweis [fɛr'vaɪs] (-es, -e) *m* reprimand, rebuke; (*Hinweis*) reference; **~en** (*unreg*) *vt* to refer; **jdn von der Schule ~en** to expel sb (from school); **jdn des Landes ~en** to deport *od* expel sb

ver'welken *vi* to fade

verwend- [fɛr'vɛnd] *zW*: **~bar** [-'vɛntbaːr] *adj* usable; **ver'wenden** (*unreg*) *vt* to use; (*Mühe, Zeit, Arbeit*) to spend ♦ *vr* to intercede; **Ver'wendung** *f* use

ver'werfen (*unreg*) *vt* to reject

verwerflich [fɛr'vɛrflɪç] *adj* reprehensible

ver'werten *vt* to utilize

Ver'wertung *f* utilization

verwesen [fɛr'veːzən] *vi* to decay

ver'wickeln *vt* to tangle (up); (*fig*) to involve ♦ *vt* to get tangled (up); **jdn in etw** *akk* **~** to involve sb in sth; **sich in etw** *akk* **~** to get involved in sth

verwickelt [fɛr'vɪkəlt] *adj* (*Situation, Fall*) difficult, complicated

verwildern [fɛr'vɪldərn] *vi* to run wild

Spelling Reform: ▲ *new spelling* △ *old spelling (to be phased out)*

verwirklichen [fɛr'vɪrklɪçən] vt to realize, to put into effect

Verwirklichung f realization

verwirren [fɛr'vɪrən] vt to tangle (up); (fig) to confuse

Verwirrung f confusion

verwittern [fɛr'vɪtərn] vi to weather

verwitwet [fɛr'vɪtvət] adj widowed

verwöhnen [fɛr'vøːnən] vt to spoil

verworren [fɛr'vɔrən] adj confused

verwundbar [fɛr'vʊntbaːr] adj vulnerable

verwunden [fɛr'vʊndən] vt to wound

verwunder- [fɛr'vʊndər] zW: **~lich** adj surprising; **V~ung** f astonishing

Verwundete(r) f(m) injured person

Verwundung f wound, injury

ver'wünschen vt to curse

verwüsten [fɛr'vyːstən] vt to devastate

verzagen [fɛr'tsaːgən] vi to despair

ver'zählen vr to miscount

verzehren [fɛr'tseːrən] vt to consume

ver'zeichnen vt to list; (Niederlage, Verlust) to register

Verzeichnis [fɛr'tsaɪçnɪs] (-ses, -se) nt list, catalogue; (in Buch) index

verzeih- [fɛr'tsaɪ] zW: **~en** (unreg) vt, vi to forgive; **jdm etw ~en** to forgive sb for sth; **~lich** adj pardonable; **V~ung** f forgiveness, pardon; **V~ung!** sorry!, excuse me!

verzichten [fɛr'tsɪçtən] vi: **~ auf** +akk to forgo, to give up

ver'ziehen (unreg) vi to move ♦ vt to put out of shape; (Kind) to spoil; (Pflanzen) to thin out ♦ vr to go out of shape; (Gesicht) to contort; (verschwinden) to disappear; **das Gesicht ~** to pull a face

verzieren [fɛr'tsiːrən] vt to decorate, to ornament

Verzierung f decoration

verzinsen [fɛr'tsɪnzən] vt to pay interest on

ver'zögern vt to delay

Ver'zögerung f delay, time lag; **~staktik** f delaying tactics pl

verzollen [fɛr'tsɔlən] vt to pay duty on

Verzug [fɛr'tsuːk] m delay

verzweif- [fɛr'tsvaɪf] zW: **~eln** vi to despair; **~elt** adj desperate; **V~lung** f despair

Veto ['veːto] (-s, -s) nt veto

Vetter ['fɛtər] (-s, -n) m cousin

vgl. abk (= vergleiche) cf.

v. H. abk (= vom Hundert) p.c.

vibrieren [vi'briːrən] vi to vibrate

Video ['viːdeo] nt video; **~gerät** nt video recorder; **~rekorder** m video recorder

Vieh [fiː] (-(e)s nt cattle pl; **v~isch** adj bestial

viel [fiːl] adj a lot of, much ♦ adv a lot, much; **~ sagend** significant; **~ versprechend** promising; **~e** pron pl a lot of, many; **~ zu wenig** much too little; **~erlei** adj a great variety of; **~es** pron a lot; **~fach** adj, adv many times; **auf ~fachen Wunsch** at the request of many people; **V~falt** (-) f variety; **~fältig** adj varied, many-sided

vielleicht [fi'laɪçt] adv perhaps

viel- zW: **V~mal(s)** adv many times; **danke ~mals** many thanks; **~mehr** adv rather, on the contrary; **~seitig** adj many-sided

vier [fiːr] num four; **V~eck** (-(e)s, -e) nt four-sided figure; (gleichseitig) square; **~eckig** adj four-sided; square; **V~taktmotor** m four-stroke engine; **~te(r, s)** ['fiːrtə(r, s)] adj fourth; **V~tel** ['fɪrtəl] (-s, -) nt quarter; **V~teljahr** nt quarter; **~teljährlich** adj quarterly; **~teln** vt to divide into four; (Kuchen usw) to divide into quarters; **V~telstunde** f quarter of an hour; **~zehn** ['fɪrtseːn] num fourteen; **in ~zehn Tagen** in a fortnight; **~zehn-tägig** adj fortnightly; **~zig** ['fɪrtsɪç] num forty

Villa ['vɪla] (-, Villen) f villa

violett [vio'lɛt] adj violet

Violin- [vio'liːn] zW: **~e** f violin; **~schlüssel** m treble clef

virtuell [vɪr'tɛl] adj (COMPUT) virtual; **~e Realität** virtual reality

Virus ['viːrʊs] (-, **Viren**) m od nt (auch COMPUT) virus

Visa ['viːza] pl von **Visum**

vis-a-vis ▲, **vis-à-vis** [viza'viː] adv opposite

Visen ['viːzən] pl von **Visum**

Visier [vi'ziːr] (-s, -e) nt gunsight; (am Helm) visor

Visite [vi'ziːtə] f (MED) visit; **~nkarte** f visiting card

Visum ['viːzʊm] (-s, **Visa** od **Visen**) nt visa

vital [vi'taːl] adj lively, full of life, vital

Vitamin [vita'miːn] (-s, -e) nt vitamin

Vogel ['foːgəl] (-s, ⸚) m bird; **einen ~ haben** (umg) to have bats in the belfry; **jdm den ~ zeigen** (umg) to tap one's forehead (meaning that one thinks sb stupid); **~bauer** m birdcage; **~perspektive** f bird's-eye view; **~scheuche** f scarecrow

Vokabel [vo'kaːbəl] (-, -n) f word

Vokabular [vokabu'laːr] (-s, -e) nt vocabulary

Vokal [vo'kaːl] (-s, -e) m vowel

Volk [fɔlk] (-(e)s, ⸚er) nt people; nation

Völker- ['fœlkər] zW: **~recht** nt international law; **v~rechtlich** adj according to international law; **~verständigung** f international understanding

---

Volkshochschule

The Volkshochschule (VHS) is an institution which offers Adult Education classes. No set qualifications are necessary to attend. For a small fee adults can attend both vocational and non-vocational classes in the day-time or evening.

Volks- zW: **~entscheid** m referendum;

~fest nt fair; **~hochschule** f adult education classes pl; **~lied** nt folksong; **~republik** f people's republic; **~schule** f elementary school; **~tanz** m folk dance; **~vertreter(in)** m(f) people's representative; **~wirtschaft** f economics sg

voll [fɔl] adj full; **etw ~ machen** to fill sth up; **~ tanken** to fill up; **~ und ganz** completely; **jdn für ~ nehmen** (umg) to take sb seriously; **~auf** adv amply; **V~bart** m full beard; **V~beschäftigung** f full employment; **~'bringen** (unreg) vt insep to accomplish; **~'enden** vt insep to finish, to complete; **~endet** adj (~kommen) completed; **~ends** ['fɔlɛnts] adv completely; **V~endung** f completion

Volleyball ['vɔliːbal] m volleyball

Vollgas nt: **mit ~** at full throttle; **~ geben** to step on it

völlig ['fœlɪç] adj complete ♦ adv completely

voll- zW: **~jährig** adj of age; **V~kaskoversicherung** ['fɔlkaskoːfɛrzɪçərʊŋ] f fully comprehensive insurance; **~'kommen** adj perfect; **V~kommenheit** f perfection; **V~kornbrot** nt wholemeal bread; **V~macht** (-, -en) f authority, full powers pl; **V~milch** f (KOCH) full-cream milk; **V~mond** m full moon; **V~pension** f full board; **~ständig** ['fɔlʃtɛndɪç] adj complete; **~'strecken** vt insep to execute; **~tanken** △ vt, vi siehe **voll**; **V~waschmittel** nt detergent; **V~wertkost** f wholefood; **~zählig** ['fɔlˈtsɛːlɪç] adj complete; in full number; **~'ziehen** (unreg) vt insep to carry out ♦ vr insep to happen; **V~'zug** m execution

Volumen [vo'luːmən] (-s, - od **Volumina**) nt volume

vom [fɔm] = **von dem**

SCHLÜSSELWORT

von [fɔn] *präp +dat* **1** (*Ausgangspunkt*) from; **von ... bis** from ... to; **von morgens bis abends** from morning till night; **von ... nach ...** from ... to ...; **von ... an** from ... to ...; **von ... aus** from ...; **von dort aus** from there; **etw von sich aus tun** to do sth of one's own accord; **von mir aus** (*umg*) if you like, I don't mind; **von wo/wann ...?** where/when ... from?

2 (*Ursache, im Passiv*) by; **ein Gedicht von Schiller** a poem by Schiller; **von etw müde** tired from sth

3 (*als Genitiv*) of; **ein Freund von mir** a friend of mine; **nett von dir** nice of you; **jeweils zwei von zehn** two out of every ten

4 (*über*) about; **er erzählte vom Urlaub** he talked about his holiday

5: von wegen! (*umg*) no way!

voneinander *adv* from each other

SCHLÜSSELWORT

vor [foːr] *präp +dat* **1** (*räumlich*) in front of; **vor der Kirche links abbiegen** turn left before the church

2 (*zeitlich*) before; **ich war vor ihm da** I was there before him; **vor 2 Tagen** 2 days ago; **5 (Minuten) vor 4** 5 (minutes) to 4; **vor kurzem** a little while ago

3 (*Ursache*) with; **vor Wut/Liebe** with rage/love; **vor Hunger sterben** to die of hunger; **vor lauter Arbeit** because of work

4: vor allem, vor allen Dingen most of all

♦ *präp +akk* (*räumlich*) in front of

♦ *adv:* **vor und zurück** backwards and forwards

Vorabend [ˈfoːrˌaːbənt] *m* evening before, eve

voran [foˈran] *adv* before, ahead;

mach ~! get on with it!; **~gehen** (*unreg*) *vi* to go ahead; **~gehen** *dat* **~gehen** to precede sth; **~kommen** (*unreg*) *vi* to come along, to make progress

Voranschlag [ˈfoːrˌanʃlaːk] *m* estimate

Vorarbeiter [ˈfoːrˌarbaitər] *m* foreman

voraus [foˈraus] *adv* ahead; (*zeitlich*) ahead; **jdm ~ sein** to be ahead of sb; **im V~** in advance; **~gehen** (*unreg*) *vi* to go (on) ahead; (*fig*) to precede; **~haben** (*unreg*) *vt:* **jdm etw ~haben** to have the edge on sb in sth; **V~sage** *f* prediction; **~sagen** *vt* to predict; **~sehen** (*unreg*) *vt* to foresee; **~setzen** *vt* to assume; **~gesetzt, dass ...** provided that ...; **V~setzung** *f* requirement, prerequisite; **V~sicht** *f* foresight; **aller V~sicht nach** in all probability; **~sichtlich** *adv* probably

Vorbehalt [ˈfoːrbəhalt] (*-(e)s, -e*) *m* reservation, proviso; **v~en** (*unreg*) *vt:* **sich/jdm etw v~en** to reserve sth (for o.s.)/for sb; **v~los** *adj* unconditional ♦ *adv* unconditionally

vorbei [foːrˈbai] *adv* by, past; **das ist ~** that's over; **~gehen** (*unreg*) *vi* to pass by, to go past; **~kommen** (*unreg*) *vi:* **bei jdm ~kommen** to drop in *od* call in on sb

vor- *zW:* **~belastet** [ˈfoːrbəlastət] *adj* (*fig*) handicapped; **~bereiten** *vt* to prepare; **V~bereitung** *f* preparation; **V~bestellung** *f* advance order; (*von Platz, Tisch etc*) advance booking; **~bestraft** [ˈfoːrbəʃtraːft] *adj* previously convicted, with a record

vorbeugen [ˈfoːrbɔygən] *vt, vr* to lean forward ♦ *vi +dat* to prevent; **~d** *adj* preventive

Vorbeugung *f* prevention; **zur ~ gegen** for the prevention of

Vorbild [ˈfoːrbilt] *nt* model; **sich** *dat* **jdn zum ~ nehmen** to model o.s. on sb; **v~lich** *adj* model, ideal

vorbringen [ˈfoːrbrıŋən] (*unreg*) *vt* to advance, to state

Vorder- ['fɔrdər] zW: **~achse** f front axle; **v~e(r, s)** adj front; **~grund** m foreground; **~mann** (pl **-männer**) m man in front; **jdn auf ~mann bringen** (umg) to get sb to shape up; **~seite** f front (side); **v~ste(r, s)** adj front

vordrängen ['fɔːrdrɛŋən] vr to push to the front

voreilig ['foːrʔailɪç] adj hasty, rash

voreinander [foːrʔaiˈnandər] adv (räumlich) in front of each other

voreingenommen ['foːrʔaingənɔmən] adj biased; **V~heit** f bias

vorenthalten ['foːrʔɛnthaltən] (unreg) vt: **jdm etw ~** to withhold sth from sb

vorerst ['foːrʔeːrst] adv for the moment od present

Vorfahr ['foːrfaːr] (**-en, -en**) m ancestor

vorfahren (unreg) vi to drive (on) ahead; (vors Haus etc) to drive up

Vorfahrt f (AUT) right of way; **~ achten!** give way!

Vorfahrts- zW: **~regel** f right of way; **~schild** nt give way sign; **~straße** f major road

Vorfall ['foːrfal] m incident; **v~en** (unreg) vi to occur

vorfinden ['foːrfɪndən] (unreg) vt to find

Vorfreude ['foːrfrɔydə] f (joyful) anticipation

vorführen ['foːrfyːrən] vt to show, to display; **dem Gericht ~** to bring before the court

Vorgabe ['foːrgaːbə] f (SPORT) start, handicap ♦ in zW (COMPUT) default

Vorgang ['foːrgaŋ] m course of events; (bes SCI) process

Vorgänger(in) ['foːrgɛŋər(ɪn)] (**-s, -**) m(f) predecessor

vorgeben ['foːrgeːbən] (unreg) vt to pretend, to use as a pretext; (SPORT) to give an advantage od a start of

vorgefertigt ['foːrgəfɛrtɪçt] adj prefabricated

vorgehen ['foːrgeːən] (unreg) vi (voraus) to go (on) ahead; (nach vorn) to go up front; (handeln) to act, to proceed; (Uhr) to be fast; (Vorrang haben) to take precedence; (passieren) to go on

Vorgehen (**-s**) nt action

Vorgeschichte ['foːrgəʃɪçtə] f past history

Vorgeschmack ['foːrgəʃmak] m foretaste

Vorgesetzte(r) ['foːrgəzɛtstə(r)] f(m) superior

vorgestern ['foːrgɛstərn] adv the day before yesterday

vorhaben ['foːrhaːbən] (unreg) vt to intend; **hast du schon was vor?** have you got anything on?; **V~** (**-s, -**) nt intention

vorhalten ['foːrhaltən] (unreg) vt to hold od put up ♦ vi to last; **jdm etw ~** (fig) to reproach sb for sth

vorhanden [foːrˈhandən] adj existing; (erhältlich) available

Vorhang ['foːrhaŋ] m curtain

Vorhängeschloss ▲ ['foːrhɛŋəʃlɔs] nt padlock

vorher [foːrˈheːr] adv before(hand); **~bestimmen** vt (Schicksal) to preordain; **~gehen** (unreg) vi to precede; **~ig** adj previous

Vorherrschaft ['foːrhɛrʃaft] f predominance, supremacy

vorherrschen ['foːrhɛrʃən] vi to predominate

vorher- [foːrˈheːr] zW: **V~sage** f forecast; **~sagen** vt to forecast, to predict; **~sehbar** adj predictable; **~sehen** (unreg) vt to foresee

vorhin [foːrˈhɪn] adv not long ago, just now; **V~ein** ▲ adv: **im V~ein** beforehand

---

Spelling Reform: ▲ *new spelling* △ *old spelling (to be phased out)*

vorig ['fo:riç] adj previous, last

Vorkämpfer(in) ['fo:rkɛmpfər(in)] m(f) pioneer

Vorkaufsrecht ['fo:rkaufsrɛçt] nt option to buy

Vorkehrung ['fo:rke:ruŋ] f precaution

vorkommen ['fo:rkɔmən] (unreg) vi to come forward; (geschehen, sich finden) to occur; (scheinen) to seem (to be); **sich** dat **dumm** etc ~ to feel stupid etc; **V~** (**-s, -**) nt occurrence

Vorkriegs- ['fo:rkri:ks] in zW prewar

Vorladung ['fo:rla:duŋ] f summons

Vorlage ['fo:rla:gə] f model, pattern; (Gesetzesvorlage) bill; (SPORT) pass

vorlassen ['fo:rlasən] (unreg) vt to admit; (vorgehen lassen) to allow to go in front

vorläufig ['fo:rlɔyfiç] adj temporary, provisional

vorlaut ['fo:rlaut] adj impertinent, cheeky

vorlesen ['fo:rle:zən] (unreg) vt to read (out)

Vorlesung f (UNIV) lecture

vorletzte(r, s) ['fo:rlɛtstə(r, s)] adj last but one

vorlieb [fo:r'li:p] adv: ~ **nehmen mit** to make do with

Vorliebe ['fo:rli:bə] f preference, partiality

vorliegen ['fo:rli:gən] (unreg) vi to be (here); **etw liegt jdm vor** sb has sth; **~d** present, at issue

vormachen ['fo:rmaxən] vt: **jdm etw** ~ to show sb how to do sth; (fig) to fool sb; to have sb on

Vormachtstellung ['fo:rmaxtʃtɛluŋ] f supremacy, hegemony

Vormarsch ['fo:rmarʃ] m advance

vormerken ['fo:rmɛrkən] vt to book

Vormittag ['fo:rmita:k] m morning; **v~s** adv in the morning, before noon

vorn [fɔrn] adv in front; **von** ~ **anfangen** to start at the beginning; **nach** ~ to the front

Vorname m first name,

Christian name

vorne ['fɔrnə] adv = **vorn**

vornehm ['fo:rne:m] adj distinguished; refined; elegant

vornehmen (unreg) vt (fig) to carry out; **sich** dat **etw** ~ to start on sth; (beschließen) to decide to do sth; **sich** dat **jdn** ~ to tell sb off

vornherein ['fɔrnhɛrain] adv: **von** ~ from the start

Vorort ['fo:rʔɔrt] m suburb

Vorrang ['fo:rraŋ] m precedence, priority; **v~ig** adj of prime importance, primary

Vorrat ['fo:rra:t] m stock, supply

vorrätig ['fo:rrɛ:tiç] adj in stock

Vorratskammer f pantry

Vorrecht ['fo:rrɛçt] nt privilege

Vorrichtung ['fo:rriçtuŋ] f device, contrivance

vorrücken ['fo:rrʏkən] vi to advance ♦ vt to move forward

Vorsaison ['fo:rzezɔ̃] f early season

Vorsatz ['fo:rzats] m intention; (JUR) intent; **einen** ~ **fassen** to make a resolution

vorsätzlich ['fo:rzɛtsliç] adj intentional; (JUR) premeditated ♦ adv intentionally

Vorschau ['fo:rʃau] f (RADIO, TV) (programme) preview; (Film) trailer

Vorschlag ['fo:rʃla:k] m suggestion, proposal; **v~en** (unreg) vt to suggest, to propose

vorschreiben ['fo:rʃraibən] (unreg) vt to prescribe, to specify

Vorschrift ['fo:rʃrift] f regulation(s); rule(s); (Anweisungen) instruction(s); **Dienst nach** ~ work-to-rule; **v~smäßig** adj as per regulations/instructions

Vorschuss ▲ ['fo:rʃʊs] m advance

vorsehen ['fo:rze:ən] (unreg) vt to provide for, to plan ♦ vt to take care, to be careful ♦ vi to be visible

Vorsehung f providence

Vorsicht ['fo:rziçt] f caution; care; ~!

look out!, take care!; *(auf Schildern)* caution!, danger!; **~, Stufe!** mind the step!; **v~ig** adj cautious, careful; **v~shalber** adv just in case

Vorsilbe ['foːɐzɪlbə] f prefix

vorsingen ['foːɐzɪŋən] vt *(vor Zuhörern)* to sing (to); *(in Prüfung, für Theater etc)* to audition (for) ♦ vi to sing

Vorsitz ['foːɐzɪts] m chair(manship); **~ende(r)** f(m) chairman(-woman)

Vorsorge ['foːɐzɔrɡə] f precaution(s), provision(s); **v~n** vi: **v~n für** to make provision(s) for; **~untersuchung** f check-up

vorsorglich ['foːɐzɔrklɪç] adv as a precaution

Vorspeise ['foːɐʃpaɪzə] f hors d'oeuvre, appetizer

Vorspiel ['foːɐʃpiːl] nt prelude

vorspielen vt: **jdm etw ~** *(MUS)* to play sth for od to sb ♦ vi *(zur Prüfung etc)* to play for od to sb

vorsprechen ['foːɐʃprɛçən] *(unreg)* vt to say out loud, to recite ♦ vi: **bei jdm ~** to call on sb

Vorsprung ['foːɐʃprʊŋ] m projection, ledge; *(fig)* advantage, start

Vorstadt ['foːɐʃtat] f suburbs pl

Vorstand ['foːɐʃtant] m executive committee; *(COMM)* board (of directors); *(Person)* director, head

vorstehen ['foːɐʃteːən] *(unreg)* vi to project; **einer Sache** dat **~** *(fig)* to be the head of sth

vorstell- ['foːɐʃtɛl] zW: **~bar** adj conceivable; **~en** vt to put forward; *(bekannt machen)* to introduce; *(darstellen)* to represent; **~en vor** +akk to put in front of; **sich** dat **etw ~en** to imagine sth; **V~ung** f *(Bekanntmachung)* introduction; *(THEAT etc)* performance; *(Gedanke)* idea, thought

vorstoßen ['foːɐʃtoːsən] *(unreg)* vi *(ins Unbekannte)* to venture (forth)

Vorstrafe ['foːɐʃtraːfə] f previous conviction

Vortag ['foːɐtak] m: **am ~ einer Sache** gen on the day before sth

vortäuschen ['foːɐtɔysən] vt to feign, to pretend

Vorteil ['foːɐtaɪl] *(-s, -e)* m: **~ (gegenüber)** advantage (over); **im ~ sein** to have the advantage; **v~haft** adj advantageous

Vortrag ['foːɐtraːk] *(-(e)s, Vorträge)* m talk, lecture; **v~en** *[-ɡən]* *(unreg)* vt to carry forward; *(fig)* to recite; *(Rede)* to deliver; *(Lied)* to perform; *(Meinung etc)* to express

vortreten ['foːɐtreːtən] *(unreg)* vi to step forward; *(Augen etc)* to protrude

vorüber [fo'ryːbar] adv past, over; **~gehen** *(unreg)* vi to pass (by); **~gehen an** +dat *(fig)* to pass over; **~gehend** adj temporary, passing

Vorurteil ['foːɐʔʊrtaɪl] nt prejudice

Vorverkauf ['foːɐfɛrkaʊf] m advance booking

Vorwahl ['foːɐvaːl] f preliminary election; *(TEL)* dialling code

Vorwand ['foːɐvant] *(-(e)s, Vorwände)* m pretext

vorwärts ['foːɐvɛrts] adv forward; **~ gehen** to progress; **V~gang** m *(AUT etc)* forward gear; **~ kommen** to get on, to make progress

Vorwäsche f prewash

vorweg [foːɐ'vɛk] adv in advance; **~nehmen** *(unreg)* vt to anticipate

vorweisen ['foːɐvaɪzən] *(unreg)* vt to show, to produce

vorwerfen ['foːɐvɛrfən] *(unreg)* vt: **jdm etw ~** to reproach sb for sth, to accuse sb of sth; **sich** dat **nichts vorzuwerfen haben** to have nothing to reproach o.s. with

vorwiegend ['foːɐviːɡənt] adj predominant ♦ adv predominantly

vorwitzig ['foːɐvɪtsɪç] adj *(Mensch, Bemerkung)* cheeky

Spelling Reform: ▲ *new spelling* △ *old spelling (to be phased out)*

Vorwort ['fo:rvɔrt] (-(e)s, -e) nt preface

Vorwurf ['fo:rvʊrf] m reproach; jdm/sich Vorwürfe machen to reproach sb/o.s.; **v~svoll** adj reproachful

vorzeigen ['fo:rtsaɪgən] vt to show, to produce

vorzeitig ['fo:rtsaɪtɪç] adj premature

vorziehen ['fo:rtsi:ən] (unreg) vt to pull forward; (Gardinen) to draw; (lieber haben) to prefer

Vorzimmer ['fo:rtsɪmər] nt (Büro) outer office

Vorzug ['fo:rtsu:k] m preference; (gute Eigenschaft) merit, good quality; (Vorteil) advantage

vorzüglich [fo:r'tsy:klɪç] adj excellent

Vorzugspreis m special discount price

vulgär [vʊl'gɛ:r] adj vulgar

Vulkan [vʊl'ka:n] (-s, -e) m volcano

W, w

Waage ['va:gə] f scales pl; (ASTROL) Libra; **w~recht** adj horizontal

Wabe ['va:bə] f honeycomb

wach [vax] adj awake; (fig) alert; **W~e** f guard, watch; **W~e halten** to keep watch; **W~e stehen** to stand guard; **~en** vi to be awake; (Wache halten) to guard

Wachs [vaks] (-es, -e) nt wax

wachsam ['vaxza:m] adj watchful, vigilant, alert

wachsen (unreg) vi to grow

Wachstuch ['vakstu:x] nt oilcloth

Wachstum ['vakstu:m] (-s) nt growth

Wächter ['vɛçtər] (-s, -) m guard, warden, keeper; (Parkplatzwächter) attendant

wackel- ['vakəl] zW: **~ig** adj shaky, wobbly; **W~kontakt** m loose connection; **~n** vi to shake; (fig: Position) to be shaky

wacker ['vakər] adj valiant, stout ♦ adv well, bravely

Wade ['va:də] f (ANAT) calf

Waffe ['vafə] f weapon

Waffel ['vafəl] (-, -n) f waffle; wafer

Waffen- zW: **~schein** m gun licence; **~stillstand** m armistice, truce

Wagemut ['va:gəmu:t] m daring

wagen ['va:gən] vt to venture, to dare

Wagen ['va:gən] (-s, -) m vehicle; (Auto) car; (EISENB) carriage; (Pferdewagen) cart; **~heber** (-s, -) m jack

Waggon [va'gõ:] (-s, -s) m carriage; (Güterwaggon) goods van, freight truck (US)

Wagnis ['va:knɪs] (-ses, -se) nt risk

Wagon ▲ [va'gõ:, va'go:n] (-s, -s) m = Waggon

Wahl [va:l] (-, -en) f choice; (POL) election; **zweite ~** (COMM) seconds pl

wähl- ['vɛ:l] zW: **~bar** adj eligible; **~en** vt, vi to choose; (POL) to elect, to vote (for); (TEL) to dial; **W~er(in)** (-s, -) m(f) voter; **~erisch** adj fastidious, particular

Wahl- zW: **~fach** nt optional subject; **~gang** m ballot; **~kabine** f polling booth; **~kampf** m election campaign; **~kreis** m constituency; **~lokal** nt polling station; **~los** adv at random; **~recht** nt franchise; **~spruch** m motto; **~urne** f ballot box

Wahn [va:n] (-(e)s) m delusion; folly; **~sinn** m madness; **w~sinnig** adj insane, mad ♦ adv (umg) incredibly

wahr [va:r] adj true

wahren vt to maintain, to keep

während ['vɛ:rənt] präp +gen during ♦ konj while; **~dessen** adv meanwhile

wahr- zW: **~haben** (unreg) vt: etw nicht **~haben wollen** to refuse to admit sth; **~haft** adv (tatsächlich) truly; **~haftig** [va:r'haftɪç] adj true, real ♦ adv really; **W~heit** f truth; **~nehmen** (unreg) vt to perceive, to observe; **W~nehmung** f perception; **~sagen** vi to prophesy, to tell fortunes; **W~sager(in)** (-s, -) m(f) fortune teller; **~scheinlich** [va:r'ʃaɪnlɪç] adj probable ♦ adv probably; **W~'scheinlichkeit** f

Währung probability; **aller W~scheinlichkeit nach** in all probability

Währung ['vɛːrʊŋ] f currency

Wahrzeichen nt symbol

Waise ['vaizə] f orphan; **~nhaus** nt orphanage

Wald [valt] (-(e)s, "er) m wood(s); (*groß*) forest; **~brand** m forest fire; **~sterben** nt trees dying due to pollution

Wales [weɪlz] (-) nt Wales

Wal(fisch) ['vaːl(fɪʃ)] (-(e)s, -e) m whale

Waliser [va'liːzər] (-s, -) m Welshman; **Waliserin** [va'liːzərɪn] f Welshwoman; **walisisch** ['va'liːzɪʃ] adj Welsh

Walkman ['wɔːkman] ® -s, Walkmen) m Walkman ®, personal stereo

Wall [val] (-(e)s, "e) m embankment; (*Bollwerk*) rampart

Wallfahr- zW: **~er(in)** m(f) pilgrim; **~t** f pilgrimage

Walnuss ▲ ['valnʊs] f walnut

Walross ▲ ['valrɔs] nt walrus

Walze ['valtsə] f (*Gerät*) cylinder; (*Fahrzeug*) roller; **w~n** vt to roll (out)

wälzen ['vɛltsən] vt to roll (over); (*Bücher*) to hunt through; (*Probleme*) to deliberate on ♦ vr to wallow; (*vor Schmerzen*) to roll about; (*im Bett*) to toss and turn

Walzer ['valtsər] (-s, -) m waltz

Wand [vant] (-, "e) f wall; (*Trennwand*) partition; (*Bergwand*) precipice

Wandel ['vandəl] (-s) m change; **w~bar** adj changeable, variable; **w~n** vt, vr to change ♦ vi (*gehen*) to walk

Wander- ['vandər] zW: **~er** (-s, -) m hiker, rambler; **~karte** f map of country walks; **w~n** vi to hike; (*Blick*) to wander; (*Gedanken*) to stray; **~schaft** f travelling; **~ung** f walk, hike; **~weg** m trail, walk

Wandlung f change, transformation

Wange ['vaŋə] f cheek

wanken ['vankən] vi to stagger; (*fig*) to waver

wann [van] adv when

Wanne ['vanə] f tub

Wanze ['vantsə] f bug

Wappen ['vapən] (-s, -) nt coat of arms, crest; **~kunde** f heraldry

war etc [vaːr] vb siehe **sein**

Ware ['vaːrə] f ware

Waren- zW: **~haus** nt department store; **~lager** nt stock, store; **~muster** nt trade sample; **~probe** f sample; **~sendung** f trade sample (*sent by post*); **~zeichen** nt: (*eingetragenes*) **~zeichen** (registered) trademark

warf etc [varf] vb siehe **werfen**

warm [varm] adj warm; (*Essen*) hot

Wärm- ['vɛrm] zW: **~e** f warmth; **w~en** vt, vr to warm (up), to heat (up); **~flasche** f hot-water bottle

Warn- ['varn] zW: **~blinkanlage** f (AUT) hazard warning lights pl; **~dreieck** nt warning triangle; **w~en** vt to warn; **~ung** f warning

warten ['vartən] vi; **~ (auf** +akk) to wait (for); **auf sich** ~ **lassen** to take a long time

Wärter(in) ['vɛrtər(ɪn)] (-s, -) m(f) attendant

Warte- ['vartə] zW: **~saal** m (EISENB) waiting room; **~zimmer** nt waiting room

Wartung f servicing; service; **~ und Instandhaltung** maintenance

warum [va'rʊm] adv why

Warze ['vartsə] f wart

was [vas] pron what; (*umg: etwas*) something; **~ für (ein)** ... what sort of ...

waschbar adj washable

Waschbecken nt washbasin

Wäsche ['vɛʃə] f wash(ing); (*Bettwäsche*) linen; (*Unterwäsche*) underclothing

waschecht adj colourfast; (*fig*) genu-

Spelling Reform: ▲ *new spelling* △ *old spelling (to be phased out)*

ine

Wäsche- zW: **~klammer** f clothes peg (BRIT), clothespin (US); **~leine** f washing line (BRIT)

waschen ['vaʃən] (unreg) vt, vi to wash ♦ vr to (have a) wash; **sich** dat **die Hände** ~ to wash one's hands

Wäsche'rei f laundry

Wasch- zW: **~gelegenheit** f washing facilities; **~küche** f laundry room; **~lappen** m face flannel, washcloth (US); (umg) sissy; **~maschine** f washing machine; **~mittel** nt detergent, washing powder; **~pulver** nt detergent, washing powder; **~raum** m washroom; **~salon** m Launderette ®

Wasser ['vasər] (-s, -) nt water; **~ball** m water polo; **w~dicht** adj waterproof; **~fall** m waterfall; **~farbe** f watercolour; **~hahn** m tap, faucet (US); **~kraftwerk** nt hydroelectric power station; **~leitung** f water pipe; **~mann** m (ASTROL) Aquarius

wässern ['vesərn] vt, vi to water

Wasser- zW: **w~scheu** adj afraid of (the) water; **~ski** ['vasərʃi:] nt waterskiing; **~stoff** m hydrogen; **~waage** f spirit level; **~zeichen** nt watermark

wässrig ▲ ['vesrɪç] adj watery

Watt [vat] (-(e)s, -en) nt mud flats pl

Watte f cotton wool, absorbent cotton (US)

WC ['ve:'tse:] (-s, -s) nt abk (= water closet) W.C.

Web- ['ve:b] zW: **w~en** (unreg) vt to weave; **~er** (-s, -) m weaver; **~e'rei** f (Betrieb) weaving mill; **~stuhl** m loom

Wechsel ['veksəl] (-s, -) m change; (COMM) bill of exchange; **~geld** nt change; **w~haft** adj (Wetter) variable; **~jahre** pl change of life sg; **~kurs** m rate of exchange; **w~n** vt to change; (Blicke) to exchange ♦ vi to change; (Geldwechseln) to have change; **~strom** m alternating current; **~stube** f bureau de change; **~wirkung** f interaction

Weck- ['vek] zW: **~dienst** m alarm call service; **w~en** vt to wake (up); to call; **~er** (-s, -) m alarm clock

wedeln ['ve:dəln] vi (mit Schwanz) to wag; (mit Fächer etc) to wave

weder ['ve:dər] konj neither; **~ ... noch ...** neither ... nor ...

Weg [ve:k] (-(e)s, -e) m way; (Pfad) path; (Route) route; **sich auf den ~ machen** to be on one's way; **jdm aus dem ~ gehen** to keep out of sb's way; siehe zuwege

weg [vek] adv away, off; **über etw** akk **~ sein** to be over sth; **er war schon ~** he had already left; **Finger ~!** hands off!

wegbleiben (unreg) vi to stay away

wegen ['ve:gən] präp +gen (umg: +dat) because of

Weg- [ve:k] zW: **w~fallen** (unreg) vi to be left out; (Ferien, Bezahlung) to be cancelled; (aufhören) to cease; **~gehen** (unreg) vi to go away; to leave; **~lassen** (unreg) vt to leave out; **~laufen** (unreg) vi to run away od off; **~legen** vt to put aside; **~machen** (umg) vt to get rid of; **~müssen** (unreg; umg) vi to have to go; **~nehmen** (unreg) vt to take away; **~tun** (unreg) vt to put away; **W~weiser** (-s, -) m road sign, signpost; **~werfen** (unreg) vt to throw away

weh [ve:] adj sore; **~(e)** excl: **~(e),** **wenn du ...** woe betide you if ...; **o ~!** oh dear!; **~e!** just you dare!

wehen vt, vi to blow; (Fahnen) to flutter

weh- zW: **~leidig** adj whiny, whining; **~mütig** adj melancholy

Wehr [ve:r] (-, -en) f: **sich zur ~ setzen** to defend o.s.; **~dienst** m military service; **~dienstverweigerer** m = conscientious objector; **w~en** vt to defend o.s.; **w~los** adj defenceless; **~pflicht** f compulsory military service; **w~pflichtig** adj liable for military service

Wehrdienst

Wehrdienst is military service which is still compulsory in Germany. All young men receive their call-up papers at 18 and all those pronounced physically fit are required to spend 10 months in the Bundeswehr. Conscientious objectors are allowed to do Zivildienst as an alternative, after attending a hearing and presenting their case.

wehtun ▲ ['ve:tu:n] (unreg) vt to hurt, to be sore; **jdm/sich ~** to hurt sb/o.s.

Weib [vaıp] (-(e)s, -er) nt woman, female; wife; **~chen** nt female; **w~lich** adj feminine

weich [vaıç] adj soft; **W~e** f (EISENB) points pl; **~en** (unreg) vi to yield, to give way; **W~heit** f softness; **~lich** adj soft, namby-pamby

Weide ['vaıdə] f (Baum) willow; (Gras) pasture; **w~n** vi to graze ♦ vr: **sich an etw** dat **w~n** to delight in sth

weigern ['vaıgərn] vr to refuse

Weigerung ['vaıgərʊŋ] f refusal

Weihe ['vaıə] f consecration; (Priesterweihe) ordination; **w~n** vt to consecrate; to ordain

Weihnacht zW: **~en** (-) nt Christmas; **w~lich** adj Christmas cpd

Weihnachts- zW: **~abend** m Christmas Eve; **~lied** nt Christmas carol; **~mann** m Father Christmas, Santa Claus; **~markt** m Christmas fair; **~tag** m Christmas Day; **zweiter ~tag** Boxing Day

Weihnachtsmarkt

The Weihnachtsmarkt is a market held in most large towns in Germany in the weeks prior to Christmas. People visit it to buy presents, toys and Christmas decorations, and to enjoy the festive atmosphere. Traditional Christmas food and drink can also be consumed there, for example, Lebkuchen and Glühwein.

Weihwasser nt holy water

weil [vaıl] konj because

Weile ['vaılə] (-) f while, short time

Wein [vaın] (-(e)s, -e) m wine; (Pflanze) vine; **~bau** m cultivation of vines; **~berg** m vineyard; **~bergschnecke** f snail; **~brand** m brandy

weinen vt, vi to cry; **das ist zum W~** it's enough to make you cry ♦ weep

Wein- zW: **~glas** nt wine glass; **~karte** f wine list; **~lese** f vintage; **~probe** f wine-tasting; **~rebe** f vine; **w~rot** adj burgundy, claret, wine-red; **~stock** m vine; **~stube** f wine bar; **~traube** f grape

weise ['vaızə] adj wise

Weise f manner, way; (Lied) tune; **auf diese ~** in this way

weisen (unreg) vt to show

Weisheit ['vaıshaıt] f wisdom; **~zahn** m wisdom tooth

weiß [vaıs] adj white ♦ vb siehe **wissen**; **W~bier** nt weissbier (light, fizzy beer made using top-fermentation yeast); **W~brot** nt white bread; **~en** vt to whitewash; **W~glut** f (TECH) incandescence; **jdn bis zur W~glut bringen** (fig) to make sb see red; **W~kohl** m (white) cabbage; **W~wein** m white wine; **W~wurst** f veal sausage

weit [vaıt] adj wide; (Begriff) broad; (Reise, Wurf) long ♦ adv far; **wie ~ ist es ...?** how far is it ...?; **in ~er Ferne** in the far distance; **~ blickend** far-seeing; **~ reichend** long-range; (fig) far-reaching; **~ verbreitet** widespread; **das geht zu ~** that's going too far; **~aus** adv by far; **~blickend** adj far-seeing; **W~e** f width; (Raum) space; (von Entfernung) distance; **~en** vt, vr to widen

weiter ['vaɪtar] adj wider; broader; farther (away); (zusätzlich) further ♦ adv further; **ohne ~es** without further ado; just like that; ~ **nichts/niemand** nothing/nobody else; **~arbeiten** vi to go on working; **~bilden** vr to continue one's education; **~empfehlen** (unreg) vr to recommend (to others); **W~fahrt** f continuation of the journey; **~führen** vt (in Straße) to lead on (to) ♦ vt (fortsetzen) to continue, carry on; **~gehen** (unreg) vi to go on; **~hin** adv: **etw ~hin tun** to go on doing sth; **~kommen** (unreg) vi (fig: mit Arbeit) to make progress; **~leiten** vt to pass on; **~machen** vt, vi to continue

weit- zW: **~gehend** adj considerable ♦ adv largely; **~läufig** adj (Gebäude) spacious; (Erklärung) lengthy; (Verwandter) distant; **~reichend** adj long-range; (fig) far-reaching; **~schweifig** adj long-winded; **~sichtig** adj (MED) long-sighted; (fig) far-sighted; **W~sprung** m long jump; **~verbreitet** adj widespread

Weizen ['vaɪtsən] (-s, -) m wheat

SCHLÜSSELWORT

welche(r, s) interrogativ pron which; **welcher von beiden?** which (one) of the two?; **welchen hast du genommen?** which (one) did you take?; **welche eine ...!** what a ...!; **welche Freude!** what joy!

♦ indef pron some; (in Fragen) any; **ich habe welche** I have some; **haben Sie welche?** do you have any?

♦ relativ pron (bei Menschen) who; (bei Sachen) which, that; **welche(r, s) auch immer** whoever/whichever/whatever

welk [vɛlk] adj withered; **~en** vi to wither

Welle ['vɛlə] f wave; (TECH) shaft

Wellen- zW: **~bereich** m waveband;

~länge f (auch fig) wavelength; **~linie** f wavy line; **~sittich** m budgerigar

Welt [vɛlt] (-, -en) f world; **~all** nt universe; **~anschauung** f philosophy of life; **w~berühmt** adj world-famous; **~krieg** m world war; **w~lich** adj worldly; (nicht kirchlich) secular; **~macht** f world power; **~meister** m world champion; **~raum** m space; **~reise** f trip round the world; **~stadt** f metropolis; **w~weit** adj world-wide

wem [veːm] (dat von wer) pron to whom

wen [veːn] (akk von wer) pron whom

Wende ['vɛndə] f turn; (Veränderung) change; **~kreis** m (GEOG) tropic; (AUT) turning circle; **~treppe** f spiral staircase; **w~n** (unreg) vt, vi, vr to turn; **sich an jdn w~n** to go/come to sb

wendig ['vɛndɪç] adj (Auto etc) manoeuvrable; (fig) agile

Wendung f turn; (Redewendung) idiom

wenig ['veːnɪç] adj, adv little; **~e** pron pl few pl; **~er** adj less; (mit pl) fewer ♦ adv less; **~ste(r, s)** adj least; **am ~sten** least; **~stens** adv at least

SCHLÜSSELWORT

wenn [vɛn] konj 1 (falls, bei Wünschen) if; **wenn auch ..., selbst wenn ...** even if ...; **wenn ich doch ...** if only I ...

2 (zeitlich) when; **immer wenn** whenever

wennschon ['vɛnʃoːn] adv: **na ~** so what?; **~, dennschon!** in for a penny, in for a pound

wer [veːr] pron who

Werbe- ['vɛrbə] zW: **~fernsehen** nt commercial television; **~geschenk** nt gift (from company); (zu Gekauftem) free gift; **w~n** (unreg) vt to win; (Mitglied) to recruit ♦ vi to advertise; **um jdn/etw w~n** to try to win sb/sth; **für jdn/etw w~n** to promote sb/sth

Werbung f advertising; (von Mitglie-

dern) recruitment; ~ **um jdn/etw** promotion of sb/sth

Werdegang ['veːrdəɡaŋ] *m* (*Laufbahn*) development; (*beruflich*) career

SCHLÜSSELWORT

werden ['veːrdən] (*pt* **wurde**, *pp* **geworden** *od* (*bei Passiv*) **worden**) *vi* to become; **was ist aus ihm/aus der Sache geworden?** what became of him/it?; **es ist nichts/gut geworden** it came to nothing/turned out well; **es wird Nacht/Tag** it's getting dark/light; **mir wird kalt** I'm getting cold; **mir wird schlecht** I feel ill; **Erster werden** to come *od* be first; **das muss anders werden** that'll have to change; **rot/zu Eis werden** to turn red/to ice; **was willst du (mal) werden?** what do you want to be?; **die Fotos sind gut geworden** the photos have come out nicely

♦ *als Hilfsverb* 1 (*bei Futur*): **er wird es tun** he will *od* he'll do it; **er wird das nicht tun** he will not *od* he won't do it; **es wird gleich regnen** it's going to rain

2 (*bei Konjunktiv*): **ich würde** ... I would ...; **er würde gern** ... he would *od* he'd like to ...; **ich würde lieber** ... I would *od* I'd rather ...

3 (*bei Vermutung*): **sie wird in der Küche sein** she will be in the kitchen

4 (*bei Passiv*): **gebraucht werden** to be used; **er ist erschossen worden** he has *od* he's been shot; **mir wurde gesagt, dass** ... I was told that ...

werfen ['vɛrfən] (*unreg*) *vt* to throw
Werft [vɛrft] (-, -en) *f* shipyard, dockyard
Werk [vɛrk] (-(e)s, -e) *nt* work; (*Tätigkeit*) job; (*Fabrik, Mechanismus*) works *pl*; **ans ~ gehen** to set to work; **~statt** (-, -stätten) *f* workshop; (*AUT*)

garage; **~tag** *m* working day; **w~tags** *adv* on working days; **w~tätig** *adj* working; **~zeug** *nt* tool
Wermut ['veːrmuːt] (-(e)s) *m* wormwood; (*Wein*) vermouth
Wert [veːrt] (-(e)s, -e) *m* worth; (*FIN*) value; ~ **legen auf** +*akk* to attach importance to; **es hat doch keinen ~** it's useless; **w~** *adj* worth; (*geschätzt*) dear; worthy; **das ist nichts/viel w~** it's not worth anything/it's worth a lot; **das ist es/er mir w~** it's/he's worth that to me; **~angabe** *f* declaration of value; **~brief** *m* registered letter (*containing sth of value*); **w~en** *vt* to rate; **~gegenstände** *mpl* valuables; **w~los** *adj* worthless; **~papier** *nt* security; **w~voll** *adj* valuable
Wesen ['veːzən] (-s, -) *nt* (*Geschöpf*) being; (*Natur, Charakter*) nature; **w~tlich** *adj* significant; (*beträchtlich*) considerable
weshalb [vɛs'halp] *adv* why
Wespe ['vɛspə] *f* wasp
wessen ['vɛsən] (*gen von* **wer**) *pron* whose
Weste ['vɛstə] *f* waistcoat, vest (*US*); (*Wollweste*) cardigan
West- *zW*: **~en** (-s) *m* west; **~europa** *nt* Western Europe; **w~lich** *adj* western ♦ *adv* to the west
weswegen [vɛs'veːɡən] *adv* why
wett [vɛt] *adj* even; **W~bewerb** *m* competition; **W~e** *f* bet, wager; **~en** *vt, vi* to bet
Wetter ['vɛtər] (-s, -) *nt* weather; **~bericht** *m* weather report; **~dienst** *m* meteorological service; **~lage** *f* (weather) situation; **~vorhersage** *f* weather forecast; **~warte** *f* weather station
Wett- *zW*: **~kampf** *m* contest; **~lauf** *m* race; **w~machen** *vt* to make good
wichtig ['vɪçtɪç] *adj* important; **W~keit** *f* importance

Spelling Reform: ▲ *new spelling* △ *old spelling (to be phased out)*

wickeln 294 Wiese

wickeln ['vɪkəln] vt to wind; (Haare) to set; (Kind) to change; **jdn/etw in etw akk ~** to wrap sb/sth in sth

Wickelraum m mothers' (and babies') room

Widder ['vɪdər] (-s, -) m ram; (ASTROL) Aries

wider ['vi:dər] präp +akk against; **~'fahren** (unreg) vi to happen; **~'legen** vt to refute

widerlich ['vi:dərlɪç] adj disgusting, repulsive

wider- ['vi:dər] zW: **~'rechtlich** adj unlawful; **W~rede** f contradiction; **~'rufen** (unreg) vt insep to retract; (Anordnung) to revoke; (Befehl) to countermand; **~'setzen** vr insep: **sich jdm/etw ~setzen** to oppose sb/sth

widerspenstig ['vi:dərʃpɛnstɪç] adj wilful

wider- ['vi:dər] zW: **~'spiegeln** vt (Entwicklung, Erscheinung) to mirror, to reflect ♦ vr to be reflected; **~'sprechen** (unreg) vi insep: **jdm ~sprechen** to contradict sb

Widerspruch ['vi:dərʃprɔx] m contradiction; **w~slos** adv without arguing

Widerstand ['vi:dərʃtant] m resistance

Widerstands- zW: **~bewegung** f resistance (movement); **w~fähig** adj resistant, tough; **w~los** adj unresisting

wider'stehen vi insep: **jdm/etw ~** to withstand sb/sth

wider- ['vi:dər] zW: **~wärtig** adj nasty, horrid; **W~wille** m: **W~wille (gegen)** aversion (to); **~willig** adj unwilling, reluctant

widmen ['vɪtmən] vt to dedicate; to devote ♦ vr to devote o.s.

widrig ['vi:drɪç] adj (Umstände) adverse

SCHLÜSSELWORT
---

wie [vi:] adv how; **wie groß/schnell?** how big/fast?; **wie wärs?** how about it?; **wie ist er?** what's he like?; **wie gut du das kannst!** you're very good at it; **wie bitte?** pardon?; (entrüstet) I

beg your pardon!; **und wie!** and how!; **wie viel** how much; **wie viel Menschen** how many people; **wie weit** to what extent

♦ konj 1 (bei Vergleichen): **so schön wie ...** as beautiful as ...; **wie ich schon sagte** as I said; **wie du** like you; **singen wie ein ...** to sing like a ...; **wie (zum Beispiel)** such as (for example)

2 (zeitlich): **wie er das hörte, ging er** when he heard that he left; **er hörte, wie der Regen fiel** he heard the rain falling

---

wieder ['vi:dər] adv again; **~ da sein** to be back (again); **~ aufbereiten** to recycle; **~ aufnehmen** to resume; **~ erkennen** to recognize; **~ gutmachen** to make up for; (Fehler) to put right; **~ herstellen** (Ruhe, Frieden etc) to restore; **~ vereinigen** to reunite; (POL) to reunify; **~ verwerten** to recycle; **gehst du schon ~?** are you off again?; **~ ein(e) ...** another ...; **W~aufbau** m rebuilding; **~bekommen** (unreg) vt to get back; **W~gabe** f reproduction; **~geben** (unreg) vt (zurückgeben) to return; (Erzählung etc) to repeat; (Gefühle etc) to convey; **W~gutmachung** f reparation; **~herstellen** vt (Gesundheit, Gebäude) to restore; **~holen** vt insep to repeat; **W~holung** f repetition; **W~hören** nt: **auf W~hören** (TEL) goodbye; **W~kehr** (-) f return; (von Vorfall) repetition, recurrence; **W~sehen** (unreg) vt to see again; **auf W~sehen** goodbye; **~um** adv again; (andererseits) on the other hand; **W~vereinigung** f (POL) reunification; **W~wahl** f re-election

Wiege ['vi:gə] f cradle; **w~n¹** vt (schaukeln) to rock

wiegen² (unreg) vt, vi (Gewicht) to weigh

Wien [vi:n] nt Vienna

Wiese ['vi:zə] f meadow

Wiesel ['viːzəl] (-s, -) nt weasel
wieso [viˈzoː] adv why
wieviel △ [viˈfiːl] adj siehe **wie**
wievielmal [viˈfiːlmaːl] adv how often
wievielte(r, s) adj: **zum ~n Mal?** how
many times?; **den W~n haben wir?**
what's the date?; **an ~ Stelle?** in
what place?; **der ~ Besucher war er?**
how many visitors were there before
him?
wild [vɪlt] adj wild; **W~** (-(e)s) nt game;
W~e(r) ['vɪldə(r)] f(m) savage; **~ern** vi
to poach; **~'fremd** (umg) adj quite
strange and unknown; **W~heit** f wild-
ness; **W~leder** nt suede; **W~nis** (-,
-se) f wilderness; **W~schwein** nt
(wild) boar
will etc [vɪl] vb siehe **wollen**
Wille ['vɪlə] (-ns, -n) m will; **w~n** präp
+gen: **um ... w~n** for the sake of ...;
w~nsstark adj strong-willed
will- zW: **~ig** adj willing; **W~kommen**
[vɪlˈkɔmən] (-s, -) nt welcome; **~kom-
men** adj welcome; **jdn ~kommen heißen** to welcome sb; **~kürlich** adj arbitrary; (Bewegung) voluntary
wimmeln ['vɪməln] vi: **~ (von)** to
swarm (with)
wimmern ['vɪmərn] vi to whimper
Wimper ['vɪmpər] (-, -n) f eyelash
Wimperntusche ['vɪmpərntʊʃə] f mascara
Wind [vɪnt] (-(e)s, -e) m wind; **~beu-
tel** m cream puff; (fig) rake; **~e** f (TECH)
winch, windlass; (BOT) bindweed; **~el**
['vɪndəl] (-, -n) f nappy, diaper (US);
w~en vi unpers to be windy ♦ vt (unreg) to wind; (Kranz) to weave; (entwinden) to twist ♦ vr (unreg) to wind;
(Person) to writhe; **~energie** f wind
energy; **w~ig** ['vɪndɪç] adj windy; (fig)
dubious; **~jacke** f windcheater;
~mühle f windmill; **~pocken** pl
chickenpox sg; **~schutzscheibe** f
(AUT) windscreen (BRIT), windshield
(US); **~stärke** f wind force; **w~still** adj

(Tag) still, windless; (Platz) sheltered;
~stille f calm; **~stoß** m gust of wind
Wink [vɪŋk] (-(e)s, -e) m (mit Hand)
wave; (mit Kopf) nod; (Hinweis) hint
Winkel ['vɪŋkəl] (-s, -) m (MATH) angle;
(Gerät) set square; (in Raum) corner
winken ['vɪŋkən] vt, vi to wave
winseln ['vɪnzəln] vi to whine
Winter ['vɪntər] (-s, -) m winter;
w~fest adj (Pflanze) hardy; **~garten** m
conservatory; **w~lich** adj wintry; **~rei-
fen** m winter tyre; **~sport** m winter
sports pl
Winzer ['vɪntsər] (-s, -) m vine grower
winzig ['vɪntsɪç] adj tiny
Wipfel ['vɪpfəl] (-s, -) m treetop
wir [viːr] pron we; **~ alle** all of us, we all
Wirbel ['vɪrbəl] (-s, -) m whirl, swirl;
(Trubel) hurly-burly; (Aufsehen) fuss;
(ANAT) vertebra; **w~n** vi to whirl, to
swirl; **~säule** f spine
wird [vɪrt] vb siehe **werden**
wirfst etc [vɪrfst] vb siehe **werfen**
wirken ['vɪrkən] vi to have an effect;
(erfolgreich sein) to work; (scheinen) to
seem ♦ vt (Wunder) to work
wirklich ['vɪrklɪç] adj real ♦ adv really;
~keit f reality
wirksam ['vɪrkzaːm] adj effective
Wirkstoff m (biologisch, chemisch,
pflanzlich) active substance
Wirkung ['vɪrkʊŋ] f effect; **w~slos** adj
ineffective; **w~slos bleiben** to have
no effect; **w~svoll** adj effective
wirr [vɪr] adj confused, wild; **W~warr**
(-s) m disorder, chaos
wirst [vɪrst] vb siehe **werden**
Wirt(in) [vɪrt(ɪn)] (-(e)s, -e) m(f) land-
lord(lady); **~schaft** f (Gaststätte) pub;
(Haushalt) housekeeping; (eines
Landes) economy; (umg: Durcheinander) mess; **w~schaftlich** adj economical; (POL) economic
Wirtschafts- zW: **~krise** f economic
crisis; **~politik** f economic policy;

~prüfer *m* chartered accountant;
~wunder *nt* economic miracle
Wirtshaus *nt* inn
wischen ['vɪʃən] *vt* to wipe
Wischer (-s, -) *m* (AUT) wiper
Wissbegier(de) ▲ ['vɪsbəgiːr(də)] *f* thirst for knowledge; **wissbegierig** ▲ *adj* inquisitive, eager for knowledge
wissen ['vɪsən] (*unreg*) *vt* to know; **was weiß ich!** I don't know!; **W~** (-s) *nt* knowledge; **W~schaft** *f* science; **W~schaftler(in)** (-s, -) *m(f)* scientist; **~schaftlich** *adj* scientific; **~swert** *adj* worth knowing
wittern ['vɪtərn] *vt* to scent; (*fig*) to suspect
Witterung *f* weather; (*Geruch*) scent
Witwe ['vɪtvə] *f* widow; **~r** (-s, -) *m* widower
Witz [vɪts] (-es, -e) *m* joke; **~bold** (-[e]s, -e) *m* joker, wit; **w~ig** *adj* funny
wo [voː] *adv* where; (*umg: irgendwo*) somewhere; **im Augenblick, ~** ... the moment (that) ...; **die Zeit, ~** ... the time when ...; **~anders** [voːˈʔandɐs] *adv* elsewhere; **~bei** [-ˈbaɪ] *adv* (*relativ*) by/with which; (*interrogativ*) what ... in/by/with
Woche ['vɔxə] *f* week
Wochen- *zW*: **~ende** *nt* weekend; **w~lang** *adj, adv* for weeks; **~markt** *m* weekly market; **~schau** *f* newsreel
wöchentlich ['vœçəntlɪç] *adj, adv* weekly
wodurch [voˈdʊrç] *adv* (*relativ*) through which; (*interrogativ*) what through
wofür [voˈfyːr] *adv* (*relativ*) for which; (*interrogativ*) what ... for
wog *etc* [voːk] *vb siehe* **wiegen**
wo- [voː] *zW*: **~gegen** *adv* (*relativ*) against which; (*interrogativ*) what ... against; **~her** [-ˈheːr] *adv* where ... from; **~hin** [-ˈhɪn] *adv* where ... to

SCHLÜSSELWORT

wohl [voːl] *adv* **1: sich wohl fühlen**

(*zufrieden*) to feel happy; (*gesundheitlich*) to feel well; **jdm wohl tun** to do sb good; **wohl oder übel** whether one likes it or not
2 (*wahrscheinlich*) probably; (*gewiss*) certainly; (*vielleicht*) perhaps; **sie ist wohl zu Hause** she's probably at home; **das ist doch wohl nicht dein Ernst!** surely you're not serious!; **das mag wohl sein** that may well be; **ob das wohl stimmt?** I wonder if that's true; **er weiß das sehr wohl** he knows that perfectly well

Wohl [voːl] (-[e]s) *nt* welfare; **zum ~!** cheers!; **w~auf** *adv* well; **~behagen** *nt* comfort; **~fahrt** *f* welfare; **~fahrtsstaat** *m* welfare state; **w~habend** *adj* wealthy; **w~ig** *adj* contented, comfortable; **w~schmeckend** *adj* delicious; **~stand** *m* prosperity; **~standsgesellschaft** *f* affluent society; **~tat** *f* relief; act of charity; **~täter(in)** *m(f)* benefactor; **w~tätig** *adj* charitable; **~tätigkeits-** *zW* charity, charitable; **w~verdient** *adj* well-earned, well-deserved; **w~weislich** *adv* prudently; **~wollen** (-s) *nt* good will; **w~wollend** *adj* benevolent
wohn- [voːn] *zW*: **~en** *vi* to live; **W~gemeinschaft** *f* (*Menschen*) people sharing a flat; *adj* resident; **W~heim** *nt* (*für Studenten*) hall of residence; (*für Senioren*) home; (*bes für Arbeiter*) hostel; **~lich** *adj* comfortable; **W~mobil** (-s, -e) *nt* camper; **W~ort** *m* domicile; **W~sitz** *m* place of residence; **W~ung** *f* house; (*Etagenwohnung*) flat, apartment (*us*); **W~wagen** *m* caravan; **W~zimmer** *nt* living room
wölben ['vœlbən] *vt, vr* to curve
Wolf [vɔlf] (-[e]s, *⁓e*) *m* wolf
Wolke ['vɔlkə] *f* cloud; **~nkratzer** *m* skyscraper
wolkig ['vɔlkɪç] *adj* cloudy
Wolle ['vɔlə] *f* wool; **w~n¹** *adj* woollen

---SCHLÜSSELWORT---

wollen² ['vɔlən] (*pt* **wollte**, *pp* **gewollt** *od* (*als Hilfsverb*) **wollen**) *vt*, *vi* to want; **ich will nach Hause** I want to go home; **er will nicht** he doesn't want to; **er wollte das nicht** he didn't want it; **wenn du willst** if you like; **ich will, dass du mir zuhörst** I want you to listen to me

♦ *Hilfsverb:* **er will ein Haus kaufen** he wants to buy a house; **ich wollte ... ich wäre ...** I wish I were ...; **etw gerade tun wollen** to be going to do sth

wollüstig ['vɔlʏstɪç] *adj* lusty, sensual
wo- *zW:* **~mit** *adv* (*relativ*) with which; (*interrogativ*) what ... with; **~möglich** *adv* probably, I suppose; **~nach** *adv* (*relativ*) after/for which; (*interrogativ*) what ... for/after; **~ran** *adv* (*relativ*) on/at which; (*interrogativ*) what ... on/at; **~rauf** *adv* (*relativ*) on which; (*interrogativ*) what ... on; **~raus** *adv* (*relativ*) from/out of which; (*interrogativ*) what ... from/out of; **~rin** *adv* (*relativ*) in which; (*interrogativ*) what ... in

Wort [vɔrt] (**-(e)s**, **-er** *od* **-e**) *nt* word; **jdn beim ~ nehmen** to take sb at his word; **mit anderen ~en** in other words; **w~brüchig** *adj* not true to one's word
Wörterbuch ['vœrtərbuːx] *nt* dictionary
Wort- *zW:* **~führer** *m* spokesman; **w~karg** *adj* taciturn; **~laut** *m* wording
wörtlich ['vœrtlɪç] *adj* literal
Wort- *zW:* **w~los** *adj* mute; **w~reich** *adj* wordy, verbose; **~schatz** *m* vocabulary; **~spiel** *nt* play on words, pun
wo- *zW:* **~rüber** *adv* (*relativ*) over/about which; (*interrogativ*) what ... over/about; **~rum** *adv* (*relativ*) about/round which; (*interrogativ*) what ... about/round; **~runter** *adv* (*relativ*) un-

der which; (*interrogativ*) what ... under; **~von** *adv* (*relativ*) from which; (*interrogativ*) what ... from; **~vor** *adv* (*relativ*) in front of/before which; (*interrogativ*) in front of/before what; of what; **~zu** *adv* (*relativ*) to/for which; (*interrogativ*) what ... for/to; (*warum*) why
Wrack [vrak] (**-(e)s**, **-s**) *nt* wreck
Wucher ['vuːxər] (**-s**) *m* profiteering; **~er** (**-s**, **-**) *m* profiteer; **w~isch** *adj* profiteering; **w~n** *vi* (*Pflanzen*) to grow wild; (*Geld*) to make a profit; **~ung** *f* (MED) growth, tumour
Wuchs [vuːks] (**-es**) *m* (*Wachstum*) growth; (*Statur*) build
Wucht [voxt] (**-**) *f* force
wühlen ['vyːlən] *vi* to scrabble; (*Tier*) to root; (*Maulwurf*) to burrow; (*umg: arbeiten*) to slave away ♦ *vt* to dig
Wulst [volst] (**-es**, **⁻e**) *m* bulge; (*an Wunde*) swelling
wund [vont] *adj* sore, raw; **W~e** *f* wound
Wunder ['vondər] (**-s**, **-**) *nt* miracle; **es ist kein ~** it's no wonder; **w~bar** *adj* wonderful, marvellous; **~kerze** *f* sparkler; **~kind** *nt* infant prodigy; **w~lich** *adj* odd, peculiar; **w~n** *vt* to surprise; **sich w~n über** *+akk* to be surprised at; **w~schön** *adj* beautiful; **w~voll** *adj* wonderful
Wundstarrkrampf ['vontʃtarkrampf] *m* tetanus, lockjaw
Wunsch [vonʃ] (**-(e)s**, **⁻e**) *m* wish
wünschen ['vʏnʃən] *vt* to wish; **sich** *dat* **etw ~** to want sth, to wish for sth; **w~swert** *adj* desirable
wurde *etc* ['vorda] *vb siehe* **werden**
Würde ['vʏrda] *f* dignity; (*Stellung*) honour; **w~voll** *adj* dignified
würdig ['vʏrdɪç] *adj* worthy; (*würdevoll*) dignified; **~en** *vt* to appreciate
Wurf [vorf] (**-s**, **⁻e**) *m* throw; (*Junge*) litter

Würfel ['vyrfəl] (-s, -) m dice; (MATH) cube; **~becher** m (dice) cup; **w~n** vi to play dice ♦ vt to dice; **~zucker** m lump sugar

würgen ['vyrgən] vt, vi to choke

Wurm [vorm] (-(e)s, *er) m worm; **w~stichig** adj worm-ridden

Wurst [vorst] (-, *e) f sausage; **das ist mir ~** (umg) I don't care, I don't give a damn

Würstchen ['vyrstçən] nt sausage

Würze ['vyrtsə] f seasoning, spice

Wurzel ['vortsəl] (-, -n) f root

würzen ['vyrtsən] vt to season, to spice

würzig adj spicy

wusch etc [vuʃ] vb siehe **waschen**

wusste etc ['vostə] vb siehe **wissen**

wüst [vy:st] adj untidy, messy; (ausschweifend) wild; (öde) waste; (umg: heftig) terrible; **W~e** f desert

Wut [vu:t] (-) f rage, fury; **~anfall** m fit of rage

wüten ['vy:tən] vi to rage; **~d** adj furious, mad

X, x

X-Beine ['ɪksbaɪnə] pl knock-knees

x-beliebig [ɪksbə'li:bɪç] adj any (whatever)

xerokopieren [kseroko'pi:rən] vt to xerox, to photocopy

x-mal ['ɪksma:l] adv any number of times, n times

Xylofon ▲, **Xylophon** [ksylo'fo:n] (-s, -e) nt xylophone

Y, y

Yacht (-, -en) f siehe **Jacht**

Ypsilon ['ypsilɔn] (-(s), -s) nt the letter Y

Z, z

Zacke ['tsakə] f point; (Bergzacke) jagged peak; (Gabelzacke) prong; (Kammzacke) tooth

zackig ['tsakɪç] adj jagged; (umg) smart; (Tempo) brisk

zaghaft ['tsa:khaft] adj timid

zäh [tse:] adj tough; (Mensch) tenacious; (Flüssigkeit) thick; (schleppend) sluggish; **Z~igkeit** f toughness; tenacity

Zahl [tsa:l] (-, -en) f number; **z~bar** adj payable; **z~en** vt, vi to pay; **z~en bitte!** the bill please!

zählen ['tse:lən] vt, vi to count; **~ auf** +akk to count on; **~ zu** to be numbered among

Zahlenschloss ▲ nt combination lock

Zähler ['tse:lər] (-s, -) m (TECH) meter; (MATH) numerator

Zahl- zW: **z~los** adj countless; **z~reich** adj numerous; **~tag** m payday; **~ung** f payment; **~ungsanweisung** f giro transfer order; **~ungsfähig** adj solvent; **~wort** nt numeral

zahm [tsa:m] adj tame

zähmen ['tse:mən] vt to tame; (fig) to curb

Zahn [tsa:n] (-(e)s, *e) m tooth; **~arzt** m dentist; **~ärztin** f (female) dentist; **~bürste** f toothbrush; **~fleisch** nt gums pl; **~pasta** f toothpaste; **~rad** nt cog(wheel); **~schmerzen** pl toothache sg; **~stein** m tartar; **~stocher** (-s, -) m toothpick

Zange ['tsaŋə] f pliers pl; (Zuckerzange etc) tongs pl; (Beißzange, ZOOL) pincers pl; (MED) forceps pl

zanken ['tsaŋkən] vi, vr to quarrel

zänkisch ['tsɛŋkɪʃ] adj quarrelsome

Zäpfchen ['tsɛpfçən] nt (ANAT) uvula; (MED) suppository

Zapfen ['tsapfən] (-s, -) m plug; (BOT) cone; (Eiszapfen) icicle

zappeln ['tsapəln] vi to wriggle; to fidget

zart [tsart] adj (weich, leise) soft; (Fleisch) tender; (fein, schwächlich) delicate; **Z~heit** f softness; tenderness; delicacy

zärtlich ['tsɛːrtlɪç] adj tender, affectionate

Zauber ['tsaubər] (-s, -) m magic; (~bann) spell; **~ei** f magic; **~er** (-s, -) m magician; conjuror; **z~haft** adj magical, enchanting; **~künstler** m conjuror; **~kunststück** nt conjuring trick; **z~n** vi to conjure, to practise magic

zaudern ['tsaudərn] vi to hesitate

Zaum [tsaum] (-(e)s, Zäume) m bridle; **etw im ~ halten** to keep sth in check

Zaun [tsaun] (-(e)s, Zäune) m fence

z. B. abk (= zum Beispiel) e.g.

Zebra ['tseːbra] nt zebra; **~streifen** m zebra crossing

Zeche ['tsɛçə] f (Rechnung) bill; (Bergbau) mine

Zeh [tseː] (-s, -en) m toe

Zehe [tseːə] f toe; (Knoblauchzehe) clove

zehn [tseːn] num ten; **~te(r, s)** adj tenth; **Z~tel** (-s, -) nt tenth (part)

Zeich- ['tsaɪç] zW: **~en** (-s, -) nt sign; **z~nen** vt to draw; (kennzeichnen) to mark; (unterzeichnen) to sign ♦ vi to draw; to sign; **~ner** (-s, -) m artist; **technischer ~ner** draughtsman; **~nung** f drawing; (Markierung) markings pl

Zeige- ['tsaɪɡə] zW: **~finger** m index finger; **z~n** vt to show ♦ vi to point ♦ vr to show o.s.; **z~n auf** +akk to point to; to point at; **es wird sich z~n** time will tell; **es zeigte sich, dass ...** it turned out that ...; **~r** (-s, -) m pointer; (Uhrzeiger) hand

Zeile ['tsaɪlə] f line; (Häuserzeile) row

Zeit [tsaɪt] (-, -en) f time; (GRAM) tense; **sich** dat ~ **lassen** to take one's time;

von ~ zu ~ from time to time; siehe **zurzeit**; **~alter** nt age; **~ansage** f (TEL) speaking clock; **~arbeit** f (COMM) temporary job; **z~gemäß** adj in keeping with the times; **~genosse** m contemporary; **z~ig** adj early; **z~lich** adj temporal; **~lupe** f slow motion; **z~raubend** adj time-consuming; **~raum** m period; **~rechnung** f time, era; **nach/vor unserer ~rechnung** A.D./B.C.; **~schrift** f periodical; **~ung** f newspaper; **~vertreib** m pastime, diversion; **z~weilig** adj temporary; **z~weise** adv for a time; **~wort** nt verb

Zelle ['tsɛlə] f cell; (Telefonzelle) callbox

Zellstoff m cellulose

Zelt [tsɛlt] (-(e)s, -e) nt tent; **z~en** vi to camp; **~platz** m camp site

Zement [tse'mɛnt] (-(e)s, -e) m cement; **z~ieren** vt to cement

zensieren [tsɛn'ziːrən] vt to censor; (SCH) to mark

Zensur [tsɛn'zuːr] f censorship; (SCH) mark

Zentimeter [tsɛnti'meːtər] m od nt centimetre

Zentner ['tsɛntnər] (-s, -) m hundredweight

zentral [tsɛn'traːl] adj central; **Z~e** f central office; (TEL) exchange; **Z~heizung** f central heating

Zentrum ['tsɛntrʊm] (-s, Zentren) nt centre

zerbrechen [tsɛr'brɛçən] (unreg) vt, vi to break

zerbrechlich adj fragile

zer'drücken vt to squash, to crush; (Kartoffeln) to mash

Zeremonie [tseremo'niː] f ceremony

Zerfall [tsɛr'fal] m decay; **z~en** (unreg) vi to disintegrate, to decay; (sich gliedern): **z~en (in** +akk) to fall (into)

zer'gehen (unreg) vi to melt, to dissolve

zerkleinern [tsɛr'klaɪnərn] vt to reduce

to small pieces

zerlegbar [tsɛr'le:kba:r] *adj* able to be dismantled

zerlegen [tsɛr'le:gən] *vt* to take to pieces; (*Fleisch*) to carve; (*Satz*) to analyse

zermürben [tsɛr'myrbən] *vt* to wear down

zerquetschen [tsɛr'kvɛtʃən] *vt* to squash

zer'reißen (*unreg*) *vt* to tear to pieces ♦ *vi* to tear, to rip

zerren ['tsɛrən] *vt* to drag ♦ *vi*: ~ (**an** +*dat*) to tug (at)

zer'rinnen (*unreg*) *vi* to melt away

zerrissen [tsɛr'rɪsən] *adj* torn, tattered; **Z~heit** *f* tattered state; (*POL*) disunion, discord; (*innere Z~heit*) disintegration

Zerrung *f* (*MED*): **eine ~** pulled muscle

zerrütten [tsɛr'rʏtən] *vt* to wreck, to destroy

zer'schlagen (*unreg*) *vt* to shatter, to smash ♦ *vr* to fall through

zer'schneiden (*unreg*) *vt* to cut up

zer'setzen *vt, vr* to decompose, to dissolve

zer'springen (*unreg*) *vi* to shatter, to burst

Zerstäuber [tsɛr'ʃtɔybər] (**-s, -**) *m* atomizer

zerstören [tsɛr'ʃtø:rən] *vt* to destroy

Zerstörung *f* destruction

zerstreu- [tsɛr'ʃtrɔy] *zW*: **~en** *vt* to disperse, to scatter; (*unterhalten*) to divert; (*Zweifel etc*) to dispel ♦ *vr* to disperse, to scatter; to be dispelled; **~t** *adj* scattered; (*Mensch*) absentminded; **Z~theit** *f* absentmindedness; **Z~ung** *f* dispersion; (*Ablenkung*) diversion

zerstückeln [tsɛr'ʃtʏkəln] *vt* to cut into pieces

zer'teilen *vt* to divide into parts

Zertifikat [tsɛrtifi'ka:t] (**-(e)s, -e**) *nt* certificate

zer'treten (*unreg*) *vt* to crush underfoot

zertrümmern [tsɛr'trʏmərn] *vt* to

shatter; (*Gebäude etc*) to demolish

Zettel ['tsɛtəl] (**-s, -**) *m* piece of paper, slip; (*Notizzettel*) note; (*Formular*) form

Zeug [tsɔyk] (**-(e)s, -e**) (*umg*) *nt* stuff; (*Ausrüstung*) gear; **dummes ~** (*stupid*) nonsense; **das ~ haben zu** to have the makings of; **sich ins ~ legen** to put one's shoulder to the wheel

Zeuge ['tsɔygə] (**-n, -n**) *m* witness; **z~n** *vi* to bear witness, to testify ♦ *vt* (*Kind*) to father; **es zeugt von ...** it testifies to ...; **~naussage** *f* evidence; **Zeugin** ['tsɔygɪn] *f* witness

Zeugnis ['tsɔygnɪs] (**-ses, -se**) *nt* certificate; (*SCH*) report; (*Referenz*) reference; (*Aussage*) evidence, testimony; **geben von** to be evidence of, to testify to

z. H(d). *abk* (*= zu Händen*) attn.

Zickzack ['tsɪktsak] (**-(e)s, -e**) *m* zigzag

Ziege ['tsi:gə] *f* goat

Ziegel ['tsi:gəl] (**-s, -**) *m* brick; (*Dachziegel*) tile

ziehen ['tsi:ən] (*unreg*) *vt* to draw; (*zerren*) to pull; (*SCHACH etc*) to move; (*züchten*) to rear ♦ *vi* to draw; (*umziehen, wandern*) to move; (*Rauch, Wolke etc*) to drift; (*reißen*) to pull ♦ *vb unpers*: **es zieht** there is a draught, it's draughty ♦ *vr* (*Gummi*) to stretch; (*Grenze etc*) to run; (*Gespräche*) to be drawn out; **etw nach sich ~** to lead to sth, to entail sth

Ziehung ['tsi:ʊŋ] *f* (*Losziehung*) drawing

Ziel [tsi:l] (**-(e)s, -e**) *nt* (*einer Reise*) destination; (*SPORT*) finish; (*MIL*) target; (*Absicht*) goal; **z~bewusst** ▲ *adj* decisive; **z~en** *vi*: **z~en** (**auf** +*akk*) to aim (at); **z~los** *adj* aimless; **~scheibe** *f* target; **z~strebig** *adj* purposeful

ziemlich ['tsi:mlɪç] *adj* quite a; fair ♦ *adv* rather; quite a bit

zieren ['tsi:rən] *vr* to act coy

zierlich ['tsi:rlɪç] *adj* dainty

Ziffer ['tsɪfər] (**-, -n**) *f* figure, digit; **~blatt** *nt* dial, clock-face

zig [tsɪk] (*umg*) *adj* umpteen
Zigarette [tsiga'rɛtə] *f* cigarette
Zigaretten- *zW*: **~automat** *m* cigarette machine; **~schachtel** *f* cigarette packet; **~spitze** *f* cigarette holder
Zigarre [tsi'garə] *f* cigar
Zigeuner(in) [tsi'gɔʏnər(ɪn)] **(-s, -)** *m(f)* gipsy
Zimmer ['tsɪmər] **(-s, -)** *nt* room; **~lautstärke** *f* reasonable volume; **~mädchen** *nt* chambermaid; **~mann** *m* carpenter; **z~n** *vt* to make (from wood); **~nachweis** *m* accommodation office; **~pflanze** *f* indoor plant; **~service** *m* room service
zimperlich ['tsɪmpərlɪç] *adj* squeamish; (*pingelig*) fussy, finicky
Zimt [tsɪmt] **(-(e)s, -e)** *m* cinnamon
Zink [tsɪŋk] **(-(e)s)** *nt* zinc
Zinn [tsɪn] **(-(e)s)** *nt* (*Element*) tin; (*in ~waren*) pewter; **~soldat** *m* tin soldier
Zins [tsɪns] **(-es, -en)** *m* interest; **~eszins** *m* compound interest; **~fuß** *m* rate of interest; **z~los** *adj* interest-free; **~satz** *m* rate of interest
Zipfel ['tsɪpfəl] **(-s, -)** *m* corner; (*spitz*) tip; (*Hemdzipfel*) tail; (*Wurstzipfel*) end
zirka ['tsɪrka] *adv* (round) about
Zirkel ['tsɪrkəl] **(-s, -)** *m* circle; (*MATH*) pair of compasses
Zirkus ['tsɪrkʊs] **(-, -se)** *m* circus
zischen ['tsɪʃən] *vi* to hiss
Zitat [tsi'ta:t] **(-(e)s, -e)** *nt* quotation, quote
zitieren [tsi'ti:rən] *vt* to quote
Zitrone [tsi'tro:nə] *f* lemon; **~nlimonade** *f* lemonade; **~nsaft** *m* lemon juice
zittern ['tsɪtərn] *vi* to tremble
zivil [tsi'vi:l] *adj* civil; (*Preis*) moderate; **Z~ (-s)** *nt* plain clothes *pl*; (*MIL*) civilian clothing; **Z~courage** *f* courage of one's convictions; **Z~dienst** *m* community service; **Z~isation** [tsivilizatsi'o:n] *f* civilization; **Z~isationskrankheit** *f* disease peculiar to civilization; **~i'sieren** *vt* to civilize

Zivildienst

A young German has to complete his 13 months' **Zivildienst** *or service to the community if he has opted out of military service as a conscientious objector. This is usually done in a hospital or old people's home. About 18% of young Germans choose to do this as an alternative to the* **Wehrdienst**.

Zivilist [tsivi'lɪst] *m* civilian
zögern ['tsø:gərn] *vi* to hesitate
Zoll [tsɔl] **(-(e)s, ¨e)** *m* customs *pl*; (*Abgabe*) duty; **~abfertigung** *f* customs clearance; **~amt** *nt* customs office; **~beamte(r)** *m* customs official; **~erklärung** *f* customs declaration; **z~frei** *adj* duty-free; **~kontrolle** *f* customs check; **z~pflichtig** *adj* liable to duty, dutiable
Zone ['tso:nə] *f* zone
Zoo [tso:] **(-s, -s)** *m* zoo; **~loge** [tsoo'lo:gə] **(-n, -n)** *m* zoologist; **~lo'gie** *f* zoology; **z~'logisch** *adj* zoological
Zopf [tsɔpf] **(-(e)s, ¨e)** *m* plait; pigtail; **alter ~** antiquated custom
Zorn [tsɔrn] **(-(e)s)** *m* anger; **z~ig** *adj* angry
zottig ['tsɔtɪç] *adj* shaggy
z. T. *abk* = **zum Teil**

SCHLÜSSELWORT

zu [tsu:] *präp +dat* **1** (*örtlich*) to; **zum Bahnhof/Arzt gehen** to go to the station/doctor; **zur Schule/Kirche gehen** to go to school/church; **sollen wir zu euch gehen?** shall we go to your place?; **sie sah zu ihm hin** she looked towards him; **zum Fenster herein** through the window; **zu mei-**

ner Linken to od on my left

2 (zeitlich) at; **zu Ostern** at Easter; **bis zum 1. Mai** until May 1st; (nicht später als) by May 1st; **zu meiner Zeit** in my time

3 (Zusatz) with; **Wein zum Essen trinken** to drink wine with one's meal; **sich zu jdm setzen** to sit down beside sb; **setz dich doch zu uns** (come and) sit with us; **Anmerkungen zu etw** notes on sth

4 (Zweck) for; **Wasser zum Waschen** water for washing; **Papier zum Schreiben** paper to write on; **etw zum Geburtstag bekommen** to get sth for one's birthday

5 (Veränderung) into; **zu etw werden** to turn into sth; **jdn zu etw machen** to make sb (into) sth; **zu Asche verbrennen** to burn to ashes

6 (mit Zahlen) **zu 2** (SPORT) 3-2; **das Stück zu 2 Mark** at 2 marks each; **zum ersten Mal** for the first time

7: zu meiner Freude etc to my joy etc; **zum Glück** luckily; **zu Fuß** on foot; **es ist zum Weinen** it's enough to make you cry

♦ konj to; **etw zu essen** sth to eat; **um besser sehen zu können** in order to see better; **ohne es zu wissen** without knowing it; **noch zu bezahlende Rechnungen** bills that are still to be paid

♦ adv **1** (allzu) too; **zu sehr** too much; **zu viel** too much; **zu wenig** too little

2 (örtlich) toward(s); **er kam auf mich zu** he came up to me

3 (geschlossen) shut, closed; **die Geschäfte haben zu** the shops are closed; **„auf/zu"** (Wasserhahn etc) "on/off"

4 (umg: los): **nur zu!** just keep on!; **mach zu!** hurry up!

zualler- [tsu'ʔalər] zW: **~erst** [-'ʔe:rst] adv first of all; **~letzt** [-'lɛtst] adv last of all

Zubehör ['tsu:bəhø:r] (-(e)s, -e) nt accessories pl

zubereiten ['tsu:bəraɪtən] vt to prepare

zubilligen ['tsu:bɪlɪɡən] vt to grant

zubinden ['tsu:bɪndən] (unreg) vt to tie up

zubringen ['tsu:brɪŋən] (unreg) vt (Zeit) to spend

Zubringer (-s, -) m (Straße) approach od slip road

Zucchini [tsu'ki:ni] pl (BOT, KOCH) courgette (BRIT), zucchini (US)

Zucht [tsʊxt] (-, -en) f (von Tieren) breeding; (von Pflanzen) cultivation; (Rasse) breed; (Erziehung) raising; (Disziplin) discipline

züchten ['tsʏçtən] vt (Tiere) to breed; (Pflanzen) to cultivate, to grow; **Züchter** (-s, -) m breeder, grower

Zuchthaus nt prison, penitentiary (US)

züchtigen ['tsʏçtɪɡən] vt to chastise

Züchtung ['tsʏçtʊŋ] f (Zuchtart, Sorte: von Tier) breed; (: von Pflanze) variety

zucken ['tsʊkən] vi to jerk, to twitch; (Strahl etc) to flicker ♦ vt (Schultern) to shrug

Zucker ['tsʊkər] (-s, -) m sugar; (MED) diabetes; **~guss** ▲ m icing; **z~krank** adj diabetic; **~krankheit** f (MED) diabetes; **z~n** vt to sugar; **~rohr** nt sugar cane; **~rübe** f sugar beet

Zuckung ['tsʊkʊŋ] f convulsion, spasm; (leicht) twitch

zudecken ['tsu:dɛkən] vt to cover (up)

zudem [tsu'de:m] adv in addition (to this)

zudringlich ['tsu:drɪŋlɪç] adj forward, pushing, obtrusive

zudrücken ['tsu:drʏkən] vt to close; **ein Auge ~** to turn a blind eye

zueinander [tsuʔaɪ'nandər] adv to one other; (in Verbindung) together

zuerkennen ['tsu:ʔɛrkɛnən] (unreg) vt to award; **jdm etw ~** to award sth to sb, to award sb sth

zuerst [tsu'ʔe:rst] adv first; (zu Anfang)

at first; ~ einmal first of all

Zufahrt ['tsu:fa:rt] f approach; **~stra-ße** f approach road; (von Autobahn etc) slip road

Zufall ['tsu:fal] m chance; (Ereignis) coincidence; **durch ~** by accident; **so ein ~** what a coincidence; **z~en** (unreg) vi to close, to shut; (Anteil, Aufgabe) to fall

zufällig ['tsu:fɛlɪç] adj chance ♦ adv by chance; (in Frage) by any chance

Zuflucht ['tsu:floxt] f recourse; (Ort) refuge

zufolge [tsu'fɔlgə] präp (+dat od gen) judging by; (laut) according to

zufrieden [tsu'fri:dən] adj content(ed), satisfied; **~ geben** to be content of satisfied (with); **~ stellen** to satisfy

zufrieren [tsu'fri:rən] (unreg) vi to freeze up od over

zufügen ['tsu:fy:gən] vt to add; (Leid etc) (jdm) etw ~ to cause (sb) sth

Zufuhr ['tsu:fu:r] f (-, -en) f (Herbeibringen) supplying; (MET) influx

Zug [tsu:k] m (-(e)s, ¨e) m (EISENB) train; (Luftzug) draught; (Ziehen) pull(ing); (Gesichtszug) feature; (SCHACH etc) move; (Schriftzug) stroke; (Atemzug) breath; (Charakterzug) trait; (an Zigarette) puff, pull, drag; (Schluck) gulp; (Menschengruppe) procession; (von Vögeln) flight; (MIL) platoon; **etw in vollen Zügen genießen** to enjoy sth to the full

Zu- ['tsu:] zW: **~gabe** f extra; (in Konzert etc) encore; **~gang** m access, approach; **z~gänglich** adj accessible; (Mensch) approachable

zugeben ['tsu:ge:bən] (unreg) vt (beifügen) to add, to throw in; (zugestehen) to admit; (erlauben) to permit

zugehen ['tsu:ge:ən] (unreg) vi (schließen) to shut; **es geht dort seltsam zu** there are strange goings-on there; **auf jdn/etw ~** to walk towards

sb/sth; **dem Ende ~** to be finishing

Zugehörigkeit ['tsu:gəhø:rɪçkaɪt] f: **~ (zu)** membership (of), belonging (to)

Zügel ['tsy:gəl] (-s, -) m rein(s); (fig) curb; **z~n** vt to curb; (Pferd) to rein in

zuge- ['tsu:gə-] zW: **Z~ständnis** (-ses, -se) nt concession; **~stehen** (unreg) vt to concede

Zugführer m (EISENB) guard

zugig ['tsu:gɪç] adj draughty

zügig ['tsy:gɪç] adj speedy, swift

zugreifen ['tsu:graɪfən] (unreg) vi to seize od grab at; (helfen) to help; (beim Essen) to help o.s.

Zugrestaurant nt dining car

zugrunde, zu Grunde [tsu'grʊndə] adv: **~ gehen** to collapse; (Mensch) to perish; **einer Sache** dat **etw ~ legen** to base sth on sth; **einer Sache** dat **~ liegen** to be based on sth; **~ richten** to ruin, to destroy

zugunsten, zu Gunsten [tsu'gʊnstən] präp (+gen od dat) in favour of

zugute [tsu'gu:tə] adv: **jdm etw ~ halten** to concede sth to sb; **jdm ~ kommen** to be of assistance to sb

Zugvogel m migratory bird

zuhalten ['tsu:haltən] (unreg) vt to keep closed ♦ vi: **auf jdn/etw ~** to make a beeline for sb/sth

Zuhälter ['tsu:hɛltər] (-s, -) m pimp

Zuhause ['tsu:haozə] (-) nt home

zuhause ['tsu:haozə] adv (österreichisch, schweizerisch) at home

zuhören ['tsu:hø:rən] vi to listen

Zuhörer (-s, -) m listener

zukleben ['tsu:kle:bən] vt to paste up

zukommen ['tsu:kɔmən] (unreg) vi to come up; **auf jdn ~** to come up to sb; **jdm etw ~ lassen** to give sb sth; **etw auf sich ~ lassen** to wait and see; **jdm ~** (sich gehören) to be fitting for sb

Zukunft ['tsu:kʊnft] (-, Zukünfte) f future; **zukünftig** ['tsu:kʏnftɪç] adj future ♦ adv in future; **mein zukünftiger Mann** my husband to be

Zulage ['tsu:la:gə] f bonus

zulassen ['tsu:lasən] vt (unreg) (hereinlassen) to admit; (erlauben) to permit; (Auto) to license; (umg: nicht öffnen) to keep shut

zulässig ['tsu:lɛsɪç] adj permissible, permitted

Zulassung f (amtlich) authorization; (von Kfz) licensing

zulaufen ['tsu:laufən] vi (unreg) (subj: Mensch): ~ **auf jdn/etw** to run up to sb/sth; (: Straße): ~ **auf** to lead towards

zuleide, zu Leide [tsu:laɪdə] adv: **jdm etw ~ tun** to hurt od harm sb

zuletzt [tsu:lɛtst] adv finally, at last

zuliebe [tsu:li:bə] adv: **jdm ~** to please sb

zum [tsʊm] = zu dem; ~ **dritten Mal** for the third time; ~ **Scherz** as a joke; ~ **Trinken** for drinking

zumachen ['tsu:maxən] vt to shut; (Kleidung) to do up, to fasten ♦ vi to shut; (umg) to hurry up

zu- zW: **~mal** [tsu:'ma:l] konj especially (as); **~meist** [tsu:'maɪst] adv mostly; **~mindest** [tsu:'mɪndəst] adv at least

zumutbar [tsu:mu:tba:r] adj reasonable

zumute, zu Mute [tsu:'mu:tə] adv: **wie ist ihm ~?** how does he feel?

zumuten ['tsu:mu:tən] vt: **(jdm) etw ~** to expect od ask sth (of sb)

Zumutung ['tsu:mu:tʊŋ] f unreasonable expectation od demand, impertinence

zunächst [tsu:nɛ:çst] adv first of all; ~ **einmal** to start with

Zunahme ['tsu:na:mə] f increase

Zuname ['tsu:na:mə] m surname

Zünd- [tsʏnd] zW: **~en** vi (Feuer) to light, to ignite; (Motor) to fire; (begeistern): **bei jdm z~en** to fire sb (with enthusiasm); **z~end** adj fiery; **~er** (**-s**, -) m fuse; (MIL) detonator; **~holz**

[tsʏnt] nt match; **~kerze** f (AUT) spark(ing) plug; **~schloss** ▲ nt ignition lock; **~schlüssel** m ignition key; **~schnur** f fuse wire; **~stoff** m (fig) inflammatory stuff; **~ung** f ignition

zunehmen ['tsu:ne:mən] vi (unreg) to increase, to grow; (Mensch) to put on weight

Zuneigung ['tsu:naɪgʊŋ] f affection

Zunft [tsʊnft] (**-**, **¨e**) f guild

zünftig ['tsʏnftɪç] adj proper, real; (Handwerk) decent

Zunge ['tsʊŋə] f tongue

zunichte [tsu:nɪçtə] adv: ~ **machen** to ruin, to destroy; ~ **werden** to come to nothing

zunutze, zu Nutze [tsu:nʊtsə] adv: **sich** dat **etw ~ machen** to make use of sth

zuoberst [tsu:'o:bərst] adv at the top

zupfen ['tsʊpfən] vt to pull, to pick, to pluck; (Gitarre) to pluck

zur [tsu:r] = zu der

zurate, zu Rate [tsu:'ra:tə] adv: **jdn ~ ziehen** to consult sb

zurechnungsfähig ['tsu:rɛçnʊŋsfɛ:ɪç] adj responsible, accountable

zurecht- [tsu:'rɛçt] zW: **~finden** (unreg) vr to find one's way (about); **~kommen** (unreg) vi to (be able to) cope, to manage; **~legen** vt to get ready; (Ausrede etc) to have ready; **~machen** vt to prepare ♦ vr to get ready; **~weisen** (unreg) vt to reprimand

zureden ['tsu:re:dən] vi: **jdm ~** to persuade od urge sb

zurück [tsu:rʏk] adv back; **~behalten** (unreg) vt to keep back; **~bekommen** (unreg) vt to get back; **~bleiben** (unreg) vi (Mensch) to remain behind; (nicht nachkommen) to fall behind, to lag; (Schaden) to remain; **~bringen** (unreg) vt to bring back; **~fahren** (unreg) vi to travel back; (vor Schreck) to recoil, to start ♦ vt to drive back; **~finden** (unreg) vi to find one's way back; **~fordern** vt to demand back; **~führen** vt to to lead back; **etw auf etw** *akk* ~**führen** to trace sth back to sth; ~**geben** (*unreg*) *vt* to give back; (*antworten*) to retort with; ~**geblieben** *adj* retarded; ~**gehen** (*unreg*) *vi* to go back; (*fallen*) to go down, to fall; (*zeitlich*) ~**gehen (auf** +*akk*) to date back (to); ~**gezogen** *adj* retired, withdrawn; ~**halten** (*unreg*) *vt* to hold back; (*Mensch*) to restrain; (*hindern*) to prevent ♦ *vr* (*reserviert sein*) to be reserved; (*im Essen*) to hold back; ~**haltend** *adj* reserved; **Z~haltung** *f* reserve; ~**kehren** *vi* to return; ~**kommen** (*unreg*) *vi* to come back; **auf etw** *akk* ~**kommen** to return to sth; ~**lassen** (*unreg*) *vt* to leave behind; ~**legen** *vt* to put back; (*Geld*) to put by; (*reservieren*) to keep back; (*Strecke*) to cover; ~**nehmen** (*unreg*) *vt* to take back; ~**stellen** *vt* to put back, to replace; (*aufschieben*) to put off, to postpone; (*Interessen*) to defer; (*Ware*) to keep; ~**treten** (*unreg*) *vi* to step back; (*vom Amt*) to retire; **gegenüber etw od hinter etw** *dat* ~**treten** to diminish in importance in view of sth; ~**weisen** (*unreg*) *vt* to turn down; (*Mensch*) to reject; ~**zahlen** *vt* to repay, to pay back; ~**ziehen** (*unreg*) *vt* to pull back; (*Angebot*) to withdraw ♦ *vr* to retire

Zuruf ['tsu:ru:f] *m* shout, cry

zurzeit [tsur'tsait] *adv* at the moment

Zusage ['tsu:za:gə] *f* promise; (*Annahme*) consent; **z~n** *vt* to promise ♦ *vi* to accept; **jdm z~n** (*gefallen*) to agree with *od* please sb

zusammen [tsu'zamən] *adv* together; **Z~arbeit** *f* cooperation; ~**arbeiten** *vi* to cooperate; ~**beißen** (*unreg*) *vt* (*Zähne*) to clench; ~**brechen** (*unreg*) *vi* to collapse; (*Mensch auch*) to break down; ~**bringen** (*unreg*) *vt* to bring *od* get together; (*Geld*) to get; (*Sätze*) to put together; **Z~bruch** *m* collapse;

~**fassen** *vt* to summarize; (*vereinigen*) to unite; **Z~fassung** *f* summary, résumé; ~**fügen** *vt* to join (together), to unite; ~**halten** (*unreg*) *vi* to stick together; **Z~hang** *m* connection; **im/aus dem Z~hang** in/out of context; ~**hängen** (*unreg*) *vi* to be connected *od* linked; ~**kommen** (*unreg*) *vi* to meet, to assemble; (*sich ereignen*) to occur at once *od* together; ~**legen** *vt* to put together; (*stapeln*) to pile up; (*falten*) to fold; (*verbinden*) to combine, to unite; (*Termine, Fest*) to amalgamate; (*Geld*) to collect; ~**nehmen** (*unreg*) *vt* to summon up ♦ *vr* to pull o.s. together; **alles** ~**genommen** all in all; ~**passen** *vi* to go well together; to match; ~**schließen** (*unreg*) *vt*, *vr* to join (together); **Z~schluss** ▲ *m* amalgamation; ~**schreiben** (*unreg*) *vt* to write as one word; (*Bericht*) to put together; **Z~sein** (-s) *nt* get-together; ~**setzen** *vt* to put together ♦ *vr* (*Stoff*) to be composed of; (*Menschen*) to get together; **Z~setzung** *f* composition; ~**stellen** *vt* to put together; to compile; **Z~stoß** *m* collision; ~**stoßen** (*unreg*) *vi* to collide; (*Menschen*) to coincide; (*treffen*) (*unreg*) *vi* to meet; ~**treffen** *vt* coincidence; meeting; ~**zählen** *vt* to add up; ~**ziehen** (*unreg*) *vt* (*verengern*) to draw together; (*vereinigen*) to bring together; (*addieren*) to add up ♦ *vr* to shrink; (*sich bilden*) to form, to develop

zusätzlich ['tsu:zɛtslɪç] *adj* additional ♦ *adv* in addition

zuschauen ['tsu:ʃauən] *vi* to watch, to look on; **Zuschauer(in)** (-s, -) *m(f)* spectator ♦ *pl* (THEAT) audience *sg*

zuschicken ['tsu:ʃɪkən] *vt*: (**jdm etw**) ~ to send *od* to forward (sth to sb)

Zuschlag ['tsu:ʃla:k] *m* extra charge, surcharge; **z~en** (*unreg*) *vt* (*Tür*) to slam; (*Ball*) to hit; (*bei Auktion*) to knock down; (Steine etc) to knock into shape ♦ vi (Fenster, Tür) to shut; (Mensch) to hit, to punch; **~karte** f (EISENB) surcharge ticket; **z~pflichtig** adj subject to surcharge

zuschneiden ['tsu:ʃnaɪdən] (unreg) vt to cut out; to cut to size

zuschrauben ['tsu:ʃraʊbən] vt to screw down od up

zuschreiben ['tsu:ʃraɪbən] (unreg) vt (fig) to ascribe, to attribute; (COMM) to credit

Zuschrift ['tsu:ʃrɪft] f letter, reply

zuschulden, zu Schulden [tsu:ʃʊldən] adv: **sich dat etw ~ kommen lassen** to make o.s. guilty of sth

Zuschuss ▲ ['tsu:ʃʊs] m subsidy, allowance

zusehen ['tsu:ze:ən] (unreg) vi to watch; (dafür sorgen) to take care; **jdm/etw ~** to watch sb/sth; **~ds** adv visibly

zusenden ['tsu:zɛndən] (unreg) vt to forward, to send on

zusichern ['tsu:zɪçərn] vt: **jdm etw ~** to assure sb of sth

zuspielen ['tsu:ʃpi:lən] vt, vi to pass

zuspitzen ['tsu:ʃpɪtsən] vt to sharpen ♦ vr (Lage) to become critical

zusprechen ['tsu:ʃprɛçən] (unreg) vt (zuerkennen) to award ♦ vi to speak; **jdm etw ~** to award sb sth od sth to sb; **jdm Trost ~** to comfort sb; **dem Essen/Alkohol ~** to eat/drink a lot

Zustand ['tsu:ʃtant] m state, condition

zustande, zu Stande [tsu:ʃtandə] adv: **~ bringen** to bring about; **~ kommen** to come about

zuständig ['tsu:ʃtɛndɪç] adj responsible; **Z~keit** f competence, responsibility

zustehen ['tsu:ʃte:ən] (unreg) vi: **jdm ~** to be sb's right

zustellen ['tsu:ʃtɛlən] vt (verstellen) to block; (Post etc) to send

Zustellung f delivery

zustimmen ['tsu:ʃtɪmən] vi to agree

Zustimmung f agreement, consent

zustoßen ['tsu:ʃto:sən] (unreg) vi (fig) to happen

zutage, zu Tage [tsu:ta:gə] adv: **~ bringen** to bring to light; **~ treten** to come to light

Zutaten ['tsu:ta:tən] pl ingredients

zuteilen ['tsu:taɪlən] vt (Arbeit, Rolle) to designate, assign; (Aktien, Wohnung) to allocate

zutiefst [tsu:ti:fst] adv deeply

zutragen ['tsu:tra:gən] (unreg) vt to bring; (Klatsch) to tell ♦ vr to happen

zutrau- ['tsu:trau] zW: **Z~en (-s)** nt: **Z~en (zu)** trust (in); **~en** vt: **jdm etw ~en** to credit sb with sth; **~lich** adj trusting, friendly

zutreffen ['tsu:trɛfən] vi to be correct; to apply; **~d** adj (richtig) accurate; **Z~des bitte unterstreichen** please underline where applicable

Zutritt ['tsu:trɪt] m access, admittance

Zutun ['tsu:tu:n] (-s) nt assistance

zuverlässig [tsu:fɛrlɛsɪç] adj reliable; **Z~keit** f reliability

zuversichtlich [tsu:fɛrzɪçtlɪç] adj confident

zuvor [tsu:fo:r] adv before, previously; **~kommen** (unreg) vi +dat to anticipate; **jdm ~kommen** to beat sb to it; **~kommend** adj obliging, courteous

Zuwachs ['tsu:vaks] (-es) m increase, growth; (umg) addition; **z~en** (unreg) vi to become overgrown; (Wunde) to heal (up)

zuwege, zu Wege [tsu:ve:gə] adv: **etw ~ bringen** to accomplish sth

zuweilen [tsu:vaɪlən] adv at times, now and then

zuweisen ['tsu:vaɪzən] (unreg) vt to assign, to allocate

zuwenden ['tsu:vɛndən] (unreg) vt (+dat) to turn (towards) ♦ vr: **sich jdm/etw ~** to devote o.s. to sb/sth; to turn to sb/sth

zuwider [tsu:vi:dər] adv: **etw ist jdm ~** sb loathes sth, sb finds sth repugnant; **~handeln** vi: einer Sache dat **~handeln** to act contrary to sth; einem Gesetz **~handeln** to contravene a law

zuziehen ['tsu:tsi:ən] (unreg) vt (schließen: Vorhang) to draw, to close; (herbeirufen: Experten) to call in ♦ vi to move in, to come; **sich** dat **etw ~** (Krankheit) to catch sth; (Zorn) to incur sth

zuzüglich ['tsu:tsy:klıç] präp +gen plus, with the addition of

Zwang [tsvaŋ] (-(e)s, ⁼e) m compulsion, coercion

zwängen ['tsvɛŋən] vt, vr to squeeze

zwanglos adj informal

Zwangs- zW: **~arbeit** f forced labour; (Strafe) hard labour; **~lage** f predicament, tight corner; **z~läufig** adj necessary, inevitable

zwanzig ['tsvantsıç] num twenty

zwar [tsva:r] adv to be sure, indeed; **das ist ~ ..., aber ...** that may be ... but ...; **und ~ am Sonntag** on Sunday to be precise; **und ~ so schnell, dass ...** in fact so quickly that ...

Zweck [tsvɛk] (-(e)s, -e) m purpose, aim; **es hat keinen ~** there's no point; **z~dienlich** adj practical; expedient

Zwecke f hobnail; (Heftzwecke) drawing pin, thumbtack (US)

Zweck- zW: **z~los** adj pointless; **z~mäßig** adj suitable, appropriate; **z~s** präp +gen for the purpose of

zwei [tsvaı] num two; **Z~bettzimmer** nt twin room; **~deutig** adj ambiguous; (unanständig) suggestive; **~erlei** adj: **~erlei Stoff** two different kinds of material; **~erlei Meinung** of differing opinions; **~fach** adj double

Zweifel ['tsvaıfəl] (-s, -) m doubt; **z~haft** adj doubtful, dubious; **z~los** adj doubtless; **z~n** vi: **(an etw** dat**) z~n** to doubt (sth)

Zweig [tsvaık] (-(e)s, -e) m branch; **~stelle** f branch (office)

zwei- zW: **~hundert** num two hundred; **~mal** adv twice; **~sprachig** bilingual; **~spurig** adj (AUT) two-lane; **~stimmig** adj for two voices

zweit [tsvaıt] adv: **zu ~** together; (bei mehreren Paaren) in twos

zweitbeste(r, s) adj second best

zweite(r, s) adj second

zweiteilig ['tsvaıtaılıç] adj (Gruppe) two-piece; (Fernsehfilm) two-part; (Kleidung) two-piece

zweit- zW: **~ens** adv secondly; **~größte(r, s)** adj second largest; **~klassig** adj second-class; **~letzte(r, s)** adj last but one, penultimate; **~rangig** adj second-rate

Zwerchfell ['tsvɛrçfɛl] nt diaphragm

Zwerg [tsvɛrk] (-(e)s, -e) m dwarf

Zwetsch(g)e ['tsvɛtʃ(g)ə] f plum

Zwieback ['tsvi:bak] (-(e)s, -e) m rusk

Zwiebel ['tsvi:bəl] (-, -n) f onion; (Blumenzwiebel) bulb

Zwie- ['tsvi:] zW: **z~lichtig** adj shady, dubious; **z~spältig** adj (Gefühle) conflicting; (Charakter) contradictory; **~tracht** f discord, dissension

Zwilling ['tsvılıŋ] (-s, -e) m twin; **~e** pl (ASTROL) Gemini

zwingen ['tsvıŋən] (unreg) vt to force; **~d** adj (Grund etc) compelling

zwinkern ['tsvıŋkarn] vi to blink; (absichtlich) to wink

Zwirn [tsvırn] (-(e)s, -e) m thread

zwischen ['tsvıʃən] präp (+akk od dat) between; **Z~bemerkung** f (incidental) remark; **Z~ding** nt cross; **~durch** [-'dʊrç] adv in between; (räumlich) here and there; **Z~ergebnis** nt intermediate result; **Z~fall** m incident; **Z~frage** f question; **Z~handel** m middlemen pl; middleman's trade; **Z~landung** f (AVIAT) stopover; **~menschlich** adj in-

---

Spelling Reform: ▲ new spelling △ old spelling (to be phased out)

terpersonal; **Z~raum** *m* space; **Z~ruf** *m* interjection; **Z~stecker** *m* adaptor (plug); **Z~zeit** *f* interval; **in der Z~zeit** in the interim, meanwhile

zwitschern ['tsvɪtʃərn] *vt, vi* to twitter, to chirp

zwo [tsvoː] *num* two

zwölf [tsvœlf] *num* twelve

Zyklus ['tsyːklʊs] (-, **Zyklen**) *m* cycle

Zylinder [tsi'lɪndər] (**-s, -**) *m* cylinder; (*Hut*) top hat

Zyniker ['tsyːnikər] (**-s, -**) *m* cynic

zynisch ['tsyːnɪʃ] *adj* cynical

Zypern ['tsyːpərn] *nt* Cyprus

Zyste ['tsʏstə] *f* cyst

zz., zzt. *abk* = **zurzeit**

ENGLISH – GERMAN
ENGLISCH – DEUTSCH

A, a

A [eɪ] n (MUS) A nt; **~ road** Hauptverkehrsstraße f

a [eɪ, ə] (before vowel or silent h: an) indef art 1 ein; eine; **a woman** eine Frau; **a book** ein Buch; **an eagle** ein Adler; **she's a doctor** sie ist Ärztin

2 (instead of the number "one") ein, eine; **a year ago** vor einem Jahr; **a hundred/thousand** etc **pounds** (ein) hundert/(ein) tausend etc Pfund

3 (in expressing ratios, prices etc) pro; **3 a day/week** 3 pro Tag/Woche, 3 am Tag/in der Woche; **10 km an hour** 10 km pro Stunde/in der Stunde

A.A. n abbr = **Alcoholics Anonymous**; (BRIT) = **Automobile Association**

A.A.A. (US) n abbr = **American Automobile Association**

aback [əˈbæk] adv: **to be taken ~** verblüfft sein

abandon [əˈbændən] vt (give up) aufgeben; (desert) verlassen ♦ n Hingabe f

abate [əˈbeɪt] vi nachlassen, sich legen

abattoir [ˈæbətwɑː] (BRIT) n Schlachthaus nt

abbey [ˈæbɪ] n Abtei f

abbot [ˈæbət] n Abt m

abbreviate [əˈbriːvɪeɪt] vt abkürzen; **abbreviation** [əbriːvɪˈeɪʃən] n Abkürzung f

abdicate [ˈæbdɪkeɪt] vt aufgeben ♦ vi abdanken

abdomen [ˈæbdəmən] n Unterleib m

abduct [æbˈdʌkt] vt entführen

aberration [æbəˈreɪʃən] n (geistige) Verwirrung f

abet [əˈbet] vt see **aid**

abeyance [əˈbeɪəns] n: **in ~** in der Schwebe; (disuse) außer Kraft

abide [əˈbaɪd] vt vertragen; leiden; **~ by** vt sich halten an +acc

ability [əˈbɪlɪtɪ] n (power) Fähigkeit f; (skill) Geschicklichkeit f

abject [ˈæbdʒekt] adj (liar) übel; (poverty) größte(r, s); (apology) zerknirscht

ablaze [əˈbleɪz] adj in Flammen

able [ˈeɪbl] adj geschickt, fähig; **to be ~ to do sth** etw tun können; **~-bodied** [ˈeɪblˈbɒdɪd] adj kräftig; (seaman) Voll-; **ably** [ˈeɪblɪ] adv geschickt

abnormal [æbˈnɔːməl] adj regelwidrig, abnorm

aboard [əˈbɔːd] adv, prep an Bord +gen

abode [əˈbəʊd] n: **of no fixed ~** ohne festen Wohnsitz

abolish [əˈbɒlɪʃ] vt abschaffen; **abolition** [æbəˈlɪʃən] n Abschaffung f

abominable [əˈbɒmɪnəbl] adj scheußlich

aborigine [æbəˈrɪdʒɪnɪ] n Ureinwohner m

abort [əˈbɔːt] vt abtreiben; fehlgebären; **~ion** [əˈbɔːʃən] n Abtreibung f; (miscarriage) Fehlgeburt f; **~ive** adj misslungen

abound [əˈbaʊnd] vi im Überfluss vorhanden sein; **to ~ in** Überfluss haben an +dat

about [əˈbaʊt] adv 1 (approximately) etwa, ungefähr; **about a hundred/thousand** etc etwa hundert/tausend etc; **at about 2 o'clock** etwa um 2 Uhr; **I've just about finished** ich bin gerade fertig

2 (referring to place) herum, umher; **to**

leave things lying about Sachen herumliegen lassen; **to run/walk** etc **about** herumrennen/gehen etc

3: to be about to do sth im Begriff sein, etw zu tun; **he was about to go to bed** er wollte gerade ins Bett gehen

♦ prep **1** (relating to) über +acc; **a book about London** ein Buch über London; **what is it about?** worum geht es?; (book etc) wovon handelt es?; **we talked about it** wir haben darüber geredet; **what** or **how about doing this?** wollen wir das machen?

2 (referring to place) um (... herum); **to walk about the town** in der Stadt herumgehen; **her clothes were scattered about the room** ihre Kleider waren über das ganze Zimmer verstreut

about-turn [ə'baut'tə:n] n Kehrtwendung f

above [ə'bʌv] adv oben ♦ prep über; **~ all** vor allem; **~ board** adj offen, ehrlich

abrasive [ə'breɪzɪv] adj Abschleif-; (personality) zermürbend, aufreibend

abreast [ə'brest] adv nebeneinander; **to keep ~ of** Schritt halten mit

abroad [ə'brɔːd] adv (be) im Ausland; (go) ins Ausland

abrupt [ə'brʌpt] adj (sudden) abrupt, jäh; (curt) schroff; **~ly** adv abrupt

abscess ['æbsɪs] n Geschwür nt

abscond [əb'skɒnd] vi flüchten, sich davonmachen

abseil ['æbseɪl] vi (also: **~ down**) sich abseilen

absence ['æbsəns] n Abwesenheit f

absent ['æbsənt] adj abwesend, nicht da; (lost in thought) geistesabwesend; **~-minded** adj zerstreut

absolute ['æbsəluːt] adj absolut; (power) unumschränkt; (rubbish) vollkommen, rein; **~ly** [æbsə'luːtlɪ] adv absolut, vollkommen; **~ly!** ganz bestimmt!

absolve [əb'zɒlv] vt entbinden; freisprechen

absorb [əb'zɔːb] vt aufsaugen, absorbieren; (fig) ganz in Anspruch nehmen, fesseln; **to be ~ed in a book** in ein Buch vertieft sein; **~ent cotton** (US) n Verbandwatte f; **~ing** adj aufsaugend; (fig) packend; **absorption** [əb'sɔːpʃən] n Aufsaugung f, Absorption f; (fig) Versunkenheit f

abstain [əb'steɪn] vi (in vote) sich enthalten; **to ~ from** (keep from) sich enthalten +gen

abstemious [əb'stiːmɪəs] adj enthaltsam

abstinence ['æbstɪnəns] n Enthaltsamkeit f

abstract ['æbstrækt] adj abstrakt

absurd [əb'səːd] adj absurd

abundance [ə'bʌndəns] n: **~ (of)** Überfluss m (an +dat); **abundant** [ə'bʌndənt] adj reichlich

abuse [n ə'bjuːs, vb ə'bjuːz] n (rude language) Beschimpfung f; (ill usage) Missbrauch m; (bad practice) (Amts)missbrauch m ♦ vt (misuse) missbrauchen; **abusive** [ə'bjuːsɪv] adj beleidigend, Schimpf-

abysmal [ə'bɪzməl] adj scheußlich; (ignorance) bodenlos

abyss [ə'bɪs] n Abgrund m

AC abbr (= alternating current) Wechselstrom m

academic [ækə'demɪk] adj akademisch; (theoretical) theoretisch ♦ n Akademiker(in) m(f)

academy [ə'kædəmɪ] n (school) Hochschule f; (society) Akademie f

accelerate [æk'seləreɪt] vi schneller werden; (AUT) Gas geben ♦ vt beschleunigen; **acceleration** [æksələ'reɪʃən] n Beschleunigung f; **accelerator** [æk'seləreɪtə] n Gas(pedal) nt

accent ['æksənt] n Akzent m, Tonfall m; (mark) Akzent m; (stress) Betonung f

accept [ək'sept] vt (take) annehmen,

(*agree to*) akzeptieren; **~able** *adj* annehmbar; **~ance** *n* Annahme *f*

access ['ækses] *n* Zugang *m*; **~ible** [æk'sesəbl] *adj* (*easy to approach*) zugänglich; (*within reach*) (leicht) erreichbar

accessory [æk'sesərɪ] *n* Zubehörteil *nt*; **toilet accessories** Toilettenartikel *pl*

accident ['æksɪdənt] *n* Unfall *m*; (*coincidence*) Zufall *m*; **by ~** zufällig; **~al** [æksɪ'dentl] *adj* unbeabsichtigt; **~ally** [æksɪ'dentəlɪ] *adv* zufällig; **~ insurance** *n* Unfallversicherung *f*; **~-prone** *adj*: **to be ~-prone** zu Unfällen neigen

acclaim [ə'kleɪm] *vt* zujubeln +*dat* ♦ *n* Beifall *m*

acclimatize [ə'klaɪmətaɪz] *vt*: **to become ~d (to)** sich gewöhnen (an +*acc*), sich akklimatisieren (in +*dat*)

accommodate [ə'kɒmədeɪt] *vt* unterbringen; (*hold*) Platz haben für; (*oblige*) (aus)helfen +*dat*

accommodating [ə'kɒmədeɪtɪŋ] *adj* entgegenkommend

accommodation [əkɒmə'deɪʃən] (*US* **accommodations** *pl*) *n* Unterkunft *f*

accompany [ə'kʌmpənɪ] *vt* begleiten

accomplice [ə'kʌmplɪs] *n* Helfershelfer *m*, Komplize *m*

accomplish [ə'kʌmplɪʃ] *vt* (*fulfil*) durchführen; (*finish*) vollenden; (*aim*) erreichen; **~ed** *adj* vollendet, ausgezeichnet; **~ment** *n* (*skill*) Fähigkeit *f*; (*completion*) Vollendung *f*; (*feat*) Leistung *f*

accord [ə'kɔːd] *n* Übereinstimmung *f* ♦ *vt* gewähren; **of one's own ~** freiwillig; **~ing to** nach, laut +*gen*; **~ance** *n*: **in ~ance with** in Übereinstimmung mit; **~ingly** *adv* danach, dementsprechend

accordion [ə'kɔːdɪən] *n* Akkordeon *nt*

accost [ə'kɒst] *vt* ansprechen

account [ə'kaʊnt] *n* (*bill*) Rechnung *f*; (*narrative*) Bericht *m*; (*report*) Rechenschaftsbericht *m*; (*in bank*) Konto *nt*; (*importance*) Geltung *f*; **~s** *npl* (*FIN*)

Bücher *pl*; **on ~** auf Rechnung; **of no ~** ohne Bedeutung; **on no ~** keinesfalls; **on ~ of** wegen; **to take into ~** berücksichtigen; **~ for** *vt fus* (*expenditure*) Rechenschaft ablegen für; **how do you ~ for that?** wie erklären Sie (sich) das?; **~able** *adj* verantwortlich; **~ancy** [ə'kaʊntənsɪ] *n* Buchhaltung *f*; **~ant** [ə'kaʊntənt] *n* Wirtschaftsprüfer(in) *m(f)*; **~ number** *n* Kontonummer *f*

accumulate [ə'kjuːmjuleɪt] *vt* ansammeln ♦ *vi* sich ansammeln

accuracy ['ækjʊrəsɪ] *n* Genauigkeit *f*

accurate ['ækjurɪt] *adj* genau; **~ly** *adv* genau, richtig

accusation [ækjuː'zeɪʃən] *n* Anklage *f*, Beschuldigung *f*

accuse [ə'kjuːz] *vt* anklagen, beschuldigen; **~d** *n* Angeklagte(r) *f(m)*

accustom [ə'kʌstəm] *vt*: **to ~ sb (to sth)** jdn (an etw *acc*) gewöhnen; **~ed** *adj* gewohnt

ace [eɪs] *n* Ass *nt*; (*inf*) Ass *nt*, Kanone *f*

ache [eɪk] *n* Schmerz *m* ♦ *vi* (*be sore*) schmerzen, wehtun

achieve [ə'tʃiːv] *vt* zustande *or* zu Stande bringen; (*aim*) erreichen; **~ment** *n* Leistung *f*; (*act*) Erreichen *nt*

acid ['æsɪd] *n* Säure *f* ♦ *adj* sauer, scharf; **~ rain** *n* saure(r) Regen *m*

acknowledge [ək'nɒlɪdʒ] *vt* (*receipt*) bestätigen; (*admit*) zugeben; **~ment** *n* Anerkennung *f*; (*letter*) Empfangsbestätigung *f*

acne ['æknɪ] *n* Akne *f*

acorn ['eɪkɔːn] *n* Eichel *f*

acoustic [ə'kuːstɪk] *adj* akustisch; **~s** *npl* Akustik *f*

acquaint [ə'kweɪnt] *vt* vertraut machen; **to be ~ed with** mit jdm bekannt sein; **~ance** *n* (*person*) Bekannte(r) *f(m)*; (*knowledge*) Kenntnis *f*

acquire [ə'kwaɪə] *vt* erwerben; **acquisition** [ækwɪ'zɪʃən] *n* Errungenschaft *f*; (*act*) Erwerb *m*

acquit [ə'kwɪt] *vt* (*free*) freisprechen; **to**

~ **o.s. well** sich bewähren; **~tal** n Freispruch m

acre ['eɪkə'] n Morgen m

acrid ['ækrɪd] adj (smell, taste) bitter; (smoke) beißend

acrobat ['ækrəbæt] n Akrobat m

across [ə'krɒs] prep über +acc ♦ adv hinüber, herüber; **he lives ~ the river** er wohnt auf der anderen Seite des Flusses; **ten metres ~** zehn Meter breit; **he lives ~ from us** er wohnt uns gegenüber; **to run/swim ~** hinüberlaufen/schwimmen

acrylic [ə'krɪlɪk] adj Acryl-

act [ækt] n (deed) Tat f; (JUR) Gesetz nt; (THEAT) Akt m; (: turn) Nummer f ♦ vi (take ~ion) handeln; (behave) sich verhalten; (pretend) vorgeben; (THEAT) spielen ♦ vt (in play) spielen; **to ~ as** fungieren als; **~ing** adj stellvertretend ♦ n Schauspielkunst f; (performance) Aufführung f

action ['ækʃən] n (deed) Tat f; Handlung f; (motion) Bewegung f; (way of working) Funktionieren nt; (battle) Einsatz m, Gefecht nt; (lawsuit) Klage f, Prozess m; **out of ~** (person) nicht einsatzfähig; (thing) außer Betrieb; **to take ~** etwas unternehmen; **~ replay** n (TV) Wiederholung f

activate ['æktɪveɪt] vt (mechanism) betätigen; (CHEM, PHYS) aktivieren

active ['æktɪv] adj (brisk) rege, tatkräftig; (working) aktiv; (GRAM) aktiv, Tätigkeits-; **~ly** adv aktiv; (dislike) offen

activity [æk'tɪvɪtɪ] n Aktivität f; (doings) Unternehmungen pl; (occupation) Tätigkeit f; **~ holiday** n Aktivurlaub m

actor ['æktə'] n Schauspieler m

actress ['æktrɪs] n Schauspielerin f

actual ['æktjʊəl] adj wirklich; **~ly** adv tatsächlich; (in fact) eigentlich

acumen ['ækjʊmən] n Scharfsinn m

acute [ə'kjuːt] adj (severe) heftig, akut; (keen) scharfsinnig

ad [æd] n abbr = **advertisement**

A.D. adv abbr (= Anno Domini) n. Chr.

adamant ['ædəmənt] adj eisern; hartnäckig

adapt [ə'dæpt] vt anpassen ♦ vi: **to ~ (to)** sich anpassen (an +acc); **~able** adj anpassungsfähig; **~ation** [ædæp'teɪʃən] n (THEAT etc) Bearbeitung f; (adjustment) Anpassung f; **~er, ~or** n (ELEC) Zwischenstecker m

add [æd] vt (join) hinzufügen; (numbers: also: **~ up**) addieren; **~ up** vi (make sense) stimmen; **~ up to** vt fus ausmachen

adder ['ædə'] n Kreuzotter f, Natter f

addict ['ædɪkt] n Süchtige(r) f(m); **~ed** [ə'dɪktɪd] adj: **~ed to** -süchtig; **~ion** [ə'dɪkʃən] n Sucht f; **~ive** [ə'dɪktɪv] adj: **to be ~ive** süchtig machen

addition [ə'dɪʃən] n Anhang m, Addition f; (MATH) Addition f, Zusammenzählen nt; **in ~** zusätzlich, außerdem; **~al** adj zusätzlich, weiter

additive ['ædɪtɪv] n Zusatz m

address [ə'dres] n Adresse f; (speech) Ansprache f ♦ vt (letter) adressieren; (speak to) ansprechen; (make speech to) eine Ansprache halten an +acc

adept ['ædept] adj geschickt; **to be ~ at** gut sein in +dat

adequate ['ædɪkwɪt] adj angemessen

adhere [əd'hɪə'] vi: **to ~ to** haften an +dat; (fig) festhalten an +dat

adhesive [əd'hiːzɪv] adj klebend; Kleb(e)- ♦ n Klebstoff m; **~ tape** n (BRIT) Klebestreifen m; (US) Heftpflaster nt

ad hoc [æd'hɔk] adj (decision, committee) Ad-hoc- ♦ adv ad hoc

adjacent [ə'dʒeɪsənt] adj benachbart; **~ to** angrenzend an +acc

adjective ['ædʒektɪv] n Adjektiv nt, Eigenschaftswort nt

adjoining [ə'dʒɔɪnɪŋ] adj benachbart, Neben-

adjourn [ə'dʒɜːn] vt vertagen ♦ vi abbrechen

adjudicate [ə'dʒuːdɪkeɪt] vi entscheiden, ein Urteil fällen

adjust [əˈdʒʌst] vt (alter) anpassen; (put right) regulieren, richtig stellen ♦ vi sich anpassen; **~able** adj verstellbar

ad-lib [ædˈlɪb] vt, vi improvisieren ♦ adv: **ad lib** aus dem Stegreif

administer [ədˈmɪnɪstəʳ] vt (manage) verwalten; (dispense) ausüben; (justice) sprechen; (medicine) geben; **administration** [ədmɪnɪsˈtreɪʃən] n Verwaltung f; (POL) Regierung f; **administrative** [ədˈmɪnɪstrətɪv] adj Verwaltungs-; **administrator** [ədˈmɪnɪstreɪtəʳ] n Verwaltungsbeamte(r) f(m)

Admiralty [ˈædmərəltɪ] (BRIT) n Admiralität f

admiration [ædməˈreɪʃən] n Bewunderung f

admire [ədˈmaɪəʳ] vt (respect) bewundern; (love) verehren; **~r** n Bewunderer m

admission [ədˈmɪʃən] n (entrance) Einlass m; (fee) Eintritt(spreis m) m; (confession) Geständnis n; **~ charge** n Eintritt(spreis) m

admit [ədˈmɪt] vt (let in) einlassen; (confess) gestehen; (accept) anerkennen; **~tance** n Zulassung f; **~tedly** adv zugegebenermaßen

admonish [ədˈmɒnɪʃ] vt ermahnen

ad nauseam [ædˈnɔːsɪæm] adv (repeat, talk) endlos

ado [əˈduː] n: **without more ~** ohne weitere Umstände

adolescence [ædəʊˈlesns] n Jugendalter nt; **adolescent** [ædəʊˈlesnt] adj jugendlich ♦ n Jugendliche(r) f(m)

adopt [əˈdɒpt] vt (child) adoptieren; (idea) übernehmen; **~ion** [əˈdɒpʃən] n Adoption f; Übernahme f

adore [əˈdɔːʳ] vt anbeten; verehren

adorn [əˈdɔːn] vt schmücken

Adriatic [eɪdrɪˈætɪk] n: **the ~ (Sea)** die Adria

adrift [əˈdrɪft] adv Wind und Wellen preisgegeben

adult [ˈædʌlt] n Erwachsene(r) f(m)

adultery [əˈdʌltərɪ] n Ehebruch m

advance [ədˈvɑːns] n (progress) Vorrücken nt; (money) Vorschuss m ♦ vt (move forward) vorrücken; (money) vorschießen; (argument) vorbringen ♦ vi vorwärts gehen; **in ~** im Voraus; **~ booking** n Vorverkauf m; **~d** adj (ahead) vorgerückt; (modern) fortgeschritten; (study) für Fortgeschrittene

advantage [ədˈvɑːntɪdʒ] n Vorteil m; **to have an ~ over sb** jdm gegenüber im Vorteil sein; **to take ~ of** (misuse) ausnutzen; (profit from) Nutzen ziehen aus; **~ous** [ædvənˈteɪdʒəs] adj vorteilhaft

advent [ˈædvənt] n Ankunft f; **A~** Advent m

adventure [ədˈventʃəʳ] n Abenteuer nt; **adventurous** adj abenteuerlich, waghalsig

adverb [ˈædvɜːb] n Adverb nt, Umstandswort nt

adversary [ˈædvəsərɪ] n Gegner m

adverse [ˈædvɜːs] adj widrig; **adversity** [ədˈvɜːsɪtɪ] n Widrigkeit f, Missgeschick nt

advert [ˈædvɜːt] n Anzeige f; **~ise** [ˈædvətaɪz] vt werben für ♦ vi annoncieren; **to ~ise for sth** etw (per Anzeige) suchen; **~isement** [ədˈvɜːtɪsmənt] n Anzeige f, Inserat nt, Reklame f; **~iser** n (in newspaper etc) Inserent m; **~ising** n Werbung f

advice [ədˈvaɪs] n Rat(schlag) m; ratsam

advisable [ədˈvaɪzəbl] adj ratsam

advise [ədˈvaɪz] vt: **to ~ (sb)** (jdm) raten; **~dly** [ədˈvaɪzɪdlɪ] adv (deliberately) bewusst; **~r** n Berater m; **advisory** [ədˈvaɪzərɪ] adj beratend, Beratungs-

advocate [vb ˈædvəkeɪt, n ˈædvəkət] vt vertreten ♦ n Befürworter(in) m(f)

Aegean [iːˈdʒiːən] n: **the ~ (Sea)** die Ägäis

aerial [ˈeərɪəl] n Antenne f ♦ adj Luft-

aerobics [eəˈrəʊbɪks] n Aerobic nt

aerodynamic [ˈeərəʊdaɪˈnæmɪk] adj aerodynamisch

aeroplane ['ɛərəpleɪn] n Flugzeug nt

aerosol ['ɛərəsɒl] n Aerosol nt; Sprühdose f

aesthetic [iːsˈθetɪk] adj ästhetisch

afar [əˈfɑːʳ] adv: **from ~** aus der Ferne

affable ['æfəbl] adj umgänglich

affair [əˈfɛəʳ] n (concern) Angelegenheit f; (event) Ereignis nt; (love ~) Verhältnis nt; **~s** npl (business) Geschäfte pl

affect [əˈfekt] vt (influence) (ein)wirken auf +acc; (move deeply) bewegen; **this change doesn't ~ us** diese Änderung betrifft uns nicht; **~ed** adj affektiert, gekünstelt

affection [əˈfekʃən] n Zuneigung f; **~ate** adj liebevoll

affiliated [əˈfɪleɪtɪd] adj angeschlossen

affinity [əˈfɪnɪtɪ] n (attraction) gegenseitige Anziehung f; (relationship) Verwandtschaft f

affirmative [əˈfɜːmətɪv] adj bestätigend

afflict [əˈflɪkt] vt quälen, heimsuchen

affluence ['æfluəns] n (wealth) Wohlstand m; **affluent** adj wohlhabend, Wohlstands-

afford [əˈfɔːd] vt sich dat leisten; (yield) bieten, einbringen

afield [əˈfiːld] adv: **far ~** weit fort

afloat [əˈfləut] adj: **to be ~** schwimmen

afoot [əˈfut] adv im Gang

afraid [əˈfreɪd] adj ängstlich; **to be ~ of** Angst haben vor +dat; **to be ~ to do sth** sich scheuen, etw zu tun; **I am ~ I have ...** ich habe leider ...; **I'm ~ so/ not** leider/leider nicht; **I am ~ that ...** ich fürchte(, dass) ...

afresh [əˈfreʃ] adv von neuem

Africa ['æfrɪkə] n Afrika nt; **~n** adj afrikanisch ♦ n Afrikaner(in) m(f)

after [ˈɑːftəʳ] prep nach; (following, seeking) hinter ... dat ... her; (in imitation) nach, im Stil von ♦ adv: **soon ~** bald danach ♦ conj nachdem; **what are you ~?** was wollen Sie?; **~ he left** nachdem er gegangen war; **~ you!**

nach Ihnen!; **~ all** letzten Endes; **~ having shaved** als er sich rasiert hatte; **~effects** npl Nachwirkungen pl; **~math** n Auswirkungen pl; **~noon** n Nachmittag m; **~s** (inf) n (dessert) Nachtisch m; **~sales service** (BRIT) n Kundendienst m; **~shave (lotion)** n Rasierwasser nt; **~sun** n Aftersunlotion f; **~thought** n nachträgliche(r) Einfall m; **~wards** adv danach, nachher

again [əˈgen] adv wieder, noch einmal; (besides) außerdem, ferner; **~ and ~** immer wieder

against [əˈgenst] prep gegen

age [eɪdʒ] n (of person) Alter nt; (in history) Zeitalter nt ♦ vi altern, alt werden ♦ vt alter machen; **to come of ~** mündig werden; **20 years of ~** 20 Jahre alt; **it's been ~s since** ... es ist ewig her, seit ...

aged[1] [eɪdʒd] adj: ... Jahre alt, -jährig

aged[2] [ˈeɪdʒɪd] adj (elderly) betagt ♦ npl: **the ~** die Alten pl

age group n Altersgruppe f

age limit n Altersgrenze f

agency [ˈeɪdʒənsɪ] n Agentur f; (CHEM) Wirkung f; **through** or **by the ~ of** ... mithilfe or mit Hilfe von ...

agenda [əˈdʒendə] n Tagesordnung f

agent [ˈeɪdʒənt] n (COMM) Vertreter m; (spy) Agent m

aggravate [ˈægrəveɪt] vt (make worse) verschlimmern; (irritate) reizen

aggregate [ˈægrɪgɪt] n Summe f

aggression [əˈgreʃən] n Aggression f; **aggressive** [əˈgresɪv] adj aggressiv

aghast [əˈgɑːst] adj entsetzt

agile [ˈædʒaɪl] adj flink; agil; (mind) rege

agitate [ˈædʒɪteɪt] vt rütteln; **to ~ for** sich stark machen für

AGM n abbr (= annual general meeting) JHV f

ago [əˈgəu] adv: **two days ~** vor zwei Tagen; **not long ~** vor kurzem; **it's so long ~** es ist schon so lange her

agog [əˈgɔg] adj gespannt

agonizing [ˈægənaɪzɪŋ] adj quälend

agony [ˈægənɪ] n Qual f; **to be in ~** in Qualen leiden

agree [əˈgriː] vt (date) vereinbaren ♦ vi (have same opinion, correspond) übereinstimmen; (consent) zustimmen; (be in harmony) sich vertragen; **to ~ to sth** einer Sache dat zustimmen; **to ~ that** ... (admit) zugeben, dass ...; **to ~ to do sth** sich bereit erklären, etw zu tun; **garlic doesn't ~ with me** Knoblauch vertrage ich nicht; **I ~** einverstanden, ich stimme zu; **to ~ on sth** sich auf etw acc einigen; **~able** adj (pleasing) liebenswürdig; (willing to consent) einverstanden; **~d** adj (time) vereinbart; **~ment** n (~ing) Übereinstimmung f; (contract) Vereinbarung f, Vertrag m; **to be in ~ment** übereinstimmen

agricultural [ægrɪˈkʌltʃərəl] adj landwirtschaftlich, Landwirtschafts-

agriculture [ˈægrɪkʌltʃər] n Landwirtschaft f

aground [əˈgraʊnd] adv: **to run ~** auf Grund laufen

ahead [əˈhed] adv vorwärts; **to be ~** voraus sein; **~ of time** der Zeit voraus; **go right** or **straight ~** gehen Sie geradeaus; fahren Sie geradeaus

aid [eɪd] n (assistance) Hilfe f, Unterstützung f; (person) Hilfe f; (thing) Hilfsmittel nt ♦ vt unterstützen, helfen +dat; **in ~ of** zugunsten or zu Gunsten +gen; **to ~ and abet sb** jdm Beihilfe leisten

aide [eɪd] n (person) Gehilfe m; (MIL) Adjutant m

AIDS [eɪdz] n abbr (= acquired immune deficiency syndrome) Aids nt; **AIDS-related** aidsbedingt

ailing [ˈeɪlɪŋ] adj kränkelnd

ailment [ˈeɪlmənt] n Leiden nt

aim [eɪm] vt (gun, camera) richten ♦ vi (with gun: also: **take ~**) zielen; (intend) beabsichtigen ♦ n (intention) Absicht f;

Ziel nt; (pointing) Zielen nt, Richten nt; **to ~ at sth** auf etw dat richten; (fig) etw anstreben; **to ~ to do sth** vorhaben, etw zu tun; **~less** adj ziellos; **~lessly** adv ziellos

ain't [eɪnt] (inf) = **am not; are not; is not; has not; have not**

air [eər] n Luft f; (manner) Miene f, Anschein m; (MUS) Melodie f ♦ vt lüften; (fig) an die Öffentlichkeit bringen ♦ cpd Luft-; **by ~** (travel) auf dem Luftweg; **to be on the ~** (RADIO, TV: programme) gesendet werden; **~bed** (BRIT) n Luftmatratze f; **~conditioned** adj mit Klimaanlage; **~conditioning** n Klimaanlage f; **~craft** n Flugzeug nt, Maschine f; **~craft carrier** n Flugzeugträger m; **~field** n Flugplatz m; **~ force** n Luftwaffe f; **~ freshener** n Raumspray m; **~gun** n Luftgewehr nt; **~ hostess** (BRIT) n Stewardess f; **~ letter** (BRIT) n Luftpostbrief m; **~lift** n Luftbrücke f; **~line** n Luftverkehrsgesellschaft f; **~liner** n Verkehrsflugzeug nt; **~lock** n Luftblase f; **~mail** n: **by ~mail** mit Luftpost; **~ miles** npl ~ Flugkilometer pl; **~plane** (US) n Flugzeug nt; **~port** n Flughafen m, Flugplatz m; **~ raid** n Luftangriff m; **~sick** adj luftkrank; **~space** n Luftraum m; **~strip** n Landestreifen m; **~ terminal** n Terminal m; **~tight** adj luftdicht; **~ traffic controller** n Fluglotse m; **~y** adj luftig; (manner) leichtfertig

aisle [aɪl] n Gang m; **~ seat** n Sitz m am Gang

ajar [əˈdʒɑːr] adv angelehnt; einen Spalt offen

alarm [əˈlɑːm] n (warning) Alarm m; (bell etc) Alarmanlage f; (anxiety) Sorge f ♦ vt erschrecken; **~ call** n (in hotel etc) Weckruf m; **~ clock** n Wecker m

Albania [ælˈbeɪnɪə] n Albanien nt

albeit [ɔːlˈbiːɪt] conj obgleich

album [ˈælbəm] n Album nt

alcohol [ˈælkəhɒl] n Alkohol m; **~free** adj alkoholfrei; **~ic** n [ælkəˈhɒlɪk] adj (*drink*) alkoholisch ♦ *n* Alkoholiker(in) *m(f)*; **~ism** *n* Alkoholismus *m*

alert ['lɔːt] *adj* wachsam ♦ *n* Alarm *m* ♦ *vt* alarmieren; **to be on the ~** wachsam sein

Algeria [æl'dʒɪərɪə] *n* Algerien *nt*

alias ['eɪlɪəs] *adv* alias ♦ *n* Deckname *m*

alibi ['ælɪbaɪ] *n* Alibi *nt*

alien ['eɪlɪən] *n* Ausländer *m* ♦ *adj* (*foreign*) ausländisch; (*strange*) fremd; **~ to** fremd *+dat*; **~ate** *vt* entfremden

alight [ə'laɪt] *adj* brennend; (*of building*) in Flammen ♦ *vi* (*descend*) aussteigen; (*bird*) sich setzen

align [ə'laɪn] *vt* ausrichten

alike [ə'laɪk] *adj* gleich, ähnlich ♦ *adv* gleich, ebenso; **to look ~** sich *dat* ähnlich sehen

alimony ['ælɪmənɪ] *n* Unterhalt *m*, Alimente *pl*

alive [ə'laɪv] *adj* (*living*) lebend; (*lively*) lebendig, aufgeweckt; **~ with** (*full of*) voll (von), wimmelnd (von)

all [ɔːl] *adj* alle(r, s); **all day/night** den ganzen Tag/die ganze Nacht; **all men are equal** alle Menschen sind gleich; **all five came** alle fünf kamen; **all the books/food** die ganzen Bücher/das ganze Essen; **all the time** die ganze Zeit (über); **all his life** sein ganzes Leben (lang)
♦ *pron* 1 alles; **I ate it all, I ate all of it** ich habe alles gegessen; **all of us/the boys went** wir gingen alle/alle Jungen gingen; **we all sat down** wir setzten uns alle

2 (*in phrases*): **above all** vor allem; **after all** schließlich; **at all: not at all** (*in answer to question*) überhaupt nicht; (*in answer to thanks*) gern geschehen; **I'm not at all tired** ich bin überhaupt nicht müde; **anything at all will do** es ist egal, welche(r, s); **all in all** alles in allem
♦ *adv* ganz; **all alone** ganz allein; **it's**

not as hard as all that so schwer ist es nun auch wieder nicht; **all the more/the better** umso mehr/besser; **all but fast**; **the score is 2 all** es steht 2 zu 2

allay [ə'leɪ] *vt* (*fears*) beschwichtigen

all clear *n* Entwarnung *f*

allegation [ælɪ'geɪʃən] *n* Behauptung *f*

allege [ə'ledʒ] *vt* (*declare*) behaupten; (*falsely*) vorgeben; **~dly** *adv* angeblich

allegiance [ə'liːdʒəns] *n* Treue *f*

allergic [ə'lɔːdʒɪk] *adj:* **~ (to)** allergisch (gegen)

allergy ['ælədʒɪ] *n* Allergie *f*

alleviate [ə'liːvɪeɪt] *vt* lindern

alley ['ælɪ] *n* Gasse *f*, Durchgang *m*

alliance [ə'laɪəns] *n* Bund *m*, Allianz *f*

allied ['ælaɪd] *adj* vereinigt; (*powers*) alliiert; **~ (to)** verwandt (mit)

all: **~-in** (*BRIT*) *adj, adv* alles inbegriffen, Gesamt-; **~-in wrestling** *n* Freistilringen *nt*; **~-night** *adj* (*café, cinema*) die ganze Nacht geöffnet, Nacht-

allocate ['æləkeɪt] *vt* zuteilen

allot [ə'lɔt] *vt* zuteilen; **~ment** *n* (*share*) Anteil *m*; (*plot*) Schrebergarten *m*

all-out ['ɔːlaut] *adj* total; **all out** *adv* mit voller Kraft

allow [ə'lau] *vt* (*permit*) erlauben, gestatten; (*grant*) bewilligen; (*deduct*) abziehen; (*concede*): **to ~ that ...** annehmen, dass ...; **to ~ sb to do sth** jdm etw erlauben, jdm etw gestatten; **to ~ sb to do sth** jdm erlauben or gestatten, etw zu tun; **~ for** *vt fus* berücksichtigen, einplanen; **~ance** *n* Beihilfe *f*; **to make ~ances for** berücksichtigen

alloy ['ælɔɪ] *n* Metalllegierung *f*

all: **~ right** *adv* (*well*) gut; (*correct*) richtig; (*as answer*) okay; **~-round** *adj* (*sportsman*) allseitig, Allround-; (*view*) Rundum-; **~-time** *adj* (*record, high*) ... aller Zeiten, Höchst-

allude [ə'luːd] *vi:* **to ~ to** hinweisen auf *+acc*, anspielen auf *+acc*

alluring [ə'ljuərɪŋ] *adj* verlockend

ally [n 'ælaɪ, vb ə'laɪ] n Verbündete(r) f(m); (POL) Alliierte(r) f(m) ♦ vr: **to ~ o.s. with** sich verbünden mit

almighty [ɔːl'maɪtɪ] adj allmächtig

almond ['ɑːmənd] n Mandel f

almost ['ɔːlməust] adv fast, beinahe

alms [ɑːmz] npl Almosen nt

alone [ə'ləun] adj, adv allein; **to leave sth ~** etw sein lassen; **let ~ ...** geschweige denn ...

along [ə'lɔŋ] prep entlang, längs ♦ adv (onward) vorwärts, weiter; **~ with** zusammen mit; **he was limping ~** er humpelte einher; **all ~** (all the time) die ganze Zeit; **~side** adv (walk) nebenher; (come) nebendran; (be) daneben ♦ prep (walk, compared with) neben +dat; (come) neben +acc; (be) entlang, neben +dat; (of ship) längsseits +gen

aloof [ə'luːf] adj zurückhaltend ♦ adv fern; **to stand ~** abseits stehen

aloud [ə'laud] adv laut

alphabet ['ælfəbet] n Alphabet nt; **~ical** [ælfə'betɪkl] adj alphabetisch

alpine ['ælpaɪn] adj alpin, Alpen-

Alps [ælps] npl: **the ~** die Alpen pl

already [ɔːl'redɪ] adv schon, bereits

alright ['ɔːl'raɪt] (BRIT) adv = **all right**

Alsatian [æl'seɪʃən] n (dog) Schäferhund m

also ['ɔːlsəu] adv auch, außerdem

altar ['ɔːltəʳ] n Altar m

alter ['ɔːltəʳ] vt ändern; (dress) umändern; **~ation** [ɔːltə'reɪʃən] n Änderung f; Umänderung f; (to building) Umbau m

alternate [adj ɔːl'tɜːnɪt, vb 'ɔːltəːneɪt] adj abwechselnd ♦ vi abwechseln; on **~ days** jeden zweiten Tag

alternating ['ɔːltəːneɪtɪŋ] adj: **~ current** Wechselstrom m; **alternative** [ɔːl'tɜːnətɪv] adj andere(r, s) ♦ n Alternative f; **alternative medicine** Alternativmedizin f; **alternatively** adv in anderen Falle; **alternatively one could ...** oder man könnte ...; **alternator** ['ɔːltəːneɪtəʳ] n (AUT) Lichtma-

schine f

although [ɔːl'ðəu] conj obwohl

altitude ['æltɪtjuːd] n Höhe f

alto ['æltəu] n Alt m

altogether [ɔːltə'geðəʳ] adv (on the whole) im Ganzen genommen; (entirely) ganz und gar

aluminium [ælju'mɪnɪəm] (BRIT) n Aluminium nt

aluminum [ə'luːmɪnəm] (US) n Aluminium nt

always ['ɔːlweɪz] adv immer

Alzheimer's (disease) ['æltshaɪməz-] n (MED) Alzheimerkrankheit f

a.m. adv abbr (= ante meridiem) vormittags

amalgamate [ə'mælgəmeɪt] vi (combine) sich vereinigen ♦ vt (mix) amalgamieren

amass [ə'mæs] vt anhäufen

amateur ['æmətəʳ] n Amateur m; (pej) Amateur m, Stümper m; **~ish** (pej) adj dilettantisch, stümperhaft

amaze [ə'meɪz] vt erstaunen; **to be ~d (at)** erstaunt sein (über); **~ment** n höchste(s) Erstaunen nt; **amazing** adj höchst erstaunlich

Amazon ['æməzən] n (GEOG) Amazonas m

ambassador [æm'bæsədəʳ] n Botschafter m

amber ['æmbəʳ] n Bernstein m; **at ~** (BRIT: AUT) auf Gelb, gelb

ambiguous [æm'bɪgjuəs] adj zweideutig; (not clear) unklar

ambition [æm'bɪʃən] n Ehrgeiz m; **ambitious** adj ehrgeizig

amble ['æmbl] vi (usu: ~ along) schlendern

ambulance ['æmbjuləns] n Krankenwagen m; **~ man** (irreg) n Sanitäter m

ambush ['æmbuʃ] n Hinterhalt m ♦ vt (aus dem Hinterhalt) überfallen

amenable [ə'miːnəbl] adj gefügig; **~ (to)** (reason) zugänglich (+dat); (flattery) empfänglich (für)

amend [ə'mɛnd] vt (law etc) abändern, ergänzen; **to make ~s** etw wieder gutmachen; **~ment** n Abänderung f

amenities [ə'mi:nɪtɪz] npl Einrichtungen pl

America [ə'mɛrɪkə] n Amerika nt; **~n** adj amerikanisch ♦ n Amerikaner(in) m(f)

amiable ['eɪmɪəbl] adj liebenswürdig

amicable ['æmɪkəbl] adj freundschaftlich; (settlement) gütlich

amid(st) [ə'mɪd(st)] prep mitten in or unter +dat

amiss [ə'mɪs] adv: **to take sth ~** etw übel nehmen; **there's something ~** da stimmt irgendetwas nicht

ammonia [ə'məunɪə] n Ammoniak nt

ammunition [æmju'nɪʃən] n Munition f

amnesia [æm'ni:zɪə] n Gedächtnisverlust m

amnesty ['æmnɪstɪ] n Amnestie f

amok [ə'mɔk] adv: **to run ~** Amok laufen

among(st) [ə'mʌŋ(st)] prep unter

amoral [æ'mɔrəl] adj unmoralisch

amorous ['æmərəs] adj verliebt

amount [ə'maunt] n (of money) Betrag m; (of water, sand) Menge f ♦ vi: **to ~ to** (total) sich belaufen auf +acc; **a great ~ of time/energy** ein großer Aufwand an Zeit/Energie (dat); **this ~s to treachery** das kommt Verrat gleich; **he won't ~ to much** aus ihm wird nie was

amp(ere) ['æmp(ɛəʳ)] n Ampere nt

amphibian [æm'fɪbɪən] n Amphibie f

ample ['æmpl] adj (portion) reichlich; (dress) weit, groß; **~ time** genügend Zeit

amplifier ['æmplɪfaɪəʳ] n Verstärker m

amuse [ə'mju:z] vt (entertain) unterhalten; (make smile) belustigen; **~ment** n (feeling) Unterhaltung f; (recreation) Zeitvertreib m; **~ment arcade** n Spielhalle f; **~ment park** n Vergnügungspark m

an [æn, ən] see **a**

anaemia [ə'ni:mɪə] n Anämie f; **anaemic** adj blutarm

anaesthetic [ænɪs'θetɪk] n Betäubungsmittel nt; **under ~** unter Narkose; **anaesthetist** [æ'ni:sθɪtɪst] n Anästhesist(in) m(f)

analgesic [ænæl'dʒi:sɪk] n schmerzlindernde(s) Mittel nt

analog(ue) ['ænəlɔg] adj Analog-

analogy [ə'nælədʒɪ] n Analogie f

analyse ['ænəlaɪz] (BRIT) vt analysieren

analyses [ə'næləsi:z] (BRIT) npl of **analysis**

analysis [ə'næləsɪs] (pl **analyses**) n Analyse f

analyst ['ænəlɪst] n Analytiker(in) m(f)

analytic(al) [ænə'lɪtɪk(l)] adj analytisch

analyze ['ænəlaɪz] (US) vt = **analyse**

anarchy ['ænəkɪ] n Anarchie f

anatomy [ə'nætəmɪ] n (structure) anatomische(r) Aufbau m; (study) Anatomie f

ancestor ['ænsɪstəʳ] n Vorfahr m

anchor ['æŋkəʳ] n Anker m ♦ vi (also: **to drop ~**) ankern, vor Anker gehen ♦ vt verankern; **to weigh ~** den Anker lichten

anchovy ['æntʃəvɪ] n Sardelle f

ancient ['eɪnʃənt] adj alt; (car etc) uralt

ancillary [æn'sɪlərɪ] adj Hilfs-

and [ænd] conj und; **~ so on** und so weiter; **try ~ come** versuche zu kommen; **better ~ better** immer besser

Andes ['ændi:z] npl: **the ~** die Anden pl

anemia etc [ə'ni:mɪə] (US) n = **anaemia** etc

anesthetic etc [ænɪs'θetɪk] (US) n = **anaesthetic** etc

anew [ə'nju:] adv von neuem

angel ['eɪndʒəl] n Engel m

anger ['æŋgəʳ] n Zorn m ♦ vt ärgern

angina [æn'dʒaɪnə] n Angina f

angle ['æŋgl] n Winkel m; (point of view) Standpunkt m

angler ['æŋgləʳ] n Angler m

Anglican ['æŋglɪkən] adj anglikanisch ♦ n Anglikaner(in) m(f)

angling ['æŋglɪŋ] n Angeln nt

angrily ['æŋgrɪlɪ] adv ärgerlich, böse

angry ['æŋgrɪ] adj ärgerlich, ungehalten, böse; (wound) entzündet; **to be ~ with sb** auf jdn böse sein; **to be ~ at sth** über etw acc verärgert sein

anguish ['æŋgwɪʃ] n Qual f

angular ['æŋgjulə*] adj eckig, winkelförmig; (face) kantig

animal ['ænɪml] n Tier nt; (living creature) Lebewesen nt ♦ adj tierisch

animate [vb 'ænɪmeɪt, adj 'ænɪmɪt] vt beleben ♦ adj lebhaft; **~d** adj lebendig; (film) Zeichentrick-

animosity [ænɪ'mɒsɪtɪ] n Feindseligkeit f, Abneigung f

aniseed ['ænɪsiːd] n Anis m

ankle ['æŋkl] n (Fuß)knöchel m; **~ sock** n Söckchen nt

annex [n 'æneks, vb ə'neks] n (BRIT: also: **~e**) Anbau m ♦ vt anfügen; (POL) annektieren, angliedern

annihilate [ə'naɪəleɪt] vt vernichten

anniversary [ænɪ'vɜːsərɪ] n Jahrestag m

announce [ə'nauns] vt ankündigen, anzeigen; **~ment** n Ankündigung f; (official) Bekanntmachung f; **~r** n Ansager(in) m(f)

annoy [ə'nɔɪ] vt ärgern; **don't get ~ed!** reg dich nicht auf!; **~ance** n Ärgernis nt, Störung f; **~ing** adj ärgerlich; (person) lästig

annual ['ænjuəl] adj jährlich; (salary) Jahres- ♦ n (plant) einjährige Pflanze f; (book) Jahrbuch nt; **~ly** adv jährlich

annul [ə'nʌl] vt aufheben, annullieren

annum ['ænəm] n see **per**

anonymous [ə'nɒnɪməs] adj anonym

anorak ['ænəræk] n Anorak m, Windjacke f

anorexia [ænə'reksɪə] n (MED) Magersucht f

another [ə'nʌðə*] adj, pron (different) eine(n) andere(r, s); (additional) noch eine(r, s); see also **one**

answer ['ɑːnsə*] n Antwort f ♦ vi antworten; (on phone) sich melden ♦ vt (person) antworten +dat; (letter, question) beantworten; (telephone) gehen an +acc, abnehmen; (door) öffnen; **in ~ to your letter** in Beantwortung Ihres Schreibens; **to ~ the phone** ans Telefon gehen; **to ~ the bell** or **the door** aufmachen; **~ back** vi frech sein; **~ for** vt fus: **to ~ for sth** für etw verantwortlich sein; **~able** adj: **to be ~able to sb for sth** jdm gegenüber für etw verantwortlich sein; **~ing machine** n Anrufbeantworter m

ant [ænt] n Ameise f

antagonism [æn'tægənɪzəm] n Antagonismus m

antagonize [æn'tægənaɪz] vt reizen

Antarctic [ænt'ɑːktɪk] adj antarktisch ♦ n: **the ~** die Antarktis

antelope ['æntɪləup] n Antilope f

antenatal ['æntɪ'neɪtl] adj vor der Geburt; **~ clinic** n Sprechstunde f für werdende Mütter

antenna [æn'tenə] n (BIOL) Fühler m; (RAD) Antenne f

antennae [æn'teniː] npl of **antenna**

anthem ['ænθəm] n Hymne f; **national ~** Nationalhymne f

anthology [æn'θɒlədʒɪ] n Gedichtsammlung f, Anthologie f

anti- ['æntɪ] prefix Gegen-, Anti-

anti-aircraft ['æntɪ'ɛəkrɑːft] adj Flugabwehr-

antibiotic ['æntɪbaɪ'ɒtɪk] n Antibiotikum nt

antibody ['æntɪbɒdɪ] n Antikörper m

anticipate [æn'tɪsɪpeɪt] vt (expect: trouble, question) erwarten, rechnen mit; (look forward to) sich freuen auf +acc; (do first) vorwegnehmen; (foresee) ahnen, vorhersehen; **anticipation** [æntɪsɪ'peɪʃən] n Erwartung f; (foreshadowing) Vorwegnahme f

anticlimax ['æntɪ'klaɪmæks] n Ernüchterung f

anticlockwise ['æntɪ'klɔkwaɪz] *adv* entgegen dem Uhrzeigersinn

antics ['æntɪks] *npl* Possen *pl*

anti: ~**cyclone** *n* Hoch *nt*, Hochdruckgebiet *nt*; ~**dote** *n* Gegenmittel *nt*; ~**freeze** *n* Frostschutzmittel *nt*; ~**histamine** *n* Antihistamin *n*

antiquated ['æntɪkweɪtɪd] *adj* antiquiert

antique [æn'tiːk] *n* Antiquität *f* ♦ *adj* antik; (*old-fashioned*) altmodisch; ~ **shop** *n* Antiquitätenladen *m*; **antiquity** [æn'tɪkwɪtɪ] *n* Altertum *nt*

antiseptic [æntɪ'septɪk] *n* Antiseptikum *nt* ♦ *adj* antiseptisch

antisocial ['æntɪ'səufəl] *adj* (*person*) ungesellig; (*law*) unsozial

antlers ['æntləz] *npl* Geweih *nt*

anus ['eɪnəs] *n* After *m*

anvil ['ænvɪl] *n* Amboss *m*

anxiety [æŋ'zaɪətɪ] *n* Angst *f*; (*worry*) Sorge *f*; **anxious** ['æŋkʃəs] *adj* ängstlich; (*worried*) besorgt; **to be anxious to do sth** etw unbedingt tun wollen

┌─────────────┐
│ **KEYWORD** │
└─────────────┘

any ['enɪ] *adj* **1** (*in questions etc*): **have you any butter?** haben Sie (etwas) Butter?; **have you any children?** haben Sie Kinder?; **if there are any tickets left** falls noch Karten da sind

2 (*with negative*): **I haven't any money/books** ich habe kein Geld/keine Bücher

3 (*no matter which*) jede(r, s) (beliebige); **any colour (at all)** jede beliebige Farbe; **choose any book you like** nehmen Sie ein beliebiges Buch

4 (*in phrases*): **in any case** in jedem Fall; **any day now** jeden Tag; **at any moment** jeden Moment; **at any rate** auf jeden Fall

♦ *pron* **1** (*in questions etc*): **have you got any?** haben Sie welche?; **can any of you sing?** kann (irgend)einer von euch singen?

2 (*with negative*): **I haven't any (of them)** ich habe keinen/keines (davon)

3 (*no matter which one(s)*): **take any of those books (you like)** nehmen Sie irgendeines dieser Bücher

♦ *adv* **1** (*in questions etc*): **do you want any more soup/sandwiches?** möchten Sie noch Suppe/Brote?; **are you feeling any better?** fühlen Sie sich etwas besser?

2 (*with negative*): **I can't hear him any more** ich kann ihn nicht mehr hören

anybody ['enɪbɔdɪ] *pron* (*no matter who*) jede(r); (*in questions etc*) (irgend)jemand, (irgend)eine(r); (*with negative*): **I can't see** ~ ich kann niemanden sehen

anyhow ['enɪhau] *adv* (*at any rate*): **I shall go** ~ ich gehe sowieso; (*haphazardly*): **do it** ~ machen Sie es, wie Sie wollen

anyone ['enɪwʌn] *pron* = **anybody**

┌─────────────┐
│ **KEYWORD** │
└─────────────┘

anything ['enɪθɪŋ] *pron* **1** (*in questions etc*) (irgend)etwas; **can you see anything?** können Sie etwas sehen?

2 (*with negative*): **I can't see anything** ich kann nichts sehen

3 (*no matter what*): **you can say anything you like** Sie können sagen, was Sie wollen; **anything will do** irgendetwas (wird genügen), irgendeine(r, s) (wird genügen); **he'll eat anything** er isst alles

anyway ['enɪweɪ] *adv* (*at any rate*) auf jeden Fall; (*besides*): ~, **I couldn't come even if I wanted to** jedenfalls könnte ich nicht kommen, selbst wenn ich wollte; **why are you phoning,** ~? warum rufst du überhaupt an?

anywhere ['enɪwɛə] *adv* (*in questions etc*) irgendwo; (: *with direction*) irgendwohin; (*no matter where*) überall, (: *with direction*) überallhin; (*with nega-*

tive): **I can't see him ~** ich kann ihn nirgendwo *or* nirgends sehen; **can you see him ~?** siehst du ihn irgendwo?; **put the books down ~** leg die Bücher irgendwohin

apart [ə'pɑːt] *adv* (*parted*) auseinander; (*away*) beiseite, abseits; **10 miles ~** 10 Meilen auseinander; **to take ~** auseinander nehmen; **~ from** *prep* außer

apartheid [ə'pɑːteɪt] *n* Apartheid *f*

apartment [ə'pɑːtmənt] *n* (*US*) *n* Wohnung *f*; **~ building** (*US*) *n* Wohnhaus *nt*

apathy ['æpəθɪ] *n* Teilnahmslosigkeit *f*, Apathie *f*

ape [eɪp] *n* (Menschen)affe *m* ♦ *vt* nachahmen

aperitif [ə'perɪtɪf] *n* Aperitif *m*

aperture ['æpətʃʊər] *n* Öffnung *f*; (*PHOT*) Blende *f*

APEX ['eɪpeks] *n abbr* (*AVIAT*: = *advance purchase excursion*) APEX (*im Voraus reservierte(r) Fahrkarte/Flugschein zu reduzierten Preisen*)

apex ['eɪpeks] *n* Spitze *f*

apiece [ə'piːs] *adv* pro Stück; (*per person*) pro Kopf

apologetic [əpɒlə'dʒetɪk] *adj* entschuldigend; **to be ~** sich sehr entschuldigen

apologize [ə'pɒlədʒaɪz] *vi*: **to ~ (for sth to sb)** sich (für etw bei jdm) entschuldigen; **apology** *n* Entschuldigung *f*

apostle [ə'pɒsl] *n* Apostel *m*

apostrophe [ə'pɒstrəfɪ] *n* Apostroph *m*

appal [ə'pɔːl] *vt* erschrecken; **~ling** *adj* schrecklich

apparatus [æpə'reɪtəs] *n* Gerät *nt*

apparel [ə'pærəl] (*US*) *n* Kleidung *f*

apparent [ə'pærənt] *adj* offenbar; **~ly** *adv* anscheinend

apparition [æpə'rɪʃən] *n* (*ghost*) Erscheinung *f*, Geist *m*

appeal [ə'piːl] *vi* dringend ersuchen; (*JUR*) Berufung einlegen ♦ *n* Aufruf *m*; (*JUR*) Berufung *f*; **to ~ for** dringend bit-

ten um; **to ~ to** sich wenden an +*acc*; (*to public*) appellieren an +*acc*; **it doesn't ~ to me** es gefällt mir nicht; **~ing** *adj* ansprechend

appear [ə'pɪər] *vi* (*come into sight*) erscheinen; (*be seen*) auftauchen; (*seem*) scheinen; **it would ~ that ...** anscheinend ...; **~ance** *n* (*coming into sight*) Erscheinen *nt*; (*outward show*) Äußere(s) *nt*

appease [ə'piːz] *vt* beschwichtigen

appendices [ə'pendɪsiːz] *npl of* **appendix**

appendicitis [əpendɪ'saɪtɪs] *n* Blinddarmentzündung *f*

appendix [ə'pendɪks] (*pl* **appendices**) *n* (*in book*) Anhang *m*; (*MED*) Blinddarm *m*

appetite ['æpɪtaɪt] *n* Appetit *m*; (*fig*) Lust *f*

appetizer ['æpɪtaɪzər] *n* Appetitanreger *m*; **appetizing** ['æpɪtaɪzɪŋ] *adj* appetitanregend

applaud [ə'plɔːd] *vi* Beifall klatschen, applaudieren ♦ *vt* Beifall klatschen +*dat*; **applause** [ə'plɔːz] *n* Beifall *m*, Applaus *m*

apple ['æpl] *n* Apfel *m*; **~ tree** *n* Apfelbaum *m*

appliance [ə'plaɪəns] *n* Gerät *nt*

applicable [ə'plɪkəbl] *adj* anwendbar; (*in forms*) zutreffend

applicant ['æplɪkənt] *n* Bewerber(in) *m(f)*

application [æplɪ'keɪʃən] *n* (*request*) Antrag *m*; (*for job*) Bewerbung *f*; (*putting into practice*) Anwendung *f*; (*hard work*) Fleiß *m*; **~ form** *n* Bewerbungsformular *nt*

applied [ə'plaɪd] *adj* angewandt

apply [ə'plaɪ] *vi* (*be suitable*) zutreffen; (*ask*): **to ~ (to)** sich wenden an +*acc*; (*request*): **to ~ for** sich melden für +*acc* ♦ *vt* (*place on*) auflegen; (*cream*) auftragen; (*put into practice*) anwenden; **to ~ for sth** sich um etw bewerben; **to ~ o.s. to sth** sich bei etw anstrengen

appoint [ə'pɔɪnt] vt (to office) ernennen, berufen; (settle) festsetzen; **~ment** n (meeting) Verabredung f; (at hairdresser etc) Bestellung f; (in business) Termin m; (choice for a position) Ernennung f; (UNIV) Berufung f

appraisal [ə'preɪzl] n Beurteilung f

appreciable [ə'priːʃəbl] adj (perceptible) merklich; (able to be estimated) abschätzbar

appreciate [ə'priːʃɪeɪt] vt (value) zu schätzen wissen; (understand) einsehen ♦ vi (increase in value) im Wert steigen; **appreciation** [əpriːʃɪ'eɪʃən] n Wertschätzung f; (COMM) Wertzuwachs m; **appreciative** [ə'priːʃɪətɪv] adj (showing thanks) dankbar; (showing liking) anerkennend

apprehend [æprɪ'hend] vt (arrest) festnehmen; (understand) erfassen

apprehension [æprɪ'henʃən] n Angst f

apprehensive [æprɪ'hensɪv] adj furchtsam

apprentice [ə'prentɪs] n Lehrling m; **~ship** n Lehrzeit f

approach [ə'prəʊtʃ] vi sich nähern ♦ vt herantreten an +acc; (problem) herangehen an +acc ♦ n Annäherung f; (to problem) Ansatz m; (path) Zugang m, Zufahrt f; **~able** adj zugänglich

appropriate [adj ə'prəʊprɪɪt, vb ə'prəʊprɪeɪt] adj angemessen; (remark) angebracht ♦ vt (take for o.s.) sich aneignen; (set apart) bereitstellen

approval [ə'pruːvl] n (show of satisfaction) Beifall m; (permission) Billigung f; **on ~** (COMM) bei Gefallen

approve [ə'pruːv] vt, vi billigen; **I don't ~ of it/him** ich halte nichts davon/von ihm; **~d school** (BRIT) n Erziehungsheim nt

approximate [adj ə'prɒksɪmɪt, vb ə'prɒksɪmeɪt] adj annähernd, ungefähr ♦ vi nahe kommen +dat; **~ly** adv rund, ungefähr

apricot ['eɪprɪkɒt] n Aprikose f

April ['eɪprəl] n April m; **~ Fools' Day**

n der erste April

apron ['eɪprən] n Schürze f

apt [æpt] adj (suitable) passend; (able) begabt; (likely): **to be ~ to do sth** dazu neigen, etw zu tun

aptitude ['æptɪtjuːd] n Begabung f

aqualung ['ækwəlʌŋ] n Unterwasseratmungsgerät nt

aquarium [ə'kweərɪəm] n Aquarium nt

Aquarius [ə'kweərɪəs] n Wassermann m

aquatic [ə'kwætɪk] adj Wasser-

Arab ['ærəb] n Araber(in) m(f)

Arabia [ə'reɪbɪə] n Arabien nt; **~n** adj arabisch

Arabic ['ærəbɪk] adj arabisch ♦ n Arabisch nt

arable ['ærəbl] adj bebaubar, Kultur-

arbitrary ['ɑːbɪtrərɪ] adj willkürlich

arbitration [ɑːbɪ'treɪʃən] n Schlichtung f

arc [ɑːk] n Bogen m

arcade [ɑː'keɪd] n Säulengang m; (with video games) Spielhalle f

arch [ɑːtʃ] n Bogen m ♦ vt überwölben; (back) krumm machen

archaeologist [ɑːkɪ'ɒlədʒɪst] n Archäologe m

archaeology [ɑːkɪ'ɒlədʒɪ] n Archäologie f

archaic [ɑː'keɪɪk] adj altertümlich

archbishop [ɑːtʃ'bɪʃəp] n Erzbischof m

archenemy [ɑːtʃ'enəmɪ] n Erzfeind m

archeology etc [ɑːkɪ'ɒlədʒɪ] (US) = **archaeology** etc

archery ['ɑːtʃərɪ] n Bogenschießen nt

architect ['ɑːkɪtekt] n Architekt(in) m(f); **~ural** [ɑːkɪ'tektʃərəl] adj architektonisch; **~ure** n Architektur f

archives ['ɑːkaɪvz] npl Archiv nt

archway ['ɑːtʃweɪ] n Bogen m

Arctic ['ɑːktɪk] adj arktisch ♦ n: **the ~** die Arktis

ardent ['ɑːdənt] adj glühend

arduous ['ɑːdjuəs] adj mühsam

are [ɑː] see **be**

area ['eərɪə] n Fläche f; (of land) Gebiet

nt; (part of sth) Teil m, Abschnitt m

arena [əˈriːnə] n Arena f

aren't [ɑːnt] = are not

Argentina [ɑːdʒənˈtiːnə] n Argentinien nt; **Argentinian** [ɑːdʒənˈtɪnɪən] adj argentinisch ♦ n Argentinier(in) m(f)

arguably [ˈɑːɡjuəblɪ] adv wohl

argue [ˈɑːɡjuː] vi diskutieren, (angrily) streiten; **argument** n (theory) Argument nt; (reasoning) Argumentation f; (row) Auseinandersetzung f, Streit m; **to have an argument** sich streiten; **argumentative** [ɑːɡjuˈmɛntətɪv] adj streitlustig

aria [ˈɑːrɪə] n Arie f

Aries [ˈɛərɪz] n Widder m

arise [əˈraɪz] (pt arose, pp arisen) vi aufsteigen; (get up) aufstehen; (difficulties etc) entstehen; (case) vorkommen; **to ~ from sth** herrühren von etw; **~n** [əˈrɪzn] pp of arise

aristocracy [ærɪsˈtɒkrəsɪ] n Adel m, Aristokratie f; **aristocrat** [ˈærɪstəkræt] n Adlige(r) f(m), Aristokrat(in) m(f)

arithmetic [əˈrɪθmətɪk] n Rechnen nt, Arithmetik f

arm [ɑːm] n Arm m; (branch of military service) Zweig m ♦ vt bewaffnen; **~s** npl (weapons) Waffen pl

armaments [ˈɑːməmənts] npl Aus-rüstung f

armchair [ˈɑːmtʃɛəʳ] n Lehnstuhl m

armed [ɑːmd] adj (forces) Streit-, be-waffnet; **~ robbery** n bewaffnete(r) Raubüberfall m

armistice [ˈɑːmɪstɪs] n Waffenstillstand m

armour [ˈɑːməʳ] n (US **armor**) n (knight's) Rüstung f; (MIL) Panzerplatte f; **~ed car** n Panzerwagen m

armpit [ˈɑːmpɪt] n Achselhöhle f

armrest [ˈɑːmrɛst] n Armlehne f

army [ˈɑːmɪ] n Armee f, Heer nt; (host) Heer nt

aroma [əˈrəumə] n Duft m, Aroma nt; **~therapy** [ərəuməˈθerəpɪ] n Aroma-therapie f; **~tic** [ærəˈmætɪk] adj aroma-

tisch, würzig

arose [əˈrəuz] pt of **arise**

around [əˈraund] adv ringsherum; (al-most) ungefähr ♦ prep um ... herum; **is he ~?** ist er hier?

arrange [əˈreɪndʒ] vt (time, meeting) festsetzen; (holidays) festlegen; (flow-ers, hair, objects) anordnen; **I ~d to meet him** ich habe mit ihm ausge-macht, ihn zu treffen; **it's all ~d** es ist alles arrangiert; **~ment** n (order) Rei-henfolge f; (agreement) Vereinbarung f; **~ments** npl (plans) Pläne pl

array [əˈreɪ] n (collection) Ansammlung f

arrears [əˈrɪəz] npl (of debts) Rückstand m; (of work) Unerledigte(s) nt; **in ~** im Rückstand

arrest [əˈrɛst] vt (person) verhaften; (stop) aufhalten ♦ n Verhaftung f; **un-der ~** in Haft

arrival [əˈraɪvl] n Ankunft f

arrive [əˈraɪv] vi ankommen; **to ~ at** ankommen in +dat, ankommen bei

arrogance [ˈærəɡəns] n Überheblichkeit f, Arroganz f; **arro-gant** [ˈærəɡənt] adj überheblich, arro-gant

arrow [ˈærəu] n Pfeil m

arse [ɑːs] (inf!) n Arsch m (!)

arsenal [ˈɑːsɪnl] n Waffenlager nt, Zeughaus nt

arsenic [ˈɑːsnɪk] n Arsen nt

arson [ˈɑːsn] n Brandstiftung f

art [ɑːt] n Kunst f; **A~s** npl (UNIV) Geisteswissenschaften pl

artery [ˈɑːtərɪ] n Schlagader f, Arterie f

art gallery n Kunstgalerie f

arthritis [ɑːˈθraɪtɪs] n Arthritis f

artichoke [ˈɑːtɪtʃəuk] n Artischocke f; **Jerusalem ~** Erdartischocke f

article [ˈɑːtɪkl] n (PRESS, GRAM) Artikel m; (thing) Gegenstand m, Artikel m; (clause) Abschnitt m, Paragraf m; **~ of clothing** Kleidungsstück nt

articulate [adj ɑːˈtɪkjulɪt, vb ɑːˈtɪkjuleɪt] adj (able to express o.s.) redegewandt; (*speaking clearly*) deutlich, verständlich ♦ *vt* (*connect*) zusammenfügen, gliedern; **to be ~** sich gut ausdrücken können; **~d vehicle** *n* Sattelschlepper *m*

artificial [ɑːtɪˈfɪʃəl] *adj* künstlich, Kunst-; **~ respiration** *n* künstliche Atmung *f*

artisan [ˈɑːtɪzæn] *n* gelernte(r) Handwerker *m*

artist [ˈɑːtɪst] *n* Künstler(in) *m(f)*; **~ic** [ɑːˈtɪstɪk] *adj* künstlerisch; **~ry** *n* künstlerische(s) Können *nt*

art school *n* Kunsthochschule *f*

KEYWORD

as [æz] *conj* **1** (*referring to time*) als; **as the years went by** mit den Jahren; **he came in as I was leaving** als er hereinkam, ging ich gerade; **as from tomorrow** ab morgen

2 (*in comparisons*): **as big as** so groß wie; **twice as big as** zweimal so groß wie; **as much/many as** so viel/so viele wie; **as soon as** sobald

3 (*since, because*) da; **he left early as he had to be home by 10** er ging früher, da er um 10 zu Hause sein musste

4 (*referring to manner, way*) wie; **do as you wish** mach was du willst; **as she said** wie sie sagte

5 (*concerning*): **as for** *or* **though as** das betrifft *or* angeht

6: **as if** *or* **though** als ob

♦ *prep als; see also* **long**; **he works as a driver** er arbeitet als Fahrer; *see also* **such**; **he gave it to me as a present** er hat es mir als Geschenk gegeben; *see also* **well**

---

a.s.a.p. *abbr* = **as soon as possible**

asbestos [æzˈbestəs] *n* Asbest *m*

ascend [əˈsend] *vi* aufsteigen ♦ *vt* besteigen; **ascent** *n* Aufstieg *m*; Besteigung *f*

ascertain [æsəˈteɪn] *vt* feststellen

ascribe [əˈskraɪb] *vt*: **to ~ sth to sth /sth to sb** etw einer Sache/jdm etw zuschreiben

ash [æʃ] *n* Asche *f*; (*tree*) Esche *f*

ashamed [əˈʃeɪmd] *adj* beschämt; **to be ~ of** sich für etw schämen

ashen [ˈæʃən] *adj* (*pale*) aschfahl

ashore [əˈʃɔː] *adv* an Land

ashtray [ˈæʃtreɪ] *n* Aschenbecher *m*

Ash Wednesday *n* Aschermittwoch *m*

Asia [ˈeɪʃə] *n* Asien *nt*; **~n** *adj* asiatisch ♦ *n* Asiat(in) *m(f)*

aside [əˈsaɪd] *adv* beiseite

ask [ɑːsk] *vt* fragen; (*permission*) bitten um; **~ him his name** frage ihn nach seinem Namen; **he ~ed to see you** er wollte dich sehen; **to ~ sb to do sth** jdn bitten, etw zu tun; **to ~ sb about sth** jdn nach etw fragen; **to ~ (sb) a question** (jdn) etwas fragen; **to ~ sb out to dinner** jdn zum Essen einladen; **~ after** *vt fus* fragen nach; **~ for** *vt fus* bitten um

askance [əˈskɑːns] *adv*: **to look ~ at sb** jdn schief ansehen

asking price [ˈɑːskɪŋ-] *n* Verkaufspreis *m*

asleep [əˈsliːp] *adj*: **to be ~** schlafen; **to fall ~** einschlafen

asparagus [əsˈpærəgəs] *n* Spargel *m*

aspect [ˈæspekt] *n* Aspekt *m*

aspersions [əsˈpɜːʃənz] *npl*: **to cast ~ on sb/sth** sich abfällig über jdn/etw äußern

asphyxiation [æsfɪksɪˈeɪʃən] *n* Erstickung *f*

aspirations [æspəˈreɪʃənz] *npl*: **to have ~ towards sth** etw anstreben

aspire [əsˈpaɪə] *vi*: **to ~ to** streben nach

aspirin [ˈæsprɪn] *n* Aspirin *nt*

ass [æs] *n* (*also fig*) Esel *m*; (*US: inf!*) Arsch *m* (*!*)

assailant [əˈseɪlənt] *n* Angreifer *m*

assassin [əˈsæsɪn] *n* Attentäter(in) *m(f)*; **~ate** *vt* ermorden; **~ation** [əsæsɪˈneɪʃən] *n* (geglückte(s)) Attentat *nt*

assault [ə'sɔːlt] *n* Angriff *m* ♦ *vt* überfallen; *(woman)* herfallen über +acc

assemble [ə'sɛmbl] *vt* versammeln; *(parts)* zusammensetzen ♦ *vi* sich versammeln; **assembly** *n (meeting)* Versammlung *f*, *(construction)* Zusammensetzung *f*, Montage *f*; **assembly line** *n* Fließband *nt*

assent [ə'sɛnt] *n* Zustimmung *f*

assert [ə'sɜːt] *vt* erklären; **~ion** *n* Behauptung *f*

assess [ə'sɛs] *vt* schätzen; **~ment** *n* Bewertung *f*, Einschätzung *f*; **~or** *n* Steuerberater *m*

asset [ˈæset] *n* Vorteil *m*, Wert *m*; **~s** *pl* *(FIN)* Vermögen *nt*; *(estate)* Nachlass *m*

assign [ə'saɪn] *vt* zuweisen; **~ment** *n* Aufgabe *f*, Auftrag *m*

assimilate [ə'sɪmɪleɪt] *vt* sich aneignen, aufnehmen

assist [ə'sɪst] *vt* beistehen +*dat*; **~ance** *n* Unterstützung *f*, Hilfe *f*; **~ant** *n* Assistent(in) *m(f)*, Mitarbeiter(in) *m(f)*; *(BRIT: also:* **shop ~ant)** Verkäufer(in) *m(f)*

associate [*n* ə'səʊʃɪt, *vb* ə'səʊʃɪeɪt] *n (partner)* Kollege *m*, Teilhaber *m*; *(member)* außerordentliche(s) Mitglied *nt* ♦ *vt* verbinden ♦ *vi (keep company)* verkehren; **association** [əsəʊsɪ'eɪʃən] *n* Verband *m*, Verein *m*; *(PSYCH)* Assoziation *f*; *(link)* Verbindung *f*

assorted [ə'sɔːtɪd] *adj* gemischt

assortment [ə'sɔːtmənt] *n* Sammlung *f*; *(COMM):* **~ (of)** Sortiment *nt* (von), Auswahl *f* (an +*dat*)

assume [ə'sjuːm] *vt (take for granted)* annehmen; *(put on)* annehmen, sich geben; **~d name** *n* Deckname *m*

assumption [ə'sʌmpʃən] *n* Annahme *f*

assurance [ə'ʃʊərəns] *n (firm statement)* Versicherung *f*, *(confidence)* Selbstsicherheit *f*; *(insurance)* (Lebens)versicherung *f*

assure [ə'ʃʊə^r] *vt (make sure)* sicherstel-

len; *(convince)* versichern +*dat*; *(life)* versichern

asterisk [ˈæstərɪsk] *n* Sternchen *nt*

asthma [ˈæsmə] *n* Asthma *nt*

astonish [ə'stɒnɪʃ] *vt* erstaunen; **~ment** *n* Erstaunen *nt*

astound [ə'staʊnd] *vt* verblüffen

astray [ə'streɪ] *adv* in die Irre; auf Abwege; **to go ~** *(go wrong)* sich vertun; **to lead ~** irreführen

astride [ə'straɪd] *adv* rittlings ♦ *prep* rittlings auf

astrologer [əs'trɒlədʒə^r] *n* Astrologe *m*, Astrologin *f*; **astrology** *n* Astrologie *f*

astronaut [ˈæstrənɔːt] *n* Astronaut(in) *m(f)*

astronomer [əs'trɒnəmə^r] *n* Astronom *m*

astronomical [æstrə'nɒmɪkl] *adj* astronomisch; *(success)* riesig

astronomy [əs'trɒnəmɪ] *n* Astronomie *f*

astute [əs'tjuːt] *adj* scharfsinnig; schlau, gerissen

asylum [ə'saɪləm] *n (home)* Heim *nt*; *(refuge)* Asyl *nt*

KEYWORD

at [æt] *prep* **1** *(referring to position, direction)* an +*dat*, bei +*dat*; *(with place)* in +*dat*; **at the top** an der Spitze; **at home/school** zu Hause/in der Schule; **at the baker's** beim Bäcker; **to look at sth** auf etw *acc* blicken; **to throw sth at sb** etw nach jdm werfen

2 *(referring to time):* **at 4 o'clock** um 4 Uhr; **at night** bei Nacht; **at Christmas** zu Weihnachten; **at times** manchmal

3 *(referring to rates, speed etc):* **at £1 a kilo** zu £1 pro Kilo; **two at a time** zwei auf einmal; **at 50 km/h** mit 50 km/h

4 *(referring to manner):* **at a stroke** mit einem Schlag; **at peace** in Frieden

5 *(referring to activity):* **to be at work** bei der Arbeit sein; **to play at cow-**

boys Cowboy spielen; **to be good at sth** gut in etw dat sein
6 (referring to cause): **shocked/ surprised/annoyed at sth** schockiert/überrascht/verärgert über etw acc; **I went at his suggestion** ich ging auf seinen Vorschlag hin

ate [eɪt] pt of **eat**
atheist ['eɪθɪɪst] n Atheist(in) m(f)
Athens ['æθɪnz] n Athen nt
athlete ['æθliːt] n Athlet m, Sportler m
athletic [æθ'letɪk] adj sportlich, athletisch; **~s** n Leichtathletik f
Atlantic [ət'læntɪk] adj atlantisch ♦ n: **the ~ (Ocean)** der Atlantik
atlas ['ætləs] n Atlas m
ATM abbr (= automated teller machine) Geldautomat m
atmosphere ['ætməsfɪə'] n Atmosphäre f
atom ['ætəm] n Atom nt; (fig) bisschen nt; **~ic** [ə'tɒmɪk] adj atomar, Atom-; **~(ic) bomb** n Atombombe f
atomizer ['ætəmaɪzə'] n Zerstäuber m
atone [ə'təun] vi sühnen; **to ~ for sth** etw sühnen
atrocious [ə'trəʊʃəs] adj grässlich
atrocity [ə'trɒsɪtɪ] n Scheußlichkeit f; (deed) Gräueltat f
attach [ə'tætʃ] vt (fasten) befestigen; **to be ~ed to sb/sth** an jdm/etw hängen; **to ~ importance** etc **to sth** Wichtigkeit etc auf etw acc legen, einer Sache dat Wichtigkeit etc beimessen
attaché case [ə'tæʃeɪ] n Aktenkoffer m
attachment [ə'tætʃmənt] n (tool) Zubehörteil nt; (love): **~ (to sb)** Zuneigung f (zu jdm)
attack [ə'tæk] vt angreifen ♦ n Angriff m; (MED) Anfall m; **~er** n Angreifer(in) m(f)
attain [ə'teɪn] vt erreichen; **~ments** npl Kenntnisse pl
attempt [ə'tempt] n Versuch m ♦ vt versuchen; **~ed murder** Mordversuch m

attend [ə'tend] vt (go to) teilnehmen (an +dat); (lectures) besuchen; **to ~ to** (needs) nachkommen +dat; (person) sich kümmern um; **~ance** n (presence) Anwesenheit f; (people present) Besucherzahl f; **good ~ance** gute Teilnahme; **~ant** n (companion) Begleiter(in) m(f); Gesellschafter(in) m(f); (in car park etc) Wächter(in) m(f); (servant) Bedienstete(r) mf ♦ adj begleitend; (fig) damit verbunden
attention [ə'tenʃən] n Aufmerksamkeit f; (care) Fürsorge f; (for machine etc) Pflege f ♦ excl (MIL) Achtung!; **for the ~ of ...** zu Händen (von) ...
attentive [ə'tentɪv] adj aufmerksam
attic ['ætɪk] n Dachstube f, Mansarde f
attitude ['ætɪtjuːd] n (mental) Einstellung f
attorney [ə'tɜːnɪ] n (solicitor) Rechtsanwalt m; **A~ General** n Justizminister m
attract [ə'trækt] vt anziehen; (attention) erregen; **~ion** n Anziehungskraft f; (thing) Attraktion f; **~ive** adj attraktiv
attribute [n 'ætrɪbjuːt, vb ə'trɪbjuːt] n Eigenschaft f, Attribut nt ♦ vt zuschreiben
attrition [ə'trɪʃən] n: **war of ~** Zermürbungskrieg m
aubergine ['əʊbəʒiːn] n Aubergine f
auburn ['ɔːbən] adj kastanienbraun
auction ['ɔːkʃən] n (also: **sale by ~**) Versteigerung f, Auktion f ♦ vt versteigern; **~eer** [ɔːkʃə'nɪə'] n Versteigerer m
audacity [ɔː'dæsɪtɪ] n (boldness) Wagemut m; (impudence) Unverfrorenheit f
audible ['ɔːdɪbl] adj hörbar
audience ['ɔːdɪəns] n Zuhörer pl, Zuschauer pl; (with queen) Audienz f
audiotypist ['ɔːdɪəʊ'taɪpɪst] n Phonotypistin f, Fonotypistin f
audiovisual ['ɔːdɪəʊ'vɪzjuəl] adj audiovisuell
audit ['ɔːdɪt] vt prüfen
audition [ɔː'dɪʃən] n Probe f
auditor ['ɔːdɪtə'] n (accountant) Rech-

nungsprüfer(in) m(f), Buchprüfer m

auditorium [ɔːdɪˈtɔːrɪəm] n Zuschauerraum m

augment [ɔːgˈment] vt vermehren

augur [ˈɔːɡəˈ] vi bedeuten, voraussagen; **this ~s well** das ist ein gutes Omen

August [ˈɔːɡəst] n August m

aunt [ɑːnt] n Tante f; **~ie** n Tantchen nt; **~y** n = **auntie**

au pair [ˈəuˈpeəˈ] n (also: ~ **girl**) Aupairmädchen nt, Au-pair-Mädchen nt

aura [ˈɔːrə] n Nimbus m

auspicious [ɔːsˈpɪʃəs] adj günstig; verheißungsvoll

austere [ɒsˈtɪəˈ] adj streng; (room) nüchtern; **austerity** [ɒsˈterɪtɪ] n Strenge f; (POL) wirtschaftliche Einschränkung f

Australia [ɒsˈtreɪlɪə] n Australien f; **~n** adj australisch ♦ n Australier(in) m(f)

Austria [ˈɒstrɪə] n Österreich nt; **~n** adj österreichisch ♦ n Österreicher(in) m(f)

authentic [ɔːˈθentɪk] adj echt, authentisch

author [ˈɔːθəˈ] n Autor m, Schriftsteller m; (beginner) Urheber m, Schöpfer m

authoritarian [ɔːθɔrɪˈteərɪən] adj autoritär

authoritative [ɔːˈθɔrɪtətɪv] adj (account) maßgeblich; (manner) herrisch

authority [ɔːˈθɔrɪtɪ] n (power) Autorität f; (expert) Autorität f, Fachmann m; **the authorities** npl (ruling body) die Behörden pl

authorize [ˈɔːθəraɪz] vt bevollmächtigen; (permit) genehmigen

auto [ˈɔːtəu] (US) n Auto nt, Wagen m

autobiography [ɔːtəbaɪˈɔɡrəfɪ] n Autobiografie f

autograph [ˈɔːtəɡrɑːf] n (of celebrity) Autogramm nt ♦ vt mit Autogramm versehen

automatic [ɔːtəˈmætɪk] adj automatisch ♦ n (gun) Selbstladepistole f; (car) Automatik m; **~ally** adv automatisch

automation [ɔːtəˈmeɪʃən] n Automati-

sierung f

automobile [ˈɔːtəməbiːl] (US) n Auto(mobil) nt

autonomous [ɔːˈtɔnəməs] adj autonom; **autonomy** n Autonomie f

autumn [ˈɔːtəm] n Herbst m

auxiliary [ɔːɡˈzɪlɪərɪ] adj Hilfs-

Av. abbr = **avenue**

avail [əˈveɪl] vt: **to ~ o.s. of sth** sich einer Sache gen bedienen ♦ n: **to no ~** nutzlos

availability [əveɪləˈbɪlɪtɪ] n Erhältlichkeit f, Vorhandensein nt

available [əˈveɪləbl] adj erhältlich; zur Verfügung stehend; (person) erreichbar, abkömmlich

avalanche [ˈævəlɑːnʃ] n Lawine f

Ave. abbr = **avenue**

avenge [əˈvendʒ] vt rächen, sühnen

avenue [ˈævənjuː] n Allee f

average [ˈævərɪdʒ] n Durchschnitt m ♦ adj durchschnittlich, Durchschnitts- ♦ vt (figures) den Durchschnitt nehmen von; (perform) durchschnittlich leisten; (in car etc) im Schnitt fahren; **on ~** im Durchschnitt; **~ out** vi: **to ~ out at** im Durchschnitt betragen

averse [əˈvəːs] adj: **to be ~ to doing sth** eine Abneigung dagegen haben, etw zu tun

avert [əˈvəːt] vt (turn away) abkehren; (prevent) abwehren

aviary [ˈeɪvɪərɪ] n Vogelhaus m

aviation [eɪvɪˈeɪʃən] n Luftfahrt f, Flugwesen nt

avid [ˈævɪd] adj: **~ (for)** gierig (auf +acc)

avocado [ævəˈkɑːdəu] n (BRIT: also: ~ **pear**) Avocado(birne) f

avoid [əˈvɔɪd] vt vermeiden

await [əˈweɪt] vt erwarten, entgegensehen +dat

awake [əˈweɪk] (pt **awoke**, pp **awoken** or **awaked**) adj wach ♦ vt (auf)wecken ♦ vi aufwachen; **to be ~** wach sein; **~ning** n Erwachen nt

award [əˈwɔːd] n (prize) Preis m ♦ vt: **to**

~ (sb sth) (jdm etw) zuerkennen

aware [ə'wɛə*] adj bewusst; **to be ~** sich bewusst sein; **~ness** n Bewusstsein nt

awash [ə'wɒʃ] adj überflutet

away [ə'weɪ] adv weg, fort; **two hours ~ by car** zwei Autostunden entfernt; **the holiday was two weeks ~** es war noch zwei Wochen bis zum Urlaub; **two kilometres ~** zwei Kilometer entfernt; **~ match** (SPORT) Auswärtsspiel nt

awe [ɔː] n Ehrfurcht f; **~-inspiring** adj Ehrfurcht gebietend; **~some** adj Ehrfurcht gebietend

awful ['ɔːfəl] adj (very bad) furchtbar; **~ly** adv furchtbar, sehr

awhile [ə'waɪl] adv eine Weile

awkward ['ɔːkwəd] adj (clumsy) ungeschickt, linkisch; (embarrassing) peinlich

awning ['ɔːnɪŋ] n Markise f

awoke [ə'wəʊk] pt of **awake**; **~n** pp of **awake**

awry [ə'raɪ] adv schief; (plans) schief gehen

axe [æks] (US **ax**) n Axt f, Beil nt ♦ vt (end suddenly) streichen

axes[1] ['æksɪz] npl of **axe**

axes[2] ['æksiːz] npl of **axis**

axis ['æksɪs] (pl **axes**) n Achse f

axle ['æksl] n Achse f

ay(e) [aɪ] excl (yes) ja

azalea [ə'zeɪlɪə] n Azalee f

B, b

B [biː] n (MUS) H nt; **~ road** (BRIT) Landstraße f

B.A. n abbr = **Bachelor of Arts**

babble ['bæbl] vi schwätzen

baby ['beɪbɪ] n Baby nt; **~ carriage** (US) n Kinderwagen m; **~ food** n Babynahrung f; **~-sit** vi Kinder hüten, babysitten; **~-sitter** n Babysitter m; **~-sitting** n Babysitten nt, Babysitting nt; **~ wipe**

n Ölpflegetuch nt

bachelor ['bætʃələ*] n Junggeselle m; **B~ of Arts** Bakkalaureus m der philosophischen Fakultät; **B~ of Science** Bakkalaureus m der Naturwissenschaften

back [bæk] n (of person, horse) Rücken m; (of house) Rückseite f; (of train) Ende nt; (FOOTBALL) Verteidiger m ♦ vt (support) unterstützen; (bet) wetten auf +acc; (car) rückwärts fahren ♦ vi (go ~wards) rückwärts gehen or fahren ♦ adj hintere(r, s) ♦ adv zurück; (to the rear) nach hinten; **~ down** vi zurückstecken; **~ out** vi sich zurückziehen; (inf) kneifen; **~ up** vt (support) unterstützen; (car) zurücksetzen; (COMPUT) eine Sicherungskopie machen von; **~ache** n Rückenschmerzen pl; **~bencher** (BRIT) n Parlamentarier(in) m(f); **~bone** n Rückgrat nt; **~cloth** n Hintergrund m; **~date** vt rückdatieren; **~drop** n (THEAT) = **backcloth**; (~ground) Hintergrund m; **~fire** vi (plan) fehlschlagen; (TECH) fehlzünden; **~ground** n Hintergrund m; (person's education) Vorbildung f; **~ family ~ground** Familienverhältnisse pl; **~hand** n (TENNIS: also: **~hand stroke**) Rückhand f; **~hander** (BRIT) n (bribe) Schmiergeld nt; **~ing** n (support) Unterstützung f; **~lash** n (fig) Gegenschlag m; **~log** n (of work) Rückstand m; **~ number** n (PRESS) alte Nummer f; **~pack** n Rucksack m; **~packer** n Rucksacktourist(in) m(f); **~ pain** n Rückenschmerzen pl; **~ pay** n (Gehalts- or Lohn)nachzahlung f; **~ payments** npl Zahlungsrückstände pl; **~ seat** n (AUT) Rücksitz m; **~side** (inf) n Hintern m; **~stage** adv hinter den Kulissen; **~stroke** n Rückenschwimmen nt; **~up** adj (COMPUT) Sicherungs- ♦ n (COMPUT) Sicherungskopie f; **~ward** adj (less developed) zurückgeblieben; (primitive) rückständig; **~wards**

rückwärts; **~water** n (fig) Kaff nt; **~yard** n Hinterhof m

bacon ['beɪkən] n Schinkenspeck m

bacteria [bæk'tɪərɪə] npl Bakterien pl

bad [bæd] adj schlecht, schlimm; **to go ~** schlecht werden

bade [bæd] pt of **bid**

badge [bædʒ] n Abzeichen nt

badger ['bædʒə'] n Dachs m

badly ['bædlɪ] adv schlecht, schlimm; **~ wounded** schwer verwundet; **he needs it ~** er braucht es dringend; **to be ~ off (for money)** dringend Geld nötig haben

badminton ['bædmɪntən] n Federball m, Badminton nt

bad-tempered ['bæd'tempəd] adj schlecht gelaunt

baffle ['bæfl] vt (puzzle) verblüffen

bag [bæg] n (sack) Beutel m; (paper) Tüte f; (handbag) Tasche f; (suitcase) Koffer m; (inf: old woman) alte Schachtel f ♦ vt (put in sack) in einen Sack stecken; (hunting) erlegen; **~s of** (inf: lots of) eine Menge +acc; **~gage** ['bægɪdʒ] n Gepäck nt; **~ allowance** n Freigepäck nt; **~ reclaim** n Gepäckausgabe f; **~gy** ['bægɪ] adj bauschig, sackartig

bagpipes ['bægpaɪps] npl Dudelsack m

bail [beɪl] n (money) Kaution f ♦ vt (prisoner: usu: grant ~ to) gegen Kaution freilassen; (boat: also: ~ out) ausschöpfen; **on ~** (prisoner) gegen Kaution freigelassen; **to ~ sb out** die Kaution für jdn stellen; see also **bale**

bailiff ['beɪlɪf] n Gerichtsvollzieher(in) m(f)

bait [beɪt] n Köder m ♦ vt mit einem Köder versehen; (fig) ködern

bake [beɪk] vt, vi backen; **~d beans** gebackene Bohnen pl; **~d potatoes** npl in der Schale gebackene Kartoffeln pl; **~r** n Bäcker m; **~ry** n Bäckerei f; **baking** n Backen nt; **baking powder** n Backpulver nt

balance ['bæləns] n (scales) Waage f;

(equilibrium) Gleichgewicht nt; (FIN: state of account) Saldo m; (difference) Bilanz f; (amount remaining) Restbetrag m ♦ vt (weigh) wägen; (make equal) ausgleichen; **~ of trade/payments** Handels-/Zahlungsbilanz f; **~d** adj ausgeglichen; **~ sheet** n Bilanz f, Rechnungsabschluss m

balcony ['bælkənɪ] n Balkon m

bald [bɔːld] adj kahl; (statement) knapp

bale [beɪl] n Ballen m; **bale out** vi (from a plane) abspringen

ball [bɔːl] n Ball m; **~ bearing** n Kugellager m

ballet ['bæleɪ] n Ballett nt; **~ dancer** n Ballett(tänzer(in) m(f); **~ shoe** n Ballettschuh m

balloon [bə'luːn] n (Luft)ballon m

ballot ['bælət] n (geheime) Abstimmung f

ballpoint (pen) ['bɔːlpɔɪnt-] n Kugelschreiber m

ballroom ['bɔːlrum] n Tanzsaal m

Baltic ['bɔːltɪk] n: **the ~ (Sea)** die Ostsee

bamboo [bæm'buː] n Bambus m

ban [bæn] n Verbot nt ♦ vt verbieten

banana [bə'nɑːnə] n Banane f

band [bænd] n Band f; (group) Gruppe f; (of criminals) Bande f; (MUS) Kapelle f, Band f; **~ together** vi sich zusammentun

bandage ['bændɪdʒ] n Verband m; (elastic) Bandage f ♦ vt (cut) verbinden; (broken limb) bandagieren

Bandaid ['bændeɪd] n (® US) Heftpflaster nt

bandit ['bændɪt] n Bandit m, Räuber m

bandwagon ['bændwægən] n: **to jump on the ~** (fig) auf den fahrenden Zug aufspringen

bandy ['bændɪ] vt wechseln; **~-legged** adj o-beinig, O-beinig

bang [bæŋ] n (explosion) Knall m; (blow) Hieb m ♦ vt, vi knallen

Bangladesh [bæŋglə'deʃ] n Bangladesch nt

bangle

bangle ['bæŋgl] n Armspange f

bangs [bæŋz] (US) npl (fringe) Pony m

banish ['bænɪʃ] vt verbannen

banister(s) ['bænɪstə(z)] n(pl) (Treppen)geländer nt

bank [bæŋk] n (raised ground) Erdwall m; (of lake etc) Ufer nt; (FIN) Bank f ♦ vt (tilt: AVIAT) in die Kurve bringen; (money) einzahlen; ~ **on** vt fus: **to ~ on** sth mit etw rechnen; ~ **account** n Bankkonto nt; ~ **card** n Scheckkarte f; ~**er** n Bankier m; ~**er's card** (BRIT) n = **bank card; B~ holiday** (BRIT) n gesetzliche(r) Feiertag m; ~**ing** n Bankwesen nt; ~**note** n Banknote f; ~ **rate** n Banksatz m

---

bank holiday

Als **bank holiday** wird in Großbritannien ein gesetzlicher Feiertag bezeichnet, an dem die Banken geschlossen sind. Die meisten dieser Feiertage, abgesehen von Weihnachten und Ostern, fallen auf Montage im Mai und August. An diesen langen Wochenenden (bank holiday weekends) fahren viele Briten in Urlaub, so dass dann auf den Straßen, Flughäfen und bei der Bahn sehr viel Betrieb ist.

---

bankrupt ['bæŋkrʌpt] adj: **to be ~** bankrott sein; **to go ~** Bankrott machen; ~**cy** n Bankrott m

bank statement n Kontoauszug m

banned [bænd] adj: **he was ~ from driving** (BRIT) ihm wurde Fahrverbot erteilt

banner ['bænə] n Banner nt

banns [bænz] npl Aufgebot nt

baptism ['bæptɪzəm] n Taufe f

baptize [bæp'taɪz] vt taufen

bar [bɑː] n (rod) Stange f; (obstacle) Hindernis nt; (of chocolate) Tafel f; (of soap) Stück nt; (for food, drink) Buffet nt, Bar f; (pub) Wirtschaft f; (MUS) Takt(strich) m ♦ vt (fasten) verriegeln; (hinder) versperren; (exclude) ausschlie-

barrister

ßen; **behind ~s** hinter Gittern; **the B~: to be called to the B~** als Anwalt zugelassen werden; ~ **none** ohne Ausnahme

barbaric [bɑː'bærɪk] adj primitiv, unkultiviert

barbecue ['bɑːbɪkjuː] n Barbecue nt

barbed wire ['bɑːbd-] n Stacheldraht m

barber ['bɑːbə] n Herrenfriseur m

bar code n (COMM) Registrierkode f

bare [bɛə] adj nackt; (trees, country) kahl; (mere) bloß ♦ vt entblößen; ~**back** adv ungesattelt; ~**faced** adj unverfroren; ~**foot** adj, adv barfuß; ~**ly** adv kaum, knapp

bargain ['bɑːgɪn] n (sth cheap) günstiger Kauf; (agreement: written) Kaufvertrag m; (: oral) Geschäft nt; **into the ~** obendrein; ~ **for** vt: **he got more than he ~ed for** er erlebte sein blaues Wunder

barge [bɑːdʒ] n Lastkahn m; ~ **in** vi hereinplatzen; ~ **into** vt rennen gegen

bark [bɑːk] n (of tree) Rinde f; (of dog) Bellen nt ♦ vi (dog) bellen

barley ['bɑːlɪ] n Gerste f; ~ **sugar** n Malzbonbon nt

bar: ~maid n Bardame f; ~**man** (irreg) n Barkellner m; ~ **meal** n einfaches Essen in einem Pub

barn [bɑːn] n Scheune f

barometer [bə'rɒmɪtə] n Barometer nt

baron ['bærən] n Baron m; ~**ess** n Baronin f

barracks ['bærəks] npl Kaserne f

barrage ['bærɑːʒ] n (gunfire) Sperrfeuer nt; (dam) Staudamm m; Talsperre f

barrel ['bærəl] n Fass nt; (of gun) Lauf m

barren ['bærən] adj unfruchtbar

barricade [bærɪ'keɪd] n Barrikade f ♦ vt verbarrikadieren

barrier ['bærɪə] n (obstruction) Hindernis nt; (fence) Schranke f

barring ['bɑːrɪŋ] prep außer im Falle +gen

barrister ['bærɪstə] (BRIT) n Rechtsanwalt m

barrow ['bærəʊ] n (cart) Schubkarren m

bartender ['bɑːtɛndər] (US) n Barmann or -kellner m

barter ['bɑːtər] vt handeln

base [beɪs] n (bottom) Boden m, Basis f; (MIL) Stützpunkt m ♦ vt gründen; (opinion, theory): **to be ~d on** basieren auf +dat ♦ adj (low) gemein; **I'm ~d in London** ich wohne in London; **~ball** ['beɪsbɔːl] n Baseball nt; **~ment** ['beɪsmənt] n Kellergeschoss nt

bases¹ ['beɪsɪz] npl of **base**

bases² ['beɪsiːz] npl of **basis**

bash [bæʃ] (inf) vt (heftig) schlagen

bashful ['bæʃfʊl] adj schüchtern

basic ['beɪsɪk] adj grundlegend; **~s** npl: **the ~s** das Wesentliche sg; **~ally** adv im Grunde

basil ['bæzl] n Basilikum nt

basin ['beɪsn] n (dish) Schüssel f; (for washing, also valley) Becken nt; (dock) (Trocken)becken nt

basis ['beɪsɪs] (pl **bases**) n Basis f, Grundlage f

bask [bɑːsk] vi: **to ~ in the sun** sich sonnen

basket ['bɑːskɪt] n Korb m; **~ball** n Basketball m

bass [beɪs] n (MUS, also instrument) Bass m; (voice) Bassstimme f; **~ drum** n große Trommel

bassoon [bə'suːn] n Fagott nt

bastard ['bɑːstəd] n Bastard m; (inf!) Arschloch nt (!)

bat [bæt] n (SPORT) Schlagholz nt, Schläger m; (ZOOL) Fledermaus f ♦ vt: **he didn't ~ an eyelid** er hat nicht mit der Wimper gezuckt

batch [bætʃ] n (of letters) Stoß m; (of samples) Satz m

bated ['beɪtɪd] adj: **with ~ breath** mit angehaltenem Atem

bath [bɑːθ] n Bad nt; (~ tub) Badewanne f ♦ vt baden; **to have a ~** baden; see also **baths**

bathe [beɪð] vt, vi baden; **~r** n Badende(r) f(m)

bathing ['beɪðɪŋ] n Baden nt; **~ cap** n Badekappe f; **~ costume** n Badeanzug m; **~ suit** (US) n Badeanzug m; **~ trunks** (BRIT) npl Badehose f

bath: ~robe n Bademantel m; **~room** n Bad(ezimmer nt) nt; **~s** npl (Schwimm)bad nt; **~ towel** n Badetuch nt

baton ['bætən] n (of police) Gummiknüppel m; (MUS) Taktstock m

batter ['bætər] vt verprügeln ♦ n Schlagteig m; (for cake) Biskuitteig m; **~ed** adj (hat, pan) verbeult

battery ['bætərɪ] n (ELEC) Batterie f; (MIL) Geschützbatterie f

battery farming n (Hühner- etc)batterien pl

battle ['bætl] n Schlacht f; (small) Gefecht nt ♦ vi kämpfen; **~field** n Schlachtfeld nt; **~ship** n Schlachtschiff nt

Bavaria [bə'vɛərɪə] n Bayern nt; **~n** adj bay(e)risch ♦ n (person) Bayer(in) m(f)

bawdy ['bɔːdɪ] adj unflätig

bawl [bɔːl] vi brüllen

bay [beɪ] n (of sea) Bucht f ♦ vi bellen; **to keep at ~** unter Kontrolle halten; **~ window** n Erkerfenster nt

bazaar [bə'zɑːr] n Basar m

B. & B. abbr = **bed and breakfast**

BBC n abbr (= British Broadcasting Corporation) BBC f or m

B.C. adv abbr (= before Christ) v. Chr.

KEYWORD

be [biː] (pt **was**, **were**, pp **been**) aux vb 1 (with present participle: forming continuous tenses): **what are you doing?** was machst du (gerade)?; **it is raining** es regnet; **I've been waiting for you for hours** ich warte schon seit Stunden auf dich

2 (with pp: forming passives): **to be killed** getötet werden; **the thief was nowhere to be seen** der Dieb war

nirgendwo zu sehen
3 (in tag questions): **it was fun, wasn't it?** es hat Spaß gemacht, nicht wahr?
4 (+to +infin): **the house is to be sold** das Haus soll verkauft werden; **he's not to open it** er darf es nicht öffnen
♦ vb +complement **1** (usu) sein; **I'm tired** ich bin müde; **I'm hot/cold** mir ist heiß/kalt; **he's a doctor** er ist Arzt; **2 and 2 are 4** 2 und 2 ist or sind 4; **she's tall/pretty** sie ist groß/hübsch; **be careful/quiet** sei vorsichtig/ruhig
2 (of health): **how are you?** wie geht es dir?; **he's very ill** er ist sehr krank; **I'm fine now** jetzt geht es mir gut
3 (of age): **how old are you?** wie alt bist du?; **I'm sixteen (years old)** ich bin sechzehn (Jahre alt)
4 (cost): **how much was the meal?** was or wie viel hat das Essen gekostet?; **that'll be £5.75, please** das macht £5.75, bitte
♦ vi **1** (exist, occur etc) sein; **is there a God?** gibt es einen Gott?; **be that as it may** wie dem auch sei; **so be it** also gut
2 (referring to place) sein; **I won't be here tomorrow** ich werde morgen nicht hier sein
3 (referring to movement): **where have you been?** wo bist du gewesen?; **I've been in the garden** ich war im Garten
♦ impers vb **1** (referring to time, distance, weather) sein; **it's 5 o'clock** es ist 5 Uhr; **it's 10 km to the village** es sind 10 km bis zum Dorf; **it's too hot/cold** es ist zu heiß/kalt
2 (emphatic): **it's me** ich bins; **it's the postman** es ist der Briefträger

beach [bi:tʃ] n Strand m ♦ vt (ship) auf den Strand setzen
beacon ['bi:kən] n (signal) Leuchtfeuer nt; (traffic ~) Bake f
bead [bi:d] n Perle f; (drop) Tropfen m
beak [bi:k] n Schnabel m

beaker ['bi:kər] n Becher m
beam [bi:m] n (of wood) Balken m; (of light) Strahl m; (smile) strahlende(s) Lächeln nt ♦ vi strahlen
bean [bi:n] n Bohne f; (also: **baked ~s**) gebackene Bohnen pl; **~ sprouts** npl Sojasprossen pl
bear [beər] (pt **bore**, pp **borne**) n Bär m ♦ vt (weight, crops) tragen; (tolerate) ertragen; (young) gebären ♦ vi: **to ~ right/left** sich rechts/links halten; **~ out** vt (suspicions etc) bestätigen; **~ up** vi sich halten
beard [biəd] n Bart m; **~ed** adj bärtig
bearer ['beərə] n Träger m
bearing ['beəriŋ] n (posture) Haltung f; (relevance) Relevanz f; (relation) Bedeutung f; (TECH) Kugellager nt; **~s** npl (direction) Orientierung f; (also: **ball ~s**) (Kugel)lager nt
beast [bi:st] n Tier nt, Vieh nt; (person) Biest nt
beat [bi:t] (pt **beat**, pp **beaten**) n (stroke) Schlag m; (pulsation) (Herz)-schlag m; (police round) Runde f; Revier nt; (MUS) Takt m; Beat m ♦ vt, vi schlagen; **to ~ it** abhauen; **off the ~en track** abgelegen; **~ off** vt abschlagen; **~ up** vt zusammenschlagen; **~en** pp of **beat**; **~ing** n Prügel pl
beautiful ['bju:tiful] adj schön; **~ly** adv ausgezeichnet
beauty ['bju:ti] n Schönheit f; **~ salon** n Schönheitssalon m; **~ spot** n Schönheitsfleck m; (BRIT: TOURISM) (besonders) schöne(r) Ort m
beaver ['bi:və] n Biber m
became [bi'keim] pt of **become**
because [bi'kɔz] conj weil ♦ prep: **~ of** wegen +gen, wegen +dat (inf)
beck [bek] n: **to be at the ~ and call of sb** nach jds Pfeife tanzen
beckon ['bekən] vt, vi: **to ~ to sb** jdm ein Zeichen geben
become [bi'kʌm] (irreg: like **come**) vi werden ♦ vt werden; (clothes) stehen +dat

becoming [bɪ'kʌmɪŋ] *adj* (*suitable*) schicklich; (*clothes*) kleidsam

bed [bed] *n* Bett *nt*; (*of river*) Flussbett *nt*; (*foundation*) Schicht *f*; (*in garden*) Beet *nt*; **to go to ~** zu Bett gehen; **~ and breakfast** *n* Übernachtung *f* mit Frühstück; **~clothes** *npl* Bettwäsche *f*; **~ding** *n* Bettzeug *nt*

Bed and Breakfast

Bed and Breakfast bedeutet „Übernachtung mit Frühstück", wobei sich dies in Großbritannien nicht auf Hotels, sondern auf kleinere Pensionen, Privathäuser und Bauernhöfe bezieht, wo man wesentlich preisgünstiger übernachten kann als in Hotels. Oft wird für Bed and Breakfast, auch B & B genannt, durch ein entsprechendes Schild im Garten oder an der Einfahrt geworben.

---

bedlam ['bedləm] *n* (*uproar*) tolle(s) Durcheinander *nt*

bed linen *n* Bettwäsche *f*

bedraggled [bɪ'dræɡld] *adj* ramponiert

bed: ~ridden *adj* bettlägerig; **~room** *n* Schlafzimmer *nt*; **~side** *n*: **at the ~side** am Bett; **~sit(ter)** (*BRIT*) *n* Einzimmerwohnung *f*, möblierte(s) Zimmer *nt*; **~spread** *n* Tagesdecke *f*; **~time** *n* Schlafenszeit *f*

bee [biː] *n* Biene *f*

beech [biːtʃ] *n* Buche *f*

beef [biːf] *n* Rindfleisch *nt*; **roast ~** Roastbeef *nt*; **~burger** *n* Hamburger *m*

beehive ['biːhaɪv] *n* Bienenstock *m*

beeline ['biːlaɪn] *n*: **to make a ~** for schnurstracks zugehen auf +*acc*

been [biːn] *pp* of **be**

beer [bɪə*] *n* Bier *nt*

beet [biːt] *n* (*vegetable*) Rübe *f*; (*US: also:* **red ~**) Rote Bete *f* or Rübe *f*

beetle ['biːtl] *n* Käfer *m*

beetroot ['biːtruːt] (*BRIT*) *n* Rote Bete *f*

before [bɪ'fɔː*] *prep vor* ♦ *conj* bevor ♦ *adv* (*of time*) zuvor; früher; **the week**

~ die Woche zuvor or vorher; **I've done it ~** das hab ich schon mal getan; **~ going** bevor er/sie *etc* geht/ ging; **~ she goes** bevor sie geht; **~hand** *adv* im Voraus

beg [beg] *vt, vi* (*implore*) dringend bitten; (*alms*) betteln

began [bɪ'ɡæn] *pt* of **begin**

beggar ['beɡə*] *n* Bettler(in) *m(f)*

begin [bɪ'ɡɪn] (*pt* **began**, *pp* **begun**) *vt, vi* anfangen, beginnen; (*found*) gründen; **to ~ doing** or **to do sth** anfangen or beginnen, etw zu tun; **to ~ with** zunächst (einmal); **~ner** *n* Anfänger *m*; **~ning** *n* Anfang *m*

begun [bɪ'ɡʌn] *pp* of **begin**

behalf [bɪ'hɑːf] *n*: **on ~ of** im Namen +*gen*; **on my ~** für mich

behave [bɪ'heɪv] *vi* sich benehmen; **behaviour** [bɪ'heɪvjə*] (*US* **behavior**) *n* Benehmen *nt*

beheld [bɪ'held] *pt, pp* of **behold**

behind [bɪ'haɪnd] *prep* hinter ♦ *adv* (*late*) im Rückstand; (*in the rear*) hinten ♦ *n* (*inf*) Hinterteil *nt*; **~ the scenes** (*fig*) hinter den Kulissen

behold [bɪ'həuld] (*irreg: like* **hold**) *vt* erblicken

beige [beɪʒ] *adj* beige

Beijing [beɪ'dʒɪŋ] *n* Peking *nt*

being ['biːɪŋ] *n* (*existence*) (Da)sein *nt*; (*person*) Wesen *nt*; **to come into ~** entstehen

Belarus [belə'rus] *n* Weißrussland *nt*

belated [bɪ'leɪtɪd] *adj* verspätet

belch [beltʃ] *vi* rülpsen ♦ *vt* (*smoke*) ausspeien

belfry ['belfrɪ] *n* Glockenturm *m*

Belgian ['beldʒən] *adj* belgisch ♦ *n* Belgier(in) *m(f)*

Belgium ['beldʒəm] *n* Belgien *nt*

belie [bɪ'laɪ] *vt* Lügen strafen +*acc*

belief [bɪ'liːf] *n* Glaube *m*; (*conviction*) Überzeugung *f*; **in sb/sth** Glaube an jdn/etw

believe [bɪ'liːv] *vt* glauben +*dat*; (*think*) glauben, meinen, denken ♦ *vi* (*have* *faith*) glauben; **to ~ in** sth an etw *acc* glauben; **~r** *n* Gläubige(r) *f(m)*

belittle [bɪˈlɪtl] *vt* herabsetzen

bell [bel] *n* Glocke *f*

belligerent [bɪˈlɪdʒərənt] *adj* (*person*) streitsüchtig; (*country*) Krieg führend

bellow [ˈbeləu] *vt, vi* brüllen

bellows [ˈbeləuz] *npl* (*TECH*) Gebläse *nt*; (*for fire*) Blasebalg *m*

belly [ˈbelɪ] *n* Bauch *m*

belong [bɪˈlɔŋ] *vi* gehören; **to ~ to sb** jdm gehören; **to ~ to a club** *etc* einem Klub *etc* angehören; **~ings** *npl* Habe *f*

beloved [bɪˈlʌvɪd] *adj* innig geliebt ♦ *n* Geliebte(r) *f(m)*

below [bɪˈləu] *prep* unter ♦ *adv* unten

belt [belt] *n* (*band*) Riemen *m*; (*round waist*) Gürtel *m* ♦ *vt* (*fasten*) mit Riemen befestigen; (*inf: beat*) schlagen; **~way** (*US*) *n* (*AUT: ring road*) Umgehungsstraße *f*

bemused [bɪˈmjuːzd] *adj* verwirrt

bench [bentʃ] *n* (*seat*) Bank *f*; (*workshop*) Werkbank *f*; (*judge's seat*) Richterbank *f*; (*judges*) Richter *pl*

bend [bend] (*pt, pp* bent) *vt* (*curve*) biegen; (*stoop*) beugen ♦ *vi* sich biegen; sich beugen ♦ *n* Biegung *f*; (*BRIT: in road*) Kurve *f*; **~ down** or **over** *vi* sich bücken

beneath [bɪˈniːθ] *prep* unter ♦ *adv* darunter

benefactor [ˈbenɪfæktər] *n* Wohltäter(in) *m(f)*

beneficial [benɪˈfɪʃl] *adj* vorteilhaft; (*to health*) heilsam

benefit [ˈbenɪfɪt] *n* (*advantage*) Nutzen *m* ♦ *vt* fördern ♦ *vi*: **to ~ (from)** Nutzen ziehen (aus)

Benelux [ˈbenɪlʌks] *n* Beneluxstaaten *pl*

benevolent [bɪˈnevələnt] *adj* wohlwollend

benign [bɪˈnaɪn] *adj* (*person*) gütig; (*climate*) mild

bent [bent] *pt, pp of* **bend** ♦ *n* (*inclination*) Neigung *f* ♦ *adj* (*inf: dishonest*)

unehrlich; **to be ~ on** versessen sein auf +*acc*

bequest [bɪˈkwest] *n* Vermächtnis *nt*

bereaved [bɪˈriːvd] *npl*: **the ~** die Hinterbliebenen *pl*

beret [ˈbereɪ] *n* Baskenmütze *f*

Berlin [bɜːˈlɪn] *n* Berlin *nt*

berm [bɜːm] (*US*) *n* (*AUT*) Seitenstreifen *m*

berry [ˈberɪ] *n* Beere *f*

berserk [bəˈsɜːk] *adj*: **to go ~** wild werden

berth [bɜːθ] *n* (*for ship*) Ankerplatz *m*; (*in ship*) Koje *f*; (*in train*) Bett *nt* ♦ *vt* am Kai festmachen ♦ *vi* anlegen

beseech [bɪˈsiːtʃ] (*pt, pp* besought) *vt* anflehen

beset [bɪˈset] (*pt, pp* beset) *vt* bedrängen

beside [bɪˈsaɪd] *prep* neben, bei; (*except*) außer; **to be ~ o.s. (with)** außer sich sein (vor +*dat*); **that's ~ the point** das tut nichts zur Sache

besides [bɪˈsaɪdz] *prep* außer, neben ♦ *adv* außerdem

besiege [bɪˈsiːdʒ] *vt* (*MIL*) belagern; (*surround*) umlagern, bedrängen

besought [bɪˈsɔːt] *pt, pp of* **beseech**

best [best] *adj* beste(r, s) ♦ *adv* am besten; **the ~ part of** (*quantity*) das meiste +*gen*; **at ~** höchstens; **to make the ~ of** it das Beste daraus machen; **to do one's ~** sein Bestes tun; **to the ~ of my knowledge** meines Wissens; **to the ~ of my ability** so gut ich kann; **for the ~** zum Besten; **~-before date** *n* Mindesthaltbarkeitsdatum *nt*; **~ man** *n* Trauzeuge *m*

bestow [bɪˈstəu] *vt* verleihen

bet [bet] (*pt, pp* bet *or* betted) *n* Wette *f* ♦ *vt, vi* wetten

betray [bɪˈtreɪ] *vt* verraten

better [ˈbetər] *adj, adv* besser ♦ *vt* verbessern ♦ *n*: **to get the ~ of** jdn überwinden; **he thought ~ of it** er hat sich eines Besseren besonnen; **you had ~ leave** Sie gehen jetzt wohl besser; **to get ~** (MED) gesund werden; **~ off** aid (richer) wohlhabender

betting ['betɪŋ] n Wetten nt; **~ shop** (BRIT) n Wettbüro nt

between [bɪ'twiːn] prep zwischen; (among) unter ♦ adv dazwischen

beverage ['bevərɪdʒ] n Getränk nt

bevy ['bevɪ] n Schar f

beware [bɪ'weə'] vt, vi sich hüten vor +dat; **"~ of the dog"** "Vorsicht, bissiger Hund!"

bewildered [bɪ'wɪldəd] adj verwirrt

beyond [bɪ'jɔnd] prep (place) jenseits +gen; (time) über ... hinaus; (out of reach) außerhalb +gen ♦ adv darüber hinaus; **~ doubt** ohne Zweifel; **~ repair** nicht mehr zu reparieren

bias ['baɪəs] n (slant) Neigung f; (prejudice) Vorurteil nt; **~(s)ed** adj voreingenommen

bib [bɪb] n Latz m

Bible ['baɪbl] n Bibel f

bicarbonate of soda [baɪ'kɑːbənɪt-] n Natron nt

bicker ['bɪkə'] vi zanken

bicycle ['baɪsɪkl] n Fahrrad nt

bid [bɪd] (pt **bade** or **bid**, pp **bid(den)**) n (offer) Gebot nt; (attempt) Versuch m ♦ vt, vi (offer) bieten; **to ~ farewell** Lebewohl sagen; **~der** n (person) Steigerer m; **the highest ~der** der der Meistbietende; **~ding** n (command) Geheiß nt

bide [baɪd] vt: **to ~ one's time** abwarten

bifocals [baɪ'fəuklz] npl Bifokalbrille f

big [bɪg] adj groß; **~ dipper** ['-'dɪpə'] n Achterbahn f; **~headed** ['bɪg'hedɪd] adj eingebildet

bigot ['bɪgət] n Frömmler m; **~ed** adj bigott; **~ry** n Bigotterie f

big top n Zirkuszelt nt

bike [baɪk] n Rad nt

bikini [bɪ'kiːnɪ] n Bikini m

bile [baɪl] n (BIOL) Galle f

bilingual [baɪ'lɪŋgwəl] adj zweisprachig

bill [bɪl] n (account) Rechnung f; (POL)

Gesetzentwurf m; (US: FIN) Geldschein m; **to fit** or **fill the ~** (fig) der/die/das Richtige sein; **"post no ~s"** "Plakate ankleben verboten"; **~board** ['bɪlbɔːd] n Reklameschild nt

billet ['bɪlɪt] n Quartier nt

billfold ['bɪlfəuld] (US) n Geldscheintasche f

billiards ['bɪljədz] n Billard nt

billion ['bɪljən] n (BRIT) Billion f; (US) Milliarde f

bimbo ['bɪmbəu] (inf: pej) n Puppe f, Häschen n

bin [bɪn] n Kasten m; (dustbin) (Abfall)eimer m

bind [baɪnd] (pt, pp **bound**) vt (tie) binden; (tie together) zusammenbinden; (oblige) verpflichten; **~ing** n (Buch)einband m ♦ adj verbindlich

binge [bɪndʒ] (inf) n Sauferei f

bingo ['bɪŋgəu] n Bingo nt

binoculars [bɪ'nɔkjuləz] npl Fernglas nt

bio... [baɪəu] prefix: **~chemistry** n Biochemie f; **~degradable** adj biologisch abbaubar; **~graphy** n Biografie f; **~logical** [baɪə'lɔdʒɪkl] adj biologisch; **~logy** [baɪ'ɔlədʒɪ] n Biologie f

birch [bəːtʃ] n Birke f

bird [bəːd] n Vogel m; (BRIT: inf: girl) Mädchen nt; **~'s-eye view** n Vogelschau f; **~ watcher** n Vogelbeobachter(in) m(f); **~ watching** n Vogelbeobachten nt

Biro ['baɪərəu] ® n Kugelschreiber m

birth [bəːθ] n Geburt f; **to give ~ to** zur Welt bringen; **~ certificate** n Geburtsurkunde f; **~ control** n Geburtenkontrolle f; **~day** n Geburtstag m; **~day card** n Geburtstagskarte f; **~place** n Geburtsort m; **~ rate** n Geburtenrate f

biscuit ['bɪskɪt] n Keks m

bisect [baɪ'sekt] vt halbieren

bishop ['bɪʃəp] n Bischof m

bit [bɪt] pt of **bite** ♦ n bisschen, Stückchen nt; (horse's) Gebiss nt; (COMPUT) Bit nt; **a ~ tired** etwas müde

bitch [bɪtʃ] n (dog) Hündin f; (unpleasant woman) Weibsstück nt

bite [baɪt] (pt **bit**, pp **bitten**) vt, vi beißen ♦ n Biss m; (mouthful) Bissen m; to ~ one's nails Nägel kauen; let's have a ~ to eat lass uns etwas essen

bitten ['bɪtn] pp of **bite**

bitter ['bɪtər] adj bitter; (memory etc) schmerzlich; (person) verbittert ♦ n (BRIT: beer) dunkle(s) Bier nt; **~ness** n Bitterkeit f

blab [blæb] vi klatschen ♦ vt (also: ~ out) ausplaudern

black [blæk] adj schwarz; (night) finster ♦ vt schwärzen; (shoes) wichsen; (eye) blau schlagen; **to give sb a ~ eye** jdm ein blaues Auge schlagen; **in the ~** (bank account) in den schwarzen Zahlen; **~ and blue** adj grün und blau; **~berry** n Brombeere f; **~bird** n Amsel f; **~board** n (Wand)tafel f; **~ coffee** n schwarze(r) Kaffee m; **~currant** n schwarze Johannisbeere f; **~en** vt schwärzen; (fig) verunglimpfen; **B~ Forest** n Schwarzwald m; **~ ice** n Glatteis nt; **~leg** (BRIT) n Streikbrecher(in) m(f); **~list** n schwarze Liste f; **~mail** n Erpressung f ♦ vt erpressen; **~ market** n Schwarzmarkt m; **~out** n Verdunklung f; (MED): **to have a ~out** bewusstlos werden; **~ pudding** n ≈ Blutwurst f; **B~ Sea** n: **the B~ Sea** das Schwarze Meer; **~ sheep** n schwarze(s) Schaf nt; **~smith** n Schmied m; **~ spot** n (AUT) Gefahrenstelle f; (for unemployment etc) schwer betroffene(s) Gebiet nt

bladder ['blædər] n Blase f

blade [bleɪd] n (of weapon) Klinge f; (of grass) Halm m; (of oar) Ruderblatt nt

blame [bleɪm] n Tadel m, Schuld f ♦ vt Vorwürfe machen +dat; **to ~ sb for sth** jdm die Schuld an etw dat geben; **he is to ~** er ist daran schuld

bland [blænd] adj mild

blank [blæŋk] adj leer, unbeschrieben; (look) verdutzt; (verse) Blank- ♦ n

(space) Lücke f; Zwischenraum m; (cartridge) Platzpatrone f; **~ cheque** n Blankoscheck m; (fig) Freibrief m

blanket ['blæŋkɪt] n (Woll)decke f

blare [bleər] vi (radio) plärren; (horn) tuten; (MUS) schmettern

blasé ['blɑːzeɪ] adj blasiert

blast [blɑːst] n Explosion f; (of wind) Windstoß m ♦ vt (blow up) sprengen; **~!** (inf) verflixt!; **~off** n (SPACE) (Raketen)abschuss m

blatant ['bleɪtənt] adj offenkundig

blaze [bleɪz] n (fire) lodernde(s) Feuer nt ♦ vi lodern ♦ vt: **to ~ a trail** Bahn brechen

blazer ['bleɪzər] n Blazer m

bleach [bliːtʃ] n (also: **household ~**) Bleichmittel nt ♦ vt bleichen; **~ed** adj gebleicht

bleachers ['bliːtʃəz] (US) npl (SPORT) unüberdachte Tribüne f

bleak [bliːk] adj kahl, rau; (future) trostlos

bleary-eyed ['blɪərˌaɪd] adj triefäugig; (on waking up) mit verschlafenen Augen

bleat [bliːt] vi blöken; (fig: complain) meckern

bled [bled] pt, pp of **bleed**

bleed [bliːd] (pt, pp **bled**) vi bluten ♦ vt (draw blood) zur Ader lassen; **to ~ to death** verbluten

bleeper ['bliːpər] n (of doctor etc) Funkrufempfänger m

blemish ['blemɪʃ] n Makel m ♦ vt verunstalten

blend [blend] n Mischung f ♦ vt mischen ♦ vi sich mischen; **~er** n Mixer m, Mixgerät nt

bless [bles] (pt, pp **blessed**) vt segnen; (give thanks) preisen; (make happy) glücklich machen; **~ you!** Gesundheit!; **~ing** n Segen m; (at table) Tischgebet nt; (happiness) Wohltat f; Segen m; (good wish) Glück nt

blew [bluː] pt of **blow**

blimey ['blaɪmɪ] (BRIT: inf) excl verflucht

blind [blaɪnd] adj blind; (corner) unübersichtlich ♦ n (for window) Rouleau nt ♦ vt blenden; **~ alley** n Sackgasse f; **~fold** n Augenbinde f ♦ adj, adv mit verbundenen Augen ♦ vt: **to ~fold sb** jdm die Augen verbinden; **~ly** adv blind; (fig) blindlings; **~ness** n Blindheit f; **~ spot** n (AUT) tote(r) Winkel m; (fig) schwache(r) Punkt m

blink [blɪŋk] vi blinzeln; **~ers** npl Scheuklappen pl

bliss [blɪs] n (Glück)seligkeit f

blister ['blɪstər] n Blase f ♦ vi Blasen werfen

blitz [blɪts] n Luftkrieg m

blizzard ['blɪzəd] n Schneesturm m

bloated ['bləʊtɪd] adj aufgedunsen; (inf: full) nudelsatt

blob [blɒb] n Klümpchen nt

bloc [blɒk] n (POL) Block m

block [blɒk] n (of wood) Block m, Klotz m; (of houses) Häuserblock m ♦ vt hemmen; **~ade** [blɒ'keɪd] n Blockade f ♦ vt blockieren; **~age** n Verstopfung f; **~buster** n Knüller m; **~ letters** npl Blockbuchstaben pl; **~ of flats** (BRIT) n Häuserblock m

bloke [bləʊk] (BRIT: inf) n Kerl m, Typ m

blond(e) [blɒnd] adj blond ♦ n Blondine f

blood [blʌd] n Blut nt; **~ donor** n Blutspender m; **~ group** n Blutgruppe f; **~ poisoning** n Blutvergiftung f; **~ pressure** n Blutdruck m; **~shed** n Blutvergießen nt; **~shot** adj blutunterlaufen; **~ sports** npl Jagdsport, Hahnenkampf etc; **~stained** adj blutbefleckt; **~stream** n Blut nt, Blutkreislauf m; **~ test** n Blutprobe f; **~thirsty** adj blutrünstig; **~ vessel** n Blutgefäß nt; **~y** adj (BRIT: inf) verdammt; **~y-minded** (BRIT: inf) adj stur

bloom [bluːm] n Blüte f; (freshness) Glanz m ♦ vi blühen

blossom ['blɒsəm] n Blüte f ♦ vi blühen

blot [blɒt] n Klecks m ♦ vt beklecksen;

(ink) (ab)löschen; **~ out** vt auslöschen

blotchy ['blɒtʃi] adj fleckig

blotting paper ['blɒtɪŋ-] n Löschpapier nt

blouse [blaʊz] n Bluse f

blow [bləʊ] (pt blew, pp blown) n Schlag m ♦ vi blasen ♦ vi (wind) wehen; **to ~ one's nose** sich dat die Nase putzen; **~ away** vt wegblasen; **~ down** vt umwehen; **~ off** vi wegwehen ♦ vi wegfliegen; **~ out** vi ausgehen; **~ over** vi vorüberziehen; **~ up** vi explodieren ♦ vt sprengen; **~-dry** n to **have a ~-dry** sich föhnen lassen ♦ vt föhnen; **~lamp** (BRIT) n Lötlampe f; **~n** pp of **blow**; **~-out** n (AUT) geplatzte(r) Reifen m; **~torch** n = **blowlamp**

blue [bluː] adj blau; (inf: unhappy) niedergeschlagen; (obscene) pornografisch; (joke) anzüglich ♦ n: **out of the ~** (fig) aus heiterem Himmel; **to have the ~s** traurig sein; **~bell** n Glockenblume f; **~bottle** n Schmeißfliege f; **~film** n Pornofilm m; **~print** n (fig) Entwurf m

bluff [blʌf] vi bluffen, täuschen ♦ n (deception) Bluff m; **to call sb's ~** es darauf ankommen lassen

blunder ['blʌndər] n grobe(r) Fehler m, Schnitzer m ♦ vi einen groben Fehler machen

blunt [blʌnt] adj (knife) stumpf; (talk) unverblümt ♦ vt abstumpfen

blur [bləːr] n Fleck m ♦ vt verschwommen machen

blurb [bləːb] n Waschzettel m

blush [blʌʃ] vi erröten

blustery ['blʌstəri] adj stürmisch

boar [bɔːr] n Keiler m, Eber m

board [bɔːd] n (of wood) Brett nt; (of card) Pappe f; (committee) Ausschuss m; (of firm) Aufsichtsrat m; (SCH) Direktorium f ♦ vt (train) einsteigen in +acc; (ship) an Bord gehen +gen; on **~** (AVIAT, NAUT) an Bord; **~ and lodging** Unterkunft f und Verpflegung; **full/half ~** (BRIT) Voll-/Halbpension f; **to go by**

the ~ flachfallen, über Bord gehen; **~ up** vt mit Brettern vernageln; **~er** n Kostgänger m; (SCH) Internatsschüler(in) m(f); **~ game** n Brettspiel nt; **~ing card** n (AVIAT, NAUT) Bordkarte f; **~ing house** n Pension f; **~ing school** n Internat nt; **~ room** n Sitzungszimmer nt

boast [bəust] vi prahlen ♦ vt sich rühmen +gen ♦ n Großtuerei f, Prahlerei f; **to ~ about** or **of sth** mit etw prahlen

boat [bəut] n Boot nt; (ship) Schiff nt; **~er** n (hat) Kreissäge f; **~swain** n = **bosun**; **~ train** n Zug m mit Fährenanschluss

bob [bɔb] vi sich auf und nieder bewegen; **~ up** vi auftauchen

bobbin ['bɔbɪn] n Spule f

bobby ['bɔbɪ] (BRIT: inf) n Bobby m

bobsleigh ['bɔbsleɪ] n Bob m

bode [bəud] vi: **to ~ well/ill** ein gutes/schlechtes Zeichen sein

bodily ['bɔdɪlɪ] adj, adv körperlich

body ['bɔdɪ] n Körper m; (dead) Leiche f; (group) Mannschaft f; (AUT) Karosserie f; (trunk) Rumpf m; **~ building** n Bodybuilding nt; **~guard** n Leibwache f; **~work** n Karosserie f

bog [bɔg] n Sumpf m ♦ vt: **to get ~ged down** sich festfahren

boggle ['bɔgl] vi stutzen; **the mind ~s** es ist kaum auszumalen

bog-standard adj stinknormal (inf)

bogus ['bəugəs] adj unecht, Schein-

boil [bɔɪl] vt, vi kochen ♦ n (MED) Geschwür nt; **to come to the** (BRIT) or **a** (US) **~** zu kochen anfangen; **to ~ down to** (fig) hinauslaufen auf +acc; **~ over** vi überkochen; **~ed egg** n (weich) gekochte(s) Ei nt; **~ed potatoes** npl Salzkartoffeln pl; **~er** n Boiler m; **~er suit** (BRIT) n Arbeitsanzug m; **~ing point** n Siedepunkt m

boisterous ['bɔɪstərəs] adj ungestüm

bold [bəuld] adj (fearless) unerschrocken; (handwriting) fest und klar

bollard ['bɔləd] n (NAUT) Poller m; (BRIT: AUT) Pfosten m

bolt [bəult] n Bolzen m; (lock) Riegel m ♦ adv: **~ upright** kerzengerade ♦ vt verriegeln; (swallow) verschlingen ♦ vi (horse) durchgehen

bomb [bɔm] n Bombe f ♦ vt bombardieren; **~ard** [bɔm'ba:d] vt bombardieren; **~ardment** [bɔm'ba:dmənt] n Beschießung f; **~ disposal** n: **~ disposal unit** Bombenräumkommando nt; **~er** n Bomber m; (terrorist) Bombenattentäter(in) m(f); **~ing** n Bomben nt; **~shell** n (fig) Bombe f

bona fide ['bəunə'faɪdɪ] adj echt

bond [bɔnd] n (link) Band nt; (FIN) Schuldverschreibung f

bondage ['bɔndɪdʒ] n Sklaverei f

bone [bəun] n Knochen m; (of fish) Gräte f; (piece of ~) Knochensplitter m ♦ vt die Knochen herausnehmen +dat; (fish) entgräten; **~ dry** adj (inf) knochentrocken; **~ idle** adj stinkfaul; **~ marrow** n (ANAT) Knochenmark nt

bonfire ['bɔnfaɪə*] n Feuer nt im Freien

bonnet ['bɔnɪt] n Haube f; (for baby) Häubchen nt; (BRIT: AUT) Motorhaube f

bonus ['bəunəs] n Bonus m; (annual ~) Prämie f

bony ['bəunɪ] adj knochig, knochendürr

boo [bu:] vt auspfeifen

booby trap ['bu:bɪ-] n Falle f

book [buk] n Buch nt ♦ vt (ticket etc) vorbestellen; (person) verwarnen; **~s** npl (COMM) Bücher pl; **~case** n Bücherregal nt, Bücherschrank nt; **~ing office** (BRIT) n (RAIL) Fahrkartenschalter m; (THEAT) Vorverkaufsstelle f; **~keeping** n Buchhaltung f; **~let** n Broschüre f; **~maker** n Buchmacher m; **~seller** n Buchhändler m; **~shelf** n Bücherbord nt; **~shop** ['bukʃɔp], **~store** n Buchhandlung f

boom [bu:m] n (noise) Dröhnen nt; (busy period) Hochkonjunktur f ♦ vi dröhnen

boon [buːn] n Wohltat f, Segen m

boost [buːst] n Auftrieb m; (fig) Reklame f ♦ vt Auftrieb geben; **~er** n (MED) Wiederholungsimpfung f

boot [buːt] n Stiefel m; (BRIT: AUT) Kofferraum m ♦ vt (kick) einen Fußtritt geben; (COMPUT) laden; **to ~** (in addition) obendrein

booth [buːð] n (at fair) Bude f; (telephone ~) Zelle f; (voting ~) Kabine f

booze [buːz] (inf) n Alkohol m, Schnaps m ♦ vi saufen

border ['bɔːdər] n Grenze f; (edge) Kante f; (in garden) (Blumen)rabatte f ♦ adj Grenz-; **the B~s** Grenzregion zwischen England und Schottland; **~ on** vt grenzen an +acc; **~line** n Grenze f; **~line case** n Grenzfall m

bore [bɔːr] pt of **bear** ♦ vt bohren; (weary) langweilen ♦ n (person) Langweiler m; (thing) langweilige Sache f; (of gun) Kaliber nt; **I am ~d** ich langweile mich; **~dom** n Langeweile f

boring ['bɔːrɪŋ] adj langweilig

born [bɔːn] adj: **to be ~** geboren werden

borne [bɔːn] pp of **bear**

borough ['bʌrə] n Stadt(gemeinde) f, Stadtbezirk m

borrow ['bɔrəu] vt borgen

Bosnia (and) Herzegovina ['bɔznɪə (ənd) hɜːtsəgəu'viːnə] n Bosnien und Herzegowina nt; **~n** n Bosnier(in) m(f) ♦ adj bosnisch

bosom ['buzəm] n Busen m

boss [bɔs] n Chef m, Boss m ♦ vt: **to ~ around** or **about** herumkommandieren; **~y** adj herrisch

bosun ['bəusn] n Bootsmann m

botany ['bɔtənɪ] n Botanik f

botch [bɔtʃ] vt (also: **~ up**) verpfuschen

both [bəuθ] adj beide(s) ♦ pron beide(s) ♦ adv: **~ X and Y** sowohl X wie or als auch Y; **~ (of)** the books both of us went, **we ~** went wir gingen beide

bother ['bɔðər] vt (pester) quälen ♦ vi

(fuss) sich aufregen ♦ n Mühe f, Umstand m; **to ~ doing sth** sich dat die Mühe machen, etw zu tun; **what a ~!** wie ärgerlich!

bottle ['bɔtl] n Flasche f ♦ vt (in Flaschen) abfüllen; **~ up** vt aufstauen; **~bank** n Altglascontainer m; **~d beer** n Flaschenbier nt; **~d water** n in Flaschen abgefülltes Wasser; **~neck** n (also fig) Engpass m; **~ opener** n Flaschenöffner m

bottom ['bɔtəm] n Boden m; (of person) Hintern m; (riverbed) Flussbett m ♦ adj unterste(r, s)

bough [bau] n Zweig m, Ast m

bought [bɔːt] pt, pp of **buy**

boulder ['bəuldər] n Felsbrocken m

bounce [bauns] vi (person) herumhüpfen; (ball) hochspringen; (cheque) platzen ♦ vt (auf)springen lassen ♦ n (rebound) Aufprall m; **~r** n Rausschmeißer m

bound [baund] pt, pp of **bind** ♦ n Grenze f; (leap) Sprung m ♦ vi (spring, leap) (auf)springen ♦ adj (obliged) gebunden, verpflichtet; **out of ~s** Zutritt verboten; **to be ~ to do sth** verpflichtet sein, etw zu tun; **it's ~ to happen** es muss so kommen; **to be ~ for** … nach … fahren

boundary ['baundrɪ] n Grenze f

bouquet ['bukeɪ] n Strauß m; (of wine) Blume f

bourgeois ['buəʒwɑː] adj kleinbürgerlich, bourgeois ♦ n Spießbürger(in) m

bout [baut] n (of illness) Anfall m; (of contest) Kampf m

bow¹ [bəu] n (ribbon) Schleife f; (weapon, MUS) Bogen m

bow² [bau] n (with head, body) Verbeugung f; (of ship) Bug m ♦ vi sich verbeugen; (submit): **to ~ to** sich beugen +dat

bowels ['bauəlz] npl (ANAT) Darm m

bowl [bəul] n (basin) Schüssel f; (of pipe) (Pfeifen)kopf m; (wooden ball)

(Holz)kugel f ♦ vt, vi (die Kugel) rollen

bow-legged ['bəʊ'legɪd] adj o-beinig, O-beinig

bowler ['bəʊləʳ] n Werfer m; (BRIT: also: ~ **hat**) Melone f

bowling ['bəʊlɪŋ] n Kegeln nt; **~ alley** n Kegelbahn f; **~ green** n Rasen m zum Bowlingspiel

bowls n (game) Bowlsspiel nt

bow tie [bəʊ-] n Fliege f

box [bɒks] n (also: **cardboard ~**) Schachtel f; (bigger) Kasten m; (THEAT) Loge f ♦ vt einpacken ♦ vi boxen; **~er** n Boxer m; **~er shorts** pl Boxershorts pl; **~ing** n (SPORT) Boxen nt; **B~ing Day** (BRIT) n zweite(r) Weihnachtsfeiertag m; **~ing gloves** npl Boxhandschuhe pl; **~ing ring** n Boxring m; **~ office** n (Theater)kasse f; **~room** n Rumpelkammer f

---

Boxing Day

Boxing Day (26.12.) ist ein Feiertag in Großbritannien. Wenn Weihnachten auf ein Wochenende fällt, wird der Feiertag am nächsten darauf folgenden Wochentag nachgeholt. Der Name geht auf einen alten Brauch zurück; früher erhielten Händler und Lieferanten an diesem Tag ein Geschenk, die sogenannte Christmas Box.

---

boy [bɔɪ] n Junge m

boycott ['bɔɪkɒt] n Boykott m ♦ vt boykottieren

boyfriend ['bɔɪfrend] n Freund m

boyish ['bɔɪɪʃ] adj jungenhaft

B.R. n abbr = British Rail

bra [brɑː] n BH m

brace [breɪs] n (TECH) Stütze f; (MED) Klammer f ♦ vt stützen; **~s** npl (BRIT) Hosenträger pl; **to ~ o.s. for sth** (fig) sich auf etw acc gefasst machen

bracelet ['breɪslɪt] n Armband nt

bracing ['breɪsɪŋ] adj kräftigend

bracken ['brækən] n Farnkraut nt

bracket ['brækɪt] n Halter m, Klammer

f; (in punctuation) Klammer f; (group) Gruppe f ♦ vt einklammern; (fig) in dieselbe Gruppe einordnen

brag [bræg] vi sich rühmen

braid [breɪd] n (hair) Flechte f; (trim) Borte f

Braille [breɪl] n Blindenschrift f

brain [breɪn] n (ANAT) Gehirn nt; (intellect) Intelligenz f, Verstand m; (person) kluge(r) Kopf m; **~s** npl (intelligence) Verstand m; **~child** n Erfindung f; **~wash** vt eine Gehirnwäsche vornehmen bei; **~wave** n Geistesblitz m; **~y** adj gescheit

braise [breɪz] vt schmoren

brake [breɪk] n Bremse f ♦ vt, vi bremsen; **~ fluid** n Bremsflüssigkeit f; **~ light** n Bremslicht nt

bramble ['bræmbl] n Brombeere f

bran [bræn] n Kleie f; (food) Frühstücksflocken pl

branch [brɑːntʃ] n Ast m; (division) Zweig m ♦ vi (also: ~ **out**: road) sich verzweigen

brand [brænd] n (COMM) Marke f, Sorte f; (on cattle) Brandmal nt ♦ vt brandmarken; (COMM) ein Warenzeichen geben +dat

brandish ['brændɪʃ] vt (drohend) schwingen

brand-new ['brænd'njuː] adj funkelnagelneu

brandy ['brændɪ] n Weinbrand m, Kognak m

brash [bræʃ] adj unverschämt

brass [brɑːs] n Messing nt; **the ~** (MUS) das Blech; **~ band** n Blaskapelle f

brassière ['bræsɪəʳ] n Büstenhalter m

brat [bræt] n Gör nt

bravado [brə'vɑːdəʊ] n Tollkühnheit f

brave [breɪv] adj tapfer ♦ vt die Stirn bieten +dat; **~ry** n Tapferkeit f

brawl [brɔːl] n Rauferei f

brawn [brɔːn] n (ANAT) Muskeln pl; (strength) Muskelkraft f

bray [breɪ] vi schreien

brazen ['breɪzn] adj (shameless) unver-

brazier ['breɪzɪəʳ] *n* (*of workmen*) offene(r) Kohlenofen *m*

Brazil [brə'zɪl] *n* Brasilien *nt*; **~ian** *adj* brasilianisch ♦ *n* Brasilianer(in) *m(f)*

breach [briːtʃ] *n* (*gap*) Lücke *f*; (*MIL*) Durchbruch *m*; (*of discipline*) Verstoß *m* (*gegen die Disziplin*); (*of faith*) Vertrauensbruch *m* ♦ *vt* durchbrechen; **~ of contract** Vertragsbruch *m*; **~ of the peace** öffentliche Ruhestörung *f*

bread [brɛd] *n* Brot *nt*; **~ and butter** Butterbrot *nt*; **~bin** *n* Brotkasten *m*; **~box** (*US*) *n* Brotkasten *m*; **~crumbs** *npl* Brotkrumen *pl*; (*COOK*) Paniermehl *nt*; **~line** *n*: **to be on the ~line** sich gerade so durchschlagen

breadth [brɛtθ] *n* Breite *f*

breadwinner ['brɛdwɪnəʳ] *n* Ernährer *m*

break [breɪk] (*pt* **broke**, *pp* **broken**) *vt* (*destroy*) (ab- or zer)brechen; (*promise*) brechen, nicht einhalten ♦ *vi* (*fall apart*) auseinander brechen; (*collapse*) zusammenbrechen; (*dawn*) anbrechen ♦ *n* (*gap*) Lücke *f*; (*chance*) Chance *f*, Gelegenheit *f*; (*fracture*) Bruch *m*; (*rest*) Pause *f*; **~ down** *vt* (*figures, data*) aufschlüsseln; (*undermine*) überwinden ♦ *vi* (*car*) eine Panne haben; (*person*) zusammenbrechen; **~ even** *vi* die Kosten decken; **~ free** *vi* sich losreißen; **~ in** *vt* (*horse*) zureiten ♦ *vi* (*burglar*) einbrechen in +*acc*; **~ into** *vt fus* (*house*) einbrechen in +*acc*; **~ loose** *vi* sich losreißen; **~ off** *vi* abbrechen; **~ open** *vt* (*door etc*) aufbrechen; **~ out** *vi* ausbrechen; **to ~ out in spots** Pickel bekommen; **~ up** *vi* zerbrechen; (*fig*) sich zerstreuen; (*BRIT: SCH*) in die Ferien gehen ♦ *vt* brechen; **~age** *n* Bruch *m*, Beschädigung *f*; **~down** *n* (*TECH*) Panne *f*; (*MED: also:* **nervous ~down**) Zusammenbruch *m*; **~down van** (*BRIT*) *n* Abschleppwagen *m*; **~er** *n* Brecher *m*

breakfast ['brɛkfəst] *n* Frühstück *nt*

break: **~-in** *n* Einbruch *m*; **~ing** *n*: **~ing and entering** (*JUR*) Einbruch *m*; **~through** *n* Durchbruch *m*; **~water** *n* Wellenbrecher *m*

breast [brɛst] *n* Brust *f*; **~-feed** (*irreg: like* **feed**) *vt*, *vi* stillen; **~-stroke** *n* Brustschwimmen *nt*

breath [brɛθ] *n* Atem *m*; **out of ~** außer Atem; **under one's ~** flüsternd

Breathalyzer ['brɛθəlaɪzəʳ] ® *n* Röhrchen *n*

breathe [briːð] *vt*, *vi* atmen; **~ in** *vt*, *vi* einatmen; **~ out** *vt*, *vi* ausatmen; **~r** *n* Verschnaufpause *f*; **breathing** *n* Atmung *f*

breathless ['brɛθlɪs] *adj* atemlos

breathtaking ['brɛθteɪkɪŋ] *adj* atemberaubend

bred [brɛd] *pt*, *pp of* **breed**

breed [briːd] (*pt*, *pp* **bred**) *vi* sich vermehren ♦ *vt* züchten ♦ *n* (*race*) Rasse *f*, Zucht *f*; **~ing** *n* Züchtung *f*; (*upbringing*) Erziehung *f*

breeze [briːz] *n* Brise *f*; **breezy** *adj* windig; (*manner*) munter

brevity ['brɛvɪtɪ] *n* Kürze *f*

brew [bruː] *vt* (*beer*) brauen ♦ *vi* (*storm*) sich zusammenziehen; **~ery** *n* Brauerei *f*

bribe [braɪb] *n* Bestechungsgeld *nt*, Bestechungsgeschenk *nt* ♦ *vt* bestechen; **~ry** ['braɪbərɪ] *n* Bestechung *f*

bric-a-brac ['brɪkəbræk] *n* Nippes *pl*

brick [brɪk] *n* Backstein *m*; **~layer** *n* Maurer *m*; **~works** *n* Ziegelei *f*

bridal ['braɪdl] *adj* Braut-

bride [braɪd] *n* Braut *f*; **~groom** *n* Bräutigam *m*; **~smaid** *n* Brautjungfer *f*

bridge [brɪdʒ] *n* Brücke *f*; (*NAUT*) Kommandobrücke *f*; (*CARDS*) Bridge *nt*; (*ANAT*) Nasenrücken *m* ♦ *vt* eine Brücke schlagen über +*acc*; (*fig*) überbrücken

bridle ['braɪdl] *n* Zaum *m*; (*fig*) zügeln; (*horse*) aufzäumen; **~ path** *n* Reitweg *m*

brief [briːf] *adj* kurz ♦ *n* (*JUR*) Akten *pl* ♦ *vt* instruieren; **~s** *npl* (*underwear*)

Schlüpfer m, Slip m; **~case** n Aktentasche f; **~ing** n (genaue) Anweisung f; **~ly** adv kurz

brigadier [brɪgəˈdɪəˈ] n Brigadegeneral m

bright [braɪt] adj hell; (cheerful) heiter; (idea) klug; **~en (up)** [ˈbraɪtn-] vt aufhellen; (person) aufheitern ♦ vi sich aufheitern

brilliance [ˈbrɪljəns] n Glanz m; (of person) Scharfsinn m

brilliant [ˈbrɪljənt] adj glänzend

brim [brɪm] n Rand m

brine [braɪn] n Salzwasser nt

bring [brɪŋ] (pt, pp brought) vt bringen; **~ about** vt zustande or zu Standebringen; **~ back** vt zurückbringen; **~ down** vt (price) senken; **~ forward** vt (meeting) vorverlegen; (COMM) übertragen; **~ in** vt hereinbringen; (harvest) einbringen; **~ off** vt davontragen; (success) erzielen; **~ out** vt (object) herausbringen; **~ round** or **to** vt wieder zu sich bringen; **~ up** vt aufziehen; (question) zur Sprache bringen

brink [brɪŋk] n Rand m

brisk [brɪsk] adj lebhaft

bristle [ˈbrɪsl] n Borste f ♦ vi sich sträuben; **bristling with** strotzend vor +dat

Britain [ˈbrɪtən] n (also: **Great ~**) Großbritannien nt

British [ˈbrɪtɪʃ] adj britisch ♦ npl: **the ~** die Briten pl; **~ Isles** npl: **the ~ Isles** die Britischen Inseln pl; **~ Rail** n die Britische Eisenbahnen

Briton [ˈbrɪtən] n Brite m, Britin f

Brittany [ˈbrɪtənɪ] n die Bretagne

brittle [ˈbrɪtl] adj spröde

broach [brəʊtʃ] vt (subject) anschneiden

broad [brɔːd] adj breit; (hint) deutlich; (general) allgemein; (accent) stark; **in ~ daylight** am hellichten Tag; **~cast** (pt, pp broadcast) n Rundfunkübertragung f ♦ vt, vi übertragen, senden; **~en** vt erweitern ♦ vi sich er-

weitern; **~ly** adv allgemein gesagt; **~-minded** adj tolerant

broccoli [ˈbrɒkəlɪ] n Brokkoli pl

brochure [ˈbrəʊʃjuəˈ] n Broschüre f

broil [brɔɪl] vt (grill) grillen

broke [brəʊk] pt of **break** ♦ adj (inf) pleite

broken [ˈbrəʊkən] pp of **break** ♦ adj: **~ leg** gebrochenes Bein; **in ~ English** in gebrochenem Englisch; **~-hearted** adj untröstlich

broker [ˈbrəʊkəˈ] n Makler m

brolly [ˈbrɒlɪ] (BRIT: inf) n Schirm m

bronchitis [brɒŋˈkaɪtɪs] n Bronchitis f

bronze [brɒnz] n Bronze f

brooch [brəʊtʃ] n Brosche f

brood [bruːd] n Brut f ♦ vi brüten

brook [brʊk] n Bach m

broom [brʊm] n Besen m

Bros. abbr = **Brothers**

broth [brɒθ] n Suppe f, Fleischbrühe f

brothel [ˈbrɒθl] n Bordell m

brother [ˈbrʌðəˈ] n Bruder m; **~-in-law** n Schwager m

brought [brɔːt] pt, pp of **bring**

brow [braʊ] n (eyebrow) (Augen)braue f; (forehead) Stirn f; (of hill) Bergkuppe f

brown [braʊn] adj braun ♦ n Braun nt ♦ vt bräunen; **~ bread** n Mischbrot nt; **B~ie** n Wichtel m; **~ paper** n Packpapier nt; **~ sugar** n braune(r) Zucker m

browse [braʊz] vi (in books) blättern; (in shop) schmökern, herumschauen

bruise [bruːz] n Bluterguss m, blaue(r) Fleck m ♦ vt einen blauen Fleck geben ♦ vi einen blauen Fleck bekommen

brunt [brʌnt] n volle Wucht f

brush [brʌʃ] n Bürste f; (for sweeping) Handbesen m; (for painting) Pinsel m; (fight) kurze(r) Kampf m; (MIL) Scharmützel nt; (fig) Auseinandersetzung f ♦ vt (clean) bürsten; (sweep) fegen; (usu: ~ past, ~ against) streifen; **~ aside** vt abtun; **~ up** vt (knowledge) auffrischen; **~wood** n Gestrüpp nt

brusque [bruːsk] adj schroff

Brussels ['brʌslz] n Brüssel nt; ~ **sprout** n Rosenkohl m

brutal ['bru:tl] adj brutal

brute [bru:t] n (person) Scheusal nt ♦ adj: **by ~ force** mit roher Kraft

B.Sc. n abbr = **Bachelor of Science**

BSE n abbr (= bovine spongiform encephalopathy) BSE f

bubble ['bʌbl] n (Luft)blase f ♦ vi sprudeln; (with joy) übersprudeln; ~ **bath** n Schaumbad nt; ~ **gum** n Kaugummi m or nt

buck [bʌk] n Bock m; (US: inf) Dollar m ♦ vi bocken; **to pass the ~ (to sb)** die Verantwortung (auf jdn) abschieben; ~ **up** (inf) vi sich zusammenreißen

bucket ['bʌkɪt] n Eimer m

Buckingham Palace

Buckingham Palace ist die offizielle Londoner Residenz der britischen Monarchen und liegt am St James Park. Der Palast wurde 1703 für den Herzog von Buckingham erbaut, 1762 von George III. gekauft, zwischen 1821 und 1836 von John Nash umgebaut, und Anfang des 20. Jahrhunderts teilweise neu gestaltet. Teile des Buckingham Palace sind heute der Öffentlichkeit zugänglich.

buckle ['bʌkl] n Schnalle f ♦ vt (an- or zusammen)schnallen ♦ vi (bend) sich verziehen

bud [bʌd] n Knospe f ♦ vi knospen, keimen

Buddhism ['budɪzəm] n Buddhismus m; **Buddhist** adj buddhistisch ♦ n Buddhist(in) m(f)

budding ['bʌdɪŋ] adj angehend

buddy ['bʌdɪ] (inf) n Kumpel m

budge [bʌdʒ] vt, vi (sich) von der Stelle rühren

budgerigar ['bʌdʒərɪgɑːr] n Wellensittich m

budget ['bʌdʒɪt] n Budget nt; (POL) Haushalt m ♦ vi: **to ~ for sth** etw ein-

planen

budgie ['bʌdʒɪ] n = **budgerigar**

buff [bʌf] adj (colour) lederfarben ♦ n (enthusiast) Fan m

buffalo ['bʌfələu] (pl ~ or ~es) n (BRIT) Büffel m; (US: bison) Bison m

buffer ['bʌfər] n Puffer m; (COMPUT) Pufferspeicher m; ~ **zone** n Pufferzone f

buffet¹ ['bʌfɪt] n (blow) Schlag m ♦ vt (herum)stossen

buffet² ['bufeɪ] (BRIT) n (bar) Imbissraum m, Erfrischungsraum m; (food) (kaltes) Büffett nt; ~ **car** (BRIT) n Speisewagen m

bug [bʌg] n (also fig) Wanze f ♦ vt verwanzen; **the room is bugged** das Zimmer ist verwanzt

bugle ['bju:gl] n Jagdhorn nt; (MIL: MUS) Bügelhorn nt

build [bɪld] (pt, pp built) vt bauen ♦ n Körperbau m; ~ **up** vt aufbauen; ~**er** n Bauunternehmer m; ~**ing** n Gebäude nt; ~**ing society** (BRIT) n Bausparkasse f

built [bɪlt] pt, pp of **build**; ~**-in** adj (cupboard) eingebaut; ~**-up area** n Wohngebiet nt

bulb [bʌlb] n (BOT) (Blumen)zwiebel f; (ELEC) Glühlampe f, Birne f

Bulgaria [bʌl'gɛərɪə] n Bulgarien nt; ~n adj bulgarisch ♦ n Bulgare m, Bulgarin f; (LING) Bulgarisch nt

bulge [bʌldʒ] n Wölbung f ♦ vi sich wölben

bulk [bʌlk] n Größe f, Masse f; (greater part) Großteil m; **in ~** (COMM) en gros; **the ~ of** der größte Teil +gen; ~**head** n Schott nt; ~**y** adj (sehr) umfangreich; (goods) sperrig

bull [bul] n Bulle m; (cattle) Stier m; ~**dog** n Bulldogge f

bulldozer ['buldəuzər] n Planierraupe f

bullet ['bulɪt] n Kugel f

bulletin ['bulɪtɪn] n Bulletin nt, Bekanntmachung f

bulletproof ['bulɪtpru:f] adj kugelsicher

bullfight ['bulfaɪt] n Stierkampf m; **~er** n Stierkämpfer m; **~ing** n Stierkampf m

bullion ['buljən] n Barren m

bullock ['bulək] n Ochse m

bullring n Stierkampfarena f

bull's-eye ['bulzaɪ] n Zentrum nt

bully ['bulɪ] n Raufbold m ♦ vt einschüchtern

bum [bʌm] n (inf: backside) Hintern m; (tramp) Landstreicher m

bumblebee ['bʌmblbiː] n Hummel f

bump [bʌmp] n (blow) Stoß m; (swelling) Beule f ♦ vt, vi stoßen, prallen; **~ into** vt fus stoßen gegen +acc, vt (person) treffen; **~er** n (AUT) Stoßstange f ♦ adj (edition) dick; (harvest) Rekord-

bumpy ['bʌmpɪ] adj holprig

bun [bʌn] n Korinthenbrötchen nt

bunch [bʌntʃ] n (of flowers) Strauß m; (of keys) Bund m; (of people) Haufen m; **~es** npl (in hair) Zöpfe pl

bundle ['bʌndl] n Bündel nt ♦ vt (also: **~ up**) bündeln

bungalow ['bʌŋgələu] n einstöckige(s) Haus nt, Bungalow m

bungle ['bʌŋgl] vt verpfuschen

bunion ['bʌnjən] n entzündete(r) Fußballen m

bunk [bʌŋk] n Schlafkoje f; **~ beds** npl Etagenbett nt

bunker ['bʌŋkər] n (coal store) Kohlenbunker m; (GOLF) Sandloch nt

bunny ['bʌnɪ] n (also: **~ rabbit**) Häschen nt

bunting ['bʌntɪŋ] n Fahnentuch nt

buoy [bɔɪ] n Boje f; (lifebuoy) Rettungsboje f; **~ant** adj (floating) schwimmend; (fig) heiter

burden ['bɜːdn] n (weight) Ladung f, Last f; (fig) Bürde f ♦ vt belasten

bureau ['bjuərəu] n (pl **~x**) n (BRIT: writing desk) Sekretär m; (us: chest of drawers) Kommode f; (for information etc) Büro nt

bureaucracy [bjuə'rɔkrəsɪ] n Bürokratie f

bureaucrat ['bjuərəkræt] n Büro-
krat(in) m(f)

bureaux ['bjuərəuz] npl of **bureau**

burglar ['bɜːglər] n Einbrecher m; **~ alarm** n Einbruchssicherung f; **~y** n Einbruch m

burial ['berɪəl] n Beerdigung f

burly ['bɜːlɪ] adj stämmig

Burma ['bɜːmə] n Birma nt

burn [bɜːn] (pt, pp **burned** or **burnt**) vt verbrennen ♦ vi brennen ♦ n Brandwunde f; **~ down** vt, vi abbrennen; **~er** n Brenner m; **~ing** adj brennend; **~t** [bɜːnt] pt, pp of **burn**

burrow ['bʌrəu] n (of fox) Bau m; (of rabbit) Höhle f ♦ vt eingraben

bursar ['bɜːsər] n Kassenverwalter m, Quästor m; **~y** (BRIT) n Stipendium nt

burst [bɜːst] (pt, pp **burst**) vt zerbrechen ♦ vi platzen ♦ n Explosion f; (outbreak) Ausbruch m; (in pipe) Bruch(stelle f) m; **to ~ into flames** in Flammen aufgehen; **to ~ into tears** in Tränen ausbrechen; **to ~ out laughing** in Gelächter ausbrechen; **~ into** vt fus (room etc) platzen in +acc; **~ open** vi aufbrechen

bury ['berɪ] vt vergraben; (in grave) beerdigen

bus [bʌs] n (Auto)bus m, Omnibus m

bush [buʃ] n Busch m; **to beat about the ~** wie die Katze um den heißen Brei herumgehen; **~y** ['buʃɪ] adj buschig

busily ['bɪzɪlɪ] adv geschäftig

business ['bɪznɪs] n Geschäft nt; (concern) Angelegenheit f; **it's none of your ~** es geht dich nichts an; **to mean ~** es ernst meinen; **to be away on ~** geschäftlich verreist sein; **it's my ~ to ...** es ist meine Sache, zu ...; **~like** adj geschäftsmäßig; **~man** (irreg) n Geschäftsmann m; **~ trip** n Geschäftsreise f; **~woman** (irreg) n Geschäftsfrau f

busker ['bʌskər] (BRIT) n Straßenmusikant m

bus: ~ shelter n Wartehäuschen nt; **~**

station n Busbahnhof m; **~ stop** n Bushaltestelle f

bust [bʌst] n Büste f ♦ adj (broken) kaputt(gegangen); (business) pleite: **to go ~** Pleite machen

bustle ['bʌsl] n Getriebe nt ♦ vi hasten

bustling ['bʌslɪŋ] adj geschäftig

busy ['bɪzɪ] adj beschäftigt; (road) belebt ♦ vt: **to ~ o.s.** sich beschäftigen; **~body** n Übereifrige(r) mf; **~ signal** (US) n (TEL) Besetzzeichen nt

KEYWORD

but [bʌt] conj 1 (yet) aber; **not X but Y** nicht X sondern Y

2 (however): **I'd love to come, but I'm busy** ich würde gern kommen, bin aber beschäftigt

3 (showing disagreement, surprise etc): **but that's fantastic!** (aber) das ist ja fantastisch!

♦ prep (apart from, except): **nothing but trouble** nichts als Ärger; **no-one but him can do it** niemand außer ihn kann es machen; **but for you/your help** ohne dich/deine Hilfe; **anything but that** alles, nur das nicht

♦ adv (just, only): **she's but a child** sie ist noch ein Kind; **had I but known** wenn ich es nur gewusst hätte; **I can but try** ich kann es immerhin versuchen; **all but finished** so gut wie fertig

butcher ['bʊtʃə*] n Metzger m; (murderer) Schlächter m ♦ vt schlachten; (kill) abschlachten; **~'s (shop)** n Metzgerei f

butler ['bʌtlə*] n Butler m

butt [bʌt] n (cask) große(s) Fass nt; (BRIT: fig: target) Zielscheibe f; (of gun) Kolben m; (of cigarette) Stummel m ♦ vt (mit dem Kopf) stoßen; **~ in** vi sich einmischen

butter ['bʌtə*] n Butter f ♦ vt buttern; **~ bean** n Wachsbohne f; **~cup** n Butterblume f

butterfly ['bʌtəflaɪ] n Schmetterling m; (SWIMMING: also: **~ stroke**) Butterflystil m

buttocks ['bʌtəks] npl Gesäß nt

button ['bʌtn] n Knopf m ♦ vt, vi (also: **~ up**) zuknöpfen

buttress ['bʌtrɪs] n Strebepfeiler m; Stützbogen m

buxom ['bʌksəm] adj drall

buy [baɪ] (pt, pp bought) vt kaufen ♦ n Kauf m; **to ~ sb a drink** jdm einen Drink spendieren; **~er** n Käufer(in) m(f)

buzz [bʌz] n Summen nt ♦ vi summen; **~er** n Summer m; **~ word** n Modewort nt

KEYWORD

by [baɪ] prep 1 (referring to cause, agent) of, durch; **killed by lightning** vom Blitz getötet; **a painting by Picasso** ein Gemälde von Picasso

2 (referring to method, manner): **by bus/car/train** mit dem Bus/Auto/Zug; **to pay by cheque** mit per Scheck bezahlen; **by moonlight** bei Mondschein; **by saving hard**, ... indem er einen sparte, ... er ...

3 (via, through) über +acc; **he came in by the back door** er kam durch die Hintertür herein

4 (close to, past) bei, an +dat; **a holiday by the sea** ein Urlaub am Meer; **she rushed by me** sie eilte an mir vorbei

5 (not later than): **by 4 o'clock** bis 4 Uhr; **by this time tomorrow** morgen um diese Zeit; **by the time I got here it was too late** als ich hier ankam, war es zu spät

6 (during): **by day** bei Tag

7 (amount): **by the kilo/metre** kiloweise/meterweise; **paid by the hour** stundenweise bezahlt

8 (MATH, measure): **to divide by 3** durch 3 teilen; **to multiply by 3** mit 3 malnehmen; **a room 3 metres by 4** ein Zimmer 3 mal 4 Meter; **it's broad-**

er by a metre es ist (um) einem Meter breiter

9 (according to) nach; **it's all right by me** von mir aus gern

10: (all) by oneself etc ganz allein

11: by the way übrigens

♦ *adv 1 see* **go; pass** *etc*

2: by and by irgendwann; (with past tenses) nach einiger Zeit; **by and large** (on the whole) im Großen und Ganzen

bye(-bye) ['baɪ('baɪ)] *excl* (auf) Wiedersehen

by(e)-law ['baɪlɔː] *n* Verordnung *f*

by-election ['baɪlekʃən] (BRIT) *n* Nachwahl *f*

bygone ['baɪgɔn] *adj* vergangen ♦ *n:* **let ~s be ~s** lass(t) das Vergangene vergangen sein

bypass ['baɪpɑːs] *n* Umgehungsstraße *f* ♦ *vt* umgehen

by-product ['baɪprɔdʌkt] *n* Nebenprodukt *nt*

bystander ['baɪstændə*] *n* Zuschauer *m*

byte [baɪt] *n* (COMPUT) Byte *nt*

byword ['baɪwɔːd] *n* Inbegriff *m*

C, c

C [siː] *n* (MUS) C *nt*

C. *abbr* (= centigrade) C

C.A. *abbr* = **chartered accountant**

cab [kæb] *n* Taxi *nt*; (of train) Führerstand *m*; (of truck) Führersitz *m*

cabaret ['kæbəreɪ] *n* Kabarett *nt*

cabbage ['kæbɪdʒ] *n* Kohl(kopf) *m*

cabin ['kæbɪn] *n* Hütte *f*; (NAUT) Kajüte *f*; (AVIAT) Kabine *f*; **~ crew** (AVIAT) Flugbegleitpersonal *nt*; **~ cruiser** *n* Motorjacht *f*

cabinet ['kæbɪnɪt] *n* Schrank *m*; (for china) Vitrine *f*; (POL) Kabinett *nt*; **~maker** *n* Kunsttischler *m*

cable ['keɪbl] *n* Drahtseil *nt*, Tau *nt*; (TEL) (Leitungs)kabel *nt*; (telegram) Kabel *nt* ♦ *vt* kabeln, telegrafieren; **~ car** *n* Seilbahn *f*; **~ television** *n* Kabelfernsehen *nt*

cache [kæʃ] *n* geheime(s) (Waffen)lager *nt*; geheime(s) (Proviant)lager *nt*

cackle ['kækl] *vi* gackern

cacti ['kæktaɪ] *npl of* **cactus**

cactus ['kæktəs] (*pl* **cacti**) *n* Kaktus *m*, Kaktee *f*

caddie ['kædɪ] *n* (GOLF) Golfjunge *m*;

caddy ['kædɪ] *n* = **caddie**

cadet [kə'det] *n* Kadett *m*

cadge [kædʒ] *vt* schmarotzen

Caesarean [sɪ'zɛərɪən] *adj:* **~ (section)** Kaiserschnitt *m*

café ['kæfeɪ] *n* Café *nt*, Restaurant *nt*

cafeteria [kæfɪ'tɪərɪə] *n* Selbstbedienungsrestaurant *nt*

caffein(e) ['kæfiːn] *n* Koffein *nt*

cage [keɪdʒ] *n* Käfig *m* ♦ *vt* einsperren

cagey ['keɪdʒɪ] *adj* geheimnistuerisch, zurückhaltend

cagoule [kə'guːl] *n* Windhemd *nt*

Cairo ['kaɪərəu] *n* Kairo *nt*

cajole [kə'dʒəul] *vt* überreden

cake [keɪk] *n* Kuchen *m*; (of soap) Stück *nt*; **~d** *adj* verkrustet

calamity [kə'læmɪtɪ] *n* Unglück *nt*, (Schicksals)schlag *m*

calcium ['kælsɪəm] *n* Kalzium *nt*

calculate ['kælkjuleɪt] *vt* berechnen, kalkulieren; **calculating** *adj* berechnend; **calculation** [kælkju'leɪʃən] *n* Berechnung *f*; **calculator** *n* Rechner *m*

calendar ['kælɪndə*] *n* Kalender *m*; **~ month** *n* Kalendermonat *m*

calf [kɑːf] (*pl* **calves**) *n* Kalb *nt*; (also: **~skin**) Kalbsleder *nt*; (ANAT) Wade *f*

calibre ['kælɪbə*] (US **caliber**) *n* Kaliber *nt*

call [kɔːl] *vt* rufen; (name) nennen; (meeting) einberufen; (awaken) wecken; (TEL) anrufen ♦ *vi* (shout) rufen; (visit: also: **~ in, ~ round**) vorbeikommen ♦ *n* (shout) Ruf *m*; (TEL) Anruf *m*; **to be ~ed** heißen; **on ~** in Bereitschaft; **~ back** vi (return) wiederkommen; (TEL) zurückrufen; **~ for** vt fus (demand) erfordern, verlangen; (fetch) abholen; **~ off** vt (cancel) absagen; **~ on** vt fus (visit) besuchen; (turn to) bitten; **~ out** vt rufen; **~ up** vt (MIL) einberufen; **~box** (BRIT) n Telefonzelle f; **~ centre** n Telefoncenter nt, Callcenter nt; **~er** n Besucher(in) m(f); (TEL) Anrufer m; **~ girl** n Callgirl nt; **~-in** (US) n (phone-in) Phone-in nt; **~ing** n (vocation) Berufung f; **~ing card** (US) n Visitenkarte f

callous ['kæləs] adj herzlos

calm [kɑːm] n Ruhe f; (NAUT) Flaute f ♦ vt beruhigen ♦ adj ruhig; (person) gelassen; **~ down** vi sich beruhigen ♦ vt beruhigen

Calor gas ['kælər-] ® n Propangas nt

calorie ['kælərɪ] n Kalorie f

calves [kɑːvz] npl of **calf**

Cambodia [kæm'bəʊdɪə] n Kambodscha m

camcorder ['kæmkɔːdər] n Camcorder m

came [keɪm] pt of **come**

cameo ['kæmɪəʊ] n Kamee f

camera ['kæmərə] n Fotoapparat m, (CINE, TV) Kamera f; **in ~** unter Ausschluss der Öffentlichkeit; **~man** (irreg) n Kameramann m

camouflage ['kæməflɑːʒ] n Tarnung f ♦ vt tarnen

camp [kæmp] n Lager nt ♦ vi zelten, campen ♦ adj affektiert

campaign [kæm'peɪn] n Kampagne f, (MIL) Feldzug m ♦ vi (MIL) Krieg führen; (fig) werben, Propaganda machen; (POL) den Wahlkampf führen

camp: **~ bed** ['kæmp'bed] (BRIT) n Campingbett nt; **~er** ['kæmpər] n Camper(in) m(f); (vehicle) Campingwagen m; **~ing** ['kæmpɪŋ] n: **to go ~ing** zelten, Camping machen; **~ing gas** (US) n Campinggas nt; **~site** ['kæmpsaɪt] n Campingplatz m

campus ['kæmpəs] n Universi-

tätsgelände nt, Campus m

can¹ [kæn] n Büchse f, Dose f; (for water) Kanne f ♦ vt konservieren, in Büchsen einmachen

can² [kæn] (negative **cannot, can't**, conditional **could**) aux vb 1 (be able to, know how to) können; **I can see you tomorrow, if you like** ich kann Sie morgen sehen, wenn Sie wollen; **I can swim** ich kann schwimmen; **can you speak German?** sprechen Sie Deutsch?

2 (may) können, dürfen; **could I have a word with you?** könnte ich Sie kurz sprechen?

Canada ['kænədə] n Kanada nt; **Canadian** [kə'neɪdɪən] adj kanadisch ♦ n Kanadier(in) m(f)

canal [kə'næl] n Kanal m

canapé ['kænəpeɪ] n Cocktail- or Appetithappen m

canary [kə'nɛərɪ] n Kanarienvogel m

cancel ['kænsəl] vt absagen; (delete) durchstreichen; (train) streichen; **~lation** [kænsə'leɪʃən] n Absage f, Streichung f

cancer ['kænsər] n (ASTROL: C~) Krebs m

candid ['kændɪd] adj offen, ehrlich

candidate ['kændɪdeɪt] n Kandidat(in) m(f)

candle ['kændl] n Kerze f; **~light** n Kerzenlicht nt; **~stick** n (also: **~ holder**) Kerzenhalter m

candour ['kændər] (US **candor**) n Offenheit f

candy ['kændɪ] n Kandis(zucker) m; (US) Bonbons pl; **~floss** (BRIT) n Zuckerwatte f

cane [keɪn] n (BOT) Rohr nt; (stick) Stock m ♦ vt (BRIT: beat) schlagen

canine ['keɪnaɪn] adj Hunde-

canister ['kænɪstər] n Blechdose f

cannabis ['kænəbɪs] n Hanf m, Haschisch nt

canned [kænd] *adj* Büchsen-, eingemacht

cannon ['kænən] (*pl* ~ *or* ~**s**) *n* Kanone *f*

cannot ['kænɒt] = **can not**

canny ['kænɪ] *adj* schlau

canoe [kə'nuː] *n* Kanu *nt*; ~**ing** *n* Kanusport *m*, Kanufahren *nt*

canon ['kænən] *n* (*clergyman*) Domherr *m*; (*standard*) Grundsatz *m*

can-opener ['kænəʊpnə'] *n* Büchsenöffner *m*

canopy ['kænəpɪ] *n* Baldachin *m*

can't [kænt] = **can not**

cantankerous [kæn'tæŋkərəs] *adj* zänkisch, mürrisch

canteen [kæn'tiːn] *n* Kantine *f*; (*BRIT: of cutlery*) Besteckkasten *m*

canter ['kæntə'] *n* Kanter *m* ♦ *vi* in kurzem Galopp reiten

canvas ['kænvəs] *n* Segeltuch *nt*; (*sail*) Segel *nt*; (*for painting*) Leinwand *f*; **under** ~ (*camping*) in Zelten

canvass ['kænvəs] *vi* um Stimmen werben; ~**ing** *n* Wahlwerbung *f*

canyon ['kænjən] *n* Felsenschlucht *f*

cap [kæp] *n* Mütze *f*; (*of pen*) Kappe *f*; (*of bottle*) Deckel *m* ♦ *vt* (*surpass*) übertreffen; (*SPORT*) aufstellen; (*put limit on*) einen Höchstsatz festlegen für

capability [keɪpə'bɪlɪtɪ] *n* Fähigkeit *f*

capable ['keɪpəbl] *adj* fähig

capacity [kə'pæsɪtɪ] *n* Fassungsvermögen *nt*; (*ability*) Fähigkeit *f*; (*position*) Eigenschaft *f*

cape [keɪp] *n* (*garment*) Cape *nt*, Umhang *m*; (*GEOG*) Kap *nt*

caper ['keɪpə'] *n* (*COOK: usu:* ~**s**) Kaper *f*; (*prank*) Kapriole *f*

capital ['kæpɪtl] *n* (~ *city*) Hauptstadt *f*; (*FIN*) Kapital *nt*; (~ *letter*) Großbuchstabe *m*; ~ **gains tax** *n* Kapitalertragssteuer *f*; ~**ism** *n* Kapitalismus *m*; ~**ist** *adj* kapitalistisch ♦ *n* Kapitalist(in) *m(f)*; ~**ize**: *vi*: **to** ~**ize on** Kapital schlagen aus; ~ **punishment** *n* Todesstrafe *f*

Capitol *ist das Gebäude in Washington auf dem Capitol Hill, in dem der Kongress der USA zusammentritt. Die Bezeichnung wird in vielen amerikanischen Bundesstaaten auch für das Parlamentsgebäude des jeweiligen Staates verwendet.*

Capricorn ['kæprɪkɔːn] *n* Steinbock *m*

capsize [kæp'saɪz] *vt, vi* kentern

capsule ['kæpsjuːl] *n* Kapsel *f*

captain ['kæptɪn] *n* Kapitän *m*; (*MIL*) Hauptmann *m* ♦ *vt* anführen

caption ['kæpʃən] *n* (*heading*) Überschrift *f*; (*to picture*) Unterschrift *f*

captivate ['kæptɪveɪt] *vt* fesseln

captive ['kæptɪv] *n* Gefangene(r) *f(m)* ♦ *adj* gefangen (gehalten); **captivity** [kæp'tɪvɪtɪ] *n* Gefangenschaft *f*

capture ['kæptʃə'] *vt* gefangen nehmen; (*place*) erobern; (*attention*) erregen ♦ *n* Gefangennahme *f*; (*data* ~) Erfassung *f*

car [kɑː'] *n* Auto *nt*, Wagen *m*; (*RAIL*) Wagen *m*

caramel ['kærəməl] *n* Karamelle *f*, Karamellbonbon *m or nt*; (*burnt sugar*) Karamell *m*

carat ['kærət] *n* Karat *nt*

caravan ['kærəvæn] *n* (*BRIT*) Wohnwagen *m*; (*in desert*) Karawane *f*; ~**ning** *n* Caravaning *nt*, Urlaub *m* im Wohnwagen; ~ **site** *n* (*BRIT*) Campingplatz *m* für Wohnwagen

carbohydrate [kɑːbəʊ'haɪdreɪt] *n* Kohlenhydrat *nt*

carbon ['kɑːbən] *n* Kohlenstoff *m*; ~ **copy** *n* Durchschlag *m*; ~ **dioxide** *n* Kohlendioxyd *nt*; ~ **monoxide** *n* Kohlenmonoxyd *nt*; ~ **paper** *n* Kohlepapier *nt*

car boot sale *n* auf einem Parkplatz stattfindender Flohmarkt mit dem Kofferraum als Auslage

carburettor [kɑːbju'retə'] (*US* **carbure-**

tor) n Vergaser m

carcass ['kɑːkəs] n Kadaver m

card [kɑːd] n Karte f; **~board** n Pappe f; **~ game** n Kartenspiel nt

cardiac ['kɑːdɪæk] adj Herz-

cardigan ['kɑːdɪgən] n Strickjacke f

cardinal ['kɑːdɪnl] adj: **~ number** Kardinalzahl f ♦ n (REL) Kardinal m

card index n Kartei f; (in library) Katalog m

cardphone n Kartentelefon nt

care [kɛəʳ] n (of teeth, car etc) Pflege f; (of children) Fürsorge f; (~fulness) Sorgfalt f; (worry) Sorge f ♦ vi: **to ~ about** sich kümmern um; (*like*) **to be in sb's ~** in jds Obhut; **I don't ~** das ist mir egal; **I couldn't ~ less** es ist mir doch völlig egal; **to take ~** aufpassen; **to take ~ of** sorgen für; **to take ~ to do sth** sich bemühen, etw zu tun; **~ for** vt sorgen für; (*like*) mögen

career [kəˈrɪəʳ] n Karriere f, Laufbahn f ♦ vi (*also*: **~ along**) rasen; **~ woman** (irreg) n Karrierefrau f

care: **~free** adj sorgenfrei; **~ful** adj sorgfältig; (be) **~ful!** pass auf!; **~fully** adv vorsichtig; (methodically) sorgfältig; **~less** adj nachlässig; **~lessness** n Nachlässigkeit f; **~r** n (MED) Betreuer(in) m(f)

caress [kəˈrɛs] n Liebkosung f ♦ vt liebkosen

caretaker ['kɛəteɪkəʳ] n Hausmeister m

car ferry n Autofähre f

cargo ['kɑːgəu] (pl **~es**) n Schiffsladung f

car hire n Autovermietung f

Caribbean [kærɪˈbiːən] n: **the ~ (Sea)** die Karibik

caricature ['kærɪkətjuəʳ] n Karikatur f

caring ['kɛərɪŋ] adj (society, organization) sozial eingestellt; (person) liebevoll

carnage ['kɑːnɪdʒ] n Blutbad nt

carnation [kɑːˈneɪʃən] n Nelke f

carnival ['kɑːnɪvl] n Karneval m, Fasching m; (US: fun fair) Kirmes f

carnivorous [kɑːˈnɪvərəs] adj Fleisch fressend

carol ['kærəl] n: **(Christmas) ~** (Weihnachts)lied nt

carp [kɑːp] n (fish) Karpfen m

car park (BRIT) n Parkplatz m; (covered) Parkhaus nt

carpenter ['kɑːpɪntəʳ] n Zimmermann m; **carpentry** ['kɑːpɪntrɪ] n Zimmerei f

carpet ['kɑːpɪt] n Teppich m ♦ vt mit einem Teppich auslegen; **~ bombing** n Flächenbombardierung f; **~ slippers** npl Pantoffeln pl; **~ sweeper** ['kɑːpɪtswiːpəʳ] n Teppichkehrer m

car phone n (TEL) Autotelefon nt

car rental (US) n Autovermietung f

carriage ['kærɪdʒ] n Kutsche f, (RAIL, of typewriter) Wagen m; (of goods) Beförderung f; (bearing) Haltung f; **~ return** n (on typewriter) Rücklauftaste f; **~way** (BRIT) n (part of road) Fahrbahn f

carrier ['kærɪəʳ] n Träger(in) m(f); (COMM) Spediteur m; **~ bag** (BRIT) n Tragetasche m

carrot ['kærət] n Möhre f, Karotte f

carry ['kærɪ] vt, vi tragen; **to get carried away** (fig) sich nicht mehr bremsen können; **~ on** vi (continue) weitermachen; (inf: complain) Theater machen; **~ out** vt (orders) ausführen; (investigation) durchführen; **~cot** (BRIT) n Babytragetasche f; **~-on** (inf) n (fuss) Theater nt

cart [kɑːt] n Wagen m, Karren m ♦ vt schleppen

cartilage ['kɑːtɪlɪdʒ] n Knorpel m

carton ['kɑːtən] n Karton m; (of milk) Tüte f

cartoon [kɑːˈtuːn] n (PRESS) Karikatur f; (comic strip) Comics pl; (CINE) (Zeichen)trickfilm m

cartridge ['kɑːtrɪdʒ] n Patrone f

carve [kɑːv] vt (wood) schnitzen; (stone) meißeln; (meat) (vor)schneiden; **~ up** vt aufschneiden; **carving** ['kɑːvɪŋ] n Schnitzerei f; **carving knife** n Tran(s)chiermesser nt

car wash n Autowäsche f

cascade ['kæs'keɪd] n Wasserfall m ♦ vi kaskadenartig herabfallen

case [keɪs] n (box) Kasten m; (BRIT: also: **suitcase**) Koffer m; (JUR, matter) Fall m; **in ~** falls, im Falle; **in any ~** jedenfalls, auf jeden Fall

cash [kæʃ] n (Bar)geld nt ♦ vt einlösen; **~ on delivery** per Nachnahme; **~ book** n Kassenbuch nt; **~ card** n Scheckkarte f; **~ desk** (BRIT) n Kasse f; **~ dispenser** n Geldautomat m

cashew [kæˈʃuː] n (also: **~ nut**) Cashewnuss f

cash flow n Cashflow m

cashier [kæˈʃɪə] n Kassierer(in) m(f)

cashmere ['kæʃmɪə] n Kaschmirwolle f

cash register n Registrierkasse f

casing ['keɪsɪŋ] n Gehäuse nt

casino [kəˈsiːnəʊ] n Kasino nt

casket ['kɑːskɪt] n Kästchen nt; (US: coffin) Sarg m

casserole ['kæsərəʊl] n Kasserolle f; (food) Auflauf m

cassette [kæˈset] n Kassette f; **~ player** n Kassettengerät nt

cast [kɑːst] (pt, pp **cast**) vt werfen; (horns) verlieren; (metal) gießen; (THEAT) besetzen; (vote) abgeben ♦ n (THEAT) Besetzung f; (also: **plaster ~**) Gipsverband m; **~ off** vi (NAUT) losmachen

castaway ['kɑːstəweɪ] n Schiffbrüchige(r) f(m)

caste [kɑːst] n Kaste f

caster sugar ['kɑːstə-] (BRIT) n Raffinade f

casting vote ['kɑːstɪŋ-] (BRIT) n entscheidende Stimme f

cast iron n Gusseisen nt

castle ['kɑːsl] n Burg f; Schloss nt; (CHESS) Turm m

castor ['kɑːstə] n (wheel) Laufrolle f

castor oil n Rizinusöl nt

castrate [kæsˈtreɪt] vt kastrieren

casual ['kæʒjʊl] adj (attitude) nachlässig; (dress) leger; (meeting) zufällig; (work) Gelegenheits-; **~ly** adv (dress) zwanglos, leger; (remark) beiläufig

casualty ['kæʒjʊltɪ] n Verletzte(r) f(m); (dead) Tote(r) f(m); (also: **~ department**) Unfallstation f

cat [kæt] n Katze f

catalogue ['kætəlɒg] (US **catalog**) n Katalog m ♦ vt katalogisieren

catalyst ['kætəlɪst] n Katalysator m

catalytic converter [kætəˈlɪtɪk kənˈvɜːtə] n Katalysator m

catapult ['kætəpʌlt] n Schleuder f

cataract ['kætərækt] n (MED) graue(r) Star m

catarrh [kəˈtɑː] n Katarr(h) m

catastrophe [kəˈtæstrəfɪ] n Katastrophe f

catch [kætʃ] (pt, pp **caught**) vt fangen; (arrest) fassen; (train) erreichen; (person: by surprise) ertappen; (also: **~ up**) einholen ♦ vi (fire) in Gang kommen; (in branches etc) hängen bleiben ♦ n (fish etc) Fang m; (trick) Haken m; (of lock) Sperrhaken m; **to ~ an illness** sich auf eine Krankheit holen; **to ~ fire** Feuer fangen; **~ on** vi (understand) begreifen; (grow popular) ankommen; **~ up** vi (fig) aufholen; **~ing** ['kætʃɪŋ] adj ansteckend; **~ment area** ['kætʃmənt-] (BRIT) n Einzugsgebiet nt; **~ phrase** n Slogan m; **~y** ['kætʃɪ] adj (tune) eingängig

categoric(al) [kætɪˈgɒrɪk(l)] adj kategorisch

category ['kætɪgərɪ] n Kategorie f

cater ['keɪtə] vi versorgen; **~ for** (BRIT) vt fus (party) ausrichten; (needs) eingestellt sein auf +acc; **~er** n Lieferant(in) m(f) von Speisen und Getränken; **~ing** n Gastronomie f

caterpillar ['kætəpɪlə] n Raupe f; **~ track** ® n Gleiskette f

cathedral [kəˈθiːdrəl] n Kathedrale f, Dom m

Catholic ['kæθəlɪk] adj (REL) katholisch ♦ n Katholik(in) m(f); **c~** adj (tastes etc) vielseitig

CAT scan [kæt-] n Computertomografie f

Catseye ['kætsaɪ] (BRIT: ®) n (AUT) Katzenauge nt

cattle ['kætl] npl Vieh nt

catty ['kætɪ] adj gehässig

caucus ['kɔːkəs] n (POL) Gremium nt; (US: meeting) Sitzung f

caught [kɔːt] pt, pp of **catch**

cauliflower ['kɔlɪflauə'] n Blumenkohl m

cause [kɔːz] n Ursache f; (purpose) Sache f ♦ vt verursachen

causeway ['kɔːzweɪ] n Damm m

caustic ['kɔːstɪk] adj ätzend; (fig) bissig

caution ['kɔːʃən] n Vorsicht f; (warning) Verwarnung f ♦ vt verwarnen; **cautious** ['kɔːʃəs] adj vorsichtig

cavalry ['kævəlrɪ] n Kavallerie f

cave [keɪv] n Höhle f; **~ in** vi einstürzen; **~man** (irreg) n Höhlenmensch m

cavern ['kævən] n Höhle f

caviar(e) ['kævɪɑː'] n Kaviar m

cavity ['kævɪtɪ] n Loch nt

cavort [kə'vɔːt] vi umherspringen

C.B. n abbr (= Citizens' Band (Radio)) CB

C.B.I. n abbr (= Confederation of British Industry) ≃ BDI m

cc n abbr = **carbon copy; cubic centimetres**

CD n abbr (= compact disc) CD f

CDI n abbr (= Compact Disk Interactive) CD-I f

CD player n CD-Spieler m

CD-ROM n abbr (= compact disc readonly memory) CD-Rom f

cease [siːs] vi aufhören ♦ vt beenden; **~fire** n Feuereinstellung f; **~less** adj unaufhörlich

cedar ['siːdə'] n Zeder f

ceiling ['siːlɪŋ] n Decke f; (fig) Höchstgrenze f

celebrate ['sɛlɪbreɪt] vt, vi feiern; **~d** adj gefeiert; **celebration** [sɛlɪ'breɪʃən] n Feier f

celebrity [sɪ'lɛbrɪtɪ] n gefeierte Persönlichkeit f

celery ['sɛlərɪ] n Sellerie m or f

celibacy ['sɛlɪbəsɪ] n Zölibat nt or m

cell [sɛl] n Zelle f; (ELEC) Element nt

cellar ['sɛlə'] n Keller m

cello ['tʃɛləu] n Cello nt

Cellophane ['sɛləfeɪn] ® n Cellophan nt ®

cellphone ['sɛlfaun] n Funktelefon nt

cellular ['sɛljulə'] adj zellular

cellulose ['sɛljuləus] n Zellulose f

Celt [kɛlt, sɛlt] n Kelte m, Keltin f; **~ic** ['kɛltɪk, 'sɛltɪk] adj keltisch

cement [sə'mɛnt] n Zement m ♦ vt zementieren; **~ mixer** n Betonmischmaschine f

cemetery ['sɛmɪtrɪ] n Friedhof m

censor ['sɛnsə'] n Zensor m ♦ vt zensieren; **~ship** n Zensur f

censure ['sɛnʃə'] vt rügen

census ['sɛnsəs] n Volkszählung f

cent [sɛnt] n (US: coin) Cent m; see also **per cent**

centenary [sɛn'tiːnərɪ] n Jahrhundertfeier f

center ['sɛntə'] (US) n = **centre**

centigrade ['sɛntɪgreɪd] adj Celsius

centimetre ['sɛntɪmiːtə'] (US **centimeter**) n Zentimeter m

centipede ['sɛntɪpiːd] n Tausendfüßler m

central ['sɛntrəl] adj zentral; **C~ America** n Mittelamerika nt; **~ heating** n Zentralheizung f; **~ize** vt zentralisieren; **~ reservation** (BRIT) n (AUT) Mittelstreifen m

centre ['sɛntə'] (US **center**) n Zentrum nt ♦ vt zentrieren; **~-forward** n (SPORT) Mittelstürmer m; **~-half** n; (SPORT) Stopper m

century ['sɛntjurɪ] n Jahrhundert nt

ceramic [sɪ'ræmɪk] adj keramisch; **~s** npl Keramiken pl

cereal ['siːrɪəl] n (grain) Getreide nt; (at breakfast) Getreideflocken pl

cerebral ['sɛrɪbrəl] adj zerebral; (intel-

lectual) geistig

ceremony ['serɪmənɪ] *n* Zeremonie *f*; **to stand on ~** förmlich sein

certain ['sɜːtən] *adj* sicher; *(particular)* gewiß; **for ~** ganz bestimmt; **~ly** *adv* sicher, bestimmt; **~ty** *n* Gewißheit *f*

certificate [sə'tɪfɪkɪt] *n* Bescheinigung *f*; *(SCH etc)* Zeugnis *nt*

certified mail ['sɜːtɪfaɪd-] *(US)* *n* Einschreiben *nt*

certified public accountant ['sɜːtɪfaɪd-] *(US)* *n* geprüfte(r) Buchhalter *m*

certify ['sɜːtɪfaɪ] *vt* bescheinigen

cervical ['sɜːvɪkl] *adj* *(smear, cancer)* Gebärmutterhals-

cervix ['sɜːvɪks] *n* Gebärmutterhals *m*

cf. *abbr (= compare)* vgl.

CFC *n abbr (= chlorofluorocarbon)* FCKW *m*

ch. *abbr (= chapter)* Kap.

chafe [tʃeɪf] *vt* scheuern

chaffinch ['tʃæfɪntʃ] *n* Buchfink *m*

chain [tʃeɪn] *n* Kette *f* ♦ *vt (also: ~ up)* anketten; **~ reaction** *n* Kettenreaktion *f*; **~-smoke** *vi* kettenrauchen; **~ store** *n* Kettenladen *m*

chair [tʃeə*] *n* Stuhl *m*; *(armchair)* Sessel *m*; *(UNIV)* Lehrstuhl *m* ♦ *vt (meeting)* den Vorsitz führen bei; **~lift** *n* Sessellift *m*; **~man** *(irreg)* *n* Vorsitzende(r) *m*

chalet ['ʃæleɪ] *n* Chalet *nt*

chalk [tʃɔːk] *n* Kreide *f*

challenge ['tʃælɪndʒ] *n* Herausforderung *f* ♦ *vt* herausfordern; *(contest)* bestreiten; **challenging** *adj (tone)* herausfordernd; *(work)* anspruchsvoll

chamber ['tʃeɪmbə*] *n* Kammer *f*; **~ of commerce** Handelskammer *f*; **~maid** *n* Zimmermädchen *nt*; **~ music** *n* Kammermusik *f*

chamois ['ʃæmwɑː] *n* Gämse *f*

champagne [ʃæm'peɪn] *n* Champagner *m*, Sekt *m*

champion ['tʃæmpɪən] *n (SPORT)* Meister(in) *m(f)*; *(of cause)* Verfechter(in) *m(f)*; **~ship** *n* Meisterschaft *f*

chance [tʃɑːns] *n (luck)* Zufall *m*; *(possibility)* Möglichkeit *f*; *(opportunity)* Gelegenheit *f*, Chance *f*; *(risk)* Risiko *nt* ♦ *adj* zufällig ♦ *vt*: **to ~ it** es darauf ankommen lassen; **by ~** zufällig; **to take a ~** ein Risiko eingehen

chancellor ['tʃɑːnsələ*] *n* Kanzler *m*; **C~ of the Exchequer** *(BRIT)* *n* Schatzkanzler *m*

chandelier [ʃændə'lɪə*] *n* Kronleuchter *m*

change [tʃeɪndʒ] *vt* ändern; *(replace, COMM: money)* wechseln; *(exchange)* umtauschen; *(transform)* verwandeln ♦ *vi* sich ändern; *(~ trains)* umsteigen; *(~ clothes)* sich umziehen ♦ *n* Veränderung *f*; *(money returned)* Wechselgeld *nt*; *(coins)* Kleingeld *nt*; **to ~ one's mind** es sich dat anders überlegen; **to ~ into sth** *(be transformed)* sich in etw *acc* verwandeln; **for a ~** zur Abwechslung; **~able** *adj (weather)* wechselhaft; **~ machine** *n* Geldwechselautomat *m*; **~over** *n* Umstellung *f*

changing ['tʃeɪndʒɪŋ] *adj* veränderlich; **~ room** *(BRIT)* *n* Umkleideraum *m*

channel ['tʃænl] *n (stream)* Bachbett *nt*; *(NAUT)* Straße *f*; *(TV)* Kanal *m*; *(fig)* Weg *m* ♦ *vt (of efforts)* lenken; **the (English) C~** der Ärmelkanal; **~-hopping** *n (TV)* ständiges Umschalten; **C~ Islands** *npl*: **the C~ Islands** die Kanalinseln *pl*; **C~ Tunnel** *n*: **the C~ Tunnel** der Kanaltunnel

chant [tʃɑːnt] *n* Gesang *m*; *(of fans)* Sprechchor *m* ♦ *vt* intonieren

chaos ['keɪɒs] *n* Chaos *nt*

chap [tʃæp] *(inf)* *n* Kerl *m*

chapel ['tʃæpl] *n* Kapelle *f*

chaperon ['ʃæpərəʊn] *n* Anstandsdame *f*

chaplain ['tʃæplɪn] *n* Kaplan *m*

chapped [tʃæpt] *adj (skin, lips)* spröde

chapter ['tʃæptə*] *n* Kapitel *nt*

char [tʃɑː*] *vt (burn)* verkohlen

character ['kærɪktə*] *n* Charakter *m*, Wesen *nt*; *(in novel, film)* Figur *f*; **~istic**

[kærɪktə'rɪstɪk] *adj* **~istic (of sb/sth)** (für jdn/etw) charakteristisch ♦ *n* Kennzeichen, kennzeichnen ♦ **~ize** *vt* charakterisieren, kennzeichnen

charade [ʃə'rɑːd] *n* Scharade *f*

charcoal ['tʃɑːkəʊl] *n* Holzkohle *f*

charge [tʃɑːdʒ] *n* (*cost*) Preis *m*; (*JUR*) Anklage *f*; (*explosive*) Ladung *f*; (*attack*) Angriff *m* ♦ *vt* (*gun, battery*) laden; (*price*) verlangen; (*JUR*) anklagen; (*MIL*) angreifen ♦ *vi* (*rush*) (an)stürmen; **bank ~s** Bankgebühren *pl*; **free of ~** kostenlos; **to reverse the ~s** (*TEL*) ein R-Gespräch führen; **to be in ~ of** verantwortlich sein für; **to take ~** (die Verantwortung) übernehmen; **to ~ sth (up) to sb's account** jdm etw in Rechnung stellen; **~ card** *n* Kundenkarte *f*

charitable ['tʃærɪtəbl] *adj* wohltätig; (*lenient*) nachsichtig

charity ['tʃærɪtɪ] *n* (*institution*) Hilfswerk *nt*; (*attitude*) Nächstenliebe *f*

charm [tʃɑːm] *n* Charme *m*; (*spell*) Bann *m*; (*object*) Talisman *m* ♦ *vt* bezaubern; **~ing** *adj* reizend

chart [tʃɑːt] *n* Tabelle *f*; (*NAUT*) Seekarte *f* ♦ *vt* (*course*) abstecken

charter ['tʃɑːtə'] *vt* chartern ♦ *n* Schutzbrief *m*; **~ed accountant** *n* Wirtschaftsprüfer(in) *m(f)*; **~ flight** *n* Charterflug *m*

chase [tʃeɪs] *vt* jagen, verfolgen ♦ *n* Jagd *f*

chasm ['kæzəm] *n* Kluft *f*

chassis ['ʃæsɪ] *n* Fahrgestell *nt*

chat [tʃæt] *vi* (*also:* **have a ~**) plaudern ♦ *n* Plauderei *f*; **~ show** (*BRIT*) *n* Talkshow *f*

chatter ['tʃætə'] *vi* schwatzen; (*teeth*) klappern ♦ *n* Geschwätz *nt*; **~box** *n* Quasselstrippe *f*

chatty ['tʃætɪ] *adj* geschwätzig

chauffeur ['ʃəʊfə'] *n* Chauffeur *m*

chauvinist ['ʃəʊvɪnɪst] *n* (*male* **~**) Chauvi *m* (*inf*)

cheap [tʃiːp] *adj, adv* billig; **~ day re-**

turn *n* Tagesrückfahrkarte *f* (*zu einem günstigeren Tarif*); **~ly** *adv* billig

cheat [tʃiːt] *vt, vi* betrügen; (*SCH*) mogeln ♦ *n* Betrüger(in) *m(f)*

check [tʃek] *vt* (*examine*) prüfen; (*make sure*) kontrollieren; (*control*) kontrollieren; (*restrain*) zügeln; (*stop*) anhalten ♦ *n* (*examination, restraint*) Kontrolle *f*; (*bill*) Rechnung *f*; (*pattern*) Karo(muster) *nt*; (*US*) = **cheque** ♦ *adj* (*pattern, cloth*) kariert; **~ in** *vi* (*in hotel, airport*) sich anmelden ♦ *vt* (*luggage*) abfertigen lassen; **~ out** *vi* (*of hotel*) abreisen; **~ up** *vi* nachschauen; **~ up on** *vt* kontrollieren; **~ered** (*US*) *adj* = **chequered**; **~ers** (*US*) *n* (*draughts*) Damespiel *nt*; **~in (desk)** *n* Abfertigung *f*; **~ing account** *n* (*US*) (*current account*) Girokonto *nt*; **~mate** *n* Schachmatt *nt*; **~out** *n* Kasse *f*; **~point** *n* Kontrollpunkt *m*; **~room** (*US*) *n* (*left-luggage office*) Gepäckaufbewahrung *f*; **~up** *n* (Nach)prüfung *f*; (*MED*) (ärztliche) Untersuchung *f*

cheek [tʃiːk] *n* Backe *f*; (*fig*) Frechheit *f*; **~bone** *n* Backenknochen *m*; **~y** *adj* frech

cheep [tʃiːp] *vi* piepsen

cheer [tʃɪə'] *n* (*usu pl*) Hurra- or Beifallsruf *m* ♦ *vt* zujubeln; (*encourage*) aufmuntern ♦ *vi* jauchzen; **~s!** Prost!; **~ up** *vi* bessere Laune bekommen ♦ *vt* aufmuntern; **~ up!** nun lach doch mal!; **~ful** *adj* fröhlich

cheerio [tʃɪərɪ'əʊ] (*BRIT*) *excl* tschüss!

cheese [tʃiːz] *n* Käse *m*; **~board** *n* (gemischte) Käseplatte *f*

cheetah ['tʃiːtə] *n* Gepard *m*

chef [ʃef] *n* Küchenchef *m*

chemical ['kemɪkl] *adj* chemisch ♦ *n* Chemikalie *f*

chemist ['kemɪst] *n* (*BRIT: pharmacist*) Apotheker *m*, Drogist *m*; (*scientist*) Chemiker *m*; **~ry** *n* Chemie *f*; **~'s (shop)** (*BRIT*) *n* Apotheke *f*, Drogerie *f*

cheque [tʃek] (*BRIT*) *n* Scheck *m*; **~book** *n* Scheckbuch *nt*; **~ card** *n* Scheckkarte

f

chequered ['tʃɛkəd] *adj* (*fig*) bewegt

cherish ['tʃɛrɪʃ] *vt* (*person*) lieben; (*hope*) hegen

cherry ['tʃɛrɪ] *n* Kirsche f

chess [tʃɛs] *n* Schach *nt*; **~board** *n* Schachbrett *nt*; **~man** (*irreg*) *n* Schachfigur f

chest [tʃɛst] *n* (*ANAT*) Brust f; (*box*) Kiste f; **~ of drawers** *n* Kommode f

chestnut ['tʃɛsnʌt] *n* Kastanie f

chew [tʃuː] *vt, vi* kauen; **~ing gum** *n* Kaugummi *m*

chic [ʃiːk] *adj* schick, elegant

chick [tʃɪk] *n* Küken *nt*; (*inf: girl*) Biene f

chicken ['tʃɪkɪn] *n* Huhn *nt*; (*food*) Hähnchen *nt*; **~ out** (*inf*) *vi* kneifen

chickenpox ['tʃɪkɪnpɒks] *n* Windpocken *pl*

chicory ['tʃɪkərɪ] *n* (*in coffee*) Zichorie f; (*plant*) Chicorée f, Schikoree f

chief [tʃiːf] *n* (*of tribe*) Häuptling *m*; (*COMM*) Chef *m* ♦ *adj* Haupt-; **~ executive** *n* Geschäftsführer(in) *m(f)*; **~ly** *adv* hauptsächlich

chilblain ['tʃɪlbleɪn] *n* Frostbeule f

child [tʃaɪld] (*pl* **~ren**) *n* Kind *nt*; **~birth** *n* Entbindung f; **~hood** *n* Kindheit f; **~ish** *adj* kindisch; **~like** *adj* kindlich; **~minder** (*BRIT*) *n* Tagesmutter f; **~ren** ['tʃɪldrən] *npl* *of* **child**; **~ seat** *n* Kindersitz *m*

Chile ['tʃɪlɪ] *n* Chile *nt*; **~an** *adj* chilenisch

chill [tʃɪl] *n* Kühle f; (*MED*) Erkältung f ♦ *vt* (*COOK*) kühlen

chilli ['tʃɪlɪ] *n* Peperoni *pl*; (*meal, spice*) Chili *m*

chilly ['tʃɪlɪ] *adj* kühl, frostig

chime [tʃaɪm] *n* Geläut *nt* ♦ *vi* ertönen

chimney ['tʃɪmnɪ] *n* Schornstein *m*; **~ sweep** *n* Schornsteinfeger(in) *m(f)*

chimpanzee [tʃɪmpæn'ziː] *n* Schimpanse *m*

chin [tʃɪn] *n* Kinn *nt*

China ['tʃaɪnə] *n* China *nt*

china ['tʃaɪnə] *n* Porzellan *nt*

Chinese [tʃaɪ'niːz] *adj* chinesisch ♦ *n* (*inv*) Chinese *m*, Chinesin f; (*LING*) Chinesisch *nt*

chink [tʃɪŋk] *n* (*opening*) Ritze f; (*noise*) Klirren *nt*

chip [tʃɪp] *n* (*of wood etc*) Splitter *m*; (*in poker etc: spec*) Chip *m* ♦ *vt* absplittern; **~s** *npl* (*BRIT: COOK*) Pommes frites *pl*; **~ in** *vi* Zwischenbemerkungen machen

---

Chip shop

Chip shop, auch fish-and-chip shop, ist die traditionelle britische Imbissbude, in der vor allem frittierte Fischfilets und Pommes frites, aber auch andere einfache Mahlzeiten angeboten werden. Früher wurde das Essen zum Mitnehmen in Zeitungspapier verpackt. Manche chip shops haben auch einen Essraum.

---

chiropodist [kɪ'rɒpədɪst] (*BRIT*) *n* Fußpfleger(in) *m(f)*

chirp [tʃɜːp] *vi* zwitschern

chisel ['tʃɪzl] *n* Meißel *m*

chit [tʃɪt] *n* Notiz f

chivalrous ['ʃɪvəlrəs] *adj* ritterlich; **chivalry** ['ʃɪvəlrɪ] *n* Ritterlichkeit f

chives [tʃaɪvz] *npl* Schnittlauch *m*

chlorine ['klɔːriːn] *n* Chlor *nt*

chock-a-block ['tʃɒk'blɒk] *adj* voll gepfropft

chock-full [tʃɒk'ful] *adj* voll gepfropft

chocolate ['tʃɒklɪt] *n* Schokolade f

choice [tʃɔɪs] *n* Wahl f; (*of goods*) Auswahl f ♦ *adj* Qualitäts-

choir ['kwaɪə²] *n* Chor *m*; **~boy** *n* Chorknabe *m*

choke [tʃəuk] *vi* ersticken ♦ *vt* erdrosseln; (*block*) (ab)drosseln *n* (*AUT*) Starterklappe f

cholera ['kɒlərə] *n* Cholera f

cholesterol [kə'lɛstərɒl] *n* Cholesterin *nt*

choose [tʃuːz] (*pt* **chose**, *pp* **chosen**) *vt*

wählen; **choosy** ['tʃuːzi] *adj* wählerisch

chop [tʃɒp] *vt* (*wood*) spalten; (*COOK: also:* ~ **up**) (zer)hacken ♦ *n* Hieb *m*; (*COOK*) Kotelett *nt*; ~**s** *npl* (*jaws*) Lefzen *pl*

chopper ['tʃɒpə'] *n* (*helicopter*) Hubschrauber *m*

choppy ['tʃɒpɪ] *adj* (*sea*) bewegt

chopsticks ['tʃɒpstɪks] *npl* (Ess)stäbchen *pl*

choral ['kɔːrəl] *adj* Chor-

chord [kɔːd] *n* Akkord *m*

chore [tʃɔː'] *n* Pflicht *f*; ~**s** *npl* (*housework*) Hausarbeit *f*

choreographer [kɔrɪ'ɒɡrəfə'] *n* Choreograf(in) *m(f)*

chorister ['kɒrɪstə'] *n* Chorsänger(in) *m(f)*

chortle ['tʃɔːtl] *vi* glucksen

chorus ['kɔːrəs] *n* Chor *m*; (*in song*) Refrain *m*

chose [tʃəuz] *pt of* **choose**

chosen ['tʃəuzn] *pp of* **choose**

chowder ['tʃaudə'] *n* (*US*) sämige Fischsuppe *f*

Christ [kraɪst] *n* Christus *m*

christen ['krɪsn] *vt* taufen; ~**ing** *n* Taufe *f*

Christian ['krɪstɪən] *adj* christlich ♦ *n* Christ(in) *m(f)*; ~**ity** [krɪstɪ'ænɪtɪ] *n* Christentum *nt*; ~ **name** *n* Vorname *m*

Christmas ['krɪsməs] *n* Weihnachten *pl*; **Happy** *or* **Merry** ~! frohe *or* fröhliche Weihnachten!; ~ **card** *n* Weihnachtskarte *f*; ~ **Day** *n* der erste Weihnachtstag; ~ **Eve** *n* Heiligabend *m*; ~ **tree** *n* Weihnachtsbaum *m*

chrome [krəum] *n* Verchromung *f*

chromium ['krəumɪəm] *n* Chrom *nt*

chronic ['krɒnɪk] *adj* chronisch

chronicle ['krɒnɪkl] *n* Chronik *f*

chronological [krɒnə'lɒdʒɪkl] *adj* chronologisch

chubby ['tʃʌbɪ] *adj* rundlich

chuck [tʃʌk] *vt* werfen; (*BRIT: also:* ~ **up**) hinwerfen; ~ **out** *vt* (*person*) rauswerfen; (*old clothes etc*) wegwerfen

chuckle ['tʃʌkl] *vi* in sich hineinlachen

chug [tʃʌɡ] *vi* tuckern

chunk [tʃʌŋk] *n* Klumpen *m*; (*of food*) Brocken *m*

church [tʃəːtʃ] *n* Kirche *f*; ~**yard** *n* Kirchhof *m*

churn [tʃəːn] *n* (*for butter*) Butterfass *nt*; (*for milk*) Milchkanne *f*; ~ **out** (*inf*) *vt* produzieren

chute [ʃuːt] *n* Rutsche *f*; (*rubbish* ~) Müllschlucker *m*

chutney ['tʃʌtnɪ] *n* Chutney *nt*

CIA (*US*) *n abbr* (= *Central Intelligence Agency*) CIA *m*

CID (*BRIT*) *n abbr* (= *Criminal Investigation Department*) ≈ Kripo *f*

cider ['saɪdə'] *n* Apfelwein *m*

cigar [sɪ'ɡɑː'] *n* Zigarre *f*

cigarette [sɪɡə'ret] *n* Zigarette *f*; ~ **case** *n* Zigarettenetui *nt*; ~ **end** *n* Zigarettenstummel *m*

Cinderella [sɪndə'relə] *n* Aschenbrödel *nt*

cinders ['sɪndəz] *npl* Asche *f*

cine camera ['sɪnɪ-] (*BRIT*) *n* Filmkamera *f*

cine film (*BRIT*) *n* Schmalfilm *m*

cinema ['sɪnəmə] *n* Kino *nt*

cinnamon ['sɪnəmən] *n* Zimt *m*

circle ['səːkl] *n* Kreis *m*; (*in cinema etc*) Rang *m* ♦ *vi* kreisen ♦ *vt* (*surround*) umgeben; (*move round*) kreisen um

circuit ['səːkɪt] *n* (*track*) Rennbahn *f*; (*lap*) Runde *f*; (*ELEC*) Stromkreis *m*

circular ['səːkjulə'] *adj* rund ♦ *n* Rundschreiben *nt*

circulate ['səːkjuleɪt] *vi* zirkulieren ♦ *vt* in Umlauf setzen; **circulation** [səːkju'leɪʃən] *n* (*of blood*) Kreislauf *m*; (*of newspaper*) Auflage *f*; (*of money*) Umlauf *m*

circumcise ['səːkəmsaɪz] *vt* beschneiden

circumference [sə'kʌmfərəns] *n* (Kreis)umfang *m*

circumspect ['səːkəmspekt] *adj* umsichtig

circumstances ['sɜːkəmstənsɪz] *npl* Umstände *pl*; *(financial)* Verhältnisse *pl*

circumvent [sɜːkəm'vent] *vt* umgehen

circus ['sɜːkəs] *n* Zirkus *m*

CIS *n abbr* (= *Commonwealth of Independent States*) GUS *f*

cistern ['sɪstən] *n* Zisterne *f*; *(of W.C.)* Spülkasten *m*

cite [saɪt] *vt* zitieren, anführen

citizen ['sɪtɪzn] *n* Bürger(in) *m(f)*; ~**ship** *n* Staatsbürgerschaft *f*

citrus fruit ['sɪtrəs-] *n* Zitrusfrucht *f*

city ['sɪtɪ] *n* Großstadt *f*; **the C~** die City, das Finanzzentrum Londons

city technology college *n* ≈ Technische Fachschule *f*

civic ['sɪvɪk] *adj* (*of town*) städtisch; *(of citizen)* Bürger-; ~ **centre** (*BRIT*) *n* Stadtverwaltung *f*

civil ['sɪvl] *adj* bürgerlich; (*not military*) zivil; (*polite*) höflich; ~ **engineer** *n* Bauingenieur *m*; ~**ian** [sɪ'vɪlɪən] *n* Zivilperson *f* ♦ *adj* zivil, Zivil-

civilization [sɪvɪlaɪ'zeɪʃən] *n* Zivilisation *f*

civilized ['sɪvɪlaɪzd] *adj* zivilisiert

civil: ~ **law** *n* Zivilrecht *nt*; ~ **servant** *n* Staatsbeamte(r) *m*; **C~ Service** *n* Staatsdienst *m*; ~ **war** *n* Bürgerkrieg *m*

clad [klæd] *adj*: ~ **in** gehüllt in +*acc*

claim [kleɪm] *vt* beanspruchen; (*have opinion*) behaupten ♦ *vi* (*for insurance*) Ansprüche geltend machen ♦ *n* (*demand*) Forderung *f*; (*right*) Anspruch *m*; (*pretension*) Behauptung *f*; ~**ant** *n* Antragsteller(in) *m(f)*

clairvoyant [kleə'vɔɪənt] *n* Hellseher(in) *m(f)*

clam [klæm] *n* Venusmuschel *f*

clamber ['klæmbə*] *vi* kraxeln

clammy ['klæmɪ] *adj* klamm

clamour ['klæmə*] *vi*: **to ~ for sth** nach etw verlangen

clamp [klæmp] *n* Schraubzwinge *f* ♦ *vt* einspannen; (*AUT: wheel*) krallen; ~ **down on** *vt fus* Maßnahmen ergrei-

fen gegen

clan [klæn] *n* Clan *m*

clandestine [klæn'destɪn] *adj* geheim

clang [klæŋ] *vi* scheppern

clap [klæp] *vi* klatschen ♦ *vt* Beifall klatschen +*dat* ♦ *n* (*of hands*) Klatschen *nt*; (*of thunder*) Donnerschlag *m*; ~**ping** *n* Klatschen *nt*

claret ['klærət] *n* rote(r) Bordeaux(wein) *m*

clarify ['klærɪfaɪ] *vt* klären, erklären

clarinet [klærɪ'net] *n* Klarinette *f*

clarity ['klærɪtɪ] *n* Klarheit *f*

clash [klæʃ] *n* (*fig*) Konflikt *m* ♦ *vi* zusammenprallen; (*colours*) sich beißen; (*argue*) sich streiten

clasp [klɑːsp] *n* (*on jewels, bag*) Verschluss *m* ♦ *vt* umklammern

class [klɑːs] *n* Klasse *f* ♦ *vt* einordnen; ~**conscious** *adj* klassenbewusst

classic ['klæsɪk] *n* Klassiker *m* ♦ *adj* klassisch; ~**al** *adj* klassisch

classified ['klæsɪfaɪd] *adj* (*information*) Geheim-; ~ **advertisement** *n* Kleinanzeige *f*

classify ['klæsɪfaɪ] *vt* klassifizieren

classmate ['klɑːsmeɪt] *n* Klassenkamerad(in) *m(f)*

classroom ['klɑːsrum] *n* Klassenzimmer *nt*

clatter ['klætə*] *vi* klappern; (*feet*) trappeln

clause [klɔːz] *n* (*JUR*) Klausel *f*; (*GRAM*) Satz *m*

claustrophobia [klɔːstrə'fəʊbɪə] *n* Platzangst *f*

claw [klɔː] *n* Kralle *f* ♦ *vt* (*zer*)kratzen

clay [kleɪ] *n* Lehm *m*; (*for pots*) Ton *m*

clean [kliːn] *adj* sauber ♦ *vt* reinigen; (*clothes*) reinigen; ~ **out** *vt* gründlich putzen; ~ **up** *vt* aufräumen; ~**cut** *adj* (*person*) adrett; (*clear*) klar; ~**er** *n* (*person*) Putzfrau *f*; ~**er's** *n* (*also: dry ~er's*) Reinigung *f*; ~**ing** *n* Putzen *nt*, Reinigung *f*; ~**liness** ['klenlɪnɪs] *n* Reinlichkeit *f*

cleanse [klenz] *vt* reinigen; ~**r** *n* (*for*

face) Reinigungsmilch f

clean-shaven ['kli:n'ʃeɪvn] adj glatt rasiert

cleansing department ['klenzɪŋ-] (BRIT) n Stadtreinigung f

clear [klɪəʳ] adj klar; (road) frei ♦ vt (road etc) freimachen; (obstacle) beseitigen; (JUR: suspect) freisprechen ♦ vi klar werden; (fog) sich lichten ♦ adv: ~ of von ... entfernt; to ~ the table den Tisch abräumen; ~ up vt aufräumen; (solve) aufklären; ~ance ['klɪərəns] n (removal) Räumung f; (free space) Lichtung f; (permission) Freigabe f; ~cut adj (case) eindeutig; ~ing n Lichtung f; ~ing bank (BRIT) n Clearingbank f; ~ly adv klar; (obviously) eindeutig; ~way (BRIT) n (Straße f mit) Halteverbot nt

cleaver ['kli:vəʳ] n Hackbeil f

cleft [kleft] n (in rock) Spalte f

clementine ['klemntaɪn] n (fruit) Klementine f

clench [klentʃ] vt (teeth) zusammenbeißen; (fist) ballen

clergy ['klɜ:dʒɪ] n Geistliche(n) pl; ~man (irreg) n Geistliche(r) m

clerical ['klerɪkl] adj (office) Schreib-, Büro-; (REL) geistlich

clerk [klɑ:k, (US) klɜ:rk] n (in office) Büroangestellte(r) mf; (US: sales person) Verkäufer(in) m(f)

clever ['klevəʳ] adj klug; (crafty) schlau

cliché ['kli:ʃeɪ] n Klischee nt

click [klɪk] vt (tongue) schnalzen mit; (heels) zusammenklappen

client ['klaɪənt] n Klient(in) m(f); ~ele [kli:ɑ:n'tel] n Kundschaft f

cliff [klɪf] n Klippe f

climate ['klaɪmɪt] n Klima nt

climax ['klaɪmæks] n Höhepunkt m

climb [klaɪm] vt besteigen ♦ vi steigen, klettern ♦ n Aufstieg m; ~down n Abstieg m; ~er n Bergsteiger(in) m(f); ~ing n Bergsteigen nt

clinch [klɪntʃ] vt (decide) entscheiden; (deal) festmachen

cling [klɪŋ] (pt, pp **clung**) vi (clothes) eng anliegen; to ~ to sich festklammern an +dat

clinic ['klɪnɪk] n Klinik f; ~al adj klinisch

clink [klɪŋk] vi klimpern

clip [klɪp] n Spange f; (also: **paper ~**) Klammer f ♦ vt (papers) heften; (hair, hedge) stutzen; ~**pers** npl (for hedge) Heckenschere f; (for hair) Haarschneidemaschine f; ~**ping** n Ausschnitt m

cloak [kləʊk] n Umhang m ♦ vt hüllen; ~**room** n (for coats) Garderobe f; (BRIT: W.C.) Toilette f

clock [klɒk] n Uhr f; ~ **in** or **on** vi stempeln; ~ **off** or **out** vi stempeln; ~**wise** adv im Uhrzeigersinn; ~**work** n Uhrwerk nt ♦ adj zum Aufziehen

clog [klɒg] n Holzschuh m ♦ vt verstopfen

cloister ['klɔɪstəʳ] n Kreuzgang m

clone [kləʊn] n Klon m

close[1] [kləʊs] adj (near) in der Nähe; (friend, connection, print) eng; (relative) nahe; (result) knapp; (examination) eingehend; (weather) schwül; (room) stickig ♦ adv nahe, dicht; ~ **by** in der Nähe; ~ **at hand** in der Nähe; **to have a ~ shave** (fig) mit knapper Not davonkommen

close[2] [kləʊz] vt (shut) schließen; (end) beenden ♦ vi (shop etc) schließen; (door etc) sich schließen ♦ n Ende nt; ~ **down** vi (shop etc) schließen; ~**d** adj (shop etc) geschlossen; ~**d shop** n Gewerkschaftszwang m

close-knit ['kləʊs'nɪt] adj eng zusammengewachsen

closely ['kləʊslɪ] adv eng; (carefully) genau

closet ['klɒzɪt] n Schrank m

close-up ['kləʊsʌp] n Nahaufnahme f

closure ['kləʊʒəʳ] n Schließung f

clot [klɒt] n (of blood) Blutgerinnsel nt; (fool) Blödmann m ♦ vi gerinnen

cloth [klɒθ] n (material) Tuch nt; (rag) Lappen m

clothe [kləʊð] vt kleiden

clothes [kləuðz] *npl* Kleider *pl*; ~
brush *n* Kleiderbürste *f*; ~ **line** *n*
Wäscheleine *f*; ~ **peg**, ~ **pin** (*US*) *n*
Wäscheklammer *f*

clothing ['kləuðɪŋ] *n* Kleidung *f*

clotted cream ['klɔtɪd-] (*BRIT*) *n* Sahne
aus erhitzter Milch

cloud [klaud] *n* Wolke *f*; **~burst** *n* Wol-
kenbruch *m*; **~y** *adj* bewölkt; (*liquid*)
trüb

clout [klaut] *vt* hauen

clove [kləuv] *n* Gewürznelke *f*; ~ **of**
garlic Knoblauchzehe *f*

clover ['kləuvər] *n* Klee *m*

clown [klaun] *n* Clown *m* ♦ *vi* (*also: ~*
about, ~ *around*) kaspern

cloying ['klɔɪŋ] *adj* (*taste, smell*)
übersüß

club [klʌb] *n* (*weapon*) Knüppel *m*; (*so-*
ciety) Klub *m*; (*also: golf* ~) Golfschläger *m* ♦ *vt* prügeln ♦ *vi*: **to ~ to-**
gether zusammenlegen; **~s** *npl* (*CARDS*)
Kreuz *nt*; ~ **car** (*US*) *n* (*RAIL*) Speisewagen *m*; ~ **class** *n* (*AVIAT*) Club-Klasse *f*;
~house *n* Klubhaus *nt*

cluck [klʌk] *vi* glucken

clue [klu:] *n* Anhaltspunkt *m*; (*in cross-*
words) Frage *f*; **I haven't a ~** (ich hab)
keine Ahnung

clump [klʌmp] *n* Gruppe *f*

clumsy ['klʌmzi] *adj* (*person*) unbeholfen; (*shape*) unförmig

clung [klʌŋ] *pt, pp of* **cling**

cluster ['klʌstər] *n* (*of trees etc*) Gruppe
f ♦ *vi* sich drängen, sich scharen

clutch [klʌtʃ] *n* Griff *m*; (*AUT*) Kupplung
f ♦ *vt* sich festklammern an +*dat*

clutter ['klʌtər] *vt* voll propfen; (*desk*)
übersäen

CND *n abbr* = **Campaign for Nuclear**
Disarmament

Co. *abbr* = **county; company**

c/o *abbr* (= *care of*) c/o

coach [kəutʃ] *n* (*bus*) Reisebus *m*;
(*horse-drawn*) Kutsche *f*; (*RAIL*) (Personen)wagen *m*; (*trainer*) Trainer *m* ♦ *vt*
(*SCH*) Nachhilfeunterricht geben +*dat*;

(*SPORT*) trainieren; ~ **trip** *n* Busfahrt *f*

coal [kəul] *n* Kohle *f*; ~ **face** *n* Streb *m*

coalition [kəuə'lɪʃən] *n* Koalition *f*

coalman ['kəulmən] (*irreg*) *n* Kohlen-
händler *m*

coal mine *n* Kohlenbergwerk *nt*

coarse [kɔ:s] *adj* grob; (*fig*) ordinär

coast [kəust] *n* Küste *f* ♦ *vi* dahinrollen;
(*AUT*) im Leerlauf fahren; **~al** *adj*
Küsten-; **~guard** *n* Küstenwache *f*;
~line *n* Küste(nlinie) *f*

coat [kəut] *n* Mantel *m*; (*on animals*)
Fell *nt*; (*of paint*) Schicht *f* ♦ *vt*
überstreichen; **~hanger** *n* Kleiderbügel *m*; **~ing** *n* Überzug *m*; (*of paint*)
Schicht *f*; ~ **of arms** *n* Wappen *nt*

coax [kəuks] *vt* beschwatzen

cob [kɔb] *n* see **corn**

cobbler ['kɔblər] *n* Schuster *m*

cobbles ['kɔblz] *npl* Pflastersteine *pl*

cobweb ['kɔbweb] *n* Spinnennetz *nt*

cocaine [kə'keɪn] *n* Kokain *nt*

cock [kɔk] *n* Hahn *m* ♦ *vt* (*gun*) entsi-
chern; **~erel** ['kɔkərəl] *n* junge(r) Hahn
m; **~eyed** *adj* (*fig*) verrückt

cockle ['kɔkl] *n* Herzmuschel *f*

cockney ['kɔkni] *n* echte(r) Londoner
m

cockpit ['kɔkpɪt] *n* (*AVIAT*) Pilotenkanzel
f

cockroach ['kɔkrəutʃ] *n* Küchenschabe
f

cocktail ['kɔkteɪl] *n* Cocktail *m*; ~
cabinet *n* Hausbar *f*; ~ **party** *n* Cock-
tailparty *f*

cocoa ['kəukəu] *n* Kakao *m*

coconut ['kəukənʌt] *n* Kokosnuss *f*

cocoon [kə'ku:n] *n* Kokon *m*

cod [kɔd] *n* Kabeljau *m*

C.O.D. *abbr* = **cash on delivery**

code [kəud] *n* Kode *m*; (*JUR*) Kodex *m*

cod-liver oil ['kɔdlɪvə-] *n* Lebertran *m*

coercion [kəu'ə:ʃən] *n* Zwang *m*

coffee ['kɔfi] *n* Kaffee *m*; ~ **bar** (*BRIT*) *n*
Café *nt*; ~ **bean** *n* Kaffeebohne *f*; ~
break *n* Kaffeepause *f*; **~pot** *n* Kaffeekanne *f*; ~ **table** *n* Couchtisch *m*

coffin ['kɔfɪn] n Sarg m

cog [kɔg] n (Rad)zahn m

cognac ['kɔnjæk] n Kognak m

coherent [kəu'hɪərənt] adj zusammenhängend; (person) verständlich

coil [kɔɪl] n Rolle f; (ELEC) Spule f; (contraceptive) Spirale f ♦ vt aufwickeln

coin [kɔɪn] n Münze f ♦ vt prägen; **~age** ['kɔɪnɪdʒ] n (word) Prägung f; **~box** (BRIT) n Münzfernsprecher m

coincide [kəuɪn'saɪd] vi (happen together) zusammenfallen; (agree) übereinstimmen; **~nce** [kəu'ɪnsɪdəns] n Zufall m

coinphone ['kɔɪnfəun] n Münzfernsprecher m

Coke [kəuk] ® n (drink) Coca-Cola ® f

coke [kəuk] n Koks m

colander ['kɔləndə] n Durchschlag m

cold [kəuld] adj kalt ♦ n Kälte f; (MED) Erkältung f; **I'm ~** mir ist kalt; **to catch ~** sich erkälten; **in ~ blood** kaltblütig; **to give sb the ~ shoulder** jdm die kalte Schulter zeigen; **~ly** adv kalt; **~shoulder** vt die kalte Schulter zeigen +dat; **~ sore** n Erkältungsbläschen nt

coleslaw ['kəulslɔ:] n Krautsalat m

colic ['kɔlɪk] n Kolik f

collaborate [kə'læbəreɪt] vi zusammenarbeiten

collapse [kə'læps] vi (people) zusammenbrechen; (things) einstürzen ♦ n Zusammenbruch m; Einsturz m; **collapsible** adj zusammenklappbar, Klapp-

collar ['kɔlə] n Kragen m; **~bone** n Schlüsselbein nt

collateral [kə'lætərl] n (zusätzliche) Sicherheit f

colleague ['kɔli:g] n Kollege m, Kollegin f

collect [kə'lekt] vt sammeln; (BRIT call and pick up) abholen ♦ vi (people) sich sammeln ♦ adv: **to call** ~ (US: TEL) ein R-Gespräch führen; **~ion** [kə'lekʃən] n Sammlung f; (REL) Kollekte f; (of post)

Leerung f; **~ive** [kə'lektɪv] adj gemeinsam; (POL) kollektiv; **~or** [kə'lektə] n Sammler m; (tax ~or) (Steuer)einnehmer m

college ['kɔlɪdʒ] n (UNIV) College nt; (TECH) Fach-, Berufsschule f

collide [kə'laɪd] vi zusammenstoßen

collie ['kɔlɪ] n Collie m

colliery ['kɔlɪərɪ] (BRIT) n Zeche f

collision [kə'lɪʒən] n Zusammenstoß m

colloquial [kə'ləukwɪəl] adj umgangssprachlich

colon ['kəulən] n Doppelpunkt m; (MED) Dickdarm m

colonel ['kə:nl] n Oberst m

colonial [kə'ləunɪəl] adj Kolonial-

colonize ['kɔlənaɪz] vt kolonisieren

colony ['kɔlənɪ] n Kolonie f

colour ['kʌlə] (US color) n Farbe f ♦ vt (also dye) färben ♦ vi sich verfärben; **~s** npl (of club) Fahne f; **~ bar** n Rassenschranke f; **~blind** adj farbenblind; **~ed** adj farbig; **~ film** n Farbfilm m; **~ful** adj bunt; (personality) schillernd; **~ing** (complexion) Gesichtsfarbe f; (substance) Farbstoff m; **~ scheme** n Farbgebung f; **~ television** n Farbfernsehen nt

colt [kəult] n Fohlen nt

column ['kɔləm] n Säule f; (MIL) Kolonne f; (of print) Spalte f; **~ist** ['kɔləmnɪst] n Kolumnist m

coma ['kəumə] n Koma nt

comb [kəum] n Kamm m ♦ vt kämmen; (search) durchkämmen

combat ['kɔmbæt] n Kampf m ♦ vt bekämpfen

combination [kɔmbɪ'neɪʃən] n Kombination f

combine [vb kəm'baɪn, n 'kɔmbaɪn] vt verbinden ♦ vi sich vereinigen ♦ n (COMM) Konzern m; **~ (harvester)** n Mähdrescher m

combustion [kəm'bʌstʃən] n Verbrennung f

come [kʌm] (pt came, pp come) vi kommen; **to ~ undone** aufgehen; **~**

about vi geschehen; **~ across** vt fus (find) stoßen auf +acc; **~ away** vi (person) weggehen; (handle etc) abgehen; **~ back** vi zurückkommen; **~ by** vt (find): **to ~ by sth** zu etw kommen; **~ down** vi (price) fallen; **~ forward** vi (volunteer) sich melden; **~ from** vt fus (result) kommen von; **where do you ~ from?** wo kommen Sie her?; **I ~ from London** ich komme aus London; **~ in** vi hereinkommen; (train) einfahren; **~ in for** vt fus abkriegen; **~ into** vt fus (inherit) erben; **~ off** vi (handle) abgehen; (succeed) klappen; **~ on** vi (progress) vorankommen; **~ on!** komm!; (hurry) beeil dich!; **~ out** vi herauskommen; **~ round** vi (MED) wieder zu sich kommen; **to ~** vi (MED) wieder zu sich kommen ♦ vt fus (bill) sich belaufen auf +acc; **~ up** vi hochkommen; (sun) aufgehen; (problem) auftauchen; **~ up against** vt fus (resistance, difficulties) stoßen auf +acc; **~ upon** vt fus stoßen auf +acc; **~ up with** vt fus sich einfallen lassen

comedian [kə'mi:dɪən] n Komiker m; **comedienne** [kəmi:dɪ'en] n Komikerin f

comedown ['kʌmdaun] n Abstieg m

comedy ['kɒmɪdɪ] n Komödie f

comet ['kɒmɪt] n Komet m

comeuppance [kʌm'ʌpəns] n: **to get one's ~** seine Quittung bekommen

comfort ['kʌmfət] n Komfort m; (consolation) Trost m ♦ vt trösten; **~able** adj bequem; **~ably** adv (sit etc) bequem; (live) angenehm; **~ station** (US) n öffentliche Toilette f

comic ['kɒmɪk] n Comic(heft) nt; (comedian) Komiker m ♦ adj (also: **~al**) komisch; **~ strip** n Comicstrip m

coming ['kʌmɪŋ] n Kommen nt; **~(s) and going(s)** n(pl) Kommen und Gehen nt

comma ['kɒmə] n Komma nt

command [kə'mɑ:nd] n Befehl m; (control) Führung f; (MIL) Kommando nt; (mastery) Beherrschung f ♦ vt befehlen +dat; (MIL) kommandieren; (be able to get) verfügen über +acc; **~er** n (MIL) Befehlshaber m; (MIL) Kommandant m; **~ment** n (REL) Gebot nt

commando [kə'mɑ:ndəu] n Kommandotruppe nt; (person) Mitglied nt einer Kommandotruppe

commemorate [kə'meməreɪt] vt gedenken +gen

commence [kə'mens] vt, vi beginnen

commend [kə'mend] vt (recommend) empfehlen; (praise) loben

commensurate [kə'menʃərɪt] adj: **~ with sth** einer Sache dat entsprechend

comment ['kɒmənt] n Bemerkung f ♦ vi: **to ~ (on)** sich äußern (zu); **~ary** n Kommentar m; **~ator** n Kommentator m; (TV) Reporter(in) m(f)

commerce ['kɒmə:s] n Handel m

commercial [kə'mə:ʃəl] adj kommerziell, geschäftlich; (training) kaufmännisch ♦ n (TV) Fernsehwerbung f; **~ break** n Werbespot m; **~ize** vt kommerzialisieren

commiserate [kə'mɪzəreɪt] vi: **to ~ with** Mitleid haben mit

commission [kə'mɪʃən] n (act) Auftrag m; (fee) Provision f; (body) Kommission f ♦ vt beauftragen; (MIL) zum Offizier ernennen; (work of art) in Auftrag geben; **out of ~** außer Betrieb; **~er** n (POLICE) Polizeipräsident m

commit [kə'mɪt] vt (crime) begehen; (entrust) anvertrauen; **to ~ o.s.** sich festlegen; **~ment** n Verpflichtung f

committee [kə'mɪtɪ] n Ausschuss m

commodity [kə'mɒdɪtɪ] n Ware f

common ['kɒmən] adj (cause) gemeinsam; (pej) gewöhnlich; (widespread) üblich, häufig ♦ n Gemeindeland nt; (BRIT) **C~s** npl: **the C~s** das Unterhaus; **~er** n Bürgerliche(r) mf; **~ law** n Gewohnheitsrecht nt; **~ly** adv gewöhnlich; **C~ Market** n Gemeinsame(r) Markt m; **~place** adj alltäglich;

room n Gemeinschaftsraum m; ~
sense n gesunde(r) Menschenverstand m; **C~wealth** n: the **C~wealth** das Commonwealth

commotion [kə'məʊʃən] n Aufsehen nt

communal ['kɔmjuːnl] adj Gemeinde-; Gemeinschafts-

commune [n 'kɔmjuːn, vb kə'mjuːn] n Kommune f ♦ vi: **to ~ with** sich mitteilen +dat

communicate [kə'mjuːnɪkeɪt] vt (transmit) übertragen ♦ vi (be in touch) in Verbindung stehen; (make self understood) sich verständigen; **communication** [kɔmjuːnɪ'keɪʃən] n (message) Mitteilung f; (make understood) Kommunikation f; **communication cord** (BRIT) n Notbremse f

communion [kə'mjuːnɪən] n (also: Holy C~) Abendmahl nt, Kommunion f

communism ['kɔmjunɪzəm] n Kommunismus m; **communist** ['kɔmjunɪst] n Kommunist(in) m(f) ♦ adj kommunistisch

community [kə'mjuːnɪtɪ] n Gemeinschaft f; ~ **centre** n Gemeinschaftszentrum nt; ~ **chest** (US) n Wohltätigkeitsfonds m; ~ **home** (BRIT) n Erziehungsheim nt

commutation ticket [kɔmju'teɪʃən-] (US) n Zeitkarte f

commute [kə'mjuːt] vi pendeln ♦ vt umwandeln; **~r** n Pendler m

compact [adj kəm'pækt, n 'kɔmpækt] adj kompakt ♦ n (for make-up) Puderdose f; ~ **disc** n Compactdisc f, Compact Disc f; ~ **disc player** n CD-Spieler m

companion [kəm'pænjən] n Begleiter(in) m(f); **~ship** n Gesellschaft f

company ['kʌmpənɪ] n Gesellschaft f; (COMM) Firma f, Gesellschaft f; **to keep sb ~** jdm Gesellschaft leisten; ~ **secretary** (BRIT) n ≈ Prokurist(in) m(f)

comparable ['kɔmpərəbl] adj ver-

gleichbar

comparative [kəm'pærətɪv] adj (relative) relativ; **~ly** adv verhältnismäßig

compare [kəm'peə'] vt vergleichen ♦ vi sich vergleichen lassen; **comparison** [kəm'pærɪsn] n Vergleich m; **in comparison (with)** im Vergleich (mit or zu)

compartment [kəm'pɑːtmənt] n (RAIL) Abteil nt; (in drawer) Fach nt

compass ['kʌmpəs] n Kompaß m; **~es** npl (MATH etc: also: **pair of ~es**) Zirkel m

compassion [kəm'pæʃən] n Mitleid nt; **~ate** adj mitfühlend

compatible [kəm'pætɪbl] adj vereinbar; (COMPUT) kompatibel

compel [kəm'pel] vt zwingen

compensate ['kɔmpenseɪt] vt entschädigen ♦ vi: **to ~ for** Ersatz leisten für; **compensation** [kɔmpən'seɪʃən] n Entschädigung f

compère ['kɔmpeə'] n Conférencier m

compete [kəm'piːt] vi (take part) teilnehmen; (vie with) konkurrieren

competent ['kɔmpɪtənt] adj kompetent

competition [kɔmpɪ'tɪʃən] n (contest) Wettbewerb m; (COMM, rivalry) Konkurrenz f; **competitive** [kəm'petɪtɪv] adj Konkurrenz-; (COMM) konkurrenzfähig; **competitor** [kəm'petɪtə'] n (COMM) Konkurrent(in) m(f); (participant) Teilnehmer(in) m(f)

compile [kəm'paɪl] vt zusammenstellen

complacency [kəm'pleɪsnsɪ] n Selbstzufriedenheit f

complacent [kəm'pleɪsnt] adj selbstzufrieden

complain [kəm'pleɪn] vi sich beklagen; (formally) sich beschweren; **~t** n Klage f; (formal ~t) Beschwerde f; (MED) Leiden nt

complement [n 'kɔmplɪmənt, vb 'kɔmplɪmənt] n Ergänzung f; (ship's crew etc) Bemannung f ♦ vt ergänzen; **~ary** [kɔmplɪ'mentərɪ] adj (sich) ergänzend

complete [kəm'pli:t] adj (full) vollkommen, ganz; (finished) fertig ♦ vt vervollständigen; (finish) beenden; (fill in: form) ausfüllen; **~ly** adv ganz; **completion** [kəm'pli:ʃən] n Fertigstellung f, (of contract etc) Abschluss m

complex ['kɒmpleks] adj kompliziert

complexion [kəm'plekʃən] n Gesichtsfarbe f; (fig) Aspekt m

complexity [kəm'pleksɪtɪ] n Kompliziertheit f

compliance [kəm'plaɪəns] n Fügsamkeit f, Einwilligung f; **in ~ with** sth einer Sache dat gemäß

complicate ['kɒmplɪkeɪt] vt komplizieren; **~d** adj kompliziert; **complication** [kɒmplɪ'keɪʃən] n Komplikation f

compliment [n 'kɒmplɪmənt, vb 'kɒmplɪmənt] n Kompliment nt ♦ vt ein Kompliment machen; **~s** npl (greetings) Grüße pl; **to pay sb a ~** jdm ein Kompliment machen; **~ary** [kɒmplɪ'mentərɪ] adj schmeichelhaft; (free) Frei-, Gratis-

comply [kəm'plaɪ] vi: **to ~ with** erfüllen +acc; entsprechen +dat

component [kəm'pəʊnənt] adj Teil- ♦ n Bestandteil m

compose [kəm'pəʊz] vt (music) komponieren; (poetry) verfassen; **to ~ o.s.** sich sammeln; **~d** adj gefasst; **~r** n Komponist(in) m(f); **composition** [kɒmpə'zɪʃən] n (MUS) Komposition f; (SCH) Aufsatz m; (structure) Zusammensetzung f, Aufbau m

composure [kəm'pəʊʒə*] n Fassung f

compound ['kɒmpaʊnd] n (CHEM) Verbindung f; (enclosure) Lager nt; (LING) Kompositum nt ♦ adj zusammengesetzt; (fracture) kompliziert; **~ interest** n Zinseszins m

comprehend [kɒmprɪ'hend] vt begreifen; **comprehension** n Verständnis nt

comprehensive [kɒmprɪ'hensɪv] adj umfassend ♦ n = **comprehensive school**; **~ insurance** n Vollkasko nt;

school (BRIT) n Gesamtschule f

compress [vb kəm'pres, n 'kɒmpres] vt komprimieren ♦ n (MED) Kompresse f

comprise [kəm'praɪz] vt (also: **be ~d of**) umfassen, bestehen aus

compromise ['kɒmprəmaɪz] n Kompromiss m ♦ vt kompromittieren ♦ vi einen Kompromiss schließen

compulsion [kəm'pʌlʃən] n Zwang m; **compulsive** [kəm'pʌlsɪv] adj zwanghaft; **compulsory** [kəm'pʌlsərɪ] adj obligatorisch

computer [kəm'pju:tə*] n Computer, Rechner m; **~ game** n Computerspiel nt; **~-generated** adj computergeneriert; **~ize** vt (information) computerisieren; (company, accounts) auf Computer umstellen; **~ programmer** n Programmierer(in) m(f); **~ programming** n Programmieren nt; **~ science** n Informatik f; **computing** [kəm'pju:tɪŋ] n (science) Informatik f; (work) Computerei f

comrade ['kɒmrɪd] n Kamerad m, (POL) Genosse m

con [kɒn] n hereinlegen ♦ n Schwindel nt

concave ['kɒnkeɪv] adj konkav

conceal [kən'si:l] vt (secret) verschweigen; (hide) verbergen

concede [kən'si:d] vt (grant) gewähren; (point) zugeben ♦ vi (admit defeat) nachgeben

conceit [kən'si:t] n Einbildung f; **~ed** adj eingebildet

conceivable [kən'si:vəbl] adj vorstellbar

conceive [kən'si:v] vt (idea) ausdenken; (imagine) sich vorstellen; (baby) empfangen ♦ vi empfangen

concentrate ['kɒnsəntreɪt] vi sich konzentrieren; **to ~ on** sth sich auf etw acc konzentrieren; **concentration** [kɒnsən'treɪʃən] n Konzentration f; **concentration camp** n Konzentrationslager nt, KZ nt

concept ['kɒnsept] n Begriff m

conception [kənˈsepʃən] n (idea) Vorstellung f; (BIOL) Empfängnis f

concern [kənˈsɜːn] n (affair) Angelegenheit f; (COMM) Unternehmen nt; (worry) Sorge f ♦ vt (interest) angehen; (be about) handeln von; (have connection with) betreffen; **to be ~ed (about)** sich Sorgen machen (um); **~ing** prep hinsichtlich +gen

concert [ˈkɔnsət] n Konzert nt

concerted [kənˈsɜːtɪd] adj gemeinsam

concert hall n Konzerthalle f

concertina [kɔnsəˈtiːnə] n Handharmonika f

concerto [kənˈtʃɜːtəʊ] n Konzert nt

concession [kənˈseʃən] n (yielding) Zugeständnis nt; **tax ~** Steuerkonzession f

conciliation [kənsɪlɪˈeɪʃən] n Versöhnung f; (official) Schlichtung f

concise [kənˈsaɪs] adj präzis

conclude [kənˈkluːd] vt (end) beenden; (treaty) (ab)schließen; (decide) schließen, folgern; **conclusion** [kənˈkluːʒən] n (Ab)schluss m; (deduction) Schluss m; **conclusive** [kənˈkluːsɪv] adj schlüssig

concoct [kənˈkɔkt] vt zusammenbrauen; **~ion** [kənˈkɔkʃən] n Gebräu nt

concourse [ˈkɔnkɔːs] n (Bahnhofs)halle f, Vorplatz m

concrete [ˈkɔnkriːt] n Beton m ♦ adj konkret

concur [kənˈkɜːʳ] vi übereinstimmen

concurrently [kənˈkʌrntlɪ] adv gleichzeitig

concussion [kənˈkʌʃən] n (Gehirn)erschütterung f

condemn [kənˈdem] vt (JUR) verurteilen; (building) abbruchreif erklären

condensation [kɔndenˈseɪʃən] n Kondensation f

condense [kənˈdens] vi (CHEM) kondensieren ♦ vt (fig) zusammendrängen; **~d milk** n Kondensmilch f

condescending [kɔndɪˈsendɪŋ] adj herablassend

condition [kənˈdɪʃən] n (state) Zustand m; (presupposition) Bedingung f ♦ vt (hair etc) behandeln; (accustom) gewöhnen; **~s** npl (circumstances) Verhältnisse pl; **on ~ that** ... unter der Bedingung, dass ...; **~al** adj bedingt; **~er** n (for hair) Spülung f; (for fabrics) Weichspüler m

condolences [kənˈdəʊlənsɪz] npl Beileid nt

condom [ˈkɔndəm] n Kondom nt or m

condominium [kɔndəˈmɪnɪəm] (US) n Eigentumswohnung f; (block) Eigentumsblock m

condone [kənˈdəʊn] vt gutheißen

conducive [kənˈdjuːsɪv] adj: **~ to** dienlich +dat

conduct [n ˈkɔndʌkt, vb kənˈdʌkt] n (behaviour) Verhalten nt; (management) Führung f ♦ vt führen; (MUS) dirigieren; **~ed tour** n Führung f; **~or** [kənˈdʌktəʳ] n (of orchestra) Dirigent m; (in bus, US: on train) Schaffner m; (ELEC) Leiter m; **~ress** [kənˈdʌktrɪs] n (in bus) Schaffnerin f

cone [kəʊn] n (MATH) Kegel m; (for ice cream) (Waffel)tüte f; (BOT) Tannenzapfen m

confectioner's (shop) [kənˈfekʃənəz-] n Konditorei f; **~y** [kənˈfekʃənrɪ] n Süßigkeiten pl

confederation [kənfedəˈreɪʃən] n Bund m

confer [kənˈfɜːʳ] vt (degree) verleihen ♦ vi (discuss) konferieren, verhandeln; **~ence** [ˈkɔnfərəns] n Konferenz f

confess [kənˈfes] vt, vi gestehen; (ECCL) beichten; **~ion** [kənˈfeʃən] n Geständnis nt; (ECCL) Beichte f; **~ional** n Beichtstuhl m

confide [kənˈfaɪd] vi: **to ~ in** (sich) anvertrauen +dat

confidence [ˈkɔnfɪdns] n Vertrauen nt; (assurance) Selbstvertrauen nt; (secret) Geheimnis nt; **in ~** (speak, write) vertraulich; **~ trick** n Schwindel m

confident [ˈkɔnfɪdənt] adj (sure)

überzeugt; (self-assured) selbstsicher

confidential [kɒnfɪˈdenʃəl] adj vertraulich

confine [kənˈfaɪn] vt (limit) beschränken; (lock up) einsperren; **~d** adj (space) eng; **~ment** (in prison) Haft f; (MED) Wochenbett nt; **~s** [ˈkɒnfaɪnz] npl Grenzen pl

confirm [kənˈfɜːm] vt bestätigen; **~ation** [kɒnfəˈmeɪʃən] n Bestätigung f; (REL) Konfirmation f; **~ed** adj unverbesserlich; (bachelor) eingefleischt

confiscate [ˈkɒnfɪskeɪt] vt beschlagnahmen

conflict [n ˈkɒnflɪkt, vb kənˈflɪkt] n Konflikt m ♦ vi im Widerspruch stehen; **~ing** [kənˈflɪktɪŋ] adj widersprüchlich

conform [kənˈfɔːm] vi: **to ~ (to)** (things) entsprechen +dat; (people) sich anpassen +dat; (to rules) sich richten (nach)

confound [kənˈfaʊnd] vt verblüffen; (confuse) durcheinander bringen

confront [kənˈfrʌnt] vt (enemy) entgegentreten +dat; (problems) sich stellen +dat; **to ~ sb with sth** jdn mit etw konfrontieren; **~ation** [kɒnfrənˈteɪʃən] n Konfrontation f

confuse [kənˈfjuːz] vt verwirren; (sth with sth) verwechseln; **~d** adj verwirrt; **confusing** adj verwirrend; **confusion** [kənˈfjuːʒən] n (perplexity) Verwirrung f; (mixing up) Verwechslung f; (tumult) Aufruhr m

congeal [kənˈdʒiːl] vi (freeze) gefrieren; (clot) gerinnen

congested [kənˈdʒestɪd] adj überfüllt

congestion [kənˈdʒestʃən] n Stau m

conglomerate [kənˈglɒmərɪt] n (COMM, GEOL) Konglomerat nt

conglomeration [kɒŋglɒməˈreɪʃən] n Anhäufung f

congratulate [kənˈgrætjuleɪt] vt: **to ~ sb (on sth)** jdn (zu etw) beglückwünschen; **congratulations** [kəngrætjuˈleɪʃənz] npl Glückwünsche pl; **congratulations!** gratuliere!, herzlichen Glückwunsch!

congregate [ˈkɒŋgrɪgeɪt] vi sich versammeln; **congregation** [kɒŋgrɪˈgeɪʃən] n Gemeinde f

congress [ˈkɒŋgres] n Kongress m; **C~man** (irreg: US) n Mitglied nt des amerikanischen Repräsentantenhauses

conifer [ˈkɒnɪfə*] n Nadelbaum m

conjunction [kənˈdʒʌŋkʃən] n Verbindung f; (GRAM) Konjunktion f

conjunctivitis [kəndʒʌŋktɪˈvaɪtɪs] n Bindehautentzündung f

conjure [ˈkʌndʒə*] vi zaubern; **~ up** vt heraufbeschwören; **~r** n Zauberkünstler(in) m(f)

conk out [kɒŋk-] (inf) vi den Geist aufgeben

con man (irreg) n Schwindler m

connect [kəˈnekt] vt verbinden; (ELEC) anschließen; **to be ~ed with** eine Beziehung haben zu; (be related to) verwandt sein mit; **~ion** [kəˈnekʃən] n Verbindung f; (relation) Zusammenhang m; (ELEC, TEL, RAIL) Anschluss m

connive [kəˈnaɪv] vi: **to ~ at** stillschweigend dulden

connoisseur [kɒnɪˈsɜː*] n Kenner m

conquer [ˈkɒŋkə*] vt (feelings) überwinden; (enemy) besiegen; (country) erobern; **~or** n Eroberer m

conquest [ˈkɒŋkwest] n Eroberung f

cons [kɒnz] npl see **convenience**; **pro**

conscience [ˈkɒnʃəns] n Gewissen nt

conscientious [kɒnʃɪˈenʃəs] adj gewissenhaft

conscious [ˈkɒnʃəs] adj bewusst; (MED) bei Bewusstsein; **~ness** n Bewusstsein nt

conscript [ˈkɒnskrɪpt] n Wehrpflichtige(r) m; **~ion** [kənˈskrɪpʃən] n Wehrpflicht f

consecutive [kənˈsekjutɪv] adj aufeinander folgend

consensus [kənˈsensəs] n allgemeine Übereinstimmung f

consent [kənˈsent] n Zustimmung f ♦ vi zustimmen

consequence ['kɔnsɪkwəns] *n* (*importance*) Bedeutung *f*; (*effect*) Folge *f*

consequently ['kɔnsɪkwəntlɪ] *adv* folglich

conservation [kɔnsə'veɪʃən] *n* Erhaltung *f*; (*nature* ~) Umweltschutz *m*

conservative [kən'sɜːvətɪv] *adj* konservativ; **C~** *adj* konservativ ♦ *n* Konservative(r) *mf*

conservatory [kən'sɜːvətrɪ] *n* (*room*) Wintergarten *m*

conserve [kən'sɜːv] *vt* erhalten

consider [kən'sɪdə*] *vt* überlegen; (*take into account*) in Betracht ziehen; (*regard as*) halten für; **to ~ doing sth** daran denken, etw zu tun; **~able** [kən'sɪdərəbl] *adj* beträchtlich; **~ably** *adv* beträchtlich; **~ate** *adj* rücksichtsvoll; **~ation** [kənsɪdə'reɪʃən] *n* Rücksicht(nahme) *f*; (*thought*) Erwägung *f*; **~ing** *prep* in Anbetracht +*gen*

consign [kən'saɪn] *vt* übergeben; **~ment** *n* Sendung *f*

consist [kən'sɪst] *vi*: **to ~ of** bestehen aus

consistency [kən'sɪstənsɪ] *n* (*of material*) Konsistenz *f*; (*of argument, person*) Konsequenz *f*

consistent [kən'sɪstənt] *adj* (*person*) konsequent; (*argument*) folgerichtig

consolation [kɔnsə'leɪʃən] *n* Trost *m*

console[1] [kən'səul] *vt* trösten

console[2] ['kɔnsəul] *n* Kontrollpult *nt*

consolidate [kən'sɔlɪdeɪt] *vt* festigen

consommé [kən'sɔmeɪ] *n* Fleischbrühe *f*

consonant ['kɔnsənənt] *n* Konsonant *m*, Mitlaut *m*

conspicuous [kən'spɪkjuəs] *adj* (*prominent*) auffällig; (*visible*) deutlich sichtbar

conspiracy [kən'spɪrəsɪ] *n* Verschwörung *f*

conspire [kən'spaɪə*] *vi* sich verschwören

constable ['kʌnstəbl] (*BRIT*) *n* Poli-

zist(in) *m(f)*; **chief ~** Polizeipräsident *m*; **constabulary** [kən'stæbjulərɪ] *n* Polizei *f*

constant ['kɔnstənt] *adj* (*continuous*) ständig; (*unchanging*) konstant; **~ly** *adv* ständig

constellation [kɔnstə'leɪʃən] *n* Sternbild *nt*

consternation [kɔnstə'neɪʃən] *n* Bestürzung *f*

constipated ['kɔnstɪpeɪtɪd] *adj* verstopft; **constipation** [kɔnstɪ'peɪʃən] *n* Verstopfung *f*

constituency [kən'stɪtjuənsɪ] *n* Wahlkreis *m*

constituent [kən'stɪtjuənt] *n* (*person*) Wähler *m*; (*part*) Bestandteil *m*

constitute ['kɔnstɪtjuːt] *vt* (*make up*) bilden; (*amount to*) darstellen

constitution [kɔnstɪ'tjuːʃən] *n* Verfassung *f*; **~al** *adj* Verfassungs-

constraint [kən'streɪnt] *n* Zwang *m*; (*shyness*) Befangenheit *f*

construct [kən'strʌkt] *vt* bauen; **~ion** [kən'strʌkʃən] *n* Konstruktion *f*; (*building*) Bau *m*; **~ive** *adj* konstruktiv

construe [kən'struː] *vt* deuten

consul ['kɔnsl] *n* Konsul *m*; **~ate** ['kɔnsjulɪt] *n* Konsulat *nt*

consult [kən'sʌlt] *vt* um Rat fragen; (*doctor*) konsultieren; (*book*) nachschlagen in +*dat*; **~ant** *n* (*MED*) Facharzt *m*; (*other specialist*) Gutachter *m*; **~ation** [kɔnsl'teɪʃən] *n* Beratung *f*; (*MED*) Konsultation *f*; **~ing room** *n* Sprechzimmer *nt*

consume [kən'sjuːm] *vt* verbrauchen; (*food*) konsumieren; **~r** *n* Verbraucher *m*; **~r goods** *npl* Konsumgüter *pl*; **~rism** *n* Konsum *m*; **~r society** *n* Konsumgesellschaft *f*

consummate ['kɔnsʌmeɪt] *vt* (*marriage*) vollziehen

consumption [kən'sʌmpʃən] *n* Verbrauch *m*; (*of food*) Konsum *m*

cont. *abbr* (= *continued*) Forts.

contact ['kɔntækt] *n* (*touch*) Berührung

f; *(connection)* Verbindung *f*; *(person)* Kontakt *m* ♦ *vt* sich in Verbindung setzen mit; **~ lenses** *npl* Kontaktlinsen *pl*

contagious [kən'teɪdʒəs] *adj* ansteckend

contain [kən'teɪn] *vt* enthalten; **to ~ o.s.** sich zügeln; **~er** *n* Behälter *m*; *(transport)* Container *m*

contaminate [kən'tæmɪneɪt] *vt* verunreinigen

cont'd *abbr* (= *continued*) Forts.

contemplate ['kɒntəmpleɪt] *vt (look at)* (nachdenklich) betrachten; *(think about)* überdenken; *(plan)* vorhaben

contemporary [kən'tempərərɪ] *adj* zeitgenössisch ♦ *n* Zeitgenosse *m*

contempt [kən'tempt] *n* Verachtung *f*; **~ of court** *(JUR)* Missachtung *f* des Gerichts; **~ible** *adj* verachtenswert; **~uous** *adj* verächtlich

contend [kən'tend] *vt (argue)* behaupten ♦ *vi* kämpfen; **~er** *n (for post)* Bewerber(in) *m(f)*; *(SPORT)* Wettkämpfer(in) *m(f)*

content [*adj, vb* kən'tent, *n* 'kɒntent] *adj* zufrieden ♦ *vt* befriedigen ♦ *n (also:* **~s)** Inhalt *m*; **~ed** *adj* zufrieden

contention [kən'tenʃən] *n (dispute)* Streit *m*; *(argument)* Behauptung *f*

contentment [kən'tentmənt] *n* Zufriedenheit *f*

contest [*n* 'kɒntest, *vb* kən'test] *n* (Wett)kampf *m* ♦ *vt (dispute)* bestreiten; *(JUR)* anfechten; *(POL)* kandidieren in **+dat**; **~ant** [kən'testənt] *n* Bewerber(in) *m(f)*

context ['kɒntekst] *n* Zusammenhang *m*

continent ['kɒntɪnənt] *n* Kontinent *m*; **the C~** *(BRIT)* das europäische Festland; **~al** [kɒntɪ'nentl] *adj* kontinental; **~al breakfast** *n* kleines Frühstück *nt*; **~al quilt** *(BRIT)* *n* Federbett *nt*

contingency [kən'tɪndʒənsɪ] *n* Möglichkeit *f*

contingent [kən'tɪndʒənt] *n* Kontingent *nt*

continual [kən'tɪnjuəl] *adj (endless)* fortwährend; *(repeated)* immer wiederkehrend; **~ly** *adv* immer wieder

continuation [kəntɪnju'eɪʃən] *n* Fortsetzung *f*

continue [kən'tɪnju:] *vi (person)* weitermachen; *(thing)* weitergehen ♦ *vt* fortsetzen

continuity [kɒntɪ'nju:ɪtɪ] *n* Kontinuität *f*

continuous [kən'tɪnjuəs] *adj* ununterbrochen; **~ stationery** *n* Endlospapier *nt*

contort [kən'tɔ:t] *vt* verdrehen; **~ion** [kən'tɔ:ʃən] *n* Verzerrung *f*

contour ['kɒntuə] *n* Umriss *m*; *(also:* **~ line)** Höhenlinie *f*

contraband ['kɒntrəbænd] *n* Schmuggelware *f*

contraception [kɒntrə'sepʃən] *n* Empfängnisverhütung *f*

contraceptive [kɒntrə'septɪv] *n* empfängnisverhütende(s) Mittel *nt* ♦ *adj* empfängnisverhütend

contract [*n* 'kɒntrækt, *vb* kən'trækt] *n* Vertrag *m* ♦ *vi (muscle, metal)* sich zusammenziehen; *vt* zusammenziehen; **to ~ to do sth** *(COMM)* sich vertraglich verpflichten, etw zu tun; **~ion** [kən'trækʃən] *n (shortening)* Verkürzung *f*; **~or** [kən'træktə*] *n* Unternehmer *m*

contradict [kɒntrə'dɪkt] *vt* widersprechen **+dat**; **~ion** [kɒntrə'dɪkʃən] *n* Widerspruch *m*

contraflow ['kɒntrəfləʊ] *n (AUT)* Gegenverkehr *m*

contraption [kən'træpʃən] *(inf)* *n* Apparat *m*

contrary[1] ['kɒntrərɪ] *adj (opposite)* entgegengesetzt ♦ *n* Gegenteil *nt*; **on the ~** im Gegenteil

contrary[2] [kən'treərɪ] *adj (obstinate)* widerspenstig

contrast [*n* 'kɒntrɑ:st, *vb* kən'trɑ:st] *n* Kontrast *m* ♦ *vt* entgegensetzen; **~ing** [kən'trɑ:stɪŋ] *adj* Kontrast-

contravene [kɔntrə'vi:n] vt verstoßen gegen

contribute [kən'trɪbju:t] vt, vi: **to ~ to** beitragen zu; **contribution** [kɔntrɪ'bju:ʃən] n Beitrag m; **contributor** [kən'trɪbjutə'] n Beitragende(r) f(m)

contrive [kən'traɪv] vt ersinnen ♦ vi: **to ~ to do sth** es schaffen, etw zu tun

control [kən'trəul] vt (direct, test) kontrollieren ♦ n Kontrolle f; **~s** npl (of vehicle) Steuerung f; (of engine) Schaltafel f; **to be in ~ of** (business, office) leiten; (group of children) beaufsichtigen; **out of ~** außer Kontrolle; **under ~** unter Kontrolle; **~led substance** n verschreibungspflichtiges Medikament; **~ panel** n Schalttafel f; **~ room** n Kontrollraum m; **~ tower** n (AVIAT) Kontrollturm m

controversial [kɔntrə'vɜ:ʃl] adj umstritten; **controversy** ['kɔntrəvɜ:sɪ] n Kontroverse f

conurbation [kɔnə'beɪʃən] n Ballungsgebiet nt

convalesce [kɔnvə'les] vi genesen; **~nce** [kɔnvə'lesns] n Genesung f

convector [kən'vektə'] n Heizlüfter m

convene [kən'vi:n] vt zusammenrufen ♦ vi sich versammeln

convenience [kən'vi:nɪəns] n Annehmlichkeit f; **all modern ~s** or (BRIT) **mod cons** mit allem Komfort; **at your ~** wann es Ihnen passt

convenient [kən'vi:nɪənt] adj günstig

convent ['kɔnvənt] n Kloster nt

convention [kən'venʃən] n Versammlung f; (custom) Konvention f; **~al** adj konventionell

convent school n Klosterschule f

converge [kən'vɜ:dʒ] vi zusammenlaufen

conversant [kən'vɜ:snt] adj: **to be ~ with** bewandert sein in +dat

conversation [kɔnvə'seɪʃən] n Gespräch nt; **~al** adj Unterhaltungs-

converse [n 'kɔnvɜ:s, vb kən'vɜ:s] n

Gegenteil nt ♦ vi sich unterhalten

conversion [kən'vɜ:ʃən] n Umwandlung f; (REL) Bekehrung f

convert [vb kən'vɜ:t, n 'kɔnvɜ:t] vt (change) umwandeln; (REL) bekehren ♦ n Bekehrte(r) mf; Konvertit(in) m(f); **~ible** n (AUT) Kabriolett nt ♦ adj umwandelbar; (FIN) konvertierbar

convex ['kɔnveks] adj konvex

convey [kən'veɪ] vt (carry) befördern; (feelings) vermitteln; **~or belt** n Fließband nt

convict [vb kən'vɪkt, n 'kɔnvɪkt] vt verurteilen ♦ n Häftling m; **~ion** [kən'vɪkʃən] n (verdict) Verurteilung f; (belief) Überzeugung f

convince [kən'vɪns] vt überzeugen; **~d** adj: **~d that** überzeugt davon, dass; **convincing** adj überzeugend

convoluted ['kɔnvəlu:tɪd] adj verwickelt; (style) gewunden

convoy ['kɔnvɔɪ] n (of vehicles) Kolonne f; (protected) Konvoi m

convulse [kən'vʌls] vt zusammenzucken lassen; **to be ~d with laughter** sich vor Lachen krümmen; **convulsion** [kən'vʌlʃən] n (esp MED) Zuckung f, Krampf m

coo [ku:] vi gurren

cook [kuk] vt, vi kochen ♦ n Koch m, Köchin f; **~ book** n Kochbuch nt; **~er** n Herd m; **~ery** n Kochkunst f; **~ery book** (BRIT) n = **cook book**; **~ie** (US) n Plätzchen nt; **~ing** n Kochen nt

cool [ku:l] adj kühl ♦ vt, vi (ab)kühlen; **~ down** vt, vi (fig) (sich) beruhigen; **~ness** n Kühle f; (of temperament) kühle(r) Kopf m

coop [ku:p] n Hühnerstall m ♦ vt: **~ up** (fig) einpferchen

cooperate [kəu'ɔpəreɪt] vi zusammenarbeiten; **cooperation** [kəuɔpə'reɪʃən] n Zusammenarbeit f

cooperative [kəu'ɔpərətɪv] adj hilfsbereit; (COMM) genossenschaftlich ♦ n (of farmers) Genossenschaft f; (~ store) Konsumladen m

coordinate [vb kəu'ɔːdɪneɪt, kəu'ɔːdɪnət] vt koordinieren ♦ n (MATH) Koordinate f; ~s npl (clothes) Kombinationen pl; **coordination** [kəuɔːdɪ'neɪʃən] n Koordination f

cop [kɔp] (inf) n Polyp m, Bulle m

cope [kəup] vi: **to ~ with** fertig werden mit

copious ['kəupɪəs] adj reichhaltig

copper ['kɔpər] n (metal) Kupfer nt; (inf: policeman) Polyp m, Bulle m; ~s npl (money) Kleingeld nt

copse [kɔps] n Unterholz nt

copy ['kɔpɪ] n (imitation) Kopie f; (of book etc) Exemplar nt; (of newspaper) Nummer f ♦ vt kopieren, abschreiben; ~**right** n Copyright nt

coral ['kɔrəl] n Koralle f; ~ **reef** n Korallenriff nt

cord [kɔːd] n Schnur f; (ELEC) Kabel nt

cordial ['kɔːdɪəl] adj herzlich ♦ n Fruchtsaft m

cordon ['kɔːdn] n Absperrkette f; ~ **off** vt abriegeln

corduroy ['kɔːdərɔɪ] n Kord(samt) m

core [kɔː*] n Kern m ♦ vt entkernen

cork [kɔːk] n (bark) Korkrinde f; (stopper) Korken m; ~**screw** n Korkenzieher m

corn [kɔːn] n (BRIT: wheat) Getreide nt, Korn nt; (US: maize) Mais m; (on foot) Hühnerauge nt; ~ **on the cob** Maiskolben m

corned beef ['kɔːnd-] n Cornedbeef nt, Corned Beef nt

corner ['kɔːnər] n Ecke f; (on road) Kurve f ♦ vt in die Enge treiben; (market) monopolisieren ♦ vi (AUT) in die Kurve gehen; ~**stone** n Eckstein m

cornet ['kɔːnɪt] n (MUS) Kornett nt, (BRIT: of ice cream) Eistüte f

corn: ~**flakes** ['kɔːnfleɪks] npl Cornflakes pl ®; ~**flour** ['kɔːnflauə*] (BRIT) n Maizena nt ®; ~**starch** ['kɔːnstɑːtʃ] (US) n Maizena nt ®

corny ['kɔːnɪ] adj (joke) blöd(e)

coronary ['kɔrənərɪ] n (also: ~ thrombosis) Herzinfarkt m

coronation [kɔrə'neɪʃən] n Krönung f

coroner ['kɔrənər] n Untersuchungsrichter m

corporal ['kɔːpərl] n Obergefreite(r) m ♦ adj: ~ **punishment** Prügelstrafe f

corporate ['kɔːpərɪt] adj gemeinschaftlich, korporativ

corporation [kɔːpə'reɪʃən] n (of town) Gemeinde f; (COMM) Körperschaft f, Aktiengesellschaft f

corps [kɔː*] (pl ~) n (Armee)korps nt

corpse [kɔːps] n Leiche f

corral [kə'rɑːl] n Pferch m, Korral m

correct [kə'rekt] adj (accurate) richtig; (proper) korrekt ♦ vt korrigieren; ~**ion** [kə'rekʃən] n Berichtigung f

correlation [kɔrɪ'leɪʃən] n Wechselbeziehung f

correspond [kɔrɪs'pɔnd] vi (agree) übereinstimmen; (exchange letters) korrespondieren; ~**ence** n (similarity) Entsprechung f; (letters) Briefwechsel m, Korrespondenz f; ~**ence course** n Fernkurs m; ~**ent** n (PRESS) Berichterstatter m

corridor ['kɔrɪdɔː*] n Gang m

corroborate [kə'rɔbəreɪt] vt bestätigen

corrode [kə'rəud] vt zerfressen ♦ vi rosten

corrosion [kə'rəuʒən] n Korrosion f

corrugated ['kɔrəgeɪtɪd] adj gewellt; ~ **iron** n Wellblech nt

corrupt [kə'rʌpt] adj korrupt ♦ vt verderben; (bribe) bestechen; ~**ion** [kə'rʌpʃən] n Verdorbenheit f; (bribery) Bestechung f

corset ['kɔːsɪt] n Korsett nt

Corsica ['kɔːsɪkə] n Korsika nt

cosmetics [kɔz'metɪks] npl Kosmetika pl

cosmic ['kɔzmɪk] adj kosmisch

cosmonaut ['kɔzmənɔːt] n Kosmonaut(e) m(f)

cosmopolitan [kɔzmə'pɔlɪtn] adj international; (city) Welt-

cosmos ['kɔzmɔs] n Kosmos m

cost [kɒst] (*pt, pp* **cost**) *n* Kosten *pl*, Preis *m* ♦ *vt, vi* kosten; **~s** *npl* (*JUR*) Kosten *pl*; **how much does it ~?** wie viel kostet das?; **at all ~s** um jeden Preis

co-star ['kəʊstɑːʳ] *n* zweite(r) *or* weitere(r) Hauptdarsteller(in) *m(f)*

cost: **~-effective** *adj* rentabel; **~ly** ['kɒstlɪ] *adj* kostspielig; **~-of-living** ['kɒstəv'lɪvɪŋ] *adj* (*index*) Lebenshaltungskosten-; **~ price** (*BRIT*) *n* Selbstkostenpreis *m*

costume ['kɒstjuːm] *n* Kostüm nt; (*fancy dress*) Maskenkostüm nt; (*BRIT: also:* **swimming ~**) Badeanzug *m*; **~ jewellery** *n* Modeschmuck *m*

cosy ['kəʊzɪ] (*BRIT*) *adj* behaglich; (*atmosphere*) gemütlich

cot [kɒt] *n* (*BRIT: child's*) Kinderbett(chen) nt; (*US: camp bed*) Feldbett nt

cottage ['kɒtɪdʒ] *n* kleine(s) Haus nt; **~ cheese** *n* Hüttenkäse *m*; **~ industry** *n* Heimindustrie *f*; **~ pie** *n* Auflauf mit Hackfleisch und Kartoffelbrei

cotton ['kɒtn] *n* Baumwolle *f*; (*thread*) Garn nt; **~ on to** (*inf*) *vt* kapieren; **~ wool** (*BRIT*) *n* Watte *f*

couch [kaʊtʃ] *n* Couch *f*

couchette [kuː'ʃet] *n* (*on train, boat*) Liegewagenplatz *m*

cough [kɒf] *vi* husten ♦ *n* Husten *m*; **~ drop** *n* Hustenbonbon *m*

could [kʊd] *pt of* **can**[2]

couldn't ['kʊdnt] = **could not**

council ['kaʊnsl] *n* (*of town*) Stadtrat *m*; **~ estate** (*BRIT*) *n* Siedlung *f* des sozialen Wohnungsbaus; **~ house** (*BRIT*) *n* Haus nt des sozialen Wohnungsbaus; **~lor** ['kaʊnsləʳ] *n* Stadtrat *m*/-rätin *f*

counsel ['kaʊnsl] *n* (*barrister*) Anwalt *m*; (*advice*) Rat(schlag) *m* ♦ *vt* beraten; **~lor** ['kaʊnsləʳ] *n* Berater *m*

count [kaʊnt] *vt, vi* zählen ♦ *n* (*reckoning*) Abrechnung *f*; (*nobleman*) Graf *m*; **~ on** *vt* zählen auf +*acc*

countenance ['kaʊntɪnəns] *n* (*old*)

Antlitz nt ♦ *vt* (*tolerate*) gutheißen

counter ['kaʊntəʳ] *n* (*in shop*) Ladentisch *m*; (*in café*) Theke *f*; (*in bank, post office*) Schalter *m* ♦ *vt* entgegnen

counteract ['kaʊntər'ækt] *vt* entgegenwirken +*dat*

counterfeit ['kaʊntəfɪt] *n* Fälschung *f* ♦ *vt* fälschen ♦ *adj* gefälscht

counterfoil ['kaʊntəfɔɪl] *n* (*Kontroll*)abschnitt *m*

counterpart ['kaʊntəpɑːt] *n* (*object*) Gegenstück nt; (*person*) Gegenüber nt

counterproductive ['kaʊntəprə'dʌktɪv] *adj* destruktiv

countersign ['kaʊntəsaɪn] *vt* gegenzeichnen

countess ['kaʊntɪs] *n* Gräfin *f*

countless ['kaʊntlɪs] *adj* zahllos, unzählig

country ['kʌntrɪ] *n* Land nt; **~ dancing** (*BRIT*) *n* Volkstanz *m*; **~ house** *n* Landhaus nt; **~man** (*irreg*) *n* (*national*) Landsmann *m*; (*rural*) Bauer *m*; **~side** *n* Landschaft *f*

county ['kaʊntɪ] *n* Landkreis *m*; (*BRIT*) Grafschaft *f*

coup [kuː] (*pl* **~s**) *n* Coup *m*; (*also:* **~ d'état**) Staatsstreich *m*, Putsch *m*

couple ['kʌpl] *n* Paar nt ♦ *vt* koppeln; **a ~ of** ein paar

coupon ['kuːpɒn] *n* Gutschein *m*

coups [kuː] *npl of* **coup**

courage ['kʌrɪdʒ] *n* Mut *m*; **~ous** [kə'reɪdʒəs] *adj* mutig

courgette [kʊə'ʒet] (*BRIT*) *n* Zucchini *f* *or pl*

courier ['kʊrɪəʳ] *n* (*for holiday*) Reiseleiter *m*; (*messenger*) Kurier *m*

course [kɔːs] *n* (*race*) Bahn *f*; (*of stream*) Lauf *m*; (*golf* ~) Platz *m*; (*NAUT, SCH*) Kurs *m*; (*in meal*) Gang *m*; **of ~** natürlich

court [kɔːt] *n* (*royal*) Hof *m*; (*JUR*) Gericht *m* ♦ *vt* (*woman*) gehen mit; (*danger*) herausfordern; **to take to ~** vor Gericht bringen

courteous ['kɜːtɪəs] *adj* höflich

courtesy ['kə:təsɪ] n Höflichkeit f

courtesy bus, courtesy coach n gebührenfreier Bus m

court: ~ **house** (US) n Gerichtsgebäude nt; ~**ier** ['kɔ:tɪə'] n Höfling m; ~ **martial** ['kɔ:t'mɑ:ʃəl] (pl ~**s martial**) n Kriegsgericht nt ♦ vt vor ein Kriegsgericht stellen; ~**room** n Gerichtssaal m; ~**s martial** npl of **court martial**; ~**yard** ['kɔ:tjɑ:d] n Hof m

cousin ['kʌzn] n Cousin m, Vetter m; Kusine f

cove [kəʊv] n kleine Bucht f

covenant ['kʌvənənt] n (ECCL) Bund m; (JUR) Verpflichtung f

cover ['kʌvə'] vt (spread over) bedecken; (shield) abschirmen; (include) sich erstrecken über +acc; (protect) decken; (distance) zurücklegen; (report on) berichten über +acc ♦ n (lid) Deckel m; (for bed) Decke f; (MIL) Bedeckung f; (of book) Einband m; (of magazine) Umschlag m; (insurance) Versicherung f; **to take ~** (from rain) sich unterstellen; (MIL) in Deckung gehen; **under ~** (indoors) drinnen; **under ~ of** im Schutze +gen; **under separate ~** (COMM) mit getrennter Post; **to ~ up for sb** jdn decken; ~**age** n (PRESS: reports) Berichterstattung f; (distribution) Verbreitung f; ~ **charge** n Bedienungsgeld nt; ~**ing** n Bedeckung f; ~**ing letter** (US ~ **letter**) n Begleitbrief m; ~ **note** n (INSURANCE) vorläufige(r) Versicherungsschein m

covert ['kʌvət] adj geheim

cover-up ['kʌvərʌp] n Vertuschung f

cow [kaʊ] n Kuh f ♦ vt einschüchtern

coward ['kaʊəd] n Feigling m; ~**ice** ['kaʊədɪs] n Feigheit f; ~**ly** adj feige

cower ['kaʊə'] vi kauern

coy [kɔɪ] adj schüchtern

coyote [kɔɪ'əʊtɪ] n Präriewolf m

cozy ['kəʊzɪ] (US) adj = **cosy**

CPA (US) n abbr = **certified public accountant**

crab [kræb] n Krebs m

crab apple n Holzapfel m

crack [kræk] n Riss m, Sprung m; (noise) Knall m; (drug) Crack nt ♦ vt (break) springen lassen; (joke) reißen; (nut, safe) knacken; (whip) knallen lassen ♦ vi springen ♦ adj erstklassig; (troops) Elite-; ~ **down** vi: **to ~ down (on)** hart durchgreifen (bei); ~ **up** vi (fig) zusammenbrechen

cracked [krækt] adj (glass, plate, ice) gesprungen; (rib, bone) gebrochen, angeknackst (umg); (broken) gebrochen; (surface, walls) rissig; (inf: mad) übergeschnappt

cracker ['krækə'] n (firework) Knallkörper m, Kracher m; (biscuit) Keks m; (Christmas ~) Knallbonbon m

crackle ['krækl] vi knistern; (fire) prasseln

cradle ['kreɪdl] n Wiege f

craft [krɑ:ft] n (skill) (Hand- or Kunst)fertigkeit f; (trade) Handwerk nt; (NAUT) Schiff nt; ~**sman** (irreg) n Handwerker m; ~**smanship** n (quality) handwerkliche Ausführung f; (ability) handwerkliche(s) Können nt

crafty ['krɑ:ftɪ] adj schlau

crag [kræg] n Klippe f

cram [kræm] vt voll stopfen ♦ vi (learn) pauken; **to ~ sth into sth** etw in etw acc stopfen

cramp [kræmp] n Krampf m ♦ vt (limit) einengen; (hinder) hemmen; ~**ed** adj (position) verkrampft; (space) eng

crampon ['kræmpən] n Steigeisen nt

cranberry ['krænbərɪ] n Preiselbeere f

crane [kreɪn] n (machine) Kran m; (bird) Kranich m

crank [kræŋk] n (lever) Kurbel f; (person) Spinner m; ~**shaft** n Kurbelwelle f

cranny ['krænɪ] n see **nook**

crash [kræʃ] n (noise) Krachen nt; (with cars) Zusammenstoß m; (with plane) Absturz m; (COMM) Zusammenbruch m ♦ vt (plane) abstürzen mit ♦ vi (cars) zusammenstoßen; (plane) abstürzen; (economy) zusammenbrechen; (noise) knallen; **~ course** n Schnellkurs m; **~ helmet** n Sturzhelm m; **~ landing** n Bruchlandung f

crass [kræs] adj krass

crate [kreɪt] n (also fig) Kiste f

crater ['kreɪtə'] n Krater m

cravat(e) [krə'væt] n Halstuch nt

crave [kreɪv] vt verlangen nach

crawl [krɔːl] vi kriechen; (baby) krabbeln ♦ n Kriechen nt; (swim) Kraul m

crayfish ['kreɪfɪʃ] n inv (freshwater) Krebs m; (saltwater) Languste f

crayon ['kreɪən] n Buntstift m

craze [kreɪz] n Fimmel m

crazy ['kreɪzɪ] adj verrückt

creak [kriːk] vi knarren

cream [kriːm] n (from milk) Rahm m, Sahne f; (polish, cosmetic) Creme f; (fig: people) Elite f ♦ adj cremefarbig; **~ cake** n Sahnetorte f; **~ cheese** n Rahmquark m; **~y** adj sahnig

crease [kriːs] n Falte f ♦ vt falten; (wrinkle) zerknittern ♦ vi (wrinkle up) knittern; **~d** adj zerknittert, faltig

create [kriː'eɪt] vt erschaffen; (cause) verursachen; **creation** [kriː'eɪʃən] n Schöpfung f; **creative** adj kreativ; **creator** n Schöpfer m

creature ['kriːtʃə'] n Geschöpf nt

crèche [kreʃ] n Krippe f

credence ['kriːdns] n: **to lend** or **give ~ to sth** etw dat Glauben schenken

credentials [krɪ'denʃlz] npl Beglaubigungsschreiben nt

credibility [kredɪ'bɪlɪtɪ] n Glaubwürdigkeit f

credible ['kredɪbl] adj (person) glaubwürdig; (story) glaubhaft

credit ['kredɪt] n (also COMM) Kredit m ♦ vt Glauben schenken +dat; (COMM) gutschreiben; **~s** npl (of film) Mitwirkende pl; **~able** adj rühmlich; **~ card** n Kreditkarte f; **~or** n Gläubiger m

creed [kriːd] n Glaubensbekenntnis nt

creek [kriːk] n (inlet) kleine Bucht f; (US: river) kleine(r) Wasserlauf m

creep [kriːp] (pt, pp **crept**) vi kriechen;

~er n Kletterpflanze f; **~y** adj (frightening) gruselig

cremate [krɪ'meɪt] vt einäschern; **cremation** [krɪ'meɪʃən] n Einäscherung f;

crematorium [kremə'tɔːrɪəm] n Krematorium nt

crêpe [kreɪp] n Krepp m; **~ bandage** (BRIT) n Elastikbinde f

crept [krept] pt, pp of **creep**

crescent ['kresnt] n (of moon) Halbmond m

cress [kres] n Kresse f

crest [krest] n (of cock) Kamm m; (of wave) Wellenkamm m; (coat of arms) Wappen nt

crestfallen ['krestfɔːlən] adj niedergeschlagen

Crete [kriːt] n Kreta nt

crevice ['krevɪs] n Riss m

crew [kruː] n Besatzung f, Mannschaft f; **~-cut** n Bürstenschnitt m; **~ neck** n runde(r) Ausschnitt m

crib [krɪb] n (bed) Krippe f ♦ vt (inf) spicken

crick [krɪk] n Muskelkrampf m

cricket ['krɪkɪt] n (insect) Grille f; (game) Kricket m

crime [kraɪm] n Verbrechen nt

criminal ['krɪmɪnl] n Verbrecher m ♦ adj kriminell; (act) strafbar

crimson ['krɪmzn] adj leuchtend rot

cringe [krɪndʒ] vi sich ducken

crinkle ['krɪŋkl] vt zerknittern

cripple ['krɪpl] n Krüppel m ♦ vt lahm legen; (MED) verkrüppeln

crisis ['kraɪsɪs] (pl **crises**) n Krise f

crisp [krɪsp] adj knusprig; **~s** (BRIT) npl Chips pl

crisscross ['krɪskrɔs] adj gekreuzt, Kreuz-

criteria [kraɪ'tɪərɪə] npl of **criterion**

criterion [kraɪ'tɪərɪən] (pl **criteria**) n Kriterium nt

critic ['krɪtɪk] n Kritiker(in) m(f); **~al** adj kritisch; **~ally** adv kritisch; (ill) gefährlich; **~ism** ['krɪtɪsɪzəm] n Kritik f; **~ize** ['krɪtɪsaɪz] vt kritisieren

croak [krəʊk] vi krächzen; (frog) quaken

Croatia [krəʊ'eɪʃə] n Kroatien nt

crochet ['krəʊʃeɪ] n Häkelei f

crockery ['krɔkərɪ] n Geschirr nt

crocodile ['krɔkədaɪl] n Krokodil nt

crocus ['krəʊkəs] n Krokus m

croft [krɔft] (BRIT) n kleine(s) Pachtgut nt

crony ['krəʊnɪ] (inf) n Kumpel m

crook [krʊk] n (criminal) Gauner m; (stick) Hirtenstab m

crooked ['krʊkɪd] adj krumm

crop [krɔp] n (harvest) Ernte f; (riding ~) Reitpeitsche f ♦ vt ernten; ~ **up** vi passieren

croquet ['krəʊkeɪ] n Krocket nt

croquette [krə'ket] n Krokette f

cross [krɔs] n Kreuz nt ♦ vt (road) überqueren; (legs) übereinander legen; kreuzen ♦ adj (annoyed) böse; ~ **out** vt streichen; ~ **over** vi hinübergehen; ~**bar** n Querstange f; ~-**country** (race) n Geländelauf m; ~-**examine** ♦ vt ins Kreuzverhör nehmen; ~-**eyed** adj: to be ~-eyed schielen; ~**fire** n Kreuzfeuer nt; ~**ing** n (~roads) (Straßen)kreuzung f; (of ship) Überfahrt f; (for pedestrians) Fußgängerübergang m; ~**ing guard** (US) n Schülerlotse m; ~ **purposes** npl: to be at ~ purposes aneinander vorbeireden; ~-**reference** n Querverweis m; ~**roads** n Straßenkreuzung f; (fig) Scheideweg m; ~ **section** n Querschnitt m; ~**walk** (US) n Fußgängerübergang m; ~**wind** n Seitenwind m; ~**word** (puzzle) n Kreuzworträtsel nt

crotch [krɔtʃ] n Zwickel m; (ANAT) Unterleib m

crouch [kraʊtʃ] vi hocken

crow [krəʊ] n (bird) Krähe f; (of cock) Krähen nt ♦ vi krähen

crowbar ['krəʊbɑː] n Stemmeisen nt

crowd [kraʊd] n Menge f ♦ vt (fill) überfüllen ♦ vi drängen; ~**ed** adj überfüllt

crown [kraʊn] n Krone f; (of head, hat) Kopf m ♦ vt krönen; ~ **jewels** npl Kronjuwelen pl; ~ **prince** n Kronprinz m

crow's-feet ['krəʊzfiːt] npl Krähenfüße pl

crucial ['kruːʃl] adj entscheidend

crucifix ['kruːsɪfɪks] n Kruzifix nt; ~**ion** [kruːsɪ'fɪkʃən] n Kreuzigung f

crude [kruːd] adj (raw) roh; (humour, behaviour) grob; (basic) primitiv; ~ (**oil**) n Rohöl nt

cruel ['krʊəl] adj grausam; ~**ty** n Grausamkeit f

cruise [kruːz] n Kreuzfahrt f ♦ vi kreuzen; ~**r** n (MIL) Kreuzer m

crumb [krʌm] n Krume f

crumble ['krʌmbl] vt, vi zerbröckeln; **crumbly** adj krümelig

crumpet ['krʌmpɪt] n Tee(pfann)-kuchen m

crumple ['krʌmpl] vt zerknittern

crunch [krʌntʃ] n: the ~ (fig) der Knackpunkt ♦ vt knirschen; ~**y** adj knusprig

crusade [kruː'seɪd] n Kreuzzug m

crush [krʌʃ] n Gedränge nt ♦ vt zerdrücken; (rebellion) unterdrücken

crust [krʌst] n Kruste f

crutch [krʌtʃ] n Krücke f

crux [krʌks] n springende(r) Punkt m

cry [kraɪ] vi (shout) schreien; (weep) weinen ♦ n (call) Schrei m; ~ **off** vi (plötzlich) absagen

crypt [krɪpt] n Krypta f

cryptic ['krɪptɪk] adj hintergründig

crystal ['krɪstl] n Kristall m; (glass) Kristallglas nt; (mineral) Bergkristall m; ~-**clear** adj kristallklar

crystallize ['krɪstəlaɪz] vt, vi kristallisieren; (fig) klären

CSA n abbr (= Child Support Agency) Amt zur Regelung von Unterhaltszahlungen für Kinder

CTC (BRIT) n abbr = **city technology college**

cub [kʌb] n Junge(s) nt; (also: **C~ scout**) Wölfling m

Cuba ['kju:bə] n Kuba nt; **~n** adj kubanisch ♦ n Kubaner(in) m(f)

cubbyhole ['kʌbɪhəul] n Eckchen nt

cube [kju:b] n Würfel m ♦ vt (MATH) hoch drei nehmen

cubic ['kju:bɪk] adj würfelförmig; (centimetre etc) Kubik-; **~ capacity** n Fassungsvermögen nt

cubicle ['kju:bɪkl] n Kabine f

cuckoo ['kuku:] n Kuckuck m; **~ clock** n Kuckucksuhr f

cucumber ['kju:kʌmbər] n Gurke f

cuddle ['kʌdl] vt, vi herzen, drücken (inf)

cue [kju:] n (THEAT) Stichwort nt; (snooker ~) Billardstock m

cuff [kʌf] n (BRIT: of shirt, coat etc) Manschette f; Aufschlag m; (US) = **turn-up**; **off the ~** aus dem Handgelenk; **~link** n Manschettenknopf m

cuisine [kwɪ'zi:n] n Kochkunst f, Küche f

cul-de-sac ['kʌldəsæk] n Sackgasse f

culinary ['kʌlɪnərɪ] adj Koch-

cull [kʌl] vt (select) auswählen

culminate ['kʌlmɪneɪt] vi gipfeln; **culmination** [kʌlmɪ'neɪʃən] n Höhepunkt m

culottes [kju:'lɒts] npl Hosenrock m

culpable ['kʌlpəbl] adj schuldig

culprit ['kʌlprɪt] n Täter m

cult [kʌlt] n Kult m

cultivate ['kʌltɪveɪt] vt (AGR) bebauen; (mind) bilden; **cultivation** [kʌltɪ'veɪʃən] n (AGR) Bebauung f; (of person) Bildung f

cultural ['kʌltʃərəl] adj kulturell, Kultur-

culture ['kʌltʃər] n Kultur f; **~d** adj gebildet

cumbersome ['kʌmbəsəm] adj (object) sperrig

cumulative ['kju:mjulətɪv] adj gehäuft

cunning ['kʌnɪŋ] n Verschlagenheit f ♦ adj schlau

cup [kʌp] n Tasse f; (prize) Pokal m

cupboard ['kʌbəd] n Schrank m

cup tie n (BRIT) Pokalspiel nt

curate ['kjuərɪt] n (Catholic) Kurat m; (Protestant) Vikar m

curator [kjuə'reɪtər] n Kustos m

curb [kə:b] vt zügeln ♦ n (on spending etc) Einschränkung f; (US) Bordstein m

curdle ['kə:dl] vi gerinnen

cure [kjuər] n Heilmittel nt; (process) Heilverfahren nt ♦ vt heilen

curfew ['kə:fju:] n Ausgangssperre f, Sperrstunde f

curio ['kjuərɪəu] n Kuriosität f

curiosity [kjuərɪ'ɒsɪtɪ] n Neugier f

curious ['kjuərɪəs] adj neugierig; (strange) seltsam

curl [kə:l] n Locke f ♦ vt locken ♦ vi sich locken; **~ up** vi sich zusammenrollen; (person) sich anschmiegen; **~er** n Lockenwickler m; **~y** ['kə:lɪ] adj lockig

currant ['kʌrnt] n Korinthe f

currency ['kʌrnsɪ] n Währung f; **to gain ~** an Popularität gewinnen

current ['kʌrnt] n Strömung f ♦ adj (expression) gängig, üblich; (issue) neueste; **~ account** (BRIT) n Girokonto nt; **~ affairs** npl Zeitgeschehen nt; **~ly** adv zurzeit

curricula [kə'rɪkjulə] npl of **curriculum**

curriculum [kə'rɪkjuləm] (pl **~s** or **curricula**) n Lehrplan m; **~ vitae** [-'vi:taɪ] n Lebenslauf m

curry ['kʌrɪ] n Currygericht nt ♦ vt: **to ~ favour with** sich einschmeicheln bei; **~ powder** n Curry(pulver) nt

curse [kə:s] vi (swear): **to ~ (at)** fluchen (auf or über +acc) ♦ vt (insult) verwünschen ♦ n Fluch m

cursor ['kə:sər] n (COMPUT) Cursor m

cursory ['kə:sərɪ] adj flüchtig

curt [kə:t] adj schroff

curtail [kə:'teɪl] vt abkürzen; (rights) einschränken

curtain ['kə:tn] n Vorhang m

curts(e)y ['kə:tsɪ] n Knicks m ♦ vi knicksen

curve [kə:v] n Kurve f; (of body, vase

etc) Rundung f ♦ vi sich biegen; *(hips, breasts)* sich runden; *(road)* einen Bogen machen

cushion ['kuʃən] n Kissen nt ♦ vt dämpfen

custard ['kʌstəd] n Vanillesoße f

custodian [kʌs'təudiən] n Kustos m, Verwalter(in) m(f)

custody ['kʌstədi] n Aufsicht f; *(police ~)* Haft f; **to take into ~** verhaften

custom ['kʌstəm] n *(tradition)* Brauch m; *(COMM)* Kundschaft f; **~ary** adj üblich

customer ['kʌstəmə'] n Kunde m, Kundin f

customized ['kʌstəmaizd] adj *(car etc)* mit Spezialausrüstung

custom-made ['kʌstəm'meid] adj speziell angefertigt

customs ['kʌstəmz] npl Zoll m; **~ duty** n Zollabgabe f; **~ officer** n Zollbeamte(r) m, Zollbeamtin f

cut [kʌt] *(pt, pp* **cut)** vt schneiden; *(wages)* kürzen; *(prices)* heruntersetzen ♦ vi schneiden; *(intersect)* sich schneiden ♦ n Schnitt m; *(wound)* Schnittwunde f; *(in income etc)* Kürzung f; *(share)* Anteil m; **to ~ a tooth** zahnen; **~ down** vt *(tree)* fällen; *(reduce)* einschränken; **~ off** vt *(also fig)* abschneiden; *(allowance)* sperren; **~ out** vt *(shape)* ausschneiden; *(delete)* streichen; **~ up** vt *(meat)* aufschneiden; **~back** n Kürzung f

cute [kju:t] adj niedlich

cuticle ['kju:tikl] n Nagelhaut f

cutlery ['kʌtləri] n Besteck nt

cutlet ['kʌtlit] n *(pork)* Kotelett nt; *(veal)* Schnitzel nt

cut- **~out** n *(cardboard ~out)* Ausschneidemodell nt; **~-price, ~-rate** *(US)* adj verbilligt; **~throat** n Verbrechertyp m ♦ adj mörderisch

cutting ['kʌtiŋ] adj schneidend ♦ n *(BRIT: PRESS)* Ausschnitt m; *(: RAIL)* Durchstich m

CV n abbr = **curriculum vitae**

cwt abbr = **hundredweight(s)**

cyanide ['saiənaid] n Zyankali m

cyberspace ['saibəspeis] n Cyberspace m

cycle ['saikl] n Fahrrad nt; *(series)* Reihe f ♦ vi Rad fahren; **~ lane, ~ path** n *(Fahr)radweg* m; **cycling** n Radfahren nt; **cyclist** n Radfahrer(in) m(f)

cyclone ['saikləun] n Zyklon m

cygnet ['ssignit] n junge(r) Schwan m

cylinder ['silində'] n Zylinder m; *(TECH)* Walze f; **~ head gasket** n Zylinderkopfdichtung f

cymbals ['simblz] npl Becken nt

cynic ['sinik] n Zyniker(in) m(f); **~al** adj zynisch; **~ism** ['sinisizəm] n Zynismus m

cypress ['saiprəs] n Zypresse f

Cyprus ['saiprəs] n Zypern nt

cyst [sist] n Zyste f

cystitis [sis'taitis] n Blasenentzündung f

czar [zɑ:'] n Zar m

Czech [tʃek] adj tschechisch ♦ n Tscheche m, Tschechin f

Czechoslovakia [tʃekəslə'vækiə] *(HIST)* n die Tschechoslowakei; **~n** adj tschechoslowakisch ♦ n Tschechoslowake m, Tschechoslowakin f

D, d

D [di:] n *(MUS)* D nt

dab [dæb] vt *(wound, paint)* betupfen ♦ n *(little bit)* bisschen nt; *(of paint)* Tupfer m

dabble ['dæbl] vi: **to ~ in sth** in etw dat machen

dad [dæd] n Papa m, Vati m; **~dy** ['dædi] n Papa m, Vati m; **~dy-long-legs** n Weberknecht m

daffodil ['dæfədil] n Osterglocke f

daft [dɑ:ft] *(inf)* adj blöd(e), doof

dagger ['dægə'] n Dolch m

daily ['deili] adj täglich ♦ n *(PRESS)* Tageszeitung f; (BRIT: cleaner) Haushaltshilfe f ♦ adv täglich

dainty ['deɪntɪ] adj zierlich

dairy ['dɛərɪ] n (shop) Milchgeschäft nt; (on farm) Molkerei f ♦ adj Milch-; ~ **farm** n Hof m mit Milchwirtschaft; ~ **produce** n Molkereiprodukte pl; ~ **products** npl Milchprodukte pl, Molkereiprodukte pl; ~ **store** (US) n Milchgeschäft nt

dais ['deɪɪs] n Podium nt

daisy ['deɪzɪ] n Gänseblümchen nt

dale [deɪl] n Tal nt

dam [dæm] n (Stau)damm m ♦ vt stauen

damage ['dæmɪdʒ] n Schaden m ♦ vt beschädigen; ~s npl (JUR) Schaden(s)ersatz m

damn [dæm] vt verdammen ♦ n (inf): I don't give a ~ das ist mir total egal ♦ adj (inf: also: ~ed) verdammt; ~ it! verflucht!; ~ing adj vernichtend

damp [dæmp] adj feucht ♦ n Feuchtigkeit f ♦ vt (also: ~en) befeuchten; (discourage) dämpfen

damson ['dæmzən] n Damaszenerpflaume f

dance [dɑːns] n Tanz m ♦ vi tanzen; ~ **hall** n Tanzlokal nt; ~r n Tänzer(in) m(f); **dancing** n Tanzen nt

dandelion ['dændɪlaɪən] n Löwenzahn m

dandruff ['dændrəf] n (Kopf)schuppen pl

Dane [deɪn] n Däne m, Dänin f

danger ['deɪndʒə*] n Gefahr f; ~! (sign) Achtung!; **to be in ~ of doing sth** Gefahr laufen, etw zu tun; ~**ous** adj gefährlich

dangle ['dæŋgl] vi baumeln ♦ vt herabhängen lassen

Danish ['deɪnɪʃ] adj dänisch ♦ n Dänisch nt

dare [dɛə*] vt herausfordern ♦ vi: ~ (to) do sth es wagen, etw zu tun; I ~ say ich würde sagen; **daring** ['dɛərɪŋ] adj (audacious) verwegen; (bold) wage-

mutig; (dress) gewagt ♦ n Mut m

dark [dɑːk] adj dunkel; (fig) düster, trübe; (deep colour) dunkel- ♦ n Dunkelheit f; **to be left in the ~ about** im Dunkeln sein über +acc; **after** ~ nach Anbruch der Dunkelheit; ~**en** vt, vi verdunkeln; ~ **glasses** npl Sonnenbrille f; ~**ness** n Finsternis nt; ~**room** n Dunkelkammer f

darling ['dɑːlɪŋ] n Liebling m ♦ adj lieb

darn [dɑːn] vt stopfen

dart [dɑːt] n (weapon) Pfeil m; (in sewing) Abnäher m ♦ vi sausen; ~s n (game) Pfeilwerfen nt; ~**board** n Zielscheibe f

dash [dæʃ] n Sprung m; (mark) (Gedanken)strich m; (small amount) bisschen nt ♦ vt (hopes) zunichte machen ♦ vi stürzen; ~ **away** vi davonstürzen; ~ **off** vi davonstürzen

dashboard ['dæʃbɔːd] n Armaturenbrett nt

dashing ['dæʃɪŋ] adj schneidig

data ['deɪtə] npl Einzelheiten pl, Daten pl; ~**base** n Datenbank f; ~ **processing** n Datenverarbeitung f

date [deɪt] n Datum nt; (for meeting etc) Termin m; (with person) Verabredung f; (fruit) Dattel f ♦ vt (letter etc) datieren; (person) gehen mit; ~ **of birth** Geburtsdatum nt; **to** ~ bis heute; **out of** ~ überholt; **up to** ~ (clothes) modisch; (report) up-to-date; (with news) auf dem Laufenden; ~**d** adj altmodisch; ~ **rape** n Vergewaltigung f nach einem Rendezvous

daub [dɔːb] vt beschmieren; (paint) schmieren

daughter ['dɔːtə*] n Tochter f; ~-**in-law** n Schwiegertochter f

daunting ['dɔːntɪŋ] adj entmutigend

dawdle ['dɔːdl] vi trödeln

dawn [dɔːn] n Morgendämmerung f ♦ vi dämmern; (fig): **it ~ed on him that ...** es dämmerte ihm, dass ...

day [deɪ] n Tag m; **the ~ before/after** am Tag zuvor/danach; **the ~ after to-**

daze 376 **decide**

morrow übermorgen; **the ~ before yesterday** vorgestern; **by ~** am Tage; **~break** n Tagesanbruch m; **~dream** vi mit offenen Augen träumen; **~light** n Tageslicht nt; **~ return** (BRIT) n Tagesrückfahrkarte f; **~time** n Tageszeit f; **~-to-~** adj alltäglich

daze [deɪz] vt betäuben ♦ n Betäubung f; **in a ~** benommen

dazzle ['dæzl] vt blenden

DC abbr (= direct current) Gleichstrom m

D-day ['diːdeɪ] n (HIST) Tag der Invasion durch die Alliierten (6.6.44); (fig) der Tag X

deacon ['diːkən] n Diakon m

dead [ded] adj tot; (without feeling) gefühllos ♦ adv ganz; (exactly) genau ♦ npl: **the ~** die Toten pl; **to shoot sb ~** jdn erschießen; **~ tired** todmüde; **to stop ~** abrupt stehen bleiben; **~en** vt (pain) abtöten; (sound) ersticken; **~ end** n Sackgasse f; **~ heat** n tote(s) Rennen nt; **~line** n Stichtag m; **~lock** n Stillstand m; **~ loss** (inf) n: **to be a ~ loss** ein hoffnungsloser Fall sein; **~ly** adj tödlich; **~pan** adj undurchdringlich; **D~ Sea** n: **the D~ Sea** das Tote Meer

deaf [def] adj taub; **~en** vt taub machen; **~ening** adj (noise) ohrenbetäubend; (noise) lautstark; **~-mute** n Taubstumme(r) mf; **~ness** n Taubheit f

deal [diːl] (pt, pp **dealt**) n Geschäft nt ♦ vt austeilen; (CARDS) geben; **a great ~ of** sehr viel; **~ in** vt fus handeln mit; **~ with** vt fus (person) behandeln; (subject) sich befassen mit; (problem) in Angriff nehmen; **~er** n (COMM) Händler m; (CARDS) Kartengeber m; **~ings** npl (FIN) Geschäfte pl; (relations) Beziehungen pl; **~t** [delt] pt, pp of **deal**

dean [diːn] n (Protestant) Superintendent m; (Catholic) Dechant m; (UNIV) Dekan m

dear [dɪə*] adj lieb; (expensive) teuer ♦ n Liebling m ♦ excl: **~ me!** du liebe Zeit!;

D~ Sir Sehr geehrter Herr!; **D~ John** Lieber John!; **~ly** adv (love) herzlich; (pay) teuer

death [deθ] n Tod m; (statistic) Todesfall m; **~ certificate** n Totenschein m; **~ly** adj totenähnlich, Toten-; **~ penalty** n Todesstrafe f; **~ rate** n Sterblichkeitsziffer f

debar [dɪˈbɑː*] vt ausschließen

debase [dɪˈbeɪs] vt entwerten

debatable [dɪˈbeɪtəbl] adj anfechtbar

debate [dɪˈbeɪt] n Debatte f ♦ vt debattieren, diskutieren; (consider) überlegen

debilitating [dɪˈbɪlɪteɪtɪŋ] adj schwächend

debit ['debɪt] n Schuldposten m ♦ vt belasten

debris ['debriː] n Trümmer pl

debt [det] n Schuld f; **to be in ~** verschuldet sein; **~or** n Schuldner m

debunk [diːˈbʌŋk] vt entlarven

decade [dekeɪd] n Jahrzehnt nt

decadence ['dekədəns] n Dekadenz f

decaff ['diːkæf] (inf) n koffeinfreier Kaffee

decaffeinated [dɪˈkæfɪneɪtɪd] adj koffeinfrei

decanter [dɪˈkæntə*] n Karaffe f

decay [dɪˈkeɪ] n Verfall m; (tooth ~) Karies m ♦ vi verfallen; (teeth, meat etc) faulen; (leaves etc) verrotten

deceased [dɪˈsiːst] adj verstorben

deceit [dɪˈsiːt] n Betrug m; **~ful** adj falsch

deceive [dɪˈsiːv] vt täuschen

December [dɪˈsembə*] n Dezember m

decency ['diːsənsɪ] n Anstand m

decent ['diːsənt] adj (respectable) anständig; (pleasant) annehmbar

deception [dɪˈsepʃən] n Betrug m

deceptive [dɪˈseptɪv] adj irreführend

decibel ['desɪbel] n Dezibel nt

decide [dɪˈsaɪd] vt entscheiden ♦ vi sich entscheiden; **to ~ on sth** etw beschließen; **~d** adj entschieden; **~dly** [dɪˈsaɪdɪdlɪ] adv entschieden

deciduous [dɪˈsɪdjuəs] adj Laub-

decimal [ˈdesɪməl] adj dezimal ♦ n Dezimalzahl f; **~ point** n Liegestuhl m

decipher [dɪˈsaɪfəʳ] vt entziffern

decision [dɪˈsɪʒən] n Entscheidung f, Entschluss m

decisive [dɪˈsaɪsɪv] adj entscheidend; (person) entschlossen

deck [dek] n (NAUT) Deck nt; (of cards) Pack m; **~chair** n Liegestuhl m

declaration [dekləˈreɪʃən] n Erklärung f

declare [dɪˈkleəʳ] vt erklären; (CUSTOMS) verzollen

decline [dɪˈklaɪn] n (decay) Verfall m; (lessening) Rückgang m; (of invitation) ablehnen ♦ vi (say no) ablehnen; (of strength) nachlassen

decode [ˈdiːˈkəud] vt entschlüsseln; **~r** n (TV) Decoder m

decompose [diːkəmˈpəuz] vi (sich) zersetzen

décor [ˈdeɪkɔːʳ] n Ausstattung f

decorate [ˈdekəreɪt] vt (room: paper) tapezieren; (: paint) streichen; (adorn) (aus)schmücken; (cake) verzieren; (honour) auszeichnen; **decoration** [dekəˈreɪʃən] n (of house) (Wand)dekoration f; (medal) Orden m; **decorator** [ˈdekəreɪtəʳ] n Maler m, Anstreicher m

decorum [dɪˈkɔːrəm] n Anstand m

decoy [ˈdiːkɔɪ] n Lockvogel m

decrease [n ˈdiːkriːs, vb diːˈkriːs] n Abnahme f ♦ vt vermindern ♦ vi abnehmen

decree [dɪˈkriː] n Erlass m; **~ nisi** n vorläufige(s) Scheidungsurteil nt

decrepit [dɪˈkrepɪt] adj hinfällig

dedicate [ˈdedɪkeɪt] vt widmen; (devote) hingebungsvoll, engagiert; (COMPUT) dedizieren; **dedication** [dedɪˈkeɪʃən] n (devotion) Ergebenheit f; (in book) Widmung f

deduce [dɪˈdjuːs] vt: **to ~ sth (from sth)** etw (aus etw) ableiten, etw (aus etw) schließen

deduct [dɪˈdʌkt] vt abziehen; **~ion** n

deed [diːd] n Tat f; (document) Urkunde f

deem [diːm] vt: **to ~ sb/sth (to be)** jdn/etw für etw halten

deep [diːp] adj tief ♦ adv: **the spectators stood 20 ~** die Zuschauer standen in 20 Reihen hintereinander; **to be 4m ~** 4 Meter tief sein; **~en** vt vertiefen ♦ vi (darkness) tiefer werden; **~ end** n: **the ~ end** (of swimming pool) das Tiefe; **~-freeze** n Tiefkühlung f; **~-fry** vt frittieren; **~ly** adv tief; **~-sea diving** n Tiefseetauchen nt; **~-seated** adj tief sitzend

deer [dɪəʳ] n Reh nt; **~skin** n Hirsch-/Rehleder nt

deface [dɪˈfeɪs] vt entstellen

defamation [defəˈmeɪʃən] n Verleumdung f

default [dɪˈfɔːlt] n Versäumnis nt; (COMPUT) Standardwert m ♦ vi versäumen; **by ~** durch Nichterscheinen

defeat [dɪˈfiːt] n Niederlage f ♦ vt schlagen; **~ist** adj defätistisch ♦ n Defätist m

defect [n ˈdiːfekt, vb dɪˈfekt] n Fehler m ♦ vi überlaufen; **~ive** [dɪˈfektɪv] adj fehlerhaft

defence [dɪˈfens] n Verteidigung f; **~less** adj wehrlos

defend [dɪˈfend] vt verteidigen; **~ant** n Angeklagte(r) m; **~er** n Verteidiger m

defense [dɪˈfens] (US) n = **defence**

defensive [dɪˈfensɪv] adj defensiv ♦ n: **on the ~** in der Defensive

defer [dɪˈfɜːʳ] vt verschieben

deference [ˈdefərəns] n Rücksichtnahme f

defiance [dɪˈfaɪəns] n Trotz m, Unnachgiebigkeit f; **in ~ of sth** einer Sache dat zum Trotz

defiant [dɪˈfaɪənt] adj trotzig, unnachgiebig

deficiency [dɪˈfɪʃənsɪ] n (lack) Mangel m; (weakness) Schwäche f

decimal [ˈdesɪməl] adj dezimal ♦ n Dezimalzahl f; **~ point** nt

deficient [dɪ'fɪʃnt] *adj* mangelhaft

deficit ['defɪsɪt] *n* Defizit *nt*

defile [*vb* dɪ'faɪl, *n* 'di:faɪl] *vt* beschmutzen ♦ *n* Hohlweg *m*

define [dɪ'faɪn] *vt* bestimmen; (*explain*) definieren

definite ['defɪnɪt] *adj* (*fixed*) definitiv; (*clear*) eindeutig; **~ly** *adv* bestimmt

definition [defɪ'nɪʃən] *n* Definition *f*

deflate [di:'fleɪt] *vt* die Luft ablassen aus

deflect [dɪ'flekt] *vt* ablenken

deformity [dɪ'fɔ:mɪtɪ] *n* Missbildung *f*

defraud [dɪ'frɔ:d] *vt* betrügen

defrost [di:'frɔst] *vt* (*fridge*) abtauen; (*food*) auftauen; **~er** (*US*) *n* (*demister*) Gebläse *nt*

deft [deft] *adj* geschickt

defunct [dɪ'fʌŋkt] *adj* verstorben

defuse [di:'fju:z] *vt* entschärfen

defy [dɪ'faɪ] *vt* (*disobey*) sich widersetzen +*dat*; (*orders, death*) trotzen +*dat*; (*challenge*) herausfordern

degenerate [*v* dɪ'dʒenəreɪt, *adj* dɪ'dʒenərɪt] *vi* degenerieren ♦ *adj* degeneriert

degrading [dɪ'ɡreɪdɪŋ] *adj* erniedrigend

degree [dɪ'ɡri:] *n* Grad *m*; (*UNIV*) Universitätsabschluss *m*; **by ~s** allmählich; **to some ~** zu einem gewissen Grad

dehydrated [di:haɪ'dreɪtɪd] *adj* (*person*) ausgetrocknet

de-ice ['di:'aɪs] *vt* enteisen

deign [deɪn] *vi* sich herablassen

deity ['di:ɪtɪ] *n* Gottheit *f*

dejected [dɪ'dʒektɪd] *adj* niedergeschlagen

delay [dɪ'leɪ] *vt* (*hold back*) aufschieben ♦ *vi* (*linger*) sich aufhalten ♦ *n* Aufschub *m*, Verzögerung *f*; (*of train etc*) Verspätung *f*; **to be ~ed** (*train*) Verspätung haben; **without ~** unverzüglich

delectable [dɪ'lektəbl] *adj* köstlich; (*fig*) reizend

delegate [*n* 'delɪɡɪt, *vb* 'delɪɡeɪt] *n* De-

legierte(r) *mf* ♦ *vt* delegieren

delete [dɪ'li:t] *vt* (aus)streichen

deliberate [*adj* dɪ'lɪbərɪt, *vb* dɪ'lɪbəreɪt] *adj* (*intentional*) absichtlich; (*slow*) bedächtig ♦ *vi* (*consider*) überlegen; (*debate*) sich beraten; **~ly** *adv* absichtlich

delicacy ['delɪkəsɪ] *n* Zartheit *f*; (*weakness*) Anfälligkeit *f*; (*food*) Delikatesse *f*

delicate ['delɪkɪt] *adj* (*fine*) fein; (*fragile*) zart; (*situation*) heikel; (*MED*) empfindlich

delicatessen [delɪkə'tesn] *n* Feinkostgeschäft *nt*

delicious [dɪ'lɪʃəs] *adj* lecker

delight [dɪ'laɪt] *n* Wonne *f* ♦ *vt* entzücken; **to take ~ in sth** Freude an etw *dat* haben; **~ed** *adj*: **~ed (at** or **with sth)** entzückt (über +*acc* etw); **~ed to do sth** etw sehr gern tun; **~ful** *adj* entzückend, herrlich

delinquency [dɪ'lɪŋkwənsɪ] *n* Kriminalität *f*

delinquent [dɪ'lɪŋkwənt] *n* Straffällige(r) *mf* ♦ *adj* straffällig

delirious [dɪ'lɪrɪəs] *adj* im Fieberwahn

deliver [dɪ'lɪvər] *vt* (*goods*) (ab)liefern; (*letter*) zustellen; (*speech*) halten; **~y** *n* (Ab)lieferung *f*; (*of letter*) Zustellung *f*; (*of speech*) Vortragsweise *f*; (*MED*) Entbindung *f*; **to take ~y of** in Empfang nehmen

delude [dɪ'lu:d] *vt* täuschen

deluge ['delju:dʒ] *n* Überschwemmung *f*; (*fig*) Flut *f* ♦ *vt* (*fig*) überfluten

delusion [dɪ'lu:ʒən] *n* (Selbst)täuschung *f*

de luxe [də'lʌks] *adj* Luxus-

delve [delv] *vi*: **to ~ into** sich vertiefen in +*acc*

demand [dɪ'mɑ:nd] *vt* verlangen ♦ *n* (*request*) Verlangen *nt*; (*COMM*) Nachfrage *f*; **in ~** gefragt; **on ~** auf Verlangen; **~ing** *adj* anspruchsvoll

demean [dɪ'mi:n] *vt*: **to ~ o.s.** sich erniedrigen

demeanour [dɪ'mi:nər] (*US* **de**

meanor) n Benehmen nt

demented [dɪ'mɛntɪd] adj wahnsinnig

demister [diː'mɪstəʳ] n (AUT) Gebläse nt

demo ['dɛməʊ] (inf) n abbr (= demonstration) Demo f

democracy [dɪ'mɒkrəsɪ] n Demokratie f

democrat ['dɛməkræt] n Demokrat m; **democratic** [dɛmə'krætɪk] adj demokratisch

demolish [dɪ'mɒlɪʃ] vt abreißen; (fig) vernichten

demolition [dɛmə'lɪʃən] n Abbruch m

demon ['diːmən] n Dämon m

demonstrate ['dɛmənstreɪt] vt, vi demonstrieren; **demonstration** [dɛmən'streɪʃən] n Demonstration f; **demonstrator** ['dɛmənstreɪtəʳ] n (POL) Demonstrant(in) m(f)

demote [dɪ'məʊt] vt degradieren

demure [dɪ'mjʊəʳ] adj ernst

den [dɛn] n (of animal) Höhle f; (study) Bude f

denatured alcohol [diː'neɪtʃəd-] (US) n ungenießbar gemachte(r) Alkohol m

denial [dɪ'naɪəl] n Leugnung f; **official** ~ Dementi nt

denim ['dɛnɪm] adj Denim-; ~s npl Denimjeans pl

Denmark ['dɛnmɑːk] n Dänemark nt

denomination [dɪnɒmɪ'neɪʃən] n (ECCL) Bekenntnis nt; (type) Klasse f; (FIN) Wert m

denote [dɪ'nəʊt] vt bedeuten

denounce [dɪ'naʊns] vt brandmarken

dense [dɛns] adj dicht; (stupid) schwer von Begriff; **~ly** adv dicht; **density** ['dɛnsɪtɪ] n Dichte f; **single/double density disk** Diskette f mit einfacher/doppelter Dichte

dent [dɛnt] n Delle f ♦ vt (also: make a ~ in) einbeulen

dental ['dɛntl] adj Zahn-; ~ **surgeon** = **dentist**

dentist ['dɛntɪst] n Zahnarzt(ärztin) m(f)

dentures ['dɛntʃəz] npl Gebiss nt

deny [dɪ'naɪ] vt leugnen; (officially) dementieren; (help) abschlagen

deodorant [diː'əʊdərənt] n Deodorant nt

depart [dɪ'pɑːt] vi abfahren; **to ~ from** (fig: differ from) abweichen von

department [dɪ'pɑːtmənt] n (COMM) Abteilung f; (UNIV) Seminar nt; (POL) Ministerium nt; ~ **store** n Warenhaus nt

departure [dɪ'pɑːtʃəʳ] n (of person) Abreise f; (of train) Abfahrt f; (of plane) Abflug m; **new** ~ Neuerung f; ~ **lounge** n (at airport) Abflughalle f

depend [dɪ'pɛnd] vi: **to ~ on** ab hängen von; (rely on) angewiesen sein auf +acc; **it ~s** es kommt darauf an; **~ing on the result ...** abhängend vom Resultat ...; **~able** adj zuverlässig; **~ant** n Angehörige(r) f(m); **~ence** n Abhängigkeit f; **~ent** adj abhängig ♦ n = **dependant**; **~ent on** abhängig von

depict [dɪ'pɪkt] vt schildern

depleted [dɪ'pliːtɪd] adj aufgebraucht

deplorable [dɪ'plɔːrəbl] adj bedauerlich

deploy [dɪ'plɔɪ] vt einsetzen

depopulation [diːpɒpju'leɪʃən] n Entvölkerung f

deport [dɪ'pɔːt] vt deportieren; **~ation** [diːpɔː'teɪʃən] n Abschiebung f

deportment [dɪ'pɔːtmənt] n Betragen nt

deposit [dɪ'pɒzɪt] n (in bank) Guthaben nt; (down payment) Anzahlung f; (security) Kaution f; (CHEM) Niederschlag m ♦ vt (in bank) deponieren; (put down) niederlegen; ~ **account** n Sparkonto nt

depot ['dɛpəʊ] n Depot nt

depraved [dɪ'preɪvd] adj verkommen

depreciate [dɪ'priːʃɪeɪt] vi im Wert sinken; **depreciation** [dɪpriːʃɪ'eɪʃən] n Wertminderung f

depress [dɪ'prɛs] vt (press down) niederdrücken; (in mood) deprimieren; **~ed** adj deprimiert; **~ion** [dɪ'prɛʃən] n (mood) Depression f; (in trade) Wirtschaftskrise f; (hollow) Vertiefung f; (MET) Tief(druckgebiet) nt

deprivation [depriˈveiʃən] n Not f

deprive [diˈpraiv] vt: to ~ sb of sth jdn einer Sache gen berauben; ~d adj (child) sozial benachteiligt; (area) unterentwickelt

depth [depθ] n Tiefe f; in the ~s of despair in tiefster Verzweiflung

deputation [depjuˈteiʃən] n Abordnung f

deputize [ˈdepjutaiz] vi: to ~ (for sb) (jdn) vertreten

deputy [ˈdepjuti] adj stellvertretend ♦ n (Stell)vertreter m; ~ head (BRIT: SCOL) n Konrektor(in) m(f)

derail [diˈreil] vt: to be ~ed entgleisen; ~ment n Entgleisung f

deranged [diˈreindʒd] adj verrückt

derby [ˈdɑːbi] (US) n Melone f

derelict [ˈderilikt] adj verlassen

deride [diˈraid] vt auslachen

derisory [diˈraisəri] adj spöttisch

derivative [diˈrivətiv] n Derivat nt ♦ adj abgeleitet

derive [diˈraiv] vt (get) gewinnen; (deduce) ableiten ♦ vi (come from) abstammen

dermatitis [dəːməˈtaitis] n Hautentzündung f

derogatory [diˈrɔgətəri] adj geringschätzig

derrick [ˈderik] n Drehkran m

descend [diˈsend] vt, vi hinuntersteigen; to ~ from abstammen von; ~ant n Nachkomme m; **descent** [diˈsent] n (coming down) Abstieg m; (origin) Abstammung f

describe [disˈkraib] vt beschreiben

description [disˈkripʃən] n Beschreibung f; (sort) Art f

descriptive [disˈkriptiv] adj beschreibend; (word) anschaulich

desecrate [ˈdesikreit] vt schänden

desert [n ˈdezət, vb dˈzəːt] n Wüste f ♦ vt verlassen; (temporarily) im Stich

lassen ♦ vi (MIL) desertieren; ~s npl (what one deserves): **to get one's just ~s** seinen gerechten Lohn bekommen; **~er** n Deserteur m; **~ion** [diˈzəːʃən] n (of wife) Verlassen nt; (MIL) Fahnenflucht f; **~ island** n einsame Insel f

deserve [diˈzəːv] vt verdienen; **deserving** adj verdienstvoll

design [diˈzain] n (plan) Entwurf m; (planning) Design nt ♦ vt entwerfen

designate [vb ˈdezigneit, adj ˈdezignit] vt bestimmen ♦ adj designiert

designer [diˈzainəʳ] n Designer(in) m(f); (TECH) Konstrukteur(in) m(f); (fashion ~) Modeschöpfer(in) m(f)

desirable [diˈzaiərəbl] adj wünschenswert

desire [diˈzaiəʳ] n Wunsch m, Verlangen nt ♦ vt (lust) begehren; (ask for) wollen

desk [desk] n Schreibtisch m; (BRIT: in shop, restaurant) Kasse f; **~top publishing** n Desktop-Publishing nt

desolate [ˈdesəlit] adj öde; (sad) trostlos; **desolation** [desəˈleiʃən] n Trostlosigkeit f

despair [disˈpɛəʳ] n Verzweiflung f ♦ vi: **to ~ (of)** verzweifeln (an +dat)

despatch [disˈpætʃ] n, vt = dispatch

desperate [ˈdespərit] adj verzweifelt; **~ly** adv verzweifelt; **desperation** [despəˈreiʃən] n Verzweiflung f

despicable [disˈpikəbl] adj abscheulich

despise [disˈpaiz] vt verachten

despite [disˈpait] prep trotz +gen

despondent [disˈpɔndənt] adj mutlos

dessert [diˈzəːt] n Nachtisch m, ~**spoon** n Dessertlöffel m

destination [destiˈneiʃən] n (of person) (Reise)ziel nt; (of goods) Bestimmungsort m

destiny [ˈdestini] n Schicksal nt

destitute [ˈdestitjuːt] adj Not leidend

destroy [disˈtrɔi] vt zerstören; **~er** n (NAUT) Zerstörer m

destruction [disˈtrʌkʃən] n Zerstörung f

destructive [dɪsˈtrʌktɪv] *adj* zerstörend

detach [dɪˈtætʃ] *vt* loslösen; **~able** *adj* abtrennbar; **~ed** *adj* (attitude) distanziert; (house) Einzel-; **~ment** *nt* (fig) Abstand *m*; (MIL) Sonderkommando *nt*

detail [ˈdiːteɪl] *n* Einzelheit *f*, Detail *nt* ♦ *vt* (relate) ausführlich berichten; (appoint) abkommandieren; **in ~** im Detail; **~ed** *adj* detailliert

detain [dɪˈteɪn] *vt* aufhalten; (imprison) in Haft halten

detect [dɪˈtekt] *vt* entdecken; **~ion** [dɪˈtekʃən] *n* Aufdeckung *f*; **~ive** *n* Detektiv *m*; **~ive story** *n* Kriminalgeschichte *f*, Krimi *m*

détente [deɪˈtɑːnt] *n* Entspannung *f*

detention [dɪˈtenʃən] *n* Haft *f*; (SCH) Nachsitzen *nt*

deter [dɪˈtɜːʳ] *vt* abschrecken

detergent [dɪˈtɜːdʒənt] *n* Waschmittel *nt*

deteriorate [dɪˈtɪərɪəreɪt] *vi* sich verschlechtern; **deterioration** [dɪtɪərɪəˈreɪʃən] *n* Verschlechterung *f*

determination [dɪtɜːmɪˈneɪʃən] *n* Entschlossenheit *f*

determine [dɪˈtɜːmɪn] *vt* bestimmen; **~d** *adj* entschlossen

deterrent [dɪˈterənt] *n* Abschreckungsmittel *nt*

detest [dɪˈtest] *vt* verabscheuen

detonate [ˈdetəneɪt] *vt* explodieren lassen ♦ *vi* detonieren

detour [ˈdiːtʊəʳ] *n* Umweg *m*; (US: AUT: diversion) Umleitung *f* ♦ *vt* (US: AUT: traffic) umleiten

detract [dɪˈtrækt] *vi*: **to ~ from** schmälern

detriment [ˈdetrɪmənt] *n*: **to the ~ of** zum Schaden +gen; **~al** [detrɪˈmentl] *adj* schädlich

devaluation [diːvæljʊˈeɪʃən] *n* Abwertung *f*

devastate [ˈdevəsteɪt] *vt* verwüsten; (fig: shock): **to be ~d by** niedergeschmettert sein von; **devastating** *adj* verheerend

develop [dɪˈveləp] *vt* entwickeln; (resources) erschließen ♦ *vi* sich entwickeln; **~ing country** *n* Entwicklungsland *nt*; **~ment** *n* Entwicklung *f*

deviate [ˈdiːvɪeɪt] *vi* abweichen

device [dɪˈvaɪs] *n* Gerät *nt*

devil [ˈdevl] *n* Teufel *m*

devious [ˈdiːvɪəs] *adj* (means) krumm; (person) verschlagen

devise [dɪˈvaɪz] *vt* entwickeln

devoid [dɪˈvɔɪd] *adj*: **~ of** ohne

devolution [diːvəˈluːʃən] *n* (POL) Dezentralisierung *f*

devote [dɪˈvəʊt] *vt*: **to ~ sth (to sth)** etw (einer Sache *dat*) widmen; **~d** *adj* ergeben; **~e** [devəʊˈtiː] *n* Anhänger(in) *m(f)*, Verehrer(in) *m(f)*; **devotion** [dɪˈvəʊʃən] *n* (piety) Andacht *f*; (loyalty) Ergebenheit *f*, Hingabe *f*

devour [dɪˈvaʊəʳ] *vt* verschlingen

devout [dɪˈvaʊt] *adj* andächtig

dew [djuː] *n* Tau *m*

dexterity [deksˈterɪtɪ] *n* Geschicklichkeit *f*

DHSS (BRIT) *n abbr* = **Department of Health and Social Security**

diabetes [daɪəˈbiːtiːz] *n* Zuckerkrankheit *f*

diabetic [daɪəˈbetɪk] *adj* zuckerkrank; (food) Diabetiker- ♦ *n* Diabetiker *m*

diabolical [daɪəˈbɒlɪkl] (inf) *adj* (weather, behaviour) saumäßig

diagnose [daɪəgˈnəʊz] *vt* diagnostizieren

diagnoses [daɪəgˈnəʊsiːz] *npl of* **diagnosis**

diagnosis [daɪəgˈnəʊsɪs] *n* Diagnose *f*

diagonal [daɪˈægənl] *adj* diagonal ♦ *n* Diagonale *f*

diagram [ˈdaɪəgræm] *n* Diagramm *nt*, Schaubild *nt*

dial [ˈdaɪəl] *n* (TEL) Wählscheibe *f*; (of clock) Zifferblatt *nt* ♦ *vt* wählen

dialect [ˈdaɪəlekt] *n* Dialekt *m*

dialling code [ˈdaɪəlɪŋ-] *n* Vorwahl *f*

dialling tone *n* Amtszeichen *nt*

dialogue [ˈdaɪəlɔg] *n* Dialog *m*

dial tone (US) n = **dialling tone**

diameter [daɪˈæmɪtə*] n Durchmesser m

diamond [ˈdaɪəmənd] n Diamant m; **~s** npl (CARDS) Karo nt

diaper [ˈdaɪpə*] (US) n Windel f

diaphragm [ˈdaɪəfræm] n Zwerchfell m

diarrhoea [daɪəˈriːə] (US **diarrhea**) n Durchfall m

diary [ˈdaɪərɪ] n Taschenkalender m; (account) Tagebuch nt

dice [daɪs] n Würfel pl ♦ vt in Würfel schneiden

dictate [dɪkˈteɪt] vt diktieren; **~s** [ˈdɪkteɪts] npl Gebote pl; **dictation** [dɪkˈteɪʃən] n Diktat nt

dictator [dɪkˈteɪtə*] n Diktator m; **~ship** [dɪkˈteɪtəʃɪp] n Diktatur f

dictionary [ˈdɪkʃənrɪ] n Wörterbuch nt

did [dɪd] pt of **do**

didn't [ˈdɪdnt] = **did not**

die [daɪ] vi sterben; **to be dying for sth** etw unbedingt haben wollen; **to be dying to do sth** darauf brennen, etw zu tun; **~ away** vi schwächer werden; **~ down** vi nachlassen; **~ out** vi aussterben

diesel [ˈdiːzl] n (car) Diesel m; **~ engine** n Dieselmotor m; **~ oil** n Dieselkraftstoff m

diet [ˈdaɪət] n Nahrung f; (special food) Diät f; (slimming) Abmagerungskur f ♦ vi (also: **be on a ~**) eine Abmagerungskur machen

differ [ˈdɪfə*] vi sich unterscheiden; (disagree) anderer Meinung sein; **~ence** n Unterschied m; **~ent** adj anders; (two things) verschieden; **~entiate** [dɪfəˈrenʃieɪt] vt, vi unterscheiden; **~ently** adv anders; (from one another) unterschiedlich

difficult [ˈdɪfɪkəlt] adj schwierig; **~y** n Schwierigkeit f

diffident [ˈdɪfɪdənt] adj schüchtern

diffuse [adj dɪˈfjuːs, vb dɪˈfjuːz] adj langatmig ♦ vt verbreiten

dig [dɪg] (pt, pp **dug**) vt graben ♦ vi

(prod) Stoß m; (remark) Spitze f; (archaeological) Ausgrabung f; **~ in** vi (MIL) sich eingraben; **~ into** vt fus (savings) angreifen; **~ up** vt ausgraben; (fig) aufgabeln

digest [vb daɪˈdʒest, n ˈdaɪdʒest] vt verdauen ♦ n Auslese f; **~ion** [dɪˈdʒestʃən] n Verdauung f

digit [ˈdɪdʒɪt] n Ziffer f; (ANAT) Finger m; **~al** adj digital, Digital-; **~al TV** n Digitalfernsehen nt

dignified [ˈdɪgnɪfaɪd] adj würdevoll

dignity [ˈdɪgnɪtɪ] n Würde f

digress [daɪˈgres] vi abschweifen

digs [dɪgz] (BRIT: inf) npl Bude f

dilapidated [dɪˈlæpɪdeɪtɪd] adj baufällig

dilate [daɪˈleɪt] vt weiten ♦ vi sich weiten

dilemma [daɪˈlemə] n Dilemma nt

diligent [ˈdɪlɪdʒənt] adj fleißig

dilute [daɪˈluːt] vt verdünnen

dim [dɪm] adj trübe; (stupid) schwer von Begriff ♦ vt verdunkeln; **to ~ one's headlights** (esp US) abblenden

dime [daɪm] (US) n Zehncentstück nt

dimension [daɪˈmenʃən] n Dimension f

diminish [dɪˈmɪnɪʃ] vt, vi verringern

diminutive [dɪˈmɪnjutɪv] adj winzig ♦ n Verkleinerungsform f

dimmer [ˈdɪmə*] (US) n (AUT) Abblendschalter m; **~s** npl Abblendlicht nt; (sidelights) Begrenzungsleuchten pl

dimple [ˈdɪmpl] n Grübchen nt

din [dɪn] n Getöse nt

dine [daɪn] vi speisen; **~r** n Tischgast m; (RAIL) Speisewagen m

dinghy [ˈdɪŋgɪ] n Dingi nt; **rubber ~** Schlauchboot nt

dingy [ˈdɪndʒɪ] adj armselig

dining car (BRIT) n Speisewagen m

dining room [ˈdaɪnɪŋ-] n Esszimmer nt; (in hotel) Speisezimmer nt

dinner [ˈdɪnə*] n (lunch) Mittagessen nt; (evening) Abendessen nt; (public) Festessen nt; **~ jacket** n Smoking m

party n Tischgesellschaft f; **~ time** n Tischzeit f

dinosaur ['daɪnəsɔːʳ] n Dinosaurier m

int [dɪnt] n: **by ~ of** durch

iocese ['daɪəsɪs] n Diözese f

ip [dɪp] n (hollow) Senkung f ♦ vt (bathe) kurze(s) Baden nt ♦ vt eintauchen; (BRIT: AUT) abblenden ♦ vi (slope) sich senken, abfallen

iploma [dɪ'pləumə] n Diplom nt

iplomacy [dɪ'pləuməsɪ] n Diplomatie f

iplomat ['dɪpləmæt] n Diplomat(in) m(f); **~ic** [dɪplə'mætɪk] adj diplomatisch

ip stick n Ölmessstab m

ipswitch ['dɪpswɪtʃ] (BRIT) n (AUT) Abblendschalter m

ire [daɪəʳ] adj schrecklich

irect [daɪ'rɛkt] adj direkt ♦ vt leiten; (film) die Regie führen +gen; (aim) richten; (order) anweisen; **can you ~ me to ...?** können Sie mir sagen, wo ich zu ... komme?; **~ debit** n (BRIT) Einzugsauftrag m; (transaction) automatische Abbuchung f

irection [dɪ'rɛkʃən] n Richtung f; (CINE) Regie f; Leitung f; **~s** npl (for use) Gebrauchsanleitung f; (orders) Anweisungen pl; **sense of ~** Orientierungssinn m

irectly [dɪ'rɛktlɪ] adv direkt; (at once) sofort

irector [dɪ'rɛktəʳ] n Direktor m; (of film) Regisseur m

irectory [dɪ'rɛktərɪ] n (TEL) Telefonbuch nt; **~ enquiries** n, **~ assistance** (US) n (Fernsprech)auskunft f

irt [dɜːt] n Schmutz m, Dreck m; **~cheap** adj spottbillig; **~y** adj schmutzig ♦ vt beschmutzen; **~y trick** n gemeine(r) Trick m

isability [dɪsə'bɪlɪtɪ] n Körperbehinderung f

isabled [dɪs'eɪbld] adj körperbehindert

isadvantage [dɪsəd'vɑːntɪdʒ] n Nachteil m

disagree [dɪsə'griː] vi nicht übereinstimmen; (quarrel) (sich) streiten; (food): **to ~ with sb** jdm nicht bekommen; **~able** adj unangenehm; **~ment** n (between persons) Streit m; (between things) Widerspruch m

disallow ['dɪsə'lau] vt nicht zulassen

disappear [dɪsə'pɪəʳ] vi verschwinden; **~ance** n Verschwinden nt

disappoint [dɪsə'pɔɪnt] vt enttäuschen; **~ed** adj enttäuscht; **~ment** n Enttäuschung f

disapproval [dɪsə'pruːvəl] n Missbilligung f

disapprove [dɪsə'pruːv] vi: **to ~ of** missbilligen

disarm [dɪs'ɑːm] vt entwaffnen; (POL) abrüsten; **~ament** n Abrüstung f

disarray [dɪsə'reɪ] n: **to be in ~** (army) in Auflösung (begriffen) sein; (clothes) in unordentlichem Zustand sein

disaster [dɪ'zɑːstəʳ] n Katastrophe f; **disastrous** [dɪ'zɑːstrəs] adj verhängnisvoll

disband [dɪs'bænd] vt auflösen ♦ vi auseinander gehen

disbelief ['dɪsbə'liːf] n Ungläubigkeit f

disc [dɪsk] n Scheibe f; (record) (Schall)platte f; (COMPUT) = disk

discard [dɪs'kɑːd] vt ablegen

discern [dɪ'sɜːn] vt erkennen; **~ing** adj scharfsinnig

discharge [vb dɪs'tʃɑːdʒ, n 'dɪstʃɑːdʒ] vt (ship) entladen; (duties) nachkommen +dat; (dismiss) entlassen; (gun) abschießen; (JUR) freisprechen ♦ n (of ship, ELEC) Entladung f; (dismissal) Entlassung f; (MED) Ausfluss m

disciple [dɪ'saɪpl] n Jünger m

discipline ['dɪsɪplɪn] n Disziplin f ♦ vt (train) schulen; (punish) bestrafen

disc jockey n Diskjockey m

disclaim [dɪs'kleɪm] vt nicht anerkennen

disclose [dɪs'kləuz] vt enthüllen; **disclosure** [dɪs'kləuʒəʳ] n Enthüllung f

disco ['dɪskəʊ] n abbr = **discotheque**

discoloured [dɪs'kʌləd] (US **discol-ored**) adj verfärbt

discomfort [dɪs'kʌmfət] n Unbehagen nt

disconcert [dɪskən'sɜːt] vt aus der Fassung bringen

disconnect [dɪskə'nekt] vt abtrennen

disconnected [dɪskə'nektɪd] adj Unzufriedenheit f; **~ed** adj unzufrieden

discontinue [dɪskən'tɪnjuː] vt einstellen

discord ['dɪskɔːd] n Zwietracht f; (noise) Dissonanz f

discotheque ['dɪskəʊtek] n Diskothek f

discount [n 'dɪskaʊnt, vb dɪs'kaʊnt] n Rabatt m ♦ vt außer Acht lassen

discourage [dɪs'kʌrɪdʒ] vt entmutigen; (prevent) abraten

discourteous [dɪs'kɜːtɪəs] adj unhöflich

discover [dɪs'kʌvəʳ] vt entdecken; **~y** n Entdeckung f

discredit [dɪs'kredɪt] vt in Verruf bringen

discreet [dɪs'kriːt] adj diskret

discrepancy [dɪs'krepənsɪ] n Diskrepanz f

discriminate [dɪs'krɪmɪneɪt] vi unterscheiden; **to ~ against** diskriminieren; **discriminating** adj anspruchsvoll; **discrimination** [dɪskrɪmɪ'neɪʃən] n Urteilsvermögen nt; (pej) Diskriminierung f

discuss [dɪs'kʌs] vt diskutieren, besprechen; **~ion** [dɪs'kʌʃən] n Diskussion f, Besprechung f

disdain [dɪs'deɪn] n Verachtung f

disease [dɪ'ziːz] n Krankheit f

disembark [dɪsɪm'bɑːk] vi von Bord gehen

disenchanted ['dɪsɪn'tʃɑːntɪd] adj desillusioniert

disengage [dɪsɪn'geɪdʒ] vt (AUT) auskuppeln

disentangle [dɪsɪn'tæŋgl] vt entwirren

disfigure [dɪs'fɪgəʳ] vt entstellen

disgrace [dɪs'greɪs] n Schande f ♦ vt Schande bringen über +acc; **~ful** adj unerhört

disgruntled [dɪs'grʌntld] adj verärgert

disguise [dɪs'gaɪz] vt verkleiden; (feelings) verhehlen ♦ n Verkleidung f; **in ~** verkleidet, maskiert

disgust [dɪs'gʌst] n Abscheu f ♦ vt anwidern; **~ed** adj angeekelt; (at sb's behaviour) empört; **~ing** adj widerlich

dish [dɪʃ] n Schüssel f; (food) Gericht nt **to do** or **wash the ~es** abwaschen; **~ up** vt auftischen; **~ cloth** n Spüllappen m

dishearten [dɪs'hɑːtn] vt entmutigen

dishevelled [dɪ'ʃevəld] adj (hair) zerzaust; (clothing) ungepflegt

dishonest [dɪs'ɒnɪst] adj unehrlich

dishonour [dɪs'ɒnəʳ] (US **dishonor**) n Unehre f; **~able** adj unehrenhaft

dishtowel ['dɪʃtaʊəl] n Geschirrtuch nt

dishwasher ['dɪʃwɒʃəʳ] n Geschirrspülmaschine f

disillusion [dɪsɪ'luːʒən] vt enttäuschen, desillusionieren

disincentive [dɪsɪn'sentɪv] n Entmutigung f

disinfect [dɪsɪn'fekt] vt desinfizieren, **~ant** n Desinfektionsmittel nt

disintegrate [dɪs'ɪntɪgreɪt] vi sich auflösen

disinterested [dɪs'ɪntrəstɪd] adj uneigennützig; (inf) uninteressiert

disjointed [dɪs'dʒɔɪntɪd] adj unzusammenhängend

disk [dɪsk] n (COMPUT) Diskette f, **single/double sided ~** einseitige, beidseitige Diskette; **~ drive** n Diskettenlaufwerk nt; **~ette** [dɪs'ket] (US) n = **disk**

dislike [dɪs'laɪk] n Abneigung f ♦ vt nicht leiden können

dislocate ['dɪsləkeɪt] vt auskugeln

dislodge [dɪs'lɒdʒ] vt verschieben; (MIL) aus der Stellung werfen

disloyal [dɪs'lɔɪəl] adj treulos

dismal ['dɪzml] adj trostlos, trübe

dismantle [dɪsˈmæntl] vt demontieren

dismay [dɪsˈmeɪ] n Bestürzung f ♦ vt bestürzen

dismiss [dɪsˈmɪs] vt (employee) entlassen; (idea) von sich weisen; (send away) wegschicken; (JUR) abweisen; **~al** n Entlassung f

dismount [dɪsˈmaunt] vi absteigen

disobedience [dɪsəˈbiːdɪəns] n Ungehorsam m; **disobedient** adj ungehorsam

disobey [dɪsəˈbeɪ] vt nicht gehorchen +dat

disorder [dɪsˈɔːdər] n (confusion) Verwirrung f; (commotion) Aufruhr m; (MED) Erkrankung f

disorderly [dɪsˈɔːdəlɪ] adj (untidy) unordentlich; (unruly) ordnungswidrig

disorganized [dɪsˈɔːgənaɪzd] adj unordentlich

disorientated [dɪsˈɔːrɪəntɪtɪd] adj (person: after journey) verwirrt

disown [dɪsˈəun] vt (child) verstoßen

disparaging [dɪsˈpærɪdʒɪŋ] adj geringschätzig

dispassionate [dɪsˈpæʃənɪt] adj objektiv

dispatch [dɪsˈpætʃ] vt (goods) abschicken, abfertigen ♦ n Absendung f; (esp MIL) Meldung f

dispel [dɪsˈpel] vt zerstreuen

dispensary [dɪsˈpensərɪ] n Apotheke f

dispense [dɪsˈpens] vt verteilen, austeilen; **~ with** vt fus verzichten auf +acc; **~r** n (container) Spender m; **dispensing** adj: **dispensing chemist** (BRIT) Apotheker m

dispersal [dɪsˈpəːsl] n Zerstreuung f

disperse [dɪsˈpəːs] vt zerstreuen ♦ vi sich verteilen

dispirited [dɪsˈpɪrɪtɪd] adj niedergeschlagen

displace [dɪsˈpleɪs] vt verschieben; **~d person** n Verschleppte(r) mf

display [dɪsˈpleɪ] n (of goods) Auslage f; (of feeling) Zurschaustellung f ♦ vt zeigen; (ostentatiously) vorführen; (goods) ausstellen

displease [dɪsˈpliːz] vt missfallen +dat

displeasure [dɪsˈpleʒər] n Missfallen nt

disposable [dɪsˈpəuzəbl] adj Wegwerf-; **~ nappy** n Papierwindel f

disposal [dɪsˈpəuzl] n (of property) Verkauf m; (throwing away) Beseitigung f; **to be at one's ~** einem zur Verfügung stehen

dispose [dɪsˈpəuz] vi: **to ~ of** loswerden; **~d** adj geneigt

disposition [dɪspəˈzɪʃən] n Wesen nt

disproportionate [dɪsprəˈpɔːʃənət] adj unverhältnismäßig

disprove [dɪsˈpruːv] vt widerlegen

dispute [dɪsˈpjuːt] n Streit m; (also: **industrial ~**) Arbeitskampf m ♦ vt bestreiten

disqualify [dɪsˈkwɒlɪfaɪ] vt disqualifizieren

disquiet [dɪsˈkwaɪət] n Unruhe f

disregard [dɪsrɪˈgɑːd] vt nicht (be)achten

disrepair [ˈdɪsrɪˈpeər] n: **to fall into ~** verfallen

disreputable [dɪsˈrepjutəbl] adj verrufen

disrespectful [dɪsrɪˈspektful] adj respektlos

disrupt [dɪsˈrʌpt] vt stören; (service) unterbrechen; **~ion** [dɪsˈrʌpʃən] n Störung f; Unterbrechung f

dissatisfaction [dɪssætɪsˈfækʃən] n Unzufriedenheit f; **dissatisfied** [dɪsˈsætɪsfaɪd] adj unzufrieden

dissect [dɪˈsekt] vt zerlegen, sezieren

dissent [dɪˈsent] n abweichende Meinung f

dissertation [dɪsəˈteɪʃən] n wissenschaftliche Arbeit f; (Ph.D.) Doktorarbeit f

disservice [dɪsˈsəːvɪs] n: **to do sb a ~** jdm einen schlechten Dienst erweisen

dissident [ˈdɪsɪdənt] adj anders denkend ♦ n Dissident m

dissimilar [dɪˈsɪmɪlər] adj: **~ (to sb/sth)** (jdm/etw) unähnlich

dissipate 386 **do**

dissipate ['dɪsɪpeɪt] vt (waste) verschwenden; (scatter) zerstreuen

dissociate [dɪ'səʊʃɪeɪt] vt trennen

dissolve [dɪ'zɒlv] vt auflösen ♦ vi sich auflösen

dissuade [dɪ'sweɪd] vt: to ~ sb from doing sth jdn davon abbringen, etw zu tun

distance ['dɪstns] n Entfernung f; in the ~ in der Ferne; **distant** adj entfernt, fern; (with time) fern

distaste [dɪs'teɪst] n Abneigung f; **~ful** adj widerlich

distended [dɪs'tendɪd] adj (stomach) aufgebläht

distil [dɪs'tɪl] vt destillieren; **~lery** n Brennerei f

distinct [dɪs'tɪŋkt] adj (separate) getrennt; (clear) klar, deutlich; **as ~ from** im Unterschied zu; **~ion** [dɪs'tɪŋkʃən] n Unterscheidung f; (eminence) Auszeichnung f; **~ive** adj bezeichnend

distinguish [dɪs'tɪŋgwɪʃ] vt unterscheiden; **~ed** adj (eminent) berühmt; **~ing** adj bezeichnend

distort [dɪs'tɔːt] vt verdrehen; (misrepresent) entstellen; **~ion** [dɪs'tɔːʃən] n Verzerrung f

distract [dɪs'trækt] vt ablenken; **~ing** adj verwirrend; **~ion** [dɪs'trækʃən] n (distress) Raserei f; (diversion) Zerstreuung f

distraught [dɪs'trɔːt] adj bestürzt

distress [dɪs'tres] n Not f; (suffering) Qual f ♦ vt quälen; **~ing** adj erschütternd; **~ signal** n Notsignal nt

distribute [dɪs'trɪbjuːt] vt verteilen; **distribution** [dɪstrɪ'bjuːʃən] n Verteilung f; **distributor** n Verteiler m

district ['dɪstrɪkt] n (of country) Kreis m; (of town) Bezirk m; **~ attorney** (US) n Oberstaatsanwalt m; **~ nurse** n Kreiskrankenschwester f

distrust [dɪs'trʌst] n Misstrauen nt ♦ vt misstrauen +dat

disturb [dɪs'tɜːb] vt stören; (agitate) erregen; **~ance** n Störung f; **~ed** adj

beunruhigt; **emotionally ~ed** emotional gestört; **~ing** adj beunruhigend

disuse [dɪs'juːs] n: to fall into ~ außer Gebrauch kommen; **~d** [dɪs'juːzd] adj außer Gebrauch; (mine, railway line) stillgelegt

ditch [dɪtʃ] n Graben m ♦ vt (person) loswerden; (plan) fallen lassen

dither ['dɪðə*] vi verdattert sein

ditto ['dɪtəʊ] adv dito, ebenfalls

divan [dɪ'væn] n Liegesofa nt

dive [daɪv] n (into water) Kopfsprung m; (AVIAT) Sturzflug m ♦ vi tauchen; **~r** n Taucher m

diverge [daɪ'vɜːdʒ] vi auseinander gehen

diverse [daɪ'vɜːs] adj verschieden

diversion [daɪ'vɜːʃən] n Ablenkung f; (BRIT: AUT) Umleitung f

diversity [daɪ'vɜːsɪti] n Vielfalt f

divert [daɪ'vɜːt] vt ablenken; (traffic) umleiten

divide [dɪ'vaɪd] vt teilen ♦ vi sich teilen; **~d highway** (US) n Schnellstraße f

divine [dɪ'vaɪn] adj göttlich

diving ['daɪvɪŋ] n (SPORT) Turmspringen nt; (underwater ~) Tauchen nt; **~board** n Sprungbrett nt

divinity [dɪ'vɪnɪtɪ] n Gottheit f; (subject) Religion f

division [dɪ'vɪʒən] n Teilung f; (MIL) Division f; (part) Abteilung f; (in opinion) Uneinigkeit f; (BRIT: POL) (Abstimmung f durch) Hammelsprung f

divorce [dɪ'vɔːs] n (Ehe)scheidung f ♦ vt scheiden; **~d** adj geschieden; **~e** [dɪvɔː'siː] n Geschiedene(r) f(m)

divulge [daɪ'vʌldʒ] vt preisgeben

DIY (BRIT) n abbr = **do-it-yourself**

dizzy ['dɪzɪ] adj schwindlig

DJ n abbr = **disc jockey**

DNA fingerprinting n genetische Fingerabdrücke pl

⌐ KEYWORD ¬

do [duː] (pt **did**, pp **done**) n (inf: party etc) Fete f

♦ **aux vb** 1 (in negative constructions and questions): **I don't understand** ich verstehe nicht; **didn't you know?** wusstest du das nicht?; **what do you think?** was meinen Sie?

2 (for emphasis, in polite phrases): **she does seem rather tired** sie scheint wirklich sehr müde zu sein; **do sit down/help yourself** setzen Sie sich doch hin/greifen Sie doch zu

3 (used to avoid repeating vb): **she swims better than I do** sie schwimmt besser als ich; **she lives in Glasgow - so do I** sie wohnt in Glasgow - ich auch

4 (in tag questions): **you like him, don't you?** du magst ihn doch, oder?

♦ **vt** 1 (carry out, perform etc) tun, machen; **what are you doing tonight?** was machst du heute Abend?; **I've got nothing to do** ich habe nichts zu tun; **to do one's hair/nails** sich die Haare/Nägel machen

♦ (AUT etc) fahren

♦ **vi** 1 (act, behave): **do as I do** mach es wie ich

2 (get on, fare): **he's doing well/badly at school** er ist gut/schlecht in der Schule; **how do you do?** guten Tag

3 (be suitable) gehen; (be sufficient) reichen; **to make do (with)** auskommen mit

do away with vt (kill) umbringen; (abolish: law etc) abschaffen

do up vt (laces, dress, buttons) zumachen; (room, house) renovieren

do with vt (need) brauchen; (be connected) zu tun haben mit

do without vt, vi auskommen ohne

docile ['dəʊsaɪl] adj gefügig

dock [dɒk] n Dock nt; (JUR) Anklagebank f ♦ vi ins Dock gehen; **~er** n Hafenarbeiter m; **~yard** n Werft f

doctor ['dɒktə*] n Arzt m, Ärztin f; (UNIV) Doktor m ♦ vt (fig) fälschen; (drink etc) etw beimischen +dat; **D~ of**

Philosophy n Doktor m der Philosophie

document ['dɒkjumənt] n Dokument nt; **~ary** [dɒkju'mentərɪ] n Dokumentarbericht m; (film) Dokumentarfilm m ♦ adj dokumentarisch; **~ation** [dɒkjumən'teɪʃən] n dokumentarische(r) Nachweis m

dodge [dɒdʒ] n Kniff m ♦ vt ausweichen +dat

dodgems ['dɒdʒəmz] (BRIT) npl Autoskooter m

doe [dəʊ] n (roe deer) Ricke f; (red deer) Hirschkuh f; (rabbit) Weibchen nt

does [dʌz] vb see do; **~n't = does not**

dog [dɒg] n Hund m; **~ collar** n Hundehalsband nt; (ECCL) Kragen m des Geistlichen; **~-eared** adj mit Eselsohren

dogged ['dɒgɪd] adj hartnäckig

dogsbody ['dɒgzbɒdɪ] n Mädchen nt für alles

doings ['duːɪŋz] npl (activities) Treiben nt

do-it-yourself ['duːɪtjɔː'self] n Do-it-yourself nt

doldrums ['dɒldrəmz] npl: **to be in the ~** (business) Flaute haben; (person) deprimiert sein

dole [dəʊl] (BRIT) n Stempelgeld nt; **to be on the ~** stempeln gehen; **~ out** vt ausgeben, austeilen

doleful ['dəʊlful] adj traurig

doll [dɒl] n Puppe f ♦ vt: **to ~ o.s. up** sich aufdonnern

dollar ['dɒlə*] n Dollar m

dolphin ['dɒlfɪn] n Delfin m, Delphin m

dome [dəʊm] n Kuppel f

domestic [də'mestɪk] adj häuslich; (within country) Innen-, Binnen-; (animal) Haus-; **~ated** adj (person) häuslich; (animal) zahm

dominant ['dɒmɪnənt] adj vorherrschend

dominate ['dɒmɪneɪt] vt beherrschen

domineering [dɒmɪ'nɪərɪŋ] adj herrisch

dominion [də'mɪnɪən] n (rule) Regierungsgewalt f; (land) Staatsgebiet nt mit Selbstverwaltung

domino ['dɒmɪnəʊ] (pl **-es**) n Dominostein m; **~es** n (game) Domino(spiel) nt

don [dɒn] (BRIT) n akademische(r) Lehrer m

donate [də'neɪt] vt (blood, money) spenden; (lot of money) stiften; **donation** [də'neɪʃən] n Spende f

done [dʌn] pp of **do**

donkey ['dɒŋkɪ] n Esel m

donor ['dəʊnəʳ] n Spender m; **~ card** n Organspenderausweis m

don't [dəʊnt] = **do not**

doodle ['duːdl] vi kritzeln

doom [duːm] n böse(s) Geschick nt; (downfall) Verderben nt ♦ vt: **to be ~ed** zum Untergang verurteilt sein; **~sday** n der Jüngste Tag

door [dɔːʳ] n Tür f; **~bell** n Türklingel f; **~ handle** n Türklinke f; **~man** (irreg) n Türsteher m; **~mat** n Fußmatte f; **~step** n Türstufe f; **~way** n Türöffnung f

dope [dəʊp] n (drug) Aufputschmittel nt ♦ vt (horse) dopen

dopey ['dəʊpɪ] (inf) adj bekloppt

dormant ['dɔːmənt] adj latent

dormitory ['dɔːmɪtrɪ] n Schlafsaal m

dormouse ['dɔːmaʊs] (pl **-mice**) n Haselmaus f

DOS [dɒs] n abbr (= disk operating system) DOS nt

dosage ['dəʊsɪdʒ] n Dosierung f

dose [dəʊs] n Dosis f

dosh [dɒʃ] (inf) n (money) Moos nt, Knete f

doss house ['dɒs-] (BRIT) n Bleibe f

dot [dɒt] n Punkt m; **~ted with** übersät mit; **on the ~** pünktlich

dote [dəʊt]: **to ~ on** vt fus vernarrt sein in +acc

dotted line ['dɒtɪd-] n punktierte Linie f

double ['dʌbl] adj, adv doppelt ♦ n Doppelgänger m ♦ vt verdoppeln ♦ vi

sich verdoppeln; **~s** npl (TENNIS) Doppel nt; **on** or **at the ~** im Laufschritt; **~ bass** n Kontrabass m; **~ bed** n Doppelbett nt; **~ bend** (BRIT) n S-Kurve f; **~-breasted** adj zweireihig; **~-cross** vt hintergehen; **~-decker** n Doppeldecker m; **~ glazing** (BRIT) n Doppelverglasung f; **~ room** n Doppelzimmer nt

doubly ['dʌblɪ] adv doppelt

doubt [daʊt] n Zweifel m ♦ vt bezweifeln; **~ful** adj zweifelhaft; **~less** adv ohne Zweifel

dough [dəʊ] n Teig m; **~nut** n Berliner m

douse [daʊz] vt (drench) mit Wasser begießen, durchtränken; (extinguish) ausmachen

dove [dʌv] n Taube f

dovetail ['dʌvteɪl] vi (plans) übereinstimmen

dowdy ['daʊdɪ] adj unmodern

down [daʊn] n (fluff) Flaum m; (hill) Hügel m ♦ adv unten; (motion) herunter; hinunter ♦ prep: **to go ~ the street** die Straße hinuntergehen ♦ vt niederschlagen; **~ with X!** nieder mit X!; **~-and-out** n Tramp m; **~-at-heel** adj schäbig; **~cast** adj niedergeschlagen; **~fall** n Sturz m; **~hearted** adj niedergeschlagen; **~hill** adv bergab; **~ payment** n Anzahlung f; **~pour** n Platzregen m; **~right** adj ausgesprochen; **~size** vi (ECON: company) sich verkleinern

---

Downing Street

Downing Street ist die Straße in London, die von Whitehall zum St James Park führt und in der sich der offizielle Wohnsitz des Premierministers (Nr. 10) und des Finanzministers (Nr. 11) befindet. Im weiteren Sinne bezieht sich der Begriff Downing Street auf die britische Regierung.

Down's syndrome [daʊnz-] n (MED) Down-Syndrom nt

down: ~stairs adv unten; (motion) nach unten; **~stream** adv flussabwärts; **~-to-earth** adj praktisch; **~town** adv in der Innenstadt; (motion) in die Innenstadt; **~ under** (BRIT: inf) adv in/nach Australien/Neuseeland; **~ward** adj Abwärts-, nach unten ♦ adv abwärts, nach unten; **~wards** adv abwärts, nach unten

dowry ['dauri] n Mitgift f

doz. abbr (= dozen) Dtzd.

doze [dəuz] vi dösen; **~ off** vi einnicken

dozen ['dʌzn] n Dutzend nt; **a ~ books** ein Dutzend Bücher; **~s of** dutzende or Dutzende von

Dr. abbr = **doctor; drive**

drab [dræb] adj düster, eintönig

draft [drɑːft] n Entwurf m; (FIN) Wechsel m; (US: MIL) Einberufung f ♦ vt skizzieren; see also **draught**

draftsman ['drɑːftsmən] (US: irreg) n = **draughtsman**

drag [dræg] vt schleppen; (river) mit einem Schleppnetz absuchen ♦ vi sich (dahin)schleppen ♦ n (bore) etwas Blödes; **in ~** als Tunte; **a man in ~** eine Tunte; **~ on** vi sich in die Länge ziehen; **~ and drop** n (COMPUT) Drag & Drop nt

dragon ['drægən] n Drache m; **~fly** n ['drægənflai] Libelle f

drain [drein] n Abfluss m; (fig: burden) Belastung f ♦ vt ableiten; (exhaust) erschöpfen ♦ vi (of water) abfließen; **~age** n Kanalisation f; **~ing board** (US **~board**) n Ablaufbrett nt; **~pipe** n Abflussrohr nt

dram [dræm] n Schluck m

drama ['drɑːmə] n Drama nt; **~tic** [drə'mætik] adj dramatisch; **~tist** ['dræmətist] n Dramatiker m; **~tize** ['dræmətaiz] vt (events) dramatisieren; (for TV etc) bearbeiten

drank [dræŋk] pt of **drink**

drape [dreip] vt drapieren; **~s** (US) npl Vorhänge pl

drastic ['dræstik] adj drastisch

draught [drɑːft] (US **draft**) n Zug m; (NAUT) Tiefgang m; **~s** n Damespiel nt; **on ~** (beer) vom Fass; **~ beer** n Bier nt vom Fass; **~board** (BRIT) n Zeichenbrett nt

draughtsman ['drɑːftsmən] (irreg) n technische(r) Zeichner m

draw [drɔː] (pt **drew**, pp **drew**) vt ziehen; (crowd) anlocken; (picture) zeichnen; (money) abheben; (water) schöpfen ♦ vi (SPORT) unentschieden spielen ♦ n (SPORT) Unentschieden nt; (lottery) Ziehung f; **~ near** vi näher rücken; **~ out** vi (train) ausfahren; (lengthen) sich hinziehen; **~ up** vi (stop) halten ♦ vt (document) aufsetzen

drawback ['drɔːbæk] n Nachteil m

drawbridge ['drɔːbridʒ] n Zugbrücke f

drawer [drɔːr] n Schublade f

drawing ['drɔːiŋ] n Zeichnung f, Zeichnen nt; **~ board** n Reißbrett nt; **~pin** (BRIT) n Reißzwecke f; **~ room** n Salon m

drawl [drɔːl] n schleppende Sprechweise f

drawn [drɔːn] pp of **draw**

dread [dred] n Furcht f ♦ vt fürchten; **~ful** adj furchtbar

dream [driːm] (pt, pp **dreamed** or **dreamt**) n Traum m ♦ vt träumen ♦ vi: **to ~ (about)** träumen (von); **~er** n Träumer m; **~t** [dremt] pt, pp of **dream**; **~y** adj verträumt

dreary ['driəri] adj trostlos, öde

dredge [dredʒ] vt ausbaggern

dregs [dregz] npl Bodensatz m; (fig) Abschaum m

drench [drentʃ] vt durchnässen

dress [dres] n Kleidung f; (garment) Kleid nt ♦ vt anziehen; (MED) verbinden; **to get ~ed** sich anziehen; **~ up** vi sich fein machen; **~ circle** (BRIT) n erste(r) Rang m; **~er** n (furniture) Anrichte f; **~ing** n (MED) Verband m; (COOK) Soße f; **~ing gown** (BRIT) n Morgenrock m; **~ing room** n (THEAT)

Garderobe f; (SPORT) Umkleideraum m; **~ing table** n Toilettentisch m; **~maker** n Schneiderin f; **~ rehearsal** n Generalprobe f

drew [dru:] pt of **draw**

dribble ['drɪbl] vi sabbern ♦ vt (ball) dribbeln

dried [draɪd] adj getrocknet; (fruit) Dörr-, gedörrte(r, s); **~ milk** n Milchpulver nt

drier ['draɪə'] n = **dryer**

drift [drɪft] n Strömung f; (snowdrift) Schneewehe f; (fig) Richtung f ♦ vi sich treiben lassen; **~wood** n Treibholz n

drill [drɪl] n Bohrer m; (MIL) Drill m ♦ vt bohren; (MIL) ausbilden ♦ vi: **to ~ (for)** bohren (nach)

drink [drɪŋk] (pt **drank**, pp **drunk**) n Getränk nt; (spirits) Drink m ♦ vt, vi trinken; **to have a ~** etwas trinken; **~er** n Trinker m; **~ing water** n Trinkwasser nt

drip [drɪp] n Tropfen m ♦ vi tropfen; **~dry** adj bügelfrei; **~ping** n Bratenfett nt

drive [draɪv] (pt **drove**, pp **driven**) n Fahrt f; (road) Einfahrt f; (campaign) Aktion f; (energy) Schwung m; (SPORT) Schlag m; (also: **disk ~**) Diskettenlaufwerk nt ♦ vt (car) fahren; (animals, people, objects) treiben; (power) antreiben ♦ vi fahren; **left-/right-hand ~** Links-/Rechtssteuerung f; **to ~ sb mad** jdn verrückt machen; **~by shooting** n Schusswaffenangriff aus einem vorbeifahrenden Wagen

drivel ['drɪvl] n Faselei f

driven ['drɪvn] pp of **drive**

driver ['draɪvə'] n Fahrer m; **~'s license** (US) n Führerschein m

driveway ['draɪvweɪ] n Auffahrt f; (longer) Zufahrtsstraße f

driving ['draɪvɪŋ] adj (rain) stürmisch; **~ instructor** n Fahrlehrer m; **~ lesson** n Fahrstunde f; **~ licence** (BRIT) n Führerschein m; **~ school** n Fahrschule f; **~ test** n Fahrprüfung f

drizzle ['drɪzl] n Nieselregen m ♦ vi nieseln

droll [drəul] adj drollig

drone [drəun] n (sound) Brummen nt; (bee) Drohne f

drool [dru:l] vi sabbern

droop [dru:p] vi (schlaff) herabhängen

drop [drɒp] n (of liquid) Tropfen m; (fall) Fall m ♦ vt fallen lassen; (lower) senken; (abandon) fallen lassen ♦ vi (fall) herunterfallen; **~s** npl (MED) Tropfen pl; **~ off** vi (sleep) einschlafen ♦ vt (passenger) absetzen; **~ out** vi (withdraw) ausscheiden; **~out** n Aussteiger m; **~per** n Pipette f; **~pings** npl Kot m

drought [draut] n Dürre f

drove [drəuv] pt of **drive**

drown [draun] vt ertränken; (sound) übertönen ♦ vi ertrinken

drowsy ['drauzɪ] adj schläfrig

drudgery ['drʌdʒərɪ] n Plackerei f

drug [drʌg] n (MED) Arznei f; (narcotic) Rauschgift nt ♦ vt betäuben; **~ addict** n Rauschgiftsüchtige(r) f(m); **~gist** (US) n Drogist(in) m(f); **~store** (US) n Drogerie f

drum [drʌm] n Trommel f ♦ vi trommeln; **~s** npl (MUS) Schlagzeug nt; **~mer** n Trommler m

drunk [drʌŋk] pp of **drink** ♦ adj betrunken ♦ n (also: **~ard**) Trinker(in) m(f); **~en** adj betrunken

dry [draɪ] adj trocken ♦ vt (ab)trocknen ♦ vi trocknen; **~ up** vi austrocknen ♦ vt (dishes) abtrocknen; **~ cleaner's** n chemische Reinigung f; **~ cleaning** n chemische Reinigung f; **~er** n Trockner m; (US: spin-dryer) (Wäsche)schleuder f; **~ goods store** (US) n Kurzwarengeschäft nt; **~ness** n Trockenheit f; **~ rot** n Hausschwamm m

DSS (BRIT) n abbr (= Department of Social Security) ≈ Sozialministerium nt

DTP n abbr (= desktop publishing) DTP nt

dual ['djuəl] adj doppelt; **~ carriageway** (BRIT) n zweispurige Fahrbahn f

nationality n doppelte Staatsangehörigkeit f; **~purpose** adj Mehrzweck-

dubbed [dʌbd] adj (film) synchronisiert

dubious ['dju:bɪəs] adj zweifelhaft

duchess ['dʌtʃɪs] n Herzogin f

duck [dʌk] n Ente f ♦ vi sich ducken; **~ling** n Entchen nt

duct [dʌkt] n Röhre f

dud [dʌd] n Niete f ♦ adj (cheque) ungedeckt

due [dju:] adj fällig; (fitting) angemessen ♦ n Gebühr f; (right) Recht nt ♦ adv (south etc) genau; **~s** npl (for club) Beitrag m; (NAUT) Gebühren pl; **~ to** wegen +gen

duel ['djuəl] n Duell nt

duet [dju:'et] n Duett nt

duffel ['dʌfl] adj: **~ bag** Matchbeutel m, Matchsack m

dug [dʌg] pt, pp of **dig**

duke [dju:k] n Herzog m

dull [dʌl] adj (colour, weather) trübe; (stupid) schwer von Begriff; (boring) langweilig ♦ vt abstumpfen

duly ['dju:lɪ] adv ordnungsgemäß

dumb [dʌm] adj stumm; (inf: stupid) doof, blöde; **~founded** [dʌm'faundɪd] adj verblüfft

dummy ['dʌmɪ] n Schneiderpuppe f; (substitute) Attrappe f; (BRIT: for baby) Schnuller m ♦ adj Schein-

dump [dʌmp] n Abfallhaufen m; (MIL) Stapelplatz m; (inf: place) Nest m ♦ vt abladen, auskippen; **~ing** n (COMM) Schleuderexport m; (of rubbish) Schuttabladen nt

dumpling ['dʌmplɪŋ] n Kloß m, Knödel m

dumpy ['dʌmpɪ] adj pummelig

dunce [dʌns] n Dummkopf m

dune [dju:n] n Düne f

dung [dʌŋ] n Dünger m

dungarees [dʌŋgə'ri:z] npl Latzhose f

dungeon ['dʌndʒən] n Kerker m

dupe [dju:p] n Gefoppte(r) m ♦ vt hintergehen, anführen

duplex ['dju:pleks] (US) n zweistöckige Wohnung f

duplicate [n 'dju:plɪkət, vb 'dju:plɪkeɪt] n Duplikat nt ♦ vt verdoppeln; (make copies) kopieren; **in ~** in doppelter Ausführung

duplicity [dju:'plɪsɪtɪ] n Doppelspiel nt

durable ['djuərəbl] adj haltbar

duration [djuə'reɪʃən] n Dauer f

duress [djuə'res] n: **under ~** unter Zwang

during ['djuərɪŋ] prep während +gen

dusk [dʌsk] n Abenddämmerung f

dust [dʌst] n Staub m ♦ vt abstauben; (sprinkle) bestäuben; **~bin** (BRIT) n Mülleimer m; **~er** n Staubtuch nt; **~ jacket** n Schutzumschlag m; **~man** (BRIT: irreg) n Müllmann m; **~y** adj staubig

Dutch [dʌtʃ] adj holländisch, niederländisch ♦ n (LING) Holländisch nt, Niederländisch nt; **the ~** npl (people) die Holländer pl, die Niederländer pl; **to go ~** getrennte Kasse machen; **~man/woman** (irreg) n Holländer(in) m(f), Niederländer(in) m(f)

dutiful ['dju:tɪful] adj pflichtbewusst

duty ['dju:tɪ] n Pflicht f; (job) Aufgabe f; (tax) Einfuhrzoll m; **on ~** im Dienst; **~ chemist's** n Apotheke f im Bereitschaftsdienst; **~-free** adj zollfrei

duvet ['du:veɪ] (BRIT) n Daunendecke f

dwarf [dwɔ:f] (pl **dwarves**) n Zwerg m ♦ vt überragen

dwell [dwel] (pt, pp **dwelt**) vi wohnen; **~ on** vt fus verweilen bei; **~ing** n Wohnung f

dwelt [dwelt] pt, pp of **dwell**

dwindle ['dwɪndl] vi schwinden

dye [daɪ] n Farbstoff m ♦ vt färben

dying ['daɪɪŋ] adj (person) sterbend; (moments) letzt

dyke [daɪk] (BRIT) n (channel) Kanal m; (barrier) Deich m, Damm m

dynamic [daɪ'næmɪk] adj dynamisch

dynamite ['daɪnəmaɪt] n Dynamit nt

dynamo ['daɪnəməu] n Dynamo m

dyslexia [dɪs'leksɪə] n Legasthenie f

E, e

E [iː] n (MUS) E nt
each [iːtʃ] adj jeder/jede/jedes ♦ pron (ein) jeder/(eine) jede/(ein) jedes; ~ **other** einander, sich; **they have two books** ~ sie haben je 2 Bücher
eager ['iːgə*] adj eifrig
eagle ['iːgl] n Adler m
ear [ɪə*] n Ohr nt; (of corn) Ähre f; ~**ache** n Ohrenschmerzen pl; ~**drum** n Trommelfell nt
earl [əːl] n Graf m
earlier ['əːlɪə*] adj, adv früher; **I can't come any** ~ ich kann nicht früher or eher kommen
early ['əːlɪ] adj, adv früh; ~ **retirement** n vorzeitige Pensionierung
earmark ['ɪəmɑːk] vt vorsehen
earn [əːn] vt verdienen
earnest ['əːnɪst] adj ernst; **in** ~ im Ernst
earnings ['əːnɪŋz] npl Verdienst m
ear: ~**phones** ['ɪəfəunz] npl Kopfhörer pl; ~**ring** ['ɪərɪŋ] n Ohrring m; ~**shot** ['ɪəʃɒt] n Hörweite f
earth [əːθ] n Erde f; (BRIT: ELEC) Erdung f ♦ vt erden; ~**enware** n Steingut nt; ~**quake** n Erdbeben nt; ~**y** adj roh
earwig ['ɪəwɪg] n Ohrwurm m
ease [iːz] n (simplicity) Leichtigkeit f; (social) Ungezwungenheit f ♦ vt (pain) lindern; (burden) erleichtern; **at** ~ ungezwungen; (MIL) rührt euch!; ~ **off** or **up** vi nachlassen
easel ['iːzl] n Staffelei f
easily ['iːzɪlɪ] adv leicht
east [iːst] n Osten m ♦ adj östlich ♦ adv nach Osten
Easter ['iːstə*] n Ostern nt; ~ **egg** n Osterei nt
east: ~**erly** adj östlich, Ost-; ~**ern** adj östlich; ~**ward(s)** adv ostwärts
easy ['iːzɪ] adj (task) einfach; (life) be-

quem; (manner) ungezwungen, natürlich ♦ adv leicht; ~ **chair** n Sessel m; ~-**going** adj gelassen; (lax) lässig
eat [iːt] (pt **ate**, pp **eaten**) vt essen; (animals) fressen; (destroy) (zer)fressen ♦ vi essen; fressen; ~ **away** vt zerfressen; ~ **into** vt fus zerfressen; ~**en** pp of **eat**
eau de Cologne ['əudəkə'ləun] n Kölnischwasser nt
eaves [iːvz] npl Dachrand m
eavesdrop ['iːvzdrɒp] vi lauschen; **to** ~ **on sb** jdn belauschen
ebb [eb] n Ebbe f ♦ vi (fig: also: ~ **away**) (ab)ebben
ebony ['ebənɪ] n Ebenholz nt
EC n abbr (= European Community) EG f
eccentric [ɪk'sentrɪk] adj exzentrisch ♦ n Exzentriker(in) m(f)
ecclesiastical [ɪkliːzɪ'æstɪk] adj kirchlich
echo ['ekəu] (pl ~**es**) n Echo nt ♦ vt zurückwerfen; (fig) nachbeten ♦ vi widerhallen
eclipse [ɪ'klɪps] n Finsternis f ♦ vt verfinstern
ecology [ɪ'kɒlədʒɪ] n Ökologie f
economic [iːkə'nɒmɪk] adj wirtschaftlich; ~**al** adj wirtschaftlich; (person) sparsam; ~ **refugee** n Wirtschaftsflüchtling m; ~**s** n Volkswirtschaft f
economist [ɪ'kɒnəmɪst] n Volkswirt(schaftler) m
economize [ɪ'kɒnəmaɪz] vi sparen
economy [ɪ'kɒnəmɪ] n (thrift) Sparsamkeit f; (of country) Wirtschaft f; ~ **class** n Touristenklasse f
ecstasy ['ekstəsɪ] n Ekstase f; (drug) Ecstasy nt; **ecstatic** [eks'tætɪk] adj hingerissen
ECU ['eɪkjuː] n abbr (= European Currency Unit) ECU m
eczema ['eksɪmə] n Ekzem nt
edge [edʒ] n Rand m; (of knife) Schneide f ♦ vt (SEWING) einfassen; **on** ~ (fig) = **edgy**; **to** ~ **away from** langsam abrücken von; ~**ways** adv: **he couldn't get a word in** ~**ways** er kam

überhaupt nicht zu Wort

edgy ['edʒɪ] *adj* nervös

edible ['edɪbl] *adj* essbar

edict ['iːdɪkt] *n* Erlass *m*

edit ['edɪt] *vt* redigieren; **~ion** [ɪ'dɪʃən] *n* Ausgabe *f*; **~or** *n* (*of newspaper*) Redakteur *m*; (*of book*) Lektor *m*

editorial [edɪ'tɔːrɪəl] *adj* Redaktions- ♦ *n* Leitartikel *m*

educate ['edjukeɪt] *vt* erziehen, (aus)bilden; **~d** *adj* gebildet; **education** [edju'keɪʃən] *n* (*teaching*) Unterricht *m*; (*system*) Schulwesen *nt*; (*schooling*) Erziehung *f*; Bildung *f*; **educational** *adj* pädagogisch

eel [iːl] *n* Aal *m*

eerie ['ɪərɪ] *adj* unheimlich

effect [ɪ'fekt] *n* Wirkung *f* ♦ *vt* bewirken; **~s** *npl* (*sound, visual*) Effekte *pl*; **in ~** in der Tat; **to take ~** (*law*) in Kraft treten; (*drug*) wirken; **~ive** *adj* wirksam, effektiv; **~ively** *adv* wirksam, effektiv

effeminate [ɪ'femɪnɪt] *adj* weibisch

effervescent [efə'vesnt] *adj* (*also fig*) sprudelnd

efficiency [ɪ'fɪʃənsɪ] *n* Leistungsfähigkeit *f*

efficient [ɪ'fɪʃənt] *adj* tüchtig; (*TECH*) leistungsfähig; (*method*) wirksam

effigy ['efɪdʒɪ] *n* Abbild *nt*

effort ['efət] *n* Anstrengung *f*; **~less** *adj* mühelos

effusive [ɪ'fjuːsɪv] *adj* überschwänglich

e.g. *adv abbr* (= *exempli gratia*) z. B.

egalitarian [ɪgælɪ'teərɪən] *adj* Gleichheits-, egalitär

egg [eg] *n* Ei *nt*; **~ on** *vt* anstacheln; **~cup** *n* Eierbecher *m*; **~plant** (*esp US*) *n* Aubergine *f*; **~shell** *n* Eierschale *f*

ego ['iːgəu] *n* Ich *nt*, Selbst *nt*; **~tism** ['egəutɪzəm] *n* Ichbezogenheit *f*; **~tist** ['egəutɪst] *n* Egozentriker *m*

Egypt ['iːdʒɪpt] *n* Ägypten *nt*; **~ian** [ɪ'dʒɪpʃən] *adj* ägyptisch ♦ *n* Ägypter(in) *m(f)*

eiderdown ['aɪdədaun] *n* Daunende-

cke *f*

eight [eɪt] *num* acht; **~een** *num* achtzehn; **~h** [eɪtθ] *adj* achte(r, s) ♦ *n* Achtel *nt*; **~y** *num* achtzig

Eire ['eərə] *n* Irland *nt*

either ['aɪðə*] *conj*: **~ ... or** entweder ... oder ♦ *pron*: **~ of the two** eine(r, s) von beiden ♦ *adj*: **on ~ side** auf beiden Seiten ♦ *adv*: **I don't ~** ich auch nicht; **I don't want ~** ich will keins von beiden

eject [ɪ'dʒekt] *vt* ausstoßen, vertreiben

eke [iːk] *vt*: **to ~ out** strecken

elaborate [*adj* ɪ'læbərɪt, *vb* ɪ'læbəreɪt] *adj* sorgfältig ausgearbeitet, ausführlich ♦ *vt* sorgfältig ausarbeiten ♦ *vi* ausführlich darstellen

elapse [ɪ'læps] *vi* vergehen

elastic [ɪ'læstɪk] *n* Gummiband *nt* ♦ *adj* elastisch; **~ band** (*BRIT*) *n* Gummiband *nt*

elated [ɪ'leɪtɪd] *adj* froh

elation [ɪ'leɪʃən] *n* gehobene Stimmung *f*

elbow ['elbəu] *n* Ellbogen *m*

elder ['eldə*] *adj* älter ♦ *n* Ältere(r) *f(m)*; **~ly** *adj* ältere(r, s) ♦ *npl*: **the ~ly** die Älteren *pl*; **eldest** ['eldɪst] *adj* älteste(r, s) ♦ *n* Älteste(r) *f(m)*

elect [ɪ'lekt] *vt* wählen ♦ *adj* zukünftig; **~ion** [ɪ'lekʃən] *n* Wahl *f*; **~ioneering** [ɪlekʃə'nɪərɪŋ] *n* Wahlpropaganda *f*; **~or** *n* Wähler *m*; **~oral** *adj* Wahl-; **~orate** *n* Wähler *pl*, Wählerschaft *f*

electric [ɪ'lektrɪk] *adj* elektrisch, Elektro-; **~al** *adj* elektrisch; **~ blanket** *n* Heizdecke *f*; **~ chair** *n* elektrische(r) Stuhl *m*; **~ fire** *n* elektrische(r) Heizofen *m*

electrician [ɪlek'trɪʃən] *n* Elektriker *m*

electricity [ɪlek'trɪsɪtɪ] *n* Elektrizität *f*

electrify [ɪ'lektrɪfaɪ] *vt* elektrifizieren; (*fig*) elektrisieren

electrocute [ɪ'lektrəkjuːt] *vt* durch elektrischen Strom töten

electronic [ɪlek'trɔnɪk] *adj* elektronisch, Elektronen-; **~ mail** *n* elektronische(r) Briefkasten *m*; **~s** in Elektronik *f*

elegance ['eligəns] *n* Eleganz *f*; **elegant** ['eligənt] *adj* elegant

element ['elimənt] *n* Element *nt*; **~ary** [eli'mentəri] *adj* einfach; (*primary*) Grund-

elephant ['elifənt] *n* Elefant *m*

elevate ['eliveit] *vt* emporheben; **elevation** [eli'veiʃən] *n* (*height*) Erhebung *f*, (*ARCHIT*) (Quer)schnitt *m*; **elevator** (*US*) *n* Fahrstuhl *m*, Aufzug *m*

eleven [i'levn] *num* elf; **~ses** (*BRIT*) *npl* ≈ zweite(s) Frühstück *nt*; **~th** *adj* elfte(r, s)

elicit [i'lisit] *vt* herausbekommen

eligible ['elidʒəbl] *adj* wählbar; **to be ~ for a pension** pensionsberechtigt sein

eliminate [i'limineit] *vt* ausschalten

elite [ei'li:t] *n* Elite *f*

elm [elm] *n* Ulme *f*

elocution [elə'kju:ʃən] *n* Sprecherziehung *f*

elongated ['i:lɒŋgeitid] *adj* verlängert

elope [i'ləup] *vi* entlaufen

eloquence ['eləkwəns] *n* Beredsamkeit *f*; **eloquent** *adj* redegewandt

else [els] *adv* sonst; **who ~?** wer sonst?; **somebody ~** jemand anders; **or ~** sonst; **~where** *adv* anderswo, woanders

elude [i'lu:d] *vt* entgehen +*dat*

elusive [i'lu:siv] *adj* schwer fassbar

emaciated [i'meisieitid] *adj* abgezehrt

E-mail ['i:meil] *n abbr* (= *electronic mail*) E-Mail *f*

emancipation [imænsi'peiʃən] *n* Emanzipation *f*; Freilassung *f*

embankment [im'bæŋkmənt] *n* (*of river*) Uferböschung *f*; (*of road*) Straßendamm *m*

embargo [im'bɑ:gəu] (*pl* **~es**) *n* Embargo *nt*

embark [im'bɑ:k] *vi* sich einschiffen; **~ on** *vt fus* unternehmen; **~ation** [embɑ:'keiʃən] *n* Einschiffung *f*

embarrass [im'bærəs] *vt* in Verlegenheit bringen; **~ed** *adj* verlegen; **~ing** *adj* peinlich; **~ment** *n* Verlegenheit *f*

embassy ['embəsi] *n* Botschaft *f*

embed [im'bed] *vt* einbetten

embellish [im'beliʃ] *vt* verschönern

embers ['embəz] *npl* Glut(asche) *f*

embezzle [im'bezl] *vt* unterschlagen; **~ment** *n* Unterschlagung *f*

embitter [im'bitə*r*] *vt* verbittern

embody [im'bɒdi] *vt* (*ideas*) verkörpern; (*new features*) (in sich) vereinigen

embossed [im'bɒst] *adj* geprägt

embrace [im'breis] *vt* umarmen; (*include*) einschließen ♦ *vi* sich umarmen ♦ *n* Umarmung *f*

embroider [im'brɔidə*r*] *vt* (be)sticken; (*story*) ausschmücken; **~y** *n* Stickerei *f*

emerald ['emərəld] *n* Smaragd *m*

emerge [i'mɜ:dʒ] *vi* auftauchen; (*truth*) herauskommen; **~nce** *n* Erscheinen *nt*

emergency [i'mɜ:dʒənsi] *n* Notfall *m*; **~ cord** (*US*) *n* Notbremse *f*; **~ exit** *n* Notausgang *m*; **~ landing** *n* Notlandung *f*; **~ services** *npl* Notdienste *pl*

emery board ['eməri-] *n* Papiernagelfeile *f*

emigrant ['emigrənt] *n* Auswanderer *m*

emigrate ['emigreit] *vi* auswandern; **emigration** [emi'greiʃən] *n* Auswanderung *f*

eminence ['eminəns] *n* hohe(r) Rang *m*

eminent ['eminənt] *adj* bedeutend

emission [i'miʃən] *n* Ausströmen *nt*; **~s** *npl* Emissionen *fpl*

emit [i'mit] *vt* von sich *dat* geben

emotion [i'məuʃən] *n* Emotion *f*, Gefühl *nt*; **~al** *adj* (*person*) emotional; (*scene*) emotive

emotive [i'məutiv] *adj* gefühlsbetont

emperor ['empərə*r*] *n* Kaiser *m*

emphases ['emfəsi:z] *npl* of **emphasis**

emphasis ['emfəsis] *n* (*in LING*) Betonung *f*; (*fig*) Nachdruck *m*; **emphasize** ['emfəsaiz] *vt* betonen

emphatic [em'fætik] *adj* nachdrücklich; **~ally** *adv* nachdrücklich

empire ['ɛmpaɪə'] *n* Reich *nt*

empirical [ɛm'pɪrɪkl] *adj* empirisch

employ [ɪm'plɔɪ] *vt* (*hire*) anstellen; (*use*) verwenden; **~ee** [ɪmplɔɪ'iː] *n* Angestellte(r) *f(m)*; **~er** *n* Arbeitgeber(in) *m(f)*; **~ment** *n* Beschäftigung *f*; **~ment agency** *n* Stellenvermittlung *f*

empower [ɪm'pauə'] *vt*: **to ~ sb to do sth** jdn ermächtigen, etw zu tun

empress ['ɛmprɪs] *n* Kaiserin *f*

emptiness ['ɛmptɪnɪs] *n* Leere *f*

empty ['ɛmptɪ] *adj* leer ♦ *vt* (*bottle*) Leergut *nt* ♦ *vt* (*contents*) leeren; (*container*) ausleeren ♦ *vi* (*water*) abfließen; (*river*) münden; (*house*) sich leeren; **~-handed** *adj* mit leeren Händen

EMU ['iːmjuː] *n abbr* (= *economic and monetary union*) EWU *f*

emulate ['ɛmjuleɪt] *vt* nacheifern +*dat*

emulsion [ɪ'mʌlʃən] *n* Emulsion *f*

enable [ɪ'neɪbl] *vt*: **to ~ sb to do sth** es jdm ermöglichen, etw zu tun

enact [ɪ'nækt] *vt* (*law*) erlassen; (*play*) aufführen; (*role*) spielen

enamel [ɪ'næməl] *n* Email *nt*; (*of teeth*) (Zahn)schmelz *m*

encased [ɪn'keɪst] *adj*: **~ in** (*enclosed*) eingeschlossen in +*dat*; (*covered*) verkleidet mit

enchant [ɪn'tʃɑːnt] *vt* bezaubern; **~ing** *adj* entzückend

encircle [ɪn'sɜːkl] *vt* umringen

encl. *abbr* (= *enclosed*) Anl.

enclose [ɪn'kləʊz] *vt* einschließen; **to ~ sth** (*in* or *with a letter*) etw (einem Brief) beilegen; **~d** (*in letter*) beiliegend, anbei; **enclosure** [ɪn'kləʊʒə'] *n* Einfriedung *f*; (*in letter*) Anlage *f*

encompass [ɪn'kʌmpəs] *vt* (*include*) umfassen

encore [ɔŋ'kɔː'] *n* Zugabe *f*

encounter [ɪn'kaʊntə'] *n* Begegnung *f*; (*MIL*) Zusammenstoß *m* ♦ *vt* treffen; (*resistance*) stoßen auf +*acc*

encourage [ɪn'kʌrɪdʒ] *vt* ermutigen; **~ment** *n* Ermutigung *f*, Förderung *f*;

encouraging *adj* ermutigend, viel versprechend

encroach [ɪn'krəʊtʃ] *vi*: **to ~ (up)on** eindringen in +*acc*; (*time*) in Anspruch nehmen

encrusted [ɪn'krʌstɪd] *adj*: **~ with** besetzt mit

encyclop(a)edia [ɛnsaɪkləu'piːdɪə] *n* Konversationslexikon *nt*

end [ɛnd] *n* Ende *nt*, Schluss *m*; (*purpose*) Zweck *m* ♦ *vt* (*also*: **bring to an ~**, **put an ~ to**) beenden ♦ *vi* zu Ende gehen; **in the ~** zum Schluss; **on ~** (*object*) hochkant; **to stand on ~** (*hair*) zu Berge stehen; **for hours on ~** stundenlang; **~ up** *vi* landen

endanger [ɪn'deɪndʒə'] *vt* gefährden; **~ed species** *n* eine vom Aussterben bedrohte Art

endearing [ɪn'dɪərɪŋ] *adj* gewinnend

endeavour [ɪn'dɛvə'] (*US* **endeavor**) *n* Bestrebung *f* ♦ *vi* sich bemühen

ending ['ɛndɪŋ] *n* Ende *nt*

endless ['ɛndlɪs] *adj* endlos

endorse [ɪn'dɔːs] *vt* unterzeichnen; (*approve*) unterstützen; **~ment** *n* (*AUT*) Eintrag *m*

endow [ɪn'dau] *vt*: **to ~ sb with sth** jdm etw verleihen; (*with money*) jdm etw stiften

endurance [ɪn'djuərəns] *n* Ausdauer *f*

endure [ɪn'djuə'] *vt* ertragen ♦ *vi* (*last*) (fort)dauern

enemy ['ɛnəmɪ] *n* Feind *m* ♦ *adj* feindlich

energetic [ɛnə'dʒɛtɪk] *adj* tatkräftig

energy ['ɛnədʒɪ] *n* Energie *f*

enforce [ɪn'fɔːs] *vt* durchsetzen

engage [ɪn'geɪdʒ] *vt* (*employ*) einstellen; (*in conversation*) verwickeln; (*TECH*) einschalten ♦ *vi* (*TECH*) ineinander greifen; (*clutch*) fassen; **to ~ in** sich beteiligen an +*dat*; **~d** *adj* verlobt; (*BRIT: TEL, toilet*) besetzt; (: *busy*) beschäftigt; **to get ~d** sich verloben; **~d tone** (*BRIT*) *n* (*TEL*) Besetztzeichen *nt*; **~ment** *n* (*appointment*) Verabredung *f*; (*to marry*)

Verlobung f; (MIL) Gefecht nt; ~ment
ring n Verlobungsring m; **engaging**
adj gewinnend

engender [ɪnˈdʒɛndəʳ] vt hervorrufen

engine [ˈendʒɪn] n (AUT) Motor m;
(RAIL) Lokomotive f; ~ **driver** n
Lok(omotiv)führer(in) m(f)

engineer [endʒɪˈnɪəʳ] n Ingenieur m;
(US: RAIL) Lok(omotiv)führer(in) m(f);
~ing [endʒɪˈnɪərɪŋ] n Technik f

England [ˈɪŋɡlənd] n England nt

English [ˈɪŋɡlɪʃ] adj englisch ♦ n (LING)
Englisch nt; the ~ npl (people) die
Engländer pl; ~ **Channel** n: the ~
Channel der Ärmelkanal m; ~**man/
woman** (irreg) n Engländer(in) m(f)

engraving [ɪnˈɡreɪvɪŋ] n Stich m

engrossed [ɪnˈɡrəʊst] adj vertieft

engulf [ɪnˈɡʌlf] vt verschlingen

enhance [ɪnˈhɑːns] vt steigern, heben

enigma [ɪˈnɪɡmə] n Rätsel nt; ~**tic**
[enɪɡˈmætɪk] adj rätselhaft

enjoy [ɪnˈdʒɔɪ] vt genießen; (privilege)
besitzen; to ~ o.s. sich amüsieren;
~**able** adj erfreulich; ~**ment** n Genuss
m, Freude f

enlarge [ɪnˈlɑːdʒ] vt erweitern; (PHOT)
vergrößern ♦ vi: to ~ on sth eine weiter ausführen; ~**ment** n Vergrößerung
f

enlighten [ɪnˈlaɪtn] vt aufklären;
~**ment** n: the E~**ment** (HIST) die Aufklärung

enlist [ɪnˈlɪst] vt gewinnen ♦ vi (MIL)
sich melden

enmity [ˈenmɪtɪ] n Feindschaft f

enormity [ɪˈnɔːmɪtɪ] n Ungeheuerlichkeit f

enormous [ɪˈnɔːməs] adj ungeheuer

enough [ɪˈnʌf] adj, adv genug; **funnily
~** komischerweise

enquire [ɪnˈkwaɪəʳ] vt, vi = **inquire**

enrage [ɪnˈreɪdʒ] vt wütend machen

enrich [ɪnˈrɪtʃ] vt bereichern

enrol [ɪnˈrəʊl] vt einschreiben ♦ vi (register) sich anmelden; ~**ment** n (for
course) Anmeldung f

en route [ɒnˈruːt] adv unterwegs

ensign [ˈensaɪn, ˈensən] n (NAUT) Flagge f; (MIL) Fähnrich m

enslave [ɪnˈsleɪv] vt versklaven

ensue [ɪnˈsjuː] vi folgen, sich ergeben

en suite [ɒnswiːt] adj: **room with ~
bathroom** Zimmer nt mit eigenem
Bad

ensure [ɪnˈʃʊəʳ] vt garantieren

entail [ɪnˈteɪl] vt mit sich bringen

entangle [ɪnˈtæŋɡl] vt verwirren, ver-
stricken; ~**d** adj: **to become ~d (in)** (in
net, rope etc) sich verfangen (in +dat)

enter [ˈentəʳ] vt eintreten in +dat, betreten; (club) beitreten +dat; (in book)
eintragen ♦ vi hereinkommen, hineingehen; ~ **for** vt fus sich beteiligen an
+dat; ~ **into** vt fus (agreement) eingehen; (plans) eine Rolle spielen bei; ~
(**up**)**on** vt fus beginnen

enterprise [ˈentəpraɪz] n (in person)
Initiative f; (COMM) Unternehmen nt;
enterprising [ˈentəpraɪzɪŋ] adj unter-
nehmungslustig

entertain [entəˈteɪn] vt (guest) bewirten; (amuse) unterhalten; ~**er** n Unter-
haltungskünstler(in) m(f); ~**ing** adj
unterhaltsam; ~**ment** n Unterhaltung
f

enthralled [ɪnˈθrɔːld] adj gefesselt

enthusiasm [ɪnˈθuːzɪæzm] n Begeisterung f

enthusiast [ɪnˈθuːzɪæst] n Enthusiast
m; ~**ic** [ɪnθuːzɪˈæstɪk] adj begeistert

entice [ɪnˈtaɪs] vt verlocken

entire [ɪnˈtaɪəʳ] adj ganz; ~**ly** adv ganz,
völlig; ~**ty** [ɪnˈtaɪərɪtɪ] n: **in its ~ty** in
seiner Gesamtheit

entitle [ɪnˈtaɪtl] vt (allow) berechtigen;
(name) betiteln; ~**d** adj (book) mit dem
Titel; **to be ~d to sth** das Recht auf
etw acc haben; **to be ~d to do sth** das
Recht haben, etw zu tun

entity [ˈentɪtɪ] n Ding nt, Wesen nt

entourage [ɒntuˈrɑːʒ] n Gefolge nt

entrails [ˈentreɪlz] npl Eingeweide pl

entrance [n ˈentrns, vb ɪnˈtrɑːns] n Eingang m; (entering) Eintritt m ♦ vt hinreißen; **~ examination** n Aufnahmeprüfung f; **~ fee** n Eintrittsgeld nt; **~ ramp** (US) n (AUT) Einfahrt f

entrant ['entrnt] n (for exam) Kandidat m; (in race) Teilnehmer m

entreat [en'tri:t] vt anflehen

entrenched [en'trentʃt] adj (fig) verwurzelt

entrepreneur ['ɔntrəprə'nə:r] n Unternehmer(in) m(f)

entrust [in'trʌst] vt: **to ~ sb with sth** or **sth to sb** jdm etw anvertrauen

entry ['entri] n Eingang m; (THEAT) Auftritt m; (in account) Eintragung f; (in dictionary) Eintrag m; **"no ~"** „Eintritt verboten"; (for cars) „Einfahrt verboten"; **~ form** n Anmeldeformular nt; **~ phone** n Sprechanlage f

enumerate [i'nju:mǝreit] vt aufzählen

enunciate [i'nʌnsieit] vt aussprechen

envelop [in'velǝp] vt einhüllen

envelope ['envǝlǝup] n Umschlag m

enviable ['enviǝbl] adj beneidenswert

envious ['enviǝs] adj neidisch

environment [in'vaiǝnmǝnt] n Umgebung f; (ECOLOGY) Umwelt f; **~al** [invaiǝn'mentl] adj Umwelt-; **~-friendly** adj umweltfreundlich

envisage [in'vizidʒ] vt sich etw vorstellen

envoy ['envoi] n Gesandte(r) mf

envy ['envi] n Neid m ♦ vt: **to ~ sb sth** jdn um etw beneiden

enzyme ['enzaim] n Enzym nt

epic ['epik] n Epos m ♦ adj episch

epidemic [epi'demik] n Epidemie f

epilepsy ['epilepsi] n Epilepsie f; **epileptic** [epi'leptik] adj epileptisch ♦ n Epileptiker(in) m(f)

episode ['episǝud] n (incident) Vorfall m; (story) Episode f

epitaph ['epita:f] n Grabinschrift f

epitomize [i'pitǝmaiz] vt verkörpern

equable ['ekwǝbl] adj ausgeglichen

equal ['i:kwl] adj gleich ♦ n Gleichgestellte(r) mf ♦ vt gleichkommen +dat; **~ to the task** der Aufgabe gewachsen; **equality** [i:'kwɔliti] n Gleichheit f; (equal rights) Gleichberechtigung f; **~ize** vt gleichmachen ♦ vi (SPORT) ausgleichen; **~izer** n (SPORT) Ausgleich(streffer) m; **~ly** adv gleich

equanimity [ekwǝ'nimiti] n Gleichmut m

equate [i'kweit] vt gleichsetzen

equation [i'kweiʒǝn] n Gleichung f

equator [i'kweitǝr] n Äquator m

equestrian [i'kwestriǝn] adj Reit-

equilibrium [i:kwi'libriǝm] n Gleichgewicht nt

equinox ['i:kwinɔks] n Tagundnachtgleiche f

equip [i'kwip] vt ausrüsten; **to be well ~ped** gut ausgerüstet sein; **~ment** n Ausrüstung f; (TECH) Gerät nt

equitable ['ekwitǝbl] adj gerecht, billig

equities ['ekwitiz] (BRIT) npl (FIN) Stammaktien pl

equivalent [i'kwivǝlǝnt] adj gleichwertig, entsprechend ♦ n Äquivalent nt; (in money) Gegenwert m; **~ to** gleichwertig +dat, entsprechend +dat

equivocal [i'kwivǝkl] adj zweideutig

era ['iǝrǝ] n Epoche f, Ära f

eradicate [i'rædikeit] vt ausrotten

erase [i'reiz] vt ausradieren; (tape) löschen; **~r** n Radiergummi m

erect [i'rekt] adj aufrecht ♦ vt errichten; **~ion** [i'rekʃǝn] n Errichtung f; (ANAT) Erektion f

ERM n abbr (= Exchange Rate Mechanism) Wechselkursmechanismus m

erode [i'rǝud] vt zerfressen; (land) auswaschen

erotic [i'rɔtik] adj erotisch

err [ǝ:r] vi sich irren

errand ['erǝnd] n Besorgung f

erratic [i'rætik] adj unberechenbar

erroneous [i'rǝuniǝs] adj irrig

error ['erǝr] n Fehler m

erupt [i'rʌpt] vi ausbrechen; **~ion** [i'rʌpʃǝn] n Ausbruch m

escalate ['eskǝleit] vi sich steigern

escalator [ˈɛskəleɪtə] n Rolltreppe f

escape [ɪsˈkeɪp] n Flucht f; (of gas) Entweichen nt ♦ vi entkommen; (prisoners) fliehen; (leak) entweichen ♦ vt entkommen +dat; **escapism** n Flucht f (vor der Wirklichkeit)

escort [n ˈɛskɔːt, vb ɪsˈkɔːt] n (person accompanying) Begleiter m; (guard) Eskorte f ♦ vt (lady) begleiten; (MIL) eskortieren

Eskimo [ˈɛskɪməʊ] n Eskimo(frau) m(f)

especially [ɪsˈpɛʃlɪ] adv besonders

espionage [ˈɛspɪənɑːʒ] n Spionage f

esplanade [ɛspləˈneɪd] n Promenade f

Esquire [ɪsˈkwaɪə] n: **J. Brown ~** Herrn J. Brown

essay [ˈɛseɪ] n Aufsatz m; (LITER) Essay m

essence [ˈɛsns] n (quality) Wesen nt; (extract) Essenz f

essential [ɪˈsɛnʃl] adj (necessary) unentbehrlich; (basic) wesentlich ♦ n Allernötigste(s) nt; **~ly** adv eigentlich

establish [ɪsˈtæblɪʃ] vt (set up) gründen; (prove) nachweisen; **~ed** adj anerkannt; (belief, laws etc) herrschend; **~ment** n (setting up) Einrichtung f

estate [ɪsˈteɪt] n Gut nt; (BRIT: housing ~) Siedlung f; (will) Nachlass m; **~ agent** (BRIT) n Grundstücksmakler m; **~ car** (BRIT) n Kombiwagen m

esteem [ɪsˈtiːm] n Wertschätzung f

esthetic [ɪsˈθɛtɪk] (US) adj = **aesthetic**

estimate [n ˈɛstɪmət, vb ˈɛstɪmeɪt] n Schätzung f; (of price) (Kosten)voranschlag m ♦ vt schätzen; **estimation** [ɛstɪˈmeɪʃən] n Einschätzung f; (esteem) Achtung f

estranged [ɪsˈtreɪndʒd] adj entfremdet

estuary [ˈɛstjʊərɪ] n Mündung f

etc abbr (= et cetera) usw

etching [ˈɛtʃɪŋ] n Kupferstich m

eternal [ɪˈtɜːnl] adj ewig

eternity [ɪˈtɜːnɪtɪ] n Ewigkeit f

ether [ˈiːθə] n Äther m

ethical [ˈɛθɪkl] adj ethisch

ethics [ˈɛθɪks] n Ethik f ♦ npl Moral f

Ethiopia [iːθɪˈəʊpɪə] n Äthiopien nt

ethnic [ˈɛθnɪk] adj Volks-, ethnisch; **~ minority** n ethnische Minderheit f

ethos [ˈiːθɒs] n Gesinnung f

etiquette [ˈɛtɪkɛt] n Etikette f

EU abbr (= European Union) EU f

euphemism [ˈjuːfəmɪzəm] n Euphemismus m

euro [ˈjʊərəʊ] n (FIN) Euro m

Eurocheque [ˈjʊərəʊtʃɛk] n Euroscheck m

Europe [ˈjʊərəp] n Europa nt; **~an** [jʊərəˈpiːən] adj europäisch ♦ n Europäer(in) m(f); **~an Community** n: the **~an Community** die Europäische Gemeinschaft

Euro-sceptic [ˈjʊərəʊskɛptɪk] n Kritiker der Europäischen Gemeinschaft

evacuate [ɪˈvækjʊeɪt] vt (place) -räumen; (people) evakuieren; **evacuation** [ɪvækjuˈeɪʃən] n Räumung f; Evakuierung f

evade [ɪˈveɪd] vt (escape) entkommen +dat; (avoid) meiden; (duty) sich entziehen +dat

evaluate [ɪˈvæljʊeɪt] vt (information) auswerten

evaporate [ɪˈvæpəreɪt] vi verdampfen ♦ vt verdampfen lassen; **~d milk** n Kondensmilch f

evasion [ɪˈveɪʒən] n Umgehung f

evasive [ɪˈveɪsɪv] adj ausweichend

eve [iːv] n: on the **~ of** am Vorabend +gen

even [ˈiːvn] adj eben; gleichmäßig; (score etc) unentschieden; (number) gerade ♦ adv: **~ you** sogar du; te gute **~ with sb** jdm heimzahlen; **~ if** selbst wenn; **~ so** dennoch; **~ though** obwohl; **~ more** sogar noch mehr; **~ out** vi sich ausgleichen

evening [ˈiːvnɪŋ] n Abend m; in the **~** abends, am Abend; **~ class** n Abendschule f; **~ dress** n (man's) Gesellschaftsanzug m; (woman's) Abendkleid nt

event [ɪˈvɛnt] n (happening) Ereignis nt;

(SPORT) Disziplin f; **in the ~** im Falle +gen; **~ful** adj ereignisreich

eventual [ɪ'ventʃuəl] adj (final) schließlich; **~ity** [ɪventʃu'ælɪtɪ] n Möglichkeit f; **~ly** adv am Ende; (given time) schließlich

ever ['evə*] adv (always) immer; (at any time) je(mals) ♦ conj seit; **~ since** seitdem; **have you ~ seen it?** haben Sie es je gesehen?; **~green** n Immergrün nt; **~lasting** adj immer während

every ['evrɪ] adj jede(r, s); **~ other/third day** jeden zweiten/dritten Tag; **~ one of them** alle; **I have ~ confidence in him** ich habe uneingeschränktes Vertrauen in ihn; **we wish you ~ success** wir wünschen Ihnen viel Erfolg; **he's ~ bit as clever as his brother** er ist genauso klug wie sein Bruder; **~ now and then** ab und zu; **~body** pron = **everyone**; **~day** adj (daily) täglich; (commonplace) alltäglich, Alltags-; **~one** pron jeder, alle pl; **~thing** pron alles; **~where** adv überall(hin); (wherever) wohin; **~where you go** wohin du auch gehst

evict [ɪ'vɪkt] vt ausweisen; **~ion** [ɪ'vɪkʃən] n Ausweisung f

evidence ['evɪdns] n (sign) Spur f; (proof) Beweis m; (testimony) Aussage f

evident ['evɪdnt] adj augenscheinlich; **~ly** adv offensichtlich

evil ['i:vl] adj böse ♦ n Böse nt

evocative [ɪ'vɒkətɪv] adj: **to be ~ of sth** an etw acc erinnern

evoke [ɪ'vəuk] vt hervorrufen

evolution [i:və'lu:ʃən] n Entwicklung f; (of life) Evolution f

evolve [ɪ'vɒlv] vt entwickeln ♦ vi sich entwickeln

ewe [ju:] n Mutterschaf nt

ex- [eks] prefix Ex-, Alt-, ehemalig

exacerbate [eks'æsəbeɪt] vt verschlimmern

exact [ɪg'zækt] adj genau ♦ vt (demand) verlangen; **~ing** adj anspruchsvoll; **~ly** adv genau

exaggerate [ɪg'zædʒəreɪt] vt, vi übertreiben; **exaggeration** [ɪgzædʒə-'reɪʃən] n Übertreibung f

exalted [ɪg'zɔ:ltɪd] adj (position, style) hoch; (person) exaltiert

exam [ɪg'zæm] n abbr (SCH) = **examination**

examination [ɪgzæmɪ'neɪʃən] n Untersuchung f; (SCH) Prüfung f, Examen nt; (customs) Kontrolle f

examine [ɪg'zæmɪn] vt untersuchen; (SCH) prüfen; (consider) erwägen; **~r** n Prüfer m

example [ɪg'zɑ:mpl] n Beispiel nt; **for ~** zum Beispiel

exasperate [ɪg'zɑ:spəreɪt] vt zur Verzweiflung bringen; **exasperating** adj ärgerlich, zum Verzweifeln bringend; **exasperation** [ɪgzɑ:spə'reɪʃən] n Verzweiflung f

excavate ['ekskəveɪt] vt ausgraben; **excavation** [ekskə'veɪʃən] n Ausgrabung f

exceed [ɪk'si:d] vt überschreiten; (hopes) übertreffen; **~ingly** adv äußerst

excel [ɪk'sel] vi sich auszeichnen; **~lence** ['eksələns] n Vortrefflichkeit f; **E~lency** ['eksələnsɪ] n: **His E~lency** Seine Exzellenz f; **~lent** ['eksələnt] adj ausgezeichnet

except [ɪk'sept] prep (also: **~ for, ~ing**) außer +dat ♦ vt ausnehmen; **~ion** [ɪk'sepʃən] n Ausnahme f; **to take ~ion to** Anstoß nehmen an +dat; **~ional** [ɪk'sepʃənl] adj außergewöhnlich

excerpt ['eksə:pt] n Auszug m

excess [ɪk'ses] n Übermaß nt; **an ~ of** ein Übermaß an +dat; **~ baggage** n Mehrgepäck nt; **~ fare** n Nachlösegebühr f; **~ive** adj übermäßig

exchange [ɪks'tʃeɪndʒ] n Austausch m; (also: **telephone ~**) Zentrale f ♦ vt (goods) tauschen; (greetings) austauschen; (money, blows) wechseln; **~ rate** n Wechselkurs m

Exchequer [ɪks'tʃekə*] (BRIT) n: **the ~** das Schatzamt

excise ['eksaız] n Verbrauchssteuer f

excite [ık'saıt] vt erregen; **to get ~d** sich aufregen; **~ment** n Aufregung f; **exciting** adj spannend

exclaim [ıks'kleım] vi ausrufen

exclamation [ekskləʹmeıʃən] n Ausruf m; **~ mark** n Ausrufezeichen nt

exclude [ıks'klu:d] vt ausschließen

exclusion [ıks'klu:ʒən] n Ausschluss m; **~ zone** n Sperrzone f

exclusive [ıks'klu:sıv] adj (select) exklusiv; (sole) ausschließlich, Allein-; **~ of** exklusive +gen; **~ly** adv nur, ausschließlich

excommunicate [ekskəʹmju:nıkeıt] vt exkommunizieren

excrement ['ekskrəmənt] n Kot m

excruciating [ıks'kru:ʃıeıtıŋ] adj qualvoll

excursion [ıks'kɜ:ʃən] n Ausflug m

excusable [ıks'kju:zəbl] adj entschuldbar

excuse [n ıks'kju:s, vb ıks'kju:z] n Entschuldigung f ♦ vt entschuldigen; **~ me!** entschuldigen Sie!

ex-directory [eksdı'rektərı] (BRIT) adj: **to be ~** nicht im Telefonbuch stehen

execute ['eksıkju:t] vt (carry out) ausführen; (kill) hinrichten; **execution** [eksıʹkju:ʃən] n Ausführung f; (killing) Hinrichtung f; **executioner** [eksıʹkju:ʃnə*] n Scharfrichter m

executive [ıg'zekjutıv] n (COMM) Geschäftsführer m; (POL) Exekutive f ♦ adj Exekutiv-, ausführend

executor [ıg'zekjutə*] n Testamentsvollstrecker m

exemplary [ıg'zemplərı] adj musterhaft

exemplify [ıg'zemplıfaı] vt veranschaulichen

exempt [ıg'zempt] adj befreit ♦ vt befreien; **~ion** [ıg'zempʃən] n Befreiung f

exercise [n 'eksəsaız] n Übung f ♦ vt (power) ausüben; (muscle, patience) üben; (dog) ausführen ♦ vi Sport treiben; **~ bike** n Heimtrainer m; **~ book**

n (Schul)heft nt

exert [ıg'zɜ:t] vt (influence) ausüben; **to ~ o.s.** sich anstrengen; **~ion** [ıg'zɜ:ʃən] n Anstrengung f

exhale [eks'heıl] vt, vi ausatmen

exhaust [ıg'zɔ:st] n (fumes) Abgase pl; (pipe) Auspuffrohr nt ♦ vt erschöpfen; **~ed** adj erschöpft; **~ion** [ıg'zɔ:stʃən] n Erschöpfung f; **~ive** adj erschöpfend

exhibit [ıg'zıbıt] n (JUR) Beweisstück nt; (ART) Ausstellungsstück nt ♦ vt ausstellen; **~ion** [eksıʹbıʃən] n (ART) Ausstellung f; (of temper etc) Zurschaustellung f; **~ionist** [eksıʹbıʃənıst] n Exhibitionist m

exhilarating [ıg'zıləreıtıŋ] adj erhebend

ex-husband n Ehemann m

exile ['eksaıl] n Exil nt; (person) Verbannte(r) f(m) ♦ vt verbannen

exist [ıg'zıst] vi existieren; **~ence** n Existenz f; **~ing** adj bestehend

exit ['eksıt] n Ausgang m; (THEAT) Abgang m ♦ vi (THEAT) abtreten; (COMPUT) aus einem Programm herausgehen; **~ poll** n bei Wahlen unmittelbar nach Verlassen der Wahllokale durchgeführte Umfrage; **~ ramp** (US) n (AUT) Ausfahrt f

exodus ['eksədəs] n Auszug m

exonerate [ıg'zonəreıt] vt entlasten

exorbitant [ıg'zɔ:bıtnt] adj übermäßig; (price) Fantasie-

exotic [ıg'zotık] adj exotisch

expand [ıks'pænd] vt ausdehnen ♦ vi sich ausdehnen

expanse [ıks'pæns] n Fläche f

expansion [ıks'pænʃən] n Erweiterung f

expatriate [eks'pætrıət] n Ausländer(in) m(f)

expect [ıks'pekt] vt erwarten; (suppose) annehmen ♦ vi: **to be ~ing** ein Kind erwarten; **~ancy** n Erwartung f; **~ant mother** n werdende Mutter f; **~ation** [ekspek'teıʃən] n Hoffnung f

expedient [ıks'pi:dıənt] adj zweckdienlich ♦ n (Hilfs)mittel nt

expedition [ɛkspə'dɪʃən] n Expedition f

expel [ɪks'pɛl] vt ausweisen; (student) (ver)weisen

expend [ɪks'pɛnd] vt (effort) aufwenden; **~iture** n Ausgaben pl

expense [ɪks'pɛns] n Kosten pl; **~s** npl (COMM) Spesen pl; **at the ~ of** auf Kosten von; **~ account** n Spesenkonto nt; **expensive** [ɪks'pɛnsɪv] adj teuer

experience [ɪks'pɪərɪəns] n (incident) Erlebnis nt; (practice) Erfahrung f ♦ vt erleben; **~d** adj erfahren

experiment [ɪks'pɛrɪmənt] n Versuch m, Experiment nt ♦ vi experimentieren; **~al** [ɪkspɛrɪ'mɛntl] adj experimentell

expert ['ɛkspəːt] n Fachmann m; (official) Sachverständige(r) m ♦ adj erfahren; **~ise** [ɛkspəː'tiːz] n Sachkenntnis f

expire [ɪks'paɪər] vi (end) ablaufen; (ticket) verfallen; (die) sterben; **expiry** n Ablauf m

explain [ɪks'pleɪn] vt erklären

explanation [ɛksplə'neɪʃən] n Erklärung f; **explanatory** [ɪks'plænətrɪ] adj erklärend

explicit [ɪks'plɪsɪt] adj ausdrücklich

explode [ɪks'pləʊd] vi explodieren ♦ vt (bomb) sprengen

exploit [n 'ɛksplɔɪt, vb ɪks'plɔɪt] n (Helden)tat f ♦ vt ausbeuten; **~ation** [ɛksplɔɪ'teɪʃən] n Ausbeutung f

exploration [ɛksplɔ'reɪʃən] n Erforschung f

exploratory [ɪks'plɔrətrɪ] adj Probe-

explore [ɪks'plɔːr] vt (travel) erforschen; (search) untersuchen; **~r** n Erforscher(in) m(f)

explosion [ɪks'pləʊʒən] n Explosion f; (fig) Ausbruch m

explosive [ɪks'pləʊsɪv] adj explosiv, Spreng- ♦ n Sprengstoff m

export [vb ɛks'pɔːt, n 'ɛkspɔːt] vt exportieren ♦ n Export m ♦ cpd (trade) Export-; **~er** [ɛks'pɔːtər] n Exporteur m

expose [ɪks'pəʊz] vt (to danger etc) aussetzen; (impostor) entlarven; **to ~ sb to sth** jdn einer Sache dat aussetzen; **~d** adj (position) exponiert

exposure [ɪks'pəʊʒər] n (MED) Unterkühlung f; (PHOT) Belichtung f; **exposure meter** n Belichtungsmesser m

express [ɪks'prɛs] adj ausdrücklich; (speedy) Express-, Eil- ♦ n (RAIL) Schnellzug m ♦ adv (send) per Express ♦ vt ausdrücken; **to ~ o.s.** sich ausdrücken; **~ion** [ɪks'prɛʃən] n Ausdruck m; **~ive** adj ausdrucksvoll; **~ly** adv ausdrücklich; **~way** (US) n (urban motorway) Schnellstraße f

expulsion [ɪks'pʌlʃən] n Ausweisung f

exquisite [ɛks'kwɪzɪt] adj erlesen

extend [ɪks'tɛnd] vt (visit etc) verlängern; (building) ausbauen; (hand) ausstrecken; (welcome) bieten ♦ vi (land) sich erstrecken

extension [ɪks'tɛnʃən] n Erweiterung f; (of building) Anbau m; (TEL) Apparat m

extensive [ɪks'tɛnsɪv] adj (knowledge) umfassend; (use) weitgehend, weitgehend

extent [ɪks'tɛnt] n Ausdehnung f; (fig) Ausmaß nt; **to a certain ~** bis zu einem gewissen Grade; **to such an ~ that ...** dermaßen, dass ...; **to what ~?** inwieweit?

extenuating [ɪks'tɛnjʊeɪtɪŋ] adj mildernd

exterior [ɛks'tɪərɪər] adj äußere(r, s), Außen- ♦ n Äußere(s) nt

exterminate [ɪks'tɜːmɪneɪt] vt ausrotten

external [ɛks'tɜːnl] adj äußere(r, s), Außen-

extinct [ɪks'tɪŋkt] adj ausgestorben; **~ion** [ɪks'tɪŋkʃən] n Aussterben nt

extinguish [ɪks'tɪŋgwɪʃ] vt (aus)löschen

extort [ɪks'tɔːt] vt erpressen; **~ion** [ɪks'tɔːʃən] n Erpressung f; **~ionate** [ɪks'tɔːʃnɪt] adj überhöht, erpresserisch

extra ['ɛkstrə] adj zusätzlich ♦ adv besonders ♦ n (for car etc) Extra nt;

(*charge*) Zuschlag *m*; (*THEAT*) Statist *m*
♦ *prefix* außer...

extract [*v* ɪks'trækt, *n* 'ekstrækt] *vt* (heraus)ziehen ♦ *n* (*from book etc*) Auszug
m; (*COOK*) Extrakt *m*

extracurricular ['ekstrəkə'rɪkjuləʳ] *adj*
außerhalb des Stundenplans

extradite ['ekstrədaɪt] *vt* ausliefern

extramarital ['ekstrə'mærɪtl] *adj*
außerehelich

extramural ['ekstrə'mjuərl] *adj* (*course*)
Volkshochschul-

extraordinary [ɪks'trɔ:dnrɪ] *adj* außerordentlich; (*amazing*) erstaunlich

extravagance [ɪks'trævəgəns] *n* Verschwendung *f*; (*lack of restraint*)
Zügellosigkeit *f*; (*an* ~) Extravaganz *f*

extravagant [ɪks'trævəgənt] *adj* extravagant

extreme [ɪks'tri:m] *adj* (*edge*)
äußerste(r, s), hinterste(r, s); (*cold*)
äußerste(r, s); (*behaviour*) außergewöhnlich, übertrieben ♦ *n* Extrem *nt*;
~ly *adv* äußerst, höchst; **extremist** *n*
Extremist(in) *m(f)*

extremity [ɪks'tremɪtɪ] *n* (*end*) Spitze *f*,
äußerste(s) Ende *nt*; (*hardship*) bitterste Not *f*; (*ANAT*) Hand *f*, Fuß *m*

extricate ['ekstrɪkeɪt] *vt* losmachen,
befreien

extrovert ['ekstrəvə:t] *n* extrovertierte(r) Mensch *m*

exuberant [ɪg'zju:bərnt] *adj* ausgelassen

exude [ɪg'zju:d] *vt* absondern

eye [aɪ] *n* Auge *nt*; (*of needle*) Öhr *nt*
♦ *vt* betrachten; (*up and down*) mustern; **to keep an** ~ **on** aufpassen auf
+acc; **~ball** *n* Augapfel *m*; **~bath** *n* Augenbad *nt*; **~brow** *n* Augenbraue *f*;
~brow pencil *n* Augenbrauenstift *m*;
~drops *npl* Augentropfen *pl*; **~lash** *n*
Augenwimper *f*; **~lid** *n* Augenlid *nt*;
~liner *n* Eyeliner *m*; **~opener** *n* das
was an ~**opener** das hat mir/ihm *etc*
die Augen geöffnet; **~shadow** *n* Lidschatten *m*; **~sight** *n* Sehkraft *f*; **~sore**

n Schandfleck *m*; ~ **witness** *n* Augenzeuge *m*

F, f

F [ef] *n* (*MUS*) F *nt*

F. *abbr* (= *Fahrenheit*) F

fable ['feɪbl] *n* Fabel *f*

fabric ['fæbrɪk] *n* Stoff *m*; (*fig*) Gefüge
nt

fabrication [fæbrɪ'keɪʃən] *n* Erfindung *f*

fabulous ['fæbjuləs] *adj* sagenhaft

face [feɪs] *n* Gesicht *nt*; (*surface*) Oberfläche *f*; (*of clock*) Zifferblatt *nt*; (*fig*)
(*point towards*) liegen nach; (*situation,
difficulty*) sich stellen *+dat*; ~ **down**
(*person*) mit dem Gesicht nach unten;
(*card*) mit der Vorderseite nach unten;
to make *or* **pull a** ~ das Gesicht verziehen; in the ~ of angesichts *+gen*; **on
the** ~ **of it** so, wie es aussieht; ~ **to** ~
Auge in Auge; **to** ~ **up to sth** einer Sache *dat* ins Auge sehen; ~ **cloth** (*BRIT*)
n Waschlappen *m*; ~ **cream** *n* Gesichtscreme *f*; ~ **lift** *n* Facelifting *nt*; ~
powder *n* (Gesichts)puder *m*

facet ['fæsɪt] *n* Aspekt *m*; (*of gem*) Facette *f*, Fassette *f*

facetious [fə'si:ʃəs] *adj* witzig

face value *n* Nennwert *m*; **to take sth
at (its)** ~ (*fig*) etw für bare Münze
nehmen

facial ['feɪʃl] *adj* Gesichts-

facile ['fæsaɪl] *adj* (*easy*) leicht

facilitate [fə'sɪlɪteɪt] *vt* erleichtern

facilities [fə'sɪlɪtɪz] *npl* Einrichtungen
pl; **credit** ~ Kreditmöglichkeiten *pl*

facing ['feɪsɪŋ] *adj* zugekehrt ♦ *prep*
gegenüber

facsimile [fæk'sɪmɪlɪ] *n* Faksimile *nt*;
(*machine*) Telekopierer *m*

fact [fækt] *n* Tatsache *f*; **in** ~ in der Tat

faction ['fækʃən] *n* Splittergruppe *f*

factor ['fæktəʳ] *n* Faktor *m*

factory ['fæktərɪ] *n* Fabrik *f*

factual ['fæktjuəl] *adj* sachlich

faculty ['fækəltɪ] n Fähigkeit f; (UNIV) Fakultät f; (US: teaching staff) Lehrpersonal nt

fad [fæd] n Tick m; (fashion) Masche f

fade [feɪd] vi (lose colour) verblassen; (dim) nachlassen; (sound, memory) schwächer werden; (wilt) verwelken

fag [fæg] (inf) n (cigarette) Kippe f

fail [feɪl] vt (exam) nicht bestehen; (student) durchfallen lassen; (courage) verlassen; (memory) im Stich lassen ♦ vi (supplies) zu Ende gehen; (student) durchfallen; (eyesight) nachlassen; (light) schwächer werden; (crop) fehlschlagen; (remedy) nicht wirken; **~ to do sth** (neglect) es unterlassen, etw zu tun; (be unable) es nicht schaffen, etw zu tun; **without ~** unbedingt; **~ing** n Schwäche f ♦ prep mangels +gen; **~ure** ['feɪljəʳ] n (person) Versager m; (act) Versagen nt; (TECH) Defekt m

faint [feɪnt] adj schwach ♦ n Ohnmacht f ♦ vi ohnmächtig werden

fair [fɛəʳ] adj (just) gerecht, fair; (hair) blond; (skin) hell; (weather) schön; (not very good) mittelmäßig; (sizeable) ansehnlich ♦ adv (play) fair ♦ n (COMM) Messe f; (BRIT: funfair) Jahrmarkt m; **~ly** adv (honestly) gerecht, fair; (rather) ziemlich; **~ness** n Fairness f

fairy ['fɛərɪ] n Fee f; **~ tale** n Märchen nt

faith [feɪθ] n Glaube m; (trust) Vertrauen nt; (sect) Bekenntnis nt; **~ful** adj treu; **~fully** adv treu; **yours ~fully** (BRIT) hochachtungsvoll

fake [feɪk] n Fälschung f; (person) Schwindler m ♦ adj vorgetäuscht ♦ vt fälschen

falcon ['fɔːlkən] n Falke m

fall [fɔːl] (pt **fell**, pp **fallen**) n Fall m, Sturz m; (decrease) Fallen nt; (of snow) (Schnee)fall m; (US: autumn) Herbst m ♦ vi (also fig) fallen; (night) hereinbrechen; **~s** npl (waterfall) Fälle pl; **to ~ flat** platt hinfallen; (joke) nicht ankommen; **~ back** vi zurückweichen; **~**

back on vt fus zurückgreifen auf +acc; **~ behind** vi zurückbleiben; **~ down** vi (person) hinfallen; (building) einstürzen; **~ for** vt fus (trick) hereinfallen auf +acc; (person) sich verknallen in +acc; **~ in** vi (roof) einstürzen; **~ off** vi herunterfallen; (diminish) sich vermindern; **~ out** vi sich streiten; (MIL) wegtreten; **~ through** vi (plan) ins Wasser fallen

fallacy ['fæləsɪ] n Trugschluss m

fallen ['fɔːlən] pp of **fall**

fallible ['fæləbl] adj fehlbar

fallout ['fɔːlaʊt] n radioaktive(r) Niederschlag m; **~ shelter** n Atombunker m

fallow ['fæləʊ] adj brach(liegend)

false [fɔːls] adj falsch; (artificial) künstlich; **under ~ pretences** unter Vorspiegelung falscher Tatsachen; **~ alarm** n Fehlalarm m; **~ teeth** (BRIT) npl Gebiss nt

falter ['fɔːltəʳ] vi schwanken; (in speech) stocken

fame [feɪm] n Ruhm m

familiar [fə'mɪlɪəʳ] adj bekannt; (intimate) familiär; **to be ~ with** vertraut sein mit; **~ize** vt vertraut machen

family ['fæmɪlɪ] n Familie f; (relations) Verwandtschaft f; **~ business** n Familienunternehmen nt; **~ doctor** n Hausarzt m

famine ['fæmɪn] n Hungersnot f

famished ['fæmɪʃt] adj ausgehungert

famous ['feɪməs] adj berühmt

fan [fæn] n (folding) Fächer m; (ELEC) Ventilator m; (admirer) Fan m ♦ vt fächeln; **~ out** vi sich (fächerförmig) ausbreiten

fanatic [fə'nætɪk] n Fanatiker(in) m(f)

fan belt n Keilriemen m

fanciful ['fænsɪful] adj (odd) seltsam; (imaginative) fantasievoll

fancy ['fænsɪ] n (liking) Neigung f; (imagination) Einbildung f ♦ adj schick ♦ vt (like) gern haben; wollen; (imagine) sich einbilden; **he fancies her** er

mag sie; **~ dress** n Maskenkostüm nt;
~-dress ball n Maskenball m

fang [fæŋ] n Fangzahn m; (of snake)
Giftzahn m

fantastic [fæn'tæstɪk] adj fantastisch

fantasy ['fæntəsɪ] n Fantasie f

far [fɑːʳ] adj weit ♦ adv weit entfernt;
(very much) weitaus; **by ~** bei weitem;
so ~ so weit; bis jetzt; **go as ~ as the
station** gehen Sie bis zum Bahnhof;
as ~ as I know soweit or soviel ich
weiß; **~away** adj weit entfernt

farce [fɑːs] n Farce f; **farcical** ['fɑːsɪkəl]
adj lächerlich

fare [fɛəʳ] n Fahrpreis m; Fahrgeld n;
(food) Kost f; **half/full ~** halber/voller
Fahrpreis m

Far East n: **the ~** der Ferne Osten

farewell [fɛə'wɛl] n Abschied(sgruß) m
♦ excl leben wohl!

farm [fɑːm] n Bauernhof m, Farm f ♦ vt
bewirtschaften; **~er** n Bauer m, Land-
wirt m; **~hand** n Landarbeiter m;
~house n Bauernhaus nt; **~ing** n
Landwirtschaft f; **~land** n Ackerland
nt; **~yard** n Hof m

far-reaching ['fɑː'riːtʃɪŋ] adj (reform,
effect) weitreichend, weit reichend

fart [fɑːt] (inf!) n Furz m ♦ vi furzen

farther ['fɑːðəʳ] adv weiter; **farthest**
['fɑːðɪst] adj fernste(r, s) ♦ adv am wei-
testen

fascinate ['fæsɪneɪt] vt faszinieren; **fascinating** adj faszinierend; **fascination**
[fæsɪ'neɪʃən] n Faszination f

fascism ['fæʃɪzəm] n Faschismus m

fashion ['fæʃən] n (of clothes) Mode f;
(manner) Art f (und Weise f) ♦ vt machen; **in ~** in Mode; **out of ~** unmo-
disch; **~able** (clothes) modisch; (place)
elegant; **~ show** n
Mode(n)schau f

fast [fɑːst] adj schnell; (firm) fest ♦ adv
schnell; fest ♦ n Fasten nt ♦ vi fasten;
to be ~ (clock) vorgehen

fasten ['fɑːsn] vt (attach) befestigen;
(with rope) zuschnüren; (seat belt) fest-

machen; (coat) zumachen ♦ vi sich
schließen lassen; **~er** n Verschluss m;
~ing n Verschluss m

fast food n Fastfood nt, Fast Food nt

fastidious [fæs'tɪdɪəs] adj wählerisch

fat [fæt] adj dick ♦ n Fett nt

fatal ['feɪtl] adj tödlich; (disastrous) verhängnisvoll; **~ity** [fə'tælɪtɪ] n (road
death etc) Todesopfer nt; **~ly** adv
tödlich

fate [feɪt] n Schicksal nt; **~ful** adj (pro-
phetic) schicksalsschwer; (important)
schicksalhaft

father ['fɑːðəʳ] n Vater m; (REL) Pater m;
~-in-law n Schwiegervater m; **~ly** adj
väterlich

fathom ['fæðəm] n Klafter m ♦ vt auslo-
ten; (fig) ergründen

fatigue [fə'tiːg] n Ermüdung f

fatten ['fætn] vt dick machen; (animals)
mästen ♦ vi dick werden

fatty ['fætɪ] adj fettig ♦ n (inf) Dicker-
chen nt

fatuous ['fætjuəs] adj albern, affig

faucet ['fɔːsɪt] (US) n Wasserhahn m

fault [fɔːlt] n (defect) Defekt m; (ELEC)
Störung f; (blame) Schuld f; (GEOG)
Verwerfung f; **it's your ~** du bist daran schuld; **to find ~ with** (sth/sb) etwas auszusetzen haben an (etw/jdm);
at ~ im Unrecht; **~less** adj tadellos;
~y adj fehlerhaft, defekt

fauna ['fɔːnə] n Fauna f

favour ['feɪvəʳ] (US **favor**) n (approval)
Wohlwollen nt; (kindness) Gefallen m
♦ vt (prefer) vorziehen; **in ~ of** für; zugunsten or zu Gunsten +gen; **to find ~
with sb** bei jdm Anklang finden;
~able ['feɪvrəbl] adj günstig; **~ite**
['feɪvrɪt] adj Lieblings- ♦ n (child) Liebling m; (SPORT) Favorit m

fawn [fɔːn] adj rehbraun ♦ n (animal)
(Reh)kitz n ♦ vi: **to ~ (up)on** (fig) katz-
buckeln vor +dat

fax [fæks] n (document) Fax nt; (machine) Telefax nt ♦ vt: **to ~ sth to sb**
jdm etw faxen

FBI (US) n abbr (= Federal Bureau of Investigation) FBI nt

fear [fɪəʳ] n Furcht f ♦ vt fürchten; **~ful** adj (timid) furchtsam; (terrible) fürchterlich; **~less** adj furchtlos

feasible ['fiːzəbl] adj durchführbar

feast [fiːst] n Festmahl nt; (REL: also: **~day**) Feiertag m ♦ vi: to **~** (on) sich gütlich tun (an +dat)

feat [fiːt] n Leistung f

feather ['fɛðəʳ] n Feder f

feature ['fiːtʃəʳ] n (Gesichts)zug m; (important part) Grundzug m; (CINE, PRESS) Feature nt ♦ vt darstellen; (advertising etc) groß herausbringen ♦ vi vorkommen; **featuring X** mit X; **~ film** n Spielfilm m

February ['fɛbruəri] n Februar m

fed [fɛd] pt, pp of **feed**

federal ['fɛdərəl] adj Bundes-

federation [fɛdə'reɪʃən] n (society) Verband m; (of states) Staatenbund m

fed up adj: to be **~** with sth etw satt haben; **I'm ~** ich habe die Nase voll

fee [fiː] n Gebühr f

feeble ['fiːbl] adj (person) schwach; (excuse) lahm

feed [fiːd] (pt, pp **fed**) n (for animals) Futter nt ♦ vt füttern; (support) ernähren; (data) eingeben; to **~** on fressen; **~back** n (information) Feed-back nt, Feedback nt; **~ing bottle** (BRIT) n Flasche f

feel [fiːl] (pt, pp **felt**) n: it has a soft **~** es fühlt sich weich an ♦ vt (sense) fühlen; (touch) anfassen; (think) meinen ♦ vi (person) sich fühlen; (thing) sich anfühlen; to **get the ~ of sth** sich an etw acc gewöhnen; **I ~ cold** mir ist kalt; **I ~ like a cup of tea** ich habe Lust auf eine Tasse Tee; **~ about or around** vi herumsuchen; **~er** n Fühler m; **~ing** n Gefühl nt; (opinion) Meinung f

feet [fiːt] npl of **foot**

feign [feɪn] vt vortäuschen

feline ['fiːlaɪn] adj katzenartig

fell [fɛl] pt of **fall** ♦ vt (tree) fällen

fellow ['fɛləu] n (man) Kerl m; ~ citizen n Mitbürger(in) m(f); ~ countryman (irreg) n Landsmann m; ~ men npl Mitmenschen pl; ~ship n (group) Körperschaft f; (friendliness) Kameradschaft f; (scholarship) Forschungsstipendium nt; ~ student n Kommilitone m, Kommilitonin f

felony ['fɛləni] n schwere(s) Verbrechen nt

felt [fɛlt] pt, pp of **feel** ♦ n Filz m; **~-tip pen** n Filzstift m

female ['fiːmeɪl] n (of animals) Weibchen nt ♦ adj weiblich

feminine ['fɛmɪnɪn] adj (LING) weiblich; (qualities) fraulich

feminist ['fɛmɪnɪst] n Feminist(in) m(f)

fence [fɛns] n Zaun m ♦ vt (also: **~ in**) einzäunen ♦ vi fechten; **fencing** ['fɛnsɪŋ] n Zaun m; (SPORT) Fechten nt

fend [fɛnd] vi: to **~ for o.s.** sich (allein) durchschlagen; **~ off** vt abwehren

fender ['fɛndəʳ] n Kaminvorsetzer m; (US: AUT) Kotflügel m

ferment [vb fə'mɛnt, n 'fɜːmɛnt] vi (CHEM) gären n (unrest) Unruhe f

fern [fɜːn] n Farn m

ferocious [fə'rəuʃəs] adj wild, grausam

ferret ['fɛrɪt] n Frettchen nt ♦ vt: to **~ out** aufspüren

ferry ['fɛrɪ] n Fähre f ♦ vt übersetzen

fertile ['fɜːtaɪl] adj fruchtbar

fertilize ['fɜːtɪlaɪz] vt (AGR) düngen; (BIOL) befruchten; **~r** n (Kunst)dünger m

fervent ['fɜːvənt] adj (admirer) glühend; (hope) innig

fervour ['fɜːvəʳ] (US fervor) n Leidenschaft f

fester ['fɛstəʳ] vi eitern

festival ['fɛstɪvəl] n (REL etc) Fest nt; (ART, MUS) Festspiele pl

festive ['fɛstɪv] adj festlich; **the ~ season** (Christmas) die Festzeit; **festivities** [fɛs'tɪvɪtɪz] npl Feierlichkeiten pl

festoon [fɛs'tuːn] vt: to **~** with

schmücken mit

fetch [fetʃ] vt holen; (in sale) einbringen

fetching ['fetʃɪŋ] adj reizend

fête [feit] n Fest nt

fetus (esp US) n = **foetus**

feud [fju:d] n Fehde f

feudal ['fju:dl] adj Feudal-

fever ['fi:vər] n Fieber nt; **~ish** adj (MED) fiebrig; (fig) fieberhaft

few [fju:] adj wenig; **a ~** einige; **~er** adj weniger(s); **~est** adj wenigste(r,s)

fiancé [fɪ'ɑ:ŋseɪ] n Verlobte(r) m; **~e** n Verlobte f

fib [fɪb] n Flunkerei f ♦ vi flunkern

fibre ['faɪbər] (US **fiber**) n Faser f; **~glass** n Glaswolle f

fickle ['fɪkl] adj unbeständig

fiction ['fɪkʃən] n (novels) Romanliteratur f; (story) Erdichtung f; **~al** adj erfunden

fictitious [fɪk'tɪʃəs] adj erfunden, fingiert

fiddle ['fɪdl] n Geige f; (trick) Schwindelei f ♦ vt (BRIT: accounts) frisieren; **~ with** vt fus herumfummeln an +dat

fidelity [fɪ'delɪtɪ] n Treue f

fidget ['fɪdʒɪt] vi zappeln

field [fi:ld] n Feld nt; (range) Gebiet nt; **~ marshal** n Feldmarschall m; **~work** n Feldforschung f

fiend [fi:nd] n Teufel m

fierce [fɪəs] adj wild

fiery ['faɪərɪ] adj (person) hitzig

fifteen [fɪf'ti:n] num fünfzehn

fifth [fɪfθ] adj fünfte(r, s) ♦ n Fünftel nt

fifty ['fɪftɪ] num fünfzig; **~-fifty** adj, adv halbe-halbe, fifty-fifty (inf)

fig [fɪg] n Feige f

fight [faɪt] (pt, pp **fought**) n Kampf m; (brawl) Schlägerei f; (argument) Streit m ♦ vt kämpfen gegen; sich schlagen mit; (fig) bekämpfen ♦ vi kämpfen; sich schlagen; streiten; **~er** n Kämpfer m(f); (plane) Jagdflugzeug nt; **~ing** n Kämpfen nt; (war) Kampfhandlungen pl

figment ['fɪgmənt] n: **~ of the imagination** reine Einbildung f

figurative ['fɪgjurətɪv] adj bildlich

figure ['fɪgər] n (of person) Figur f; (person) Gestalt f; (number) Ziffer f ♦ vt (US: imagine) glauben ♦ vi (appear) erscheinen; **~ out** vt herausbekommen; **~head** n (NAUT, fig) Galionsfigur f; **~ of speech** n Redensart f

file [faɪl] n (tool) Feile f; (dossier) Akte f; (folder) Aktenordner m; (COMPUT) Datei f; (row) Reihe f ♦ vt (metal, nails) feilen; (papers) abheften; (claim) einreichen ♦ vi: **to ~ in/out** hintereinander hereinkommen/hinausgehen; **to ~ past** vorbeimarschieren; **filing** ['faɪlɪŋ] n Ablage f; **filing cabinet** n Aktenschrank m

fill [fɪl] vt füllen; (occupy) ausfüllen; (satisfy) sättigen ♦ vi: **to eat one's ~** sich richtig satt essen; **~ in** vt (hole) (auf)füllen; (form) ausfüllen; **~ up** vt (container) auffüllen; (form) ausfüllen ♦ vi (AUT) tanken

fillet ['fɪlɪt] n Filet nt; **~ steak** n Filetsteak nt

filling ['fɪlɪŋ] n (COOK) Füllung f; (for tooth) (Zahn)plombe f; **~ station** n Tankstelle f

film [fɪlm] n Film m ♦ vt (scene) filmen; **~ star** n Filmstar m

filter ['fɪltər] n Filter m ♦ vt filtern; **~ lane** (BRIT) n Abbiegespur f; **~-tipped** adj Filter-

filth [fɪlθ] n Dreck m; **~y** adj dreckig; (weather) scheußlich

fin [fɪn] n Flosse f

final ['faɪnl] adj letzte(r, s); End-; (conclusive) endgültig ♦ n (FOOTBALL etc) Endspiel nt; **~s** npl (UNIV) Abschlussexamen nt; (SPORT) Schlussrunde f

finale [fɪ'nɑ:lɪ] n (MUS) Finale nt

final: ~ist n (SPORT) Schlussrundenteilnehmer m; **~ize** vt endgültig festlegen; (form geben +dat); abschließen; **~ly** adv (lastly) zuletzt; (eventually) endlich; (irrevocably) endgültig

finance [faɪˈnæns] n Finanzwesen nt ♦ vt finanzieren; **~s** npl (funds) Finanzen pl; **financial** [faɪˈnænʃəl] adj Finanz-; finanziell

find [faɪnd] (pt, pp **found**) vt finden ♦ n Fund m; **to ~ sb guilty** jdn für schuldig erklären; **~ out** vt herausfinden; **~ings** npl (JUR) Ermittlungsergebnis nt; (of report) Befund m

fine [faɪn] adj fein; (good) gut; (weather) schön ♦ adv (well) gut; (small) klein ♦ n (JUR) Geldstrafe f ♦ vt (JUR) mit einer Geldstrafe belegen; **~ arts** npl schöne(n) Künste pl

finger [ˈfɪŋgəʳ] n Finger m ♦ vt befühlen; **~nail** n Fingernagel m; **~print** n Fingerabdruck m; **~tip** n Fingerspitze f

finicky [ˈfɪnɪkɪ] adj pingelig

finish [ˈfɪnɪʃ] n Ende nt; (SPORT) Ziel nt; (of object) Verarbeitung f; (of paint) Oberflächenwirkung f ♦ vt beenden; (book) zu Ende lesen ♦ vi aufhören; (SPORT) ans Ziel kommen; **to be ~ed with sth** fertig sein mit etw; **to ~ doing sth** mit etw fertig werden; **~ off** vt (complete) fertig machen; (kill) den Gnadenstoß geben ♦ abst; (knock out) erledigen (umg); **~ up** vt (food) aufessen; (drink) austrinken ♦ vi (end up) enden; **~ing line** n Ziellinie f; **~ing school** n Mädchenpensionat nt

finite [ˈfaɪnaɪt] adj endlich, begrenzt

Finland [ˈfɪnlənd] n Finnland nt

Finn [fɪn] n Finne m, Finnin f; **~ish** ♦ n finnisch ♦ n (LING) Finnisch nt

fir [fɜːʳ] n Tanne f

fire [ˈfaɪəʳ] n Feuer nt; (in house etc) Brand m ♦ vt (gun) abfeuern; (imagination) entzünden; (dismiss) hinauswerfen ♦ vi (AUT) zünden; **to be on ~** brennen; **~ alarm** n Feueralarm m; **~arm** n Schusswaffe f; **~ brigade** (BRIT) n Feuerwehr f; **~ department** (US) n Feuerwehr f; **~ engine** n Feuerwehrauto nt; **~ escape** n Feuerleiter f; **~ extinguisher** n Löschgerät nt;

~man (irreg) n Feuerwehrmann m; **~place** n Kamin m; **~side** n Kamin m; **~ station** n Feuerwache f; **~wood** n Brennholz nt; **~works** npl Feuerwerk nt; **~ squad** n Exekutionskommando nt

firm [fɜːm] adj fest ♦ n Firma f; **~ly** [ˈfɜːmlɪ] adv (grasp, speak) fest; (push, tug) energisch; (decide) endgültig

first [fɜːst] adj erste(r, s) ♦ adv zuerst; (arrive) als Erste(r); (happen) zum ersten Mal ♦ n (person: in race) Erste(r) mf; (UNIV) Eins f; (AUT) erste(r) Gang m; **at ~** zuerst; **~ of all** zuallererst; **~ aid** n Erste Hilfe f; **~-aid kit** n Verbandskasten m; **~-class** adj erstklassig; (travel) erster Klasse; **~-hand** adj aus erster Hand; **~ lady** (US) n First Lady f; **~ly** adv erstens; **~ name** n Vorname m; **~-rate** adj erstklassig

fiscal [ˈfɪskl] adj Finanz-

fish [fɪʃ] n inv Fisch m ♦ vi fischen; angeln; **to go ~ing** angeln gehen; (in sea) fischen gehen; **~erman** (irreg) n Fischer m; **~ farm** n Fischzucht f; **~ fingers** (BRIT) npl Fischstäbchen pl; **~ing boat** n Fischerboot nt; **~ing line** n Angelschnur f; **~ing rod** n Angel(rute) f; **~ing tackle** n (for sport) Angelgeräte pl; **~monger's (shop)** n Fischhändler m; **~ slice** n Fischvorlegemesser nt; **~ sticks** (US) npl = **fish fingers**

fishy [ˈfɪʃɪ] (inf) adj (suspicious) faul

fission [ˈfɪʃən] n Spaltung f

fissure [ˈfɪʃəʳ] n Riss m

fist [fɪst] n Faust f

fit [fɪt] adj (MED) gesund; (SPORT) in Form, fit; (suitable) geeignet ♦ vt passen +dat; (insert, attach) einsetzen ♦ vi passen; (in space, gap) hineinpassen ♦ n (of clothes) Sitz m; (MED, of anger) Anfall m; (of laughter) Krampf m; **by ~s and starts** (move) ruckweise; (work) unregelmäßig; **~ in** vi hineinpassen; (fig: person) passen; **~ out** vt (also: **~ up**) ausstatten; **~ful** adj (sleep) unruhig; **~ment** n Einrichtungsgegenstand m; **~ness** n (suitability) Eignung f; (MED) Gesundheit f; (SPORT) Fitness f; **~ted carpet** n Teppichboden m; **~ted kitchen** n Einbauküche f; **~ter** n (TECH) Monteur m; **~ting** adj passend ♦ n (of dress) Anprobe f; (piece of equipment) (Ersatz)teil m; **~tings** npl (equipment) Zubehör nt; **~ting room** n Anproberaum m

five [faɪv] num fünf; **~r** (inf) n (BRIT) Fünfpfundnote f; (US) Fünfdollarnote f

fix [fɪks] vt befestigen; (settle) festsetzen; (repair) reparieren ♦ n: **in a ~** in der Klemme; **~ up** vt (meeting) arrangieren; **to ~ sb up with sth** jdm etw acc verschaffen; **~ation** [fɪk'seɪʃən] n Fixierung f; **~ed** [fɪkst] adj fest; **~ture** ['fɪkstʃəʳ] n Installationsteil m; (SPORT) Spiel nt

fizzy ['fɪzɪ] adj Sprudel-, sprudelnd

flabbergasted ['flæbəgɑːstɪd] (inf) adj platt

flabby ['flæbɪ] adj wabbelig

flag [flæg] n Fahne f ♦ vi (strength) nachlassen; (spirit) erlahmen; **~ down** vt anhalten; **~pole** [flægpəul] n Fahnenstange f

flair [flɛəʳ] n Talent nt

flak [flæk] n Flakfeuer nt

flake [fleɪk] n (of snow) Flocke f; (of rust) Schuppe f ♦ vi (also: **~ off**) abblättern

flamboyant [flæm'bɔɪənt] adj extravagant

flame [fleɪm] n Flamme f

flamingo [flə'mɪŋgəu] n Flamingo m

flammable ['flæməbl] adj brennbar

flan [flæn] (BRIT) n Obsttorte f

flank [flæŋk] n Flanke f ♦ vt flankieren

flannel ['flænl] n Flanell m; (BRIT: also: **face ~**) Waschlappen m; (: inf) Geschwafel nt; **~s** npl (trousers) Flanellhose f

flap [flæp] n Klappe f; (inf: crisis) (helle) Aufregung f ♦ vt (wings) schlagen mit ♦ vi flattern

flare [flɛəʳ] n (signal) Leuchtsignal nt; (in skirt etc) Weite f; **~ up** vi aufflammen; (fig) aufbrausen; (revolt) (plötzlich) ausbrechen

flash [flæʃ] n Blitz m; (also: **news ~**) Kurzmeldung f; (PHOT) Blitzlicht nt ♦ vt aufleuchten lassen ♦ vi aufleuchten; **in a ~** im Nu; **~ by** or **past** vi vorbeirasen; **~back** n Rückblende f; **~bulb** n Blitzlichtbirne f; **~ cube** n Blitzwürfel m; **~light** n Blitzlicht nt

flashy ['flæʃɪ] (pej) adj knallig

flask [flɑːsk] n (CHEM) Kolben m; (also: **vacuum ~**) Thermosflasche f ®

flat [flæt] adj flach; (dull) matt; (MUS) erniedrigt; (beer) schal; (tyre) platt ♦ n (BRIT: rooms) Wohnung f; (MUS) b nt; (AUT) Platte(r) m; **to work ~ out** auf Hochtouren arbeiten; **~ly** adv glatt; **~screen** adj (TV, COMPUT) mit flachem Bildschirm; **~ten** vt (also: **~ten out**) ebnen

flatter ['flætəʳ] vt schmeicheln +dat; **~ing** adj schmeichelhaft; **~y** n Schmeichelei f

flatulence ['flætjuləns] n Blähungen pl

flaunt [flɔːnt] vt prunken mit

flavour ['fleɪvəʳ] (US **flavor**) n Geschmack m ♦ vt würzen; **~ed** adj: **strawberry-~ed** mit Erdbeergeschmack; **~ing** n Würze f

flaw [flɔː] n Fehler m; **~less** adj einwandfrei

flax [flæks] n Flachs m; **~en** adj flachsfarben

flea [fliː] n Floh m

fleck [flek] n (mark) Fleck m; (pattern) Tupfen m

fled [fled] pt, pp of **flee**

flee [fliː] (pt, pp **fled**) vi fliehen ♦ vt fliehen vor +dat; (country) fliehen aus

fleece [fliːs] n Vlies nt ♦ vt (inf) schröpfen

fleet [fliːt] n Flotte f

fleeting ['fliːtɪŋ] adj flüchtig

Flemish ['flemɪʃ] adj flämisch

flesh [fleʃ] n Fleisch nt; **~ wound** n

Fleischwunde f

flew [fluː] pt of fly

flex [fleks] n Kabel nt ♦ vt beugen; **~ibility** [fleksɪ'bɪlɪtɪ] n Biegsamkeit f; (fig) Flexibilität f; **~ible** adj biegsam; (plans) flexibel

flick [flɪk] n leichte(r) Schlag m ♦ vt leicht schlagen; **~ through** vt fus durchblättern

flicker ['flɪkə^r] n Flackern nt ♦ vi flackern

flier ['flaɪə^r] n Flieger m

flight [flaɪt] n Flug m; (fleeing) Flucht f; (also: **~ of steps**) Treppe f; **to take ~** die Flucht ergreifen; **~ attendant** (US) n Steward(ess) m(f); **~ deck** n Flugdeck nt

flimsy ['flɪmzɪ] adj (thin) hauchdünn; (excuse) fadenscheinig

flinch [flɪntʃ] vi: **to ~ (away from)** zurückschrecken (vor +dat)

fling [flɪŋ] (pt, pp **flung**) vt schleudern

flint [flɪnt] n Feuerstein m

flip [flɪp] vt werfen

flippant ['flɪpənt] adj schnippisch

flipper ['flɪpə^r] n Flosse f

flirt [fləːt] vi flirten ♦ n: **he/she is a ~** er/sie flirtet gern

flit [flɪt] vi flitzen

float [fləʊt] n (FISHING) Schwimmer m; (esp in procession) Plattformwagen m ♦ vi schwimmen; (in air) schweben ♦ vt (COMM) gründen; (currency) floaten

flock [flɒk] n (of sheep, REL) Herde f; (of birds) Schwarm m

flog [flɒg] vt prügeln; (inf: sell) verkaufen

flood [flʌd] n Überschwemmung f; (fig) Flut f ♦ vt überschwemmen; **~ing** n Überschwemmung f; **~light** n Flutlicht nt

floor [flɔː^r] n (Fuß)boden m; (storey) Stock m ♦ vt (person) zu Boden schlagen; **ground ~** (BRIT) Erdgeschoss nt; **first ~** (BRIT) erste(r) Stock m; (US) Erdgeschoss nt; **~board** n Diele f; **~ show** n Kabarettvorstellung f

flop [flɒp] n Plumps m; (failure) Reinfall m ♦ vi (fail) durchfallen

floppy ['flɒpɪ] adj hängend; **~ (disk)** n (COMPUT) Diskette f

flora ['flɔːrə] n Flora f; **~l** adj Blumen-

florist ['flɒrɪst] n Blumenhändler(in) m(f); **~'s (shop)** n Blumengeschäft nt

flotation [fləʊ'teɪʃən] n (FIN) Auflegung f

flounce [flaʊns] n Volant m

flounder ['flaʊndə^r] vi (fig) ins Schleudern kommen ♦ n (ZOOL) Flunder f

flour ['flaʊə^r] n Mehl nt

flourish ['flʌrɪʃ] vi blühen; gedeihen ♦ n (waving) Schwingen nt; (of trumpets) Tusch m, Fanfare f

flout [flaʊt] vt missachten

flow [fləʊ] n Fließen nt; (of sea) Flut f ♦ vi fließen; **~ chart** n Flussdiagramm nt

flower ['flaʊə^r] n Blume f ♦ vi blühen; **~ bed** n Blumenbeet nt; **~pot** n Blumentopf m; **~y** adj (style) blumenreich

flown [fləʊn] pp of fly

flu [fluː] n Grippe f

fluctuate ['flʌktjʊeɪt] vi schwanken; **fluctuation** [flʌktjʊ'eɪʃən] n Schwankung f

fluency ['fluːənsɪ] n Flüssigkeit f

fluent ['fluːənt] adj fließend; **~ly** adv fließend

fluff [flʌf] n Fussel f; **~y** adj flaumig

fluid ['fluːɪd] n Flüssigkeit f ♦ adj flüssig; (fig: plans) veränderbar

fluke [fluːk] n (inf) Dusel m

flung [flʌŋ] pt, pp of fling

fluoride ['flʊəraɪd] n Fluorid nt; **~ toothpaste** n Fluorzahnpasta f

flurry ['flʌrɪ] n (of snow) Gestöber nt; (of activity) Aufregung f

flush [flʌʃ] n Erröten nt; (of excitement) Glühen nt ♦ vt (aus)spülen ♦ vi erröten ♦ adj glatt; **~ out** vt aufstöbern; **~ed** adj rot

flustered ['flʌstəd] adj verwirrt

flute [fluːt] n Querflöte f

flutter ['flʌtə^r] n Flattern nt ♦ vi flattern

flux [flʌks] n: **in a state of ~** im Fluss

fly [flaɪ] (*pt* **flew**, *pp* **flown**) *n* (*insect*) Fliege *f*; (*on trousers: also*: **flies**) (Hosen)schlitz *m* ♦ *vi* fliegen; (*flee*) fliehen; (*flag*) wehen; ~ **away** or **off** *vi* (*bird, insect*) wegfliegen; ~**drive** *n*: ~**drive holiday** Fly & Drive-Urlaub *m*; ~**ing** *n* Fliegen *nt* ♦ *adj*: **with ~ing colours** mit fliegenden Fahnen; ~**ing start** gute(r) Start *m*; ~**ing visit** Stippvisite *f*; ~**ing saucer** *n* fliegende Untertasse *f*; ~**over** *n* (BRIT) Überführung *f*; ~**sheet** *n* (*for tent*) Regendach *nt*

foal [fəʊl] *n* Fohlen *nt*

foam [fəʊm] *n* Schaum *m* ♦ *vi* schäumen; ~ **rubber** *n* Schaumgummi *m*

fob [fɒb] *vt*: **to ~ sb off with sth** jdm etw andrehen; (*with promise*) jdn mit etw abspeisen

focal [ˈfəʊkl] *adj* Brenn-; ~ **point** *n* (*of room, activity*) Mittelpunkt *m*

focus [ˈfəʊkəs] (*pl* ~**es**) *n* Brennpunkt *m* ♦ *vt* (*attention*) konzentrieren; (*camera*) scharf einstellen ♦ *vi*: **to ~ (on)** sich konzentrieren (auf +*acc*); **in ~** scharf eingestellt; **out of ~** unscharf

fodder [ˈfɒdəʳ] *n* Futter *nt*

foe [fəʊ] *n* Feind *m*

foetus [ˈfiːtəs] (US **fetus**) *n* Fötus *m*

fog [fɒg] *n* Nebel *m*; ~**gy** *adj* neblig; ~ **lamp** (BRIT), ~ **light** (US) (AUT) Nebelscheinwerfer *m*

foil [fɔɪl] *vt* vereiteln ♦ *n* (*metal, also fig*) Folie *f*; (FENCING) Florett *nt*

fold [fəʊld] *n* (*bend, crease*) Falte *f*; (AGR) Pferch *m* ♦ *vt* falten; ~ **up** *vi* (*map etc*) zusammenfalten ♦ *vt* (*business*) eingehen; ~**er** *n* Schnellhefter *m*; ~**ing** *adj* (*chair etc*) Klapp-

foliage [ˈfəʊlɪɪdʒ] *n* Laubwerk *nt*

folk [fəʊk] *npl* Leute *pl* ♦ *adj* Volks-; ~**s** *npl* (*family*) Leute *pl*; ~**lore** [ˈfəʊklɔːʳ] *n* (*study*) Volkskunde *f*; (*tradition*) Folklore *f*; ~ **song** *n* Volkslied *nt*; (*modern*) Folksong *m*

follow [ˈfɒləʊ] *vt* folgen +*dat*; (*fashion*)

mitmachen ♦ *vi* folgen; ~ **up** *vt* verfolgen; ~**er** *n* Anhänger(in) *m(f)*; ~**ing** *adj* folgend ♦ *n* (*people*) Gefolgschaft *f*; ~ **on call** *n* weiteres Gespräch in einer Telefonzelle um Guthaben zu verbrauchen

folly [ˈfɒlɪ] *n* Torheit *f*

fond [fɒnd] *adj*: **to be ~ of** gern haben

fondle [ˈfɒndl] *vt* streicheln

font [fɒnt] *n* Taufbecken *nt*

food [fuːd] *n* Essen *nt*; (*fodder*) Futter *nt*; ~ **mixer** *n* Küchenmixer *m*; ~ **poisoning** *n* Lebensmittelvergiftung *f*; ~ **processor** *n* Küchenmaschine *f*; ~**stuffs** *npl* Lebensmittel *pl*

fool [fuːl] *n* Narr *m*, Närrin *f* ♦ *vt* (*deceive*) hereinlegen ♦ *vi* (*also*: ~ **around**) (herum)albern; ~**hardy** *adj* tollkühn; ~**ish** *adj* albern; ~**proof** *adj* idiotensicher

foot [fʊt] (*pl* **feet**) *n* Fuß *m* ♦ *vt* (*bill*) bezahlen; **on ~** zu Fuß

footage [ˈfʊtɪdʒ] *n* (CINE) Filmmaterial *nt*

football [ˈfʊtbɔːl] *n* Fußball *m*; (*game*: BRIT) Fußball *nt*; (: US) Football *m*; ~ **player** *n* (BRIT: *also*: ~**er**) Fußballspieler *m*, Fußballer *m*; (US) Footballer *m*

Football Pools

Football Pools, umgangssprachlich auch die pools genannt, ist das in Großbritannien sehr beliebte Fußballtoto, bei dem auf die Ergebnisse der samstäglichen Fußballspiele gewettet wird. Teilnehmer schicken ihren ausgefüllten Totoschein vor den Spielen an die Totogesellschaft und vergleichen nach den Spielen die Ergebnisse mit ihrem Schein. Die Gewinne können sehr hoch sein und gelegentlich Millionen von Pfund betragen.

foot: ~**brake** *n* Fußbremse *f*; ~**bridge** *n* Fußgängerbrücke *f*; ~**hills** *npl* Ausläufer *pl*; ~**hold** *n* Halt *m*; ~**ing** *n* Halt *m*; (*fig*) Verhältnis *nt*; ~**lights** *npl* Rampenlicht nt; **~man** (irreg) n Bediensteter(r) m; **~note** n Fußnote f; **~path** n Fußweg m; **~print** n Fußabdruck m; **~sore** adj fußkrank; **~step** n Schritt m; **~wear** n Schuhzeug nt

---

KEYWORD

for [fɔːʳ] prep 1 für; **is this for me?** ist das für mich?; **the train for London** der Zug nach London; **he went for the paper** er ging die Zeitung holen; **give it to me – what for?** gib es mir – warum?

2 (because of) wegen; **for this reason** aus diesem Grunde

3 (referring to distance): **there are roadworks for 5 km** die Baustelle ist 5 km lang; **we walked for miles** wir sind meilenweit gegangen

4 (referring to time) seit; (: with future sense) für; **he was away for 2 years** er war zwei Jahre lang weg

5 (+infin clauses): **it is not for me to decide** das kann ich nicht entscheiden; **for this to be possible ...** damit dies möglich wird/wurde ...

6 (in spite of) trotz +gen or (inf) dat; **for all his complaints** obwohl er sich ständig beschwert

♦ conj denn

---

forage ['fɔrɪdʒ] n (Vieh)futter nt

foray ['fɔreɪ] n Raubzug m

forbad(e) [fə'bæd] pt of **forbid**

forbid [fə'bɪd] (pt **forbad(e)**, pp **forbidden**) vt verbieten; **~ding** adj einschüchternd

force [fɔːs] n Kraft f; (compulsion) Zwang m ♦ vt zwingen; (lock) aufbrechen; **the F~s** npl (BRIT) die Streitkräfte; **in ~** (rule) gültig; (group) in großer Stärke; **~d** adj (smile) gezwungen; (landing) Not-; **~-feed** vt zwangsernähren; **~ful** adj (speech) kraftvoll; (personality) resolut

forceps ['fɔːseps] npl Zange f

forcibly ['fɔːsəblɪ] adv zwangsweise

ford [fɔːd] n Furt f ♦ vt durchwaten

fore [fɔːʳ] n: **to the ~** in den Vordergrund; **~arm** ['fɔːrɑːm] n Unterarm m; **~boding** [fɔː'bəʊdɪŋ] n Vorahnung f; **~cast** [fɔːkɑːst] (irreg: like **cast**) n (of weather) Vorhersage f ♦ vt voraussagen; **~court** ['fɔːkɔːt] n (of garage) Vorplatz m; **~fathers** ['fɔːfɑːðəz] npl Vorfahren pl; **~finger** ['fɔːfɪŋɡəʳ] n Zeigefinger m; **~front** ['fɔːfrʌnt] n Spitze f

forego [fɔː'ɡəʊ] (irreg: like **go**) vt verzichten auf +acc

fore: **~gone** ['fɔːɡɔn] adj: **it's a ~gone conclusion** es steht von vornherein fest; **~ground** ['fɔːɡraʊnd] n Vordergrund m; **~head** ['fɔrɪd] n Stirn f

foreign ['fɔrɪn] adj Auslands-; (accent) ausländisch; (trade) Außen-; (body) Fremd-; **~er** n Ausländer(in) m(f); **~ exchange** n Devisen pl; **F~ Office** (BRIT) n Außenministerium nt; **F~ Secretary** (BRIT) n Außenminister m

fore [fɔː-]: **~leg** n Vorderbein nt; **~man** (irreg) n Vorarbeiter m, **~most** adj erste(r, s) ♦ adv: **first and ~most** vor allem

forensic [fə'rensɪk] adj gerichtsmedizinisch

fore [fɔː-]: **~runner** n Vorläufer m; **~see** [fɔː'siː] (irreg: like **see**) vt vorhersehen; **~seeable** adj absehbar; **~shadow** [fɔː'ʃædəʊ] vt andeuten; **~sight** ['fɔːsaɪt] n Voraussicht f

forest ['fɔrɪst] n Wald m

forestall [fɔː'stɔːl] vt zuvorkommen +dat

forestry ['fɔrɪstrɪ] n Forstwirtschaft f

foretaste ['fɔːteɪst] n Vorgeschmack m

foretell [fɔː'tel] (irreg: like **tell**) vt vorhersagen

forever [fə'revəʳ] adv für immer

foreword ['fɔːwɜːd] n Vorwort m

forfeit ['fɔːfɪt] n Einbuße f ♦ vt verwirken

forgave [fə'ɡeɪv] pt of **forgive**

forge [fɔːdʒ] n Schmiede f ♦ vt fälschen; (iron) schmieden; **~ ahead**

vi Fortschritte machen; **~d** *adj* gefälscht; **~d banknotes** Blüten (*inf*) *pl*; **~r** *n* Fälscher *m*; **~ry** *n* Fälschung *f*

forget [fə'gɛt] (*pt* **forgot**, *pp* **forgotten**) *vt, vi* vergessen; **~ful** *adj* vergesslich; **~-me-not** *n* Vergissmeinnicht *nt*

forgive [fə'gɪv] (*pt* **forgave**, *pp* **forgiven**) *vt* verzeihen; **to ~ sb (for sth)** jdm (etw) verzeihen; **~ness** *n* Verzeihung *f*

forgot [fə'gɒt] *pt of* **forget**; **~ten** *pp of* **forget**

fork [fɔːk] *n* Gabel *f*; (*in road*) Gabelung *f* ♦ *vi* (*road*) sich gabeln; **~ out** (*inf*) *vt* (*pay*) blechen; **~-lift truck** *n* Gabelstapler *m*

forlorn [fə'lɔːn] *adj* (*person*) verlassen; (*hope*) vergeblich

form [fɔːm] *n* Form *f*; (*type*) Art *f*; (*figure*) Gestalt *f*; (*SCH*) Klasse *f*; (*bench*) (Schul)bank *f*; (*document*) Formular *nt* ♦ *vt* formen; (*be part of*) bilden

formal ['fɔːməl] *adj* formell; (*occasion*) offiziell; **~ly** *adv* (*ceremoniously*) formell; (*officially*) offiziell

format ['fɔːmæt] *n* Format *nt* ♦ *vt* (*COMPUT*) formatieren

formation [fɔː'meɪʃən] *n* Bildung *f*; (*AVIAT*) Formation *f*

formative ['fɔːmətɪv] *adj* (*years*) formend

former ['fɔːmə*] *adj* früher; (*opposite of latter*) erstere(r, s); **~ly** *adv* früher

formidable ['fɔːmɪdəbl] *adj* furchtbar

formula ['fɔːmjʊlə] (*pl* **~e** *or* **~s**) *n* Formel *f*; **~e** ['fɔːmjuːliː] *npl of* **formula**; **~te** ['fɔːmjuleɪt] *vt* formulieren

fort [fɔːt] *n* Feste *f*, Fort *nt*

forte ['fɔːtɪ] *n* Stärke *f*, starke Seite *f*

forth [fɔːθ] *adv*: **and so ~** und so weiter; **~coming** *adj* kommend; (*character*) entgegenkommend; **~right** *adj* offen; **~with** *adv* umgehend

fortify ['fɔːtɪfaɪ] *vt* (ver)stärken; (*protect*) befestigen

fortitude ['fɔːtɪtjuːd] *n* Seelenstärke *f*

fortnight ['fɔːtnaɪt] (*BRIT*) *n* vierzehn

Tage *pl*; **~ly** (*BRIT*) *adj* zweiwöchentlich ♦ *adv* alle vierzehn Tage

fortress ['fɔːtrɪs] *n* Festung *f*

fortunate ['fɔːtʃənɪt] *adj* glücklich; **~ly** *adv* glücklicherweise, zum Glück

fortune ['fɔːtʃən] *n* Glück *nt*; (*money*) Vermögen *nt*; **~-teller** *n* Wahrsager(in) *m(f)*

forty ['fɔːtɪ] *num* vierzig

forum ['fɔːrəm] *n* Forum *nt*

forward ['fɔːwəd] *adj* vordere(r, s); (*movement*) Vorwärts-; (*person*) vorlaut; (*planning*) Voraus- ♦ *adv* vorwärts ♦ *n* (*SPORT*) Stürmer *m* ♦ *vt* (*send*) schicken; (*help*) fördern; **~s** *adv* vorwärts

fossil ['fɒsl] *n* Fossil *nt*, Versteinerung *f*

foster ['fɒstə*] *vt* (*talent*) fördern; **~ child** *n* Pflegekind *nt*; **~ mother** *n* Pflegemutter *f*

fought [fɔːt] *pt, pp of* **fight**

foul [faul] *n* schmutzig; (*language*) gemein; (*weather*) schlecht ♦ *n* (*SPORT*) Foul *nt* ♦ *vt* (*mechanism*) blockieren; (*SPORT*) foulen; **~ play** *n* (*SPORT*) Foulspiel *nt*; (*LAW*) Verbrechen *nt*

found [faund] *pt, pp of* **find** ♦ *vt* gründen; **~ation** [faun'deɪʃən] *n* (*act*) Gründung *f*; (*fig*) Fundament *nt*; (*also*: **~ation cream**) Grundierungscreme *f*; **~ations** *npl* (*of house*) Fundament *nt*; **~er** *n* Gründer(in) *m(f)* ♦ *vi* sinken

foundry ['faundri] *n* Gießerei *f*

fountain ['fauntɪn] *n* (Spring)brunnen *m*; **~ pen** *n* Füllfederhalter *m*

four [fɔː*] *num* vier; **on all ~s** auf allen vieren; **~-poster** *n* Himmelbett *nt*; **~some** *n* Quartett *nt*; **~teen** *num* vierzehn; **~teenth** *adj* vierzehnte(r, s); **~th** *adj* vierte(r, s)

fowl [faul] *n* Huhn *nt*; (*food*) Geflügel *nt*

fox [fɒks] *n* Fuchs *m* ♦ *vt* täuschen

foyer ['fɔɪeɪ] *n* Foyer *nt*, Vorhalle *f*

fraction ['frækʃən] *n* (*MATH*) Bruch *m*; (*part*) Bruchteil *m*

fracture ['fræktʃə*] *n* (*MED*) Bruch *m* ♦ *vt* brechen

fragile ['frædʒaɪl] *adj* zerbrechlich

fragment

413

fragment ['frægmənt] n Bruchstück nt; (small part) Splitter m

fragrance ['freɪɡrəns] n Duft m; **fragrant** ['freɪɡrənt] adj duftend

frail [freɪl] adj schwach, gebrechlich

frame [freɪm] n Rahmen m; (of spectacles: also: **~s**) Gestell nt; (body) Gestalt f ♦ vt einrahmen; **to ~ sb** (inf: incriminate) jdm etwas anhängen; **~ of mind** Verfassung f; **~work** n Rahmen m; (of society) Gefüge nt

France [frɑ:ns] n Frankreich nt

franchise ['fræntʃaɪz] n (POL) (aktives) Wahlrecht nt; (COMM) Lizenz f

frank [fræŋk] adj offen ♦ vt (letter) frankieren; **~ly** adv offen gesagt

frantic ['fræntɪk] adj verzweifelt

fraternal [frə'tɜ:nl] adj brüderlich

fraternity [frə'tɜ:nɪtɪ] n (club) Vereinigung f; (spirit) Brüderlichkeit f; (US: SCH) Studentenverbindung f

fraternize ['frætənaɪz] vi fraternisieren

fraud [frɔ:d] n (trickery) Betrug m; (person) Schwindler(in) m(f); **~ulent** ['frɔ:djulənt] adj betrügerisch

fraught [frɔ:t] adj: **~ with** voller +gen

fray [freɪ] vt, vi ausfransen; **tempers were ~ed** die Gemüter waren erhitzt

freak [fri:k] n Monstrosität f ♦ cpd (storm etc) anormal

freckle ['frekl] n Sommersprosse f

free [fri:] adj frei; (loose) lose; (liberal) freigebig ♦ vt (set ~) befreien; (unblock) freimachen; **~ (of charge)** gratis, umsonst; **for ~** gratis, umsonst; **~dom** ['fri:dəm] n Freiheit f; **F~fone** ® n: **call F~fone 0800 ...** rufen Sie gebührenfrei 0800 ... an; **~-for-all** n (fight) allgemeine(s) Handgemenge nt; **~ gift** n Geschenk nt; **~ kick** n Freistoß m; **~lance** adj frei; (artist) freischaffend; **~ly** adv frei; (admit) offen; **F~post** ® n ≃ Gebühr zahlt Empfänger; **~-range** adj (hen) Freiland-; (eggs) Land-; **~ trade** n Freihandel m; **~way** (US) n Autobahn f; **~wheel** vi im Freilauf fahren; **~ will** n: **of one's**

own **~ will** aus freien Stücken

freeze [fri:z] (pt froze, pp frozen) vi gefrieren; (feel cold) frieren ♦ vt (also fig) einfrieren ♦ n (fig, FIN) Stopp m; **~r** n Tiefkühltruhe f; (in fridge) Gefrierfach nt; **freezing** adj eisig; **freezing cold** eiskalt; **freezing point** n Gefrierpunkt m

freight [freɪt] n Fracht f; **~ train** n Güterzug m

French [frentʃ] adj französisch ♦ n (LING) Französisch nt; **the ~** npl (people) die Franzosen pl; **~ bean** n grüne Bohne f; (COMM) Lizenz f; **~ fried potatoes** (BRIT) npl Pommes frites pl; **~ fries** (US) npl Pommes frites pl; **~ horn** n (MUS) (Wald)horn nt; **~ kiss** n Zungenkuss m; **~ loaf** n Baguette f; **~man/woman** (irreg) n Franzose m/Französin f; **~ window** n Verandatür f

frenzy ['frenzɪ] n Raserei f

frequency ['fri:kwənsɪ] n Häufigkeit f; (PHYS) Frequenz f

frequent [adj 'fri:kwənt, vb frɪ'kwent] adj häufig ♦ vt (regelmäßig) besuchen; **~ly** adv (often) häufig, oft

fresh [freʃ] adj frisch; **~en** vi (also: **~en up**) sich auffrischen; (person) sich frisch machen; **~er** (inf: BRIT) n (UNIV) Erstsemester nt; **~ly** adv gerade; **~man** (irreg) (US) n = fresher; **~ness** n Frische f; **~water** adj (fish) Süßwasser-

fret [fret] vi sich der Sorgen machen

friar ['fraɪə*] n Klosterbruder m

friction ['frɪkʃən] n (also fig) Reibung f

Friday ['fraɪdɪ] n Freitag m

fridge [frɪdʒ] (BRIT) n Kühlschrank m

fried [fraɪd] adj gebraten

friend [frend] n Freund(in) m(f); **~ly** adj freundlich; (relations) freundschaftlich; **~ly fire** n Beschuss m durch die eigene Seite; **~ship** n Freundschaft f

frieze [fri:z] n Fries m

frigate ['frɪɡɪt] n Fregatte f

fright [fraɪt] n Schrecken m; **to take ~** es mit der Angst zu tun bekommen; **~en** vt erschrecken; **to be ~ened**

Angst haben; **~ening** adj schrecklich;
~ful (inf) adj furchtbar

frigid ['frɪdʒɪd] adj frigide

frill [frɪl] n Rüsche f

fringe [frɪndʒ] n Besatz m; (BRIT: of hair)
Pony m; (fig) Peripherie f; **~ benefits**
npl zusätzliche Leistungen pl

Frisbee ['frɪzbi] ® n Frisbee ® nt

frisk [frɪsk] vt durchsuchen

frisky ['frɪskɪ] adj lebendig, ausgelassen

fritter ['frɪtə'] vt: **to ~ away** vergeuden

frivolous ['frɪvələs] adj frivol

frizzy ['frɪzɪ] adj kraus

fro [frəʊ] adv see to

frock [frɒk] n Kleid nt

frog [frɒg] n Frosch m; **~man** (irreg) n
Froschmann m

frolic ['frɒlɪk] vi ausgelassen sein

KEYWORD

---

from [frɒm] prep **1** (indicating starting
place) of; (indicating origin etc) aus +dat;
**a letter/telephone call from my sis-
ter** ein Brief/Anruf von meiner Schwester;
where do you come from? wo-
her kommen Sie?; **to drink from the
bottle** aus der Flasche trinken

2 (indicating time) von ... an; (: past)
seit; **from one o'clock to** or **until** or **till
two** von ein Uhr bis zwei; **from
January (on)** ab Januar

3 (indicating distance) von ... (entfernt)

4 (indicating number etc) ab +dat;
from £10 ab £10; **there were from
20 to 30 people there** es waren zwischen 20 und 30 Leute da

5 (indicating difference) **he can't tell
red from green** er kann nicht zwischen Rot und Grün unterscheiden; **to
be different from sb/sth** anders sein
als jd/etw

6 (because of, based on): **from what he
says** aus dem, was er sagt; **weak
from hunger** schwach vor Hunger

front [frʌnt] n Vorderseite f; (of house)
Fassade f; (promenade: also: **sea ~**)

Strandpromenade f; (MIL, POL, MET)
Front f; (fig: appearances) Fassade f
♦ adj (forward) vordere(r, s), Vorder-;
(first) vorderste(r, s) adj; **in ~** vorne; **in ~
of** vor; **~age** ['frʌntɪdʒ] n Vorderfront
f; **~ door** n Haustür f; **~ier** ['frʌntɪə'] n
Grenze f; **~ page** n Titelseite f; **~
room** n Wohnzimmer nt; **~
wheel drive** n Vorderradantrieb m

frost [frɒst] n Frost m; **~bite** n Erfrie-
rung f; **~ed** adj (glass) Milch-; **~y** adj
frostig

froth [frɒθ] n Schaum m

frown [fraʊn] n Stirnrunzeln nt ♦ vi die
Stirn runzeln

froze [frəʊz] pt of freeze

frozen ['frəʊzn] pp of freeze

frugal ['fruːgl] adj sparsam, bescheiden

fruit [fruːt] n inv (as collective) Obst nt;
(particular) Frucht f; **~ful** adj fruchtbar;
~ion [fruːˈɪʃən] n: **to come to ~** in
Erfüllung gehen; **~ juice** n Fruchtsaft
m; **~ machine** (BRIT) n Spielautomat
m; **~ salad** n Obstsalat m

frustrate [frʌsˈtreɪt] vt vereiteln; **~d** adj
gehemmt; (PSYCH) frustriert

fry [fraɪ] (pt, pp **fried**) vt braten ♦ npl:
small ~ kleine Fische pl; **~ing pan** n
Bratpfanne f

ft. abbr = foot; feet

fuddy-duddy ['fʌdɪdʌdɪ] n altmodi-
sche(r) Kauz m

fudge [fʌdʒ] n Fondant m

fuel ['fjuəl] n Treibstoff m; (for heating)
Brennstoff m; (for lighter) Benzin nt; **~
oil** n (diesel fuel) Heizöl nt; **~ tank** n
Tank m

fugitive ['fjuːdʒɪtɪv] n Flüchtling m

fulfil [fʊlˈfɪl] vt (duty) erfüllen; (promise)
einhalten; **~ment** n Erfüllung f

full [fʊl] adj (box, bottle, price) voll; (person: satisfied) satt; (member, power, employment) Voll-; (complete) vollständig,
Voll-; (speed) höchste(r, s); (skirt) weit
♦ adv: **~ well** sehr wohl; **in ~** vollständig; **a ~ two hours** volle zwei
Stunden; **~-length** adj (lifesize) lebens-

groß; **a ~-length photograph** eine Ganzaufnahme; **~ moon** n Vollmond m; **~-scale** adj (attack) General-; (drawing) in Originalgröße; **~ stop** n Punkt m; **~-time** adj (job) Ganztags- ♦ adv (work) ganztags ♦ n (SPORT) Spielschluss nt; **~y** adv völlig; **~ fledged** adj (also fig) flügge; **~ licensed** adj (hotel, restaurant) mit voller Schankkonzession or -erlaubnis

fumble ['fʌmbl] vi: **to ~ (with)** herumfummeln (an +dat)

fume [fju:m] vi qualmen; (fig) kochen (inf); **~s** npl (of fuel, car) Abgase pl

fumigate ['fju:mɪgeɪt] vt ausräuchern

fun [fʌn] n Spaß m; **to make ~ of** sich lustig machen über +acc

function ['fʌŋkʃən] n Funktion f; (occasion) Veranstaltung f ♦ vi funktionieren; **~al** adj funktionell

fund [fʌnd] n (money) Geldmittel pl, Fonds m; (store) Vorrat m; **~s** npl (resources) Mittel pl

fundamental [fʌndə'mentl] adj fundamental, grundlegend

funeral ['fju:nərəl] n Beerdigung f; **~ parlour** n Leichenhalle f; **~ service** n Trauergottesdienst m

funfair ['fʌnfɛəʳ] (BRIT) n Jahrmarkt m

fungi ['fʌŋgaɪ] npl of **fungus**

fungus ['fʌŋgəs] n Pilz m

funnel ['fʌnl] n Trichter m; (NAUT) Schornstein m

funny ['fʌnɪ] adj komisch

fur [fəːʳ] n Pelz m; **~ coat** n Pelzmantel m

furious ['fjʊərɪəs] adj wütend; (attempt) heftig

furlong ['fəːlɒŋ] n = 201.17 m

furnace ['fəːnɪs] n (Brenn)ofen m

furnish ['fəːnɪʃ] vt einrichten; (supply) versehen; **~ings** npl Einrichtung f

furniture ['fəːnɪtʃəʳ] n Möbel pl; **piece of ~** Möbelstück nt

furrow ['fʌrəʊ] n Furche f

furry ['fəːrɪ] adj (tongue) pelzig; (animal) Pelz-

further ['fəːðəʳ] adj weitere(r, s) ♦ adv weiter ♦ vt fördern; **~ education** n Weiterbildung f; Erwachsenenbildung f; **~more** adv ferner

furthest ['fəːðɪst] superl of **far**

furtive ['fəːtɪv] adj verstohlen

fury ['fjʊərɪ] n Wut f, Zorn m

fuse [fju:z] (US **fuze**) n (ELEC) Sicherung f; (of bomb) Zünder m ♦ vt verschmelzen ♦ vi (BRIT: ELEC) durchbrennen; **~ box** n Sicherungskasten m

fuselage ['fju:zəlɑːʒ] n Flugzeugrumpf m

fusion ['fju:ʒən] n Verschmelzung f

fuss [fʌs] n Theater nt; **~y** adj kleinlich

futile ['fju:taɪl] adj zwecklos, sinnlos; **futility** [fju:'tɪlɪtɪ] n Zwecklosigkeit f

future ['fju:tʃəʳ] adj zukünftig ♦ n Zukunft f; **in (the) ~** in Zukunft

fuze [fju:z] (US) = **fuse**

fuzzy ['fʌzɪ] adj (indistinct) verschwommen; (hair) kraus

G, g

G [dʒiː] n (MUS) G nt

G7 n abbr (= Group of Seven) G7 f

gabble ['gæbl] vi plappern

gable ['geɪbl] n Giebel m

gadget ['gædʒɪt] n Vorrichtung f

Gaelic ['geɪlɪk] adj gälisch ♦ n (LING) Gälisch nt

gaffe [gæf] n Fauxpas m

gag [gæg] n Knebel m; (THEAT) Gag m ♦ vt knebeln

gaiety ['geɪtɪ] n Fröhlichkeit f

gain [geɪn] vt (obtain) erhalten; (win) gewinnen ♦ vi (clock) vorgehen ♦ vt Gewinn m; **to ~ in sth** an etw dat gewinnen; **~ on** vt fus einholen

gait [geɪt] n Gang m

gal. abbr = **gallon**

gala ['gɑːlə] n Fest nt

galaxy ['gæləksɪ] n Sternsystem nt

gale [geɪl] n Sturm m

gallant ['gælənt] adj tapfer; (polite) galant

gallbladder [ˈgɔːl-] n Gallenblase f

gallery [ˈgælərɪ] n (also: **art** ~) Galerie f

galley [ˈgælɪ] n (ship's kitchen) Kombüse f; (ship) Galeere f

gallon [ˈgælən] n Gallone f

gallop [ˈgæləp] n Galopp m ♦ vi galoppieren

gallows [ˈgæləʊz] n Galgen m

gallstone [ˈgɔːlstəʊn] n Gallenstein m

galore [gəˈlɔːr] adv in Hülle und Fülle

galvanize [ˈgælvənaɪz] vt (metal) galvanisieren; (fig) elektrisieren

gambit [ˈgæmbɪt] n (fig: **opening** ~) (einleitende(r)) Schachzug m

gamble [ˈgæmbl] vi (um Geld) spielen ♦ vt (risk) aufs Spiel setzen ♦ n Risiko nt; ~**r** n Spieler(in) m(f); **gambling** n Glücksspiel nt

game [geɪm] n Spiel nt; (hunting) Wild nt ♦ adj: ~ (**for**) bereit (zu); ~**keeper** n Wildhüter m; ~**s console** n (COMPUT) Gameboy m ®, Konsole f

gammon [ˈgæmən] n geräucherte(r) Schinken m

gamut [ˈgæmət] n Tonskala f

gang [gæŋ] n (of criminals, youths) Bande f; (of workmen) Kolonne f ♦ vi: **to ~ up on sb** sich gegen jdn verschwören

gangrene [ˈgæŋgriːn] n Brand m

gangster [ˈgæŋstər] n Gangster m

gangway [ˈgæŋweɪ] n (NAUT) Laufplanke f; (aisle) Gang m

gaol [dʒeɪl] (BRIT) n, vt = **jail**

gap [gæp] n Lücke f

gape [geɪp] vi glotzen; **gaping** [ˈgeɪpɪŋ] adj (wound) klaffend; (hole) gähnend

garage [ˈgæraːʒ] n Garage f; (for repair) (Auto)reparaturwerkstatt f; (for petrol) Tankstelle f

garbage [ˈgaːbɪdʒ] n Abfall m; ~ **can** (US) n Mülltonne f

garbled [ˈgaːbld] adj (story) verdreht

garden [ˈgaːdn] n Garten m; ~**s** npl (public park) Park m; (private) Gartenanlagen pl; ~**er** n Gärtner(in) m(f);

~**ing** n Gärtnern nt

gargle [ˈgaːgl] vi gurgeln

gargoyle [ˈgaːgɔɪl] n Wasserspeier m

garish [ˈgeərɪʃ] adj grell

garland [ˈgaːlənd] n Girlande f

garlic [ˈgaːlɪk] n Knoblauch m

garment [ˈgaːmənt] n Kleidungsstück nt

garnish [ˈgaːnɪʃ] vt (food) garnieren

garrison [ˈgærɪsn] n Garnison f

garter [ˈgaːtər] n Strumpfband nt; (US) Strumpfhalter m

gas [gæs] n Gas nt; (esp US: petrol) Benzin nt ♦ vt vergasen; ~ **cooker** (BRIT) n Gasherd m; ~ **cylinder** n Gasflasche f; ~ **fire** n Gasofen m

gash [gæʃ] n klaffende Wunde f ♦ vt tief verwunden

gasket [ˈgæskɪt] n Dichtungsring m

gas mask n Gasmaske f

gas meter n Gaszähler m

gasoline [ˈgæsəliːn] (US) n Benzin nt

gasp [gaːsp] vi keuchen; (in surprise) tief Luft holen ♦ n Keuchen nt

gas: ~ ring n Gasring m; ~ **station** (US) n Tankstelle f; ~ **tap** n Gashahn m

gastric [ˈgæstrɪk] adj Magen-

gate [geɪt] n Tor nt; (barrier) Schranke f

gateau [ˈgætəʊ] (pl ~**x**) n Torte f

gatecrash [ˈgeɪtkræʃ] (BRIT) vt (party) platzen in +acc

gateway [ˈgeɪtweɪ] n Toreingang m

gather [ˈgæðər] vt (people) versammeln; (things) sammeln; (understand) annehmen ♦ vi (assemble) sich versammeln; **to ~ speed** schneller werden; **to ~ (from)** schließen (aus); ~**ing** n Versammlung f

gauche [gəʊʃ] adj linkisch

gaudy [ˈgɔːdɪ] adj schreiend

gauge [geɪdʒ] n (instrument) Messgerät nt; (RAIL) Spurweite f; (dial) Anzeiger m; (measure) Maß nt ♦ vt (ab)messen; (fig) abschätzen

gaunt [gɔːnt] adj hager

gauze [gɔːz] n Gaze f

gave [geɪv] pt of **give**

gay [geɪ] adj (homosexual) schwul; (lively) lustig

gaze [geɪz] n Blick m ♦ vi starren; **to ~ at sth** etw dat anstarren

gazelle [gə'zel] n Gazelle f

gazumping [gə'zʌmpɪŋ] (BRIT) n Hausverkauf an Höherbietenden trotz Zusage an anderen

GB n abbr = **Great Britain**

GCE (BRIT) n abbr = **General Certificate of Education**

GCSE (BRIT) n abbr = **General Certificate of Secondary Education**

gear [gɪə] n Getriebe nt; (equipment) Ausrüstung f; (AUT) Gang m ♦ vt (fig: adapt): **to be ~ed to** ausgerichtet sein auf +acc; **top ~** höchste(r) Gang m; **high ~** (US) höchste(r) Gang m; **low ~** niedrige(r) Gang m; **in ~** eingekuppelt; **~ box** n Getriebe(gehäuse) nt; **~ lever** n Schalthebel m; **~ shift** (US) n Schalthebel m

geese [giːs] npl of **goose**

gel [dʒel] n Gel nt

gelatin(e) ['dʒelətiːn] n Gelatine f

gem [dʒem] n Edelstein m; (fig) Juwel nt

Gemini ['dʒemɪnaɪ] n Zwillinge pl

gender ['dʒendə] n (GRAM) Geschlecht nt

gene [dʒiːn] n Gen nt

general ['dʒenərəl] n General m ♦ adj allgemein; **~ delivery** (US) n Ausgabe(schalter) m postlagernder Sendungen; **~ election** n allgemeine Wahlen pl; **~ize** vi verallgemeinern; **~ knowledge** n Allgemeinwissen nt; **~ly** adv allgemein, im Allgemeinen; **~ practitioner** n praktische(r) Arzt m, praktische Ärztin f

generate ['dʒenəreɪt] vt erzeugen

generation [dʒenə'reɪʃən] n Generation f; (act) Erzeugung f

generator ['dʒenəreɪtə] n Generator m

generosity [dʒenə'rɔsɪtɪ] n Großzügigkeit f

generous ['dʒenərəs] adj großzügig

genetic [dʒɪ'netɪk] adj genetisch; **~ally** adv genetisch; **~ally modified** genmanipuliert; **~ engineering** n Gentechnik f; **~ fingerprinting** ['fɪŋɡəprɪntɪŋ] n genetische Fingerabdrücke pl

genetics [dʒɪ'netɪks] n Genetik f

Geneva [dʒɪ'niːvə] n Genf nt

genial ['dʒiːnɪəl] adj freundlich, jovial

genitals ['dʒenɪtlz] npl Genitalien pl

genius ['dʒiːnɪəs] n Genie nt

genocide ['dʒenəsaɪd] n Völkermord m

gent [dʒent] n abbr = **gentleman**

genteel [dʒen'tiːl] adj (polite) wohlanständig; (affected) affektiert

gentle ['dʒentl] adj sanft, zart

gentleman ['dʒentlmən] (irreg) n Herr m; (polite) Gentleman m

gentleness ['dʒentlnɪs] n Zartheit f, Milde f

gently ['dʒentlɪ] adv zart, sanft

gentry ['dʒentrɪ] n Landadel m

gents [dʒents] n: **G~** (lavatory) Herren pl

genuine ['dʒenjuɪn] adj echt

geographic(al) [dʒɪə'ɡræfɪk(l)] adj geografisch

geography [dʒɪ'ɔɡrəfɪ] n Geografie f

geological [dʒɪə'lɔdʒɪkl] adj geologisch

geology [dʒɪ'ɔlədʒɪ] n Geologie f

geometric(al) [dʒɪə'metrɪk(l)] adj geometrisch

geometry [dʒɪ'ɔmɪtrɪ] n Geometrie f

geranium [dʒɪ'reɪnɪəm] n Geranie f

geriatric [dʒerɪ'ætrɪk] adj Alten- ♦ n Greis(in) m(f)

germ [dʒɜːm] n Keim m; (MED) Bazillus m

German ['dʒɜːmən] adj deutsch ♦ n Deutsche(r) f(m); (LING) Deutsch nt; **~ measles** n Röteln pl; **~y** n Deutschland nt

germination [dʒɜːmɪ'neɪʃən] n Keimen nt

gesticulate [dʒes'tɪkjuleɪt] vi gestiku-
lieren
gesture ['dʒestʃəʳ] n Geste f

> KEYWORD

get [get] (pt, pp **got**, pp **gotten** (US)) vi 1
(become, be) werden; **to get old/tired**
alt/müde werden; **to get married** heiraten
2 (go) (an)kommen, gehen
3 (begin): **to get to know sb** jdn kennen lernen; **let's get going** or **started!**
fangen wir an!
4 (modal aux vb): **you've got to do it**
du musst es tun
♦ vt 1: **to get sth done** (do) etw machen; (have done) etw machen lassen;
to get sth going or **to get sth in Gang
bringen** or bekommen; **to get sb to
do sth** jdn dazu bringen, etw zu tun
2 (obtain: money, permission, results) erhalten; (find: job, flat) finden; (fetch:
person, object) holen; **to get sth for sb**
jdm etw besorgen; **get me Mr Jones,
please** (TEL) verbinden Sie mich bitte
mit Mr Jones
3 (receive: present, letter) bekommen,
kriegen; (acquire: reputation etc) erwerben
4 (catch) bekommen, kriegen; (hit: target etc) treffen, erwischen; **get him!**
(to dog) fass!
5 (take, move) bringen; **to get sth to
sb** jdm etw bringen
6 (understand) verstehen; (hear) mitbekommen; **I've got it!** ich hab's!
7 (have, possess): **to have got sth** etw
haben
get about vi herumkommen; (news)
sich verbreiten
get along vi (people) (gut) zurechtkommen; (depart) sich acc auf den
Weg machen
get at vt (facts) herausbekommen; **to
get at sb** (nag) an jdm herumnörgeln
get away vi (leave) sich acc davonmachen; (escape): **to get away from sth**

von etw dat entkommen; **to get away
with sth** mit etw davonkommen
get back vi (return) zurückkommen
♦ vt zurückbekommen
get by vi (pass) vorbeikommen;
(manage) zurechtkommen
get down vi (her)untergehen ♦ vt
(depress) fertig machen; **to get down
to** in Angriff nehmen; (find time to do)
kommen zu
get in vi (train) ankommen; (arrive
home) heimkommen
get into vt (enter) hinein-/
hereinkommen in +acc; (: car, train etc)
einsteigen in +acc; (clothes) anziehen
get off vi (from train etc) aussteigen;
(from horse) absteigen ♦ vt aussteigen
aus; absteigen von
get on vi (progress) vorankommen;
(be friends) auskommen; (age) alt werden; (onto train etc) einsteigen; (onto
horse) aufsteigen ♦ vt einsteigen in
+acc; etw auf etw acc aufsteigen
get out vi (of house) herauskommen;
(of vehicle) aussteigen ♦ vt (take out)
herausholen
get out of vt (duty etc) herumkommen um
get over vt (illness) sich acc erholen
von; (surprise) verkraften; (news) fassen; (loss) sich abfinden mit
get round vt herumkommen; (fig:
person) herumkriegen
get through to vi (TEL) durchkommen zu
get together vi zusammenkommen
get up vi aufstehen ♦ vt hinaufbrin-
gen; (go up) hinaufgehen; (organize)
auf die Beine stellen
get up to vt (reach) erreichen; (prank
etc) anstellen

getaway ['getəweɪ] n Flucht f
get-up ['getʌp] (inf) n Aufzug m
geyser ['giːzəʳ] n Geiser m; (heater)
Durchlauferhitzer m

ghastly ['gɑːstlɪ] adj grässlich

gherkin ['gə:kɪn] n Gewürzgurke f

ghetto ['gɛtəu] n G(h)etto nt; **~ blaster** n (große(r)) Radiorekorder m

ghost [gəust] n Gespenst nt

giant ['dʒaɪənt] n Riese m ♦ adj riesig, Riesen-

gibberish ['dʒɪbərɪʃ] n dumme(s) Geschwätz nt

gibe [dʒaɪb] n spöttische Bemerkung f

giblets ['dʒɪblɪts] npl Geflügelinnereien pl

giddiness ['gɪdɪnɪs] n Schwindelgefühl nt

giddy ['gɪdɪ] adj schwindlig

gift [gɪft] n Geschenk nt; (ability) Begabung f; **~ed** adj begabt; **~ shop** n Geschenkladen m; **~ token, ~ voucher** n Geschenkgutschein m

gigantic [dʒaɪ'gæntɪk] adj riesenhaft

giggle ['gɪgl] vi kichern ♦ n Gekicher nt

gild [gɪld] vt vergolden

gill [dʒɪl] n (1/4 pint) Viertelpinte f

gills [gɪlz] npl (of fish) Kiemen pl

gilt [gɪlt] n Vergoldung f ♦ adj vergoldet; **~-edged** adj mündelsicher

gimmick ['gɪmɪk] n Gag m

gin [dʒɪn] n Gin m

ginger ['dʒɪndʒər] n Ingwer m; **~ ale** n Ingwerbier nt; **~ beer** n Ingwerbier nt; **~bread** n Pfefferkuchen m; **~-haired** adj rothaarig

gingerly ['dʒɪndʒəlɪ] adv behutsam

gipsy ['dʒɪpsɪ] n Zigeuner(in) m(f)

giraffe [dʒɪ'rɑːf] n Giraffe f

girder ['gə:dər] n Eisenträger m

girdle ['gə:dl] n Hüftgürtel m

girl [gə:l] n Mädchen nt; **an English ~** eine (junge) Engländerin; **~friend** n Freundin f; **~ish** adj mädchenhaft

giro ['dʒaɪrəu] n (bank ~) Giro nt; (post office ~) Postscheckverkehr m

girth [gə:θ] n (measure) Umfang m; (strap) Sattelgurt m

gist [dʒɪst] n Wesentliche(s) nt

give [gɪv] (pt **gave**, pp **given**) vt geben ♦ vi (break) nachgeben; **~ away** vt verschenken; (betray) verraten; **~**

back vt zurückgeben; **~ in** vi nachgeben ♦ vt (hand in) abgeben; **~ off** vt abgeben; **~ out** vt verteilen; (announce) bekannt geben; **~ up** vt, vi aufgeben; **to ~ o.s. up** sich stellen; (after siege) sich ergeben; **~ way** vi (BRIT: traffic) Vorfahrt lassen; (to feelings): **to ~ way to** nachgeben +dat

glacier ['glæsɪər] n Gletscher m

glad [glæd] adj froh; **~ly** ['glædlɪ] adv gern(e)

glamorous ['glæmərəs] adj reizvoll

glamour ['glæmər] n Glanz m

glance [glɑːns] n Blick m ♦ vi: **to ~ (at)** (hin)blicken (auf +acc); **~ off** vt fus (fly off) abprallen von; **glancing** ['glɑːnsɪŋ] adj (blow) Streif-

gland [glænd] n Drüse f

glare [glɛər] n (light) grelle(s) Licht nt; (stare) wilde(r) Blick m ♦ vi grell scheinen; (angrily): **to ~ at** böse ansehen; **glaring** ['glɛərɪŋ] adj (injustice) schreiend; (mistake) krass

glass [glɑːs] n Glas nt; (mirror: also: **looking ~**) Spiegel m; **~es** npl (spectacles) Brille f; **~house** n Gewächshaus nt; **~ware** n Glaswaren pl; **~y** adj glasig

glaze [gleɪz] vt verglasen; (finish with a ~) glasieren ♦ n Glasur f; **~d** adj (eye) glasig; (pot) glasiert; **glazier** ['gleɪzɪər] n Glaser m

gleam [gliːm] n Schimmer m ♦ vi schimmern

glean [gliːn] vt (fig) ausfindig machen

glen [glɛn] n Bergtal nt

glib [glɪb] adj oberflächlich

glide [glaɪd] vi gleiten; **~r** n (AVIAT) Segelflugzeug nt; **gliding** ['glaɪdɪŋ] n Segelfliegen nt

glimmer ['glɪmər] n Schimmer m

glimpse [glɪmps] n flüchtige(r) Blick m ♦ vt flüchtig erblicken

glint [glɪnt] n Glitzern nt ♦ vi glitzern

glisten ['glɪsn] vi glänzen

glitter ['glɪtər] vi funkeln ♦ n Funkeln nt

gloat [gləut] vi: **to ~ over** sich weiden an +dat

global ['gləʊbl] adj: ~ **warming** globale(r) Temperaturanstieg m

globe [gləʊb] n Erdball m; (sphere) Globus m

gloom [gluːm] n (darkness) Dunkel nt; (depression) düstere Stimmung f; **~y** adj düster

glorify ['glɔːrɪfaɪ] vt verherrlichen

glorious ['glɔːrɪəs] adj glorreich

glory ['glɔːrɪ] n Ruhm m

gloss [glɒs] n (shine) Glanz m; ~ **over** vt fus übertünchen

glossary ['glɒsərɪ] n Glossar m

glossy ['glɒsɪ] adj (surface) glänzend

glove [glʌv] n Handschuh m; ~ **compartment** n (AUT) Handschuhfach nt

glow [gləʊ] vi Glühen nt

glower ['glaʊər] vi: **to ~** at finster anblicken

glucose ['gluːkəʊs] n Traubenzucker m

glue [gluː] n Klebstoff m ♦ vt kleben

glum [glʌm] adj bedrückt

glut [glʌt] n Überfluss m

glutton ['glʌtn] n Vielfraß m; **a ~ for work** ein Arbeitstier nt

glycerin(e) ['glɪsəriːn] n Glyzerin nt

GM abbr = **genetically modified**

gnarled [nɑːld] adj knorrig

gnat [næt] n Stechmücke f

gnaw [nɔː] vt nagen an +dat

gnome [nəʊm] n Gnom m

go [gəʊ] (pt **went**, pp **gone**, pl **~es**) vi gehen; (travel) reisen, fahren; (depart: train) (ab)fahren; (be sold) verkauft werden; (work) gehen, funktionieren; (fit, suit) passen; (become) werden; (break etc) nachgeben ♦ n (energy) Schwung m; (attempt) Versuch m; **he's ~ing to do it** er wird es tun; **to ~ for a walk** spazieren gehen; **to ~ dancing** tanzen gehen; **how did I ~?** wie war's?; **to ~ with** (be suitable) passen zu; **to have a ~ at sth** sich versuchen an +dat; **to be on the ~** auf Trab sein; **whose ~ is it?** wer ist dran?; **~ about** vi (rumour) umgehen ♦ vt fus: **how do I ~ about this?** wie packe ich das an?; **~ after** vt fus (pursue: person) nachgehen +dat; **~ ahead** vi (proceed) weitergehen; **~ along** vi dahingehen, dahinfahren ♦ vt entlanggehen, entlangfahren; **to ~ along with** (support) zustimmen +dat; **~ away** vi (depart) weggehen; **~ back** vi (return) zurückgehen; **~ back on** vt fus (promise) nicht halten; **~ by** vi (years, time) vergehen ♦ vt fus sich richten nach; **~ down** vi (sun) untergehen ♦ vt fus hinuntergehen, hinunterfahren; **~ for** vt fus (fetch) holen (gehen); (like) mögen; (attack) sich stürzen auf +acc; **~ in** vi hineingehen; **~ in for** vt fus (competition) teilnehmen an; **~ into** vt fus (enter) hineingehen in +acc; (study) sich befassen mit; **~ off** vi (depart) weggehen; (lights) ausgehen; (milk etc) sauer werden; (explode) losgehen ♦ vt fus (dislike) nicht mehr mögen; **~ on** vi (continue) weitergehen; (inf: complain) meckern; (lights) angehen; **to ~ on with sth** mit etw weitermachen; **~ out** vi (fire, light) ausgehen; (of house) hinausgehen; **~ over** vi (ship) kentern ♦ vt fus (examine, check) durchgehen; **~ past** vi: **to ~ past sth** an etw vorbeigehen; **~ round** vi (visit): **to ~ round (to sb's)** (bei jdm) vorbeigehen; **~ through** vt fus (town etc) durchgehen, durchfahren; **~ up** vi (price) steigen; **~ with** vt fus (suit) zu etw passen; **~ without** vt fus sich behelfen ohne; (food) entbehren

goad [gəʊd] vt anstacheln

go-ahead ['gəʊəhed] adj zielstrebig; (progressive) fortschrittlich ♦ n grüne(s) Licht nt

goal [gəʊl] n Ziel nt; (SPORT) Tor nt; **~keeper** n Torwart m; **~ post** n Torpfosten m

goat [gəʊt] n Ziege f

gobble ['gɒbl] vt (also: **~ down, ~ up**) hinunterschlingen

go-between ['gəʊbɪtwiːn] n Mittelsmann m

god [gɔd] n Gott m; **G~** n Gott m; **~child** n Patenkind nt; **~daughter** n Patentochter f; **~dess** n Göttin f; **~father** n Pate m; **~forsaken** adj gottverlassen; **~mother** n Patin f; **~send** n Geschenk nt des Himmels; **~son** n Patensohn m

goggles ['gɔglz] npl Schutzbrille f

going ['gəʊɪŋ] n (HORSE-RACING) Bahn f ♦ adj (rate) gängig; (concern) gut gehend; **it's hard ~** es ist schwierig

gold [gəʊld] n Gold nt ♦ adj golden; **~en** adj golden, Gold-; **~fish** n Goldfisch m; **~ mine** n Goldgrube f; **~plated** adj vergoldet; **~smith** n Goldschmied(in) m(f)

golf [gɔlf] n Golf nt; **~ ball** n Golfball m; (on typewriter) Kugelkopf m; **~ club** n (society) Golfklub m; (stick) Golfschläger m; **~ course** n Golfplatz m; **~er** n Golfspieler(in) m(f)

gondola ['gɔndələ] n Gondel f

gone [gɔn] pp of **go**

gong [gɔŋ] n Gong m

good [gʊd] n (benefit) Wohl nt; (moral excellence) Güte f ♦ adj gut; **~s** npl (merchandise etc) Waren pl, Güter pl; **a ~ deal (of)** ziemlich viel; **a ~ many** ziemlich viele; **~ morning!** guten Morgen!; **~ afternoon!** guten Tag!; **~ evening!** guten Abend!; **~ night!** gute Nacht!; **would you be ~ enough to ...?** könnten Sie bitte ...?

goodbye [gʊd'baɪ] excl auf Wiedersehen!

good: G~ Friday n Karfreitag m; **~-looking** adj gut aussehend; **~natured** adj gutmütig; (joke) harmlos; **~ness** n Güte f; (virtue) Tugend f; **~s train** (BRIT) n Güterzug m; **~will** n (favour) Wohlwollen nt; (COMM) Firmenansehen nt

goose [guːs] (pl **geese**) n Gans f

gooseberry ['gʊzbərɪ] n Stachelbeere f

gooseflesh ['guːsfleʃ] n Gänsehaut f

goose pimples npl Gänsehaut f

gore [gɔːʳ] vt aufspießen ♦ n Blut nt

gorge [gɔːdʒ] n Schlucht f ♦ vt: **to ~ o.s.** (sich voll) fressen

gorgeous ['gɔːdʒəs] adj prächtig

gorilla [gə'rɪlə] n Gorilla m

gorse [gɔːs] n Stechginster m

gory ['gɔːrɪ] adj blutig

go-slow ['gəʊ'sləʊ] (BRIT) n Bummelstreik m

gospel ['gɔspl] n Evangelium nt

gossip ['gɔsɪp] n Klatsch m; (person) Klatschbase f ♦ vi klatschen

got [gɔt] pt, pp of **get**

gotten ['gɔtn] (US) pp of **get**

gout [gaʊt] n Gicht f

govern ['gʌvən] vt regieren; verwalten

governess ['gʌvənɪs] n Gouvernante f

government ['gʌvnmənt] n Regierung f

governor ['gʌvənəʳ] n Gouverneur m

gown [gaʊn] n Gewand nt; (UNIV) Robe f

G.P. n abbr = **general practitioner**

grab [græb] vt packen

grace [greɪs] n Anmut f; (blessing) Gnade f; (prayer) Tischgebet nt ♦ vt (adorn) zieren; (honour) auszeichnen; **5 days' ~** 5 Tage Aufschub; **~ful** adj anmutig

gracious ['greɪʃəs] adj gnädig; (kind) freundlich

grade [greɪd] n Grad m; (slope) Gefälle nt ♦ vt (classify) einstufen; **~ crossing** (US) n Bahnübergang m; **~ school** (US) n Grundschule f

gradient ['greɪdɪənt] n Steigung f; Gefälle nt

gradual ['grædjʊəl] adj allmählich; **~ly** adv allmählich

graduate [n 'grædjuət, vb 'grædjueɪt] n: **to be a ~** das Staatsexamen haben ♦ vi das Staatsexamen machen; **graduation** [grædju'eɪʃən] n Abschlussfeier f

graffiti [grə'fiːtɪ] n Graffiti pl

graft [grɑːft] n (hard work) Schufterei f; (MED) Verpflanzung f ♦ vt pfropfen; (fig) aufpfropfen; (MED) verpflanzen

grain [greɪn] n Korn nt; (in wood) Maserung f

gram [græm] n Gramm nt

grammar ['græmə*] n Grammatik f; **~ school** (BRIT) n Gymnasium nt; **grammatical** [grə'mætɪkl] adj grammat(ikal)isch

gramme [græm] n = **gram**

granary ['grænərɪ] n Kornspeicher m

grand [grænd] adj großartig; **~child** (pl **~children**) n Enkelkind nt, Enkel(in) m(f); **~dad** n Opa m; **~daughter** n Enkelin f; **~eur** ['grændjə*] n Erhabenheit f; **~father** n Großvater m; **~iose** ['grændɪəus] adj (imposing) großartig; (pompous) schwülstig; **~ma** n Oma f; **~mother** n Großmutter f; **~pa** n = **granddad**; **~parents** npl Großeltern pl; **~ piano** n Flügel m; **~son** n Enkel m; **~stand** n Haupttribüne f

granite ['grænɪt] n Granit m

granny ['grænɪ] n Oma f

grant [grɑːnt] vt gewähren ♦ n Unterstützung f; (UNIV) Stipendium nt; **to take sth for ~ed** etw als selbstverständlich (an)nehmen

granulated sugar ['grænjuleitid-] n Zuckerraffinade f

granule ['grænjuːl] n Körnchen nt

grape [greɪp] n (Wein)traube f

grapefruit ['greɪpfruːt] n Pampelmuse f, Grapefruit f

graph [grɑːf] n Schaubild nt; **~ic** ['græfɪk] adj (descriptive) anschaulich; (drawing) grafisch; **~ics** npl Grafik f

grapple ['græpl] vi: **to ~ with** kämpfen mit

grasp [grɑːsp] vt ergreifen; (understand) begreifen ♦ n Griff m; (of subject) Beherrschung f; **~ing** adj habgierig

grass [grɑːs] n Gras nt; **~hopper** n Heuschrecke f; **~land** nt Weideland nt; **~roots** adj an der Basis; **~ snake** n Ringelnatter f

grate [greɪt] n Kamin m ♦ vi (sound) knirschen ♦ vt (cheese etc) reiben; **to ~ on the nerves** auf die Nerven gehen

grateful ['greɪtful] adj dankbar

grater ['greɪtə*] n Reibe f

gratify ['grætɪfaɪ] vt befriedigen; **~ing** adj erfreulich

grating ['greɪtɪŋ] n (iron bars) Gitter nt ♦ adj (noise) knirschend

gratitude ['grætɪtjuːd] n Dankbarkeit f

gratuity [grə'tjuːɪtɪ] n Gratifikation f

grave [greɪv] n Grab nt ♦ adj (serious) ernst

gravel ['grævl] n Kies m

gravestone ['greɪvstəun] n Grabstein m

graveyard ['greɪvjɑːd] n Friedhof m

gravity ['grævɪtɪ] n Schwerkraft f; (seriousness) Schwere f

gravy ['greɪvɪ] n (Braten)soße f

gray [greɪ] adj = **grey**

graze [greɪz] vi grasen ♦ vt (touch) streifen; (MED) abschürfen ♦ n Abschürfung f

grease [griːs] n (in fat) Fett nt; (lubricant) Schmiere f ♦ vt (ab)schmieren; **~proof** (BRIT) adj (paper) Butterbrot-; **greasy** ['griːsɪ] adj fettig

great [greɪt] adj groß; (inf: good) prima; **G~ Britain** n Großbritannien nt; **~-grandfather** n Urgroßvater m; **~-grandmother** n Urgroßmutter f; **~-ly** adv sehr

Greece [griːs] n Griechenland nt

greed [griːd] n (also: **~iness**) Gier f; (meanness) Geiz m; **~(iness) for** Gier nach; **~y** adj gierig

Greek [griːk] adj griechisch ♦ n Grieche m, Griechin f; (LING) Griechisch nt

green [griːn] adj grün ♦ n (village ~) Dorfwiese f; **~ belt** n Grüngürtel m; **~ card** n (AUT) grüne Versicherungskarte f; **~ery** n Grün nt; grüne(s) Laub nt; **~gage** n Reneklode f, Reineclaude f; **~grocer** (BRIT) n Obst- und Gemüsehändler m; **~house** n Gewächshaus nt; **~house effect** n Treibhauseffekt m; **~house gas** n Treibhausgas nt

Greenland ['griːnlənd] n Grönland nt

greet [griːt] vt grüßen; **~ing** n Gruß m

~ing(s) card n Glückwunschkarte f

gregarious [grə'gɛərɪəs] adj gesellig

grenade [grə'neɪd] n Granate f

grew [gruː] pt of **grow**

grey [greɪ] adj grau; **~-haired** adj grauhaarig; **~hound** n Windhund m

grid [grɪd] n Gitter nt; (ELEC) Leitungsnetz nt; (on map) Gitternetz nt

gridlock ['grɪdlɔk] n (AUT: traffic jam) totale(r) Stau m; **~ed** adj: **to be ~ed** (roads) total verstopft sein; (talks etc) festgefahren sein

grief [griːf] n Gram m, Kummer m

grievance ['griːvəns] n Beschwerde f

grieve [griːv] vi sich grämen ♦ vt betrüben

grievous ['griːvəs] adj: **~ bodily harm** (JUR) schwere Körperverletzung f

grill [grɪl] n Grill m ♦ vt (BRIT) grillen; (question) in die Mangel nehmen

grille [grɪl] n (AUT) (Kühler)gitter nt

grim [grɪm] adj grim, (situation) düster

grimace [grɪ'meɪs] n Grimasse f ♦ vi Grimassen schneiden

grime [graɪm] n Schmutz m; **grimy** ['graɪmɪ] adj schmutzig

grin [grɪn] n Grinsen nt ♦ vi grinsen

grind [graɪnd] (pt, pp **ground**) vt mahlen; (US: meat) durch den Fleischwolf drehen; (sharpen) schleifen; (teeth) knirschen mit ♦ n (fig) Plackerei f

grip [grɪp] n Griff m; (suitcase) Handkoffer m ♦ vt packen; **~ping** adj (exciting) spannend

grisly ['grɪzlɪ] adj grässlich

gristle ['grɪsl] n Knorpel m

grit [grɪt] n Splitt m; (courage) Mut m ♦ vt (teeth) zusammenbeißen; (road) (mit Splitt be)streuen

groan [grəʊn] n Stöhnen nt ♦ vi stöhnen

grocer ['grəʊsə'] n Lebensmittelhändler m; **~ies** npl Lebensmittel pl; **~'s (shop)** n Lebensmittelgeschäft nt

groggy ['grɔgɪ] adj benommen

groin [grɔɪn] n Leistengegend f

groom [gruːm] n (also: **bridegroom**) Bräutigam m; (for horses) Pferdeknecht m ♦ vt (horse) striegeln; **(well-)~ed** adj gepflegt

groove [gruːv] n Rille f, Furche f

grope [grəʊp] vi tasten; **~ for** vt fus suchen nach

gross [grəʊs] adj (coarse) dick, plump; (bad) grob, schwer; (COMM) brutto; **~ly** adv höchst

grotesque [grə'tɛsk] adj grotesk

grotto ['grɔtəʊ] n Grotte f

ground [graʊnd] pt, pp of **grind** ♦ n Boden m; (land) Grundbesitz m; (reason) Grund m; (US: also: **~ wire**) Endleitung f ♦ vt (run ashore) stranden, auflaufen; **~s** npl (dregs) Bodensatz m; (around house) (Garten)anlagen pl; on the **~** am Boden; to the **~** zu Boden; **to gain/lose ~** Boden gewinnen/verlieren; **~ cloth** (US) n = **groundsheet**; **~ing** n (instruction) Anfangsunterricht m; **~less** adj grundlos; **~sheet** (BRIT) n Zeltboden m; **~ staff** n Bodenpersonal nt; **~work** n Grundlage f

group [gruːp] n Gruppe f ♦ vt (also: **~ together**) gruppieren ♦ vi sich gruppieren

grouse [graʊs] n inv (bird) schottische(s) Moorhuhn m

grove [grəʊv] n Gehölz m, Hain m

grovel ['grɔvl] vi (fig) kriechen

grow [grəʊ] (pt **grew**, pp **grown**) vi wachsen; (become) werden ♦ vt (raise) anbauen; **~ up** vi aufwachsen; **~er** n Züchter m; **~ing** adj zunehmend

growl [graʊl] vi knurren

grown [graʊn] pp of **grow**; **~-up** n Erwachsene(r) mf

growth [grəʊθ] n Wachstum nt; (increase) Zunahme f; (of beard etc) Wuchs m

grub [grʌb] n Made f, Larve f; (inf: food) Futter nt; **~by** ['grʌbɪ] adj schmutzig

grudge [grʌdʒ] n Groll m ♦ vt: **to ~ sb sth** jdm etw missgönnen; **to bear sb**

a ~ einen Groll gegen jdn hegen
gruelling ['gruəlɪŋ] *adj* (climb, race) mörderisch
gruesome ['gruːsəm] *adj* grauenhaft
gruff [grʌf] *adj* barsch
grumble ['grʌmbl] *vi* murren
grumpy ['grʌmpɪ] *adj* verdrießlich
grunt [grʌnt] *vi* grunzen ♦ *n* Grunzen *nt*
G-string ['dʒiːstrɪŋ] *n* Minislip *m*
guarantee [gærən'tiː] *n* Garantie *f* ♦ *vt* garantieren
guard [gɑːd] *n* (sentry) Wache *f*; (BRIT: RAIL) Zugbegleiter *m* ♦ *vt* bewachen; **~ed** *adj* vorsichtig; **~ian** *n* Vormund *m*; (keeper) Hüter *m*; **~'s van** (BRIT) *n* (RAIL) Dienstwagen *m*
guerrilla [gə'rɪlə] *n* Guerilla(kämpfer) *m*; **~ warfare** *n* Guerillakrieg *m*
guess [ges] *vt, vi* (er)raten, schätzen ♦ *n* Vermutung *f*; **~work** *n* Raterei *f*
guest [gest] *n* Gast *m*; **~ house** *n* Pension *f*; **~ room** *n* Gastzimmer *nt*
guffaw [gʌ'fɔː] *vi* schallend lachen
guidance ['gaɪdəns] *n* (control) Leitung *f*; (advice) Beratung *f*
guide [gaɪd] *n* Führer *m*; (also: **girl ~**) Pfadfinderin *f* ♦ *vt* führen; **~book** *n* Reiseführer *m*; **~ dog** *n* Blindenhund *m*; **~lines** *npl* Richtlinien *pl*
guild [gɪld] *n* (HIST) Gilde *f*
guillotine ['gɪlətiːn] *n* Guillotine *f*
guilt [gɪlt] *n* Schuld *f*; **~y** *adj* schuldig
guinea pig ['gɪnɪ-] *n* Meerschweinchen *nt*; (fig) Versuchskaninchen *nt*
guise [gaɪz] *n*: **in the ~ of** in der Form +gen
guitar [gɪ'tɑː] *n* Gitarre *f*
gulf [gʌlf] *n* Golf *m*; (fig) Abgrund *m*
gull [gʌl] *n* Möwe *f*
gullet ['gʌlɪt] *n* Schlund *m*
gullible ['gʌlɪbl] *adj* leichtgläubig
gully ['gʌlɪ] *n* (Wasser)rinne *f*
gulp [gʌlp] *vt* (also: **~ down**) hinunterschlucken ♦ *vi* (gasp) schlucken
gum [gʌm] *n* (around teeth) Zahnfleisch *nt*; (glue) Klebstoff *m*; (also: **chewing** ~)

Kaugummi *m* ♦ *vt* gummieren;
~boots (BRIT) *npl* Gummistiefel *pl*
gun [gʌn] *n* Schusswaffe *f*; **~boat** *n* Kanonenboot *nt*; **~fire** *n* Geschützfeuer *nt*; **~man** (irreg) *n* bewaffnete(r) Verbrecher *m*; **~point** *n*: **at ~point** mit Waffengewalt; **~powder** *n* Schießpulver *nt*; **~shot** *n* Schuss *m*
gurgle ['gɜːgl] *vi* gluckern
gush [gʌʃ] *vi* (rush out) hervorströmen; (fig) schwärmen
gust [gʌst] *n* Windstoß *m*, Bö *f*
gusto ['gʌstəu] *n* Genuss *m*, Lust *f*
gut [gʌt] *n* (ANAT) Gedärme *pl*; (string) Darm *m*; **~s** *npl* (fig) Schneid *m*
gutter ['gʌtə] *n* Dachrinne *f*; (in street) Gosse *f*
guttural ['gʌtərəl] *adj* guttural, Kehl-
guy [gaɪ] *n* (also: **~rope**) Halteseil *nt*; (man) Typ *m*, Kerl *m*

Guy Fawkes' Night

Guy Fawkes' Night, *auch bonfire night genannt, erinnert an den Gunpowder Plot, einen Attentatsversuch auf James I. und sein Parlament am 5. November 1605. Einer der Verschwörer, Guy Fawkes, wurde auf frischer Tat ertappt, als er das Parlamentsgebäude in die Luft sprengen wollte. Vor der Guy Fawkes' Night basteln Kinder in Großbritannien eine Puppe des Guy Fawkes, mit der sie Geld für Feuerwerkskörper von Passanten erbetteln, und die dann am 5. November auf einem Lagerfeuer mit Feuerwerk verbrannt wird.*

guzzle ['gʌzl] *vt, vi* (drink) saufen; (eat) fressen
gym [dʒɪm] *n* (also: **~nasium**) Turnhalle *f*; (also: **~nastics**) Turnen *nt*; **~nast** ['dʒɪmnæst] *n* Turner(in) *m(f)*; **~nastics** [dʒɪm'næstɪks] *n* Turnen *nt*, Gymnastik *f*; **~ shoes** *npl* Turnschuhe *pl*
gynaecologist [gaɪnɪ'kɔlədʒɪst] *n* (US **gynecologist**) *n* Frauenarzt(ärztin) *m(f)*

gypsy ['dʒɪpsɪ] n = gipsy

gyrate [dʒaɪ'reɪt] vi kreisen

H, h

haberdashery ['hæbə'dæʃərɪ] (BRIT) n Kurzwaren pl

habit ['hæbɪt] n (An)gewohnheit f; (monk's) Habit nt or m

habitable ['hæbɪtəbl] adj bewohnbar

habitat ['hæbɪtæt] n Lebensraum m

habitual ['hə'bɪtjuəl] adj gewohnheitsmäßig; **~ly** adv gewöhnlich

hack [hæk] vt hacken ♦ n Hieb m; (writer) Schreiberling m

hacker ['hækə'] n (COMPUT) Hacker m

hackneyed ['hæknɪd] adj abgedroschen

had [hæd] pt, pp of **have**

haddock ['hædək] (pl ~ or ~s) n Schellfisch m

hadn't ['hædnt] = **had not**

haemorrhage ['hemərɪdʒ] (US **hemorrhage**) n Blutung f

haemorrhoids ['hemərɔɪdz] (US **hemorrhoids**) npl Hämorr(ho)iden pl

haggard ['hægəd] adj abgekämpft

haggle ['hægl] vi feilschen

Hague [heɪg] n: **The ~** Den Haag nt

hail [heɪl] n Hagel m ♦ vt umjubeln ♦ vi hageln; **~stone** n Hagelkorn nt

hair [heə'] n Haar nt, Haare pl; (one ~) Haar nt; **~brush** n Haarbürste f; **~cut** n Haarschnitt m; **to get a ~cut** sich dat die Haare schneiden lassen; **~do** n Frisur f; **~dresser** n Friseur m, Friseuse f; **~dresser's** n Friseursalon m; **~ dryer** n Trockenhaube f; (hand-held) Föhn m, Fön m ®; **~ gel** n Haargel nt; **~grip** n Klemme f; **~net** n Haarnetz nt; **~pin** n Haarnadel f; **~pin bend** (US **~pin curve**) n Haarnadelkurve f; **~raising** adj haarsträubend; **~ removing cream** n Enthaarungscreme f; **~ spray** n Haarspray nt; **~style** n Frisur f; **~y** adj haarig

hake [heɪk] n Seehecht m

half [hɑːf] (pl **halves**) n Hälfte f ♦ adj halb ♦ adv halb, zur Hälfte; **~ an hour** eine halbe Stunde; **two and a ~** zweieinhalb; **~ a dozen** ein halbes Dutzend; **sechs; ~ board** n Halbpension f; **~ caste** n Mischling m; **~ fare** n halbe(r) Fahrpreis m; **~-hearted** adj lustlos; **~ hour** n halbe Stunde f; **~-price** n: (at) **~price** zum halben Preis; **~ term** (BRIT) n (SCH) Ferien pl in der Mitte des Trimesters; **~time** n Halbzeit f; **~way** adv halbwegs, auf halbem Wege

halibut ['hælɪbət] n inv Heilbutt m

hall [hɔːl] n Saal m; (entrance ~) Hausflur m; (building) Halle f; **~ of residence** (BRIT) n Studentenwohnheim nt

hallmark ['hɔːlmɑːk] n Stempel m

hallo [hə'ləu] excl = **hello**

Hallowe'en ['hæləu'iːn] n Tag m vor Allerheiligen

Hallowe'en ist der 31. Oktober, der Vorabend von Allerheiligen und nach altem Glauben der Abend, an dem man Geister und Hexen sehen kann. In Großbritannien und vor allem in den USA feiern die Kinder Hallowe'en, indem sie sich verkleiden und mit selbst gemachten Laternen aus Kürbissen von Tür zu Tür ziehen.

hallucination [həluːsɪ'neɪʃən] n Halluzination f

hallway ['hɔːlweɪ] n Korridor m

halo ['heɪləu] n Heiligenschein m

halt [hɔːlt] n Halt m ♦ vt, vi anhalten

halve [hɑːv] vt halbieren

halves [hɑːvz] pl of **half**

ham [hæm] n Schinken m

hamburger ['hæmbɜːgə'] n Hamburger m

hamlet ['hæmlɪt] n Weiler m

hammer ['hæmə'] n Hammer m ♦ vt, vi hämmern

hammock ['hæmək] n Hängematte f

hamper ['hæmpə^r] vt (be)hindern ♦ n Picknickkorb m

hamster ['hæmstə^r] n Hamster m

hand [hænd] n Hand f; (of clock) (Uhr)zeiger m; (worker) Arbeiter m ♦ vt (pass) geben; **to give sb a ~** jdm helfen; **at ~** nahe; **to ~** zur Hand; **in ~** (under control) unter Kontrolle; (being done) im Gange; (extra) übrig; **on ~** zur Verfügung; **on the one ~ ..., on the other ~ ...** einerseits ..., andererseits ...; **~ in** abgeben; (forms) einreichen; **~ out** vt austeilen; **~ over** vt (deliver) übergeben; (surrender) abgeben; (: prisoner) ausliefern; **~bag** n Handtasche f; **~book** n Handbuch nt; **~brake** n Handbremse f; **~cuffs** npl Handschellen pl; **~ful** n Hand f voll; (inf: person) Plage f

handicap ['hændɪkæp] n Handikap nt ♦ vt benachteiligen; **mentally/physically ~ped** geistig/körperlich behindert

handicraft ['hændɪkrɑːft] n Kunsthandwerk nt

handiwork ['hændɪwɜːk] n Arbeit f; (fig) Werk nt

handkerchief ['hæŋkətʃɪf] n Taschentuch nt

handle ['hændl] n (of door etc) Klinke f; (of cup etc) Henkel m; (for winding) Kurbel f ♦ vt (touch) anfassen; (deal with: things) sich befassen mit; (: people) umgehen mit; **~bar(s)** n(pl) Lenkstange f

hand-: ~ luggage n Handgepäck nt; **~made** adj handgefertigt; **~out** n (for distribution) Verteilung f; (charity) Geldzuwendung f; (leaflet) Flugblatt nt; **~rail** n Geländer nt; (on ship) Reling f; **~set** n (TEL) Hörer m; **please replace the ~set** bitte legen Sie auf; **~shake** n Händedruck f

handsome ['hænsəm] adj gut aussehend

handwriting ['hændraɪtɪŋ] n Handschrift f

handy ['hændɪ] adj praktisch; (shops) leicht erreichbar; **~man** ['hændɪmæn] (irreg) n Bastler m

hang [hæŋ] (pt, pp **hung**) vt aufhängen; (pt, pp **hanged**: criminal) hängen ♦ vi hängen ♦ n: **to get the ~ of sth** (inf) den richtigen Dreh bei etw herauskriegen; **~ about, ~ around** vi sich herumtreiben; **~ on** vi (wait) warten; **~ up** vi (TEL) auflegen

hangar ['hæŋə^r] n Hangar m

hanger ['hæŋə^r] n Kleiderbügel m

hanger-on [hæŋər'ɔn] n Anhänger(in) m(f)

hang [hæŋ-]: **~-gliding** n Drachenfliegen nt; **~over** n Kater m; **~up** n Komplex m

hanker ['hæŋkə^r] vi: **to ~ for** or **after** sich sehnen nach

hankie ['hæŋkɪ] n abbr = **handkerchief**

hanky ['hæŋkɪ] n abbr = **handkerchief**

haphazard [hæp'hæzəd] adj zufällig

happen ['hæpən] vi sich ereignen, passieren; **as it ~s I'm going there today** zufällig(erweise) gehe ich heute (dort)hin; **~ing** n Ereignis nt

happily ['hæpɪlɪ] adv glücklich; (fortunately) glücklicherweise

happiness ['hæpɪnɪs] n Glück nt

happy ['hæpɪ] adj glücklich; **~ birthday!** alles Gute zum Geburtstag!; **~-go-lucky** adj sorglos; **~ hour** n Happy Hour f

harass ['hærəs] vt plagen; **~ment** n Belästigung f

harbour ['hɑːbə^r] (US **harbor**) n Hafen m ♦ vt (hope etc) hegen; (criminal etc) Unterschlupf gewähren

hard [hɑːd] adj (firm) hart; (difficult) schwer; (harsh) hart(herzig) ♦ adv (work) hart; (try) sehr; (push, hit) fest; **no ~ feelings!** ich nehme es dir nicht übel; **~ of hearing** schwerhörig; **to be ~ done by** übel dran sein; **~back** n kartonierte Ausgabe f; **~ cash** n Bargeld nt; **~ disk** n (COMPUT) Festplatte f;

~en vt erhärten; (fig) verhärten ♦ vi hart werden; (fig) sich verhärten; **~-headed** adj nüchtern; **~ labour** n Zwangsarbeit f

hardly ['hɑːdlɪ] adv kaum

hard: **~ship** n Not f; **~ shoulder** (BRIT) n (AUT) Seitenstreifen m; **~ up** adj knapp bei Kasse; **~ware** n Eisenwaren pl; (COMPUT) Hardware f; **~ware shop** n Eisenwarenhandlung f; **~-wearing** adj strapazierfähig; **~-working** adj fleißig

hardy ['hɑːdɪ] adj widerstandsfähig

hare [heər] n Hase m; **~-brained** adj schwachsinnig

harm [hɑːm] n Schaden m ♦ vt schaden +dat; **out of ~'s way** in Sicherheit; **~ful** adj schädlich; **~less** adj harmlos

harmonica [hɑːˈmɒnɪkə] n Mundharmonika f

harmonious [hɑːˈməʊnɪəs] adj harmonisch

harmonize ['hɑːmənaɪz] vt abstimmen ♦ vi harmonieren

harmony ['hɑːmənɪ] n Harmonie f

harness ['hɑːnɪs] n Geschirr nt ♦ vt (horse) anschirren; (fig) nutzbar machen

harp [hɑːp] n Harfe f ♦ vi: **to ~ on about sth** auf etw dat herumreiten

harpoon [hɑːˈpuːn] n Harpune f

harrowing ['hærəʊɪŋ] adj nervenaufreibend

harsh [hɑːʃ] adj (rough) rau; (severe) streng; **~ness** n Härte f

harvest ['hɑːvɪst] n Ernte f ♦ vt, vi ernten

has [hæz] vb see **have**

hash [hæʃ] n klein hacken ♦ n (mess) Kuddelmuddel m

hashish ['hæʃiːʃ] n Haschisch nt

hasn't ['hæznt] = **has not**

hassle ['hæsl] (inf) n Theater nt

haste [heɪst] n Eile f; **~n** ['heɪsn] vt beschleunigen ♦ vi eilen; **hasty** adj hastig; (rash) vorschnell

hat [hæt] n Hut m

hatch [hætʃ] n (NAUT: also: **~way**) Luke f; (in house) Durchreiche f ♦ vi (young) ausschlüpfen ♦ vt (brood) ausbrüten; (plot) aushecken; **~back** ['hætʃbæk] n (AUT) Auto nt mit Heckklappe f

hate [heɪt] vt hassen ♦ n Hass m; **~ful** adj verhasst

hatred ['heɪtrɪd] n Hass m

haughty ['hɔːtɪ] adj hochnäsig, überheblich

haul [hɔːl] vt ziehen ♦ n (catch) Fang m; **~age** n Spedition f; **~ier** (US **hauler**) n Spediteur m

haunch [hɔːntʃ] n Lende f

haunt [hɔːnt] vt (ghost) spuken in +dat; (memory) verfolgen; (pub) häufig besuchen ♦ n Lieblingsplatz m; **the castle is ~ed** in dem Schloss spukt es

---

KEYWORD

have [hæv] (pt, pp **had**) aux vb 1 haben; (esp with vbs of motion) sein; **to have arrived/slept** angekommen sein/geschlafen haben; **to have been** gewesen sein; **having eaten** or **when he had eaten**, **he left** nachdem er gegessen hatte, ging er

2 (in tag questions): **you've done it, haven't you?** du hast es doch gemacht, oder nicht?

3 (in short answers and questions): **you've made a mistake – so I have/no I haven't** du hast einen Fehler gemacht – ja, stimmt/nein; **we haven't paid – yes we have!** wir haben nicht bezahlt – doch; **I've been there before, have you?** ich war schon einmal da, du auch?

♦ modal aux vb (be obliged): **to have (got) to do sth** etw tun müssen; **you haven't to tell her** or **du darfst es ihr nicht erzählen**

♦ vt 1 (possess) haben; **he has (got) blue eyes** er hat blaue Augen; **I have (got) an idea** ich habe eine Idee

2 (referring to meals etc): **to have**

breakfast/a cigarette frühstücken/ eine Zigarette rauchen

3 (*receive, obtain etc*) haben; **may I have your address?** kann ich Ihre Adresse haben?; **to have a baby** ein Kind bekommen

4 (*maintain, allow*): **he will have it that he is right** er besteht darauf, dass er Recht hat; **I won't have it** that das lasse ich nicht mit anhören

5: to have sth done etw machen lassen; **to have sb do sth** jdn etw machen lassen; **he soon had them all laughing** er brachte sie alle zum Lachen

6 (*experience, suffer*): **she had her bag stolen** man hat ihr die Tasche gestohlen; **he had his arm broken** er hat sich den Arm gebrochen

7 (*+noun: take, hold etc*): **to have a walk/rest** spazieren gehen/sich ausruhen; **to have a meeting/party** haben eine Besprechung/Party haben

have out *vt*: **to have it out with sb** (*settle problem*) etw mit jdm bereden

haven ['heɪvn] *n* Zufluchtsort *m*

haven't ['hævnt] = **have not**

havoc ['hævək] *n* Verwüstung *f*

hawk [hɔːk] *n* Habicht *m*

hay [heɪ] *n* Heu *nt*; **~ fever** *n* Heuschnupfen *m*; **~stack** *n* Heuschober *m*

haywire ['heɪwaɪə] (*inf*) *adj* durcheinander

hazard ['hæzəd] *n* Risiko *nt* ♦ *vt* aufs Spiel setzen; **~ous** *adj* gefährlich; **~ (warning) lights** *npl* (*AUT*) Warnblinklicht *nt*

haze [heɪz] *n* Dunst *m*

hazelnut ['heɪzlnʌt] *n* Haselnuss *f*

hazy ['heɪzɪ] *adj* (*misty*) dunstig; (*vague*) verschwommen

he [hiː] *pron er*

head [hed] *n* Kopf *m*; (*leader*) Leiter *m* ♦ *vt* (an)führen, leiten; (*ball*) köpfen; **~s (or tails)** Kopf (oder Zahl); **~ first** mit dem Kopf nach unten; **~ over**

heels kopfüber; **~ for** *vt fus* zugehen auf +*acc*; **~ache** *n* Kopfschmerzen *pl*; **~dress** *n* Kopfschmuck *m*; **~ing** *n* Überschrift *f*; **~lamp** (*BRIT*) *n* Scheinwerfer *m*; **~land** *n* Landspitze *f*; **~light** *n* Scheinwerfer *m*; **~line** *n* Schlagzeile *f*; **~long** *adv* kopfüber; **~master** *n* (*of primary school*) Rektor *m*; (*of secondary school*) Direktor *m*; **~mistress** *n* Rektorin *f*; Direktorin *f*; **~ office** *n* Zentrale *f*; **~-on** *adj* Frontal-; **~phones** *npl* Kopfhörer *pl*; **~quarters** *npl* Zentrale *f*; (*MIL*) Hauptquartier *nt*; **~rest** *n* Kopfstütze *f*; **~room** *n* (*of bridges etc*) lichte Höhe *f*; **~scarf** *n* Kopftuch *nt*; **~strong** *adj* eigenwillig; **~teacher** (*BRIT*) *n* Schulleiter(in) *m(f)*; (*of secondary school*) Direktor(in) *m*; **~waiter** *n* Oberkellner *m*; **~way** *n* Fortschritte *pl*; **~wind** *n* Gegenwind *m*; **~y** *adj* berauschend

heal [hiːl] *vt* heilen ♦ *vi* verheilen

health [helθ] *n* Gesundheit *f*; **~ food** *n* Reformkost *f*; **H~ Service** (*BRIT*) *n*: **the H~ Service** das Gesundheitswesen; **~y** *adj* gesund

heap [hiːp] *n* Haufen *m* ♦ *vt* häufen

hear [hɪə] (*pt, pp heard*) *vt* hören; (*listen to*) anhören ♦ *vi* hören; **~d** [hɜːd] *pt, pp of* **hear**; **~ing** *n* Gehör *nt*; (*JUR*) Verhandlung *f*; **~ing aid** *n* Hörapparat *m*; **~say** *n* Hörensagen *nt*

hearse [hɜːs] *n* Leichenwagen *m*

heart [hɑːt] *n* Herz *nt*; **~s** *npl* (*CARDS*) Herz *nt*; **by ~** auswendig; **~ attack** *n* Herzanfall *m*; **~beat** *n* Herzschlag *m*; **~breaking** *adj* herzzerbrechend; **~broken** *adj* untröstlich; **~burn** *n* Sodbrennen *nt*; **~ failure** *n* Herzschlag *m*; **~felt** *adj* aufrichtig

hearth [hɑːθ] *n* Herd *m*

heartily ['hɑːtɪlɪ] *adv* herzlich; (*eat*) herzhaft

heartless ['hɑːtlɪs] *adj* herzlos

hearty ['hɑːtɪ] *adj* kräftig; (*friendly*) freundlich

heat [hiːt] *n* Hitze *f*; (*of food, water etc*)

Wärme f; (SPORT: also: **qualifying ~**) Ausscheidungsrunde f ♦ vt (house) heizen; (substance) heiß machen, erhitzen; **~ up** vi warm werden ♦ vt aufwärmen; **~ed** adj erhitzt; (fig) hitzig; **~er** n (Heiz)ofen m

heath [hi:θ] (BRIT) n Heide f

heathen ['hi:ðn] n Heide m/Heidin f ♦ adj heidnisch, Heiden-

heather ['hɛðə'] n Heidekraut nt

heat: **~ing** n Heizung f; **~-seeking** adj Wärme suchend; **~stroke** n Hitzschlag m; **~ wave** n Hitzewelle f

heave [hi:v] vt hochheben; (sigh) ausstoßen ♦ vi wogen; (breast) sich heben ♦ n Heben nt

heaven ['hɛvn] n Himmel m; **~ly** adj himmlisch

heavily ['hɛvɪlɪ] adv schwer

heavy ['hɛvɪ] adj schwer; **~ goods vehicle** n Lastkraftwagen m; **~weight** n (SPORT) Schwergewicht nt

Hebrew ['hi:bru:] adj hebräisch ♦ n (LING) Hebräisch nt

Hebrides ['hɛbrɪdi:z] npl Hebriden pl

heckle ['hɛkl] vt unterbrechen

hectic ['hɛktɪk] adj hektisch

he'd [hi:d] = he had; he would

hedge [hɛdʒ] n Hecke f ♦ vt einzäunen ♦ vi (fig) ausweichen; **to ~ one's bets** sich absichern

hedgehog ['hɛdʒhɔg] n Igel m

heed [hi:d] vt (also: **take ~ of**) beachten ♦ n Beachtung f; **~less** adj achtlos

heel [hi:l] n Ferse f; (of shoe) Absatz m ♦ vt mit Absätzen versehen

hefty ['hɛftɪ] adj (person) stämmig; (portion) reichlich

heifer ['hɛfə'] n Färse f

height [haɪt] n (of person) Größe f; (of object) Höhe f; **~en** vt erhöhen

heir [ɛə'] n Erbe m; **~ess** ['ɛəres] n Erbin f; **~loom** n Erbstück nt

held [held] pt, pp of **hold**

helicopter ['hɛlɪkɔptə'] n Hubschrauber m

heliport ['hɛlɪpɔ:t] n Hubschrauberlan-

deplatz m

hell [hɛl] n Hölle f ♦ excl verdammt!

he'll [hi:l] = he will; he shall

hellish ['hɛlɪʃ] adj höllisch, verteufelt

hello [hə'ləu] excl hallo!

helm [hɛlm] n Ruder nt, Steuer nt

helmet ['hɛlmɪt] n Helm m

help [hɛlp] n Hilfe f ♦ vt helfen +dat; I can't **~ it** ich kann nichts dafür; **~ yourself** bedienen Sie sich; **~er** n Helfer m; **~ful** adj hilfreich; **~ing** n Portion f; **~less** adj hilflos

hem [hɛm] n Saum m ♦ vt säumen; **~ in** vt einengen

hemorrhage ['hɛmərɪdʒ] (US) n = **haemorrhage**

hemorrhoids ['hɛmərɔɪdz] (US) npl = **haemorrhoids**

hen [hɛn] n Henne f

hence [hɛns] adv von jetzt an; (therefore) daher; **~forth** adv von nun an; (from then on) von da an

henchman ['hɛntʃmən] (irreg) n Gefolgsmann m

her [hə:'] pron (acc) sie; (dat) ihr ♦ adj ihr; see also **me**; **my**

herald ['hɛrəld] n (Vor)bote m ♦ vt verkünden

heraldry ['hɛrəldrɪ] n Wappenkunde f

herb [hə:b] n Kraut nt

herd [hə:d] n Herde f

here [hɪə'] adv hier; (to this place) hierher; **~after** [hɪər'ɑ:ftə'] adv hernach, künftig ♦ n Jenseits nt; **~by** [hɪə'baɪ] adv hiermit

hereditary [hɪ'rɛdɪtrɪ] adj erblich

heredity [hɪ'rɛdɪtɪ] n Vererbung f

heritage ['hɛrɪtɪdʒ] n Erbe nt

hermit ['hə:mɪt] n Einsiedler m

hernia ['hə:nɪə] n Bruch m

hero ['hɪərəu] (pl **~es**) n Held m; **~ic** [hɪ'rəuɪk] adj heroisch

heroin ['hɛrəuɪn] n Heroin nt

heroine ['hɛrəuɪn] n Heldin f

heroism ['hɛrəuɪzəm] n Heldentum nt

heron ['hɛrən] n Reiher m

herring ['hɛrɪŋ] n Hering m

hers [həːz] *pron* ihre(r, s); *see also* mine²

herself [həːˈself] *pron* sich (selbst); *(emphatic)* selbst; *see also* **oneself**

he's [hiːz] = **he is**; **he has**

hesitant [ˈhezɪtənt] *adj* zögernd

hesitate [ˈhezɪteɪt] *vi* zögern; **hesitation** [hezɪˈteɪʃən] *n* Zögern *nt*

heterosexual [ˈhetərəuˈseksjuəl] *adj* heterosexuell ♦ *n* Heterosexuelle(r) *mf*

hew [hjuː] *(pt* **hewed**, *pp* **hewn)** *vt* hauen, hacken

hexagonal [hekˈsægənl] *adj* sechseckig

heyday [ˈheɪdeɪ] *n* Blüte *f*, Höhepunkt *m*

HGV *n abbr* = **heavy goods vehicle**

hi [haɪ] *excl* he, hallo

hibernate [ˈhaɪbəneɪt] *vi* Winterschlaf *m* halten; **hibernation** [haɪbəˈneɪʃən] *n* Winterschlaf *m*

hiccough [ˈhɪkʌp] *vi* den Schluckauf haben; **~s** *npl* Schluckauf *m*

'hiccup [ˈhɪkʌp] = **hiccough**

hid [hɪd] *pt of* **hide**; **~den** [ˈhɪdn] *pp of* **hide**

hide [haɪd] *(pt* **hid**, *pp* **hidden)** *n (skin)* Haut *f*, Fell *nt* ♦ *vt* verstecken ♦ *vi* sich verstecken; **~-and-seek** *n* Versteckspiel *nt*; **~away** *n* Versteck *nt*

hideous [ˈhɪdɪəs] *adj* abscheulich

hiding [ˈhaɪdɪŋ] *n (beating)* Tracht *f* Prügel; **to be in ~** *(concealed)* sich versteckt halten; **~ place** *n* Versteck *nt*

hi-fi [ˈhaɪfaɪ] *n* Hi-Fi *nt* ♦ *adj* Hi-Fi-

high [haɪ] *adj* hoch; *(wind)* stark ♦ *adv* hoch; **it is 20m ~** es ist 20 Meter hoch; **~brow** *adj* (betont) intellektuell; **~chair** *n* Hochstuhl *m*; **~er education** *n* Hochschulbildung *f*; **~-handed** *adj* eigenmächtig; **~-heeled** *adj* hochhackig; **~ jump** *n (SPORT)* Hochsprung *m*; **H~lands** *npl* the H~lands *das* schottische Hochland; **~light** *n (fig)* Höhepunkt *m* ♦ *vt* hervorheben; **~ly** *adv* höchst; **~ly strung** *adj* überempfindlich; **~ness** *n* Höhe *f*; **Her H~ness** Ihre Hoheit *f*; **~-pitched** *adj*

hoch; **~-rise block** *n* Hochhaus *nt*; **~ school** *(US) n* Oberschule *f*; **~ season** *(BRIT) n* Hochsaison *f*; **~ street** *(BRIT) n* Hauptstraße *f*

highway [ˈhaɪweɪ] *n* Landstraße *f*; **H~ Code** *(BRIT) n* Straßenverkehrsordnung *f*

hijack [ˈhaɪdʒæk] *vt* entführen; **~er** *n* Entführer(in) *m(f)*

hike [haɪk] *vi* wandern ♦ *n* Wanderung *f*; **~r** *n* Wanderer *m*; **hiking** *n* Wandern *nt*

hilarious [hɪˈlɛərɪəs] *adj* lustig

hill [hɪl] *n* Berg *m*; **~side** *n* (Berg)hang *m*; **~ walking** *n* Bergwandern *nt*; **~y** *adj* hügelig

hilt [hɪlt] *n* Heft *nt*; **(up) to the ~** ganz und gar

him [hɪm] *pron (acc)* ihn; *(dat)* ihm; *see also* **me**; **~self** *pron* sich (selbst); *(emphatic)* selbst; *see also* **oneself**

hind [haɪnd] *adj* hinter, Hinter-

hinder [ˈhɪndə*] *vt (stop)* hindern; *(delay)* behindern; **hindrance** *n (delay)* Behinderung *f*; *(obstacle)* Hindernis *nt*

hindsight [ˈhaɪndsaɪt] *n*: **with ~** im nachhinein

Hindu [ˈhɪnduː] *n* Hindu *m*

hinge [hɪndʒ] *n* Scharnier *nt*; *(on door)* Türangel *f* ♦ *vi (fig)*: **to ~ on** abhängen von

hint [hɪnt] *n* Tipp *m*; *(trace)* Anflug *m* ♦ *vt*: **to ~ that** andeuten, dass ♦ *vi*: **to ~ at** andeuten

hip [hɪp] *n* Hüfte *f*

hippie [ˈhɪpɪ] *n* Hippie *m*

hippo [ˈhɪpəu] *(inf) n* Nilpferd *nt*

hippopotamus [hɪpəˈpɔtəmɪ] *npl of* **hippopotamus**

hippopotamus [hɪpəˈpɔtəməs] *(pl* **~es** *or* **hippopotami)** *n* Nilpferd *nt*

hire [ˈhaɪə*] *vt (worker)* anstellen; *(BRIT: car)* mieten ♦ *n* Miete *f*; **for ~** *(taxi)* frei; **~(d) car** *(BRIT) n* Mietwagen *m*, Leihwagen *m*; **~ purchase** *(BRIT) n* Teilzahlungskauf *m*

his [hɪz] *adj* sein ♦ *pron* seine(r, s); *see*

also **my; mine²**

hiss [hɪs] *vi* zischen ♦ *n* Zischen *nt*

historian [hɪ'stɔːrɪən] *n* Historiker *m*

historic [hɪ'stɒrɪk] *adj* historisch; **~al** *adj* historisch, geschichtlich

history ['hɪstərɪ] *n* Geschichte *f*

hit [hɪt] (*pt, pp* **hit**) *vt* schlagen; (*injure*) treffen ♦ *n* (*blow*) Schlag *m*; (*success*) Erfolg *m*; (*MUS*) Hit *m*; **to ~ it off with sb** prima mit jdm auskommen; **~-and-run driver** *n* jemand, der Fahrerflucht begeht

hitch [hɪtʃ] *vt* festbinden; (*also*: **~ up**) hochziehen ♦ *n* (*difficulty*) Haken *m*; **to ~ a lift** trampen; **~hike** *vi* trampen; **~hiker** *n* Tramper *m*; **~hiking** *n* Trampen *nt*

hi-tech ['haɪ'tek] *adj* Hightech- ♦ *n* Spitzentechnologie *f*

hitherto [hɪðə'tuː] *adv* bislang

hit man (*inf*) *n* Killer *m*

HIV *n abbr*: **HIV-negative/-positive** HIV-negativ/-positiv

hive [haɪv] *n* Bienenkorb *m*

HMS *abbr* = **His/Her Majesty's Ship**

hoard [hɔːd] *n* Schatz *m* ♦ *vt* horten, hamstern

hoarding ['hɔːdɪŋ] *n* Bretterzaun *m*; (*BRIT: for posters*) Reklamewand *f*

hoarse [hɔːs] *adj* heiser, rau

hoax [həʊks] *n* Streich *m*

hob [hɒb] *n* Kochmulde *f*

hobble ['hɒbl] *vi* humpeln

hobby ['hɒbɪ] *n* Hobby *nt*

hobby-horse ['hɒbɪhɔːs] *n* (*fig*) Steckenpferd *nt*

hobo ['həʊbəʊ] (*US*) *n* Tippelbruder *m*

hockey ['hɒkɪ] *n* Hockey *nt*

hoe [həʊ] *n* Hacke *f* ♦ *vt* hacken

hog [hɒg] *n* Schlachtschwein *nt* ♦ *vt* mit Beschlag belegen; **to go the whole ~** aufs Ganze gehen

hoist [hɔɪst] *n* Winde *f* ♦ *vt* hochziehen

hold [həʊld] (*pt, pp* **held**) *vt* halten; (*contain*) enthalten; (*be able to contain*) fassen; (*breath*) anhalten; (*meeting*) abhalten ♦ *vi* (*withstand pressure*) aushal-

ten ♦ *n* (*grasp*) Halt *m*; (*NAUT*) Schiffsraum *m*; **~ the line!** (*TEL*) bleiben Sie am Apparat!; **to ~ one's own** sich behaupten; **~ back** *vt* zurückhalten; **~ down** *vt* niederhalten; (*job*) behalten; **~ off** *vt* (*enemy*) abwehren; **~ on** *vi* sich festhalten; (*resist*) durchhalten; (*wait*) warten; **~ on to** *vt fus* festhalten an +*dat*; (*keep*) behalten; **~ out** *vt* hinhalten ♦ *vi* aushalten; **~ up** *vt* (*delay*) aufhalten; (*rob*) überfallen; **~all** (*BRIT*) *n* Reisetasche *f*; **~er** *n* Behälter *m*; (*share*) (Aktien)anteil *m*; **~up** *n* (*BRIT: in traffic*) Stockung *f*; (*robbery*) Überfall *m*; (*delay*) Verzögerung *f*

hole [həʊl] *n* Loch *nt*; **~ in the wall** (*inf*) (*cash dispenser*) Geldautomat *m*

holiday ['hɒlədeɪ] *n* (*day*) Feiertag *m*; freie(r) Tag *m*; (*vacation*) Urlaub *m*; (*SCH*) Ferien *pl*; **~maker** (*BRIT*) *n* Urlauber(in) *m(f)*; **~ resort** *n* Ferienort *m*

Holland ['hɒlənd] *n* Holland *nt*

hollow ['hɒləʊ] *adj* hohl; (*fig*) leer ♦ *n* Vertiefung *f*; **~ out** *vt* aushöhlen

holly ['hɒlɪ] *n* Stechpalme *f*

holocaust ['hɒləkɔːst] *n* Inferno *nt*

holster ['həʊlstə*] *n* Pistolenhalfter *m*

holy ['həʊlɪ] *adj* heilig; **H~ Ghost** *or* **Spirit** *n*: **the H~ Ghost** *or* **Spirit** der Heilige Geist

homage ['hɒmɪdʒ] *n* Huldigung *f*; **to pay ~ to** huldigen +*dat*

home [həʊm] *n* Zuhause *nt*; (*institution*) Heim *nt*, Anstalt *f* ♦ *adj* einheimisch; (*POL*) inländ *m* ♦ *adv* heim, nach Hause; **at ~** zu Hause; **~ address** *n* Heimatadresse *f*; **~coming** *n* Heimkehr *f*; **~land** *n* Heimat(land) *nt(f)*; **~less** *adj* obdachlos; **~ly** *adj* häuslich; (*US: ugly*) unscheinbar; **~-made** *adj* selbst gemacht; **~ match** *n* Heimspiel *nt*; **H~ Office** (*BRIT*) *n* Innenministerium *nt*; **~ rule** *n* Selbstverwaltung *f*; **H~ Secretary** (*BRIT*) *n* Innenminister(in) *m(f)*; **~sick** *adj*: **to be ~sick** Heimweh haben; **~ town** *n* Heimatstadt *f*; **~ward** *adj* (*journey*) Heim-;

~work n Hausaufgaben pl

homicide ['hɒmɪsaɪd] (US) n Totschlag m

homoeopathic [həʊmɪə'pæθɪk] (US **homeopathic**) adj homöopathisch; **homoeopathy** [həʊmɪ'ɒpəθɪ] n (US **homeopathy**) n Homöopathie f

homogeneous [hɒmə'dʒi:nɪəs] adj homogen

homosexual [hɒmə'seksjʊəl] adj homosexuell ♦ n Homosexuelle(r) mf

honest ['ɒnɪst] adj ehrlich; **~ly** adv ehrlich; **~y** n Ehrlichkeit f

honey ['hʌnɪ] n Honig m; **~comb** n Honigwabe f; **~moon** n Flitterwochen pl, Hochzeitsreise f; **~suckle** ['hʌnɪsʌkl] n Geißblatt nt

honk [hɒŋk] vi hupen

honor etc ['ɒnə'] (US) vt, n = **honour** etc

honorary ['ɒnərərɪ] adj Ehren-

honour ['ɒnə'] (US **honor**) vt ehren; (cheque) einlösen ♦ n Ehre f; **~able** adj ehrenwert; (intention) ehrenhaft; **~s degree** n (UNIV) akademischer Grad mit Prüfung im Spezialfach

hood [hʊd] n Kapuze f; (BRIT: AUT) Verdeck nt; (US: AUT) Kühlerhaube f

hoof [hu:f] (pl **hooves**) n Huf m

hook [hʊk] n Haken m ♦ vt einhaken

hooligan ['hu:lɪgən] n Rowdy m

hoop [hu:p] n Reifen m

hooray [hu:'reɪ] excl = **hurrah**

hoot [hu:t] vi (AUT) hupen; **~er** n (NAUT) Dampfpfeife f; (BRIT: AUT) (Auto)hupe f

Hoover ['hu:və'] ®) n Staubsauger m ♦ vt: **to h~** staubsaugen, Staub saugen

hooves [hu:vz] pl of **hoof**

hop [hɒp] vi hüpfen, hopsen ♦ n (jump) Hopser m

hope [həʊp] vt, vi hoffen ♦ n Hoffnung f; **I ~ so/not** hoffentlich/hoffentlich nicht; **~ful** adj hoffnungsvoll; (promising) viel versprechend; **~fully** adv hoffentlich; **~less** adj hoffnungslos

hops [hɒps] npl Hopfen m

horizon [hə'raɪzn] n Horizont m; **~tal** [hɒrɪ'zɒntl] adj horizontal

hormone ['hɔ:məʊn] n Hormon nt

horn [hɔ:n] n Horn nt; (AUT) Hupe f

hornet ['hɔ:nɪt] n Hornisse f

horny ['hɔ:nɪ] adj schwielig; (US: inf) scharf

horoscope ['hɒrəskəʊp] n Horoskop nt

horrendous [hə'rendəs] adj (crime) abscheulich; (error) schrecklich

horrible ['hɒrɪbl] adj fürchterlich

horrid ['hɒrɪd] adj scheußlich

horrify ['hɒrɪfaɪ] vt entsetzen

horror ['hɒrə'] n Schrecken m; **~ film** n Horrorfilm m

hors d'oeuvre [ɔ:'də:vrə] n Vorspeise f

horse [hɔ:s] n Pferd nt; **~back** n: on **~back** berittten; **~ chestnut** n Rosskastanie f; **~man/woman** (irreg) n Reiter(in) m(f); **~power** n Pferdestärke f; **~-racing** n Pferderennen nt; **~radish** n Meerrettich m; **~shoe** n Hufeisen nt

horticulture ['hɔ:tɪkʌltʃə'] n Gartenbau m

hose [həʊz] n (also: **~pipe**) Schlauch m

hosiery ['həʊzɪərɪ] n Strumpfwaren pl

hospitable ['hɒspɪtəbl] adj gastfreundlich

hospital ['hɒspɪtl] n Krankenhaus nt

hospitality [hɒspɪ'tælɪtɪ] n Gastfreundschaft f

host [həʊst] n Gastgeber m; (innkeeper) (Gast)wirt m; (large number) Heerschar f; (ECCL) Hostie f

hostage ['hɒstɪdʒ] n Geisel f

hostel ['hɒstl] n Herberge f; (also: **youth ~**) Jugendherberge f

hostess ['həʊstɪs] n Gastgeberin f

hostile ['hɒstaɪl] adj feindlich; **hostility** [hɒ'stɪlɪtɪ] n Feindschaft f; **hostilities** npl (fighting) Feindseligkeiten pl

hot [hɒt] adj heiß; (food, water) warm; (spiced) scharf; **I'm ~** mir ist heiß; **~bed** n (fig) Nährboden m; **~ dog** n heiße(s) Würstchen m

hotel [həʊ'tel] n Hotel nt; **~ier** [həʊ'telɪə'] n Hotelier m

hot: ~house n Treibhaus nt; **~ line** n

(POL) heiße(r) Draht m; **~ly** adv (argue) hitzig; **~plate** n Kochplatte f; **~pot** ['hɔtpɔt] (BRIT) n Fleischeintopf m; **~water bottle** n Wärmflasche f

hound [haund] n Jagdhund m ♦ vt hetzen

hour ['auəʳ] n Stunde f; (time of day) (Tages)zeit f; **~ly** adj, adv stündlich

house [n haus, vb hauz] n Haus nt ♦ vt unterbringen; **on the ~** auf Kosten des Hauses; **~ arrest** n (POL, MIL) Hausarrest m; **~boat** n Hausboot nt; **~breaking** n Einbruch m; **~coat** n Morgenmantel m; **~hold** n Haushalt m; **~keeper** n Haushälterin f; **~keeping** n Haushaltung f; **~warming party** n Einweihungsparty f; **~wife** (irreg) n Hausfrau f; **~work** n Hausarbeit f

housing ['hauzɪŋ] n (act) Unterbringung f; (houses) Wohnungen pl; (POL) Wohnungsbau m; (covering) Gehäuse nt; **~ estate** (US **~ development**) n (Wohn)siedlung f

hovel ['hɔvl] n elende Hütte f

hover ['hɔvəʳ] vi (bird) schweben; (person) herumstehen; **~craft** n Luftkissenfahrzeug nt

how [hau] adv wie; **~ are you?** wie geht es Ihnen?; **~ much milk?** wie viel Milch?; **~ many people?** wie viele Leute?

however [hau'evəʳ] adv (but) (je)doch, aber; **~ you phrase it** wie Sie es auch ausdrücken

howl [haul] n Heulen nt ♦ vi heulen

H.P. abbr = **hire purchase**

h.p. abbr = **horsepower**

H.Q. abbr = **headquarters**

hub [hʌb] n Radnabe f

hubbub ['hʌbʌb] n Tumult m

hubcap ['hʌbkæp] n Radkappe f

huddle ['hʌdl] vi: **to ~ together** sich zusammendrängen

hue [hju:] n Färbung f; **~ and cry** n Zetergeschrei n

huff [hʌf] n: **to go into a ~** einschnappen

hug [hʌg] vt umarmen ♦ n Umarmung f

huge [hju:dʒ] adj groß, riesig

hulk [hʌlk] n (ship) abgetakelte(s) Schiff nt; (person) Koloss m

hull [hʌl] n Schiffsrumpf m

hullo [hʌ'ləu] excl = **hello**

hum [hʌm] n, vi summen

human ['hju:mən] adj menschlich ♦ n (also: **~ being**) Mensch m

humane [hju:'meɪn] adj human

humanitarian [hju:mænɪ'teərɪən] adj humanitär

humanity [hju:'mænɪtɪ] n Menschheit f; (kindliness) Menschlichkeit f

humble ['hʌmbl] adj demütig; (modest) bescheiden ♦ vt demütigen

humbug ['hʌmbʌg] n Humbug m; (BRIT: sweet) Pfefferminzbonbon nt

humdrum ['hʌmdrʌm] adj stumpfsinnig

humid ['hju:mɪd] adj feucht; **~ity** [hju:'mɪdɪtɪ] n Feuchtigkeit f

humiliate [hju:'mɪlɪeɪt] vt demütigen; **humiliation** [hju:mɪlɪ'eɪʃən] n Demütigung f

humility [hju:'mɪlɪtɪ] n Demut f

humor ['hju:məʳ] (US) n, vt = **humour**

humorous ['hju:mərəs] adj humorvoll

humour ['hju:məʳ] (US **humor**) n (fun) Humor m; (mood) Stimmung f ♦ vt bei Stimmung halten

hump [hʌmp] n Buckel m

hunch [hʌntʃ] n Buckel m; (premonition) (Vor)ahnung f; **~back** n Bucklige(r) mf; **~ed** adj gekrümmt

hundred ['hʌndrəd] num hundert; **~weight** n Zentner m (BRIT = 50.8 kg; US = 45.3 kg)

hung [hʌŋ] pt, pp of **hang**

Hungarian [hʌŋ'geərɪən] adj ungarisch ♦ n Ungar(in) m(f); (LING) Ungarisch nt

Hungary ['hʌŋgərɪ] n Ungarn nt

hunger ['hʌŋgəʳ] n Hunger m ♦ vi hungern

hungry ['hʌŋgrɪ] adj hungrig; **to be ~** Hunger haben

hunk [hʌŋk] n (of bread) Stück nt
hunt [hʌnt] vt, vi jagen ♦ n Jagd f; **to ~ for** suchen; **~er** n Jäger m; **~ing** n Jagd f
hurdle [ˈhɜːdl] n (also fig) Hürde f
hurl [hɜːl] vt schleudern
hurrah [huˈrɑː] n Hurra nt
hurray [huˈreɪ] n Hurra nt
hurricane [ˈhʌrɪkən] n Orkan m
hurried [ˈhʌrɪd] adj eilig; (hasty) übereilt; **~ly** adv übereilt, hastig
hurry [ˈhʌrɪ] n Eile f ♦ vi sich beeilen ♦ vt (an)treiben; (job) übereilen; **to be in a ~** es eilig haben; **~ up** vi sich beeilen ♦ vt (person) zur Eile antreiben; (work) vorantreiben
hurt [hɜːt] (pt, pp hurt) vt wehtun +dat; (injure, fig) verletzen ♦ vi wehtun; **~ful** adj schädlich; (remark) verletzend
hurtle [ˈhɜːtl] vi sausen
husband [ˈhʌzbənd] n (Ehe)mann m
hush [hʌʃ] n Stille f ♦ vt zur Ruhe bringen ♦ excl pst, still
husky [ˈhʌskɪ] adj (voice) rau ♦ n Eskimohund m
hustle [ˈhʌsl] vt (push) stoßen; (hurry) antreiben ♦ n: **~ and bustle** Geschäftigkeit f
hut [hʌt] n Hütte f
hutch [hʌtʃ] n (Kaninchen)stall m
hyacinth [ˈhaɪəsɪnθ] n Hyazinthe f
hydrant [ˈhaɪdrənt] n (also: **fire ~**) Hydrant m
hydraulic [haɪˈdrɔːlɪk] adj hydraulisch
hydroelectric [ˈhaɪdrəʊɪˈlektrɪk] adj (energy) durch Wasserkraft erzeugt; **~ power station** n Wasserkraftwerk nt
hydrofoil [ˈhaɪdrəfɔɪl] n Tragflügelboot nt
hydrogen [ˈhaɪdrədʒən] n Wasserstoff m
hyena [haɪˈiːnə] n Hyäne f
hygiene [ˈhaɪdʒiːn] n Hygiene f; **hygienic** [haɪˈdʒiːnɪk] adj hygienisch
hymn [hɪm] n Kirchenlied nt
hype [haɪp] (inf) n Publicity f
hypermarket [ˈhaɪpəmɑːkɪt] (BRIT) n Hypermarkt m
hyphen [ˈhaɪfn] n Bindestrich m
hypnosis [hɪpˈnəʊsɪs] n Hypnose f
hypnotize [ˈhɪpnətaɪz] vt hypnotisieren
hypocrisy [hɪˈpɒkrɪsɪ] n Heuchelei f
hypocrite [ˈhɪpəkrɪt] n Heuchler m; **hypocritical** [hɪpəˈkrɪtɪkl] adj scheinheilig, heuchlerisch
hypothermia [haɪpəˈθɜːmɪə] n Unterkühlung f
hypotheses [haɪˈpɒθɪsiːz] npl of **hypothesis**
hypothesis [haɪˈpɒθɪsɪs] n (pl **hypotheses**) n Hypothese f
hypothetic(al) [haɪpəʊˈθetɪk(l)] adj hypothetisch
hysterical [hɪˈsterɪkl] adj hysterisch
hysterics [hɪˈsterɪks] npl hysterische(r) Anfall m

I, i

I [aɪ] pron ich
ice [aɪs] n Eis nt ♦ vt (COOK) mit Zuckerguss überziehen ♦ vi (also: **~ up**) vereisen; **~ axe** n Eispickel m; **~berg** n Eisberg m; **~box** (US) n Kühlschrank m; **~ cream** n Eis nt; **~ cube** n Eiswürfel m; **~d** [aɪst] adj (cake) mit Zuckerguss überzogen, glasiert; (tea, coffee) Eis-; **~ hockey** n Eishockey nt
Iceland [ˈaɪslənd] n Island nt
ice: ~ lolly (BRIT) n Eis nt am Stiel; **~ rink** n (Kunst)eisbahn f; **~ skating** n Schlittschuhlaufen nt
icicle [ˈaɪsɪkl] n Eiszapfen m
icing [ˈaɪsɪŋ] n (on cake) Zuckerguss m; (on window) Vereisung f; **~ sugar** (BRIT) n Puderzucker m
icon [ˈaɪkɒn] n Ikone f
icy [ˈaɪsɪ] adj (slippery) vereist; (cold) eisig
I'd [aɪd] = **I would**; **I had**
idea [aɪˈdɪə] n Idee f
ideal [aɪˈdɪəl] n Ideal nt ♦ adj ideal

identical [aɪˈdentɪkl] *adj* identisch; (*twins*) eineiig

identification [aɪdentɪfɪˈkeɪʃən] *n* Identifizierung *f*; **means of ~** Ausweispapiere *pl*

identify [aɪˈdentɪfaɪ] *vt* identifizieren; (*regard as the same*) gleichsetzen

Identikit [aɪˈdentɪkɪt] ® *n*: **~ picture** Phantombild *nt*

identity [aɪˈdentɪtɪ] *n* Identität *f*; **~ card** *n* Personalausweis *m*

ideology [aɪdɪˈɒlədʒɪ] *n* Ideologie *f*

idiom [ˈɪdɪəm] *n* (*expression*) Redewendung *f*; (*dialect*) Idiom *nt*; **~atic** [ɪdɪəˈmætɪk] *adj* idiomatisch

idiosyncrasy [ɪdɪəˈsɪŋkrəsɪ] *n* Eigenart *f*

idiot [ˈɪdɪət] *n* Idiot(in) *m(f)*; **~ic** [ɪdɪˈɒtɪk] *adj* idiotisch

idle [ˈaɪdl] *adj* (*doing nothing*) untätig; (*lazy*) faul; (*useless*) nutzlos; (*machine*) still(stehend); (*threat, talk*) leer ♦ *vi* (*machine*) leer laufen ♦ *vt*: **to ~ away the time** die Zeit vertrödeln; **~ness** *n* Müßiggang *m*; Faulheit *f*

idol [ˈaɪdl] *n* Idol *nt*; **~ize** *vt* vergöttern

i.e. *abbr* (= *id est*) d. h.

KEYWORD

if [ɪf] *conj* **1** wenn; (*in case also*) falls; **if I were you** wenn ich ich wäre

2 (*although*): (**even**) **if** (selbst *or* auch) wenn

3 (*whether*) ob

4: **if so/not** wenn ja/nicht; **if only ...** wenn ... doch nur ...; **if only I could** wenn ich doch nur könnte; *see also* **as**

ignite [ɪgˈnaɪt] *vt* (an)zünden ♦ *vi* sich entzünden; **ignition** [ɪgˈnɪʃən] *n* Zündung *f*; **to switch on/off the ignition** den Motor anlassen/abstellen; **ignition key** *n* (*AUT*) Zündschlüssel *m*

ignorance [ˈɪgnərəns] *n* Unwissenheit *f*

ignorant [ˈɪgnərənt] *adj* unwissend; **to be ~ of** nicht wissen

ignore [ɪgˈnɔːr] *vt* ignorieren

I'll [aɪl] = **I will; I shall**

ill [ɪl] *adj* krank ♦ *n* Übel *nt* ♦ *adv* schlecht; **~-advised** *adj* unklug; **~-at-ease** *adj* unbehaglich

illegal [ɪˈliːgl] *adj* illegal

illegible [ɪˈledʒɪbl] *adj* unleserlich

illegitimate [ɪlɪˈdʒɪtɪmət] *adj* unehelich

ill-fated [ɪlˈfeɪtɪd] *adj* unselig

ill feeling *n* Verstimmung *f*

illicit [ɪˈlɪsɪt] *adj* verboten

illiterate [ɪˈlɪtərət] *adj* ungebildet

ill-mannered [ɪlˈmænəd] *adj* ungehobelt

illness [ˈɪlnɪs] *n* Krankheit *f*

illogical [ɪˈlɒdʒɪkl] *adj* unlogisch

ill-treat [ɪlˈtriːt] *vt* misshandeln

illuminate [ɪˈluːmɪneɪt] *vt* beleuchten; **illumination** [ɪluːmɪˈneɪʃən] *n* Beleuchtung *f*; **illuminations** *pl* (*decorative lights*) festliche Beleuchtung *f*

illusion [ɪˈluːʒən] *n* Illusion *f*; **to be under the ~ that ...** sich der Illusion hingeben, dass ...

illustrate [ˈɪləstreɪt] *vt* (*book*) illustrieren; (*explain*) veranschaulichen; **illustration** [ɪləˈstreɪʃən] *n* Illustration *f*; (*explanation*) Veranschaulichung *f*

illustrious [ɪˈlʌstrɪəs] *adj* berühmt

I'm [aɪm] = **I am**

image [ˈɪmɪdʒ] *n* Bild *nt*; (*public ~*) Image *nt*; **~ry** *n* Symbolik *f*

imaginary [ɪˈmædʒɪnərɪ] *adj* eingebildet; (*world*) Fantasie-

imagination [ɪmædʒɪˈneɪʃən] *n* Einbildung *f*; (*creative*) Fantasie *f*

imaginative [ɪˈmædʒɪnətɪv] *adj* fantasiereich, einfallsreich

imagine [ɪˈmædʒɪn] *vt* sich vorstellen; (*wrongly*) sich einbilden

imbalance [ɪmˈbæləns] *n* Unausgeglichenheit *f*

imbecile [ˈɪmbəsiːl] *n* Schwachsinnige(r) *mf*

imitate [ˈɪmɪteɪt] *vt* imitieren; **imitation** [ɪmɪˈteɪʃən] *n* Imitation *f*

immaculate [ɪˈmækjulət] *adj* makellos; (*dress*) tadellos; (*ECCL*) unbefleckt

immaterial [ɪmə'tɪərɪəl] adj unwesentlich; **it is ~ whether ...** es ist unwichtig, ob ...

immature [ɪmə'tjʊəʳ] adj unreif

immediate [ɪ'miːdɪət] adj (instant) sofortig; (near) unmittelbar; (relatives) nächste(r, s); (needs) dringlich; **~ly** adv sofort; **~ly next to** direkt neben

immense [ɪ'mens] adj unermesslich

immerse [ɪ'məːs] vt eintauchen; **to be ~d in** (fig) vertieft sein in +acc

immersion heater [ɪ'məːʃən-] (BRIT) n Boiler m

immigrant ['ɪmɪgrənt] n Einwanderer m

immigrate ['ɪmɪgreɪt] vi einwandern; **immigration** [ɪmɪ'greɪʃən] n Einwanderung f

imminent ['ɪmɪnənt] adj bevorstehend

immobile [ɪ'məʊbaɪl] adj unbeweglich; **immobilize** [ɪ'məʊbɪlaɪz] vt lähmen

immoral [ɪ'mɒrl] adj unmoralisch; **~ity** [ɪmə'rælɪtɪ] n Unsittlichkeit f

immortal [ɪ'mɔːtl] adj unsterblich

immune [ɪ'mjuːn] adj (secure) sicher; (MED) immun; **~ from** sicher vor +dat; **immunity** n (MED, JUR) Immunität f; (fig) Freiheit f; **immunize** ['ɪmjunaɪz] vt immunisieren

impact ['ɪmpækt] n Aufprall m; (fig) Wirkung f

impair [ɪm'peəʳ] vt beeinträchtigen

impart [ɪm'pɑːt] vt mitteilen; (knowledge) vermitteln; (exude) abgeben

impartial [ɪm'pɑːʃl] adj unparteiisch

impassable [ɪm'pɑːsəbl] adj unpassierbar

impassive [ɪm'pæsɪv] adj gelassen

impatience [ɪm'peɪʃəns] n Ungeduld f; **impatient** adj ungeduldig; **impatiently** adv ungeduldig

impeccable [ɪm'pekəbl] adj tadellos

impede [ɪm'piːd] vt (be)hindern; **impediment** [ɪm'pedɪmənt] n Hindernis nt; **speech impediment** Sprachfehler m

impending [ɪm'pendɪŋ] adj bevorstehend

impenetrable [ɪm'penɪtrəbl] adj (also fig) undurchdringlich

imperative [ɪm'perətɪv] adj (necessary) unbedingt erforderlich

imperceptible [ɪmpə'septɪbl] adj nicht wahrnehmbar

imperfect [ɪm'pəːfɪkt] adj (faulty) fehlerhaft; **~ion** [ɪmpə'fekʃən] n Unvollkommenheit f; (fault) Fehler m

imperial [ɪm'pɪərɪəl] adj kaiserlich

impersonal [ɪm'pəːsənl] adj unpersönlich

impersonate [ɪm'pəːsəneɪt] vt sich ausgeben als; (for fun) imitieren

impertinent [ɪm'pəːtɪnənt] adj unverschämt, frech

impervious [ɪm'pəːvɪəs] adj (fig): **~ (to)** unempfänglich (für)

impetuous [ɪm'petjuəs] adj ungestüm

impetus ['ɪmpətəs] n Triebkraft f; (fig) Auftrieb m

impinge [ɪm'pɪndʒ]: **~ on** vt beeinträchtigen

implacable [ɪm'plækəbl] adj unerbittlich

implement [n 'ɪmplɪmənt, vb 'ɪmplɪment] n Werkzeug nt ♦ vt ausführen

implicate ['ɪmplɪkeɪt] vt verwickeln; **implication** [ɪmplɪ'keɪʃən] n (effect) Auswirkung f; (in crime) Verwicklung f

implicit [ɪm'plɪsɪt] adj (suggested) unausgesprochen; (utter) vorbehaltlos

implore [ɪm'plɔːʳ] vt anflehen

imply [ɪm'plaɪ] vt (hint) andeuten; (be evidence for) schließen lassen auf +acc

impolite [ɪmpə'laɪt] adj unhöflich

import [vb ɪm'pɔːt, n 'ɪmpɔːt] vt einführen ♦ n Einfuhr f; (meaning) Bedeutung f

importance [ɪm'pɔːtns] n Bedeutung f

important [ɪm'pɔːtənt] adj wichtig; **it's not ~** es ist unwichtig

importer [ɪm'pɔːtəʳ] n Importeur m

impose [ɪm'pəʊz] vt, vi: **to ~ (on)** auferlegen (+dat); (penalty, sanctions) verhängen (gegen); **to ~ (o.s.) on sb** sich jdm aufdrängen

imposing [ɪm'pəʊzɪŋ] *adj* eindrucksvoll

imposition [ɪmpə'zɪʃən] *n* (*of burden, fine*) Auferlegung *f*; **to be an ~** (*on person*) eine Zumutung sein

impossible [ɪm'pɒsɪbl] *adj* unmöglich

impostor [ɪm'pɒstə*] *n* Hochstapler *m*

impotent ['ɪmpətnt] *adj* machtlos; (*sexually*) impotent

impound [ɪm'paʊnd] *vt* beschlagnahmen

impoverished [ɪm'pɒvərɪʃt] *adj* verarmt

impracticable [ɪm'præktɪkəbl] *adj* undurchführbar

impractical [ɪm'præktɪkl] *adj* unpraktisch

imprecise [ɪmprɪ'saɪs] *adj* ungenau

impregnable [ɪm'pregnəbl] *adj* (*castle*) uneinnehmbar

impregnate ['ɪmpregneɪt] *vt* (*saturate*) sättigen; (*fertilize*) befruchten

impress [ɪm'pres] *vt* (*influence*) beeindrucken; (*imprint*) (auf)drücken; **to ~ sth on sb** jdm etw einschärfen; **~ed** *adj* beeindruckt; **~ion** [ɪm'preʃən] *n* Eindruck *m*; (*on wax, footprint*) Abdruck *m*; (*of book*) Auflage *f*; (*take-off*) Nachahmung *f*; **I was under the ~ion** ich hatte den Eindruck; **~ionable** *adj* leicht zu beeinflussen; **~ive** *adj* eindrucksvoll

imprint ['ɪmprɪnt] *n* Abdruck *m*

imprison [ɪm'prɪzn] *vt* ins Gefängnis schicken; **~ment** *n* Inhaftierung *f*

improbable [ɪm'prɒbəbl] *adj* unwahrscheinlich

impromptu [ɪm'prɒmptju:] *adj, adv* aus dem Stegreif, improvisiert

improper [ɪm'prɒpə*] *adj* (*indecent*) unanständig; (*unsuitable*) unpassend

improve [ɪm'pru:v] *vt* verbessern ♦ *vi* besser werden; **~ment** *n* (Ver)besserung *f*

improvise ['ɪmprəvaɪz] *vt, vi* improvisieren

imprudent [ɪm'pru:dnt] *adj* unklug

impudent ['ɪmpjudnt] *adj* unverschämt

impulse ['ɪmpʌls] *n* Impuls *m*; **to act on ~** spontan handeln; **impulsive** [ɪm'pʌlsɪv] *adj* impulsiv

impure [ɪm'pjʊə*] *adj* (*dirty*) verunreinigt; (*bad*) unsauber; **impurity** [ɪm'pjʊərɪtɪ] *n* Unreinheit *f*; (*TECH*) Verunreinigung *f*

KEYWORD

---

in [ɪn] *prep* **1** (*indicating place, position*) in +*dat*; (*with motion*) in +*acc*; **in here/ there** hier/dort; **in London** in London; **in the United States** in den Vereinigten Staaten

2 (*indicating time: during*) in +*dat*; **in summer** im Sommer; **in 1988** (im Jahre) 1988 (im Jahre) 1988; **in the afternoon** nachmittags, am Nachmittag

3 (*indicating time: in the space of*) innerhalb von; **I'll see you in 2 weeks** *or* **in 2 weeks' time** ich sehe Sie in zwei Wochen

4 (*indicating manner, circumstances, state etc*) in +*dat*; **in the sun/rain** in der Sonne/im Regen; **in English/French** auf Englisch/Französisch; **in a loud/ soft voice** mit lauter/leiser Stimme

5 (*with ratios, numbers*): **1 in 10** jeder Zehnte; **20 pence in the pound** 20 Pence pro Pfund; **they lined up in twos** sie stellten sich in Zweierreihe auf

6 (*referring to people, works*): **the disease is common in children** die Krankheit ist bei Kindern häufig; **in Dickens** bei Dickens; **we have a loyal friend in him** er ist uns ein treuer Freund

7 (*indicating profession etc*): **to be in teaching/the army** Lehrer(in)/beim Militär sein; **to be in publishing** im Verlagswesen arbeiten

8 (*with present participle*): **in saying this, I ...** wenn ich das sage, ... ich; **in**

accepting this view, he ... weil er diese Meinung akzeptiere, ...

♦ *adv*: **to be in** (*person: at home, work*) da sein; (*train, ship, plane*) angekommen sein; (*in fashion*) in sein; **to ask sb in** jdn hereinbitten; **to run/limp** *etc* **in** hereingerannt/gehumpelt *etc* kommen

♦ *n*: **the ins and outs** (*of proposal, situation etc*) die Feinheiten

in. *abbr* = **inch**

inability [ɪnə'bɪlɪtɪ] *n* Unfähigkeit *f*

inaccessible [ɪnək'sesɪbl] *adj* unzugänglich

inaccurate [ɪn'ækjʊrət] *adj* ungenau; (*wrong*) unrichtig

inactivity [ɪnæk'tɪvɪtɪ] *n* Untätigkeit *f*

inadequate [ɪn'ædɪkwət] *adj* unzulänglich

inadvertently [ɪnəd'vɜːtntlɪ] *adv* unabsichtlich

inadvisable [ɪnəd'vaɪzəbl] *adj* nicht ratsam

inane [ɪ'neɪn] *adj* dumm, albern

inanimate [ɪn'ænɪmət] *adj* leblos

inappropriate [ɪnə'prəʊprɪət] *adj* (*clothing*) ungeeignet; (*remark*) unangebracht

inarticulate [ɪnɑː'tɪkjʊlət] *adj* unklar

inasmuch as [ɪnəz'mʌtʃ-] *adv* da; (*in so far as*) so weit

inaudible [ɪn'ɔːdɪbl] *adj* unhörbar

inauguration [ɪnɔːɡjʊ'reɪʃən] *n* Eröffnung *f*; (*feierliche*) Amtseinführung *f*

inborn [ɪn'bɔːn] *adj* angeboren

inbred [ɪn'bred] *adj* angeboren

Inc. *abbr* = **incorporated**

incalculable [ɪn'kælkjʊləbl] *adj* (*consequences*) unabsehbar

incapable [ɪn'keɪpəbl] *adj*: **~ (of doing sth)** unfähig(, etw zu tun)

incapacitate [ɪnkə'pæsɪteɪt] *vt* untauglich machen

incapacity [ɪnkə'pæsɪtɪ] *n* Unfähigkeit *f*

incarcerate [ɪn'kɑːsəreɪt] *vt* einkerkern

incarnation [ɪnkɑː'neɪʃən] *n* (*ECCL*) Menschwerdung *f*; (*fig*) Inbegriff *m*

incendiary [ɪn'sendɪərɪ] *adj* Brand-

incense [*n* 'ɪnsens, *vb* ɪn'sens] *n* Weihrauch *m* ♦ *vt* erzürnen

incentive [ɪn'sentɪv] *n* Anreiz *m*

incessant [ɪn'sesnt] *adj* unaufhörlich

incest ['ɪnsest] *n* Inzest *m*

inch [ɪntʃ] *n* Zoll *m* ♦ *vi*: **to ~ forward** sich Stückchen für Stückchen vorwärts bewegen; **to be within an ~ of** kurz davor sein; **he didn't give an ~** er gab keinen Zentimeter nach

incidence ['ɪnsɪdns] *n* Auftreten *nt*; (*of crime*) Quote *f*

incident ['ɪnsɪdnt] *n* Vorfall *m*; (*disturbance*) Zwischenfall *m*

incidental [ɪnsɪ'dentl] *adj* (*music*) Begleit-; (*unimportant*) nebensächlich; (*remark*) beiläufig; **~ly** *adv* übrigens

incinerator [ɪn'sɪnəreɪtə] *n* Verbrennungsofen *m*

incision [ɪn'sɪʒən] *n* Einschnitt *m*

incisive [ɪn'saɪsɪv] *adj* (*style*) treffend; (*person*) scharfsinnig

incite [ɪn'saɪt] *vt* anstacheln

inclination [ɪnklɪ'neɪʃən] *n* Neigung *f*

incline [*n* 'ɪnklaɪn, *vb* ɪn'klaɪn] *n* Abhang *m* ♦ *vt* neigen; (*fig*) veranlassen ♦ *vi* sich neigen; **to be ~d to do sth** dazu neigen, etw zu tun

include [ɪn'kluːd] *vt* einschließen; (*on list, in group*) aufnehmen; **including** *prep*: **including X X** inbegriffen; **inclusion** [ɪn'kluːʒən] *n* Aufnahme *f*; **inclusive** [ɪn'kluːsɪv] *adj* einschließlich; (*COMM*) inklusive; **inclusive of** einschließlich +*gen*

incoherent [ɪnkəʊ'hɪərənt] *adj* zusammenhanglos

income ['ɪnkʌm] *n* Einkommen *nt*; (*from business*) Einkünfte *pl*; **~ tax** *n* Lohnsteuer *f*; (*of self-employed*) Einkommenssteuer *f*

incoming ['ɪnkʌmɪŋ] *adj*: **~ flight** eintreffende Maschine *f*

incomparable [ɪn'kɒmpərəbl] *adj* unvergleichlich

incompatible [ɪnkəm'pætɪbl] *adj* unvereinbar; (*people*) unverträglich

incompetence [ɪn'kɒmpɪtns] *n* Unfähigkeit *f;* **incompetent** *adj* unfähig

incomplete [ɪnkəm'pli:t] *adj* unvollständig

incomprehensible [ɪnkɒmprɪ'hensɪbl] *adj* unverständlich

inconceivable [ɪnkən'si:vəbl] *adj* unvorstellbar

incongruous [ɪn'kɒŋɡruəs] *adj* seltsam; (*remark*) unangebracht

inconsiderate [ɪnkən'sɪdərət] *adj* rücksichtslos

inconsistency [ɪnkən'sɪstənsɪ] *n* Widersprüchlichkeit *f;* (*state*) Unbeständigkeit *f*

inconsistent [ɪnkən'sɪstnt] *adj* (*action, speech*) widersprüchlich; (*person, work*) unbeständig; **~ with** nicht übereinstimmend mit

inconspicuous [ɪnkən'spɪkjuəs] *adj* unauffällig

incontinent [ɪn'kɒntɪnənt] *adj* (MED) nicht fähig, Stuhl und Harn zurückzuhalten

inconvenience [ɪnkən'vi:njəns] *n* Unbequemlichkeit *f;* (*trouble to others*) Unannehmlichkeiten *pl*

inconvenient [ɪnkən'vi:njənt] *adj* ungelegen; (*journey*) unbequem

incorporate [ɪn'kɔ:pəreɪt] *vt* (*include*) aufnehmen; (*contain*) enthalten; **~d** *adj:* **~d company** (US) eingetragene Aktiengesellschaft *f*

incorrect [ɪnkə'rekt] *adj* unrichtig

incorrigible [ɪn'kɒrɪdʒɪbl] *adj* unverbesserlich

incorruptible [ɪnkə'rʌptɪbl] *adj* unzerstörbar; (*person*) unbestechlich

increase [*n* 'ɪnkri:s, *vb* ɪn'kri:s] *n* Zunahme *f;* (*pay* ~) Gehaltserhöhung *f;* (*in size*) Vergrößerung *f* ♦ *vt* erhöhen; (*wealth, rage*) vermehren; (*business*) erweitern ♦ *vi* zunehmen; (*prices*) steigen; (*in size*) größer werden; (*in num-*

ber) sich vermehren; **increasing** *adj* (*number*) steigend; **increasingly** [ɪn'kri:sɪŋlɪ] *adv* zunehmend

incredible [ɪn'kredɪbl] *adj* unglaublich

incredulous [ɪn'kredjuləs] *adj* ungläubig

increment ['ɪnkrɪmənt] *n* Zulage *f*

incriminate [ɪn'krɪmɪneɪt] *vt* belasten

incubation [ɪnkju'beɪʃən] *n* Ausbrüten *nt*

incubator ['ɪnkjubeɪtəʳ] *n* Brutkasten *m*

incumbent [ɪn'kʌmbənt] *n* ♦ *adj:* **it is ~ on him to ...** es obliegt ihm, ...

incur [ɪn'kɜ:ʳ] *vt* sich zuziehen; (*debts*) machen

incurable [ɪn'kjuərəbl] *adj* unheilbar

indebted [ɪn'detɪd] *adj* (*obliged*): **~ (to sb)** (jdm) verpflichtet

indecent [ɪn'di:snt] *adj* unanständig; **~ assault** (BRIT) *n* Notzucht *f;* **~ exposure** *n* Exhibitionismus *m*

indecisive [ɪndɪ'saɪsɪv] *adj* (*battle*) nicht entscheidend; (*person*) unentschlossen

indeed [ɪn'di:d] *adv* tatsächlich, in der Tat; **yes ~!** allerdings!

indefinite [ɪn'defɪnɪt] *adj* unbestimmt; **~ly** *adv* auf unbestimmte Zeit; (*wait*) unbegrenzt lange

indelible [ɪn'delɪbl] *adj* unauslöschlich

indemnity [ɪn'demnɪtɪ] *n* (*insurance*) Versicherung *f;* (*compensation*) Entschädigung *f*

independence [ɪndɪ'pendns] *n* Unabhängigkeit *f;* **independent** *adj* unabhängig

---

Independence Day

Independence Day (*der 4. Juli*) ist in den USA ein gesetzlicher Feiertag zum Gedenken an die Unabhängigkeitserklärung am 4. Juli 1776, mit der die 13 amerikanischen Kolonien ihre Freiheit und Unabhängigkeit von Großbritannien erklärten.

indestructible [ˌɪndɪs'trʌktəbl] *adj* unzerstörbar

indeterminate [ˌɪndɪ'tɜːmɪnɪt] *adj* unbestimmt

index ['ɪndeks] (*pl* **~es** *or* **indices**) *n* Index *m*; **~ card** *n* Karteikarte *f*; **~ finger** *n* Zeigefinger *m*; **~-linked** (*US* **~ed**) *adj* (*salaries*) der Inflationsrate *dat* angeglichen; (*pensions*) dynamisch

India ['ɪndɪə] *n* Indien *nt*; **~n** *adj* indisch ♦ *n* Inder(in) *m(f)*; **American ~n** Indianer(in) *m(f)*; **~n Ocean** *n*: the **~n Ocean** der Indische Ozean

indicate ['ɪndɪkeɪt] *vt* anzeigen; (*hint*) andeuten; **indication** [ˌɪndɪ'keɪʃən] *n* Anzeichen *nt*; (*information*) Angabe *f*; **indicative** [ɪn'dɪkətɪv] *adj*: **indicative of** bezeichnend für; **indicator** *n* (An)zeichen *nt*; (*AUT*) Richtungsanzeiger *m*

indict [ɪn'daɪt] *vt* anklagen; **~ment** *n* Anklage *f*

indifference [ɪn'dɪfrəns] *n* Gleichgültigkeit *f*; Unwichtigkeit *f*; **indifferent** *adj* gleichgültig; (*mediocre*) mäßig

indigenous [ɪn'dɪdʒɪnəs] *adj* einheimisch

indigestion [ˌɪndɪ'dʒestʃən] *n* Verdauungsstörung *f*

indignant [ɪn'dɪgnənt] *adj*: **to be ~ about sth** über etw *acc* empört sein

indignation [ˌɪndɪg'neɪʃən] *n* Entrüstung *f*

indignity [ɪn'dɪgnɪtɪ] *n* Demütigung *f*

indirect [ˌɪndɪ'rekt] *adj* indirekt

indiscreet [ˌɪndɪs'kriːt] *adj* (*insensitive*) taktlos; (*telling secrets*) indiskret; **indiscretion** [ˌɪndɪs'kreʃən] *n* Taktlosigkeit *f*; Indiskretion *f*

indiscriminate [ˌɪndɪs'krɪmɪnət] *adj* wahllos; kritiklos

indispensable [ˌɪndɪs'pensəbl] *adj* unentbehrlich

indisposed [ˌɪndɪs'pəʊzd] *adj* unpässlich

indisputable [ˌɪndɪs'pjuːtəbl] *adj* unbestreitbar; (*evidence*) unanfechtbar

indistinct [ˌɪndɪs'tɪŋkt] *adj* undeutlich

individual [ˌɪndɪ'vɪdjuəl] *n* Individuum *nt* ♦ *adj* individuell; (*case*) Einzel-; (*for one person*) eigen, individuell; (*characteristic*) eigentümlich; **~ly** *adv* einzeln, individuell

indivisible [ˌɪndɪ'vɪzɪbl] *adj* unteilbar

indoctrinate [ɪn'dɒktrɪneɪt] *vt* indoktrinieren

Indonesia [ˌɪndə'niːzɪə] *n* Indonesien *nt*

indoor ['ɪndɔːr] *adj* Haus-; Zimmer-; Innen-; (*SPORT*) Hallen-; **~s** [ɪn'dɔːz] *adv* drinnen, im Haus

induce [ɪn'djuːs] *vt* dazu bewegen; (*reaction*) herbeiführen

induction course [ɪn'dʌkʃən-] (*BRIT*) *n* Einführungskurs *m*

indulge [ɪn'dʌldʒ] *vt* (*give way*) nachgeben +*dat*; (*gratify*) frönen +*dat* ♦ *vi*: **to ~ (in)** frönen (+*dat*); **~nce** *n* Nachsicht *f*; (*enjoyment*) Genuss *m*; **~nt** *adj* nachsichtig; (*pej*) nachgiebig

industrial [ɪn'dʌstrɪəl] *adj* Industrie-, industriell; (*dispute, injury*) Arbeits-; **~ action** *n* Arbeitskampfmaßnahmen *pl*; **~ estate** (*BRIT*) *n* Industriegebiet *nt*; **~ist** *n* Industrielle(r) *mf*; **~ize** *vt* industrialisieren; **~ park** (*US*) *n* Industriegebiet *nt*

industrious [ɪn'dʌstrɪəs] *adj* fleißig

industry ['ɪndəstrɪ] *n* Industrie *f*; (*diligence*) Fleiß *m*

inebriated [ɪ'niːbrɪeɪtɪd] *adj* betrunken

inedible [ɪn'edɪbl] *adj* ungenießbar

ineffective [ˌɪnɪ'fektɪv] *adj* unwirksam; (*person*) untauglich

ineffectual [ˌɪnɪ'fektʃuəl] *adj* = **ineffective**

inefficiency [ˌɪnɪ'fɪʃənsɪ] *n* Ineffizienz *f*

inefficient [ˌɪnɪ'fɪʃənt] *adj* ineffizient; (*ineffective*) unwirksam

inept [ɪ'nept] *adj* (*remark*) unpassend; (*person*) ungeeignet

inequality [ˌɪnɪ'kwɒlɪtɪ] *n* Ungleichheit *f*

inert [ɪ'nɜːt] *adj* träge; (*CHEM*) inaktiv; (*motionless*) unbeweglich

inescapable [ˌɪnɪˈskeɪpəbl] adj unvermeidbar

inevitable [ɪnˈevɪtəbl] adj unvermeidlich; **inevitably** adv zwangsläufig

inexcusable [ˌɪnɪksˈkjuːzəbl] adj unverzeihlich

inexhaustible [ˌɪnɪgˈzɔːstɪbl] adj unerschöpflich

inexpensive [ˌɪnɪkˈspensɪv] adj preiswert

inexperience [ˌɪnɪkˈspɪərɪəns] n Unerfahrenheit f; **~d** adj unerfahren

inexplicable [ˌɪnɪkˈsplɪkəbl] adj unerklärlich

inextricably [ˌɪnɪkˈstrɪkəbl] adv untrennbar

infallible [ɪnˈfælɪbl] adj unfehlbar

infamous [ˈɪnfəməs] adj (deed) schändlich; (person) niederträchtig

infancy [ˈɪnfənsɪ] n frühe Kindheit f; (fig) Anfangsstadium nt

infant [ˈɪnfənt] n kleine(s) Kind nt, Säugling m; **~ile** [-aɪl] adj kindisch, infantil; **~ school** (BRIT) n Vorschule f

infatuated [ɪnˈfætjʊeɪtɪd] adj vernarrt; **to become ~ with** sich vernarren in +acc; **infatuation** [ɪnˌfætjuˈeɪʃən] n: **~ (with)** Vernarrtheit f (in +acc)

infect [ɪnˈfekt] vt anstecken (also fig); **~ed with** (illness) infiziert mit; **~ion** [ɪnˈfekʃən] n Infektion f; **~ious** [ɪnˈfekʃəs] adj ansteckend

infer [ɪnˈfɜːr] vt schließen

inferior [ɪnˈfɪərɪər] adj (rank) untergeordnet; (quality) minderwertig ♦ n Untergebene(r) m; **~ity** [ɪnˌfɪərɪˈɔrɪtɪ] n Minderwertigkeit f; (in rank) untergeordnete Stellung f; **~ity complex** n Minderwertigkeitskomplex m

infernal [ɪnˈfɜːnl] adj höllisch

infertile [ɪnˈfɜːtaɪl] adj unfruchtbar; **infertility** [ɪnfəˈtɪlɪtɪ] n Unfruchtbarkeit f

infested [ɪnˈfestɪd] adj: **to be ~ with** wimmeln von

infidelity [ɪnfɪˈdelɪtɪ] n Untreue f

infighting [ˈɪnfaɪtɪŋ] n Nahkampf m

infiltrate [ˈɪnfɪltreɪt] vt infiltrieren; (spies) einschleusen ♦ vi (MIL, liquid) einsickern; (POL): **to ~ (into)** unterwandern (+acc)

infinite [ˈɪnfɪnɪt] adj unendlich

infinitive [ɪnˈfɪnɪtɪv] n Infinitiv m

infinity [ɪnˈfɪnɪtɪ] n Unendlichkeit f

infirm [ɪnˈfɜːm] adj gebrechlich; **~ary** n Krankenhaus nt

inflamed [ɪnˈfleɪmd] adj entzündet

inflammable [ɪnˈflæməbl] (BRIT) adj feuergefährlich

inflammation [ɪnfləˈmeɪʃən] n Entzündung f

inflatable [ɪnˈfleɪtəbl] adj aufblasbar

inflate [ɪnˈfleɪt] vt aufblasen; (tyre) aufpumpen; (prices) hoch treiben; **inflation** [ɪnˈfleɪʃən] n Inflation f; **inflationary** [ɪnˈfleɪʃənərɪ] adj (increase) inflationistisch; (situation) inflationär

inflexible [ɪnˈfleksɪbl] adj (person) nicht flexibel; (opinion) starr; (thing) unbiegsam

inflict [ɪnˈflɪkt] vt: **to ~ sth on sb** jdm etw zufügen; (wound) jdm etw beibringen

influence [ˈɪnfluəns] n Einfluss m ♦ vt beeinflussen

influential [ɪnfluˈenʃl] adj einflussreich

influenza [ɪnfluˈenzə] n Grippe f

influx [ˈɪnflʌks] n (of people) Zustrom m; (of ideas) Eindringen nt

infomercial [ˈɪnfəʊmɜːʃl] n Werbeinformationssendung f

inform [ɪnˈfɔːm] vt informieren ♦ vi: **to ~ on sb** jdn denunzieren; **to keep sb ~ed** jdn auf dem Laufenden halten

informal [ɪnˈfɔːml] adj zwanglos; **~ity** [ɪnfɔːˈmælɪtɪ] n Ungezwungenheit f

informant [ɪnˈfɔːmənt] n Informant(in) m(f)

information [ɪnfəˈmeɪʃən] n Auskunft f, Information f; **a piece of ~** eine Auskunft, eine Information; **~ desk** n Auskunftsschalter m; **~ office** n Informationsbüro nt

informative [ɪnˈfɔ:mətɪv] adj informativ; (person) mitteilsam

informer [ɪnˈfɔ:məʳ] n Denunziant(in) m(f)

infra-red [ɪnfrəˈred] adj infrarot

infrequent [ɪnˈfri:kwənt] adj selten

infringe [ɪnˈfrɪndʒ] vt (law) verstoßen gegen; ~ **upon** vt verletzen; **~ment** n Verstoß m, Verletzung f

infuriating [ɪnˈfjuərɪeɪtɪŋ] adj ärgerlich

ingenuity [ɪndʒɪˈnju:ɪtɪ] n Genialität f

ingenuous [ɪnˈdʒenjuəs] adj aufrichtig; (naive) naiv

ingot [ˈɪŋɡət] n Barren m

ingrained [ɪnˈɡreɪnd] adj tief sitzend

ingratiate [ɪnˈɡreɪʃɪeɪt] vt: **to ~ o.s. with sb** sich bei jdm einschmeicheln

ingratitude [ɪnˈɡrætɪtju:d] n Undankbarkeit f

ingredient [ɪnˈɡri:dɪənt] n Bestandteil m; (cook) Zutat f

inhabit [ɪnˈhæbɪt] vt bewohnen; **~ant** n Bewohner(in) m(f); (of island, town) Einwohner(in) m(f)

inhale [ɪnˈheɪl] vt einatmen; (MED, cigarettes) inhalieren

inherent [ɪnˈhɪərənt] adj: **~ (in)** innewohnend (+dat)

inherit [ɪnˈherɪt] vt erben; **~ance** n Erbe nt, Erbschaft f

inhibit [ɪnˈhɪbɪt] vt hemmen; **to ~ sb from doing sth** jdn daran hindern, etw zu tun; **~ion** [ɪnhɪˈbɪʃən] n Hemmung f

inhospitable [ɪnhɒsˈpɪtəbl] adj (person) ungastlich; (country) unwirtlich

inhuman [ɪnˈhju:mən] adj unmenschlich

initial [ɪˈnɪʃl] adj anfänglich, Anfangs- ♦ n Initiale f ♦ vt abzeichnen; (POL) paraphieren; **~ly** adv anfangs

initiate [ɪˈnɪʃɪeɪt] vt einführen; (negotiations) einleiten; **to ~ proceedings against sb** (JUR) gerichtliche Schritte gegen jdn einleiten; **initiation** [ɪnɪʃɪˈeɪʃən] n Einführung f; Einleitung f

initiative [ɪˈnɪʃɪətɪv] n Initiative f

inject [ɪnˈdʒekt] vt einspritzen; (fig) einflößen; **~ion** [ɪnˈdʒekʃən] n Spritze f

injunction [ɪnˈdʒʌŋkʃən] n Verfügung f

injure [ˈɪndʒəʳ] vt verletzen; **~d** adj (person, arm) verletzt; **injury** [ˈɪndʒərɪ] n Verletzung f; **to play injury time** (SPORT) nachspielen

injustice [ɪnˈdʒʌstɪs] n Ungerechtigkeit f

ink [ɪŋk] n Tinte f

inkling [ˈɪŋklɪŋ] n (dunkle) Ahnung f

inlaid [ˈɪnleɪd] adj eingelegt, Einlege-

inland [adj ˈɪnlənd, adv ɪnˈlænd] adj Binnen-; (domestic) Inlands- ♦ adv landeinwärts; **~ revenue** (BRIT) n Fiskus m

in-laws [ˈɪnlɔ:z] npl (parents-in-law) Schwiegereltern pl; (others) angeheiratete Verwandte pl

inlet [ˈɪnlet] n Einlass m; (bay) kleine Bucht f

inmate [ˈɪnmeɪt] n Insasse m

inn [ɪn] n Gasthaus nt, Wirtshaus nt

innate [ɪˈneɪt] adj angeboren

inner [ˈɪnəʳ] adj inner, Innen-; (fig) verborgen; **~ city** n Innenstadt f; **~ tube** n (of tyre) Schlauch m

innings [ˈɪnɪŋz] n (CRICKET) Innenrunde f

innocence [ˈɪnəsns] n Unschuld f; (ignorance) Unkenntnis f

innocent [ˈɪnəsnt] adj unschuldig

innocuous [ɪˈnɒkjuəs] adj harmlos

innovation [ɪnəʊˈveɪʃən] n Neuerung f

innuendo [ɪnjuˈendəʊ] n (versteckte) Anspielung f

innumerable [ɪˈnju:mrəbl] adj unzählig

inoculation [ɪnɒkjuˈleɪʃən] n Impfung f

inopportune [ɪnˈɒpətju:n] adj (remark) unangebracht; (visit) ungelegen

inordinately [ɪˈnɔ:dɪnətlɪ] adv unmäßig

inpatient [ˈɪnpeɪʃənt] n stationäre(r) Patient m/stationäre Patientin f

input [ˈɪnput] n (COMPUT) Eingabe f

(*power* ~) Energiezufuhr *f*; (*of energy, work*) Aufwand *m*

inquest ['ɪnkwest] *n* gerichtliche Untersuchung *f*

inquire [ɪn'kwaɪə'] *vi* sich erkundigen ♦ *vt* (*price*) sich erkundigen nach; ~ **into** *vt* untersuchen; **inquiry** [ɪn'kwaɪərɪ] *n* (*question*) Erkundigung *f*; (*investigation*) Untersuchung *f*; **inquiries** Auskunft *f*; **inquiry office** (*BRIT*) *n* Auskunft(sbüro *nt*) *f*

inquisitive [ɪn'kwɪzɪtɪv] *adj* neugierig

ins. *abbr* = **inches**

insane [ɪn'seɪn] *adj* wahnsinnig; (*MED*) geisteskrank; **insanity** [ɪn'sænɪtɪ] *n* Wahnsinn *m*

insatiable [ɪn'seɪʃəbl] *adj* unersättlich

inscribe [ɪn'skraɪb] *vt* eingravieren; **inscription** [ɪn'skrɪpʃən] *n* (*on stone*) Inschrift *f*; (*in book*) Widmung *f*

insect ['ɪnsekt] *n* Insekt *nt*; **~icide** [ɪn'sektɪsaɪd] *n* Insektenvertilgungsmittel *nt*; **~ repellent** *n* Insektenbekämpfungsmittel *nt*

insecure [ɪnsɪ'kjuə'] *adj* (*person*) unsicher; (*thing*) nicht fest or sicher; **insecurity** [ɪnsɪ'kjuərɪtɪ] *n* Unsicherheit *f*

insemination [ɪnsemɪ'neɪʃən] *n*: **artificial ~** künstliche Befruchtung *f*

insensible [ɪn'sensɪbl] *adj* (*unconscious*) bewusstlos

insensitive [ɪn'sensɪtɪv] *adj* (*to pain*) unempfindlich; (*unfeeling*) gefühllos

inseparable [ɪn'seprəbl] *adj* (*people*) unzertrennlich; (*word*) untrennbar

insert [*vb* ɪn'sɜːt, *n* 'ɪnsɜːt] *vt* einfügen; (*coin*) einwerfen; (*stick into*) hineinstecken; (*advertisement*) aufgeben ♦ *n* (*in book*) Einlage *f*; (*in magazine*) Beilage *f*; **~ion** [ɪn'sɜːʃən] *n* Einfügung *f*; (*PRESS*) Inserat *nt*

in-service ['ɪn'sɜːvɪs] *adj* (*training*) berufsbegleitend

inshore ['ɪn'ʃɔː'] *adj* Küsten- ♦ *adv* an der Küste

inside ['ɪn'saɪd] *n* Innenseite *f*, Innere(s) *nt* ♦ *adj* innere(r, s), Innen- ♦ *adv*

(*place*) innen; (*direction*) nach innen, hinein ♦ *prep* (*place*) in +*dat*; (*direction*) in +*acc* ... hinein; (*time*) innerhalb +*gen*; **~s** *npl* (*inf*) Eingeweide *nt*; **~ 10 minutes** unter 10 Minuten; **~ information** *n* interne Informationen *pl*; **~ lane** *n* (*AUT*: *in Britain*) linke Spur; **~ out** *adv* linksherum; (*know*) in- und auswendig

insider dealing, insider trading [ɪn'saɪdə'-] *n* (*STOCK EXCHANGE*) Insiderhandel *m*

insidious [ɪn'sɪdɪəs] *adj* heimtückisch

insight ['ɪnsaɪt] *n* Einsicht *f*, +*acc*; **~ into** Einblick *m* in +*acc*

insignificant [ɪnsɪg'nɪfɪkənt] *adj* unbedeutend

insincere [ɪnsɪn'sɪə'] *adj* unaufrichtig

insinuate [ɪn'sɪnjueɪt] *vt* (*hint*) andeuten

insipid [ɪn'sɪpɪd] *adj* fad(e)

insist [ɪn'sɪst] *vi*: **to ~ (on)** bestehen (auf +*acc*); **~ence** *n* Bestehen *nt*; **~ent** *adj* hartnäckig; (*urgent*) dringend

insole ['ɪnsəul] *n* Einlegesohle *f*

insolence ['ɪnsələns] *n* Frechheit *f*

insolent ['ɪnsələnt] *adj* frech

insoluble [ɪn'sɔljubl] *adj* unlösbar; (*CHEM*) unlöslich

insolvent [ɪn'sɔlvənt] *adj* zahlungsunfähig

insomnia [ɪn'sɔmnɪə] *n* Schlaflosigkeit *f*

inspect [ɪn'spekt] *vt* prüfen; (*officially*) inspizieren; **~ion** [ɪn'spekʃən] *n* Inspektion *f*; **~or** *n* (*official*) Inspektor *m*; (*police*) Polizeikommissar *m*; (*BRIT*: *on buses, trains*) Kontrolleur *m*

inspiration [ɪnspə'reɪʃən] *n* Inspiration *f*

inspire [ɪn'spaɪə'] *vt* (*person*) inspirieren; **to ~ sth in sb** (*respect*) jdm etw einflößen; (*hope*) etw in jdm wecken

instability [ɪnstə'bɪlɪtɪ] *n* Unbeständigkeit *f*, Labilität *f*

install [ɪn'stɔːl] *vt* (*put in*) installieren; (*telephone*) anschließen; (*establish*) einsetzen; **~ation** [ɪnstə'leɪʃən] n (of person) (Amts)einsetzung f; (of machinery) Installierung f; (machines etc) Anlage f

instalment [ɪn'stɔːlmənt] (US **installment**) n Rate f; (of story) Fortsetzung f; **to pay in ~s** in Raten zahlen

instance ['ɪnstəns] n Fall m; (example) Beispiel nt; **for ~** zum Beispiel; **in the first ~** zunächst

instant ['ɪnstənt] n Augenblick m ♦ adj augenblicklich, sofortig; **~aneous** [ɪnstən'teɪnɪəs] adj unmittelbar; **~ coffee** n Pulverkaffee m; **~ly** adv sofort

instead [ɪn'sted] adv stattdessen; **~ of** prep anstatt +gen

instep ['ɪnstep] n Spann m; (of shoe) Blatt nt

instil [ɪn'stɪl] vt (fig): **to ~ sth in sb** jdm etw beibringen

instinct ['ɪnstɪŋkt] n Instinkt m; **~ive** [ɪn'stɪŋktɪv] adj instinktiv

institute ['ɪnstɪtjuːt] n Institut nt ♦ vt einführen; (search) einleiten

institution [ɪnstɪ'tjuːʃən] n Institution f; (home) Anstalt f

instruct [ɪn'strʌkt] vt anweisen; (officially) instruieren; **~ion** [ɪn'strʌkʃən] n Unterricht m; **~ions** npl (orders) Anweisungen pl; (for use) Gebrauchsanweisung f; **~or** n Lehrer m

instrument ['ɪnstrəmənt] n Instrument nt; **~al** [ɪnstrʊ'mentl] adj (MUS) Instrumental-; (helpful): **~al (in)** behilflich (bei); **~ panel** n Armaturenbrett nt

insubordinate [ɪnsə'bɔːdənɪt] adj aufsässig, widersetzlich

insufferable [ɪn'sʌfrəbl] adj unerträglich

insufficient [ɪnsə'fɪʃnt] adj ungenügend

insular ['ɪnsjələ] adj (fig) engstirnig

insulate ['ɪnsjʊleɪt] vt (ELEC) isolieren; (fig): **to ~ (from)** abschirmen (vor +dat); **insulating tape** n Isolierband nt; **insulation** [ɪnsjʊ'leɪʃən] n Isolierung f

insulin ['ɪnsjʊlɪn] n Insulin nt

insult [n 'ɪnsʌlt, vb ɪn'sʌlt] n Beleidigung f ♦ vt beleidigen

insurance [ɪn'ʃuərəns] n Versicherung f; **fire/life ~** Feuer-/Lebensversicherung; **~ agent** n Versicherungsvertreter m; **~ policy** n Versicherungspolice f

insure [ɪn'ʃuə] vt versichern

intact [ɪn'tækt] adj unversehrt

intake ['ɪnteɪk] n (place) Einlassöffnung f; (act) Aufnahme f; (BRIT: SCH): **an ~ of 200 a year** ein Neuzugang von 200 im Jahr

intangible [ɪn'tændʒɪbl] adj nicht greifbar

integral ['ɪntɪgrəl] adj (essential) wesentlich; (complete) vollständig; (MATH) Integral-

integrate ['ɪntɪgreɪt] vt integrieren ♦ vi sich integrieren

integrity [ɪn'tegrɪtɪ] n (honesty) Redlichkeit f, Integrität f

intellect ['ɪntəlekt] n Intellekt m; **~ual** [ɪntə'lektjuəl] adj geistig, intellektuell ♦ n Intellektuelle(r) mf

intelligence [ɪn'telɪdʒəns] n (understanding) Intelligenz f; (news) Information f; (MIL) Geheimdienst m; **~ service** n Nachrichtendienst m, Geheimdienst m

intelligent [ɪn'telɪdʒənt] adj intelligent; **~ly** adv klug; (write, speak) verständlich

intelligentsia [ɪntelɪ'dʒentsɪə] n Intelligenz f

intelligible [ɪn'telɪdʒɪbl] adj verständlich

intend [ɪn'tend] vt beabsichtigen; **that was ~ed for you** das war für dich gedacht

intense [ɪn'tens] adj stark, intensiv; (person) ernsthaft; **~ly** adv äußerst; (study) intensiv

intensify [ɪn'tensɪfaɪ] vt verstärken, intensivieren

intensity [ɪn'tensɪtɪ] n Intensität f

intensive [ɪnˈtɛnsɪv] adj intensiv; ~ **care unit** n Intensivstation f

intent [ɪnˈtɛnt] n Absicht f ♦ adj: **to be ~ on doing sth** fest entschlossen sein, etw zu tun; **to all ~s and purposes** praktisch

intention [ɪnˈtɛnʃən] n Absicht f; **~al** adj absichtlich

intently [ɪnˈtɛntlɪ] adv konzentriert

interact [ɪntərˈækt] vi aufeinander einwirken; **~ion** [ɪntərˈækʃən] n Wechselwirkung f; **~ive** ad [COMPUT] interaktiv

intercept [ɪntəˈsɛpt] vt abfangen

interchange [n ˈɪntətʃeɪndʒ, vb ɪntəˈtʃeɪndʒ] n (exchange) Austausch m; (on roads) Verkehrskreuz nt ♦ vt austauschen; **~able** [ɪntəˈtʃeɪndʒəbl] adj austauschbar

intercom [ˈɪntəkɔm] n (Gegen)sprechanlage f

intercourse [ˈɪntəkɔːs] n (exchange) Beziehungen pl; (sexual) Geschlechtsverkehr m

interest [ˈɪntrɪst] n Interesse nt; (FIN) Zinsen pl; (COMM: share) Anteil m; (group) Interessengruppe f ♦ vt interessieren; **~ed** adj (having claims) beteiligt; (attentive) interessiert; **to be ~ed in sich** interessieren für; **~ing** adj interessant; **~ rate** n Zinssatz m

interface [ˈɪntəfeɪs] n (COMPUT) Schnittstelle f, Interface nt

interfere [ɪntəˈfɪər] vi: **to ~ (with)** (meddle) sich einmischen (in +acc); (disrupt) stören +acc; **~nce** [ɪntəˈfɪərəns] n Einmischung f; (TV) Störung f

interim [ˈɪntərɪm] n: **in the ~** inzwischen

interior [ɪnˈtɪərɪər] n Innere(s) nt ♦ adj innere(r, s), Innen-; **~ designer** n Innenarchitekt(in) m(f)

interjection [ɪntəˈdʒɛkʃən] n Ausruf m

interlock [ɪntəˈlɔk] vi ineinander greifen

interlude [ˈɪntəluːd] n Pause f

intermediary [ɪntəˈmiːdɪərɪ] n Ver-

mittler m

intermediate [ɪntəˈmiːdɪət] adj Zwischen-, Mittel-

interminable [ɪnˈtəːmɪnəbl] adj endlos

intermission [ɪntəˈmɪʃən] n Pause f

intermittent [ɪntəˈmɪtnt] adj periodisch, stoßweise

intern [vb ɪnˈtəːn, n ˈɪntəːn] vt internieren ♦ n (US) Assistenzarzt m/-ärztin f

internal [ɪnˈtəːnl] adj (inside) innere(r, s); (domestic) Inlands-; **~ly** adv innen; (MED) innerlich; **"not to be taken ~ly"** "nur zur äußerlichen Anwendung"; **Internal Revenue Service** (US) n Finanzamt nt

international [ɪntəˈnæʃənl] adj international ♦ n (SPORT) Nationalspieler(in) m(f); (: match) internationale(s) Spiel nt

Internet [ˈɪntənɛt] n: **the ~** das Internet; **~ café** n Internet-Café nt

interplay [ˈɪntəpleɪ] n Wechselspiel nt

interpret [ɪnˈtəːprɪt] vt (explain) auslegen, interpretieren; (translate) dolmetschen; **~er** n Dolmetscher(in) m(f)

interrelated [ɪntərɪˈleɪtɪd] adj untereinander zusammenhängend

interrogate [ɪnˈtɛrəugeɪt] vt verhören; **interrogation** [ɪntɛrəuˈgeɪʃən] n Verhör nt

interrupt [ɪntəˈrʌpt] vt unterbrechen; **~ion** [ɪntəˈrʌpʃən] n Unterbrechung f

intersect [ɪntəˈsɛkt] vi (a. durch)schneiden ♦ vi sich schneiden; **~ion** [ɪntəˈsɛkʃən] n (of roads) Kreuzung f; (of lines) Schnittpunkt m

intersperse [ɪntəˈspəːs] vt: **to ~ sth with sth** etw mit etw durchsetzen

intertwine [ɪntəˈtwaɪn] vt verflechten ♦ vi sich verflechten

interval [ˈɪntəvl] n Abstand m; (BRIT: THEAT, SPORT) Pause f; **at ~s** in Abständen

intervene [ɪntəˈviːn] vi (intervene) dazwischenliegen; (act): **to ~ (in)** einschreiten (gegen); **intervention** [ɪntəˈvɛnʃən] n Eingreifen nt, Intervention f

interview [ˈɪntəvjuː] n (PRESS etc) Interview *nt*; *(for job)* Vorstellungsgespräch *nt* ♦ *vt* interviewen; **~er** *n* Interviewer *m*

intestine [ɪnˈtestɪn] *n*: **large/small ~** Dick-/Dünndarm *m*

intimacy [ˈɪntɪməsɪ] *n* Intimität *f*

intimate [*adj* ˈɪntɪmɪt, *vb* ˈɪntɪmeɪt] *adj* *(inmost)* innerste(r, s); *(knowledge)* eingehend; *(familiar)* vertraut; *(friends)* eng ♦ *vt* andeuten

intimidate [ɪnˈtɪmɪdeɪt] *vt* einschüchtern

into [ˈɪntu] *prep* *(motion)* in *+acc* ... hinein; **5 ~ 25** 25 durch 5

intolerable [ɪnˈtɔlərəbl] *adj* unerträglich

intolerant [ɪnˈtɔlərnt] *adj*: **~ of** unduldsam gegen(über)

intoxicate [ɪnˈtɔksɪkeɪt] *vt* berauschen; **~d** *adj* betrunken; **intoxication** [ɪntɔksɪˈkeɪʃən] *n* Rausch *m*

intractable [ɪnˈtræktəbl] *adj* schwer zu handhaben; *(problem)* schwer lösbar

intransitive [ɪnˈtrænsɪtɪv] *adj* intransitiv

intravenous [ɪntrəˈviːnəs] *adj* intravenös

in-tray [ˈɪntreɪ] *n* Eingangskorb *m*

intrepid [ɪnˈtrepɪd] *adj* unerschrocken

intricate [ˈɪntrɪkət] *adj* kompliziert

intrigue [ɪnˈtriːg] *n* Intrige *f* ♦ *vt* faszinieren ♦ *vi* intrigieren

intrinsic [ɪnˈtrɪnsɪk] *adj* innere(r, s); *(difference)* wesentlich

introduce [ɪntrəˈdjuːs] *vt* *(person)* vorstellen; *(sth new)* einführen; *(subject)* anschneiden; **to ~ sb to sb** jdn jdm vorstellen; **to ~ sb to sth** jdn in etw *acc* einführen; **introduction** [ɪntrəˈdʌkʃən] *n* Einführung *f*; *(to book)* Einleitung *f*; **introductory** [ɪntrəˈdʌktərɪ] *adj* Einführungs-, Vor-

introspective [ɪntrəuˈspektɪv] *adj* nach innen gekehrt

introvert [ˈɪntrəuvɜːt] *n* Introvertierte(r) *mf* ♦ *adj* introvertiert

intrude [ɪnˈtruːd] *vi*: **to ~ (on sb/sth)**

(jdn/etw) stören; **~r** *n* Eindringling *m*

intrusion [ɪnˈtruːʒən] *n* Störung *f*

intrusive [ɪnˈtruːsɪv] *adj* aufdringlich

intuition [ɪntjuːˈɪʃən] *n* Intuition *f*

inundate [ˈɪnʌndeɪt] *vt* *(also fig)* überschwemmen

invade [ɪnˈveɪd] *vt* einfallen in *+acc*; **~r** *n* Eindringling *m*

invalid¹ [ˈɪnvəlɪd] *n* *(disabled)* Invalide *m* ♦ *adj* *(disabled)* invalide

invalid² [ɪnˈvælɪd] *adj* *(not valid)* ungültig

invaluable [ɪnˈvæljuəbl] *adj* unschätzbar

invariable [ɪnˈvɛərɪəbl] *adj* unveränderlich; **invariably** *adv* ausnahmslos

invent [ɪnˈvent] *vt* erfinden; **~ion** [ɪnˈvenʃən] *n* Erfindung *f*; **~ive** *adj* erfinderisch; **~or** *n* Erfinder *m*

inventory [ˈɪnvəntrɪ] *n* Inventar *nt*

inverse [ɪnˈvɜːs] *n* Umkehrung *f* ♦ *adj* umgekehrt

invert [ɪnˈvɜːt] *vt* umdrehen; **~ed commas** (*BRIT*) *npl* Anführungsstriche *pl*

invest [ɪnˈvest] *vt* investieren

investigate [ɪnˈvestɪgeɪt] *vt* untersuchen; **investigation** [ɪnvestɪˈgeɪʃən] *n* Untersuchung *f*; **investigator** [ɪnˈvestɪgeɪtə*r*] *n* Untersuchungsbeamte(r) *m*

investiture [ɪnˈvestɪtʃə*r*] *n* Amtseinsetzung *f*

investment [ɪnˈvestmənt] *n* Investition *f*

investor [ɪnˈvestə*r*] *n* (Geld)anleger *m*

invigilate [ɪnˈvɪdʒɪleɪt] *vi* *(in exam)* Aufsicht führen ♦ *vt* Aufsicht führen bei; **invigilator** *n* Aufsicht *f*

invigorating [ɪnˈvɪgəreɪtɪŋ] *adj* stärkend

invincible [ɪnˈvɪnsɪbl] *adj* unbesiegbar

invisible [ɪnˈvɪzɪbl] *adj* unsichtbar

invitation [ɪnvɪˈteɪʃən] *n* Einladung *f*

invite [ɪnˈvaɪt] *vt* einladen

invoice [ˈɪnvɔɪs] *n* Rechnung *f* ♦ *vt*

(goods): **to ~ sb for sth** jdm etw acc in Rechnung stellen

nvoke [ɪn'vəʊk] vt anrufen

nvoluntary [ɪn'vɒləntrɪ] adj unabsichtlich

nvolve [ɪn'vɒlv] vt (entangle) verwickeln; (entail) mit sich bringen; **~d** adj verwickelt; **~ment** n Verwicklung f

nward ['ɪnwəd] adj innere(r, s); (curve) Innen- ♦ adv nach innen; **~ly** adv im Innern; **~s** adv nach innen

/O abbr (COMPUT) (= input/output) I/O

odine ['aɪəʊdiːn] n Jod nt

oniser ['aɪənaɪzə⁰] n Ionisator m

ota [aɪ'əʊtə] n (fig) bisschen n

OU n abbr (= I owe you) Schuldschein m

IQ n abbr (= intelligence quotient) IQ m

IRA n abbr (= Irish Republican Army) IRA f

Iran [ɪ'rɑːn] n Iran m; **~ian** [ɪ'reɪnɪən] adj iranisch ♦ n Iraner(in) m(f); (LING) Iranisch nt

Iraq [ɪ'rɑːk] n Irak m; **~i** adj irakisch ♦ n Iraker(in) m(f)

irate [aɪ'reɪt] adj zornig

Ireland ['aɪələnd] n Irland nt

iris ['aɪrɪs] (pl ~es) n Iris f

Irish ['aɪrɪʃ] adj irisch ♦ npl: **the ~** die Iren pl, die Irländer pl; **~man** (irreg) n Ire m, Irländer m; **~ Sea** n: **the ~ Sea** die Irische See f; **~woman** (irreg) n Irin f, Irländerin f

irksome ['ɜːksəm] adj lästig

iron ['aɪən] n Eisen nt; (for ~ing) Bügeleisen nt ♦ adj eisern ♦ vt bügeln; **~ out** vt (also fig) ausbügeln; **Iron Curtain** n (HIST) Eiserne(r) Vorhang m

ironic(al) [aɪ'rɒnɪk(l)] adj ironisch; (coincidence etc) witzig

iron: ~ing n Bügeln nt; (laundry) Bügelwäsche f; **~ing board** n Bügelbrett nt; **~monger's (shop)** n Eisen- und Haushaltswarenhandlung f

irony ['aɪrənɪ] n Ironie f

irrational [ɪ'ræʃənl] adj irrational

irreconcilable [ɪrekən'saɪləbl] adj unvereinbar

irrefutable [ɪrɪ'fjuːtəbl] adj unwider-

legbar

irregular [ɪ'regjʊlə⁰] adj unregelmäßig; (shape) ungleich(mäßig); (fig) unüblich; (: behaviour) ungehörig

irrelevant [ɪ'reləvənt] adj belanglos, irrelevant

irreparable [ɪ'reprəbl] adj nicht wieder gutzumachen

irreplaceable [ɪrɪ'pleɪsəbl] adj unersetzlich

irresistible [ɪrɪ'zɪstɪbl] adj unwiderstehlich

irrespective [ɪrɪ'spektɪv]: **~ of** prep ungeachtet +gen

irresponsible [ɪrɪ'spɒnsɪbl] adj verantwortungslos

irreverent [ɪ'revərnt] adj respektlos

irrevocable [ɪ'revəkəbl] adj unwiderruflich

irrigate ['ɪrɪgeɪt] vt bewässern

irritable ['ɪrɪtəbl] adj reizbar

irritate ['ɪrɪteɪt] vt irritieren, reizen (also MED); **irritating** adj ärgerlich, irritierend; **he is irritating** er kann einem auf die Nerven gehen; **irritation** [ɪrɪ'teɪʃən] n (anger) Ärger m; (MED) Reizung f

IRS n abbr = Internal Revenue Service

is [ɪz] vb see be

Islam ['ɪzlɑːm] n Islam m; **~ic** [ɪz'læmɪk] adj islamisch

island ['aɪlənd] n Insel f; **~er** n Inselbewohner(in) m(f)

isle [aɪl] n (kleine) Insel f

isn't ['ɪznt] = is not

isolate ['aɪsəleɪt] vt isolieren; **~d** adj isoliert; (case) Einzel-; **isolation** [aɪsə'leɪʃən] n Isolierung f

Israel ['ɪzreɪl] n Israel nt; **~i** [ɪz'reɪlɪ] adj israelisch ♦ n Israeli mf

issue ['ɪʃjuː] n (matter) Frage f; (outcome) Ausgang m; (of newspaper, shares) Ausgabe f; (offspring) Nachkommenschaft f ♦ vt ausgeben; (warrant) erlassen; (documents) ausstellen; (orders) erteilen; (books) herausgeben; (verdict) aussprechen; **to be at ~** zur Debatte

stehen; **to take ~ with sb over sth**
jdm in etw *dat* widersprechen

KEYWORD
---

it [ɪt] *pron* **1** (*specific: subject*) er/sie/es;
(*: direct object*) ihn/sie/es; (*: indirect object*) ihm/ihr/ihm; **about/from/in/of it**
darüber/davon/darin/davon
2 (*impers*) es; **it's raining** es regnet;
it's Friday tomorrow morgen ist Freitag; **who is it? – it's me** wer ist da? –
ich (bins)

Italian [ɪ'tæljən] *adj* italienisch ♦ *n* Italiener(in) *m(f)*; (*LING*) Italienisch *nt*
italic [ɪ'tælɪk] *adj* kursiv; **~s** *npl* Kursivschrift *f*
Italy ['ɪtəlɪ] *n* Italien *nt*
itch [ɪtʃ] *n* Juckreiz *m*; (*fig*) Lust *f* ♦ *vi*
jucken; **to be ~ing to do sth** darauf
brennen, etw zu tun; **~y** *adj* juckend
it'd ['ɪtd] = **it would**; **it had**
item ['aɪtəm] *n* Gegenstand *m*; (*on list*)
Posten *m*; (*in programme*) Nummer *f*;
(*in agenda*) (Programm)punkt *m*; (*in newspaper*) (Zeitungs)notiz *f*; **~ize** *vt*
verzeichnen
itinerant [ɪ'tɪnərənt] *adj* (*person*) umherreisend
itinerary [aɪ'tɪnərərɪ] *n* Reiseroute *f*
it'll ['ɪtl] = **it will**; **it shall**
its [ɪts] *adj* (*masculine, neuter*) sein; *f*,
(*feminine*) ihr
it's [ɪts] = **it is**; **it has**
itself [ɪt'sɛlf] *pron* sich (selbst); (*emphatic*) selbst
ITV (*BRIT*) *n abbr* = **Independent Television**
I.U.D. *n abbr* (= *intra-uterine device*) Pessar *nt*
I've [aɪv] = **I have**
ivory ['aɪvərɪ] *n* Elfenbein *nt*
ivy ['aɪvɪ] *n* Efeu *nt*

J, j

jab [dʒæb] *vt* (hinein)stechen ♦ *n* Stich
m, Stoß *m*; (*inf*) Spritze *f*
jack [dʒæk] *n* (*AUT*) (Wagen)heber *m*;
(*CARDS*) Bube *m*; **~ up** *vt* aufbocken
jackal ['dʒækl] *n* (*ZOOL*) Schakal *m*
jackdaw ['dʒækdɔː] *n* Dohle *f*
jacket ['dʒækɪt] *n* Jacke *f*; (*of book*)
Schutzumschlag *m*; (*TECH*) Ummantelung *f*; **~ potatoes** *npl* in der Schale
gebackene Kartoffeln *pl*
jackknife ['dʒæknaɪf] *vi* (*truck*) sich zusammenschieben
jack plug (*ELEC*) *n* Buchsenstecker *m*
jackpot ['dʒækpɔt] *n* Haupttreffer *m*
jaded ['dʒeɪdɪd] *adj* ermattet
jagged ['dʒægɪd] *adj* zackig
jail [dʒeɪl] *n* Gefängnis *nt* ♦ *vt* einsperren; **~er** *n* Gefängniswärter *m*
jam [dʒæm] *n* Marmelade *f*; (*also:*
traffic ~) (Verkehrs)stau *m*; (*inf: trouble*) Klemme *f* ♦ *vt* (*wedge*) einklemmen; (*cram*) hineinzwängen; (*obstruct*)
blockieren ♦ *vi* sich verklemmen; **to ~**
sth into sth etw in etw *acc* hineinstopfen
Jamaica [dʒə'meɪkə] *n* Jamaika *nt*
jam jar *n* Marmeladenglas *nt*
jammed [dʒæmd] *adj*: **it's ~** es klemmt
jam-packed [dʒæm'pækt] *adj* überfüllt,
proppenvoll
jangle ['dʒæŋgl] *vt, vi* klimpern
janitor ['dʒænɪtə*] *n* Hausmeister *m*
January ['dʒænjuərɪ] *n* Januar *m*
Japan [dʒə'pæn] *n* Japan *nt*; **~ese**
[dʒæpə'niːz] *adj* japanisch ♦ *n inv* Japaner(in) *m(f)*; (*LING*) Japanisch *nt*
jar [dʒɑː*] *n* Glas *nt* ♦ *vi* kreischen; (*colours etc*) nicht harmonieren
jargon ['dʒɑːgən] *n* Fachsprache *f*, Jargon *m*
jaundice ['dʒɔːndɪs] *n* Gelbsucht *f*; **~d**
adj (*fig*) missgünstig
jaunt [dʒɔːnt] *n* Spritztour *f*

avelin ['dʒævlɪn] n Speer m

aw [dʒɔː] n Kiefer m

ay [dʒeɪ] n (ZOOL) Eichelhäher m

aywalker ['dʒeɪwɔːkə] n unvorsichtige(r) Fußgänger m

azz [dʒæz] n Jazz m; ~ **up** vt (MUS) verjazzen; (enliven) aufpolieren

ealous ['dʒeləs] adj (envious) missgünstig; (husband) eifersüchtig; ~**y** n Missgunst f; Eifersucht f

eans [dʒiːnz] npl Jeans pl

Jeep [dʒiːp] ® n Jeep m ®

eer [dʒɪə] vi: **to ~ (at sb)** (über jdn) höhnisch lachen, (jdn) verspotten

Jehovah's Witness [dʒɪ'həʊvəz-] n Zeuge m/Zeugin f Jehovas

elly ['dʒelɪ] n Gelee nt; (dessert) Grütze f; ~**fish** n Qualle f

eopardize ['dʒepədaɪz] vt gefährden

eopardy ['dʒepədɪ] n: **to be in jeopardy** in Gefahr sein

erk [dʒɜːk] n Ruck m; (inf: idiot) Trottel m ♦ vt ruckartig bewegen ♦ vi sich ruckartig bewegen

erky ['dʒɜːkɪ] adj (movement) ruckartig; (ride) rüttelnd

ersey ['dʒɜːzɪ] n Pullover m

est [dʒest] n Scherz m ♦ vi spaßen; **in ~** im Spaß

Jesus ['dʒiːzəs] n Jesus m

et [dʒet] n (stream: of water etc) Strahl m; (spout) Düse f; (AVIAT) Düsenflugzeug nt; ~-**black** adj rabenschwarz; ~ **engine** n Düsenmotor m; ~ **lag** n jetlag m

jettison ['dʒetɪsn] vt über Bord werfen

jetty ['dʒetɪ] n Landesteg m, Mole f

Jew [dʒuː] n Jude m

jewel ['dʒuːəl] n (also fig) Juwel nt; ~**ler** (US **jeweler**) n Juwelier m; ~**ler's (shop)** n Juwelier m; ~**lery** (US **jewelry**) n Schmuck m

Jewess ['dʒuːɪs] n Jüdin f

Jewish ['dʒuːɪʃ] adj jüdisch

jibe [dʒaɪb] n spöttische Bemerkung f

jiffy ['dʒɪfɪ] (inf) n: **in a ~** sofort

jigsaw ['dʒɪgsɔː] n (also: ~ **puzzle**) Puzzle(spiel) nt

jilt [dʒɪlt] vt den Laufpass geben +dat

jingle ['dʒɪŋgl] n (advertisement) Werbesong m ♦ vi klimpern; (bells) bimmeln ♦ vt klimpern mit; bimmeln lassen

jinx [dʒɪŋks] n: **there's a ~ on it** es ist verhext

jitters ['dʒɪtəz] (inf) npl: **to get the ~** einen Bammel kriegen

job [dʒɒb] n (piece of work) Arbeit f; (position) Stellung f; (duty) Aufgabe f; (difficulty) Mühe f; **it's a good ~ he** ... es ist ein Glück, dass er ...; **just the ~** genau das Richtige; **J~centre** (BRIT) n Arbeitsamt nt; ~**less** adj arbeitslos

jockey ['dʒɒkɪ] n Jockei m, Jockey m ♦ vi: **to ~ for position** sich in eine gute Position drängen

jocular ['dʒɒkjʊlə] adj scherzhaft

jog [dʒɒg] vt (an)stoßen ♦ vi (run) joggen; **to ~ along** vor sich acc hinwursteln; (work) seinen Gang gehen; ~**ging** n Jogging nt

join [dʒɔɪn] vt (club) beitreten +dat; (person) sich anschließen +dat; (fasten) **to ~ (sth to sth)** (etw mit etw) verbinden ♦ vi (unite) sich vereinigen ♦ n Verbindungsstelle f, Naht f; **in** vt, vi: **to ~ in (sth)** bei etw mitmachen; ~ **up** vi (MIL) zur Armee gehen

joiner ['dʒɔɪnə] n Schreiner m; ~**y** n Schreinerei f

joint [dʒɔɪnt] n (TECH) Fuge f; (of bones) Gelenk nt; (of meat) Braten m; (inf: place) Lokal nt ♦ adj gemeinsam; ~ **account** n (with bank etc) gemeinsame(s) Konto nt; ~**ly** adv gemeinsam

joke [dʒəʊk] n Witz m ♦ vi Witze machen; **to play a ~ on sb** jdm einen Streich spielen; ~**r** n Witzbold m; (CARDS) Joker m

jolly ['dʒɒlɪ] adj lustig ♦ adv (inf) ganz schön

jolt [dʒəʊlt] n (shock) Schock m; (jerk) Stoß m ♦ vt (push) stoßen; (shake) durchschütteln; (fig) aufrütteln ♦ vi holpern

Jordan ['dʒɔːdən] n Jordanien nt

jostle ['dʒɒsl] vt anrempeln

jot [dʒɒt] n: **not one** ~ kein Jota nt; ~ **down** nt notieren; **~ter** (BRIT) n Notizblock m

journal ['dʒɜːnl] n (diary) Tagebuch nt; (magazine) Zeitschrift f; **~ism** n Journalismus m; **~ist** n Journalist(in) m(f)

journey ['dʒɜːnl] n Reise f

jovial ['dʒəuvɪəl] adj jovial

joy [dʒɔl] n Freude f; **~ful** adj freudig; **~ous** adj freudig; ~ **ride** n Schwarzfahrt f; **~rider** n Autodieb, der den Wagen nur für eine Spritztour stiehlt; **~stick** n Steuerknüppel m; (COMPUT) Joystick m

J.P. n abbr = **Justice of the Peace**

Jr abbr = **junior**

jubilant ['dʒuːbɪlnt] adj triumphierend

jubilee ['dʒuːbɪliː] n Jubiläum nt

judge [dʒʌdʒ] n Richter m; (fig) Kenner m ♦ vt (JUR: person) die Verhandlung führen über +acc; (case) verhandeln; (assess) beurteilen; (estimate) einschätzen; **~ment** n (JUR) Urteil nt; (ECCL) Gericht nt; (ability) Urteilsvermögen nt

judicial [dʒuːˈdɪʃl] adj gerichtlich, Justiz-

judiciary [dʒuːˈdɪʃɪərɪ] n Gerichtsbehörden pl; (judges) Richterstand m

judicious [dʒuːˈdɪʃəs] adj weise

judo ['dʒuːdəu] n Judo nt

jug [dʒʌg] n Krug m

juggernaut ['dʒʌgənɔːt] (BRIT) n (huge truck) Schwertransporter m

juggle ['dʒʌgl] vi, vt jonglieren; **~r** n Jongleur m

Jugoslav etc ['juːgəuˈslɑːv] = **Yugoslav** etc

juice [dʒuːs] n Saft m; **juicy** ['dʒuːsɪ] adj (also fig) saftig

jukebox ['dʒuːkbɒks] n Musikautomat m

July [dʒuːˈlaɪ] n Juli m

jumble ['dʒʌmbl] n Durcheinander nt

♦ vt (also: ~ **up**) durcheinander werfen; (facts) durcheinander bringen; ~ **sale** (BRIT) n Basar m, Flohmarkt m

---

Jumble sale

Jumble sale ist ein Wohltätigkeitsbasar, meist in einer Aula oder einem Gemeindehaus abgehalten, bei dem alle möglichen Gebrauchtwaren (vor allem Kleidung, Spielzeug, Bücher, Geschirr und Möbel) verkauft werden. Der Erlös fließt entweder einer Wohltätigkeitsorganisation zu oder wird für örtliche Zwecke verwendet, z.B. die Pfadfinder, die Grundschule, Reparatur der Kirche usw.

---

jumbo (jet) ['dʒʌmbəu-] n Jumbo(jet) m

jump [dʒʌmp] vi springen; (nervously) zusammenzucken ♦ vt überspringen ♦ n Sprung m; **to** ~ **the queue** (BRIT) sich vordrängeln

jumper ['dʒʌmpə'] n (BRIT: pullover) Pullover m; (US: dress) Trägerkleid nt

jump leads, **jumper cables** US npl Überbrückungskabel nt

jumpy ['dʒʌmpɪ] adj nervös

Jun. abbr = **junior**

junction ['dʒʌŋkʃən] n (BRIT: of roads) (Straßen)kreuzung f; (RAIL) Knotenpunkt m

juncture ['dʒʌŋktʃə'] n: **at this** ~ in diesem Augenblick

June [dʒuːn] n Juni m

jungle ['dʒʌŋgl] n Dschungel m

junior ['dʒuːnɪə'] adj (younger) jünger; (after name) junior; (SPORT) Junioren-; (lower position) untergeordnet; (for young people) Junioren- ♦ n jüngere(r) m/f; ~ **school** (BRIT) n Grundschule f

junk [dʒʌŋk] n (rubbish) Plunder m; (ship) Dschunke f; ~ **bond** n (COMM) niedrig eingestuftes Wertpapier mit hohen Ertragschancen bei erhöhtem Risiko; ~ **food** n Junk food nt; ~ **mail** n Reklame, die unangefordert in den

Briefkasten gesteckt wird; **~ shop** n
Ramschladen m

Junr abbr = **junior**

urisdiction [dʒʊərɪs'dɪkʃən] n Gerichtsbarkeit f; (range of authority) Zuständigkeit(sbereich m) f

uror ['dʒʊərə*] n Geschworene(r) mf; (in competition) Preisrichter m

ury ['dʒʊərɪ] n (court) Geschworene pl; (panel) Jury f

ust [dʒʌst] adj gerecht ♦ adv (recently, now) gerade, eben; (barely) gerade noch; (exactly) genau, gerade; (only) nur, bloß; (a small distance) gleich; (absolutely) einfach; **~ as I arrived** gerade als ich ankam; **~ as nice** genauso nett; **~ as well** umso besser; **~ now** soeben, gerade; **~ try** versuch es mal; **she's ~ left** sie ist gerade or (so)eben gegangen; **he's ~ done it** er hat es gerade or (so)eben getan; **~ before** gerade or kurz bevor; **~ enough** gerade genug; **he ~ missed** er hat fast or beinahe getroffen

justice ['dʒʌstɪs] n (fairness) Gerechtigkeit f; **J~ of the Peace** n Friedensrichter m

justifiable [dʒʌstɪ'faɪəbl] adj berechtigt

justification [dʒʌstɪfɪ'keɪʃən] n Rechtfertigung f

justify ['dʒʌstɪfaɪ] vt rechtfertigen; (text) justieren

justly ['dʒʌstlɪ] adv (say) mit Recht; (condemn) gerecht

jut [dʒʌt] vi (also: **~ out**) herausragen, vorstehen

juvenile ['dʒuːvənaɪl] adj (young) jugendlich; (for the young) jugend- ♦ n Jugendliche(r) mf

juxtapose ['dʒʌkstəpəʊz] vt nebeneinander stellen

K, k

K [keɪ] abbr (= one thousand) Tsd.; (= kilobyte) K

kangaroo [kæŋgə'ruː] n Känguru nt

karate [kə'rɑːtɪ] n Karate nt

kebab [kə'bæb] n Kebab m

keel [kiːl] n Kiel m; **on an even ~** (fig) im Lot

keen [kiːn] adj begeistert; (wind, blade, intelligence) scharf; (sight, hearing) gut; **to be ~ to do** or **on doing sth** etw unbedingt tun wollen; **to be ~ on sth/ sb** scharf auf etw/jdn sein

keep [kiːp] (pt, pp **kept**) vt (retain) behalten; (have) haben; (animals, one's word) halten; (support) versorgen; (maintain in state) halten; (preserve) aufbewahren; (restrain) abhalten ♦ vi (continue in direction) sich halten; (food) sich halten; (remain: quiet etc) bleiben ♦ n Unterhalt m; (tower) Burgfried m; (inf): **for ~s** für immer; **to ~ sth to o.s.** etw für sich behalten; **it ~s happening** es passiert immer wieder; **~ back** vt fern halten; (information) verschweigen; **~ on** vi: **~ on doing sth** etw immer weiter tun; **~ out** vt nicht hereinlassen; **"~ out"** „Eintritt verboten!"; **~ up** vi Schritt halten ♦ vt aufrechterhalten; (continue) weitermachen; **to ~ up with** Schritt halten mit; **~er** n Wärter(in) m(f); (goalkeeper) Torhüter(in) m(f); **~-fit** n Keep-fit nt; **~ing** n (care) Obhut f; **in ~ing with** in Übereinstimmung mit; **~sake** n Andenken nt

keg [keg] n Fass nt

kennel ['kenl] n Hundehütte f; **~s** npl: **to put a dog in ~s** (for boarding) einen Hund in Pflege geben

Kenya ['kenjə] n Kenia nt; **~n** adj kenianisch ♦ n Kenianer(in) m(f)

kept [kept] pt, pp of **keep**

kerb [kɜːb] (BRIT) n Bordstein m

kernel ['kə:nl] n Kern m

kerosene ['kerəsi:n] n Kerosin nt

kettle ['ketl] n Kessel m; (for tea) Pauke f

key [ki:] n Schlüssel m; (of piano, typewriter) Taste f; (MUS) Tonart f ♦ vt (also: ~ **in**) eingeben; **~board** n Tastatur f; **~ed up** adj (person) überdreht; **~hole** n Schlüsselloch nt; **~hole surgery** n minimal invasive Chirurgie f, Schlüssellochchirurgie f; **~note** n Grundton m; **~ ring** n Schlüsselring m

khaki ['kɑ:kɪ] n K(h)aki nt ♦ adj k(h)aki(farben)

kick [kɪk] vt einen Fußtritt geben +dat, treten ♦ vi treten; (baby) strampeln; (horse) ausschlagen ♦ n (of foot) Tritt m; (thrill) Spaß m; **he does it for ~s** er macht das aus Jux; **~ off** vi (SPORT) anstoßen; **~-off** n (SPORT) Anstoß m

kid [kɪd] n (inf: child) Kind nt; (goat) Zicklein nt; (leather) Glacéleder nt, Glaceeleder nt ♦ vi (inf) Witze machen

kidnap ['kɪdnæp] vt entführen; **~per** n Entführer m; **~ping** n Entführung f

kidney ['kɪdnɪ] n Niere f

kill [kɪl] vt töten, umbringen ♦ vi töten ♦ n (hunting) (Jagd)beute f; **~er** n Mörder(in) m(f); **~ing** n Mord m; **~joy** n Spaßverderber(in) m(f)

kiln [kɪln] n Brennofen m

kilo ['ki:ləu] n Kilo nt; **~byte** n (COMPUT) Kilobyte nt; **~gram(me)** ['kɪləugræm] n Kilogramm nt; **~metre** ['kɪləmi:tər] (US **kilometer**) n Kilometer m; **~watt** n Kilowatt nt

kilt [kɪlt] n Schottenrock m

kind [kaɪnd] adj freundlich ♦ n Art f; a ~ **of** eine Art von; **(two) of a ~** (zwei) von der gleichen Art; **in** ~ auf dieselbe Art; (in goods) in Naturalien

kindergarten ['kɪndəgɑ:tn] n Kindergarten m

kind-hearted [kaɪnd'hɑ:tɪd] adj gutherzig

kindle ['kɪndl] vt (set on fire) anzünden; (rouse) reizen, (er)wecken

kindly ['kaɪndlɪ] adj freundlich ♦ adv liebenswürdig(erweise); **would you** ~ ...? wären Sie so freundlich und ...?

kindness ['kaɪndnɪs] n Freundlichkeit f

kindred ['kɪndrɪd] adj: ~ **spirit** Gleichgesinnte(r) mf

king [kɪŋ] n König m; **~dom** n Königreich nt

kingfisher ['kɪŋfɪʃər] n Eisvogel m

king-size(d) ['kɪŋsaɪz(d)] adj (cigarette) Kingsize

kinky ['kɪŋkɪ] (inf) adj (person, ideas) verrückt; (sexual) abartig

kiosk ['ki:ɔsk] (BRIT) n (TEL) Telefonhäuschen nt

kipper ['kɪpər] n Räucherhering m

kiss [kɪs] n Kuss m ♦ vt küssen ♦ vi: **they ~ed** sie küssten sich; **~ of life** (BRIT) n: **the ~ of life** Mund-zu-Mund-Beatmung f

kit [kɪt] n Ausrüstung f; (tools) Werkzeug nt

kitchen ['kɪtʃɪn] n Küche f; ~ **sink** n Spülbecken nt

kite [kaɪt] n Drachen m

kitten ['kɪtn] n Kätzchen nt

kitty ['kɪtɪ] n (money) Kasse f

km abbr (= kilometre) km

knack [næk] n Dreh m, Trick m

knapsack ['næpsæk] n Rucksack m; (MIL) Tornister m

knead [ni:d] vt kneten

knee [ni:] n Knie nt; **~cap** n Kniescheibe f

kneel [ni:l] (pt, pp **knelt**) vi (also: ~ **down**) knien

knelt [nelt] pt, pp of **kneel**

knew [nju:] pt of **know**

knickers ['nɪkəz] (BRIT) npl Schlüpfer m

knife [naɪf] (pl **knives**) n Messer nt ♦ vt erstechen

knight [naɪt] n Ritter m; (chess) Springer m; **~hood** n (title): **to get a ~hood** zum Ritter geschlagen werden

knit [nɪt] vt stricken ♦ vi stricken; (bones) zusammenwachsen; **~ting** n (occupation) Stricken nt; (work) Strickzeug nt; **~ting needle** n Stricknadel f;

~**wear** n Strickwaren pl

knives [naɪvz] pl of **knife**

knob [nɔb] n Knauf m; (on instrument) Knopf m; (BRIT: of butter etc) kleine(s) Stück nt

knock [nɔk] vt schlagen; (criticize) heruntermachen ♦ vi: to ~ at or on the **door** an die Tür klopfen ♦ n Schlag m; (on door) Klopfen nt; ~ **down** vt umwerfen; (with car) anfahren; ~ **off** vt (do quickly) hinhauen; (inf: steal) klauen ♦ vi (finish) Feierabend machen; ~ **out** vt ausschlagen; (BOXING) k. o. schlagen; ~ **over** vt (person, object) umwerfen; (with car) anfahren; ~**er** n (on door) Türklopfer m; ~**out** n K.-o.-Schlag m; (fig) Sensation f

knot [nɔt] n Knoten m ♦ vt (ver)knoten

knotty ['nɔtɪ] adj (fig) kompliziert

know [nəʊ] (pt **knew**, pp **known**) vt, vi wissen; (be able to) können; (be acquainted with) kennen; (recognize) erkennen; to ~ **how to do sth** wissen, wie man etw macht, etw tun können; to ~ **about** or **of sth/sb** etw/jdn kennen; ~-**all** n Alleswisser m; ~-**how** n Kenntnis f, Know-how nt; ~**ing** adj (look, smile) wissend; ~**ingly** adv wissend; (intentionally) wissentlich

knowledge ['nɔlɪdʒ] n Wissen nt, Kenntnis f; ~**able** adj informiert

known [nəʊn] pp of **know**

knuckle ['nʌkl] n Fingerknöchel m

K.O. n abbr = **knockout**

Koran [kɔ'rɑːn] n Koran m

Korea [kə'rɪə] n Korea nt

kosher ['kəʊʃəʳ] adj koscher

L, l

L [el] abbr (BRIT: AUT) (= learner) am Auto angebrachtes Kennzeichen für Fahrschüler; = **lake**; (= large) gr.; (= left) l.

l. abbr = **litre**

lab [læb] (inf) n Labor nt

label ['leɪbl] n Etikett nt ♦ vt etikettieren

labor etc ['leɪbəʳ] (US) = **labour** etc

laboratory [lə'bɔrətərɪ] n Laboratorium nt

laborious [lə'bɔːrɪəs] adj mühsam

labour ['leɪbəʳ] (US **labor**) n Arbeit f; (workmen) Arbeitskräfte pl; (MED) Wehen pl ♦ vi: to ~ (**at**) sich abmühen (mit) ♦ vt breittreten (inf); **in** ~ (MED) in den Wehen; **L**~ (BRIT: also: **the L**~ **party**) die Labour Party; ~**ed** adj (movement) gequält; (style) schwerfällig; ~**er** n Arbeiter m; **farm** ~**er** n (Land)arbeiter m

lace [leɪs] n (fabric) Spitze f; (of shoe) Schnürsenkel m; (braid) Litze f ♦ vt (also: ~ **up**) (zu)schnüren

lack [læk] n Mangel m ♦ vt nicht haben; **sb** ~**s sth** jdm fehlt etw nom; **to be** ~**ing** fehlen; **sb is** ~**ing in sth** es fehlt jdm an etw dat; **for** or **through** ~ **of** aus Mangel an +dat

lacquer ['lækəʳ] n Lack m

lad [læd] n Junge m

ladder ['lædəʳ] n Leiter f; (BRIT: in tights) Laufmasche f ♦ vt (BRIT: tights) Laufmaschen bekommen in +dat

laden ['leɪdn] adj beladen, voll

ladle ['leɪdl] n Schöpfkelle f

lady ['leɪdɪ] n Dame f; (title) Lady f; **young** ~ (also: ~ **behind**) junge Dame; **the ladies' (room)** die Damentoilette; ~**bird** (US ~**bug**) n Marienkäfer m; ~**like** adj damenhaft, vornehm; ~**ship** n: **your L**~**ship** Ihre Ladyschaft

lag [læg] vi (also: ~ **behind**) zurückbleiben ♦ vt (pipes) verkleiden

lager ['lɑːgəʳ] n helle(s) Bier nt

lagging ['lægɪŋ] n Isolierung f

lagoon [lə'guːn] n Lagune f

laid [leɪd] pt, pp of **lay**; ~ **back** (inf) adj cool

lain [leɪn] pp of **lie**

lair [lɛəʳ] n Lager nt

lake [leɪk] n See m

lamb [læm] n Lamm nt; (meat) Lammfleisch nt; ~ **chop** n Lammkotelett nt; ~**swool** n Lammwolle f

lame [leɪm] *adj* lahm; (*excuse*) faul

lament [lə'ment] *n* Klage *f* ♦ *vt* beklagen

laminated ['læmɪneɪtd] *adj* beschichtet

lamp [læmp] *n* Lampe *f*; (*in street*) Straßenlaterne *f*; **~post** *n* Laternenpfahl *m*; **~shade** *n* Lampenschirm *m*

lance [lɑːns] *n* Lanze *f*; **~ corporal** (*BRIT*) *n* Obergefreite(r) *m*

land [lænd] *n* Land *nt* ♦ *vi* (*from ship*) an Land gehen; (*AVIAT, and so*) landen ♦ *vt* (*obtain*) kriegen; (*passengers*) absetzen; (*goods*) abladen; (*troops, space probe*) landen; **~fill site** ['lændfɪl-] *n* Mülldeponie *f*; **~ing** *n* Landung *f*; (*on stairs*) (Treppen)absatz *m*; **~ing gear** *n* Fahrgestell *nt*; **~ing stage** (*BRIT*) *n* Landesteg *m*; **~ing strip** *n* Landebahn *f*; **~lady** *n* (Haus)wirtin *f*; **~locked** *adj* landumschlossen, Binnen-; **~lord** *n* (*of house*) Hauswirt *m*, Besitzer *m*; (*of pub*) Gastwirt *m*; (*of area*) Grundbesitzer *m*; **~mark** *n* Wahrzeichen *nt*; (*fig*) Meilenstein *m*; **~owner** *n* Grundbesitzer *m*; **~scape** *n* Landschaft *f*; **~scape gardener** *n* Landschaftsgärtner(in) *m(f)*; **~slide** (*GEOG*) *n* Erdrutsch *m*; (*POL*) überwältigende(r) Sieg *m*

lane [leɪn] *n* (*in town*) Gasse *f*; (*in country*) Weg *m*; (*of motorway*) Fahrbahn *f*, Spur *f*; (*SPORT*) Bahn *f*; **"get in ~"** „bitte einordnen"

language ['læŋgwɪdʒ] *n* Sprache *f*; **bad ~** unanständige Ausdrücke *pl*; **~ laboratory** *n* Sprachlabor *nt*

languish ['læŋgwɪʃ] *vi* schmachten

lank [læŋk] *adj* dürr

lanky ['læŋkɪ] *adj* schlaksig

lantern ['læntən] *n* Laterne *f*

lap [læp] *n* Schoß *m*; (*SPORT*) Runde *f* ♦ *vt* (*also*: **~ up**) auflecken ♦ *vi* (*water*) plätschern

lapel [lə'pel] *n* Revers *nt or m*

Lapland ['læplænd] *n* Lappland *nt*

lapse [læps] *n* (*moral*) Fehltritt *m* ♦ *vi* (*decline*) nachlassen; (*expire*) ablaufen;

(*claims*) erlöschen; **to ~ into bad habits** sich schlechte Gewohnheiten angewöhnen

laptop (computer) ['læptɔp-] *n* Laptop(-Computer) *m*

lard [lɑːd] *n* Schweineschmalz *nt*

larder ['lɑːdəʳ] *n* Speisekammer *f*

large [lɑːdʒ] *adj* groß; **at ~** auf freiem Fuß; **~ly** *adv* zum größten Teil; **~scale** *adj* groß angelegt, Groß-

lark [lɑːk] *n* (*bird*) Lerche *f*; (*joke*) Jux *m*; **~ about** (*inf*) *vi* herumalbern

laryngitis [lærɪn'dʒaɪtɪs] *n* Kehlkopfentzündung *f*

laser ['leɪzəʳ] *n* Laser *m*; **~ printer** *n* Laserdrucker *m*

lash [læʃ] *n* Peitschenhieb *m*; (*eyelash*) Wimper *f* ♦ *vt* (*rain*) schlagen gegen; (*whip*) peitschen; (*bind*) festbinden; **~ out** *vi* (*with fists*) um sich schlagen

lass [læs] *n* Mädchen *nt*

lasso [læ'suː] *n* Lasso *nt*

last [lɑːst] *adj* letzte(r, s) ♦ *adv* zuletzt; (*~ time*) das letzte Mal ♦ *vi* (*continue*) dauern; (*remain good*) sich halten; (*money*) ausreichen; **at ~** endlich; **~ night** gestern Abend; **~ week** letzte Woche; **~ but one** vorletzte(r, s); **~ditch** *adj* (*attempt*) in letzter Minute; **~ing** *adj* dauerhaft; (*shame etc*) andauernd; **~ly** *adv* schließlich; **~minute** *adj* in letzter Minute

latch [lætʃ] *n* Riegel *m*

late [leɪt] *adj* spät; (*dead*) verstorben ♦ *adv* spät; (*after proper time*) zu spät; **to be ~** zu spät kommen; **of ~** in letzter Zeit; **in ~ May** Ende Mai; **~comer** *n* Nachzügler(in) *m(f)*; **~ly** *adv* in letzter Zeit; **later** ['leɪtəʳ] *adj* (*date*) später; (*version*) neuer ♦ *adv* später

lateral ['lætərəl] *adj* seitlich

latest ['leɪtɪst] *adj* (*fashion*) neueste(r, s) ♦ *n* (*news*) Neu(e)ste(s) *nt*; **at the ~** spätestens

lathe [leɪð] *n* Drehbank *f*

lather ['lɑːðəʳ] *n* (Seifen)schaum *m* ♦ *vt* einschäumen ♦ *vi* schäumen

Latin ['lætɪn] n Latein nt ♦ adj lateinisch; (Roman) römisch; **~ America** n Lateinamerika nt; **~ American** adj lateinamerikanisch

latitude ['lætɪtjuːd] n (GEOG) Breite f; (freedom) Spielraum m

latter ['lætə*] adj (second of two) letztere; (coming at end) letzte(r, s), später ♦ n: **the ~** der/die/das letztere, die letzteren; **~ly** adv in letzter Zeit

lattice ['lætɪs] n Gitter nt

laudable ['lɔːdəbl] adj löblich

laugh [lɑːf] n Lachen nt ♦ vi lachen; **~ at** vt lachen über +acc; **~ off** vt lachend abtun; **~able** adj lachhaft; **~ing stock** n Zielscheibe f des Spottes; **~ter** n Gelächter nt

launch [lɔːntʃ] n (of ship) Stapellauf m; (of rocket) Abschuss m; (boat) Barkasse f; (of product) Einführung f ♦ vt (set afloat) vom Stapel lassen; (rocket) (ab)schießen; (product) auf den Markt bringen; **~(ing) pad** n Abschussrampe f

launder ['lɔːndə*] vt waschen

Launderette [lɔːn'dret] ® (BRIT) n Waschsalon m

Laundromat ['lɔːndrəmæt] ® (US) n Waschsalon m

laundry ['lɔːndrɪ] n (place) Wäscherei f; (clothes) Wäsche f; **to do the ~** waschen

laureate ['lɔːrɪət] adj see poet

laurel ['lɒrl] n Lorbeer m

lava ['lɑːvə] n Lava f

lavatory ['lævətərɪ] n Toilette f

lavender ['lævəndə*] n Lavendel m

lavish ['lævɪʃ] adj (extravagant) verschwenderisch; (generous) großzügig ♦ vt (money): **to ~ sth on sth** etw auf etw acc verschwenden; (attention, gifts): **to ~ sth on sb** jdn mit etw überschütten

law [lɔː] n Gesetz nt; (system) Recht nt; (as studies) jura no art; **~-abiding** adj gesetzestreu; **~ and order** n Recht und Ordnung f; **~ court** n Gerichtshof

m; **~ful** adj gesetzlich; **~less** adj gesetzlos

lawn [lɔːn] n Rasen m; **~mower** n Rasenmäher m; **~ tennis** n Rasentennis m

law: ~ school n Rechtsakademie f; **~suit** n Prozess m; **~yer** n Rechtsanwalt m, Rechtsanwältin f

lax [læks] adj (behaviour) nachlässig; (standards) locker

laxative ['læksətɪv] n Abführmittel nt

lay [leɪ] (pt, pp laid) pt of **lie** ♦ adj lai-; ♦ vt (place) legen; (table) decken; (egg) legen; (trap) stellen; (money) wetten; **~ aside** vt zurücklegen; **~ by** vt (set aside) beiseite legen; **~ down** vt hinlegen; (rules) vorschreiben; (arms) strecken; **to ~ down the law** Vorschriften machen; **~ off** vt (workers) (vorübergehend) entlassen; **~ on** vt (water, gas) anschließen; (concert etc) veranstalten; **~ out** vt (her)auslegen; (money) ausgeben; (corpse) aufbahren; **~ up** vt (subj: illness) ans Bett fesseln; **~about** n Faulenzer m; **~-by** (BRIT) n Parkbucht f; (bigger) Rastplatz m

layer ['leɪə*] n Schicht f

layman ['leɪmən] (irreg) n Laie m

layout ['leɪaʊt] n Anlage f; (ART) Lay-out nt, Layout nt

laze [leɪz] vi faulenzen

laziness ['leɪzɪnɪs] n Faulheit f

lazy ['leɪzɪ] adj faul; (slow-moving) träge

lb. abbr = **pound** (weight)

lead[1] [led] n (chemical) Blei nt; (of pencil) (Bleistift)mine f ♦ adj bleiern, Blei-

lead[2] [liːd] (pt, pp led) n (first position) Führung f; (distance, time ahead) Vorsprung f; (example) Vorbild nt; (clue) Tipp m; (of police) Spur f; (THEAT) Hauptrolle f; (dog's) Leine f ♦ vi (guide) führen; (group etc) leiten; **to be the first** führen; **in the ~** (SPORT, fig) in Führung; **~ astray** vt irreführen; **~ away** vt wegführen; (prisoner) abführen; **~ back** vi zurückführen; **~ on** vt anführen; **~ on to** vt (induce) dazu bringing; **~ to** vt (street) (hin)führen nach; (result in) führen zu; **~ up to** vt (drive) führen zu; (speaker etc) hinführen auf +acc

leaded petrol ['lɛdɪd-] n verbleites Benzin nt

leaden ['lɛdn] adj (sky, sea) bleiern; (heavy: footsteps) bleischwer

leader ['li:dəʳ] n Führer m, Leiter m; (of party) Vorsitzende(r) m; (PRESS) Leitartikel m; **~ship** n (office) Leitung f; (quality) Führerschaft f

lead-free ['lɛdfri:] adj (petrol) bleifrei

leading ['li:dɪŋ] adj führend; **~ lady** n (THEAT) Hauptdarstellerin f; **~ light** n (person) führende(r) Geist m

lead singer [li:d-] n Leadsänger(in) m(f)

leaf [li:f] (pl **leaves**) n Blatt nt ♦ vi: **to ~ through** durchblättern; **to turn over a new ~** einen neuen Anfang machen

leaflet ['li:flɪt] n (advertisement) Prospekt m; (pamphlet) Flugblatt nt; (for information) Merkblatt nt

league [li:g] n (union) Bund m; (SPORT) Liga f; **to be in ~ with** unter einer Decke stecken mit

leak [li:k] n undichte Stelle f; (in ship) Leck nt ♦ vt (liquid etc) durchlassen ♦ vi (pipe etc) undicht sein; (liquid etc) auslaufen; **the information was ~ed to the enemy** die Information wurde dem Feind zugespielt; **~ out** vi (liquid etc) auslaufen; (information) durchsickern; **~y** ['li:kɪ] adj undicht

lean [li:n] (pt, pp **leaned** or **leant**) adj mager ♦ vi sich neigen ♦ vt: **to ~ against sth** an etw dat angelehnt sein; sich an etw acc anlehnen; **~ back** vi sich zurücklehnen; **~ forward** vi sich vorbeugen; **~ on** vt fus sich stützen auf +acc; **~ out** vi sich hinauslehnen; **~ over** vi sich hinüberbeugen; **~ing** n Neigung f ♦ adj schief; **~t** [lɛnt] pt, pp of **lean**; **~-to** n Anbau m

leap [li:p] (pt, pp **leaped** or **leapt**) n Sprung m ♦ vi springen; **~frog** n Bockspringen nt; **~t** [lɛpt] pt, pp of **leap**; **~ year** n Schaltjahr nt

learn [lə:n] (pt, pp **learned** or **learnt**) vt, vi lernen; (find out) erfahren; **to ~ how to do sth** etw (er)lernen; **~ed** ['lə:nɪd] adj gelehrt; **~er** n Anfänger(in) m(f); (AUT: BRIT: also: **~er driver**) Fahrschüler(in) m(f); **~ing** n Gelehrsamkeit f; **~t** [lə:nt] pt, pp of **learn**

lease [li:s] n (of property) Mietvertrag m ♦ vt pachten

leash [li:ʃ] n Leine f

least [li:st] adj geringste(r, s) ♦ adv am wenigsten ♦ n Mindeste(s) nt; **the ~ possible effort** möglichst geringer Aufwand; **at ~** zumindest; **not in the ~!** durchaus nicht!

leather ['lɛðəʳ] n Leder nt

leave [li:v] (pt, pp **left**) vt verlassen; (~ behind) zurücklassen; (forget) vergessen; (allow to remain) lassen; (after death) hinterlassen; (entrust): **to ~ sth to sb** jdm etw überlassen ♦ vi weggehen, wegfahren; (for journey) abreisen; (bus, train) abfahren ♦ n Erlaubnis f; (MIL) Urlaub m; **to be left** (remain) übrig bleiben; **there's some milk left over** es ist noch etwas Milch übrig; **on ~** auf Urlaub; **~ behind** vt (person, object) dalassen; (forget) liegen lassen, stehen lassen; **~ out** vt auslassen; **~ of absence** n Urlaub m

leaves [li:vz] pl of **leaf**

Lebanon ['lɛbənən] n Libanon m

lecherous ['lɛtʃərəs] adj lüstern

lecture ['lɛktʃəʳ] n Vortrag m; (UNIV) Vorlesung f ♦ vi einen Vortrag halten; (UNIV) lesen ♦ vt (scold) abkanzeln; **to give a ~ on sth** einen Vortrag über etwas halten; **~r** ['lɛktʃərəʳ] n Vortragende(r) m(f); (BRIT: UNIV) Dozent(in) m(f)

led [lɛd] pt, pp of **lead²**

ledge [lɛdʒ] n Leiste f; (window ~) Sims m or nt; (of mountain) (Fels)vorsprung m

ledger ['lɛdʒər] n Hauptbuch nt

leech [li:tʃ] n Blutegel m

leek [li:k] n Lauch m

leer [lɪər] vi: **to ~ (at sb)** (nach jdm) schielen

leeway ['li:wei] n (fig): **to have some ~** etwas Spielraum haben

left [lɛft] pt, pp of **leave** ♦ adj linke(r, s) ♦ n (side) linke Seite f ♦ adv links; **on the ~** links; **to the ~** nach links; **the L~** (POL) die Linke f; **~-hand** adj: **~-hand drive** mit Linkssteuerung; **~-handed** adj linkshändig; **~-hand side** n linke Seite f; **~-luggage locker** n Gepäckschließfach nt; **~-luggage (office)** (BRIT) n Gepäckaufbewahrung f; **~-overs** npl Reste pl; **~-wing** adj linke(r, s)

leg [lɛg] n Bein nt; (of meat) Keule f; (stage) Etappe f; **1st/2nd ~** (SPORT) 1./ 2. Etappe

legacy ['lɛgəsi] n Erbe nt, Erbschaft f

legal ['li:gl] adj gesetzlich; (allowed) legal; **~ holiday** (US) n gesetzliche(r) Feiertag m; **~ize** vt legalisieren; **~ly** adv gesetzlich; legal; **~ tender** n gesetzliche(s) Zahlungsmittel nt

legend ['lɛdʒənd] n Legende f; **~ary** adj legendär

leggings ['lɛgɪnz] npl Leggings pl

legible ['lɛdʒəbl] adj leserlich

legislation [lɛdʒɪs'leɪʃən] n Gesetzgebung f; **legislative** ['lɛdʒɪslətɪv] adj gesetzgebend; **legislature** ['lɛdʒɪslətʃər] n Legislative f

legitimate [lɪ'dʒɪtɪmət] adj rechtmäßig, legitim; (child) ehelich

legroom ['lɛgru:m] n Platz m für die Beine

leisure ['lɛʒər] n Freizeit f; **to be at ~** Zeit haben; **~ centre** n Freizeitzentrum nt; **~ly** adj gemächlich

lemon ['lɛmən] n Zitrone f; (colour) Zitronengelb nt; **~ade** [lɛmə'neɪd] n Limonade f; **~ tea** n Zitronentee m

lend [lɛnd] (pt, pp lent) vt leihen; **to ~ sb sth** jdm etw leihen; **~ing library** n

Leihbibliothek f

length [lɛŋθ] n Länge f; (of road, pipe etc) Strecke f; (of material) Stück nt; **at ~** (lengthily) ausführlich; (at last) schließlich; **~en** vt verlängern ♦ vi länger werden; **~ways** adv längs; **~y** adj sehr lang, langatmig

lenient ['li:nɪənt] adj nachsichtig

lens [lɛnz] n Linse f; (PHOT) Objektiv nt

Lent [lɛnt] n Fastenzeit f

lent [lɛnt] pt, pp of **lend**

lentil ['lɛntɪl] n Linse f

Leo ['li:əu] n Löwe m

leotard ['li:əta:d] n Trikot nt, Gymnastikanzug m

leper ['lɛpər] n Leprakranke(r) f(m)

leprosy ['lɛprəsi] n Lepra f

lesbian ['lɛzbɪən] adj lesbisch ♦ n Lesbierin f

less [lɛs] adj, adv weniger ♦ n weniger ♦ pron weniger; **~ than half** weniger als die Hälfte; **~ than ever** weniger denn je; **~ and ~** immer weniger; **the ~ he works** je weniger er arbeitet; **~en** ['lɛsn] vi abnehmen ♦ vt verringern, verkleinern; **~er** ['lɛsər] adj kleiner, geringer; **to a ~er extent** in geringerem Maße

lesson ['lɛsn] n (SCH) Stunde f; (unit of study) Lektion f; (fig) Lehre f; (ECCL) Lesung f; **a maths ~** eine Mathestunde

lest [lɛst] conj: **~ it happen** damit es nicht geschieht

let [lɛt] (pt, pp let) vt lassen; (BRIT: lease) vermieten; **to ~ sb do sth** jdn etw tun lassen; **to ~ sb know sth** jdn etw wissen lassen; **~'s go!** gehen wir!; **~ him come** soll er doch kommen; **~ down** vt hinunterlassen; (disappoint) enttäuschen; **~ go** vi loslassen ♦ vt (things) loslassen; (person) gehen lassen; **~ in** vt hereinlassen; (water) durchlassen; **~ off** vt (gun) abfeuern; (steam) ablassen; (forgive) laufen lassen; **~ on** vi durchblicken lassen; (pretend) vorgeben; **~ out** vt herauslassen;

(*scream*) fahren lassen; **~ up** vi nachlassen; (*stop*) aufhören

lethal [ˈliːθl] adj tödlich

lethargic [lɛˈθɑːdʒɪk] adj lethargisch

letter [ˈlɛtər] n Brief m; (*of alphabet*) Buchstabe m; **~ bomb** n Briefbombe f; **~box** (BRIT) n Briefkasten m; **~ing** n Beschriftung f; **~ of credit** n Akkreditiv m

lettuce [ˈlɛtɪs] n (Kopf)salat m

let-up [ˈlɛtʌp] (*inf*) n Nachlassen nt

leukaemia [luːˈkiːmɪə] (US **leukemia**) n Leukämie f

level [ˈlɛvl] adj (*ground*) eben; (*at same height*) auf gleicher Höhe; (*equal*) gleich gut; (*head*) kühl ♦ adv auf gleicher Höhe ♦ n (*instrument*) Wasserwaage f; (*altitude*) Höhe f; (*flat place*) ebene Fläche f; (*position on scale*) Niveau nt; (*amount, degree*) Grad m ♦ vt (*ground*) einebnen; **to draw ~ with** gleichziehen mit; **to be ~ with** auf einer Höhe sein mit; **A ~s** (BRIT) ≃ Abitur nt; **O ~s** (BRIT) ≃ mittlere Reife f; **on the ~** (*fig: honest*) ehrlich; **to ~ at sb** (*blow*) jdm etw versetzen; (*remark*) etw gegen jdn richten; **~ off** or **out** vi flach or eben werden; (*fig*) sich ausgleichen; (*plane*) horizontal fliegen ♦ vt (*ground*) planieren; (*differences*) ausgleichen; **~ crossing** (BRIT) n Bahnübergang m; **~-headed** adj vernünftig

lever [ˈliːvər] n Hebel m; (*fig*) Druckmittel nt ♦ vt (hoch)stemmen; **~age** n Hebelkraft f; (*fig*) Einfluss m

levy [ˈlɛvɪ] n (*of taxes*) Erhebung f; (*tax*) Abgaben pl; (MIL) Aushebung f ♦ vt erheben; (MIL) ausheben

lewd [luːd] adj unzüchtig, unanständig

liability [laɪəˈbɪlɪtɪ] n (*burden*) Belastung f; (*duty*) Pflicht f; (*debt*) Verpflichtung f; (*responsibility*) Haftung f; (*proneness*) Anfälligkeit f

liable [ˈlaɪəbl] adj (*responsible*) haftbar; (*prone*) anfällig; **to be ~ for sth** etw dat unterliegen; **it's ~ to happen** es

kann leicht vorkommen

liaise [liːˈeɪz] vi: **to ~ (with sb)** (mit jdm) zusammenarbeiten; **liaison** n Verbindung f

liar [ˈlaɪər] n Lügner m

libel [ˈlaɪbl] n Verleumdung f ♦ vt verleumden

liberal [ˈlɪbərl] adj (*generous*) großzügig; (*open-minded*) aufgeschlossen; (POL) liberal

liberate [ˈlɪbəreɪt] vt befreien; **liberation** n Befreiung f

liberty [ˈlɪbətɪ] n Freiheit f; (*permission*) Erlaubnis f; **to be at ~ to do sth** etw tun dürfen; **to take the ~ of doing sth** sich dat erlauben, etw zu tun

Libra [ˈliːbrə] n Waage f

librarian [laɪˈbrɛərɪən] n Bibliothekar(in) m(f)

library [ˈlaɪbrərɪ] n Bibliothek f; (*lending ~*) Bücherei f

Libya [ˈlɪbɪə] n Libyen nt; **~n** adj libysch ♦ n Libyer(in) m(f)

lice [laɪs] npl of **louse**

licence [ˈlaɪsns] (US **license**) n (*permit*) Erlaubnis f; (*also: driving ~*, (US) **driver's ~**) Führerschein m

license [ˈlaɪsns] n (US) = **licence** ♦ vt genehmigen, konzessionieren; **~d** adj (*for alcohol*) konzessioniert (für den Alkoholausschank); **~ plate** n (US AUT) Nummernschild nt

lichen [ˈlaɪkən] n Flechte f

lick [lɪk] vt lecken ♦ n Lecken nt; **a ~ of paint** ein bisschen Farbe

licorice [ˈlɪkərɪs] (US) n = **liquorice**

lid [lɪd] n Deckel m; (*eyelid*) Lid nt

lie [laɪ] (*pt* lay, *pp* lain) vi (*rest, be situated*) liegen; (*put o.s. in position*) sich legen; (*pt, pp* lied: *tell lies*) lügen ♦ n Lüge f; **to ~ low** (*fig*) untertauchen; **~ about** vi (*things*) herumliegen; (*people*) faulenzen; **~down** (BRIT) n: **to have a ~-down** ein Nickerchen machen; **~-in** (BRIT) n: **to have a ~-in** sich ausschlafen

lieu [luː] n: **in ~ of** anstatt +gen

lieutenant [lef'tenənt, (US) lu:'tenənt] n Leutnant m

life [laɪf] (pl **lives**) n Leben nt; **~ assurance** (BRIT) n = **life insurance**; **~belt** (BRIT) n Rettungsring m; **~boat** n Rettungsboot nt; **~guard** n Rettungsschwimmer m; **~ insurance** n Lebensversicherung f; **~ jacket** n Schwimmweste f; **~less** adj (dead) leblos; (dull) langweilig; **~like** adj lebenswahr, naturgetreu; **~line** n Rettungsleine f; (fig) Rettungsanker m; **~long** adj lebenslang; **~ preserver** (US) n = **lifebelt**; **~saver** n Lebensretter(in) m(f); **~saving** adj lebensrettend, Rettungs-; **~ sentence** n lebenslängliche Freiheitsstrafe f; **~ span** n Lebensspanne f; **~style** n Lebensstil m; **~ support system** n (MED) Lebenserhaltungssystem nt; **~time** n: in his **~time** während er lebte; once in a **~time** einmal im Leben

lift [lɪft] vt hochheben ♦ vi sich heben ♦ n (BRIT: elevator) Aufzug m, Lift m; to give sb a **~** jdn mitnehmen; **~-off** n Abheben nt (vom Boden)

ligament ['lɪgəmənt] n Band nt

light [laɪt] (pt, pp **lighted** or **lit**) n Licht nt; (for cigarette etc): **have you got a ~?** haben Sie Feuer?; vt beleuchten; (lamp) anmachen; (fire, cigarette) anzünden ♦ adj (bright) hell; (pale) hell-; (not heavy, easy) leicht; (punishment) milde; (touch) leicht; **~s** npl (AUT) Beleuchtung f; **~ up** vi (lamp) angehen; (face) aufleuchten ♦ vt (illuminate) beleuchten; (~s) anmachen; **~ bulb** n Glühbirne f; **~en** vi (brighten) hell werden; (~ning) blitzen ♦ vt (give ~ to) erhellen; (hair) aufhellen; (gloom) aufheitern; (make less heavy) leichter machen; (fig) erleichtern; **~er** n Feuerzeug nt; **~-headed** adj (thoughtless) leichtsinnig; (giddy) schwindlig; **~hearted** adj leichtherzig, fröhlich; **~house** n Leuchtturm m; **~ing** n Beleuchtung f; **~ly** adv leicht; (irrespon-

sibly) leichtfertig; **to get off ~ly** mit einem blauen Auge davonkommen; **~ness** n (of weight) Leichtigkeit f; (of colour) Helle f

lightning ['laɪtnɪŋ] n Blitz m; **~ conductor** (US **~ rod**) n Blitzableiter m

light-: **~ pen** n Lichtstift m; **~weight** adj (suit) leicht ♦ n (BOXING) Leichtgewichtler m; **~ year** n Lichtjahr nt

like [laɪk] vt mögen, gern haben ♦ prep wie ♦ adj (similar) ähnlich; (equal) gleich ♦ n: **the ~** dergleichen; I **would** or I'd **~** ich möchte gern; **would you ~ a coffee?** möchten Sie einen Kaffee?; **to be** or **look ~ sb/sth** jdm/etw ähneln; **that's just ~ him** das ist typisch für ihn; **do it ~ this** mach es so; **it is nothing ~ ...** es ist nicht zu vergleichen mit ...; **what does it look ~?** wie sieht es aus?; **what does it sound ~?** wie hört es sich an?; **what does it taste ~?** wie schmeckt es?; **my ~s and dislikes** was er mag und was er nicht mag; **~able** adj sympathisch

likelihood ['laɪklɪhʊd] n Wahrscheinlichkeit f

likely ['laɪklɪ] adj wahrscheinlich; **he's ~ to leave** er geht möglicherweise; **not ~!** wohl kaum!

likeness ['laɪknɪs] n Ähnlichkeit f; (portrait) Bild nt

likewise ['laɪkwaɪz] adv ebenso

liking ['laɪkɪŋ] n Zuneigung f; (taste) Vorliebe f

lilac ['laɪlək] n Flieder m ♦ adj (colour) fliederfarben

lily ['lɪlɪ] n Lilie f; **~ of the valley** n Maiglöckchen nt

limb [lɪm] n Glied nt

limber up ['lɪmbə'-] vi sich auflockern; (fig) sich vorbereiten

limbo ['lɪmbəʊ] n: **to be in ~** (fig) in der Schwebe sein

lime [laɪm] n (tree) Linde f; (fruit) Limone f; (substance) Kalk m

limelight ['laɪmlaɪt] n: **to be in the ~**

(fig) im Rampenlicht stehen

limestone ['laɪmstəʊn] *n* Kalkstein *m*

limit ['lɪmɪt] *n* Grenze *f*; *(inf)* Höhe *f*
♦ *vt* begrenzen, einschränken; **~ation**
[lɪmɪ'teɪʃən] *n* Einschränkung *f*; **~ed**
adj beschränkt; **to be ~ed to** sich
beschränken auf +*acc*; **~ed (liability)
company** *(BRIT)* *n* Gesellschaft *f* mit
beschränkter Haftung

limousine ['lɪməziːn] *n* Limousine *f*

limp [lɪmp] *n* Hinken *nt* ♦ *vi* hinken
♦ *adj* schlaff

limpet ['lɪmpɪt] *n (fig)* Klette *f*

line [laɪn] *n* Linie *f*; *(rope)* Leine *f*; *(on
face)* Falte *f*; *(row)* Reihe *f*; *(of hills)* Kette *f*; *(US: queue)* Schlange *f*; *(company)*
Linie *f*, Gesellschaft *f*; *(TEL)* Leitung *f*;
(written) Zeile *f*; *(direc-
tion)* Richtung *f*; *(fig: business)* Branche
f; *(range of items)* Kollektion *f* ♦ *vt
(coat)* füttern; *(border)* säumen; **~s** *npl
(RAIL)* Gleise *pl*; **in ~ with** in
Übereinstimmung mit; **~ up** *vi* sich
aufstellen ♦ *vt* aufstellen; *(prepare)* sorgen für; *(support)* mobilisieren; *(surprise)* planen; **~ar** ['lɪnɪəᵊ] *adj* gerade;
(measure) Längen-; **~d** *adj (face)* faltig;
(paper) liniert

linen ['lɪnɪn] *n* Leinen *nt*; *(sheets etc)*
Wäsche *f*

liner ['laɪnəᵊ] *n* Überseedampfer *m*

linesman ['laɪnzmən] *(irreg)* *n (SPORT)*
Linienrichter *m*

line-up ['laɪnʌp] *n* Aufstellung *f*

linger ['lɪŋgəᵊ] *vi (remain long)* verweilen; *(taste)* (zurück)bleiben; *(delay)*
zögern, verharren

lingerie ['lænʒəriː] *n* Damenunter-
wäsche *f*

lingering ['lɪŋgərɪŋ] *adj (doubt)* zu-
rückbleibend; *(disease)* langwierig;
(taste) nachhaltend; *(look)* lang

lingo ['lɪŋgəʊ] *(pl* **~es)** *(inf)* Sprache *f*

linguist ['lɪŋgwɪst] *n* Sprachkundige(r)
mf; *(UNIV)* Sprachwissenschaftler(in)
m(f); **~ic** [lɪŋ'gwɪstɪk] *adj* sprachlich;
sprachwissenschaftlich; **~ics** *n* Sprach-

wissenschaft *f*, Linguistik *f*

lining ['laɪnɪŋ] *n* Futter *nt*

link [lɪŋk] *n* Glied *nt*; *(connection)* Verbindung *f* ♦ *vt* verbinden; **~s** *npl (GOLF)*
Golfplatz *m*; **~ up** *vt* verbinden ♦ *vi* zusammenkommen; *(companies)* sich zu-
sammenschließen; **~up** *n (TEL)* Verbindung *f*; *(of spaceships)* Kopplung *f*

lino ['laɪnəʊ] *n* = **linoleum**

linoleum [lɪ'nəʊlɪəm] *n* Linoleum *nt*

linseed oil ['lɪnsiːd-] *n* Leinöl *nt*

lion ['laɪən] *n* Löwe *m*; **~ess** *n* Löwin *f*

lip [lɪp] *n* Lippe *f*; *(of jug)* Schnabel *m*;
to pay ~ service (to) ein Lippenbe-
kenntnis ablegen (zu)

liposuction ['lɪpəʊsʌkʃən] *n* Fettabsau-
gen *nt*

lip: **~read** *(irreg)* *vi* von den Lippen
ablesen; **~ salve** *n* Lippenbalsam *m*;
~stick *n* Lippenstift *m*

liqueur [lɪ'kjʊəᵊ] *n* Likör *m*

liquid ['lɪkwɪd] *n* Flüssigkeit *f* ♦ *adj*
flüssig

liquidate ['lɪkwɪdeɪt] *vt* liquidieren

liquidize ['lɪkwɪdaɪz] *vt (COOK)* (im Mixer) pürieren; **~r** ['lɪkwɪdaɪzəᵊ] *n* Mixgerät *nt*

liquor ['lɪkəᵊ] *n* Alkohol *m*

liquorice ['lɪkərɪs] *(BRIT)* *n* Lakritze *f*

liquor store *(US)* *n* Spirituosengeschäft
nt

Lisbon ['lɪzbən] *n* Lissabon *nt*

lisp [lɪsp] *n* Lispeln *nt* ♦ *vt*, *vi* lispeln

list [lɪst] *n* Liste *f*, Verzeichnis *nt*; *(of
ship)* Schlagseite *f* ♦ *vt (write down)*
eine Liste machen von; *(verbally)* aufzählen ♦ *vi (ship)* Schlagseite haben

listen ['lɪsn] *vi* hören; **~ to** zuhören
+*dat*; **~er** *n* (Zu)hörer(in) *m(f)*

listless ['lɪstlɪs] *adj* lustlos

lit [lɪt] *pt*, *pp* of **light**

liter ['liːtəᵊ] *(US)* *n* = **litre**

literacy ['lɪtərəsɪ] *n* Fähigkeit *f* zu lesen
und zu schreiben

literal ['lɪtərəl] *adj* buchstäblich; *(translation)* wortwörtlich; **~ly** *adv* wörtlich;
buchstäblich

literary ['lɪtərərɪ] adj literarisch

literate ['lɪtərət] adj des Lesens und Schreibens kundig

literature ['lɪtrɪtʃə'] n Literatur f

litigation [lɪtɪ'geɪʃən] n Prozess m

litre ['liːtə'] (US **liter**) n Liter m

litter ['lɪtə'] n (rubbish) Abfall m; (of animals) Wurf m ♦ vt in Unordnung bringen; **to be ~ed with** übersät sein mit; **~ bin** (BRIT) n Abfalleimer m

little ['lɪtl] adj klein ♦ adv n wenig; **a ~** ein bisschen; **~ by ~** nach und nach

live¹ [laɪv] adj lebendig; (MIL) scharf; (ELEC) geladen; (broadcast) live

live² [lɪv] vi leben; (dwell) wohnen ♦ vt (life) führen; **~ down** vt: **I'll never ~ it down** das wird man mir nie vergessen; **~ on** vi weiterleben ♦ vt fus: **to ~ on sth** von etw leben; **~ together** vi zusammenleben; (share a flat) zusammenwohnen; **~ up to** vt (standards) gerecht werden +dat; (principles) anstreben; (hopes) entsprechen +dat

livelihood ['laɪvlɪhʊd] n Lebensunterhalt m

lively ['laɪvlɪ] adj lebhaft, lebendig

liven up ['laɪvn-] vt beleben

liver ['lɪvə'] n (ANAT) Leber f

lives [laɪvz] pl of **life**

livestock ['laɪvstɔk] n Vieh nt

livid ['lɪvɪd] adj bläulich; (furious) fuchsteufelswild

living ['lɪvɪŋ] n (Lebens)unterhalt m ♦ adj lebendig; (language etc) lebend; **to earn** or **make a ~** sich dat einen Lebensunterhalt verdienen; **~ conditions** npl Wohnverhältnisse pl; **~ room** n Wohnzimmer nt; **~ standards** npl Lebensstandard m; **~ wage** n ausreichender Lohn m

lizard ['lɪzəd] n Eidechse f

load [ləʊd] n (burden) Last f; (amount) Ladung f ♦ vt (also: **~ up**) (be)laden; (COMPUT) laden; (camera) Film einlegen in +acc; (gun) laden; **a ~ of, ~s of** (fig) jede Menge; **~ed** adj beladen; (dice) präpariert; (question) Fang-; (inf: rich)

steinreich; **~ing bay** n Ladeplatz m

loaf [ləʊf] (pl **loaves**) n Brot nt ♦ vi (also: **~ about, ~ around**) herumlungern, faulenzen

loan [ləʊn] n Leihgabe f; (FIN) Darlehen nt ♦ vt leihen; **on ~** geliehen

loath [ləʊθ] adj: **to be ~ to do sth** etw ungern tun

loathe [ləʊð] vt verabscheuen

loaves [ləʊvz] pl of **loaf**

lobby ['lɔbɪ] n Vorhalle f; (POL) Lobby f ♦ vt politisch beeinflussen (wollen)

lobster ['lɔbstə'] n Hummer m

local ['ləʊkl] adj ortsansässig, Orts- ♦ n (pub) Stammwirtschaft f; **the ~s** npl (people) die Ortsansässigen pl; **~ anaesthetic** n (MED) örtliche Betäubung f; **~ authority** n städtische Behörden pl; **~ call** n (TEL) Ortsgespräch nt; **~ government** n Gemeinde-/Kreisverwaltung f; **~ity** [ləʊ'kælɪtɪ] n Ort m; **~ly** adv örtlich, am Ort

locate [ləʊ'keɪt] vt ausfindig machen; (establish) errichten; **location** [ləʊ'keɪʃən] n Platz m, Lage f; **on ~** (CINE) auf Außenaufnahme

loch [lɔx] (SCOTTISH) n See m

lock [lɔk] n Schloss nt; (NAUT) Schleuse f; (of hair) Locke f ♦ vt (fasten) (ver)schließen ♦ vi (door etc) sich schließen (lassen); (wheels) blockieren; **~ up** vt (criminal, mental patient) einsperren; (house) abschließen

locker ['lɔkə'] n Spind m

locket ['lɔkɪt] n Medaillon nt

lock [lɔk-]: **~out** n Aussperrung f; **~smith** n Schlosser(in) m(f); **~up** n (jail) Gefängnis nt; (garage) Garage f

locum ['ləʊkəm] n (MED) Vertreter(in) m(f)

lodge [lɔdʒ] n (gatehouse) Pförtnerhaus nt; (freemasons') Loge f ♦ vi (get stuck) stecken (bleiben); (in Untermiete): **to ~ (with)** wohnen (bei) ♦ vt (protest) einreichen; **~r** n (Unter)mieter m; **lodgings** n (Miet)wohnung f

loft [lɒft] n (Dach)boden m

lofty ['lɒftɪ] adj hoch(ragend); (proud) hochmütig

log [lɒg] n Klotz m; (book) = **logbook**

logbook ['lɒgbʊk] n Bordbuch nt; (for lorry) Fahrtenschreiber m; (AUT) Kraftfahrzeugbrief m

loggerheads ['lɒgəhedz] npl: to be at ~ sich in den Haaren liegen

logic ['lɒdʒɪk] n Logik f; **~al** adj logisch

logistics [lɒ'dʒɪstɪks] npl Logistik f

logo ['ləʊgəʊ] n Firmenzeichen nt

loin [lɔɪn] n Lende f

loiter ['lɔɪtə] vi herumstehen

loll [lɒl] vi (also: ~ **about**) sich rekeln or räkeln

lollipop ['lɒlɪpɒp] n (Dauer)lutscher m; ~ **man/lady** (irreg; BRIT) n ≈ Schülerlotse m

Lollipop man/lady

Lollipop man/lady heißen in Großbritannien die Männer bzw. Frauen, die mit Hilfe eines runden Stoppschildes den Verkehr anhalten, damit Schulkinder die Straße gefahrlos überqueren können. Der Name bezieht sich auf die Form des Schildes, die an einen Lutscher erinnert.

lolly ['lɒlɪ] (inf) n (sweet) Lutscher m

London ['lʌndən] n London nt; **~er** n Londoner(in) m(f)

lone [ləʊn] adj einsam

loneliness ['ləʊnlɪnɪs] n Einsamkeit f

lonely ['ləʊnlɪ] adj einsam

loner ['ləʊnə] n Einzelgänger m

long [lɒŋ] adj lang; (distance) weit ♦ adv lange ♦ vi: to ~ for sth sich sehnen nach; before ~ bald; as ~ as solange; in the ~ run auf die Dauer; don't be ~! beeil dich!; how ~ is the street? wie lang ist die Straße?; how ~ is the lesson? wie lange dauert die Stunde?; 6 metres ~ 6 Meter lang; 6 months ~ 6 Monate lang; all night ~ die ganze Nacht; he no ~er comes er kommt

nicht mehr; ~ ago vor langer Zeit; ~ before lange vorher; at ~ last endlich; **~distance** adj Fern-

longevity [lɒn'dʒevɪtɪ] n Langlebigkeit f

long: **~-haired** adj langhaarig; **~hand** n Langschrift f; **~ing** n Sehnsucht f ♦ adj sehnsüchtig

longitude ['lɒŋgɪtjuːd] n Längengrad m

long: ~ **jump** n Weitsprung m; **~-life** adj (batteries etc) mit langer Lebensdauer; **~-lost** adj längst verloren geglaubt; **~-playing record** n Langspielplatte f; **~-range** adj Langstrecken-, Fern-; **~-sighted** adj weitsichtig; **~standing** adj alt, seit langer Zeit bestehend; **~-suffering** adj schwer geprüft; **~-term** adj langfristig; ~ **wave** n Langwelle f; **~-winded** adj langatmig

loo [luː] (BRIT: inf) n Klo nt

look [lʊk] vi schauen; (seem) aussehen; (building etc): to ~ **on to the sea** aufs Meer gehen ♦ n Blick m; **~s** npl (appearance) Aussehen nt; ~ **after** vt (care for) sorgen für; (watch) aufpassen auf +acc; ~ **at** vt ansehen; (consider) sich überlegen; ~ **back** vi sich umsehen; (fig) zurückblicken; ~ **down on** vt (fig) herabsehen auf +acc; ~ **for** vt (seek) suchen; ~ **forward to** vt sich freuen auf +acc; (in letters): **we** ~ **forward to hearing from you** wir hoffen, bald von Ihnen zu hören; ~ **into** vt untersuchen; ~ **on** vi zusehen; ~ **out** vi hinaussehen; (take care) aufpassen; ~ **out for** vt Ausschau halten nach; (be careful) Acht geben auf +acc; ~ **round** vi sich umsehen; ~ **to** vt (take care of) Acht geben auf +acc; (rely on) sich verlassen auf +acc; ~ **up** vi aufblicken; (improve) sich bessern ♦ vt (word) nachschlagen; (person) besuchen; ~ **up to** vt aufsehen zu; **~out** n (watch) Ausschau f; (person) Wachposten m; (place) Ausguck m; (prospect)

Aussichten pl; **to be on the ~ out for sth** nach etw Ausschau halten

loom [luːm] n Webstuhl m ♦ vi sich abzeichnen

loony ['luːnɪ] (inf) n Verrückte(r) mf

loop [luːp] n Schlaufe f; **~hole** n (fig) Hintertürchen nt

loose [luːs] adj lose, locker; (free) frei; (inexact) unpräzise ♦ vt lösen, losbinden; **~ change** n Kleingeld nt; **~ chippings** npl (on road) Rollsplit m; **~ end** n: **to be at a ~ end** (BRIT) or **at ~ ends** (US) nicht wissen, was man tun soll; **~ly** adv locker, lose; **~n** vt lockern, losmachen

loot [luːt] n Beute f ♦ vt plündern

lop off [lɔp-] vt abhacken

lopsided ['lɔp'saɪdɪd] adj schief

lord [lɔːd] n (ruler) Herr m; (BRIT: title) Lord m; **the L~** (God) der Herr; **(the House of) L~s** das Oberhaus m; **~ship** n: **Your L~ship** Eure Lordschaft

lorry ['lɔrɪ] (BRIT) n Lastwagen m; **~ driver** (BRIT) n Lastwagenfahrer(in) m(f)

lose [luːz] (pt, pp **lost**) vt verlieren; (chance) verpassen ♦ vi verlieren; **to ~ (time)** (clock) nachgehen; **~r** n Verlierer m

loss [lɔs] n Verlust m; **at a ~** (COMM) mit Verlust; (unable) außerstande, außer Stande

lost [lɔst] pt, pp of **lose** ♦ adj verloren; **~ property** (US **~ and found**) n Fundsachen pl

lot [lɔt] n (quantity) Menge f; (fate, at auction) Los nt; (inf: people, things) Haufen m; **the ~** alles; (people) alle; **a ~ of** (with sg) viel; (with pl) viele; **~s of** massenhaft, viel(e); **I read a ~** ich lese viel; **to draw ~s for sth** etw verlosen

lotion ['ləuʃən] n Lotion f

lottery ['lɔtərɪ] n Lotterie f

loud [laud] adj laut; (showy) schreiend ♦ adv laut; **~ly** adv laut; **~speaker** n Lautsprecher m

lounge [laundʒ] n (in hotel) Gesellschaftsraum m; (in house) Wohnzim-

mer nt ♦ vi sich herumlümmeln

louse [laus] (pl **lice**) n Laus f

lousy ['lauzɪ] adj (fig) miserabel

lout [laut] n Lümmel m

louvre ['luːvər] (US **louver**) adj (door, window) Jalousie-

lovable ['lʌvəbl] adj liebenswert

love [lʌv] n Liebe f; (person) Liebling m; (SPORT) null ♦ vt (person) lieben; (activity) gerne mögen; **to be in ~ with sb** in jdn verliebt sein; **to make ~** sich lieben; **for the ~ of** aus Liebe zu; **"15 ~"** (TENNIS) "15 null"; **to ~ to do sth** etw (gerne) tun; **~ affair** n (Liebes)verhältnis nt; **~ letter** n Liebesbrief m; **~ life** n Liebesleben nt

lovely ['lʌvlɪ] adj schön

lover ['lʌvər] n Liebhaber(in) m(f)

loving ['lʌvɪŋ] adj liebend, liebevoll

low [ləu] adj niedrig; (rank) niedere(r, s); (level, note, neckline) tief; (intelligence, density) gering; (vulgar) ordinär; (not loud) leise; (depressed) gedrückt ♦ adv (not high) niedrig; (not loudly) leise ♦ n (~ point) Tiefstand m; (MET) Tief nt; **to feel ~** sich mies fühlen; **to turn (down)** ~ leiser stellen; **~ alcohol** adj alkoholarm; **~-calorie** adj kalorienarm; **~-cut** adj (dress) tief ausgeschnitten; **~er** vt herunterlassen; (eyes, gun) senken; (reduce) herabsetzen, senken ♦ vr: **to ~er o.s.** to (fig) sich herablassen zu; **~er sixth** (BRIT) n (SCOL) ≈ zwölfte Klasse; **~-fat** adj fettarm, Mager-; **~lands** npl (GEOG) Flachland nt; **~ly** adj bescheiden; **~-lying** adj tief gelegen

loyal ['lɔɪəl] adj treu; **~ty** n Treue f

lozenge ['lɔzɪndʒ] n Pastille f

L-plates ['ɛlpleɪts] (BRIT) npl L-Schild nt (für Fahrschüler)

müssen. Fahrschüler müssen einen vorläufigen Führerschein beantragen und dürfen damit unter der Aufsicht eines erfahrenen Autofahrers auf allen Straßen außer Autobahnen fahren.

Ltd *abbr* (= *limited company*) GmbH

lubricant ['lu:brɪkənt] *n* Schmiermittel *nt*

lubricate ['lu:brɪkeɪt] *vt* schmieren

lucid ['lu:sɪd] *adj* klar; (*sane*) bei klarem Verstand; (*moment*) licht

luck [lʌk] *n* Glück *nt*; **bad** or **hard** or **tough** ~! (so ein) Pech!; **good** ~! viel Glück!; **~ily** *adv* glücklicherweise, zum Glück; **~y** *adj* Glücks-; **to be ~y** Glück haben

lucrative ['lu:krətɪv] *adj* einträglich

ludicrous ['lu:dɪkrəs] *adj* grotesk

lug [lʌg] *vt* schleppen

luggage ['lʌgɪdʒ] *n* Gepäck *nt*; ~ **rack** *n* Gepäcknetz *nt*

lukewarm ['lu:kwɔ:m] *adj* lauwarm; (*indifferent*) lau

lull [lʌl] *n* Flaute *f* ♦ *vt* einlullen; (*calm*) beruhigen

lullaby ['lʌləbaɪ] *n* Schlaflied *nt*

lumbago [lʌm'beɪgəu] *n* Hexenschuss *m*

lumber ['lʌmbər] *n* Plunder *m*; (*wood*) Holz *nt*; ~**jack** *n* Holzfäller *m*

luminous ['lu:mɪnəs] *adj* Leucht-

lump [lʌmp] *n* Klumpen *m*; (MED) Schwellung *f*; (*in breast*) Knoten *m*; (*of sugar*) Stück *nt* ♦ *vt* (*also:* ~ **together**) zusammentun; (*judge together*) in einen Topf werfen; ~ **sum** *n* Pauschalsumme *f*; ~**y** *adj* klumpig

lunacy ['lu:nəsɪ] *n* Irrsinn *m*

lunar ['lu:nər] *adj* Mond-

lunatic ['lu:nətɪk] *n* Wahnsinnige(r) *mf* ♦ *adj* wahnsinnig, irr

lunch [lʌntʃ] *n* Mittagessen *nt*; ~**eon** ['lʌntʃən] *n* Mittagessen *nt*; ~**eon meat** *n* Frühstücksfleisch *nt*; ~**eon voucher** (BRIT) *n* Essenmarke *f*; ~**time** *n* Mittagszeit *f*

lung [lʌŋ] *n* Lunge *f*

lunge [lʌndʒ] *vi* (*also:* ~ **forward**) (los)stürzen; **to** ~ **at** sich stürzen auf +*acc*

lurch [lə:tʃ] *vi* taumeln; (NAUT) schlingern ♦ *n* Ruck *m*; (NAUT) Schlingern *nt*; **to leave sb in the** ~ jdn im Stich lassen

lure [luər] *n* Köder *m*; (*fig*) Lockung *f* ♦ *vt* (ver)locken

lurid ['luərɪd] *adj* (*shocking*) grausig, widerlich; (*colour*) grell

lurk [lə:k] *vi* lauern

luscious ['lʌʃəs] *adj* köstlich

lush [lʌʃ] *adj* satt; (*vegetation*) üppig

lust [lʌst] *n* Wollust *f*; (*greed*) Gier *f* ♦ *vi*: **to** ~ **after** gieren nach

lustre ['lʌstər] (US **luster**) *n* Glanz *m*

Luxembourg ['lʌksəmbə:g] *n* Luxemburg *nt*

luxuriant [lʌg'zjuərɪənt] *adj* üppig

luxurious [lʌg'zjuərɪəs] *adj* luxuriös, Luxus-

luxury ['lʌkʃərɪ] *n* Luxus *m* ♦ *cpd* Luxus-

lying ['laɪɪŋ] *n* Lügen *nt* ♦ *adj* verlogen

lynx [lɪŋks] *n* Luchs *m*

lyric ['lɪrɪk] *n* Lyrik *f* ♦ *adj* lyrisch; ~**s** *pl* (*words for song*) (Lied)text *m*; ~**al** *adj* lyrisch, gefühlvoll

M, m

m *abbr* = **metre**; **mile**; **million**

M.A. *abbr* = **Master of Arts**

mac [mæk] (BRIT: *inf*) *n* Regenmantel *m*

macaroni [mækə'rəuni] *n* Makkaroni *pl*

machine [mə'ʃi:n] *n* Maschine *f* ♦ *vt* (*dress etc*) mit der Maschine nähen; ~ **gun** *n* Maschinengewehr *nt*; ~ **language** *n* (COMPUT) Maschinensprache *f*; ~**ry** *n* Maschinerie *f*

macho ['mætʃəu] *adj* macho

mackerel ['mækrl] *n* Makrele *f*

mackintosh ['mækɪntɔʃ] (BRIT) *n* Regenmantel *m*

mad [mæd] *adj* verrückt; (*dog*) tollwütig; *(angry)* wütend; **~ about** *(fond of)* verrückt nach, versessen auf +*acc*

madam ['mædəm] *n* gnädige Frau *f*

madden ['mædn] *vt* verrückt machen; *(make angry)* ärgern

made [meɪd] *pt, pp of* **make**

made-to-measure ['meɪdtə'meʒə^r] *(BRIT) adj* Maß-

mad [mæd-]: **~ly** *adv* wahnsinnig; **~man** *(irreg) n* Verrückte(r) *m*, Irre(r) *m*; **~ness** *n* Wahnsinn *m*

magazine [mægə'ziːn] *n* Zeitschrift *f*; *(in gun)* Magazin *n*

maggot ['mægət] *n* Made *f*

magic ['mædʒɪk] *n* Zauberei *f*, Magie *f*; *(fig)* Zauber *m* ♦ *adj* magisch, Zauber-; **~al** *adj* magisch; **~ian** [mə'dʒɪʃən] *n* Zauberer *m*

magistrate ['mædʒɪstreɪt] *n* (Friedens)richter *m*

magnanimous [mæg'nænɪməs] *adj* großmütig

magnet ['mægnɪt] *n* Magnet *m*; **~ic** [mæg'netɪk] *adj* magnetisch; **~ic tape** *n* Magnetband *nt*; **~ism** *n* Magnetismus *m*; *(fig)* Ausstrahlungskraft *f*

magnificent [mæg'nɪfɪsnt] *adj* großartig

magnify ['mægnɪfaɪ] *vt* vergrößern; **~ing glass** *n* Lupe *f*

magnitude ['mægnɪtjuːd] *n (size)* Größe *f*; *(importance)* Ausmaß *nt*

magpie ['mægpaɪ] *n* Elster *f*

mahogany [mə'hɒgənɪ] *n* Mahagoni *nt* ♦ *cpd* Mahagoni-

maid [meɪd] *n* Dienstmädchen *nt*; **old ~** alte Jungfer *f*

maiden ['meɪdn] *n* Maid *f* ♦ *adj (flight, speech)* Jungfern-; **~ name** *n* Mädchenname *m*

mail [meɪl] *n* Post *f* ♦ *vt* aufgeben; **~box** *(US) n* Briefkasten *m*; **~ing list** *n* Anschreibeliste *f*; **~ order** *n* Bestellung *f* durch die Post; **~ order firm** *n* Versandhaus *nt*

maim [meɪm] *vt* verstümmeln

main [meɪn] *adj* hauptsächlich, Haupt-

♦ *n (pipe)* Hauptleitung *f*; **the ~s** *npl (ELEC)* das Stromnetz; **in the ~** im Großen und Ganzen; **~frame** *n (COMPUT)* Großrechner *m*; **~land** *n* Festland *nt*; **~ly** *adv* hauptsächlich; **~ road** *n* Hauptstraße *f*; **~stay** *n (fig)* Hauptstütze *f*; **~stream** *n* Hauptrichtung *f*

maintain [meɪn'teɪn] *vt (machine, roads)* instand *or* in Stand halten; *(support)* unterhalten; *(keep up)* aufrechterhalten; *(claim)* behaupten; *(innocence)* beteuern

maintenance ['meɪntənəns] *n (TECH)* Wartung *f*; *(of family)* Unterhalt *m*

maize [meɪz] *n* Mais *m*

majestic [mə'dʒestɪk] *adj* majestätisch

majesty ['mædʒɪstɪ] *n* Majestät *f*

major ['meɪdʒə^r] *n* Major *m* ♦ *adj (MUS)* Dur; *(more important)* Haupt-; *(bigger)* größer

Majorca [mə'jɔːkə] *n* Mallorca *nt*

majority [mə'dʒɒrɪtɪ] *n* Mehrheit *f*; *(JUR)* Volljährigkeit *f*

make [meɪk] *(pt, pp* **made)** *vt* machen; *(appoint)* ernennen (zu); *(cause to do sth)* veranlassen; *(reach)* erreichen; *(in time)* schaffen; *(earn)* verdienen ♦ *n* Marke *f*; **to ~ sth happen** etw geschehen lassen; **to ~ it** es schaffen; **what time do you ~ it?** wie spät hast du es?; **to ~ do with** auskommen mit; **~ for** *vi* gehen/fahren nach; **~ out** *vt (write out)* ausstellen; *(understand)* verstehen; **~ up** *vt* machen; *(face)* schminken; *(quarrel)* beilegen; *(story etc)* erfinden ♦ *vi* sich versöhnen; **~ up for** *vi* wieder gutmachen; **~believe** *n (COMM)* Fantasie *f*; **~r** *n (COMM)* Hersteller *m*; **~shift** *adj* behelfsmäßig, Not-; **~up** *n* Schminke *f*, Make-up *nt*; **~up remover** *n* Make-up-Entferner *m*; **making** *n:* **in the making** im Entstehen; **to have the makings of** das Zeug haben zu

malaria [mə'leərɪə] *n* Malaria *f*

Malaysia [mə'leɪzɪə] *n* Malaysia *nt*

male [meɪl] *n* Mann *m*; *(animal)*

Männchen nt ♦ adj männlich
malevolent [mə'levələnt] adj übel
wollend
malfunction [mæl'fʌŋkʃən] n (MED)
Funktionsstörung f; (of machine) Defekt m
malice ['mælɪs] n Bosheit f; **malicious**
[mə'lɪʃəs] adj böswillig, gehässig
malign [mə'laɪn] vt verleumden ♦ adj
böse
malignant [mə'lɪgnənt] adj bösartig
mall [mɔ:l] n (also: **shopping ~**) Einkaufszentrum nt
malleable ['mælɪəbl] adj formbar
mallet ['mælɪt] n Holzhammer m
malnutrition [mælnju:'trɪʃən] n Unterernährung f
malpractice [mæl'præktɪs] n Amtsvergehen nt
malt [mɔ:lt] n Malz nt
Malta ['mɔ:ltə] n Malta nt; **Maltese**
[mɔ:l'ti:z] adj inv maltesisch ♦ n inv
Malteser(in) m(f)
maltreat [mæl'tri:t] vt misshandeln
mammal ['mæml] n Säugetier nt
mammoth ['mæməθ] n Mammut nt
♦ adj Mammut-
man [mæn] (pl **men**) n Mann m; (human race) der Mensch, die Menschen
pl ♦ vt bemannen; **an old ~** ein alter
Mann, ein Greis m; **~ and wife** Mann
und Frau
manage ['mænɪdʒ] vi zurechtkommen
♦ vt (control) führen, leiten; (cope with)
fertig werden mit; **~able** adj (person,
animal) fügsam; (object) handlich;
~ment n (control) Führung f, Leitung
f; (directors) Management nt; **~r** n Geschäftsführer m; **~ress** [mænɪdʒə'res]
n Geschäftsführerin f; **~rial** [mænɪ-
'dʒɪərɪəl] adj (post) leitend; (problem
etc) Management-; **managing**
['mænɪdʒɪŋ] adj: **managing director**
Betriebsleiter m
mandarin ['mændərɪn] n (fruit) Mandarine f
mandatory ['mændətərɪ] adj obligato-

risch
mane [meɪn] n Mähne f
maneuver [mə'nu:və] (US) = **manoeuvre**
manfully ['mænfʊlɪ] adv mannhaft
mangle ['mæŋgl] vt verstümmeln ♦ n
Mangel f
mango ['mæŋgəʊ] (pl **~es**) n Mango(pflaume) f
mangy ['meɪndʒɪ] adj (dog) räudig
man ['mæn-]: **~handle** vt grob behandeln; **~hole** n (Straßen)schacht m;
~hood n Mannesalter nt; (~liness)
Männlichkeit f; **~-hour** n Arbeitsstunde f; **~hunt** n Fahndung f
mania ['meɪnɪə] n Manie f; **~c**
['meɪnɪæk] n Wahnsinnige(r) mf
manic ['mænɪk] adj (behaviour, activity)
hektisch
manicure ['mænɪkjʊə] n Maniküre f;
~ set n Necessaire nt, Nessessär nt
manifest ['mænɪfest] vt offenbaren
♦ adj offenkundig; **~ation** [mænɪfes-
'teɪʃən] n (sign) Anzeichen nt
manifesto [mænɪ'festəʊ] n Manifest nt
manipulate [mə'nɪpjʊleɪt] vt handhaben; (fig) manipulieren
man ['mæn-]: **~kind** n Menschheit f;
~ly ['mænlɪ] adj männlich; mannhaft;
~-made adj (fibre) künstlich
manner ['mænə] n Art f, Weise f; **~s**
npl (behaviour) Manieren pl; **in a ~ of
speaking** sozusagen; **~ism** n (of person) Angewohnheit f; (of style) Manieriertheit f
manoeuvre [mə'nu:və] (US **maneuver**) vt, vi manövrieren ♦ n (MIL) Feldzug m; (general) Manöver nt, Schachzug m
manor ['mænə] n Landgut nt
manpower ['mænpaʊə] n Arbeitskräfte pl
mansion ['mænʃən] n Villa f
manslaughter ['mænslɔ:tə] n Totschlag m
mantelpiece ['mæntlpi:s] n Kaminsims m

manual ['mænjuəl] adj manuell, Hand-
♦ n Handbuch nt

manufacture [mænju'fæktʃəʳ] vt herstellen ♦ n Herstellung f; **~r** n Hersteller m

manure [mə'njuəʳ] n Dünger m

manuscript ['mænjuskrɪpt] n Manuskript nt

Manx [mæŋks] adj der Insel Man

many ['menɪ] adj, pron viele; **a great ~**
sehr viele; **~ a time** oft

map [mæp] n (Land)karte f; (of town)
Stadtplan m ♦ vt eine Karte machen
von; **~ out** vt (fig) ausarbeiten

maple ['meɪpl] n Ahorn m

mar [mɑːʳ] vt verderben

marathon ['mærəθən] n (SPORT) Mara-
thonlauf m; (fig) Marathon m

marble ['mɑːbl] n Marmor m; (for
game) Murmel f

March [mɑːtʃ] n März m

march [mɑːtʃ] vi marschieren ♦ n
Marsch m

mare [mɛəʳ] n Stute f

margarine [mɑːdʒə'riːn] n Margarine f

margin ['mɑːdʒɪn] n Rand m; (extra
amount) Spielraum m; (COMM) Spanne
f; **~al** adj (note) Rand-; (difference etc)
geringfügig; **~al (seat)** n (POL) Wahlkreis, der nur mit knapper Mehrheit gehalten wird

marigold ['mærɪgəʊld] n Ringelblume
f

marijuana [mærɪ'wɑːnə] n Marihuana
nt

marina [mə'riːnə] n Jachthafen m

marinate ['mærɪneɪt] vt marinieren

marine [mə'riːn] adj Meeres-, See- ♦ n
(MIL) Marineinfanterist m

marital ['mærɪtl] adj ehelich, Ehe-; **~
status** n Familienstand m

maritime ['mærɪtaɪm] adj See-

mark [mɑːk] n (coin) Mark f; (spot)
Fleck m; (scar) Kratzer m; (sign) Zeichen nt; (target) Ziel nt; (SCH) Note f
♦ vt (make ~ on) Flecken/Kratzer machen auf +acc; (indicate) markieren;

(exam) korrigieren; **to ~ time** (also fig)
auf der Stelle treten; **~ out** vt bestimmen; (area) abstecken; **~ed** adj deutlich; **~er** n (in book) (Lese)zeichen nt;
(on road) Schild nt

market ['mɑːkɪt] n Markt m; (stock ~)
Börse f ♦ vt (COMM: new product) auf
den Markt bringen; (sell) vertreiben; **~
garden** (BRIT) n Handelsgärtnerei f;
~ing n Marketing nt; **~ research** n
Marktforschung f; **~ value** n Markt-
wert m

marksman ['mɑːksmən] (irreg) n
Scharfschütze m

marmalade ['mɑːməleɪd] n Orangen-
marmelade f

maroon [mə'ruːn] vt aussetzen ♦ adj
(colour) kastanienbraun

marquee [mɑː'kiː] n große(s) Zelt nt

marriage ['mærɪdʒ] n Ehe f; (wedding)
Heirat f; **~ bureau** n Heiratsinstitut nt;
~ certificate n Heiratsurkunde f

married ['mærɪd] adj (person) verheiratet; (couple, life) Ehe-

marrow ['mærəʊ] n (Knochen)mark nt;
(BOT) Kürbis m

marry ['mærɪ] vt (join) trauen; (take as
husband, wife) heiraten ♦ vi (also: **get
married**) heiraten

marsh [mɑːʃ] n Sumpf m

marshal ['mɑːʃl] n (US) Bezirkspolizei-
chef m ♦ vt (an)ordnen, arrangieren

marshy ['mɑːʃɪ] adj sumpfig

martial law ['mɑːʃl-] n Kriegsrecht nt

martyr ['mɑːtəʳ] n (also fig)
Märtyrer(in) m(f) ♦ vt zum Märtyrer
machen; **~dom** n Martyrium nt

marvel [mɑːvl] n Wunder nt ♦ vi: **to ~
(at)** sich wundern (über +acc); **~lous**
(US **marvelous**) adj wunderbar

Marxist ['mɑːksɪst] n Marxist(in) m(f)

marzipan ['mɑːzɪpæn] n Marzipan nt

mascara [mæs'kɑːrə] n Wimperntusche f

mascot ['mæskət] n Maskottchen nt

masculine ['mæskjulɪn] adj männlich

mash [mæʃ] n Brei m; **~ed potatoes**

npl Kartoffelbrei *m or* -püree *nt*

mask [mɑːsk] *n* (*also fig*) Maske *f* ♦ *vt* maskieren, verdecken

mason ['meɪsn] *n* (*stonemason*) Steinmetz *m*; (*freemason*) Freimaurer *m*; **~ry** *n* Mauerwerk *nt*

masquerade [mæskə'reɪd] *n* Maskerade *f* ♦ *vi*: **to ~ as** sich ausgeben als

mass [mæs] *n* Masse *f*; (*great part*) Mehrheit *f*; (*REL*) Messe *f* ♦ *vi* sich sammeln; **the ~es** *npl* (*people*) die Masse(n) *f(pl)*

massacre ['mæsəkər] *n* Blutbad *nt* ♦ *vt* niedermetzeln, massakrieren

massage ['mæsɑːʒ] *n* Massage *f* ♦ *vt* massieren

massive ['mæsɪv] *adj* gewaltig, massiv

mass media *npl* Massenmedien *pl*

mass production *n* Massenproduktion *f*

mast [mɑːst] *n* Mast *m*

master ['mɑːstər] *n* Herr *m*; (*NAUT*) Kapitän *m*; (*teacher*) Lehrer *m*; (*artist*) Meister *m* ♦ *vt* meistern; (*language etc*) beherrschen; **~ly** *adj* meisterhaft; **~mind** *n* Kapazität *f* ♦ *vt* geschickt lenken; **M~ of Arts** *n* Magister *m der* philosophischen Fakultät; **M~ of Science** *n* Magister *m der* naturwissenschaftlichen Fakultät; **~piece** *n* Meisterwerk *nt*; **~ plan** *n* kluge(r) Plan *m*; **~y** *n* Können *nt*

masturbate ['mæstəbeɪt] *vi* masturbieren, onanieren

mat [mæt] *n* Matte *f*; (*for table*) Untersetzer *m* ♦ *adj* = **matt**

match [mætʃ] *n* Streichholz *nt*; (*sth corresponding*) Pendant *nt*; (*SPORT*) Wettkampf *m*; (*ball games*) Spiel *m* ♦ *vt* (*be like, suit*) passen zu; (*equal*) gleichkommen +*dat* ♦ *vi* zusammenpassen; **it's a good ~ (for)** es passt gut (zu); **~box** *n* Streichholzschachtel *f*; **~ing** *adj* passend

mate [meɪt] *n* (*companion*) Kamerad *m*; (*spouse*) Lebensgefährte *m*; (*of animal*) Weibchen *nt*/Männchen *nt*; (*NAUT*)

Schiffsoffizier *m* ♦ *vi* (*animals*) sich paaren ♦ *vt* (*animals*) paaren

material [mə'tɪərɪəl] *n* Material *nt*; (*for book, cloth*) Stoff *m* ♦ *adj* (*important*) wesentlich; (*damage*) Sach-; (*comforts etc*) materiell; **~s** *npl* (*for building etc*) Materialien *pl*; **~istic** [mətɪərə'lɪstɪk] *adj* materialistisch; **~ize** *vi* sich verwirklichen, zustande *or* zu Stande kommen

maternal [mə'tɜːnl] *adj* mütterlich, Mutter-

maternity [mə'tɜːnɪtɪ] *adj* (*dress*) Umstands-; (*benefit*) Wochen-; **~ hospital** *n* Entbindungsheim *nt*

math [mæθ] (*US*) *n* = **maths**

mathematical [mæθə'mætɪkl] *adj* mathematisch; **mathematics** *n* Mathematik *f*; **maths** (*US* math) *n* Mathe *f*

matinée ['mætɪneɪ] *n* Matinee *f*

matrices ['meɪtrɪsiːz] *npl of* **matrix**

matriculation [mətrɪkju'leɪʃən] *n* Immatrikulation *f*

matrimonial [mætrɪ'məʊnɪəl] *adj* ehelich, Ehe-

matrimony ['mætrɪmənɪ] *n* Ehestand *m*

matrix ['meɪtrɪks] (*pl* **matrices**) *n* Matrize *f*; (*GEOL etc*) Matrix *f*

matron ['meɪtrən] *n* (*MED*) Oberin *f*; (*SCH*) Hausmutter *f*

matt [mæt] *adj* (*paint*) matt

matted ['mætɪd] *adj* verfilzt

matter ['mætər] *n* (*substance*) Materie *f*; (*affair*) Angelegenheit *f* ♦ *vi* darauf ankommen; **no ~ how/what** egal wie/was; **what is the ~?** was ist los?; **as a ~ of course** selbstverständlich; **as a ~ of fact** eigentlich; **it doesn't ~** es macht nichts; **~-of-fact** *adj* sachlich, nüchtern

mattress ['mætrɪs] *n* Matratze *f*

mature [mə'tjʊər] *adj* reif ♦ *vi* reif werden; **maturity** [mə'tjʊərɪtɪ] *n* Reife *f*

maul [mɔːl] *vt* übel zurichten

maxima ['mæksɪmə] *npl of* **maximum**

maximum ['mæksɪməm] (*pl* **maxima**) *adj* Höchst-, Maximal- ♦ *n* Maximum *nt*

May [meɪ] *n* Mai *m*

may [meɪ] *vi (be possible)* **might**) *vi (be possible)* können; *(have permission)* dürfen; **he ~ come** er kommt vielleicht; **~be** ['meɪbiː] *adv* vielleicht

May Day *n* der 1. Mai

mayhem ['meɪhem] *n* Chaos *nt; (US)* Körperverletzung *f*

mayonnaise [meɪə'neɪz] *n* Majonäse *f*, Mayonnaise *f*

mayor [mɛəʳ] *n* Bürgermeister *m;* **~ess** *n* Bürgermeisterin *f; (wife)* (die) Frau *f* Bürgermeister

maypole ['meɪpəul] *n* Maibaum *m*

maze [meɪz] *n* Irrgarten *m; (fig)* Wirrwarr *nt*

M.D. *abbr* = **Doctor of Medicine**

KEYWORD

me [miː] *pron* **1** *(direct)* mich; **it's me** ich bins

2 *(indirect)* mir; **give them to me** sie mir

3 *(after prep: +acc)* mich; *(: +dat)* mir; **with/without me** mit mir/ohne mich

---

meadow ['medəu] *n* Wiese *f*

meagre ['miːgəʳ] *(US* **meager**) *adj* dürftig, spärlich

meal [miːl] *n* Essen *nt*, Mahlzeit *f; (grain)* Schrotmehl *nt;* **to have a ~** essen (gehen); **~time** *n* Essenszeit *f*

mean [miːn] *(pt, pp* **meant**) *adj (stingy)* geizig; *(spiteful)* gemein; *(average)* durchschnittlich, Durchschnitts- ♦ *vt (signify)* bedeuten; *(intend)* vorhaben, beabsichtigen ♦ *n (average)* Durchschnitt *m;* **~s** *npl (wherewithal)* Mittel *pl; (wealth)* Vermögen *nt;* **do you ~ me?** meinst du mich?; **do you ~ it?** meinst du das ernst?; **what do you ~?** was willst du damit sagen?; **to be ~ for sb/sth** für jdn/etw bestimmt sein; **by ~s of** durch; **by all ~s** selbstverständlich; **by no ~s** keineswegs

meander [mɪ'ændəʳ] *vi* sich schlängeln

meaning ['miːnɪŋ] *n* Bedeutung *f; (of life)* Sinn *m;* **~ful** *adj* bedeutungsvoll; *(life)* sinnvoll; **~less** *adj* sinnlos

meanness ['miːnnɪs] *n (stinginess)* Geiz *m; (spitefulness)* Gemeinheit *f*

meant [ment] *pt, pp of* **mean**

meantime ['miːntaɪm] *adv* inzwischen

meanwhile ['miːnwaɪl] *adv* inzwischen

measles ['miːzlz] *n* Masern *pl*

measly ['miːzlɪ] *(inf) adj* poplig

measure ['meʒəʳ] *vt, vi* messen ♦ *n* Maß *nt; (step)* Maßnahme *f;* **~ments** *npl* Maße *pl*

meat [miːt] *n* Fleisch *nt;* **cold ~** Aufschnitt *m;* **~ ball** *n* Fleischkloß *m;* **~ pie** *n* Fleischpastete *f;* **~y** *adj* fleischig; *(fig)* gehaltvoll

Mecca ['mekə] *n* Mekka *nt (also fig)*

mechanic [mɪ'kænɪk] *n* Mechaniker *m;* **~al** *adj* mechanisch; **~s** *n* Mechanik *f* ♦ *npl* Technik *f*

mechanism ['mekənɪzəm] *n* Mechanismus *m*

mechanize ['mekənaɪz] *vt* mechanisieren

medal ['medl] *n* Medaille *f; (decoration)* Orden *m;* **~list** *(US* **medalist**) *n* Medaillengewinner(in) *m(f)*

meddle ['medl] *vi:* **to ~ (in)** sich einmischen *(in +acc);* **to ~ with sth** sich an etw *dat* zu schaffen machen

media ['miːdɪə] *npl* Medien *pl*

mediaeval [medɪ'iːvl] *adj* = **medieval**

median ['miːdɪən] *(US) n (also:* **~ strip**) Mittelstreifen *m*

mediate ['miːdɪeɪt] *vi* vermitteln; **mediator** *n* Vermittler *m*

Medicaid ['medɪkeɪd] ® *(US) n* medizinisches Versorgungsprogramm für soziale Schwache

medical ['medɪkl] *adj* medizinisch; Medizin-; ärztlich ♦ *n (ärztliche)* Untersuchung *f*

Medicare ['medɪkeəʳ] *(US) n* staatliche Krankenversicherung besonders für Ältere

medicated ['medɪkeɪtɪd] *adj* medizinisch

medication [mɛdɪˈkeɪʃən] n (drugs etc) Medikamente pl

medicinal [mɛˈdɪsɪnl] adj medizinisch, Heil-

medicine [ˈmɛdsɪn] n Medizin f; (drugs) Arznei f

medieval [mɛdɪˈiːvl] adj mittelalterlich

mediocre [miːdɪˈəukə*] adj mittelmäßig

meditate [ˈmɛdɪteɪt] vi meditieren; to ~ (on sth) (über etw acc) nachdenken; **meditation** [mɛdɪˈteɪʃən] n Nachsinnen nt; Meditation f

Mediterranean [mɛdɪtəˈreɪnɪən] adj Mittelmeer-; (person) südländisch; the ~ (Sea) das Mittelmeer

medium [ˈmiːdɪəm] adj mittlere(r, s), Mittel-, mittel- ♦ n Mitte f; (means) Mittel nt; (person) Medium nt; happy ~ goldener Mittelweg; **~-sized** adj mittelgroß; **~ wave** n Mittelwelle f

medley [ˈmɛdlɪ] n Gemisch nt

meek [miːk] adj sanft(mütig); (pej) duckmäuserisch

meet [miːt] (pt, pp **met**) vt (encounter) treffen, begegnen +dat; (by arrangement) sich treffen mit; (difficulties) stoßen auf +acc; (get to know) kennen lernen; (fetch) abholen; (join) zusammentreffen mit; (satisfy) entsprechen +dat ♦ vi sich treffen; (become acquainted) sich kennen lernen; ~ **with** (problems) stoßen auf +acc; (us: people) zusammentreffen mit; **~ing** n Treffen nt; (business ~ing) Besprechung f; (of committee) Sitzung f; (assembly) Versammlung f

mega- [ˈmɛgə-] (inf) prefix Mega-; **~byte** n (COMPUT) Megabyte nt; **~phone** n Megafon nt, Megaphon nt

melancholy [ˈmɛlənkəlɪ] n (of person) melancholisch; (sight, event) traurig

mellow [ˈmɛləu] adj mild, weich; (fruit) reif; (fig) gesetzt ♦ vi reif werden

melodious [mɪˈləudɪəs] adj wohlklingend

melody [ˈmɛlədɪ] n Melodie f

melon [ˈmɛlən] n Melone f

melt [mɛlt] vi schmelzen; (anger) verfliegen ♦ vt schmelzen; ~ **away** vi dahinschmelzen; ~ **down** vt einschmelzen; **~down** n (in nuclear reactor) Kernschmelze f; **~ing point** n Schmelzpunkt m; **~ing pot** n (fig) Schmelztiegel m

member [ˈmɛmbə*] n Mitglied nt; (of tribe, species) Angehörige(r) f(m); (ANAT) Glied nt; **M~ of Parliament** (BRIT) n Parlamentsmitglied nt; **M~ of the European Parliament** (BRIT) n Mitglied nt des Europäischen Parlaments; **~ship** n Mitgliedschaft f; to **seek ~ship** of einen Antrag auf Mitgliedschaft stellen; **~ship card** n Mitgliedskarte f

memento [məˈmɛntəu] n Andenken nt

memo [ˈmɛməu] n Mitteilung f

memoirs [ˈmɛmwɑːz] npl Memoiren pl

memorable [ˈmɛmərəbl] adj denkwürdig

memorandum [mɛməˈrændə] npl of **memorandum**

memorandum [mɛməˈrændəm] (pl **memoranda**) n Mitteilung f

memorial [mɪˈmɔːrɪəl] n Denkmal nt ♦ adj Gedenk-

memorize [ˈmɛməraɪz] vt sich einprägen

memory [ˈmɛmərɪ] n Gedächtnis nt; (of computer) Speicher m; (sth recalled) Erinnerung f

men [mɛn] pl of **man** ♦ n (human race) die Menschen pl

menace [ˈmɛnɪs] n Drohung f; Gefahr f ♦ vt bedrohen; **menacing** adj drohend

menagerie [mɪˈnædʒərɪ] n Tierschau f

mend [mɛnd] vt reparieren, flicken ♦ n (ver)heilen ♦ n ausgebesserte Stelle f; **on the ~** auf dem Wege der Besserung; **~ing** n (articles) Flickarbeit f

menial [ˈmiːnɪəl] adj niedrig

meningitis [mɛnɪnˈdʒaɪtɪs] n Hirnhautentzündung f, Meningitis f

menopause ['menəʊpɔːz] n Wechsel-jahre pl, Menopause f

menstruation [menstru'eɪʃən] n Menstruation f

mental ['mentl] adj geistig, Geistes-; (arithmetic) Kopf-; (hospital) Nerven-; (cruelty) seelisch; (inf: abnormal) verrückt; **~ity** [men'tælɪtɪ] n Mentalität f

menthol ['menθɒl] n Menthol nt

mention ['menʃən] n Erwähnung f ♦ vt erwähnen; **don't ~ it!** bitte (sehr), gern geschehen

mentor ['mentɔː'] n Mentor m

menu ['menjuː] n Speisekarte f

MEP n abbr = **Member of the European Parliament**

mercenary ['mɜːsɪnərɪ] adj (person) geldgierig ♦ n Söldner m

merchandise ['mɜːtʃəndaɪz] n (Handels)ware f

merchant ['mɜːtʃənt] n Kaufmann m; **~ bank** (BRIT) n Handelsbank f; **~ navy** (US ~ **marine**) n Handelsmarine f

merciful ['mɜːsɪful] adj gnädig

merciless ['mɜːsɪlɪs] adj erbarmungslos

mercury ['mɜːkjurɪ] n Quecksilber nt

mercy ['mɜːsɪ] n Erbarmen nt; Gnade f; **at the ~ of** ausgeliefert +dat

mere [mɪə'] adj bloß; **~ly** adv bloß

merge [mɜːdʒ] vt verbinden; (COMM) fusionieren ♦ vi verschmelzen; (roads) zusammenlaufen; (COMM) fusionieren; **~r** n (COMM) Fusion f

meringue [mə'ræŋ] n Baiser nt

merit ['merɪt] n Verdienst nt; (advantage) Vorzug m ♦ vt verdienen

mermaid ['mɜːmeɪd] n Wassernixe f

merry ['merɪ] adj fröhlich; **~-go-round** n Karussell nt

mesh [meʃ] n Masche f

mesmerize ['mezməraɪz] vt hypnotisieren; (fig) faszinieren

mess [mes] n Unordnung f; (dirt) Schmutz m; (trouble) Schwierigkeiten pl; (MIL) Messe f; **~ about** or **around** vi (play the fool) herumalbern; (do nothing in particular) herumgammeln;

~ about or **around with** vt fus (tinker with) herummurksen an +dat; **~ up** vt verpfuschen; (make untidy) in Unordnung bringen

message ['mesɪdʒ] n Mitteilung f; **to get the ~** kapieren

messenger ['mesɪndʒə'] n Bote m

Messrs ['mesəz] abbr (on letters) die Herren

messy ['mesɪ] adj schmutzig; (untidy) unordentlich

met [met] pt, pp of **meet**

metabolism [me'tæbəlɪzəm] n Stoffwechsel m

metal ['metl] n Metall nt; **~lic** adj metallisch; (made of ~) aus Metall

metaphor ['metəfɔː'] n Metapher f

meteorology [miːtɪə'rɒlədʒɪ] n Meteorologie f

meter ['miːtə'] n Zähler m; (US) = **metre**

method ['meθəd] n Methode f; **~ical** [mɪ'θɒdɪkl] adj methodisch; **M~ist** ['meθədɪst] adj methodistisch ♦ n Methodist(in) m(f); **~ology** [meθə'dɒlədʒɪ] n Methodik f

meths [meθs] (BRIT) n(pl) = **methylated spirit(s)**

methylated spirit(s) ['meθɪleɪtɪd-] (BRIT) n (Brenn)spiritus m

meticulous [mɪ'tɪkjuləs] adj (über)genau

metre ['miːtə'] (US **meter**) n Meter m or nt

metric ['metrɪk] adj (also: **~al**) metrisch

metropolitan [metrə'pɒlɪtn] adj der Großstadt; **M~ Police** (BRIT) n: **the M~ Police** die Londoner Polizei

mettle ['metl] n Mut m

mew [mjuː] vi (cat) miauen

mews [mjuːz] n: **~ cottage** ehemaliges Kutscherhäuschen

Mexican ['meksɪkən] adj mexikanisch ♦ n Mexikaner(in) m(f)

Mexico ['meksɪkəʊ] n Mexiko nt

miaow [miː'au] vi miauen

mice [maɪs] pl of **mouse**

micro ['maɪkrəʊ] n (also: **~computer**) Mikrocomputer m; **~chip** n Mikrochip m; **~cosm** ['maɪkrəʊkɒzəm] n Mikrokosmos m; **~phone** n Mikrofon m, Mikrophon nt; **~scope** n Mikroskop nt; **~wave** n (also: **~wave oven**) Mikrowelle(nherd n) f

mid [mɪd] adj: **in ~ afternoon** am Nachmittag; **in ~ air** in der Luft; **in ~ May** Mitte Mai

midday ['mɪd'deɪ] n Mittag m

middle ['mɪdl] n Mitte f; (waist) Taille f ♦ adj mittlere(r, s), Mittel-; **in the ~ of** mitten in +dat; **~-aged** adj mittleren Alters; **M~ Ages** npl: **the M~ Ages** das Mittelalter; **~-class** adj Mittelstands-; **M~ East** n: **the M~ East** der Nahe Osten; **~man** (irreg) n (COMM) Zwischenhändler m; **~ name** n zweiter Vorname m; **~ weight** n (BOXING) Mittelgewicht nt

middling ['mɪdlɪŋ] adj mittelmäßig

midge [mɪdʒ] n Mücke f

midget ['mɪdʒɪt] n Liliputaner(in) m(f)

midnight ['mɪdnaɪt] n Mitternacht f

midriff ['mɪdrɪf] n Taille f

midst [mɪdst] n: **in the ~ of** (persons) mitten unter +dat; (things) mitten in +dat

mid [mɪd'-]: **~summer** n Hochsommer m; **~way** adv auf halbem Wege ♦ adj Mittel-; **~week** adv in der Mitte der Woche

midwife ['mɪdwaɪf] (irreg) n Hebamme f; **~ry** ['mɪdwɪfərɪ] n Geburtshilfe f

midwinter [mɪd'wɪntər] n tiefste(r) Winter m

might [maɪt] vi see **may** ♦ n Macht f, Kraft f; **I ~ come** ich komme vielleicht; **~y** adj, adv mächtig

migraine ['miːɡreɪn] n Migräne f

migrant ['maɪɡrənt] adj Wander-; (bird) Zug-

migrate [maɪ'ɡreɪt] vi (ab)wandern; (birds) (fort)ziehen; **migration** [maɪ'ɡreɪʃən] n Wanderung f, Zug m

mike [maɪk] n = **microphone**

Milan [mɪ'læn] n Mailand nt

mild [maɪld] adj mild; (medicine, interest) leicht; (person) sanft ♦ n (beer) leichtes dunkles Bier

mildew ['mɪldjuː] n (on plants) Mehltau m; (on food) Schimmel m

mildly ['maɪldlɪ] adv leicht; **to put it ~** gelinde gesagt

mile [maɪl] n Meile f; **~age** n Meilenzahl f; **~ometer** n = **milometer**; **~stone** n (also fig) Meilenstein m

militant ['mɪlɪtnt] adj militant ♦ n Militante(r) mf

military ['mɪlɪtərɪ] adj militärisch, Militär-, Wehr-

militate ['mɪlɪteɪt] vi: **to ~ against** entgegenwirken +dat

militia [mɪ'lɪʃə] n Miliz f

milk [mɪlk] n Milch f ♦ vt (also fig) melken; **~ chocolate** n Milchschokolade f; **~man** (irreg) n Milchmann m; **~ shake** n Milchmixgetränk nt; **~y** adj milchig; **M~y Way** n Milchstraße f

mill [mɪl] n Mühle f; (factory) Fabrik f ♦ vt mahlen ♦ vi umherlaufen

millennia [mɪ'lenɪə] npl of **millennium**

millennium [mɪ'lenɪəm] (pl ~s or **millennia**) n Jahrtausend nt; **~ bug** n (COMPUT) Jahrtausendfehler m

miller ['mɪlər] n Müller m

milligram(me) ['mɪlɪɡræm] n Milligramm nt

millimetre ['mɪlɪmiːtər] (US **millimeter**) n Millimeter m

million ['mɪljən] n Million f; **a ~ times** tausendmal; **~aire** [mɪljə'neər] n Millionär(in) m(f)

millstone ['mɪlstəʊn] n Mühlstein m

milometer [maɪ'lɒmɪtər] n ≈ Kilometerzähler m

mime [maɪm] n Pantomime f ♦ vt, vi mimen

mimic ['mɪmɪk] n Mimiker m ♦ vt, vi nachahmen; **~ry** n Nachahmung f, (BIOL) Mimikry f

min. abbr = **minutes**; **minimum**

mince [mɪns] vt (zer)hacken ♦ n (meat)

Hackfleisch nt; **~meat** n süße Pastetenfüllung f; **~ pie** n gefüllte (süße) Pastete f; **~r** n Fleischwolf m

mind [maɪnd] n Verstand m, Geist m; (opinion) Meinung f ♦ vt aufpassen auf +acc; (object to) etwas haben gegen; **on my ~** auf dem Herzen; **to my ~** meiner Meinung nach; **to be out of one's ~** wahnsinnig sein; **to bear in keep in ~** bedenken; **to change one's ~** es sich dat anders überlegen; **to make up one's ~** sich entschließen; **I don't ~** das macht mir nichts aus; **~ you, ...** allerdings ...; **never ~!** macht nichts!; **"~ the step"** „Vorsicht Stufe"; **~ your own business** kümmern Sie sich um Ihre eigenen Angelegenheiten; **~er** n Aufpasser(in m(f)); **~ful** adj: **~ful of** achtsam auf +acc; **~less** adj sinnlos

mine¹ [maɪn] n (coalmine) Bergwerk nt; (MIL) Mine f ♦ vt abbauen; (MIL) verminen

mine² [maɪn] pron meine(r, s); **that book is ~** das Buch gehört mir; **a friend of ~** ein Freund von mir

minefield ['maɪnfiːld] n Minenfeld nt

miner ['maɪnə*] n Bergarbeiter m

mineral ['mɪnərəl] adj mineralisch, Mineral- ♦ n Mineral nt; **~s** npl (BRIT: soft drinks) alkoholfreie Getränke pl; **~ water** n Mineralwasser nt

minesweeper ['maɪnswiːpə*] n Minensuchboot nt

mingle ['mɪŋgl] vi: **to ~ (with)** sich mischen (unter +acc)

miniature ['mɪnətʃə*] adj Miniatur- ♦ n Miniatur f

minibus ['mɪnɪbʌs] n Kleinbus m

minimal ['mɪnɪml] adj minimal

minimize ['mɪnɪmaɪz] vt auf das Mindestmaß beschränken

minimum ['mɪnɪməm] (pl **minima**) n Minimum nt ♦ adj Mindest-

mining ['maɪnɪŋ] n Bergbau m ♦ adj Bergbau-, Berg-

miniskirt ['mɪnɪskɜːt] n Minirock m

minister ['mɪnɪstə*] n (BRIT: POL) Minister m; (ECCL) Pfarrer m ♦ vi: **to ~ to sb's needs** sich um jdn kümmern; **~ial** [mɪnɪs'tɪərɪəl] adj ministeriell, Minister-

ministry ['mɪnɪstrɪ] n (BRIT: POL) Ministerium nt; (ECCL: office) geistliche(s) Amt nt

mink [mɪŋk] n Nerz m

minnow ['mɪnəʊ] n Elritze f

minor ['maɪnə*] adj kleiner; (operation) leicht; (problem, poet) unbedeutend; (MUS) Moll ♦ n (BRIT: under 18) Minderjährige(r) mf

minority [maɪ'nɒrɪtɪ, maɪ'nɔːrɪtɪ] n Minderheit f

mint [mɪnt] n Minze f; (sweet) Pfefferminzbonbon nt ♦ vt (coins) prägen; **the (Royal** (BRIT) or **US** (US)) **M~** die Münzanstalt; **in ~ condition** in tadellosem Zustand

minus ['maɪnəs] n Minuszeichen nt; (amount) Minusbetrag m ♦ prep minus, weniger

minuscule ['mɪnəskjuːl] adj winzig

minute¹ [maɪ'njuːt] adj winzig; (detailed) minutiös, minuziös

minute² ['mɪnɪt] n Minute f; (moment) Augenblick m; **~s** npl (of meeting etc) Protokoll nt

miracle ['mɪrəkl] n Wunder nt

miraculous [mɪ'rækjʊləs] adj wunderbar

mirage ['mɪrɑːʒ] n Fata Morgana f

mire ['maɪə*] n Morast m

mirror ['mɪrə*] n Spiegel m ♦ vt (wider)spiegeln

mirth [mɜːθ] n Heiterkeit f

misadventure [mɪsəd'ventʃə*] n Missgeschick m, Unfall m

misanthropist [mɪ'zænθrəpɪst] n Menschenfeind m

misapprehension ['mɪsæprɪ'henʃən] n Missverständnis nt

misbehave [mɪsbɪ'heɪv] vi sich schlecht benehmen

miscalculate [mɪs'kælkjuleɪt] vt falsch

berechnen

miscarriage ['mɪskærɪdʒ] n (MED) Fehlgeburt f; **~ of justice** Fehlurteil nt

miscellaneous [mɪsɪ'leɪnɪəs] adj verschieden

mischief ['mɪstʃɪf] n Unfug m; **mischievous** ['mɪstʃɪvəs] adj (person) durchtrieben; (glance) verschmitzt; (rumour) bösartig

misconception ['mɪskən'sepʃən] n fälschliche Annahme f

misconduct [mɪs'kɒndʌkt] n Vergehen nt; **professional ~** Berufsvergehen nt

misconstrue [mɪskən'stru:] vt missverstehen

misdemeanour [mɪsdɪ'mi:nər] (US **misdemeanor**) n Vergehen nt

miser ['maɪzər] n Geizhals m

miserable ['mɪzərəbl] adj (unhappy) unglücklich; (headache, weather) fürchterlich; (poor) elend; (contemptible) erbärmlich

miserly ['maɪzəlɪ] adj geizig

misery ['mɪzərɪ] n Elend nt, Qual f

misfire [mɪs'faɪər] vi (gun) versagen; (engine) fehlzünden; (plan) fehlgehen

misfit ['mɪsfɪt] n Außenseiter m

misfortune [mɪs'fɔːtʃən] n Unglück nt

misgiving(s) [mɪs'gɪvɪŋ(z)] n(pl) Bedenken pl

misguided [mɪs'gaɪdɪd] adj fehlgeleitet; (opinions) irrig

mishandle [mɪs'hændl] vt falsch handhaben

mishap ['mɪshæp] n Missgeschick nt

misinform [mɪsɪn'fɔːm] vt falsch unterrichten

misinterpret [mɪsɪn'tɜːprɪt] vt falsch auffassen

misjudge [mɪs'dʒʌdʒ] vt falsch beurteilen

mislay [mɪs'leɪ] (irreg: like **lay**) vt verlegen

mislead [mɪs'liːd] (irreg: like **lead**²) vt (deceive) irreführen; **~ing** adj irreführend

mismanage [mɪs'mænɪdʒ] vt schlecht verwalten

misnomer [mɪs'nəʊmər] n falsche Bezeichnung f

misplace [mɪs'pleɪs] vt verlegen

misprint ['mɪsprɪnt] n Druckfehler m

Miss [mɪs] n Fräulein nt

miss [mɪs] vt (fail to hit, catch) verfehlen; (not notice) verpassen; (be too late) versäumen, verpassen; (omit) auslassen; (regret the absence of) vermissen ♦ vi fehlen ♦ n (in shot) Fehlschuss m; (failure) Fehlschlag m; **I ~ you** du fehlst mir; **~ out** vt auslassen

misshapen [mɪs'ʃeɪpən] adj missgestaltet

missile ['mɪsaɪl] n Rakete f

missing ['mɪsɪŋ] adj (person) vermisst; (thing) fehlend; **to be ~** fehlen

mission ['mɪʃən] n (work) Auftrag m; (people) Delegation f; (REL) Mission f; **~ary** n Missionar(in) m(f); **~ statement** n Kurzdarstellung f der Firmenphilosophie

misspell ['mɪs'spel] (irreg: like **spell**) vt falsch schreiben

misspent ['mɪs'spent] adj (youth) vergeudet

mist [mɪst] n Dunst m, Nebel m ♦ vi (also: **~ over, ~ up**) sich trüben; (BRIT: windows) sich beschlagen

mistake [mɪs'teɪk] (irreg: like **take**) n Fehler m ♦ vt (misunderstand) missverstehen; (mix up): **to ~** (sth for sth) (etw mit etw) verwechseln; **to make a ~** einen Fehler machen; **by ~** aus Versehen; **to ~ A for B** A mit B verwechseln; **~n** pp of **mistake** ♦ adj (idea) falsch; **to be ~n** sich irren

mister ['mɪstər] n (inf) Herr m; see **Mr**

mistletoe ['mɪsltəʊ] n Mistel f

mistook [mɪs'tʊk] pt of **mistake**

mistress ['mɪstrɪs] n (teacher) Lehrerin f; (in house) Herrin f; (lover) Geliebte f; see **Mrs**

mistrust [mɪs'trʌst] vt misstrauen +dat

misty ['mɪstɪ] adj neblig

misunderstand [mɪsʌndə'stænd] (*irreg: like* **understand**) *vt, vi* missverstehen, falsch verstehen; **~ing** *n* Missverständnis *nt*; (*disagreement*) Meinungsverschiedenheit *f*

misuse [*n* mɪs'juːs, *vb* mɪs'juːz] *n* falsche(r) Gebrauch *m* ♦ *vt* falsch gebrauchen

mitigate ['mɪtɪgeɪt] *vt* mildern

mitt(en) ['mɪt(n)] *n* Fausthandschuh *m*

mix [mɪks] *vt* (*blend*) (ver)mischen ♦ *vi* (*liquids*) sich (ver)mischen lassen; (*people: get on*) sich vertragen; (*: associate*) Kontakt haben ♦ *n* (*~ture*) Mischung *f*; **~ up** *vt* zusammenmischen; (*confuse*) verwechseln; **~ed** *adj* gemischt; **~ed-up** *adj* durcheinander; **~er** *n* (*for food*) Mixer *m*; **~ture** *n* Mischung *f*; **~up** *n* Durcheinander *nt*

mm *abbr* (= *millimetre(s)*) mm

moan [məʊn] *n* Stöhnen *nt*; (*complaint*) Klage *f* ♦ *vi* stöhnen; (*complain*) maulen

moat [məʊt] *n* (Burg)graben *m*

mob [mɒb] *n* Mob *m*; (*the masses*) Pöbel *m* ♦ *vt* herfallen über +*acc*

mobile ['məʊbaɪl] *adj* beweglich; (*library etc*) fahrbar ♦ *n* (*decoration*) Mobile *nt*; **~ home** *n* Wohnwagen *m*; **~ phone** *n* (TEL) Mobiltelefon *nt*; **mobility** [məʊ'bɪlɪtɪ] *n* Beweglichkeit *f*; **mobilize** ['məʊbɪlaɪz] *vt* mobilisieren

mock [mɒk] *vt* verspotten; (*defy*) trotzen +*dat* ♦ *adj* Schein-; **~ery** *n* Spott *m*; (*person*) Gespött *nt*

mod [mɒd] *adj see* **convenience**

mode [məʊd] *n* (Art *f und*) Weise *f*

model ['mɒdl] *n* (*example*) Vorbild *nt*; (*in fashion*) Mannequin *nt* ♦ *adj* (*railway*) Modell-; (*perfect*) Muster-; vorbildlich ♦ *vt* (*make*) bilden; (*clothes*) vorführen ♦ *vi* als Mannequin arbeiten

modem ['məʊdem] *n* (COMPUT) Modem *nt*

moderate [*adj, n* 'mɒdərət, *vb* 'mɒdəreɪt] *adj* gemäßigt ♦ *n* (POL) Gemäßigte(r) *mf* ♦ *vi* sich mäßigen ♦ *vt*

mäßigen; **moderation** [mɒdə'reɪʃən] *n* Mäßigung *f*; **in moderation** mit Maßen

modern ['mɒdən] *adj* modern; (*history, languages*) neuere(r, s); **~ize** *vt* modernisieren

modest ['mɒdɪst] *adj* bescheiden; **~y** *n* Bescheidenheit *f*

modicum ['mɒdɪkəm] *n* bisschen *nt*

modification [mɒdɪfɪ'keɪʃən] *n* (Ab-) änderung *f*

modify ['mɒdɪfaɪ] *vt* abändern

module ['mɒdjuːl] *n* (*component*) (Bau)element *nt*; (SPACE) (Raum)kapsel *f*

mogul ['məʊgl] *n* (*fig*) Mogul *m*

mohair ['məʊhɛəʳ] *n* Mohär *m*, Mohair *m*

moist [mɔɪst] *adj* feucht; **~en** ['mɔɪsn] *vt* befeuchten; **~ure** ['mɔɪstʃəʳ] *n* Feuchtigkeit *f*; **~urizer** ['mɔɪstʃəraɪzəʳ] *n* Feuchtigkeitscreme *f*

molar ['məʊləʳ] *n* Backenzahn *m*

molasses [mə'læsɪz] *n* Melasse *f*

mold [məʊld] (US) = **mould**

mole [məʊl] *n* (*spot*) Leberfleck *m*; (*animal*) Maulwurf *m*; (*pier*) Mole *f*

molest [mə'lest] *vt* belästigen

mollycoddle ['mɒlɪkɒdl] *vt* verhätscheln

molt [məʊlt] (US) *vi* = **moult**

molten ['məʊltən] *adj* geschmolzen

mom [mɒm] (US) *n* = **mum**

moment ['məʊmənt] *n* Moment *m*, Augenblick *m*; (*importance*) Tragweite *f*; **at the ~** im Augenblick; **~ary** *adj* kurz; **~ous** [məʊ'mentəs] *adj* folgenschwer

momentum [məʊ'mentəm] *n* Schwung *m*; **to gather ~** in Fahrt kommen

mommy ['mɒmɪ] (US) *n* = **mummy**

Monaco ['mɒnəkəʊ] *n* Monaco *nt*

monarch ['mɒnək] *n* Herrscher(in) *m(f)*; **~y** *n* Monarchie *f*

monastery ['mɒnəstərɪ] *n* Kloster *nt*

monastic [mə'næstɪk] *adj* klösterlich

Monday ['mʌndɪ] n Montag m

monetary ['mʌnɪtərɪ] adj Geld-; (of currency) Währungs-

money ['mʌnɪ] n Geld nt; **to make ~** Geld verdienen; **~ belt** n Geldgürtel nt; **~lender** n Geldverleiher m; **~ order** n Postanweisung f; **~-spinner** (inf) n Verkaufsschlager m

mongol ['mɔŋgəl] n (MED) mongoloide(s) Kind nt ♦ adj mongolisch; (MED) mongoloid

mongrel ['mʌŋgrəl] n Promenadenmischung f

monitor ['mɔnɪtər] n (SCH) Klassenordner m; (television ~) Monitor m ♦ vt (broadcasts) abhören; (control) überwachen

monk [mʌŋk] n Mönch m

monkey ['mʌŋkɪ] n Affe m; **~ nut** (BRIT) n Erdnuss f; **~ wrench** n (TECH) Engländer m, Franzose m

monochrome ['mɔnəkrəum] adj schwarz-weiß, schwarzweiß

monopolize [mə'nɔpəlaɪz] vt beherrschen

monopoly [mə'nɔpəlɪ] n Monopol nt

monosyllable ['mɔnəsɪləbl] n einsilbige(s) Wort nt

monotone ['mɔnətəun] n gleich bleibende(r) Ton(fall) m; **to speak in a ~** monoton sprechen; **monotonous** [mə'nɔtənəs] adj eintönig; **monotony** [mə'nɔtənɪ] n Eintönigkeit f, Monotonie f

monsoon [mɔn'suːn] n Monsun m

monster ['mɔnstər] n Ungeheuer nt; (person) Scheusal nt

monstrosity [mɔn'strɔsɪtɪ] n Ungeheuerlichkeit f; (thing) Monstrosität f

monstrous ['mɔnstrəs] adj (shocking) grässlich, ungeheuerlich; (huge) riesig

month [mʌnθ] n Monat m; **~ly** adj monatlich, Monats- ♦ adv einmal im Monat ♦ n (magazine) Monatsschrift f

monument ['mɔnjumənt] n Denkmal nt; **~al** [mɔnju'mentl] adj (huge) gewaltig; (ignorance) ungeheuer

moo [muː] vi muhen

mood [muːd] n Stimmung f, Laune f; **to be in a good/bad ~** gute/ schlechte Laune haben; **~y** adj launisch

moon [muːn] n Mond m; **~light** n Mondlicht nt; **~lighting** n Schwarzarbeit f; **~lit** adj mondhell

moor [muər] n Heide f, Hochmoor nt ♦ vt (ship) festmachen, verankern ♦ vi anlegen; **~ings** npl Liegeplatz m; **~land** ['muələnd] n Heidemoor nt

moose [muːs] n Elch m

mop [mɔp] n Mopp m ♦ vt (auf)wischen; **~ up** vt aufwischen

mope [məup] vi Trübsal blasen

moped ['məupɛd] n Moped nt

moral ['mɔrl] adj moralisch; (values) sittlich; (virtuous) tugendhaft ♦ n Moral f; **~s** npl (ethics) Moral f

morale [mɔ'rɑːl] n Moral f

morality [mə'rælɪtɪ] n Sittlichkeit f

morass [mə'ræs] n Sumpf m

morbid ['mɔːbɪd] adj krankhaft; (jokes) makaber

KEYWORD

more [mɔːr] adj (greater in number etc) mehr; (additional) noch mehr; **do you want (some) more tea?** möchten Sie noch etwas Tee?; **I have no** or **I don't have any more money** ich habe kein Geld mehr

♦ pron (greater amount) mehr; (further or additional amount) noch mehr; **is there any more?** gibt es noch mehr?; (left over) ist noch etwas da?; **there's no more** es ist nichts mehr da

♦ adv mehr; **more dangerous/easily** etc (than) gefährlicher/einfacher etc (als); **more and more** immer mehr; **more and more excited** immer aufgeregter; **more or less** mehr oder weniger; **more than ever** mehr denn je; **more beautiful than ever** schöner denn je

moreover [mɔːˈrəʊvəʳ] adv überdies

morgue [mɔːg] n Leichenschauhaus nt

Mormon [ˈmɔːmən] n Mormone m, Mormonin f

morning [ˈmɔːnɪŋ] n Morgen m; **in the ~** am Morgen; **7 o'clock in the ~** 7 Uhr morgens; **~ sickness** n (Schwangerschafts)übelkeit f

Morocco [məˈrɒkəʊ] n Marokko nt

moron [ˈmɔːrɒn] n Schwachsinnige(r) mf

morose [məˈrəʊs] adj mürrisch

morphine [ˈmɔːfiːn] n Morphium nt

Morse [mɔːs] n (also: **~ code**) Morsealphabet nt

morsel [ˈmɔːsl] n Bissen m

mortal [ˈmɔːtl] adj sterblich; (deadly) tödlich; (very great) Todes- ♦ n (human being) Sterbliche(r) mf; **~ity** [mɔːˈtælɪtɪ] n Sterblichkeit f; (death rate) Sterblichkeitsziffer f

mortar [ˈmɔːtəʳ] n (for building) Mörtel m; (MIL) Granatwerfer m

mortgage [ˈmɔːgɪdʒ] n Hypothek f ♦ vt hypothekarisch belasten; **~ company** (US) n ≈ Bausparkasse f

mortify [ˈmɔːtɪfaɪ] vt beschämen

mortuary [ˈmɔːtjʊərɪ] n Leichenhalle f

mosaic [məʊˈzeɪɪk] n Mosaik nt

Moscow [ˈmɒskəʊ] n Moskau nt

Moslem [ˈmɒzləm] = **Muslim**

mosque [mɒsk] n Moschee f

mosquito [mɒsˈkiːtəʊ] (pl **~es**) n Moskito m

moss [mɒs] n Moos nt

most [məʊst] adj viele(r, s) ♦ adv am meisten; (very) höchst ♦ n das meiste, der größte Teil; (people) die meisten; **~ men** die meisten Männer; **at the (very) ~** allerhöchstens; **to make the ~ of** das Beste machen aus; **a ~ interesting book** ein höchstinteressantes Buch; **~ly** adv größtenteils

MOT (BRIT) n abbr (= Ministry of Transport): **the MOT (test)** ≈ der TÜV

motel [məʊˈtɛl] n Motel nt

moth [mɒθ] n Nachtfalter m; (wool-eating) Motte f; **~ball** n Mottenkugel f

mother [ˈmʌðəʳ] n Mutter f ♦ vt bemuttern; **~hood** n Mutterschaft f; **~-in-law** n Schwiegermutter f; **~ly** adj mütterlich; **~-of-pearl** n Perlmutt nt; **M~'s Day** n Muttertag m; **~-to-be** n werdende Mutter f; **~ tongue** n Muttersprache f

motif [məʊˈtiːf] n Motiv nt

motion [ˈməʊʃən] n Bewegung f; (in meeting) Antrag m ♦ vt, vi: **to ~ (to) sb** jdm winken, jdm zu verstehen geben; **~less** adj regungslos; **~ picture** n Film m

motivated [ˈməʊtɪveɪtɪd] adj motiviert

motivation [məʊtɪˈveɪʃən] n Motivierung f

motive [ˈməʊtɪv] n Motiv nt, Beweggrund m ♦ adj treibend

motley [ˈmɒtlɪ] adj bunt

motor [ˈməʊtəʳ] n Motor m; (BRIT: inf: vehicle) Auto nt ♦ adj Motor-; **~bike** n Motorrad nt; **~boat** n Motorboot nt; **~car** (BRIT) n Auto nt; **~cycle** n Motorrad nt; **~cyclist** n Motorradfahrer(in) m(f); **~ing** (BRIT) n Autofahren nt ♦ adj Auto-; **~ist** n Autofahrer(in) m(f); **~ mechanic** n Kraftfahrzeugmechaniker(in) m(f), Kfz-Mechaniker(in) m(f); **~ racing** (BRIT) n Autorennen nt; **~ vehicle** n Kraftfahrzeug nt; **~way** (BRIT) n Autobahn f

mottled [ˈmɒtld] adj gesprenkelt

mould [məʊld] (US **mold**) n Form f; (mildew) Schimmel m ♦ vt (also fig) formen; **~y** adj schimmelig

moult [məʊlt] (US **molt**) vi sich mausern

mound [maʊnd] n (Erd)hügel m

mount [maʊnt] n (liter. hill) Berg m; (horse) Pferd m; (for jewel etc) Fassung f ♦ vt (horse) steigen auf +acc; (put in setting) fassen; (exhibition) veranstalten; (attack) unternehmen ♦ vi (also: **~ up**) sich häufen; (on horse) aufsitzen

mountain [ˈmaʊntɪn] n Berg m ♦ cpd

Berg-; **~ bike** n Mountainbike nt; **~eer** n Bergsteiger(in) m(f); **~eering** [maʊntɪ'nɪərɪŋ] n Bergsteigen nt; **~ous** adj bergig; **~ rescue team** n Bergwacht f; **~side** n Berg(ab)hang m

mourn [mɔːn] vt betrauern, beklagen ♦ vi: **to ~ (for sb)** (um jdn) trauern; **~er** n Trauernde(r) mf; **~ful** adj traurig; **~ing** n (grief) Trauer f ♦ cpd (dress) Trauer-; **in ~ing** (period etc) in Trauer; (dress) in Trauerkleidung f

mouse [maʊs] (pl mice) n Maus f; **~trap** n Mausefalle f

mousse [muːs] n (COOK) Creme f; (cosmetic) Schaumfestiger m

moustache [məs'tɑːʃ] n Schnurrbart m

mousy ['maʊsɪ] adj (colour) mausgrau; (person) schüchtern

mouth [maʊθ] n Mund m; (opening) Öffnung f; (of river) Mündung f; **~ful** n Mund m voll; **~ organ** n Mundharmonika f; **~piece** n Mundstück nt; (fig) Sprachrohr nt; **~wash** n Mundwasser nt; **~watering** adj lecker, appetitlich

movable ['muːvəbl] adj beweglich

move [muːv] n (~ment) Bewegung f; (in game) Zug m; (step) Schritt m; (of house) Umzug m ♦ vt bewegen; (people) transportieren; (in job) versetzen; (emotionally) bewegen ♦ vi sich bewegen; (vehicle, ship) fahren; (~ house) umziehen; **to get a ~ on** sich beeilen; **to ~ sb to do sth** jdn veranlassen, etw zu tun; **~ about** or **around** vi sich hin und her bewegen; (travel) unterwegs sein; **~ along** vi weitergehen; (cars) weiterfahren; **~ away** vi weggehen; **~ back** vi zurückgehen; (to the rear) zurückweichen; **~ forward** vi vorwärts gehen, sich vorwärts bewegen ♦ vt vorschieben; (time) vorverlegen; **~ in** vi (to house) einziehen; (troops) einrücken; **~ on** vi weitergehen ♦ vt weitergehen lassen; **~ out** vi (of house) ausziehen; (troops) abziehen; **~ over** vi zur Seite rücken; **~ up** vi aufsteigen; (in job) befördert werden ♦ vt nach

oben bewegen; (in job) befördern; **~ment** ['muːvmənt] n Bewegung f

movie ['muːvɪ] n Film m; **to go to the ~s** ins Kino gehen; **~ camera** n Filmkamera f

moving ['muːvɪŋ] adj beweglich; (touching) ergreifend

mow [məʊ] (pt mowed, pp mowed or mown) vt mähen; **~ down** vt (fig) niedermähen; **~er** n (lawnmower) Rasenmäher m; **~n** pp of **mow**

MP n abbr = **Member of Parliament**

m.p.h. abbr = **miles per hour**

Mr ['mɪstəʳ] (US **Mr.**) n Herr m

Mrs ['mɪsɪz] (US **Mrs.**) n Frau f

Ms [mɪz] (US **Ms.**) n (= Miss or Mrs) Frau f

M.Sc. n abbr = **Master of Science**

much [mʌtʃ] adj viel ♦ adv sehr; viel ♦ n viel, eine Menge; **how ~ is it?** wie viel kostet das?; **too ~** zu viel; **it's not ~** es ist nicht viel; **as ~ as** so sehr, so viel; **however ~ he tries** sosehr er es auch versucht

muck [mʌk] n Mist m; (fig) Schmutz m; **~ about** or **around** (inf) vi: **to ~ about** or **around (with sth)** (an etw dat) herumalbern; **~ up** vt (inf: ruin) vermasseln; (dirty) dreckig machen; **~y** adj (dirty) dreckig

mud [mʌd] n Schlamm m

muddle ['mʌdl] n Durcheinander nt ♦ vt (also: **~ up**) durcheinander bringen; **~ through** vi sich durchwursteln

mud ['mʌd-]: **~dy** adj schlammig; **~guard** n Schutzblech nt; **~slinging** (inf) n Verleumdung f

muesli ['mjuːzlɪ] n Müsli nt

muffin ['mʌfɪn] n süße(s) Teilchen nt

muffle ['mʌfl] vt (sound) dämpfen; (wrap up) einhüllen; **~d** adj gedämpft; **~r** (US) n (AUT) Schalldämpfer m

mug [mʌg] n (cup) Becher m; (inf: face) Visage f; (: fool) Trottel m ♦ vt überfallen und ausrauben; **~ger** n Straßenräuber m; **~ging** n Überfall m

muggy ['mʌgɪ] adj (weather) schwül

mule [mjuːl] n Maulesel m

mull [mʌl] : ~ **over** vt nachdenken über +acc

multicoloured ['mʌltɪkʌləd] (US **multicolored**) adj mehrfarbig

multi-level ['mʌltɪlevl] (US) adj = **multistorey**

multiple ['mʌltɪpl] n Vielfache(s) nt ♦ adj mehrfach; (many) mehrere; ~ **sclerosis** n multiple Sklerose f

multiplex cinema ['mʌltɪpleks-] n Kinocenter nt

multiplication [mʌltɪplɪ'keɪʃən] n Multiplikation f; (increase) Vervielfachung f

multiply ['mʌltɪplaɪ] vt: **to ~ (by)** multiplizieren (mit) ♦ vi (BIOL) sich vermehren

multistorey ['mʌltɪ'stɔːrɪ] (BRIT) adj (building, car park) mehrstöckig

multitude ['mʌltɪtjuːd] n Menge f

mum [mʌm] n (BRIT: inf) Mutti f ♦ adj: **to keep ~ (about)** den Mund halten (über +acc)

mumble ['mʌmbl] vt, vi murmeln ♦ n Gemurmel nt

mummy ['mʌmɪ] n (dead body) Mumie f; (BRIT: inf) Mami f

mumps [mʌmps] n Mumps m

munch [mʌntʃ] vt, vi mampfen

mundane [mʌn'deɪn] adj banal

municipal [mjuː'nɪsɪpl] adj städtisch, Stadt-

mural ['mjuərl] n Wandgemälde nt

murder ['mɜːdər] n Mord m ♦ vt ermorden; **~er** n Mörder m; **~ous** adj Mord-; (fig) mörderisch

murky ['mɜːkɪ] adj finster

murmur ['mɜːmər] n Murmeln nt; (of water, wind) Rauschen nt ♦ vt, vi murmeln

muscle ['mʌsl] n Muskel m; **~ in** vi mitmischen; **muscular** ['mʌskjʊlər] adj Muskel-; (strong) muskulös

museum [mjuː'zɪəm] n Museum nt

mushroom ['mʌʃrum] n Champignon m; Pilz m ♦ vi (fig) emporschießen

music ['mjuːzɪk] n Musik f; (printed) Noten pl; **~al** adj (sound) melodisch; (person) musikalisch ♦ n (show) Musical nt; **~al instrument** n Musikinstrument nt; **~ centre** n Stereoanlage f; **~ hall** (BRIT) n Varieté nt, Varieté nt; **~ian** [mjuː'zɪʃən] n Musiker(in) m(f)

Muslim ['mʌzlɪm] adj moslemisch ♦ n Moslem m

muslin ['mʌzlɪn] n Musselin m

mussel ['mʌsl] n Miesmuschel f

must [mʌst] vb aux müssen; (in negation) dürfen ♦ n Muss nt; **the film is a ~** den Film muss man einfach gesehen haben

mustard ['mʌstəd] n Senf m

muster ['mʌstər] vt (MIL) antreten lassen; (courage) zusammennehmen

mustn't ['mʌsnt] = **must not**

musty ['mʌstɪ] adj muffig

mute [mjuːt] adj stumm ♦ n (person) Stumme(r) mf; (MUS) Dämpfer m; **~d** adj gedämpft

mutilate ['mjuːtɪleɪt] vt verstümmeln

mutiny ['mjuːtɪnɪ] n Meuterei f ♦ vi meutern

mutter ['mʌtər] vt, vi murmeln

mutton ['mʌtn] n Hammelfleisch nt

mutual ['mjuːtʃuəl] adj gegenseitig; beiderseitig; **~ly** adv gegenseitig; für beide Seiten

muzzle ['mʌzl] n (of animal) Schnauze f; (for animal) Maulkorb m; (of gun) Mündung f ♦ vt einen Maulkorb anlegen +dat

my [maɪ] adj mein; **this is ~ car** das ist mein Auto; **I've washed ~ hair** ich habe mir die Haare gewaschen

myself [maɪ'self] pron mich acc; mir dat; (emphatic) selbst; see also **oneself**

mysterious [mɪs'tɪərɪəs] adj geheimnisvoll

mystery ['mɪstərɪ] n (secret) Geheimnis nt; (sth difficult) Rätsel nt

mystify ['mɪstɪfaɪ] vt ein Rätsel nt sein +dat; verblüffen

mystique [mɪs'tiːk] n geheimnisvolle

Natur f

myth [mɪθ] n Mythos m; (fig) Erfindung f; **~ology** [mɪˈθɒlədʒɪ] n Mythologie f

N, n

n/a abbr (= not applicable) nicht zutreffend

nab [næb] (inf) vt schnappen

naff [næf] (BRIT: inf) adj blöd

nag [næg] n (horse) Gaul m; (person) Nörgler(in) m(f) ♦ vt, vi: **to ~ (at) sb** an jdm herumnörgeln; **~ging** adj (doubt) nagend ♦ n Nörgelei f

nail [neɪl] n Nagel m ♦ vt nageln; **to ~ sb down to doing sth** jdn darauf festnageln, etw zu tun; **~brush** n Nagelbürste f; **~file** n Nagelfeile f; **~ polish** n Nagellack m; **~ polish remover** n Nagellackentferner m; **~ scissors** npl Nagelschere f; **~ varnish** (BRIT) n = **nail polish**

naïve [naɪˈiːv] adj naiv

naked [ˈneɪkɪd] adj nackt

name [neɪm] n Name m; (reputation) Ruf m ♦ vt nennen; (sth new) benennen; (appoint) ernennen; **by ~** mit Namen; **I know him only by ~** ich kenne ihn nur dem Namen nach; **what's your ~?** wie heißen Sie?; **in the ~ of** im Namen +gen; (for the sake of) um +gen ... willen; **~less** adj namenlos; **~ly** adv nämlich; **~sake** n Namensvetter m

nanny [ˈnænɪ] n Kindermädchen nt

nap [næp] n (sleep) Nickerchen nt; (on cloth) Strich m ♦ vi: **to be caught ~ping** (fig) überrumpelt werden

nape [neɪp] n Nacken m

napkin [ˈnæpkɪn] n (at table) Serviette f; (BRIT: for baby) Windel f

nappy [ˈnæpɪ] (BRIT) n (for baby) Windel f; **~ rash** n wunde Stellen pl

narcotic [nɑːˈkɒtɪk] adj betäubend ♦ n Betäubungsmittel nt

narrative [ˈnærətɪv] n Erzählung f ♦ adj erzählend

narrator [nəˈreɪtəʳ] n Erzähler(in) m(f)

narrow [ˈnærəu] adj eng, schmal; (limited) beschränkt ♦ vi sich verengen; **to have a ~ escape** mit knapper Not davonkommen; **to ~ sth down to sth** etw auf etw acc einschränken; **~ly** adv (miss) knapp; (escape) mit knapper Not; **~-minded** adj engstirnig

nasty [ˈnɑːstɪ] adj ekelhaft, fies; (business, wound) schlimm

nation [ˈneɪʃən] n Nation f, Volk nt; **~al** [ˈnæʃənl] adj national, National-, Landes- ♦ n Staatsangehörige(r) mf; **~al anthem** (BRIT) n Nationalhymne f; **~al dress** n Tracht f; **N~al Health Service** (BRIT) n staatliche(r) Gesundheitsdienst m; **N~al Insurance** (BRIT) n Sozialversicherung f; **~alism** [ˈnæʃnəlɪzəm] n Nationalismus m; **~alist** [ˈnæʃnəlɪst] n Nationalist(in) m(f) ♦ adj nationalistisch; **~ality** [næʃəˈnælɪtɪ] n Staatsangehörigkeit f; **~alize** [ˈnæʃnəlaɪz] vt verstaatlichen; **~ally** [ˈnæʃnəlɪ] adv national, auf Staatsebene; **~al park** (BRIT) n Nationalpark m; **~-wide** [ˈneɪʃənwaɪd] adj, adv allgemein, landesweit

---

National Trust

*Der **National Trust** ist ein 1895 gegründeter Natur- und Denkmalschutzverband in Großbritannien, der Gebäude und Gelände von besonderem historischen oder ästhetischen Interesse erhält und der Öffentlichkeit zugänglich macht. Viele Gebäude im Besitz des National Trust sind (z.T. gegen ein Eintrittsgeld) zu besichtigen.*

---

native [ˈneɪtɪv] n (born in) Einheimische(r) mf; (original inhabitant) Eingeborene(r) mf ♦ adj einheimisch; Eingeborenen-; (belonging by birth) heimatlich, Heimat-; (inborn) angeboren, natürlich; **a ~ of Germany** ein gebürtiger Deutscher; **a ~ speaker of French** ein französischer Muttersprachler; **N~ American** *n* Indianer(in) *m(f)*, Ureinwohner(in) *m(f)* Amerikas; **~ language** *n* Muttersprache *f*

Nativity [nə'tɪvɪtɪ] *n*: **the ~** Christi Geburt *no art*

NATO ['neɪtəu] *n abbr* (= North Atlantic Treaty Organization) NATO *f*

natural ['nætʃrəl] *adj* natürlich; Natur-; (*inborn*) angeboren; **~ gas** *n* Erdgas *nt*; **~ist** *n* Naturkundler(in) *m(f)*; **~ly** *adv* natürlich

nature ['neɪtʃə'] *n* Natur *f*; **by ~** von Natur (aus)

naught [nɔːt] *n* = **nought**

naughty ['nɔːtɪ] *adj* (*child*) unartig, ungezogen; (*action*) ungehörig

nausea ['nɔːsɪə] *n* (*sickness*) Übelkeit *f*; (*disgust*) Ekel *m*; **~te** ['nɔːsɪeɪt] *vt* anekeln

nautical ['nɔːtɪkl] *adj* nautisch; See-; (*expression*) seemännisch

naval ['neɪvl] *adj* Marine-, Flotten-; **~ officer** *n* Marineoffizier *m*

nave [neɪv] *n* Kirchen(haupt)schiff *nt*

navel ['neɪvl] *n* Nabel *m*

navigate ['nævɪɡeɪt] *vi* navigieren; **navigation** [nævɪ'ɡeɪʃən] *n* Navigation *f*; **navigator** ['nævɪɡeɪtə'] *n* Steuermann *m*; (AVIAT) Navigator *m*; (AUT) Beifahrer(in) *m(f)*

navvy ['nævɪ] (BRIT) *n* Straßenarbeiter *m*

navy ['neɪvɪ] *n* (Kriegs)marine *f* ♦ *adj* (*also*: **~ blue**) marineblau

Nazi ['nɑːtsɪ] *n* Nazi *m*

NB *abbr* (= nota bene) NB

near [nɪə'] *adj* nah ♦ *adv* in der Nähe ♦ *prep* (*also*: **~ to**: space) in der Nähe +gen; (*also*: : time) um +acc ... herum ♦ *vt* sich nähern +dat; **a ~ miss** knapp daneben; **~by** *adj* nahe (gelegen) ♦ *adv* in der Nähe; **~ly** *adv* fast; **I ~ly fell** ich wäre fast gefallen; **~side** *n* (AUT) Beifahrerseite *f* ♦ *adj* auf der Bei-

fahrerseite; **~sighted** *adj* kurzsichtig

neat [niːt] *adj* (tidy) ordentlich; (soluo) sauber; (pure) pur; **~ly** *adv* (tidily) ordentlich

necessarily ['nesɪsrɪlɪ] *adv* unbedingt

necessary ['nesɪsrɪ] *adj* notwendig, nötig; **he did all that was ~** er erledigte alles, was nötig war; **it is ~ to/ that ...** man muss ...

necessitate [nɪ'sesɪteɪt] *vt* erforderlich machen

necessity [nɪ'sesɪtɪ] *n* (need) Not *f*; (compulsion) Notwendigkeit *f*; **necessities** *npl* (things needed) das Notwendigste

neck [nek] *n* Hals *m* ♦ *vi* (*inf*) knutschen; **~ and ~** Kopf an Kopf; **~lace** ['neklɪs] *n* Halskette *f*; **~line** ['neklaɪn] *n* Ausschnitt *m*; **~tie** ['nektaɪ] (US) *n* Krawatte *f*

née [neɪ] *adj* geborene

need [niːd] *n* Bedürfnis *nt*; (lack) Mangel *m*; (necessity) Notwendigkeit *f*; (poverty) Not *f* ♦ *vt* brauchen; **I ~ to do it** ich muss es tun; **you don't ~ to go** du brauchst nicht zu gehen

needle ['niːdl] *n* Nadel *f* ♦ *vt* (fig: inf) ärgern

needless ['niːdlɪs] *adj* unnötig; **~ to say** natürlich

needlework ['niːdlwɜːk] *n* Handarbeit *f*

needn't ['niːdnt] = **need not**

needy ['niːdɪ] *adj* bedürftig

negative ['negətɪv] *n* (PHOT) Negativ *nt* ♦ *adj* negativ; (answer) abschlägig; **~ equity** *n* Differenz zwischen gefallenem Wert und hypothekarischer Belastung eines Wohneigentums

neglect [nɪ'ɡlekt] *vt* vernachlässigen ♦ *n* Vernachlässigung *f*; **~ed** *adj* vernachlässigt

negligee ['neɡlɪʒeɪ] *n* Negligee *nt*, Negligé *n*

negligence ['neɡlɪdʒəns] *n* Nachlässigkeit *f*

negligible ['neɡlɪdʒɪbl] *adj* unbedeutend, geringfügig

negotiable [nɪ'gəʊʃɪəbl] adj (cheque) übertragbar, einlösbar

negotiate [nɪ'gəʊʃɪeɪt] vi verhandeln ♦ vt (treaty) abschließen; (difficulty) überwinden; (corner) nehmen; **negotiation** [nɪgəʊʃɪ'eɪʃən] n Verhandlung f; **negotiator** n Unterhändler m

neigh [neɪ] vi wiehern

neighbour ['neɪbər] (US **neighbor**) n Nachbar(in) m(f); **~hood** n Nachbarschaft f; Umgebung f; **~ing** adj benachbart, angrenzend; **~ly** adj (person, attitude) nachbarlich

neither ['naɪðər] adj, pron keine(r, s) (von beiden) ♦ conj: **he can't do it, and ~** can I er kann es nicht und ich auch nicht ♦ adv: **~ good nor bad** weder gut noch schlecht; **~ story is true** keine der beiden Geschichten stimmt

neon ['niːɒn] n Neon nt; **~ light** n Neonlampe f

nephew ['nevjuː] n Neffe m

nerve [nɜːv] n Nerv m; (courage) Mut m; (impudence) Frechheit f; **to have a fit of ~s** in Panik geraten; **~-racking** adj nervenaufreibend

nervous ['nɜːvəs] adj (of the nerves) Nerven-; (timid) nervös, ängstlich; **~ breakdown** n Nervenzusammenbruch m; **~ness** n Nervosität f

nest [nest] n Nest nt ♦ vi nisten; **~ egg** n (fig) Notgroschen m

nestle ['nesl] vi sich kuscheln

net [net] n Netz nt ♦ adj netto, Netto- ♦ vt netto einnehmen; **~ball** n Netzball m

Netherlands ['neðələndz] npl: **the ~** die Niederlande pl

nett [net] adj = net

netting ['netɪŋ] n Netz(werk) nt

nettle ['netl] n Nessel f

network ['netwɜːk] n Netz nt

neurotic [njuə'rɒtɪk] adj neurotisch

neuter ['njuːtər] adj (BIOL) geschlechtslos; (GRAM) sächlich ♦ vt kastrieren

neutral ['njuːtrəl] adj neutral ♦ n (AUT)

Leerlauf m; **~ity** [njuː'trælɪtɪ] n Neutralität f; **~ize** vt (fig) ausgleichen

never ['nevər] adv nie(mals); **I ~ went** ich bin gar nicht gegangen; **~ in my life** nie im Leben; **~-ending** adj endlos; **~theless** [nevəðə'les] adv trotzdem, dennoch

new [njuː] adj neu; **N~ Age** adj Newage-, New-Age-; **~born** adj neugeboren; **~comer** ['njuːkʌmər] n Neuankömmling m; **~fangled** (pej) adj neumodisch; **~found** adj neu entdeckt; **~ly** adv frisch, neu; **~ly-weds** npl Frischvermählte pl; **~ moon** n Neumond m

news [njuːz] n Nachricht f; (RAD, TV) Nachrichten pl; **a piece of ~** eine Nachricht; **~ agency** n Nachrichtenagentur f; **~agent** (BRIT) n Zeitungshändler m; **~caster** n Nachrichtensprecher(in) m(f); **~ flash** n Kurzmeldung f; **~letter** n Rundschreiben nt; **~paper** n Zeitung f; **~print** n Zeitungspapier nt; **~reader** n = newscaster; **~reel** n Wochenschau f; **~ stand** n Zeitungsstand m

newt [njuːt] n Wassermolch m

New Year n Neujahr nt; **~'s Day** n Neujahrstag m; **~'s Eve** n Silvester(abend m) nt

New Zealand [-'ziːlənd] n Neuseeland nt; **~er** n Neuseeländer(in) m(f)

next [nekst] adj nächste(r, s) ♦ adv (after) dann, darauf; (~ time) das nächste Mal; **the ~ day** am nächsten or folgenden Tag; **~ time** das nächste Mal; **~ year** nächstes Jahr; **~ door** adv nebenan ♦ adj (neighbour, flat) von nebenan; **~ of kin** n nächste(r) Verwandte(r) mf; **~ to** prep neben; **~ to nothing** so gut wie nichts

NHS n abbr = National Health Service

nib [nɪb] n Spitze f

nibble ['nɪbl] vt knabbern an +dat

nice [naɪs] adj (person) nett; (thing) schön; (subtle) fein; **~-looking** adj gut aussehend; **~ly** adv gut, nett; **~ties**

['naɪsɪtɪz] npl Feinheiten pl

nick [nɪk] n Einkerbung f ♦ vt (inf: steal) klauen; **in the ~ of time** gerade rechtzeitig

nickel ['nɪkl] n Nickel nt; (US) Nickel m (5 cents)

nickname ['nɪkneɪm] n Spitzname m ♦ vt taufen

nicotine patch ['nɪkətiːn-] n Nikotinpflaster nt

niece [niːs] n Nichte f

Nigeria [naɪˈdʒɪəriə] n Nigeria nt

niggling ['nɪglɪŋ] adj pedantisch; (doubt, worry) quälend

night [naɪt] n Nacht f; (evening) Abend m; **the ~ before last** vorletzte Nacht; **at** or **by ~** (before midnight) abends; (after midnight) nachts; **~cap** n (drink) Schlummertrunk m; (US) n Nachtlokal nt; **~dress** n Nachthemd nt; **~fall** n Einbruch m der Nacht; **~gown** n = **nightdress**; **~ie** (inf) n Nachthemd nt

nightingale ['naɪtɪŋgeɪl] n Nachtigall f

night: ~life n Nachtleben nt; **~ly** ['naɪtlɪ] adj, adv jeden Abend; jede Nacht; **~mare** n ['naɪtmɛəʳ] n Albtraum m; **~ porter** n Nachtportier m; **~ school** n Abendschule f; **~ shift** n Nachtschicht f; **~time** n Nacht f

nil [nɪl] n Null f

Nile [naɪl] n: **the ~** der Nil

nimble ['nɪmbl] adj beweglich

nine [naɪn] num neun; **~teen** num neunzehn; **~ty** num neunzig

ninth [naɪnθ] adj neunte(r, s)

nip [nɪp] vt kneifen ♦ n Kneifen nt

nipple ['nɪpl] n Brustwarze f

nippy ['nɪpɪ] (inf) adj (person) flink; (BRIT: car) flott; (: cold) frisch

nitrogen ['naɪtrədʒən] n Stickstoff m

KEYWORD

---

no [nəʊ] (pl noes) adv (opposite of yes) nein; **to answer no** (to question) mit Nein antworten; (to request) Nein or nein sagen; **no thank you** nein, danke ♦ adj (not any) kein(e); **I have no**

money/time ich habe kein Geld/keine Zeit; **"no smoking"** „Rauchen verboten"
♦ n Nein nt; (no vote) Neinstimme f

nobility [nəʊˈbɪlɪtɪ] n Adel m

noble ['nəʊbl] adj (rank) adlig; (splendid) nobel, edel

nobody ['nəʊbədɪ] pron niemand, keiner

nocturnal [nɔkˈtɜːnl] adj (tour, visit) nächtlich; (animal) Nacht-

nod [nɔd] vi nicken ♦ n nicken mit ♦ n Nicken nt; **~ off** vi einnicken

noise [nɔɪz] n (sound) Geräusch nt; (unpleasant, loud) Lärm m; **noisy** ['nɔɪzɪ] adj laut; (crowd) lärmend

nominal ['nɔmɪnl] adj nominell

nominate ['nɔmɪneɪt] vt (suggest) vorschlagen; (in election) aufstellen; (appoint) ernennen; **nomination** [nɔmɪ'neɪʃən] n (election) Nominierung f; (appointment) Ernennung f; **nominee** [nɔmɪ'niː] n Kandidat(in) m(f)

non- [nɔn] prefix Nicht-, un-; **~alcoholic** adj alkoholfrei

nonchalant ['nɔnʃələnt] adj lässig

non-committal [nɔnkə'mɪtl] adj (reserved) zurückhaltend; (uncommitted) unverbindlich

nondescript ['nɔndɪskrɪpt] adj mittelmäßig

none [nʌn] adj, pron keine, er, es)
♦ adv: **he's the worse for it** es hat ihm nicht geschadet; **~ of you** keiner von euch; **I've ~ left** ich habe keinen mehr

nonentity [nɔˈnentɪtɪ] n Null f (inf)

nonetheless [ˈnʌnðəˈles] adv nichtsdestoweniger

non-existent [nɔnɪgˈzɪstənt] adj nicht vorhanden

non-fiction [nɔnˈfɪkʃən] n Sachbücher pl

nonplussed [nɔnˈplʌst] adj verdutzt

nonsense ['nɔnsəns] n Unsinn m

non: ~-smoker n Nichtraucher(in)

m(f); **~-smoking** *adj* Nichtraucher-; **~-stick** *adj* (pan, surface) Teflon- ®; **~-stop** *adj* Nonstop-, Non-Stop-

noodles ['nuːdlz] *npl* Nudeln *pl*

nook [nuk] *n* Winkel *m*; **~s and crannies** Ecken und Winkel

noon [nuːn] *n* (12 Uhr) Mittag *m*

no one ['nəʊwʌn] *pron* = **nobody**

noose [nuːs] *n* Schlinge *f*

nor [nɔːʳ] *conj* = **neither** ♦ *adv see* **neither**

norm [nɔːm] *n* (convention) Norm *f*; (rule, requirement) Vorschrift *f*

normal ['nɔːməl] *adj* normal; **~ly** *adv* normal; (usually) normalerweise

Normandy ['nɔːməndɪ] *n* Normandie *f*

north [nɔːθ] *n* Norden *m* ♦ *adj* nördlich, Nord- ♦ *adv* nördlich, nach or im Norden; **N~ Africa** *n* Nordafrika *nt*; **N~ America** *n* Nordamerika *nt*; **~-east** *n* Nordosten *m*; **~erly** ['nɔːðəlɪ] *adj* nördlich; **~ern** ['nɔːðən] *adj* nördlich, Nord-; **N~ern Ireland** *n* Nordirland *nt*; **N~ Pole** *n* Nordpol *m*; **N~ Sea** *n* Nordsee *f*; **~ward(s)** ['nɔːθwəd(z)] *adv* nach Norden; **~west** *n* Nordwesten *m*

Norway ['nɔːweɪ] *n* Norwegen *nt*

Norwegian [nɔːˈwiːdʒən] *adj* norwegisch ♦ *n* Norweger(in) *m(f)*; (LING) Norwegisch *nt*

nose [nəʊz] *n* Nase *f* ♦ *vi*: **to ~ about** herumschnüffeln; **~bleed** *n* Nasenbluten *nt*; **~ dive** *n* Sturzflug *m*; **~y** *adj* = **nosy**

nostalgia [nɒsˈtældʒɪə] *n* Nostalgie *f*; **nostalgic** *adj* nostalgisch

nostril ['nɒstrɪl] *n* Nasenloch *nt*

nosy ['nəʊzɪ] (inf) *adj* neugierig

not [nɒt] *adv* nicht; **he is ~ or isn't here** er ist nicht hier; **it's too late, isn't it?** es ist zu spät, oder or nicht wahr?; **~ yet/now** noch nicht/nicht jetzt; *see also* **all; only**

notably ['nəʊtəblɪ] *adv* (especially) besonders; (noticeably) bemerkenswert

notary ['nəʊtərɪ] *n* Notar(in) *m(f)*

notch [nɒtʃ] *n* Kerbe *f*, Einschnitt *m*

note [nəʊt] *n* (MUS) Note *f*, Ton *m*; (short letter) Nachricht *f*; (POL) Note *f*; (comment, attention) Notiz *f*; (of lecture etc) Aufzeichnung *f*; (banknote) Schein *m*; (fame) Ruf *m* ♦ *vt* (observe) bemerken; (also: **~ down**) notieren; **~book** *n* Notizbuch *nt*; **~d** *adj* bekannt; **~pad** *n* Notizblock *m*; **~paper** *n* Briefpapier *nt*

nothing ['nʌθɪŋ] *n* nichts; **~ new/much** nichts Neues/nicht viel; **for ~** umsonst

notice ['nəʊtɪs] *n* (announcement) Bekanntmachung *f*; (warning) Ankündigung *f*; (dismissal) Kündigung *f* ♦ *vt* bemerken; **to take ~ of** beachten; **at short ~** kurzfristig; **until further ~** bis auf weiteres; **to hand in one's ~** kündigen; **~able** *adj* merklich; **~ board** *n* Anschlagtafel *f*

notify ['nəʊtɪfaɪ] *vt* benachrichtigen

notion ['nəʊʃən] *n* Idee *f*

notorious [nəʊˈtɔːrɪəs] *adj* berüchtigt

notwithstanding [nɒtwɪðˈstændɪŋ] *adv* trotzdem; **~ this** ungeachtet dessen

nought [nɔːt] *n* Null *f*

noun [naʊn] *n* Substantiv *nt*

nourish ['nʌrɪʃ] *vt* nähren; **~ing** *adj* nahrhaft; **~ment** *n* Nahrung *f*

novel ['nɒvl] *n* Roman *m* ♦ *adj* neu(artig); **~ist** *n* Schriftsteller(in) *m(f)*; **~ty** *n* Neuheit *f*

November [nəʊˈvɛmbəʳ] *n* November *m*

novice ['nɒvɪs] *n* Neuling *m*

now [naʊ] *adv* jetzt; **right ~** jetzt, gerade; **by ~** inzwischen; **just ~** gerade; **~ and then, ~ and again** ab und zu, manchmal; **from ~ on** von jetzt an; **~adays** *adv* heutzutage

nowhere ['nəʊwɛəʳ] *adv* nirgends

nozzle ['nɒzl] *n* Düse *f*

nuclear ['njuːklɪəʳ] *adj* (energy etc) Atom-, Kern-

nuclei ['njuːklɪaɪ] *npl of* **nucleus**

nucleus ['njuːklɪəs] *n* Kern *m*

nude [nju:d] *adj* nackt ♦ *n* (*ART*) Akt *m*; **in the ~** nackt

nudge [nʌdʒ] *vt* leicht anstoßen

nudist ['nju:dɪst] *n* Nudist(in) *m(f)*

nudity ['nju:dɪtɪ] *n* Nacktheit *f*

nuisance ['nju:sns] *n* Ärgernis *nt*; **what a ~!** wie ärgerlich!

nuke [nju:k] (*inf*) *n* Kernkraftwerk *nt* ♦ *vt* atomar vernichten

null [nʌl] *adj*: **~ and void** null und nichtig

numb [nʌm] *adj* taub, gefühllos ♦ *vt* betäuben

number ['nʌmbə*r*] *n* Nummer *f*; (*numeral also*) Zahl *f*; (*quantity*) (An)zahl *f* ♦ *vt* nummerieren; (*amount to*) sein; **to be ~ed among** gezählt werden zu; **a ~ of** (*several*) einige; **they were ten in ~** sie waren zehn an der Zahl; **~ plate** (*BRIT*) *n* (*AUT*) Nummernschild *nt*

numeral ['nju:mərəl] *n* Ziffer *f*

numerate ['nju:mərɪt] *adj* rechenkundig

numerical [nju:'merɪkl] *adj* (*order*) zahlenmäßig

numerous ['nju:mərəs] *adj* zahlreich

nun [nʌn] *n* Nonne *f*

nurse [nɜ:s] *n* Krankenschwester *f*; (*for children*) Kindermädchen *nt* ♦ *vt* (*patient*) pflegen; (*doubt etc*) hegen

nursery ['nɜ:sərɪ] *n* (*for children*) Kinderzimmer *nt*; (*for plants*) Gärtnerei *f*; (*for trees*) Baumschule *f*; **~ rhyme** *n* Kinderreim *m*; **~ school** *n* Kindergarten *m*; **~ slope** (*BRIT*) *n* (*SKI*) Idiotenhügel *m* (*inf*), Anfängerhügel *m*

nursing ['nɜ:sɪŋ] *n* (*profession*) Krankenpflege *f*; **~ home** *n* Privatklinik *f*

nurture ['nɜ:tʃə*r*] *vt* aufziehen

nut [nʌt] *n* Nuss *f*; (*TECH*) Schraubenmutter *f*; (*inf*) Verrückte(r) *mf*; **he's ~s** er ist verrückt; **~crackers** ['nʌtkrækəz] *npl* Nussknacker *m*

nutmeg ['nʌtmeg] *n* Muskat(nuss *f*) *m*

nutrient ['nju:trɪənt] *n* Nährstoff *m*

nutrition [nju:'trɪʃən] *n* Nahrung *f*

nutritious [nju:'trɪʃəs] *adj* nahrhaft

nutshell ['nʌtʃel] *n* Nussschale *f*; **in a ~** (*fig*) kurz gesagt

nutter ['nʌtə*r*] (*BRIT*: *inf*) *n* Spinner(in) *m(f)*

nylon ['naɪlɔn] *n* Nylon *nt* ♦ *adj* Nylon-

O, o

oak [əuk] *n* Eiche *f* ♦ *adj* Eichen(holz)-

O.A.P. *abbr* = **old-age pensioner**

oar [ɔ:*r*] *n* Ruder *nt*

oases [əu'eɪsi:z] *npl of* **oasis**

oasis [əu'eɪsɪs] *n* Oase *f*

oath [əuθ] *n* (*statement*) Eid *m*, Schwur *m*; (*swearword*) Fluch *m*

oatmeal ['əutmi:l] *n* Haferschrot *m*

oats [əuts] *npl* Hafer *m*

obedience [ə'bi:dɪəns] *n* Gehorsam *m*

obedient [ə'bi:dɪənt] *adj* gehorsam

obesity [əu'bi:sɪtɪ] *n* Fettleibigkeit *f*

obey [ə'beɪ] *vt, vi*: **to ~ (sb)** (jdm) gehorchen

obituary [ə'bɪtjuərɪ] *n* Nachruf *m*

object [*n* 'ɔbdʒɪkt, *vb* əb'dʒekt] *n* (*thing*) Gegenstand *m*, Objekt *nt*; (*purpose*) Ziel *nt* ♦ *vi* dagegen sein; **expense is no ~** Ausgaben spielen keine Rolle; **I ~!** ich protestiere!; **to ~ to sth** Einwände gegen etw haben; (*morally*) Anstoß an etw *acc* nehmen; **to ~ that** einwenden, dass; **~ion** [əb'dʒekʃən] *n* (*reason against*) Einwand *m*, Einspruch *m*; (*dislike*) Abneigung *f*; **I have no ~ion to ...** ich habe nichts gegen ... einzuwenden; **~ionable** [əb'dʒekʃənəbl] *adj* nicht einwandfrei; (*language*) anstößig

objective [əb'dʒektɪv] *n* Ziel *nt* ♦ *adj* objektiv

obligation [ɔblɪ'geɪʃən] *n* Verpflichtung *f*; **without ~** unverbindlich; **obligatory** [ə'blɪgətərɪ] *adj* obligatorisch

oblige [ə'blaɪdʒ] *vt* (*compel*) zwingen; (*do a favour*) einen Gefallen tun +*dat*; **to be ~d to sb for sth** jdm für etw verbunden sein

obliging [ə'blaɪdʒɪŋ] adj entgegenkommend

oblique [ə'bliːk] adj schräg, schief ♦ n Schrägstrich m

obliterate [ə'blɪtəreɪt] vt auslöschen

oblivion [ə'blɪvɪən] n Vergessenheit f

oblivious [ə'blɪvɪəs] adj nicht bewußt

oblong ['ɒblɒŋ] n Rechteck nt ♦ adj länglich

obnoxious [əb'nɒkʃəs] adj widerlich

oboe ['əʊbəʊ] n Oboe f

obscene [əb'siːn] adj obszön; **obscenity** [əb'senɪtɪ] n Obszönität f; **obscenities** npl (oaths) Zoten pl

obscure [əb'skjʊə'] adj unklar; (indistinct) undeutlich; (unknown) unbekannt, obskur; (dark) düster ♦ vt verdunkeln; (view) verbergen; (confuse) verwirren; **obscurity** [əb'skjʊərɪtɪ] n Unklarheit f; (darkness) Dunkelheit f

observance [əb'zɜːvəns] n Befolgung f

observant [əb'zɜːvənt] adj aufmerksam

observation [ɒbzə'veɪʃən] n (noticing) Beobachtung f; (surveillance) Überwachung f; (remark) Bemerkung f

observatory [əb'zɜːvətrɪ] n Sternwarte f, Observatorium nt

observe [əb'zɜːv] vt (notice) bemerken; (watch) beobachten; (customs) einhalten; ~r n Beobachter(in) m(f)

obsess [əb'ses] vt verfolgen, quälen; ~ion [əb'seʃən] n Besessenheit f, Wahn m; ~ive adj krankhaft

obsolete ['ɒbsəliːt] adj überholt, veraltet

obstacle ['ɒbstəkl] n Hindernis nt; ~ race n Hindernisrennen nt

obstetrics [ɒb'stetrɪks] n Geburtshilfe f

obstinate ['ɒbstɪnɪt] adj hartnäckig, stur

obstruct [əb'strʌkt] vt versperren; (pipe) verstopfen; (hinder) hemmen; ~ion [əb'strʌkʃən] n Versperrung f; Verstopfung f; (obstacle) Hindernis nt

obtain [əb'teɪn] vt erhalten, bekommen; (result) erzielen

obtrusive [əb'truːsɪv] adj aufdringlich

obvious ['ɒbvɪəs] adj offenbar, offensichtlich; ~ly adv offensichtlich

occasion [ə'keɪʒən] n Gelegenheit f; (special event) Ereignis nt; (reason) Anlass m ♦ vt veranlassen; ~al adj gelegentlich; ~ally adv gelegentlich

occupant ['ɒkjupənt] n Inhaber(in) m(f); (of house) Bewohner(in) m(f)

occupation [ɒkju'peɪʃən] n (employment) Tätigkeit f, Beruf m; (pastime) Beschäftigung f; (of country) Besetzung f, Okkupation f; ~al hazard n Berufsrisiko nt

occupier ['ɒkjupaɪə'] n Bewohner(in) m(f)

occupy ['ɒkjupaɪ] vt (take possession of) besetzen; (seat) belegen; (live in) bewohnen; (position, office) bekleiden; (position in sb's life) einnehmen; (time) beanspruchen; to ~ o.s. with sth sich mit etw beschäftigen; to ~ o.s. by doing sth sich damit beschäftigen, etw zu tun

occur [ə'kɜː'] vi vorkommen; to ~ to sb jdm einfallen; ~rence n (event) Ereignis nt; (appearing) Auftreten nt

ocean ['əʊʃən] n Ozean m, Meer nt; ~going adj Hochsee-

o'clock [ə'klɒk] adv: **it is 5** ~ es ist 5 Uhr

OCR n abbr = **optical character reader**

octagonal [ɒk'tægənl] adj achteckig

October [ɒk'təʊbə'] n Oktober m

octopus ['ɒktəpəs] n Krake f; (small) Tintenfisch m

odd [ɒd] adj (strange) sonderbar; (not even) ungerade; (sock etc) einzeln; (surplus) übrig; **60-** ~ so um die 60; **at** ~ **times** ab und zu; **to be the** ~ **one out** (person) das fünfte Rad am Wagen sein; (thing) nicht dazugehören; ~**ity** n (strangeness) Merkwürdigkeit f; (queer person) seltsame(r) Kauz m; (thing) Kuriosität f; ~**job man** (irreg) n Mädchen nt für alles; ~ **jobs** npl gelegentlich anfallende Arbeiten; ~**ly** adv seltsam;

~ments *npl* Reste *pl*; **~s** *npl* Chancen *pl*; (betting) Gewinnchancen *pl*; **it makes no ~s** es spielt keine Rolle; **at ~s uneinig; ~s and ends** *npl* Krimskrams *m*

odometer [ɔ'dɔmitər] (esp US) *n* Tacho(meter) *m*

odour ['əudər] (US **odor**) *n* Geruch *m*

KEYWORD

of [ɒv, əv] prep 1 von +dat; use of gen; **the history of Germany** die Geschichte Deutschlands; **a friend of ours** ein Freund von uns; **a boy of 10** ein 10-jähriger Junge; **that was kind of you** das war sehr freundlich von Ihnen

2 (expressing quantity, amount, dates etc): **a kilo of flour** ein Kilo Mehl; **how much of this do you need?** wie viel brauchen Sie (davon)?; **there were 3 of them** (people) sie waren zu dritt; (objects) es gab 3 (davon); **a cup of tea/vase of flowers** eine Tasse Tee/Vase mit Blumen; **the 5th of July** der 5. Juli

3 (from, out of) aus; **a bridge made of wood** eine Holzbrücke, eine Brücke aus Holz

---

off [ɔf] adj, adv (absent) weg, fort; (switch) aus(geschaltet), ab(geschaltet); (BRIT: food: bad) schlecht; (cancelled) abgesagt ♦ prep von +dat; **to be ~** (to leave) gehen; **to be ~ sick** krank sein; **a day ~** ein freier Tag; **to have an ~ day** einen schlechten Tag haben; **he had his coat ~** er hatte seinen Mantel aus; **10% ~** (COMM) 10% Rabatt; **5 km ~ (the road)** 5 km (von der Straße) entfernt; **~ the coast** vor der Küste; **I'm ~ meat** (no longer eat it) ich esse kein Fleisch mehr; (no longer like it) mag kein Fleisch mehr; **on the ~ chance** auf gut Glück

offal ['ɔfl] *n* Innereien *pl*

off-colour ['ɔf'kʌlər] adj nicht wohl

offence [ə'fɛns] (US **offense**) *n* (crime) Vergehen *nt*, Straftat *f*; (insult) Beleidigung *f*; **to take ~ at** gekränkt sein

offend [ə'fɛnd] *vt* beleidigen; **~er** *n* Gesetzesübertreter *m*

offense [ə'fɛns] (US) *n* = **offence**

offensive [ə'fɛnsɪv] adj (unpleasant) übel, abstoßend; (weapon) Kampf-; (remark) verletzend ♦ *n* Angriff *m*

offer ['ɔfər] *n* Angebot *f* ♦ *vt* anbieten; (opinion) äußern; (resistance) leisten; **on ~** zum Verkauf angeboten; **~ing** *n* Gabe *f*

offhand [ɔf'hænd] adj lässig ♦ adv ohne weiteres

office ['ɔfɪs] *n* Büro *nt*; (position) Amt *nt*; (doctor's ~) Praxis *f*; **to take ~** sein Amt antreten; (POL) die Regierung übernehmen; **~ automation** *n* Büroautomatisierung *f*; **~ block** (US **~ building**) *n* Büro(hoch)haus *nt*; **~ hours** *npl* Dienstzeit *f*; (US: MED) Sprechstunde *f*

officer ['ɔfɪsər] *n* (MIL) Offizier *m*; (public ~) Beamte(r) *m*

official [ə'fɪʃl] adj offiziell, amtlich ♦ *n* Beamte(r) *m*; **~dom** *n* Beamtentum *nt*

officiate [ə'fɪʃieɪt] *vi* amtieren

officious [ə'fɪʃəs] adj aufdringlich

offing ['ɔfɪŋ] *n*: **in the ~** in (Aus)sicht

Off-licence

Off-licence *ist ein Geschäft (oder eine Theke in einer Gaststätte), wo man alkoholische Getränke kaufen kann, die aber anderswo konsumiert werden müssen. In solchen Geschäften, die oft von landesweiten Ketten betrieben werden, kann man auch andere Getränke, Süßigkeiten, Zigaretten und Knabbereien kaufen.*

---

off: ~licence (BRIT) *n* (shop) Wein- und Spirituosenhandlung *f*; **~line** adj (COMPUT) Offline- ♦ adv (COMPUT) offline; **~-peak** adj (charges) verbilligt; **~-putting** (BRIT) adj (person, remark etc) abstoßend; **~-road vehicle** n Geländefahrzeug nt; **~-season** adj außer Saison; **~set** (irreg: like set) vt ausgleichen ♦ n (also: **~set printing**) Offset(druck) m; **~shoot** n (fig: of organization) Zweig m; (: of discussion etc) Randergebnis nt; **~shore** adv in einiger Entfernung von der Küste ♦ adj küstennah, Küsten-; **~side** adj (SPORT) im Abseits ♦ adv abseits ♦ n (AUT) Fahrerseite f; **~spring** n Nachkommenschaft f; (one) Sprössling m; **~stage** adv hinter den Kulissen; **~-the-cuff** adj unvorbereitet, aus dem Stegreif; **~-the-peg** (US **~-the-rack**) adv von der Stange; **~-white** adj naturweiß

Oftel ['oftel] n Überwachungsgremium zum Verbraucherschutz nach Privatisierung der Telekommunikationsindustrie

often ['ofn] adv oft

Ofwat ['ofwot] n Überwachungsgremium zum Verbraucherschutz nach Privatisierung der Wasserindustrie

ogle ['əugl] vt liebäugeln mit

oil [oil] n Öl m ♦ vt ölen; **~can** n Ölkännchen nt; **~field** n Ölfeld nt; **~ filter** n (AUT) Ölfilter m; **~-fired** adj Öl-; **~ painting** n Ölgemälde nt; **~ rig** n Ölplattform f; **~skins** npl Ölzeug nt; **~ slick** n Ölteppich m; **~ tanker** n (Öl)tanker m; **~ well** n Ölquelle f; **~y** adj ölig; (dirty) ölbeschmiert

ointment ['ointment] n Salbe f

O.K. ['əu'kei] excl in Ordnung, O. K., o. k. ♦ adj in Ordnung ♦ vt genehmigen

okay ['əu'kei] = **O.K.**

old [əuld] adj alt; **how ~ are you?** wie alt bist du?; **he's 10 years ~** er ist 10 Jahre alt; **~er brother** ältere(r) Bruder m; **~ age** n Alter nt; **~age pensioner** (BRIT) n Rentner(in) m(f); **~-fashioned** adj altmodisch

olive ['ɔlɪv] n (fruit) Olive f; (colour) Oli-

ve nt ♦ adj Oliven-; (coloured) olivenfarbig; **~ oil** n Olivenöl nt

Olympic [əu'lɪmpɪk] adj olympisch; **the ~ Games, the ~s** die Olympischen Spiele

omelet(te) ['ɔmlɪt] n Omelett nt

omen ['əumen] n Omen nt

ominous ['ɔmɪnəs] adj bedrohlich

omission [əu'mɪʃən] n Auslassung f; (neglect) Versäumnis nt

omit [əu'mɪt] vt auslassen; (fail to do) versäumen

on [ɔn] prep 1 (indicating position) auf +dat; (with vb of motion) auf +acc; (on vertical surface, part of body) an +dat; **it's on the table** es ist auf dem Tisch; **she put the book on the table** sie legte das Buch auf den Tisch; **on the left** links

2 (indicating means, method, condition etc): **on foot** (go) zu Fuß; **on the train/plane** (go) mit dem Zug/Flugzeug; (be) im Zug/Flugzeug; **on the telephone/television** am Telefon/im Fernsehen; **to be on drugs** Drogen nehmen; **to be on holiday/business** im Urlaub/auf Geschäftsreise sein

3 (referring to time): **on Friday** (am) Freitag; **on Fridays** freitags; **on June 20th am** 20. Juni; **a week on Friday** Freitag in einer Woche; **on arrival** he ... als er ankam, ... er ...

4 (about, concerning) über +acc

♦ adv 1 (referring to dress): **she put her boots/hat on** sie zog ihre Stiefel an/setzte ihren Hut auf

2 (further, continuously) weiter; **to walk on** weitergehen

♦ adj 1 (functioning, in operation: machine, TV, light) an; (: tap) aufgedreht; (: brakes) angezogen; **is the meeting still on?** findet die Versammlung noch statt?; **there's a good film on** es läuft ein guter Film

2: that's not on! (*inf: of behaviour*) das liegt nicht drin!

once [wʌns] *adv* einmal ♦ *conj* wenn ~ einmal; **~ he had left/it was done** nachdem er gegangen war/es fertig war; **at** ~ sofort; (*at the same time*) gleichzeitig; **~ a week** einmal in der Woche; **~ more** noch einmal; **~ and for all** ein für alle Mal; **~ upon a time** es war einmal

oncoming ['ɒnkʌmɪŋ] *adj* (*traffic*) Gegen-, entgegenkommend

KEYWORD

one [wʌn] *num* eins; (*with noun, referring back to noun*) ein/eine/ein; **it is one (o'clock)** es ist eins, es ist ein Uhr; **one hundred and fifty** einhundertfünfzig

♦ *adj* 1 (*sole*) einzige(r, s); **the one book which** das einzige Buch, welches

2 (*same*) derselbe/dieselbe/dasselbe; **they came in the one car** sie kamen alle in dem einen Auto

3 (*indef*): **one day I discovered ...** eines Tages bemerkte ich ...

♦ *pron* 1 eine(r, s); **do you have a red one?** haben Sie einen roten/eine rote/ein rotes?; **this one** diese(r, s); **that one** der/die/das; **which one?** welche(r, s)?; **one by one** einzeln

2: **one another** einander; **do you two ever see one another?** seht ihr beide euch manchmal?

3 (*impers*): **one man; one never knows** man kann nie wissen; **to cut one's finger on** sich den Finger schneiden

one: **~-armed bandit** *n* einarmiger Bandit *m*; **~-day excursion** (*US*) *n* (*day return*) Tagesrückfahrkarte *f*; **~-man** *adj* Einmann-; **~-man band** *n* Einmannkapelle *f*; (*fig*) Einmannbetrieb *m*; **~-off** (*BRIT: inf*) *n* Einzelfall *m*

oneself [wʌn'sɛlf] *pron* reflexive: after

prep sich; (~ *personally*) sich selbst *or* selber; (*emphatic*) (sich) selbst; **to hurt** ~ sich verletzen

one: **~-sided** *adj* (*argument*) einseitig; **~-to-~** (*relationship*) eins-zu-eins; **~-upmanship** *n* die Kunst, anderen um eine Nasenlänge voraus zu sein; **~-way** *adj* (*street*) Einbahn-

ongoing ['ɒngəʊɪŋ] *adj* momentan; (*progressing*) sich entwickelnd

onion ['ʌnjən] *n* Zwiebel *f*

on-line ['ɒnlaɪn] *adj* (*COMPUT*) Online-

onlooker ['ɒnlʊkə*] *n* Zuschauer(in) *m(f)*

only ['əʊnlɪ] *adv* nur, bloß ♦ *adj* einzige(r, s) ♦ *conj* nur, bloß; **a ~ child** ein Einzelkind; **not ~ ... but also ...** nicht nur ..., sondern auch ...

onset ['ɒnsɛt] *n* (*start*) Beginn *m*

onshore ['ɒnʃɔː*] *adj* (*wind*) See-

onslaught ['ɒnslɔːt] *n* Angriff *m*

onto ['ɒntu] *prep* = **on to**

onus ['əʊnəs] *n* Last *f*, Pflicht *f*

onward(s) ['ɒnwəd(z)] *adv* (*place*) voran, vorwärts; **from that day ~** von dem Tag an; **from today ~** ab heute

ooze [uːz] *vi* sickern

opaque [əʊ'peɪk] *adj* undurchsichtig

OPEC ['əʊpɛk] *n abbr* (= *Organization of Petroleum-Exporting Countries*) OPEC *f*

open ['əʊpn] *adj* offen; (*public*) öffentlich; (*mind*) aufgeschlossen ♦ *vt* öffnen, aufmachen; (*trial, motorway, account*) eröffnen ♦ *vi* (*begin*) anfangen; (*shop*) aufmachen; (*door, flower*) aufgehen; (*play*) Premiere haben; **in the ~** (*air*) im Freien; **~ on to** *vt fus* sich öffnen auf +*acc*; **~ up** *vt* (*route*) erschließen; (*shop, prospects*) eröffnen ♦ *vi* öffnen; **~ing** (*hole*) Öffnung *f*; (*beginning*) Anfang *m*; (*good chance*) Gelegenheit *f*; **~ing hours** *npl* Öffnungszeiten *pl*; **~ learning centre** *n* Weiterbildungseinrichtung auf Teilzeitbasis; **~ly** *adv* offen; (*publicly*) öffentlich; **~-minded** *adj* aufgeschlossen; **~-necked** *adj* offen; **~-plan**

(office) Großraum-; *(flat etc)* offen angelegt

Open University

Open University *ist eine 1969 in Großbritannien gegründete Fernuniversität für Spätstudierende. Der Unterricht findet durch Fernseh- und Radiosendungen statt, schriftliche Arbeiten werden mit der Post verschickt, und der Besuch von Sommerkursen ist Pflicht. Die Studenten müssen eine bestimmte Anzahl von Unterrichtseinheiten in einem bestimmten Zeitraum absolvieren und für die Verleihung eines akademischen Grades eine Mindestzahl von Scheinen machen.*

---

opera ['ɔpərə] *n* Oper *f*; ~ **house** *n* Opernhaus *nt*

operate ['ɔpəreɪt] *vt (machine)* bedienen; *(brakes, light)* betätigen ♦ *vi (machine)* laufen, in Betrieb sein; *(person)* arbeiten; *(MED)*: **to ~ on** operieren

operatic [ɔpə'rætɪk] *adj* Opern-

operating ['ɔpəreɪtɪŋ] *adj*: ~ **table/theatre** Operationstisch *m*/-saal *m*

operation [ɔpə'reɪʃən] *n (working)* Betrieb *m*; *(MED)* Operation *f*; *(undertaking)* Unternehmen *nt*; *(MIL)* Einsatz *m*; **to be in ~** *(JUR)* in Kraft sein; *(machine)* in Betrieb sein; **to have an ~** *(MED)* operiert werden; **~al** *adj* einsatzbereit

operative ['ɔpərətɪv] *adj* wirksam

operator ['ɔpəreɪtə*] *n (of machine)* Arbeiter *m*; *(TEL)* Telefonist(in) *m(f)*

opinion [ə'pɪnjən] *n* Meinung *f*; **in my ~** meiner Meinung nach; **~ated** *adj* starrsinnig; ~ **poll** *n* Meinungsumfrage *f*

opponent [ə'pəunənt] *n* Gegner *m*

opportunity [ɔpə'tjuːnɪtɪ] *n* Gelegenheit *f*, Möglichkeit *f*; **to take the ~ of doing sth** die Gelegenheit ergreifen, etw zu tun

oppose [ə'pəuz] *vt* entgegentreten +*dat*; *(argument, idea)* ablehnen; *(plan)* bekämpfen; **to be ~d to sth** gegen etw sein; **as ~d to** im Gegensatz zu; **opposing** *adj* gegnerisch; *(points of view)* entgegengesetzt

opposite ['ɔpəzɪt] *adj (house)* gegenüberliegend; *(direction)* entgegengesetzt ♦ *adv* gegenüber ♦ *prep* gegenüber ♦ *n* Gegenteil *nt*

opposition [ɔpə'zɪʃən] *n (resistance)* Widerstand *m*; *(POL)* Opposition *f*; *(contrast)* Gegensatz *m*

oppress [ə'pres] *vt* unterdrücken; *(heat etc)* bedrücken; **~ion** [ə'preʃən] *n* Unterdrückung *f*; **~ive** *adj (authority, law)* repressiv; *(burden, thought)* bedrückend; *(heat)* drückend

opt [ɔpt] *vi*: **to ~ for** sich entscheiden für; **to ~ to do sth** sich entscheiden, etw zu tun; **to ~ out of** sich drücken vor +*dat*

optical ['ɔptɪkl] *adj* optisch; ~ **character reader** *n* optische(s) Lesegerät *nt*

optician [ɔp'tɪʃən] *n* Optiker *m*

optimist ['ɔptɪmɪst] *n* Optimist *m*; **~ic** [ɔptɪ'mɪstɪk] *adj* optimistisch

optimum ['ɔptɪməm] *adj* optimal

option ['ɔpʃən] *n* Wahl *f*; *(COMM)* Option *f*; **to keep one's ~s open** sich alle Möglichkeiten offen halten; **~al** *adj* freiwillig; *(subject)* wahlfrei; **~al extras** *npl* Extras auf Wunsch

or [ɔː*] *conj* oder; **he could not read ~ write** er konnte weder lesen noch schreiben; **~ else** sonst

oral ['ɔːrəl] *adj* mündlich ♦ *n (exam)* mündliche Prüfung *f*

orange ['ɔrɪndʒ] *n (fruit)* Apfelsine *f*, Orange *f*; *(colour)* Orange *nt* ♦ *adj* orange

orator ['ɔrətə*] *n* Redner(in) *m(f)*

orbit ['ɔːbɪt] *n* Umlaufbahn *f*

orbital (motorway) ['ɔːbɪtəl-] *n* Ringautobahn *f*

orchard ['ɔːtʃəd] *n* Obstgarten *m*

orchestra ['ɔːkɪstrə] *n* Orchester *nt*; *(US: seating)* Parkett *nt*; **~l** [ɔː'kestrəl] *adj* Orchester-, orchestral

orchid [ˈɔːkɪd] n Orchidee f

ordain [ɔːˈdeɪn] vt (ECCL) weihen

ordeal [ɔːˈdiːl] n Qual f

order [ˈɔːdəʳ] n (sequence) Reihenfolge f; (good arrangement) Ordnung f; (command) Befehl m; (JUR) Anordnung f; (peace) Ordnung f; (condition) Zustand m; (rank) Klasse f; (COMM) Bestellung f; (ECCL, honour) Orden m ♦ vt (also: **put in** ~) ordnen; (command) befehlen; (COMM) bestellen; **in** ~ in der Reihenfolge; **in (working)** ~ in gutem Zustand; **in** ~ **to do sth** um etw zu tun; **on** ~ (COMM) auf Bestellung; **to** ~ **sb to do sth** jdm befehlen, etw zu tun; **to** ~ **sth** (command) etw acc befehlen; ~ **form** Bestellschein m; ~**ly** n (MIL) Sanitäter m; (MED) Pfleger m ♦ adj (tidy) ordentlich; (well-behaved) ruhig

ordinary [ˈɔːdnrɪ] adj gewöhnlich ♦ n: **out of the** ~ außergewöhnlich

Ordnance Survey [ˈɔːdnəns] (BRIT) n amtliche(r) Kartografiedienst m

ore [ɔːʳ] n Erz nt

organ [ˈɔːgən] n (MUS) Orgel f; (BIOL, fig) Organ nt

organic [ɔːˈgænɪk] adj (food, farming etc) biodynamisch

organization [ɔːgənaɪˈzeɪʃən] n Organisation f; (make-up) Struktur f

organize [ˈɔːgənaɪz] vt organisieren; ~**r** n Organisator m, Veranstalter m

orgasm [ˈɔːgæzəm] n Orgasmus m

orgy [ˈɔːdʒɪ] n Orgie f

Orient [ˈɔːrɪənt] n Orient m; **o~al** [ɔːrɪˈɛntl] adj orientalisch

origin [ˈɔrɪdʒɪn] n Ursprung m; (of the world) Anfang m, Entstehung f; ~**al** [əˈrɪdʒɪnl] adj (first) ursprünglich; (painting) original; (idea) originell ♦ n Original nt; ~**ally** adv ursprünglich; originell; ~**ate** [əˈrɪdʒɪneɪt] vi entstehen ♦ vt ins Leben rufen; **to ~ate from** stammen aus

Orkney [ˈɔːknɪ] npl (also: **the** ~ **Islands**) die Orkneyinseln pl

ornament [ˈɔːnəmənt] n Schmuck m;

(on mantelpiece) Nippesfigur f; ~**al** [ɔːnəˈmɛntl] adj Zier-

ornate [ɔːˈneɪt] adj reich verziert

orphan [ˈɔːfn] n Waise f, Waisenkind nt ♦ vt: **to be ~ed** Waise werden; ~**age** n Waisenhaus nt

orthodox [ˈɔːθədɔks] adj orthodox; ~**y** n Orthodoxie f; (fig) Konventionalität f

orthopaedic [ɔːθəˈpiːdɪk] (US **orthopedic**) adj orthopädisch

ostentatious [ɔstɛnˈteɪʃəs] adj großtuerisch, protzig

ostracize [ˈɔstrəsaɪz] vt ausstoßen

ostrich [ˈɔstrɪtʃ] n Strauß m

other [ˈʌðəʳ] adj andere(r, s) ♦ pron andere(r, s) ♦ adv: ~ **than** anders als; **the** ~ **(one)** der/die/das andere; **the** ~ **day** neulich; ~**s** (~ people) andere; ~**wise** adv (in a different way) anders; (or else) sonst

otter [ˈɔtəʳ] n Otter m

ouch [autʃ] excl aua

ought [ɔːt] vb aux sollen; **I** ~ **to do it** ich sollte es tun; **this** ~ **to have been corrected** das hätte korrigiert werden sollen

ounce [auns] n Unze f

our [ˈauəʳ] adj unsere(r, s); see also **my**; ~**s** pron unsere(r, s); see also **mine**[2]; ~**selves** pron uns (selbst); (emphatic) (wir) selbst; see also **oneself**

oust [aust] vt verdrängen

out [aut] adv hinaus/heraus; (not indoors) draußen; (not alight) aus; (unconscious) bewusstlos; (results) bekannt gegeben; **to eat/go** ~ auswärts essen/ausgehen; ~ **there** da draußen; **he is** ~ (absent) er ist nicht da; **he was** ~ **in his calculations** seine Berechnungen waren nicht richtig; ~ **loud** laut; ~ **of** us; (away from) außerhalb +gen; **to be** ~ **of milk** etc keine Milch etc mehr haben; ~ **of order** außer Betrieb; ~**-and-**~ adj (liar, thief etc) ausgemacht; ~**back** n Hinterland nt; ~**board (motor)** n Außenbordmotor m; ~**break** n Ausbruch m; ~**burst**

n Ausbruch *m*; **~cast** *n* Ausgestoßene(r) *m(f)*; **~come** *n* Ergebnis *nt*; **~crop** *n (of rock)* Felsnase *f*; **~cry** *n* Protest *m*; **~dated** *adj* überholt; **~do** *(irreg: like do)* *vt* übertrumpfen; **~door** *adj* Außen-; *(SPORT)* im Freien; **~doors** *adv* im Freien

outer ['aʊtə'] *adj* äußere(r, s); **~ space** *n* Weltraum *m*

outfit ['aʊtfɪt] *n* Kleidung *f*

out: ~going *adj (character)* aufgeschlossen; **~goings** *(BRIT) npl* Ausgaben *pl*; **~grow** *(irreg: like grow) vt (clothes)* herauswachsen aus; *(habit)* ablegen; **~house** *n* Nebengebäude *nt*

outing ['aʊtɪŋ] *n* Ausflug *m*

outlandish [aʊt'lændɪʃ] *adj* eigenartig

out: ~law *n* Geächtete(r) *f(m)* ♦ *vt* ächten; *(thing)* verbieten; **~lay** *n* Auslage *f*; **~let** *n* Auslass *m*, Abfluss *m*; *(also: retail ~let)* Absatzmarkt *m*; *(US: ELEC)* Steckdose *f*; *(for emotions)* Ventil *nt*

outline ['aʊtlaɪn] *n* Umriss *m*

out: ~live *vt* überleben; **~look** *n (also fig)* Aussicht *f*; *(attitude)* Einstellung *f*; **~lying** *adj* entlegen; *(district)* Außen-; **~moded** *adj* veraltet; **~number** *vt* zahlenmäßig überlegen sein *+dat*; **~-of-date** *adj (passport)* abgelaufen; *(clothes etc)* altmodisch; *(ideas etc)* überholt; **~-of-the-way** *adj* abgelegen; **~patient** *n* ambulante(r) Patient *m*/ambulante Patientin *f*; **~post** *n (MIL, fig)* Vorposten *m*; **~put** *n* Leistung *f*, Produktion *f*; *(COMPUT)* Ausgabe *f*

outrage ['aʊtreɪdʒ] *n (cruel deed)* Ausschreitung *f*; *(indecency)* Skandal *m* ♦ *vt (morals)* verstoßen gegen; *(person)* empören; **~ous** [aʊt'reɪdʒəs] *adj* unerhört

outreach worker [aʊt'ri:tʃ-] *n* Streetworker(in) *m(f)*

outright [*adv* aʊt'raɪt, *adj* 'aʊtraɪt] *adv (at once)* sofort; *(openly)* ohne Umschweife ♦ *adj (denial)* völlig; *(sale)* Total-; *(winner)* unbestritten

outset ['aʊtsɛt] *n* Beginn *m*

outside [aʊt'saɪd] *n* Außenseite *f* ♦ *adj* äußere(r, s), Außen-; *(chance)* gering ♦ *adv* außen ♦ *prep* außerhalb *+gen*; **at the ~** *(fig)* maximal; *(time)* spätestens; **to go ~** nach draußen gehen; **~ lane** *n (AUT)* äußere Spur *f*; **~ line** *n (TEL)* Amtsanschluss *m*; **~r** *n* Außenseiter(in) *m(f)*

out: ~size *adj* übergroß; **~skirts** *npl* Stadtrand *m*; **~spoken** *adj* freimütig; **~standing** *adj* hervorragend; *(debts etc)* ausstehend; **~stay** *vt*: **to ~stay one's welcome** länger bleiben als erwünscht; **~stretched** *adj* ausgestreckt; **~strip** *vt* übertreffen; **~ tray** *n* Ausgangskorb *m*

outward ['aʊtwəd] *adj* äußere(r, s); *(journey)* Hin-; *(freight)* ausgehend ♦ *adv* nach außen; **~ly** *adv* äußerlich

outweigh [aʊt'weɪ] *vt (fig)* überwiegen

outwit [aʊt'wɪt] *vt* überlisten

oval ['əʊvl] *adj* oval ♦ *n* Oval *nt*

Oval Office

Oval Office, ein großer ovaler Raum im Weißen Haus, ist das private Büro des amerikanischen Präsidenten. Im weiteren Sinne bezieht sich dieser Begriff oft auf die Präsidentschaft selbst.

---

ovary ['əʊvərɪ] *n* Eierstock *m*

ovation [əʊ'veɪʃən] *n* Beifallssturm *m*

oven ['ʌvn] *n* Backofen *m*; **~proof** *adj* feuerfest

over ['əʊvə'] *adv (across)* hinüber/ herüber; *(finished)* vorüber; *(left)* übrig; *(again)* wieder, noch einmal ♦ *prep* über; **~ prefix** *(excessively)* übermäßig; **~ here** hier(hin); **~ there** dort(hin); **all ~** *(everywhere)* überall; *(finished)* vorbei; **~ and ~** immer wieder; **~ and above** darüber hinaus; **to ask sb ~** jdn einladen; **to bend ~** sich bücken

overall [*adj*, *n* 'əʊvərɔ:l; *adv* əʊvər'ɔ:l] *adj (situation)* allgemein; *(length)* Gesamt- ♦ *n (BRIT)* Kittel *m* ♦ *adv* insgesamt; **~s** *npl* (for man) Overall *m*

over: ~awe *vt* (frighten) einschüchtern; (make impression) überwältigen; **~balance** *vi* Übergewicht bekommen; **~bearing** *adj* aufdringlich; **~board** *adv* über Bord; **~book** *vi* überbuchen

overcast ['əuvəkɑ:st] *adj* bedeckt

overcharge [əuvə'tʃɑ:dʒ] *vt*: **to ~ sb** von jdm zu viel verlangen

overcoat ['əuvəkəut] *n* Mantel *m*

overcome [əuvə'kʌm] (irreg: like come) *vt* überwinden

over: ~crowded *adj* überfüllt; **~crowding** *n* Überfüllung *f*; (in reg: like do) *vt* (cook too much) verkochen; (exaggerate) (COOK) verbraten, verkocht; **~dose** *n* Überdosis *f*; **~draft** *n* (Konto)überziehung *f*; **~drawn** *adj* (account) überzogen; **~due** *adj* überfällig; *vt* überschätzen; **~estimate** *vt* überschätzen; **~excited** *adj* überreizt; (children) aufgeregt

overflow [əuvə'fləu] *vi* überfließen ♦ *n* ['əuvəfləu] (excess) Überschuss *m*; (also: ~ pipe) Überlaufrohr *nt*

overgrown [əuvə'grəun] *adj* (garden) verwildert

overhaul [*vb* əuvə'hɔ:l, *n* 'əuvəhɔ:l] *vt* (car) überholen; (plans) überprüfen ♦ *n* Überholung *f*

overhead [*adv* əuvə'hed, *adj*, *n* 'əuvəhed] *adv* oben ♦ *adj* (wire) oberirdisch; (lighting) Decken- ♦ *n* (US) = **overheads**; **~s** *npl* (costs) allgemeine Unkosten *pl*; **~ projector** *n* Overheadprojektor *m*

overhear (irreg: like hear) *vt* (mit an)hören; **~heat** *vi* (engine) heiß laufen; **~joyed** *adj* überglücklich; **~kill** *n* (fig) Rundumschlag *m*

overland ['əuvəlænd] *adj* Überland- ♦ *adv* (travel) über Land

overlap [*vb* əuvə'læp, *n* 'əuvəlæp] *vi* sich überschneiden; (objects) sich teilweise decken ♦ *n* Überschneidung *f*

over: ~leaf *adv* umseitig; **~load** *vt*

überladen; **~look** *vt* (view from above) überblicken; (not notice) übersehen; (pardon) hinwegsehen über +acc

overnight [*adv* əuvə'naɪt, *adj* 'əuvənaɪt] *adv* über Nacht ♦ *adj* (journey) Nacht-; ~ **stay** Übernachtung *f*; **to stay ~** übernachten

overpass ['əuvəpɑ:s] *n* Überführung *f*

overpower [əuvə'pauə*] *vt* überwältigen

over: ~rate *vt* überschätzen; **~ride** (irreg: like ride) *vt* (order, decision) aufheben; (objection) übergehen; **~riding** *adj* vorherrschend; **~rule** *vt* verwerfen; **~run** (irreg: like run) *vt* (country) einfallen in; (time limit) überziehen

overseas [əuvə'si:z] *adv* nach/in Übersee ♦ *adj* überseeisch, Übersee-

overseer ['əuvəsiə*] *n* Aufseher *m*

overshadow [əuvə'ʃædəu] *vt* überschatten

overshoot [əuvə'ʃu:t] (irreg: like shoot) *vt* (runway) hinausschießen über +acc

oversight ['əuvəsaɪt] *n* (mistake) Versehen *nt*

over: ~sleep (irreg: like sleep) *vi* verschlafen; **~spill** *n* (Bevölkerungs)überschuss *m*; **~state** *vt* übertreiben; **~step** *vt*: **to ~step the mark** zu weit gehen

overt [əu'vɜ:t] *adj* offen(kundig)

overtake [əuvə'teɪk] (irreg: like take) *vt*, *vi* überholen

over: ~throw (irreg: like throw) *vt* (POL) stürzen; **~time** *n* Überstunden *pl*; **~tone** *n* (fig) Note *f*

overture ['əuvətʃuə*] *n* Ouvertüre *f*

over: ~turn *vt*, *vi* umkippen; **~weight** *adj* zu dick; **~whelm** *vt* überwältigen; **~work** *n* Überarbeitung *f* ♦ *vi* sich überlasten ♦ *vi* sich überarbeiten; **~wrought** *adj* überreizt

owe [əu] *vt* schulden; **to ~ sth to sb** (money) jdm etw schulden; (favour etc) jdm etw verdanken; **owing to** *prep* wegen +gen

owl [aul] *n* Eule *f*

own [əun] vt besitzen ♦ adj eigen; **a room of my ~** mein eigenes Zimmer; **to get one's ~ back** sich rächen; **on one's ~** allein; **~ up** vi: **to ~ up (to sth)** (etw) zugeben; **~er** n Besitzer(in) m(f); **~ership** n Besitz m

ox [ɔks] (pl **~en**) n Ochse m

oxtail [ˈɔksteɪl] n: **~ soup** Ochsenschwanzsuppe f

oxygen [ˈɔksidʒən] n Sauerstoff m; **~ mask** n Sauerstoffmaske f; **~ tent** n Sauerstoffzelt nt

oyster [ˈɔɪstər] n Auster f

oz. abbr = **ounce(s)**

ozone [ˈəuzəun] n Ozon m; **~-friendly** adj (aerosol) ohne Treibgas; (fridge) FCKW-frei; **~ hole** n Ozonloch nt; **~ layer** n Ozonschicht f

P, p

p abbr = **penny; pence**

pa [pɑː] (inf) n Papa m

P.A. n abbr = **personal assistant; public address system**

p.a. abbr = **per annum**

pace [peɪs] n Schritt m; (speed) Tempo nt ♦ vi schreiten; **to keep ~ with** Schritt halten mit; **~maker** n Schrittmacher m

pacific [pəˈsɪfɪk] adj pazifisch ♦ n: **the P~ (Ocean)** der Pazifik

pacifist [ˈpæsɪfɪst] n Pazifist m

pacify [ˈpæsɪfaɪ] vt befrieden; (calm) beruhigen

pack [pæk] n (of goods) Packung f; (of hounds) Meute f; (of cards) Spiel nt; (gang) Bande f ♦ vt (case) packen; (clothes) einpacken ♦ vi packen; **to ~ sb off to ...** jdn nach ... schicken; **~ it in!** lass es gut sein!

package [ˈpækɪdʒ] n Paket nt; **~ tour** n Pauschalreise f

packed [pækt] adj abgepackt; **~ lunch** n Lunchpaket nt

packet [ˈpækɪt] n Päckchen nt

packing [ˈpækɪŋ] n (action) Packen nt; (material) Verpackung f; **~ case** n (Pack)kiste f

pact [pækt] n Pakt m, Vertrag m

pad [pæd] n (of paper) (Schreib)block m; (stuffing) Polster nt ♦ vt polstern; **~ding** n Polsterung f

paddle [ˈpædl] n Paddel nt; (US: SPORT) Schläger m ♦ vt (boat) paddeln ♦ vi (in sea) plan(t)schen; **~ steamer** n Raddampfer m

paddling pool [ˈpædlɪŋ-] n (BRIT) Plan(t)schbecken nt

paddock [ˈpædək] n Koppel f

paddy field [ˈpædɪ-] n Reisfeld nt

padlock [ˈpædlɔk] n Vorhängeschloss nt ♦ vt verschließen

paediatrics [piːdɪˈætrɪks] (US **pediatrics**) n Kinderheilkunde f

pagan [ˈpeɪgən] adj heidnisch ♦ n Heide m, Heidin f

page [peɪdʒ] n Seite f; (person) Page m ♦ vt (in hotel) ausrufen lassen

pageant [ˈpædʒənt] n Festzug m; **~ry** n Gepränge nt

pager [ˈpeɪdʒər] n (TEL) Funkrufempfänger m, Piepser m (inf)

paging device [ˈpeɪdʒɪŋ-] n (TEL) = **pager**

paid [peɪd] pt, pp of **pay** ♦ adj bezahlt; **to put ~ to** (BRIT) zunichte machen

pail [peɪl] n Eimer m

pain [peɪn] n Schmerz m; **to be in ~** Schmerzen haben; **on ~ of death** bei Todesstrafe; **to take ~s to do sth** sich dat Mühe geben, etw zu tun; **~ed** adj (expression) gequält; **~ful** adj (physically) schmerzhaft; (embarrassing) peinlich; (difficult) mühsam; **~fully** adv (fig: very) schrecklich; **~killer** n Schmerzmittel nt; **~less** adj schmerzlos; **~staking** [ˈzteɪkɪŋ] adj gewissenhaft

paint [peɪnt] n Farbe f ♦ vt anstreichen; (picture) malen; **to ~ the door blue** die Tür blau streichen; **~brush** n Pinsel m; **~er** n Maler m; **~ing** n Malerei f; (picture) Gemälde nt; **~work** n An-

strich m; (of car) Lack m
pair [peəʳ] n Paar nt; ~ **of scissors** Schere f; ~ **of trousers** Hose f
pajamas [pəˈdʒɑːməz] (US) npl Schlafanzug m
Pakistan [pɑːkɪˈstɑːn] n Pakistan nt; ~**i** adj pakistanisch ♦ n Pakistani mf
pal [pæl] (inf) n Kumpel m
palace [ˈpæləs] n Palast m, Schloss nt
palatable [ˈpælɪtəbl] adj schmackhaft
palate [ˈpælɪt] n Gaumen m
palatial [pəˈleɪʃəl] adj palastartig
pale [peɪl] adj blass, bleich ♦ n: **to be beyond the** ~ die Grenzen überschreiten
Palestine [ˈpælɪstaɪn] n Palästina nt; **Palestinian** [pælɪsˈtɪnɪən] adj palästinensisch ♦ n Palästinenser(in) m(f)
palette [ˈpælɪt] n Palette f
paling [ˈpeɪlɪŋ] n (stake) Zaunpfahl m; (fence) Lattenzaun m
pall [pɔːl] vi jeden Reiz verlieren, verblassen
pallet [ˈpælɪt] n (for goods) Palette f
pallid [ˈpælɪd] adj blass, bleich
pallor [ˈpæləʳ] n Blässe f
palm [pɑːm] n (of hand) Handfläche f; (also: ~ **tree**) Palme f ♦ vt: **to ~ sth off on sb** jdm etw andrehen; **P~ Sunday** n Palmsonntag m
palpable [ˈpælpəbl] adj (also fig) greifbar
palpitation [pælpɪˈteɪʃən] n Herzklopfen nt
paltry [ˈpɔːltrɪ] adj armselig
pamper [ˈpæmpəʳ] vt verhätscheln
pamphlet [ˈpæmflət] n Broschüre f
pan [pæn] n Pfanne f ♦ vi (CINE) schwenken
panache [pəˈnæʃ] n Schwung m
pancake [ˈpænkeɪk] n Pfannkuchen m
pancreas [ˈpæŋkrɪəs] n Bauchspeicheldrüse f
panda [ˈpændə] n Panda m; ~ **car** (BRIT) n (Funk)streifenwagen m
pandemonium [pændɪˈməʊnɪəm] n Hölle f; (noise) Höllenlärm m

pander [ˈpændəʳ] vi: **to ~ to** sich richten nach
pane [peɪn] n (Fenster)scheibe f
panel [ˈpænl] n (of wood) Tafel f; (TV) Diskussionsrunde f; ~**ling** (US **paneling**) n Täfelung f
pang [pæŋ] n: ~**s of hunger** quälende(r) Hunger m; ~**s of conscience** Gewissensbisse pl
panic [ˈpænɪk] n Panik f ♦ vi in Panik geraten; **don't** ~ (nur) keine Panik; ~**ky** adj (person) überängstlich; ~**stricken** adj von panischem Schrecken erfasst; (look) panisch
pansy [ˈpænzɪ] n Stiefmütterchen nt; (inf) Schwule(r) m
pant [pænt] vi keuchen; (dog) hecheln
panther [ˈpænθəʳ] n Pant(h)er m
panties [ˈpæntɪz] npl (Damen)slip m
pantihose [ˈpæntɪhəʊz] (US) n Strumpfhose f
pantomime [ˈpæntəmaɪm] (BRIT) n Märchenkomödie f um Weihnachten

---

Pantomime

Pantomime oder umgangssprachlich panto ist in Großbritannien ein zur Weihnachtszeit aufgeführtes Märchenspiel mit possenhaften Elementen, Musik, Standardrollen (ein als Frau verkleideter Mann, ein Junge, ein Bösewicht) und aktuellen Witzen. Publikumsbeteiligung wird gern gesehen (z.B. warnen die Kinder den Helden mit dem Ruf "He's behind you" vor einer drohenden Gefahr), und viele der Witze sprechen vor allem Erwachsene an, so dass pantomimes Unterhaltung für die ganze Familie bieten.

---

pantry [ˈpæntrɪ] n Vorratskammer f
pants [pænts] npl (BRIT: woman's) Schlüpfer m; (: man's) Unterhose f; (US: trousers) Hose f
papal [ˈpeɪpəl] adj päpstlich
paper [ˈpeɪpəʳ] n Papier nt; (newspaper) Zeitung f; (essay) Referat nt ♦ adj

Papier-, aus Papier ♦ vt (wall) tapezieren; **~s** npl (identity ~s) Ausweis(papiere pl) m; **~back** n Taschenbuch nt; **~ bag** n Tüte f; **~ clip** n Büroklammer f; **~ hankie** n Tempotaschentuch nt ®; **~weight** n Briefbeschwerer m; **~work** n Schreibarbeit f

par [pɑ:] n (COMM) Nennwert m, (GOLF) Par nt; **on a ~ with** ebenbürtig +dat

parable ['pærəbl] n (REL) Gleichnis nt

parachute ['pærəʃu:t] n Fallschirm m ♦ vi (mit dem Fallschirm) abspringen

parade [pə'reɪd] n Parade f ♦ vt aufmarschieren lassen; (fig) zur Schau stellen ♦ vi paradieren, vorbeimarschieren

paradise ['pærədaɪs] n Paradies nt

paradox ['pærədɒks] n Paradox nt; **~ically** [pærə'dɒksɪklɪ] adv paradoxerweise

paraffin ['pærəfɪn] (BRIT) n Paraffin nt

paragraph ['pærəgrɑ:f] n Absatz m

parallel ['pærəlel] adj parallel ♦ n Parallele f

paralyse ['pærəlaɪz] (US **paralyze**) vt (MED) lähmen, paralysieren; (fig: organization, production etc) lahm legen; **~d** adj gelähmt; **paralysis** [pə'rælɪsɪs] n Lähmung f

paralyze ['pærəlaɪz] (US) = **paralyse** vt

parameter [pə'ræmɪtə*] n Parameter m; **~s** npl (framework, limits) Rahmen m

paramount ['pærəmaʊnt] adj höchste(r, s), oberste(r, s)

paranoid ['pærənɔɪd] adj (person) an Verfolgungswahn leidend, paranoid; (feeling) krankhaft

parapet ['pærəpɪt] n Brüstung f

paraphernalia [pærəfə'neɪlɪə] n Zubehör nt, Utensilien pl

paraphrase ['pærəfreɪz] vt umschreiben

paraplegic [pærə'pli:dʒɪk] n Querschnittsgelähmte(r) f(m)

parasite ['pærəsaɪt] n (also fig) Schmarotzer m, Parasit m

parasol ['pærəsɒl] n Sonnenschirm m

paratrooper ['pærətru:pə*] n Fallschirmjäger m

parcel ['pɑ:sl] n Paket nt ♦ vt (also: ~ up) einpacken

parch ['pɑ:tʃ] vt (aus)dörren; **~ed** adj ausgetrocknet; (person) am Verdursten

parchment ['pɑ:tʃmənt] n Pergament nt

pardon ['pɑ:dn] n Verzeihung f ♦ vt (JUR) begnadigen; **~ me!, I beg your ~!** verzeihen Sie bitte!; **~ me?** (US) wie bitte?; **(I beg you) ~?** wie bitte?

parent ['pɛərənt] n Elternteil m; **~s** npl (mother and father) Eltern pl; **~al** [pə'rɛntl] adj elterlich, Eltern-

parentheses [pə'rɛnθɪsi:z] npl of **parenthesis**

parenthesis [pə'rɛnθɪsɪs] n Klammer f; (sentence) Parenthese f

Paris ['pærɪs] n Paris nt

parish ['pærɪʃ] n Gemeinde f

park [pɑ:k] n Park m ♦ vt, vi parken

parking ['pɑ:kɪŋ] n Parken nt; **"no ~"** "Parken verboten"; **~ lot** (US) n Parkplatz m; **~ meter** n Parkuhr f; **~ ticket** n Strafzettel m

parlance ['pɑ:ləns] n Sprachgebrauch m

parliament ['pɑ:ləmənt] n Parlament nt; **~ary** [pɑ:lə'mɛntərɪ] adj parlamentarisch, Parlaments-

parlour ['pɑ:lə*] (US **parlor**) n Salon m

parochial [pə'rəʊkɪəl] adj (narrow-minded) eng(stirnig)

parole [pə'rəʊl] n: **on ~** (prisoner) auf Bewährung

parrot ['pærət] n Papagei m

parry ['pærɪ] vt parieren, abwehren

parsley ['pɑ:slɪ] n Petersilie f

parsnip ['pɑ:snɪp] n Pastinake f

parson ['pɑ:sn] n Pfarrer m

part [pɑ:t] n (piece) Teil m; (THEAT) Rolle f; (of machine) Teil nt ♦ adv = partly; ♦ vt trennen; (hair) scheiteln ♦ vi (people) sich trennen; **to take ~ in** teilnehmen an +dat; **to take sth in good ~** etw nicht übel nehmen; **to take sb's**

~ sich auf jds Seite *acc* stellen; **for my ~** ich für meinen Teil; **for the most ~** meistens, größtenteils; **in ~ exchange** (*BRIT*) in Zahlung; **~ with** *vt fus* hergeben; (*renounce*) aufgeben; **~ial** [-ʃəl] *adj* (*incomplete*) teilweise; (*biased*) parteiisch; **to be ~ial to** eine (besondere) Vorliebe haben für

participant [pɑːˈtɪsɪpənt] *n* Teilnehmer(in) *m(f)*

participate [pɑːˈtɪsɪpeɪt] *vi*: **to ~ (in)** teilnehmen (an +*dat*); **participation** [pɑːtɪsɪˈpeɪʃən] *n* Teilnahme *f*; (*sharing*) Beteiligung *f*

participle [ˈpɑːtɪsɪpl] *n* Partizip *nt*

particle [ˈpɑːtɪkl] *n* Teilchen *nt*

particular [pəˈtɪkjulər] *adj* bestimmt; (*exact*) genau; (*fussy*) eigen; **in ~** besonders; **~ly** *adv* besonders

particulars *npl* (*details*) Einzelheiten *pl*; (*of person*) Personalien *pl*

parting [ˈpɑːtɪŋ] *n* (*separation*) Abschied *m*; (*BRIT: of hair*) Scheitel *m* ♦ *adj* Abschieds-

partition [pɑːˈtɪʃən] *n* (*wall*) Trennwand *f*; (*division*) Teilung *f* ♦ *vt* aufteilen

partly [ˈpɑːtlɪ] *adv* zum Teil, teilweise

partner [ˈpɑːtnər] *n* Partner *m* ♦ *vt* der Partner sein von; **~ship** *n* Partnerschaft *f*; (*COMM*) Teilhaberschaft *f*

partridge [ˈpɑːtrɪdʒ] *n* Rebhuhn *nt*

part-time [ˈpɑːtˈtaɪm] *adj* Teilzeit- ♦ *adv* stundenweise

party [ˈpɑːtɪ] *n* (*POL* also) Partei *f*; (*group*) Gesellschaft *f*; (*celebration*) Party *f* ♦ *adj* (*dress*) Party-; (*politics*) Partei-; **~ line** *n* (*TEL*) Gemeinschaftsanschluss *m*

pass [pɑːs] *vt* (*on foot*) vorbeigehen an +*dat*; (*driving*) vorbeifahren an +*dat*; (*surpass*) übersteigen; (*hand on*) weitergeben; (*approve*) genehmigen; (*time*) verbringen; (*exam*) bestehen ♦ *vi* (*go by*) vorbeigehen; vorbeifahren; (*years*) vergehen; (*be successful*) bestehen ♦ *n* (*in mountains, SPORT*) Pass *m*; (*permission*) Passierschein *m*; (*in exam*):

to get a ~ bestehen; **to ~ sth through sth** etw durch etw führen; **to make a ~ at sb** (*inf*) bei jdm Annäherungsversuche machen; **~ away** *vi* (*euph*) verscheiden; **~ by** *vi* vorbeigehen, vorbeifahren; (*years*) vergehen; **~ on** *vt* weitergeben; **~ out** *vi* (*faint*) ohnmächtig werden; **~ up** *vt* vorbeigehen lassen; **~able** *adj* (*road*) passierbar; (*fairly good*) passabel

passage [ˈpæsɪdʒ] *n* (*corridor*) Gang *m*; (*in book*) (Text)stelle *f*; (*voyage*) Überfahrt *f*; **~way** *n* Durchgang *m*

passbook [ˈpɑːsbuk] *n* Sparbuch *nt*

passenger [ˈpæsɪndʒər] *n* Passagier *m*; (*on bus*) Fahrgast *m*

passer-by [pɑːsəˈbaɪ] *n* Passant(in) *m(f)*

passing [ˈpɑːsɪŋ] *adj* (*car*) vorbeifahrend; (*thought, affair*) momentan ♦ *n*: **in ~** beiläufig; **~ place** *n* (*AUT*) Ausweichstelle *f*

passion [ˈpæʃən] *n* Leidenschaft *f*; **~ate** *adj* leidenschaftlich

passive [ˈpæsɪv] *adj* passiv; (*LING*) passivisch; **~ smoking** *n* Passivrauchen *nt*

Passover [ˈpɑːsəuvər] *n* Passahfest *nt*

passport [ˈpɑːspɔːt] *n* (Reise)pass *m*; **~ control** *n* Passkontrolle *f*; **~ office** *n* Passamt *nt*

password [ˈpɑːswɜːd] *n* Parole *f*, Kennwort *nt*, Losung *f*

past [pɑːst] *prep* (*motion*) an +*dat* ... vorbei; (*position*) hinter +*dat*; (*later than*) nach ♦ *adj* (*years*) vergangen; (*president etc*) ehemalig ♦ *n* Vergangenheit *f*; **he's ~ forty** er ist über vierzig; **for the ~ few/3 days** in den letzten paar/3 Tagen; **to run ~** vorbeilaufen; **ten/quarter ~ eight** zehn/Viertel nach acht

pasta [ˈpæstə] *n* Teigwaren *pl*

paste [peɪst] *n* (*fish – etc*) Paste *f*; (*glue*) Kleister *m* ♦ *vt* kleben

pasteurized [ˈpæstʃəraɪzd] *adj* pasteurisiert

pastime [ˈpɑːstaɪm] *n* Zeitvertreib *m*

pastor [ˈpɑːstər] *n* Pfarrer *m*

pastry ['peɪstrɪ] n Blätterteig m; **pastries** npl (tarts etc) Stückchen pl

pasture ['pɑːstʃər] n Weide f

pasty [n 'pæstɪ, adj 'peɪstɪ] n (Fleisch)pastete f ♦ adj blässlich, käsig

pat [pæt] n leichte(r) Schlag m, Klaps m ♦ vt tätscheln

patch [pætʃ] n Fleck m ♦ vt flicken; **(to go through) a bad ~** eine Pechsträhne (haben); **~ up** vt flicken; (quarrel) beilegen; **~ed** adj geflickt; **~y** adj (irregular) ungleichmäßig

pâté ['pæteɪ] n Pastete f

patent ['peɪtnt] n Patent nt ♦ vt patentieren lassen; (by authorities) patentieren ♦ adj offenkundig; **~ leather** n Lackleder nt

paternal [pə'tɜːnl] adj väterlich

paternity [pə'tɜːnɪtɪ] n Vaterschaft f

path [pɑːθ] n Pfad m; Weg m

pathetic [pə'θetɪk] adj (very bad) kläglich

pathological [pæθə'lɒdʒɪkl] adj pathologisch

pathology [pə'θɒlədʒɪ] n Pathologie f

pathos ['peɪθɒs] n Rührseligkeit f

pathway ['pɑːθweɪ] n Weg m

patience ['peɪʃns] n Geduld f; (BRIT: CARDS) Patience f

patient ['peɪʃnt] n Patient(in) m(f), Kranke(r) mf ♦ adj geduldig

patio ['pætɪəʊ] n Terrasse f

patriotic [pætrɪ'ɒtɪk] adj patriotisch

patrol [pə'trəʊl] n Patrouille f; (police) Streife f ♦ vt patrouillieren in +dat ♦ vi (police) die Runde machen; (MIL) patrouillieren; **~ car** n (Streifen)wagen m; **~man** (US) (irreg) n (Streifen)polizist m

patron ['peɪtrən] n (in shop) (Stamm)kunde m; (in hotel) (Stamm)gast m; (supporter) Förderer m; **~ of the arts** Mäzen m; **~age** ['pætrənɪdʒ] n Schirmherrschaft f; **~ize** ['pætrənaɪz] vt (support) unterstützen; (shop) besuchen; (treat condescendingly) von oben herab behandeln; **~ saint** n Schutzpatron(in) m(f)

patter ['pætər] n (sound: of feet) Trappeln nt; (: of rain) Prasseln nt; (sales talk) Gerede nt ♦ vi (feet) trappeln; (rain) prasseln

pattern ['pætən] n Muster nt; (SEWING) Schnittmuster nt; (KNITTING) Strickanleitung f

pauper ['pɔːpər] n Arme(r) mf

pause [pɔːz] n Pause f ♦ vi innehalten

pave [peɪv] vt pflastern; **to ~ the way for** den Weg bahnen für

pavement ['peɪvmənt] n (BRIT) Bürgersteig m

pavilion [pə'vɪlɪən] n Pavillon m; (SPORT) Klubhaus nt

paving ['peɪvɪŋ] n Straßenpflaster nt; **~ stone** n Pflasterstein m

paw [pɔː] n Pfote f; (of big cats) Tatze f, Pranke f ♦ vt (scrape) scharren; (handle) betatschen

pawn [pɔːn] n Pfand nt; (chess) Bauer m ♦ vt verpfänden; **~broker** n Pfandleiher m; **~shop** n Pfandhaus nt

pay [peɪ] (pt, pp **paid**) n Bezahlung f, Lohn m ♦ vt bezahlen ♦ vi zahlen; (be profitable) sich bezahlt machen; **to ~ attention (to)** Acht geben (auf +acc); **to ~ sb a visit** jdn besuchen; **~ back** vt zurückzahlen; **~ for** vt fus bezahlen; **~ in** vt einzahlen; **~ off** vt abzahlen ♦ vi (scheme, decision) sich bezahlt machen; **~ up** vt bezahlen; **~able** adj zahlbar, fällig; **~ee** n Zahlungsempfänger m; **~ envelope** (US) n Lohntüte f; **~ment** n Bezahlung f; **advance ~ment** Vorauszahlung f; **monthly ~ment** monatliche Rate f; **~ packet** (BRIT) n Lohntüte f; **~phone** n Münzfernsprecher m; **~roll** n Lohnliste f; **~ slip** n Lohn-/Gehaltsstreifen m; **~ television** n Abonnenten-Fernsehen nt

PC n abbr = **personal computer**

p.c. abbr = **per cent**

pea [piː] n Erbse f

peace [piːs] n Friede(n) m; **~able** adj friedlich; **~ful** adj friedlich, ruhig;

~keeping adj Friedens-

peach [piːtʃ] n Pfirsich m

peacock ['piːkɔk] n Pfau m

peak [piːk] n Spitze f; (of mountain) Gipfel m; (fig) Höhepunkt m; **~ hours** npl (traffic) Hauptverkehrszeit f; (telephone, electricity) Hauptbelastungszeit f; **~ period** n Stoßzeit f, Hauptzeit f

peal [piːl] n (Glocken)läuten nt; **~s of laughter** schallende(s) Gelächter nt

peanut ['piːnʌt] n Erdnuss f; **~ butter** n Erdnussbutter f

pear [pɛə] n Birne f

pearl [pɔːl] n Perle f

peasant ['pɛznt] n Bauer m

peat [piːt] n Torf m

pebble ['pɛbl] n Kiesel m

peck [pɛk] vt, vi picken ♦ n (with beak) Schnabelhieb m; (kiss) flüchtige(r) Kuss m; **~ing order** n Hackordnung f; **~ish** (BRIT: inf) adj ein bisschen hungrig

peculiar [pɪ'kjuːlɪə] adj (odd) seltsam; **~ to** charakteristisch für; **~ity** [pɪkjuːlɪ'ærɪtɪ] n (singular quality) Besonderheit f; (strangeness) Eigenartigkeit f

pedal ['pɛdl] n Pedal nt ♦ vt, vi (cycle) fahren, Rad fahren

pedantic [pɪ'dæntɪk] adj pedantisch

peddler ['pɛdlə] n Hausierer(in) m(f); (of drugs) Drogenhändler(in) m(f)

pedestal ['pɛdəstl] n Sockel m

pedestrian [pɪ'dɛstrɪən] n Fußgänger m ♦ adj Fußgänger-; (humdrum) langweilig; **~ crossing** (BRIT) n Fußgängerüberweg m; **~ized** n in eine Fußgängerzone umgewandelt; **~ precinct** (BRIT), **~ zone** (US) n Fußgängerzone f

pediatrics [piːdɪ'ætrɪks] (US) n = **paediatrics**

pedigree ['pɛdɪgriː] n Stammbaum m ♦ cpd (animal) reinrassig, Zucht-

pee [piː] (inf) vi pissen, pinkeln

peek [piːk] vi gucken

peel [piːl] n Schale f ♦ vt schälen ♦ vi (paint etc) abblättern; (skin) sich

schälen

peep [piːp] n (BRIT: look) kurze(r) Blick m; (sound) Piepsen nt ♦ vi (BRIT: look) gucken; **~ out** vi herausgucken; **~hole** n Gucklock nt

peer [pɪə] vi starren; (peep) gucken ♦ n (nobleman) Peer m; (equal) Ebenbürtige(r) m; **~age** n Peerswürde f

peeved [piːvd] adj (person) sauer

peg [pɛg] n (stake) Pflock m; (BRIT: also: clothes ~) Wäscheklammer f

Pekinese [piːkɪ'niːz] n (dog) Pekinese m

pelican ['pɛlɪkən] n Pelikan m; **~ crossing** (BRIT) n (AUT) Ampelübergang m

pellet ['pɛlɪt] n Kügelchen nt

pelmet ['pɛlmɪt] n Blende f

pelt [pɛlt] vt bewerfen ♦ vi (rain) schütten ♦ n Pelz m, Fell nt

pelvis ['pɛlvɪs] n Becken nt

pen [pɛn] n (fountain ~) Federhalter m; (ball-point ~) Kuli m; (for sheep) Pferch m

penal ['piːnl] adj Straf-; **~ize** vt (punish) bestrafen; (disadvantage) benachteiligen

penalty ['pɛnltɪ] n Strafe f; (FOOTBALL) Elfmeter m; **~ (kick)** n Elfmeter m

penance ['pɛnəns] n Buße f

pence [pɛns] (BRIT) npl of **penny**

pencil ['pɛnsl] n Bleistift m; **~ case** n Federmäppchen nt; **~ sharpener** n Bleistiftspitzer m

pendant ['pɛndnt] n Anhänger m

pending ['pɛndɪŋ] prep bis (zu) ♦ adj unentschieden, noch offen

pendulum ['pɛndjuləm] n Pendel nt

penetrate ['pɛnɪtreɪt] vt durchdringen; (enter into) eindringen in +acc; **penetration** [pɛnɪ'treɪʃən] n Durchdringen nt; Eindringen nt

penfriend ['pɛnfrɛnd] (BRIT) n Brieffreund(in) m(f)

penguin ['pɛŋgwɪn] n Pinguin m

penicillin [pɛnɪ'sɪlɪn] n Penizillin nt

peninsula [pɪ'nɪnsjulə] n Halbinsel f

penis ['piːnɪs] n Penis m

penitentiary [penɪ'tenʃərɪ] (US) n Zuchthaus nt

penknife ['pennaɪf] n Federmesser nt

pen name n Pseudonym nt

penniless ['penɪlɪs] adj mittellos

penny ['penɪ] (pl **pennies** or (BRIT) **pence**) n Penny m; (US) Centstück nt

penpal ['penpæl] n Brieffreund(in) m(f)

pension ['penʃən] n Rente f; **~er** (BRIT) n Rentner(in) m(f); **~ fund** n Rentenfonds m; **~ plan** n Rentenversicherung f

pensive ['pensɪv] adj nachdenklich

<hr>

Pentagon

Pentagon heißt das fünfeckige Gebäude in Arlington, Virginia, in dem das amerikanische Verteidigungsministerium untergebracht ist. Im weiteren Sinne bezieht sich dieses Wort auf die amerikanische Militärführung.

<hr>

pentathlon [pen'tæθlən] n Fünfkampf m

Pentecost ['pentɪkɔst] n Pfingsten pl or nt

penthouse ['penthaʊs] n Dachterrassenwohnung f

pent-up ['pentʌp] adj (feelings) angestaut

penultimate [pe'nʌltɪmət] adj vorletzte(r, s)

people ['piːpl] n (nation) Volk ♦ npl (persons) Leute pl; (inhabitants) Bevölkerung f ♦ vt besiedeln; **several ~ came** mehrere Leute kamen; **~ say that ...** man sagt, dass ...

pepper ['pepə'] n Pfeffer m; (vegetable) Paprika m ♦ vt (pelt) bombardieren; **~mill** n Pfeffermühle f; **~mint** n (plant) Pfefferminze f; (sweet) Pfefferminz nt

pep talk [pep] (inf) n Anstachelung f

per [pɜː'] prep pro; **~ day/person** pro Tag/Person; **~ annum** adv pro Jahr; **~ capita** adj (income) Pro-Kopf- ♦ adv pro Kopf

perceive [pə'siːv] vt (realize) wahrnehmen; (understand) verstehen

per cent n Prozent nt; **percentage** [pə'sentɪdʒ] n Prozentsatz m

perception [pə'sepʃən] n Wahrnehmung f; (insight) Einsicht f

perceptive [pə'septɪv] adj (person) aufmerksam; (analysis) tief gehend

perch [pɜːtʃ] n Stange f; (fish) Flussbarsch m ♦ vi sitzen, hocken

percolator [pə'kəleɪtə'] n Kaffeemaschine f

percussion [pə'kʌʃən] n (MUS) Schlagzeug nt

perennial [pə'renɪəl] adj wiederkehrend; (everlasting) unvergänglich

perfect [adj, n 'pɜːfɪkt, vb pə'fekt] adj vollkommen; (crime, solution) perfekt ♦ n (GRAM) Perfekt nt ♦ vt vervollkommnen; **~ion** n Vollkommenheit f; **~ly** adv vollkommen, perfekt; (quite) ganz, einfach

perforate ['pɜːfəreɪt] vt durchlöchern; **perforation** [pɜːfə'reɪʃən] n Perforieren nt; (line of holes) Perforation f

perform [pə'fɔːm] vt (carry out) durchor ausführen; (task) verrichten; (THEAT) spielen, geben ♦ vi (THEAT) auftreten; **~ance** n Durchführung f; (efficiency) Leistung f; (show) Vorstellung f; **~er** n Künstler(in) m(f)

perfume ['pɜːfjuːm] n Duft m; (lady's) Parfüm nt

perhaps [pə'hæps] adv vielleicht

peril ['perɪl] n Gefahr f

perimeter [pə'rɪmɪtə'] n Peripherie f; (of circle etc) Umfang m

period ['pɪərɪəd] n Periode f; (GRAM) Punkt m; (MED) Periode f ♦ adj (costume) historisch; **~ic** [pɪərɪ'ɔdɪk] adj periodisch; **~ical** [pɪərɪ'ɔdɪkl] n Zeitschrift f; **~ically** [pɪərɪ'ɔdɪklɪ] adv periodisch

peripheral [pə'rɪfərəl] adj Rand-, peripher ♦ n (COMPUT) Peripheriegerät nt

perish ['perɪʃ] vi umkommen; (fruit) verderben; **~able** adj leicht verderblich

perjury ['pɜːdʒərɪ] n Meineid m

perk [pɜːk] (inf) n (fringe benefit) Vergünstigung f; ~ **up** vi munter werden; ~y adj keck

perm [pɜːm] n Dauerwelle f

permanent ['pɜːmənənt] adj dauernd, ständig

permeate ['pɜːmɪeɪt] vt, vi durchdringen

permissible [pəˈmɪsɪbl] adj zulässig

permission [pəˈmɪʃən] n Erlaubnis f

permissive [pəˈmɪsɪv] adj nachgiebig; **the ~ society** die permissive Gesellschaft

permit [n pɜːˈmɪt, vb pəˈmɪt] n Zulassung f ♦ vt erlauben, zulassen

perpendicular [ˌpɜːpənˈdɪkjʊləʳ] adj senkrecht

perpetrate ['pɜːpɪtreɪt] vt begehen

perpetual [pəˈpetjʊəl] adj dauernd, ständig

perpetuate [pəˈpetjʊeɪt] vt verewigen, bewahren

perplex [pəˈpleks] vt verblüffen

persecute ['pɜːsɪkjuːt] vt verfolgen; **persecution** [pɜːsɪˈkjuːʃən] n Verfolgung f

perseverance [pɜːsɪˈvɪərns] n Ausdauer f

persevere [pɜːsɪˈvɪəʳ] vi durchhalten

Persian ['pɜːʃən] adj persisch ♦ n Perser(in) m(f); **the (Persian) Gulf** der Persische Golf

persist [pəˈsɪst] vi (in belief etc) bleiben; (rain, smell) andauern; (continue) nicht aufhören; **to ~ in** bleiben bei; ~**ence** n Beharrlichkeit f; ~**ent** adj beharrlich; (unending) ständig

person ['pɜːsn] n Person f; **in ~** persönlich; ~**able** adj gut aussehend; ~**al** adj persönlich; (private) privat; (of body) körperlich, Körper-; ~**al assistant** n Assistent(in) m(f); ~**al column** n private Kleinanzeigen pl; ~**al computer** n Personalcomputer m; ~**ality** [pɜːsəˈnælɪtɪ] n Persönlichkeit f; ~**ally** adv persönlich; ~**al organizer** n Ter-

minplaner m, Zeitplaner m; (electronic) elektronisches Notizbuch nt; ~**al stereo** n Walkman m ®; ~**ify** [pɜːˈsɒnɪfaɪ] vt verkörpern

personnel [pɜːsəˈnel] n Personal nt

perspective [pəˈspektɪv] n Perspektive f

Perspex ['pɜːspeks] ® n Acrylglas nt, Akrylglas nt

perspiration [pɜːspɪˈreɪʃən] n Transpiration f

perspire [pəˈspaɪəʳ] vi transpirieren

persuade [pəˈsweɪd] vt überreden; (convince) überzeugen

persuasion [pəˈsweɪʒən] n Überredung f; Überzeugung f

persuasive [pəˈsweɪsɪv] adj überzeugend

pert [pɜːt] adj keck

pertaining [pɜːˈteɪnɪŋ]: ~ **to** prep betreffend +acc

pertinent ['pɜːtɪnənt] adj relevant

perturb [pəˈtɜːb] vt beunruhigen

pervade [pəˈveɪd] vt erfüllen

perverse [pəˈvɜːs] adj pervers; (obstinate) eigensinnig

pervert [n pɜːvɜːt, vb pəˈvɜːt] n perverse(r) Mensch m ♦ vt verdrehen; (morally) verderben

pessimist ['pesɪmɪst] n Pessimist m; ~**ic** adj pessimistisch

pest [pest] n (insect) Schädling m; (fig: person) Nervensäge f; (: thing) Plage f; ~**er** ['pestəʳ] vt plagen; ~**icide** ['pestɪsaɪd] n Insektenvertilgungsmittel nt

pet [pet] n (animal) Haustier nt ♦ vt liebkosen, streicheln

petal ['petl] n Blütenblatt nt

peter out ['piːtə-] vi allmählich zu Ende gehen

petite [pəˈtiːt] adj zierlich

petition [pəˈtɪʃən] n Bittschrift f

petrified ['petrɪfaɪd] adj versteinert; (person) starr (vor Schreck)

petrify ['petrɪfaɪ] vt versteinern; (person) erstarren lassen

petrol ['petrǝl] (BRIT) n Benzin nt, Kraftstoff m; **two-/four-star** ~ ≃ Normal-/Superbenzin nt; ~ **can** n Benzinkanister m

petroleum [pǝ'trǝuliǝm] n Petroleum nt

petrol: ~ **pump** (BRIT) n (in car) Benzinpumpe f; (at garage) Zapfsäule f; ~ **station** (BRIT) n Tankstelle f; ~ **tank** (BRIT) n Benzintank m

petticoat ['petikǝut] n Unterrock m

petty ['peti] adj (unimportant) unbedeutend; (mean) kleinlich; ~ **cash** n Portokasse f; ~ **officer** n Maat m

pew [pju:] n Kirchenbank f

pewter ['pju:tǝr] n Zinn nt

phantom ['fæntǝm] n Phantom nt

pharmacist ['fɑ:mǝsist] n Pharmazeut m; (druggist) Apotheker m

pharmacy ['fɑ:mǝsi] n Pharmazie f; (shop) Apotheke f

phase [feiz] n Phase f ♦ vt: **to** ~ **sth in** etw allmählich einführen; **to** ~ **sth out** etw auslaufen lassen

Ph.D. n abbr = **Doctor of Philosophy**

pheasant ['feznt] n Fasan m

phenomena [fǝ'nɔminǝ] npl of **phenomenon**

phenomenon [fǝ'nɔminǝn] n Phänomen nt

philanthropist [fi'lænθrǝpist] n Philanthrop m, Menschenfreund m

Philippines ['filipi:nz] npl: **the** ~ die Philippinen pl

philosopher [fi'lɔsǝfǝr] n Philosoph m; **philosophical** [filǝ'sɔfikl] adj philosophisch; **philosophy** [fi'lɔsǝfi] n Philosophie f

phlegm [flem] n (MED) Schleim m

phobia ['fǝubjǝ] n (irrational fear of insects, flying, water etc) Phobie f

phone [fǝun] n Telefon nt ♦ vt, vi telefonieren, anrufen; **to be on the** ~ telefonieren; ~ **back** vt, vi zurückrufen; ~ **up** vt, vi anrufen; ~ **bill** n Telefonrechnung f; ~ **book** n Telefonbuch nt; ~ **booth** n Telefonzelle f; ~ **box** n Te-

lefonzelle f; ~ **call** n Telefonanruf m; ~**card** n (TEL) Telefonkarte f; ~**-in** n (RAD, TV) Phone-in nt; ~ **number** n Telefonnummer f

phonetics [fǝ'netiks] n Phonetik f

phoney ['fǝuni] (inf) adj unecht ♦ n (person) Schwindler m; (thing) Fälschung f; (banknote) Blüte f

phony ['fǝuni] adj, n = **phoney**

photo ['fǝutǝu] n Foto nt; ~**copier** ['fǝutǝukɔpiǝr] n Kopiergerät nt; ~**copy** ['fǝutǝukɔpi] n Fotokopie f ♦ vt fotokopieren; ~**genic** [fǝutǝu'dʒenik] adj fotogen; ~**graph** ['fǝutǝgræf] n Fotografie f, Aufnahme f ♦ vt fotografieren; ~**grapher** [fǝ'tɔgrǝfǝr] n Fotograf m; ~**graphic** [fǝutǝ'græfik] adj fotografisch; ~**graphy** [fǝ'tɔgrǝfi] n Fotografie f

phrase [freiz] n Satz m; (expression) Ausdruck m ♦ vt ausdrücken, formulieren; ~ **book** n Sprachführer m

physical ['fizikl] adj physikalisch; (bodily) körperlich, physisch; ~ **education** n Turnen nt; ~**ly** adv physikalisch

physician [fi'ziʃǝn] n Arzt m

physicist ['fizisist] n Physiker(in) m(f)

physics ['fiziks] n Physik f

physiotherapist [fiziǝu'θerǝpist] n Physiotherapeut(in) m(f)

physiotherapy [fiziǝu'θerǝpi] n Heilgymnastik f, Physiotherapie f

physique [fi'zi:k] n Körperbau m

pianist ['piǝnist] n Pianist(in) m(f)

piano [pi'ænǝu] n Klavier nt

pick [pik] n (tool) Pickel m; (choice) Auswahl f ♦ vt (of fruit) pflücken; (choose) aussuchen; **take your** ~ such dir etwas aus; **to** ~ **sb's pocket** jdn bestehlen; ~ **on** vt fus (person) herumhacken auf +dat; ~ **out** vt auswählen; ~ **up** vi (improve) sich erholen ♦ vt (lift up) aufheben; (learn) (schnell) mitbekommen; (collect) abholen; (girl) (sich dat) anlachen; (AUT: passenger) mitnehmen; (speed) gewinnen an +dat; ~ **o.s. up** aufstehen

picket ['pikit] n (striker) Streikposten m

♦ vt (factory) (Streik)posten aufstellen vor +dat ♦ vi (Streik)posten stehen

pickle ['pɪkl] n (salty mixture) Pökel m; (inf) Klemme f ♦ vt (in Essig) einlegen; einpökeln

pickpocket ['pɪkpɒkɪt] n Taschendieb m

pick-up ['pɪkʌp] n (BRIT: on record player) Tonabnehmer m; (small truck) Lieferwagen m

picnic ['pɪknɪk] n Picknick nt ♦ vi picknicken; ~ **area** n Rastplatz m

pictorial [pɪk'tɔːrɪəl] adj in Bildern

picture ['pɪktʃər] n Bild nt ♦ vt (visualize) sich dat vorstellen; **the ~s** (BRIT) das Kino; ~ **book** n Bilderbuch nt

picturesque [pɪktʃə'rɛsk] adj malerisch

pie [paɪ] n (meat) Pastete f; (fruit) Torte f

piece [piːs] n Stück nt ♦ vt: **to ~ together** zusammenstückeln; (fig) sich dat zusammenreimen; **to take to ~s in** Einzelteile zerlegen; ~**meal** adv stückweise, Stück für Stück; ~**work** n Akkordarbeit f

pie chart n Kreisdiagramm nt

pier [pɪər] n Pier m, Mole f

pierce [pɪəs] vt durchstechen, durchbohren (also look); ~**d** adj durchgestochen; **piercing** ['pɪəsɪŋ] adj (cry) durchdringend

pig [pɪg] n Schwein nt

pigeon ['pɪdʒən] n Taube f; ~**hole** n (compartment) Ablegefach nt

piggy bank ['pɪgɪ-] n Sparschwein nt

pig: ~**headed** ['pɪg'hɛdɪd] adj dickköpfig; ~**let** ['pɪglɪt] n Ferkel nt; ~**skin** ['pɪgskɪn] n Schweinsleder nt; ~**sty** ['pɪgstaɪ] n Schweinestall m; ~**tail** ['pɪgteɪl] n Zopf m

pike [paɪk] n Pike f; (fish) Hecht m

pilchard ['pɪltʃəd] n Sardine f

pile [paɪl] n Haufen m; (of books, wood) Stapel m; (in ground) Pfahl m; (on carpet) Flausch m ♦ vt (also: ~ **up**) anhäufen ♦ vi (also: ~ **up**) sich anhäufen

piles [paɪlz] npl Hämorrho(id)en pl

pile-up ['paɪlʌp] n (AUT) Massenzusammenstoß m

pilfering ['pɪlfərɪŋ] n Diebstahl m

pilgrim ['pɪlgrɪm] n Pilger(in) m(f); ~**age** n Wallfahrt f

pill [pɪl] n Tablette f, Pille f; **the ~** die (Antibaby)pille

pillage ['pɪlɪdʒ] vt plündern

pillar ['pɪlər] n Pfeiler m, Säule f (also fig); ~ **box** (BRIT) n Briefkasten m

pillion ['pɪljən] n Soziussitz m

pillow ['pɪləu] n Kissen nt; ~**case** n Kissenbezug m

pilot ['paɪlət] n Pilot m; (NAUT) Lotse m ♦ adj (scheme etc) Versuchs- ♦ vt führen; (ship) lotsen; ~ **light** n Zündflamme f

pimp [pɪmp] n Zuhälter m

pimple ['pɪmpl] n Pickel m

PIN n abbr (= personal identification number) PIN f

pin [pɪn] n Nadel f; (for sewing) Stecknadel f; (TECH) Stift m, Bolzen m ♦ vt stecken; (keep in one position) pressen, drücken; **to ~ sth to sth** etw an etw acc heften; **to ~ sth on sb** (fig) jdm etw anhängen; ~**s and needles** Kribbeln nt; ~ **down** vt (fig: person): **to ~ sb down (to sth)** jdn (auf etw acc) festnageln

pinafore ['pɪnəfɔːr] n Schürze f; ~ **dress** n Kleiderrock m

pinball ['pɪnbɔːl] n Flipper m

pincers ['pɪnsəz] npl Kneif- or Beißzange f; (MED) Pinzette f

pinch [pɪntʃ] n Zwicken nt, Kneifen nt; (of salt) Prise f ♦ vt zwicken, kneifen; (inf: steal) klauen ♦ vi (shoe) drücken; **at a ~** notfalls, zur Not

pincushion ['pɪnkuʃən] n Nadelkissen nt

pine [paɪn] n (also: ~ **tree**) Kiefer f ♦ vi: **to ~ for** sich sehnen nach; ~ **away** vi sich zu Tode sehnen

pineapple ['paɪnæpl] n Ananas f

ping [pɪŋ] n Klingeln nt; ~**-pong** ® n Pingpong nt

pink [pɪŋk] *adj* rosa *inv* ♦ *n* Rosa *nt*; (*BOT*) Nelke *f*

pinnacle ['pɪnəkl] *n* Spitze *f*

PIN (number) *n* Geheimnummer *f*

pinpoint ['pɪnpɔɪnt] *vt* festlegen

pinstripe ['pɪnstraɪp] *n* Nadelstreifen *m*

pint [paɪnt] *n* Pint *nt* (*BRIT: inf: of beer*) große(s) Bier *nt*

pioneer [paɪə'nɪəʳ] *n* Pionier *m*; (*fig also*) Bahnbrecher *m*

pious ['paɪəs] *adj* fromm

pip [pɪp] *n* Kern *m*; **the ~s** *npl* (*BRIT: RAD*) das Zeitzeichen

pipe [paɪp] *n* (*smoking*) Pfeife *f*; (*tube*) Rohr *nt*; (*in house*) (Rohr)leitung *f* ♦ *vt* (*durch Rohre*) leiten; (*MUS*) blasen; **~s** *npl* (*also*: **bagpipes**) Dudelsack *m*; **~ down** *vi* (*be quiet*) die Luft anhalten; **~ cleaner** *n* Pfeifenreiniger *m*; **~ dream** *n* Luftschloss *nt*; **~line** *n* (*for oil*) Pipeline *f*; **~r** *n* Pfeifer *m*; (*bagpipes*) Dudelsackbläser *m*

piping ['paɪpɪŋ] *adv*: **~ hot** siedend heiß

pique ['piːk] *n* gekränkte(r) Stolz *m*

pirate ['paɪərət] *n* Pirat *m*, Seeräuber *m*; **~d** *adj*: **~d version** Raubkopie *f*; **~ radio** (*BRIT*) *n* Piratensender *m*

Pisces ['paɪsiːz] *n* Fische *pl*

piss [pɪs] (*inf*) *vi* pissen; **~ed** (*inf*) *adj* (*drunk*) voll

pistol ['pɪstl] *n* Pistole *f*

piston ['pɪstən] *n* Kolben *m*

pit [pɪt] *n* Grube *f*; (*THEAT*) Parterre *n*; (*orchestra* ~) Orchestergraben *m* ♦ *vt* (*mark with scars*) zerfressen; (*compare*): **to ~ sb against** sb jdn an jdm messen; **the ~s** *npl* (*MOTOR RACING*) die Boxen *pl*

pitch [pɪtʃ] *n* Wurf *m*; (*of trader*) Stand *m*; (*SPORT*) Spielfeld *nt*; (*MUS*) Tonlage *f*; (*substance*) Pech *nt* ♦ *vt* werfen; (*set up*) aufschlagen ♦ *vi* rollen; **to ~ a tent** ein Zelt aufbauen; **~black** *adj* pechschwarz; **~ed battle** *n* offene Schlacht *f*

piteous ['pɪtɪəs] *adj* kläglich, erbärmlich

pitfall ['pɪtfɔːl] *n* (*fig*) Falle *f*

pith [pɪθ] *n* Mark *nt*

pithy ['pɪθɪ] *adj* prägnant

pitiful ['pɪtɪful] *adj* (*deserving pity*) bedauernswert; (*contemptible*) jämmerlich

pitiless ['pɪtɪlɪs] *adj* erbarmungslos

pittance ['pɪtns] *n* Hungerlohn *m*

pity ['pɪtɪ] *n* (*sympathy*) Mitleid *nt* ♦ *vt* Mitleid haben mit; **what a ~!** wie schade!

pivot ['pɪvət] *n* Drehpunkt *m* ♦ *vi*: **to ~ (on)** sich drehen (um)

pizza ['piːtsə] *n* Pizza *f*

placard ['plækɑːd] *n* Plakat *nt*, Anschlag *m*

placate [plə'keɪt] *vt* beschwichtigen

place [pleɪs] *n* Platz *m*; (*spot*) Stelle *f*; (*town etc*) Ort *m* ♦ *vt* setzen, stellen, legen; (*order*) aufgeben; (*SPORT*) platzieren; (*identify*) unterbringen; **to take ~** stattfinden; **out of ~** nicht am rechten Platz; (*fig: remark*) unangebracht; **in the first ~** erstens; **to change ~s with sb** mit jdm den Platz tauschen; **to be ~d third** (*in race, exam*) auf den dritten Platz kommen

placid ['plæsɪd] *adj* gelassen, ruhig

plagiarism ['pleɪdʒjərɪzəm] *n* Plagiat *nt*

plague [pleɪg] *n* Pest *f*; (*fig*) Plage *f* ♦ *vt* plagen

plaice [pleɪs] *n* Scholle *f*

plaid [plæd] *n* Plaid *nt*

plain [pleɪn] *adj* (*clear*) klar, deutlich; (*simple*) einfach, schlicht; (*not beautiful*) alltäglich ♦ *n* Ebene *f*; **in ~ clothes** (*police*) in Zivil(kleidung); **~ chocolate** *n* Bitterschokolade *f*

plaintiff ['pleɪntɪf] *n* Kläger *m*

plaintive ['pleɪntɪv] *adj* wehleidig

plait [plæt] *n* Zopf *m* ♦ *vt* flechten

plan [plæn] *n* Plan *m* ♦ *vt, vi* planen; **according to ~** planmäßig; **to ~ to do sth** vorhaben, etw zu tun

plane [pleɪn] n Ebene f; (AVIAT) Flugzeug nt; (tool) Hobel m; (tree) Platane f

planet ['plænɪt] n Planet m

plank [plæŋk] n Brett nt

planning ['plænɪŋ] n Planung f; ~ **family** ~ Familienplanung f; ~ **permission** n Baugenehmigung f

plant [plɑːnt] n Pflanze f; (TECH) (Maschinen)anlage f; (factory) Fabrik f, Werk nt ♦ vt pflanzen; (set firmly) stellen; ~**ation** [plæn'teɪʃən] n Plantage f

plaque [plæk] n Gedenktafel f; (on teeth) (Zahn)belag m

plaster ['plɑːstə'] n Gips m; (in house) Verputz m; (BRIT: also: sticking ~) Pflaster nt; (for fracture: ~ of Paris) Gipsverband m ♦ vt gipsen; (hole) zugipsen; (ceiling) verputzen; (fig: with pictures etc) bekleben, vollkleben; ~**ed** (inf) adj besoffen; ~**er** n Gipser m

plastic ['plæstɪk] n Plastik nt or f ♦ adj (made of ~) Plastik-; (ART) plastisch, bildend; ~ **bag** n Plastiktüte f

plasticine ['plæstɪsiːn] ® n Plastilin nt

plastic surgery n plastische Chirurgie f

plate [pleɪt] n Teller m; (gold/silver ~) vergoldete(s)/versilberte(s) Tafelgeschirr nt; (in book) (Bild)tafel f

plateau ['plætəʊ] (pl ~s or ~x) n (GEOG) Plateau nt, Hochebene f

plateaux ['plætəʊz] npl of **plateau**

plate glass n Tafelglas nt

platform ['plætfɔːm] n (at meeting) Plattform f, Podium nt; (RAIL) Bahnsteig m; (POL) Parteiprogramm nt; ~ **ticket** n Bahnsteigkarte f

platinum ['plætɪnəm] n Platin nt

platoon [plə'tuːn] n (MIL) Zug m

platter ['plætə'] n Platte f

plausible ['plɔːzɪbl] adj (theory, excuse, statement) plausibel; (person) überzeugend

play [pleɪ] n (also TECH) Spiel nt; (THEAT) (Theater)stück nt ♦ vt spielen; (another team) spielen gegen ♦ vi spielen; **to ~ safe** auf Nummer sicher or Sicher ge-

hen; ~ **down** vt herunterspielen; ~ **up** vi (cause trouble) frech werden; (bad leg etc) wehtun ♦ vt (person) plagen; **to ~ up to sb** jdm flattieren; ~**acting** n Schauspielerei f; ~**er** n Spieler(in) m(f); ~**ful** adj spielerisch; ~**ground** n Spielplatz m; ~**group** n Kindergarten m; ~**ing card** n Spielkarte f; ~**ing field** n Sportplatz m; ~**mate** n Spielkamerad m; ~**-off** n (SPORT) Entscheidungsspiel nt; ~**pen** n Laufstall m; ~**school** n = playgroup; ~**thing** n Spielzeug nt; ~**time** n (kleine) Pause f; ~**wright** ['pleɪraɪt] n Theaterschriftsteller m

plc abbr (= public limited company) AG

plea [pliː] n Bitte f; (general appeal) Appell m; (JUR) Plädoyer nt; ~ **bargaining** n (LAW) Aushandeln der Strafe zwischen Staatsanwaltschaft und Verteidigung

plead [pliːd] vt (poverty) als Entschuldigung anführen; (JUR: sb's case) vertreten ♦ vi (beg) dringend bitten; (JUR) plädieren; **to ~ with sb** jdn dringend bitten

pleasant ['plɛznt] adj angenehm; ~**ries** npl (polite remarks) Nettigkeiten pl

please [pliːz] vt, vi (be agreeable to) gefallen +dat; ~! bitte!; ~ **yourself!** wie du willst!; ~**d** adj zufrieden; (glad): ~**d (about sth)** erfreut (über etw acc); ~**d to meet you** angenehm; **pleasing** ['pliːzɪŋ] adj erfreulich

pleasure ['plɛʒə'] n Freude f ♦ cpd Vergnügungs-; **"it's a ~"** "gern geschehen"

pleat [pliːt] n Falte f

plectrum ['plɛktrəm] n Plektron nt

pledge [plɛdʒ] n Pfand nt; (promise) Versprechen nt ♦ vt verpfänden; (promise) geloben, versprechen

plentiful ['plɛntɪful] adj reichlich

plenty ['plɛntɪ] n Fülle f, Überfluss m; ~ **of** eine Menge, viel

pleurisy ['pluərɪsɪ] n Rippenfellentzündung f

pliable ['plaɪəbl] *adj* biegsam; (*person*) beeinflussbar

pliers ['plaɪəz] *npl* (Kneif)zange *f*

plight [plaɪt] *n* (Not)lage *f*

plimsolls ['plɪmsəlz] (*BRIT*) *npl* Turnschuhe *pl*

plinth [plɪnθ] *n* Sockel *m*

P.L.O. *n abbr* (= *Palestine Liberation Organization*) PLO *f*

plod [plɒd] *vi* (*work*) sich abplagen; (*walk*) trotten

plonk [plɒŋk] *n* (*BRIT: inf: wine*) billige(r) Wein *m* ♦ *vt*: **to ~ sth down** etw hinknallen

plot [plɒt] *n* Komplott *nt*; (*story*) Handlung *f*; (*of land*) Grundstück *nt* ♦ *vt* markieren; (*curve*) zeichnen; (*movements*) nachzeichnen ♦ *vi* (*plan secretly*) sich verschwören

plough [plaʊ] (*US* **plow**) *n* Pflug *m* ♦ *vt* pflügen; **~ back** *vt* (*COMM*) wieder in das Geschäft stecken; **~ through** *vt fus* (*water*) durchpflügen; (*book*) sich kämpfen durch

plow [plaʊ] (*US*) = **plough**

ploy [plɔɪ] *n* Masche *f*

pluck [plʌk] *vt* (*fruit*) pflücken; (*guitar*) zupfen; (*goose etc*) rupfen ♦ *n* Mut *m*; **to ~ up courage** all seinen Mut zusammennehmen

plug [plʌg] *n* Stöpsel *m*; (*ELEC*) Stecker *m*; (*inf: publicity*) Schleichwerbung *f*; (*AUT*) Zündkerze *f* ♦ *vt* (zu)stopfen; (*inf: advertise*) Reklame machen für; **~ in** *vt* (*ELEC*) anschließen

plum [plʌm] *n* Pflaume *f*, Zwetsch(g)e *f*

plumage ['pluːmɪdʒ] *n* Gefieder *nt*

plumber ['plʌmə*r*] *n* Klempner *m*, Installateur *m*; **plumbing** ['plʌmɪŋ] *n* (*craft*) Installieren *nt*; (*fittings*) Leitungen *pl*

plummet ['plʌmɪt] *vi* (ab)stürzen

plump [plʌmp] *adj* rundlich, füllig ♦ *vi* plumpsen lassen; **to ~ for** (*inf: choose*) sich entscheiden für

plunder ['plʌndə*r*] *n* Plünderung *f*;

(*loot*) Beute *f* ♦ *vt* plündern

plunge [plʌndʒ] *n* Sturz *m* ♦ *vt* stoßen ♦ *vi* (sich) stürzen; **to take the ~** den Sprung wagen; **plunging** ['plʌndʒɪŋ] *adj* (*neckline*) offenherzig

plural ['plʊərl] *n* Plural *m*, Mehrzahl *f*

plus [plʌs] *n* (*also:* **~ sign**) Plus(zeichen) *nt* ♦ *prep* plus, und; **ten/twenty ~** mehr als zehn/zwanzig

plush [plʌʃ] *adj* (*also:* **~-y:** *inf*) feudal

ply [plaɪ] *vt* (*trade*) (be)treiben; (*with questions*) zusetzen +*dat*; (*ship, taxi*) befahren ♦ *vi* (*ship, taxi*) verkehren ♦ *n*: **three-~** (*wool*) Dreifach-; **to ~ sb with drink** jdn zum Trinken animieren; **~wood** *n* Sperrholz *nt*

P.M. *n abbr* = **prime minister**

p.m. *adv abbr* (= *post meridiem*) nachmittags

pneumatic drill *n* Presslufthammer *m*

pneumonia [njuː'məʊnɪə] *n* Lungenentzündung *f*

poach [pəʊtʃ] *vt* (*COOK*) pochieren; (*game*) stehlen ♦ *vi* (*steal*) wildern; **~ed** *adj* (*egg*) verloren; **~er** *n* Wilddieb *m*

P.O. Box *n abbr* = **Post Office Box**

pocket ['pɒkɪt] *n* Tasche *f*; (*of resistance*) (Widerstands)nest *nt* ♦ *vt* einstecken; **to be out of ~** (*BRIT*) draufzahlen; **~book** *n* Taschenbuch *nt*; **~ calculator** *n* Taschenrechner *m*; **~ knife** *n* Taschenmesser *nt*; **~ money** *n* Taschengeld *nt*

pod [pɒd] *n* Hülse *f*; (*of peas also*) Schote *f*

podgy ['pɒdʒɪ] *adj* pummelig

podiatrist [pɒ'diːətrɪst] (*US*) *n* Fußpfleger(in) *m(f)*

poem ['pəʊɪm] *n* Gedicht *nt*

poet ['pəʊɪt] *n* Dichter *m*, Poet *m*; **~ic** [pəʊ'etɪk] *adj* poetisch, dichterisch; **~ laureate** *n* Hofdichter *m*; **~ry** *n* Poesie *f*; (*poems*) Gedichte *pl*

poignant ['pɔɪnjənt] *adj* (*touching*) ergreifend

point [pɔɪnt] *n* (*also in discussion, scoring*) Punkt *m*; (*spot*) Punkt *m*, Stelle *f*;

(*sharpened tip*) Spitze f; (*moment*) (Zeit)punkt m; (*purpose*) Zweck m; (*idea*) Argument nt; (*decimal*) Dezimalstelle f; (*personal characteristic*) Seite f ♦ vt zeigen mit; (*gun*) richten ♦ vi zeigen; ~s npl (*RAIL*) Weichen pl; **to be on the ~ of doing sth** drauf und dran sein, etw zu tun; **to make a ~ of sth** Wert darauf legen; **to get the ~** verstehen, worum es geht; **to come to the ~** zur Sache kommen; **there's no ~ (in doing sth)** es hat keinen Sinn(, etw zu tun); **~ out** vt hinweisen auf +acc; **~ to** vt fus zeigen auf +acc; **~-blank** adv (*at close range*) aus nächster Entfernung; (*bluntly*) unverblümt; **~ed** adj (*also fig*) spitz, scharf; **~edly** adv (*fig*) spitz; **~er** n Zeigestock m; (*on dial*) Zeiger m; **~less** adj sinnlos; **~ of view** Stand- or Gesichtspunkt m

poise [pɔɪz] n Haltung f; (*fig*) Gelassenheit f

poison ['pɔɪzn] n (*also fig*) Gift nt ♦ vt vergiften; **~ing** n Vergiftung f; **~ous** adj giftig, Gift-

poke [pəuk] vt stoßen; (*put*) stecken; (*fire*) schüren; (*hole*) bohren; **~ about** vi herumstochern; (*nose around*) herumwühlen

poker ['pəukər] n Schürhaken m; (*CARDS*) Poker nt

poky ['pəukɪ] adj eng

Poland ['pəulənd] n Polen nt

polar ['pəulər] adj Polar-, polar; **~ bear** n Eisbär m

Pole [pəul] n Pole m, Polin f

pole [pəul] n Stange f, Pfosten m; (*flagpole, telegraph ~*) Stange f, Mast m; (*ELEC, GEOG*) Pol m; (*SPORT: vaulting ~*) Stab m; (*ski ~*) Stock m; **~ bean** (*US*) n (*runner bean*) Stangenbohne f; **~ vault** n Stabhochsprung m

police [pə'liːs] n Polizei f ♦ vt kontrollieren; **~ car** n Polizeiwagen m; **~man** (*irreg*) n Polizist m; **~ state** n Polizeistaat m; **~ station** n (Polizei)revier nt, Wache f; **~woman** (*irreg*) n Polizistin f

policy ['pɒlɪsɪ] n Politik f; (*insurance*) (Versicherungs)police f

polio ['pəulɪəu] n (*spinale*) Kinderlähmung f, Polio f

Polish ['pəulɪʃ] adj polnisch ♦ n (*LING*) Polnisch nt

polish ['pɒlɪʃ] n Politur f; (*for floor*) Wachs nt; (*for shoes*) Creme f; (*for nails*) Lack m; (*shine*) Glanz m; (*of furniture*) Politur f; (*fig*) Schliff m ♦ vt polieren; (*shoes*) putzen; (*fig*) den letzten Schliff geben +dat; **~ off** vt (*inf: food*) wegputzen; (*: drink*) hinunterschütten; **~ed** adj glänzend; (*manners*) verfeinert

polite [pə'laɪt] adj höflich; **~ly** adv höflich; **~ness** n Höflichkeit f

politic: **~al** [pə'lɪtɪkl] adj politisch; **~ally** [pə'lɪtɪklɪ] adv politisch; **~ally correct** politisch korrekt; **~ian** [pɒlɪ'tɪʃən] n Politiker m; **~s** npl Politik f

polka dot ['pɒlkə-] n Tupfen m

poll [pəul] n Abstimmung f; (*in election*) Wahl f; (*votes cast*) Wahlbeteiligung f; (*opinion ~*) Umfrage f ♦ vt (*votes*) erhalten

pollen ['pɒlən] n (*BOT*) Blütenstaub m, Pollen m

polling ['pəulɪŋ-]: **~ booth** (*BRIT*) n Wahlkabine f; **~ day** (*BRIT*) n Wahltag m; **~ station** (*BRIT*) n Wahllokal nt

pollute [pə'luːt] vt verschmutzen, verunreinigen; **~d** adj verschmutzt; **pollution** [pə'luːʃən] n Verschmutzung f

polo ['pəuləu] n Polo nt; **~ neck** n (*also: ~-necked sweater*) Rollkragen m; Rollkragenpullover m; **~ shirt** n Polohemd nt

polystyrene [pɒlɪ'staɪriːn] n Styropor nt

polytechnic [pɒlɪ'teknɪk] n technische Hochschule f

polythene ['pɒlɪθiːn] n Plastik nt; **~ bag** n Plastiktüte f

pomegranate ['pɒmɪgrænɪt] n Granatapfel m

pompom ['pɒmpɒm] n Troddel f, Pompon m

pompous ['pɔmpəs] *adj* aufgeblasen; (*language*) geschwollen

pond [pɔnd] *n* Teich *m*, Weiher *m*

ponder ['pɔndə] *vt* nachdenken über *+acc*; **~ous** *adj* schwerfällig

pong [pɔŋ] (*BRIT: inf*) *n* Mief *m*

pontiff ['pɔntɪf] *n* Pontifex *m*

pontoon [pɔn'tuːn] *n* Ponton *m*; (*CARDS*) 17-und-4 *nt*

pony ['pəunɪ] *n* Pony *nt*; **~tail** *n* Pferdeschwanz *m*; **~ trekking** (*BRIT*) *n* Ponyreiten *nt*

poodle ['puːdl] *n* Pudel *m*

pool [puːl] *n* (*swimming ~*) Schwimmbad *nt*; (*: private*) Swimmingpool *m*; (*of liquid, blood*) Lache *f*; (*fund*) (gemeinsame) Kasse *f*; (*billiards*) Poolspiele *nt* ♦ *vt* (*money etc*) zusammenlegen; (*football*) **~s** Toto *nt*

poor [puə] *adj* arm; (*not good*) schlecht ♦ *npl*: **the ~** die Armen *pl*; **~ in** (*resources*) arm an *+dat*; **~ly** *adv* schlecht; (*dressed*) ärmlich ♦ *adj* schlecht

pop [pɔp] *n* Knall *m*; (*music*) Popmusik *f*; (*drink*) Limo(nade) *f*; (*us: inf*) Pa *m* ♦ *vt* (*put*) stecken; (*balloon*) platzen lassen ♦ *vi* knallen; **~ in** *vi* kurz vorbeigehen or vorbeikommen; **~ out** *vi* (*person*) kurz rausgehen; (*thing*) herausspringen; **~ up** *vi* auftauchen; **~corn** *n* Puffmais *m*

pope [pəup] *n* Papst *m*

poplar ['pɔplə] *n* Pappel *f*

poppy ['pɔpɪ] *n* Mohn *m*

Popsicle ['pɔpsɪkl] (® *US*) *n* (*ice lolly*) Eis *nt* am Stiel

populace ['pɔpjuləs] *n* Volk *nt*

popular ['pɔpjulə] *adj* beliebt, populär; (*of the people*) volkstümlich; (*widespread*) allgemein; **~ity** [pɔpju'lærɪtɪ] *n* Beliebtheit *f*, Popularität *f*; **~ly** *adv* allgemein, überall

population [pɔpju'leɪʃən] *n* Bevölkerung *f*; (*of town*) Einwohner *pl*

populous ['pɔpjuləs] *adj* dicht besiedelt

porcelain ['pɔːslɪn] *n* Porzellan *nt*

porch [pɔːtʃ] *n* Vorbau *m*, Veranda *f*

porcupine ['pɔːkjupaɪn] *n* Stachelschwein *nt*

pore [pɔː] *n* Pore *f* ♦ *vi*: **to ~ over** brüten über *+dat*

pork [pɔːk] *n* Schweinefleisch *nt*

porn [pɔːn] *n* Porno *m*; **~ographic** [pɔːnə'græfɪk] *adj* pornografisch; **~ography** [pɔː'nɔgrəfɪ] *n* Pornografie *f*

porous ['pɔːrəs] *adj* porös; (*skin*) porig

porpoise ['pɔːpəs] *n* Tümmler *m*

porridge ['pɔrɪdʒ] *n* Haferbrei *m*

port [pɔːt] *n* Hafen *m*; (*town*) Hafenstadt *f*; (*NAUT: left side*) Backbord *nt*; (*wine*) Portwein *m*; **~ of call** Anlaufhafen *m*

portable ['pɔːtəbl] *adj* tragbar

porter ['pɔːtə] *n* Pförtner(in) *m(f)*; (*for luggage*) (Gepäck)träger *m*

portfolio [pɔːt'fəulɪəu] *n* (*case*) Mappe *f*; (*POL*) Geschäftsbereich *m*; (*FIN*) Portefeuille *nt*; (*of artist*) Kollektion *f*

porthole ['pɔːthəul] *n* Bullauge *nt*

portion ['pɔːʃən] *n* Teil *m*, Stück *nt*; (*of food*) Portion *f*

portrait ['pɔːtreɪt] *n* Porträt *nt*

portray [pɔː'treɪ] *vt* darstellen; **~al** *n* Darstellung *f*

Portugal ['pɔːtjugl] *n* Portugal *nt*

Portuguese [pɔːtju'giːz] *adj* portugiesisch ♦ *n inv* Portugiese *m*, Portugiesin *f*; (*LING*) Portugiesisch *nt*

pose [pəuz] *n* Stellung *f*, Pose *f*; (*affectation*) Pose *f* ♦ *vi* posieren ♦ *vt* stellen

posh [pɔʃ] (*inf*) *adj* (piek)fein

position [pə'zɪʃən] *n* Stellung *f*; (*place*) Lage *f*; (*job*) Stelle *f*; (*attitude*) Standpunkt *m* ♦ *vt* aufstellen

positive ['pɔzɪtɪv] *adj* positiv; (*convinced*) sicher; (*definite*) eindeutig

posse ['pɔsɪ] (*US*) *n* Aufgebot *nt*

possess [pə'zes] *vt* besitzen; **~ion** [pə'zeʃən] *n* Besitz *m*; **~ive** *adj* besitzergreifend, eigensüchtig

possibility [pɔsɪ'bɪlɪtɪ] *n* Möglichkeit *f*

possible ['pɔsɪbl] *adj* möglich; **as big**

as ~ so groß wie möglich, möglichst groß; **possibly** adv möglicherweise, vielleicht; **I cannot possibly come** ich kann unmöglich kommen

post [pəʊst] n (BRIT: letters, delivery) Post f; (pole) Pfosten m, Pfahl m; (place of duty) Posten m; (job) Stelle f ♦ vt (notice) anschlagen; (BRIT: letters) aufgeben; (: appoint) versetzen; (soldiers) aufstellen; **I am at my** ~ Postgebühr f, Porto nt; **~al** adj Post-; **~al order** n Postanweisung f; **~box** (BRIT) n Briefkasten m; **~card** n Postkarte f; **~code** (BRIT) n Postleitzahl f

postdate ['pəʊst'deɪt] vt (cheque) nachdatieren

poster ['pəʊstə*] n Plakat nt, Poster nt

poste restante [pəʊst'restɑːnt] n Aufbewahrungsstelle f für postlagernde Sendungen

posterior [pɒs'tɪərɪə*] n Hintern m

posterity [pɒs'terɪtɪ] n Nachwelt f

postgraduate ['pəʊst'grædjʊət] n Weiterstudierende(r) mf

posthumous ['pɒstjʊməs] adj post(h)um

postman ['pəʊstmən] (irreg) n Briefträger m

postmark ['pəʊstmɑːk] n Poststempel m

post-mortem [pəʊst'mɔːtəm] n Autopsie f

post office n Postamt nt, Post f; (organization) Post f; **Post Office Box** n Postfach nt

postpone [pəʊs'pəʊn] vt verschieben

postscript ['pəʊstskrɪpt] n Postskript nt; (to affair) Nachspiel nt

posture ['pɒstʃə*] n Haltung f ♦ vi posieren

postwar ['pəʊst'wɔː*] adj Nachkriegs-

postwoman ['pəʊstwʊmən] (irreg) n Briefträgerin f

posy ['pəʊzɪ] n Blumenstrauß m

pot [pɒt] n Topf m; (teapot) Kanne f; (inf: marijuana) Hasch m ♦ vt (plant) eintopfen; **to go to** ~ (inf: work) auf

den Hund kommen

potato [pə'teɪtəʊ] (pl **~es**) n Kartoffel f; **~ peeler** n Kartoffelschäler m

potent ['pəʊtnt] adj stark; (argument) zwingend

potential [pə'tenʃl] adj potenziell, potentiell ♦ n Potenzial nt, Potential nt; **~ly** adv potenziell, potentiell

pothole ['pɒthəʊl] n (in road) Schlagloch nt; (: underground) Höhle f; **potholing** (BRIT) n: **to go potholing** Höhlen erforschen

potion ['pəʊʃən] n Trank m

potluck [pɒt'lʌk] n: **to take** ~ **with sth** etw auf gut Glück nehmen

pot plant n Topfpflanze f

potter ['pɒtə*] n Töpfer m ♦ vi herumhantieren; **~y** n Töpferwaren pl; (place) Töpferei f

potty ['pɒtɪ] adj (inf: mad) verrückt ♦ n Töpfchen nt

pouch [paʊtʃ] n Beutel m

pouf(fe) [puːf] n Sitzkissen nt

poultry ['pəʊltrɪ] n Geflügel nt

pounce [paʊns] vi sich stürzen ♦ n Sprung m, Satz m; **to** ~ **on** sich stürzen auf +acc

pound [paʊnd] n (FIN, weight) Pfund nt; (for cars, animals) Auslösestelle f ♦ vt (zer)stampfen ♦ vi klopfen, hämmern; ~ **sterling** n Pfund Sterling nt

pour [pɔː*] vt gießen, schütten ♦ vi gießen; (crowds etc) strömen; ~ **away** vt abgießen; ~ **in** vi (people) hereinströmen; ~ **off** vt abgießen; ~ **out** vi (people) herausströmen ♦ vt (drink) einschenken; **~ing** adj: **~ing rain** n strömende(r) Regen m

pout [paʊt] vi schmollen

poverty ['pɒvətɪ] n Armut f; **~-stricken** adj verarmt, sehr arm

powder ['paʊdə*] n Pulver nt; (cosmetic) Puder m ♦ vt pulverisieren; **to** ~ **one's nose** sich zur die Nase pudern; ~ **compact** n Puderdose f; **~ed milk** n Milchpulver nt; ~ **room** n Damentoilette f; **~y** adj pulverig

power ['pauə'] n (also POL) Macht f; (ability) Fähigkeit f; (strength) Stärke f; (MATH) Potenz f; (ELEC) Strom m ♦ vt betreiben, antreiben; **to be in ~** (POL etc) an der Macht sein; **~ cut** n Stromausfall m; **~ed** adj: **~ed by** betrieben mit; **~ failure** (US) n Stromausfall m; **~ful** adj (person) mächtig; (engine, government) stark; **~less** adj machtlos; **~ point** (BRIT) n elektrische(r) Anschluss m; **~ station** n Elektrizitätswerk nt; **~ struggle** n Machtkampf m

p.p. abbr (= per procurationem): **p.p.** J. Smith i. A. J. Smith

PR n abbr = **public relations**

practicable ['præktɪkəbl] adj durchführbar

practical ['præktɪkl] adj praktisch; **~ity** [præktɪ'kælɪtɪ] n (of person) praktische Veranlagung f; (of situation etc) Durchführbarkeit f; **~ joke** n Streich m; **~ly** adv praktisch

practice ['præktɪs] n Übung f; (reality, also of doctor, lawyer) Praxis f; (custom) Brauch m; (in business) Usus m ♦ vt, vi (US) = **practise**; **in ~** (in reality) in der Praxis; **out of ~** außer Übung; **practicing** (US) adj = **practising**

practise ['præktɪs] (US **practice**) vt üben; (profession) ausüben ♦ vi (sich) üben; (doctor, lawyer) praktizieren; **practising** (US **practicing**) adj praktizierend; (Christian etc) aktiv

practitioner [præk'tɪʃənə'] n praktische(r) Arzt m, praktische Ärztin f

pragmatic [præg'mætɪk] adj pragmatisch

prairie ['prɛərɪ] n Prärie f, Steppe f

praise [preɪz] n Lob nt ♦ vt loben; **~worthy** adj lobenswert

pram [præm] (BRIT) n Kinderwagen m

prance [prɑːns] vi (horse) tänzeln; (person) stolzieren

prank [præŋk] n Streich m

prawn [prɔːn] n Garnele f, Krabbe f; **~ cocktail** n Krabbencocktail m

pray [preɪ] vi beten; **~er** [prɛə'] n Ge-

bet nt

preach [priːtʃ] vi predigen; **~er** n Prediger m

preamble [prɪˈæmbl] n Einleitung f

precarious [prɪˈkɛərɪəs] adj prekär, unsicher

precaution [prɪˈkɔːʃən] n (Vorsichts-) maßnahme f

precede [prɪˈsiːd] vi vorausgehen ♦ vt vorausgehen +dat; **~nce** ['presɪdəns] n Vorrang m; **~nt** ['presɪdənt] n Präzedenzfall m; **preceding** [prɪˈsiːdɪŋ] adj vorhergehend

precinct ['priːsɪŋkt] n (US: district) Bezirk m; **~s** npl (round building) Gelände nt; (area, environs) Umgebung f; **pedestrian ~** Fußgängerzone f; **shopping ~** Geschäftsviertel nt

precious ['preʃəs] adj kostbar, wertvoll; (affected) pretiös, preziös, geziert

precipice ['presɪpɪs] n Abgrund m

precipitate [adj prɪˈsɪpɪtɪt, vb prɪˈsɪpɪteɪt] adj überstürzt, übereilt ♦ vt hinunterstürzen; (events) heraufbeschwören

precise [prɪˈsaɪs] adj genau, präzis; **~ly** adv genau, präzis

precision [prɪˈsɪʒən] n Präzision f

preclude [prɪˈkluːd] vt ausschließen

precocious [prɪˈkəʊʃəs] adj frühreif

preconceived [priːkənˈsiːvd] adj (idea) vorgefasst

precondition ['priːkənˈdɪʃən] n Vorbedingung f, Voraussetzung f

precursor [prɪˈkɜːsə'] n Vorläufer m

predator ['predətə'] n Raubtier nt

predecessor ['priːdɪsesə'] n Vorgänger m

predicament [prɪˈdɪkəmənt] n missliche Lage f

predict [prɪˈdɪkt] vt voraussagen; **~able** adj vorhersagbar; **~ion** [prɪˈdɪkʃən] n Voraussage f

predominantly [prɪˈdɒmɪnəntlɪ] adv überwiegend, hauptsächlich

predominate [prɪˈdɒmɪneɪt] vi vorherrschen; (fig) vorherrschen, überwiegen

pre-eminent [prɪ'emɪnənt] adj hervorragend, herausragend

pre-empt [prɪ'emt] vt (action, decision) vorwegnehmen

preen [priːn] vt putzen; **to ~ o.s.** (person) sich brüsten

prefab ['priːfæb] n Fertighaus nt

preface ['prefəs] n Vorwort nt

prefect ['priːfekt] n Präfekt m; (SCH) Aufsichtsschüler(in) m(f)

prefer [prɪ'fɜː] vt vorziehen, lieber mögen; **to ~ to do sth** etw lieber tun; **~ably** ['prefrəblɪ] adv vorzugsweise, am liebsten; **~ence** ['prefrəns] n Präferenz f, Vorzug m; **~ential** [prefə'renʃəl] adj bevorzugt, Vorzugs-

prefix ['priːfɪks] n Vorsilbe f, Präfix nt

pregnancy ['pregnənsɪ] n Schwangerschaft f

pregnant ['pregnənt] adj schwanger

prehistoric ['priːhɪs'tɔrɪk] adj prähistorisch, vorgeschichtlich

prejudice ['predʒudɪs] n (bias) Voreingenommenheit f; (opinion) Vorurteil nt; (harm) Schaden m ♦ vt beeinträchtigen; **~d** adj (person) voreingenommen

preliminary [prɪ'lɪmɪnərɪ] adj einleitend, Vor-

prelude ['preljuːd] n Vorspiel nt; (fig) Auftakt m

premarital ['priː'mærɪtl] adj vorehelich

premature ['prematʃuə] adj vorzeitig, verfrüht; (birth) Früh-

premeditated [priː'medɪteɪtɪd] adj geplant; (murder) vorsätzlich

premenstrual syndrome [priː'menstruəl-] n prämenstruelles Syndrom nt

premier ['premɪə] adj erste(r, s) ♦ n Premier m

première [premɪeə] n Premiere f; Uraufführung f

Premier League [-liːg] n ≈ 1. Bundesliga (höchste Spielklasse im Fußball)

premise ['premɪs] n Voraussetzung f,

Prämisse f; **~s** npl (shop) Räumlichkeiten pl; (grounds) Gelände nt; **on the ~s** im Hause

premium ['priːmɪəm] n Prämie f; **to be at a ~** über pari stehen; **~ bond** (BRIT) n Prämienanleihe f

premonition [premə'nɪʃən] n Vorahnung f

preoccupation [priːˌɔkjuˈpeɪʃən] n Sorge f

preoccupied [priː'ɔkjupaɪd] adj (look) geistesabwesend

prep [prep] n (SCH) Hausaufgabe f

prepaid [priː'peɪd] adj vorausbezahlt; (letter) frankiert

preparation [prepə'reɪʃən] n Vorbereitung f

preparatory [prɪ'pærətərɪ] adj Vor(bereitungs)-; **~ school** n (BRIT) private Vorbereitungsschule für die Public School; (US) private Vorbereitungsschule für die Hochschule

prepare [prɪ'peə] vt vorbereiten ♦ vi sich vorbereiten; **to ~ for/prepare sth for** sich/etw vorbereiten auf +acc; **to be ~d to ...** bereit sein zu ...

preponderance [prɪ'pɔndərns] n Übergewicht nt

preposition [prepə'zɪʃən] n Präposition f, Verhältniswort nt

preposterous [prɪ'pɔstərəs] adj absurd

prep school n = preparatory school

prerequisite [priː'rekwɪzɪt] n (unerlässliche) Voraussetzung f

prerogative [prɪ'rɔgətɪv] n Vorrecht nt

Presbyterian [prezbɪ'tɪərɪən] adj presbyterianisch ♦ n Presbyterier(in) m(f)

preschool ['priː'skuːl] adj Vorschul-

prescribe [prɪ'skraɪb] vt vorschreiben; (MED) verschreiben

prescription [prɪ'skrɪpʃən] n (MED) Rezept nt

presence ['prezns] n Gegenwart f; **~ of mind** Geistesgegenwart f

present [adj, n 'preznt, vb prɪ'zent] adj (here) anwesend; (current) gegenwärtig ♦ n Gegenwart f; (gift) Geschenk *nt* ♦ *vt* vorlegen; *(introduce)* vorstellen; *(show)* zeigen; *(give)*: **to ~ sb with sth** jdm etw überreichen; **at ~ im Augenblick; to give sb a ~** jdm ein Geschenk machen; **~able** [prɪˈzentəbl] *adj* präsentabel; **~ation** [prezn̩ˈteɪʃən] *n* Überreichung *f*; **~-day** *adj* heutig; **~er** [prɪˈzentə*] *n (RAD, TV)* Moderator(in) *m(f)*; **~ly** *adv* bald; *(at ~)* im Augenblick

preservation [prezəˈveɪʃən] *n* Erhaltung *f*

preservative [prɪˈzɜːvətɪv] *n* Konservierungsmittel *nt*

preserve [prɪˈzɜːv] *vt* erhalten; *(food)* einmachen ♦ *n (jam)* Eingemachte(s) *nt*; *(reserve)* Schutzgebiet *nt*

preside [prɪˈzaɪd] *vi* den Vorsitz haben

president [ˈprezɪdənt] *n* Präsident *m*; **~ial** [prezɪˈdenʃl] *adj* Präsidenten-; *(election)* Präsidentschafts-; *(system)* Präsidial-

press [pres] *n* Presse *f*; *(printing house)* Druckerei *f* ♦ *vt* drücken; *(iron)* bügeln; *(urge)* (be)drängen ♦ *vi (push)* drücken; **to be ~ed for time** unter Zeitdruck stehen; **to ~ for sth** drängen auf etw *acc*; **~ on** *vi* vorwärts drängen; **~ agency** *n* Presseagentur *f*; **~ conference** *n* Pressekonferenz *f*; **~ed** *adj (clothes)* gebügelt; **~ing** *adj* dringend; **~ stud** *(BRIT)* *n* Druckknopf *m*; **~-up** *(BRIT)* *n* Liegestütz *m*

pressure [ˈpreʃə*] *n* Druck *m*; **~ cooker** *n* Schnellkochtopf *m*; **~ gauge** *n* Druckmesser *m*

pressurized [ˈpreʃəraɪzd] *adj* Druck-

prestige [presˈtiːʒ] *n* Prestige *nt*; **prestigious** [presˈtɪdʒəs] *adj* Prestige-

presumably [prɪˈzjuːməblɪ] *adv* vermutlich

presume [prɪˈzjuːm] *vt, vi* annehmen; **to ~ to do sth** sich erlauben, etw zu tun; **presumption** [prɪˈzʌmpʃən] *n* Annahme *f*; **presumptuous** [prɪˈzʌmpʃəs] *adj* anmaßend

pretence [prɪˈtens] *n (US* **pretense)** *n*

Vorgabe *f*, Vortäuschung *f*; *(false claim)* Vorwand *m*

pretend [prɪˈtend] *vt* vorgeben, so tun als ob ... ♦ *vi* so tun; **to ~ to sth** Anspruch erheben auf etw *acc*

pretense [prɪˈtens] *(US)* *n* = **pretence**

pretension [prɪˈtenʃən] *n* Anspruch *m*; *(impudent claim)* Anmaßung *f*

pretentious [prɪˈtenʃəs] *adj* angeberisch

pretext [ˈpriːtekst] *n* Vorwand *m*

pretty [ˈprɪtɪ] *adj* hübsch ♦ *adv (inf)* ganz schön

prevail [prɪˈveɪl] *vi* siegen; *(custom)* vorherrschen; **to ~ against** *or* **over** siegen über *+acc*; **to ~ (up)on sb to do sth** jdn dazu bewegen, etw zu tun; **~ing** *adj* vorherrschend

prevalent [ˈprevələnt] *adj* vorherrschend

prevent [prɪˈvent] *vt (stop)* verhindern, verhüten; **to ~ sb from doing sth** jdn (daran) hindern, etw zu tun; **~ative** *n* Vorbeugungsmittel *nt*; **~ion** [-ʃən] *n* Verhütung *f*; **~ive** *adj* vorbeugend, Schutz-

preview [ˈpriːvjuː] *n* private Voraufführung *f*; *(trailer)* Vorschau *f*

previous [ˈpriːvɪəs] *adj* früher, vorherig; **~ly** *adv* früher

prewar [priːˈwɔː*] *adj* Vorkriegs-

prey [preɪ] *n* Beute *f*; **~ on** *vt fus* Jagd machen auf *+acc*; **it was ~ing on his mind** es quälte sein Gewissen

price [praɪs] *n* Preis *m*; *(value)* Wert *m* ♦ *vt (label)* auszeichnen; **~less** *adj (also fig)* unbezahlbar; **~ list** *n* Preisliste *f*

prick [prɪk] *n* Stich *m* ♦ *vt, vi* stechen; **to ~ up one's ears** die Ohren spitzen

prickle [ˈprɪkl] *n* Stachel *m*, Dorn *m*

prickly [ˈprɪklɪ] *adj* stachelig; *(fig: person)* reizbar; **~ heat** *n* Hitzebläschen *pl*

pride [praɪd] *n* Stolz *m*; *(arrogance)* Hochmut *m* ♦ *vt*: **to ~ o.s. on sth** auf etw *acc* stolz sein

priest [priːst] *n* Priester *m*; **~hood** *n* Priesteramt *nt*

prim [prɪm] *adj* prüde

primarily ['praɪmərɪlɪ] *adv* vorwiegend

primary ['praɪmərɪ] *adj* (*main*) Haupt-; (*SCH*) Grund-; **~ school** (*BRIT*) *n* Grundschule *f*

prime [praɪm] *adj* erste(r, s); (*excellent*) erstklassig ♦ *vt* vorbereiten; (*gun*) laden; **in the ~ of life** in der Blüte der Jahre; **~ minister** *n* Premierminister *m*, Ministerpräsident *m*; **~r** ['praɪmə'] *n* Fibel *f*

primeval [praɪ'mi:vl] *adj* vorzeitlich; (*forests*) Ur-

primitive ['prɪmɪtɪv] *adj* primitiv

primrose ['prɪmrəuz] *n* (*gelbe*) Primel *f*

primus (stove) ['praɪməs] (®) *BRIT*) *n* Primuskocher *m*

prince [prɪns] *n* Prinz *m*; (*ruler*) Fürst *m*; **princess** [prɪn'ses] *n* Prinzessin *f*; Fürstin *f*

principal ['prɪnsɪpl] *adj* Haupt- ♦ *n* (*SCH*) (Schul)direktor *m*, Rektor *m*; (*money*) (Grund)kapital *nt*

principle ['prɪnsɪpl] *n* Grundsatz *m*, Prinzip *nt*; **in ~** im Prinzip; **on ~** aus Prinzip, prinzipiell

print [prɪnt] *n* Druck *m*; (*made by feet, fingers*) Abdruck *m*; (*PHOT*) Abzug *m* ♦ *vt* drucken; (*name*) in Druckbuchstaben schreiben; (*PHOT*) abziehen; **out of ~** vergriffen; **~ed matter** *n* Drucksache *f*; **~er** *n* Drucker *m*; **~ing** *n* Drucken *nt*; (*of photos*) Abziehen *nt*; **~out** *n* (*COMPUT*) Ausdruck *m*

prior ['praɪə'] *adj* früher ♦ *n* Prior *m*; **~ to sth** vor etw *dat*; **~ to going abroad, she had ...** bevor sie ins Ausland ging, hatte sie ...

priority [praɪ'ɒrɪtɪ] *n* Vorrang *m*; Priorität *f*

prise [praɪz] *vt*: **to ~ open** aufbrechen

prison ['prɪzn] *n* Gefängnis *nt* ♦ *adj* Gefängnis-; (*system etc*) Strafvollzugs-; **~er** *n* Gefangene(r) *mf*

pristine ['prɪstiːn] *adj* makellos

privacy ['prɪvəsɪ] *n* Ungestörtheit *f*,

Ruhe *f*; Privatleben *nt*

private ['praɪvɪt] *adj* privat, Privat-; (*secret*) vertraulich, geheim ♦ *n* einfache(r) Soldat *m*; **"~"** (*on envelope*) "persönlich"; (*on door*) "Privat"; **in ~** privat, unter vier Augen; **~ enterprise** *n* Privatunternehmen *nt*; **~ eye** *n* Privatdetektiv *m*; **~ property** *n* Privatbesitz *m*; **~ school** *n* Privatschule *f*; **privatize** *vt* privatisieren

privet ['prɪvɪt] *n* Liguster *m*

privilege ['prɪvɪlɪdʒ] *n* Privileg *nt*; **~d** *adj* bevorzugt, privilegiert

privy ['prɪvɪ] *adj* geheim, privat; **P~ Council** *n* Geheime(r) Staatsrat *m*

prize [praɪz] *n* Preis *m* ♦ *adj* (*example*) erstklassig; (*idiot*) Voll- ♦ *vt* (hoch)schätzen; **~-giving** *n* Preisverteilung *f*; **~winner** *n* Preisträger(in) *m(f)*

pro [prəu] *n* (*~fessional*) Profi *m*; **the ~s and cons** das Für und Wider

probability [prɒbə'bɪlɪtɪ] *n* Wahrscheinlichkeit *f*

probable ['prɒbəbl] *adj* wahrscheinlich; **probably** *adv* wahrscheinlich

probation [prə'beɪʃən] *n* Probe(zeit) *f*; (*JUR*) Bewährung *f*; **on ~** auf Probe; auf Bewährung

probe [prəub] *n* Sonde *f*; (*enquiry*) Untersuchung *f* ♦ *vt, vi* erforschen

problem ['prɒbləm] *n* Problem *nt*; **~atic** [prɒblə'mætɪk] *adj* problematisch

procedure [prə'siːdʒə'] *n* Verfahren *nt*

proceed [prə'siːd] *vi* (*advance*) vorrücken; (*start*) anfangen; (*carry on*) fortfahren; (*set about*) vorgehen; **~ings** *npl* Verfahren *nt*

proceeds ['prəusiːdz] *npl* Erlös *m*

process ['prəuses] *n* Prozess *m*; (*method*) Verfahren *nt* ♦ *vt* bearbeiten; (*food*) verarbeiten; (*film*) entwickeln; **~ing** *n* (*PHOT*) Entwickeln *nt*

procession [prə'seʃən] *n* Prozession *f*, Umzug *m*; **funeral ~** Trauerprozession *f*

pro-choice [prəʊ'tʃɔɪs] adj (movement) Pro-Abtreibungs-; ~ **campaigner** Abtreibungsbefürworter(in) m(f)

proclaim [prə'kleɪm] vt verkünden

procrastinate [prəʊ'kræstɪnɛt] vi zaudern

procure [prə'kjʊəʳ] vt beschaffen

prod [prɒd] vt stoßen ♦ n Stoß m

prodigal ['prɒdɪgl] adj: ~ **(with** or **of)** verschwenderisch (mit)

prodigy ['prɒdɪdʒɪ] n Wunder nt

produce [n 'prɒdjuːs, vb prə'djuːs] n (AGR) (Boden)produkte pl, (Natur)erzeugnis nt ♦ vt herstellen, produzieren; (cause) hervorrufen; (farmer) erzeugen; (yield) liefern, bringen; (play) inszenieren; ~**r** n Hersteller m, Produzent m (also CINE); Erzeuger m

product ['prɒdʌkt] n Produkt nt, Erzeugnis nt; ~**ion** [prə'dʌkʃən] n Produktion f, Herstellung f; (thing) Erzeugnis nt, Produkt nt; (THEAT) Inszenierung f; ~**ion line** n Fließband nt; ~**ive** [prə'dʌktɪv] adj produktiv; (fertile) ertragreich, fruchtbar

productivity [prɒdʌk'tɪvɪtɪ] n Produktivität f

profane [prə'feɪn] adj weltlich, profan; (language etc) gotteslästerlich

profess [prə'fes] vt bekennen; (show) zeigen; (claim to be) vorgeben

profession [prə'feʃən] n Beruf m; (declaration) Bekenntnis nt; ~**al** n Fachmann m; (SPORT) Berufsspieler(in) m(f) ♦ adj Berufs-; (expert) fachmännisch; (player) professionell; ~**ally** adv beruflich, fachmännisch

professor [prə'fesəʳ] n Professor m

proficiency [prə'fɪʃənsɪ] n Können nt

proficient [prə'fɪʃənt] adj fähig

profile ['prəʊfaɪl] n Profil nt; (fig: report) Kurzbiografie f

profit ['prɒfɪt] n Gewinn m ♦ vi: **to** ~ **(by** or **from)** profitieren (von); ~**ability** [prɒfɪtə'bɪlɪtɪ] n Rentabilität f; ~**able** adj einträglich, rentabel; ~**eering** [prɒfɪ'tɪərɪŋ] n Profitmacherei f

profound [prə'faʊnd] adj tief

profuse [prə'fjuːs] adj überreich; ~**ly** [prə'fjuːslɪ] adv überschwänglich; (sweat) reichlich; **profusion** [prə'fjuːʒən] n: **profusion (of)** Überfülle f (von), Überfluss m (an +dat)

program ['prəʊgræm] n (COMPUT) Programm nt ♦ vt (machine) programmieren; ~**me** (US **program**) n Programm nt ♦ vt planen; (computer) programmieren; ~**mer** (US **programer**) n Programmierer(in) m(f)

progress [n 'prəʊgres, vb prə'gres] n Fortschritt m ♦ vi fortschreiten, weitergehen; **in** ~ im Gang; ~**ion** [prə'greʃən] n Folge f; ~**ive** [prə'gresɪv] adj fortschrittlich, progressiv

prohibit [prə'hɪbɪt] vt verbieten; **to** ~ **sb from doing sth** jdm untersagen, etw zu tun; ~**ion** [prəʊɪ'bɪʃən] n Verbot nt; (US) Alkoholverbot nt, Prohibition f; ~**ive** adj unerschwinglich

project [n 'prɒdʒekt, vb prə'dʒekt] n Projekt nt ♦ vt vorausplanen; (film etc) projizieren; (personality, voice) zum Tragen bringen ♦ vi (stick out) hervorragen, (her)vorstehen

projectile [prə'dʒektaɪl] n Geschoss nt

projection [prə'dʒekʃən] n Projektion f; (sth prominent) Vorsprung m

projector [prə'dʒektəʳ] n Projektor m

proletariat [prəʊlɪ'tɛərɪət] n Proletariat nt

pro-life [prəʊ'laɪf] adj (movement) Anti-Abtreibungs-; ~ **campaigner** Abtreibungsgegner(in) m(f)

prolific [prə'lɪfɪk] adj fruchtbar; (author etc) produktiv

prologue ['prəʊlɒg] n Prolog m; (event) Vorspiel nt

prolong [prə'lɒŋ] vt verlängern

prom [prɒm] n abbr = **promenade**; **promenade concert**

Prom

Prom (promenade concert) ist in Großbritannien ein Konzert, bei dem

*ein Teil der Zuhörer steht (ur-
sprünglich spazieren ging). Die seit
1895 alljährlich stattfindenden Proms
(seit 1941 immer in der Londoner
Royal Albert Hall) zählen zu den be-
deutendsten Musikereignissen in England. Der letzte Abend der Proms steht
ganz im Zeichen des Patriotismus und
gipfelt im Singen des Lieds „Land of
Hope and Glory". In den USA und Kanada steht das Wort für* promenade*,
ein Ball an einer* High School *oder
einem* College.

promenade [prɒməˈnɑːd] *n* Promenade *f*; **~ concert** *n* Promenadenkonzert
nt

prominence [ˈprɒmɪnəns] *n* (große)
Bedeutung *f*

prominent [ˈprɒmɪnənt] *adj* bedeutend; (*politician*) prominent; (*easily
seen*) herausragend, auffallend

promiscuous [prəˈmɪskjuəs] *adj* lose

promise [ˈprɒmɪs] *n* Versprechen *nt*;
(*hope: ~ of sth*) Aussicht *f* auf etw acc
♦ *vt, vi* versprechen; **promising** *adj*
viel versprechend

promontory [ˈprɒməntrɪ] *n* Vorsprung
m

promote [prəˈməut] *vt* befördern;
(*help on*) fördern, unterstützen; **~r** *n*
(*in entertainment, sport*) Veranstalter *m*;
(*for charity etc*) Organisator *m*; **promotion** [prəˈməuʃən] *n* (*in rank*) Beförderung *f*; (*furtherance*) Förderung *f*;
(*COMM*): **promotion (of)** Werbung *f*
(*für*)

prompt [prɒmpt] *adj* prompt, schnell
♦ *adv* (*punctually*) genau ♦ *n* (*COMPUT*)
Meldung *f* ♦ *vt* veranlassen; (*THEAT*)
souflieren +*dat*; **to ~ sb to do sth** jdn
dazu veranlassen, etw zu tun; **~ly** *adv*
sofort

prone [prəun] *adj* hingestreckt; **to be ~
to sth** zu etw neigen

prong [prɒŋ] *n* Zinke *f*

pronoun [ˈprəunaun] *n* Fürwort *nt*

pronounce [prəˈnauns] *vt* aussprechen; (*JUR*) verkünden ♦ *vi*: **to ~ (on)**
sich äußern (zu)

pronunciation [prənʌnsɪˈeɪʃən] *n* Aussprache *f*

proof [pruːf] *n* Beweis *m*; (*PRINT*) Kor-
rekturfahne *f*; (*of alcohol*) Alkoholge-
halt *m* ♦ *adj* sicher

prop [prɒp] *n* (*also fig*) Stütze *f*; (*THEAT*)
Requisit *nt* ♦ *vt* (*also: ~ up*) (ab)stützen

propaganda [prɒpəˈgændə] *n* Propaganda *f*

propel [prəˈpel] *vt* (an)treiben; **~ler** *n*
Propeller *m*; **~ling pencil** (*BRIT*) *n*
Drehbleistift *m*

propensity [prəˈpensɪtɪ] *n* Tendenz *f*

proper [ˈprɒpər] *adj* richtig; (*seemly*)
schicklich; **~ly** *adv* richtig; **~ noun** *n*
Eigenname *m*

property [ˈprɒpətɪ] *n* Eigentum *nt*;
(*quality*) Eigenschaft *f*; (*land*) Grundbesitz *m*; **~ owner** *n* Grundbesitzer *m*

prophecy [ˈprɒfɪsɪ] *n* Prophezeiung *f*

prophesy [ˈprɒfɪsaɪ] *vt* prophezeien

prophet [ˈprɒfɪt] *n* Prophet *m*

proportion [prəˈpɔːʃən] *n* Verhältnis
nt; (*share*) Teil *m* ♦ *vt*: **to ~ (to)** abstimmen (auf +*acc*); **~al** *adj* proportional;
~ate *adj* verhältnismäßig

proposal [prəˈpəuzl] *n* Vorschlag *m*; (*of
marriage*) Heiratsantrag *m*

propose [prəˈpəuz] *vt* vorschlagen;
(*toast*) ausbringen ♦ *vi* (*offer marriage*)
einen Heiratsantrag machen; **to ~ to
do sth** beabsichtigen, etw zu tun

proposition [prɒpəˈzɪʃən] *n* Angebot
nt; (*statement*) Satz *m*

proprietor [prəˈpraɪətər] *n* Besitzer *m*,
Eigentümer *m*

propriety [prəˈpraɪətɪ] *n* Anstand *m*

pro rata [prəuˈrɑːtə] *adv* anteilmäßig

prose [prəuz] *n* Prosa *f*

prosecute [ˈprɒsɪkjuːt] *vt* (strafrecht-
lich) verfolgen; **prosecution** [prɒsɪ-
ˈkjuːʃən] *n* (*JUR*) strafrechtliche Verfolgung *f*; (*party*) Anklage *f*; **prosecutor**
n Vertreter *m* der Anklage; **Public**

Prosecutor Staatsanwalt *m*

prospect [*n* 'prɒspekt, *vb* prə'spekt] *n* Aussicht *f* ♦ *vt* auf Bodenschätze hin untersuchen ♦ *vi*: **to ~ (for)** suchen (nach); **~ing** ['prɒspektɪŋ] *n* (*for minerals*) Suche *f*; **~ive** [prə'spektɪv] *adj* (*son-in-law etc*) zukünftig; (*customer, candidate*) voraussichtlich

prospectus [prə'spektəs] *n* (Werbe)prospekt *m*

prosper ['prɒspər] *vi* blühen, gedeihen; (*person*) erfolgreich sein; **~ity** [prɒ'sperɪtɪ] *n* Wohlstand *m*; **~ous** *adj* wohlhabend, reich

prostitute ['prɒstɪtjuːt] *n* Prostituierte *f*

prostrate ['prɒstreɪt] *adj* ausgestreckt (liegend)

protagonist [prə'tægənɪst] *n* Hauptperson *f*, Held *m*

protect [prə'tekt] *vt* (be)schützen; **~ed species** *n* geschützte Art; **~ion** [prə'tekʃən] *n* Schutz *m*; **~ive** *adj* Schutz-, (be)schützend

protégé ['prəʊteʒeɪ] *n* Schützling *m*

protein ['prəʊtiːn] *n* Protein *nt*, Eiweiß *nt*

protest [*n* 'prəʊtest, *vb* prə'test] *n* Protest *m* ♦ *vi* protestieren ♦ *vt* (*affirm*) beteuern

Protestant ['prɒtɪstənt] *adj* protestantisch ♦ *n* Protestant(in) *m(f)*

protester [prə'testər] *n* (*demonstrator*) Demonstrant(in) *m(f)*

protracted [prə'træktɪd] *adj* sich hinziehend

protrude [prə'truːd] *vi* (her)vorstehen

proud [praʊd] *adj*: **~ (of)** stolz (auf +*acc*)

prove [pruːv] *vt* beweisen ♦ *vi*: **to ~ (to be) correct** sich als richtig erweisen; **to ~ o.s.** sich bewähren

proverb ['prɒvɜːb] *n* Sprichwort *nt*; **~ial** [prə'vɜːbɪəl] *adj* sprichwörtlich

provide [prə'vaɪd] *vt* versehen; (*supply*) besorgen; **to ~ sb with sth** jdn mit etw versorgen; **~ for** *vt fus* sorgen für; (*emergency*) Vorkehrungen treffen für;

~d (that) *conj* vorausgesetzt (, dass)

providing [prə'vaɪdɪŋ] *conj* vorausgesetzt (, dass)

province ['prɒvɪns] *n* Provinz *f*; (*division of work*) Bereich *m*; **provincial** [prə'vɪnʃəl] *adj* provinziell, Provinz-

provision [prə'vɪʒən] *n* Vorkehrung *f*; (*condition*) Bestimmung *f*; **~s** *npl* (*food*) Vorräte *pl*, Proviant *m*; **~al** *adj* provisorisch

proviso [prə'vaɪzəʊ] *n* Bedingung *f*

provocative [prə'vɒkətɪv] *adj* provozierend

provoke [prə'vəʊk] *vt* provozieren; (*cause*) hervorrufen

prowess ['praʊɪs] *n* überragende(s) Können *nt*

prowl [praʊl] *vi* herumstreichen; (*animal*) schleichen ♦ *n*: **on the ~** umherstreifend; **~er** *n* Herumtreiber(in) *m(f)*

proximity [prɒk'sɪmɪtɪ] *n* Nähe *f*

proxy ['prɒksɪ] *n* (Stell)vertreter *m*, (*authority, document*) Vollmacht *f*; **by ~** durch einen Stellvertreter

prudent ['pruːdənt] *adj* klug, umsichtig

prudish ['pruːdɪʃ] *adj* prüde

prune [pruːn] *n* Backpflaume *f* ♦ *vt* ausputzen; (*fig*) zurechtstutzen

pry [praɪ] *vi*: **to ~ (into)** seine Nase stecken (in +*acc*)

PS *n abbr* (= *postscript*) PS

pseudonym ['sjuːdənɪm] *n* Pseudonym *nt*, Deckname *m*

psychiatric [saɪkɪ'ætrɪk] *adj* psychiatrisch

psychiatrist [saɪ'kaɪətrɪst] *n* Psychiater *m*

psychic ['saɪkɪk] *adj* (*also:* **~al**) übersinnlich; (*person*) paranormal begabt

psychoanalyse [saɪkəʊ'ænəlaɪz] (*US* **psychoanalyze**) *vt* psychoanalytisch behandeln; **psychoanalyst** [saɪkəʊ'ænəlɪst] *n* Psychoanalytiker(in) *m(f)*

psychological [saɪkə'lɒdʒɪkl] *adj* psychologisch; **psychologist** [saɪ'kɒlədʒɪst] n Psychologe m, Psychologin f; **psychology** [saɪˈkɔlədʒɪ] n Psychologie f

PTO abbr = **please turn over**

pub [pʌb] n abbr (= **public house**) Kneipe f

Pub

Pub ist ein Gasthaus mit einer Lizenz zum Ausschank von alkoholischen Getränken. Ein Pub besteht meist aus verschiedenen gemütlichen (lounge, snug) oder einfacheren Räumen (public bar), in denen oft auch Spiele wie Darts, Domino und Poolbillard zur Verfügung stehen. In Pubs werden vor allem mittags oft auch Mahlzeiten angeboten. Pubs sind normalerweise von 11 bis 23 Uhr geöffnet, da manchmal nachmittags geschlossen.

---

pubic [ˈpjuːbɪk] adj Scham-
public [ˈpʌblɪk] adj öffentlich ♦ n (also: **general ~**) Öffentlichkeit f; **in ~** in der Öffentlichkeit; **~ address system** n Lautsprecheranlage f
publican [ˈpʌblɪkən] n Wirt m
publication [pʌblɪˈkeɪʃən] n Veröffentlichung f
public: **~ company** n Aktiengesellschaft f; **~ convenience** (BRIT) n öffentliche Toiletten pl; **~ holiday** n gesetzliche(r) Feiertag m; **~ house** (BRIT) n Lokal nt, Kneipe f
publicity [pʌbˈlɪsɪtɪ] n Publicity f, Werbung f
publicize [ˈpʌblɪsaɪz] vt bekannt machen; (advertise) Publicity machen für
publicly [ˈpʌblɪklɪ] adv öffentlich
public: **~ opinion** n öffentliche Meinung f; **~ relations** npl Publicrelations pl, Public Relations pl; **~ school** n (BRIT) Privatschule f; (US) staatliche Schule f; **~-spirited** adj mit Gemeinschaftssinn; **~ transport** n öffentliche Verkehrsmittel pl
publish [ˈpʌblɪʃ] vt veröffentlichen;

(event) bekannt geben; **~er** n Verleger m; **~ing** n (business) Verlagswesen nt
pub lunch n in Pubs servierter Imbiss
pucker [ˈpʌkəʳ] vt (face) verziehen; (lips) kräuseln
pudding [ˈpudɪŋ] n (BRIT: course) Nachtisch m; Pudding m; **black ~** ≃ Blutwurst f
puddle [ˈpʌdl] n Pfütze f
puff [pʌf] n (of wind etc) Stoß m; (cosmetic) Puderquaste f ♦ vt blasen, pusten; (pipe) paffen ♦ vi keuchen, schnaufen; (smoke) paffen; **to ~ out smoke** Rauch ausstoßen; **~ pastry** (US **~ paste**) n Blätterteig m; **~y** adj aufgedunsen
pull [pul] n Ruck m; (influence) Beziehung f ♦ vt ziehen; (trigger) abdrücken ♦ vi ziehen; **to ~ sb's leg** jdn auf den Arm nehmen; **to ~ to pieces** in Stücke reißen; (fig) verreißen; **to ~ one's punches** sich zurückhalten; **to ~ one's weight** sich in die Riemen legen; **to ~ o.s. together** sich zusammenreißen; **~ apart** vt (break) zerreißen; (dismantle) auseinander nehmen; (separate) trennen; **~ down** vt (house) abreißen; **~ in** vi hineinfahren; (stop) anhalten; (RAIL) einfahren; **~ off** vt (deal etc) abschließen; **~ out** vi (car) herausfahren; **~ out** vi (AUT) an die Seite fahren; (fig: partner) aussteigen ♦ vt he. heraušziehen; **~ over** vi (AUT) an die Seite fahren; **~ through** vi durchkommen; **~ up** vi anhalten ♦ vt (uproot) herausreißen; (stop) anhalten
pulley [ˈpulɪ] n Rolle f, Flaschenzug m
pullover [ˈpuləuvəʳ] n Pullover m
pulp [pʌlp] n Brei m; (of fruit) Fruchtfleisch nt
pulpit [ˈpulpɪt] n Kanzel f
pulsate [pʌlˈseɪt] vi pulsieren
pulse [pʌls] n Puls m; **~s** npl (BOT) Hülsenfrüchte pl
pummel [ˈpʌml] vt mit den Fäusten bearbeiten
pump [pʌmp] n Pumpe f; (shoe) leichter (Tanz)schuh m; vt pumpen; **~ up**

vt (tyre) aufpumpen

pumpkin ['pʌmpkɪn] n Kürbis m

pun [pʌn] n Wortspiel nt

punch [pʌntʃ] n (tool) Locher m; (blow) (Faust)schlag m; (drink) Punsch m, Bowle f ♦ vt lochen; (strike) schlagen, boxen; **~ line** n Pointe f; **~-up** (BRIT: inf) n Keilerei f

punctual ['pʌŋktjuəl] adj pünktlich

punctuate ['pʌŋktjuet] vt mit Satzzeichen versehen; (fig) unterbrechen; **punctuation** [pʌŋktju'eɪʃən] n Zeichensetzung f, Interpunktion f

puncture ['pʌŋktʃər] n Loch nt; (AUT) Reifenpanne f ♦ vt durchbohren

pundit ['pʌndɪt] n Gelehrte(r) m

pungent ['pʌndʒənt] adj scharf

punish ['pʌnɪʃ] vt bestrafen; (in boxing etc) übel zurichten; **~ment** n Strafe f; (action) Bestrafung f

punk [pʌŋk] n (also: **~ rocker**) Punker(in) m(f); (also: **~ rock**) Punk m; (US: inf: hoodlum) Ganove m

punt [pʌnt] n Stechkahn m

punter ['pʌntər] (BRIT) n (better) Wetter m

puny ['pjuːnɪ] adj kümmerlich

pup [pʌp] n = **puppy**

pupil ['pjuːpɪl] n Schüler(in) m(f); (in eye) Pupille f

puppet ['pʌpɪt] n Puppe f; Marionette f

puppy ['pʌpɪ] n junge(r) Hund m

purchase ['pɜːtʃɪs] n Kauf m; (grip) Halt m ♦ vt kaufen, erwerben; **~r** n Käufer(in) m(f)

pure [pjuər] adj (also fig) rein; **~ly** ['pjuəlɪ] adv rein

purgatory ['pɜːgətərɪ] n Fegefeuer nt

purge [pɜːdʒ] n (also POL) Säuberung f ♦ vt reinigen; (body) entschlacken

purify ['pjuərɪfaɪ] vt reinigen

purity ['pjuərɪtɪ] n Reinheit f

purple ['pɜːpl] adj violett; (face) dunkelrot

purport [pɜː'pɔːt] vi vorgeben

purpose ['pɜːpəs] n Zweck m, Ziel nt;

(of person) Absicht f; **on ~** absichtlich; **~ful** adj zielbewusst, entschlossen

purr [pɜːr] n Schnurren nt ♦ vi schnurren

purse [pɜːs] n Portemonnaie nt, Portmonee nt, Geldbeutel m ♦ vt (lips) zusammenpressen, schürzen

purser ['pɜːsər] n Zahlmeister m

pursue [pə'sjuː] vt verfolgen; (study) nachgehen +dat; **~r** n Verfolger m;

pursuit [pə'sjuːt] n Verfolgung f; (occupation) Beschäftigung f

pus [pʌs] n Eiter m

push [pʊʃ] n Stoß m, Schub m; (MIL) Vorstoß m ♦ vt stoßen, schieben; (button) drücken; (idea) durchsetzen ♦ vi stoßen, schieben; **~ aside** vt beiseite schieben; **~ off** (inf) vi abschieben; **~ on** vi weitermachen; **~ through** vt durchdrücken; (policy) durchsetzen; **~ up** vt (total) erhöhen; (prices) hoch treiben; **~chair** (BRIT) n (Kinder)sportwagen m; **~er** n (drug dealer) Pusher m; **~over** (inf) n Kinderspiel nt; **~-up** (US) n (press-up) Liegestütz m; **~y** (inf) adj aufdringlich

puss [pʊs] n Mieze(katze) f; **~y(cat)** n Mieze(katze) f

put [pʊt] (pt, pp **put**) vt setzen, stellen, legen; (express) ausdrücken, sagen; (write) schreiben; **~ about** vi (turn back) wenden ♦ vt (spread) verbreiten; **~ across** vt (explain) erklären; **~ away** vt weglegen; (store) beiseite legen; **~ back** vt zurückstellen or -legen; **~ by** vt zurücklegen, sparen; **~ down** vt hinstellen or -legen; (rebellion) niederschlagen; (animal) einschläfern; (in writing) niederschreiben; **~ forward** vt (idea) vorbringen; (clock) vorstellen; **~ in** vt (application, complaint) einreichen; **~ off** vt verschieben; (discourage): **to ~ sb off sth** jdn von etw abbringen; **~ on** vt (clothes etc) anziehen; (light etc) anschalten, anmachen; (play etc) aufführen; (brake) anziehen; **~ out** vt (hand etc) (her)ausstrecken;

(news, rumour) verbreiten; (light etc) ausschalten, ausmachen; **~ through** vt (TEL: person) verbinden; (: call) durchstellen; **~ up** vt (tent) aufstellen; (building) errichten; (price) erhöhen; (person) unterbringen; **~ up with** vt fus sich abfinden mit

putrid ['pju:trɪd] adj faul

putt [pʌt] vt (golf) putten ♦ n (golf) Putten nt; **~ing green** n kleine(r) Golfplatz m nur zum Putten

putty ['pʌtɪ] n Kitt m; (fig) Wachs nt

put-up ['pʊtʌp] adj: **~ job** abgekartete(s) Spiel nt

puzzle ['pʌzl] n Rätsel nt; (toy) Geduldspiel nt ♦ vt verwirren ♦ vi sich den Kopf zerbrechen; **~d** adj verdutzt, verblüfft; **puzzling** adj rätselhaft, verwirrend

pyjamas [pə'dʒɑːməz] (BRIT) npl Schlafanzug m, Pyjama m

pylon ['paɪlən] n Mast m

pyramid ['pɪrəmɪd] n Pyramide f

Q, q

quack [kwæk] n Quaken nt; (doctor) Quacksalber m ♦ vi quaken

quad [kwɔd] n abbr = **quadrangle; quadruplet**

quadrangle ['kwɔdræŋgl] n (court) Hof m; (MATH) Viereck nt

quadruple [kwɔ'druːpl] adj ♦ vi sich vervierfachen ♦ vt vervierfachen

quadruplets [kwɔ'druːplɪts] npl Vierlinge pl

quagmire ['kwægmaɪər] n Morast m

quail [kweɪl] n (bird) Wachtel f ♦ vi (vor Angst) zittern

quaint [kweɪnt] adj kurios; malerisch

quake [kweɪk] vi beben, zittern ♦ n abbr = **earthquake**

qualification [kwɔlɪfɪ'keɪʃən] n Qualifikation f; (sth which limits) Einschränkung f

qualified ['kwɔlɪfaɪd] adj (competent)

qualifiziert; (limited) bedingt

qualify ['kwɔlɪfaɪ] vt (prepare) befähigen; (limit) einschränken ♦ vi sich qualifizieren; **to ~ as a doctor/lawyer** sein medizinisches/juristisches Staatsexamen machen

quality ['kwɔlɪtɪ] n Qualität f; (characteristic) Eigenschaft f

> ## Quality press
>
> Quality press bezeichnet die seriösen Tages- und Wochenzeitungen, im Gegensatz zu den Massenblättern. Diese Zeitungen sind fast alle großformatig und wenden sich an den anspruchsvolleren Leser, der voll informiert sein möchte und bereit ist, für die Zeitungslektüre viel Zeit aufzuwenden. Siehe auch tabloid press.

quality time n intensiv genutzte Zeit

qualm [kwɑːm] n Bedenken nt

quandary ['kwɔndrɪ] n: **to be in a ~** in Verlegenheit sein

quantity ['kwɔntɪtɪ] n Menge f; **~ surveyor** n Baukostenkalkulator m

quarantine ['kwɔrəntiːn] n Quarantäne f

quarrel ['kwɔrl] n Streit m ♦ vi sich streiten; **~some** adj streitsüchtig

quarry ['kwɔrɪ] n Steinbruch m; (animal) Wild nt; (fig) Opfer nt

quarter ['kwɔːtər] n Viertel nt; (of year) Quartal nt ♦ vt (divide) vierteln; (MIL) einquartieren; **~s** npl (esp MIL) Quartier nt; **~ of an hour** Viertelstunde f; **~ final** n Viertelfinale nt; **~ly** adj vierteljährlich

quartet(te) [kwɔː'tet] n Quartett nt

quartz [kwɔːts] n Quarz m

quash [kwɔʃ] vt (verdict) aufheben

quaver ['kweɪvər] vi (tremble) zittern

quay [kiː] n Kai m

queasy ['kwiːzɪ] adj übel

queen [kwiːn] n Königin f; **~ mother** n Königinmutter f

queer [kwɪər] adj seltsam ♦ n (inf: ho-

mosexual) Schwule(r) *m*

quell [kwɛl] *vt* unterdrücken

quench [kwɛntʃ] *vt (thirst)* löschen

querulous ['kwɛrʊləs] *adj* nörglerisch

query ['kwɪərɪ] *n (question)* (An)frage *f;* *(question mark)* Fragezeichen *nt* ♦ *vt* in Zweifel ziehen, infrage *or* in Frage stellen

quest [kwɛst] *n* Suche *f*

question ['kwɛstʃən] *n* Frage *f* ♦ *vt (ask)* (be)fragen; *(suspect)* verhören; *(doubt)* infrage *or* in Frage stellen, bezweifeln; **beyond ~** ohne Frage; **out of the ~** ausgeschlossen; **~able** *adj* zweifelhaft; **~ mark** *n* Fragezeichen *nt*

questionnaire [kwɛstʃə'nɛəʳ] *n* Fragebogen *m*

queue [kjuː] *(BRIT) n* Schlange *f* ♦ *vi (also: ~ up)* Schlange stehen

quibble ['kwɪbl] *vi* kleinlich sein

quick [kwɪk] *adj* schnell ♦ *n (of nail)* Nagelhaut *f;* **be ~!** mach schnell!; **cut to the ~** *(fig)* tief getroffen; **~en** *vt (hasten)* beschleunigen ♦ *vi* sich beschleunigen; **~ly** *adv* schnell; **~sand** *n* Treibsand *m;* **~-witted** *adj* schlagfertig

quid [kwɪd] *(BRIT: inf) n* Pfund *nt*

quiet ['kwaɪət] *adj (without noise)* leise; *(peaceful, calm)* still, ruhig ♦ *n* Stille *f,* Ruhe *f* ♦ *vt, vi (US) =* **quieten;** **keep ~!** sei still!; **~en** *vt (also:* **~en down)** ruhig werden ♦ *vt* beruhigen; **~ly** *adv* leise, ruhig; **~ness** *n* Ruhe *f,* Stille *f*

quilt [kwɪlt] *n (continental ~)* Steppdecke *f*

quin [kwɪn] *n abbr =* **quintuplet**

quintuplets [kwɪn'tjuːplɪts] *npl* Fünflinge *pl*

quip [kwɪp] *n* witzige Bemerkung *f*

quirk [kwɜːk] *n (oddity)* Eigenart *f*

quit [kwɪt] *(pt, pp* **quit** *or* **quitted)** *vt* verlassen ♦ *vi* aufhören

quite [kwaɪt] *adv (completely)* ganz, völlig; *(fairly)* ziemlich; **~ a few of them** ziemlich viele von ihnen; **~ (so)!** richtig!

quits [kwɪts] *adj* quitt; **let's call it ~**

lassen wirs gut sein

quiver ['kwɪvəʳ] *vi* zittern ♦ *n (for arrows)* Köcher *m*

quiz [kwɪz] *n (competition)* Quiz *nt* ♦ *vt* prüfen; **~zical** *adj* fragend

quota ['kwəʊtə] *n* Anteil *m;* *(COMM)* Quote *f*

quotation [kwəʊ'teɪʃən] *n* Zitat *nt;* *(price)* Kostenvoranschlag *m;* **~ marks** *npl* Anführungszeichen *pl*

quote [kwəʊt] *n =* **quotation** ♦ *vi (from book)* zitieren ♦ *vt* zitieren; *(price)* angeben

R, r

rabbi ['ræbaɪ] *n* Rabbiner *m;* *(title)* Rabbi *m*

rabbit ['ræbɪt] *n* Kaninchen *nt;* **~ hole** *n* Kaninchenbau *m;* **~ hutch** *n* Kaninchenstall *m*

rabble ['ræbl] *n* Pöbel *m*

rabies ['reɪbiːz] *n* Tollwut *f*

RAC *(BRIT) n abbr =* **Royal Automobile Club**

raccoon [rə'kuːn] *n* Waschbär *m*

race [reɪs] *n (species)* Rasse *f;* *(competition)* Rennen *nt;* *(on foot)* Rennen *nt,* Wettlauf *m;* *(rush)* Hetze *f* ♦ *vt* um die Wette laufen mit; *(horses)* laufen lassen ♦ *vi (run)* rennen; *(in contest)* am Rennen teilnehmen; **~ car** *(US) n =* **racing car; ~ car driver** *(US) n =* **racing driver; ~course** *n (for horses)* Rennbahn *f;* **~horse** *n* Rennpferd *nt;* **~r** *n (person)* Rennfahrer(in) *m(f);* *(car)* Rennwagen *m;* **~track** *n (for cars etc)* Rennstrecke *f*

racial ['reɪʃl] *adj* Rassen-

racing ['reɪsɪŋ] *n* Rennen *nt;* **~ car** *(BRIT) n* Rennwagen *m;* **~ driver** *(BRIT) n* Rennfahrer *m*

racism ['reɪsɪzəm] *n* Rassismus *m;* **racist** ['reɪsɪst] *n* Rassist *m* ♦ *adj* rassistisch

rack [ræk] *n* Ständer *m,* Gestell *nt* ♦ *vt*

plagen; **to go to ~ and ruin** verfallen; **to ~ one's brains** sich *dat* den Kopf zerbrechen

racket ['rækɪt] n (*din*) Krach m; (*scheme*) (Schwindel)geschäft nt; (TENNIS) (Tennis)schläger m

racquet ['rækɪt] n (Tennis)schläger m

racy ['reɪsɪ] adj gewagt; (*style*) spritzig

radar ['reɪdɑ:ʳ] n Radar m or nt

radial ['reɪdɪəl] adj (*also*: US: **-ply**) radial

radiant ['reɪdɪənt] adj strahlend; (*giving out rays*) Strahlungs-

radiate ['reɪdɪeɪt] vi ausstrahlen; (*roads, lines*) strahlenförmig wegführen ♦ vt ausstrahlen; **radiation** [reɪdɪ'eɪʃən] n (Aus)strahlung f

radiator ['reɪdɪeɪtəʳ] n (*for heating*) Heizkörper m; (AUT) Kühler m

radical ['rædɪkl] adj radikal

radii ['reɪdɪaɪ] npl of **radius**

radio ['reɪdɪəu] n Rundfunk m, Radio nt; (*set*) Radio nt, Radioapparat m; **on the ~** im Radio; **~active** ['reɪdɪəu'æktɪv] adj radioaktiv; **~ cassette** n Radiorekorder m; **~-controlled** adj ferngesteuert; **~logy** [reɪdɪ'ɔlədʒɪ] n Strahlenkunde f; **~station** n Rundfunkstation f; **~therapy** ['reɪdɪəu'θerəpɪ] n Röntgentherapie f

radish ['rædɪʃ] n (*big*) Rettich m; (*small*) Radieschen nt

radius ['reɪdɪəs] n (*pl* **radii**) n Radius m; (*area*) Umkreis m

RAF n abbr = **Royal Air Force**

raffle ['ræfl] n Verlosung f, Tombola f ♦ vt verlosen

raft [rɑ:ft] n Floß m

rafter ['rɑ:ftəʳ] n Dachsparren m

rag [ræg] n (*cloth*) Lumpen m, Lappen m; (*inf*: *newspaper*) Käseblatt nt; (UNIV: *for charity*) studentische Sammelaktion f ♦ vt (BRIT) auf den Arm nehmen; **~s** npl (*cloth*) Lumpen pl; **~ doll** n Flickenpuppe f

rage [reɪdʒ] n Wut f; (*fashion*) große Mode f ♦ vi wüten, toben

ragged ['rægɪd] adj (*edge*) gezackt; (*clothes*) zerlumpt

raid [reɪd] n Überfall m; (MIL) Angriff m; (*by police*) Razzia f ♦ vt überfallen

rail [reɪl] n (*also*: RAIL) Schiene f; (*on stair*) Geländer nt or pl; (*of ship*) Reling f; **~s** npl (RAIL) Geleise pl; **by ~** per Bahn; **~ing(s)** n(pl) Geländer nt; **~road** (US) n Eisenbahn f; **~way** (BRIT) n Eisenbahn f; **~way line** (BRIT) n (Eisen)Bahnlinie f; (*track*) Gleis nt; **~wayman** (*irreg*; BRIT) n Eisenbahner m; **~way station** (BRIT) n Bahnhof m

rain [reɪn] n Regen m ♦ vt, vi regnen; **in the ~** im Regen; **it's ~ing** es regnet; **~bow** n Regenbogen m; **~coat** n Regenmantel m; **~drop** n Regentropfen m; **~fall** n Niederschlag m; **~forest** n Regenwald m; **~y** adj (*region, season*) Regen-; (*day*) regnerisch, verregnet

raise [reɪz] n (*esp* US: *increase*) (Gehalts)erhöhung f ♦ vt (*lift*) (hoch)heben; (*increase*) erhöhen; (*question*) aufwerfen; (*doubts*) äußern; (*funds*) beschaffen; (*family*) großziehen; (*livestock*) züchten; **to ~ one's voice** die Stimme erheben

raisin ['reɪzn] n Rosine f

rake [reɪk] n Rechen m, Harke f; (*person*) Wüstling m ♦ vt rechen, harken; (*search*) (durch)suchen

rally ['rælɪ] n (POL etc) Kundgebung f; (AUT) Rallye f ♦ vt (MIL) sammeln ♦ vi Kräfte sammeln; **~ round** vt fus (sich) scharen um; (*help*) zu Hilfe kommen +dat ♦ vi zu Hilfe kommen

RAM [ræm] n abbr (= *random access memory*) RAM m

ram [ræm] n Widder m ♦ vt (*hit*) rammen; (*stuff*) (hinein)stopfen

ramble ['ræmbl] n Wanderung f ♦ vi (*talk*) schwafeln; **~r** n Wanderer m; **rambling** adj (*speech*) weitschweifig; (*town*) ausgedehnt

ramp [ræmp] n Rampe f; **on/off ~** (US: AUT) Ein-/Ausfahrt f

rampage [ræm'peɪdʒ] n: **to be on the**

~ randalieren ♦ vi randalieren

rampant ['ræmpənt] adj wild wuchernd

rampart ['ræmpɑ:t] n (Schutz)wall m

ram raid n Raubüberfall, bei dem eine Geschäftsfront mit einem Fahrzeug gerammt wird

ramshackle ['ræmʃækl] adj baufällig

ran [ræn] pt of **run**

ranch [rɑ:ntʃ] n Ranch f

rancid ['rænsɪd] adj ranzig

rancour ['ræŋkəʳ] (US **rancor**) n Verbitterung f, Groll m

random ['rændəm] adj ziellos, wahllos ♦ n: **at ~** aufs Geratewohl; **~ access** n (COMPUT) wahlfreie(r) Zugriff m

randy ['rændɪ] (BRIT: inf) adj geil, scharf

rang [ræŋ] pt of **ring**

range [reɪndʒ] n Reihe f; (of mountains) Kette f; (COMM) Sortiment nt; (reach) (Reich)weite f; (of gun) Schussweite f; (for shooting practice) Schießplatz m; (stove) (großer) Herd m ♦ vt (set in row) anordnen, aufstellen; (roam) durchstreifen ♦ vi: **to ~ over** (wander) umherstreifen in +dat; (extend) sich erstrecken auf +acc; **a ~ of** (selection) eine (große) Auswahl an +dat; **prices ranging from £5 to £10** Preise, die sich zwischen £5 und £10 bewegen; **~r** ['reɪndʒəʳ] n Förster m

rank [ræŋk] n (row) Reihe f; (BRIT: also: **taxi ~**) (Taxi)stand m; (MIL) Rang m; (social position) Stand m ♦ vi (have ~): **to ~ among** gehören zu ♦ adj (strongsmelling) stinkend; (extreme) kraß; **the ~ and file** (fig) die breite Masse

rankle ['ræŋkl] vi nagen

ransack ['rænsæk] vt (plunder) plündern; (search) durchwühlen

ransom ['rænsəm] n Lösegeld nt; **to hold sb to ~** jdn gegen Lösegeld festhalten

rant [rænt] vi hochtrabend reden

rap [ræp] n Schlag m; (music) Rap m ♦ vt klopfen

rape [reɪp] n Vergewaltigung f; (BOT)

Raps m ♦ vt vergewaltigen; **~(seed) oil** n Rapsöl nt

rapid ['ræpɪd] adj rasch, schnell; **~ity** [rə'pɪdɪtɪ] n Schnelligkeit f; **~s** npl Stromschnellen pl

rapist ['reɪpɪst] n Vergewaltiger m

rapport [ræ'pɔ:ʳ] n gute(s) Verhältnis nt

rapture ['ræptʃəʳ] n Entzücken nt; **rapturous** ['ræptʃərəs] adj (applause) stürmisch; (expression) verzückt

rare [reəʳ] adj selten, rar; (underdone) nicht durchgebraten; **~ly** ['reəlɪ] adv selten

raring ['reərɪŋ] adj: **to be ~ to go** (inf) es kaum erwarten können, bis es losgeht

rarity ['reərɪtɪ] n Seltenheit f

rascal ['rɑ:skl] n Schuft m

rash [ræʃ] adj übereilt; (reckless) unbesonnen ♦ n (Haut)ausschlag m

rasher ['ræʃəʳ] n Speckscheibe f

raspberry ['rɑ:zbərɪ] n Himbeere f

rasping ['rɑ:spɪŋ] adj (noise) kratzend; (voice) krächzend

rat [ræt] n (animal) Ratte f; (person) Halunke m

rate [reɪt] n (proportion) Rate f; (price) Tarif m; (speed) Tempo nt ♦ vt (ein)schätzen; **~s** npl (BRIT: tax) Grundsteuer f; **to ~ as** für etw halten; **~able value** (BRIT) n Einheitswert m (als Bemessungsgrundlage); **~payer** (BRIT) n Steuerzahler(in) m(f)

rather ['rɑ:ðəʳ] adv (in preference) lieber, eher; (to some extent) ziemlich; **I would** or **I'd ~ go** ich würde lieber gehen; **it's ~ expensive** (quite) es ist ziemlich teuer; (too) es ist etwas zu teuer; **there's ~ a lot** es ist ziemlich viel

ratify ['rætɪfaɪ] vt (POL) ratifizieren

rating ['reɪtɪŋ] n Klasse f

ratio ['reɪʃɪəu] n Verhältnis nt; **in the ~ of 100 to 1** im Verhältnis 100 zu 1

ration ['ræʃən] n (usu pl) Ration f ♦ vt rationieren

rational ['ræʃənl] adj rational

rationale [ræʃə'nɑːl] n Grundprinzip nt

rationalize ['ræʃnəlaɪz] vt rationalisieren

rat race n Konkurrenzkampf m

rattle ['rætl] n (sound) Rasseln nt; (toy) Rassel f ♦ vi ratteln, klappern ♦ vt rasseln mit; **~snake** n Klapperschlange f

raucous ['rɔːkəs] adj heiser, rau

rave [reɪv] vi (talk wildly) fantasieren; (rage) toben ♦ n (BRIT: inf: party) Rave m, Fete f

raven ['reɪvən] n Rabe m

ravenous ['rævənəs] adj heißhungrig

ravine [rə'viːn] n Schlucht f

raving ['reɪvɪŋ] adj: **~ lunatic** völlig Wahnsinnige(r) mf

ravishing ['rævɪʃɪŋ] adj atemberaubend

raw [rɔː] adj roh; (tender) wund (gerieben); (inexperienced) unerfahren; **to get a ~ deal** (inf) schlecht wegkommen; **~ material** n Rohmaterial nt

ray [reɪ] n (of light) Strahl m; **~ of hope** Hoffnungsschimmer m

raze [reɪz] vt (also: **~ to the ground**) dem Erdboden gleichmachen

razor ['reɪzə'] n Rasierapparat m; **~ blade** n Rasierklinge f

Rd abbr = **road**

RE (BRIT: SCH) abbr (= religious education) Religionsunterricht m

re [riː] prep (COMM) betreffs +gen

reach [riːtʃ] n Reichweite f; (of river) Strecke f ♦ vt (arrive at) erreichen; (give) reichen ♦ vi (stretch) sich erstrecken; **within ~** (shops etc) in erreichbarer Weite or Entfernung; **out of ~** außer Reichweite; **to ~ for** (try to get) langen nach; **~ out** vi die Hand ausstrecken; **to ~ out for sth** nach etw greifen

react [riː'ækt] vi reagieren; **~ion** [riː'ækʃən] n Reaktion f; **~or** [riː'æktə'] n Reaktor m

read¹ [red] pt, pp of **read²**

read² [riːd] (pt, pp **read**) vt, vi lesen; (aloud) vorlesen; **~ out** vt vorlesen;

~able adj leserlich; (worth ~ing) lesenswert; **~er** n (person) Leser(in) m(f); **~ership** n Leserschaft f

readily ['redɪlɪ] adv (willingly) bereitwillig; (easily) prompt

readiness ['redɪnɪs] n (willingness) Bereitwilligkeit f; (being ready) Bereitschaft f; **in ~** (prepared) bereit

reading ['riːdɪŋ] n Lesen nt

readjust [riːə'dʒʌst] vt neu einstellen ♦ vi (person): **to ~** to sich wieder anpassen an +acc

ready ['redɪ] adj (prepared, willing) bereit ♦ adv: **~-cooked** vorgekocht ♦ n: **at the ~** bereit; **~-made** adj gebrauchsfertig, Fertig-; (clothes) Konfektions-; **~ money** n Bargeld nt; **~-to-wear** adj Konfektions-

reckoner n Rechentabelle f; **~-to-wear** adj Konfektions-

real [rɪəl] adj wirklich; (actual) eigentlich; (not fake) echt; **in ~ terms** effektiv; **~ estate** n Grundbesitz m; **~istic** [rɪə'lɪstɪk] adj realistisch

reality [riː'ælɪtɪ] n Wirklichkeit f, Realität f; **in ~** in Wirklichkeit

realization [rɪəlaɪ'zeɪʃən] n (understanding) Erkenntnis f; (fulfilment) Verwirklichung f

realize ['rɪəlaɪz] vt (understand) begreifen; (make real) verwirklichen; **I didn't ~** ... ich wusste nicht, ...

really ['rɪəlɪ] adv wirklich; **~?** (indicating interest) tatsächlich?; (expressing surprise) wirklich?

realm [relm] n Reich nt

realtor ['rɪəltɔː'] (us) n Grundstücksmakler(in) m(f)

reap [riːp] vt ernten

reappear [riːə'pɪə'] vi wieder erscheinen

rear [rɪə'] adj hintere(r, s), Rück- ♦ n Rückseite f; (last part) Schluss m ♦ vt (bring up) aufziehen ♦ vi (horse) sich aufbäumen; **~guard** n Nachhut f

rearmament [riː'ɑːməmənt] n Wiederaufrüstung f

rearrange [riːə'reɪndʒ] vt umordnen

rear-view mirror [ˈrɪəvjuː-] n Rückspiegel m

reason [ˈriːzn] n (cause) Grund m; (ability to think) Verstand m; (sensible thoughts) Vernunft f ♦ vi (think) denken; (use arguments) argumentieren; **it stands to ~** that es ist logisch, dass; **to ~ with sb** mit jdm diskutieren; **~able** adj vernünftig; **~ably** adv vernünftig; (fairly) ziemlich; **~ed** adj (argument) durchdacht; **~ing** n Urteilen nt; (argumentation) Beweisführung f

reassurance [riːəˈʃuərəns] n Beruhigung f; (confirmation) Bestätigung f; **reassure** [riːəˈʃuəʳ] vt beruhigen; **to reassure sb of sth** jdm etw versichern

rebate [ˈriːbeɪt] n Rückzahlung f

rebel [n ˈrɛbl, vb rɪˈbɛl] n Rebell m ♦ vi rebellieren; **~lion** [rɪˈbɛljən] n Rebellion f, Aufstand m; **~lious** [rɪˈbɛljəs] adj rebellisch

rebirth [riːˈbɜːθ] n Wiedergeburt f

rebound [vb rɪˈbaʊnd, n ˈriːbaʊnd] vi zurückprallen ♦ n Rückprall m

rebuff [rɪˈbʌf] n Abfuhr f ♦ vt abblitzen lassen

rebuild [riːˈbɪld] (irreg) vt wieder aufbauen; (fig) wieder herstellen

rebuke [rɪˈbjuːk] n Tadel m ♦ vt tadeln, rügen

rebut [rɪˈbʌt] vt widerlegen

recall [vb rɪˈkɔːl, n ˈriːkɔːl] vt (call back) zurückrufen; (remember) sich erinnern an +acc ♦ n Rückruf m

recap [ˈriːkæp] vt, vi wiederholen

rec'd abbr (= received) Eing.

recede [rɪˈsiːd] vi zurückweichen; **receding** adj: **receding hairline** Stirnglatze f

receipt [rɪˈsiːt] n (document) Quittung f; (receiving) Empfang m; **~s** npl (ECON) Einnahmen pl

receive [rɪˈsiːv] vt erhalten; (visitors etc) empfangen; **~r** n (TEL) Hörer m

recent [ˈriːsnt] adj vor kurzem (geschehen), neuerlich; (modern) neu; **~ly** adv kürzlich, neulich

receptacle [rɪˈsɛptɪkl] n Behälter m

reception [rɪˈsɛpʃən] n Empfang m; **~ desk** n Empfang m; (in hotel) Rezeption f; **~ist** n (in hotel) Empfangschef m, Empfangsdame f; (MED) Sprechstundenhilfe f

receptive [rɪˈsɛptɪv] adj aufnahmebereit

recess [rɪˈsɛs] n (break) Ferien pl; (hollow) Nische f

recession [rɪˈsɛʃən] n Rezession f

recharge [riːˈtʃɑːdʒ] vt (battery) aufladen

recipe [ˈrɛsɪpɪ] n Rezept nt

recipient [rɪˈsɪpɪənt] n Empfänger m

reciprocal [rɪˈsɪprəkl] adj gegenseitig; (mutual) wechselseitig

recital [rɪˈsaɪtl] n Vortrag m

recite [rɪˈsaɪt] vt vortragen, aufsagen

reckless [ˈrɛkləs] adj leichtsinnig; (driving) fahrlässig

reckon [ˈrɛkən] vt (count) rechnen, berechnen, errechnen; (estimate) schätzen; (think): **I ~ that ...** ich nehme an, dass ...; **~ on** vt fus rechnen mit; **~ing** n (calculation) Rechnen nt

reclaim [rɪˈkleɪm] vt (expenses) zurückverlangen; (land): **to ~ (from sth)** (etw dat) gewinnen; **reclamation** [rɛkləˈmeɪʃən] n (of land) Gewinnung f

recline [rɪˈklaɪn] vi sich zurücklehnen; **reclining** adj Liege-

recluse [rɪˈkluːs] n Einsiedler m

recognition [rɛkəgˈnɪʃən] n (recognizing) Erkennen nt; (acknowledgement) Anerkennung f; **transformed beyond ~** völlig verändert

recognizable [ˈrɛkəgnaɪzəbl] adj erkennbar

recognize [ˈrɛkəgnaɪz] vt erkennen; (POL, approve) anerkennen; **to ~ as** anerkennen als; **to ~ by** erkennen an +dat

recoil [rɪˈkɔɪl] vi (in horror) zurückschrecken; (rebound) zurückprallen; (person): **to ~ from doing sth** davor zurückschrecken, etw zu tun

recollect [rekə'lekt] vt sich erinnern an +acc; **~ion** [rekə'lekʃən] n Erinnerung f

recommend [rekə'mend] vt empfehlen; **~ation** [rekəmen'deiʃən] n Empfehlung f

recompense ['rekəmpens] n (compensation) Entschädigung f; (reward) Belohnung f ♦ vt entschädigen; belohnen

reconcile ['rekənsail] vt (facts) vereinbaren; (people) versöhnen; **~ o.s. to sth** sich mit etw abfinden; **reconciliation** [rekənsili'eiʃən] n Versöhnung f

recondition [ri:kən'diʃən] vt (machine) generalüberholen

reconnoitre [rekə'nɔitə'] (US **reconnoiter**) vt erkunden ♦ vi aufklären

reconsider [ri:kən'sidə'] vt von neuem erwägen, noch einmal überdenken ♦ vi es noch einmal überdenken

reconstruct [ri:kən'strʌkt] vt wieder aufbauen; (crime) rekonstruieren

record [n 'rekɔːd, vb ri'kɔːd] n Aufzeichnung f; (MUS) Schallplatte f; (best performance) Rekord m ♦ vt aufzeichnen; (music etc) aufnehmen; **off the ~** vertraulich, im Vertrauen; **in ~ time** in Rekordzeit; **~ card** n (in file) Karteikarte f; **~ed delivery** (BRIT) n (POST) Einschreiben nt; **~er** n (TECH) Registriergerät nt; (MUS) Blockflöte f; **~ holder** n (SPORT) Rekordinhaber m; **~ing** n (MUS) Aufnahme f; **~ player** n Plattenspieler m

re-count [n 'ri:kaunt] (tell) berichten

re-count ['ri:kaunt] n Nachzählung f

recoup [ri'ku:p] vt: **to ~ one's losses** seinen Verlust wieder gutmachen

recourse [ri'kɔːs] n: **to have ~ to** Zuflucht nehmen zu or bei

recover [ri'kʌvə'] vt (get back) zurückerhalten ♦ vi sich erholen

re-cover [ri:'kʌvə'] vt (quilt etc) neu überziehen

recovery [ri'kʌvəri] n Wiedererlangung f; (of health) Erholung f

recreate [ri:kri'eit] vt wieder herstellen

recreation [rekri'eiʃən] n Erholung f; **~al** adj Erholungs-; **~al drug** n Freizeitdroge f

recrimination [rikrimi'neiʃən] n Gegenbeschuldigung f

recruit [ri'kru:t] n Rekrut m ♦ vt rekrutieren; **~ment** n Rekrutierung f

rectangle ['rektæŋgl] n Rechteck nt; **rectangular** [rek'tæŋgjulə'] adj rechteckig, rechtwinklig

rectify ['rektifai] vt berichtigen

rector ['rektə'] n (REL) Pfarrer m; (SCH) Direktor(in) m(f); **~y** ['rektəri] n Pfarrhaus nt

recuperate [ri'kju:pəreit] vi sich erholen

recur [ri'kɔː'] vi sich wiederholen; **~rence** n Wiederholung f; **~rent** adj wiederkehrend

recycle [ri:'saikl] vt wieder verwerten, wieder aufbereiten; **recycling** n Recycling nt

red [red] n Rot nt; (POL) Rote(r) m ♦ adj rot; **in the ~** in den roten Zahlen; **~ carpet treatment** n Sonderbehandlung f; **R~ Cross** n Rote(s) Kreuz nt; **~currant** n rote Johannisbeere f; **~den** vi sich röten; (blush) erröten ♦ vt röten; **~dish** adj rötlich

redecorate [ri:'dekəreit] vt neu tapezieren, neu streichen

redeem [ri'di:m] vt (COMM) einlösen; (save) retten; **~ing** adj: **~ing feature** versöhnende(s) Moment nt

redeploy [ri:di'plɔi] vt (resources) umverteilen

red: ~-haired [red'heəd] adj rothaarig; **~-handed** [red'hændid] adv: **to be caught ~-handed** auf frischer Tat ertappt werden; **~head** ['redhed] n Rothaarige(r) mf; **~ herring** n Ablenkungsmanöver nt; **~-hot** [red'hɔt] adj rot glühend

redirect [ri:dai'rekt] vt umleiten

red light n: **to go through a ~** (AUT) bei Rot über die Ampel fahren; **red-**

light district n Strichviertel nt
redo [riː'duː] (irreg: like **do**) vt nochmals machen
redolent ['redələnt] adj: ~ **of** (fig) erinnernd an +acc
redouble [riː'dʌbl] vt: **to ~ one's efforts** seine Anstrengungen verdoppeln
redress [rɪ'dres] vt wieder gutmachen
red: **R~ Sea** n: **the R~ Sea** das Rote Meer; **~skin** ['redskin] n Rothaut f; **~ tape** n Bürokratismus m
reduce [rɪ'djuːs] vt (speed, temperature) vermindern; (photo) verkleinern; **"~ speed now"** (AUT) ≈ „langsam"; **to ~ the price** (to) den Preis herabsetzen (auf +acc); **at a ~d price** zum ermäßigten Preis
reduction [rɪ'dʌkʃən] n Verminderung f; Verkleinerung f; Herabsetzung f; (amount of money) Nachlass m
redundancy [rɪ'dʌndənsɪ] n Überflüssigkeit f; (of workers) Entlassung f
redundant [rɪ'dʌndnt] adj überflüssig; (workers) ohne Arbeitsplatz; **to be made ~** arbeitslos werden
reed [riːd] n Schilf nt; (MUS) Rohrblatt nt
reef [riːf] n Riff nt
reek [riːk] vi: **to ~ (of)** stinken (nach)
reel [riːl] n Spule f, Rolle f ♦ vt (also: ~ **in**) wickeln, spulen ♦ vi (stagger) taumeln
ref [ref] (inf) n abbr (= referee) Schiri m
refectory [rɪ'fektərɪ] n (UNIV) Mensa f; (SCH) Speisesaal m; (ECCL) Refektorium nt
refer [rɪ'fɜː'] vt: **to ~ sb to sb/sth** jdn an jdn/etw verweisen ♦ vi: **to ~ to** (to book) nachschlagen in +dat; (mention) sich beziehen auf +acc
referee [refə'riː] n Schiedsrichter m; (BRIT: for job) Referenz f ♦ vt schiedsrichtern
reference ['refrəns] n (for job) Referenz f; (in book) Verweis m; (number, code) Aktenzeichen nt; (allusion): **~ (to)** An-

spielung (auf +acc); **with ~ to** in Bezug auf +acc; **~ book** n Nachschlagewerk nt; **~ number** n Aktenzeichen nt
referenda [refə'rendə] npl of **referendum**
referendum [refə'rendəm] (pl **-da**) n Volksabstimmung f
refill [vb rɪ'fɪl, n 'riːfɪl] vt nachfüllen ♦ n (for pen) Ersatzmine f
refine [rɪ'faɪn] vt (purify) raffinieren; **~d** adj kultiviert; **~ment** n Kultiviertheit f; **~ry** n Raffinerie f
reflect [rɪ'flekt] vt (light) reflektieren; (fig) widerspiegeln ♦ vi (meditate): **to ~ (on)** nachdenken (über +acc); **it ~s badly/well on him** das stellt ihn in ein schlechtes/gutes Licht; **~ion** [rɪ'flekʃən] n Reflexion f; (image) Spiegelbild nt; (thought) Überlegung f; **on ~ion** wenn man sich dat das recht überlegt
reflex ['riːfleks] adj Reflex- ♦ n Reflex m; **~ive** [rɪ'fleksɪv] adj reflexiv
reform [rɪ'fɔːm] n Reform f ♦ vt (person) bessern; **~atory** (US) n Besserungsanstalt f
refrain [rɪ'freɪn] vi: **to ~ from** unterlassen ♦ n Refrain m
refresh [rɪ'freʃ] vt erfrischen; **~er course** (BRIT) n Wiederholungskurs m; **~ing** adj erfrischend; **~ments** npl Erfrischungen pl
refrigeration [rɪfrɪdʒə'reɪʃən] n Kühlung f
refrigerator [rɪ'frɪdʒəreɪtə'] n Kühlschrank m
refuel [riː'fjuəl] vt, vi auftanken
refuge ['refjuːdʒ] n Zuflucht f; **to take ~ in** sich flüchten in +acc; **~e** [refjʊ'dʒiː] n Flüchtling m
refund [n 'riːfʌnd, vb rɪ'fʌnd] n Rückvergütung f ♦ vt zurückerstatten
refurbish [riː'fɜːbɪʃ] vt aufpolieren
refusal [rɪ'fjuːzəl] n (Ver)weigerung f; **first ~** Vorkaufsrecht nt
refuse¹ [rɪ'fjuːz] vt abschlagen ♦ vi sich weigern

refuse² [ˈrɛfjuːs] n Abfall m, Müll m; **~ collection** n Müllabfuhr f

refute [rɪˈfjuːt] vt widerlegen

regain [rɪˈgeɪn] vt wiedergewinnen; (consciousness) wiedererlangen

regal [ˈriːgl] adj königlich

regalia [rɪˈgeɪlɪə] npl Insignien pl

regard [rɪˈgɑːd] n Achtung f ♦ vt ansehen; **to send one's ~s to sb** jdn grüßen lassen; **"with kindest ~s"** "mit freundlichen Grüßen"; **~ing** as ~s or **with ~ to** bezüglich +gen, in Bezug auf +acc; **~less** adj **~less of** ohne Rücksicht auf +acc ♦ adv trotzdem

regenerate [rɪˈdʒɛnəreɪt] vt erneuern

régime [reɪˈʒiːm] n Regime nt

regiment [n ˈrɛdʒɪmənt, vb ˈrɛdʒɪment] n Regiment nt ♦ vt (fig) reglementieren; **~al** [rɛdʒɪˈmɛntl] adj Regiments-

region [ˈriːdʒən] n Region f; **in the ~ of** (fig) so um; **~al** adj örtlich, regional

register [ˈrɛdʒɪstə*] n Register nt ♦ vt (list) registrieren; (emotion) zeigen; (write down) eintragen ♦ vi (at hotel) sich eintragen; (with police) sich melden; (make impression) wirken, ankommen; **~ed** adj (letter) Einschreibe-, eingeschrieben; **~ed trademark** n eingetragenes Warenzeichen nt

registrar [ˈrɛdʒɪstrɑː*] n Standesbeamte(r) m

registration [rɛdʒɪsˈtreɪʃən] n (act) Registrierung f; (AUT: also: **~ number**) polizeiliches Kennzeichen nt

registry [ˈrɛdʒɪstrɪ] n Sekretariat nt; **~ office** (BRIT) n Standesamt nt; **to get married in a ~ office** standesamtlich heiraten

regret [rɪˈgrɛt] n Bedauern nt ♦ vt bedauern; **~fully** adv mit Bedauern, ungern; **~table** adj bedauerlich

regroup [riːˈgruːp] vt umgruppieren ♦ vi sich umgruppieren

regular [ˈrɛgjulə*] adj regelmäßig; (usual) üblich; (inf) regelrecht ♦ n (client etc) Stammkunde m; **~ity**

[rɛgjuˈlærɪtɪ] n Regelmäßigkeit f; **~ly** adv regelmäßig

regulate [ˈrɛgjuleɪt] vt regeln, regulieren; **regulation** [rɛgjuˈleɪʃən] n (rule) Vorschrift f; (control) Regulierung f

rehabilitation [ˈriːəbɪlɪˈteɪʃən] n (of criminal) Resozialisierung f

rehearsal [rɪˈhəːsəl] n Probe f

rehearse [rɪˈhəːs] vt proben

reign [reɪn] n Herrschaft f ♦ vi herrschen

reimburse [riːɪmˈbəːs] vt: **to ~ sb for sth** jdn für etw entschädigen, jdm etw zurückzahlen

rein [reɪn] n Zügel m

reincarnation [riːɪnkɑːˈneɪʃən] n Wiedergeburt f

reindeer [ˈreɪndɪə*] n Ren nt

reinforce [riːɪnˈfɔːs] vt verstärken; **~d concrete** n Stahlbeton m; **~ment** n Verstärkung f; **~ments** npl (MIL) Verstärkungstruppen pl

reinstate [riːɪnˈsteɪt] vt wieder einsetzen

reissue [riːˈɪʃuː] vt neu herausgeben

reiterate [riːˈɪtəreɪt] vt wiederholen

reject [n ˈriːdʒɛkt, vb rɪˈdʒɛkt] n (COMM) Ausschuss(artikel) m ♦ vt ablehnen; **~ion** [rɪˈdʒɛkʃən] n Zurückweisung f

rejoice [rɪˈdʒɔɪs] vi: **to ~ at** or **over** sich freuen über +acc

rejuvenate [rɪˈdʒuːvəneɪt] vt verjüngen

rekindle [riːˈkɪndl] vt wieder anfachen

relapse [rɪˈlæps] n Rückfall m

relate [rɪˈleɪt] vt (tell) erzählen; (connect) verbinden ♦ vi: **to ~ to** zusammenhängen mit; (form relationship) eine Beziehung aufbauen zu; **~d** adj: **~d** (to) verwandt (mit); **relating** prep: **relating to** bezüglich +gen; **relation** [rɪˈleɪʃən] n Verwandte(r) m/f; (connection) Beziehung f; **relationship** n Verhältnis nt, Beziehung f

relative [ˈrɛlətɪv] n Verwandte(r) m/f ♦ adj relativ; **~ly** adv verhältnismäßig

relax [rɪˈlæks] vi (slacken) sich lockern;

(*muscles, person*) sich entspannen ♦ vt (*ease*) lockern, entspannen; **~ation** [riːlækˈseɪʃən] n Entspannung f; **~ed** adj entspannt, locker; **~ing** adj entspannend

relay [n 'riːleɪ, vb rɪˈleɪ] n (SPORT) Staffel f ♦ vt (*message*) weiterleiten; (RADIO, TV) übertragen

release [rɪˈliːs] n (*freedom*) Entlassung f; (TECH) Auslöser m ♦ vt befreien; (*prisoner*) entlassen; (*report, news*) verlautbaren, bekannt geben

relegate [ˈrelɪgeɪt] vt (SPORT): **to be ~d** absteigen

relent [rɪˈlent] vi nachgeben; **~less** adj unnachgiebig

relevant [ˈreləvənt] adj wichtig, relevant; **~ to** relevant für

reliability [rɪlaɪəˈbɪlɪtɪ] n Zuverlässigkeit f

reliable [rɪˈlaɪəbl] adj zuverlässig; **reliably** adv zuverlässig; **to be reliably informed that ...** aus zuverlässiger Quelle wissen, dass ...

reliance [rɪˈlaɪəns] n: **~ (on)** Abhängigkeit f (von)

relic [ˈrelɪk] n (*from past*) Überbleibsel nt; (REL) Reliquie f

relief [rɪˈliːf] n Erleichterung f; (*help*) Hilfe f; (*person*) Ablösung f

relieve [rɪˈliːv] vt (*ease*) erleichtern; (*help*) entlasten; (*person*) ablösen; **to ~ sb of sth** jdm etw abnehmen; **to o.s.** (*euph*) sich erleichtern (*euph*); **~d** adj erleichtert

religion [rɪˈlɪdʒən] n Religion f; **religious** [rɪˈlɪdʒəs] adj religiös

relinquish [rɪˈlɪŋkwɪʃ] vt aufgeben

relish [ˈrelɪʃ] n Würze f ♦ vt genießen; **to ~ doing** gern tun

relocate [riːləʊˈkeɪt] vt verlegen ♦ vi umziehen

reluctance [rɪˈlʌktəns] n Widerstreben nt, Abneigung f

reluctant [rɪˈlʌktənt] adj widerwillig; **~ly** adv ungern

rely [rɪˈlaɪ] vt fus: **to ~ on** sich verlassen

auf +acc

remain [rɪˈmeɪn] vi (*be left*) übrig bleiben; (*stay*) bleiben; **~der** n Rest m; **~ing** adj übrig (geblieben); **~s** npl Überreste pl

remake [ˈriːmeɪk] n (CINE) Neuverfilmung f

remand [rɪˈmɑːnd] n: **on ~** in Untersuchungshaft ♦ vt: **to ~ in custody** in Untersuchungshaft schicken; **~ home** (BRIT) n Untersuchungsgefängnis nt für Jugendliche

remark [rɪˈmɑːk] n Bemerkung f ♦ vt bemerken; **~able** adj bemerkenswert; **remarkably** adv außergewöhnlich

remarry [riːˈmærɪ] vi sich wieder verheiraten

remedial [rɪˈmiːdɪəl] adj Heil-; (*teaching*) Hilfsschul-

remedy [ˈremɪdɪ] n Mittel nt ♦ vt (*pain*) abhelfen +dat; (*trouble*) in Ordnung bringen

remember [rɪˈmembə*] vt sich erinnern an +acc; **remembrance** [rɪˈmembrəns] n Erinnerung f; (*official*) Gedenken nt; **R~ Day** n ≈ Volkstrauertag m

---

Remembrance Day

Remembrance Day oder **Remembrance Sunday** ist der britische Gedenktag für die Gefallenen der beiden Weltkriege und anderer Konflikte. Er fällt auf einen Sonntag vor oder nach dem 11. November (am 11. November 1918 endete der erste Weltkrieg) und wird mit einer Schweigeminute, Kranzniederlegungen an Kriegerdenkmälern und dem Tragen von Ansteckenadeln in Form einer Mohnblume begangen.

---

remind [rɪˈmaɪnd] vt: **to ~ sb to do sth** jdn daran erinnern, etw zu tun; **to ~ sb of sth** jdn an etw acc erinnern; **she ~s me of her mother** sie erinnert mich an ihre Mutter; **~er** n Mahnung f

reminisce [remɪˈnɪs] vi in Erinnerun-

gen schwelgen; **~nt** [rɪmɪˈnɪsnt] *adj*:
to be ~nt of sth an etw *acc* erinnern

remiss [rɪˈmɪs] *adj* nachlässig

remission [rɪˈmɪʃən] *n* Nachlaß *m*; (of *debt, sentence*) Erlaß *m*

remit [rɪˈmɪt] *vt (money)*: **to ~ (to)** überweisen (an *+acc*); **~tance** *n* Geldanweisung *f*

remnant [ˈremnənt] *n* Rest *m*; **~s** *npl* (COMM) Einzelstücke *pl*

remorse [rɪˈmɔːs] *n* Gewissensbisse *pl*; **~ful** *adj* reumütig; **~less** *adj* unbarmherzig

remote [rɪˈməut] *adj* abgelegen; (*slight*) gering; **~ control** *n* Fernsteuerung *f*; **~ly** *adv* entfernt

remould [ˈriːməuld] (BRIT) *n* runderneuerte(r) Reifen *m*

removable [rɪˈmuːvəbl] *adj* entfernbar

removal [rɪˈmuːvəl] *n* Beseitigung *f*; (of *furniture*) Umzug *m*; (*from office*) Entlassung *f*; **~ van** (BRIT) *n* Möbelwagen *m*

remove [rɪˈmuːv] *vt* beseitigen, entfernen; **~rs** *npl* Möbelspedition *f*

remuneration [rɪmjuːnəˈreɪʃən] *n* Vergütung *f*, Honorar *nt*

render [ˈrendə*] *vt* machen; (*translate*) übersetzen; **~ing** *n* (MUS) Wiedergabe *f*

rendezvous [ˈrɔndɪvuː] *n* (*meeting*) Rendezvous *nt*; (*place*) Treffpunkt *m* ♦ *vi* sich treffen

renew [rɪˈnjuː] *vt* erneuern; (*contract, licence*) verlängern; (*replace*) ersetzen; **~able** *adj* regenerierbar; **~al** *n* Erneuerung *f*; Verlängerung *f*

renounce [rɪˈnauns] *vt* (*give up*) verzichten auf *+acc*; (*disown*) verstoßen

renovate [ˈrenəveɪt] *vt* renovieren; (*building*) restaurieren

renown [rɪˈnaun] *n* Ruf *m*; **~ed** *adj* namhaft

rent [rent] *n* Miete *f*; (*for land*) Pacht *f* ♦ *vt* (*hold as tenant*) mieten; pachten; (*let*) vermieten; verpachten; (*car etc*) mieten; (*firm*) vermieten; **~al** *n* Miete *f*

renunciation [rɪnʌnsɪˈeɪʃən] *n*: **~ (of)**

Verzicht *m* (auf *+acc*)

reorganize [riːˈɔːgənaɪz] *vt* umgestalten, reorganisieren

rep [rep] *n abbr* (COMM) = **representative**; (THEAT) = **repertory**

repair [rɪˈpeə*] *n* Reparatur *f* ♦ *vt* reparieren; (*damage*) wieder gutmachen; **in good/bad ~** in gutem/schlechtem Zustand; **~ kit** *n* Werkzeugkasten *m*

repartee [repɑːˈtiː] *n* Witzeleien *pl*

repatriate [riːˈpætrɪeɪt] *vt* in die Heimat zurückschicken

repay [riːˈpeɪ] (*irreg*) *vt* zurückzahlen; (*reward*) vergelten; **~ment** *n* Rückzahlung *f*; (*fig*) Vergeltung *f*

repeal [rɪˈpiːl] *vt* aufheben

repeat [rɪˈpiːt] *n* (RAD, TV) Wiederholung(ssendung) *f* ♦ *vt* wiederholen; **~edly** *adv* wiederholt

repel [rɪˈpel] *vt* (*drive back*) zurückschlagen; (*disgust*) abstoßen; **~lent** *adj* abstoßend ♦ *n*: **insect ~lent** Insektenmittel *nt*

repent [rɪˈpent] *vt, vi*: **to ~ (of)** bereuen; **~ance** *n* Reue *f*

repercussion [riːpəˈkʌʃən] *n* Auswirkung *f*; **to have ~s** ein Nachspiel haben

repertory [ˈrepətəri] *n* Repertoire *nt*

repetition [repɪˈtɪʃən] *n* Wiederholung *f*

repetitive [rɪˈpetɪtɪv] *adj* sich wiederholend

replace [rɪˈpleɪs] *vt* ersetzen; (*put back*) zurückstellen; **~ment** *n* Ersatz *m*

replay [ˈriːpleɪ] *n* (of *match*) Wiederholungsspiel *nt*; (of *tape, film*) Wiederholung *f*

replenish [rɪˈplenɪʃ] *vt* ergänzen

replica [ˈreplɪkə] *n* Kopie *f*

reply [rɪˈplaɪ] *n* Antwort *f* ♦ *vi* antworten; **~ coupon** *n* Antwortschein *m*

report [rɪˈpɔːt] *n* Bericht *m*; (BRIT: SCH) Zeugnis *nt* ♦ *vt* (*tell*) berichten; (*give information against*) melden; (*to police*) anzeigen ♦ *vi* (*make ~*) Bericht erstatten; (*present o.s.*): **to ~ (to sb)** sich (bei jdm) melden; **~ card** (US, SCOTTISH) *n*

Zeugnis nt; **~edly** adv wie verlautet; **~er** n Reporter m

reprehensible [reprɪˈhensɪbl] adj tadelnswert

represent [reprɪˈzent] vt darstellen; (speak for) vertreten; **~ation** [reprɪzenˈteɪʃən] n Darstellung f; (being ~ed) Vertretung f; **~ations** npl (protest) Vorhaltungen pl; **~ative** n (person) Vertreter m; (US: POL) Abgeordnete(r) mf ♦ adj repräsentativ

repress [rɪˈpres] vt unterdrücken; **~ion** [rɪˈpreʃən] n Unterdrückung f

reprieve [rɪˈpriːv] n (JUR) Begnadigung f; (fig) Gnadenfrist f ♦ vt (JUR) begnadigen

reprimand [ˈreprɪmɑːnd] n Verweis m ♦ vt einen Verweis erteilen +dat

reprint [nˈriːprɪnt, vb riːˈprɪnt] n Neudruck m ♦ vt wieder abdrucken

reprisal [rɪˈpraɪzl] n Vergeltung f

reproach [rɪˈprəʊtʃ] n Vorwurf m ♦ vt Vorwürfe machen +dat; **to ~ sb with sth** jdm etw vorwerfen; **~ful** adj vorwurfsvoll

reproduce [riːprəˈdjuːs] vt reproduzieren ♦ vi (have offspring) sich vermehren; **reproduction** [riːprəˈdʌkʃən] n (ART, PHOT) Reproduktion f; (breeding) Fortpflanzung f; **reproductive** [riːprəˈdʌktɪv] adj reproduktiv; (breeding) Fortpflanzungs-

reprove [rɪˈpruːv] vt tadeln

reptile [ˈreptaɪl] n Reptil nt

republic [rɪˈpʌblɪk] n Republik f

repudiate [rɪˈpjuːdɪeɪt] vt zurückweisen

repugnant [rɪˈpʌɡnənt] adj widerlich

repulse [rɪˈpʌls] vt (drive back) zurückschlagen; (reject) abweisen

repulsive [rɪˈpʌlsɪv] adj abstoßend

reputable [ˈrepjutəbl] adj angesehen

reputation [repjuˈteɪʃən] n Ruf m

reputed [rɪˈpjuːtɪd] adj angeblich; **~ly** [rɪˈpjuːtɪdlɪ] adv angeblich

request [rɪˈkwest] n Bitte f ♦ vt (thing) erbitten; **to ~ sth of** or **from sb** jdn

um etw bitten; (formally) jdn um etw ersuchen; **~ stop** (BRIT) n Bedarfshaltestelle f

require [rɪˈkwaɪəˈ] vt (need) brauchen; (demand) erfordern; **~ment** n (condition) Anforderung f; (need) Bedarf m

requisite [ˈrekwɪzɪt] adj erforderlich

requisition [rekwɪˈzɪʃən] n Anforderung f ♦ vt beschlagnahmen

rescue [ˈreskjuː] n Rettung f ♦ vt retten; **~ party** n Rettungsmannschaft f; **~r** n Retter m

research [rɪˈsɜːtʃ] n Forschung f ♦ vi forschen ♦ vt erforschen; **~er** n Forscher m

resemblance [rɪˈzembləns] n Ähnlichkeit f

resemble [rɪˈzembl] vt ähneln +dat

resent [rɪˈzent] vt übel nehmen; **~ful** adj nachtragend, empfindlich; **~ment** n Verstimmung f, Unwille m

reservation [rezəˈveɪʃən] n (booking) Reservierung f; (THEAT) Vorbestellung f; (doubt) Vorbehalt m; (land) Reservat nt

reserve [rɪˈzɜːv] n (store) Vorrat m, Reserve f; (manner) Zurückhaltung f; (game ~) Naturschutzgebiet nt; (SPORT) Ersatzspieler(in) m(f) ♦ vt reservieren; (judgement) sich dat vorbehalten; **~s** npl (MIL) Reserve f; **in ~** in Reserve; **~d** adj reserviert

reshuffle [riːˈʃʌfl] n (POL): **cabinet ~** Kabinettsumbildung f ♦ vt (POL) umbilden

reside [rɪˈzaɪd] vi wohnen, ansässig sein

residence [ˈrezɪdəns] n (house) Wohnsitz m; (living) Aufenthalt m; **~ permit** (BRIT) n Aufenthaltserlaubnis f

resident [ˈrezɪdənt] n (in house) Bewohner m; (in area) Einwohner m ♦ adj wohnhaft, ansässig; **~ial** [rezɪˈdenʃəl] adj Wohn-

residue [ˈrezɪdjuː] n Rest m; (CHEM) Rückstand m; (fig) Bodensatz m

resign [rɪˈzaɪn] vt (office) aufgeben, zurücktreten von ♦ vi (from office) zu-

resilience

rücktreten; *(employee)* kündigen; **to be ~ed to sth, to ~ o.s. to sth** sich mit etw abfinden; **~ation** [rɛzɪɡ'neɪʃən] n *(from job)* Kündigung f; *(POL)* Rücktritt m; *(submission)* Resignation f; **~ed** adj resigniert

resilience [rɪ'zɪlɪəns] n Spannkraft f; *(of person)* Unverwüstlichkeit f; **resilient** [rɪ'zɪlɪənt] adj unverwüstlich

resin ['rɛzɪn] n Harz nt

resist [rɪ'zɪst] vt widerstehen +dat; **~ance** n Widerstand m

resit [vb riː'sɪt, n 'riːsɪt] vt *(exam)* wiederholen ♦ n Wiederholung(sprüfung) f

resolute ['rɛzəluːt] adj entschlossen, resolut; **resolution** [rɛzə'luːʃən] n *(firmness)* Entschlossenheit f; *(intention)* Vorsatz m; *(decision)* Beschluss m

resolve [rɪ'zɔlv] n Entschlossenheit f ♦ vt *(decide)* beschließen ♦ vi sich lösen; **~d** adj *(test)* entschlossen

resonant ['rɛzənənt] adj voll tönend

resort [rɪ'zɔːt] n *(holiday place)* Erholungsort m; *(help)* Zuflucht f ♦ vi: **to ~ to** Zuflucht nehmen zu; **as a last ~** als letzter Ausweg

resound [rɪ'zaʊnd] vi: **to ~ (with)** widerhallen (von); **~ing** adj nachhallend; *(success)* groß

resource [rɪ'sɔːs] n Findigkeit f; **~s** npl *(financial)* Geldmittel pl; *(natural)* Bodenschätze pl; **~ful** adj findig

respect [rɪs'pɛkt] n Respekt m ♦ vt achten, respektieren; **~s** npl *(regards)* Grüße pl; **with ~ to** in Bezug auf +acc, hinsichtlich +gen; **in this ~** in dieser Hinsicht; **~able** adj anständig; *(not bad)* leidlich; *(fairly good)* ordentlich, ganz gut; **~ful** adj höflich

respective [rɪs'pɛktɪv] adj jeweilig; **~ly** adv beziehungsweise

respiration [rɛspɪ'reɪʃən] n Atmung f

respite ['rɛspaɪt] n Ruhepause f

resplendent [rɪs'plɛndənt] adj strahlend

respond [rɪs'pɔnd] vi antworten; *(react)* reagieren (auf +acc);

response [rɪs'pɔns] n Antwort f; Reaktion f; *(to advert)* Resonanz f

responsibility [rɪspɔnsɪ'bɪlɪtɪ] n Verantwortung f

responsible [rɪs'pɔnsɪbl] adj verantwortlich; *(reliable)* verantwortungsvoll

responsive [rɪs'pɔnsɪv] adj empfänglich

rest [rest] n Ruhe f; *(break)* Pause f; *(remainder)* Rest m ♦ vi sich ausruhen; *(be supported)* (auf)liegen ♦ vt *(lean)*: **to ~ sth on/against sth** etw gegen etw acc lehnen; **the ~ of them** die Übrigen; **it ~s with him to ...** es liegt bei ihm, zu ...

restaurant ['rɛstərɔn] n Restaurant nt; **~ car** (BRIT) n Speisewagen m

restful ['rɛstful] adj erholsam, ruhig

rest home n Erholungsheim nt

restive ['rɛstɪv] adj unruhig

restless ['rɛstlɪs] adj unruhig

restoration [rɛstə'reɪʃən] n Rückgabe f; *(of building etc)* Rückerstattung f

restore [rɪs'tɔː] vt *(order)* wieder herstellen; *(customs)* wieder einführen; *(person to position)* wieder einsetzen; *(give back)* zurückgeben; *(renovate)* restaurieren

restrain [rɪs'treɪn] vt zurückhalten; *(curiosity etc)* beherrschen; *(person)*: **to ~ sb from doing sth** jdn davon abhalten, etw zu tun; **~ed** adj *(style etc)* gedämpft, verhalten; **~t** n *(control)* Zurückhaltung f

restrict [rɪs'trɪkt] vt einschränken; **~ion** [rɪs'trɪkʃən] n Einschränkung f; **~ive** adj einschränkend

rest room (US) n Toilette f

restructure [riː'strʌktʃəʳ] vt umstrukturieren

result [rɪ'zʌlt] n Resultat nt, Folge f; *(of exam, game)* Ergebnis nt ♦ vi: **to ~ in sth** etw zur Folge haben; **as a ~ of** als Folge +gen

resume [rɪ'zjuːm] vt fortsetzen; *(occupy again)* wieder einnehmen ♦ vi *(work etc)* wieder beginnen

résumé ['reɪzju:meɪ] n Zusammenfassung f

resumption [rɪ'zʌmpʃən] n Wiederaufnahme f

resurgence [rɪ'sə:dʒəns] n Wiedererwachen nt

resurrection [rezə'rekʃən] n Auferstehung f

resuscitate [rɪ'sʌsɪteɪt] vt wieder beleben; **resuscitation** [rɪsʌsɪ'teɪʃən] n Wiederbelebung f

retail [n, adj 'ri:teɪl, vb 'ri:'teɪl] n Einzelhandel m ♦ adj Einzelhandels- ♦ vt im Kleinen verkaufen ♦ vi im Einzelhandel kosten; **~er** ['ri:teɪləʳ] n Einzelhändler m, Kleinhändler m; **~ price** n Ladenpreis m

retain [rɪ'teɪn] vt (keep) (zurück)behalten; **~er** n (fee) (Honorar)vorschuss m

retaliate [rɪ'tælɪeɪt] vi zum Vergeltungsschlag ausholen; **retaliation** [rɪtælɪ'eɪʃən] n Vergeltung f

retarded [rɪ'tɑ:dɪd] adj zurückgeblieben

retch [retʃ] vi würgen

retentive [rɪ'tentɪv] adj (memory) gut

reticent ['retɪsnt] adj schweigsam

retina ['retɪnə] n Netzhaut f

retire [rɪ'taɪəʳ] vi (from work) in den Ruhestand treten; (withdraw) sich zurückziehen; (go to bed) schlafen gehen; **~d** adj (person) pensioniert, im Ruhestand; **~ment** n Ruhestand m

retiring [rɪ'taɪərɪŋ] adj zurückhaltend

retort [rɪ'tɔ:t] n (reply) Erwiderung f ♦ vi (sharp) entgegnen

retrace [ri:'treɪs] vt zurückverfolgen; to **~ one's steps** denselben Weg zurückgehen

retract [rɪ'trækt] vt (statement) zurücknehmen; (claws) einziehen ♦ vi einen Rückzieher machen; **~able** adj (aerial) ausziehbar

retrain [ri:'treɪn] vt umschulen

retread ['ri:tred] n (tyre) Reifen m mit erneuerter Lauffläche

retreat [rɪ'tri:t] n Rückzug m; (place) Zufluchtsort m ♦ vi sich zurückziehen

retribution [retrɪ'bju:ʃən] n Strafe f

retrieval [rɪ'tri:vəl] n Wiedergewinnung f

retrieve [rɪ'tri:v] vt wiederbekommen; (rescue) retten; **~r** n Apportierhund m

retrograde [retrəgreɪd] adj (step) Rück-; (policy) rückschrittlich

retrospect ['retrəspekt] n: **in ~** im Rückblick, rückblickend; **~ive** [retrə'spektɪv] adj (action) rückwirkend; (look) rückblickend

return [rɪ'tə:n] n Rückkehr f; (profits) Ertrag m; (BRIT: rail ticket etc) Rückfahrkarte f; (: plane ticket) Rückflugkarte f ♦ adj (journey, match) Rück- ♦ vi zurückkehren, zurückkommen ♦ vt zurückgeben, zurücksenden; (pay back) zurückzahlen; (elect) wählen; (verdict) aussprechen; **~s** npl (COMM) Gewinn m; (receipts) Einkünfte pl; **in ~** dafür; **by ~ of post** postwendend; **many happy ~s!** herzlichen Glückwunsch zum Geburtstag!

reunion [ri:'ju:nɪən] n Wiedervereinigung f; (SCH etc) Treffen nt

reunite [ri:ju:'naɪt] vt wieder vereinigen

reuse [ri:'ju:z] vt wieder verwenden, wieder verwerten

rev [rev] n abbr (AUT: = revolution) Drehzahl f

revamp [ri:'væmp] vt aufpolieren

reveal [rɪ'vi:l] vt enthüllen; **~ing** adj aufschlussreich

revel ['revl] vi: to **~ in sth/in doing sth** seine Freude an etw dat haben/daran haben, etw zu tun

revelation [revə'leɪʃən] n Offenbarung f

revelry ['revlrɪ] n Rummel m

revenge [rɪ'vendʒ] n Rache f; to **take ~ on** sich rächen an +dat

revenue ['revənju:] n Einnahmen pl

reverberate [rɪ'və:bəreɪt] vi widerhallen

revere [rɪ'vɪəʳ] vt (ver)ehren; **~nce** ['revərəns] n Ehrfurcht f

Reverend ['revərənd] adj: **the ~ Robert Martin** ≈ Pfarrer Robert Martin

reversal [rɪ'vɜ:sl] n Umkehrung f

reverse [rɪ'vɜ:s] n Rückseite f; (AUT: gear) Rückwärtsgang m ♦ adj (order, direction) entgegengesetzt ♦ vt umkehren ♦ vi (BRIT: AUT) rückwärts fahren; **~-charge call** (BRIT) n R-Gespräch nt; **reversing lights** npl (AUT) Rückfahrscheinwerfer pl

revert [rɪ'vɜ:t] vi: **to ~ to** zurückkehren zu; (to bad state) zurückfallen in +acc

review [rɪ'vju:] n (of book) Rezension f; (magazine) Zeitschrift f ♦ vt Rückschau halten auf +acc; (MIL) mustern; (book) rezensieren; (reexamine) von neuem untersuchen; **~er** n (critic) Rezensent m

revise [rɪ'vaɪz] vt (book) überarbeiten; (reconsider) ändern, revidieren; **revision** [rɪ'vɪʒən] n Prüfung f; (COMM) Revision f; (SCH) Wiederholung f

revitalize [ri:'vaɪtəlaɪz] vt neu beleben

revival [rɪ'vaɪvl] n Wiederbelebung f; (REL) Erweckung f; (THEAT) Wiederaufnahme f

revive [rɪ'vaɪv] vt wieder beleben; (fig) wieder auffrischen ♦ vi wieder erwachen; (fig) wieder aufleben

revoke [rɪ'vəuk] vt aufheben

revolt [rɪ'vəult] n Aufstand m, Revolte f ♦ vi sich auflehnen ♦ vt entsetzen; **~ing** adj widerlich

revolution [revə'lu:ʃən] n (turn) Umdrehung f; (POL) Revolution f; **~ary** adj revolutionär ♦ n Revolutionär m; **~ize** vt revolutionieren

revolve [rɪ'vɒlv] vi kreisen; (on own axis) sich drehen

revolver [rɪ'vɒlvəʳ] n Revolver m

revolving door [rɪ'vɒlvɪŋ-] n Drehtür f

revulsion [rɪ'vʌlʃən] n Ekel m

reward [rɪ'wɔ:d] n Belohnung f ♦ vt belohnen; **~ing** adj lohnend

rewind [ri:'waɪnd] (irreg: like wind) vt (tape etc) zurückspulen

rewire [ri:'waɪəʳ] vt (house) neu verkabeln

reword [ri:'wɜ:d] vt anders formulieren

rewrite [ri:'raɪt] (irreg: like write) vt umarbeiten, neu schreiben

rheumatism ['ru:mətɪzəm] n Rheumatismus m, Rheuma nt

Rhine [raɪn] n: **the ~** der Rhein

rhinoceros [raɪ'nɒsərəs] n Nashorn nt

Rhone [rəun] n: **the ~** die Rhone

rhubarb ['ru:bɑ:b] n Rhabarber m

rhyme [raɪm] n Reim m

rhythm ['rɪðm] n Rhythmus m

rib [rɪb] n Rippe f ♦ vt (mock) hänseln, aufziehen

ribbon ['rɪbən] n Band nt; **in ~s** (torn) in Fetzen

rice [raɪs] n Reis m; **~ pudding** n Milchreis m

rich [rɪtʃ] adj reich; (food) reichhaltig ♦ npl: **the ~** die Reichen pl; **~es** npl Reichtum m; **~ly** adv reich; (deserve) völlig

rickets ['rɪkɪts] n Rachitis f

rickety ['rɪkɪtɪ] adj wack(e)lig

rickshaw ['rɪkʃɔ:] n Rikscha f

ricochet ['rɪkəʃeɪ] n Abprallen nt; (shot) Querschläger m ♦ vi abprallen

rid [rɪd] (pt, pp **rid**) vt befreien; **to get ~ of** loswerden

riddle ['rɪdl] n Rätsel nt ♦ vt: **to be ~d with** völlig durchlöchert sein von

ride [raɪd] (pt **rode**, pp **ridden**) n (in vehicle) Fahrt f; (on horse) Ritt m ♦ vt (horse) reiten; (bicycle) fahren ♦ vi fahren, reiten; **to take sb for a ~** mit jdm eine Fahrt etc machen; (fig) jdn aufs Glatteis führen; **~r** n Reiter m

ridge [rɪdʒ] n Kamm m; (of roof) First m

ridicule ['rɪdɪkju:l] n Spott m ♦ vt lächerlich machen

ridiculous [rɪ'dɪkjuləs] adj lächerlich

riding ['raɪdɪŋ] n Reiten nt; **~ school** n Reitschule f

rife [raɪf] adj weit verbreitet; **to be ~** grassieren; **to be ~ with** voll sein von

riffraff ['rɪfræf] n Pöbel m

rifle ['raɪfl] n Gewehr nt ♦ vt berauben; **~ range** n Schießstand m

rift [rɪft] n Spalte f; (fig) Bruch m

rig [rɪg] n (oil ~) Bohrinsel f ♦ vt (election etc) manipulieren; **~ out** (BRIT) vt ausstatten; **~ up** vt zusammenbasteln; **~ging** n Takelage f

right [raɪt] adj (correct, just) richtig, recht; (~ side) rechte(r, s) ♦ n Recht nt; (not left, POL) Rechte f ♦ adv (of the ~) rechts; (to the ~) nach rechts; (look, work) richtig, recht; (directly) gerade; (exactly) genau ♦ vt in Ordnung bringen, korrigieren ♦ excl gut; **on the ~**: rechts; **to be in the ~** im Recht sein; **by ~s** von Rechts wegen; **to be ~** away sofort; **~ now** in diesem Augenblick, eben; **~ in the middle** genau in der Mitte; **~ angle** n rechte(r) Winkel m; **~eous** ['raɪtʃəs] adj rechtschaffen; **~ful** adj rechtmäßig; **~-hand** adj: **~-hand drive** mit Rechtssteuerung; **~-handed** adj rechtshändig; **~-hand man** n (irreg) n rechte Hand f; **~-hand side** n rechte Seite f; **~ly** adv mit Recht; **~ of way** n Vorfahrt f; **~-wing** adj rechtsorientiert

rigid ['rɪdʒɪd] adj (stiff) starr, steif; (strict) streng; **~ity** [rɪ'dʒɪdɪtɪ] n Starrheit f; Strenge f

rigmarole ['rɪgmərəʊl] n Gewäsch nt

rigor ['rɪgər] (US) n = **rigour**

rigorous ['rɪgərəs] adj streng

rigour ['rɪgər] (US **rigor**) n Strenge f, Härte f

rile [raɪl] vt ärgern

rim [rɪm] n (edge) Rand m; (of wheel) Felge f

rind [raɪnd] n Rinde f

ring [rɪŋ] n (pt **rang**, pp **rung**) n Ring m; (of people) Kreis m; (arena) Manege f; (of telephone) Klingeln nt ♦ vi (pt rang, pp rung) läuten; (BRIT) anrufen ♦ vt (BRIT) vt läuten; **~ back** (BRIT) vt, vi zurückrufen; **~ off** (BRIT) vi auflegen; **~ up** (BRIT) vt anrufen; **~binder** n Ringbuch nt; **~ing** n Klingeln nt; (of large bell) Läuten nt; (in ears)

Klingen nt; **~ing tone** n (TEL) Rufzeichen nt

ringleader ['rɪŋliːdər] n Anführer m, Rädelsführer m

ringlets ['rɪŋlɪts] npl Ringellocken pl

ring road (BRIT) n Umgehungsstraße f

rink [rɪŋk] n (ice ~) Eisbahn f

rinse [rɪns] n Spülen nt ♦ vt spülen

riot ['raɪət] n Aufruhr m ♦ vi randalieren; **to run ~** (people) randalieren; (vegetation) wuchern; **~er** n Aufrührer m; **~ous** adj aufrührerisch; (noisy) lärmend

rip [rɪp] n Schlitz m, Riss m ♦ vt, vi (zer)reißen; **~cord** n Reißleine f

ripe [raɪp] adj reif; **~n** vi reifen ♦ vt reifen lassen

rip-off ['rɪpɔf] (inf) n: **it's a ~~!** das ist Wucher!

ripple ['rɪpl] n kleine Welle f ♦ vi kräuseln ♦ vi sich kräuseln

rise [raɪz] (pt **rose**, pp **risen**) n (slope) Steigung f; (esp in wages: BRIT) Erhöhung f; (growth) Aufstieg m ♦ vi (sun) aufgehen; (smoke) aufsteigen; (mountain) sich erheben; (ground) ansteigen; (prices) steigen; (in revolt) sich erheben; **to give ~ to** Anlass geben zu; **to ~ to the occasion** sich der Lage gewachsen zeigen; **~n** [rɪzn] pp of **rise**; **~r** ['raɪzər] n: **to be an early ~r** ein(e) Frühaufsteher(in) m(f) sein; **rising** ['raɪzɪŋ] adj (tide, prices) steigend; (sun, moon) aufgehend ♦ n (uprising) Aufstand m

risk [rɪsk] n Gefahr f, Risiko nt ♦ vt (venture) wagen; (chance loss of) riskieren, aufs Spiel setzen; **to take** or **run the ~ of doing sth** das Risiko eingehen, etw zu tun; **at ~** in Gefahr; **at one's own ~** auf eigene Gefahr; **~y** adj riskant

risqué ['riːskeɪ] adj gewagt

rissole ['rɪsəʊl] n Fleischklößchen nt

rite [raɪt] n Ritus m; **last ~s** Letzte Ölung f

ritual ['rɪtjʊəl] n Ritual nt ♦ adj ritual, Ritual-; (fig) rituell

rival ['raɪvl] n Rivale m, Konkurrent m ♦ adj rivalisierend ♦ vt rivalisieren mit; (COMM) konkurrieren mit; **~ry** n Rivalität f, Konkurrenz f

river ['rɪvə²] n Fluss m, Strom m ♦ cpd (port, traffic) Fluss-; **up/down** ~ flussaufwärts/-abwärts; **~bank** n Flussufer nt; **~bed** n Flussbett nt

rivet ['rɪvɪt] n Niete f ♦ vt (fasten) (ver)nieten

Riviera [rɪvɪ'eərə] n: **the** ~ die Riviera

road [rəud] n Straße f ♦ cpd Straßen-; **major/minor** ~ Haupt-/Nebenstraße f; **~ accident** n Verkehrsunfall m; **~block** n Straßensperre f; **~hog** n Verkehrsrowdy m; **~ map** n Straßenkarte f; **~ rage** n Aggressivität im Straßenverkehr; **~ safety** n Verkehrssicherheit f; **~side** n Straßenrand m ♦ adj an der Landstraße (gelegen); **~ sign** n Straßenschild nt; **~ user** n Verkehrsteilnehmer m; **~way** n Fahrbahn f; **~ works** npl Straßenbauarbeiten pl; **~worthy** adj verkehrssicher

roam [rəum] vi (umher)streifen ♦ vt durchstreifen

roar [rɔː²] n Brüllen nt, Gebrüll nt ♦ vi brüllen; **to** ~ **with laughter** vor Lachen brüllen; **to do a ~ing trade** ein Riesengeschäft machen

roast [rəust] n Braten m ♦ vt braten, schmoren; ~ **beef** n Roastbeef nt

rob [rɒb] vt bestehlen, berauben; (bank) ausrauben; **to ~ sb of sth** jdm etw rauben; **~ber** n Räuber m; **~bery** n Raub m

robe [rəub] n (dress) Gewand nt; (US) Hauskleid nt; (judge's) Robe f

robin ['rɒbɪn] n Rotkehlchen nt

robot ['rəubɒt] n Roboter m

robust [rəu'bʌst] adj (person) robust; (appetite, economy) gesund

rock [rɒk] n Felsen m; (BRIT: sweet) Zuckerstange f ♦ vt, vi wiegen, schaukeln; **on the ~s** (drink) mit Eis(würfeln); (marriage) geschetert; (ship) aufgelaufen; ~ **and roll** n Rock and Roll m; ~

bottom n (fig) Tiefpunkt m; **~ery** n Steingarten m

rocket ['rɒkɪt] n Rakete f

rocking chair ['rɒkɪŋ-] n Schaukelstuhl m

rocking horse n Schaukelpferd nt

rocky ['rɒkɪ] adj felsig

rod [rɒd] n (bar) Stange f; (stick) Rute f

rode [rəud] pt of **ride**

rodent ['rəudnt] n Nagetier nt

roe [rəu] n (also: ~ **deer**) Reh nt; (of fish: also: **hard** ~) Rogen m; (**soft** ~) Milch f

rogue [rəug] n Schurke m

role [rəul] n Rolle f; ~ **play** n Rollenspiel m

roll [rəul] n Rolle f; (bread) Brötchen nt; (list) (Namens)liste f; (of drum) Wirbel m ♦ vt (turn) rollen, (herum)wälzen; (grass etc) walzen ♦ vi (swing) sich wiegen; (sound) rollen, grollen; ~ **about** or **around** vi herumkugeln; (ship) schlingern; (dog etc) sich wälzen; ~ **by** vi (time) verfließen; ~ **over** vi sich (herum)drehen; ~ **up** vi (arrive) kommen, auftauchen ♦ vt (carpet) aufrollen; ~ **call** n Namensaufruf m; **~er** n Rolle f, Walze f; (road **~er**) Straßenwalze f; **~blade** n Rollerblade m; **~er coaster** n Achterbahn f; **~er skates** npl Rollschuhe pl; **~-skating** n Rollschuhlaufen nt

rolling [rəulɪŋ] adj (landscape) wellig; ~ **pin** n Nudel- or Wellholz nt; ~ **stock** n Wagenmaterial nt

ROM [rɒm] n abbr (= read only memory) ROM m

Roman ['rəumən] adj römisch ♦ n Römer(in) m(f); ~ **Catholic** adj römisch-katholisch ♦ n Katholik(in) m(f)

romance [rə'mæns] n Romanze f; (story) (Liebes)roman m

Romania [rəu'meɪnɪə] n = **Rumania**; **~n** n = **Rumanian**

Roman numeral n römische Ziffer

romantic [rə'mæntɪk] adj romantisch; **~ism** [rə'mæntɪsɪzəm] n Romantik f

Rome [rəum] n Rom nt

romp [rɒmp] n Tollen nt ♦ vi (also: ~ about) herumtollen

rompers ['rɒmpəz] npl Spielanzug m

roof [ru:f] (pl ~s) n Dach nt; (of mouth) Gaumen m ♦ vt überdachen, überdecken; ~ing n Deckmaterial nt; ~rack n (AUT) Dachgepäckträger m

rook [ruk] n (bird) Saatkrähe f; (chess) Turm m

room [ru:m] n Zimmer n, Raum m; (space) Platz m; (fig) Spielraum m; ~s npl (accommodation) Wohnung f; "~s to let (BRIT) or for rent (US)" „Zimmer zu vermieten"; single/double ~ Einzel-/Doppelzimmer nt; ~ing house (US) n Mietshaus nt (mit möblierten Wohnungen); ~mate n Mitbewohner(in) m(f); ~ service n Zimmerbedienung f; ~y adj geräumig

roost [ru:st] n Hühnerstange f ♦ vi auf der Stange hocken

rooster ['ru:stə] n Hahn m

root [ru:t] n (also fig) Wurzel f ♦ vi wurzeln; ~ about vi (fig) herumwühlen; ~ for vt fus Stimmung machen für; ~ out vt ausjäten; (fig) ausrotten

rope [rəup] n Seil nt ♦ vt (tie) festschnüren; to know the ~s sich auskennen; to ~ sb in jdn gewinnen; ~ off vt absperren; ~ ladder n Strickleiter f

rosary ['rəuzəri] n Rosenkranz m

rose [rəuz] pt of **rise** ♦ n Rose f ♦ adj Rosen-, rosenrot

rosé ['rəuzei] n Rosé m

rosebud ['rəuzbʌd] n Rosenknospe f

rosebush ['rəuzbuʃ] n Rosenstock m

rosemary ['rəuzməri] n Rosmarin m

rosette [rəu'zet] n Rosette f

roster ['rɒstə] n Dienstplan m

rostrum ['rɒstrəm] n Rednerbühne f

rosy ['rəuzi] adj rosig

rot [rɒt] n Fäulnis f; (nonsense) Quatsch m ♦ vi verfaulen ♦ vt verfaulen lassen

rota ['rəutə] n Dienstliste f

rotary ['rəutəri] adj rotierend

rotate [rəu'teit] vt rotieren lassen; (take turns) turnusmäßig wechseln ♦ vi rotieren; **rotating** adj rotierend; **rotation** [rəu'teiʃən] n Umdrehung f

rote [rəut] n: **by** ~ auswendig

rotten ['rɒtn] adj faul; (fig) schlecht, gemein; to **feel** ~ (ill) sich elend fühlen

rotund [rəu'tʌnd] adj rundlich

rouble ['ru:bl] (US **ruble**) n Rubel m

rough [rʌf] adj (not smooth) rau; (path) uneben; (violent) roh, grob; (crossing) stürmisch; (without comforts) hart, unbequem; (unfinished, makeshift) grob; (approximate) ungefähr ♦ n (BRIT: person) Rowdy m, Rohling m; (GOLF): **in the** ~ im Rau ♦ vt: **to** ~ **it** primitiv leben; **to sleep** ~ im Freien schlafen; ~age n Ballaststoffe pl; ~and-ready adj provisorisch; (work) zusammengehauen; ~ **copy** n Entwurf m; ~ **draft** n Entwurf m; ~ly adv grob; (about) ungefähr; ~ness n Rauheit f; (of manner) Ungeschliffenheit f

roulette [ru:'let] n Roulett(e) nt

Roumania [ru:'meiniə] n = **Rumania**

round [raund] adj rund; (figures) aufgerundet ♦ adv (in a circle) rundherum ♦ prep um ... herum ♦ n Runde f; (of ammunition) Magazin nt ♦ vt (corner) biegen um; **all** ~ überall; **the long way** ~ der Umweg m; **all the year** ~ das ganze Jahr über; **it's just** ~ **the corner** (fig) es ist gerade um die Ecke; **the clock** rund um die Uhr; **to go** ~ **to sb's (house)** jdn besuchen; **to go** ~ **the back** hintenherum gehen; **enough to go** ~ genug für alle; **to go the** ~s (story) die Runde machen; **a** ~ **of applause** eine Beifall m; **a** ~ **of drinks** eine Runde Drinks; **a** ~ **of sandwiches** ein Sandwich nt or m, ein belegtes Brot; ~ **off** vt abrunden; ~ **up** vt (end) abschließen; (figures) aufrunden; (criminals) hochnehmen; ~**about** n (BRIT: traffic) Kreisverkehr m; (: merry-go-~) Karussell nt ♦ adj

Umwegen; **~ers** npl (game) ≈ Schlagball m; **~ly** adv (fig) gründlich; **~-shouldered** adj mit abfallenden Schultern; **~ trip** n Rundreise f; **~up** n Zusammentreiben nt, Sammeln nt

rouse [rauz] vt (waken) (auf)wecken; (stir up) erregen; **rousing** adj (welcome) stürmisch; (speech) zündend

route [ruːt] n Weg m, Route f ♦ **map** (BRIT) n (for journey) Streckenkarte f

routine [ruːˈtiːn] n Routine f ♦ adj Routine-

row¹ [rau] n (noise) Lärm m; (dispute) Streit m ♦ vi sich streiten

row² [rau] n (line) Reihe f ♦ vt, vi (boat) rudern; **in a ~** (fig) hintereinander; **~boat** ['rəubaut] (US) n Ruderboot nt

rowdy ['raudɪ] adj rüpelhaft ♦ n (person) Rowdy m

rowing ['rəuɪŋ] n Rudern nt; (SPORT) Rudersport m; **~ boat** (BRIT) n Ruderboot nt

royal ['rɔɪəl] adj königlich, Königs-; **R~ Air Force** n Königliche Luftwaffe f; **~ty** ['rɔɪəltɪ] n (family) königliche Familie f; (for novel etc) Tantieme f

rpm abbr (= revs per minute) U/min

R.S.V.P. abbr (= répondez s'il vous plaît) u. A. w. g.

Rt. Hon. abbr (= Right Honourable) Abgeordnete(r) mf

rub [rʌb] n (with cloth) Polieren nt; (on person) Reiben n ♦ vt reiben; **to ~ sb up** (BRIT) or **to ~ sb** (US) **the wrong way** jdn aufreizen; **~ off** vi (also fig): **to ~ off (on)** abfärben (auf +acc); **~ out** vt herausreiben; (with eraser) ausradieren

rubber ['rʌbər] n Gummi m, (BRIT) Radiergummi m; **~ band** n Gummiband nt; **~ plant** n Gummibaum m

rubbish ['rʌbɪʃ] n (waste) Abfall m; (nonsense) Blödsinn m, Quatsch m; **~ bin** (BRIT) n Mülleimer m; **~ dump** n Müllabladeplatz m

rubble ['rʌbl] n (Stein)schutt m

ruby ['ruːbɪ] n Rubin m ♦ adj rubinrot

rucksack ['rʌksæk] n Rucksack m

rudder ['rʌdər] n Steuerruder nt

ruddy ['rʌdɪ] adj (colour) rötlich; (inf: bloody) verdammt

rude [ruːd] adj unverschämt; (shock) hart; (awakening) unsanft; (unrefined, rough) grob; (**~ness** n Unverschämtheit f; Grobheit f

rudiment ['ruːdɪmənt] n Grundlage f

rueful ['ruːful] adj reuevoll

ruffian ['rʌfɪən] n Rohling m

ruffle ['rʌfl] vt kräuseln

rug [rʌg] n Brücke f; (in bedroom) Bettvorleger m; (BRIT: for knees) (Reise)decke f

rugby ['rʌgbɪ] n (also: **~ football**) Rugby nt

rugged ['rʌgɪd] adj (coastline) zerklüftet; (features) markig

rugger ['rʌgər] (BRIT: inf) n = **rugby**

ruin ['ruːɪn] n Ruine f; (downfall) Ruin m ♦ vt ruinieren; **~s** npl (fig) Trümmer pl; **~ous** adj ruinierend

rule [ruːl] n Regel f; (government) Regierung f; (for measuring) Lineal nt ♦ vt (govern) herrschen über +acc, regieren; (decide) anordnen, entscheiden; (make lines on) linieren ♦ vi herrschen, regieren; entscheiden; **as a ~** in der Regel; **~ out** vt ausschließen; **~d** adj (paper) liniert; **~r** n Lineal nt; Herrscher m; **ruling** ['ruːlɪŋ] adj (party) Regierungs-; (class) herrschend ♦ n (JUR) Entscheid m

rum [rʌm] n Rum m

Rumania [ruːˈmeɪnɪə] (US **rumor**) n Rumänien nt; **~n** adj rumänisch ♦ n Rumäne m, Rumänin f; (LING) Rumänisch nt

rumble ['rʌmbl] n Rumpeln nt; (of thunder) Grollen nt ♦ vi rumpeln; grollen

rummage ['rʌmɪdʒ] vi durchstöbern

rumour ['ruːmər] (US **rumor**) n Gerücht nt ♦ vt: **it is ~ed that** man sagt or man munkelt, dass

rump [rʌmp] n Hinterteil nt; **~ steak** n Rumpsteak nt

rumpus ['rʌmpəs] n Spektakel m

run [rʌn] (pt ran, pp run) n Lauf m; (in car) (Spazier)fahrt f; (series) Serie f, Reihe f; (ski ~) (Ski)abfahrt f; (in stocking) Laufmasche f ♦ vt (cause to ~) laufen lassen; (car, train, bus) fahren; (race, distance) laufen, rennen; (manage) leiten; (COMPUT) laufen lassen; (pass: hand, eye) gleiten lassen ♦ vi laufen; (move quickly) laufen, rennen; (bus, train) fahren; (flow) fließen, laufen; (colours) ab)färben; **there was a ~ on** (meat, tickets) es gab einen Ansturm auf +acc; **on the ~** auf der Flucht; **in the long ~** auf die Dauer; **I'll ~ you to the station** ich fahre dich zum Bahnhof; **to ~ a risk** ein Risiko eingehen; **~ about** or **around** vi (children) umherspringen; **~ across** vt fus (find) stoßen auf +acc; **~ away** vi weglaufen; **~ down** vi (clock) allmählich ♦ vt (production, factory) allmählich auflösen; (with car) überfahren; (talk against) heruntermachen; **to be ~ down** erschöpft or abgespannt sein; **~ in** (BRIT) vt (car) einfahren; **~ into** vt fus (meet: person) zufällig treffen; (trouble) bekommen; (collide with) rennen gegen; fahren gegen; **~ off** vi fortlaufen; **~ out** vi (person) hinausrennen; (liquid) auslaufen; (lease) ablaufen; (money) ausgehen; **he ran out of money/petrol** ihm ging das Geld/Benzin aus; **~ over** vt (in accident) überfahren; **~ through** vt (instructions) durchgehen; **~ up** vt (debt, bill) machen; **~ up against** vt fus (difficulties) stoßen auf +acc; **~away** adj (horse) ausgebrochen; (person) flüchtig

rung [rʌŋ] pp of ring ♦ n Sprosse f

runner ['rʌnər] n Läufer(in) m(f); (for sleigh) Kufe f; **~ bean** (BRIT) n Stangenbohne f; **~up** n Zweite(r) mf

running ['rʌnɪŋ] n (of business) Leitung f; (of machine) Betrieb m ♦ adj (water) fließend; (commentary) laufend; **to be in/out of the ~ for sth** im/aus dem

Rennen für etw sein; **3 days ~** 3 Tage lang or hintereinander; **~ costs** npl (of car, machine) Unterhaltungskosten pl

runny ['rʌnɪ] adj dünn; (nose) laufend

run-of-the-mill ['rʌnəvðə'mɪl] adj gewöhnlich, alltäglich

runt [rʌnt] n (animal) Kümmerer m

run-up ['rʌnʌp] n: **the ~~ to** (election etc) die Endphase vor +dat

runway ['rʌnweɪ] n Startbahn f

rupture ['rʌptʃər] n (MED) Bruch m

rural ['ruərl] adj ländlich, Land-

ruse [ru:z] n Kniff m, List f

rush [rʌʃ] n Eile f, Hetze f; (FIN) starke Nachfrage f; (BOT) Binse f ♦ vt (carry along) auf dem schnellsten Wege schaffen or transportieren; (attack) losstürmen auf +acc ♦ vi (hurry) eilen, stürzen; **don't ~ me** dräng mich nicht; **~ hour** n Hauptverkehrszeit f

rusk [rʌsk] n Zwieback m

Russia ['rʌʃə] n Russland nt; **~n** adj russisch ♦ n Russe m, Russin f; (LING) Russisch nt

rust [rʌst] n Rost m ♦ vi rosten

rustic ['rʌstɪk] adj bäuerlich, ländlich

rustle ['rʌsl] vi rauschen, rascheln ♦ vt rascheln lassen

rustproof ['rʌstpru:f] adj rostfrei

rusty ['rʌstɪ] adj rostig

rut [rʌt] n (in track) Radspur f; **to be in a ~** im Trott stecken

ruthless ['ru:θlɪs] adj rücksichtslos

rye [raɪ] n Roggen m; **~ bread** n Roggenbrot m

S, s

sabbath ['sæbəθ] n Sabbat m

sabotage ['sæbətɑ:ʒ] n Sabotage f ♦ vt sabotieren

saccharin ['sækərɪn] n Sa(c)charin nt

sachet ['sæʃeɪ] n (of shampoo etc) Briefchen nt, Kissen nt

sack [sæk] n Sack m ♦ vt (inf) hinauswerfen; (pillage) plündern; **to get the**

~ **rausfliegen;** ~**ing** n (material) Sackleinen nt; (inf) Rausschmiss m

sacrament ['sækrəmənt] n Sakrament nt

sacred ['seɪkrɪd] adj heilig

sacrifice ['sækrɪfaɪs] n Opfer nt ♦ vt (also fig) opfern

sacrilege ['sækrɪlɪdʒ] n Schändung f

sad [sæd] adj traurig; ~**den** vt traurig machen, betrüben

saddle ['sædl] n Sattel m ♦ vt (burden): **to ~ sb with sth** jdm etw aufhalsen; ~**bag** n Satteltasche f

sadistic [sə'dɪstɪk] adj sadistisch

sadly ['sædlɪ] adv traurig; (unfortunately) leider

sadness ['sædnɪs] n Traurigkeit f

s.a.e. abbr (= stamped addressed envelope) adressierte(r) Rückumschlag m

safe [seɪf] adj (careful) vorsichtig ♦ n Safe m; ~ **and sound** gesund und wohl; (just) **to be on the ~ side** um ganz sicherzugehen; ~ **from** (attack) sicher vor +dat; ~**conduct** n freie(s) Geleit nt; ~**deposit** n (vault) Tresorraum m; (box) Banksafe m; ~**guard** n Sicherung f ♦ vt sichern, schützen; ~**keeping** n sichere Verwahrung f; ~**ly** adv sicher; (arrive) wohlbehalten; ~ **sex** n geschützter Sex m

safety ['seɪftɪ] n Sicherheit f; ~ **belt** n Sicherheitsgurt m; ~ **pin** n Sicherheitsnadel f; ~ **valve** n Sicherheitsventil nt

sag [sæg] vi (durch)sacken

sage [seɪdʒ] n (herb) Salbei m; (person) Weise(r) mf

Sagittarius [sædʒɪ'tɛərɪəs] n Schütze m

Sahara [sə'hɑːrə] n: **the ~ (Desert)** die (Wüste) Sahara

said [sed] pt, pp of **say**

sail [seɪl] n Segel nt; (trip) Fahrt f ♦ vt segeln ♦ vi segeln; (begin voyage: person) abfahren; (: ship) auslaufen; (fig: cloud etc) dahinsegeln; **to go for a ~** segeln gehen; **they ~ed into Copenhagen** sie liefen in Kopenhagen ein; ~ **through** vt fus, vi (fig) es spielend

schaffen; ~**boat** (US) n Segelboot nt; ~**ing** n Segeln nt; ~**ing ship** n Segelschiff nt; ~**or** n Matrose m, Seemann m

saint [seɪnt] n Heilige(r) mf; ~**ly** adj heilig, fromm

sake [seɪk] n: **for the ~ of** um +gen willen

salad ['sæləd] n Salat m; ~ **bowl** n Salatschüssel f; ~ **cream** (BRIT) n Salatmayonnaise f; Salatmajonäse f; ~ **dressing** n Salatsoße f

salary ['sælərɪ] n Gehalt nt

sale [seɪl] n Verkauf m; (reduced prices) Schlussverkauf m; **"for ~"** "zu verkaufen"; **on ~** zu verkaufen; ~**room** n Verkaufsraum m; ~**s assistant** n Verkäufer(in) m(f); ~**s clerk** (US) n Verkäufer(in) m(f); ~**sman** (irreg) n Verkäufer m; (representative) Vertreter m; ~**s rep** n (COMM) Vertreter(in) m(f); ~**swoman** (irreg) n Verkäuferin f

salient ['seɪlɪənt] adj bemerkenswert

saliva [sə'laɪvə] n Speichel m

sallow ['sæləu] adj fahl; (face) bleich

salmon ['sæmən] n Lachs m

salon ['sælɒn] n Salon m

saloon [sə'luːn] n (BRIT: AUT) Limousine f; (ship's lounge) Salon m; ~ **car** (BRIT) n Limousine f

salt [sɔːlt] n Salz nt ♦ vt (cure) einsalzen; (flavour) salzen; ~**cellar** n Salzfass nt; ~**water** adj Salzwasser-; ~**y** adj salzig

salute [sə'luːt] n (MIL) Gruß m; (with guns) Salutschüsse pl ♦ vt (MIL) salutieren

salvage ['sælvɪdʒ] n (from ship) Bergung f; (property) Rettung f ♦ vt bergen; retten

salvation [sæl'veɪʃən] n Rettung f; **S~ Army** n Heilsarmee f

same [seɪm] adj, pron (similar) gleiche(r, s); (identical) derselbe/dieselbe/dasselbe; **the ~ book** as das gleiche Buch wie; **at the ~ time** zur gleichen Zeit, gleichzeitig; (however) zugleich, andererseits; **all** or **just the ~** trotzdem; **the ~ to you!** gleichfalls!; **to do**

the ~ (as sb) das Gleiche tun (wie jd)

sample ['sɑːmpl] n Probe f ♦ vt probieren

sanctify ['sæŋktɪfaɪ] vt weihen

sanctimonious [sæŋktɪ'məʊnɪəs] adj scheinheilig

sanction ['sæŋkʃən] n Sanktion f

sanctity ['sæŋktɪtɪ] n Heiligkeit f; (fig) Unverletzlichkeit f

sanctuary ['sæŋktjʊərɪ] n (for fugitive) Asyl nt; (refuge) Zufluchtsort m; (for animals) Schutzgebiet nt

sand [sænd] n Sand m ♦ vt (furniture) schmirgeln

sandal ['sændl] n Sandale f

sand: ~box (US) n = sandpit; **~castle** n Sandburg f; **~ dune** n (Sand)düne f; **~paper** n Sandpapier nt; **~pit** n Sandkasten m; **~stone** n Sandstein m

sandwich ['sændwɪtʃ] n Sandwich m or nt ♦ vt (also: **~ in**) einklemmen; **cheese/ham** ~ Käse-/Schinkenbrot; **~ed between** eingeklemmt zwischen; **~ board** n Reklametafel f; **~ course** (BRIT) n in Theorie und Praxis abwechselnde(r) Ausbildungsgang m

sandy ['sændɪ] adj sandig; (hair) rotblond

sane [seɪn] adj geistig gesund or normal; (sensible) vernünftig, gescheit

sang [sæŋ] pt of **sing**

sanitary ['sænɪtərɪ] adj hygienisch; **~ towel** n (Monats)binde f

sanitation [sænɪ'teɪʃən] n sanitäre Einrichtungen pl; **~ department** (US) n Stadtreinigung f

sanity ['sænɪtɪ] n geistige Gesundheit f; (sense) Vernunft f

sank [sæŋk] pt of **sink**

Santa Claus [sæntə'klɔːz] n Nikolaus m, Weihnachtsmann m

sap [sæp] n (of plants) Saft m ♦ vt (strength) schwächen

sapling ['sæplɪŋ] n junge(r) Baum m

sapphire ['sæfaɪə*] n Saphir m

sarcasm ['sɑːkæzm] n Sarkasmus m

sarcastic [sɑː'kæstɪk] adj sarkastisch

sardine [sɑː'diːn] n Sardine f

Sardinia [sɑː'dɪnɪə] n Sardinien nt

sardonic [sɑː'dɒnɪk] adj zynisch

sash [sæʃ] n Schärpe f

sat [sæt] pt, pp of **sit**

Satan ['seɪtn] n Satan m

satchel ['sætʃl] n (for school) Schulmappe f

satellite ['sætəlaɪt] n Satellit m; **~ dish** n (TECH) Parabolantenne f, Satellitenantenne f; **~ television** n Satellitenfernsehen nt

satisfaction [sætɪs'fækʃən] n Befriedigung f, Genugtuung f; **satisfactory** [sætɪs'fæktərɪ] adj zufrieden stellend, befriedigend; **satisfied** adj befriedigt

satisfy ['sætɪsfaɪ] vt befriedigen, zufrieden stellen; (convince) überzeugen; (conditions) erfüllen; **~ing** adj befriedigend; (meal) sättigend

saturate ['sætʃəreɪt] vt (durch)tränken

Saturday ['sætədɪ] n Samstag m, Sonnabend m

sauce [sɔːs] n Soße f, Sauce f; **~pan** n Kasserolle f

saucer ['sɔːsə*] n Untertasse f

saucy ['sɔːsɪ] adj frech, keck

Saudi: ['saudɪ] **~ Arabia** n Saudi-Arabien nt; **~ (Arabian)** adj saudiarabisch ♦ n Saudi-Araber(in) m(f)

sauna ['sɔːnə] n Sauna f

saunter ['sɔːntə*] vi schlendern

sausage ['sɒsɪdʒ] n Wurst f; **~ roll** n Wurst f im Schlafrock, Wurstpastete f

sauté ['səʊteɪ] adj Röst-

savage ['sævɪdʒ] adj wild ♦ n Wilde(r) mf ♦ vt (animals) zerfleischen

save [seɪv] vt retten; (money, electricity etc) sparen; (strength etc) aufsparen; (COMPUT) speichern ♦ vi (also: **~ up**) sparen ♦ n (SPORT) (Ball)abwehr f ♦ prep, conj außer, ausgenommen

saving ['seɪvɪŋ] adj: **the ~ grace of** das Versöhnende an +dat ♦ n Sparen nt, Ersparnis f; **~s** npl (money) Ersparnisse pl; **~s account** n Sparkonto nt; **~s bank** n Sparkasse f

saviour ['seɪvjə^r] *n* (*US* **savior**) *n* (*REL*) Erlöser *m*

savour ['seɪvə^r] (*US* **savor**) *vt* (*taste*) schmecken; (*fig*) genießen; **~y** *adj* pikant, würzig

saw [sɔː] (*pt* **sawed**, *pp* **sawed** *or* **sawn**) *pt of* **see** ♦ *n* (*tool*) Säge *f* ♦ *vt, vi* sägen; **~dust** *n* Sägemehl *nt*; **~mill** *n* Sägewerk *nt*; **~n** *pp of* **saw**; **~n-off shotgun** *n* Gewehr *nt* mit abgesägtem Lauf

sax [sæks] (*inf*) *n* Saxofon *nt*, Saxophon *nt*

saxophone ['sæksəfəun] *n* Saxofon *nt*, Saxophon *nt*

say [seɪ] (*pt, pp* **said**) *n*: to have a/no **~ in sth** Mitspracherecht/kein Mitspracherecht bei etw haben ♦ *vt, vi* sagen; **let him have his ~** laß ihn doch reden; **to ~ yes/no** Ja/Nein *or* ja/nein sagen; **that goes without ~ing** das versteht sich von selbst; **that is to ~** das heißt; **~ing** *n* Sprichwort *nt*

scab [skæb] *n* Schorf *m*; (*pej*) Streikbrecher *m*

scaffold ['skæfəld] *n* (*for execution*) Schafott *nt*; **~ing** *n* (Bau)gerüst *nt*

scald [skɔːld] *n* Verbrühung *f* ♦ *vt* (*burn*) verbrühen

scale [skeɪl] *n* (*of fish*) Schuppe *f*; (*MUS*) Tonleiter *f*; (*on map, size*) Maßstab *m*; (*gradation*) Skala *f* ♦ *vt* (*climb*) erklimmen; **~s** *npl* (*balance*) Waage *f*; **on a large ~** (*fig*) im Großen, in großem Umfang; **~ of charges** Gebührenordnung *f*; **~ down** *vt* verkleinern; **~ model** *n* maßstabgetreue(s) Modell *nt*

scallop ['skɔləp] *n* Kammmuschel *f*

scalp [skælp] *n* Kopfhaut *f*

scamper ['skæmpə^r] *vi*: **to ~ away** *or* **off** sich davonmachen

scampi ['skæmpɪ] *npl* Scampi *pl*

scan [skæn] *vt* genau prüfen; (*quickly*) überfliegen; (*horizon*) absuchen

scandal ['skændl] *n* Skandal *m*; (*piece of gossip*) Skandalgeschichte *f*

Scandinavia [skændɪ'neɪvɪə] *n* Skandinavien *nt*; **~n** *adj* skandinavisch ♦ *n* Skandinavier(in) *m(f)*

scant [skænt] *adj* knapp; **~ily** *adv* knapp, dürftig; **~y** *adj* knapp, unzureichend

scapegoat ['skeɪpgəut] *n* Sündenbock *m*

scar [skɑː^r] *n* Narbe *f* ♦ *vt* durch Narben entstellen

scarce [skɛəs] *adj* selten, rar; (*goods*) knapp; **~ly** *adv* kaum; **scarcity** *n* Mangel *m*

scare [skɛə^r] *n* Schrecken *m* ♦ *vt* erschrecken; **bomb ~** Bombendrohung *f*; **to ~ sb stiff** jdn zu Tode erschrecken; **to be ~d** Angst haben; **~ away** *vt* (*animal*) verscheuchen; **~ off** *vt* = **scare away**; **~crow** *n* Vogelscheuche *f*

scarf [skɑːf] (*pl* **scarves**) *n* Schal *m*; (*headscarf*) Kopftuch *nt*

scarlet ['skɑːlɪt] *adj* scharlachrot ♦ *n* Scharlachrot *nt*; **~ fever** *n* Scharlach *m*

scarves [skɑːvz] *npl of* **scarf**

scary ['skɛərɪ] (*inf*) *adj* schaurig

scathing ['skeɪðɪŋ] *adj* scharf, vernichtend

scatter ['skætə^r] *vt* (*sprinkle*) (ver)streuen; (*disperse*) zerstreuen ♦ *vi* sich zerstreuen; **~brained** *adj* flatterhaft, schusselig

scavenger ['skævəndʒə^r] *n* (*animal*) Aasfresser *m*

scenario [sɪ'nɑːrɪəu] *n* (*THEAT, CINE*) Szenarium *nt*; (*fig*) Szenario *nt*

scene [siːn] *n* (*of happening*) Ort *m*; (*of play, incident*) Szene *f*; (*view*) Anblick *m*; (*argument*) Szene *f*, Auftritt *m*; **~ry** ['siːnərɪ] *n* (*THEAT*) Bühnenbild *nt*; (*landscape*) Landschaft *f*

scenic ['siːnɪk] *adj* landschaftlich

scent [sɛnt] *n* Parfüm *nt*; (*smell*) Duft *m* ♦ *vt* parfümieren

sceptical ['skɛptɪkl] (*US* **skeptical**) *adj* skeptisch

schedule ['ʃɛdjuːl], (*US*) 'skɛdjuːl] *n* (*list*) Liste *f*; (*plan*) Programm *nt*; (*of work*)

scheme 542 **scrap**

Zeitplan m ♦ vt planen; **on ~** pünktlich; **to be ahead of/behind ~** dem Zeitplan voraus/im Rückstand sein; **~d flight** n (not charter) Linienflug m

scheme [skiːm] n Schema nt; (dishonest) Intrige f; (plan of action) Plan m ♦ vi intrigieren ♦ vt planen; **scheming** ['skiːmɪŋ] adj intrigierend

scholar ['skɔlə'] n Gelehrte(r) m; (holding ~ship) Stipendiat m; **~ly** adj gelehrt; **~ship** n Gelehrsamkeit f; (grant) Stipendium nt

school [skuːl] n Schule f; (UNIV) Fakultät f ♦ vt schulen; **~ age** n schulpflichtige(s) Alter nt; **~book** n Schulbuch nt; **~boy** n Schüler m; **~children** npl Schüler pl, Schulkinder pl; **~days** npl (alte) Schulzeit f; **~girl** n Schülerin f; **~ing** n Schulung f, Ausbildung f; **~master** n Lehrer m; **~mistress** n Lehrerin f; **~teacher** n Lehrer(in) m(f)

sciatica [saɪˈætɪkə] n Ischias m or nt

science ['saɪəns] n Wissenschaft f; (natural ~) Naturwissenschaft f; **~ fiction** n Sciencefiction f; **scientific** [saɪənˈtɪfɪk] adj wissenschaftlich; (natural ~s) naturwissenschaftlich; **scientist** ['saɪəntɪst] n Wissenschaftler(in) m(f)

scintillating ['sɪntɪleɪtɪŋ] adj sprühend

scissors ['sɪzəz] npl Schere f; **a pair of ~** eine Schere

scoff [skɔf] vt (eat) (BRIT: inf: eat) fressen ♦ vi (mock): **to ~ (at)** spotten (über +acc)

scold [skəʊld] vt schimpfen

scone [skɔn] n weiche(s) Teegebäck nt

scoop [skuːp] n Schaufel f; (news) sensationelle Erstmeldung f; **~ out** vt herausschaufeln; **~ up** vt aufschaufeln; (liquid) aufschöpfen

scooter ['skuːtə'] n Motorroller m; (child's) Roller m

scope [skəʊp] n Ausmaß nt; (opportunity) Spiel)raum m

scorch [skɔːtʃ] n Brandstelle f ♦ vt versengen; **~ing** adj brennend

score [skɔː'] n (in game) Punktzahl f;

(final ~) (Spiel)ergebnis nt; (MUS) Partitur f; (line) Kratzer m; (twenty) zwanzig, zwanzig Stück s ♦ vt (goal) schießen; (points) machen; (mark) einritzen ♦ vi (keep record) Punkte zählen; **on that ~** in dieser Hinsicht; **what's the ~?** wie stehts?; **to ~ 6 out of 10** 6 von 10 Punkten erzielen; **~ out** vt ausstreichen; **~board** n Anschreibetafel f; **~r** n Torschütze m; (recorder) (Auf)schreiber m

scorn [skɔːn] n Verachtung f ♦ vt verhöhnen; **~ful** adj verächtlich

Scorpio ['skɔːpɪəʊ] n Skorpion m

Scot [skɔt] n Schotte m, Schottin f

Scotch [skɔtʃ] n Scotch m

scotch [skɔtʃ] vt (end) unterbinden

scot-free ['skɔt'friː] adv: **to get off ~~** (unpunished) ungeschoren davonkommen

Scotland ['skɔtlənd] n Schottland nt

Scots [skɔts] adj schottisch; **~man/woman** (irreg) n Schotte m/Schottin f

Scottish ['skɔtɪʃ] adj schottisch

scoundrel ['skaʊndrl] n Schuft m

scour ['skaʊə'] vt (search) absuchen; (clean) schrubben

scourge [skɜːdʒ] n (whip) Geißel f; (plague) Qual f

scout [skaʊt] n (MIL) Späher m; (also: boy ~) Pfadfinder m; **~ around** vi: **to ~ around (for)** sich umsehen (nach)

scowl [skaʊl] n finstere(r) Blick m ♦ vi finster blicken

scrabble ['skræbl] vi (also: **~ around:** search) (herum)tasten; (claw): **to ~ (at)** kratzen (an +dat) ♦ n: **S~ ®** Scrabble nt ®

scraggy ['skrægɪ] adj dürr, hager

scram [skræm] (inf) vi abhauen

scramble ['skræmbl] n (climb) Kletterei f; (struggle) Kampf m ♦ vi klettern; (fight) sich schlagen; **to ~ out/through** krabbeln aus/durch; **to ~ for** sth sich um etw raufen; **~d eggs** npl Rührei nt

scrap [skræp] n (bit) Stückchen nt;

(fight) Keilerei f; *(also: ~ iron)* Schrott m ♦ vt verwerfen ♦ vi *(fight)* streiten, sich prügeln; *(waste)* Abfall m; **~book** n Einklebealbum nt; **~ dealer** n Schrotthändler(in) m(f)

scrape [skreɪp] n Kratzen nt; *(trouble)* Klemme f ♦ vt kratzen; *(car)* zerkratzen; *(clean)* abkratzen ♦ vi *(make harsh noise)* kratzen; **to ~ through** gerade noch durchkommen; **~r** n Kratzer m

scrap: ~ heap n Schrotthaufen m; **on the ~ heap** *(fig)* beim alten Eisen; **~ iron** n Schrott m; **~ merchant** *(BRIT)* n Altwarenhändler(in) m(f); **~ paper** n Schmierpapier nt

scrappy ['skræpɪ] adj zusammengestoppelt

scratch [skrætʃ] n *(wound)* Kratzer m, Schramme f ♦ adj: **~ team** zusammengewürfelte Mannschaft ♦ vt kratzen; *(car)* zerkratzen ♦ vi *(sich)* kratzen; **to start from ~** ganz von vorne anfangen; **to be up to ~** den Anforderungen entsprechen

scrawl [skrɔːl] n Gekritzel nt ♦ vt, vi kritzeln

scrawny ['skrɔːnɪ] adj *(person, neck)* dürr

scream [skriːm] n Schrei m ♦ vi schreien

scree [skriː] n Geröll(halde f) nt

screech [skriːtʃ] n Schrei m ♦ vi kreischen

screen [skriːn] n *(protective)* Schutzschirm m; *(CINE)* Leinwand f; *(TV)* Bildschirm m ♦ vt *(shelter)* (be)schirmen; *(film)* zeigen, vorführen; **~ing** n *(MED)* Untersuchung f; **~play** n Drehbuch nt; **~ saver** n *(COMPUT)* Bildschirmschoner m

screw [skruː] n Schraube f ♦ vt *(fasten)* schrauben; *(vulgar)* bumsen; **~ up** n *(paper etc)* zerknüllen; *(inf: ruin)* vermasseln *(inf)*; **~driver** n Schraubenzieher m

scribble ['skrɪbl] n Gekritzel nt ♦ vt krit-

zeln

script [skrɪpt] n *(handwriting)* Handschrift f; *(for film)* Drehbuch nt; *(THEAT)* Manuskript nt, Text m

Scripture ['skrɪptʃə*] n Heilige Schrift f

scroll [skrəʊl] n Schriftrolle f

scrounge [skraʊndʒ] *(inf)* vt: **to ~ sth off or from sb** etw bei jdm abstauben ♦ n: **on the ~** beim Schnorren

scrub [skrʌb] n *(clean)* Schrubben nt; *(in countryside)* Gestrüpp nt ♦ vt *(clean)* schrubben

scruff [skrʌf] n: **by the ~ of the neck** am Genick

scruffy ['skrʌfɪ] adj unordentlich, vergammelt

scrum(mage) ['skrʌm(ɪdʒ)] n Getümmel nt

scruple ['skruːpl] n Skrupel m, Bedenken nt

scrupulous ['skruːpjələs] adj peinlich genau, gewissenhaft

scrutinize ['skruːtɪnaɪz] vt genau prüfen; **scrutiny** ['skruːtɪnɪ] n genaue Untersuchung f

scuff [skʌf] vt *(shoes)* abstoßen

scuffle ['skʌfl] n Handgemenge nt

sculptor ['skʌlptə*] n Bildhauer(in) m(f)

sculpture ['skʌlptʃə*] n *(ART)* Bildhauerei f; *(statue)* Skulptur f

scum [skʌm] n *(also fig)* Abschaum m

scurry ['skʌrɪ] vi huschen

scuttle ['skʌtl] n *(also: coal ~)* Kohleneimer m ♦ vt *(ship)* versenken ♦ vi *(scamper)*: **to ~ away or off** sich davonmachen

scythe [saɪð] n Sense f

SDP *(BRIT)* n abbr = **Social Democratic Party**

sea [siː] n Meer nt, See f; *(fig)* Meer nt ♦ adj Meeres-, See-; **by ~** *(travel)* auf dem Seeweg; **on the ~** *(boat)* auf dem Meer; *(town)* am Meer; **out to ~** aufs Meer hinaus; **out at ~** aufs Meer; **~board** n Küste f; **~food** n Meeresfrüchte pl; **~ front** n Strandpromenade f; **~going** adj seetüchtig, Hochsee-;

~gull n Möwe f

seal [si:l] n (animal) Robbe f, Seehund m; (stamp, impression) Siegel nt ♦ vt versiegeln; **~ off** vt (place) abriegeln

sea level n Meeresspiegel m

sea lion n Seelöwe m

seam [si:m] n Saum m; (edges joining) Naht f; (of coal) Flöz nt

seaman [ˈsi:mən] (irreg) n Seemann m

seaplane [ˈsi:pleɪn] n Wasserflugzeug nt

seaport [ˈsi:pɔ:t] n Seehafen m

search [sɜ:tʃ] n (for person, thing) Suche f; (of drawer, pockets, house) Durchsuchung f ♦ vi suchen ♦ vt durchsuchen; **in ~ of** auf der Suche nach; **to ~ for** suchen nach; **~ through** vt fus durchsuchen; **~ing** adj (look) forschend; **~light** n Scheinwerfer m; **~ party** n Suchmannschaft f; **~ warrant** n Durchsuchungsbefehl m

sea: **~shore** n Meeresküste f; **~sick** [ˈsi:sɪk] adj seekrank; **~side** [ˈsi:saɪd] n Küste f; **~side resort** n Badeort m

season [ˈsi:zn] n Jahreszeit f; (Christmas etc) Zeit f, Saison f ♦ vt (flavour) würzen; **~al** adj Saison-; **~ed** adj (fig) erfahren; **~ing** n Gewürz nt, Würze f; **~ ticket** n (RAIL) Zeitkarte f; (THEAT) Abonnement nt

seat [si:t] n Sitz m, Platz m; (in Parliament) Sitz m; (part of body) Gesäß nt; (of trousers) Hosenboden m ♦ vt (place) setzen; (have space for) Sitzplätze bieten für; **to be ~ed** sitzen; **~ belt** n Sicherheitsgurt m

sea: **~ water** n Meerwasser nt; **~weed** [ˈsi:wi:d] n (See)tang m; **~worthy** [ˈsi:wɜ:ðɪ] adj seetüchtig

sec. abbr (= second(s)) Sek.

secluded [sɪˈklu:dɪd] adj abgelegen

seclusion [sɪˈklu:ʒən] n Zurückgezogenheit f

second [ˈsekənd] adj zweite(r,s) ♦ adv (in ~ position) an zweiter Stelle ♦ n Sekunde f; (person) Zweite(r) mf; (COMM:

imperfect) zweite Wahl f; (SPORT) Sekundant m; (AUT: also: ~ **gear**) zweite(r) Gang m; (BRIT: UNIV: degree) mittlere Note bei Abschlussprüfungen ♦ vt (support) unterstützen; **~ary** adj zweitrangig; **~ary school** n höhere Schule f; Mittelschule f; **~-class** n zweiter Klasse; **~hand** adj aus zweiter Hand; (car etc) gebraucht; **~ hand** n (on clock) Sekundenzeiger m; **~ly** adv zweitens

secondment [sɪˈkɔndmənt] (BRIT) n Abordnung f

second-rate [ˈsekəndˈreɪt] adj mittelmäßig

second thoughts npl: **to have ~** es sich dat anders überlegen; **on ~** (BRIT) or **thought** (US) oder lieber (nicht)

secrecy [ˈsi:krəsɪ] n Geheimhaltung f

secret [ˈsi:krɪt] n Geheimnis nt ♦ adj geheim, Geheim-; **in ~** geheim

secretarial [sekrɪˈtɛərɪəl] adj Sekretärinnen-

secretary [ˈsekrətərɪ] n Sekretär(in) m(f); **S~ of State** (BRIT) or (POL): **S~ of State (for)** Minister(in) m(f) (für)

secretion [sɪˈkri:ʃən] n Absonderung f

secretive [ˈsi:krətɪv] adj geheimtuerisch

secretly [ˈsi:krɪtlɪ] adv geheim

sectarian [sekˈtɛərɪən] adj (riots etc) Konfessions-, zwischen den Konfessionen

section [ˈsekʃən] n Teil m; (department) Abteilung f; (of document) Abschnitt m

sector [ˈsektə*] n Sektor m

secular [ˈsekjulə*] adj weltlich, profan

secure [sɪˈkjuə*] adj (safe) sicher; (firmly fixed) fest ♦ vt (make firm) befestigen, sichern; (obtain) sichern; **security** [sɪˈkjuərɪtɪ] n Sicherheit f; (pledge) Pfand nt; (document) Wertpapier nt; (national security) Staatssicherheit f; **security guard** n Sicherheitsbeamte(r) m, Wächter m, Wache f

sedan [səˈdæn] (US) n (AUT) Limousine f

sedate [sɪˈdeɪt] adj gesetzt ♦ vt (MED)

ein Beruhigungsmittel geben +dat; **se-dation** [sɪˈdeɪʃən] n (MED) Einfluss m von Beruhigungsmitteln; **sedative** [ˈsedɪtɪv] n Beruhigungsmittel n ♦ adj beruhigend, einschläfernd

sediment [ˈsedɪmənt] n (Boden)satz m

seduce [sɪˈdjuːs] vt verführen; **seductive** [sɪˈdʌktɪv] adj verführerisch

see [siː] (pt **saw**, pp **seen**) vt sehen; (understand) (ein)sehen, erkennen; (visit) besuchen ♦ vi (be aware) sehen; (find out) nachsehen ♦ n (ECCL: R.C.) Bistum nt; (: Protestant) Kirchenkreis m; **to ~ sb to the door** jdn hinausbegleiten; **to ~ that** (ensure) dafür sorgen, dass; **~ you soon!** bis bald!; **~ about** vt fus sich kümmern um; **~ off** vt: **to ~ sb off** jdn zum Zug etc begleiten; **~ through** vt: **to ~ sth through** vt/w durchfechten; **to ~ through sb/sth** jdn/etw durchschauen; **~ to** vt fus: **~ to it** dafür sorgen

seed [siːd] n Samen m ♦ vt (TENNIS) platzieren; **to go to ~** (plant) schießen; (fig) herunterkommen; **~ling** n Setzling m; **~y** adj (café) übel; (person) zweifelhaft

seeing [ˈsiːɪŋ] conj: **~ (that) da**

seek [siːk] (pt, pp **sought**) vt suchen

seem [siːm] vi scheinen; **it ~s that ...** es scheint, dass ...; **~ingly** adv anscheinend

seen [siːn] pp of **see**

seep [siːp] vi sickern

seesaw [ˈsiːsɔː] n Wippe f

seethe [siːð] vi: **to ~ with anger** vor Wut kochen

see-through [ˈsiːθruː] adj (dress etc) durchsichtig

segment [ˈsegmənt] n Teil m; (of circle) Ausschnitt m

segregate [ˈsegrɪgeɪt] vt trennen

seize [siːz] vt (grasp) (er)greifen, packen; (power) ergreifen; (take legally) beschlagnahmen; **~ (up)on** vt fus sich stürzen auf +acc; **~ up** vi (TECH) sich festfressen; **seizure** [ˈsiːʒəʳ] n (illness)

Anfall m

seldom [ˈseldəm] adv selten

select [sɪˈlekt] adj ausgewählt ♦ vt auswählen; **~ion** [sɪˈlekʃən] n Auswahl f; **~ive** adj (person) wählerisch

self [self] (pl **selves**) pron selbst ♦ n Selbst nt, Ich nt; **the ~** das Ich; **~-assured** adj selbstbewusst; **~-catering** (BRIT) adj für Selbstversorger; **~-centred** (US **self-centered**) adj egozentrisch; **~-coloured** (US **self-colored**) adj (of one colour) einfarbig, uni; **~-confidence** n Selbstvertrauen nt, Selbstbewusstsein nt; **~-conscious** adj gehemmt, befangen; **~-contained** adj (complete) (in sich) geschlossen; (person) verschlossen; (BRIT: flat) separat; **~-control** n Selbstbeherrschung f; **~-defence** (US **self-defense**) n Selbstverteidigung f; (JUR) Notwehr f; **~-discipline** n Selbstdisziplin f; **~-employed** adj frei(schaffend); **~-evident** adj offensichtlich; **~-governing** adj selbst verwaltet; **~-indulgent** adj zügellos; **~-interest** n Eigennutz m

selfish [ˈselfɪʃ] adj egoistisch, selbstsüchtig; **~ness** n Egoismus m, Selbstsucht f

self-: **~lessly** adv selbstlos; **~-made** adj: **~-made man** Selfmademan m; **~-pity** n Selbstmitleid nt; **~-portrait** n Selbstbildnis nt; **~-possessed** adj selbstbeherrscht; **~-preservation** n Selbsterhaltung f; **~-reliant** adj unabhängig; **~-respect** n Selbstachtung f; **~-righteous** adj selbstgerecht; **~-sacrifice** n Selbstaufopferung f; **~-satisfied** adj selbstzufrieden; **~-service** adj Selbstbedienungs-; **~-sufficient** adj selbstgenügsam; **~-taught** adj selbst erlernt; **~-taught person** Autodidakt m

sell [sel] (pt, pp **sold**) vt verkaufen ♦ vi verkaufen; (goods) sich verkaufen; **to ~ at** or **for £10** für £10 verkaufen; **~ off** vt verkaufen; **~ out** vi alles verkaufen;

~by date n Verfallsdatum nt; **~er** n Verkäufer m; **~ing price** n Verkaufspreis m

Sellotape ['seləʊteɪp] (® BRIT) n Tesafilm m ®

sellout ['selaʊt] n (of tickets): **it was a ~** es war ausverkauft

selves [selvz] npl of **self**

semaphore ['seməfɔːʳ] n Winkzeichen pl

semblance ['sembləns] n Anschein m

semen ['siːmən] n Sperma nt

semester [sɪ'mestəʳ] (US) n Semester nt

semi ['semɪ] n = semidetached house; **~circle** n Halbkreis m; **~colon** n Semikolon nt; **~conductor** n Halbleiter m; **~detached house** (BRIT) n halbe(s) Doppelhaus nt; **~final** n Halbfinale nt

seminary ['semɪnərɪ] n (REL) Priesterseminar nt

semiskilled [semɪ'skɪld] adj angelernt

semi-skimmed [semɪ'skɪmd] adj (milk) teilentrahmt, Halbfett-

senate ['senɪt] n Senat m; **senator** n Senator m

send [send] (pt, pp **sent**) vt senden, schicken; (inf: inspire) hinreißen; **~ away** vt wegschicken; **~ away for** vt fus anfordern; **~ back** vt zurückschicken; **~ for** vt fus holen lassen; **~ off** vt (goods) abschicken; (BRIT: SPORT: player) vom Feld schicken; **~ out** vt (invitation) aussenden; **~ up** vt hinaufsenden; (BRIT: parody) verulken; **~er** n Absender m; **~-off** n: **to give sb a good ~-off** jdn (ganz) groß verabschieden

senior ['siːnɪəʳ] adj (older) älter; (higher rank) Ober- ♦ n (older person) Ältere(r) mf; (higher ranking) Rangälteste(r) mf; **~ citizen** n ältere(r) Mitbürger(in) m(f); **~ity** [siːnɪ'ɒrɪtɪ] n (of age) höhere(s) Alter nt; (in rank) höhere(r) Dienstgrad m

sensation [sen'seɪʃən] n Gefühl nt; (excitement) Sensation f, Aufsehen nt; **~al** adj (wonderful) wunderbar; (result) sen-

sationell; (headlines etc) reißerisch

sense [sens] n Sinn m; (understanding) Verstand m, Vernunft f; (feeling) Gefühl nt ♦ vt fühlen, spüren; **~ of humour** Humor m; **to make ~** Sinn ergeben; **~less** adj sinnlos; (unconscious) besinnungslos

sensibility [sensɪ'bɪlɪtɪ] n Empfindsamkeit f; (feeling hurt) Empfindlichkeit f; **sensibilities** npl (feelings) Zartgefühl nt

sensible ['sensɪbl] adj vernünftig

sensitive ['sensɪtɪv] adj: **~ (to)** empfindlich (gegen); **sensitivity** [sensɪ'tɪvɪtɪ] n Empfindlichkeit f; (artistic) Feingefühl nt; (tact) Einfühligkeit f

sensual ['sensjʊəl] adj sinnlich

sensuous ['sensjʊəs] adj sinnlich

sent [sent] pt, pp of **send**

sentence ['sentns] n Satz m; (JUR) Strafe f; Urteil nt ♦ vt: **to ~ sb to death/to 5 years** jdn zum Tode/zu 5 Jahren verurteilen

sentiment ['sentɪmənt] n Gefühl nt; (thought) Gedanke m; **~al** [sentɪ'mentl] adj sentimental; (of feelings rather than reason) gefühlsmäßig

sentry ['sentrɪ] n (Schild)wache f

separate [adj 'seprɪt, vb 'sepəreɪt] adj getrennt, separat ♦ vt trennen ♦ vi sich trennen; **~ly** adv getrennt; **~s** npl (clothes) Röcke, Pullover etc; **separation** [sepə'reɪʃən] n Trennung f

September [sep'tembəʳ] n September m

septic ['septɪk] adj vereitert, septisch; **~ tank** n Klärbehälter m

sequel ['siːkwl] n Folge f

sequence ['siːkwəns] n (Reihen)folge f

sequin ['siːkwɪn] n Paillette f

Serbia ['sɜːbɪə] n Serbien nt

serene [sɪ'riːn] adj heiter

sergeant ['sɑːdʒənt] n Feldwebel m; (POLICE) (Polizei)wachtmeister m

serial ['sɪərɪəl] n Fortsetzungsroman m; (TV) Fernsehserie f ♦ adj (number) (fort)laufend; **~ize** vt in Fortsetzungen veröffentlichen; in Fortsetzungen senden

series ['sɪərɪz] *n inv* Serie *f*, Reihe *f*

serious ['sɪərɪəs] *adj* ernst; (*injury*) schwer; **~ly** *adv* ernst(haft); (*hurt*) schwer; **~ness** *n* Ernst *m*, Ernsthaftigkeit *f*

sermon ['sɜːmən] *n* Predigt *f*

serrated [sɪ'reɪtɪd] *adj* gezackt

servant ['sɜːvənt] *n* Diener(in) *m(f)*

serve [sɜːv] *vt* dienen +*dat*; (*guest, customer*) bedienen; (*food*) servieren ♦ *vi* dienen, nützen; (*at table*) servieren; (*TENNIS*) geben, aufschlagen; **it ~s him right** das geschieht ihm recht; **that'll ~ as a table** das geht als Tisch; **to ~ a summons** (*on sb*) (jdn) vor Gericht laden; **~ out** *or* **up** *vt* (*food*) auftragen, servieren

service ['sɜːvɪs] *n* (*help*) Dienst *m*; (*trains etc*) Verbindung *f*; (*hotel*) Service *m*, Bedienung *f*; (*set of dishes*) Service *nt*; (*REL*) Gottesdienst *m*; (*car*) Inspektion *f*; (*for TVs etc*) Kundendienst *m*; (*TENNIS*) Aufschlag *m* ♦ *vt* (*AUT, TECH*) warten, überholen; **the S~s** *npl* (*armed forces*) die Streitkräfte *pl*; **to be of ~ to sb** jdm einen großen Dienst erweisen; **~ included/not included** Bedienung inbegriffen/nicht inbegriffen; **~able** *adj* brauchbar; **~ area** *n* (*on motorway*) Raststätte *f*; **~ charge** (*BRIT*) *n* Bedienung *f*; **~man** (*irreg*) *n* (*soldier etc*) Soldat *m*; **~ station** *n* (Groß)tankstelle *f*

serviette [sɜːvɪ'et] *n* Serviette *f*

servile ['sɜːvaɪl] *adj* unterwürfig

session ['seʃən] *n* Sitzung *f*; (*POL*) Sitzungsperiode *f*; **to be in ~** tagen

set [set] (*pt, pp* **set**) *n* (*collection of things*) Satz *m*, Set *nt*; (*RAD, TV*) Apparat *m*; (*TENNIS*) Satz *m*; (*group of people*) Kreis *m*; (*CINE*) Szene *f*; (*THEAT*) Bühnenbild *nt* ♦ *adj* festgelegt; (*ready*) bereit ♦ *vt* (*place*) setzen, stellen, legen; (*arrange*) (an)ordnen; (*table*) decken; (*time, price*) festsetzen; (*alarm, watch, task*) stellen; (*jewels*)

(*ein*)fassen; (*exam*) ausarbeiten ♦ *vi* (*sun*) untergehen; (*become hard*) fest werden; (*bone*) zusammenwachsen; **to be ~ on doing sth** etw unbedingt tun wollen; **to ~ to music** vertonen; **to ~ on fire** anstecken; **to ~ free** freilassen; **to ~ sth going** etw in Gang bringen; **to ~ sail** losfahren; **~ about** *vt fus* (*task*) anpacken; **~ aside** *vt* beiseite legen; **~ back** *vt*: **to ~ back (by)** zurückwerfen (um); **~ off** *vi* aufbrechen ♦ *vt* (*explode*) sprengen; (*alarm*) losgehen lassen; (*show up well*) hervorheben; **~ out** *vi*: **to ~ out to do sth** vorhaben, etw zu tun ♦ *vt* (*arrange*) anlegen, arrangieren; (*state*) darlegen; **~ up** *vt* (*organization*) aufziehen; (*record*) aufstellen; (*monument*) erstellen; **~back** *n* Rückschlag *m*; **~ meal** *n* Menü *nt*; **~ menu** *n* Tageskarte *f*

settee [se'tiː] *n* Sofa *nt*

setting ['setɪŋ] *n* Hintergrund *m*

settle ['setl] *vt* beruhigen; (*pay*) begleichen, bezahlen; (*agree*) regeln ♦ *vi* sich einleben; (*come to rest*) sich niederlassen; (*sink*) sich setzen; (*calm down*) sich beruhigen; **to ~ for sth** sich mit etw zufrieden geben; **to ~ on sth** sich für etw entscheiden; **to ~ up with sb** mit jdm abrechnen; **~ down** *vi* (*feel at home*) sich einleben; (*calm down*) sich beruhigen; **~ in** *vi* sich eingewöhnen; **~ment** *n* Regelung *f*; (*payment*) Begleichung *f*; (*colony*) Siedlung *f*; **~r** *n* Siedler *m*

setup ['setʌp] *n* (*situation*) Lage *f*

seven ['sevn] *num* sieben; **~teen** *num* siebzehn; **~th** *adj* siebte(r, s) ♦ *n* Siebtel *nt*; **~ty** *num* siebzig

sever ['sevər] *vt* abtrennen

several ['sevrəl] *adj* mehrere, verschiedene ♦ *pron* mehrere; **~ of us** einige von uns

severance ['sevərəns] *n*: **~ pay** Abfindung *f*

severe [sɪ'vɪər] *adj* (*strict*) streng; (*serious*) schwer; (*climate*) rau; **severity**

[ʃɪˈverɪt] n Strenge f; Schwere f; Rauheit f

sew [səu] (pt **sewed**, pp **sewn**) vt, vi nähen; **~ up** vt zunähen

sewage [ˈsuːɪdʒ] n Abwässer pl

sewer [ˈsuːəʳ] n (Abwasser)kanal m

sewing [ˈsəuɪŋ] n Näharbeit f; **~ machine** n Nähmaschine f

sewn [səun] pp of **sew**

sex [seks] n Sex m; (gender) Geschlecht nt; **to have ~ with sb** mit jdm Geschlechtsverkehr haben; **~ism** n Sexismus m; **~ist** adj sexistisch ♦ n Sexist(in) m(f); **~ual** [ˈseksjuəl] adj sexuell, geschlechtlich, Geschlechts-; **~uality** [seksjuˈælɪtɪ] n Sexualität f; **~y** adj sexy

shabby [ˈʃæbɪ] adj (also fig) schäbig

shack [ʃæk] n Hütte f

shackles [ˈʃæklz] npl (also fig) Fesseln pl, Ketten pl

shade [ʃeɪd] n Schatten m; (for lamp) Lampenschirm m; (colour) Farbton m ♦ vt abschirmen; **in the ~** im Schatten; **a ~ smaller** ein bisschen kleiner

shadow [ˈʃædəu] n Schatten m ♦ vt (follow) beschatten ♦ adj: **~ cabinet** (BRIT: POL) Schattenkabinett nt; **~y** adj schattig

shady [ˈʃeɪdɪ] adj schattig; (fig) zwielichtig

shaft [ʃɑːft] n (of spear etc) Schaft m; (in mine) Schacht m; (TECH) Welle f; (of light) Strahl m

shaggy [ˈʃægɪ] adj struppig

shake [ʃeɪk] (pt **shook**, pp **shaken**) vt schütteln, rütteln; (shock) erschüttern ♦ vi (move) schwanken; (tremble) zittern, beben ♦ n (jerk) Schütteln nt, Rütteln nt; **to ~ hands with** die Hand geben +dat; **to ~ one's head** den Kopf schütteln; **~ off** vt abschütteln; **~ up** vt aufschütteln; (fig) aufrütteln; **~n** [ˈʃeɪkn] pp of **shake**; **shaky** [ˈʃeɪkɪ] adj zittrig; (weak) unsicher

shall [ʃæl] vb aux: **I ~ go** ich werde gehen; **~ I open the door?** soll ich die Tür öffnen?; **I'll buy some cake, ~ I?**

soll ich Kuchen kaufen?, ich kaufe Kuchen, oder?

shallow [ˈʃæləu] adj seicht

sham [ʃæm] n Schein m ♦ adj unecht, falsch

shambles [ˈʃæmblz] n Durcheinande nt

shame [ʃeɪm] n Scham f; (disgrace, pity) Schande f ♦ vt beschämen; **it is a ~ that** es ist schade, dass; **it is a ~ to** ... es ist eine Schande, ... zu tun; **what a ~!** wie schade!; **~faced** adj beschämt; **~ful** adj schändlich; **~less** ad schamlos

shampoo [ʃæmˈpuː] n Shampoo(n) r ♦ vt (hair) waschen; **~ and set** n Waschen nt und Legen

shamrock [ˈʃæmrɔk] n Kleeblatt nt

shandy [ˈʃændɪ] n Bier mit Limonade

shan't [ʃɑːnt] = **shall not**

shantytown [ˈʃæntɪtaun] n Bidonville

shape [ʃeɪp] n Form f ♦ vt formen, gestalten ♦ vi (also: **~ up**) sich entwickeln; **to take ~** Gestalt annehmen; **~d** suffix: **heart~d** herzförmig; **~less** adj formlos; **~ly** adj wohlproportioniert

share [ʃɛəʳ] n (An)teil m; (FIN) Aktie ♦ vt teilen; **to ~ out** (among, between) verteilen (unter/zwischen); **~holder** n Aktionär(in) m(f)

shark [ʃɑːk] n Hai(fisch) m; (swindler Gauner m

sharp [ʃɑːp] adj scharf; (pin) spitz; (person) clever; (MUS) erhöht ♦ n Kreuz n ♦ adv zu hoch; **nine o'clock ~** Punk neun; **~en** vt schärfen; (pencil) spitzen; **~ener** n (also: **pencil ~ener**) Anspitzer m; **~-eyed** adj scharfsichtig; **~ly** adv (turn, stop) plötzlich; (stand out, contrast) deutlich; (criticize, retort) scharf

shatter [ˈʃætəʳ] vt zerschmettern; (fig zerstören ♦ vi zerspringen

shave [ʃeɪv] n Rasur f ♦ vt rasieren ♦ vi sich rasieren; **to have a ~** sich rasieren (lassen); **~r** n (also: **electric ~r**) Rasierapparat m

shaving [ˈʃeɪvɪŋ] n (action) Rasieren m

~s npl (of wood etc) Späne pl; **~ brush** n Rasierpinsel m; **~ cream** n Rasiercreme f; **~ foam** n Rasierschaum m

shawl [ʃɔːl] n Schal m, Umhang m

she [ʃiː] pron sie ♦ adj weiblich

sheaf [ʃiːf] (pl **sheaves**) n Garbe f

shear [ʃɪər] (pt **sheared**, pp **sheared** or **shorn**) vt scheren; **~ off** vi abbrechen; **~s** npl Heckenschere f

sheath [ʃiːθ] n Scheide f; (condom) Kondom m or nt

sheaves [ʃiːvz] npl of **sheaf**

shed [ʃɛd] (pt, pp **shed**) n Schuppen m; (for animals) Stall m ♦ vt (leaves etc) verlieren; (tears) vergießen

she'd [ʃiːd] = **she had**; **she would**

sheen [ʃiːn] n Glanz m

sheep [ʃiːp] n inv Schaf nt; **~dog** n Schäferhund m; **~ish** adj verlegen; **~skin** n Schaffell nt

sheer [ʃɪər] adj bloß, rein; (steep) steil; (transparent) hauchdünn ♦ adv (directly) direkt

sheet [ʃiːt] n Betttuch nt, Bettlaken nt; (of paper) Blatt nt; (of metal etc) Platte f; (of ice) Fläche f

sheik(h) [ʃeɪk] n Scheich m

shelf [ʃɛlf] (pl **shelves**) n Bord nt, Regal nt

shell [ʃɛl] n Schale f; (seashell) Muschel f; (explosive) Granate f ♦ vt (peas) schälen; (fire on) beschießen

she'll [ʃiːl] = **she will**; **she shall**

shellfish [ʃɛlfɪʃ] n Schalentier nt; (as food) Meeresfrüchte pl

shell suit n Ballonseidenanzug m

shelter [ʃɛltər] n Schutz m; (air-raid ~) Bunker m ♦ vt schützen, bedecken; (refugees) aufnehmen ♦ vi sich unterstellen; **~ed** adj (life) behütet; (spot) geschützt; **~ housing** n (for old people) Altenwohnungen pl; (for handicapped people) Behindertenwohnungen pl

shelve [ʃɛlv] vt aufschieben ♦ vi abfallen

shelves [ʃɛlvz] npl of **shelf**

shepherd [ʃɛpəd] n Schäfer m ♦ vt trei-

ben, führen; **~'s pie** n Auflauf aus Hackfleisch und Kartoffelbrei

sheriff [ʃɛrɪf] n Sheriff m; (SCOTTISH) Friedensrichter m

she's [ʃiːz] = **she is**; **she has**

Shetland [ʃɛtlənd] n (also: **the ~s, the ~ Isles**) die Shetlandinseln pl

shield [ʃiːld] n Schild m; (fig) Schirm m ♦ vt (be)schirmen; (TECH) abschirmen

shift [ʃɪft] n Verschiebung f; (work) Schicht f ♦ vt (ver)rücken, verschieben; (arm) wegnehmen ♦ vi sich verschieben; **~less** adj (person) träge; **~ work** n Schichtarbeit f; **~y** adj verschlagen

shilly-shally [ʃɪlɪʃælɪ] vi zögern

shin [ʃɪn] n Schienbein nt

shine [ʃaɪn] (pt, pp **shone**) n Glanz m, Schein m ♦ vt polieren ♦ vi scheinen; (fig) glänzen; **to ~ a torch on sb** jdn (mit einer Lampe) anleuchten

shingle [ʃɪŋgl] n Strandkies m; **~s** npl (MED) Gürtelrose f

shiny [ʃaɪnɪ] adj glänzend

ship [ʃɪp] n Schiff nt ♦ vt verschiffen; **~building** n Schiffbau m; **~ment** n Schiffsladung f; **~per** n Verschiffer m; **~ping** n (act) Verschiffung f; (~s) Schiffahrt f; **~wreck** n Schiffbruch m; (destroyed) Wrack nt ♦ vt: **to be ~wrecked** Schiffbruch erleiden; **~yard** n Werft f

shire [ʃaɪər] (BRIT) n Grafschaft f

shirk [ʃɜːk] vt ausweichen +dat

shirt [ʃɜːt] n (Ober)hemd nt; **in ~ sleeves** in Hemdsärmeln

shit [ʃɪt] (inf!) excl Scheiße (!)

shiver [ʃɪvər] n Schauer m ♦ vi frösteln, zittern

shoal [ʃəul] n (Fisch)schwarm m

shock [ʃɔk] n Erschütterung f; (mental) Schock m; (ELEC) Schlag m ♦ vt erschüttern; (offend) schockieren; **~ absorber** n Stoßdämpfer m; **~ed** adj geschockt, schockiert, erschüttert; **~ing** adj unerhört

shod [ʃɔd] pt, pp of **shoe**

shoddy [ʃɔdɪ] adj schäbig

shoe [ʃuː] (*pt, pp* **shod**) *n* Schuh *m*; (*of horse*) Hufeisen *nt* ♦ *vt* (*horse*) beschlagen; **~brush** *n* Schuhbürste *f*; **~horn** *n* Schuhlöffel *m*; **~lace** *n* Schnürsenkel *m*; **~ polish** *n* Schuhcreme *f*; **~ shop** *n* Schuhgeschäft *nt*; **~string** *n* (*fig*): **on a ~string** mit sehr wenig Geld

shone [ʃɔn] *pt, pp of* **shine**

shoo [ʃuː] *excl* sch; (*to dog etc*) pfui

shook [ʃuk] *pt of* **shake**

shoot [ʃuːt] (*pt, pp* **shot**) *n* (*branch*) Schössling *m* ♦ *vt* (*gun*) abfeuern; (*goal, arrow*) schießen; (*person*) anschießen; (*kill*) erschießen; (*film*) drehen ♦ *vi* (*move quickly*) schießen; **to ~ (at)** schießen (auf +*acc*); **~ down** *vt* abschießen; **~ in** *vi* hineinschießen; **~ out** *vi* hinausschießen; **~ up** *vi* (*fig*) aus dem Boden schießen; **~ing** *n* Schießerei *f*; **~ing star** *n* Sternschnuppe *f*

shop [ʃɔp] *n* (*esp BRIT*) Geschäft *nt*, Laden *m*; (*workshop*) Werkstatt *f* ♦ *vi* (*also:* **go shopping**) einkaufen gehen; **~ assistant** (*BRIT*) *n* Verkäufer(in) *m(f)*; **~ floor** (*BRIT*) *n* Werkstatt *f*; **~keeper** *n* Geschäftsinhaber *m*; **~lifting** *n* Ladendiebstahl *m*; **~per** *n* Käufer(in) *m(f)*; **~ping** *n* Einkaufen *nt*, Einkauf *m*; **~ping bag** *n* Einkaufstasche *f*; **~ping centre** (*US* **shopping center**) *n* Einkaufszentrum *nt*; **~-soiled** *adj* angeschmutzt; **~ steward** (*BRIT*) *n* (*INDUSTRY*) Betriebsrat *m*; **~ window** *n* Schaufenster *nt*

shore [ʃɔːʳ] *n* Ufer *nt*; (*of sea*) Strand *m* ♦ *vt*: **to ~ up** abstützen

shorn [ʃɔːn] *pp of* **shear**

short [ʃɔːt] *adj* kurz; (*person*) klein; (*curt*) kurz angebunden; (*measure*) zu knapp ♦ *n* (*also:* **~ film**) Kurzfilm *m* ♦ *adv* (*suddenly*) plötzlich ♦ *vi* (*ELEC*) einen Kurzschluss haben; **~s** *npl* (*clothes*) Shorts *pl*; **to be ~ of etw** nicht genug von etw haben; **in ~** kurz gesagt; **~ of doing sth** ohne zu weit zu gehen, etw zu tun; **everything ~ of ...** alles

außer ; **it is ~ for** das ist die Kurzform von; **to cut ~** abkürzen; **to fall ~ of sth** etw nicht erreichen; **to stop ~** plötzlich anhalten; **to stop ~ of** Halt machen vor; **~age** *n* Knappheit *f*, Mangel *m*; **~bread** *n* Mürbegebäck *nt*; **~change** *vt*: **to ~change sb** jdm zu wenig herausgeben; **~circuit** *n* Kurzschluss *m* ♦ *vi* einen Kurzschluss haben ♦ *vt* kurzschließen; **~coming** *n* Mangel *m*; **~(crust) pastry** (*BRIT*) *n* Mürbeteig *m*; **~ cut** *n* Abkürzung *f*; **~en** *vt* (ab)kürzen; (*clothes*) kürzer machen; **~fall** *n* Defizit *nt*; **~hand** (*BRIT*) *n* Stenografie *f*; **~hand typist** (*BRIT*) *n* Stenotypistin *f*; **~ list** (*BRIT*) *n* (*for job*) engere Wahl *f*; **~lived** *adj* kurzlebig; **~ly** *adv* bald; **~ notice** *n*: **at ~ notice** kurzfristig; **~sighted** (*BRIT*) *adj* (*also: fig*) kurzsichtig; **~staffed** *adj*: **to be ~staffed** zu wenig Personal haben; **~stay** *n* (*car park*) Kurzparken *nt*; **~ story** *n* Kurzgeschichte *f*; **~ tempered** *adj* leicht aufbrausend; **~ term** *adj* (*effect*) kurzfristig; **~ wave** (*RAD*) Kurzwelle *f*

shot [ʃɔt] *pt, pp of* **shoot** ♦ *n* (*from gun*) Schuss *m*; (*person*) Schütze *m*; (*try*) Versuch *m*; (*injection*) Spritze *f*; (*PHOT*) Aufnahme *f*; **like a ~** wie der Blitz; **~gun** *n* Schrotflinte *f*

should [ʃud] *vb aux*: **I ~ go now** ich sollte jetzt gehen; **he ~ be there now** er sollte eigentlich schon da sein; **I ~ go if I were you** ich würde gehen wenn ich du wäre; **I ~ like to** ich möchte gerne

shoulder [ˈʃəuldəʳ] *n* Schulter *f*; (*of road*): **hard ~** Seitenstreifen *m* ♦ *vt* (*rifle*) schultern; (*fig*) auf sich nehmen; **~ bag** *n* Umhängetasche *f*; **~ blade** *n* Schulterblatt *nt*; **~ strap** *n* (*of dress etc*) Träger *m*

shouldn't [ˈʃudnt] = **should not**

shout [ʃaut] *n* Schrei *m*; (*call*) Ruf *m* ♦ *vt* rufen ♦ *vi* schreien; **~ down** *vt* niederbrüllen; **~ing** *n* Geschrei *nt*

shove [ʃʌv] n Schubs m, Stoß m ♦ vt
schieben, stoßen, schubsen; (*inf*: *put*)
to ~ sth in(to) sth etw in etw *acc* hi-
neinschieben; **~ off** vi (NAUT) abstoßen; (*fig*: *inf*) abhauen

shovel [ʃʌvl] n Schaufel f ♦ vt schau-
feln

show [ʃəu] (*pt* **showed**, *pp* **shown**) n
(*display*) Schau f; (*exhibition*) Ausstellung f; (CINE, THEAT) Vorstellung f, Show
f ♦ vt zeigen; (*kindness*) erweisen ♦ vi
zu sehen sein; **to be on ~** (*exhibits
etc*) ausgestellt sein; **to ~ sb in** jdn
hereinführen; **to ~ sb out** jdn hinausbegleiten; **~ off** vi (*pej*) angeben ♦ vt
(*display*) ausstellen; **~ up** vi (*stand out*)
sich abheben; (*arrive*) erscheinen ♦ vt
aufzeigen; (*unmask*) bloßstellen; **~
business** n Showbusiness nt; **~down**
n Kraftprobe f

shower [ʃauə*] n Schauer m; (*of
stones*) (Stein)hagel m; (~ *bath*) Dusche f ♦ vi duschen ♦ vt: **to ~ sb with
sth** jdn mit etw überschütten; **~proof**
adj Wasser abstoßend

showing [ʃəuɪŋ] n Vorführung f

show jumping n Turnierreiten nt

shown [ʃəun] *pp of* **show**

show: **~-off** [ʃəuɔf] n Angeber(in) m(f);
~piece [ʃəupiːs] n Paradestück nt;
~room [ʃəurum] n Ausstellungsraum
m

shrank [ʃræŋk] *pt of* **shrink**

shred [ʃred] n Fetzen m ♦ vt zerfetzen;
(COOK) raspeln; **~der** n (COOK) Ge-
müseschneider m; (*for documents*)
Reißwolf m

shrewd [ʃruːd] *adj* clever

shriek [ʃriːk] n Schrei m ♦ vt, vi kreischen, schreien

shrill [ʃrɪl] *adj* schrill

shrimp [ʃrɪmp] n Krabbe f, Garnele f

shrine [ʃraɪn] n Schrein m; (*fig*) Ge-
denkstätte f

shrink [ʃrɪŋk] (*pt* **shrank**, *pp* **shrunk**) vi
schrumpfen, eingehen ♦ vt ein-
schrumpfen lassen; **to ~ from doing**

sth davor zurückschrecken, etw zu
tun; **~age** n Schrumpfung f; **~-wrap**
vt einschweißen

shrivel [ʃrɪvl] vt, vi (*also*: **~ up**)
schrumpfen, schrumpeln

shroud [ʃraud] n Leichentuch nt ♦ vt:
~ed in mystery mit einem Geheimnis
umgeben

Shrove Tuesday [ʃrəuv-] n Fast-
nachtsdienstag m

shrub [ʃrʌb] n Busch m, Strauch m;
~bery n Gebüsch nt

shrug [ʃrʌg] n Achselzucken nt ♦ vt, vi:
to ~ (one's shoulders) die Achseln
zucken; **~ off** vt auf die leichte Schulter nehmen

shrunk [ʃrʌŋk] *pp of* **shrink**

shudder [ʃʌdə*] n Schauder m ♦ vi
schaudern

shuffle [ʃʌfl] vt (*cards*) mischen; **to ~
(one's feet)** scharren

shun [ʃʌn] vt scheuen, (ver)meiden

shunt [ʃʌnt] vt rangieren

shut [ʃʌt] (*pt*, *pp* **shut**) vt schließen, zumachen ♦ vi sich schließen (lassen); **~
down** vt, vi schließen; **~ off** vt (*supply*)
abdrehen; **~ up** vi (*keep quiet*) den
Mund halten ♦ vt (*close*) zuschließen;
~ter n Fensterladen m; (PHOT) Verschluss m

shuttle [ʃʌtl] n (*plane, train etc*) Pen-
delflugzeug nt/-zug nt etc; (*space* ~)
Raumtransporter m; (*also*: **~ service**)
Pendelverkehr m; **~cock** [ʃʌtlkɔk] n
Federball m; **~ diplomacy** n Pendeldi-
plomatie f

shy [ʃaɪ] *adj* schüchtern; **~ness** n
Schüchternheit f

Siamese [saɪəmiːz] *adj*: **~ cat** Siamkat-
ze f

Siberia [saɪbɪərɪə] n Sibirien nt

sibling [sɪblɪŋ] n Geschwister nt

Sicily [sɪsɪlɪ] n Sizilien nt

sick [sɪk] *adj* krank; (*joke*) makaber; **I
feel ~** mir ist schlecht; **I was ~** ich
habe gebrochen; **to be ~ of sb/sth**
jdn/etw satt haben; **~ bay** n

(Schiffs)lazarett nt; **~en** vt (disgust) krank machen ♦ vi krank werden; **~ening** (annoying) zum Weinen

sickle ['sɪkl] n Sichel f

sick: ~ leave n: **to be on ~ leave** krankgeschrieben sein; **~ly** adj kränklich, blass; (causing nausea) widerlich; **~ness** n Krankheit f; (vomiting) Übelkeit f, Erbrechen nt; **~ note** n Arbeitsunfähigkeitsbescheinigung f; **~ pay** n Krankengeld nt

side [saɪd] n Seite f ♦ adj (door, entrance) Seiten-, Neben- ♦ vi: **to ~ with sb** jds Partei ergreifen; **by the ~ of** neben; **~ by ~** nebeneinander; **on all ~s** von allen Seiten; **to take ~s (with)** Partei nehmen (für); **from all ~s** von allen Seiten; **~board** n Sideboard nt; **~boards** npl Koteletten pl; **~burns** npl Koteletten pl; **~car** n Beiwagen m; **~ drum** n (MUS) kleine Trommel; **~ effect** n Nebenwirkung f; **~light** n (AUT) Parkleuchte f; **~line** n (SPORT) Seitenlinie f; (fig: hobby) Nebenbeschäftigung f; **~long** adj Seiten-; **~ order** n Beilage f; **~saddle** adv im Damensattel; **~ show** n Nebenausstellung f; **~step** vt (fig) ausweichen; **~ street** n Seitenstraße f; **~track** vt (fig) ablenken; **~walk** (US) n Bürgersteig m; **~ways** adv seitwärts

siding ['saɪdɪŋ] n Nebengleis nt

sidle ['saɪdl] vi: **to ~ up (to)** sich heranmachen (an +acc)

siege [siːdʒ] n Belagerung f

sieve [sɪv] n Sieb nt ♦ vt sieben

sift [sɪft] vt sieben; (fig) sichten

sigh [saɪ] n Seufzer m ♦ vi seufzen

sight [saɪt] n (power of seeing) Sehvermögen nt; (look) Blick m; (fact of seeing) Anblick m; (of gun) Visier nt ♦ vt sichten; **in ~** in Sicht; **out of ~** außer Sicht; **~seeing** n Besuch m von Sehenswürdigkeiten; **to go ~seeing** Sehenswürdigkeiten besichtigen

sign [saɪn] n Zeichen nt; (notice, road ~ etc) Schild nt ♦ vt unterschreiben; **to ~**

sth over to sb jdm etw überschreiben; **~ on** vi (as unemployed) sich (arbeitslos) melden ♦ (employee) sich anstellen; **~ up** vi (MIL) sich verpflichten ♦ vt verpflichten

signal ['sɪgnl] n Signal nt ♦ vt ein Zeichen geben +dat; **~man** (irreg) n (RAIL) Stellwerkswärter m

signature ['sɪgnətʃə*] n Unterschrift f; **~ tune** n Erkennungsmelodie f

signet ring ['sɪgnət-] n Siegelring m

significance [sɪg'nɪfɪkəns] n Bedeutung f

significant [sɪg'nɪfɪkənt] adj (meaningful) bedeutsam; (important) bedeutend

signify ['sɪgnɪfaɪ] vt bedeuten; (show) andeuten, zu verstehen geben

sign language n Zeichensprache f, Fingersprache f

signpost ['saɪnpəʊst] n Wegweiser m

silence ['saɪləns] n Stille f; (of person) Schweigen nt ♦ vt zum Schweigen bringen; **~r** n (on gun) Schalldämpfer m; (BRIT: AUT) Auspufftopf m

silent ['saɪlənt] adj still; (person) schweigsam; **to remain ~** schweigen; **~ partner** n (COMM) stille(r) Teilhaber m

silicon chip ['sɪlɪkən-] n Siliciumchip m, Siliziumchip m

silk [sɪlk] n Seide f ♦ adj seiden, Seiden-; **~y** adj seidig

silly ['sɪlɪ] adj dumm, albern

silt [sɪlt] n Schlamm m, Schlick m

silver ['sɪlvə*] n Silber nt ♦ adj silbern, Silber-; **~ paper** (BRIT) n Silberpapier nt; **~-plated** adj versilbert; **~smith** n Silberschmied m; **~ware** n Silber nt; **~y** adj silbern

similar ['sɪmɪlə*] adj: **~ (to)** ähnlich (+dat); **~ity** [sɪmɪ'lærɪtɪ] n Ähnlichkeit f; **~ly** adv in ähnlicher Weise

simmer ['sɪmə*] vi sieden ♦ vt sieden lassen

simple ['sɪmpl] adj einfach; **~(-minded)** adj einfältig

simplicity [sɪm'plɪsɪtɪ] n Einfachheit f; (of person) Einfältigkeit f

simplify ['sɪmplɪfaɪ] vt vereinfachen

simply ['sɪmplɪ] adv einfach

simulate ['sɪmjʊleɪt] vt simulieren

simultaneous [sɪməl'teɪnɪəs] adj gleichzeitig

sin [sɪn] n Sünde f ♦ vi sündigen

since [sɪns] adv seither ♦ prep seit, seitdem ♦ conj (time) seit; (because) da, weil; ~ **then** seitdem

sincere [sɪn'sɪər] adj aufrichtig; **~ly** adv: **yours ~ly** mit freundlichen Grüßen; **sincerity** [sɪn'serɪtɪ] n Aufrichtigkeit f

sinew ['sɪnjuː] n Sehne f

sinful ['sɪnful] adj sündig, sündhaft

sing [sɪŋ] (pt **sang**, pp **sung**) vt, vi singen

Singapore [sɪŋgə'pɔːr] n Singapur nt

singe [sɪndʒ] vt versengen

singer ['sɪŋər] n Sänger(in) m(f)

singing ['sɪŋɪŋ] n Singen nt, Gesang m

single ['sɪŋgl] adj (one only) einzig; (bed, room) Einzel-, einzeln; (unmarried) ledig; (BRIT: ticket) einfach; (having one part only) einzeln ♦ n (BRIT: also: ~ **ticket**) einfache Fahrkarte f; **in ~ file** hintereinander; **~ out** vt aussuchen, auswählen; **~ bed** n Einzelbett nt; **~-breasted** adj einreihig; **~-handed** adj allein; **~-minded** adj zielstrebig; **~ parent** n Alleinerziehende(r) f(m); **~ room** n Einzelzimmer nt; **~s** n (TENNIS) Einzel nt; **~-track road** n einspurige Straße (mit Ausweichstellen); **singly** adv einzeln, allein

singular ['sɪŋgjʊlər] adj (odd) merkwürdig, seltsam ♦ n (GRAM) Einzahl f, Singular m

sinister ['sɪnɪstər] adj (evil) böse; (ghostly) unheimlich

sink [sɪŋk] (pt **sank**, pp **sunk**) n Spülbecken nt ♦ vt (ship) versenken ♦ vi sinken; **to ~ sth into** (teeth, claws) etw schlagen in +acc; **~ in** vi (news etc) eingehen

sinner ['sɪnər] n Sünder(in) m(f)

sinus ['saɪnəs] n (ANAT) Sinus m

sip [sɪp] n Schlückchen nt ♦ vt nippen an +dat

siphon ['saɪfən] n Siphon(flasche f) m; **~ off** vt absaugen; (fig) abschöpfen

sir [sɜːr] n (respect) Herr m; (knight) Sir m; **S~ John Smith** Sir John Smith; **yes ~** ja(wohl, mein Herr)

siren ['saɪərn] n Sirene f

sirloin ['sɜːlɔɪn] n Lendenstück nt

sissy ['sɪsɪ] n (inf) Waschlappen m

sister ['sɪstər] n Schwester f; (BRIT: nurse) Oberschwester f; (nun) Ordensschwester f; **~-in-law** n Schwägerin f

sit [sɪt] (pt, pp **sat**) vi sitzen; (hold session) tagen ♦ vt (exam) machen; **~ down** vi sich hinsetzen; **~ in on** vt fus dabei sein bei; **~ up** vi (after lying) sich aufsetzen; (straight) sich gerade setzen; (at night) aufbleiben

sitcom ['sɪtkɒm] n abbr (= situation comedy) Situationskomödie f

site [saɪt] n Platz m; (also: **building ~**) Baustelle f ♦ vt legen

sitting ['sɪtɪŋ] n (meeting) Sitzung f; **~ room** n Wohnzimmer nt

situated ['sɪtjʊeɪtɪd] adj: **to be ~** liegen

situation [sɪtjʊ'eɪʃən] n Situation f, Lage f; (place) Lage f; (employment) Stelle f; **"~s vacant"** (BRIT) "Stellenangebote" pl

six [sɪks] num sechs; **~teen** num sechzehn; **~th** adj sechste(r, s) ♦ n Sechstel nt; **~ty** num sechzig

size [saɪz] n Größe f; (of project) Umfang m; **~ up** vt (assess) abschätzen, einschätzen; **~able** adj ziemlich groß, ansehnlich

sizzle ['sɪzl] vi zischen; (COOK) brutzeln

skate [skeɪt] n Schlittschuh m; (fish: pl inv) Rochen m ♦ vi Schlittschuh laufen; **~board** n Skateboard nt; **~boarding** n Skateboardfahren nt; **~r** n Schlittschuhläufer(in) m(f); **skating** ['skeɪtɪŋ] n Eislauf m; **to go skating** Eis laufen gehen; **skating rink** n Eisbahn f

skeleton ['skɛlɪtn] n Skelett nt; (fig) Gerüst nt; ~ **key** n Dietrich m; ~ **staff** n Notbesetzung f

skeptical ['skɛptɪkl] (US) adj = **sceptical**

sketch [skɛtʃ] n Skizze f; (THEAT) Sketch m ♦ vt skizzieren; ~**book** n Skizzenbuch nt; ~**y** adj skizzenhaft

skewer ['skju:ə^r] n Fleischspieß m

ski [ski:] n Ski m, Schi m ♦ vi Ski or Schi laufen; ~ **boot** n Skistiefel m

skid [skɪd] n (AUT) Schleudern nt ♦ vi rutschen; (AUT) schleudern

ski: ~**er** ['ski:ə^r] n Skiläufer(in) m(f); ~**ing** ['ski:ɪŋ] n: **to go** ~**ing** Ski laufen gehen; ~**jump** n Sprungschanze f ♦ vi Ski springen

skilful ['skɪlful] adj geschickt

ski-lift n Skilift m

skill [skɪl] n Können nt; ~**ed** adj geschickt; (worker) Fach-, gelernt

skim [skɪm] vt (liquid) abschöpfen; (glide over) gleiten über +acc ♦ vi: ~ **through** (book) überfliegen; ~**med milk** n Magermilch f

skimp [skɪmp] vt (do carelessly) oberflächlich tun; ~**y** adj (dress) knapp

skin [skɪn] n Haut f; (peel) Schale f ♦ vt abhäuten; schälen; ~ **cancer** n Hautkrebs m; ~**deep** adj oberflächlich; ~**diving** n Schwimmtauchen nt; ~**head** n Skinhead m; ~**ny** adj dünn; ~**tight** adj (dress etc) hauteng

skip [skɪp] n Sprung m ♦ vi hüpfen; (with rope) Seil springen ♦ vt (pass over) übergehen

ski: ~ **pants** npl Skihosen pl; ~ **pass** n Skipass m; ~ **pole** n Skistock m

skipper ['skɪpə^r] n Kapitän m ♦ vt führen

skipping rope ['skɪpɪŋ-] (BRIT) n Hüpfseil nt

skirmish ['skə:mɪʃ] n Scharmützel nt

skirt [skə:t] n Rock m ♦ vt herumgehen um; (fig) umgehen; ~**ing board** (BRIT) n Fußleiste f

ski suit n Skianzug m

skit [skɪt] n Parodie f

ski tow n Schlepplift m

skittle ['skɪtl] n Kegel m; ~s n (game) Kegeln nt

skive [skaɪv] (BRIT: inf) vi schwänzen

skulk [skʌlk] vi sich herumdrücken

skull [skʌl] n Schädel m

skunk [skʌŋk] n Stinktier nt

sky [skaɪ] n Himmel m; ~**light** n Oberlicht nt; ~**scraper** n Wolkenkratzer m

slab [slæb] n (of stone) Platte f

slack [slæk] adj (loose) locker; (business) flau; (careless) nachlässig, lasch ♦ vi nachlässig sein ♦ n: **to take up the** ~ straff ziehen; ~**s** npl (trousers) Hose(n pl) f; ~**en** vi (also: ~**en off**) locker werden; (: slow down) stocken, nachlassen ♦ vt (: loosen) lockern

slag [slæg] (BRIT) n: ~ **off** (criticize) (he)runtermachen

slag heap [slæg-] n Halde f

slain [sleɪn] pp of **slay**

slam [slæm] n Knall m ♦ vt (door) zuschlagen; (throw down) knallen ♦ vi zuschlagen

slander ['slɑ:ndə^r] n Verleumdung f ♦ vt verleumden

slang [slæŋ] n Slang m; (jargon) Jargon m

slant [slɑ:nt] n Schräge f; (fig) Tendenz f ♦ vt schräg legen ♦ vi schräg liegen; ~**ed** adj schräg; ~**ing** adj schräg

slap [slæp] n Klaps m ♦ vt einen Klaps geben +dat ♦ adv (directly) geradewegs; ~**dash** adj salopp; ~**stick** n (comedy) Klamauk m; ~**up** (BRIT) adj (meal) erstklassig, prima

slash [slæʃ] n Schnittwunde f ♦ vt (auf)schlitzen

slat [slæt] n Leiste f

slate [sleɪt] n (stone) Schiefer m; (roofing) Dachziegel m ♦ vt (criticize) verreißen

slaughter ['slɔ:tə^r] n (of animals) Schlachten nt; (of people) Gemetzel nt ♦ vt schlachten; (people) niedermetzeln; ~**house** n Schlachthof m

Slav [slɑːv] *adj* slawisch

slave [sleɪv] *n* Sklave *m*, Sklavin *f* ♦ *vi* schuften, sich schinden; **~ry** *n* Sklaverei *f*

slay [sleɪ] (*pt* **slew**, *pp* **slain**) *vt* ermorden

sleazy ['sliːzɪ] *adj* (*place*) schmierig

sledge [sledʒ] *n* Schlitten *m*

sledgehammer ['sledʒhæməʳ] *n* Schmiedehammer *m*

sledging *n* Schlittenfahren *nt*

sleek [sliːk] *adj* glatt; (*shape*) rassig

sleep [sliːp] (*pt*, *pp* **slept**) *n* Schlaf *m* ♦ *vi* schlafen; **to go to ~** einschlafen; **~ in** *vi* ausschlafen; (*oversleep*) verschlafen; **~er** *n* (*person*) Schläfer *m*; (*BRIT: RAIL*) Schlafwagen *m*; (: *beam*) Schwelle *f*; **~ing bag** *n* Schlafsack *m*; **~ing car** *n* Schlafwagen *m*; **~ing partner** *n* = **silent partner**; **~ing pill** *n* Schlaftablette *f*; **~less** *adj* (*night*) schlaflos; **~walker** *n* Schlafwandler(in) *m(f)*; **~y** *adj* schläfrig

sleet [sliːt] *n* Schneeregen *m*

sleeve [sliːv] *n* Ärmel *m*; (*of record*) Umschlag *m*; **~less** *adj* ärmellos

sleigh [sleɪ] *n* Pferdeschlitten *m*

sleight [slaɪt] *n*: **~ of hand** Fingerfertigkeit *f*

slender ['slendəʳ] *adj* schlank; (*fig*) gering

slept [slept] *pt*, *pp* *of* **sleep**

slew [sluː] *vi* (*veer*) (herum)schwenken ♦ *pt of* **slay**

slice [slaɪs] *n* Scheibe *f* ♦ *vt* in Scheiben schneiden

slick [slɪk] *adj* (*clever*) raffiniert, aalglatt ♦ *n* Ölteppich *m*

slid [slɪd] *pt*, *pp of* **slide**

slide [slaɪd] (*pt*, *pp* **slid**) *n* Rutschbahn *f*; (*PHOT*) Dia(positiv) *nt*; (*BRIT: for hair*) (Haar)spange *f* ♦ *vt* schieben ♦ *vi* (*slip*) gleiten, rutschen; **sliding** ['slaɪdɪŋ] *adj* (*door*) Schiebe-; **sliding scale** *n* gleitende Skala *f*

slight [slaɪt] *adj* zierlich; (*trivial*) geringfügig; (*small*) gering ♦ *n* Kränkung *f*

♦ *vt* (*offend*) kränken; **not in the ~est** nicht im Geringsten; **~ly** *adv* etwas, ein bisschen

slim [slɪm] *adj* schlank; (*book*) dünn; (*chance*) gering ♦ *vi* eine Schlankheitskur machen

slime [slaɪm] *n* Schleim *m*

slimming ['slɪmɪŋ] *n* Schlankheitskur *f*

slimy ['slaɪmɪ] *adj* glitschig; (*dirty*) schlammig; (*person*) schmierig

sling [slɪŋ] (*pt*, *pp* **slung**) *n* Schlinge *f*; (*weapon*) Schleuder *f* ♦ *vt* schleudern

slip [slɪp] *n* (*mistake*) Flüchtigkeitsfehler *m*; (*petticoat*) Unterrock *m*; (*of paper*) Zettel *m* ♦ *vt* (*put*) stecken, schieben ♦ *vi* (*lose balance*) ausrutschen; (*move*) gleiten, rutschen; (*decline*) nachlassen; (*move smoothly*): **to ~ in/out** hinein-/hinausschlüpfen; **to give sb the ~** jdm entwischen; **~ped disc** *n* Bandscheibenschaden *m*

slipper ['slɪpəʳ] *n* Hausschuh *m*

slippery ['slɪpərɪ] *adj* glatt

slip: ~ road (*BRIT*) *n* Auffahrt *f*/Ausfahrt *f*; **~shod** *adj* schlampig; **~-up** *n* Panne *f*; **~way** *n* Auslaufbahn *f*

slit [slɪt] (*pt*, *pp* **slit**) *n* Schlitz *m* ♦ *vt* aufschlitzen

slither ['slɪðəʳ] *vi* schlittern; (*snake*) sich schlängeln

sliver ['slɪvəʳ] *n* (*of glass, wood*) Splitter *m*; (*of cheese*) Scheibchen *nt*

slob [slɒb] (*inf*) *n* Klotz *m*

slog [slɒg] *vi* (*work hard*) schuften ♦ *n*: **it was a ~** es war eine Plackerei

slogan ['sləʊgən] *n* Schlagwort *nt*; (*COMM*) Werbespruch *m*

slop [slɒp] *vi* (*also*: **~ over**) überschwappen ♦ *vt* verschütten

slope [sləʊp] *n* Neigung *f*; (*of mountains*) (Ab)hang *m* ♦ *vi*: **to ~ down**

senken; **to ~ up** ansteigen; **sloping**
['sləʊpɪŋ] adj schräg

sloppy ['slɒpɪ] adj schlampig

slot [slɒt] n Schlitz m ♦ vt: **to ~ sth in**
etw einlegen

sloth [sləʊθ] n (laziness) Faulheit f

slot machine n (BRIT) Automat m; (for
gambling) Spielautomat m

slouch [slaʊtʃ] vi: **to ~ about** (laze)
herumhängen (inf)

slovenly ['slʌvnlɪ] adj schlampig;
(speech) salopp

slow [sləʊ] adj langsam ♦ adv langsam;
to be ~ (clock) nachgehen; (stupid)
begriffsstutzig sein; **"~"** (road sign)
„Langsam"; **in ~ motion** in Zeitlupe;
~ down vi langsamer werden ♦ vt
verlangsamen; **~ up** vi sich verlangsamen, sich verzögern ♦ vt aufhalten,
langsamer machen; **~ly** adv langsam

sludge [slʌdʒ] n Schlamm m

slug [slʌg] n Nacktschnecke f; (inf: bullet) Kugel f

sluggish ['slʌgɪʃ] adj träge; (COMM)
schleppend

sluice [slu:s] n Schleuse f

slum [slʌm] n (house) Elendsquartier nt

slump [slʌmp] n Rückgang m ♦ vi fallen, stürzen

slung [slʌŋ] pt, pp of **sling**

slur [slɜ:[r]] n Undeutlichkeit f; (insult)
Verleumdung f; **~red** [slɜ:d] adj (pronunciation) undeutlich

slush [slʌʃ] n (snow) Schneematsch m;
~ fund n Schmiergeldfonds m

slut [slʌt] n Schlampe f

sly [slaɪ] adj schlau

smack [smæk] n Klaps m ♦ vt einen
Klaps geben +dat ♦ vi: **to ~ of** riechen
nach; **to ~ one's lips** schmatzen, sich
dat die Lippen lecken

small [smɔ:l] adj klein; **in the ~ hours**
in den frühen Morgenstunden; **~ ads**
(BRIT) npl Kleinanzeigen pl; **~ change** n
Kleingeld nt; **~holder** (BRIT) n Klein-
bauer m; **~pox** n Pocken pl; **~ talk** n
Geplauder nt

smart [smɑ:t] adj (fashionable) elegant,
schick; (neat) adrett; (clever) clever;
(quick) scharf ♦ vi brennen, schmerzen; **~ card** n Chipkarte f; **~en up** vi
sich in Schale werfen ♦ vt herausput-
zen

smash [smæʃ] n Zusammenstoß m,
(TENNIS) Schmetterball m ♦ vt (break)
zerschmettern; (destroy) vernichten
♦ vi (break) zersplittern, zerspringen;
~ing (inf) adj toll

smattering ['smætərɪŋ] n ober-
flächliche Kenntnis f

smear [smɪə[r]] n Fleck m ♦ vt beschmieren

smell [smɛl] (pt, pp **smelt** or **smelled**) n
Geruch m; (sense) Geruchssinn m ♦ vt
riechen ♦ vi: **to ~ (of)** riechen (nach);
(fragrantly) duften (nach); **~y** adj übel
riechend

smile [smaɪl] n Lächeln nt ♦ vi lächeln

smiling ['smaɪlɪŋ] adj lächelnd

smirk [smɜ:k] n blöde(s) Grinsen nt

smock [smɒk] n Kittel m

smoke [sməʊk] n Rauch m ♦ vi rauchen; (food) räuchern ♦ vi rauchen; **~d**
adj (bacon) geräuchert; (glass) Rauch-;
~r n Raucher(in) m(f); (RAIL) Raucherabteil nt; **~ screen** n Rauchwand f

smoking ['sməʊkɪŋ] n: **"no ~"** „Rauchen verboten"; **~ compartment**
(BRIT) ~ **car** (US) n Raucherabteil nt

smoky ['sməʊkɪ] adj rauchig; (room)
verraucht; (taste) geräuchert

smolder ['sməʊldə[r]] (US) vi = **smoulder**

smooth [smu:ð] adj glatt ♦ vt (also: ~
out) glätten, glatt streichen

smother ['smʌðə[r]] vt ersticken

smoulder ['sməʊldə[r]] (US **smolder**) vi
schwelen

smudge [smʌdʒ] n Schmutzfleck m
♦ vt beschmieren

smug [smʌg] adj selbstgefällig

smuggle ['smʌgl] vt schmuggeln; **~r** n
Schmuggler m

smuggling ['smʌglɪŋ] n Schmuggel m

smutty ['smʌtɪ] adj schmutzig

snack [snæk] n Imbiss m; ~ **bar** n Imbissstube f

snag [snæg] n Haken m

snail [sneɪl] n Schnecke f

snake [sneɪk] n Schlange f

snap [snæp] n Schnappen nt; (photograph) Schnappschuss m ♦ adj (decision) schnell ♦ vt (break) zerbrechen; (PHOT) knipsen ♦ vi (break) brechen; (speak) anfauchen; **to ~ shut** zuschnappen; **~ at** vt fus schnappen nach; **~ off** vt (break) abbrechen; **~ up** vt aufschnappen; **~shot** n Schnappschuss m

snare [sneə(r)] n Schlinge f ♦ vt mit einer Schlinge fangen

snarl [snɑːl] n Zähnefletschen nt ♦ vi (dog) knurren

snatch [snætʃ] n (small amount) Bruchteil m ♦ vt schnappen, packen

sneak [sniːk] vi schleichen ♦ n (inf) Petze(r) mf; **~ers** ['sniːkəz] (US) npl Freizeitschuhe pl; **~y** [sniːkɪ] adj raffiniert

sneer [snɪə(r)] n Hohnlächeln nt ♦ vi spötteln

sneeze [sniːz] n Niesen nt ♦ vi niesen

sniff [snɪf] n Schnüffeln nt ♦ vi schnieben; (smell) schnüffeln ♦ vt schnuppern

snigger ['snɪgə(r)] n Kichern nt ♦ vi hämisch kichern

snip [snɪp] n Schnippel m, Schnipsel m ♦ vt schnippeln

sniper ['snaɪpə(r)] n Heckenschütze m

snippet ['snɪpɪt] n Schnipsel m; (of conversation) Fetzen m

snivelling ['snɪvlɪŋ] adj weinerlich

snob [snɒb] n Snob m

snooker ['snuːkə(r)] n Snooker nt

snoop [snuːp] vi: **to ~ about** herumschnüffeln

snooze [snuːz] n Nickerchen nt ♦ vi ein Nickerchen machen, dösen

snore [snɔː(r)] vi schnarchen ♦ n Schnarchen nt

snorkel ['snɔːkl] n Schnorchel m

snort [snɔːt] n Schnauben nt ♦ vi schnauben

snout [snaʊt] n Schnauze f

snow [snəʊ] n Schnee m ♦ vi schneien; **~ball** n Schneeball m ♦ vi eskalieren; **~bound** adj eingeschneit; **~drift** n Schneewehe f; **~drop** n Schneeglöckchen nt; **~fall** n Schneefall m; **~flake** n Schneeflocke f; **~man** (irreg) n Schneemann m; **~plough** (US snowplow) n Schneepflug m; **~ shoe** n Schneeschuh m; **~storm** n Schneesturm m

snub [snʌb] vt schroff abfertigen ♦ n Verweis m; **~-nosed** adj stupsnasig

snuff [snʌf] n Schnupftabak m

snug [snʌg] adj gemütlich, behaglich

snuggle ['snʌgl] vi: **to ~ up to sb** sich an jdn kuscheln

KEYWORD

so [səʊ] adv 1 (thus) so; (likewise) auch; **so saying he walked away** indem er das sagte, ging er; **if so** wenn ja; **I didn't do it – you did so!** ich hab das nicht gemacht – hast du wohl!; **so do I, so am I** etc ich auch; **so it is!** tatsächlich!; **I hope/think so** hoffentlich/ich glaube schon; **so far** bis jetzt

2 (in comparisons etc: to such a degree) so; **so quickly/big (that)** so schnell/groß, dass; **I'm so glad to see you** ich freue mich so, dich zu sehen

3: **so many, so much; so much work** so viel Arbeit; **I love you so much** ich liebe dich so sehr

4 (phrases): **10 or so** etwa 10; **so long!** (inf: goodbye) tschüss!

♦ conj 1 (expressing purpose): **so as to** um ... zu; **so (that)** damit

2 (expressing result) also; **so I was right after all** ich hatte also doch Recht; **so you see ...** wie du siehst ...

soak [səʊk] vt durchnässen; (leave in liquid) einweichen ♦ vi (ein)weichen; ~

in *vi* einsickern; **~ up** *vt* aufsaugen; **~ed** *adj* völlig durchnässt; **~ing** *adj* klitschnass, patschnass

so-and-so ['səuənsəu] *n* (*somebody*) Soundso *m*

soap [səup] *n* Seife *f*; **~flakes** *npl* Seifenflocken *pl*; **~ opera** *n* Familienserie *f* (*im Fernsehen, Radio*); **~ powder** *n* Waschpulver *nt*; **~y** *adj* seifig, Seifen-

soar [sɔ:ʳ] *vi* aufsteigen; (*prices*) in die Höhe schnellen

sob [sɔb] *n* Schluchzen *nt* ♦ *vi* schluchzen

sober ['səubəʳ] *adj* (*also fig*) nüchtern; **~ up** *vi* nüchtern werden

so-called ['səu'kɔ:ld] *adj* so genannt

soccer ['sɔkəʳ] *n* Fußball *m*

sociable ['səuʃəbl] *adj* gesellig

social ['səuʃl] *adj* sozial; (*friendly, living with others*) gesellig ♦ *n* gesellige(r) Abend *m*; **~ club** *n* Verein *m* (*für Freizeitgestaltung*); **~ism** *n* Sozialismus *m*; **~ist** *n* Sozialist(in) *m(f)* ♦ *adj* sozialistisch; **~ize** *vt*: **to ~ize (with)** gesellschaftlich verkehren (mit); **~ly** *adv* gesellschaftlich, privat; **~ security** *n* Sozialversicherung *f*; **~ work** *n* Sozialarbeit *f*; **~ worker** *n* Sozialarbeiter(in) *m(f)*

society [sə'saiəti] *n* Gesellschaft *f*; (*fashionable world*) die große Welt

sociology [səusi'ɔlədʒi] *n* Soziologie *f*

sock [sɔk] *n* Socke *f*

socket ['sɔkit] *n* (*ELEC*) Steckdose *f*; (*of eye*) Augenhöhle *f*

sod [sɔd] *n* Rasenstück *nt*; (*inf!*) Saukerl *m* (!)

soda ['səudə] *n* Soda *f*; (*also:* **~ water**) Soda(wasser) *nt*; (*US: also:* **~ pop**) Limonade *f*

sodden ['sɔdn] *adj* durchweicht

sodium ['səudiəm] *n* Natrium *nt*

sofa ['səufə] *n* Sofa *nt*

soft [sɔft] *adj* weich; (*not loud*) leise; (*weak*) nachgiebig; **~ drink** *n* alkoholfreie(s) Getränk *nt*; **~en** ['sɔfn] *vt* weich machen; (*blow*) abschwächen,

mildern ♦ *vi* weich werden; **~ly** *adv* sanft; leise; **~ness** *n* Weichheit *f*; (*fig*) Sanftheit *f*

software ['sɔftwɛəʳ] *n* (*COMPUT*) Software *f*

soggy ['sɔgi] *adj* (*ground*) sumpfig; (*bread*) aufgeweicht

soil [sɔil] *n* Erde *f*, Boden *m* ♦ *vt* beschmutzen

solace ['sɔlis] *n* Trost *m*

solar ['səuləʳ] *adj* Sonnen-; **~ cell** *n* Solarzelle *f*, **~ energy** *n* Sonnenenergie *f*; **~ panel** *n* Sonnenkollektor *m*; **~ power** *n* Sonnenenergie *f*

sold [səuld] *pt, pp of* **sell**; **~ out** (*COMM*) ausverkauft

solder ['sɔldəʳ] *vt* löten

soldier ['səuldʒəʳ] *n* Soldat *m*

sole [səul] *n* Sohle *f*; (*fish*) Seezunge *f* ♦ *adj* alleinig, Allein-; **~ly** *adv* ausschließlich

solemn ['sɔləm] *adj* feierlich

sole trader *n* (*COMM*) Einzelunternehmen *nt*

solicit [sə'lisit] *vt* (*request*) bitten um ♦ *vi* (*prostitute*) Kunden anwerben

solicitor [sə'lisitəʳ] *n* Rechtsanwalt *m/* anwältin *f*

solid ['sɔlid] *adj* (*hard*) fest; (*of same material, not hollow*) massiv; (*without break*) voll, ganz; (*reliable, sensible*) solide ♦ *n* Festkörper *m*; **~arity** [sɔli'dæriti] *n* Solidarität *f*; **~ify** [sə'lidifai] *vi* fest werden

solitary ['sɔlitəri] *adj* einsam, einzeln; **~ confinement** *n* Einzelhaft *f*

solitude ['sɔlitju:d] *n* Einsamkeit *f*

solo ['səuləu] *n* Solo *nt*; **~ist** ['səuləuist] *n* Solist(in) *m(f)*

soluble ['sɔljubl] *adj* (*substance*) löslich; (*problem*) (auf)lösbar

solution [sə'lu:ʃən] *n* (*also fig*) Lösung *f*; (*of mystery*) Erklärung *f*

solve [sɔlv] *vt* (auf)lösen

solvent ['sɔlvənt] *adj* (*FIN*) zahlungsfähig ♦ *n* (*CHEM*) Lösungsmittel *nt*

sombre ['sɔmbəʳ] (*US* **somber**) *adj* düster

some [sʌm] adj **1** (a certain amount or number of) einige; (a few) ein paar; (with singular nouns) etwas; some tea/biscuits etwas Tee/ein paar Plätzchen; **I've got some money, but not much** ich habe ein bisschen Geld, aber nicht viel

2 (certain: in contrasts) manche(r, s); **some people say that …** manche Leute sagen, dass …

3 (unspecified) irgendein(e); **some woman was asking for you** da hat eine Frau nach Ihnen gefragt; **some day** eines Tages; **some day next week** irgendwann nächste Woche

♦ pron **1** (a certain number) einige; **have you got some?** haben Sie welche?

2 (a certain amount) etwas; **I've read some of the book** ich habe das Buch teilweise gelesen

♦ adv: **some 10 people** etwa 10 Leute

somebody ['sʌmbədi] pron = **someone**

somehow ['sʌmhaʊ] adv (in some way, for some reason) irgendwie

someone ['sʌmwʌn] pron jemand; (direct obj) jemand(en); (indirect obj) jemandem

someplace ['sʌmpleɪs] (US) adv = **somewhere**

somersault ['sʌməsɔːlt] n Salto m ♦ vi einen Salto machen

something ['sʌmθɪŋ] pron etwas

sometime ['sʌmtaɪm] adv (in future) irgend)einmal

sometimes ['sʌmtaɪmz] adv manchmal

somewhat ['sʌmwɔt] adv etwas

somewhere ['sʌmweəʳ] adv irgendwo; (to a place) irgendwohin; ~ **else** irgendwo anders

son [sʌn] n Sohn m

sonar ['səʊnɑːʳ] n Echolot nt

song [sɒŋ] n Lied nt

sonic boom ['sɒnɪk-] n Überschallknall m

son-in-law ['sʌnɪnlɔː] n Schwiegersohn m

soon [suːn] adv bald; ~ **afterwards** kurz danach; ~**er** adv (time) früher; (for preference) lieber; ~**er or later** früher oder später

soot [sʊt] n Ruß m

soothe [suːð] vt (person) beruhigen; (pain) lindern

sophisticated [səˈfɪstɪkeɪtɪd] adj (person) kultiviert; (machinery) hoch entwickelt

sophomore ['sɒfəmɔːʳ] (US) n Collegestudent m im 2. Jahr

soporific [sɒpəˈrɪfɪk] adj einschläfernd

sopping ['sɒpɪŋ] adj patschnass

soppy ['sɒpɪ] (inf) adj schmalzig

soprano [səˈprɑːnəʊ] n Sopran m

sorcerer ['sɔːsərəʳ] n Hexenmeister m

sordid ['sɔːdɪd] adj erbärmlich

sore [sɔːʳ] adj schmerzend; (point) wund ♦ n Wunde f; ~**ly** adv (tempted) stark, sehr

sorrow ['sɒrəʊ] n Kummer m, Leid nt; ~**ful** adj sorgenvoll

sorry ['sɒrɪ] adj traurig, erbärmlich; ~! Entschuldigung!; **to feel** ~ **for sb** jdn bemitleiden; **I feel** ~ **for him** er tut mir Leid; ~? (pardon) wie bitte?

sort [sɔːt] n Art f, Sorte f ♦ vt (also: ~ out: papers) sortieren; (: problems) sichten, in Ordnung bringen; ~**ing office** n Sortierstelle f

SOS n SOS nt

so-so ['səʊsəʊ] adv so(so) lala

sought [sɔːt] pt, pp of **seek**

soul [səʊl] n Seele f; (music) Soul m; ~-**destroying** adj trostlos; ~**ful** adj seelenvoll

sound [saʊnd] adj (healthy) gesund; (safe, sensible) vernünftig; (theory) stichhaltig; (thorough) tüchtig, gehörig ♦ adv: **to be** ~ **asleep** fest schlafen ♦ n (noise) Geräusch nt, Laut m; (GEOG) Sund m ♦ vt erschallen lassen; (alarm) (Alarm) schlagen ♦ vi (make a ~) schallen, tönen; (seem) klingen; **to ~ like** sich anhören wie; **~ out** vt erforschen; (person) auf den Zahn fühlen +dat; **~ barrier** n Schallmauer f; **~ bite** n (RAD, TV) prägnante(s) Zitat nt; **~ effects** npl Toneffekte pl; **~ly** adv (sleep) fest; (beat) tüchtig; **~proof** adj (room) schalldicht; **~ track** n Tonstreifen m; (music) Filmmusik f

soup [suːp] n Suppe f; **~ plate** n Suppenteller m; **~spoon** n Suppenlöffel m

sour ['sauə'] adj (also fig) sauer; **it's ~ grapes** (fig) die Trauben hängen zu hoch

source [sɔːs] n (also fig) Quelle f

south [sauθ] n Süden m ♦ adj Süd-, südlich ♦ adv nach Süden, südwärts; **S~ Africa** n Südafrika nt; **S~ African** adj südafrikanisch ♦ n Südafrikaner(in) m(f); **S~ America** n Südamerika nt; **S~ American** adj südamerikanisch ♦ n Südamerikaner(in) m(f); **~east** n Südosten m; **~erly** ['sʌðəlɪ] adj südlich; **~ern** ['sʌðən] adj südlich, Süd-; **S~ Pole** n Südpol m; **S~ Wales** n Südwales nt; **~ward(s)** adv nach Süden; **~west** n Südwesten m

souvenir [suːvə'nɪə'] n Souvenir nt

sovereign ['sɔvrɪn] n (ruler) Herrscher(in) m(f) ♦ adj (independent) souverän

soviet ['səuvɪət] adj sowjetisch; **the S~ Union** die Sowjetunion

sow¹ [sau] n Sau f

sow² [səu] (pt sowed, pp sown) vt (also fig) säen

soya ['sɔɪə] (US **soy**) n: **~ bean** Sojabohne f; **~ sauce** Sojasauce f

spa [spɑː] n (place) Kurort m

space [speɪs] n Platz m, Raum m; (universe) Weltraum m, All nt; (of time) Abstand m ♦ vt (also: **~ out**) verteilen; **~craft** n Raumschiff nt; **~man** (irreg) n Raumfahrer m; **~ ship** n Raum-

schiff nt

spacing ['speɪsɪŋ] n Abstand m; (also: **~ out**) Verteilung f

spacious ['speɪʃəs] adj geräumig, weit

spade [speɪd] n Spaten m; **~s** npl (CARDS) Pik nt

Spain [speɪn] n Spanien nt

span [spæn] n Spanne f; (of bridge etc) Spannweite f ♦ vt überspannen

Spaniard ['spænjəd] n Spanier(in) m(f)

spaniel ['spænjəl] n Spaniel m

Spanish ['spænɪʃ] adj spanisch ♦ n (LING) Spanisch nt; **the ~** npl (people) die Spanier pl

spank [spæŋk] vt verhauen, versohlen

spanner ['spænə'] (BRIT) n Schraubenschlüssel m

spar [spɑː'] n (NAUT) Sparren m ♦ vi (BOXING) einen Sparring machen

spare [spɛə'] adj Ersatz- ♦ n = **spare part** ♦ vt (lives, feelings) verschonen; (trouble) ersparen; **to ~** (surplus) übrig; **~ part** n Ersatzteil nt; **~ time** n Freizeit f; **~ wheel** n (AUT) Reservereifen m

sparing ['spɛərɪŋ] adj: **to be ~ with** geizen mit; **~ly** adv sparsam; (eat, spend etc) in Maßen

spark [spɑːk] n Funken m; **~(ing) plug** n Zündkerze f

sparkle ['spɑːkl] n Funkeln nt; (gaiety) Schwung m ♦ vi funkeln; **sparkling** adj funkelnd; (wine) Schaum-; (mineral water) mit Kohlensäure; (conversation) spritzig, geistreich

sparrow ['spærəu] n Spatz m

sparse [spɑːs] adj spärlich

spasm ['spæzəm] n (MED) Krampf m; (fig) Anfall m; **~odic** [spæz'mɔdɪk] adj (fig) sprunghaft

spastic ['spæstɪk] (old) n Spastiker(in) m(f) ♦ adj spastisch

spat [spæt] pt, pp of **spit**

spate [speɪt] n (fig) Flut f, Schwall m; **in ~** (river) angeschwollen

spatter ['spætə'] vt bespritzen, verspritzen

spatula ['spætjulə] n Spatel m

spawn [spɔːn] vi laichen ♦ n Laich m

speak [spiːk] (pt **spoke**, pp **spoken**) vt sprechen, reden; (truth) sagen; (language) sprechen ♦ vi: to ~ (to) sprechen (mit or zu); to ~ to sb of or about sth mit jdm über etw acc sprechen; ~ up! sprich lauter!; ~er n Sprecher(in) m(f), Redner(in) m(f); (loudspeaker) Lautsprecher m; (POL): the S~er der Vorsitzende des Parlaments (BRIT) or des Kongresses (US)

spear [spɪəʳ] n Speer m ♦ vt aufspießen; ~head vt (attack etc) anführen

spec [spek] (inf) n: on ~ auf gut Glück

special ['speʃl] adj besondere(r, s); ~ist n (TECH) Fachmann m; (MED) Facharzt m/Fachärztin f; ~ity [speʃi'ælɪtɪ] n Spezialgebiet nt; (study) Spezialität f; ~ize vi: to ~ize (in) sich spezialisieren (auf +acc); ~ly adv besonders; (explicitly) extra; ~ needs adj: ~ needs children behinderte Kinder pl; ~ty (esp US) n = speciality

species ['spiːʃiːz] n Art f

specific [spə'sɪfɪk] adj spezifisch; ~ally adv spezifisch

specification [spesɪfɪ'keɪʃən] n Angabe f; (stipulation) Bedingung f; ~s npl (TECH) technische Daten pl

specify ['spesɪfaɪ] vt genau angeben

specimen ['spesɪmən] n Probe f

speck [spek] n Fleckchen nt

speckled ['spekld] adj gesprenkelt

specs [speks] (inf) npl Brille f

spectacle ['spektəkl] n Schauspiel nt; ~s npl (glasses) Brille f

spectacular [spek'tækjuləʳ] adj sensationell; (success etc) spektakulär

spectator [spek'teɪtəʳ] n Zuschauer(in) m(f)

spectre ['spektəʳ] (US **specter**) n Geist m, Gespenst nt

speculate ['spekjuleɪt] vi spekulieren

speech [spiːtʃ] n Sprache f; (address) Rede f; (way one speaks) Sprechweise f; ~less adj sprachlos

speed [spiːd] n Geschwindigkeit f; (gear) Gang m ♦ vi (JUR) (zu) schnell fahren; at full or top ~ mit Höchstgeschwindigkeit; ~ up vt beschleunigen ♦ vi: schneller werden; schneller fahren; ~boat n Schnellboot nt; ~ily adv schleunigst; ~ing n Geschwindigkeitsüberschreitung f; ~ limit n Geschwindigkeitsbegrenzung f; ~ometer [spɪ'dɒmɪtəʳ] n Tachometer m; ~way n (bike racing) Motorradrennstrecke f; ~y adj schnell

spell [spel] (pt, pp **spelt** (BRIT) or **spelled**) n (magic) Bann m; (period of time) (eine) Zeit lang ♦ vt buchstabieren; (imply) bedeuten; to cast a ~ on sb jdn verzaubern; ~bound adj (wie) gebannt; ~ing n Rechtschreibung f

spelt [spelt] (BRIT) pt, pp of **spell**

spend [spend] (pt, pp **spent**) vt (money) ausgeben; (time) verbringen; ~thrift n Verschwender(in) m(f)

spent [spent] pt, pp of **spend**

sperm [spɜːm] n (BIOL) Samenflüssigkeit f

spew [spjuː] vt (er)brechen

sphere [sfɪəʳ] n (globe) Kugel f; (fig) Sphäre f, Gebiet nt; **spherical** ['sferɪkl] adj kugelförmig

spice [spaɪs] n Gewürz nt ♦ vt würzen

spick-and-span ['spɪkən'spæn] adj blitzblank

spicy ['spaɪsɪ] adj (food) stark gewürzt; (fig) pikant

spider ['spaɪdəʳ] n Spinne f

spike [spaɪk] n Dorn m, Spitze f

spill [spɪl] (pt, pp **spilt** or **spilled**) vt verschütten ♦ vi sich ergießen; ~ over vi überlaufen; (fig) sich ausbreiten

spilt [spɪlt] pt, pp of **spill**

spin [spɪn] (pt, pp **spun**) n (trip in car) Spazierfahrt f; (AVIAT) (Ab)trudeln nt; (on ball) Drall m ♦ vt (thread) spinnen; (like top) (herum)wirbeln ♦ vi sich drehen; ~ out vt in die Länge ziehen

spinach ['spɪnɪtʃ] n Spinat m

spinal ['spaɪnl] adj Rückgrat-; ~ cord n

Rückenmark nt

spindly ['spɪndlɪ] adj spindeldürr

spin doctor n PR-Fachmann m, PR-Fachfrau f

spin-dryer [spɪn'draɪəʳ] (BRIT) n Wäscheschleuder f

spine [spaɪn] n Rückgrat nt; (thorn) Stachel m; **~less** adj (also fig) rückgratlos

spinning ['spɪnɪŋ] n Spinnen nt; **~ top** n Kreisel m; **~ wheel** n Spinnrad nt

spin-off ['spɪnɒf] n Nebenprodukt nt

spinster ['spɪnstəʳ] n unverheiratete Frau f; (pej) alte Jungfer f

spiral ['spaɪərl] n Spirale f ♦ adj spiralförmig; (movement etc) in Spiralen ♦ vi sich (hoch)winden; **~ staircase** n Wendeltreppe f

spire [spaɪəʳ] n Turm m

spirit ['spɪrɪt] n Geist m; (humour, mood) Stimmung f; (courage) Mut m; (verve) Elan m; (alcohol) Alkohol m; **~s** npl (drink) Spirituosen pl; **in good ~s** gut aufgelegt; **~ed** adj beherzt; **~level** n Wasserwaage f

spiritual ['spɪrɪtjuəl] adj geistig, seelisch; (REL) geistlich ♦ n Spiritual nt

spit [spɪt] (pt, pp **spat**) n (for roasting) (Brat)spieß m; (saliva) Spucke f ♦ vi spucken; (rain) sprühen; (make a sound) zischen; (cat) fauchen

spite [spaɪt] n Gehässigkeit f ♦ vt kränken; **in ~ of** trotz; **~ful** adj gehässig

spittle ['spɪtl] n Speichel m, Spucke f

splash [splæʃ] n Spritzer m; (of colour) (Farb)fleck m ♦ vt bespritzen ♦ vi spritzen

spleen [spli:n] n (ANAT) Milz f

splendid ['splendɪd] adj glänzend

splendour ['splendəʳ] (US **splendor**) n Pracht f

splint [splɪnt] n Schiene f

splinter ['splɪntəʳ] n Splitter m ♦ vi (zer)splittern

split [splɪt] (pt, pp **split**) n Spalte f; (fig) Spaltung f; (division) Trennung f ♦ vt spalten vi ♦ vi (divide) reißen; **~ up** vi

sich trennen

splutter ['splʌtəʳ] vi stottern

spoil [spɔɪl] (pt, pp **spoilt** or **spoiled**) vt (ruin) verderben; (child) verwöhnen; **~s** npl Beute f; **~sport** n Spielverderber m; **~t** pt, pp of **spoil**

spoke [spəʊk] pt of **speak** ♦ n Speiche f; **~n** pp of **speak**

spokesman ['spəʊksmən] (irreg) n Sprecher m; **spokeswoman** ['spəʊkswumən] (irreg) n Sprecherin f

sponge [spʌndʒ] n Schwamm m ♦ vt abwaschen ♦ vi: **to ~ on** auf Kosten +gen leben; **~ bag** (BRIT) n Kulturbeutel m; **~ cake** n Rührkuchen m

sponsor ['spɒnsəʳ] n Sponsor m ♦ vt fördern; **~ship** n Finanzierung f; (public) Schirmherrschaft f

spontaneous [spɒn'teɪnɪəs] adj spontan

spooky ['spu:kɪ] (inf) adj gespenstisch

spool [spu:l] n Spule f, Rolle f

spoon [spu:n] n Löffel m; **~-feed** (irreg) vt mit dem Löffel füttern; (fig) hochpäppeln; **~ful** n Löffel m (voll)

sport [spɔ:t] n Sport m; (person) feine(r) Kerl m; **~ing** adj (fair) sportlich, fein; **to give sb a ~ing chance** jdm eine faire Chance geben; **~ jacket** (US) n = **sports jacket**; **~s car** n Sportwagen m; **~s jacket** n Sportjackett nt; **~sman** (irreg) n Sportler m; **~smanship** n Sportlichkeit f; **~swear** n Sportkleidung f; **~swoman** (irreg) n Sportlerin f; **~y** adj sportlich

spot [spɒt] n Punkt m; (dirty) Fleck(en) m; (place) Stelle f; (MED) Pickel m ♦ vt erspähen; (mistake) bemerken; **on the ~** an Ort und Stelle; (at once) auf der Stelle; **~ check** n Stichprobe f; **~less** adj fleckenlos; **~light** n Scheinwerferlicht nt; (lamp) Scheinwerfer m; **~ted** adj gefleckt; **~ty** adj (face) pickelig

spouse [spaus] n Gatte m/Gattin f

spout [spaut] n (of pot) Tülle f; (jet) Wasserstrahl m ♦ vi speien

sprain [spreɪn] (pt, pp **sprained**) n Verrenkung f ♦ vt verrenken

sprang [spræŋ] *pt of* **spring**

sprawl [sprɔ:l] *vi* sich strecken

spray [spreɪ] *n* Spray *nt*; *(off sea)* Gischt *f*; *(of flowers)* Zweig *m* ♦ *vt* besprühen, sprayen

spread [spred] *(pt, pp* **spread***) n (extent)* Verbreitung *f*; *(inf: meal)* Schmaus *m*; *(for bread)* Aufstrich *m* ♦ *vt* ausbreiten; *(scatter)* verbreiten; *(butter)* streichen ♦ *vi* sich ausbreiten; **~-eagled** ['spredi:gld] *adj*: **to be ~-eagled** alle viere von sich strecken; **~ out** *vi (move apart)* sich verteilen; **~sheet** *n* Tabellenkalkulation *f*

spree [spri:] *n (shopping)* Einkaufsbummel *m*; **to go on a ~** einen draufmachen

sprightly ['spraɪtlɪ] *adj* munter, lebhaft

spring [sprɪŋ] *(pt* **sprang***, pp* **sprung***) n (leap)* Sprung *m*; *(TECH)* Feder *f*; *(season)* Frühling *m*; *(water)* Quelle *f* ♦ *vi (leap)* springen; **~ up** *vi (problem)* auftauchen; **~board** *n* Sprungbrett *nt*; **~-clean** *n (also:* **~-cleaning***)* Frühjahrsputz *m*; **~time** *n* Frühling *m*; **~y** *adj* federnd, elastisch

sprinkle ['sprɪŋkl] *vt (salt)* streuen; *(liquid)* sprenkeln; **to ~ water on, to ~ with water** mit Wasser besprengen; **~r** ['sprɪŋklə*] *n (for lawn)* Sprenger *m*; *(for fire fighting)* Sprinkler *m*

sprint [sprɪnt] *n (race)* Sprint *m* ♦ *vi (run fast)* rennen; *(SPORT)* sprinten; **~er** *n* Sprinter(in) *m(f)*

sprout [spraʊt] *vi* sprießen

sprouts [spraʊts] *npl (also:* **Brussels ~***)* Rosenkohl *m*

spruce [spru:s] *n* Fichte *f* ♦ *adj* schmuck, adrett

sprung [sprʌŋ] *pp of* **spring**

spry [spraɪ] *adj* flink, rege

spun [spʌn] *pt, pp of* **spin**

spur [spə:*] *n* Sporn *m*; *(fig)* Ansporn *m* ♦ *vt (also:* **~ on***: fig)* anspornen; **on the ~ of the moment** spontan

spurious ['spjʊərɪəs] *adj* falsch

spurn [spə:n] *vt* verschmähen

spurt [spə:t] *n (jet)* Strahl *m*; *(acceleration)* Spurt *m* ♦ *vi (liquid)* schießen

spy [spaɪ] *n* Spion(in) *m(f)* ♦ *vi* spionieren; *vt* erspähen; **~ing** *n* Spionage *f*

sq. *abbr* = **square**

squabble ['skwɒbl] *n* Zank *m* ♦ *vi* sich zanken

squad [skwɒd] *n (MIL)* Abteilung *f*; *(POLICE)* Kommando *nt*

squadron ['skwɒdrn] *n (cavalry)* Schwadron *f*; *(NAUT)* Geschwader *nt*; *(air force)* Staffel *f*

squalid ['skwɒlɪd] *adj* verkommen

squall [skwɔ:l] *n* Bö(e) *f*, Windstoß *m*

squalor ['skwɒlə*] *n* Verwahrlosung *f*

squander ['skwɒndə*] *vt* verschwenden

square [skwεə*] *n* Quadrat *nt*; *(open space)* Platz *m*; *(instrument)* Winkel *m*; *(inf: person)* Spießer *m* ♦ *adj* viereckig; *(inf: ideas, tastes)* spießig ♦ *vt (arrange)* ausmachen; *(MATH)* ins Quadrat erheben ♦ *vi (agree)* übereinstimmen; **all ~** quitt; **a ~ meal** eine ordentliche Mahlzeit; **2 metres ~** 2 Meter im Quadrat; **1 ~ metre** 1 Quadratmeter; **~ly** *adv* fest, gerade

squash [skwɒʃ] *n (BRIT: drink)* Saft *m*; *(game)* Squash *nt* ♦ *vt* zerquetschen

squat [skwɒt] *adj* untersetzt ♦ *vi* hocken; **~ter** *n* Hausbesetzer *m*

squawk [skwɔ:k] *vi* kreischen

squeak [skwi:k] *vi* quiek(s)en; *(spring, door etc)* quietschen

squeal [skwi:l] *vi* schrill schreien

squeamish ['skwi:mɪʃ] *adj* empfindlich

squeeze [skwi:z] *vt* pressen, drücken; *(orange)* auspressen; **~ out** *vt* ausquetschen

squelch [skweltʃ] *vi* platschen

squib [skwɪb] *n* Knallfrosch *m*

squid [skwɪd] *n* Tintenfisch *m*

squiggle ['skwɪgl] *n* Schnörkel *m*

squint [skwɪnt] *vi* schielen ♦ *n*: **to have a ~** schielen; **to ~ at sb/sth** nach jdm/etw schielen

squirm [skwɜːm] vi sich winden

squirrel ['skwɪrəl] n Eichhörnchen nt

squirt [skwɜːt] vt, vi spritzen

Sr abbr (= senior) sen.

St abbr (= saint) hl., St.; (= street) Str.

stab [stæb] n (blow) Stich m; (inf: try) Versuch m ♦ vt erstechen

stabilize ['steɪbəlaɪz] vt stabilisieren ♦ vi sich stabilisieren

stable ['steɪbl] adj stabil ♦ n Stall m

stack [stæk] n Stapel m ♦ vt stapeln

stadium ['steɪdɪəm] n Stadion nt

staff [stɑːf] n (stick, MIL) Stab m; (personnel) Personal nt; (BRIT: SCH) Lehrkräfte pl ♦ vt besetzen

stag [stæg] n Hirsch m

stage [steɪdʒ] n Bühne f; (of journey) Etappe f; (degree) Stufe f; (point) Stadium nt ♦ vt (put on) aufführen; (simulate) inszenieren; (demonstration) veranstalten; **in ~s** stufenweise; **~coach** n Postkutsche f; **~ door** n Bühneneingang m; **~ manager** n Intendant m

stagger ['stægə*] vi wanken, taumeln ♦ vt (amaze) verblüffen; (hours) staffeln; **~ing** adj unglaublich

stagnant ['stægnənt] adj stagnierend; (water) stehend; **stagnate** [stæg'neɪt] vi stagnieren

stag party n Männerabend m (vom Bräutigam vor der Hochzeit gegeben)

staid [steɪd] adj gesetzt

stain [steɪn] n Fleck m ♦ vt beflecken; **~ed glass window** n buntes Glasfenster nt; **~less** adj (steel) rostfrei; **~ remover** n Fleckentferner m

stair [steə*] n (Treppen)stufe f; **~s** npl (flight of steps) Treppe f; **~case** n Treppenhaus nt, Treppe f; **~way** n Treppenaufgang m

stake [steɪk] n (post) Pfahl m; (money) Einsatz m ♦ vt (bet: money) setzen; **to be at ~** auf dem Spiel stehen

stale [steɪl] adj alt; (bread) altbacken

stalemate ['steɪlmeɪt] n (CHESS) Patt nt; (fig) Stillstand m

stalk [stɔːk] n Stängel m, Stiel m ♦ vt (game) jagen; **~ off** vi abstolzieren

stall [stɔːl] n (in stable) Stand m, Box f; (in market) (Verkaufs)stand m ♦ (AUT) abwürgen ♦ vi (AUT) stehen bleiben; (fig) Ausflüchte machen; **~s** npl (BRIT: THEAT) Parkett nt

stallion ['stæljən] n Zuchthengst m

stalwart ['stɔːlwət] n treue(r) Anhänger m

stamina ['stæmɪnə] n Durchhaltevermögen nt, Zähigkeit f

stammer ['stæmə*] n Stottern nt ♦ vt, vi stottern, stammeln

stamp [stæmp] n Briefmarke f; (for document) Stempel m ♦ vi stampfen ♦ vt (mark) stempeln; (mail) frankieren; (foot) stampfen mit; **~ album** n Briefmarkenalbum nt; **~ collecting** n Briefmarkensammeln nt

stampede [stæm'piːd] n panische Flucht f

stance [stæns] n Haltung f

stand [stænd] (pt, pp stood) n (for objects) Gestell nt; (seats) Tribüne f ♦ vi stehen; (rise) aufstehen; (decision) feststehen ♦ vt setzen, stellen; (endure) aushalten; (person) ausstehen; (nonsense) dulden; **to make a ~** Widerstand leisten; **to ~ for parliament** (BRIT) für das Parlament kandidieren; **~ by** vi (be ready) bereitstehen ♦ vt fus (opinion) treu bleiben +dat; **~ down** vi (withdraw) zurücktreten; **~ for** vt fus (signify) stehen für; (permit, tolerate) hinnehmen; **~ in for** vt fus einspringen für; **~ out** vi (be prominent) hervorstechen; **~ up** vi (rise) aufstehen; **~ up for** vt fus sich einsetzen für; **~ up to** vt fus: **to ~ up to sth** einer Sache dat gewachsen sein; **to ~ up to sb** sich jdm gegenüber behaupten

standard ['stændəd] n (measure) Norm f; (flag) Fahne f ♦ adj (size etc) Normal-; **~s** npl (morals) Maßstäbe pl; **~ize** vt vereinheitlichen; **~ lamp** (BRIT) n Stehlampe f; **~ of living** n Lebensstandard *m*

stand: **~by** *n* Reserve *f*; **to be on ~by** in Bereitschaft sein; **~by ticket** *n* (AVIAT) Standbyticket *nt*; **~in** [ˈstændɪn] *n* Ersatz *m*

standing [ˈstændɪŋ] *adj* (erect) stehend; (permanent) ständig; (invitation) offen ♦ *n* (duration) Dauer *f*; (reputation) Ansehen *nt*; **of many years'** ~ langjährig ♦ *adj*; **~ order** *n* (at bank) Dauerauftrag *m*; **~ room** *n* Stehplatz *m*

stand: **~offish** [stændˈɔfɪʃ] *adj* zurückhaltend, sehr reserviert; **~point** [ˈstændpɔɪnt] *n* Standpunkt *m*; **~still** [ˈstændstɪl] *n*: **to be at a ~still** stillstehen; **to come to a ~still** zum Stillstand kommen

stank [stæŋk] *pt* of **stink**

staple [ˈsteɪpl] *n* (in paper) Heftklammer *f*; (article) Haupterzeugnis *nt* ♦ *adj* Grund-, Haupt- ♦ *vt* (fest)klammern; **~r** *n* Heftmaschine *f*

star [staːⁱ] *n* Stern *m*; (person) Star *m* ♦ *vi* die Hauptrolle spielen ♦ *vt*: **~ring ...** in der Hauptrolle/den Hauptrollen ...

starboard [ˈstaːbɔːd] *n* Steuerbord *nt*

starch [staːtʃ] *n* Stärke *f*

stardom [ˈstaːdəm] *n* Berühmtheit *f*

stare [steəⁱ] *n* starre(r) Blick *m* ♦ *vi*: **to ~ at** starren auf +*acc*, anstarren

starfish [ˈstaːfɪʃ] *n* Seestern *m*

stark [staːk] *adj* öde ♦ *adv*: **~ naked** splitternackt

starling [ˈstaːlɪŋ] *n* Star *m*

starry [ˈstaːrɪ] *adj* Sternen-; **~-eyed** *adj* (innocent) blauäugig

start [staːt] *n* Anfang *m*; (SPORT) Start *m*; (lead) Vorsprung *m* ♦ *vt* in Gang setzen; (car) anlassen ♦ *vi* anfangen; (car) anspringen; (on journey) aufbrechen; (SPORT) starten; (with fright) zusammenfahren; **to ~ doing** or **to do sth** anfangen, etw zu tun; **~ off** *vi* anfangen; (begin moving) losgehen; losfahren; **~ up** *vi* anfangen ♦ *vt* beginnen; (car) anlassen; (engine) anlassen;

standard *m*

~er *n* (AUT) Anlasser *m*; (for race) Starter *m*; (BRIT: COOK) Vorspeise *f*; **~ing point** *n* Ausgangspunkt *m*

startle [ˈstaːtl] *vt* erschrecken; **startling** *adj* erschreckend

starvation [staːˈveɪʃən] *n* Verhungern *nt*

starve [staːv] *vi* verhungern ♦ *vt* verhungern lassen; **I'm starving** ich sterbe vor Hunger

state [steɪt] *n* (condition) Zustand *m*; (POL) Staat *m* ♦ *vt* erklären; (facts) angeben; **the S~s** (USA) die Staaten; **to be in a ~** durchdrehen; **~ly** *adj* würdevoll; **~ly home** *n* herrschaftliches Anwesen *nt*, Schloss *nt*; **~ment** *n* Aussage *f*; (POL) Erklärung *f*; **~sman** (*irreg*) *n* Staatsmann *m*

static [ˈstætɪk] *n* (also: **~ electricity**) Reibungselektrizität *f*

station [ˈsteɪʃən] *n* (RAIL etc) Bahnhof *m*; (police etc) Wache *f*; (in society) Stand *m* ♦ *vt* stationieren

stationary [ˈsteɪʃnərɪ] *adj* stillstehend; (car) parkend

stationer's (shop) *n* Schreibwarengeschäft *nt*; **~y** *n* Schreibwaren *pl*

station master *n* Bahnhofsvorsteher *m*

station wagon *n* Kombiwagen *m*

statistics [stəˈtɪstɪks] *n* Statistik *f*

statue [ˈstætjuː] *n* Statue *f*

stature [ˈstætʃəⁱ] *n* Größe *f*

status [ˈsteɪtəs] *n* Status *m*

statute [ˈstætjuːt] *n* Gesetz *nt*; **statutory** [ˈstætjutrɪ] *adj* gesetzlich

staunch [stɔːntʃ] *adj* standhaft

stay [steɪ] *n* Aufenthalt *m* ♦ *vi* bleiben; (reside) wohnen; **to ~ put** an Ort und Stelle bleiben; **to ~ the night** übernachten; **~ behind** *vi* zurückbleiben; **~ in** *vi* (at home) zu Hause bleiben; **~ on** *vi* (continue) länger bleiben; **~ out** *vi* (of house) wegbleiben; **~ up** *vi* (at night) aufbleiben; **~ing power** *n* Durchhaltevermögen *nt*

stead [sted] *n*: **in sb's ~** an jds Stelle *dat*; **to stand sb in good ~** jdm zugute kommen

steadfast ['stedfɑːst] *adj* standhaft, treu

steadily ['stedɪlɪ] *adv* stetig, regelmäßig

steady ['stedɪ] *adj* (*firm*) fest, stabil; (*regular*) gleichmäßig; (*reliable*) beständig; (*hand*) ruhig; (*job, boyfriend*) fest ♦ *vt* festigen; **to ~ o.s. on/against sth** sich stützen auf/gegen etw *acc*

steak [steɪk] *n* Steak *nt*; (*fish*) Filet *nt*

steal [stiːl] (*pt* **stole**, *pp* **stolen**) *vt* stehlen ♦ *vi* stehlen; (*go quietly*) sich stehlen

stealth [stelθ] *n* Heimlichkeit *f*; **~y** *adj* verstohlen, heimlich

steam [stiːm] *n* Dampf *m* ♦ *vt* (COOK) im Dampfbad erhitzen ♦ *vi* dampfen; **~ engine** *n* Dampfmaschine *f*; **~er** *n* Dampfer *m*; **~roller** *n* Dampfwalze *f*; **~ship** *n* = **steamer**; **~y** *adj* dampfig

steel [stiːl] *n* Stahl *m* ♦ *adj* Stahl-; (*fig*) stählern; **~works** *n* Stahlwerke *pl*

steep [stiːp] *adj* steil; (*price*) gepfeffert ♦ *vt* einweichen

steeple ['stiːpl] *n* Kirchturm *m*; **~chase** *n* Hindernisrennen *nt*

steer [stɪəʳ] *vt, vi* steuern; (*car etc*) lenken; **~ing** *n* (AUT) Steuerung *f*; **~ing wheel** *n* Steuer- or Lenkrad *nt*

stem [stem] *n* Stiel *m* ♦ *vt* aufhalten; **~ from** *vt fus* abstammen von

stench [stentʃ] *n* Gestank *m*

stencil ['stensl] *n* Schablone *f* ♦ *vt* (auf)drucken

stenographer [ste'nɔgrəfəʳ] (US) *n* Stenograf(in) *m(f)*

step [step] *n* Schritt *m*; (*stair*) Stufe *f* ♦ *vi* treten, schreiten; **~s** *npl* (BRIT) = **stepladder; to take ~s** Schritte unternehmen; **in/out of ~ (with)** im/nicht im Gleichklang (mit); **~ down** *vi* (*fig*) abtreten; **~ off** *vt fus* aussteigen aus; **~ up** *vt* steigern

stepbrother ['stepbrʌðəʳ] *n* Stiefbruder *m*

stepdaughter ['stepdɔːtəʳ] *n* Stieftochter *f*

stepfather ['stepfɑːðəʳ] *n* Stiefvater *m*

stepladder ['steplædəʳ] *n* Trittleiter *f*

stepmother ['stepmʌðəʳ] *n* Stiefmutter *f*

stepping stone ['stepɪŋ-] *n* Stein *m*; (*fig*) Sprungbrett *nt*

stepsister ['stepsɪstəʳ] *n* Stiefschwester *f*

stepson ['stepsʌn] *n* Stiefsohn *m*

stereo ['stɪərɪəu] *n* Stereoanlage *f* ♦ *adj* (*also:* **~phonic**) stereofonisch, stereophonisch

stereotype ['stɪərɪətaɪp] *n* (*fig*) Klischee *nt* ♦ *vt* stereotypieren; (*fig*) stereotyp machen

sterile ['steraɪl] *adj* steril; (*person*) unfruchtbar; **sterilize** *vt* sterilisieren

sterling ['stɜːlɪŋ] *adj* (FIN) Sterling-; (*character*) gediegen ♦ *n* (ECON) das Pfund Sterling; **a pound ~** ein Pfund Sterling

stern [stɜːn] *adj* streng ♦ *n* Heck *nt*, Achterschiff *nt*

stew [stjuː] *n* Eintopf *m* ♦ *vt, vi* schmoren

steward ['stjuːəd] *n* Steward *m*; **~ess** *n* Stewardess *f*

stick [stɪk] (*pt, pp* **stuck**) *n* Stock *m*; (*of chalk etc*) Stück *nt* ♦ *vt* (*stab*) stechen; (*fix*) stecken; (*put*) stellen; (*gum*) (an)kleben; (*inf: tolerate*) vertragen ♦ *vi* (*stop*) stecken bleiben; (*get stuck*) klemmen; (*hold fast*) kleben, haften; **~ out** *vi* (*project*) hervorstehen; **~ up** *vi* (*project*) in die Höhe stehen; **~ up for** *vt fus* (*defend*) eintreten für; **~er** *n* Aufkleber *m*; **~ing plaster** *n* Heftpflaster *nt*

stickler ['stɪkləʳ] *n*: **~ (for)** Pedant *m* (in *+acc*)

stick-up ['stɪkʌp] (*inf*) *n* (*Raub*)überfall *m*

sticky ['stɪkɪ] *adj* klebrig; (*atmosphere*) stickig

stiff [stɪf] *adj* steif; *(difficult)* hart; *(paste)* dick; *(drink)* stark; **to have a ~ neck** einen steifen Hals haben; **~en** *vt* versteifen, (ver)stärken ♦ *vi* sich versteifen

stifle ['staɪfl] *vt* unterdrücken; **stifling** *adj* drückend

stigma ['stɪgmə] *(pl* BOT, MED, **~ta;** *fig* **~s)** *n* Stigma *nt*

stigmata [stɪg'mɑːtə] *npl of* **stigma**

stile [staɪl] *n* Steige *f*

stiletto [stɪ'letəu] *(BRIT) n (also: ~ heel)* Pfennigabsatz *m*

still [stɪl] *adj* still ♦ *adv* (immer) noch; *(anyhow)* immerhin; **~born** *adj* tot geboren; **~ life** *n* Stilleben *nt*

stilt [stɪlt] *n* Stelze *f*

stilted ['stɪltɪd] *adj* gestelzt

stimulate ['stɪmjuleɪt] *vt* anregen, stimulieren

stimuli ['stɪmjulaɪ] *npl of* **stimulus**

stimulus ['stɪmjuləs] *(pl* **-li)** *n* Anregung *f*, Reiz *m*

sting [stɪŋ] *(pt, pp* **stung)** *n* Stich *m*; *(organ)* Stachel *m* ♦ *vi* stechen; *(on skin)* brennen ♦ *vt* stechen

stingy ['stɪndʒɪ] *adj* geizig, knauserig

stink [stɪŋk] *(pt* **stank,** *pp* **stunk)** *n* Gestank *m* ♦ *vi* stinken; **~ing** *adj (fig)* widerlich

stint [stɪnt] *n (period)* Betätigung *f*; **to do one's ~** seine Arbeit tun; *(share)* seinen Teil beitragen

stipulate ['stɪpjuleɪt] *vt* festsetzen

stir [stɜː] *n* Bewegung *f*, *(COOK)* Rühren *nt*; *(sensation)* Aufsehen *nt* ♦ *vt* (um)rühren ♦ *vi* sich rühren; **~ up** *vt (mob)* aufhetzen; *(mixture)* umrühren; *(dust)* aufwirbeln

stirrup ['stɪrəp] *n* Steigbügel *m*

stitch [stɪtʃ] *n (with needle)* Stich *m*; *(MED)* Faden *m*; *(of knitting)* Masche *f*; *(pain)* Stich *m* ♦ *vt* nähen

stoat [stəut] *n* Wiesel *nt*

stock [stɔk] *n* Vorrat *m*, *(COMM)* (Waren)lager *nt*; *(livestock)* Vieh *nt*; *(COOK)* Brühe *f*; *(FIN)* Grundkapital *nt* ♦ *adj* stets vorrätig; *(standard)* Normal- ♦ *vt*

(in shop) führen; **~s** *npl (FIN)* Aktien *pl*; **in/out of ~** vorrätig/nicht vorrätig; **to take ~ of** Inventur machen von; *(fig)* Bilanz ziehen aus; **~s and shares** Effekten *pl*; **~ up** *vi:* **to ~ up (with)** Reserven anlegen (von); **~broker** ['stɔkbrəukə] *n* Börsenmakler *m*; **~ cube** *n* Brühwürfel *m*; **~ exchange** *n* Börse *f*

stocking ['stɔkɪŋ] *n* Strumpf *m*

stock: **~ market** *n* Börse *f*; **~ phrase** *n* Standardsatz *m*; **~pile** *n* Vorrat *m* ♦ *vt* aufstapeln; **~taking** *(BRIT) n (COMM)* Inventur *f*, Bestandsaufnahme *f*

stocky ['stɔkɪ] *adj* untersetzt

stodgy ['stɔdʒɪ] *adj* pampig

stoke [stəuk] *vt* schüren

stole [stəul] *pt of* **steal** ♦ *n* Stola *f*

stolen ['stəuln] *pp of* **steal**

stomach ['stʌmək] *n* Bauch *m*, Magen *m* ♦ *vt* vertragen; **~ache** *n* Magen- *or* Bauchschmerzen *pl*

stone [stəun] *n* Stein *m*; *(BRIT: weight)* Gewichtseinheit = 6.35 kg ♦ *vt (olive)* entkernen; *(kill)* steinigen; **~cold** *adj* eiskalt; **~deaf** *adj* stocktaub; **~work** *n* Mauerwerk *nt*; **stony** ['stəunɪ] *adj* steinig

stood [stud] *pt, pp of* **stand**

stool [stuːl] *n* Hocker *m*

stoop [stuːp] *vi* sich bücken

stop [stɔp] *n* Halt *m*, *(BRIT)* Haltestelle *f*; *(punctuation)* Punkt *m* ♦ *vt* anhalten; *(bring to an end)* aufhören (mit), sein lassen ♦ *vi* aufhören; *(clock)* stehen bleiben; *(remain)* bleiben; **to ~ doing sth** aufhören, etwas zu tun; **to ~ dead** innehalten; **~ off** *vi* kurz Halt machen; **~ up** *vt (hole)* zustopfen; **~gap** *n* Notlösung *f*; **~lights** *npl (AUT)* Bremslichter *pl*; **~over** *n (on journey)* Zwischenaufenthalt *m*; *(AVIAT)* Zwischenlandung *f*; **~page** ['stɔpɪdʒ] *n (An)halten nt*; *(traffic)* Verkehrsstockung *f*; *(strike)* Arbeitseinstellung *f*; **~per** ['stɔpə] *n* Propfen *m*, Stöpsel *m*; **~ press** *n* letzte Meldung *f*; **~watch** ['stɔpwɔtʃ] *n* Stoppuhr *f*

storage ['stɔːrɪdʒ] n Lagerung f; **~-heater** n (Nachtstrom)speicherofen m

store [stɔː] n Vorrat m; (place) Lager nt, Warenhaus nt; (BRIT: large shop) Kaufhaus nt; (US) Laden m ♦ vt lagern; **~s** npl (supplies) Vorräte pl; **~ up** vt sich eindecken mit; **~room** n Lagerraum m, Vorratsraum m

storey ['stɔːrɪ] (US story) n Stock m

stork [stɔːk] n Storch m

storm [stɔːm] n (also fig) Sturm m ♦ vt, vi stürmen; **~y** adj stürmisch

story ['stɔːrɪ] n Geschichte f; (lie) Märchen nt; (US) = storey; **~book** n Geschichtenbuch nt; **~teller** n Geschichtenerzähler m

stout [staut] adj (bold) tapfer; (fat) beleibt ♦ n Starkbier nt; (also: **sweet** ~) Malzbier nt

stove [stauv] n (Koch)herd m; (for heating) Ofen m

stow [stau] vt verstauen; **~away** n blinde(r) Passagier m

straddle ['strædl] vt (horse, fence) rittlings sitzen auf +dat; (fig) überbrücken

straggle ['strægl] vi (people) nachhinken; **~r** n Nachzügler m; **~straggly** adj (hair) zottig

straight [streit] adj gerade; (honest) offen, ehrlich; (drink) pur ♦ adv (direkt); (drink) pur ♦ adv direkt, geradewegs; **to put** or **get sth** ~ etw in Ordnung bringen; **~ away** sofort; **~ off** sofort; **~en** vt (also: **~en out**) gerade machen; (fig) klarstellen; **~faced** adv ohne die Miene zu verziehen ♦ adj: **to be ~-faced** keine Miene verziehen; **~forward** adj einfach, unkompliziert

strain [strein] n Belastung f; (streak, trace) Zug m; (of music) Fetzen m ♦ vt überanstrengen; (stretch) anspannen; (muscle) zerren; (filter) (durch)seihen ♦ vi sich anstrengen; **~ed** adj (laugh) gezwungen; (relations) gespannt; **~er** n Sieb nt

strait [streit] n Straße f, Meerenge f; **~jacket** n Zwangsjacke f; **~-laced** adj engherzig, streng

strand [strænd] n (of hair) Strähne f; (also fig) Faden m

stranded ['strændɪd] adj (also fig) gestrandet

strange [streindʒ] adj fremd; (unusual) seltsam; **~r** n Fremde(r) mf

strangle ['strængl] vt erwürgen; **~hold** n (fig) Umklammerung f

strap [stræp] n Riemen m; (on clothes) Träger m ♦ vt (fasten) festschnallen

strapping ['stræpɪŋ] adj stramm

strata ['strɑːtə] npl of stratum

strategic [strə'tiːdʒɪk] adj strategisch

strategy ['strætɪdʒɪ] n (fig) Strategie f

stratum ['strɑːtəm] (pl -ta) n Schicht f

straw [strɔː] n Stroh nt; (single stalk, drinking ~) Strohhalm m; **that's the last ~!** das ist der Gipfel!

strawberry ['strɔːbərɪ] n Erdbeere f

stray [strei] adj (animal) verirrt ♦ vi herumstreunen

streak [striːk] n Streifen m; (in character) Einschlag m; (in hair) Strähne f ♦ vt streifen ♦ vi zucken; (move quickly) flitzen; **~ of bad luck** Pechsträhne f; **~y** adj gestreift; (bacon) durchwachsen

stream [striːm] n (brook) Bach m; (fig) Strom m ♦ vt (SCH) in (Leistungs)gruppen einteilen ♦ vi strömen; **to ~ in/out** (people) hinein-/hinausströmen

streamer ['striːmər] n (flag) Wimpel m; (of paper) Luftschlange f

streamlined ['striːmlaɪnd] adj stromlinienförmig; (effective) rationell

street [striːt] n Straße f ♦ adj Straßen-; **~car** (US) n Straßenbahn f; **~ lamp** n Straßenlaterne f; **~ plan** n Stadtplan m; **~wise** (inf) adj: **to be ~wise** wissen, wo es langgeht

strength [streŋθ] n (also fig) Stärke f, Kraft f; **~en** vt (ver)stärken

strenuous ['strenjuəs] adj anstrengend

stress [stres] n Druck m; (mental) Stress m; (GRAM) Betonung f ♦ vt betonen

stretch [stretʃ] n Strecke f ♦ vt ausdehnen, strecken ♦ vi sich erstrecken; (person) sich strecken; **~ out** vi sich ausstrecken ♦ vt ausstrecken

stretcher ['strɛtʃə'] n Tragbahre f

stretchy ['strɛtʃi] adj elastisch, dehnbar

strewn [struːn] adj: **~ with** übersät mit

stricken ['strɪkən] adj (person) ergriffen; (city, country) heimgesucht; **~ with** (disease) leidend unter +dat

strict [strɪkt] adj (exact) genau; (severe) streng; **~ly** adv streng, genau

stride [straɪd] (pt **strode**, pp **stridden**) n lange(r) Schritt m ♦ vi schreiten

strident ['straɪdnt] adj schneidend, durchdringend

strife [straɪf] n Streit m

strike [straɪk] (pt, pp **struck**) n Streik m; (attack) Schlag m ♦ vt (hit) schlagen; (collide) stoßen gegen; (come to mind) einfallen +dat; (stand out) auffallen +dat; (find) finden ♦ vi (stop work) streiken; (attack) zuschlagen; (clock) schlagen; **on ~** (workers) im Streik; **to ~ a match** ein Streichholz anzünden; **~ down** vt (lay low) niederschlagen; **~ out** vt (cross out) ausstreichen; **~ up** vt (music) anstimmen; (friendship) schließen; **~r** n Streikende(r) mf; **striking** ['straɪkɪŋ] adj auffallend

string [strɪŋ] (pt, pp **strung**) n Schnur f; (row) Reihe f; (MUS) Saite f; **to ~ together** aneinander reihen ♦ vi: **to ~ out** sich verteilen; **the ~s** npl (MUS) die Streichinstrumente pl; **to pull ~s** (fig) Fäden ziehen; **~ bean** n grüne Bohne f; **~(ed) instrument** n (MUS) Saiteninstrument nt

stringent ['strɪndʒənt] adj streng

strip [strɪp] n Streifen m ♦ vt (uncover) abstreifen, abziehen; (clothes) ausziehen; (TECH) auseinander nehmen ♦ vi (undress) sich ausziehen; **~ cartoon** n Bildserie f

stripe [straɪp] n Streifen m; **~d** adj gestreift

strip lighting n Neonlicht nt

stripper ['strɪpə'] n Stripteasetänzerin f

strip-search ['strɪpsɜːtʃ] n Leibesvisitation f (bei der man sich ausziehen muss) ♦ vt: **to be ~~ed** sich ausziehen müssen und durchsucht werden

stripy ['straɪpi] adj gestreift

strive [straɪv] (pt **strove**, pp **striven**) vi: **to ~ (for)** streben (nach)

strode [strəud] pt of **stride**

stroke [strəuk] n Schlag m; (SWIMMING, ROWING) Stoß m; (MED) Schlaganfall m; (caress) Streicheln nt ♦ vt streicheln; **at a ~** mit einem Schlag

stroll [strəul] n Spaziergang m ♦ vi schlendern; **~er** (US) n (pushchair) Sportwagen m

strong [strɒŋ] adj stark; (firm) fest; **they are 50 ~** sie sind 50 Mann stark; **~box** n Kassette f; **~hold** n Hochburg f; **~ly** adv stark; **~room** n Tresor m

strove [strəuv] pt of **strive**

struck [strʌk] pt, pp of **strike**

structure ['strʌktʃə'] n Struktur f, Aufbau m; (building) Bau m

struggle ['strʌgl] n Kampf m ♦ vi (fight) kämpfen

strum [strʌm] vt (guitar) klimpern auf +dat

strung [strʌŋ] pt, pp of **string**

strut [strʌt] n Strebe f, Stütze f ♦ vi stolzieren

stub [stʌb] n Stummel m; (of cigarette) Kippe f ♦ vt: **to ~ one's toe** sich dat den Zeh anstoßen; **~ out** vt ausdrücken

stubble ['stʌbl] n Stoppel f

stubborn ['stʌbən] adj hartnäckig

stuck [stʌk] pt, pp of **stick** ♦ adj (jammed) klemmend; **~-up** adj hochnäsig

stud [stʌd] n (button) Kragenknopf m; (place) Gestüt n ♦ vt (fig): **~ded with** übersät mit

student ['stjuːdənt] n Student(in) m(f); (US) Schüler(in) m(f), Schüler(in) m(f) ♦ adj Studenten-; **~ driver** (US) n Fahrschüler(in) m(f)

studio ['stjuːdɪəu] n Studio nt; (for artist] Atelier nt; ~ **apartment** (US) n Appartement nt; ~ **flat** n Appartement nt

studious ['stjuːdɪəs] adj lernbegierig

study ['stʌdɪ] n Studium nt; (investigation) Studium nt, Untersuchung f; (room) Arbeitszimmer nt; (essay etc) Studie f ♦ vt studieren; (face) erforschen; (evidence) prüfen ♦ vi studieren

stuff [stʌf] n Stoff m; (inf) Zeug nt ♦ vt stopfen, füllen; (animal) ausstopfen; ~**ing** n Füllung f; ~**y** adj (room) schwül; (person) spießig

stumble ['stʌmbl] vi stolpern; **to ~ across** (fig) zufällig stoßen auf +acc

stumbling block ['stʌmblɪŋ-] n Hindernis nt

stump [stʌmp] n Stumpf m

stun [stʌn] vt betäuben; (shock) niederschmettern

stung [stʌŋ] pt, pp of **sting**

stunk [stʌŋk] pp of **stink**

stunned adj benommen, fassungslos

stunning ['stʌnɪŋ] adj betäubend; (news) überwältigend, umwerfend

stunt [stʌnt] n Kunststück nt, Trick m

stunted ['stʌntɪd] adj verkümmert

stuntman ['stʌntmæn] (irreg) n Stuntman m

stupefy ['stjuːpɪfaɪ] vt betäuben; (by news) bestürzen

stupendous [stjuːˈpendəs] adj erstaunlich, enorm

stupid ['stjuːpɪd] adj dumm; ~**ity** [stjuːˈpɪdɪtɪ] n Dummheit f

stupor ['stjuːpəʳ] n Betäubung f

sturdy ['stɜːdɪ] adj kräftig, robust

stutter ['stʌtəʳ] n Stottern nt ♦ vi stottern

sty [staɪ] n Schweinestall m

stye [staɪ] n Gerstenkorn nt

style [staɪl] n Stil m; (fashion) Mode f; **stylish** adj modisch; **stylist** ['staɪlɪst] n (hair stylist) Friseur m, Friseuse f

stylus ['staɪləs] n (Grammofon)nadel f

suave [swɑːv] adj zuvorkommend

sub... [sʌb] prefix Unter...; ~**conscious** adj unterbewußt ♦ n: **the ~conscious**

das Unterbewusste; ~**contract** vt (vertraglich) untervermitteln; ~**divide** vt unterteilen; ~**dued** adj (lighting) gedämpft; (person) still

subject [n, adj 'sʌbdʒɪkt, vb səbˈdʒɛkt] n (of kingdom) Untertan m; (citizen) Staatsangehörige(r) mf; (topic) Thema nt; (SCH) Fach nt; (GRAM) Subjekt nt ♦ adj: **to be ~ to** unterworfen sein +dat; (exposed) ausgesetzt sein +dat ♦ vt (subdue) unterwerfen; (expose) aussetzen; ~**ive** [səbˈdʒɛktɪv] adj subjektiv; ~ **matter** n Thema nt

sublet [sʌbˈlet] (irreg: like **let**) vt untervermieten

sublime [səˈblaɪm] adj erhaben

submachine gun ['sʌbməˈʃiːn-] n Maschinenpistole f

submarine [sʌbməˈriːn] n Unterseeboot m, U-Boot nt

submerge [səbˈmɜːdʒ] vt untertauchen; (flood) überschwemmen ♦ vi untertauchen

submission [səbˈmɪʃən] n (obedience) Gehorsam m; (claim) Behauptung f; (of plan) Unterbreitung f; **submissive** [səbˈmɪsɪv] adj demütig, unterwürfig (pej)

submit [səbˈmɪt] vt behaupten; (plan) unterbreiten ♦ vi sich ergeben

subnormal [sʌbˈnɔːml] adj minderbegabt

subordinate [səˈbɔːdɪnət] adj untergeordnet ♦ n Untergebene(r) mf

subpoena [səbˈpiːnə] n Vorladung f ♦ vt vorladen

subscribe [səbˈskraɪb] vi: **to ~ to** (view etc) unterstützen; (newspaper) abonnieren; ~ **r** n (to periodical) Abonnent m; (TEL) Telefonteilnehmer m

subscription [səbˈskrɪpʃən] n Abonnement nt; (money subscribed) (Mitglieds)beitrag m

subsequent ['sʌbsɪkwənt] adj folgend, später; ~**ly** adv später

subside [səbˈsaɪd] vi sich senken; ~**nce** [səbˈsaɪdns] n Senkung f

subsidiarity [səbsɪdɪ'ærɪtɪ] n (POL) Subsidiarität f

subsidiary [səb'sɪdɪərɪ] adj Neben- ♦ n Tochtergesellschaft f

subsidize ['sʌbsɪdaɪz] vt subventionieren

subsidy ['sʌbsɪdɪ] n Subvention f

subsistence [səb'sɪstəns] n Unterhalt m

substance ['sʌbstəns] n Substanz f

substantial [səb'stænʃl] adj (strong) fest, kräftig; (important) wesentlich; **~ly** adv erheblich

substantiate [səb'stænʃɪeɪt] vt begründen, belegen

substitute ['sʌbstɪtjuːt] n Ersatz m ♦ vt ersetzen; **substitution** [sʌbstɪ'tjuːʃən] n Ersetzung f

subterfuge ['sʌbtəfjuːdʒ] n Vorwand m; (trick) Trick m

subterranean [sʌbtə'reɪnɪən] adj unterirdisch

subtitle ['sʌbtaɪtl] n Untertitel m; **~d** adj untertitelt, mit Untertiteln versehen

subtle ['sʌtl] adj fein; **~ty** n Feinheit f

subtotal [sʌb'təutl] n Zwischensumme f

subtract [səb'trækt] vt abziehen; **~ion** [səb'trækʃən] n Abziehen nt, Subtraktion f

suburb ['sʌbə:b] n Vorort m; the **~s** die Außenbezirke pl; **~an** [sə'bə:bən] adj Vorort(s)-, Stadtrand-; **~ia** [sə'bə:bɪə] n Vorstadt f

subversive [səb'vɜ:sɪv] adj subversiv

subway ['sʌbweɪ] n (US) U-Bahn f; (BRIT) Unterführung f

succeed [sək'siːd] vi (person) erfolgreich sein, Erfolg haben; (plan etc: also) gelingen ♦ vt (nach)folgen +dat; he **~ed in doing it** es gelang ihm, es zu tun; **~ing** adj (nach)folgend

success [sək'ses] n Erfolg m; **~ful** adj erfolgreich; **to be ~ful (in doing sth)** Erfolg haben (bei etw); **~fully** adv erfolgreich

succession [sək'seʃən] n (Aufeinan-

derfolge f; (to throne) Nachfolge f

successive [sək'sesɪv] adj aufeinander folgend

successor [sək'sesə] n Nachfolger(in) m(f)

succinct [sək'sɪŋkt] adj knapp

succulent ['sʌkjulənt] adj saftig

succumb [sə'kʌm] vi: **to ~ (to)** erliegen (+dat); (yield) nachgeben (+dat)

such [sʌtʃ] adj solche(r, s); **~ a book** so ein Buch; **~ books** solche Bücher; **~ courage** so ein Mut; **~ a long trip** so eine lange Reise; **~ a lot of** so viel(e); **~ as** wie; **a noise ~ as** so ein derartiger Lärm, dass; **as ~** an sich; **~-and-a time** die und die Zeit

suck [sʌk] vt saugen; (lollipop etc) lutschen

sucker ['sʌkə] n Idiot m

suction ['sʌkʃən] n Saugkraft f

sudden ['sʌdn] adj plötzlich; **all of a ~** auf einmal; **~ly** adv plötzlich

suds [sʌdz] npl Seifenlauge f; (lather) Seifenschaum m

sue [suː] vt verklagen

suede [sweɪd] n Wildleder nt

suet ['suɪt] n Nierenfett nt

Suez ['suːɪz] n: the **~ Canal** der Suezkanal

suffer ['sʌfə] vt (er)leiden ♦ vi leiden; **~er** n Leidende(r) mf; **~ing** n Leiden nt

suffice [sə'faɪs] vi genügen

sufficient [sə'fɪʃənt] adj ausreichend; **~ly** adv ausreichend

suffix ['sʌfɪks] n Nachsilbe f

suffocate ['sʌfəkeɪt] vt, vi ersticken

suffrage ['sʌfrɪdʒ] n Wahlrecht nt

sugar ['ʃugə] n Zucker m ♦ vt zuckern; **~ beet** n Zuckerrübe f; **~ cane** n Zuckerrohr nt; **~y** adj süß

suggest [sə'dʒest] vt vorschlagen; (show) schließen lassen auf +acc; **~ion** [sə'dʒestʃən] n Vorschlag m; **~ive** adj anregend; (indecent) zweideutig

suicide ['suɪsaɪd] n Selbstmord m; **to commit ~** Selbstmord begehen

suit [suːt] n Anzug m; (CARDS) Farbe f

♦ *vt* passen +*dat*; *(clothes)* stehen +*dat*; **well ~ed** *(well matched)* **~able** *adj* geeignet, passend; **~ably** *adv* passend, angemessen

suitcase ['su:tkeɪs] *n* (Hand)koffer *m*

suite [swi:t] *n* *(of rooms)* Zimmerflucht *f*; *(of furniture)* Einrichtung *f*; *(MUS)* Suite *f*

suitor ['su:tə^r] *n* *(JUR)* Kläger(in) *m(f)*

sulfur ['sʌlfə^r] *(US)* *n* = **sulphur**

sulk [sʌlk] *vi* schmollen; **~y** *adj* schmollend

sullen ['sʌlən] *adj* mürrisch

sulphur ['sʌlfə^r] *(US* sulfur) *n* Schwefel *m*

sultana [sʌl'tɑ:nə] *n* *(fruit)* Sultanine *f*

sultry ['sʌltrɪ] *adj* schwül

sum [sʌm] *n* Summe *f*; *(money)* Betrag *m*, Summe *f*; *(arithmetic)* Rechenaufgabe *f*; **~ up** *vt, vi* zusammenfassen

summarize ['sʌməraɪz] *vt* kurz zusammenfassen

summary ['sʌmərɪ] *n* Zusammenfassung *f* ♦ *adj* *(justice)* kurzerhand erteilt

summer ['sʌmə^r] *n* Sommer *m* ♦ *adj* Sommer-; **~house** *n* *(in garden)* Gartenhaus *m*; **~time** *n* Sommerzeit *f*

summit ['sʌmɪt] *n* Gipfel *m*; **~ (conference)** *n* Gipfelkonferenz *f*

summon ['sʌmən] *vt* herberufen; *(JUR)* vorladen; *(gather up)* aufbringen; **~s** *(JUR)* *n* Vorladung *f* ♦ *vt* vorladen

sump [sʌmp] *(BRIT)* *n* *(AUT)* Ölwanne *f*

sumptuous ['sʌmptjuəs] *adj* prächtig

sun [sʌn] *n* Sonne *f*; **~bathe** *vi* sich sonnen; **~block** *n* Sonnenschutzcreme *f*; **~burn** *n* Sonnenbrand *m*; **~burnt** *adj* sonnenverbrannt, sonnengebräunt; **to be ~burnt** *(painfully)* einen Sonnenbrand haben

Sunday ['sʌndɪ] *n* Sonntag *m*; **~ school** *n* Sonntagsschule *f*

sundial ['sʌndaɪəl] *n* Sonnenuhr *f*

sundown ['sʌndaun] *n* Sonnenuntergang *m*

sundries ['sʌndrɪz] *npl* Verschiedene(s) *nt*

sundry ['sʌndrɪ] *adj* verschieden; **all and ~** alle

sunflower ['sʌnflauə^r] *n* Sonnenblume *f*

sung [sʌŋ] *pp of* **sing**

sunglasses ['sʌnglɑ:sɪz] *npl* Sonnenbrille *f*

sunk [sʌŋk] *pp of* **sink**

sun: **~light** ['sʌnlaɪt] *n* Sonnenlicht *nt*; **~lit** ['sʌnlɪt] *adj* sonnenbeschienen; **~ny** ['sʌnɪ] *adj* sonnig; **~rise** *n* Sonnenaufgang *m*; **~roof** *n* *(AUT)* Schiebedach *nt*; **~screen** ['sʌnskri:n] *n* Sonnenschutzcreme *f*; **~set** ['sʌnset] *n* Sonnenuntergang *m*; **~shade** ['sʌnʃeɪd] *n* Sonnenschirm *m*; **~shine** ['sʌnʃaɪn] *n* Sonnenschein *m*; **~stroke** ['sʌnstrəuk] *n* Hitzschlag *m*; **~tan** ['sʌntæn] *n* (Sonnen)bräune *f*; **~tan oil** *n* Sonnenöl *nt*

super ['su:pə^r] *(inf)* *adj* prima, klasse

superannuation [su:pərænju'eɪʃən] *n* Pension *f*

superb [su:'pə:b] *adj* ausgezeichnet, hervorragend

supercilious [su:pə'sɪlɪəs] *adj* herablassend

superficial [su:pə'fɪʃəl] *adj* oberflächlich

superfluous [su'pə:fluəs] *adj* überflüssig

superhuman [su:pə'hju:mən] *adj* *(effort)* übermenschlich

superimpose ['su:pərɪm'pəuz] *vt* übereinander legen

superintendent [su:pərɪn'tendənt] *n* Polizeichef *m*

superior [su'pɪərɪə^r] *adj* überlegen; *(better)* besser ♦ *n* Vorgesetzte(r) *mf*; **~ity** [supɪərɪ'ɔrɪtɪ] *n* Überlegenheit *f*

superlative [su'pə:lətɪv] *adj* überragend

super: **~man** *(irreg)* *n* Übermensch *m*; **~market** ['su:pə:mɑ:kɪt] *n* Supermarkt *m*; **~natural** [su:pə'nætʃərəl] *adj* übernatürlich; **~power** ['su:pəpauə^r] *n* Weltmacht

f

supersede [suːpəˈsiːd] *vt* ersetzen

supersonic [ˈsuːpəˈsɔnɪk] *adj* Überschall-

superstition [suːpəˈstɪʃən] *n* Aberglaube *m*; **superstitious** [suːpəˈstɪʃəs] *adj* abergläubisch

supervise [ˈsuːpəvaɪz] *vt* beaufsichtigen, kontrollieren; **supervision** [suːpəˈvɪʒən] *n* Aufsicht *f*; **supervisor** [ˈsuːpəvaɪzəʳ] *n* Aufsichtsperson *f*; **supervisory** [ˈsuːpəvaɪzərɪ] *adj* Aufsichts-

supper [ˈsʌpəʳ] *n* Abendessen *nt*

supplant [səˈplɑːnt] *vt* (person, thing) ersetzen

supple [ˈsʌpl] *adj* geschmeidig

supplement [*n* ˈsʌplɪmənt, *vb* ˌsʌplɪˈment] *n* Ergänzung *f*; (in book) Nachtrag *m* ♦ *vt* ergänzen; **~ary** [ˌsʌplɪˈmentərɪ] *adj* ergänzend; **~ary benefit** (BRIT: old) *n* ≈ Sozialhilfe *f*

supplier [səˈplaɪəʳ] *n* Lieferant *m*

supplies [səˈplaɪz] *npl* (food) Vorräte *pl*; (MIL) Nachschub *m*

supply [səˈplaɪ] *vt* liefern ♦ *n* Vorrat *m*; (~ing) Lieferung *f*; *see also* **supplies**; **~ teacher** (BRIT) *n* Vertretung *f*

support [səˈpɔːt] *n* Unterstützung *f*; (TECH) Stütze *f* ♦ *vt* (hold up) stützen, tragen; (provide for) ernähren; (be in favour of) unterstützen; **~er** *n* Anhänger(in) *m(f)*

suppose [səˈpəuz] *vt, vi* annehmen; **to be ~d to do sth** etw tun sollen; **~dly** [səˈpəuzɪdlɪ] *adv* angeblich; **supposing** *conj* angenommen; **supposition** [sʌpəˈzɪʃən] *n* Voraussetzung *f*

suppress [səˈpres] *vt* unterdrücken

supremacy [suˈpreməsɪ] *n* Vorherrschaft *f*, Oberhoheit *f*

supreme [suˈpriːm] *adj* oberste(r, s), höchste(r, s)

surcharge [ˈsɜːtʃɑːdʒ] *n* Zuschlag *m*

sure [ʃuəʳ] *adj* sicher, gewiss; **~!** (of course) klar!; **to make ~ of sth/that** sich einer Sache *gen* vergewissern/

vergewissern, dass; **~ enough** (with past) tatsächlich; (with future) ganz bestimmt; **~-footed** *adj* sicher (auf den Füßen); **~ly** *adv* (certainly) sicherlich, gewiss; **~ly it's wrong** das ist doch wohl falsch

surety [ˈʃuərətɪ] *n* Sicherheit *f*

surf [sɜːf] *n* Brandung *f*

surface [ˈsɜːfɪs] *n* Oberfläche *f* ♦ *vt* (roadway) teeren ♦ *vi* auftauchen; **~ mail** *n* gewöhnliche Post *f*

surfboard [ˈsɜːfbɔːd] *n* Surfbrett *nt*

surfeit [ˈsɜːfɪt] *n* Übermaß *nt*

surfing [ˈsɜːfɪŋ] *n* Surfen *nt*

surge [sɜːdʒ] *n* Woge *f* ♦ *vi* wogen

surgeon [ˈsɜːdʒən] *n* Chirurg(in) *m(f)*

surgery [ˈsɜːdʒərɪ] *n* (BRIT: place) Praxis *f*; (: time) Sprechstunde *f*; (treatment) Operation *f*; **to undergo ~** operiert werden; **~ hours** (BRIT) *npl* Sprechstunden *pl*

surgical [ˈsɜːdʒɪkl] *adj* chirurgisch; **~ spirit** (BRIT) *n* Wundbenzin *nt*

surly [ˈsɜːlɪ] *adj* verdrießlich, grob

surmount [sɜːˈmaunt] *vt* überwinden

surname [ˈsɜːneɪm] *n* Zuname *m*

surpass [sɜːˈpɑːs] *vt* übertreffen

surplus [ˈsɜːpləs] *n* Überschuss *m* ♦ *adj* überschüssig, Über(schuss)-

surprise [səˈpraɪz] *n* Überraschung *f* ♦ *vt* überraschen; **~d** *adj* überrascht; **surprising** *adj* überraschend; **surprisingly** *adv* überraschend(erweise)

surrender [səˈrendəʳ] *n* Kapitulation *f* ♦ *vi* sich ergeben

surreptitious [sʌrəpˈtɪʃəs] *adj* heimlich; (look also) verstohlen

surrogate [ˈsʌrəgɪt] *n* Ersatz *m*; **~ mother** *n* Leihmutter *f*

surround [səˈraund] *vt* umgeben; **~ing** *adj* (countryside) umliegend; **~ings** *npl* Umgebung *f*; (environment) Umwelt *f*

surveillance [sɜːˈveɪləns] *n* Überwachung *f*

survey [*n* ˈsɜːveɪ, *vb* sɜːˈveɪ] *n* Übersicht *f* ♦ *vt* überblicken; (land) vermessen;

~or [sə'veɪəʳ] n Land(ver)messer(in) m(f)

survival [sə'vaɪvl] n Überleben nt

survive [sə'vaɪv] vt, vi überleben; **survivor** [sə'vaɪvəʳ] n Überlebende(r) mf

susceptible [sə'septəbl] adj: **~ (to)** empfindlich (gegen); (charms etc) empfänglich (für)

suspect [n 'sʌspekt, vb səs'pekt] n Verdächtige(r) mf ♦ adj verdächtig ♦ vt verdächtigen; (think) vermuten

suspend [səs'pend] vt verschieben; (from work) suspendieren; (hang up) aufhängen; (SPORT) sperren; **~ed sentence** n (JUR) zur Bewährung ausgesetzte Strafe; **~er belt** n Strumpf(halter)gürtel m; **~ers** npl (BRIT) Strumpfhalter m; (US) Hosenträger m

suspense [səs'pens] n Spannung f

suspension [səs'penʃən] n (from work) Suspendierung f; (AUT) Federung f; **~ bridge** n Hängebrücke f

suspicion [səs'pɪʃən] n Misstrauen nt; Verdacht m; **suspicious** [səs'pɪʃəs] adj misstrauisch; (causing ~) verdächtig

sustain [səs'teɪn] vt (maintain) aufrechterhalten; (confirm) bestätigen; (injury) davontragen; **~able** adj (development, growth etc) aufrechtzuerhalten; **~ed** adj (effort) anhaltend

sustenance ['sʌstɪnəns] n Nahrung f

swab [swɔb] n (MED) Tupfer m

swagger ['swægəʳ] vi stolzieren

swallow ['swɔləu] n (bird) Schwalbe f; (of food etc) Schluck m ♦ vt (ver)schlucken; **~ up** vt verschlingen

swam [swæm] pt of **swim**

swamp [swɔmp] n Sumpf m ♦ vt überschwemmen

swan [swɔn] n Schwan m

swap [swɔp] n Tausch m ♦ vt: **to ~ sth (for sth)** etw (gegen etw) tauschen or eintauschen

swarm [swɔːm] n Schwarm m ♦ vi: **to ~ or be ~ing with** wimmeln von

swarthy ['swɔːðɪ] adj dunkel, braun

swastika ['swɔstɪkə] n Hakenkreuz nt

swat [swɔt] vt totschlagen

sway [sweɪ] vi schwanken; (branches) schaukeln, sich wiegen ♦ vt schwenken; (influence) beeinflussen

swear [sweəʳ] (pt swore, pp sworn) vi (promise) schwören; (curse) fluchen; **to ~ to sth** schwören auf etw acc; **~word** n Fluch m

sweat [swet] n Schweiß m ♦ vi schwitzen

sweater ['swetəʳ] n Pullover m

sweatshirt ['swetʃɜːt] n Sweatshirt nt

sweaty ['swetɪ] adj verschwitzt

Swede [swiːd] n Schwede m, Schwedin f

swede [swiːd] n (BRIT) n Steckrübe f

Sweden ['swiːdn] n Schweden nt

Swedish ['swiːdɪʃ] adj schwedisch ♦ n (LING) Schwedisch nt

sweep [swiːp] (pt, pp swept) n (chimney ~) Schornsteinfeger m ♦ vt fegen, kehren; **~ away** vt wegfegen; **~ past** vi vorbeisausen; **~ up** vi zusammenkehren; **~ing** adj (gesture) schwungvoll; (statement) verallgemeinernd

sweet [swiːt] n (course) Nachtisch m; (candy) Bonbon nt ♦ adj süß; **~corn** n Zuckermais m; **~en** vt süßen; (fig) versüßen; **~heart** n Liebste(r) mf; **~ness** n Süße f; **~ pea** n Gartenwicke f

swell [swel] (pt swelled, pp swollen or swelled) n Seegang m ♦ adj (inf) todschick ♦ vt (numbers) vermehren ♦ vi (also: **~ up**) (an)schwellen; **~ing** n Schwellung f

sweltering ['sweltərɪŋ] adj drückend

swept [swept] pt, pp of **sweep**

swerve [swɜːv] vt, vi ausscheren

swift [swɪft] n Mauersegler m ♦ adj geschwind, schnell, rasch; **~ly** adv geschwind, schnell, rasch

swig [swɪg] n Zug m

swill [swɪl] n (for pigs) Schweinefutter nt ♦ vt spülen

swim [swɪm] (pt swam, pp swum) n: **to go for a ~** schwimmen gehen ♦ vi

swindle ['swindl] n Schwindel m, Betrug m ♦ vt betrügen

swine [swain] n (also fig) Schwein nt

swing [swiŋ] (pt, pp **swung**) n (child's) Schaukel f; (movement) Schwung m ♦ vi schwingen, schaukeln; (turn quickly) schwenken; **in full ~** in vollem Gange f; **~ bridge** n Drehbrücke f; **~ door** (BRIT) n Schwingtür f

swingeing ['swindʒiŋ] (BRIT) adj hart; (taxation, cuts) extrem

swinging door ['swiŋiŋ-] (US) n Schwingtür f

swipe [swaip] n Hieb m ♦ vt (inf: hit) hart schlagen; (: steal) klauen

swirl [swə:l] vi wirbeln

swish [swiʃ] (adj: inf: smart) schick ♦ vi zischen; (grass, skirts) rascheln

Swiss [swis] adj Schweizer, schweizerisch ♦ n Schweizer(in) m(f); **the ~** npl (people) die Schweizer pl

switch [switʃ] n (ELEC) Schalter m; (change) Wechsel m ♦ vt (ELEC) schalten; (change) wechseln ♦ vi wechseln; **~ off** vt ab- or ausschalten; **~ on** vt an- or einschalten; **~board** n Zentrale f; (board) Schaltbrett nt

Switzerland ['switsələnd] n die Schweiz

swivel ['swivl] vt (also: ~ round) drehen ♦ vi (also: ~ round) sich drehen

swollen ['swəulən] pp of **swell**

swoon [swu:n] vi (old) in Ohnmacht fallen

swoop [swu:p] n Sturzflug m; (esp by police) Razzia f ♦ vi (also: ~ down) stürzen

swop [swɒp] = **swap**

schwimmen ♦ vt (cross) (durch)-schwimmen; **~mer** n Schwimmer(in) m(f); **~ming** n Schwimmen nt; **~ming cap** n Badehaube f, Badekappe f; **~ming costume** (BRIT) n Badeanzug m; **~ming pool** n Schwimmbecken nt, (private) Swimmingpool m; **~ming trunks** npl Badehose f; **~suit** n Badeanzug m

swindle ['swindl] n Schwindel m, Betrug m ♦ vt betrügen

swine [swain] n (also fig) Schwein nt

sword [sɔ:d] n Schwert nt; **~fish** n Schwertfisch m

swore [swɔ:r] pt of **swear**

sworn [swɔ:n] pp of **swear**

swot [swɒt] vt, vi pauken

swum [swʌm] pp of **swim**

swung [swʌŋ] pt, pp of **swing**

sycamore ['sikəmɔ:r] n (US) Platane f; (BRIT) Bergahorn m

syllable ['siləbl] n Silbe f

syllabus ['siləbəs] n Lehrplan m

symbol ['simbl] n Symbol nt; **~ic(al)** [sim'bɒlik(l)] adj symbolisch

symmetry ['simitri] n Symmetrie f

sympathetic [simpə'θetik] adj mitfühlend

sympathize ['simpəθaiz] vi mitfühlen; **~r** n (POL) Sympathisant(in) m(f)

sympathy ['simpəθi] n Mitleid nt, Mitgefühl nt; (condolence) Beileid nt; **with our deepest ~** mit tief empfundenem Beileid

symphony ['simfəni] n Sinfonie f

symptom ['simptəm] n Symptom nt; **~atic** [simptə'mætik] adj (fig): **~atic of** bezeichnend für

synagogue ['sinəgɒg] n Synagoge f

synchronize ['siŋkrənaiz] vt synchronisieren

syndicate ['sindikit] n Konsortium nt

synonym ['sinənim] n Synonym nt; **~ous** [si'nɒniməs] adj gleichbedeutend

synopsis [si'nɒpsis] n Zusammenfassung f

synthetic [sin'θetik] adj synthetisch; **~s** npl (man-made fabrics) Synthetik f

syphon ['saifən] = **siphon**

Syria ['siriə] n Syrien nt

syringe [si'rindʒ] n Spritze f

syrup ['sirəp] n Sirup m; (of sugar) Melasse f

system ['sistəm] n System nt; **~atic** [sistə'mætik] adj systematisch; **~ disk** n (COMPUT) Systemdiskette f; **~s analyst** n Systemanalytiker(in) m(f)

T, t

ta [tɑː] (BRIT: inf) excl danke!

tab [tæb] n Aufhänger m; (name ~) Schild nt; **to keep ~s on** (fig) genau im Auge behalten

tabby ['tæbɪ] n (also: ~ **cat**) getigerte Katze f

table ['teɪbl] n Tisch m; (list) Tabelle f ♦ vt (PARL: propose) vorlegen, einbringen; **to lay** or **set the ~** den Tisch decken; **~cloth** n Tischtuch nt; **~ d'hôte** [tɑːbl'dəut] n Tagesmenü nt; **~ lamp** n Tischlampe f; **~mat** n Untersatz m; **~ of contents** n Inhaltsverzeichnis nt; **~spoon** n Esslöffel m; **~spoonful** n Esslöffel m (voll)

tablet ['tæblɪt] n (MED) Tablette f

table tennis n Tischtennis nt

table wine n Tafelwein m

tabloid ['tæblɔɪd] n Zeitung f in kleinem Format; (pej) Boulevardzeitung f

---

tabloid press
Der Ausdruck **tabloid press** *bezieht sich auf kleinformatige Zeitungen (ca 30 x 40cm); sie sind in Großbritannien fast ausschließlich Massenblätter. Im Gegensatz zur* **quality press** *verwenden diese Massenblätter viele Fotos und einen knappen, oft reißerischen Stil. Sie kommen den Lesern entgegen, die mehr Wert auf Unterhaltung legen.*

---

tabulate ['tæbjuleɪt] vt tabellarisch ordnen

tacit ['tæsɪt] adj stillschweigend

taciturn ['tæsɪtəːn] adj wortkarg

tack [tæk] n (small nail) Stift m; (US: thumbtack) Reißzwecke f; (stitch) Heftstich m; (NAUT) Lavieren nt; (course) Kurs m ♦ vt (nail) nageln; (stitch) heften ♦ vi aufkreuzen

tackle ['tækl] n (for lifting) Flaschenzug

m; (NAUT) Takelage f; (SPORT) Tackling nt ♦ vt (deal with) anpacken, in Angriff nehmen; (person) festhalten; (player) angehen

tacky ['tækɪ] adj klebrig

tact [tækt] n Takt m; **~ful** adj taktvoll

tactical ['tæktɪkl] adj taktisch

tactics ['tæktɪks] npl Taktik f

tactless ['tæktlɪs] adj taktlos

tadpole ['tædpəul] n Kaulquappe f

taffy ['tæfɪ] (US) n Sahnebonbon nt

tag [tæg] n (label) Schild nt, Anhänger m; (maker's name) Etikett nt; **~ along** vi mitkommen

tail [teɪl] n Schwanz m; (of list) Schluss m ♦ vt folgen +dat; **~ away** or **off** vi abfallen, schwinden; **~back** (BRIT) n (AUT) (Rück)stau m; **~ coat** n Frack m; **~ end** n Schluss m, Ende nt; **~gate** n (AUT) Heckklappe f

tailor ['teɪlə*] n Schneider m; **~ing** n Schneidern nt; **~-made** adj maßgeschneidert; (fig): **~-made for sb** jdm wie auf den Leib geschnitten

tailwind ['teɪlwɪnd] n Rückenwind m

tainted ['teɪntɪd] adj verdorben

take [teɪk] (pt **took**, pp **taken**) vt nehmen; (trip, exam, PHOT) machen; (capture: person) fassen; (: town: also COMM, FIN) einnehmen; (carry to a place) bringen; (get for o.s.) sich dat nehmen; (gain, obtain) bekommen; (put up with) hinnehmen; (respond to) aufnehmen; (interpret) auffassen; (assume) annehmen; (contain) Platz haben für; **to ~ sth from sb** jdm etw wegnehmen; **to ~ sth from sth** (MATH: subtract) etw von etw abziehen; (extract, quotation) etw einer Sache dat entnehmen; **~ after** vt fus ähnlich sein +dat; **~ apart** vt auseinander nehmen; **~ away** vt (remove) wegnehmen; (carry off) wegbringen; **~ back** vt (return) zurückbringen; (retract) zurücknehmen; **~ down** vt (pull down) abreißen; (write down) aufschreiben; **~ in** vt (deceive) hereinlegen; (under-

stand) begreifen; *(include)* einschließen; **~ off** *vi (plane)* starten ♦ *vt (remove)* wegnehmen; *(clothing)* ausziehen; *(imitate)* nachmachen; **~ on** *vt
(undertake)* übernehmen; *(engage)*
einstellen; *(opponent)* antreten gegen;
~ out *vt (girl, dog)* ausführen; *(extract)*
herausnehmen; *(insurance)* abschlie-
ßen; *(licence)* sich dat geben lassen;
(book) ausleihen; *(remove)* entfernen;
~ to sth out of sth *(drawer, pocket etc)*
etw aus etw herausnehmen; **~over** *vt*
übernehmen ♦ *vi:* **to ~ over from sb**
jdn ablösen; **~ to** *vt fus (like)* mögen;
(adopt as practice) sich dat angewöhnen; **~ up** *vt (raise)* aufnehmen;
(dress etc) kürzer machen; *(occupy)* in
Anspruch nehmen; *(engage in)* sich
befassen mit; **~away** *adj zum Mitnehmen;* **~home pay** *n* Nettolohn *m;* **~n**
pp of take; **~off** *n (AVIAT)* Start *m;* (imitation) Nachahmung *f;* **~out** *(US) adj =*
takeaway; **~over** *n (COMM)*
Übernahme *f;* **takings** ['teɪkɪŋz] *npl
(COMM)* Einnahmen *pl*

alc [tælk] *n (also:* **~um powder**) Tal-
kumpuder *m*

ale [teɪl] *n* Geschichte *f*, Erzählung *f;*
to tell ~s *(fig: lie)* Geschichten erfinden

alent ['tælnt] *n* Talent *nt;* **~ed** *adj* begabt

alk [tɔːk] *n (conversation)* Gespräch *nt;*
(rumour) Gerede *f;* (speech) Vortrag *m*
♦ *vi* sprechen, reden; **~s** *npl (POL etc)*
Gespräche *pl;* **to ~ about** sprechen
von *+dat* or über *+acc;* **to ~ sb into
doing sth** jdn überreden, etw zu tun;
to ~ sb out of doing sth jdn davon ab-
den, etw zu tun; **~ shop** fachsim-
peln; **~ over** *vt* besprechen; **~ative**
['tɔːkətɪv] *adj* gesprächig

all [tɔːl] *adj* groß; *(building)* hoch; **to
be 1 m 80 ~** 1,80 m groß sein; **~boy**
(BRIT) n Kommode *f;* **~ story** *n*
übertriebene Geschichte *f*

ally ['tælɪ] *n* Abrechnung *f* ♦ *vi*

übereinstimmen

talon ['tælən] *n* Kralle *f*

tame [teɪm] *adj* zahm; *(fig)* fade

tamper ['tæmpə'] *vi:* **to ~ with** herumpfuschen an *+dat*

tampon ['tæmpɔn] *n* Tampon *m*

tan [tæn] *n* (Sonnen)bräune *f; (colour)*
Gelbbraun *nt* ♦ *adj (colour)* (gelb)braun
♦ *vt* bräunen ♦ *vi* braun werden

tang [tæŋ] *n* Schärfe *f*

tangent ['tændʒənt] *n* Tangente *f;* **to
go off at a ~** *(fig)* vom Thema abkommen

tangerine [tændʒə'riːn] *n* Mandarine *f*

tangible ['tændʒəbl] *adj* greifbar

tangle ['tæŋgl] *n* Durcheinander *nt;*
(trouble) Schwierigkeiten *pl;* **to get
in(to) a ~** sich verheddern

tank [tæŋk] *n (container)* Tank *m*, Behälter *m;* (MIL) Panzer *m;* **~er** ['tæŋkə']
n (ship) Tanker *m;* (vehicle) Tankwagen
m

tanned [tænd] *adj* gebräunt

tantalizing ['tæntəlaɪzɪŋ] *adj* verlockend; *(annoying)* quälend

tantamount ['tæntəmaunt] *adj:* **~ to**
gleichbedeutend mit

tantrum ['tæntrəm] *n* Wutanfall *m*

tap [tæp] *n* Hahn *m; (gentle blow)* Klopfen *nt* ♦ *vt (strike)* klopfen; *(supply)* an-
zapfen; *(telephone)* abhören; **~s** *(fig:
resources)* zur Hand; **~-dancing** *n*
Steppen *nt*

tape [teɪp] *n* Band *nt; (magnetic)*
(Ton)band *nt; (adhesive)* Klebstreifen *m*
♦ *vt (record)* aufnehmen; **~ deck** *n* Tape-
deck *nt;* **~ measure** *n* Maßband *nt*

taper ['teɪpə'] *vi* spitz zulaufen

tape recorder *n* Tonbandgerät *nt*

tapestry ['tæpɪstrɪ] *n* Wandteppich *m*

tar [tɑː] *n* Teer *m*

target ['tɑːgɪt] *n* Ziel *nt; (board)* Zielscheibe *f*

tariff ['tærɪf] *n (duty paid)* Zoll *m; (list)*
Tarif *m*

tarmac ['tɑːmæk] *n (AVIAT)* Rollfeld *nt*

tarnish ['tɑːnɪʃ] *vt* matt machen; *(fig)*

beflecken

tarpaulin [tɑː'pɔːlɪn] n Plane f

tarragon ['tærəgən] n Estragon m

tart [tɑːt] n (Obst)torte f; (inf) Nutte f ♦ adj scharf; **~ up** (inf) vt aufmachen; (person) auftakeln

tartan ['tɑːtn] n Schottenkaro m ♦ adj mit Schottenkaro

tartar ['tɑːtəʳ] n Zahnstein m

tartar(e) sauce ['tɑːtə-] n Remouladensoße f

task [tɑːsk] n Aufgabe f; **to take sb to ~** sich dat jdn vornehmen; **~ force** n Sondertrupp m

tassel ['tæsl] n Quaste f

taste [teɪst] n Geschmack m; (sense) Geschmackssinn m; (small quantity) Kostprobe f; (liking) Vorliebe f ♦ vt schmecken; (try) probieren ♦ vi schmecken; **can I have a ~ of this wine?** kann ich diesen Wein probieren?; **to have a ~ for sth** etw mögen; **in good/bad ~** geschmackvoll/ geschmacklos; **you can ~ the garlic (in it)** man kann den Knoblauch herausschmecken; **to ~ of sth** nach einer Sache schmecken; **~ful** adj geschmackvoll; **~less** adj (insipid) fade; (in bad ~) geschmacklos; **tasty** [teɪstɪ] adj schmackhaft

tattered ['tætəd] adj = **in tatters**

tatters ['tætəz] npl: **in ~** in Fetzen

tattoo [tə'tuː] n (MIL) Zapfenstreich m; (on skin) Tätowierung f ♦ vt tätowieren

tatty ['tætɪ] (BRIT: inf) adj schäbig

taught [tɔːt] pt, pp of **teach**

taunt [tɔːnt] n höhnische Bemerkung f ♦ vt verhöhnen

Taurus ['tɔːrəs] n Stier m

taut [tɔːt] adj straff

tawdry ['tɔːdrɪ] adj (bunt und) billig

tax [tæks] n Steuer f ♦ vt besteuern; (strain) strapazieren; (strength) angreifen; **~able** adj (income) steuerpflichtig; **~ation** [tæk'seɪʃən] n Besteuerung f; **~ avoidance** n Steuerumgehung f; **~ disc** (BRIT) n (AUT) Kraftfahrzeugsteuer-

plakette f; **~ evasion** n Steuerhinterziehung f; **~-free** adj steuerfrei

taxi ['tæksɪ] n Taxi nt ♦ vi (plane) rollen ♦ **~ driver** n Taxifahrer m; **~ rank** (BRIT) n Taxistand m; **~ stand** n Taxistand m

tax: **~payer** n Steuerzahler m; **~ relief** n Steuerermäßigung f; **~ return** n Steuererklärung f

TB n abbr (= tuberculosis) Tb f, Tbc f

tea [tiː] n Tee m; (meal) (frühes) Abendessen nt; **high ~** (BRIT) Abendessen nt; **~ bag** n Teebeutel m; **~ break** (BRIT) n Teepause f

teach [tiːtʃ] (pt, pp **taught**) vt lehren, (SCH) lehren, unterrichten; (show): **to sb sth** jdm etw beibringen ♦ vi lehren, unterrichten; **~er** n Lehrer(in) m(f); **~er's pet** n Lehrer's Liebling m; **~ing** n (~er's work) Unterricht m; (doctrine) Lehre f

tea: **~ cloth** n Geschirrtuch nt; **~ cosy** n Teewärmer m; **~cup** n Teetasse f; **~ leaves** npl Teeblätter pl

team [tiːm] n (workers) Team nt; (SPORT) Mannschaft f; (animals) Gespann n; **~work** n Gemeinschaftsarbeit f, Teamarbeit f

teapot ['tiːpɔt] n Teekanne f

tear¹ [tɛəʳ] (pt **tore**, pp **torn**) n Riss m ♦ vt zerreißen; (muscle) zerren ♦ vi (zer)reißen; (rush) rasen; **~ along** (rush) entlangrasen; **~ up** vt (sheet of paper etc) zerreißen

tear² [tɪəʳ] n Träne f; **~ful** ['tɪəful] adj weinend; (voice) weinerlich; **~ gas** ['tɪəgæs] n Tränengas nt

tearoom ['tiːruːm] n Teestube f

tease [tiːz] n Hänsler m ♦ vt necken

tea set n Teeservice nt

teaspoon ['tiːspuːn] n Teelöffel m

teat [tiːt] n Brustwarze f; (of animal) Zitze f; (of bottle) Sauger m

tea time n (in the afternoon) Teestunde f; (mealtime) Abendessen nt

tea towel n Geschirrtuch nt

technical ['teknɪkl] adj technisch; (knowledge, terms) Fach-; **~ity**

technician [tɛknɪˈkælɪti] n technische Einzelheit f; (JUR) Formsache f; **~ly** adv technisch; (speak) spezialisiert; (fig) genau genommen

technician [tɛkˈnɪʃən] n Techniker m

technique [tɛkˈniːk] n Technik f

techno [ˈtɛknəʊ] n Techno m

technological [tɛknəˈlɒdʒɪkl] adj technologisch

technology [tɛkˈnɒlədʒɪ] n Technologie f

teddy (bear) [ˈtɛdɪ-] n Teddybär m

tedious [ˈtiːdɪəs] adj langweilig, ermüdend

tee [tiː] n (GOLF: object) Tee nt

teem [tiːm] vi (swarm): **to ~ (with)** wimmeln (von); **it is ~ing (with rain)** es gießt in Strömen

teenage [ˈtiːneɪdʒ] adj (fashions etc) Teenager-, jugendlich; **~r** n Teenager m, Jugendliche(r) mf

teens [tiːnz] npl Teenageralter nt

tee-shirt [ˈtiːʃɜːt] n T-Shirt nt

teeter [ˈtiːtər] vi schwanken

teeth [tiːθ] npl of **tooth**

teethe [tiːð] vi zahnen; **teething ring** n Beißring m; **teething troubles** npl (fig) Kinderkrankheiten pl

teetotal [ˈtiːˈtəʊtl] adj abstinent

tele-: ~communications npl Fernmeldewesen nt; **~conferencing** n Telefon- or Videokonferenz f; **~gram** n Telegramm nt; **~graph** n Telegraf m; **~graph pole** n Telegrafenmast m

telephone [ˈtɛlɪfəʊn] n Telefon nt, Fernsprecher m ♦ vt anrufen; (message) telefonisch mitteilen; **to be on the ~** (talking) telefonieren; (possessing phone) Telefon haben; **~ booth** n Telefonzelle f; **~ box** (BRIT) n Telefonzelle f; **~ call** n Telefongespräch nt, Anruf m; **~ directory** n Telefonbuch nt; **~ number** n Telefonnummer f; **telephonist** [təˈlɛfənɪst] (BRIT) n Telefonist(in) m(f)

telephoto lens [ˈtɛliˈfəʊtəʊ-] n Teleobjektiv nt

telescope [ˈtɛlɪskəʊp] n Teleskop nt,

Fernrohr nt ♦ vt ineinander schieben

televise [ˈtɛlɪvaɪz] vt durch das Fernsehen übertragen

television [ˈtɛlɪvɪʒən] n Fernsehen nt; **on ~** im Fernsehen; **~ (set)** n Fernsehapparat m, Fernseher m

teleworking [ˈtɛliwɜːkɪŋ] n Telearbeit f

telex [ˈtɛlɛks] n Telex nt ♦ vt per Telex schicken

tell [tɛl] (pt, pp **told**) vt (story) erzählen; (secret) ausplaudern; (say, make known) sagen; (distinguish) erkennen; (be sure) wissen ♦ vi (talk) sprechen; (be sure) wissen; (divulge) es verraten; (have effect) sich auswirken; **to ~ sb to do sth** jdm sagen, dass er etw tun soll; **to ~ sb sth** or **sth to sb** jdm etw sagen; **to ~ sb by sth** jdn an etw akt erkennen; **to ~ sth from** etw unterscheiden von; **to ~ of sth** von etw sprechen; **~ off** vt: **to ~ sb off** jdn ausschimpfen

teller [ˈtɛlər] n Kassenbeamte(r) mf

telling [ˈtɛlɪŋ] adj verräterisch; (blow) hart

telltale [ˈtɛlteɪl] adj verräterisch

telly [ˈtɛlɪ] (BRIT: inf) n abbr (= television) TV nt

temp [tɛmp] n abbr (= temporary) Aushilfssekretärin f

temper [ˈtɛmpər] n (disposition) Temperament nt; (anger) Zorn m ♦ vt (tone down) mildern; (metal) härten; **to be in a (bad) ~** wütend sein; **to lose one's ~** die Beherrschung verlieren

temperament [ˈtɛmprəmənt] n Temperament nt; **~al** [tɛmprəˈmɛntl] adj (moody) launisch

temperate [ˈtɛmprɪt] adj gemäßigt

temperature [ˈtɛmprətʃər] n Temperatur f; (MED: high ~) Fieber nt; **to have** or **run a ~** Fieber haben

template [ˈtɛmplɪt] n Schablone f

temple [ˈtɛmpl] n Tempel m; (ANAT) Schläfe f

temporal [ˈtɛmpərl] adj (of time) zeitlich; (worldly) irdisch, weltlich

temporarily ['tempərəlɪ] adv zeitweilig, vorübergehend

temporary ['tempərɪ] adj vorläufig; (road, building) provisorisch

tempt [tempt] vt (persuade) verleiten; (attract) reizen, (ver)locken; **to ~ sb into doing sth** jdn dazu verleiten, etw zu tun; **~ation** [temp'teɪʃən] n Versuchung f; **~ing** adj (person) verführerisch; (object, situation) verlockend

ten [ten] num zehn

tenable ['tenəbl] adj haltbar

tenacious [tə'neɪʃəs] adj zäh, hartnäckig

tenacity [tə'næsɪtɪ] n Zähigkeit f, Hartnäckigkeit f

tenancy ['tenənsɪ] n Mietverhältnis nt

tenant ['tenənt] n Mieter m; (of larger property) Pächter m

tend [tend] vt (look after) sich kümmern um ♦ vi: **to ~ to do sth** etw gewöhnlich tun

tendency ['tendənsɪ] n Tendenz f; (of person) Tendenz f, Neigung f

tender ['tendə'] adj zart; (loving) zärtlich ♦ n (COMM: offer) Kostenanschlag m ♦ vt (an)bieten; (resignation) einreichen; **~ness** n Zartheit f; (being loving) Zärtlichkeit f

tendon ['tendən] n Sehne f

tenement ['tenəmənt] n Mietshaus nt

tennis ['tenɪs] n Tennis nt; **~ ball** n Tennisball m; **~ court** n Tennisplatz m; **~ player** n Tennisspieler(in) m(f); **~ racket** n Tennisschläger m; **~ shoes** npl Tennisschuhe pl

tenor ['tenə'] n Tenor m

tenpin bowling ['tenpɪn-] n Bowling nt

tense [tens] adj angespannt ♦ n Zeitform f

tension ['tenʃən] n Spannung f

tent [tent] n Zelt nt

tentacle ['tentəkl] n Fühler m; (of sea animals) Fangarm m

tentative ['tentətɪv] adj (movement)

unsicher; (offer) Probe-; (arrangement) vorläufig; (suggestion) unverbindlich; **~ly** adv versuchsweise; (try, move) vorsichtig

tenterhooks ['tentəhuks] npl: **to be on ~** auf die Folter gespannt sein

tenth [tenθ] adj zehnte(r, s)

tent peg n Hering m

tent pole n Zeltstange f

tenuous ['tenjuəs] adj schwach

tenure ['tenjuə'] n (of land) Besitz m; (of office) Amtszeit f

tepid ['tepɪd] adj lauwarm

term [tɜːm] n (period of time) Zeit(raum m) f; (limit) Frist f; (SCH) Quartal nt; (UNIV) Trimester nt; (expression) Ausdruck m ♦ vt (be)nennen; **~s** npl (conditions) Bedingungen pl; **in the short/long ~** auf kurze/lange Sicht; **to be on good ~s with sb** gut mit jdm auskommen; **to come to ~s with** (person) sich einigen mit; (problem) sich abfinden mit

terminal ['tɜːmɪnl] n (BRIT: also: **coach ~**) Endstation f; (AVIAT) Terminal m; (COMPUT) Terminal nt or m ♦ adj (MED) unheilbar; **~ly** adv (MED): **~ly ill** unheilbar krank

terminate ['tɜːmɪneɪt] vt beenden ♦ vi enden, aufhören

termini ['tɜːmɪnaɪ] npl of **terminus**

terminus ['tɜːmɪnəs] (pl **termini**) n Endstation f

terrace ['terəs] n (BRIT: row of houses) Häuserreihe f; (in garden etc) Terrasse f; **the ~s** (BRIT: SPORT) die Ränge; **~d** adj (garden) terrassenförmig angelegt; (house) Reihen-

terrain [te'reɪn] n Gelände nt

terrible ['terɪbl] adj schrecklich, entsetzlich, fürchterlich; **terribly** adv fürchterlich

terrier ['terɪə'] n Terrier m

terrific [tə'rɪfɪk] adj unwahrscheinlich; **~!** klasse!

terrified adj: **to be ~ of sth** vor etw schreckliche Angst haben

terrify ['terɪfaɪ] vt erschrecken

territorial [terɪ'tɔːrɪəl] adj Gebiets-, territorial

territory ['terɪtərɪ] n Gebiet nt

terror ['terər] n Schrecken m

terrorism ['terərɪzəm] n Terrorismus m; **~ist** n Terrorist(in) m(f); **~ize** vt terrorisieren

terse [tɜːs] adj knapp, kurz, bündig

test [test] n Probe f; (examination) Prüfung f; (PSYCH, TECH) Test m ♦ vt prüfen; (PSYCH) testen

testicle ['testɪkl] n (ANAT) Hoden m

testify ['testɪfaɪ] vi aussagen; **to ~ to** sth etw bezeugen

testimony ['testɪmənɪ] n (JUR) Zeugenaussage f; (fig) Zeugnis nt

test match n (SPORT) Länderkampf m

test tube n Reagenzglas nt

tetanus ['tetənəs] n Wundstarrkrampf m, Tetanus m

tether ['teðər] vt anbinden ♦ n: **at the end of one's ~** völlig am Ende

text [tekst] n Text m; (of document) Wortlaut m; **~book** n Lehrbuch nt

textiles ['tekstaɪlz] npl Textilien pl

texture ['tekstʃər] n Beschaffenheit f

Thai [taɪ] adj thailändisch ♦ n Thailänder(in) m(f); **~land** n Thailand nt

Thames [temz] n: **the ~** die Themse

than [ðæn, ðən] prep (in comparisons) als

thank [θæŋk] vt danken +dat; **you've him to ~ for your success** Sie haben Ihren Erfolg ihm zu verdanken; **~ you (very much)** danke (vielmals), danke schön; **~ful** adj dankbar; **~less** adj undankbar; **~s** npl Dank m ♦ excl danke!; **~s to** dank +gen; **T~sgiving (Day)** (US) n Thanksgiving Day m

Kanada gibt es einen ähnlichen Erntedanktag (der aber nichts mit den Pilgervätern zu tun hat) am zweiten Montag im Oktober.

that [ðæt, ðət] adj (demonstrative: pl those) der/die/das; jene(r, s); **that one** das da
♦ pron 1 (demonstrative: pl those) das; **who's/what's that?** wer ist da/was ist das?; **is that you?** bist du das?; **that's what he said** genau das hat er gesagt; **what happened after that?** was passierte danach?; **that is** das heißt

2 (relative: subj) der/die/das, die; (: direct obj) den/die/das, die; (: indirect obj) dem/der/dem, denen; **all (that) I have** alles, was ich habe

3 (relative: of time): **the day (that) an** dem Tag, als; **the winter (that) he came** in dem Winter, in dem er kam
♦ conj dass; **he thought that I was ill** er dachte, dass ich krank sei, er dachte, ich sei krank
♦ adv (demonstrative) so; **I can't work that much** ich kann nicht so viel arbeiten

thatched [θætʃt] adj strohgedeckt; (cottage) mit Strohdach

thaw [θɔː] n Tauwetter nt ♦ vi tauen; (frozen foods, fig: people) auftauen ♦ vt (auf)tauen lassen

the [ðiː, ðə] def art 1 der/die/das; **to play the piano/violin** Klavier/Geige spielen; **I'm going to the butcher's/ the cinema** ich gehe zum Fleischer/ ins Kino; **Elizabeth the First** Elisabeth die Erste

2 (+adj to form noun) das, die; **the rich and the poor** die Reichen und die Armen

3 (in comparisons): **the more he**

works the more he earns je mehr er arbeitet, desto mehr verdient er

theatre ['θɪətə*] (*US* theater) *n* Theater *nt*; (*for lectures etc*) Saal *m*; (*MED*) Operationssaal *m*; **~goer** *n* Theaterbesucher(in) *m(f)*; **theatrical** [θɪ'ætrɪkl] *adj* Theater-; (*career*) Schauspieler-; (*showy*) theatralisch

theft [θɛft] *n* Diebstahl *m*

their [ðɛə*] *adj* ihr; *see also* **my**; **~s** pron ihre(r, s); *see also* **mine[1]**

them [ðɛm, ðəm] *pron* (*acc*) sie; (*dat*) ihnen; *see also* **me**

theme [θiːm] *n* Thema *nt*; (*MUS*) Motiv *nt*; **~ park** *n* (thematisch gestalteter) Freizeitpark *m*; **~ song** *n* Titelmusik *f*

themselves [ðəm'sɛlvz] *pl pron* (*reflexive*) sich (selbst); (*emphatic*) selbst; *see also* **oneself**

then [ðɛn] *adv* (*at that time*) damals; (*next*) dann ♦ *conj* also, folglich; (*furthermore*) ferner ♦ *adj* damalig; **from ~ on** von da an; **by ~** bis dahin; **the ~ president** der damalige Präsident

theology [θɪ'ɔlədʒɪ] *n* Theologie *f*

theoretical [θɪə'rɛtɪkl] *adj* theoretisch; **~ly** *adv* theoretisch

theory ['θɪərɪ] *n* Theorie *f*

therapist ['θɛrəpɪst] *n* Therapeut(in) *m(f)*

therapy ['θɛrəpɪ] *n* Therapie *f*

KEYWORD
---

there [ðɛə*] *adv* **1**: **there is**, **there are** es *or* da ist/sind; (*there exists/exist also*) es gibt; **there are 3 of them** (*people, things*) es gibt 3 davon; **there has been an accident** da war ein Unfall **2** (*place*) da, dort; (*direction*) dahin, dorthin; **put it in/on there** leg es da dahinein/dorthinauf **3**: **there, there** (*esp to child*) na, na

there: **~abouts** ['ðɛərə'bauts] *adv* (*place*) dort in der Nähe, dort irgendwo; (*amount*): **20 or ~abouts** unge-

fähr 20; **~after** [ðɛər'ɑːftə*] *adv* danach; **~by** ['ðɛəbaɪ] *adv* dadurch, damit

therefore ['ðɛəfɔː*] *adv* deshalb, daher

there's ['ðɛəz] = **there is**; **there has**

thermometer [θə'mɔmɪtə*] *n* Thermometer *nt*

Thermos ['θɜːməs] ® *n* Thermosflasche *f*

thesaurus [θɪ'sɔːrəs] *n* Synonymwörterbuch *nt*

these [ðiːz] *pron, adj* (*pl*) diese

theses ['θiːsiːz] *npl of* **thesis**

thesis ['θiːsɪs] (*pl* **theses**) *n* (*for discussion*) These *f*; (*UNIV*) Dissertation *f*, Doktorarbeit *f*

they [ðeɪ] *pl pron* sie; (*people in general*) man; **~ say that ...** (*it is said that*) es wird gesagt, dass ...; **~'d = they had**; **they would**; **~'ll = they shall**; **they will**; **~'re = they are**; **~'ve = they have**

thick [θɪk] *adj* dick; (*forest*) dicht; (*liquid*) dickflüssig; (*slow, stupid*) dumm, schwer von Begriff ♦ *n*: **in the ~ of** mitten in *+dat*; **it's 20 cm ~** es ist 20 cm dick *or* stark; **~en** *vi* (*fog*) dichter werden ♦ *vt* (*sauce etc*) verdicken; **~ness** *n* Dicke *f*, Dichte *f*; Dickflüssigkeit *f*; **~set** *adj* untersetzt; **~skinned** *adj* dickhäutig

thief [θiːf] (*pl* **thieves**) *n* Dieb(in) *m(f)*

thieves [θiːvz] *npl of* **thief**

thieving ['θiːvɪŋ] *n* Stehlen *nt* ♦ *adj* diebisch

thigh [θaɪ] *n* Oberschenkel *m*

thimble ['θɪmbl] *n* Fingerhut *m*

thin [θɪn] *adj* dünn; (*person*) dünn, mager; (*excuse*) schwach ♦ *vt*: **to ~ (down)** (*sauce, paint*) verdünnen

thing [θɪŋ] *n* Ding *nt*; (*affair*) Sache *f*; **my ~s** meine Sachen *pl*; **the best ~ would be to ...** das Beste wäre, ...; **how are ~s?** wie gehts?

think [θɪŋk] (*pt, pp* **thought**) *vt, vi* denken; **what did you ~ of them?** was halten Sie von ihnen?; **to ~ about sth/sb** nachdenken über etw/jdn; **I'll**

~ about it ich überlege es mir; **to ~ of doing sth** vorhaben or beabsichtigen, etw zu tun; **to ~ so/not** ich glaube (schon)/glaube nicht; **to ~ well of sb** viel von jdm halten; **~ over** vt überdenken; **~ up** vt sich dat ausdenken; **~ tank** n Expertengruppe f

thinly ['θɪnlɪ] adv dünn; (disguised) kaum

third [θɜːd] adj dritte(r, s) ♦ n (person) Dritte(r) mf; (part) Drittel nt; **~ly** adv drittens; **~ party insurance** (BRIT) n Haftpflichtversicherung f; **~-rate** adj minderwertig; **T~ World** n: **the T~ World** die Dritte Welt f

thirst [θɜːst] n (also fig) Durst m; **~y** adj (person) durstig; (work) durstig machend; **to be ~y** Durst haben

thirteen [θɜː'tiːn] num dreizehn

thirty ['θɜːtɪ] num dreißig

this [ðɪs] adj (demonstrative: pl these) diese(r, s); **this evening** heute Abend; **this one** diese(r, s) (da)
♦ pron (demonstrative: pl these) dies, das; **who/what is this?** wer/was ist das?; **this is where I live** hier wohne ich; **this is what he said** das hat er gesagt; **this is Mr Brown** dies ist Mr Brown; (on telephone) hier ist Mr Brown
♦ adv (demonstrative): **this high/long** etc so groß/lang etc

thistle ['θɪsl] n Distel f

thorn [θɔːn] n Dorn m; **~y** adj dornig; (problem) schwierig

thorough ['θʌrə] adj gründlich; (person) gründlich; n Vollblut nt ♦ adj reinrassig, Vollblut-; **~fare** n Straße f; **"no ~fare"** „Durchfahrt verboten"; **~ly** adv gründlich; (extremely) äußerst

those [ðəʊz] pl pron die (da), jene ♦ adj die, jene

though [ðəʊ] conj obwohl ♦ adv trotzdem

thought [θɔːt] pt, pp of **think** ♦ n (idea) Gedanke m; (thinking) Denken nt, Denkvermögen nt; **~ful** adj (thinking) gedankenvoll, nachdenklich; (kind) rücksichtsvoll, aufmerksam; **~less** adj gedankenlos, unbesonnen; (unkind) rücksichtslos

thousand ['θaʊzənd] num tausend; **two ~** zweitausend; **~s of** tausende (von); **~th** adj tausendste(r, s)

thrash [θræʃ] vt verdreschen; (fig) vernichtend) schlagen; **~ about** vi um sich schlagen; **~ out** vt ausdiskutieren

thread [θred] n Faden m, Garn nt; (TECH) Gewinde nt; (in story) Faden m ♦ vt (needle) einfädeln; **~bare** adj fadenscheinig

threat [θret] n Drohung f; (danger) Gefahr f; **~en** vt bedrohen ♦ vi drohen; **to ~en sb with sth** jdm etw androhen

three [θriː] num drei; **~-dimensional** adj dreidimensional; **~-piece suite** n dreiteilige Polstergarnitur f; **~-wheeler** n Dreiradwagen m

thresh [θreʃ] vt, vi dreschen

threshold ['θreʃhəʊld] n Schwelle f

threw [θruː] pt of **throw**

thrift [θrɪft] n Sparsamkeit f; **~y** adj sparsam

thrill [θrɪl] n Reiz m, Erregung f ♦ vt begeistern, packen; **to be ~ed with** (gift etc) sich unheimlich freuen über +acc; **~er** n Krimi m; **~ing** adj spannend; (news) aufregend

thrive [θraɪv] (pt thrived, pp thrived) vi: **to ~ (on)** gedeihen (bei); **thriving** ['θraɪvɪŋ] adj blühend

throat [θrəʊt] n Hals m, Kehle f; **to have a sore ~** Halsschmerzen haben

throb [θrɒb] vi klopfen, pochen

throes [θrəʊz] npl: **in the ~ of** mitten in +dat

throne [θrəʊn] n Thron m; **on the ~** auf dem Thron

throng ['θrɒŋ] n (Menschen)schar f ♦ vt sich drängen in +dat

throttle ['θrɔtl] n Gashebel m ♦ vt erdrosseln

through [θru:] prep durch; (time) während +gen; (because of) aus, durch ♦ adv durch ♦ adj (ticket, train) durchgehend; (finished) fertig; **to put sb ~ (to)** jdn verbinden (mit); **to be ~** (TEL) eine Verbindung haben; (have finished) fertig sein; **no ~ way** (BRIT) Sackgasse f; **~out** [θru:'aut] prep (place) überall in +dat; (time) während +gen ♦ adv überall; die ganze Zeit

throw [θrəu] (pt **threw**, pp **thrown**) n Wurf m ♦ vt werfen; **to ~ a party** eine Party geben; **~ away** vt wegwerfen; (waste) verschwenden; (money) verschwenden; **~ off** vt abwerfen; (pursuer) abschütteln; **~ out** vt hinauswerfen; (rubbish) wegwerfen; (plan) verwerfen; **~ up** vt, vi (vomit) speien; **~away** adj Wegwerf-; **~-in** n Einwurf m; **~n** pp of **throw**

thru [θru:] (US) = **through**

thrush [θrʌʃ] n Drossel f

thrust [θrʌst] (pt, pp **thrust**) vt, vi (push) stoßen

thud [θʌd] n dumpfe(r) (Auf)schlag m

thug [θʌg] n Schlägertyp m

thumb [θʌm] n Daumen m ♦ vt (book) durchblättern; **to ~ a lift** per Anhalter fahren (wollen); **~tack** (US) n Reißzwecke f

thump [θʌmp] n (blow) Schlag m; (noise) Bums m ♦ vi hämmern, pochen ♦ vt schlagen auf +acc

thunder ['θʌndər] n Donner m ♦ vi donnern; (train etc): **to ~ past** vorbeidonnern ♦ vt brüllen; **~bolt** n Blitz m; **~clap** n Donnerschlag m; **~storm** n Gewitter nt, Unwetter nt; **~y** adj gewitterschwül

Thursday ['θəːzdɪ] n Donnerstag m

thus [ðʌs] adv (in this way) so; (therefore) somit, also, folglich

thwart [θwɔːt] vt vereiteln, durchkreuzen; (person) hindern

thyme [taɪm] n Thymian m

thyroid ['θaɪrɔɪd] n Schilddrüse f

tiara [tɪ'ɑːrə] n Diadem nt

tic [tɪk] n Tick m

tick [tɪk] n (sound) Ticken nt; (mark) Häkchen n ♦ vi ticken ♦ vt abhaken; **in a ~** (BRIT: inf) sofort; **~ off** vt abhaken; (person) ausschimpfen; **~ over** vi (engine) im Leerlauf laufen; (fig) auf Sparflamme laufen

ticket ['tɪkɪt] n (for travel) Fahrkarte f; (for entrance) (Eintritts)karte f; (price ~) Preisschild nt; (luggage ~) Gepäckschein m; (raffle ~) Los nt; (parking ~) Strafzettel m; (in car park) Parkschein m; **~ collector** n Fahrkartenkontrolleur m; **~ inspector** n Fahrkartenkontrolleur m; **~ office** n (THEAT etc) Kasse f; (RAIL etc) Fahrkartenschalter m

tickle ['tɪkl] n Kitzeln nt ♦ vt kitzeln; (amuse) amüsieren; **ticklish** ['tɪklɪʃ] adj (also fig) kitzlig

tidal ['taɪdl] adj Flut-, Tide-; **~ wave** n Flutwelle f

tidbit ['tɪdbɪt] (US) n Leckerbissen m

tiddlywinks ['tɪdlɪwɪŋks] n Floh(hüpf)spiel nt

tide [taɪd] n Gezeiten pl; **high/low ~** Flut f/Ebbe f

tidy ['taɪdɪ] adj ordentlich ♦ vt aufräumen, in Ordnung bringen

tie [taɪ] n (BRIT: necktie) Krawatte f, Schlips m; (sth connecting) Band nt; (SPORT) Unentschieden nt ♦ vt (fasten, restrict) binden ♦ vi (SPORT) unentschieden spielen; (in competition) punktgleich sein; **to ~ in a bow** zur Schleife binden; **to ~ a knot in sth** einen Knoten in etw acc machen; **~ down** vt festbinden; **to ~ sb down to** jdn binden auf +acc; **~ up** vt (dog) anbinden; (parcel) verschnüren; (boat) festmachen; (person) fesseln; **to be ~d up** (busy) beschäftigt sein

tier [tɪə] n Rang m; (of cake) Etage f

tiff [tɪf] n Krach m

tiger ['taɪgə] n Tiger m

tight [taɪt] adj (close) eng, knapp;

(schedule) gedrängt; (firm) fest; (control) streng; (stretched) stramm, (an)gespannt; (inf: drunk) blau, stramm ♦ adv (squeeze) fest; **~en** vt anziehen, anspannen; (restrictions) verschärfen ♦ vi sich spannen; **~-fisted** adj knauserig; **~ly** adv eng; fest; (stretched) straff; **~-rope** n Seil nt; **~s** npl (esp BRIT) Strumpfhose f

tile [taɪl] n (on roof) Dachziegel m; (on wall or floor) Fliese f; **~d** adj (roof) gedeckt, Ziegel-; (floor, wall) mit Fliesen belegt

till [tɪl] n Kasse f ♦ vt bestellen ♦ prep, conj = **until**

tiller ['tɪlər] n Ruderpinne f

tilt [tɪlt] vt kippen, neigen ♦ vi sich neigen

timber ['tɪmbər] n (wood) Holz nt

time [taɪm] n Zeit f; (occasion) Mal nt; (rhythm) Takt m ♦ vt zur rechten Zeit tun, zeitlich einrichten; (SPORT) stoppen; **in 2 weeks' ~** in 2 Wochen; **a long ~** lange; **for the ~ being** vorläufig; **4 at a ~** zu jeweils 4; **from ~ to ~** gelegentlich; **to have a good ~** sich amüsieren; **in ~** (soon enough) rechtzeitig; (after some ~) mit der Zeit; (MUS) im Takt; **in no ~** im Handumdrehen; **any ~** jederzeit; **on ~** pünktlich, rechtzeitig; **five ~s 5** fünfmal 5; **what ~ is it?** wie viel Uhr ist es?, wie spät ist es?; **at ~s** manchmal; **~ bomb** n Zeitbombe f; **~less** adj (beauty) zeitlos; **~ limit** n Frist f; **~ly** adj rechtzeitig; günstig; **~ off** n freie Zeit f; **~r** n (~ switch: in kitchen) Schaltuhr f; **~ scale** n Zeitspanne f; **~-share** adj Timesharing-; **~ switch** (BRIT) n Zeitschalter m; **~table** n Fahrplan m; (SCH) Stundenplan m; **~ zone** n Zeitzone f

timid ['tɪmɪd] adj ängstlich, schüchtern

timing ['taɪmɪŋ] n Wahl f des richtigen Zeitpunkts, Timing f

timpani ['tɪmpənɪ] npl Kesselpauken pl

tin [tɪn] n (metal) Blech nt; (BRIT: can)

Büchse f, Dose f; **~foil** n Stanniolpapier nt

tinge [tɪndʒ] n (colour) Färbung f; (fig) Anflug m ♦ vt färben; **~d with** mit einer Spur von

tingle ['tɪŋgl] n Prickeln nt ♦ vi prickeln

tinker ['tɪŋkər] n Kesselflicker m; **~ with** vt fus herumpfuschen an +dat

tinkle ['tɪŋkl] vi klingeln

tinned [tɪnd] (BRIT) adj (food) Dosen-, Büchsen-

tin opener [-əupnər] (BRIT) n Dosen- or Büchsenöffner m

tinsel ['tɪnsl] n Rauschgold f

tint [tɪnt] n (colour) Färbung f; (slight colour) Anflug m; (hair) Tönung f; **~ed** adj getönt

tiny ['taɪnɪ] adj winzig

tip [tɪp] n (pointed end) Spitze f; (money) Trinkgeld nt; (hint) Wink m, Tipp m ♦ vt (slant) kippen; (hat) antippen; (~ over) umkippen; (waiter) ein Trinkgeld geben +dat; **~-off** n Hinweis m, Tipp m; **~ped** (BRIT) adj (cigarette) Filter-

tipsy ['tɪpsɪ] adj beschwipst

tiptoe ['tɪptəu] n: **on ~** auf Zehenspitzen

tiptop ['tɪp'tɔp] adj: **in ~ condition** tipptopp, erstklassig

tire ['taɪər] n (US) = **tyre** ♦ vt, vi ermüden, müde machen/werden; **~d** adj müde; **to be ~d of sth** etw satt haben; **~less** adj unermüdlich; **~some** adj lästig

tiring ['taɪərɪŋ] adj ermüdend

tissue ['tɪʃuː] n (paper) Gewebe nt; (paper handkerchief) Papiertaschentuch nt; **~ paper** n Seidenpapier nt

tit [tɪt] n (bird) Meise f; **~ for tat** wie du mir, so ich dir

titbit ['tɪtbɪt] (US **tidbit**) n Leckerbissen m

titillate ['tɪtɪleɪt] vt kitzeln

title ['taɪtl] n Titel m; **~ deed** n Eigentumsurkunde f; **~ role** n Hauptrolle f

titter ['tɪtər] vi kichern

titular ['tɪtjʊlə'] *adj* (*in name only*) nominell

TM *abbr* (= *trademark*) Wz

KEYWORD
---

to [tuː, tə] *prep* **1** (*direction*) zu, nach; **I go to France/school** ich gehe nach Frankreich/zur Schule; **to the left** nach links

2 (*as far as*) bis

3 (*with expressions of time*) vor; **a quarter to 5** Viertel vor 5

4 (*for, of*) für; **secretary to the director** Sekretärin des Direktors

5 (*expressing indirect object*): **to give sth to sb** jdm etw geben; **to talk to sb** mit jdm sprechen; **I sold it to a friend** ich habe es einem Freund verkauft

6 (*in relation to*) zu; **30 miles to the gallon** 30 Meilen pro Gallone

7 (*purpose, result*) zu; **to my surprise** zu meiner Überraschung

♦ *with vb* **1** (*infin*): **to go/eat** gehen/essen; **to want to do sth** etw tun wollen; **to try/start to do sth** versuchen/anfangen, etw zu tun; **he has a lot to lose** er hat viel zu verlieren

2 (*with vb omitted*): **I don't want to** ich will (es) nicht

3 (*purpose, result*) um; **I did it to help you** ich tat es, um dir zu helfen

4 (*after adj etc*): **ready to use** gebrauchsfertig; **too old/young to ...** zu alt/jung, um ...

♦ *adv*: **push/pull the door to** die Tür zuschieben/zuziehen

toad [təʊd] *n* Kröte *f*; **~stool** *n* Giftpilz *m*

toast [təʊst] *n* (*bread*) Toast *m*; (*drinking*) Trinkspruch *m* ♦ *vt* trinken auf +*acc*; (*bread*) toasten; (*warm*) wärmen; **~er** *n* Toaster *m*

tobacco [tə'bækəʊ] *n* Tabak *m*; **~nist** [tə'bækənɪst] *n* Tabakhändler *m*;

~nist's (shop) *n* Tabakladen *m*

toboggan [tə'bɒɡən] *n* (Rodel)schlitten *m*; **~ing** *n* Rodeln *nt*

today [tə'deɪ] *adv* heute; (*at the present time*) heutzutage

toddler ['tɒdlə'] *n* Kleinkind *nt*

toddy ['tɒdɪ] *n* (Whisky)grog *m*

to-do [tə'duː] *n* Theater *nt*

toe [təʊ] *n* Zehe *f*; (*of sock, shoe*) Spitze *f* ♦ *vt*: **to ~ the line** (*fig*) sich einfügen; **~nail** *n* Zehennagel *m*

toffee ['tɒfɪ] *n* Sahnebonbon *nt*; **~ apple** (*BRIT*) *n* kandierte(r) Apfel *m*

together [tə'ɡeðə'] *adv* zusammen; (*at the same time*) gleichzeitig; **~ with** zusammen mit; gleichzeitig mit

toil [tɔɪl] *n* harte Arbeit *f*, Plackerei *f* ♦ *vi* sich abmühen, sich plagen

toilet ['tɔɪlət] *n* Toilette *f* ♦ *cpd* Toiletten-; **~ bag** *n* Waschbeutel *m*; **~ paper** *n* Toilettenpapier *nt*; **~ries** ['tɔɪlətrɪz] *npl* Toilettenartikel *pl*; **~ roll** *n* Rolle *f* Toilettenpapier; **~ water** *n* Toilettenwasser *nt*

token ['təʊkən] *n* Zeichen *nt*; (*gift ~*) Gutschein *m*; **book/record ~** (*BRIT*) *n* Bücher-/Plattengutschein *m*

Tokyo ['təʊkjəʊ] *n* Tokio *nt*

told [təʊld] *pt, pp of* **tell**

tolerable ['tɒlərəbl] *adj* (*bearable*) erträglich; (*fairly good*) leidlich

tolerant ['tɒlərnt] *adj*: **be ~ (of)** vertragen +*acc*

tolerate ['tɒləreɪt] *vt* dulden; (*noise*) ertragen

toll [təʊl] *n* Gebühr *f* ♦ *vi* (*bell*) läuten

tomato [tə'mɑːtəʊ] (*pl* **~es**) *n* Tomate *f*

tomb [tuːm] *n* Grab(mal) *nt*

tomboy ['tɒmbɔɪ] *n* Wildfang *m*

tombstone ['tuːmstəʊn] *n* Grabstein *m*

tomcat ['tɒmkæt] *n* Kater *m*

tomorrow [tə'mɒrəʊ] *n* Morgen *nt* ♦ *adv* morgen; **the day after ~** übermorgen; **~ morning** morgen früh; **a week ~** morgen in einer Woche

ton [tʌn] n Tonne f (BRIT = 1016kg; US = 907kg); ~s of (inf) eine Unmenge von

tone [təun] n Ton m; ~ **down** vt (criticism, demands) mäßigen; (colours) abtonen; ~ **up** vt in Form bringen; ~-**deaf** adj ohne musikalisches Gehör

tongs [tɔŋz] npl Zange f; (curling ~) Lockenstab m

tongue [tʌŋ] n Zunge f; (language) Sprache f; **with ~ in cheek** scherzhaft; ~-**tied** adj stumm, sprachlos; ~-**twister** n Zungenbrecher m

tonic [ˈtɔnɪk] n (drink) Tonic nt; (MED) Stärkungsmittel nt

tonight [təˈnaɪt] adv heute abend

tonsil [ˈtɔnsl] n Mandel f; ~**litis** [tɔnsɪˈlaɪtɪs] n Mandelentzündung f

too [tu:] adv zu; (also) auch; ~ **bad!** Pech!; ~ **many** zu viele

took [tuk] pt of **take**

tool [tu:l] n (also fig) Werkzeug nt; ~**box** n Werkzeugkasten m

toot [tu:t] n Hupen nt ♦ vi tuten; (AUT) hupen

tooth [tu:θ] n (pl teeth) Zahn m; ~**ache** n Zahnschmerzen pl, Zahnweh nt; ~**brush** n Zahnbürste f; ~**paste** n Zahnpasta f; ~**pick** n Zahnstocher m

top [tɔp] n Spitze f; (of mountain) Gipfel m; (of tree) Wipfel m; (toy) Kreisel m; (~ gear) vierte(r)/fünfte(r) Gang m ♦ adj oberste(r, s) ♦ vt (list) an erster Stelle stehen auf +dat; **on ~ of** oben auf +dat; **from ~ to bottom** von oben bis unten; ~ **off** (US) vt auffüllen; ~ **up** vt auffüllen; ~ **floor** n oberste(s) Stockwerk nt; ~ **hat** n Zylinder m; ~-**heavy** adj kopflastig

topic [ˈtɔpɪk] n Thema nt, Gesprächsgegenstand m; ~**al** adj aktuell

top: ~**less** [ˈtɔplɪs] adj (bather etc) oben ohne; ~-**level** [ˈtɔplevl] adj auf höchster Ebene; ~**most** [ˈtɔpməust] adj oberste(r, s)

topple [ˈtɔpl] vi, vt stürzen, kippen

top-secret [ˈtɔpˈsi:krɪt] adj streng geheim

topsy-turvy [ˈtɔpsɪˈtə:vɪ] adv durcheinander ♦ adj auf den Kopf gestellt

torch [tɔːtʃ] n (BRIT: ELEC) Taschenlampe f; (with flame) Fackel f

tore [tɔː] pt of **tear**[1]

torment [n ˈtɔːment, vb tɔːˈment] n Qual f ♦ vt (distress) quälen

torn [tɔːn] pp of **tear**[1] ♦ adj hin- und hergerissen

torrent [ˈtɔrənt] n Sturzbach m; ~**ial** [tɔˈrenʃl] adj wolkenbruchartig

torrid [ˈtɔrɪd] adj heiß

tortoise [ˈtɔːtəs] n Schildkröte f; ~**shell** [ˈtɔːtəʃel] n Schildpatt m

torture [ˈtɔːtʃə] n Folter f ♦ vt foltern

Tory [ˈtɔːrɪ] (BRIT) n (POL) Tory m ♦ adj Tory-, konservativ

toss [tɔs] vt schleudern; **to ~ a coin** or **to ~ up for sth** etw mit einer Münze entscheiden; **to ~ and turn** (in bed) sich hin und her werfen

tot [tɔt] n (small quantity) bisschen nt; (small child) Knirps m

total [ˈtəutl] n Gesamtheit f; (money) Endsumme f ♦ adj Gesamt-, total ♦ vt (add up) zusammenzählen; (amount to) sich belaufen auf

totalitarian [təutælɪˈtɛərɪən] adj totalitär

totally [ˈtəutəlɪ] adv total

totter [ˈtɔtə] vi wanken, schwanken

touch [tʌtʃ] n Berührung f; (sense of feeling) Tastsinn m ♦ vt (feel) berühren; (come against) leicht anstoßen; (emotionally) rühren; ~ **a ~ of** (fig) eine Spur von; **to get in ~ with** sich mit jdm in Verbindung setzen; **to lose ~** (friends) Kontakt verlieren; ~ **on** vt fus (topic) berühren, erwähnen; ~ **up** vt (paint) auffrischen; ~-**and-go** adj riskant, knapp; ~**down** n Landen nt, Niedergehen nt; ~**ed** adj (moved) gerührt; ~**ing** adj rührend; ~**line** n Seitenlinie f; ~-**sensitive screen** n (COMPUT) berührungsempfindlicher Bildschirm m; ~**y** adj empfindlich, reizbar

tough [tʌf] adj zäh; (difficult) schwierig

♦ n Schläger(typ) m; **~en** vt zäh machen; (make strong) abhärten

toupee ['tu:peɪ] n Toupet nt

tour ['tuəʳ] ♦ n Tour f ♦ vi umherreisen; (THEAT) auf Tour sein; auf Tour gehen; **~ guide** n Reiseleiter(in) m(f)

tourism ['tuərɪzm] n Fremdenverkehr m, Tourismus m

tourist ['tuərɪst] n Tourist(in) m(f) ♦ cpd (class) Touristen-; **~ office** n Verkehrsamt nt

tournament ['tuənəmənt] n Turnier nt

tousled ['tauzld] adj zerzaust

tout [taut] vi: **to ~ for** auf Kundenfang gehen ♦ n: **ticket ~** Kundenschlepper(in) m(f)

tow [təu] n vt (ab)schleppen; **on** (BRIT) or **in** (US) ~ (AUT) im Schlepp

toward(s) [tə'wɔ:d(z)] prep (with time) gegen; (in direction of) nach

towel ['tauəl] n Handtuch nt; **~ling** n (fabric) Frottee nt or m; **~ rack** (US) n Handtuchstange f; **~ rail** n Handtuchstange f

tower ['tauəʳ] n Turm m; **~ block** (BRIT) n Hochhaus nt; **~ing** adj hochragend

town [taun] n Stadt f; **to go to ~** (fig) sich ins Zeug legen; **~ centre** n Stadtzentrum nt; **~ clerk** n Stadtdirektor m; **~ council** n Stadtrat m; **~ hall** n Rathaus nt; **~ plan** n Stadtplan m; **~ planning** n Stadtplanung f

towrope ['təurəup] n Abschlepptau nt

tow truck (US) n Abschleppwagen m

toxic ['tɒksɪk] adj giftig, Gift-

toy [tɔɪ] n Spielzeug nt; **~ with** vt fus spielen mit; **~shop** n Spielwarengeschäft nt

trace [treɪs] ♦ n Spur f ♦ vt (follow a course) nachspüren +dat; (find out) aufspüren; (copy) durchpausen; **tracing paper** n Pauspapier nt

track [træk] n (mark) Spur f; (path) Weg m; (racetrack) Rennbahn f; (RAIL) Gleis nt ♦ vt verfolgen; **to keep ~ of sb** jdn im Auge behalten; **~ down** vt aufspüren; **~suit** n Trainingsanzug m

tract [trækt] n (of land) Gebiet nt

traction ['trækʃən] n (power) Zugkraft f; (AUT: grip) Bodenhaftung f; (MED): **in ~** im Streckverband

tractor ['træktəʳ] n Traktor m

trade [treɪd] n (commerce) Handel m; (business) Geschäft nt, Gewerbe nt; (people) Geschäftsleute pl; (skilled manual work) Handwerk nt ♦ vi: **to ~ (in)** handeln (mit) ♦ vt tauschen; **~ in** vt in Zahlung geben; **~ fair** n Messe nt; **~-in price** n Preis, zu dem etw in Zahlung genommen wird; **~mark** n Warenzeichen nt; **~ name** n Handelsbezeichnung f; **~r** n Händler m; **~sman** (irreg) n (shopkeeper) Geschäftsmann m; (workman) Handwerker m; (delivery man) Lieferant m; **~ union** n Gewerkschaft f; **~ unionist** n Gewerkschaftler(in) m(f)

trading ['treɪdɪŋ] n Handel m; **~ estate** (BRIT) n Industriegelände nt

tradition [trə'dɪʃən] n Tradition f; **~al** adj traditionell, herkömmlich

traffic ['træfɪk] n Verkehr m; (esp in drugs): **~ (in)** Handel m (mit) ♦ vi: **to ~ in** (esp drugs) handeln mit; **~ calming** n Verkehrsberuhigung f; **~ circle** (US) n Kreisverkehr m; **~ jam** n Verkehrsstauung f; **~ lights** npl Verkehrsampel f; **~ warden** n Verkehrspolizist m (ohne amtliche Befugnisse), Politesse f (ohne amtliche Befugnisse)

tragedy ['trædʒədɪ] n Tragödie f

tragic ['trædʒɪk] adj tragisch

trail [treɪl] n (track) Spur f; (of smoke) Rauchfahne f; (of dust) Staubwolke f; (road) Pfad m, Weg m ♦ vt (animal) verfolgen; (person) folgen +dat; (drag) schleppen ♦ vi (hang loosely) schleifen; (plants) sich ranken; (be behind) hinterherhinken; (SPORT) weit zurückliegen; (walk) zuckeln; **~ behind** vi zurückbleiben; **~er** n Anhänger m; (US: caravan) Wohnwagen m; (for film) Vorschau f; **~er truck** (US) n Sattelschlepper m

rain [treɪn] n Zug m; (of dress) Schleppe f; (series) Folge f ♦ vt (teach: person) ausbilden; (: animal) abrichten; (: mind) schulen; (SPORT) trainieren; (aim) richten ♦ vi (exercise) trainieren; (study) ausgebildet werden; **~ of thought** Gedankengang m; **to ~ sth on** (aim) etw richten auf +acc; **~ed** adj (eye) geschult; (person, voice) ausgebildet; **~ee** n Lehrling m, Praktikant(in) m(f); **~er** n Ausbilder m; (SPORT) Trainer m; **~ers** npl Turnschuhe pl; **~ing** n (for occupation) Ausbildung f; (SPORT) Training nt; **in ~ing** im Training; **~ing college** n pädagogische Hochschule f, Lehrerseminar nt; **~ing shoes** npl Turnschuhe pl

raipse [treɪps] vi latschen

rait [treɪt] n Zug m, Merkmal nt

raitor ['treɪtə*] n Verräter m

rajectory [trə'dʒektəri] n Flugbahn f

ram [træm] (BRIT) n (also: **~car**) Straßenbahn f

ramp [træmp] n Landstreicher m ♦ vi (trudge) stampfen, stapfen

rample ['træmpl] vt (nieder)trampeln ♦ vi (herum)trampeln; **to ~ (underfoot)** herumtrampeln auf +dat

rampoline ['træmpəliːn] n Trampolin nt

ranquil ['træŋkwɪl] adj ruhig, friedlich; **~lity** [træŋ'kwɪlɪti] (US **tranquility**) n Ruhe f; **~lizer** (US **tranquilizer**) n Beruhigungsmittel nt

ransact [træn'zækt] vt abwickeln; **~ion** [træn'zækʃən] n Abwicklung f; (piece of business) Geschäft nt, Transaktion f

ranscend [træn'send] vt übersteigen

ranscription [træn'skrɪpʃən] n Transkription f; (product) Abschrift f

ransfer [n 'trænsfɜː*, vb træns'fɜː*] n (~ring) Übertragung f; (of business) Umzug m; (being ~red) Versetzung f; (design) Abziehbild nt; (SPORT) Transfer m ♦ vt (business) verlegen; (person) versetzen; (prisoner) überführen; (drawing)

übertragen; (money) überweisen; **to ~ the charges** (BRIT: TEL) ein R-Gespräch führen; **~ desk** n (AVIAT) Transitschalter m

transform [træns'fɔːm] vt umwandeln; **~ation** [trænsfə'meɪʃən] n Umwandlung f, Verwandlung f

transfusion [træns'fjuːʒən] n Blutübertragung f, Transfusion f

transient ['trænzɪənt] adj kurz(lebig)

transistor [træn'zɪstə*] n (ELEC) Transistor m; (RAD) Transistorradio nt

transit ['trænzɪt] n: **in ~** unterwegs

transition [træn'zɪʃən] n Übergang m; **~al** adj Übergangs-

transit lounge n Warteraum m

translate [trænz'leɪt] vt, vi übersetzen; **translation** [trænz'leɪʃən] n Übersetzung f; **translator** [trænz'leɪtə*] n Übersetzer(in) m(f)

transmission [trænz'mɪʃən] n (of information) Übermittlung f; (ELEC, MED, TV) Übertragung f; (AUT) Getriebe nt

transmit [trænz'mɪt] vt (message) übermitteln; (ELEC, MED, TV) übertragen; **~ter** n Sender m

transparency [træns'pɛərnsi] n Durchsichtigkeit f; (BRIT: PHOT) Dia(positiv) nt

transparent [træns'pærnt] adj durchsichtig; (fig) offenkundig

transpire [træns'paɪə*] vi (turn out) sich herausstellen; (happen) passieren

transplant [vb træns'plɑːnt, n 'trænsplɑːnt] vt umpflanzen; (MED, also fig: person) verpflanzen ♦ n (MED) Transplantation f; (organ) Transplantat nt

transport [n 'trænspɔːt, vb træns'pɔːt] n Transport m, Beförderung f ♦ vt befördern; transportieren; **means of ~** Transportmittel nt; **~ation** ['trænspɔː'teɪʃən] n Transport m, Beförderung f; (means) Beförderungsmittel nt; (cost) Transportkosten pl; **~ café** (BRIT) n Fernfahrerlokal nt

trap [træp] n Falle f; (carriage) zweirädrige(r) Einspänner *m*; (*inf: mouth*) Klappe *f* ♦ *vt* fangen; (*person*) in eine Falle locken; **~door** *n* Falltür *f*

trappings ['træpɪŋz] *npl* Aufmachung *f*

trash [træʃ] *n* (*rubbish*) Plunder *m*; (*nonsense*) Mist *m*; **~ can** (*US*) *n* Mülleimer *m*; **~y** (*inf*) *adj* minderwertig, wertlos; (*novel*) Schund-

traumatic [trɔː'mætɪk] *adj* traumatisch

travel ['trævl] *n* Reisen *nt* ♦ *vi* reisen ♦ *vt* (*distance*) zurücklegen; (*country*) bereisen; **~s** *npl* (*journeys*) Reisen *pl*; **~ agency** *n* Reisebüro *nt*; **~ agent** *n* Reisebürokaufmann(-frau) *m(f)*; **~ler** (*US* **traveler**) *n* Reisende(r) *m*; (*salesman*) Handlungsreisende(r) *m*; **~ler's cheque** (*US* **traveler's check**) *n* Reisescheck *m*; **~ling** (*US* **traveling**) *n* Reisen *nt*; **~sick** *adj* reisekrank; **~ sickness** *n* Reisekrankheit *f*

trawler ['trɔːləʳ] *n* (*NAUT, FISHING*) Fischdampfer *m*, Trawler *m*

tray [treɪ] *n* (*tea* ~) Tablett *nt*; (*for mail*) Ablage *f*

treacherous ['tretʃərəs] *adj* verräterisch; (*road*) tückisch

treachery ['tretʃərɪ] *n* Verrat *m*

treacle ['triːkl] *n* Sirup *m*, Melasse *f*

tread [tred] (*pt* **trod**, *pp* **trodden**) *n* Schritt *m*, Tritt *m*; (*of stair*) Stufe *f*; (*on tyre*) Profil *nt* ♦ *vi* treten; **~ on** *vt fus* treten auf +*acc*

treason ['triːzn] *n* Verrat *m*

treasure ['treʒəʳ] *n* Schatz *m* ♦ *vt* schätzen

treasurer ['treʒərəʳ] *n* Kassenverwalter *m*, Schatzmeister *m*

treasury ['treʒərɪ] *n* (*POL*) Finanzministerium *nt*

treat [triːt] *n* besondere Freude *f* ♦ *vt* (*deal with*) behandeln; **to ~ sb to sth** jdm etw spendieren

treatise ['triːtɪz] *n* Abhandlung *f*

treatment ['triːtmənt] *n* Behandlung *f*

treaty ['triːtɪ] *n* Vertrag *m*

treble ['trebl] *adj* dreifach ♦ *vt* verdreifachen; **~ clef** *n* Violinschlüssel *m*

tree [triː] *n* Baum *m*; **~ trunk** *n* Baumstamm *m*

trek [trek] *n* Treck *m*, Zug *m*; (*inf*) anstrengende(r) Weg *m* ♦ *vi* trecken

trellis ['trelɪs] *n* Gitter *nt*; (*for gardening*) Spalier *nt*

tremble ['trembl] *vi* zittern; (*ground*) beben

tremendous [trɪ'mendəs] *adj* gewaltig, kolossal; (*inf: good*) prima

tremor ['tremɔʳ] *n* Zittern *nt*; (*of earth*) Beben *nt*

trench [trentʃ] *n* Graben *m*; (*MIL*) Schützengraben *m*

trend [trend] *n* Tendenz *f*; **~y** (*inf*) *adj* modisch

trepidation [trepɪ'deɪʃən] *n* Beklommenheit *f*

trespass ['trespəs] *vi*: **to ~ on** widerrechtlich betreten; **"no ~ing"** „Betreten verboten"

trestle ['tresl] *n* Bock *m*; **~ table** *n* Klapptisch *m*

trial ['traɪəl] *n* (*JUR*) Prozess *m*; (*test*) Versuch *m*, Probe *f*; (*hardship*) Prüfung *f*; **by ~ and error** durch Ausprobieren; **~ period** *n* Probezeit *f*

triangle ['traɪæŋgl] *n* Dreieck *nt*; (*MUS*) Triangel *f*; **triangular** [traɪ'æŋgjuləʳ] *adj* dreieckig

tribal ['traɪbl] *adj* Stammes-

tribe [traɪb] *n* Stamm *m*; **~sman** (*irreg*) *n* Stammesangehörige(r) *m*

tribulation [trɪbju'leɪʃən] *n* Not *f*, Mühsal *f*

tribunal [traɪ'bjuːnl] *n* Gericht *nt*; (*inquiry*) Untersuchungsausschuss *m*

tributary ['trɪbjutərɪ] *n* Nebenfluss *m*

tribute ['trɪbjuːt] *n* (*admiration*) Zeichen *nt* der Hochachtung; **to pay ~ to sb/sth** jdm/einer Sache Tribut zollen

trick [trɪk] *n* Trick *m*; (*CARDS*) Stich *m* ♦ *vt* überlisten, beschwindeln; **to play a ~ on sb** jdm einen Streich spielen; **that should do the ~** dass müsste eigentlich klappen; **~ery** *n* Tricks *pl*

trickle ['trɪkl] *n* Tröpfeln *nt*; (*small river*)

tricky ['trɪkɪ] *adj* (*problem*) schwierig; (*situation*) kitzlig

tricycle ['traɪsɪkl] *n* Dreirad *nt*

trifle ['traɪfl] *n* Kleinigkeit *f*; (COOK) Trifle *m* ♦ *adv*: **a ~** ... ein bisschen ...; **trifling** *adj* geringfügig

trigger ['trɪgə'] *n* Drücker *m*; **~ off** *vt* auslösen

trim [trɪm] *adj* gepflegt; (*figure*) schlank ♦ *n* (gute) Verfassung *f*; (*embellishment, on car*) Verzierung *f* ♦ *vt* (*clip*) schneiden; (*trees*) stutzen; (*decorate*) besetzen; (*sails*) trimmen; **~mings** *npl* (*decorations*) Verzierung *f*, Verzierungen *pl*; (*extras*) Zubehör *nt*

Trinity ['trɪnɪtɪ] *n*: **the ~** die Dreieinigkeit *f*

trinket ['trɪŋkɪt] *n* kleine(s) Schmuckstück *nt*

trip [trɪp] *n* (*kurze*) Reise *f*; (*outing*) Ausflug *m*; (*stumble*) Stolpern *nt* ♦ *vi* (*stumble*) stolpern; **on a ~** auf Reisen; **~ up** *vi* stolpern; (*fig*) stolpern, einen Fehler machen ♦ *vt* zu Fall bringen; (*fig*) hereinlegen

tripe [traɪp] *n* (*food*) Kutteln *pl*; (*rubbish*) Mist *m*

triple ['trɪpl] *adj* dreifach

triplets ['trɪplɪts] *npl* Drillinge *pl*

triplicate ['trɪplɪkət] *n*: **in ~** in dreifacher Ausfertigung

tripod ['traɪpɒd] *n* (PHOT) Stativ *nt*

trite [traɪt] *adj* banal

triumph ['traɪʌmf] *n* Triumph *m* ♦ *vi* **to ~ (over)** triumphieren (über +*acc*); **~ant** [traɪ'ʌmfənt] *adj* triumphierend

trivia ['trɪvɪə] *npl* Trivialitäten *pl*

trivial ['trɪvɪəl] *adj* gering(fügig), trivial

trod [trɒd] *pt of* tread; **~den** *pp of* tread

trolley ['trɒlɪ] *n* Handwagen *m*; (*in shop*) Einkaufswagen *m*; (*for luggage*) Kofferkuli *m*; (*table*) Teewagen *m*; **~ bus** *n* Oberleitungsbus *m*, Obus *m*

trombone [trɒm'bəun] *n* Posaune *f*

troop [tru:p] *n* Schar *f*; (MIL) Trupp *m*; **~s** *npl* (MIL) Truppen *pl*; **~ in/out** *vi* hinein-/hinausströmen; **~ing the colour** *n* (*ceremony*) Fahnenparade *f*

trophy ['trəufɪ] *n* Trophäe *f*

tropic ['trɒpɪk] *n* Wendekreis *m*; **~al** *adj* tropisch

trot [trɒt] *n* Trott *m* ♦ *vi* trotten; **on the ~** (BRIT: fig: *inf*) in einer Tour

trouble ['trʌbl] *n* (*problems*) Ärger *m*; (*worry*) Sorge *f*; (*in country, industry*) Unruhen *pl*; (*effort*) Mühe *f*; (MED): **stomach ~** Magenbeschwerden *pl* ♦ *vt* (*disturb*) stören; **~s** *npl* (POL *etc*) Unruhen *pl*; **to ~ to do sth** sich bemühen, etw zu tun; **to be in ~** Probleme *or* Ärger haben; **to go to the ~ of doing sth** sich die Mühe machen, etw zu tun; **what's the ~?** was ist los?; (*to sick person*) wo fehlts?; **~d** *adj* (*person*) beunruhigt; (*country*) geplagt; **~-free** *adj* sorglos; **~maker** *n* Unruhestifter *m*; **~shooter** *n* Vermittler *m*; **~some** *adj* lästig, unangenehm; (*child*) schwierig

trough [trɒf] *n* Trog *m*; (*channel*) Rinne *f*, Kanal *m*; (MET) Tief *nt*

trousers ['trauzəz] *npl* Hose *f*

trout [traut] *n* Forelle *f*

trowel ['trauəl] *n* Kelle *f*

truant ['truənt] *n*: **to play ~** (BRIT) (die Schule) schwänzen

truce [tru:s] *n* Waffenstillstand *m*

truck [trʌk] *n* Lastwagen *m*; (RAIL) offene(r) Güterwagen *m*; **~ driver** *n* Lastwagenfahrer *m*; **~ farm** (US) *n* Gemüsegärtnerei *f*

trudge [trʌdʒ] *vi* sich (mühselig) dahinschleppen

true [tru:] *adj* (*exact*) wahr; (*genuine*) echt; (*friend*) treu

truffle ['trʌfl] *n* Trüffel *f or m*

truly ['tru:lɪ] *adv* wirklich; **yours ~** Ihr sehr ergebener

trump [trʌmp] *n* (CARDS) Trumpf *m*

trumpet ['trʌmpɪt] *n* Trompete *f*

truncheon ['trʌntʃən] *n* Gummiknüppel *m*

trundle ['trʌndl] *vt* schieben ♦ *vi*: **to ~**

along entlangrollen

trunk [trʌŋk] n (of tree) (Baum)stamm m; (ANAT) Rumpf m; (box) Truhe f, Überseekoffer m; (of elephant) Rüssel m; (US: AUT) Kofferraum m; **~s** npl (US: swimming **~s**) Badehose f

truss [trʌs] vt (also: **~ up**) fesseln

trust [trʌst] n (confidence) Vertrauen nt; (for land etc) Treuhandvermögen nt ♦ vt (rely on) vertrauen +dat, sich verlassen auf +acc; (hope) hoffen; (entrust): **to ~ sth to sb** jdm etw anvertrauen; **~ed** adj treu; **~ee** [trʌsˈtiː] n Vermögensverwalter m; **~ful** adj vertrauensvoll; **~ing** adj vertrauensvoll; **~worthy** adj vertrauenswürdig; (account) glaubwürdig

truth [truːθ] n Wahrheit f; **~ful** adj ehrlich

try [traɪ] n Versuch m ♦ vt (attempt) versuchen; (test) (aus)probieren; (JUR: person) unter Anklage stellen; (: case) verhandeln; (courage, patience) auf die Probe stellen ♦ vi (make effort) versuchen, sich bemühen; **to have a ~** es versuchen; **to ~ to do sth** versuchen, etw zu tun; **~ on** vt (dress) anprobieren; (hat) aufprobieren; **~ out** vt ausprobieren; **~ing** adj schwierig

T-shirt [ˈtiːʃɜːt] n T-Shirt nt

T-square [ˈtiːskwɛər] n Reißschiene f

tub [tʌb] n Wanne f, Kübel m; (for margarine etc) Becher m

tubby [ˈtʌbɪ] adj rundlich

tube [tjuːb] n Röhre f, Rohr nt; (for toothpaste etc) Tube f; (underground) U-Bahn f; (AUT) Schlauch m

tuberculosis [tjubəːkjuˈləʊsɪs] n Tuberkulose f

tube station n (in London) U-Bahnstation f; **tubing** [ˈtjuːbɪŋ] n Schlauch m; **tubular** [ˈtjuːbjulər] adj röhrenförmig

TUC (BRIT) n abbr = **Trades Union Congress**

tuck [tʌk] n (fold) Falte f, Einschlag m ♦ vt (put) stecken; (gather) fälteln, ein-

schlagen; **~ away** vt wegstecken; **~ in** vt hineinstecken; (blanket etc) fest stecken; (person) zudecken ♦ vi (eat) hineinhauen, zulangen; **~ up** vt (child) warm zudecken; **~ shop** n Süßwarenladen m

Tuesday [ˈtjuːzdɪ] n Dienstag m

tuft [tʌft] n Büschel m

tug [tʌg] n (jerk) Zerren nt, Ruck m; (NAUT) Schleppdampfer m ♦ vt, vi zerren, ziehen; (boat) schleppen; **~ o' war** n Tauziehen nt

tuition [tjuːˈɪʃən] n (BRIT) Unterricht m (: private ~) Privatunterricht m; (US school fees) Schulgeld nt

tulip [ˈtjuːlɪp] n Tulpe f

tumble [ˈtʌmbl] n (fall) Sturz m ♦ vi fallen, stürzen; **~ to** vt fus kapieren; **~down** adj baufällig; **~ dryer** (BRIT) n Trockner m; **~r** [ˈtʌmblər] n (glass) Trinkglas nt

tummy [ˈtʌmɪ] (inf) n Bauch m; **~ upset** n Magenverstimmung f

tumour [ˈtjuːmər] (US tumor) n Geschwulst f, Tumor m

tumultuous [tjuːˈmʌltjuəs] adj (welcome, applause etc) stürmisch

tuna [ˈtjuːnə] n T(h)unfisch m

tune [tjuːn] n Melodie f ♦ vt (MUS) stimmen; (AUT) richtig einstellen; **to sing in ~/out of ~** richtig/falsch singen; **to be out of ~ with** nicht harmonieren mit; **~ in** vi einschalten; **~ up** vi (MUS) stimmen; **~ful** adj melodisch; **~r** n (RAD) Tuner m; (person) (Instrumenten)stimmer m; **piano ~r** Klavierstimmer(in) m(f)

tunic [ˈtjuːnɪk] n Waffenrock m; (loose garment) lange Bluse f

tuning [ˈtjuːnɪŋ] n (RAD, AUT) Einstellen nt; (MUS) Stimmen nt; **~ fork** n Stimmgabel f

Tunisia [tjuːˈnɪzɪə] n Tunesien nt

tunnel [ˈtʌnl] n Tunnel m, Unterführung f ♦ vi einen Tunnel anlegen

turbulent [ˈtɜːbjulənt] adj stürmisch

tureen [təˈriːn] n Terrine f

turf [təːf] n Rasen m; (piece) Sode f ♦ vt mit Grassoden belegen; **~ out** (inf) vt rauswerfen
turgid ['təːdʒɪd] adj geschwollen
Turk [təːk] n Türke m, Türkin f
Turkey ['təːkɪ] n Türkei f
turkey ['təːkɪ] n Puter m, Truthahn m
Turkish ['təːkɪʃ] adj türkisch ♦ n (LING) Türkisch nt
turmoil ['təːmɔɪl] n Aufruhr m, Tumult m

turn [təːn] n (rotation) (Um)drehung f; (performance) (Programm)nummer f; (MED) Schock m ♦ vt (rotate) drehen; (change position of) umdrehen, wenden; (page) umblättern; (transform): **to ~ sth into sth** etw in etw acc verwandeln; (direct) zuwenden ♦ vi (rotate) sich drehen; (change direction: in car) abbiegen; (: wind) drehen; (~ round) umdrehen, wenden; (become) werden; (leaves) sich verfärben; (milk) sauer werden; (weather) umschlagen; **to do sb a good ~** jdm etwas Gutes tun; **it's your ~** du bist dran or an der Reihe; **in ~, by ~s** abwechselnd; **to take ~s** sich abwechseln; **it gave me quite a ~** das hat mich ziemlich erschreckt; **"no left ~"** (AUT) "Linksabbiegen verboten"; **~ away** vi sich abwenden; **~ back** vt umdrehen; (person) zurückschicken; (clock) zurückstellen ♦ vi umkehren; **~ down** vt (refuse) ablehnen; (fold down) umschlagen; **~ in** vi (go to bed) ins Bett gehen ♦ vt (fold inwards) einwärts biegen; **~ off** vi abbiegen ♦ vt ausschalten; (tap) zudrehen; (machine, electricity) abstellen; **~ on** vt (light) anschalten, einschalten; (tap) aufdrehen; (machine) anstellen; **~ out** vi (prove to be) sich erweisen; (people) sich entwickeln ♦ vt (light) ausschalten; (gas) abstellen; (produce) produzieren; **how did the cake ~ out?** wie ist der Kuchen geworden?; **~ over** vi (person) sich umdrehen ♦ vt (object) umdrehen, wenden; (page) umblättern; **~ round**

vi (person, vehicle) sich herumdrehen; (rotate) sich drehen; **~ up** vi auftauchen ♦ vt (collar) hochklappen, hochstellen; (nose) rümpfen; (increase: radio) lauter stellen; (: heat) höher drehen; **~ing** n (in road) Abzweigung f; **~ing point** n Wendepunkt m
turnip ['təːnɪp] n Steckrübe f
turnout ['təːnaut] n (Besucher)zahl f
turnover ['təːnəuvə] n Umsatz m; (of staff) Wechsel m
turnpike ['təːnpaɪk] (US) n gebührenpflichtige Straße f
turn-stile ['təːnstaɪl] n Drehkreuz nt; **~table** [-teɪbl] n (of record player) Plattenteller m; (RAIL) Drehscheibe f; **~-up** ['təːnʌp] (BRIT) n (on trousers) Aufschlag m
turpentine ['təːpəntaɪn] n Terpentin nt
turquoise ['təːkwɔɪz] n (gem) Türkis m; (colour) Türkis nt ♦ adj türkisfarben
turret ['tʌrɪt] n Turm m
turtle ['təːtl] n Schildkröte f; **~ neck (sweater)** n Pullover m mit Schildkrötkragen
tusk [tʌsk] n Stoßzahn m
tussle ['tʌsl] n Balgerei f
tutor ['tjuːtə] n (teacher) Privatlehrer m; (college instructor) Tutor m; **~ial** [tjuːˈtɔːrɪəl] n (UNIV) Kolloquium nt, Seminarübung f
tuxedo [tʌkˈsiːdəu] (US) n Smoking m
TV [tiːˈviː] n abbr (= television) TV nt
twang [twæŋ] n scharfe(r) Ton m; (of voice) Näseln nt
tweezers ['twiːzəz] npl Pinzette f
twelfth [twelfθ] adj zwölfte(r, s)
twelve [twelv] num zwölf; **at ~ o'clock** (midday) um 12 Uhr; (midnight) um null Uhr
twentieth ['twentɪəθ] adj zwanzigste(r, s)
twenty ['twentɪ] num zwanzig
twice [twaɪs] adv zweimal; **~ as much** doppelt so viel
twiddle ['twɪdl] vt, vi: **to ~ (with) sth** an etw dat herumdrehen; **to ~ one's**

thumbs (fig) Däumchen drehen

twig [twɪg] n dünne(r) Zweig m ♦ vt (inf) kapieren, merken

twilight ['twaɪlaɪt] n Zwielicht nt

twin [twɪn] n Zwilling m ♦ adj Zwillings-; (very similar) Doppel- ♦ vt (towns) zu Partnerstädten machen; ~-**bedded room** n Zimmer nt mit zwei Einzelbetten; ~ **beds** npl zwei (gleiche) Einzelbetten pl

twine [twaɪn] n Bindfaden m ♦ vi (plants) sich ranken

twinge [twɪndʒ] n stechende(r) Schmerz m, Stechen nt

twinkle ['twɪŋkl] n Funkeln nt, Blitzen nt ♦ vi funkeln

twirl [twɜːl] n Wirbel m ♦ vt, vi (herum)wirbeln

twist [twɪst] n (~ing) Drehung f; (bend) Kurve f ♦ vt (turn) drehen; (make crooked) verbiegen; (distort) verdrehen ♦ vi (wind) sich drehen; (curve) sich winden

twit [twɪt] (inf) n Idiot m

twitch [twɪtʃ] n Zucken nt ♦ vi zucken

two [tuː] num zwei; **to put ~ and ~ together** seine Schlüsse ziehen; ~-**door** adj zweitürig; ~-**faced** adj falsch; ~-**fold** adj, adv zweifach, doppelt; **to increase** ~-**fold** verdoppeln; ~-**piece** n zweiteilig; ~-**piece (suit)** n Zweiteiler m; ~-**piece (swimsuit)** n zweiteilige(r) Badeanzug m; ~-**seater** n (plane, car) Zweisitzer m; ~-**some** n Paar nt; ~-**way** adj (traffic) Gegen-

tycoon [taɪˈkuːn] n: **(business)** ~ (Industrie)magnat m

type [taɪp] n Typ m, Art f; (PRINT) Type f ♦ vt, vi Maschine schreiben, tippen; ~-**cast** adj (THEAT, TV) auf eine Rolle festgelegt; ~-**face** n Schrift f; ~-**script** n maschinegeschriebene(r) Text m; ~-**writer** n Schreibmaschine f; ~-**written** adj maschinegeschrieben

typhoid ['taɪfɔɪd] n Typhus m

typical ['tɪpɪkl] adj: ~ **(of)** typisch (für)

typify ['tɪpɪfaɪ] vt typisch sein für

typing ['taɪpɪŋ] n Maschineschreiben nt

typist ['taɪpɪst] n Maschinenschreiber(in) m(f), Tippse f(inf)

tyrant ['taɪərnt] n Tyrann m

tyre [taɪəʳ] (US **tire**) n Reifen m; ~ **pressure** n Reifendruck m

U, u

U-bend ['juːbend] n (in pipe) U-Bogen m

udder ['ʌdəʳ] n Euter nt

UFO ['juːfəu] n abbr (= unidentified flying object) UFO nt

ugh [əːh] excl hu

ugliness ['ʌglɪnɪs] n Hässlichkeit f

ugly ['ʌglɪ] adj hässlich; (bad) böse, schlimm

UHT abbr (= ultra heat treated): **UHT milk** H-Milch f

UK n abbr = **United Kingdom**

ulcer ['ʌlsəʳ] n Geschwür nt

Ulster ['ʌlstəʳ] n Ulster m

ulterior [ʌlˈtɪərɪəʳ] adj: ~ **motive** Hintergedanke m

ultimate ['ʌltɪmət] adj äußerste(r, s), allerletzte(r, s); ~**ly** adv schließlich, letzten Endes

ultrasound ['ʌltrəsaund] n (MED) Ultraschall m

umbilical cord [ʌmˈbɪlɪkl-] n Nabelschnur f

umbrella [ʌmˈbrelə] n Schirm m

umpire ['ʌmpaɪəʳ] n Schiedsrichter m ♦ vt, vi schiedsrichtern

umpteenth [ʌmpˈtiːnθ] (inf) adj zig; **for the ~ time** zum x-ten Mal

UN n abbr = **United Nations**

unable [ʌnˈeɪbl] adj: **to be ~ to do sth** etw nicht tun können

unacceptable [ʌnəkˈseptəbl] adj unannehmbar, nicht akzeptabel

unaccompanied [ʌnəˈkʌmpənɪd] adj ohne Begleitung

unaccountably [ʌnə'kauntəblɪ] *adv* unerklärlich

unaccustomed [ʌnə'kʌstəmd] *adj* nicht gewöhnt; (*unusual*) ungewohnt; **~ to** nicht gewöhnt an *+acc*

unanimous [juː'nænɪməs] *adj* einmütig; (*vote*) einstimmig; **~ly** *adv* einmütig; einstimmig

unarmed [ʌn'ɑːmd] *adj* unbewaffnet

unashamed [ʌnə'ʃeɪmd] *adj* schamlos

unassuming [ʌnə'sjuːmɪŋ] *adj* bescheiden

unattached [ʌnə'tætʃt] *adj* ungebunden

unattended [ʌnə'tendɪd] *adj* (*person*) unbeaufsichtigt; (*thing*) unbewacht

unauthorized [ʌn'ɔːθəraɪzd] *adj* unbefugt

unavoidable [ʌnə'vɔɪdəbl] *adj* unvermeidlich

unaware [ʌnə'weər] *adj:* **to be ~ of sth** sich *dat* einer Sache *gen* nicht bewusst sein; **~s** *adv* unversehens

unbalanced [ʌn'bælənst] *adj* unausgeglichen; (*mentally*) gestört

unbearable [ʌn'beərəbl] *adj* unerträglich

unbeatable [ʌn'biːtəbl] *adj* unschlagbar

unbeknown(st) [ʌnbɪ'nəun(st)] *adv:* **~ to me** ohne mein Wissen

unbelievable [ʌnbɪ'liːvəbl] *adj* unglaublich

unbend [ʌn'bend] (*irreg: like* bend) *vt* gerade biegen ♦ *vi* aus sich herausgehen

unbias(s)ed [ʌn'baɪəst] *adj* unparteiisch

unborn [ʌn'bɔːn] *adj* ungeboren

unbreakable [ʌn'breɪkəbl] *adj* unzerbrechlich

unbridled [ʌn'braɪdld] *adj* ungezügelt

unbroken [ʌn'brəukən] *adj* (*period*) ununterbrochen; (*spirit*) ungebrochen; (*record*) unübertroffen

unburden [ʌn'bɜːdn] *vt:* **to ~ o.s.** (jdm) sein Herz ausschütten

unbutton [ʌn'bʌtn] *vt* aufknöpfen

uncalled-for [ʌn'kɔːldfɔːr] *adj* unnötig

uncanny [ʌn'kænɪ] *adj* unheimlich

unceasing [ʌn'siːsɪŋ] *adj* unaufhörlich

unceremonious [ʌnserɪ'məunɪəs] *adj* (*abrupt, rude*) brüsk; (*exit, departure*) überstürzt

uncertain [ʌn'sɜːtn] *adj* unsicher; (*doubtful*) ungewiss; (*unreliable*) unbeständig; (*vague*) undeutlich, vag(e); **~ty** *n* Ungewissheit *f*

unchanged [ʌn'tʃeɪndʒd] *adj* unverändert

unchecked [ʌn'tʃekt] *adj* ungeprüft; (*not stopped: advance*) ungehindert

uncivilized [ʌn'sɪvɪlaɪzd] *adj* unzivilisiert

uncle ['ʌŋkl] *n* Onkel *m*

uncomfortable [ʌn'kʌmfətəbl] *adj* unbequem, ungemütlich

uncommon [ʌn'kɒmən] *adj* ungewöhnlich; (*outstanding*) außergewöhnlich

uncompromising [ʌn'kɒmprəmaɪzɪŋ] *adj* kompromisslos, unnachgiebig

unconcerned [ʌnkən'sɜːnd] *adj* unbekümmert; (*indifferent*) gleichgültig

unconditional [ʌnkən'dɪʃənl] *adj* bedingungslos

unconscious [ʌn'kɒnʃəs] *adj* (MED) bewusstlos; (*not meant*) unbeabsichtigt ♦ *n:* **the ~** das Unbewusste; **~ly** *adv* unbewusst

uncontrollable [ʌnkən'trəuləbl] *adj* unkontrollierbar, unbändig

unconventional [ʌnkən'venʃənl] *adj* unkonventionell

uncouth [ʌn'kuːθ] *adj* grob

uncover [ʌn'kʌvər] *vt* aufdecken

undecided [ʌndɪ'saɪdɪd] *adj* unschlüssig

undeniable [ʌndɪ'naɪəbl] *adj* unleugbar

under ['ʌndər] *prep* unter ♦ *adv* darunter; **~ there** da drunter; **~ repair** in Reparatur

underage [ʌndər'eɪdʒ] *adj* minderjährig

undercarriage ['ʌndəkærɪdʒ] (BRIT) n (AVIAT) Fahrgestell nt

undercharge [ʌndə'tʃɑːdʒ] vt: **to ~ sb** jdm zu wenig berechnen

undercoat ['ʌndəkəʊt] n (paint) Grundierung f

undercover [ʌndə'kʌvər] adj Geheim-

undercurrent ['ʌndəkʌrnt] n Unterströmung f

undercut [ʌndə'kʌt] (irreg: like cut) vt unterbieten

underdeveloped [ʌndədɪ'veləpt] adj Entwicklungs-, unterentwickelt

underdog ['ʌndədɒg] n Unterlegene(r) mf

underdone [ʌndə'dʌn] adj (COOK) nicht gar, nicht durchgebraten

underestimate ['ʌndər'estɪmeɪt] vt unterschätzen

underexposed ['ʌndərɪks'pəʊzd] adj unterbelichtet

underfoot [ʌndə'fʊt] adv am Boden

undergo [ʌndə'gəʊ] (irreg: like go) vt (experience) durchmachen; (test, operation) sich unterziehen +dat

undergraduate [ʌndə'grædjuɪt] n Student(in) m(f)

underground ['ʌndəgraʊnd] n U-Bahn f ♦ adj Untergrund-

undergrowth ['ʌndəgrəʊθ] n Gestrüpp nt, Unterholz nt

underhand(ed) [ʌndə'hænd(ɪd)] adj hinterhältig

underlie [ʌndə'laɪ] (irreg: like lie) vt zugrunde or zu Grunde liegen +dat

underline [ʌndə'laɪn] vt unterstreichen; (emphasize) betonen

underling ['ʌndəlɪŋ] n Handlanger m

undermine [ʌndə'maɪn] vt untergraben

underneath [ʌndə'niːθ] adv darunter ♦ prep unter

underpaid [ʌndə'peɪd] adj unterbezahlt

underpants ['ʌndəpænts] npl Unterhose f

underpass ['ʌndəpɑːs] (BRIT) n Unterführung f

underprivileged [ʌndə'prɪvɪlɪdʒd] adj benachteiligt, unterprivilegiert

underrate [ʌndə'reɪt] vt unterschätzen

undershirt ['ʌndəʃɜːt] (US) n Unterhemd nt

undershorts ['ʌndəʃɔːts] (US) npl Unterhose f

underside ['ʌndəsaɪd] n Unterseite f

underskirt ['ʌndəskɜːt] (BRIT) n Unterrock m

understand [ʌndə'stænd] (irreg: like stand) vt, vi verstehen; **I ~ that ...** ich habe gehört, dass ...; **am I to ~ that ...?** soll das (etwa) heißen, dass ...?; **what do you ~ by that?** was verstehen Sie darunter?; **it is understood that ...** es wurde vereinbart, dass ...; **to make o.s. understood** sich verständlich machen; **is that understood?** ist das klar?; **~able** adj verständlich; **~ing** n Verständnis nt ♦ adj verständnisvoll

understatement ['ʌndəsteɪtmənt] n (quality) Untertreibung f; **that's an ~!** das ist untertrieben!

understood [ʌndə'stʊd] pt, pp of **understand** ♦ adj klar; (implied) angenommen

understudy ['ʌndəstʌdɪ] n Ersatz(schau)spieler(in) m(f)

undertake [ʌndə'teɪk] (irreg: like take) vt unternehmen ♦ vi: **to ~ to do sth** sich verpflichten, etw zu tun

undertaker ['ʌndəteɪkər] n Leichenbestatter m

undertaking ['ʌndəteɪkɪŋ] n (enterprise) Unternehmen nt; (promise) Verpflichtung f

undertone ['ʌndətəʊn] n: **in an ~** mit gedämpfter Stimme

underwater ['ʌndə'wɔːtə] adv unter Wasser ♦ adj Unterwasser-

underwear ['ʌndəweə] n Unterwäsche f

underworld ['ʌndəwɜːld] n (of crime)

Unterwelt f

underwriter ['Andəraitə'] n Assekurant m

undesirable [Andi'zaiərəbl] adj unerwünscht

undies ['Andiz] (inf) npl (Damen)unterwäsche f

undisputed ['Andis'pju:tid] adj unbestritten

undo [An'du:] (irreg: like **do**) vt (unfasten) öffnen, aufmachen; (work) zunichte machen; **~ing** n Verderben nt

undoubted [An'dautid] adj unbezweifelt; **~ly** adv zweifellos, ohne Zweifel

undress [An'dres] vt ausziehen ♦ vi sich ausziehen

undue [An'dju:] adj übermäßig

undulating ['Andjuleitiŋ] adj wellenförmig; (country) wellig

unduly [An'dju:li] adv übermäßig

unearth [An'ə:θ] vt (dig up) ausgraben; (discover) ans Licht bringen

unearthly [An'ə:θli] adj (hour) nachtschlafen

uneasy [An'i:zi] adj (worried) unruhig; (feeling) ungut

uneconomic(al) [Ani:kə'nɔmik(l)] adj unwirtschaftlich

uneducated [An'edjukeitid] adj ungebildet

unemployed [Anim'plɔid] adj arbeitslos ♦ npl: **the ~** die Arbeitslosen pl

unemployment [Anim'plɔimənt] n Arbeitslosigkeit f

unending [An'endiŋ] adj endlos

unerring [An'ə:riŋ] adj unfehlbar

uneven [An'i:vn] adj (surface) uneben; (quality) ungleichmäßig

unexpected [Aniks'pektid] adj unerwartet; **~ly** adv unerwartet

unfailing [An'feiliŋ] adj nie versagend

unfair [An'feə'] adj ungerecht, unfair

unfaithful [An'feiθful] adj untreu

unfamiliar [Anfə'miliə'] adj ungewohnt; (person, subject) unbekannt; **to be ~ with** nicht kennen +acc, nicht vertraut sein mit

unfashionable [An'fæʃnəbl] adj unmodern; (area etc) nicht in Mode

unfasten [An'fɑ:sn] vt öffnen, aufmachen

unfavourable [An'feivrəbl] (US **unfavorable**) adj ungünstig

unfeeling [An'fi:liŋ] adj gefühllos, kalt

unfinished [An'finiʃt] adj unvollendet

unfit [An'fit] adj ungeeignet; (in bad health) nicht fit; **~ for sth** zu or für etw ungeeignet

unfold [An'fəuld] vt entfalten; (paper) auseinander falten ♦ vi (develop) sich entfalten

unforeseen ['Anfɔ:'si:n] adj unvorhergesehen

unforgettable [Anfə'getəbl] adj unvergesslich

unforgivable [Anfə'givəbl] adj unverzeihlich

unfortunate [An'fɔ:tʃənət] adj unglücklich, bedauerlich; **~ly** adv leider

unfounded [An'faundid] adj unbegründet

unfriendly [An'frendli] adj unfreundlich

ungainly [An'geinli] adj linkisch

ungodly [An'gɔdli] adj (hour) nachtschlafend; (row) heillos

ungrateful [An'greitful] adj undankbar

unhappiness [An'hæpinis] n Unglück nt, Unglückseligkeit f

unhappy [An'hæpi] adj unglücklich; **~ with** (arrangements etc) unzufrieden mit

unharmed [An'hɑ:md] adj wohlbehalten, unversehrt

UNHCR n abbr (= United Nations High Commission for Refugees) Flüchtlingshochkommissariat der Vereinten Nationen

unhealthy [An'helθi] adj ungesund

unheard-of [An'hə:dɔv] adj unerhört

unhurt [An'hə:t] adj unverletzt

unidentified [Anai'dentifaid] adj unbekannt, nicht identifiziert

uniform ['ju:nifɔ:m] n Uniform f ♦ adj

einheitlich; **~ity** [ju:nı'fɔːmıtı] n Einheitlichkeit f

unify ['ju:nıfaı] vt vereinigen

unilateral [ju:nı'lætərəl] adj einseitig

uninhabited [ʌnın'hæbıtıd] adj unbewohnt

unintentional [ʌnın'tenʃənəl] adj unabsichtlich

union ['ju:nıən] n (uniting) Vereinigung f; (alliance) Bund m, Union f; (trade ~) Gewerkschaft f; **U~ Jack** n Union Jack m

unique [ju:'ni:k] adj einzig(artig)

UNISON n Gewerkschaft der Angestellten im öffentlichen Dienst

unison ['ju:nısn] n Einstimmigkeit f; **in ~** einstimmig

unit ['ju:nıt] n Einheit f; **kitchen ~** Küchenelement nt

unite [ju:'naıt] vt vereinigen ♦ vi sich vereinigen; **~d** adj vereinigt; (together) vereint; **U~d Kingdom** n Vereinigte(s) Königreich nt; **U~d Nations (Organization)** n Vereinte Nationen pl; **U~d States (of America)** n Vereinigte Staaten pl (von Amerika)

unit trust (BRIT) n Treuhandgesellschaft f

unity ['ju:nıtı] n Einheit f; (agreement) Einigkeit f

universal [ju:nı'vɜːsl] adj allgemein

universe ['ju:nıvɜːs] n (Welt)all nt

university [ju:nı'vɜːsıtı] n Universität f

unjust [ʌn'dʒʌst] adj ungerecht

unkempt [ʌn'kempt] adj ungepflegt

unkind [ʌn'kaınd] adj unfreundlich

unknown [ʌn'nəun] adj: **~ (to sb)** (jdm) unbekannt

unlawful [ʌn'lɔːful] adj illegal

unleaded ['ʌn'ledıd] adj bleifrei, unverbleit; **I use ~** ich fahre bleifrei

unleash [ʌn'liːʃ] vt entfesseln

unless [ʌn'les] conj wenn nicht, es sei denn; **~ he comes** es sei denn, er kommt; **~ otherwise stated** sofern nicht anders angegeben

unlike [ʌn'laık] adj unähnlich ♦ prep im

Gegensatz zu

unlikely [ʌn'laıklı] adj (not likely) unwahrscheinlich; (unexpected: combination etc) merkwürdig

unlimited [ʌn'lımıtıd] adj unbegrenzt

unlisted ['ʌn'lıstıd] (US) adj nicht im Telefonbuch stehend

unload [ʌn'ləud] vt entladen

unlock [ʌn'lɔk] vt aufschließen

unlucky [ʌn'lʌkı] adj unglücklich; (person) unglückselig; **to be ~** Pech haben

unmarried [ʌn'mærıd] adj unverheiratet, ledig

unmask [ʌn'mɑːsk] vt entlarven

unmistakable [ʌnmıs'teıkəbl] adj unverkennbar

unmitigated [ʌn'mıtıgeıtıd] adj ungemildert, ganz

unnatural [ʌn'nætʃrəl] adj unnatürlich

unnecessary [ʌn'nesəsərı] adj unnötig

unnoticed [ʌn'nəutıst] adj: **to go ~** unbemerkt bleiben

UNO ['ju:nəu] n abbr = United Nations Organization

unobtainable [ʌnəb'teınəbl] adj: **this number is ~** kein Anschluss unter dieser Nummer

unobtrusive [ʌnəb'tru:sıv] adj unauffällig

unofficial [ʌnə'fıʃl] adj inoffiziell

unpack [ʌn'pæk] vt, vi auspacken

unparalleled [ʌn'pærəleld] adj beispiellos

unpleasant [ʌn'pleznt] adj unangenehm

unplug [ʌn'plʌg] vt den Stecker herausziehen von

unpopular [ʌn'pɔpjulə*] adj (person) unbeliebt; (decision etc) unpopulär

unprecedented [ʌn'presıdentıd] adj beispiellos

unpredictable [ʌnprı'dıktəbl] adj unvorhersehbar; (weather, person) unberechenbar

unprofessional [ʌnprə'feʃənl] adj unprofessionell

UNPROFOR n abbr (= United Nations Protection Force) UNPROFOR f

unqualified [ʌn'kwɒlɪfaɪd] adj (success) uneingeschränkt, voll; (person) unqualifiziert

unquestionably [ʌn'kwestʃənəblɪ] adv fraglos

unravel [ʌn'rævl] vt (disentangle) ausfasern, entwirren; (solve) lösen

unreal [ʌn'rɪəl] adj unwirklich

unrealistic ['ʌnrɪə'lɪstɪk] adj unrealistisch

unreasonable [ʌn'riːznəbl] adj unvernünftig; (demand) übertrieben

unrelated [ʌnrɪ'leɪtɪd] adj ohne Beziehung; (family) nicht verwandt

unrelenting [ʌnrɪ'lentɪŋ] adj unerbittlich

unreliable [ʌnrɪ'laɪəbl] adj unzuverlässig

unremitting [ʌnrɪ'mɪtɪŋ] adj (efforts, attempts) unermüdlich

unreservedly [ʌnrɪ'zɜːvɪdlɪ] adv offen; (believe, trust) uneingeschränkt; (cry) rückhaltlos

unrest [ʌn'rest] n (discontent) Unruhe f; (fighting) Unruhen pl

unroll [ʌn'rəʊl] vt aufrollen

unruly [ʌn'ruːlɪ] adj (child) undiszipliniert; schwer lenkbar

unsafe [ʌn'seɪf] adj nicht sicher

unsaid [ʌn'sed] adj: **to leave sth ~** etw ungesagt lassen

unsatisfactory ['ʌnsætɪs'fæktərɪ] adj unbefriedigend; unzulänglich

unsavoury [ʌn'seɪvərɪ] (US **unsavory**) adj (fig) widerwärtig

unscathed [ʌn'skeɪðd] adj unversehrt

unscrew [ʌn'skruː] vt aufschrauben

unscrupulous [ʌn'skruːpjʊləs] adj skrupellos

unsettled [ʌn'setld] adj (person) rastlos; (weather) wechselhaft

unshaven [ʌn'ʃeɪvn] adj unrasiert

unsightly [ʌn'saɪtlɪ] adj unansehnlich

unskilled [ʌn'skɪld] adj ungelernt

unspeakable [ʌn'spiːkəbl] adj (joy)

unsagbar; (crime) scheußlich

unstable [ʌn'steɪbl] adj instabil; (mentally) labil

unsteady [ʌn'stedɪ] adj unsicher

unstuck [ʌn'stʌk] adj: **to come ~** sich lösen; (fig) ins Wasser fallen

unsuccessful [ʌnsək'sesful] adj erfolglos

unsuitable [ʌn'suːtəbl] adj unpassend

unsure [ʌn'ʃʊə] adj unsicher; **to be ~ of o.s.** unsicher sein

unsuspecting [ʌnsəs'pektɪŋ] adj nichts ahnend

unsympathetic ['ʌnsɪmpə'θetɪk] adj gefühllos; (response) abweisend; (unlikeable) unsympathisch

untapped [ʌn'tæpt] adj (resources) ungenützt

unthinkable [ʌn'θɪŋkəbl] adj unvorstellbar

untidy [ʌn'taɪdɪ] adj unordentlich

untie [ʌn'taɪ] vt aufschnüren

until [ən'tɪl] prep, conj bis; **~ he comes** bis er kommt; **~ then** bis dann; **~ now** bis jetzt

untimely [ʌn'taɪmlɪ] adj (death) vorzeitig

untold [ʌn'təʊld] adj unermesslich

untoward [ʌntə'wɔːd] adj widrig

untranslatable [ʌntrænz'leɪtəbl] adj unübersetzbar

unused [ʌn'juːzd] adj unbenutzt

unusual [ʌn'juːʒʊəl] adj ungewöhnlich

unveil [ʌn'veɪl] vt enthüllen

unwanted [ʌn'wɒntɪd] adj unerwünscht

unwavering [ʌn'weɪvərɪŋ] adj standhaft, unerschütterlich

unwelcome [ʌn'welkəm] adj (at a bad time) unwillkommen; (unpleasant) unerfreulich

unwell [ʌn'wel] adj: **to feel** or **be ~** sich nicht wohl fühlen

unwieldy [ʌn'wiːldɪ] adj sperrig

unwilling [ʌn'wɪlɪŋ] adj: **to be ~ to do sth** nicht bereit sein, etw zu tun; **~ly** adv widerwillig

unwind [ʌn'waɪnd] (*irreg: like* **wind²**) *vt* abwickeln ♦ *vi* (*relax*) sich entspannen

unwise [ʌn'waɪz] *adj* unklug

unwitting [ʌn'wɪtɪŋ] *adj* unwissentlich

unworkable [ʌn'wə:kəbl] *adj* (*plan*) undurchführbar

unworthy [ʌn'wə:ðɪ] *adj* (*person*): ~ (**of** **sth**) (einer Sache *gen*) nicht wert

unwrap [ʌn'ræp] *vt* auspacken

unwritten [ʌn'rɪtn] *adj* ungeschrieben

up [ʌp] *prep*: **to be up sth** oben auf etw *dat* sein; **to go up sth** (auf) etw *acc* hinaufgehen; **go up that road** ge- hen Sie die Straße hinauf

♦ *adv* 1 (*upwards, higher*) oben; **put it** **up a bit higher** stell es etwas weiter nach oben; **up there** da oben, dort oben; **up above** hoch oben

2: **to be up** (*out of bed*) auf sein; (*prices, level*) gestiegen sein; (*building, tent*) stehen

3: **up to** (*as far as*) bis; **up to now** bis jetzt

4: **to be up to** (*depending on*): **it's up to you** das hängt von dir ab; (*equal to*): **he's not up to it** (*job, task etc*) er ist dem nicht gewachsen; (*inf: be do- ing: showing disapproval, suspicion*): **what is he up to?** was führt er im Schilde?; **it's not up to me to decide** die Entscheidung liegt nicht bei mir; **his work is not up to the required** **standard** seine Arbeit entspricht nicht dem geforderten Niveau

♦ *n*: **ups and downs** (*in life, career*) Höhen und Tiefen *pl*

up-and-coming [ʌpənd'kʌmɪŋ] *adj* aufstrebend

upbringing ['ʌpbrɪŋɪŋ] *n* Erziehung *f*

update [ʌp'deɪt] *vt* auf den neuesten Stand bringen

upgrade [ʌp'greɪd] *vt* höher einstufen

upheaval [ʌp'hi:vl] *n* Umbruch *m*

uphill ['ʌp'hɪl] *adj* ansteigend; (*fig*)

mühsam ♦ *adv*: **to go** ~ bergauf gehen/fahren

uphold [ʌp'həʊld] (*irreg: like* **hold**) *vt* unterstützen

upholstery [ʌp'həʊlstərɪ] *n* Polster *nt*; Polsterung *f*

upkeep ['ʌpki:p] *n* Instandhaltung *f*

upon [ə'pɒn] *prep* auf

upper ['ʌpə'] *n* (*on shoe*) Oberleder *nt* ♦ *adj* obere(r, s), höhere(r, s); **to have** **the ~ hand** die Oberhand haben; **~** **class** *adj* vornehm; **~most** *adj* ober- ste(r, s), höchste(r, s); **what was** **~most in my mind** was mich in erster Linie beschäftigte; **~ sixth** (*BRIT: SCOL*) *n* Abschlussklasse *f*

upright ['ʌpraɪt] *adj* aufrecht

uprising ['ʌpraɪzɪŋ] *n* Aufstand *m*

uproar ['ʌprɔ:'] *n* Aufruhr *m*

uproot [ʌp'ru:t] *vt* ausreißen

upset [*n* 'ʌpset, *vb, adj* ʌp'set] (*irreg: like* **set**) *n* Aufregung *f* ♦ *vt* (*overturn*) um- werfen; (*disturb*) aufregen, bestürzen; (*plans*) durcheinander bringen ♦ *adj* (*person*) aufgeregt; (*stomach*) verdor- ben

upshot ['ʌpʃɒt] *n* (End)ergebnis *nt*

upside-down ['ʌpsaɪd-] *adv* verkehrt herum

upstairs [ʌp'steəz] *adv* oben; (*go*) nach oben ♦ *adj* (*room*) obere(r, s), Ober- ♦ *n* obere(s) Stockwerk *nt*

upstart ['ʌpstɑ:t] *n* Emporkömmling *m*

upstream [ʌp'stri:m] *adv* stromauf- wärts

uptake ['ʌpteɪk] *n*: **to be quick on the** **~** schnell begreifen; **to be slow on** **the ~** schwer von Begriff sein

uptight [ʌp'taɪt] (*inf*) *adj* (*nervous*) ner- vös; (*inhibited*) verklemmt

up-to-date ['ʌptə'deɪt] *adj* (*clothes*) modisch, modern; (*information*) neu- este(r, s)

upturn ['ʌptɜ:n] *n* Aufschwung *m*

upward ['ʌpwəd] *adj* nach oben ge- richtet; **~(s)** *adv* aufwärts

uranium [juə'reɪnɪəm] *n* Uran *nt*

urban ['ə:bən] *adj* städtisch, Stadt-; **~ clearway** *n* Stadtautobahn *f*

urchin ['ə:tʃɪn] *n* (*boy*) Schlingel *m*; (*sea* ~) Seeigel *m*

urge [ə:dʒ] *n* Drang *m* ♦ *vt*: **to ~ sb to do sth** jdn (dazu) drängen, etw zu tun

urgency ['ə:dʒənsɪ] *n* Dringlichkeit *f*

urgent ['ə:dʒənt] *adj* dringend

urinal ['juərɪnl] *n* (*public*) Pissoir *nt*

urinate ['juərɪneɪt] *vi* urinieren

urine ['juərɪn] *n* Urin *m*, Harn *m*

urn [ə:n] *n* Urne *f*; (*tea* ~) Teemaschine *f*

US *n abbr* = **United States**

us [ʌs] *pron* uns; *see also* **me**

USA *n abbr* = **United States of America**

usage ['ju:zɪdʒ] *n* Gebrauch *m*; (*esp* LING) Sprachgebrauch *m*

use [*n* ju:s, *vb* ju:z] *n* (*employment*) Gebrauch *m*; (*point*) Zweck *m* ♦ *vt* gebrauchen; **in ~** in Gebrauch; **out of ~** außer Gebrauch; **to be of ~** nützlich sein; **it's no ~** es hat keinen Zweck; **what's the ~?** was solls?; **~d to** (*accustomed to*) gewöhnt an +*acc*; **she ~d to live here** (*formerly*) sie hat früher mal hier gewohnt; **~ up** *vt* aufbrauchen, verbrauchen; **~d** *adj* (*car*) Gebraucht-; **~ful** *adj* nützlich; **~fulness** *n* Nützlichkeit *f*; **~less** *adj* nutzlos, unnütz; **~r** *n* Benutzer *m*; **~r-friendly** (*computer*) benutzerfreundlich

usher ['ʌʃə*] *n* Platzanweiser *m*; **~ette** [ʌʃə'ret] *n* Platzanweiserin *f*

usual ['ju:ʒuəl] *adj* gewöhnlich, üblich; **as ~** wie üblich; **~ly** *adv* gewöhnlich

usurp [ju:'zə:p] *vt* an sich reißen

utensil [ju:'tensl] *n* Gerät *nt*; **kitchen ~s** Küchengeräte *pl*

uterus ['ju:tərəs] *n* Gebärmutter *f*

utilitarian [ju:tɪlɪ'teərɪən] *adj* Nützlichkeits-

utility [ju:'tɪlɪtɪ] *n* (*usefulness*) Nützlichkeit *f*; (*also*: **public ~**) öffentliche(r) Versorgungsbetrieb *m*; **~**

room *n* Hauswirtschaftsraum *m*

utilize ['ju:tɪlaɪz] *vt* benützen

utmost ['ʌtməust] *adj* äußerste(r, s) ♦ *n*: **to do one's ~** sein Möglichstes tun

utter ['ʌtə*] *adj* äußerste(r, s), höchste(r, s), völlig ♦ *vt* äußern, aussprechen; **~ance** *n* Äußerung *f*; **~ly** *adv* äußerst, absolut, völlig

U-turn ['ju:'tə:n] *n* (AUT) Kehrtwendung *f*

V, v

v. *abbr* = **verse**; **versus**; **volt**; (= *vide*) **see**

vacancy ['veɪkənsɪ] *n* (BRIT: *job*) offene Stelle *f*; (*room*) freie(s) Zimmer *nt*; **"no vacancies"** „belegt"

vacant ['veɪkənt] *adj* leer; (*unoccupied*) frei; (*house*) leer stehend, unbewohnt; (*stupid*) (gedanken)leer; **~ lot** (US) *n* unbebaute(s) Grundstück *nt*

vacate [və'keɪt] *vt* (*seat*) frei machen; (*room*) räumen

vacation [və'keɪʃən] *n* Ferien *pl*, Urlaub *m*; **~ist** (US) *n* Ferienreisende(r) *f(m)*

vaccinate ['væksɪneɪt] *vt* impfen

vaccine ['væksi:n] *n* Impfstoff *m*

vacuum ['vækjum] *n* Vakuum *nt*; **~ bottle** (US) *n* Thermosflasche *f*; **~ cleaner** *n* Staubsauger *m*; **~ flask** (BRIT) *n* Thermosflasche *f*; **~-packed** *adj* vakuumversiegelt

vagina [və'dʒaɪnə] *n* Scheide *f*

vague [veɪg] *adj* vag(e); (*absentminded*) geistesabwesend; **~ly** *adv* unbestimmt, vag(e)

vain [veɪn] *adj* eitel; (*attempt*) vergeblich; **in ~** vergebens, umsonst

valentine ['væləntaɪn] *n* (*also*: **~ card**) Valentinsgruß *m*; **V~'s Day** *n* Valentinstag *m*

valet ['vælɪt] *n* Kammerdiener *m*

valiant ['væliənt] *adj* tapfer

valid ['vælɪd] *adj* gültig; (*argument*) stichhaltig; (*objection*) berechtigt; **~ity**

[vəˈlɪdɪt] n Gültigkeit f

valley [ˈvælɪ] n Tal nt

valour [ˈvælə*] (US **valor**) n Tapferkeit f

valuable [ˈvæljuəbl] adj wertvoll; (time) kostbar; **~s** npl Wertsachen pl

valuation [væljuˈeɪʃən] n (FIN) Schätzung f; Beurteilung f

value [ˈvæljuː] n Wert m; (usefulness) Nutzen m ♦ vt (prize) (hoch) schätzen, werthalten; (estimate) schätzen; **~ added tax** (BRIT) n Mehrwertsteuer f; **~d** adj (hoch) geschätzt

valve [vælv] n Ventil n; (BIOL) Klappe f; (RAD) Röhre f

van [væn] n Lieferwagen m; (BRIT: RAIL) Waggon m

vandal [ˈvændl] n Rowdy m; **~ism** n mutwillige Beschädigung f; **~ize** vt mutwillig beschädigen

vanguard [ˈvængɑːd] n (fig) Spitze f

vanilla [vəˈnɪlə] n Vanille f; **~ ice cream** n Vanilleeis nt

vanish [ˈvænɪʃ] vi verschwinden

vanity [ˈvænɪtɪ] n Eitelkeit f; **~ case** n Schminkkoffer m

vantage [ˈvɑːntɪdʒ] n: **~ point** gute(r) Aussichtspunkt m

vapour [ˈveɪpə*] (US **vapor**) n (mist) Dunst m; (gas) Dampf m

variable [ˈveərɪəbl] adj wechselhaft, veränderlich; (speed, height) regulierbar

variance [ˈveərɪəns] n: **to be at ~ (with)** nicht übereinstimmen (mit)

variation [veərɪˈeɪʃən] n Variation f; (in prices etc) Schwankung f

varicose [ˈværɪkəus] adj: **~ veins** Krampfadern pl

varied [ˈveərɪd] adj unterschiedlich; (life) abwechslungsreich

variety [vəˈraɪətɪ] n (difference) Abwechslung f; (varied collection) Vielfalt f; (COMM) Auswahl f; (sort) Sorte f, Art f; **~ show** n Varietee nt, Varieté nt

various [ˈveərɪəs] adj verschieden; (several) mehrere

varnish [ˈvɑːnɪʃ] n Lack m; (on pottery)

Glasur f ♦ vt lackieren

vary [ˈveərɪ] vt (alter) verändern; (give variety to) abwechslungsreicher gestalten ♦ vi sich (ver)ändern; (prices) schwanken; (weather) unterschiedlich sein

vase [vɑːz] n Vase f

Vaseline [ˈvæsɪliːn] ® n Vaseline f

vast [vɑːst] adj weit, groß, riesig

VAT [væt] n abbr (= value added tax) MwSt f

vat [væt] n große(s) Fass nt

vault [vɔːlt] n (of roof) Gewölbe nt; (tomb) Gruft f; (in bank) Tresorraum m; (leap) Sprung m ♦ vt (also: **~ over**) überspringen

vaunted [ˈvɔːntɪd] adj: **much~** viel gerühmt

VCR n abbr = **video cassette recorder**

VD n abbr = **venereal disease**

VDU n abbr = **visual display unit**

veal [viːl] n Kalbfleisch nt

veer [vɪə*] vi sich drehen; (of car) ausscheren

vegan [ˈviːgən] n Vegan m, radikale(r) Vegetarier(in) m(f)

vegeburger [ˈvedʒɪbɜːgə*] n vegetarische Frikadelle f

vegetable [ˈvedʒtəbl] n Gemüse nt ♦ adj Gemüse-; **~s** npl (CULIN) Gemüse nt

vegetarian [vedʒɪˈteərɪən] n Vegetarier(in) m(f) ♦ adj vegetarisch

vegetate [ˈvedʒɪteɪt] vi (dahin)vegetieren

veggieburger [ˈvedʒɪbɜːgə*] n = **vegeburger**

vehement [ˈviːɪmənt] adj heftig

vehicle [ˈviːɪkl] n Fahrzeug nt; (fig) Mittel nt

veil [veɪl] n (also fig) Schleier m ♦ vt verschleiern

vein [veɪn] n Ader f; (mood) Stimmung f

velocity [vɪˈlɒsɪtɪ] n Geschwindigkeit f

velvet [ˈvelvɪt] n Samt m ♦ adj Samt-

vendetta [venˈdetə] n Fehde f; (in family) Blutrache f

vending machine ['vendɪŋ-] n Automat m

vendor ['vendə'] n Verkäufer m

veneer [və'nɪə'] n Furnier(holz) nt; (fig) äußere(r) Anstrich m

venereal disease [vɪ'nɪərɪəl-] n Geschlechtskrankheit f

Venetian blind [vɪ'niːʃən-] n Jalousie f

vengeance ['vendʒəns] n Rache f; **with a ~** gewaltig

venison ['venɪsn] n Reh(fleisch) nt

venom ['venəm] n Gift nt

vent [vent] n Öffnung f; (in coat) Schlitz m; (fig) Ventil nt ♦ vt (emotion) abreagieren

ventilate ['ventɪleɪt] vt belüften; **ventilator** ['ventɪleɪtə'] n Ventilator m

ventriloquist [ven'trɪləkwɪst] n Bauchredner m

venture ['ventʃə'] n Unternehmung f, Projekt nt ♦ vt wagen; (life) aufs Spiel setzen ♦ vi sich wagen

venue ['venjuː] n Schauplatz m

verb [vɜːb] n Zeitwort m, Verb nt; **~al** adj (spoken) mündlich; (translation) wörtlich; **~ally** adv mündlich

verbatim [vɜː'beɪtɪm] adv Wort für Wort ♦ adj wortwörtlich

verbose [vɜː'bəus] adj wortreich

verdict ['vɜːdɪkt] n Urteil nt

verge [vɜːdʒ] n (BRIT) Rand m ♦ vi: **to ~ on** grenzen an +acc; **"soft ~s"** (BRIT, AUT) „Seitenstreifen nicht befahrbar"; **on the ~ of doing sth** im Begriff, etw zu tun

verify ['verɪfaɪ] vt (über)prüfen; (confirm) bestätigen; (theory) beweisen

veritable ['verɪtəbl] adj wirklich, echt

vermin ['vɜːmɪn] npl Ungeziefer nt

vermouth ['vɜːməθ] n Wermut m

versatile ['vɜːsətaɪl] adj vielseitig

verse [vɜːs] n (poetry) Poesie f; (stanza) Strophe f; (of Bible) Vers m; **in ~** in Versform

version ['vɜːʃən] n Version f; (of car) Modell nt

versus ['vɜːsəs] prep gegen

vertebrate ['vɜːtɪbrɪt] adj Wirbel-

vertical ['vɜːtɪkl] adj senkrecht

vertigo ['vɜːtɪgəu] n Schwindel m

very ['verɪ] adv sehr ♦ adj (extreme) äußerste(r, s); **the ~ book** which genau das Buch, welches; **the ~ last** ... der/die/das allerletzte ...; **at the ~ least** allerwenigstens; **~ much** sehr

vessel ['vesl] n (ship) Schiff nt; (container) Gefäß nt

vest [vest] n (BRIT) Unterhemd nt; (US: waistcoat) Weste f

vested interests ['vestɪd-] npl finanzielle Beteiligung f; (people) finanziell Beteiligte pl; (fig) persönliche(s) Interesse nt

vestige ['vestɪdʒ] n Spur f

vestry ['vestrɪ] n Sakristei f

vet [vet] n abbr (= veterinary surgeon) Tierarzt(-ärztin) m(f)

veteran ['vetərn] n Veteran(in) m(f)

veterinarian [vetrɪ'neərɪən] n (US) Tierarzt m/-ärztin f

veterinary ['vetrɪnərɪ] adj Veterinär-; **~ surgeon** (BRIT) n Tierarzt m/-ärztin f

veto ['viːtəu] (pl **~es**) n Veto nt ♦ vt sein Veto einlegen gegen

vex [veks] vt ärgern; **~ed** adj verärgert; **~ed question** umstrittene Frage f

VHF abbr (= very high frequency) UKW f

via ['vaɪə] prep über +acc

viable ['vaɪəbl] adj (plan) durchführbar; (company) rentabel

vibrant ['vaɪbrnt] adj (lively) lebhaft; (bright) leuchtend; (full of emotion: voice) bebend

vibrate [vaɪ'breɪt] vi zittern, beben; (machine, string) vibrieren; **vibration** [vaɪ'breɪʃən] n Schwingung f; (of machine) Vibrieren nt

vicar ['vɪkə'] n Pfarrer m; **~age** n Pfarrhaus nt

vice [vaɪs] n (evil) Laster nt; (TECH) Schraubstock m

vice-chairman [vaɪs'tʃeəmən] n stellvertretende(r) Vorsitzende(r) m

vice-president [vaɪs'prezɪdənt] n Vizepräsident m

vice squad n ≃ Sittenpolizei f

vice versa ['vaisi'və:sə] adv umgekehrt

vicinity [vɪ'sɪnɪtɪ] n Umgebung f; (closeness) Nähe f

vicious ['vɪʃəs] adj gemein, böse; ~ **circle** n Teufelskreis m

victim ['vɪktɪm] n Opfer nt

victor ['vɪktər] n Sieger m

Victorian [vɪk'tɔ:rɪən] adj viktorianisch; (fig) (sitten)streng

victorious [vɪk'tɔ:rɪəs] adj siegreich

victory ['vɪktərɪ] n Sieg m

video ['vɪdɪəʊ] adj Fernseh-, Bild- ♦ n (~ film) Video nt; (also: ~ **cassette**) Videokassette f; (also: ~ **cassette recorder**) Videorekorder m; ~ **tape** n Videoband nt; ~ **wall** n Videowand f

vie [vaɪ] vi wetteifern

Vienna [vɪ'enə] n Wien nt

Vietnam ['vjet'næm] n Vietnam nt; **~ese** adj vietnamesisch ♦ n inv (person) Vietnamese m, Vietnamesin f

view [vju:] n (sight) Sicht f, Blick m; (scene) Aussicht f; (opinion) Ansicht f; (intention) Absicht f ♦ vt (situation) betrachten; (house) besichtigen; **to have sth in ~** etw beabsichtigen; **on ~** ausgestellt; **in ~ of** wegen +gen, angesichts +gen; **~er** n (PHOT: small projector) Gucki m; (TV) Fernsehzuschauer(in) m(f); **~finder** n Sucher m; **~point** n Standpunkt m

vigil ['vɪdʒɪl] n (Nacht)wache f; **~ant** adj wachsam

vigorous ['vɪɡərəs] adj kräftig; (protest) energisch, heftig

vile [vaɪl] adj (mean) gemein; (foul) abscheulich

villa ['vɪlə] n Villa f

village ['vɪlɪdʒ] n Dorf nt; **~r** n Dorfbewohner(in) m(f)

villain ['vɪlən] n Schurke m

vindicate ['vɪndɪkeɪt] vt rechtfertigen

vindictive [vɪn'dɪktɪv] adj nachtragend, rachsüchtig

vine [vaɪn] n Rebstock m, Rebe f

vinegar ['vɪnɪɡər] n Essig m

vineyard ['vɪnjɑːd] n Weinberg m

vintage ['vɪntɪdʒ] n (of wine) Jahrgang m; ~ **car** n Oldtimer m (zwischen 1919 und 1930 gebaut); ~ **wine** n edle(r) Wein m

viola [vɪ'əʊlə] n Bratsche f

violate ['vaɪəleɪt] vt (law) übertreten; (rights, rule, neutrality) verletzen; (sanctity, woman) schänden; **violation** [vaɪə'leɪʃən] n Übertretung f; Verletzung f

violence ['vaɪələns] n (force) Heftigkeit f; (brutality) Gewalttätigkeit f

violent ['vaɪələnt] adj (strong) heftig; (brutal) gewalttätig, brutal; (contrast) krass; (death) gewaltsam

violet ['vaɪələt] n Veilchen n ♦ adj veilchenblau, violett

violin [vaɪə'lɪn] n Geige f, Violine f; **~ist** n Geiger(in) m(f)

VIP n abbr (= very important person) VIP m

virgin ['vɜːdʒɪn] n Jungfrau f ♦ adj jungfräulich, unberührt; **~ity** [vɜː'dʒɪnɪtɪ] n Unschuld f

Virgo ['vɜːɡəʊ] n Jungfrau f

virile ['vɪraɪl] adj männlich; **virility** [vɪ'rɪlɪtɪ] n Männlichkeit f

virtually ['vɜːtjʊəlɪ] adv praktisch, fast

virtual reality ['vɜːtjʊəl-] n (COMPUT) virtuelle Realität f

virtue ['vɜːtju:] n (moral goodness) Tugend f; (good quality) Vorteil m, Vorzug m; **by ~ of** aufgrund or auf Grund +gen

virtuous ['vɜːtjʊəs] adj tugendhaft

virulent ['vɪrʊlənt] adj (poisonous) bösartig; (bitter) scharf, geharnischt

virus ['vaɪərəs] n (also COMPUT) Virus m

visa ['vi:zə] n Visum nt

vis-à-vis [vi:zə'vi:] prep gegenüber

viscous ['vɪskəs] adj zähflüssig

visibility [vɪzɪ'bɪlɪtɪ] n (MET) Sicht(weite) f

visible ['vɪzəbl] adj sichtbar; **visibly** adv sichtlich

vision ['vɪʒən] n (ability) Sehvermögen nt; (foresight) Weitblick m; (in dream, image) Vision f

visit ['vɪzɪt] n Besuch m ♦ vt besuchen; (town, country) fahren nach; **~ing hours** npl (in hospital etc) Besuchszeiten pl; **~or** n (in house) Besucher(in) m(f); (in hotel) Gast m; **~or centre** n Touristeninformation f

visor ['vaɪzə*] n Visier nt; (on cap) Schirm m; (AUT) Blende f

vista ['vɪstə] n Aussicht f

visual ['vɪzjuəl] adj Seh-, visuell; **~ aid** n Anschauungsmaterial nt; **~ display unit** n Bildschirm(gerät nt) m; **~ize** vt sich +dat vorstellen; **~ly-impaired** adj sehbehindert

vital ['vaɪtl] adj (important) unerlässlich; (necessary for life) lebens-, lebenswichtig; (lively) vital; **~ity** [var'tælɪtɪ] n Vitalität f; **~ly** adv: **~ly important** adj wichtig; **~ statistics** npl (fig) Maße pl

vitamin ['vɪtəmɪn] n Vitamin nt

vivacious [vɪ'veɪʃəs] adj lebhaft

vivid ['vɪvɪd] adj (graphic) lebendig; (memory) lebhaft; (bright) leuchtend; **~ly** adv lebendig; lebhaft; leuchtend

V-neck ['viːnɛk] n V-Ausschnitt m

vocabulary [vəu'kæbjulərɪ] n Wortschatz m, Vokabular nt

vocal ['vəukl] n Vokal-, Gesang-; (fig) lautstark; **~ cords** npl Stimmbänder pl

vocation [vəu'keɪʃən] n (calling) Berufung f; **~al** adj Berufs-

vociferous [vəu'sɪfərəs] adj lautstark

vodka ['vɒdkə] n Wodka m

vogue [vəug] n Mode f

voice [vɔɪs] n Stimme f; (fig) Mitspracherecht nt ♦ vt äußern

void [vɔɪd] n Leere f ♦ adj (invalid) nichtig, ungültig; (empty): **~ of** ohne, bar +gen; see null

volatile ['vɒlətaɪl] adj (gas) flüchtig; (person) impulsiv; (situation) brisant

volcano [vɒl'keɪnəu] n Vulkan m

volition [və'lɪʃən] n Wille m; **of one's own ~** aus freiem Willen

volley ['vɒlɪ] n (of guns) Salve f; (of stones) Hagel m; (tennis) Flugball m; **~ball** n Volleyball m

volt [vəult] n Volt nt; **~age** n (Volt)spannung f

volume ['vɒljuːm] n (book) Band m; (size) Umfang m; (space) Rauminhalt m; (of sound) Lautstärke f

voluntarily ['vɒləntrɪlɪ] adv freiwillig

voluntary ['vɒləntərɪ] adj freiwillig

volunteer [vɒlən'tɪə*] n Freiwillige(r) mf ♦ vi sich freiwillig melden; **to ~ to do sth** sich anbieten, etw zu tun

vomit ['vɒmɪt] n Erbrochene(s) nt ♦ vt spucken ♦ vi sich übergeben

vote [vəut] n Stimme f; (ballot) Abstimmung f; (result) Abstimmungsergebnis nt; (franchise) Wahlrecht nt ♦ vt, vi wählen; **~ of thanks** n Dankesworte pl; **~r** n Wähler(in) m(f); **voting** ['vəutɪŋ] n Wahl f

voucher ['vautʃə*] n Gutschein m

vouch for [vautʃ-] vt bürgen für

vow [vau] n Versprechen nt; (REL) Gelübde nt ♦ vt geloben

vowel ['vauəl] n Vokal m

voyage ['vɔɪdʒ] n Reise f

vulgar ['vʌlgə*] adj (rude) vulgär; **~ity** [vʌl'gærɪtɪ] n Vulgarität f

vulnerable ['vʌlnərəbl] adj (easily injured) verwundbar; (sensitive) verletzlich

vulture ['vʌltʃə*] n Geier m

W, w

wad [wɒd] n (bundle) Bündel nt; (of paper) Stoß m; (of money) Packen m

waddle ['wɒdl] vi watscheln

wade [weɪd] vi: **to ~ through** waten durch

wafer ['weɪfə*] n Waffel f; (REL) Hostie f; (COMPUT) Wafer f

waffle ['wɒfl] n Waffel f; (inf: empty talk) Geschwafel nt ♦ vi schwafeln

waft [wɒft] vt, vi wedeln mit ♦ vi we-

wag [wæg] vt (tail) wedeln mit ♦ vi wedeln

wage [weɪdʒ] n (also: **~s**) (Arbeits)lohn m ♦ vt: **to ~ war** Krieg führen; **~ earner** n Lohnempfänger(in) m(f)); **~ packet** n Lohntüte f

wager ['weɪdʒə'] n Wette f ♦ vt, vi wetten

waggle ['wægl] vi wackeln

wag(g)on ['wægən] n (horse-drawn) Fuhrwerk nt; (US: AUT) Wagen m; (BRIT: RAIL) Wag(g)on m

wail [weɪl] n Wehgeschrei nt ♦ vi wehklagen, jammern

waist [weɪst] n Taille f; **~coat** (BRIT) n Weste f; **~line** n Taille f

wait [weɪt] n Wartezeit f ♦ vi warten; **to lie in ~ for sb** jdm auflauern; **I can't ~ to see him** ich kanns kaum erwarten ihn zu sehen; **"no ~ing"** (BRIT: AUT) „Halteverbot"; **~ behind** vi zurückbleiben; **~ for** vt fus warten auf +acc; **~ on** vt fus bedienen; **~er** n Kellner m; **~ing list** n Warteliste f; **~ing room** n (MED) Wartezimmer nt; (RAIL) Wartesaal m; **~ress** n Kellnerin f

waive [weɪv] vt verzichten auf +acc

wake [weɪk] n (pt **woke**, **waked**, pp **woken**) vt wecken ♦ vi (also: **~ up**) aufwachen ♦ n (NAUT) Kielwasser nt; (for dead) Totenwache f; **to ~ up to** (fig) sich bewusst werden +gen

waken ['weɪkn] vt aufwecken

Wales [weɪlz] n Wales nt

walk [wɔːk] n Spaziergang m; (gait) Gang m; (route) Weg m ♦ vi (spazieren) gehen; (longer) wandern; **~s of life** Sphären pl; **a 10-minute ~** 10 Minuten zu Fuß; **to ~ out on sb** (inf) jdn sitzen lassen; **~er** n Spaziergänger m; (hiker) Wanderer m; **~ie-talkie** ['wɔːkɪ'tɔːkɪ] n tragbare(s) Sprechfunkgerät nt; **~ing** n Gehen nt; (hiking) Wandern nt ♦ adj Wander-; **~ing shoes** npl Wanderschuhe pl; **~ing stick** n Spazierstock m; **W~man** ['wɔːkmən] ® n Walkman m ®; **~out** n Streik m; **~over** (inf) n leichte(r) Sieg

m; **~way** n Fußweg m

wall [wɔːl] n (inside) Wand f; (outside) Mauer f; **~ed** adj von Mauern umgeben

wallet ['wɔlɪt] n Brieftasche f

wallflower ['wɔːlflauə'] n Goldlack m; **to be a ~** (fig) ein Mauerblümchen sein

wallop ['wɔləp] (inf) vt schlagen, verprügeln

wallow ['wɔləu] vi sich wälzen

wallpaper ['wɔːlpeɪpə'] n Tapete f

walnut ['wɔːlnʌt] n Walnuss f

walrus ['wɔːlrəs] n Walross nt

waltz [wɔːls] n Walzer m ♦ vi Walzer tanzen

wan [wɔn] adj bleich

wand [wɔnd] n (also: **magic ~**) Zauberstab m

wander ['wɔndə'] vi (roam) (herum)wandern; (fig) abschweifen

wane [weɪn] vi abnehmen; (fig) schwinden

wangle ['wæŋgl] (BRIT: inf) vt: **to ~ sth** etw richtig hindrehen

want [wɔnt] n (lack) Mangel m ♦ vt (need) brauchen; (desire) wollen; (lack) nicht haben; **~s** npl (needs) Bedürfnisse pl; **for ~ of** aus Mangel an +dat; mangels +gen; **to ~ to do sth** etw tun wollen; **to ~ sb to do sth** wollen, dass jd etw tut; **~ed** adj (criminal etc) gesucht; **"cook ~ed"** (in adverts) „Koch/Köchin gesucht"; **~ing** adj: **to be found ~ing** sich als unzulänglich erweisen

wanton ['wɔntən] adj mutwillig, zügellos

war [wɔː'] n Krieg m; **to make ~** Krieg führen

ward [wɔːd] n (in hospital) Station f; (of city) Bezirk m; (child) Mündel nt; **~ off** vt abwenden, abwehren

warden ['wɔːdn] n (guard) Wächter m, Aufseher m; (BRIT: in youth hostel) Herbergsvater m; (UNIV) Heimleiter m; (BRIT: also: **traffic ~**) ≈ Verkehrspolizist m, ≈ Politesse f

warder ['wɔːdə*] (BRIT) n Gefängniswärter m

wardrobe ['wɔːdrəub] n Kleiderschrank m; (clothes) Garderobe f

warehouse ['wɛəhaus] n Lagerhaus nt

wares [wɛəz] npl Ware f

warfare ['wɔːfɛə*] n Krieg m; Kriegsführung f

warhead ['wɔːhed] n Sprengkopf m

warily ['wɛərɪlɪ] adv vorsichtig

warlike ['wɔːlaɪk] adj kriegerisch

warm [wɔːm] adj warm; (welcome) herzlich ♦ vt wärmen; **I'm ~** mir ist warm; **it's ~** es ist warm; **~ up** vt aufwärmen ♦ vi warm werden; **~-hearted** adj warmherzig; **~ly** adv warm; herzlich; **~th** n Wärme f; Herzlichkeit f

warn [wɔːn] vt: to ~ (of or against) warnen (vor +dat); **~ing** n Warnung f; **without ~ing** unerwartet; **~ing light** n Warnlicht nt; **~ing triangle** n (AUT) Warndreieck nt

warp [wɔːp] vt verziehen; **~ed** adj wellig; (fig) pervers

warrant ['wɔrənt] n (for arrest) Haftbefehl m

warranty ['wɔrəntɪ] n Garantie f

warren ['wɔrən] n Labyrinth nt

Warsaw ['wɔːsɔː] n Warschau nt

warship ['wɔːʃɪp] n Kriegsschiff nt

wart [wɔːt] n Warze f

wartime ['wɔːtaɪm] n Krieg m

wary ['wɛərɪ] adj misstrauisch

was [wɔz] pt of **be**

wash [wɔʃ] n Wäsche f ♦ vt waschen; (dishes) abwaschen ♦ vi sich waschen; (do ~ing) waschen; **to have a ~** sich waschen; **~ away** vt abwaschen, wegspülen; **~ off** vt abwaschen; **~ up** vi (BRIT) spülen; (US) sich waschen; **~able** adj waschbar; **~basin** n Waschbecken nt; **~ bowl** (US) n Waschbecken nt; **~ cloth** (US) n (face cloth) Waschlappen m; **~er** n (TECH) Dichtungsring m; (machine) Waschmaschine f; **~ing** n Wäsche f; **~ing machine** n Waschmaschine f; **~ing powder** (BRIT) n Waschpulver nt; **~ing-up** n Abwasch m; **~ing-up liquid** n Spülmittel nt; **~-out** (inf) n (event) Reinfall m; (person) Niete f; **~room** n Waschraum m

wasn't ['wɔznt] = was not

wasp [wɔsp] n Wespe f

wastage ['weɪstɪdʒ] n Verlust m; **natural ~** Verschleiß m

waste [weɪst] n (wasting) Verschwendung f; (what is ~d) Abfall m ♦ adj (useless) überschüssig, Abfall- ♦ vt (object) verschwenden; (time, life) vergeuden ♦ vi: to ~ away verfallen, verkümmern; **~s** npl (land) Einöde f; **~ disposal unit** (BRIT) n Müllschlucker m; **~ful** adj verschwenderisch; (process) aufwändig, aufwendig; **~ ground** (BRIT) n unbebaute(s) Grundstück nt; **~land** n Ödland nt; **~paper basket** n Papierkorb m; **~ pipe** n Abflussrohr nt

watch [wɔtʃ] n Wache f; (for time) Uhr f ♦ vt ansehen; (observe) beobachten; (be careful of) aufpassen auf +acc; (guard) bewachen ♦ vi zusehen; **to be on the ~ (for sth)** (auf etw acc) aufpassen; **to ~ TV** fernsehen; **to ~ sb doing sth** jdm bei etw zuschauen; **~ out** vi Ausschau halten; (be careful) aufpassen; **~ out!** pass auf!; **~dog** n Wachhund m; (fig) Wächter m; **~ful** adj wachsam; **~maker** n Uhrmacher m; **~man** (irreg) n (also: night ~man) (Nacht)wächter m; **~ strap** n Uhrarmband nt

water ['wɔːtə*] n Wasser nt ♦ vt (be)gießen; (river) bewässern; (horses) tränken ♦ vi (eye) tränen; **~s** npl (of sea, river etc) Gewässer nt; **~ down** vt verwässern; **~ closet** (BRIT) n (Wasser)klosett nt; **~colour** (US **watercolor**) n (painting) Aquarell nt; (paint) Wasserfarbe f; **~cress** n (Brunnen)kresse f; **~fall** n Wasserfall m; **~ heater** n Heißwassergerät nt; **~ing can** n Gießkanne f; **~ level** n Wasserstand m; **~lily** n Seerose f; **~line** n Wasserlinie f;

~logged adj (ground) voll Wasser; ~
main n Haupt(wasser)leitung f;
~mark n Wasserzeichen nt; (on wall)
Wasserstandsmarke f; **~melon** n Wassermelone f; **~ polo** n Wasserball(spiel) nt; **~proof** adj wasserdicht;
~shed n Wasserscheide f; **~skiing** n
Wasserskilaufen nt; **~ tank** n Wassertank m; **~tight** adj wasserdicht; **~way**
n Wasserweg m; **~works** npl Wasserwerk nt; **~y** adj wäss(e)rig

watt [wɔt] n Watt nt

wave [weɪv] n Welle f; (with hand) Winken nt ♦ vi (move to and fro) schwenken; (hand, flag) winken mit ♦ vi (person) winken; (flag) wehen; **~length** n
(also fig) Wellenlänge f

waver ['weɪvə'] vi schwanken

wavy ['weɪvɪ] adj wellig

wax [wæks] n Wachs nt; (sealing ~) Siegellack m; (in ear) Ohrenschmalz m
♦ vt (floor) (ein)wachsen ♦ vi (moon)
zunehmen; **~works** npl Wachsfigurenkabinett nt

way [weɪ] n Weg m; (method) Art und
Weise f; (direction) Richtung f; (habit)
Gewohnheit f; (distance) Entfernung f;
(condition) Zustand m; **which ~?** - this
~ welche Richtung? - hier entlang; **on
the ~** (en route) unterwegs; **to be in
the ~** im Weg sein; **to go out of
one's ~ to do sth** sich besonders anstrengen, um etw zu tun; **to lose
one's ~** sich verirren; **"give ~"** (BRIT:
AUT) „Vorfahrt achten!"; **in a ~** in gewisser Weise; **by the ~** übrigens; **in
some ~s** in gewisser Hinsicht; **"~ in"**
(BRIT) „Eingang"; **"~ out"** (BRIT) „Ausgang"

waylay [weɪ'leɪ] (irreg: like lay) vt auflauern +dat

wayward ['weɪwəd] adj eigensinnig

W.C. (BRIT) n WC nt

we [wiː] pl pron wir

weak [wiːk] adj schwach; **~en** vt
schwächen ♦ vi schwächer werden;
~ling n Schwächling m; **~ness** n

Schwäche f

wealth [welθ] n Reichtum m; (abundance) Fülle f; **~y** adj reich

wean [wiːn] vt entwöhnen

weapon ['wepən] n Waffe f

wear [weə'] n (pt **wore**, pp **worn**) n
(clothing): **sports/baby ~** Sport-/
Babykleidung f; (use) Verschleiß m ♦ vt
(have on) tragen; (smile etc) haben;
(use) abnutzen ♦ vi (last) halten; (become old) (sich) verschleißen; **evening
~** Abendkleidung f; **~ and tear** Verschleiß m; **~ away** vt verbrauchen ♦ vi
schwinden; **~ down** vt (people) zermürben; **~ off** vi sich verlieren; **~ out**
vt verschleißen; (person) erschöpfen

weary ['wɪərɪ] adj müde ♦ vt ermüden
♦ vi überdrüssig werden

weasel ['wiːzl] n Wiesel nt

weather ['weðə'] n Wetter nt ♦ vt wittern lassen; (resist) überstehen; **under the ~** (fig: ill) angeschlagen (inf);
~beaten adj verwittert; **~cock** n Wetterhahn m; **~ forecast** n Wettervorhersage f; **~ vane** n Wetterfahne f

weave [wiːv] (pt **wove**, pp **woven**) vt
weben; **~r** n Weber(in) m(f); **weaving**
n (craft) Webkunst f

web [web] n Netz nt; (membrane)
Schwimmhaut f; **~ site** n (COMPUT)
Website f, Webseite f

wed [wed] (pt, pp **wedded**) vt heiraten
♦ n: **the newly-~s** npl die Frischvermählten pl

we'd [wiːd] = we had; we would

wedding ['wedɪŋ] n Hochzeit f;
silver/golden ~ anniversary Silberhochzeit f/goldene Hochzeit f; **~ day**
n Hochzeitstag m; **~ dress** n Hochzeitskleid nt; **~ present** n Hochzeitsgeschenk nt; **~ ring** n Trauring m, Ehering m

wedge [wedʒ] n Keil m; (of cheese etc)
Stück nt ♦ vt (fasten) festklemmen;
(pack tightly) einkeilen

Wednesday ['wednzdɪ] n Mittwoch m

wee [wiː] (SCOTTISH) adj klein, winzig

weed [wiːd] n Unkraut nt ♦ vt jäten; **~killer** n Unkrautvertilgungsmittel nt

weedy [ˈwiːdɪ] adj (person) schmächtig

week [wiːk] n Woche f; **a ~ today/on Friday** heute/Freitag in einer Woche; **~day** n Wochentag m; **~end** n Wochenende nt; **~ly** adj wöchentlich; (wages, magazine) Wochen- ♦ adv wöchentlich

weep [wiːp] (pt, pp **wept**) vi weinen; **~ing willow** n Trauerweide f

weigh [weɪ] vt, vi wiegen; **to ~ anchor** den Anker lichten; **~ down** vt niederdrücken; **~ up** vt abschätzen

weight [weɪt] n Gewicht nt; **to lose/put on ~** abnehmen/zunehmen; **~ing** n (allowance) Zulage f; **~lifter** n Gewichtheber m; **~lifting** n Gewichtheben nt; **~y** adj (heavy) gewichtig; (important) schwerwiegend, schwer wiegend

weir [wɪəʳ] n (Stau)wehr nt

weird [wɪəd] adj seltsam

welcome [ˈwelkəm] n Willkommen nt, Empfang m ♦ vt begrüßen; **thank you - you're ~!** danke - nichts zu danken

welder [ˈweldəʳ] n (person) Schweißer(in) m(f)

welding [ˈweldɪŋ] n Schweißen nt

welfare [ˈwelfɛəʳ] n Wohl nt; (social) Fürsorge f; **~ state** n Wohlfahrtsstaat m; **~ work** n Fürsorge f

well [wel] n Brunnen m; (oil ~) Quelle f ♦ adj (in good health) gesund ♦ adv gut ♦ excl nun!, na schön!; **I'm ~** es geht mir gut; **get ~ soon!** gute Besserung!; **as ~** auch; **as ~ as** sowohl als auch; **~ done!** gut gemacht!; **to do ~** (person) gut zurechtkommen; (business) gut gehen; **~ up** vi emporsteigen; (fig) aufsteigen

we'll [wiːl] = we will; we shall

well: **~-behaved** [ˈwelbɪˈheɪvd] adj wohlerzogen; **~-being** n Wohl nt; **~-built** [ˈwelˈbɪlt] adj kräftig gebaut; **~-deserved** [ˈweldɪˈzɜːvd] adj wohlverdient; **~-dressed** [ˈwelˈdrest]

adj gut gekleidet; **~-heeled** [ˈwelˈhiːld] (inf) adj (wealthy) gut gepolstert

wellingtons [ˈwelɪŋtənz] npl (also: **wellington boots**) Gummistiefel pl

well: **~-known** [ˈwelˈnəʊn] adj bekannt; **~-mannered** [ˈwelˈmænəd] adj wohlerzogen; **~-meaning** [ˈwelˈmiːnɪŋ] adj (person) wohlmeinend; (action) gut gemeint; **~-off** [ˈwelˈɒf] adj gut situiert; **~-read** [ˈwelˈred] adj (sehr) belesen; **~-to-do** [ˈweltuːˈduː] adj wohlhabend; **~-wisher** [ˈwelwɪʃəʳ] n Gönner m

Welsh [welʃ] adj walisisch ♦ n (LING) Walisisch nt; **the ~** npl (people) die Waliser pl; **~man/woman** (irreg) n Waliser(in) m(f)

went [went] pt of go

wept [wept] pt, pp of weep

were [wɜːʳ] pt pl of be

we're [wɪəʳ] = we are

weren't [wɜːnt] = were not

west [west] n Westen m ♦ adj West-, westlich ♦ adv westwärts, nach Westen; the **W~** der Westen; **W~ Country** (BRIT) n: **the W~ Country** der Südwesten Englands; **~erly** adj westlich; **~ern** adj westlich, West- ♦ n (CINE) Western m; **W~ Indian** adj westindisch ♦ n Westindier(in) m(f); **W~ Indies** npl Westindische Inseln pl; **~ward(s)** adv westwärts

wet [wet] adj nass; **to get ~** nass werden; **"~ paint"** „frisch gestrichen"; **~ blanket** n (fig) Triefel m; **~ suit** n Taucheranzug m

we've [wiːv] = we have

whack [wæk] n Schlag m ♦ vt schlagen

whale [weɪl] n Wal m

wharf [wɔːf] n Kai m

wharves [wɔːvz] npl of wharf

what [wɒt] adj **1** (in questions) welche(r, s), was für ein(e); **what size is it?** welche Größe ist das?

2 (*in exclamations*) was für ein(e); **what a mess!** was für ein Durcheinander!
♦ *pron* (*interrogative/relative*) was; **what are you doing?** was machst du gerade?; **what are you talking about?** wovon reden Sie?; **what is it called?** wie heißt das?; **what about ...?** wie wärs mit ...?; **I saw what you did** ich habe gesehen, was du gemacht hast ♦ *excl* (*disbelieving*) wie, was; **what, no coffee!** wie, kein Kaffee?; **I've crashed the car - what!** ich hatte einen Autounfall - was!

whatever [wɔt'evər] *adj*: ~ **book** welches Buch auch immer ♦ *pron*: **do ~ is necessary** tu, was (immer auch) nötig ist; ~ **happens** egal, was passiert; **nothing ~** überhaupt *or* absolut gar nichts; **do ~ you want** tu, was (immer) du (auch) möchtest; **no reason ~** *or* **whatsoever** überhaupt *or* absolut kein Grund

whatsoever [wɔtsəu'evər] *adj see* **whatever**

wheat [wi:t] *n* Weizen *m*

wheedle ['wi:dl] *vt*: **to ~ sb into doing sth** jdn dazu überreden, etw zu tun; **to ~ sth out of sb** jdm etw abluchsen

wheel [wi:l] *n* Rad *nt*; (*steering* ~) Lenkrad *nt*; (*disc*) Scheibe *f* ♦ *vt* schieben; **~barrow** *n* Schubkarren *m*; **~chair** *n* Rollstuhl *m*; ~ **clamp** *n* (*AUT*) Parkkralle *f*

wheeze [wi:z] *vi* keuchen

KEYWORD ────────

when [wɛn] *adv* wann
♦ *conj* **1** (*at, during, after the time that*) wenn; (*in past*) als; **she was reading when I came in** sie las, als ich hereinkam; **be careful when you cross the road** seien Sie vorsichtig, wenn Sie über die Straße gehen
2 (*on, at which*) als; **on the day when**

I met him an dem Tag, an dem ich ihn traf
3 (*whereas*) wo ... doch

whenever [wɛn'evər] *adv* wann (auch) immer; (*every time that*) jedes Mal wenn ♦ *conj* (*any time*) wenn

where [wɛər] *adv* (*place*) wo; (*direction*) wohin; ~ **from** woher; **this is ~ ...** hier ...; **~abouts** ['wɛərəbauts] *adv* wo ♦ *n* Aufenthaltsort *m*; **nobody knows his ~abouts** niemand weiß, wo er ist; **~as** [wɛər'æz] *conj* während, wo ... doch; **~by** *pron* woran, wodurch, womit, wovon; **~upon** *conj* worauf, wonach; (*at beginning of sentence*) daraufhin; **~ver** [wɛər'evər] *adv* wo (immer)

wherewithal ['wɛəwiðɔːl] *n* nötige (Geld)mittel *pl*

whet [wɛt] *vt* (*appetite*) anregen

whether ['wɛðər] *conj* ob; **I don't know ~ to accept or not** ich weiß nicht, ob ich es annehmen soll oder nicht; **~ you go or not** ob du gehst oder nicht; **it's doubtful/unclear ~ ...** es ist zweifelhaft/nicht klar, ob ...

KEYWORD ────────

which [wɪtʃ] *adj* **1** (*interrogative: direct, indirect*) welche(r, s); **which one?** welche(r, s)?
2: in which case in diesem Fall; **by which time** zu dieser Zeit
♦ *pron* **1** (*interrogative*) welche(r, s); (*of people also*) wer
2 (*relative*) der/die/das; (*referring to people*) was; **the apple which you ate/which is on the table** der Apfel, den du gegessen hast/der auf dem Tisch liegt; **he said he saw her, which is true** er sagte, er habe sie gesehen, was auch stimmt

whichever [wɪtʃ'evər] *adj* welche(r, s) auch immer; (*no matter which*) ganz gleich welche(r, s); ~ **book you take** welches Buch du auch nimmst; ~ **car**

you prefer egal welches Auto du vorziehst

whiff [wɪf] n Hauch m

while [waɪl] n Weile f ♦ conj während; **for a ~** eine Zeit lang; **~ away** vt (time) sich dat vertreiben

whim [wɪm] n Laune f

whimper ['wɪmpə] n Wimmern nt ♦ vi wimmern

whimsical ['wɪmzɪkəl] adj launisch

whine [waɪn] n Gewinsel nt, Gejammer nt ♦ vi heulen, winseln

whip [wɪp] n Peitsche f; (POL) Fraktionsführer m ♦ vt (beat) peitschen; (snatch) reißen; **~ped cream** n Schlagsahne f

whip-round ['wɪpraund] (BRIT: inf) n Geldsammlung f

whirl [wɜːl] n Wirbel m ♦ vt, vi (herum)wirbeln; **~pool** n Wirbel m; **~wind** n Wirbelwind m

whirr [wɜː] vi schwirren, surren

whisk [wɪsk] n Schneebesen m ♦ vt (cream etc) schlagen; **to ~ sb away** or **off** mit jdm davon sausen

whisker ['wɪskə] n: **~s** (of animal) Barthaare pl; (of man) Backenbart m

whisky ['wɪskɪ] (US, IRISH **whiskey**) n Whisky m

whisper ['wɪspə] n Flüstern nt ♦ vt, vi flüstern

whistle ['wɪsl] n Pfiff m; (instrument) Pfeife f ♦ vt, vi pfeifen

white [waɪt] n Weiß nt; (of egg) Eiweiß nt ♦ adj weiß; **~ coffee** (BRIT) n Kaffee m mit Milch; **~-collar worker** n Angestellte(r) mf; **~ elephant** n (fig) Fehlinvestition f; **~ lie** n Notlüge f; **~ paper** n (POL) Weißbuch nt; **~wash** n (paint) Tünche f; (fig) Ehrenrettung f ♦ vt weißen, tünchen; (fig) rein waschen

whiting ['waɪtɪŋ] n Weißfisch m

Whitsun ['wɪtsn] n Pfingsten nt

whittle ['wɪtl] vt: **to ~ away** or **down** stutzen, verringern

whizz [wɪz] vi: **to ~ past** or **by** vorbeizischen, vorbeischwirren; **~ kid** (inf) n Kanone f

---

KEYWORD

who [huː] pron **1** (interrogative) wer; (acc) wen; (dat) wem; **who is it?**, **who's there?** wer ist da?

2 (relative) der/die/das; **the woman/man who spoke to me** die Frau/der Mann, die/der mit mir sprach

---

whodu(n)nit [huːˈdʌnɪt] (inf) n Krimi m

whoever [huːˈɛvə] pron wer/wen/wem auch immer; (no matter who) ganz gleich wer/wen/wem

whole [həʊl] adj ganz ♦ n Ganze(s) nt; **the ~ of the town** die ganze Stadt; **on the ~**, **as a ~** im Großen und Ganzen; **~food(s)** ['həʊlfuːd(z)] n(pl) Vollwertkost f; **~hearted** [həʊl'hɑːtɪd] adj rückhaltlos; **~heartedly** adv von ganzem Herzen; **~meal** adj (bread, flour) Vollkorn-; **~sale** n Großhandel m ♦ adj (trade) Großhandels-; (destruction) Massen-; **~saler** n Großhändler m; **~some** adj bekömmlich, gesund; **~wheat** adj = wholemeal

wholly ['həʊlɪ] adv ganz, völlig

KEYWORD

whom [huːm] pron **1** (interrogative: acc) wen; (: dat) wem; **whom did you see?** wen haben Sie gesehen?; **to whom did you give it?** wem haben Sie es gegeben?

2 (relative: acc) den/die/das; (: dat) dem/der/dem; **the man whom I saw/to whom I spoke** der Mann, den ich sah/mit dem ich sprach

---

whooping cough ['huːpɪŋ-] n Keuchhusten m

whore [hɔː] n Hure f

whose [huːz] adj (possessive: interrogative) wessen; (: relative) dessen; (after f and pl) deren ♦ pron wessen; **~ book is this?**, **~ is this book?** wessen Buch ist dies?

dies?; **~ is this?** wem gehört das?

why [waɪ] *adv* warum, weshalb
♦ *conj* warum, weshalb; **that's not why I'm here** ich bin nicht deswegen hier; **that's the reason why** deshalb
♦ *excl* (*expressing surprise, shock*) na so was; (*explaining*) also dann; **why, it's you!** na so was, du bist es!

wick [wɪk] *n* Docht *m*

wicked ['wɪkɪd] *adj* böse

wicker ['wɪkə] *n* (*also:* **~work**) Korbgeflecht *nt*

wicket ['wɪkɪt] *n* Tor *nt*, Dreistab *m*

wide [waɪd] *adj* breit; (*plain*) weit; (*in firing*) daneben ♦ *adv:* **to open ~** weit öffnen; **to shoot ~** danebenschießen; **~-angle lens** *n* Weitwinkelobjektiv *nt*; **~-awake** *adj* hellwach; **~ly** *adv* weit; (*known*) allgemein; **~n** *vt* erweitern; **~ open** *adj* weit geöffnet; **~spread** *adj* weitverbreitet, weit verbreitet

widow ['wɪdəu] *n* Witwe *f*; **~ed** *adj* verwitwet; **~er** *n* Witwer *m*

width [wɪdθ] *n* Breite *f*, Weite *f*

wield [wi:ld] *vt* schwingen, handhaben

wife [waɪf] (*pl* **wives**) *n* (Ehe)frau *f*, Gattin *f*

wig [wɪg] *n* Perücke *f*

wiggle ['wɪgl] *n* Wackeln *nt* ♦ *vt* wackeln mit ♦ *vi* wackeln

wild [waɪld] *adj* wild; (*violent*) heftig; (*plan, idea*) verrückt; **~erness** ['wɪldənɪs] *n* Wildnis *f*, Wüste *f*; **~-goose chase** *n* (*fig*) fruchtlose(s) Unternehmen *nt*; **~life** *n* Tierwelt *f*; **~ly** *adv* wild, ungestüm; (*exaggerated*) irrsinnig; **~s** *npl*: **the ~s** die Wildnis *f*

wilful ['wɪlful] (*US* **willful**) *adj* (*intended*) vorsätzlich; (*obstinate*) eigensinnig

will [wɪl] *aux vb* **1** (*forms future tense*) werden; **I will finish it tomorrow** ich mache es morgen zu Ende

2 (*in conjectures, predictions*): **he will** *or* **he'll be there by now** er dürfte jetzt da sein; **that will be the postman** das wird der Postbote sein

3 (*in commands, requests, offers*): **will you be quiet!** sei endlich still!; **will you help me?** hilfst du mir?; **will you have a cup of tea?** trinken Sie eine Tasse Tee?; **I won't put up with it!** das lasse ich mir nicht gefallen!
♦ *vt* wollen
♦ *n* Wille *m*; (*JUR*) Testament *nt*

willing ['wɪlɪŋ] *adj* gewillt, bereit; **~ly** *adv* bereitwillig, gern; **~ness** *n* (Bereit)willigkeit *f*

willow ['wɪləu] *n* Weide *f*

willpower ['wɪl'pauə] *n* Willenskraft *f*

willy-nilly ['wɪlɪ'nɪlɪ] *adv* einfach so

wilt [wɪlt] *vi* (ver)welken

wily ['waɪlɪ] *adj* gerissen

win [wɪn] (*pt, pp* **won**) *n* Sieg *m* ♦ *vt* gewinnen; **to ~ sb over** *or* **round** jdn gewinnen, jdn dazu bringen

wince [wɪns] *vi* zusammenzucken

winch [wɪntʃ] *n* Winde *f*

wind¹ [wɪnd] *n* Wind *m*; (*MED*) Blähungen *pl*

wind² [waɪnd] (*pt, pp* **wound**) *vt* (*rope*) winden; (*bandage*) wickeln ♦ *vi* (*turn*) sich winden; **~ up** *vt* (*clock*) aufziehen; (*debate*) (ab)schließen

windfall ['wɪndfɔ:l] *n* unverhoffte(r) Glücksfall *m*

winding ['waɪndɪŋ] *adj* (*road*) gewunden

wind instrument ['wɪnd-] *n* Blasinstrument *nt*

windmill ['wɪndmɪl] *n* Windmühle *f*

window ['wɪndəu] *n* Fenster *nt*; **~ box** *n* Blumenkasten *m*; **~ cleaner** *n* Fensterputzer *m*; **~ envelope** *n* Fensterbriefumschlag *m*; **~ ledge** *n* Fenstersims *m*; **~ pane** *n* Fensterscheibe *f*; **~ shopping** *n* Schaufensterbummel *m*; **to go ~-shopping** einen Schaufensterbummel machen; **~sill** *n* Fensterbank *f*

wind: **~pipe** n Luftröhre f; **~ power** n Windenergie f; **~screen** (BRIT) n Windschutzscheibe f; **~screen washer** n Scheibenwaschanlage f; **~screen wiper** n Scheibenwischer m; **~shield** (US) n = windscreen; **~swept** adj vom Wind gepeitscht; (person) zerzaust; **~y** adj windig

wine [waɪn] n Wein m; **~ bar** n Weinlokal nt; **~ cellar** n Weinkeller m; **~glass** n Weinglas nt; **~ list** n Weinkarte f; **~ merchant** n Weinhändler m; **~ tasting** n Weinprobe f; **~ waiter** n Weinkellner m

wing [wɪŋ] n Flügel m; (MIL) Gruppe f; **~s** npl (THEAT) Seitenkulisse f; **~er** n (SPORT) Flügelstürmer m

wink [wɪŋk] n Zwinkern nt ♦ vi zwinkern, blinzeln

winner ['wɪnəʳ] n Gewinner m; (SPORT) Sieger m

winning ['wɪnɪŋ] adj (team) siegreich, Sieger-; (goal) entscheidend; **~ post** n Ziel nt; **~s** npl Gewinn m

winter ['wɪntəʳ] n Winter m ♦ adj (clothes) Winter- ♦ vi überwintern; **~ sports** npl Wintersport m; **wintry** ['wɪntrɪ] adj Winter-, winterlich

wipe [waɪp] n: **to give sth a ~** etw (ab)wischen ♦ vt wischen; **~ off** vt abwischen; **~ out** vt (debt) löschen; (destroy) auslöschen; **~ up** vt aufwischen

wire ['waɪəʳ] n Draht m; (telegram) Telegramm nt ♦ vt telegrafieren; **to ~ sb** jdm telegrafieren; **~less** ['waɪəlɪs] (BRIT) n Radio(apparat m) nt

wiring ['waɪərɪŋ] n elektrische Leitungen pl

wiry ['waɪərɪ] adj drahtig

wisdom ['wɪzdəm] n Weisheit f; (of decision) Klugheit f; **~ tooth** n Weisheitszahn m

wise [waɪz] adj klug, weise ♦ suffix: **timewise** zeitlich gesehen

wisecrack ['waɪzkræk] n Witzelei f

wish [wɪʃ] n Wunsch m ♦ vt wünschen; **best ~es** (on birthday etc) alles Gute;

with best **~es** herzliche Grüße; **to ~ sb goodbye** jdn verabschieden; **he ~ed me well** er wünschte mir Glück; **to ~ to do sth** etw tun wollen; **~ for** vt fus sich dat wünschen; **~ful thinking** n Wunschdenken nt

wishy-washy ['wɪʃɪwɒʃɪ] (inf) adj (ideas, argument) verschwommen

wisp [wɪsp] n (Haar)strähne f; (of smoke) Wölkchen nt

wistful ['wɪstfʊl] adj sehnsüchtig

wit [wɪt] n (also: **~s**) Verstand m no pl; (amusing ideas) Witz m; (person) Witzbold m

witch [wɪtʃ] n Hexe f; **~craft** n Hexerei f

KEYWORD

with [wɪð, wɪθ] prep 1 (accompanying, in the company of) mit; **we stayed with friends** wir übernachteten bei Freunden; **I'll be with you in a minute** einen Augenblick, ich bin sofort da; **I'm not with you** (I don't understand) das verstehe ich nicht; **to be with it** (inf: up-to-date) auf dem Laufenden sein; (: alert) (voll) da sein (inf)

2 (descriptive, indicating manner etc) mit; **the man with the grey hat** der Mann mit dem grauen Hut; **red with anger** rot vor Wut

---

withdraw [wɪθ'drɔː] (irreg: like **draw**) vt zurückziehen; (money) abheben; (remark) zurücknehmen ♦ vi sich zurückziehen; **~al** n Zurückziehung f; Abheben nt; Zurücknahme f; **~n** adj (person) verschlossen

wither ['wɪðəʳ] vi (ver)welken

withhold [wɪθ'həʊld] (irreg: like **hold**) vt: **to ~ sth (from sb)** (jdm) etw vorenthalten

within [wɪð'ɪn] prep innerhalb +gen ♦ adv innen; **~ sight of** in Sichtweite von; **~ the week** innerhalb dieser Woche; **~ a mile of** weniger als eine Meile von

without [wɪð'aut] *prep* ohne; **~ sleeping** *etc* ohne zu schlafen *etc*

withstand [wɪθ'stænd] (*irreg: like stand*) *vt* widerstehen +*dat*

witness ['wɪtnɪs] *n* Zeuge *m*, Zeugin *f* ♦ *vt* (*see*) sehen, miterleben; (*document*) beglaubigen; **~ box** *n* Zeugenstand *m*; **~ stand** (*US*) *n* Zeugenstand *m*

witticism ['wɪtɪsɪzəm] *n* witzige Bemerkung *f*

witty ['wɪtɪ] *adj* witzig, geistreich

wives [waɪvz] *pl of* **wife**

wk *abbr* = **week**

wobble ['wɒbl] *vi* wackeln

woe [wəu] *n* Kummer *m*

woke [wəuk] *pt of* **wake**

woken ['wəukn] *pp of* **wake**

wolf [wulf] (*pl* **wolves**) *n* Wolf *m*

woman ['wumən] (*pl* **women**) *n* Frau *f*; **~ doctor** *n* Ärztin *f*; **~ly** *adj* weiblich

womb [wu:m] *n* Gebärmutter *f*

women ['wɪmɪn] *npl of* **woman**; **~'s lib** (*inf*) *n* Frauenrechtsbewegung *f*

won [wʌn] *pt, pp of* **win**

wonder ['wʌndə*r*] *n* (*marvel*) Wunder *nt*; (*surprise*) Staunen *nt*, Verwunderung *f* ♦ *vi* sich wundern ♦ *vt*: **I ~ whether ...** ich frage mich, ob ...; **it's no ~ that** es ist kein Wunder, dass; **to ~ at** sich wundern über +*acc*; **to ~ about** sich Gedanken machen über +*acc*; **~ful** *adj* wunderbar, herrlich

won't [wəunt] = **will not**

woo [wu:] *vt* (*audience etc*) umwerben

wood [wud] *n* Holz *nt*; (*forest*) Wald *m*; **~ carving** *n* Holzschnitzerei *f*; **~ed** *adj* bewaldet; **~en** *adj* (*also: fig*) hölzern; **~pecker** *n* Specht *m*; **~wind** *n* Blasinstrumente *pl*; **~work** *n* Holzwerk *nt*; (*craft*) Holzarbeiten *pl*; **~worm** *n* Holzwurm *m*

wool [wul] *n* Wolle *f*; **to pull the ~ over sb's eyes** (*fig*) jdm Sand in die Augen streuen; **~len** (*US* **woolen**) *adj* Woll-; **~lens** *npl* Wollsachen *pl*; **~ly** (*US* **wooly**) *adj* wollig; (*fig*) schwammig

word [wə:d] *n* Wort *nt*; (*news*) Bescheid *m* ♦ *vt* formulieren; **in other ~s** anders gesagt; **to break/keep one's ~** sein Wort brechen/halten; **~ing** *n* Wortlaut *m*; **~ processing** *n* Textverarbeitung *f*; **~ processor** *n* Textverarbeitung *f*

wore [wɔ:*r*] *pt of* **wear**

work [wə:k] *n* Arbeit *f*; (*ART, LITER*) Werk *nt* ♦ *vi* arbeiten; (*machine*) funktionieren; (*medicine*) wirken; (*succeed*) klappen; **~s** *n sg* (*BRIT: factory*) Fabrik *f*, Werk *nt* ♦ *npl* (*of watch*) Werk *nt*; **to be out of ~** arbeitslos sein; **in ~ing order** in betriebsfähigem Zustand; **~ loose** *vi* sich lockern; **~ on** *vi* weiterarbeiten ♦ *vt fus* arbeiten an +*dat*; (*influence*) bearbeiten; **~ out** *vi* (*sum*) aufgehen; (*plan*) klappen ♦ *vt* (*problem*) lösen; (*plan*) ausarbeiten; **it ~s out at £100** das gibt or macht £100; **~ up** *vt*: **to get ~ed up** sich aufregen; **~able** *adj* (*soil*) bearbeitbar; (*plan*) ausführbar; **~aholic** [wə:kə'hɒlɪk] *n* Arbeitssüchtige(r) *f(m)*; **~er** *n* Arbeiter(in) *m(f)*; **~ experience** *n* Praktikum *nt*; **~force** *n* Arbeiterschaft *f*; **~ing class** *n* Arbeiterklasse *f*; **~ing-class** *adj* Arbeiter-; **~man** (*irreg*) *n* Arbeiter *m*; **~manship** *n* Arbeit *f*, Ausführung *f*; **~sheet** *n* Arbeitsblatt *nt*; **~shop** *n* Werkstatt *f*; **~ station** *n* Arbeitsplatz *m*; **~-to-rule** (*BRIT*) *n* Dienst *m* nach Vorschrift

world [wə:ld] *n* Welt *f*; **to think the ~ of sb** große Stücke auf jdn halten; **~ly** *adj* weltlich, irdisch; **~-wide** *adj* weltweit

World-Wide Web ['wə:ld'waɪd] *n* World Wide Web *nt*

worm [wə:m] *n* Wurm *m*

worn [wɔ:n] *pp of* **wear** ♦ *adj* (*clothes*) abgetragen; **~-out** *adj* (*object*) abgenutzt; (*person*) völlig erschöpft

worried ['wʌrɪd] *adj* besorgt, beunruhigt

worry ['wʌrɪ] *n* Sorge *f* ♦ *vt* beunruhigen ♦ *vi* (*feel uneasy*) sich sorgen, sich

dat Gedanken machen; **~ing** adj beunruhigend

worse [wəːs] adj schlechter, schlimmer
♦ adv schlimmer, ärger ♦ n Schlimme-
re(s) nt, Schlechtere(s) nt; **a change
for the ~** eine Verschlechterung; **~n**
vt verschlimmern ♦ vi sich verschlechtern; **~ off** adj (fig) schlechter dran

worship ['wəːʃip] n Verehrung f ♦ vt
anbeten; **Your W~** (BRIT: to mayor)
Herr/Frau Bürgermeister; (: to judge)
Euer Ehren

worst [wəːst] adj schlimmste(r, s),
schlechteste(r, s) ♦ adv am schlimm-
sten, am ärgsten ♦ n Schlimmste(s) nt,
Ärgste(s) nt; **at ~** schlimmstenfalls

worth [wəːθ] n Wert m ♦ adj wert; **it's
~ it** es lohnt sich; **to be ~ one's while
(to do sth)** der Mühe wert sein; (**es
zu tun**); **~less** adj wertlos; (person)
nichtsnutzig; **~while** adj lohnend, der
Mühe wert; **~y** adj wert, würdig

KEYWORD

---

would [wud] aux vb **1** (conditional
tense): **if you asked him he would do
it** wenn du ihn fragtest, würde er es
tun; **if you had asked him he would
have done it** wenn du ihn gefragt
hättest, hätte er es getan

2 (in offers, invitations, requests): **would
you like a biscuit?** möchten Sie ein
Plätzchen?; **would you ask him to
come in?** würden Sie ihn bitte hinein-
bitten?

3 (in indirect speech): **I said I would do
it** ich sagte, ich würde es tun

4 (emphatic): **it WOULD have to
snow today!** es musste ja ausgerechnet heute schneien!

5 (insistence): **she wouldn't behave**
sie wollte sich partout nicht anständig
benehmen

6 (conjecture): **it would have been
midnight** es mag ungefähr Mitternacht gewesen sein; **it would seem
so** es sieht wohl so aus

7 (indicating habit): **he would go
there on Mondays** er ging jeden
Montag dorthin

would-be ['wudbiː] (pej) adj
Möchtegern-

wound¹ [wuːnd] n (also fig) Wunde f
♦ vt verwunden, verletzen (also fig)

wound² [waund] pt, pp of **wind²**

wove [wauv] pt of **weave**; **~n** pp of
weave

wrangle ['ræŋgl] n Streit m ♦ vi sich
zanken

wrap [ræp] vt einwickeln; **~ up** vt einwickeln; (deal) abschließen; **~per** n
Umschlag m, Schutzhülle f; **~ping paper** n Einwickelpapier nt

wrath [rɔθ] n Zorn m

wreak [riːk] vt (havoc) anrichten;
(vengeance) üben

wreath [riːθ] n Kranz m

wreck [rek] n (ship) Wrack nt; (sth
ruined) Ruine f ♦ vt zerstören; **~age** n
Trümmer pl

wren [ren] n Zaunkönig m

wrench [rentʃ] n (spanner) Schraubenschlüssel m; (twist) Ruck m ♦ vt reißen,
zerren; **to ~ sth from sb** jdm etw entreißen or entwinden

wrestle ['resl] vi: **to ~ (with sb)** (mit
jdm) ringen; **~r** n Ringer(in) m(f);
wrestling n Ringen nt

wretched ['retʃid] adj (inf) verflixt

wriggle ['rɪgl] n Schlängeln nt ♦ vi sich
winden

wring [rɪŋ] (pt, pp **wrung**) vt wringen

wrinkle ['rɪŋkl] n Falte f, Runzel f ♦ vt
runzeln ♦ vi sich runzeln; (material)
knittern; **~d** adj faltig, schrumpelig

wrist [rist] n Handgelenk nt; **~watch** n
Armbanduhr f

writ [rit] n gerichtliche(r) Befehl m

write [rait] (pt **wrote**, pp **written**) vt, vi
schreiben; **~ down** vt aufschreiben; **~
off** vt (dismiss) abschreiben; **~ out**
(essay) abschreiben; (cheque) ausstel-

len; **~ up** vt schreiben; **~-off** n: **it is a ~-off** das kann man abschreiben; **~r** n Schriftsteller m

writhe [raɪð] vi sich winden

writing ['raɪtɪŋ] n (act) Schreiben nt; (handwriting) (Hand)schrift f; **in ~** schriftlich; **~ paper** n Schreibpapier nt

written ['rɪtn] pp of **write**

wrong [rɒŋ] adj (incorrect) falsch; (morally) unrecht ♦ n Unrecht nt ♦ vt Unrecht tun +dat; **he was ~ in doing that** es war nicht recht von ihm, das zu tun; **you are ~ about that, you've got it ~** da hast du Unrecht; **to be in the ~** im Unrecht sein; **what's ~ with your leg?** was ist mit deinem Bein los?; **to go ~** (plan) schief gehen; (person) einen Fehler machen; **~ful** adj unrechtmäßig; **~ly** adv falsch; (accuse) zu Unrecht

wrong number n (TEL): **you've got the ~** Sie sind falsch verbunden

wrote [rəʊt] pt of **write**

wrought [rɔːt] adj: **~ iron** Schmiedeeisen nt

wrung [rʌŋ] pt, pp of **wring**

wry [raɪ] adj ironisch

wt. abbr = **weight**

X, x

Xmas ['eksməs] n abbr = **Christmas**

X-ray ['eksreɪ] n Röntgenaufnahme f ♦ vt röntgen; **~-s** npl Röntgenstrahlen pl

xylophone ['zaɪləfəʊn] n Xylofon nt, Xylophon nt

Y, y

yacht [jɒt] n Jacht f; **~ing** n (Sport)segeln nt; **~sman** (irreg) n Sportsegler m

Yank [jæŋk] (inf) n Ami m

yap [jæp] vi (dog) kläffen

yard [jɑːd] n Hof m; (measure) (engli-

sche) Elle f, Yard nt (0,91 m); **~stick** n (fig) Maßstab m

yarn [jɑːn] n (thread) Garn nt; (story) (Seemanns)garn nt

yawn [jɔːn] n Gähnen nt ♦ vi gähnen; **~ing** adj (gap) gähnend

yd. abbr = **yard(s)**

yeah [jeə] (inf) adv ja

year [jɪə*] n Jahr nt; **to be 8 ~s old** acht Jahre alt sein; **an eight-year-old child** ein achtjähriges Kind; **~ly** adj, adv jährlich

yearn [jɜːn] vi: **to ~ (for)** sich sehnen (nach); **~ing** n Verlangen nt, Sehnsucht f

yeast [jiːst] n Hefe f

yell [jel] n gellende(r) Schrei m ♦ vi laut schreien

yellow ['jeləʊ] adj gelb ♦ n Gelb nt

yelp [jelp] n Gekläff nt ♦ vi kläffen

yes [jes] adv ja ♦ n Ja nt, Jawort nt; **to say ~ to** ja or ja sagen; **to answer ~** mit Ja antworten

yesterday ['jestədɪ] adv gestern ♦ n Gestern nt; **~ morning/evening** gestern Morgen/Abend; **all day ~** gestern den ganzen Tag; **the day before ~** vorgestern

yet [jet] adv noch; (in question) schon; (up to now) bis jetzt ♦ conj doch, dennoch; **it is not finished ~** es ist noch nicht fertig; **as ~** bis jetzt; **the best ~** das bisher Beste; **as ~** bis jetzt; (in past) bis dahin

yew [juː] n Eibe f

yield [jiːld] n Ertrag m ♦ vt (result, crop) hervorbringen; (interest, profit) abwerfen; (concede) abtreten ♦ vi nachgeben; (MIL) sich ergeben; **"~"** (US: AUT) „Vorfahrt gewähren"

YMCA n abbr = **Young Men's Christian Association**) CVJM m

yob [jɒb] (BRIT: inf) n Halbstarke(r) f(m), Rowdy m

yoga ['jəʊgə] n Joga m

yoghourt ['jɒgət] n Jog(h)urt m

yog(h)urt ['jɒgət] n = **yoghourt**

yoke [jəʊk] n (also fig) Joch nt

yolk [jəuk] n Eidotter m, Eigelb nt

KEYWORD

you [juː] pron 1 (subj, in comparisons: familiar form: sg) du; (: pl) ihr; (in letters also) du, ihr; (: polite form) Sie; **you Germans** ihr Deutschen; **she's younger than you** sie ist jünger als du/Sie

2 (direct object, after prep +acc: familiar form: sg) dich; (: pl) euch; (in letters also) dich, euch; (: polite form) Sie; **I know you** ich kenne dich/euch/Sie

3 (indirect object, after prep +dat: familiar form: sg) dir; (: pl) euch; (in letters also) dir, euch; (: polite form) Ihnen; **I gave it to you** ich gab es dir/euch/Ihnen

4 (impers: one: subj) man; (: direct object) einen; (: indirect object) einem; **fresh air does you good** frische Luft tut gut

you'd [juːd] = you had; you would

you'll [juːl] = you will; you shall

young [jʌŋ] adj jung ♦ npl: **the ~** die Jungen pl; **~ster** n Junge m, junge(r) Bursche m, junge(s) Mädchen nt

your [jɔː] adj (familiar: sg) dein; (: pl) euer, eure pl; (polite) Ihr; see also **my**

you're [juə] = you are

yours [jɔːz] pron (familiar: sg) deine(r, s); (: pl) eure(r, s); (polite) Ihre(r, s); see also **mine²**

yourself [jɔːˈsɛlf] pron (emphatic) selbst; (familiar: sg: acc) dich (selbst); (: dat) dir (selbst); (: pl) euch (selbst); (polite) sich (selbst); see also **oneself**; **yourselves** pl pron (reflexive: familiar) euch; (: polite) sich (selbst); (emphatic) selbst; see also **oneself**

youth [juːθ] n Jugend f; (young man) junge(r) Mann m; **~s** npl (young people) Jugendliche pl; **~ club** n Jugendzentrum nt; **~ful** adj jugendlich; **~ hostel** n Jugendherberge f

you've [juːv] = you have

YTS (BRIT) n abbr (= Youth Training Scheme) staatliches Förderprogramm für arbeitslose Jugendliche

Yugoslav ['juːgəuslɑːv] adj jugoslawisch ♦ n Jugoslawe m, Jugoslawin f; **~ia** [juːgəuˈslɑːvɪə] n Jugoslawien nt

yuppie ['jʌpɪ] (inf) n Yuppie m ♦ adj yuppiehaft, Yuppie-

YWCA n abbr (= Young Women's Christian Association) CVJF m

Z, z

zany ['zeɪnɪ] adj (ideas, sense of humour) verrückt

zap [zæp] vt (COMPUT) löschen

zeal [ziːl] n Eifer m; **~ous** ['zɛləs] adj eifrig

zebra ['ziːbrə] n Zebra nt; **~ crossing** (BRIT) n Zebrastreifen m

zero ['zɪərəu] n Null f; (on scale) Nullpunkt m

zest [zɛst] n Begeisterung f

zigzag ['zɪgzæg] n Zickzack m

Zimbabwe [zɪmˈbɑːbwɪ] n Zimbabwe nt

Zimmer frame ['zɪmə-] n Laufgestell nt

zip [zɪp] n Reißverschluss m ♦ vt (also: **~ up**) den Reißverschluss zumachen +gen

zip code (US) n Postleitzahl f

zipper ['zɪpə] (US) n Reißverschluss m

zit [zɪt] (inf) n Pickel m

zodiac ['zəudɪæk] n Tierkreis m

zombie ['zɒmbɪ] n: **like a ~** (fig) wie im Tran

zone [zəun] n (also MIL) Zone f, Gebiet nt; (in town) Bezirk m

zoo [zuː] n Zoo m

zoology [zuːˈɒlədʒɪ] n Zoologie f

zoom [zuːm] vi: **to ~ past** vorbeisausen; **~ lens** n Zoomobjektiv nt

zucchini [zuːˈkiːnɪ] (US) npl Zucchini pl

GERMAN IRREGULAR VERBS
*with 'sein'

infinitive	present indicative (2nd, 3rd sg.)	imperfect	past participle
aufschrecken*	schrickst auf, schrickt auf	schrak or schreckte auf	aufgeschreckt
ausbedingen	bedingst aus, bedingt aus	bedang or bedingte aus	ausbedungen
backen	bäckst, bäckt	backte or buk	gebacken
befehlen	befiehlst, befiehlt	befahl	befohlen
beginnen	beginnst, beginnt	begann	begonnen
beißen	beißt, beißt	biss	gebissen
bergen	birgst, birgt	barg	geborgen
bersten*	birst, birst	barst	geborsten
bescheißen	bescheißt, bescheißt	beschiss	beschissen
bewegen	bewegst, bewegt	bewog	bewogen
biegen	biegst, biegt	bog	gebogen
bieten	bietest, bietet	bot	geboten
binden	bindest, bindet	band	gebunden
bitten	bittest, bittet	bat	gebeten
blasen	bläst, bläst	blies	geblasen
bleiben*	bleibst, bleibt	blieb	geblieben
braten	brätst, brät	briet	gebraten
brechen*	brichst, bricht	brach	gebrochen
brennen	brennst, brennt	brannte	gebrannt
bringen	bringst, bringt	brachte	gebracht
denken	denkst, denkt	dachte	gedacht
dreschen	drisch(e)st, drischt	drasch	gedroschen
dringen*	dringst, dringt	drang	gedrungen
dürfen	darfst, darf	durfte	gedurft
empfehlen	empfiehlst, empfiehlt	empfahl	empfohlen
erbleichen*	erbleichst, erbleicht	erbleichte	erblichen
erlöschen*	erlischst, erlischt	erlosch	erloschen
erschrecken*	erschrickst, erschrickt	erschrak	erschrocken
essen	isst, isst	aß	gegessen
fahren*	fährst, fährt	fuhr	gefahren

infinitive	present indicative (2nd, 3rd sg.)	imperfect	past participle
fallen*	fällst, fällt	fiel	gefallen
fangen	fängst, fängt	fing	gefangen
fechten	fichtst, ficht	focht	gefochten
finden	findest, findet	fand	gefunden
flechten	flichtst, flicht	flocht	geflochten
fliegen*	fliegst, fliegt	flog	geflogen
fliehen*	fliehst, flieht	floh	geflohen
fließen*	fließt, fließt	floß	geflossen
fressen	frisst, frisst	fraß	gefressen
frieren	frierst, friert	fror	gefroren
gären*	gärst, gärt	gor	gegoren
gebären	gebierst, gebiert	gebar	geboren
geben	gibst, gibt	gab	gegeben
gedeihen*	gedeihst, gedeiht	gedieh	gediehen
gehen*	gehst, geht	ging	gegangen
gelingen*	——, gelingt	gelang	gelungen
gelten	giltst, gilt	galt	gegolten
genesen*	gene(se)st, genest	genas	genesen
genießen	genießt, genießt	genoss	genossen
geraten*	gerätst, gerät	geriet	geraten
geschehen*	——, geschieht	geschah	geschehen
gewinnen	gewinnst, gewinnt	gewann	gewonnen
gießen	gießt, gießt	goss	gegossen
gleichen	gleichst, gleicht	glich	geglichen
gleiten*	gleitest, gleitet	glitt	geglitten
glimmen	glimmst, glimmt	glomm	geglommen
graben	gräbst, gräbt	grub	gegraben
greifen	greifst, greift	griff	gegriffen
haben	hast, hat	hatte	gehabt
halten	hältst, hält	hielt	gehalten
hängen	hängst, hängt	hing	gehangen
hauen	haust, haut	haute	gehauen
heben	hebst, hebt	hob	gehoben
heißen	heißt, heißt	hieß	geheißen
helfen	hilfst, hilft	half	geholfen
kennen	kennst, kennt	kannte	gekannt
klimmen*	klimmst, klimmt	klomm	geklommen
klingen	klingst, klingt	klang	geklungen
kneifen	kneifst, kneift	kniff	gekniffen

620

infinitive	present indicative (2nd, 3rd sg.)	imperfect	past participle
kommen*	kommst, kommt	kam	gekommen
können	kannst, kann	konnte	gekonnt
kriechen*	kriechst, kriecht	kroch	gekrochen
laden	lädst, lädt	lud	geladen
lassen	lässt, lässt	ließ	gelassen
laufen*	läufst, läuft	lief	gelaufen
leiden	leidest, leidet	litt	gelitten
leihen	leihst, leiht	lieh	geliehen
lesen	liest, liest	las	gelesen
liegen*	liegst, liegt	lag	gelegen
lügen	lügst, lügt	log	gelogen
mahlen	mahlst, mahlt	mahlte	gemahlen
meiden	meidest, meidet	mied	gemieden
melken	melkst, melkt	melkte	gemolken
messen	misst, misst	maß	gemessen
misslingen*	——, misslingt	misslang	misslungen
mögen	magst, mag	mochte	gemocht
müssen	musst, muss	musste	gemusst
nehmen	nimmst, nimmt	nahm	genommen
nennen*	nennst, nennt	nannte	genannt
pfeifen	pfeifst, pfeift	pfiff	gepfiffen
preisen	preist, preist	pries	gepriesen
quellen*	quillst, quillt	quoll	gequollen
raten	rätst, rät	riet	geraten
reiben	reibst, reibt	rieb	gerieben
reißen*	reißt, reißt	riss	gerissen
reiten*	reitest, reitet	ritt	geritten
rennen*	rennst, rennt	rannte	gerannt
riechen*	riechst, riecht	roch	gerochen
ringen	ringst, ringt	rang	gerungen
rinnen*	rinnst, rinnt	rann	geronnen
rufen	rufst, ruft	rief	gerufen
salzen	salzt, salzt	salzte	gesalzen
saufen	säufst, säuft	soff	gesoffen
saugen	saugst, saugt	sog	gesogen
schaffen	schaffst, schafft	schuf	geschaffen
scheiden	scheidest, scheidet	schied	geschieden
scheinen	scheinst, scheint	schien	geschienen
schelten	schiltst, schilt	schalt	gescholten
scheren	scherst, schert	schor	geschoren

infinitive	present indicative (2nd, 3rd sg.)	imperfect	past participle
schieben	schiebst, schiebt	schob	geschoben
schießen	schießt, schießt	schoss	geschossen
schinden	schindest, schindet	schindete	geschunden
schlafen	schläfst, schläft	schlief	geschlafen
schlagen	schlägst, schlägt	schlug	geschlagen
schleichen*	schleichst, schleicht	schlich	geschlichen
schleifen	schleifst, schleift	schliff	geschliffen
schließen	schließt, schließt	schloss	geschlossen
schlingen	schlingst, schlingt	schlang	geschlungen
schmeißen	schmeißt, schmeißt	schmiss	geschmissen
schmelzen*	schmilzt, schmilzt	schmolz	geschmolzen
schneiden	schneidest, schneidet	schnitt	geschnitten
schreiben	schreibst, schreibt	schrieb	geschrieben
schreien	schreist, schreit	schrie	geschrie(e)n
schreiten	schreitest, schreitet	schritt	geschritten
schweigen	schweigst, schweigt	schwieg	geschwiegen
schwellen*	schwillst, schwillt	schwoll	geschwollen
schwimmen*	schwimmst, schwimmt	schwamm	geschwommen
schwinden*	schwindest, schwindet	schwand	geschwunden
schwingen	schwingst, schwingt	schwang	geschwungen
schwören	schwörst, schwört	schwor	geschworen
sehen	siehst, sieht	sah	gesehen
sein*	bist, ist	war	gewesen
senden	sendest, sendet	sandte	gesandt
singen	singst, singt	sang	gesungen
sinken*	sinkst, sinkt	sank	gesunken
sinnen	sinnst, sinnt	sann	gesonnen

infinitive	present indicative (2nd, 3rd sg.)	imperfect	past participle
sitzen*	sitzt, sitzt	saß	gesessen
sollen	sollst, soll	sollte	gesollt
speien	speist, speit	spie	gespie(e)n
spinnen	spinnst, spinnt	spann	gesponnen
sprechen	sprichst, spricht	sprach	gesprochen
sprießen*	sprießt, sprießt	sproß	gesprossen
springen*	springst, springt	sprang	gesprungen
stechen	stichst, sticht	stach	gestochen
stecken	steckst, steckt	steckte or stak	gesteckt
stehen	stehst, steht	stand	gestanden
stehlen	stiehlst, stiehlt	stahl	gestohlen
steigen*	steigst, steigt	stieg	gestiegen
sterben*	stirbst, stirbt	starb	gestorben
stinken	stinkst, stinkt	stank	gestunken
stoßen*	stößt, stößt	stieß	gestoßen
streichen	streichst, streicht	strich	gestrichen
streiten*	streitest, streitet	stritt	gestritten
tragen	trägst, trägt	trug	getragen
treffen	triffst, trifft	traf	getroffen
treiben*	treibst, treibt	trieb	getrieben
treten*	trittst, tritt	trat	getreten
trinken	trinkst, trinkt	trank	getrunken
trügen	trügst, trügt	trog	getrogen
tun	tust, tut	tat	getan
verderben	verdirbst, verdirbt	verdarb	verdorben
verdrießen	verdrießt, verdrießt	verdross	verdrossen
vergessen	vergisst, vergisst	vergaß	vergessen
verlieren	verlierst, verliert	verlor	verloren
verschleißen*	verschleißt, verschleißt	verschliss	verschlissen
wachsen*	wächst, wächst	wuchs	gewachsen
wägen	wägst, wägt	wog	gewogen
waschen	wäschst, wäscht	wusch	gewaschen
weben	webst, webt	webte or wob	gewoben
weichen*	weichst, weicht	wich	gewichen
weisen	weist, weist	wies	gewiesen
wenden	wendest, wendet	wandte	gewandt
werben	wirbst, wirbt	warb	geworben
werden*	wirst, wird	wurde	geworden

infinitive	present indicative (2nd, 3rd sg.)	imperfect	past participle
werfen	wirfst, wirft	warf	geworfen
wiegen	wiegst, wiegt	wog	gewogen
winden	windest, windet	wand	gewunden
wissen	weißt, weiß	wusste	gewusst
wollen	willst, will	wollte	gewollt
wringen	wringst, wringt	wrang	gewrungen
zeihen	zeihst, zeiht	zieh	geziehen
ziehen*	ziehst, zieht	zog	gezogen
zwingen	zwingst, zwingt	zwang	gezwungen